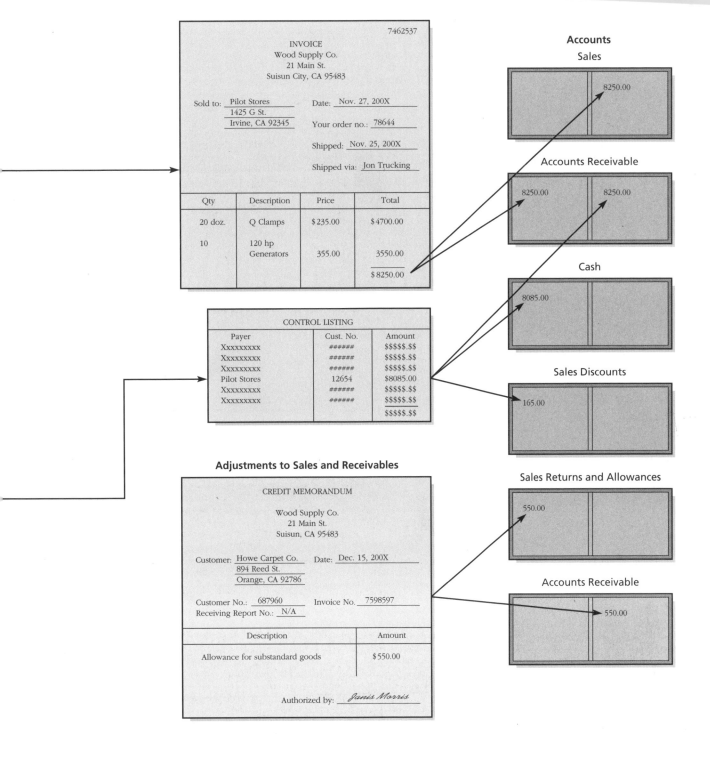

Principles of Auditing and Other Assurance Services

Principles of Auditing and Other Assurance Services

Fifteenth Edition

O. Ray Whittington
CIA, CMA, CPA
DePaul University

Kurt Pany
CFE, CPA
Arizona State University

Boston   Burr Ridge, IL   Dubuque, IA   Madison, WI   New York   San Francisco   St. Louis
Bangkok   Bogotá   Caracas   Kuala Lumpur   Lisbon   London   Madrid   Mexico City
Milan   Montreal   New Delhi   Santiago   Seoul   Singapore   Sydney   Taipei   Toronto

McGraw-Hill
Irwin

PRINCIPLES OF AUDITING AND OTHER ASSURANCE SERVICES

Published by McGraw-Hill/Irwin, a business unit of The McGraw-Hill Companies, Inc., 1221 Avenue of the Americas, New York, NY, 10020. Copyright © 2006 by The McGraw-Hill Companies, Inc. All rights reserved. No part of this publication may be reproduced or distributed in any form or by any means, or stored in a database or retrieval system, without the prior written consent of The McGraw-Hill Companies, Inc., including, but not limited to, in any network or other electronic storage or transmission, or broadcast for distance learning.

Some ancillaries, including electronic and print components, may not be available to customers outside the United States.

This book is printed on acid-free paper.

2 3 4 5 6 7 8 9 0 QPD/QPD 0 9 8 7 6

ISBN-13: 978-0-07-301084-7
ISBN-10: 0-07-301084-7

Editorial director: *Brent Gordon*
Publisher: *Stewart Mattson*
Executive editor: *Tim Vertovec*
Managing developmental editor: *Gail Korosa*
Marketing manager: *Marc Chernoff*
Media producer: *Elizabeth Mavetz*
Project manager: *Dana M. Pauley*
Production supervisor: *Gina Hangos*
Designer: *Kami Carter*
Senior media project manager: *Rose M. Range*
Senior supplement producer: *Carol Loreth*
Developer, Media technology: *Brian Nacik*
Cover design: *Jenny El-Shamy*
Interior design: *Jenny El-Shamy*
Typeface: *10/12 Times New Roman*
Compositor: *Interactive Composition Corporation*
Printer: *Quebecor World Dubuque Inc.*

Library of Congress Cataloging-in-Publication Data

Whittington, Ray, 1948–
    Principles of auditing and other assurance services / O. Ray Whittington, Kurt Pany.—
15th ed.
        p. cm.
    Includes index.
    ISBN 0-07-301084-7 (alk. paper)
    1. Auditing. I. Pany, Kurt. II. Title.
HF5667.W39 2006
657′.45—dc22

2005049113

www.mhhe.com

About the Authors

O. Ray Whittington

O. Ray Whittington, CIA, CMA, CPA, serves as the Ledger and Quill Director of the School of Accountancy at DePaul University. He received his B.B.A., M.S., and Ph.D. degrees from Sam Houston State University, Texas Tech University, and the University of Houston, respectively. Professor Whittington is an active textbook author on the subjects of auditing and audit sampling. He has also published in a variety of journals, including *The Accounting Review, The Journal of Accounting Research,* and *Auditing: A Journal of Practice and Theory.* He has served as a member of the Board of Regents of the Institute of Internal Auditors and has served as Chairman on the Auditing Standards Committee of the Auditing Section and the Bylaws Committee, both of the American Accounting Association. Professor Whittington was until recently a member of the AICPA Auditing Standards Board, and currently he is the President-elect of the Auditing Section of the American Accounting Association.

Kurt Pany

Kurt Pany, CPA, CFE, is a Professor of Accounting at Arizona State University. He received his B.S., M.B.A., and Ph.D. degrees from the University of Arizona, the University of Minnesota, and the University of Illinois, respectively. He has also served as a staff accountant with Arthur Andersen and Touche Ross, as a member of the Auditing Standards Board, and as an academic fellow with the American Institute of Certified Public Accountants. Professor Pany has published articles on auditing in such journals as *The Journal of Accounting Research, The Accounting Review, Auditing: A Journal of Practice and Theory, The Journal of Accountancy,* and *The CPA Journal.* He is a member of and has served on various committees of the American Accounting Association, the American Institute of Certified Public Accountants, and the Arizona Society of Certified Public Accountants.

Preface

The past few years we have seen unprecedented changes in the auditing profession. These changes were precipitated by the revelation that management of a number of large public companies, including Enron and WorldCom, systematically misstated the financial statements of the companies over a number of years. As a result, we have witnessed congressional hearings about the accounting profession, the criminal conviction and liquidation of the international accounting firm of Arthur Andersen LLP, the passage of the Sarbanes-Oxley Act of 2002, and the creation of the Public Company Accounting Oversight Board, which takes from the profession the major portion of its self-regulatory authority. The goal of the fifteenth edition of *Principles of Auditing and Other Assurance Services* is to provide you with a **clear perspective of this new auditing environment.**

How do we do this?

1. **Balanced presentation.** This text provides a carefully balanced presentation of auditing and assurance theory and practice. The concepts are written in a clear, concise, and understandable manner suitable for students who have not had significant audit experience. Real company examples are integrated throughout the text to bring this material to life. Lastly, Keystone Computers & Networks, Inc., the text's illustrative audit case, is integrated into selected chapters, providing students with hands-on audit experience.

2. **Clarifying the changes to the profession.** The authors have included all the new legal and standards changes affecting the auditing profession to provide students with the most current and up-to-date auditing text available.

3. **CPA Exam Support.** The text includes both multiple choice questions and simulations aimed at helping students pass the new computerized CPA exam.

4. **Maintaining a clear perspective.** The Online Learning Center provides instructors and students with a wealth of material to help keep students up-to-date. The OLC also contains quizzes and other resources to help students in this course.

Just as the cover provides a clear perspective of the environment outside, *Principles of Auditing and Other Assurance Services,* 15/e, will provide students with a clear perspective of the new auditing environment.

O. Ray Whittington

Kurt Pany

Key Features of the Book

Sarbanes-Oxley Act of 2002 and the resulting **Public Company Accounting Oversight Board** profoundly affect public accountants, CPA firms, and their clients. Most notably, the public accounting profession is no longer largely self-regulating, CPAs must issue a publicly available report on the internal control of each publicly traded client, and top management must certify the company's financial statements, and provide an assessment of internal control over financial reporting. The text carefully integrates coverage of the act's nature and effects on the profession in selected chapters. Also included is coverage of financial frauds, such as those involving Enron and WorldCom, which led to passage of the act.

The first 9 chapters of the text emphasize the philosophy and environment of the profession, with special attention paid to the nature and economic purpose of auditing and assurance services, professional standards, professional conduct, legal liability, audit evidence, audit planning, consideration of internal control, audit sampling, audit documentation, and general records.

Auditor legal liability in Chapter 4 is updated based on suggestions by legal scholar Professor Marianne Jennings of Arizona State University.

Chapter 6 includes the dramatic changes required by *Statement on Auditing Standards No. 99,* "The Auditor's Consideration of Fraud in a Financial Statement Audit."

Chapters 7 and 8 reflect the profession's most recent pronouncements relating to information technology and internal control.

1. The Role of the Public Accountant in the American Economy
2. Professional Standards
3. Professional Ethics
4. Legal Liability of CPAs
5. Audit Evidence and Documentation
6. Planning the Audit; Linking Audit Procedures to Risk
7. Internal Control
8. Consideration of Internal Control in an Information Technology Environment
9. Audit Sampling

Keystone Computers & Networks, Inc., is the text's **Illustrative Audit Case.** This feature has been updated in this edition and illustrates audit methods and provides realistic, thought-provoking case exercises. Although each portion of the case is designed to stand alone, if used in combination, the case will help the student develop problem-solving skills in planning (Chapter 6), in considering internal control and testing account balances (Chapters 11 and 14), and in completing the audit (Chapter 16). The case incorporates the use of computerized accounting applications and also integrates the fundamentals of audit sampling from Chapter 9.

International Auditing Standards are discussed as appropriate. These standards are becoming increasingly significant with the development of international markets for securities.

Chapters 10 through 16 (the "procedural chapters") deal with internal control and obtaining evidence about the various financial statement accounts; they emphasize a risk-based approach to selecting appropriate auditing procedures. They also provide a description of the business risk approach to audits that has been adopted by many large CPA firms and is the approach included in the recently issued exposure draft of the proposed Statement on Auditing Standards on Risk Assessment. Chapters 10 through 16 also thoroughly integrate the requirements of SAS No. 99. Chapters 10, 11, 12, and 14 include a set of interrelated simulations similar to those included on the uniform CPA exam.

Chapter 17 presents the auditors' reporting responsibilities for audits of financial statements for both public and nonpublic companies.

Chapter 18, new to this edition, presents the details of the audit of internal control over financial reporting required for public companies.

Chapter 19 covers special reports and reports arising from accounting and review engagements.

Chapter 20 presents a variety of attestation and other assurance services. The material on attestation services describes the current professional standards. Other assurance services are included at both a conceptual and practical level.

Chapter 21's discussion of compliance auditing has been modified based on the suggestions of Mr. Norwood J. Jackson, former Deputy Controller, Office of Federal Management, U.S. Office of Management and Budget.

NEW IN THIS EDITION

The Auditing & Attestation section of the Uniform Certified Public Accountant Exam represents 4½ hours of that 14-hour examination. The AICPA indicates that each Auditing & Attestation exam will consist of multiple choice questions and two condensed case studies referred to as simulations.

New to this edition, we have prepared four interrelated simulations. These simulations are comparable in requirements to that provided by the AICPA and are included in the text itself. They are included in Chapters 10, 11, 12, and 14. Three additional interrelated simulations on the text's Web site, www.mhhe.com/whittington15e. Two of the simulations are available to students, and all three to instructors. Because they are MS Excel based, they do not require the extensive computer downloads necessary for the AICPA simulation.

CPA Simulation	10–50.	The following simulation has three parts:

- Company profile
- Industry information
- Financial statements
- Questions

The company profile, industry information, and financial statements are also used as the basis for the simulations in Chapters 11, 12, and 14. Each of those chapters has a different set of questions.

Company profile: In 20X1, Gary Sherwood founded Sherwood Stone Company (SSC). In the middle of its second year of existence, the company completed development of a large extraction pit area and constructed an aggregate processing plant which is equipped to crush, screen, and wash aggregate products. By 20X4 the sand and gravel operation was profitable and growing market conditions justified modifications and expansion. Currently, SSC produces a wide range of sand and stone products from its pit near Bisbee, Arizona. The materials it develops are composed of sand and stone materials for commercial construction and highway projects.

SSC sells to a wide variety of commercial and governmental customers, with only one of its numerous customers—Wingo Corporation—accounting for more than 5 percent of total sales. In total, Wingo has represented approximately 30 percent of sales (and receivables) for the past few years. Wingo Corporation is by far Arizona's largest street and road contractor and

Reviewers asked for multiple choice questions similar to those on the CPA exam. We have doubled the number of this type of question in each chapter, and highlighted them in the problem material.

We have added a new chapter on integrated audits of public companies (Chapter 18) and have changed the sequencing of the last chapters in the book.

Chapter 20 now includes coverage of internal auditing for Sarbanes-Oxley and the services that are performed by internal auditors.

The book is now 2-color to help highlight material in the illustrations.

We have added subtitles to the Illustrative Cases for easy reference.

We now include numbered learning objectives at the beginning of each chapter and reference them within the chapter.

 Because fraud is such an important aspect of auditing today, we've included a logo wherever we talk about its implications on the auditing process.

All of the text figures are now included on the Instructor's Resource CD for easy classroom presentations.

The great volume of coverage included in the text make it ideal as the basis for not only a basic auditing course, but also for a major portion of a second semester (or quarter) course included in either a four or five year program.

FEATURES OF THIS EDITION

This text includes a variety of features to enhance the learning experience:

Illustrative Cases

Actual business and accounting examples are used to illustrate key chapter concepts. The cases are boxed and appear throughout the text. New cases have been added for recent alleged audit failures. They are now subtitled for easy reference.

Illustrative Case
Employment with Clients

The situation in which audit clients hire audit firm personnel is difficult. On the one hand, it provides great professional opportunities for individuals who enter the public accounting profession. On the other, independence concerns have led to the restrictions presented in this section.

Questions were raised about the number of ex–Arthur Andersen employees hired by Enron Corporation prior to its collapse (see Chapter 1). Although both firms refused to disclose details, the positions and numbers of ex–Arthur Andersen employees hired by Enron seem significant. *The Wall Street Journal* reported that Enron executives who had previously worked with Arthur Andersen in auditing included its chief accounting officer, its chief financial officer, and the vice president of corporate development. The *Washington Post* indicated that, over the years Arthur

Andersen served as auditor, 86 employees left the firm and accepted positions at Enron.

In addition, questions arose as to the nature of the relationship between continuing Arthur Andersen employees and those of Enron. Again, *The Wall Street Journal* reported that Arthur Andersen auditors and consultants "shared in office birthdays, frequented lunch-time parties in a nearby park and participated in weekend fundraisers for charities. They even went on Enron employees' ski trips to Beaver Creek, Colorado." One Enron employee suggested that "People just thought they were Enron employees . . . they walked and talked the same way." Consistently, the *Washington Post* reported that the chief accounting officer was the Arthur Andersen partner's "regular golfing buddy," and that people at Enron referred to Andersen as "Enron Prep."

Industry Focus Cases

These cases use examples from specific industries to provide students with a detailed, "real world" illustration of points being emphasized in the text. These cases show the importance of having a thorough knowledge of the audit client's business and industry. Like the illustrative cases, these cases are boxed and appear throughout the text.

Focus on the Airline Industry
Electronic ticketing has become basic to the airline industry. Under these systems a passenger may book a flight over the telephone or by computer and be assigned a reservation number rather than being issued a physical ticket. Since no ticket is created until the passenger checks in for the flight, the auditor is limited in the extent to which he or she can examine "paper" support for transactions. Accordingly, audit procedures must be developed relating to the associated revenues and receivables. Auditors often choose to test the computer controls in such situations.

Illustrative Documents

Documents included in the various procedural chapters (Chapters 10 through 16) provide concise, realistic examples of the documents associated with the various transaction cycles. See the front endpapers of this text for the complete figure.

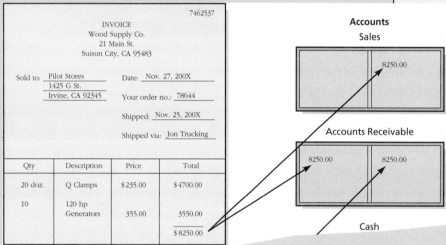

Audit Objectives

The use of Audit Objectives is a basic tool in audit program design. These help the auditor focus on the *reason* a procedure is being done and provide a check to assure that all management assertions in the financial statements are audited.

Learning Objective 6

Primary Audit Objective:

Valuation ☑

Primary Audit Objectives:

Existence ☑
Rights ☑

C. Perform Substantive Tests of Cash Transactions and Balances.

1. Obtain Analyses of Cash Balances and Reconcile to the General Ledger.

The auditors will prepare or obtain a schedule that lists all of the client's cash accounts. For cash in bank accounts, this schedule will typically list the bank, the account number, the account type, and the year-end balance per books. The auditors will trace and reconcile all accounts to the general ledger as necessary.

2. Send Standard Confirmation Forms to Financial Institutions to Verify Amounts on Deposit.

One of the objectives of the auditors' work on cash is to substantiate the existence of the amount of cash shown on the balance sheet. A direct approach to this objective is to confirm amounts on deposit and obtain or prepare reconciliations between bank statements and the accounting records.

Illustrations, Tables, and Flowcharts

These are used throughout to enhance and clarify the presentation. In this edition, flowcharts have been color-coded consistently to help students see and better understand the concepts.

Chapter Learning Objectives

These objectives provide a concise presentation of each chapter's most important concepts. They are now numbered and referenced in the chapter.

Chapter learning objectives

After studying this chapter, you should be able to:

LO1. Describe the sources and nature of cash.

LO2. Identify the auditors' objectives for the audit of cash.

LO3. Explain the nature of the cash receipts and disbursements cycles, and describe the fundamental controls over the business processes related to cash.

LO4. Assess inherent and fraud risks for cash.

LO5. Assess control risk and design typical tests of controls used by auditors to support the assessed levels of control risk for cash.

LO6. Explain how the auditors design substantive audit procedures and address the risks of material misstatement of cash.

Learning Objective 4

A. Consider the Inherent Risks of Cash, Including Fraud Risks.

Risks of material misstatement arise jointly from inherent risk and control risk. Most inherent risks relate to business risks faced by the client's management. In the area of cash and financial investments, management is particularly concerned with business risks related to the possible theft of these liquid assets. This is also a significant concern of the auditors as most misstatements of assets involve overstatement.

In addition to concerns about the overstatement of cash, auditors are aware that cash may have been improperly abstracted during the period, even though the year-end cash may be properly stated. To distinguish between the situations, assume that the client's balance sheet

---

Key Terms Introduced or Emphasized in the Chapter

This is a glossary of each chapter's most important terms. The terms are in color within the chapter and are defined at the end of the chapter. Placing the definitions at the end of each chapter allows the student to quickly find the meaning of unfamiliar terms while reading the material. The glossary also serves as an excellent review tool and helps the student see how well he or she understands the major ideas presented.

END-OF-CHAPTER MATERIAL

The questions, problems, case material, and simulation exercises at the end of each chapter are divided as follows: Review Questions; Questions Requiring Analysis; Multiple Choice Questions; Problems; In-Class Team Cases; Ethics Cases; Research and Discussion Cases; and CPA Simulations (selected chapters only). Appendixes to Chapters 6, 11, 14, and 16 include the case material and exercises for the Keystone Computers & Networks, Inc., illustrative audit case.

Review Questions

The Review Questions are closely related to the material in the chapter and provide a convenient means of determining whether students have grasped the major concepts and details contained in that chapter.

Questions Requiring Analysis

The Questions Requiring Analysis require thoughtful consideration of a realistic auditing situation and the application of professional standards. A number of these questions are taken from CPA and CIA examinations, and others describe actual practice situations. These questions, which are generally shorter than the problems, tend to stress value judgments and conflicting opinions.

Multiple Choice Questions

In this edition, we have highlighted Multiple Choice Questions by grouping them in a separate section. As are the Questions Requiring Analysis, many of these questions are drawn from CPA and CIA examinations.

Problems

Many of the Problems are drawn from CPA and CIA examinations. In selecting these problems, special consideration was given to ones appearing in recent professional exams. However, older questions are included when they are superior to others available.

Research and Discussion Cases

These cases involve controversial situations that do not lend themselves to clear-cut answers. Students are required to research appropriate professional literature and to then apply critical thinking skills to logically formulate and justify their personal positions on the issues involved in each case. The cases acquaint students with the professional literature, develop research and communication skills required on the new CPA exam, and demonstrate that several diverse, yet defensible, positions may be argued persuasively in a given situation.

Research and Discussion Case

4–41. You are a partner in the Denver office of a national public accounting firm. During the audit of Mountain Resources, you learn that this audit client is negotiating to sell some of its unproved oil and gas properties to SuperFund, a large investment company. SuperFund is an audit client of your New York office.

Mountain Resources acquired these properties several years ago at a cost of $15 million. The company drilled several exploratory wells but found no developable resources. Last year, you and Mountain Resources agreed that the value of these unproved properties had been "impaired" as defined in paragraph 28 of *FASB 19*. The company wrote the carrying value of the properties down to an estimated realizable value of $9 million and recognized a $6 million loss. You concurred with this treatment and issued an unqualified auditors' report on the company's financial statements.

Illustrative Audit Case Exercises

These exercises all pertain to the text's updated continuing integrated case, **Keystone Computers & Networks, Inc.** While each exercise may "stand alone," when used in combination, these case exercises take the student from the original planning of an audit through the testing of controls, substantive testing, and accumulation and analysis of uncorrected misstatements. Exercises are included in Chapters 6, 11, 14, and 16.

Appendix 6C

Illustrative Audit Case: Keystone Computers & Networks, Inc.

Part I: Audit Planning

The Keystone Computers & Networks, Inc. (KCN) case is used throughout the text to illustrate audit procedures and methodology. KCN is a company that sells and installs microcomputers and networking software to business customers. The CPA firm of Adams, Barnes & Co. has audited the financial statements of KCN for the past three years. This part of the case illustrates selective audit planning working papers prepared by the staff of Adams, Barnes & Co. for this year's audit. You should read through the information to obtain an understanding of the nature of the information that is important to planning an audit engagement. The working papers include:

Spreadsheet Templates

Spreadsheet templates are available on the text's Web site to be used in conjunction with selected audit case exercises. The exercises with templates are identified by a logo in the margin.

6C–4.   A partially completed analytical ratios working paper for Keystone Computers & Networks, Inc., is presented on page 218.

Required: a. Complete the working paper by computing the financial ratios for 20X5.

    b. After completing part (*a*), review the ratios and identify financial statement accounts that should be investigated because the related ratios are not comparable to prior-year ratios and industry averages.
    c. For each account identified in part (*b*), list potential reasons for the unexpected account balances and related ratios.

Ethics Cases

Ethics Cases allow the instructor to discuss ethical issues in an integrated manner throughout the course. The cases present a series of situations which result in ethical dilemmas of the type that beginning accountants may expect to encounter in practice. These cases are included in selected chapters.

Ethics Case   6–42.   Tammy Potter, a new partner with the regional CPA firm of Tower & Tower, was recently appointed to the board of directors of a local civic organization. The chairman of the board of the civic organization is Lewis Edmond, who is also the owner of a real estate development firm, Tierra Corporation.

Potter was quite excited when Edmond indicated that his corporation needed an audit, and he wished to discuss the matter with her. During the discussion, Potter was told that Tierra Corporation needed the audit to obtain a substantial amount of additional financing to acquire another company. Presently, Tierra Corporation is successful, profitable, and committed to growth. The audit fee for the engagement should be substantial.

In-Class Team Cases

These cases are meant to be solved in class either by teams of students or, if the instructor prefers, by individuals. They help provide the student with an active learning environment in which to apply key concepts included in each chapter.

In-Class Team Case

5–56. Houseco, an audit client of Jones, CPA, for the past five years, is a manufacturer of various household products. Approximately four years ago Houseco developed a better toaster than had been available and sales took off, especially during the most recent two years, 20X7 and 20X8. Currently, the company controls approximately 25 percent of the toaster market in the United States. In addition, the company manufactures other products, including vacuum cleaners, floor polishers, and electric fondue pots.

Much of the increased sales performance is due to Donald Skaldon, who became the chief executive officer in 20X4. Donald and several other officers were able to accomplish a leveraged stock buyout in 20X6. This seems to have worked out very well since Donald suggests that his net worth grew from less than $300,000 to well over $5 million due to increases in the value of the common stock he holds in the company. He is also excited since the company's unaudited results show earnings per share of $1.21, one cent more than the most optimistic analysts had projected. He points out to Jones that sales are up over 38 percent compared to the previous year and net income has increased by 54 percent. All is well.

Internet Assignments

Internet assignments are included among the end-of-chapter problem material for selected chapters. These assignments require students to use the *Internet* to do audit research and are identified with a logo in the margin.

6–33. SEC filings of certain public companies can be accessed from EDGAR (Electronic Data Gathering and Retrieval System), which has the following Internet address:

www.sec.gov/edgar.shtml.

Required:

a. Use EDGAR to locate a company in the software industry.

b. Access the latest Form 10-K for the company and read "Management's Discussion and Analysis" from Form 10-K.

c. Describe four significant business risks of the company as described in "Management's Discussion and Analysis."

SUPPLEMENTS

Web Site

Online Learning Center (OLC)
(www.mhhe.com/whittington15e)

The text Web site includes links to various sites referenced in the text and updates that reflect changes in auditing standards that have occurred subsequent to publication of the text. The student site includes interactive quizzes and solutions for each chapter to allow them to measure their mastery of key concepts. It also contains PowerPoint slides, Audit Simulations, and the Keystone Computers & Networks Case spreadsheets. The instructor site contains the text's downloadable supplements.

Study Guide

A Study Guide (ISBN 0073127612), written by the text's authors, enables students to review text material and to test their understanding. The guide includes a summary of each chapter's highlights and an abundance of objective questions and exercises. Since the guide includes answers to the questions and exercises, it provides immediate feedback to students.

Instructor's Resource CD-ROM

The Instructor's Resource CD-ROM (ISBN 0073127620) allows you to access the text's ancillary materials in one convenient CD. This includes the Instructor's Lecture Guide, the Solutions Manual, Test Bank, Computerized Test Bank, Spreadsheets, all text figures, and PowerPoint presentations.

Instructor's Lecture Guide and Solutions Manual

Our Instructor's Lecture Guide includes topical outlines of each chapter, the authors' comments on each chapter, and numerous instructional aids. A Solutions Manual includes thorough and up-to-date solutions to the text's questions, problems, and exercises. These are included on the Instructor's Resource CD and on the text's Web site.

Test Bank

The Test Bank includes both original questions and problems, and questions adapted from various professional examinations. It has been significantly expanded in this edition by the inclusion of approximately 180 additional multiple-choice and essay-type questions. This is included on the Instructor's Resource CD.

Computerized Test Bank

McGraw-Hill's EZ Test is a flexible and easy-to-use electronic testing program. The program allows instructors to create tests from book specific items. It accommodates a wide range of question types and instructors may add their own questions. Multiple versions of the test can be created and any test can be exported for use with course management systems such as WebCT, BlackBoard or PageOut. EZ Test Online is a new service and gives you a place to easily administer your EZ Test created exams and quizzes online. The program is available for Windows and Macintosh environments.

PowerPoint Presentations

PowerPoint presentations are available to assist in classroom presentations and are located on the Web site and Instructor's Resource CD.

Online Course Management
WebCT, eCollege, and Blackboard

We offer Principles of Auditing content for complete online courses. You can customize the Online Learning Center content and author your own course materials. No matter which online course solution you choose, you can count on the highest level of support.

REFERENCES TO AUTHORITATIVE SOURCES

Numerous references are made to the pronouncements of the American Institute of Certified Public Accountants (AICPA), the Institute of Internal Auditors (IIA), the Financial Accounting Standards Board (FASB), the Governmental Accounting Standards Board (GASB), the Public Company Accounting Oversight Board (PCAOB), and the Securities and Exchange Commission (SEC). Special attention is given to the *Code of Professional Conduct, Statements on Standards for Accounting and Review Services, Statements on Standards for Attestation Engagements, Statements on Auditing Standards,* and guidelines developed for other types of assurance services. The cooperation of the AICPA and the IIA in permitting the use of their published materials and of questions from the CPA and CIA examinations brings to the text an element of authority not otherwise available.

Acknowledgements

The work of Donald A. Schwartz, JD, CPA, of National University, in developing the software supplement for the illustrative audit case exercises is especially appreciated. We thank Norwood Jackson (U.S. Office of Management and Budget) for his guidance on compliance auditing.

We express our sincere thanks to the following professors who provided extensive reviews for the fifteenth edition:

Joseph Aubert
Bemidji State University

Gary Bridges
University of Texas at San Antonio

Laurel Cobb
St. Leo University

Martha Doran
San Diego State University

Hans Dykxhoorn
Western Michigan University

Thomas English
Boise State University

Mary Beth Goodrich
University of Texas at Dallas

William Huffman
Missouri Southern State University

Russell Jacques
St. Leo University

Pamela Legner
College of DuPage

Kathy MacLellan

Michael Milliren
Milwaukee Area Technical College

Marshall Pitman
University of Texas at San Antonio

Abe Qastin
Lakeland College

Alan Reinstein
Wayne State University

Shirley Rockel
Iowa Wesleyan College

Michael Trebesh
Alma College

Valerie Trott
Duquesne University

Allan Unseth
Norfolk State University

Donna Whitten
Purdue University North Central

Jian Zhang
Long Beach State University

We also express our appreciation to the many people who reviewed the preceding edition and offered helpful suggestions. They include:

Jeffrey J. Archambault
Marshall University

Barbara Arel
Arizona State University

Anthony T. Barbera
SUNY College at Old Westbury

Michael Broihahn
Barry University

Al Case
Southern Oregon University

John Corless
California State University at Sacramento

Thomas English
Boise State University

Lori R. Fuller
University of Delaware

Jongsoo Han
Rutgers University at Camden

Theresa Hrncir
Southeastern Oklahoma State University

Perry Moore
Lipscomb University

Margaret P. Pollard
American River College

Julie Ann Gardner Treloar
UCLA

Patricia Villafana
College of St. Catherine

Judith C. Walo
Central Connecticut State University

Finally, we would like to thank the staff at McGraw-Hill/Irwin: Brent Gordon, Editorial Director; Stewart Mattson, Publisher; Tim Vertovec, Executive Editor; Gail Korosa, Managing Developmental Editor; Marc Chernoff, Marketing Manager; Elizabeth Mavetz, Media Producer; Dana Pauley, Project Manager; Gina Hangos, Production Supervisor; Kami Carter, Designer; Rose Range, Senior Media Project Manager; and Carol Loreth, Senior Supplement Producer.

O. Ray Whittington

Kurt Pany

Brief Contents

Contents

Chapter 7
Internal Control 223

Chapter 8
Consideration of Internal Control in an
Information Technology Environment 269

Chapter 15
Debt and Equity Capital   561

Chapter 16
Auditing Operations and Completing
the Audit   587

Chapter 17
Auditors' Reports   623

Chapter 18
Integrated Audits of Public Companies   657

Chapter 19
Additional Assurance Services: Historical Financial Information   687

Chapter 20
Additional Assurance Services: Other Information   713

Chapter 21
Internal, Operational, and Compliance Auditing   737

Chapter 1

The Role of the Public Accountant in the American Economy

Chapter learning objectives

After studying this chapter, you should be able to:

LO1. Describe the nature of assurance services.

LO2. Identify assurance services that involve attestation.

LO3. Describe the nature of financial statement audits.

LO4. Explain why audits are demanded by society.

LO5. Describe how the credibility of the accounting profession was affected by the large number of companies reporting accounting irregularities in the beginning of this century.

LO6. Contrast the various types of audits and types of auditors.

LO7. Explain the regulatory process for auditors of public companies and auditors of nonpublic companies.

LO8. Describe how public accounting firms are typically organized and the responsibilities of auditors at the various levels in the organization.

Dependable information is essential to the very existence of our society. The investor making a decision to buy or sell securities, the banker deciding whether to approve a loan, the government in obtaining revenue based on income tax returns—all are relying upon information provided by others. In many of these situations, the goals of the providers of information run directly counter to those of the users of the information. Implicit in this line of reasoning is recognition of the social need for independent public accountants—individuals of professional competence and integrity who can tell us whether the information that we use constitutes a fair picture of what is really going on.

Our primary purpose in this chapter is to make clear the nature of independent audits and the accounting profession. We begin with a discussion of the broader concept of assurance services. Next, we describe those assurance services that involve attestation, of which audits of financial statements are an important type. Another purpose of this chapter is to summarize the influence exerted on the public accounting profession by the American Institute of Certified Public Accountants (AICPA), the Financial Accounting Standards Board (FASB), the Governmental Accounting Standards Board (GASB), the Federal Accounting Standards Advisory Board (FASAB), the Public Company Accounting Oversight Board (PCAOB), and the Securities and Exchange Commission (SEC). We will also explore various types of audits and note the impact of the Institute of Internal Auditors (IIA) and the General Accounting Office (GAO). Finally, we will examine other types of professional services and the nature and organization of public accounting firms.

What Are Assurance Services?

The name **assurance services** is used to describe the broad range of information enhancement services that are provided by certified public accountants (CPAs). In general, assurance services consist of two types—those that increase the reliability of information and those that involve putting information in a form or context that facilitates decision making. In this chapter we will focus on the first type—audit and assurance services that involve reliability enhancement.

The Attest Function

A major subset of assurance services is called *attestation services*. To attest to information means to provide assurance as to its reliability. More formally, an **attest engagement** is one in which:

> a practitioner is engaged to issue or does issue an examination, a review, or an agreed-upon procedures report on subject matter or an assertion about subject matter that is the responsibility of another party (e.g., management).

CPAs attest to many types of subject matter (or assertions about subject matter), including financial forecasts, internal control, compliance with laws and regulations, and advertising claims.

Figure 1.1 describes the attest function, which begins with the subject matter that is the responsibility of another party, usually management. As an example, consider the situation in which the CPAs attest to a company's internal control over financial reporting. The subject matter of this engagement is internal control over financial reporting—internal control is the responsibility of management. The CPAs may be engaged to report directly on the internal control and express an opinion on whether a company's internal control over financial reporting follows certain *standards* (benchmarks). Alternatively, they may report on an assertion made by management that the company's internal control follows certain standards. In this second case the audit report would include an opinion on whether management's **assertion** is accurate. Management of public companies are now required to include in their annual reports an assertion about the effectiveness of internal control over financial reporting and to engage their auditors to attest to both the assertion and the effectiveness of internal control. This form of reporting is described in detail in Chapters 7 and 18.

Illustrative Case
The Value of Attest Services

CPAs have attested that a supermarket chain in Phoenix has the lowest overall prices in that city. The CPAs selected a sample of approximately 1,000 items and compared the prices to those of the various other major supermarkets.

Representatives of the supermarket chain stated that the credibility added by the CPAs has helped to convince consumers that the chain's prices are indeed the lowest.

What standards must the subject matter follow? The standards are those established or developed by groups composed of experts and are referred to as **suitable criteria.** In an internal control engagement, the standards may be those that have been established by a committee of experts on internal control. In a financial statement audit, the standards may be **generally accepted accounting principles (GAAP);** the CPAs perform an audit to gather sufficient evidence to issue their audit report which attests to the fairness of the financial statements (the subject matter).

The definition of an attest engagement refers to reports arising from three forms of engagements—examinations, reviews, and the performance of agreed-upon procedures. An **examination,** referred to as an *audit* when it involves historical financial statements, provides the highest form of assurance that CPAs provide. In an examination the CPAs select from

FIGURE 1.1   The Attest Function

*If the criteria are not generally available to the users, they should be presented in the CPA's report or management's presentation.

FIGURE 1.2   **Forms of Attestation** *—These are all assurance services* (handwritten)

Type of Engagement	Level of Assurance Provided	Nature of the Report	Procedures
Examination*	High; provides reasonable assurance	Expresses an opinion	Select from all available procedures any combination that can limit attestation risk to an appropriately low level
Review	Moderate or limited assurance	Expresses negative assurance	Generally limited to inquiry and analytical procedures
Agreed-upon procedures	Varies with nature and extent of the procedures performed	States findings	Procedures agreed upon with the specified user or users

*Referred to as an *audit* when the subject matter is historical financial statements.

FIGURE 1.3
Relationships among Assurance Services, Attestation Services, and Nonassurance Services

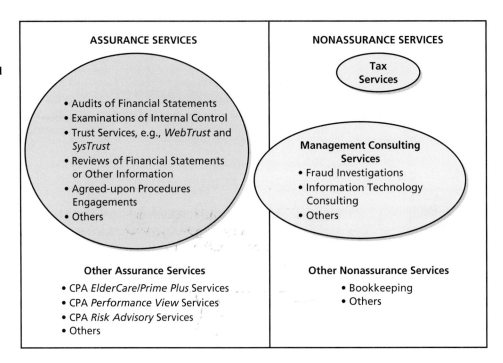

all available evidence a combination that limits to a *low level* the risk of undetected misstatement and provides *reasonable assurance* that the subject matter (or assertion) is materially correct. A **review** is substantially lesser in scope of procedures than an examination and is designed to lend only a limited degree of assurance—a moderate risk of misstatement remains. If an examination or review does not meet the client's needs, the CPAs and specified user or users of the information may mutually decide on specific agreed-upon procedures that the CPAs will perform. An **agreed-upon procedures engagement** results in a report by the CPAs that describes those procedures and their findings. Figure 1.2 summarizes the three forms of attestation engagements.

Assurance and Nonassurance Services

It is important to understand the relationships among the range of services that are offered by CPAs, because different professional standards apply to each type of service. Figure 1.3 illustrates the universe of services that may be offered by CPAs and the relationships among these services. As shown, CPAs provide both assurance and nonassurance services but a few, specifically of the management consulting type, overlap. Certain management consulting services have assurance aspects. Later in this chapter, we will provide a brief description of the prevalent types of nonassurance services offered by CPA firms.

Figure 1.3 also illustrates that attestation services are only a portion of the assurance services that are offered by CPAs. A few examples of assurance services that do not involve attestation include:

- CPA *ElderCare/Prime Plus* services—providing assurance to individuals that their elderly family members' needs are being met by institutions and other professionals.
- CPA *Performance View*—assisting in the development of performance measurement systems, or providing assurance about the effectiveness of the systems.
- CPA *Risk Advisory* services—assisting in the development of enterprise risk management systems, or providing assurance about the effectiveness of the systems.

Throughout the first 17 chapters of this textbook, we will focus primarily on the attest function as it relates to the audit of financial statements. Other types of attestation and assurance services are discussed in Chapters 18 through 21.

Financial Statement Audits

Learning Objective 3

In a financial statement audit, the auditors undertake to gather evidence and provide a high level of assurance that the financial statements follow generally accepted accounting principles, or some other appropriate basis of accounting. An audit involves searching and verifying the accounting records and examining other evidence supporting the financial statements. By obtaining an understanding of the company's internal control, inspecting documents, observing assets, making inquiries within and outside the company, and performing other auditing procedures, the auditors will gather the evidence necessary to issue an audit report. That audit report states that it is the auditors' opinion that the financial statements follow generally accepted accounting principles. The flowchart in Figure 1.4 illustrates an audit of financial statements.

The evidence gathered by the auditors focuses on whether the financial statements are presented in accordance with generally accepted accounting principles. More specifically, an audit addresses management's assertions that the assets listed in the balance sheet really exist,

FIGURE 1.4
Audit of Financial Statements

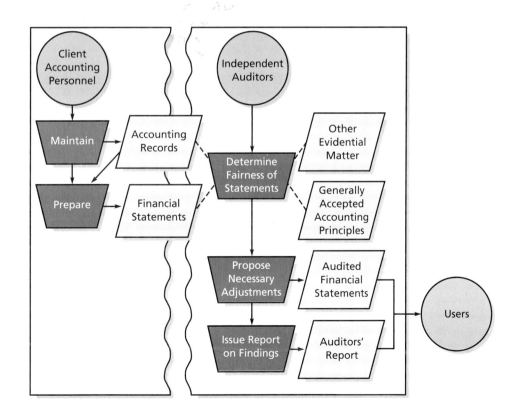

that the company has title (rights) to the assets, and that the valuations assigned to the assets have been established in conformity with generally accepted accounting principles. Evidence is gathered to show that the balance sheet contains *all the liabilities* of the company; otherwise the balance sheet might be grossly misleading because certain important liabilities had been accidentally or deliberately omitted. Similarly, the auditors gather evidence about the income statement. They demand evidence that the reported sales really occurred, that the goods were actually shipped to customers, and that the recorded costs and expenses are applicable to the current period and that all expenses have been recognized. Finally, the auditors consider whether the financial statement amounts are accurate, properly classified and summarized, and whether the notes are informative and complete. Only if sufficient evidence is gathered in support of all these significant assertions can the auditors provide an opinion on whether the financial statements are presented in accordance with generally accepted accounting principles.

The procedures composing an audit vary considerably from one engagement to the next. Many of the procedures appropriate to the audit of a small retail store would not be appropriate for the audit of a giant corporation such as General Motors. Auditors perform audits of all types of businesses, and of governmental and nonprofit organizations as well. Banks and breweries, factories and stores, colleges and churches, school districts and labor unions—all are regularly visited by auditors. The selection of the procedures best suited to each audit requires the exercise of professional skill and judgment.

What Creates the Demand for Audits?

Learning Objective 4

Reliable accounting and financial reporting aid society in allocating resources in an efficient manner. A primary goal is to allocate limited capital resources to the production of those goods and services for which demand is great. Economic resources are attracted to the industries, the geographic areas, and the organizational entities that are shown by financial measurements to be capable of using the resources to the best advantage. Inadequate accounting and reporting, on the other hand, conceal waste and inefficiency, thereby preventing an efficient allocation of economic resources.

The contribution of the independent auditor is to provide *credibility* to information. Credibility, in this usage, means that the information can be believed; that is, it can be relied upon by outsiders, such as stockholders, creditors, government regulators, customers, and other interested third parties. These third parties use the information to make various economic decisions, such as decisions about whether to invest in the organization.

Economic decisions are made under conditions of uncertainty; there is always a risk that the decision maker will select the wrong alternative and incur a significant loss. The credibility added to the information by auditors actually reduces the decision maker's risk. To be more precise, the auditors reduce **information risk,** which is the risk that the financial information used to make a decision is materially misstated.

Audited financial statements are the accepted means by which business corporations report their operating results and financial position. The word *audited,* when applied to financial statements, means that the balance sheet and the statements of income, retained earnings, and cash flows are accompanied by an audit report prepared by independent public accountants, expressing their professional opinion as to the fairness of the company's financial statements.

Financial statements prepared by management and transmitted to outsiders without first being audited by independent accountants leave a credibility gap. In reporting on its own administration of the business, management can hardly be expected to be entirely impartial and unbiased, any more than a football coach could be expected to serve as both coach and referee in the same game. Independent auditors have no material personal or financial interest in the business; their reports can be expected to be impartial and free from bias.

Unaudited financial statements may have been honestly, but carelessly, prepared. Liabilities may have been overlooked and omitted from the balance sheet. Assets may have been overstated as a result of arithmetical errors or due to a lack of knowledge of generally accepted accounting principles. Net income may have been exaggerated because expenses were capitalized or because sales transactions were recorded in advance of delivery dates.

Finally, there is the possibility that unaudited financial statements have been deliberately falsified in order to conceal theft and fraud or as a means of inducing the reader to invest in the business or to extend credit. Although deliberate falsification of financial statements is not common, it does occur and can cause devastating losses to persons who make decisions based upon such misleading statements.

For all these reasons (accidental errors, lack of knowledge of accounting principles, unintentional bias, and deliberate falsification), financial statements may depart from generally accepted accounting principles. Audits provide users with assurance that the financial statements do not materially depart from generally accepted accounting principles.

Illustrating the Demand for Auditing

A decision by a bank loan officer about whether to make a loan to a business can be used to illustrate the demand for auditing. Since the bank's objective in making the loan is to earn an appropriate rate of interest and to collect the principal of the loan at maturity, the loan officer is making two related decisions: (1) whether to make the loan at all, and (2) what rate of interest adequately compensates the bank for the level of risk assumed. The loan officer will make these decisions based on a careful study of the company's financial statements along with other information. The risk assumed by the bank related to this customer has two aspects:[1]

1. **Business risk**—the risk associated with a company's survival and profitability. This includes, for example, the risk that the company will not be able to make the interest payments and repay the principal of the loan because of economic conditions or poor management decisions. Business risk is assessed by considering factors such as the financial position of the company, the nature of its operations, the characteristics of the industry in which it operates, and the quality and integrity of its management.

2. **Information risk**—the risk that the information used to assess business risk is not accurate. Information risk includes the possibility that the financial statements might contain material departures from generally accepted accounting principles.

While auditing normally has only a limited effect on a company's business risk,[2] it can significantly affect the level of information risk. If the loan officer has assurance from the auditors that the company's financial statements are prepared in accordance with generally accepted accounting principles, he or she will have more confidence in his or her assessment of business risk. In addition, periodic audits performed after the loan has been made provide the loan officer with a way of monitoring management performance and compliance with the various loan provisions. By reducing information risk, the auditors reduce the overall risk to the bank; the loan officer is more likely to make the loan to the company and at a lower rate of interest. Therefore, management of the company has an incentive to provide audited financial statements to the loan officer to obtain the loan and to get the best possible interest rate.

A major portion of our economy is characterized by large corporate organizations that have gathered capital from millions of investors and that control economic resources spread throughout the country or even throughout the world. Top management in the corporate headquarters is often remote from the operations of company plants and branches and must rely on financial statements and other reports to control the corporation's resources. In brief, the decision makers in a large corporation cannot obtain much information on a firsthand basis. They must rely on information provided by lower-level management, and this fact creates a risk of receiving unreliable information. As in the case of the loan officer, auditing can reduce the risk of poor management decisions by reducing information risk and by monitoring the performance of management at every level within the organization.

The millions of individuals who have entrusted their savings to corporations by investing in securities rely upon annual and quarterly financial statements for investment decisions and for assurance that their invested funds are being used honestly and efficiently. Even greater numbers of people entrust their savings to banks, insurance companies, and pension funds, which in turn invest the money in corporate securities. Thus, directly or indirectly, almost everyone

---

[1] The banker also assumes *interest rate risk,* which varies depending on the terms of the loan. Interest rate risk reflects the risk due to potential changes in the "risk free" interest rate.

[2] Possible effects of an audit on business risk include modifications of management's operating decisions either due to knowledge that an audit will be performed or due to operating recommendations made by auditors. Accordingly, an audit *may* reduce business risk.

has a financial stake in corporate enterprises, and the public interest demands prompt, *reliable* financial reporting on the operations and the financial health of publicly owned corporations.

Various regulatory agencies also demand audit services. As an example, consider the income tax reporting system in our country. The information provided on tax returns is provided by taxpayers and may be biased because of the self-interest of the providers. The government attempts to compensate for this inherent weakness through verification by audits carried out by agents of the Internal Revenue Service.

Major Auditing Developments of the 20th Century

Although the objectives and concepts that guide present-day audits were almost unknown in the early years of the 20th century, audits of one type or another have been performed throughout the recorded history of commerce and government finance. The original meaning of the word *auditor* was "one who hears" and was appropriate to the era during which governmental accounting records were approved only after a public reading in which the accounts were read aloud. From medieval times on through the Industrial Revolution, audits were performed to determine whether persons in positions of official responsibility in government and commerce were acting and reporting in an honest manner.

During the Industrial Revolution, as manufacturing concerns grew in size, their owners began to use the services of hired managers. With this separation of the ownership and management groups, the absentee owners turned increasingly to auditors to protect themselves against the danger of unintentional errors as well as fraud committed by managers and employees. Bankers were the primary outside users of financial reports (usually only balance sheets), and they were also concerned with whether the reports were distorted by errors or fraud. Before 1900, consistent with this primary objective to detect errors and fraud, audits often included a study of all, or almost all, recorded transactions.

In the first half of the 20th century, the direction of audit work tended to move away from fraud detection toward a new goal of determining whether financial statements gave a full and fair picture of financial position, operating results, and changes in financial position. This shift in emphasis was a response to the increasing number of shareholders and the corresponding increased size of corporate entities. In addition to the new shareholders, auditors became more responsible to governmental agencies, stock exchanges representing these new investors, as well as to other parties who might rely upon the financial information. No longer were bankers the only important outside users of audited financial data. The fairness of reported earnings became of prime importance.

As large-scale corporate entities developed rapidly in both Great Britain and the United States, auditors began to sample selected transactions, rather than study all transactions. Auditors and business managers gradually came to accept the proposition that careful examination of relatively few selected transactions would give a cost-effective, reliable indication of the accuracy of other similar transactions.

In addition to sampling, auditors became aware of the importance of effective internal control. A company's internal control consists of the policies and procedures established to provide reasonable assurance that the objectives of the company will be achieved, including the objective of preparing accurate financial statements. Auditors found that by studying the client's internal control they could identify areas of strength as well as of weakness. *The stronger the internal control, the less testing of financial statement account balances required by the auditors.* For any significant account or any phase of financial operations in which controls were weak, the auditors expanded the nature and extent of their tests of the account balance.

With the increased reliance upon sampling and internal control, professional standards began to emphasize limitations on auditors' ability to detect **fraud.** The profession recognized that audits designed to discover fraud would be too costly. Good internal control and surety bonds were recognized as better fraud protection techniques than audits.

Beginning in the 1960s, the detection of large-scale fraud assumed a larger role in the audit process. Professional standards, which used the term *irregularities* in place of fraud, described fraudulent financial reporting and misappropriation of assets. This shift in emphasis to taking a greater responsibility for the detection of fraud resulted from (1) a dramatic increase in congressional pressure to assume more responsibility for large-scale frauds, (2) a number of successful lawsuits claiming that management fraud had improperly gone undetected by the independent auditors, and (3) a belief by public accountants that audits should be expected to detect *material* fraud.

As a result of a number of instances of fraudulent financial reporting, the major accounting organizations[3] sponsored the *National Commission on Fraudulent Financial Reporting* (the Treadway Commission) to study the causes of fraudulent reporting and make recommendations to reduce its incidence. The commission's final report, which was issued in 1987, made a number of recommendations for auditors, public companies, regulators, and educators. Many of the recommendations for auditors were enacted by the AICPA in a group of *Statements on Auditing Standards* known as the *expectation gap* standards. The commission's recommendations about internal control led to the development of an internal control framework, titled *Internal Control—Integrated Framework,* to be used to evaluate the internal control of an organization. The development of these internal control criteria increased the demand for attestation by auditors to the effectiveness of internal control. As an example, the Federal Deposit Insurance Corporation (FDIC) Improvement Act of 1991 was passed requiring management of large financial institutions to engage CPAs to attest to the effectiveness of assertions by management about the effectiveness of the institution's controls over financial reporting.

In the late 1980s and early 1990s, the billions of dollars in federal funds that were required to "bail out" the savings and loan industry caused a movement toward increased regulation of federally insured financial institutions. Congress and regulatory agencies believed that the key to preventing such problems was enacting effective laws and regulations and requiring reports by auditors on compliance with provisions of these laws and regulations. An important example of this type of legislation is the FDIC Improvement Act of 1991. This law also requires management of large financial institutions to engage its CPAs to attest to management's assertion about the institution's compliance with laws and regulations related to the safety and soundness of the institution.

In 1996, in response to a continuing expectation gap between user demands and auditor performance, the AICPA issued guidance to auditors requiring an explicit assessment of the risk of material misstatement in financial statements due to **fraud** on all audits. In 2002, this auditing standard was replaced with an even more stringent standard that requires auditors to definitively design procedures to address the risk of management fraud.

A factor overlaying a number of changes has been fast-paced changes in business technology. From small computer accounting systems to large mainframe computers to networked enterprise-wide information systems to the use of the Internet to initiate and process transactions, auditing methods have had to adapt. While technology has not changed the basic objective of the financial statement audit, it has resulted in the need to develop innovative computer testing techniques and tools to assure audit effectiveness.

Many of the ideas mentioned in this brief historical sketch of the development of auditing will be analyzed in detail in later sections of this book. Our purpose at this point is merely to orient you with a quick overall look at some of the major auditing developments of the 20th century. These many developments, while significant, may be overshadowed by what has and will occur in the 21st century as the accounting profession faces the most significant challenges to its viability.

The Accounting Profession's Credibility Crisis

In 2000, at the request of the Securities and Exchange Commission, the profession established the Panel on Audit Effectiveness. The panel was charged with the responsibility to review and evaluate how independent audits of financial statements are performed and to assess whether recent trends in audit practices serve the public interest. Recommendations from the panel resulted in changes in auditing standards related to the detection of fraud, documentation of audit evidence and judgments, risk assessments, and the linkage of audit procedures to audit risks. However, even before these changes in audit requirements could be implemented,

---

[3] The sponsoring organizations included the American Institute of Certified Public Accountants, the American Accounting Association, the Financial Executives Institute, the Institute of Internal Auditors, and the Institute of Management Accountants.

Illustrative Case
Massive Fraud at WorldCom

WorldCom reported over $11 billion in accounting irregularities, completely eliminating the company's previously reported profits for all of 2000 and 2001 and causing the company to declare bankruptcy. At one time WorldCom had reported total assets in excess of $100 billion and a market value in excess of $150 billion, making it the largest bankruptcy in American history.

a series of events in the capital markets produced a chain reaction that caused unprecedented reforms in the accounting profession.

Learning Objective 5

In December 2001 Enron Corporation filed for bankruptcy shortly after acknowledging that accounting irregularities had been used to significantly inflate earnings in the current and preceding years. Shortly thereafter, it was disclosed that WorldCom had used accounting fraud to significantly overstate its reported income. In addition to these two very visible cases, a record number of public companies restated prior-period financial statements, and almost weekly the Securities and Exchange Commission announced a new investigation into another company's accounting practices. Investor uncertainty about the reliability of financial statements rocked an already weak financial market during the latter part of 2001 and the first half of 2002. It brought into question the effectiveness of financial statement audits and created a crisis of credibility for the accounting profession. More significantly, the highly publicized conviction of Andersen LLP, one of the then "Big 5" accounting firms, on charges of destruction of documents related to the Enron case brought into question the ethical principles of the public accounting profession.

These events drew quick responses from a number of congressional committees, the SEC, and the U.S. Justice Department, as they began investigating corporate management and the accounting profession. By the summer of 2002, Congress had passed the **Sarbanes-Oxley Act of 2002,** which included a set of reforms toughening penalties for corporate fraud, restricting the types of consulting CPAs may perform for audit clients, and creating the Public Company Accounting Oversight Board (PCAOB) to oversee the accounting profession. The PCAOB, which has broad powers to develop and enforce standards for public accounting firms that audit public companies, will be described in more detail later in this chapter.

Establishment of the PCAOB eliminated a significant portion of the accounting profession's system of self-regulation. It is clear that regulation of the profession, at least with respect to the audit of public companies, is no longer primarily in the hands of the accounting profession.

Types of Audits

Audits are often viewed as falling into three major categories: (1) financial audits, (2) compliance audits, and (3) operational audits. In addition, the Sarbanes-Oxley Act requires an integrated audit for public companies.

Learning Objective 6

Financial Audits

A **financial audit** is an audit of the financial statements of an entity. An **audit of financial statements** ordinarily covers the balance sheet and the related statements of income, retained earnings, and cash flows. The goal is to determine whether these statements have been prepared in conformity with generally accepted accounting principles. Financial statement audits are normally performed by firms of certified public accountants; users of auditors' reports include management, investors, bankers, creditors, financial analysts, and government agencies. However, internal auditors often perform financial audits of departments or business segments.

Compliance Audits

The performance of a **compliance audit** is dependent upon the existence of verifiable data and of recognized criteria or standards, such as established laws and regulations, or an organization's policies and procedures. A familiar example is the audit of an income tax return by an auditor of the Internal Revenue Service (IRS). Such audits seek to determine whether a tax return is in compliance with tax laws and IRS regulations. The findings of the IRS auditors are transmitted to the taxpayer by means of the IRS auditor's report.

Another example of a compliance audit is the periodic bank examination by bank examiners employed by the Federal Deposit Insurance Corporation and the state banking departments. These audits measure compliance with banking laws and regulations and with traditional standards of sound banking practice.

Internal auditors perform audits of compliance with internal controls, other company policies and procedures, and applicable laws and regulations. Internal audit departments often are involved with documenting and testing internal control for management's reports required by the Sarbanes-Oxley Act.

Finally, many state and local governmental entities and nonprofit organizations that receive financial assistance from the federal government must arrange for compliance audits under the Single Audit Act or OMB Circular A–133. Such audits are designed to determine whether the financial assistance is spent in accordance with applicable laws and regulations. Compliance audits are described in greater detail in Chapter 21.

Operational Audits

An **operational audit** is a study of a specific unit of an organization for the purpose of measuring its performance. The operations of the receiving department of a manufacturing company, for example, may be evaluated in terms of its *effectiveness,* that is, its success in meeting its stated goals and responsibilities. Performance is also judged in terms of *efficiency,* that is, success in using to its best advantage the resources available to the department. Because the criteria for effectiveness and efficiency are not as clearly established as are generally accepted accounting principles and many laws and regulations, an operational audit tends to require more subjective judgment than do audits of financial statements or compliance audits. For example, quantifiable criteria often must be developed by the auditors to be used to measure the effectiveness or efficiency of the department. Operational auditing is also discussed in detail in Chapter 21.

Integrated Audits

The Sarbanes-Oxley Act requires that auditors of publicly traded companies in the United States perform an **integrated audit** that includes providing assurance on both the financial statements and the effectiveness of internal control over financial reporting. Accordingly, such audits combine aspects of both financial and compliance audits. The Sarbanes-Oxley Act and PCAOB Standard No. 2—which implements the integrated audit—requires company management to assess and report on the company's internal control. The auditors, in addition to providing an opinion on the company's financial statements, report on both management's assessment and internal control effectiveness.

Types of Auditors

In addition to the audit of financial statements by certified public accountants, other professional groups carry on large-scale auditing programs. Among these other well-known types of auditors are internal auditors, auditors of the General Accounting Office, and internal revenue agents.

Internal Auditors

Nearly every large corporation maintains an internal auditing staff. Internal auditors are also employed extensively by governmental and nonprofit organizations. A principal goal of the internal auditors is to investigate and appraise the effectiveness with which the various organizational units of the company are carrying out their assigned functions. Much attention is given by internal auditors to the study and appraisal of internal control.

A large part of the work of the internal auditors consists of operational audits; in addition, they may conduct numerous compliance audits. The number and kind of investigative projects vary from year to year. Unlike the CPAs, who are committed to verify each significant item in the annual financial statements, the internal auditors are not obligated to repeat their audits on an annual basis.

The internal auditing staff often reports to the audit committee of the board of directors and also to the president or another high executive. This strategic placement high in the organizational structure helps ensure that the internal auditors will have ready access to all units of the organization, and that their recommendations will be given prompt attention by department heads. It is imperative that the internal auditors be independent of the department heads and other line executives whose work they review. Thus, it would generally not be desirable for the internal auditing staff to be under the authority of the chief accountant. Regardless of their reporting level, however, the internal auditors are not independent in the same sense as the independent auditors. The internal auditors are employees of the organization in which they work, subject to the restraints inherent in the employer–employee relationship.

The Institute of Internal Auditors (IIA) is the international organization of internal auditors. It has developed various standards relating to internal auditing, and it administers the certified internal auditor (CIA) examination. Chapter 21 provides further discussion of the internal auditing profession and the CIA designation.

Government Accountability Office Auditors

Congress has long had its own auditing staff, headed by the comptroller general and known as the Government Accountability Office, or GAO.[4] The work of GAO auditors includes compliance, operational, and financial audits. These assignments include audits of government agencies to determine that spending programs follow the intent of Congress and operational audits to evaluate the effectiveness and efficiency of selected government programs. GAO auditors conduct examinations of corporations holding government contracts to verify that contract payments by the government have been proper. In addition, the financial statements of a number of federal agencies and the consolidated financial statements of the federal government are audited by the GAO.

The enormous size of many of the federal agencies has caused the GAO to stress the development of computer auditing techniques and statistical sampling plans. Its pioneering in these areas has led to the recognition of the GAO as a sophisticated professional auditing staff.

Internal Revenue Agents

The Internal Revenue Service is responsible for enforcement of the federal tax laws. Its agents conduct compliance audits of the income tax returns of individuals and corporations to determine that income has been computed and taxes paid as required by federal law. Although IRS audits include some simple individual tax returns that can be completed in an hour or so in an IRS office, they also include field audits of the nation's largest corporations and involve highly complex tax issues.

The Public Accounting Profession

Learning Objective 7

In recognition of the public trust afforded to public accountants, each state recognizes public accountancy as a profession and issues the certificate of **certified public accountant.** The CPA certificate is a symbol of technical competence. This official recognition by the state is comparable to that accorded to the legal, medical, and other professions.

The licensing of CPAs by the states reflects a belief that the public interest will be protected by an official identification of competent professional accountants who offer their services to the public. Although CPAs provide various types of services, including tax, consulting, and accounting services which are also provided by non-CPAs, the various states generally restrict performance of audits of financial statements to CPAs. It is this performance of the attest function on financial statements that is most unique to CPAs.

American Institute of Certified Public Accountants

The **American Institute of Certified Public Accountants (AICPA)** is a voluntary national organization of more than 300,000 members. The following four major areas of the AICPA's work are of particular interest to students of auditing:

1. Establishing standards and rules to guide CPAs in their conduct of professional services.
2. Carrying on a program of research and publication.

---

[4] The GAO changed its name from the General Accounting Office to the Government Accountability Office in 2004.

3. Promoting continuing professional education.
4. Contributing to the profession's self-regulation.

Establishing Standards

The AICPA has assigned to its Auditing Standards Board (ASB) responsibility for issuing official pronouncements on auditing matters. A most important series of pronouncements on auditing by the Auditing Standards Board is entitled **Statements on Auditing Standards (SASs)**. The ASB currently has the authority to issue auditing standards only for audits of nonpublic companies. As indicated previously, the Public Company Accounting Oversight Board (PCAOB) issues standards for audits of public companies. The PCAOB has adopted the Auditing Standards Board's *Statements on Auditing Standards* as interim standards for audits of publicly traded companies. The standards are "interim" in that they serve as a starting point as the PCAOB develops its own set of standards.

The AICPA also issues *Statements on Standards for Attestation Engagements* (SSAEs). These statements provide CPAs with guidance for attesting to information other than financial statements, such as financial forecasts. Chapter 2 also provides a description of the SSAEs.

The Accounting and Review Services Committee of the AICPA establishes standards for reporting on financial statements when the CPAs' role is to compile or review the financial statements rather than to perform an audit. The series of pronouncements by this committee is called *Statements on Standards for Accounting and Review Services* (SSARS). The SSARSs provide guidance for the many sensitive situations in which a public accounting firm is in some way associated with the financial statements of a nonpublic company and, therefore, needs to make clear the extent of the responsibility that the public accounting firm assumes for the fairness of the statements. SSARSs are discussed more fully in Chapter 19.

Research and Publication

In addition to the professional standards indicated above, the AICPA issues additional technical guidance. Many accounting students are familiar with the *Journal of Accountancy,* published monthly. Another AICPA monthly journal is *The Tax Advisor.* Publications bearing directly on auditing include:

- *Industry Audit and Accounting Guides.* These guides cover various industries, including, for example, *Audits of Casinos.*
- *Auditing Practice Releases.* This series is intended to keep auditors informed of new developments and advances in auditing procedures.

A number of other AICPA publications bear directly on accounting issues, including:

- *Accounting Research Studies.* The results of studies of accounting methods are described in these publications.
- *Statements of Position* of the Accounting Standards Division. These statements express the AICPA's position on the appropriate method of accounting for particular events or transactions.
- *Accounting Trends & Techniques.* This is an annual study of current reporting practices of 600 large corporations.

Continuing Professional Education

Another important activity of the AICPA is the development of a continuing professional education program. Continuing education is a necessity for CPAs to remain knowledgeable about the unending stream of changes in accounting principles, tax law, auditing, computers, and consulting services. Continuing education programs are offered by the AICPA, state societies, and other professional organizations. State laws require CPAs to participate in continuing education programs as a condition for license renewal.

Professional Regulation

Historically, most of the regulation of accounting firms has been performed by the accounting profession itself through the AICPA. While the SEC has provided oversight and some regulation, Congress has enacted limited legislation to regulate the profession. This situation changed significantly in 2002 with the passage of the Sarbanes-Oxley Act. As indicated previously, this legislation created the PCAOB which now regulates all accounting firms that audit public companies. The AICPA now provides very limited regulation for these accounting firms, but continues to regulate the accounting firms that do not audit public companies.

Regulation of Individual CPAs   The membership of the AICPA has adopted ethical rules for CPAs in the form of its goal-oriented *Code of Professional Conduct.* This ethical code sets forth positively stated principles on which CPAs can make decisions about appropriate conduct. The AICPA *Code of Professional Conduct* is described completely in Chapter 3.

Self-regulation also is apparent in the requirements for regular membership in the AICPA, which include the following:

1. Members in public practice must practice with a firm enrolled in an approved practice (peer) review program.
2. As of 2000, new members must have 150 semester hours of college education, including a bachelor's degree from an accredited college or university.
3. Members must obtain continuing education: 120 hours every three years for members in public practice and 90 hours every three years for other members.

Regulation of Public Accounting Firms   The AICPA also has a division in which the members are public accounting firms, rather than individual CPAs. The *Division for Public Accounting Firms* was created for the purpose of improving the quality of practice in public accounting firms of all sizes. The division has two sections: (1) the *Center for Public Company Audit Firms* and (2) the *PCPS/Partnering for CPA Practice Success/the AICPA Alliance for Public Accounting Firms Section.*

The *Center for Public Company Audit Firms* is a voluntary membership organization of firms that audit or are interested in auditing public companies. The Center's purpose is to promote improvement in the quality of audits of public companies through the communication of information about SEC and PCAOB developments and the development of technical and educational information for members. The Center for Public Company Audit Firms also has a peer review program for the nonpublic company accounting and auditing practices of its members, because the PCAOB inspections cover only public company audits.

The *PCPS: the AICPA Alliance for Public Accounting Firms Section* attempts to improve the quality of accounting firms that audit nonpublic companies. A major requirement for membership in the section is periodic peer (practice) review. A *peer review* involves a critical review of one public accounting firm's practices by another public accounting firm. Such an external review clearly offers a more objective evaluation of the quality of performance than could be made by self-review. The purpose of this concept is to encourage rigorous adherence to the AICPA's quality control standards. Quality control standards and the peer review process are discussed in detail in Chapter 2.

The AICPA—In Perspective

Throughout its existence, the AICPA has contributed enormously to the evolution of generally accepted accounting principles as well as to the development of professional standards. The many technical divisions and committees of the institute (such as the Auditing Standards Board) provide a means of focusing the collective experience and ability of the profession on current problems. However, with the passage of the Sarbanes-Oxley Act, the AICPA's influence and responsibility have been significantly diminished.

The CPA Examination

The **CPA examination** is a uniform national examination prepared and graded by the American Institute of Certified Public Accountants. Historically given twice each year, in May and November, the AICPA is currently in the process of changing it to a computerized exam given on demand at computer centers throughout most of the year.

Although the preparation and grading of the examination are in the hands of the AICPA, the issuance of CPA certificates is a function of each state or territory. Passing the CPA examination does not, in itself, entitle the candidate to a CPA certificate; states have experience and education requirements that must be met before the CPA certificate is awarded.

The CPA examination is essentially an academic one; in most states, candidates are not required to have any work experience to sit for the examination. In the opinion of the authors, the ideal time to take the examination is immediately after the completion of a comprehensive program of accounting courses in a college or university. The format of the CPA examination, which is entirely computerized, includes the following four parts:

1. Auditing & Attestation.
2. Financial Accounting & Reporting (business enterprises, not-for-profit organizations, and governmental entities).
3. Regulation (professional responsibilities, business law, and taxation).
4. Business Environment & Concepts.

The exam consists of multiple choice questions and simulations. The compilation of the questions and problems included in this textbook involved a review of CPA questions used during the past 20 years and the selection of representative questions and problems. Use of this material is with the consent of the AICPA. Many other problems and questions (not from CPA examinations) are also included with each chapter.

State Boards of Accountancy

Permits to practice as a CPA are granted by the state boards of accountancy in the various states. These boards also regulate the profession and may suspend or revoke an accountant's certificate. While all state boards require successful completion of the CPA examination, the requirements for education and experience vary. A few states require only a baccalaureate degree, while most require 150 semester hours of education or a master's degree to sit for the CPA examination. The experience required generally ranges from none to two years. The AICPA currently is attempting to get states to adopt the revised Uniform Accounting Act to facilitate CPA practice across state lines.

Financial Accounting Standards Board

Auditors must determine whether financial statements are prepared in conformity with generally accepted accounting principles. The AICPA has designated the Financial Accounting Standards Board as the body with power to set forth these principles for entities other than federal, state, and local governments. Thus, *FASB Statements,* exposure drafts, public hearings, and research projects are all of major concern to the public accounting profession.

The structure, history, and pronouncements of the FASB (and its predecessor, the Accounting Principles Board) are appropriately covered in introductory, intermediate, and advanced accounting courses.

Governmental Accounting Standards Board

The Governmental Accounting Standards Board (GASB) was formed in 1984 to establish and improve standards of financial accounting for state and local government entities. The operational structure of the GASB is similar to that of the FASB. Auditors of state and local government entities, such as cities and school districts, look to the GASB pronouncements for the appropriate accounting principles.

Federal Accounting Standards Advisory Board

In 1990, the federal Office of Management and Budget, the U.S. Treasury, and the General Accounting Office (recently renamed the Government Accountability Office) established the Federal Accounting Standards Advisory Board (FASAB) to develop accounting standards for the U.S. government. This body issues standards that are used to audit a number of major federal agencies and the U.S. government as a whole as required by the Government Management Reform Act of 1994.

The Public Company Accounting Oversight Board

As indicated previously, the **Public Company Accounting Oversight Board (PCAOB)** was created in 2002 to oversee and discipline CPAs and public accounting firms that audit public companies. This five-member board, under the authority of the SEC, has the responsibility to establish or adopt "auditing, attestation, quality control, ethics, and independence standards relating to the preparation of audit reports" for SEC registrants (almost all publicly traded companies in the United States). In addition, the PCAOB has the responsibility to:

- Register public accounting firms that audit public companies.
- Perform inspections of the practices of registered firms.
- Conduct investigations and disciplinary proceedings of registered firms.
- Sanction registered firms.

As indicated previously, the inspection program of the PCAOB covers only the public company audit practice of CPA firms. The results of the inspections are posted on the PCAOB's Web site at www.pcaobus.org.

Securities and Exchange Commission

The **Securities and Exchange Commission (SEC)** is an agency of the U.S. government. It administers the Securities Act of 1933, the Securities Exchange Act of 1934, and other legislation concerning securities and financial matters. In addition, the SEC has oversight responsibility for the PCAOB. The primary function of the SEC is to protect investors and the public by requiring full disclosure of financial information by companies offering securities for sale to the public. A second objective is to prevent misrepresentation, deceit, or other fraud in the sale of securities.

The term *registration statement* is an important one in any discussion of the impact of the SEC on accounting practice. To *register* securities means to qualify them for sale to the public by filing with the SEC financial statements and other data in a form acceptable to the Commission. A registration statement contains *audited financial statements,* including balance sheets for a two-year period and income statements and statements of cash flows for a three-year period.

The legislation creating the SEC made the commission responsible for determining whether the financial statements presented to it reflect proper application of accounting principles. To aid the commission in discharging this responsibility, the securities acts provide for an examination and report by a public accounting firm registered with the Public Company Accounting Oversight Board. From its beginning, the SEC has been a major user of audited financial statements and has exercised great influence upon the development of accounting principles, the strengthening of auditing standards, and the concept of auditor independence.

Protection of investors, of course, requires that the public have available the information contained in a registration statement concerning a proposed issue of securities. The issuing company is therefore required to deliver to prospective buyers of securities a *prospectus,* or selling circular, from the registration statement. The registration of securities does not insure investors against loss; the SEC does not pass on the merit of securities. There is, in fact, only one purpose of registration: to provide disclosure of the important facts so that the investor has available all pertinent information on which to base an intelligent decision on whether to buy a given security. If the SEC believes that a given registration statement does not meet its standards of disclosure, it may require amendment of the statement or may issue a stop order preventing sale of the securities.

To improve the quality of the financial statements filed with it and the professional standards of the independent accountants who report on these statements, the SEC has adopted a basic accounting regulation known as *Regulation S-X* and entitled *Form and Content of Financial Statements*. Between 1937 and 1982, the SEC issued 307 *Accounting Series Releases* (ASRs) addressing various accounting and auditing issues. In 1982 the series was replaced by two series—*Financial Reporting Releases* and *Accounting and Auditing Enforcement Releases*. *Financial Reporting Releases* present the SEC's current views on financial reporting and auditing issues. *Accounting and Auditing Enforcement Releases* summarize enforcement activities against auditors when the SEC has found deficiencies in the auditors' work.

Other Types of Professional Services

In addition to auditing and other assurance services, public accounting firms offer other types of services to their clients, including tax services, consulting services, accounting and review services, fraud investigation services, and personal financial planning. Public accounting firms tend to specialize in particular types of services depending on their size and the expertise of their personnel.

Illustrative Case
Exiting the Consulting Business

Most of the large CPA firms have now sold or spun off their consulting practices. As examples, IBM bought the consulting practice of PricewaterhouseCoopers LLP, KPMG LLP spun off its consulting practice and took it public, and Ernst & Young LLP sold its consulting practice to Cap Gemini.

Tax Services

Tax services that are performed by public accounting firms fall into two broad categories: compliance work and tax planning. Compliance work involves preparing the federal, state, and local tax returns of corporations, partnerships, individuals, and estates and trusts. Tax planning, on the other hand, involves consulting with clients on how to structure their business affairs to legally minimize the amount and postpone the payment of their taxes.

Consulting Services

Public accounting firms offer a variety of services that are designed to improve the effectiveness and efficiency of their clients' operations. Initially, these services developed as a natural extension of the audit and primarily involved consulting on accounting and internal control systems. In recent years, public accounting firms have expanded by offering a host of services that tend to be more operational in nature. Examples are developing strategic planning models and management information systems and performing executive search services.

Performance of consulting services for audit clients has been a significant issue with respect to the independence of auditors, so much so that a number of restrictions have been placed on the types and extent of consulting services that may be performed by the auditors of public companies. This issue will be discussed in more detail in Chapter 3.

Accounting and Review Services

Audits are expensive. For a small business, the cost of an audit will run into the thousands of dollars; for large corporations, the cost may exceed a million dollars. The most common reason for a small business to incur the cost of an audit is the influence exerted by a bank that insists upon audited financial statements as a condition for granting a bank loan. If a small business is not in need of a significant amount of bank credit, the cost of an audit may exceed its benefits.

An alternative is to retain a public accounting firm to perform other services, such as the compilation or review of financial statements. To compile financial statements means to prepare them; this service is often rendered when the client does not have accounting personnel capable of preparing statements. The public accounting firm issues a compilation report on the financial statements that provides *no assurance* that the statements are presented fairly in accordance with generally accepted accounting principles.

A review of financial statements by a public accounting firm is an attestation service that is substantially less in scope than an audit. It is designed to provide *limited assurance* on the credibility of the statements. A review stresses inquiries by the CPA and comparison of amounts in the statements to comparable financial and nonfinancial data. These comparisons, which are referred to as analytical procedures, are useful in bringing to light possible misstatements of financial statement amounts. Compilations and reviews are discussed in Chapter 19.

Litigation Support Services

The explosion of litigation has had one benefit for the accounting profession. It has created a fast-growing area of practice. CPAs are often used in business litigation cases as expert witnesses to calculate damages, or to explain complex business and accounting concepts to judges and juries. As a result, many public accounting firms have developed departments that specialize in litigation support services.

Fraud Investigation Services

Fraud investigation services generally involve engaging professionals to investigate suspected or known fraud. These types of services are also referred to as *forensic accounting services,* but forensic accounting is somewhat broader and includes litigation support services. Because of increased incidences of defalcation and theft, fraud investigation has become a significant part of the work performed by many internal audit departments. These types of services are also a practice specialty for many public accounting firms. To demonstrate expertise in the area of fraud investigation, the designation "Certified Fraud Examiner" has been developed by the Association of Certified Fraud Examiners.

Personal Financial Planning

Public accounting firms also may advise individuals on their personal financial affairs. For example, a public accounting firm may review a client's investment portfolio and evaluate whether the nature of the investments meets the client's financial objectives. The public accounting firm might also advise the client on the nature and amount of insurance coverage that is appropriate. The AICPA offers the designation "Personal Financial Specialist" to CPAs who satisfy certain experience requirements and pass a one-day examination on personal financial planning topics, such as income tax planning, risk management planning, investment planning, retirement planning, and estate planning.

Organization of the Public Accounting Profession

Learning Objective 8

Many public accounting firms are organized as either sole practitioners or partnerships. A CPA may also practice as a member of a professional corporation or, in many states, as a *limited liability partnership* (LLP) or a *limited liability company* (LLC).

Professional corporations differ from traditional corporations in a number of respects. For example, all shareholders and directors of a professional corporation must be engaged in the practice of public accounting. In addition, shareholders and directors of the professional corporation may be held personally liable for the corporation's actions, although they may choose to carry liability insurance to cover damages caused by negligent actions. *Limited liability partnerships (companies)* are similar to professional corporations, but they provide for the protection of the personal assets of any shareholders or partners not directly involved in providing services on engagements resulting in litigation.

In comparison with a sole proprietorship, partnerships and professional corporations with multiple owners have several advantages. When two or more CPAs join forces, the opportunity for specialization is increased, and the scope of services offered to clients may be expanded. Also, qualified members of the staff may be rewarded by admission to the partnership or issuance of stock. Providing an opportunity to become part owner of the business is an important factor in the public accounting firm's ability to attract and retain competent personnel.

Public accounting firms range in size from one person to over 100,000 on the professional staff. In terms of size, public accounting firms are often grouped into the following four categories: local firms, regional firms, national firms, and Big 4 firms.

Local Firms

Local firms typically have one or two offices, include only one CPA or a few CPAs as partners, and serve clients in a single city or area. These firms often emphasize income tax, consulting, and accounting services. Auditing is usually only a small part of the practice and tends to involve small business concerns that find need for audited financial statements to support applications for bank loans.

Regional Firms

Many local firms have become regional firms by opening additional offices in neighboring cities or states and increasing the number of professional staff. Merger with other local firms is often a route to regional status. This growth is often accompanied by an increase in the amount of auditing as compared to other services.

National Firms

Public accounting firms with offices in most major cities in the United States are called national firms. These firms may operate internationally as well, either with their own offices or through affiliations with firms in other countries.

Big 4 Firms

Often in the news are the large international public accounting firms. Until 1989, there were eight of these firms. However, mergers and the dissolution of (Arthur) Andersen LLP have reduced them to the Big 4. Since only a very large public accounting firm has sufficient staff and resources to audit a giant corporation, these firms audit nearly all of the largest American corporations. Although these firms offer a wide range of professional services, auditing represents a large, if not the largest, share of their work. Annual revenue of an international firm is in the billions of dollars. In alphabetical order, the four firms are Deloitte & Touche LLP, Ernst & Young LLP, KPMG LLP, and PricewaterhouseCoopers LLP.

Alternative Practice Structure Firms

Beginning in the late 1990s a number of publicly traded companies—including American Express, Century Business Services, and H&R Block—began purchasing public accounting firms. These companies are often referred to as "consolidators" because they purchase public accounting firms in various cities and consolidate them into the overall corporation. In essence the approach is to purchase the nonattest portion of the practice, hire public accounting firm partners and other personnel as employees of the publicly traded company, and perform those services. The attest and auditing partners retain that status in the public accounting firm, but ordinarily are also employees of the publicly traded company. The public accounting firm then provides attestation services, using partners and other staff members leased from the public company. This trend is having a profound effect on the public accounting profession, as we will indicate in several places throughout the text. For example, ethical complications are discussed in Chapter 3.

Industry Specialization

Public accounting firms have long recognized the value of industry specialization. When they possess a detailed knowledge and understanding of a client's industry, the auditors can be more effective at collecting and evaluating audit evidence. Also, they are in a better position to make valuable suggestions that will improve the client's operations and to provide the client consulting services.

A number of national and Big 4 public accounting firms have organized their firms along industry lines. Each industry group is made up of personnel involved in providing audit, tax, and consulting services for a specialized industry. The firms believe that such an organizational structure leads to the performance of higher-quality, integrated services to firms in specialized industries.

Responsibilities of the Professional Staff

Human resources—the competence, judgment, and integrity of personnel—represent the greatest asset of any public accounting firm. The professional staff of a typical public accounting firm includes partners, managers, senior accountants, and staff assistants.

Partners

The lead partner on an engagement is responsible for assuring that the audit is performed in accordance with applicable professional standards. Partners are also responsible for maintaining primary contacts with clients. These contacts include discussing with clients the objectives and scope of the audit work, resolving controversies that may arise as to how items are to be presented in the financial statements, and attending the client's stockholders' meetings to answer any questions regarding the financial statements or the auditors' report. Other responsibilities of the partner include recruiting new staff members, general supervision of the professional staff, reviewing audit working papers, and signing the audit reports.

Specialization by each partner in a different area of the firm's practice is often advantageous. One partner, for example, may become expert in tax matters and head the firm's tax department; another may specialize in SEC registrations; and a third may devote full time to design and installation of computer information systems.

The partnership level in a public accounting firm is comparable to that of top management in an industrial organization. Executives at this level are concerned with the long-run well-being of the organization and of the community it serves. They should and do contribute important amounts of time to civic, professional, and educational activities in the community. Participation in the state society of certified public accountants and in the AICPA is, of course, a requisite if the partners are to do their share in building the profession. Contribution of their specialized skills and professional judgment to leadership of civic organizations is equally necessary in developing the economic and social environment in which business and professional accomplishment is possible.

An important aspect of partners' active participation in various business and civic organizations is the prestige and recognition that may come to their firms. Many clients select a particular public accounting firm because they have come to know and respect one of the firm's partners. Thus, partners who are widely known and highly regarded within the community may be a significant factor in attracting business to the firm.

Managers

In large public accounting firms, managers or supervisors perform many of the duties that would be discharged by partners in smaller firms. A manager may be responsible for supervising two or more concurrent audit engagements. This supervisory work includes reviewing the audit working papers and discussing with the audit staff and with the client any accounting or auditing problems that may arise during the engagement. The manager is responsible for determining the audit procedures applicable to specific audits and for maintaining uniform standards of fieldwork. Often, managers have the administrative duties of compiling and collecting the firm's billings to clients.

Familiarity with tax laws, as well as a broad and current knowledge of accounting theory and practice, are essential qualifications for a successful manager. Like the partner, the audit manager may specialize in specific industries or other areas of the firm's practice.

Senior Auditors

The responsibility assumed by the senior "in-charge" auditor varies based on the size of the engagement. On a smaller engagement, the senior auditor may assume responsibility for planning and conducting the audit and drafting the audit report, subject to review and approval by the manager and partner. On larger engagements a senior auditor may assume responsibility for supervising some aspect of the audit, such as the audit of accounts receivable. In conducting the audit, the senior will delegate most audit tasks to assistants based on an appraisal of each assistant's ability to perform particular phases of the work. A well-qualified university graduate with a formal education in accounting may progress from staff assistant to senior auditor within two or three years, or even less.

One of the major responsibilities of the senior is on-the-job staff training. In assigning work to staff assistants, the senior should make clear the end objectives of the particular audit operation. By assigning assistants a wide variety of audit tasks and by providing constructive criticism of the assistants' work, the senior should try to make each audit a significant learning experience for the staff assistants.

Reviewing working papers shortly after they are completed is another duty of the senior in charge of an audit. This enables the senior to control the progress of the work and to ascertain that each phase of the engagement is adequately covered. At the conclusion of the fieldwork, the senior will make a final review, including tracing items from individual working papers to the financial statements.

The senior will also maintain a continuous record of the hours devoted by all members of the staff to the various phases of the audit. In addition to maintaining uniform professional standards of fieldwork, the senior is responsible for preventing the accumulation of excessive staff hours on inconsequential matters and for completing the entire engagement within the budgeted time, if possible.

Staff Assistants

The first position of a college graduate entering the public accounting profession is that of staff assistant. Staff assistants usually encounter a variety of assignments that fully utilize their capacity for analysis and growth. Of course some routine work must be done in every audit engagement, but college graduates with thorough training in accounting need have little fear of being assigned for long to extensive routine procedures when they enter the field of public accounting. Most firms are anxious to increase the assigned responsibility to younger staff members as rapidly as they are able to assume it. Ordinarily, the demand for accounting services is so high as to create a situation in which every incentive has existed for rapid development of promising assistants.

The audit staff members of all public accounting firms attend training programs that are either developed "in house" or sponsored by professional organizations. One of the most attractive features of the public accounting profession is the richness and variety of experience acquired even by the beginning staff member. Because of the high quality of the experience gained by certified public accountants as they move from one audit engagement to another, many business concerns select individuals from the public accounting field to fill such executive positions as controller or treasurer.

Professional Development for Public Accounting Firm Personnel

A major challenge in public accounting is keeping abreast of current developments within the profession. New business practices; new pronouncements by the Auditing Standards Board, the SEC, the FASB, and the GASB; and changes in the tax laws are only a few of the factors that require members of the profession continually to update their technical knowledge.

A public accounting firm must make certain that the professional staff remains continuously up to date on technical issues. To assist in this updating process, most large public accounting firms maintain a separate professional development section.

Professional development sections offer a wide range of seminars and educational programs to personnel of the firm. The curriculum of each program is especially designed to suit the needs and responsibilities of participants. Partners may attend programs focusing on the firm's policies on audit quality control or current developments in a specialized industry; on the other hand, programs designed for staff assistants may cover audit procedures or use of the firm's audit software. In addition to offering educational programs, the professional development section usually publishes a monthly newsletter or journal for distribution to personnel of the public accounting firm and other interested persons.

Many public accounting firms that are too small to maintain their own professional development departments have banded together into associations of public accounting firms. These associations organize educational programs, distribute information on technical issues, and engage in other professional activities that are designed to meet the needs of their members. Since the cost of the association's professional activities are shared by all members, the firms are provided with many of the benefits of having their own professional development department at a fraction of the cost.

Seasonal Fluctuations in Public Accounting Work

One of the traditional disadvantages of the public accounting profession has been the concentration of work during the "busy season" from December through April, followed by a period of slack demand during the summer months. This seasonal trend is caused by the fact that many companies keep their records on a calendar-year basis and require auditing services immediately after the December 31 closing of the accounts. Another important factor is the spring deadline for filing of federal income tax returns.

Auditors often work a considerable number of hours of overtime during the busy season. Some public accounting firms pay their staff for overtime hours. Other firms allow their staff to accumulate the overtime in an "overtime bank" and to "withdraw" these hours in the form of additional vacation time during the less busy times of the year.

Relationships with Clients

The wide-ranging scope of public accountants' activities today demands that CPAs be interested in and well informed on economic trends, political developments, and other topics that play a significant part in business and social contacts. Although an in-depth knowledge of accounting is the most important qualification of the CPA, an ability to meet people easily and to gain their confidence and goodwill may be no less important in achieving success in the profession of public accounting. The ability to work effectively with clients will be enhanced by a sincere interest in their problems and by a relaxed and cordial manner.

The question of the auditors' independence inevitably arises in considering the advisability of social activities with clients. The partner in today's public accounting firm may play golf or tennis with the executives of client companies and other business associates. These relationships actually may make it easier to resolve differences of opinions that arise during an audit, if the client has learned to know and respect the partner. This mutual understanding need not prevent the CPA from standing firm on matters of accounting principle. Alternatively, such relationships have the potential for impairing auditor independence. Auditor response to differences of opinions when such relationships exist is perhaps the "moment of truth" for the practitioners of a profession.

The CPA must always remember that the concept of independence embodies an *appearance* of independence. This appearance of independence may be impaired if an auditor becomes excessively involved in social activities with clients. For example, if a CPA frequently attends lavish parties held by a client or dates an officer or employee of a client corporation, the question might be raised as to whether the CPA will appear independent to outsiders. This dilemma is but one illustration of the continual need for judgment and perspective on the part of an auditor.

Chapter Summary

This chapter explored the nature of assurance services, the attest function, independent audits, and the auditing profession. To summarize:

1. CPAs provide a wide array of information enhancement services referred to as assurance services. Currently, the primary type of assurance services provided by CPAs involves attestation. When performing attestation services, CPAs enhance the reliability of information by issuing an examination, review, or agreed-upon procedures report on subject matter or an assertion that is the responsibility of another party. In the case of financial statement audits, the report most frequently includes an opinion about whether management's financial statements conform to generally accepted accounting principles.

2. Since audits involve examinations of financial information by independent experts, they increase the credibility of the information contained in the statements. Decision makers both within and outside the organization can use audited financial information with confidence that it is not likely to be materially misstated. Audits reduce information risk and, therefore, they reduce the overall risk of making various types of economic decisions.

3. The nature and emphasis of auditing has changed over the years. Auditing began with the objective of detecting fraud by examination of all, or most, business transactions. Today the objective of an audit is to attest to the fairness of the financial statements. Because of the large size of business organizations, audits necessarily involve the use of sampling techniques based on the auditors' consideration of the organization's controls. CPAs also are being asked to assume more responsibility for attesting to compliance with laws and regulations, and to the effectiveness of controls.

4. Due to a number of very visible instances of fraudulent financial reporting, Congress passed the Sarbanes-Oxley Act of 2002. This act significantly changed the nature of public company audits, as well as the regulation of auditors that perform such audits. The act created the Public Company Accounting Oversight Board (PCAOB) to regulate audits and auditors of public companies.

5. The auditing profession is much broader than auditors involved in public accounting; it also includes internal auditors and various governmental auditors, such as auditors of the General Accounting Office and the Internal Revenue Service.

6. Various professional and regulatory organizations have a significant influence on the auditing profession, including the American Institute of Certified Public Accountants, the Financial Accounting Standards Board, the Governmental Accounting Standards Board, the Federal Accounting Standards Advisory Board, the Public Company Accounting Oversight Board, the Securities and Exchange Commission, and the Institute of Internal Auditors.

7. In addition to performing attestation engagements, public accounting firms offer tax services, consulting services, and accounting and review services. Public accounting firms range in size from sole practitioners to the large international firms referred to as the Big 4 firms. The professional staff of a typical medium-to-large public accounting firm includes partners, managers, senior accountants, and staff assistants.

Key Terms Introduced or Emphasized in Chapter 1

Agreed-upon procedures engagement   An attest engagement in which the CPAs agree to perform procedures for a specified party and issue a report that is restricted to use by that party.

American Institute of Certified Public Accountants (AICPA)   The national professional organization of CPAs engaged in promoting high professional standards to ensure that CPAs serve the public interest.

Assertion   A representation or declaration made by the responsible party, typically management of the entity.

Assurance services   Professional services that enhance the quality of information, or its context, for decision makers. Many assurance services involve some form of attestation.

Attest engagement   An engagement in which the CPAs issue an examination, a review, or an agreed-upon procedures report on subject matter or an assertion about subject matter that is the responsibility of another party (e.g., management).

Audit of financial statements   An examination designed to provide the highest level of assurance that CPAs provide that the financial statements follow generally accepted accounting principles, or another acceptable basis of accounting.

Business risk (of the client)   The risk assumed by investors or creditors that is associated with the company's survival and profitability.

Certified public accountant   A person licensed by the state to practice public accounting as a profession, based on having passed the Uniform CPA Examination and having met certain educational and experience requirements.

Compliance audit   An audit to measure the compliance of the organization with some established criteria; for example, laws and regulations, or internal control policies and procedures.

CPA examination   A uniform examination administered by the American Institute of Certified Public Accountants for state boards of accountancy to enable them to issue CPA licenses. The examination covers the topics of accounting and reporting, auditing, business environment, regulation, and professional responsibilities.

Examination   An attest engagement designed to provide the highest level of assurance that CPAs provide on an assertion. An examination of financial statements is referred to as an *audit*.

Financial audit   An audit of the financial statements of an organization or segment of the organization.

Fraud   Intentional misstatement of financial statements by management (management fraud), or theft of assets by employees (employee fraud). Fraud also is referred to as *irregularities*.

Generally accepted accounting principles (GAAP)   Concepts or standards established by such authoritative bodies as the FASB and the GASB and accepted by the accounting profession as essential to proper financial reporting.

Information risk   The risk that the information used by investors, creditors, and others to assess business risk is not accurate.

Integrated audit   As required by the Sarbanes-Oxley Act and the Public Company Accounting Oversight Board, an audit that includes providing assurance on both the financial statements and internal control over financial reporting. Integrated audits are required of publicly traded companies in the United States.

Operational audit   An analysis of a department or other unit of a business or governmental organization to measure the effectiveness and efficiency of operations.

Public Company Accounting Oversight Board (PCAOB)   The five-member board established in 2002 to oversee the audit of public companies that are subject to the securities laws. The board has authority to establish or adopt, or both, rules for auditing, quality control, ethics, independence, and other standards relating to the preparation of audit reports.

Review   An engagement designed to lend only a limited degree of assurance relating to an assertion. As discussed in further detail in Chapter 19, the procedures performed are generally limited to inquiries and analytical procedures.

Sarbanes-Oxley Act of 2002   A set of reforms that toughened penalties for corporate fraud, restricted the kinds of consulting CPAs can perform for audit clients, and created the Public Company Accounting Oversight Board to oversee CPAs and public accounting firms.

Securities and Exchange Commission (SEC)   A government agency authorized to regulate companies seeking approval to issue securities for sale to the public.

Statements on Auditing Standards (SASs)   A series of statements issued by the Auditing Standards Board of the AICPA. These statements are considered to be interpretations of generally accepted auditing standards.

Suitable criteria   Criteria are the standards or benchmarks used to measure and present the subject matter and against which the CPA evaluates the subject matter. Suitable criteria are criteria that are established or developed by groups composed of experts that follow due process procedures, including exposure of the proposed criteria for public comment. Suitable criteria must have each of the following attributes: objectivity, measurability, completeness, and relevance.

Review Questions

1–1.   In late 2001 through 2002, the accounting profession faced a "crisis of credibility." Describe the events that led up to this crisis.

1–2.   Define assurance services. What are the two distinct types?

1–3.   What is the most common type of attest engagement? What is most frequently being "asserted" by management on this type of engagement?

1–4.   What is the principal use and significance of an audit report to a large corporation with securities listed on a stock exchange? To a small family-owned enterprise?

1–5.   Describe several business situations that would create a need for a report by an independent public accountant concerning the fairness of a company's financial statements.

1–6.   Explain the following statement: One contribution of the independent auditor is to lend *credibility* to financial statements.

1–7.   The overall risk of the investment in a business includes both business risk and information risk. Contrast these two types of risk. Which one is most directly affected by the auditors?

1–8.   Contrast the objectives of auditing at the beginning of this century with the objectives of auditing today.

1–9.   What does an operational audit attempt to measure? Does an operational audit involve more or fewer subjective judgments than a compliance audit or an audit of financial statements? Explain. To whom is the report usually directed after completion of an operational audit?

1–10.   Distinguish between a compliance audit and an operational audit.

1–11.   Is an *independent status* possible or desirable for internal auditors as compared with the independence of a public accounting firm? Explain.

1–12.   Spacecraft, Inc., is a large corporation that is audited regularly by a public accounting firm and that also maintains an internal auditing staff. Explain briefly how the relationship of the public accounting firm to Spacecraft differs from the relationship of the internal auditing staff to Spacecraft.

1–13.   Describe briefly the function of the GAO.

1–14.   List two of the important contributions to auditing literature by the AICPA.

1–15.   What is meant by a *peer review* in public accounting?

1–16.   How does the role of the SEC differ from that of the AICPA?

1–17.   Apart from auditing, what other professional services are offered by public accounting firms?

1–18.   What are the advantages of organizing a public accounting firm as a partnership rather than a sole proprietorship?

1–19.   How does a professional corporation differ from the traditional corporation?

1–20.   Public accounting firms are sometimes grouped into categories of local firms, regional firms, national firms, and international firms. Explain briefly the characteristics of each. Include in your answer the types of services stressed in each group.

1–21.   Describe the various levels or positions of accounting personnel in a large public accounting firm.

1–22.   List three of the more important responsibilities of a partner in a public accounting firm.

Questions Requiring Analysis

Required:

1–23.   As a result of a number of events that caused Congress to doubt the ability of the accounting profession to self-regulate itself, a number of reforms were made to accounting profession's system of self-regulation.

a. Provide a brief overview of the legislation that altered the self-regulation process of the accounting profession.

b. Explain the regulation process for accounting firms that audit public companies.

c. Explain the regulation process for accounting firms that do not audit public companies.

1–24.   A corporation is contemplating issuing debenture bonds to a group of investors.

Required: *a.* Explain how independent audits of the corporation's financial statements facilitate this transaction.

   b. Describe the likely effects on the transaction if the corporation decides not to obtain independent audits of its financial statements.

1–25.   The Sarbanes-Oxley Act of 2002 created the Public Company Accounting Oversight Board. Explain the major responsibilities of this board.

1–26.   The self-interest of the provider of financial information (whether an individual or a business entity) often runs directly counter to the interests of the user of the information.

Required: *a.* Give an example of such opposing interests.

   b. What may be done to compensate for the possible bias existing because of the self-interest of the individual or business entity providing the financial information?

1–27.   The role of the auditor in the American economy has changed over the years in response to changes in our economic and political institutions. Consequently, the nature of an audit today is quite different from that of an audit performed in the year 1900. Classify the following phrases into two groups: (1) phrases more applicable to an audit performed in 1900 and (2) phrases more applicable to an audit performed today.

   a. Complete review of all transactions.

   b. Assessment of internal control.

   c. Auditors' attention concentrated on balance sheet.

   d. Emphasis upon use of sampling techniques.

   e. Determination of fairness of financial statements.

   f. Audit procedures to prevent or detect fraud on the part of all employees and managers.

   g. Registration statement.

   h. Fairness of reported earnings per share.

   i. Influence of stock exchanges and the investing public upon use of independent auditors.

   j. Concern about fraudulent financial reporting.

   k. Generally accepted auditing standards.

   l. Bankers and short-term creditors as principal users of audit reports.

   m. Pressure for more disclosure.

   n. Auditing for compliance with laws and regulations.

Multiple Choice Questions

1–28.   Select the best answer for each of the following items and give reasons for your choice.

   a. Which of the following best describes the relationship between assurance services and attest services?

   (1) While attest services involve financial data, assurance services involve nonfinancial data.

   (2) While attest services require objectivity, assurance services do not have to be objective.

   (3) Attest services are a subset of assurance services.

   (4) Attest and assurance services are different terms referring to the same types of services.

   b. Which of the following has primary responsibility for the fairness of the representations made in financial statements?

   (1) Client's management.

   (2) Independent auditor.

   (3) Audit committee.

   (4) AICPA.

   c. The most important benefit of having an annual audit by a public accounting firm is to:

   (1) Provide assurance to investors and other outsiders that the financial statements are reliable.

   (2) Enable officers and directors to avoid personal responsibility for any misstatements in the financial statements.

   (3) Meet the requirements of government agencies.

   (4) Provide assurance that illegal acts, if any exist, will be brought to light.

d. The Sarbanes-Oxley Act created the Public Company Accounting Oversight Board (PCAOB). Which of the following is **not** one of responsibilities of that board?

(1) Establish independence standards for auditors of public companies.

(2) Review financial reports filed with the SEC.

(3) Establish auditing standards for audits of public companies.

(4) Sanction registered audit firms.

e. Which of these organizations has the responsibility to do inspections of auditors of public companies?

(1) American Institute of Certified Public Accountants.

(2) Securities and Exchange Commission.

(3) Financial Accounting Standards Board.

(4) Public Company Accounting Oversight Board.

f. Governmental auditing, in addition to including audits of financial statements, often includes audits of efficiency, effectiveness, and:

(1) Adequacy.

(2) Evaluation.

(3) Accuracy.

(4) Compliance.

g. In general, internal auditors' independence will be greatest when they report directly to the:

(1) Financial vice president.

(2) Corporate controller.

(3) Audit committee of the board of directors.

(4) Corporate stockholders.

h. Which of the following did not precipitate the passage of the Sarbanes-Oxley Act of 2002 to regulate public accounting firms:

(1) Disclosures related to accounting irregularities at Enron and WorldCom.

(2) Restatements of financial statements by a number of public companies.

(3) Conviction of the accounting firm of Arthur Andersen LLP.

(4) Ethical scandals at the AICPA.

i. Which of the following organizations establishes accounting standards for U.S. government agencies?

(1) The Financial Accounting Standards Board.

(2) The Governmental Accounting Standards Board.

(3) The Federal Accounting Standards Advisory Board.

(4) The Public Company Accounting Oversight Board.

j. Which of the following is correct about forensic audits?

(1) All audit engagements are forensic in nature.

(2) While forensic audits are performed by law firms, they are not performed by CPA firms.

(3) Forensic audits are equivalent to compliance audits.

(4) Forensic audits are usually performed in situations in which fraud has been found or is suspected.

k. What best describes the purpose of the auditors' consideration of internal control in a financial statement audit for a nonpublic company?

(1) To determine the nature, timing and extent of audit testing.

(2) To make recommendations to the client regarding improvements in internal control.

(3) To train new auditors on accounting and control systems.

(4) To identify opportunities for fraud within the client's operations.

l. Which of the following is an example of a compliance audit?

(1) An audit of financial statements.

(2) An audit of a company's policies and procedures for adhering to environmental laws and regulations.

     (3) An audit of a company's internal control over financial reporting.

     (4) An audit of the efficiency and effectiveness of a company's legal department.

(AICPA, adapted)

Problems

1–29. Feller, the sole owner of a small hardware business, has been told that the business should have financial statements audited by an independent CPA. Feller, having some bookkeeping experience, has personally prepared the company's financial statements and does not understand why such statements should be audited by a CPA. Feller discussed the matter with Farber, a CPA, and asked Farber to explain why an audit is considered important.

Required:

    a. Describe the objectives of an independent audit.

    b. Identify five ways in which an independent audit may be beneficial to Feller.

1–30. For the purposes of this problem, you are to assume the existence of five types of auditors: CPA, GAO, IRS, bank examiner, and internal auditor. Also assume that the work of these various auditors can be grouped into five classifications: audits of financial statements, compliance audits, operational audits, accounting services, and consulting services.

    For each of the following topics, you are to state the type of auditor most probably involved. Also identify the topic with one of the above classes of work.

    You should organize your answer in a three-column format as follows: Column 1, the number of the topic; Column 2, the type of auditor involved; and Column 3, the class of work.

1. Financial statements of a small business to be submitted to a bank in support of a loan application.

2. Financial statements of a large bank listed on the New York Stock Exchange to be distributed to stockholders.

3. Review of the management directive stating the goals and responsibilities of a corporation's mail-handling department.

4. Review of costs and accomplishments of a military research program carried on within the air force to determine whether the program was cost effective.

5. Examination on a surprise basis of Midtown State Bank. Emphasis placed on verification of cash, marketable securities, and loans receivable and on consistent observation of the banking code.

6. Analysis of the accounting system of a small business with the objective of making recommendations concerning installation of a computer-based system.

7. Determination of fairness of financial statements for public distribution by a corporation that has a professional level internal auditing staff.

8. Review of the activities of the receiving department of a large manufacturing company, with special attention to efficiency of materials inspection and promptness of reports issued.

9. Review of the tax return of the corporate president to determine whether charitable contributions are adequately substantiated.

10. Review of daily attendance during spring term at Blue Ridge Consolidated School District to ascertain whether payments received from the state were substantiated by pupil-day data, and whether disbursements by the district were within authorized limits.

11. Review of transactions of a government agency to determine whether disbursements under the Payment-In-Kind program of the U.S. Department of Agriculture followed the intent of Congress.

12. Compilation of quarterly financial statements for a small business that does not have any accounting personnel capable of preparing financial statements.

1–31. In a discussion between Peters and Ferrel, two auditing students, Peters made the following statement: "A CPA is a professional person who is licensed by the state for the purpose of providing an independent expert opinion on the fairness of financial statements. To maintain an attitude of mental independence and objectivity in all phases of audit work, it is advisable that the CPA not fraternize with client personnel. The CPA should be courteous but reserved and dignified at all times. Indulging in social contacts with clients outside business hours will make it more difficult to be firm and objective if the CPA finds evidence of fraud or of unsound accounting practices."

Ferrel replied as follows: "You are 50 years behind the times, Peters. An auditor and a client are both human beings. The auditor needs the cooperation of the client to do a good job; you're much more likely to get cooperation if you're relaxed and friendly rather than being cold and impersonal. Having a few beers or going to a football game with a client won't keep the CPA from being independent. It will make the working relationship a lot more comfortable, and will probably cause the client to recommend the CPA to other business people who need auditing services. In other words, the approach you're recommending should be called 'How to Avoid Friends and Alienate Clients.' I will admit, though, that with so many women entering public accounting and other women holding executive positions in business, a few complications may arise when auditor-client relations get pretty relaxed."

Evaluate the opposing views expressed by Peters and Ferrel.

1–32. Listed below are 10 publications in the fields of auditing and accounting.

1. *Statements on Auditing Standards* (SASs).

2. *The Journal of Accountancy.*

3. *Regulation S-X, Form and Content of Financial Statements.*

4. *Statements on Standards for Accounting and Review Services* (SSARS).

5. *Financial Reporting Releases* (FRR).

6. *Accounting and Reporting Standards for Corporate Financial Statements.*

7. *Accounting and Reporting Standards for Governmental Entities.*

8. *Industry Audit and Accounting Guides.*

9. *Auditing Practice Releases.*

10. *The Tax Advisor.*

The list of organizations shown below includes the sponsors or publishers of the above 10 publications.

a. Accounting Principles Board (APB).

b. Securities and Exchange Commission (SEC).

c. American Institute of Certified Public Accountants (AICPA).

d. Financial Accounting Standards Board (FASB).

e. Internal Revenue Service (IRS).

f. Government Accountability Office (GAO).

g. Governmental Accounting Standards Board (GASB).

Required: Identify the sponsoring organization for each of the 10 publications. (Some of the organizations may not have a publication in this list.) Organize your answer in a two-column format. In the left-hand column, list the number and name of each publication in the order shown above. In the right-hand column, list the identifying letter and the abbreviation of the sponsoring organization. For example, on line 1, list (1) *Statements on Auditing Standards* in the left column and (*c*) AICPA in the right column.

1–33. Each auditing term (or organizational name) in Column 1 below bears a close relationship to a term in Column 2.

Column 1	Column 2
1. Quality control	*a.* Regulate auditors of public companies
2. Operational audit	*b.* Attest function
3. Internal control	*c.* Material information
4. Government Accountability Office	*d.* Credibility
5. Disclosure	*e.* Peer review
6. Critical characteristic that must be maintained by the accounting profession	*f.* Registration statement
7. Public Company Accounting Oversight Board	*g.* Accounting service
8. Securities and Exchange Commission	*h.* Measurement of effectiveness and efficiency of a unit of an organization
9. Audited financial statements	*i.* Basis for sampling and testing
10. Compilation of financial statements	*j.* Auditing staff reporting to Congress

Required: Identify the most closely related terms in Columns 1 and 2. Organize your answer in a two-column format by copying the numbers and terms in Column 1 as given. Then, rearrange the sequence of terms in Column 2 so that each line of your schedule will contain two closely related terms.

In-Class Team Case

1–34. Will Williams, a college senior, has begun the interviewing process. He has discovered a great variety of organizations in search of "accounting majors." He finds that various public accounting firms, corporations, the GAO, and the IRS are all interviewing candidates at his school.

He has come to you and asked for your advice. He has suggested that although he has had only one class session of auditing, he already realizes that it is going to be a great course; but he also especially enjoyed his tax and accounting systems courses.

Required: Compare and contrast his possibilities with public accounting firms, corporations, the GAO, and the IRS if he wishes to emphasize the following areas of expertise:

a. Taxation.

b. Auditing.

c. Systems design.

For example, first compare and contrast his likely responsibilities with each of the above organizations if he chooses to emphasize taxation.

Research and Discussion Case

1–35. Smith & Co., a local Dallas public accounting firm, is incorporated as a professional corporation, with three shareholders, all CPAs. The shareholders have developed a combination of marketing, software, and professional expertise that has allowed them to perform the accounting service of compiling individuals' personal financial statements in an extremely efficient manner.

The three shareholders are interested in "going national" with their accounting service but lack the capital necessary to expand to other cities. They are currently considering the possibility of obtaining outside capital as a way to expand their business by offering their firm's services to individuals in other markets. They estimate that if they raised $4 million of capital they could open and staff 15 offices within the next 12 months.

In a recent meeting of the three shareholders, the possibility of raising the capital through incorporation as a traditional corporation and thereby selling stock to the public was discussed. The original three shareholders would retain 51 percent of the total stock, which would be traded over the counter. The only work performed through the new corporation would be the compilation of individuals' financial statements.

Subsequently, the shareholders were dismayed to learn that states do not generally allow CPAs to practice as a traditional corporation. Also, those states that do allow "limited liability companies" generally require that shareholders be involved in public accounting. Only by establishing a separate organization not held out as a public accounting firm will the current three shareholders be allowed to follow their expansion plan.

Required: *a.* Summarize the arguments for allowing public accounting firms to sell ownership interests to individuals not in public accounting through incorporation as a traditional corporation.

b. Summarize the arguments in favor of restricting public accounting firm ownership to those involved in public accounting.

c. Express your personal opinion as to whether ownership of public accounting firms should be restricted to individuals involved in public accounting.

Suggested References

AICPA, *Professional Standards,* Volume 2, Commerce Clearing House, Section ET 505 (*Code of Professional Conduct,* Rule 505).
Appropriate chapters from other accounting and business textbooks that discuss the advantages of the corporate form of business.

Chapter 2

Professional Standards

Chapter learning objectives

After studying this chapter, you should be able to:

LO1. Describe the authority of the two types of auditing standards–PCAOB standards and AICPA generally accepted auditing standards.

LO2. Identify the authoritative status of the *Statements on Auditing Standards.*

LO3. Discuss the auditors' responsibility for detecting errors, fraud, and illegal acts.

LO4. Explain the key elements of the auditors' standard report.

LO5. Discuss the other types of reports that are issued by auditors.

LO6. Describe the attestation standards.

LO7. Describe the quality control standards and their purposes.

LO8. Explain the status of international auditing standards.

Standards are established to measure the quality of performance of individuals and organizations. Standards relating to the accounting profession concern themselves with certified public accountant (CPA) professional qualities, the judgment exercised by CPAs in the performance of their professional engagements and a CPA firm's quality control.

Our purpose in this chapter is to make clear the nature of auditing standards, attestation standards, and quality control standards. In our discussion of the auditing standards, we consider in detail the nature of the independent auditors' report—that brief but important document that emerges as the end product of an audit engagement.

Auditing Standards for Public and Nonpublic Companies

Learning Objective 1

As discussed in Chapter 1, the regulatory environment for auditors and audit firms has become much more complex with the passage of the Sarbanes-Oxley Act. Previously, the AICPA's standards, based on their general acceptance, applied to audits of both public and nonpublic companies. The Sarbanes-Oxley Act created the Public Company Accounting Oversight Board (PCAOB) and charged that body with the responsibility for developing and enforcing professional standards for integrated audits of public companies. Remember that the integrated audit involves auditing both the company's financial statements and its internal control over financial reporting. The PCAOB also is charged with the responsibility of regulating the public company audit practices of registered CPA firms. To complicate matters further, the state boards of accountancy have the authority to regulate CPAs and CPA firms that practice within their state or jurisdiction. Figure 2.1 on page 34 summaries the regulatory authority of the PCAOB, the AICPA, and the state boards of accountancy.

In the majority of this textbook we will focus on the generally accepted auditing standards established by the AICPA. Currently, the AICPA standards do not differ significantly from the standards for audits of public companies because the PCAOB adopted the AICPA standards in existence at April 16, 2003, as its interim standards. As we present the audit process, we will describe situations in which PCAOB standards depart from AICPA standards. In addition, Chapter 18 specifically focuses on the integrated audit required for a public company, which involves the audit of the company's financial statements and attestation to its internal control over financial reporting.

AICPA Generally Accepted Auditing Standards (GAAS)

What are the standards developed by the public accounting profession through the AICPA? The AICPA has set forth the basic framework in the following 10 generally accepted auditing standards (emphasis added).

General Standards
1. The audit is to be performed by a person or persons having *adequate technical training and proficiency* as an auditor.
2. In all matters relating to the assignment, an *independence in mental attitude* is to be maintained by the auditor or auditors.
3. *Due professional care* is to be exercised in the planning and performance of the audit and the preparation of the report.

Standards of Fieldwork
1. The work is to be *adequately planned* and assistants, if any, are to be *properly supervised*.
2. A *sufficient understanding of internal control* is to be obtained to plan the audit and to determine the nature, timing, and extent of further audit procedures.
3. *Sufficient competent evidential matter* is to be obtained through inspection, observation, inquiries, and confirmations to afford a reasonable basis for an opinion regarding the financial statements under audit.

Standards of Reporting
1. The report shall state whether the financial statements are *presented in accordance with generally accepted accounting principles.*
2. The report shall identify those circumstances in which such *principles have not been consistently observed* in the current period in relation to the preceding period.

3. *Informative disclosures* in the financial statements are to be regarded as reasonably adequate *unless otherwise stated in the report.*

4. The report shall either contain an *expression of opinion* regarding the financial statements, taken as a whole, or an assertion to the effect that an opinion cannot be expressed. When an overall opinion cannot be expressed, the reasons therefor should be stated. In all cases where an auditor's name is associated with financial statements, the report should contain a clear-cut indication of the *character of the auditor's work* if any, and the *degree of responsibility* the auditor is taking.

[handwritten margin note: ✱ disclaimer of opinion / qualified – limited to parts / adverse – disagree]

The 10 standards set forth by the AICPA include such subjective terms of measurement as "*adequate* planning," "*sufficient* understanding of internal control," "*sufficient competent* evidential matter," and "*adequate* disclosure." To decide under the circumstances of each audit engagement what is adequate, sufficient, and competent requires the exercise of *professional judgment.* Auditing cannot be reduced to rote; the exercise of judgment by the auditor is vital at numerous points in every engagement. However, the formulation and publication of carefully worded auditing standards are of immense aid in raising the quality of audit work, even though these standards require professional judgment in their application.

General Standards— Auditor Qualifications and Quality of Work

[handwritten margin note: T I D]

The general standards are personal in nature in that they deal with auditor training and proficiency, auditor independence, and the need for due professional care. These standards apply to all parts of the audit, including fieldwork and reporting.

Training and Proficiency

How does the independent auditor achieve the "adequate technical training and proficiency" required by the first general standard? This requirement is usually interpreted to mean college or university education in accounting and auditing, participation in continuing education programs, and substantial public accounting experience. A technical knowledge of the industry in which the client operates is also part of the personal qualifications of the auditor. It follows that a CPA firm must not accept an audit engagement without first determining that members of its staff have the proficiency needed to function effectively in the particular industry.

Independence

An opinion by an independent public accountant as to the fairness of a company's financial statements is of questionable value unless the accountant is truly independent. Consequently, the auditing standard that states "in all matters relating to the assignment an **independence** in mental attitude is to be maintained by the auditor" is perhaps the most essential factor in the existence of a public accounting profession.

If auditors own shares of stock in a company that they audit, or if they serve as members of the board of directors, they might subconsciously be biased in the performance of auditing duties. An auditor should therefore avoid any relationship with a client that would cause an outsider who had knowledge of all the facts to doubt the CPA's independence. It is not enough that auditors *be* independent; they must conduct themselves in such a manner that informed members of the public will have no reason to doubt their independence. Independence is a key element of professional ethics and will be described in detail in Chapter 3.

Due Professional Care

The third general standard requires due professional care in the conduct of the audit and in the preparation of the audit report. This standard requires the auditors to plan and carry out every step of the audit engagement in an alert and diligent manner. Full compliance with this standard would rule out any negligent acts or material omissions by the auditors. Of course, auditors, as well as members of other professions, inevitably make occasional errors in judgment.

Standards of Fieldwork— Accumulating and Evaluating Evidence

The three standards of fieldwork relate to planning the audit and accumulating and evaluating evidence sufficient for the auditors to express an opinion on the financial statements. Audit planning involves developing an overall strategy relating to collecting and evaluating the evidence to be obtained. By understanding and testing **internal control,** the auditors can assess whether it offers assurance that the financial statements will be free from material errors and fraud. These assessments enable the auditors to evaluate the risks of material misstatement

FIGURE 2.1 Regulation of the Profession

Authority of Regulatory Bodies

Regulatory Bodies	Integrated Audits for Public Companies	Audits for Nonpublic Companies
Public Company Accounting Oversight Board (PCAOB)	1. Establishes standards* for the audits of public companies: • Auditing • Attestation • Quality control • Independence • Ethical behavior 2. PCAOB standards have authority based on federal legislation. 3. Registers CPA firms to audit public companies and may revoke a firm's registration or bar an individual CPA from participating in public company audits. 4. Performs inspections of the public company audit practices of registered CPA firms.	No standard-setting or regulatory responsibilities regarding CPA services for nonpublic companies.
American Institute of Certified Public Accountants (AICPA)	No standard-setting or regulatory responsibilities regarding public company audits.**	1. Establishes standards for: • Auditing • Attestation • Accounting and review • Quality control • Independence • Ethical behavior 2. AICPA standards have authority based on their general acceptance by state boards of accountancy, other legislative organizations, and the courts. 3. Firms may subject themselves to AICPA regulation by voluntarily joining one or both of the AICPA sections: (1) the PCPS: the AICPA Alliance for CPA firms, or (2) the Center for Public Company Audit Firms. Both sections have voluntary peer review programs. 4. The AICPA Center for Public Company Audit Firms' peer review program covers the nonpublic practices of firms whose public company practices are inspected by the PCAOB. 5. The individual membership requirements of the AICPA require members to practice in a firm that participates in a practice review program.
State Boards of Accountancy	1. License CPAs and CPA firms to practice public accountancy in their states or jurisdictions and can revoke the right to practice in those jurisdictions. 2. In their jurisdictions, state boards have regulatory responsibility for both public and nonpublic practice. 3. State boards adopt AICPA and PCAOB standards but may supplement them with their own requirements.	

*The PCAOB adopted AICPA professional standards issued through April 16, 2003, as its interim standards. In addition, the SEC has oversight responsibility for the PCAOB and all standards must be approved and issued by the SEC.

**Technically, the AICPA general ethics requirements also would apply to a AICPA member performing services for public companies.

of the financial statements. To address these risks, the auditors will perform procedures to substantiate the amounts on the financial statements being audited. Examples of such evidence include written confirmations from outsiders and firsthand observation of assets by the auditors. The gathering and evaluating of evidence lies at the very heart of the audit process and is a continuing theme throughout this textbook.

Adequate Planning and Supervision

Adequate planning is essential to a satisfactory audit. Some portions of the audit can be performed prior to the end of the year under audit; some information may be compiled by the client's staff and made available for the auditors' analysis. The appropriate number of audit staff with various levels of skill and the time required of each need to be determined in advance of fieldwork. These are but a few of the elements of planning the audit.

Most of the fieldwork of an audit is carried out by staff members with limited experience. The key to successful use of relatively new staff members is close supervision at every level. This concept extends from providing a specific written audit program to staff members all the way to an overall review of the work by the partner in charge of the engagement.

Sufficient Understanding of Internal Control

The auditors' understanding of the client, its environment, and internal control allows the auditors to determine what can go wrong to cause the financial statements to be materially misstated. In areas where risk is high the auditors must plan and perform more extensive audit procedures. Such procedures may be tests of internal controls or procedures to substantiate financial statement amounts.

Effective internal control provides assurance that the client's records are reliable. When the auditors find this type of internal control, the quantity of other evidence required is much less than if controls are weak. Thus, the auditors' assessment of internal control has great impact on the nature of the audit process.

Sufficient Competent Audit Evidence

The third standard of fieldwork requires that the auditors gather sufficient competent evidence to have a basis for expressing an opinion on the financial statements. The term *competent* refers to the quality of the evidence; some forms of evidence are stronger and more convincing than others. In Chapter 5, we explore at length the meaning of this standard.

Standards of Reporting

The four reporting standards establish some specific directives for preparation of the auditors' report. The report must specifically state whether the financial statements are in conformity with generally accepted accounting principles. The report must contain an opinion on the financial statements as a whole, or must disclaim an opinion. **Consistency** in the application of generally accepted accounting principles and adequate informative disclosure in the financial statements is to be assumed unless the audit report states otherwise. These basic reporting standards are considered more fully in the later part of this chapter.

AICPA Statements on Auditing Standards (SASs)

Learning Objective 2

Statements on Auditing Standards are serially numbered pronouncements issued by the AICPA's Auditing Standards Board (ASB). The first in the series, *SAS 1*, is a codification of 54 *Statements* previously issued over many years by the Committee on Auditing Procedure, a predecessor of the ASB. Since *SAS 1* was released in 1972, many additional statements on specific topics have been issued to provide more detailed guidance than is available from the 10 generally accepted auditing standards.

According to *SAS 95* (AU 150) the SASs are codified within the framework of the 10 generally accepted auditing standards. They are the most authoritative references that auditors can utilize to resolve problems encountered during the audit of a nonpublic company. The term *auditing standards* is often used in practice to refer to the SASs, to the 10 generally accepted auditing standards, or to both. The authoritative status of the SASs is derived from the AICPA *Code of Professional Conduct* (Rule 202). The code requires auditors to adhere to these pronouncements. A CPA firm must be prepared to justify any departure from the SASs, a task not to be taken lightly.

FIGURE 2.2
The GAAS Hierarchy

Category	Status	Audit Guidance
1. Standards	Auditors should be prepared to justify departures from these standards.	• The 10 generally accepted auditing standards. • Statements on Auditing Standards (SASs). • Other standards that apply for PCAOB, government audits, etc.
2. Interpretive Publications	Recommendations on the application of the SASs. If not followed, the auditors should be prepared to explain how they complied with the SAS provisions addressed by the interpretive publication.	• Appendixes to SASs. • Interpretations of SASs. • Auditing guidance in *AICPA Audit and Accounting Guides.* • AICPA auditing *Statements of Position.*
3. Other Auditing Publications	No authoritative status, but may help the auditor understand and apply the standards.	• Auditing articles in *Journal of Accountancy* and other professional journals. • Auditing articles in the *AICPA CPA Letter.* • Continuing education programs and other instruction materials. • Textbooks. • Guidebooks. • Audit programs. • Checklists.

The SASs, although more detailed and specific than the generally accepted auditing standards, do not usually prescribe specific auditing procedures to be followed. For more detailed, but less authoritative guidelines on specific audit problems, auditors can refer to *interpretive publications,* which include appendixes to the SASs, *AICPA Audit and Accounting Guides,* and AICPA auditing *Statements of Position.* The auditors should be aware of and consider the interpretive publications applicable to their audits. If the auditors fail to apply the auditing guidance in such publications, they should be prepared to explain how they complied with the related SAS.

Other auditing publications include such publications as AICPA *Auditing Practice Releases;* various technical studies published by the AICPA; auditing textbooks; and articles in professional journals, such as the *Journal of Accountancy* and *The CPA Journal.* Other auditing publications have no authoritative status but may be helpful to the auditors in understanding and applying the SASs.

The role and authority of various auditing publications are summarized in Figure 2.2. Keep in mind, however, that compliance with auditing standards does not represent an ideal level of audit performance, but rather a *minimum standard* for all engagements.

Throughout this textbook, we will be making references to individual AICPA SASs. Each SAS is identified under two numbering systems: the original SAS number and an AU number. The SAS numbering system organizes the SASs by date of issue, whereas the AU numbering system organizes them by topic. Thus, *Statement on Auditing Standards 39,* "Audit Sampling," is identified as *SAS 39* and AU 350.

In reading auditing standards it is important to understand the meaning of terms that express the auditors' responsibilities. Auditing standards use the terms "must" and "is required" to indicate unconditional responsibilities; the auditors *must* perform these steps or procedures. When the term "should" is used in auditing standards it is presumed that the auditors will perform the step or procedure. If they do not, the auditors must be prepared to demonstrate how the objective of the standard was met with other auditing procedures.

The Auditors' Responsibility for Detecting Misstatements

The auditors have a responsibility to plan and perform the audit to obtain *reasonable assurance* about whether the financial statements are free of material misstatement.[1] Reasonable assurance is achieved when **audit risk,** the risk that the auditor may unknowingly fail to appropriately modify the opinion on financial statements that are materially misstated, is at an appropriately low level. Financial statements may be misstated due to various causes, including errors, fraud, and certain illegal acts.

Errors and Fraud

SAS 47 (AU 312) defines the term **errors** as unintentional misstatements or omissions of amounts or disclosures in the financial statements. Errors may involve mistakes in gathering or processing data, unreasonable accounting estimates arising from oversight or misinterpretation of facts, or mistakes in the application of generally accepted accounting principles.

Fraud, as the term is used in *SAS 99,* "Consideration of Fraud in a Financial Statement Audit," relates to intentional acts that cause a misstatement of the financial statements. Misstatements due to fraud may occur due to either (1) fraudulent financial reporting or (2) misappropriation of assets (also referred to as "defalcation").

During the planning of an audit, the auditors are required to assess the risk of material misstatements—whether caused by error or fraud. Based on that assessment, they design and perform their audit to provide reasonable assurance of detecting such misstatements. To provide reasonable assurance, the auditors must exercise due care in planning, performing, and evaluating the results of their audit procedures. This requires auditors to exercise *professional skepticism,* which involves a questioning mind and a critical assessment of audit evidence throughout the audit process.

An audit provides reasonable, but not absolute, assurance of detecting material misstatement of the financial statements. Providing absolute assurance is not possible because available audit evidence is often less than convincing or conclusive, and due to the characteristics of fraud. For example, fraud often includes collusion among management, employees, or third parties, and is concealed by falsifying documents (including forgery). An audit rarely involves authentication of documents, nor are auditors ordinarily experts in authentication. In addition, management has the ability to override internal controls which otherwise may appear to be effective. Even if possible, audits providing absolute assurance of detecting material misstatement of financial statements would be exorbitant in price.

Illegal Acts by Clients

Laws and regulations vary in their relation to the client's financial statements. Certain laws have a direct effect on the financial statement amounts and are considered on every audit. An example is income tax law, which affects the amount of income tax expense in the financial statements of most clients. The auditors' responsibility for detecting violations of these laws is greater than their responsibility to detect **illegal acts** arising from laws that only indirectly affect the client's financial statements, such as violations of antitrust laws. Violations of these laws have an indirect effect because they may result in fines or penalties that should be disclosed as contingent liabilities in the client's financial statements.

As explained in *SAS 54* (AU 317), an audit carried out in accordance with generally accepted auditing standards should be designed to provide reasonable assurance of detecting illegal acts having a material *direct effect* on the determination of financial statement amounts—this is the same responsibility the auditors have for material errors and fraud. An audit does *not* generally provide a basis for detecting violations of laws or regulations that have an *indirect effect* on financial statement amounts.

The media and the public sometimes tend to blame auditors when illegal acts by a client company are not brought to light during an audit. Yet the very nature of audits cannot be relied on to detect all types of illegal acts by the client, particularly those with an indirect effect on

---

[1] The professional standards on these responsibilities are presented in *SAS 47* (AU 312), "Audit Risk and Materiality in Conducting an Audit," and *SAS 99* (AU 316), "Consideration of Fraud in a Financial Statement Audit."

the financial statements. On the other hand, audit procedures such as reading minutes of the board of directors and inquiring of management and the client's attorney may result in the discovery of certain indirect illegal acts. Also, the auditors are alert throughout their audit for information that raises a question regarding the possibility of illegal acts, such as transactions that are unauthorized or improperly recorded, investigations by governmental agencies, and excessive or unusual payments.

If the auditors conclude that an illegal act has or is likely to have occurred (regardless of whether it is believed to possibly have a direct effect on the financial statements), they should attempt to assess the impact of the actions on the financial statements. This usually requires consulting legal counsel or another specialist. The auditors should also discuss the situation with top management and notify the audit committee of the board of directors with respect to the illegal act, unless it is clearly inconsequential. The communication with the audit committee should describe the event, the circumstances of its occurrence, and the effect on the financial statements.

The auditors should consider whether the client has taken appropriate remedial action concerning the act. Such remedial action may include taking appropriate disciplinary actions, establishing controls to safeguard against recurrence and, if necessary, reporting the effects of the illegal acts in the financial statements. Ordinarily, if the client does not take the remedial action the auditors believe necessary in the circumstances the auditors should withdraw from the engagement.[2] This action on the part of the auditors makes clear that they will not be associated in any way with dishonorable or illegal activities.

The Auditors' Reports

Learning Objective 4

The end product of an audit of a business entity is a report expressing the auditors' opinion on the client's financial statements. The content of the auditors' report varies somewhat depending on whether it results from the audit of a nonpublic or public company. We will first present the standard audit report for a nonpublic company, followed by a discussion of how the report for a public company differs.

The auditors' *standard unqualified report* (as illustrated on the next page) consists of three paragraphs. The first paragraph clarifies the responsibilities of management and the auditors and is referred to as the *introductory paragraph.* The second paragraph, which describes the nature of the audit, is called the *scope paragraph;* and the final paragraph, the *opinion paragraph,* is a concise statement of the auditors' opinion based on the audit.

The auditors' report is addressed to the person or persons who retained the auditors. In the case of corporations, the selection of an auditing firm is usually made by the board of directors and ratified by the stockholders.

The Introductory Paragraph of the Auditors' Report

To gain a full understanding of the introductory paragraph of the auditors' report we need to emphasize the following two points:

1. *The client company is primarily responsible for the financial statements.* The management of a company has the responsibility of maintaining adequate accounting records and of preparing proper financial statements for the use of stockholders and creditors.

---

[2] The Private Securities Reform Act of 1995 places additional requirements upon public companies registered with the Securities and Exchange Commission and their auditors when (1) the illegal act has a material effect on the financial statements, (2) senior management and the board of directors have not taken appropriate remedial actions, and (3) the failure to take remedial action is reasonably expected to warrant departure from a standard audit report (or to warrant resignation). In such circumstances the auditors "shall, as soon as practicable" communicate their conclusions directly to the board of directors. Within one day the company must notify the Securities and Exchange Commission of having received such a communication and must send a copy of that notification to the auditor. If the auditors do not receive such notice within the one-day period, they must furnish the report to the SEC within one business day after the failure of the company to give the required notice.

Even though the financial statements are sometimes constructed and printed in the auditors' office, primary responsibility for the statements remains with management. The auditors' product is their report. It is a separate document from the client's financial statements, although the two are closely related and transmitted together to stockholders, creditors, and other financial statement users.

Auditors' Report for Audits of Nonpublic Companies

Independent Auditors' Report

To the Board of Directors and Stockholders, XYZ Company:

We have audited the accompanying balance sheet of XYZ Company as of December 31, 20X1, and the related statements of income, retained earnings, and cash flows for the year then ended. These financial statements are the responsibility of the Company's management. Our responsibility is to express an opinion on these financial statements based on our audit.

We conducted our audit in accordance with auditing standards generally accepted in the United States of America. Those standards require that we plan and perform the audit to obtain reasonable assurance about whether the financial statements are free of material misstatement. An audit includes examining, on a test basis, evidence supporting the amounts and disclosures in the financial statements. An audit also includes assessing the accounting principles used and significant estimates made by management, as well as evaluating the overall financial statement presentation. We believe that our audit provides a reasonable basis for our opinion.

In our opinion, the financial statements referred to above present fairly, in all material respects, the financial position of XYZ Company as of December 31, 20X1, and the results of its operations and its cash flows for the year then ended in conformity with accounting principles generally accepted in the United States of America.

Los Angeles, California

Blue, Gray & Company
Certified Public Accountants
February 26, 20X2

Once we recognize that the financial statements are the statements of the company and not of the auditors, we realize that the auditors have no right to make changes in the financial statements. What action then should the auditors take if they do not agree with the presentation of a material item in the balance sheet or income statement? Assume, for example, that the allowance for uncollectible accounts is not sufficient (in the auditors' view) to cover the probable collection losses in the accounts receivable.

The auditors will first discuss the problem with management and point out why they believe the valuation allowance to be inadequate. If management agrees to increase the allowance for uncollectible accounts, an adjusting entry will be made for that purpose, and the problem is solved. If management is not convinced by the auditors' arguments and declines to increase the allowance, the auditors will probably *qualify* their opinion by stating in the report that the financial statements reflect fairly the company's financial position and operating results, *except for the effects of not providing an adequate provision for uncollectible accounts.* Usually such issues are satisfactorily disposed of in discussions between the auditors and the client, and a qualification of the auditors' opinion is avoided. A full consideration of the use of qualifications in the auditors' report is presented in Chapter 17.

2. *The auditors render a report on the financial statements, not on the accounting records.* The primary purpose of an audit is to provide assurance to the users of the financial statements that these statements are reliable. Auditors do not express an opinion on the client's accounting records. The auditors' investigation of financial statement items includes reference to the client's accounting records, but is not limited to these records. An audit includes observation of tangible assets, inspection of such documents as purchase orders and contracts, and the gathering of evidence from outsiders (such as banks, customers, and suppliers), as well as analysis of the client's accounting records.

A principal means of establishing the validity of a balance sheet and income statement is to compare the statement figures to the accounting records and to the original evidence of transactions. However, the auditors' use of the accounting records is only a means to an end—and merely a part of the audit. It is, therefore, appropriate for the auditors to state in their report that they have made an audit of the *financial statements* rather than to say that they have made an audit of the accounting records. In the illustration, the auditors' report covers the years for which financial statements are being presented by the company. Reporting on such comparative financial statements is discussed in detail in Chapter 17.

The Scope Paragraph of the Auditors' Report

The scope paragraph describes the nature of the CPAs' audit. It states that the audit was conducted in accordance with auditing standards generally accepted in the United States of America[3] and points out that, while an audit is meant to obtain *reasonable assurance* that the financial statements are free of material misstatement, the procedures are applied on a test basis. Thus, an audit cannot provide *absolute assurance* that the financial statements are free from material misstatement; the auditors do, however, believe that the procedures performed provide a reasonable basis for their opinion.

The Opinion Paragraph of the Auditors' Report

The opinion paragraph consists of only one sentence, which is restated here with certain significant phrases shown in italics:

In our opinion, the financial statements referred to above *present fairly, in all material respects,* the financial position of XYZ Company as of December 31, 20X1, and the results of its operations and its cash flows for the year then ended in conformity with *accounting principles generally accepted in the United States of America.*

Each of the italicized phrases has a special significance. The first phrase, "in our opinion," makes clear that the auditors are expressing nothing more than an informed opinion; they are not guaranteeing or certifying that the statements are accurate, correct, or true. In an earlier period of public accounting, the wording of the audit report contained the phrase "we certify that," but this expression was discontinued on the grounds that it was misleading. To "certify" implies absolute assurance of accuracy, which an audit does not provide.

The auditors cannot guarantee the correctness of the financial statements because the statements include many estimates, not absolute facts. Furthermore, the auditors do not make a complete and detailed examination of all transactions. Their audit is limited to a program of tests that leaves the possibility of some misstatements going undetected. Because of limitations inherent in the accounting process and because of practical limitations of time and cost in performing an audit, the auditors' work culminates in the expression of an opinion and not in the issuance of a guarantee of accuracy. The growth of public accounting and the increased confidence placed in audited statements by all sectors of the economy indicate that the auditors' opinion is usually sufficient assurance that the statements may be relied upon.

The Financial Statements "Present Fairly, in All Material Respects . . ."
Since many of the items in financial statements cannot be measured exactly, the auditors cannot say that the statements present exactly or correctly the financial position or operating results. The meaning of "present fairly," as used in the context of the auditors' report, has been much discussed in court cases and in auditing literature. Some accountants believed that financial statements were fair if they conformed to GAAP; others insisted that fairness was a distinct concept, broader than mere compliance with GAAP. This discussion led to the issuance by the

---

[3] Historically, *audit reports* referred simply to generally accepted auditing standards and generally accepted accounting principles. The globalization of business resulted in a modification of the standard report which identifies the source of the standards followed (e.g., International, United States [of America], or some other country). In this text we will use the new terminology in report illustrations, but, like the standards, will refer to generally accepted auditing standards (GAAS) and generally accepted accounting principles (GAAP) in other contexts.

Auditing Standards Board of *SAS 69* (AU 411), "The Meaning of 'Present Fairly in Conformity with Generally Accepted Accounting Principles' in the Independent Auditor's Report." *SAS 69* states that fairly presented financial statements are:

1. Prepared in accordance with accounting principles that have *general acceptance* and are *appropriate* in the circumstances.
2. *Informative* of matters that may affect their use, understanding, and interpretation.
3. Presented in a manner that is *classified and summarized in a reasonable manner,* neither too detailed nor too condensed.
4. Prepared to *reflect transactions and events* within a range of reasonable limits.

What Is "Material"?

Auditors cannot issue an unqualified opinion on financial statements that contain material deficiencies. The term *material* may be defined as "sufficiently important to influence decisions made by reasonable users of financial statements." In the audit of a small client—such as a condominium property owners' association—$1,000 might be considered material. On the other hand, in the audit of a company such as IBM or Microsoft, an amount of $1 million might be considered immaterial.

In practice, one of the most significant elements of professional judgment is the ability to draw the line between material and immaterial departures from generally accepted accounting principles. The auditor who raises objections over immaterial items will soon lose the respect of both clients and associates. On the other hand, the auditor who fails to identify and disclose material deficiencies in financial statements may be liable for the losses of those who rely upon the audited statements. In short, applying the concept of materiality is one of the most complex problems faced by auditors.

Materiality depends upon both the *dollar amount* and the *nature of the item.* For example, a $500,000 error in the balance of the Cash account is ordinarily far more significant than a $500,000 error in the balance of Accumulated Depreciation. If a corporation sells assets to a member of top management and then buys the assets back at a higher price, this *related party transaction* warrants disclosure even though the dollar amounts are not large in relation to the financial statements as a whole. The reason for requiring disclosure of such a transaction is based more on the nature of the transaction than upon the dollar amount. Materiality is discussed further in Chapter 6.

Adequate Informative Disclosure

If financial statements are to present fairly, in all material respects, the financial position and operating results of a company, there must be **adequate disclosure** of all essential information. A financial statement may be misleading if it does not give a complete picture. For example, if an extraordinary item arising from an uninsured flood loss of plant and equipment were combined with operating income and not clearly identified, the reader might be misled as to the earning power of the company. Adequate disclosure means the information is accurate, complete, and has been clearly conveyed to the financial statement user.

Generally Accepted Accounting Principles (GAAP)

The next key phrase to be considered is "accounting principles generally accepted in the United States of America." The wording of the audit report implies that these accounting principles represent a concept well known to CPAs and sophisticated users of financial statements. However, no official list of accounting principles exists, and a satisfactory concise definition has yet to be developed.

In evaluating whether a particular accounting principle used by a client is generally accepted, the auditors may refer to a variety of sources, from *Statements* and *Interpretations* of the FASB, the GASB, and the FASAB to articles in accounting journals. The auditors look to these references to determine whether there is *substantial authoritative support* for the principle. Figure 2.3 illustrates the relative authority of sources of generally accepted accounting principles from the category with highest authority to that with the least. As

FIGURE 2.3 The GAAP Hierarchy

Category	Nongovernmental Entities	State and Local Governments	Federal Government
a. Authoritative Body Pronouncements	• *FASB Statements and Interpretations* • *APB Opinions* • *AICPA Accounting Research Bulletins*	• *GASB Statements and Interpretations* • *FASB and AICPA pronouncements made applicable by a GASB Statement or Interpretation*	• *FASAB Statements and Interpretations* • *AICPA, FASB, and GASB pronouncements made applicable by a FASAB Statement or Interpretation*
b. Pronouncements of Bodies Composed of Expert Accountants, Exposed for Public Comment	• *FASB Technical Bulletins* • *AICPA Industry Audit and Accounting Guides and Statements of Position* (cleared by FASB)	• *GASB Technical Bulletins* • *AICPA Industry Audit and Accounting Guides and Statements of Position* (cleared by GASB)	• *FASAB Technical Bulletins* • *AICPA Industry Audit and Accounting Guides and Statements of Position* (cleared by FASAB)
c. Pronouncements of Bodies Composed of Expert Accountants, Not Exposed for Public Comment	• *Consensus Positions of the FASB Emerging Issues Task Force* • *AICPA Practice Bulletins* (cleared by FASB)	• *Consensus Positions of the GASB Emerging Issues Task Force* • *AICPA Practice Bulletins* (cleared by GASB)	• *Technical Releases of the Accounting and Auditing Policy Committee of the FASAB* • *AICPA Practice Bulletins* (cleared by the FASAB)
d. Widely Recognized Practices and Pronouncements	• FASB staff *"Questions and Answers"* • *AICPA Accounting Interpretations* • Widely accepted industry practices	• GASB staff *"Questions and Answers"* • Widely accepted industry practices	• FASAB staff *Implementation Guides* • Widely accepted federal government practices
e. Other Accounting Literature	• *FASB Concepts Statements* • *APB Statements* • *AICPA Issues Papers and Technical Practice Aids* • *International Accounting Standards Committee Statements* • *GASB Statements, Interpretations, and Technical Bulletins* • Pronouncements of other professional associations or regulatory agencies • Accounting textbooks, handbooks, and articles	• *GASB Concepts Statements* • Pronouncements in (a) through (d) of nongovernmental hierarchy not specifically made applicable • *APB Statements* • *FASB Concepts Statements* • *AICPA Issues Papers and Technical Practice Aids* • *International Accounting Standards Committee Statements* • Pronouncements of other professional associations or regulatory agencies • Accounting textbooks, handbooks, and articles	• *FASAB Concepts Statements* • Pronouncements in (a) through (d) of GASB and FASB not specifically made applicable • *FASB and GASB Concepts Statements* • *AICPA Issues Papers and Technical Practice Aids* • *International Accounting Standards Committee Statements* • Pronouncements of other professional associations or regulatory agencies • Accounting textbooks, handbooks, and articles

Source: *SAS 69* (AU 411), "The Meaning of 'Present Fairly in Conformity with Generally Accepted Accounting Principles' in the Independent Auditor's Report."

illustrated, the pronouncements of generally accepted accounting principles differ among state and local governments, federal government entities, and businesses and not-for-profit organizations.

In situations in which there is a conflict between the accounting treatment suggested by pronouncements from two different categories, the pronouncement from the higher category should be followed. For example, authoritative body pronouncements prevail over pronouncements of other experts and widely recognized practices and pronouncements. When there is a conflict within a category, the auditors should select the accounting principle that most clearly reflects the *economic substance* of the particular transaction.

Other Types of Auditors' Reports

Learning Objective 5

The form of auditors' report discussed in this chapter is called a **standard unqualified opinion.** An unqualified opinion denotes that the audit was adequate in scope and that the financial statements present fairly the financial position, results of operations, and cash flows in conformity with generally accepted accounting principles. Under these circumstances, the auditors are taking *no exceptions* and inserting *no qualifications* in the report.

An unqualified opinion is the type of report the client wants and also the type auditors prefer to issue. In some audits, however, the circumstances do not permit the auditors to give their unqualified opinion on the financial statements. As alternatives to an unqualified opinion, auditors may issue a *qualified opinion,* an *adverse opinion,* or a *disclaimer of opinion.* In some situations, auditors also include additional *explanatory language* in an unqualified report.

Auditors issue a **qualified opinion** on financial statements when there is some limitation on their audit, or when one or more items in the financial statements are not presented in accordance with generally accepted accounting principles. The limitation or exception must be significant but not so material as to overshadow an overall opinion on the financial statements.

An **adverse opinion** states that the financial statements *are not fairly presented.* In practice an adverse opinion is rare, because it would be of little use to the client. If the financial statements contain such material departures from generally accepted accounting principles as to warrant an adverse opinion, this situation will be discussed among the auditors and the client's management. Management probably will agree to make the changes necessary to avoid an adverse opinion or will decide to terminate the audit engagement and thus avoid paying additional audit fees.

Auditors will issue a **disclaimer of opinion** if they are unable to determine the overall fairness of the financial statements. This type of report results from very significant limitations in the scope of the auditors' examination or limitations that are imposed by the client.

When a qualified, adverse, or disclaimer of opinion is issued on the financial statements, *explanatory language* is added to the report describing the matter of concern. In certain other circumstances, explanatory language may be added to what remains an unqualified opinion. For example, audit reports are modified to inform users of financial statements of changes in accounting principles in relation to the prior year, or the fact that another audit firm is responsible for a significant portion of the audit. In circumstances such as these, although the opinion may remain unqualified, the overall wording of the report itself deviates from the wording of the standard unqualified report.

Public Company Audit Reports

As discussed in Chapter 1, the Sarbanes-Oxley Act requires that auditors of publicly traded companies in the United States perform an integrated audit that includes providing assurance on both the financial statements and the effectiveness of internal control over financial reporting. In these audits, the auditors may either issue separate reports on the financial statements and internal control, or they may issue a combined report. The following separate report on the financial statements of a publicly traded company emphasizes the differences as compared to the standard audit report for the audit of a nonpublic company. Notice that "auditing standards generally accepted in the United States of America" is replaced by the standards of the "Public Company Accounting Oversight Board (United States)" and a fourth paragraph is added referring to the auditors' report on internal control. The report on internal control is illustrated in Chapter 18.

Report of Independent Registered Public Accounting Firm

To the Board of Directors and Stockholders
XYZ Company:

We have audited the accompanying balance sheet of XYZ Company as of December 31, 20X1, and the related statements of income, retained earnings, and cash flows for the year then ended. These financial statements are the responsibility of the Company's management. Our responsibility is to express an opinion on these financial statements based on our audit.

We conducted our audit in accordance with standards of the Public Company Accounting Oversight Board (United States). Those standards require that we plan and perform the audit to obtain reasonable assurance about whether the financial statements are free of material misstatement. An audit includes examining, on a test basis, evidence supporting the amounts and disclosures in the financial statements. An audit also includes assessing the accounting principles used and significant estimates made by management, as well as evaluating the overall financial statement presentation. We believe that our audit provides a reasonable basis for our opinion.

In our opinion, the financial statements referred to above present fairly, in all material respects, the financial position of XYZ Company as of December 31, 20X1, and the results of its operations and its cash flows for the year then ended in conformity with accounting principles generally accepted in the United States of America.

We also have audited, in accordance with the standards of the Public Company Accounting Oversight Board (United States), the effectiveness of XYZ Company's internal control over financial reporting as of December 31, 20X1, based on *Internal Control—Integrated Framework issued by the Committee of Sponsoring Organizations of the Treadway Commission (COSO)* and our report dated February 26, 20X2, expressed unqualified opinions.

Los Angeles, Calif.   *Blue, Gray & Company*
Certified Public Accountants
February 26, 20X2

The Attestation Standards

Learning Objective 6

The generally accepted auditing standards were adopted by the AICPA to provide guidance for the performance of audits of historical financial statements. The expansion of the attestation function has led the accounting profession to develop more general attestation standards, which are contained in *Statement on Standards for Attestation Services No. 1* (SSAE 1). These attestation standards, presented as Figure 2.4, are meant to serve as a general framework and set boundaries for the attest function. Since the issuance of SSAE 1, the Auditing Standards Board has issued a number of SSAEs that provide guidance for attesting to specific types of information, such as prospective financial statements and internal control over financial reporting. The relationship of these attestation standards is shown in Figure 2.5. The PCAOB adopted the AICPA attestation standards as interim standards for attestation engagements related to the financial reporting of public companies.

Quality Control in CPA Firms

Learning Objective 7

A CPA firm should establish adequate quality control policies and procedures to provide reasonable assurance that it follows professional standards on every engagement. To provide CPA firms with guidance in establishing quality control policies, the AICPA has issued *Statements on Quality Control Standards* which identify five "elements" of **quality control**. The elements of quality control may be regarded as the areas in which the AICPA considers it desirable for a CPA firm to establish quality control procedures.

The AICPA does not require specific quality control procedures. In fact, it states that the specific procedures should depend upon the size of the firm, the number of offices, and the nature of the firm's practice. Thus, the quality control procedures employed by a 200-office international firm will differ considerably from those employed by a single-office firm that audits only small businesses. Technically, the *Statements on Quality Control* apply only to auditing, other attestation, and accounting services for which professional standards have been

FIGURE 2.4
AICPA Attestation Standards

General Standards

1. The engagement shall be performed by a practitioner having *adequate technical training* and *proficiency in the attest function.*
2. The engagement shall be performed by a practitioner having *adequate knowledge in the subject matter.*
3. The practitioner shall perform the engagement only if he or she has reason to believe that the *subject matter is capable of evaluation or measurement* against criteria (standards or benchmarks) that are suitable and available to users.
4. In all matters relating to the engagement, an *independence* in mental attitude shall be maintained by the practitioner.
5. *Due professional care* shall be exercised in the planning and the performance of the engagement.

Standards of Fieldwork

1. The work shall be *adequately planned* and assistants, if any, shall be properly *supervised.*
2. *Sufficient evidence* shall be obtained to provide a reasonable basis for the conclusion that is expressed in the report.

Standards of Reporting

1. The report shall *identify the subject matter* or the assertion being reported on and state the *character of the engagement.*
2. The report shall state the *practitioner's conclusion* about the subject matter or the assertion based on the criteria against which the subject matter was measured.
3. The report shall state all of the practitioner's *significant reservations* about the engagement.
4. The report on an engagement to evaluate subject matter that has been prepared based on *agreed-upon criteria* or an assertion related thereto, or on an engagement to apply *agreed-upon procedures,* should contain a statement *restricting its use* to the parties who have agreed upon such criteria or procedures.

FIGURE 2.5   **Applicability of Statements on Standards for Attestation Services (SSAEs)**

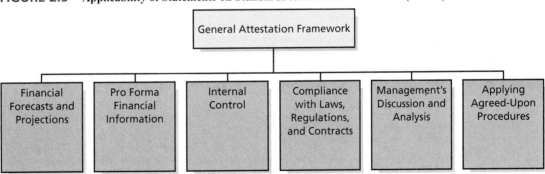

established by the AICPA. As a practical matter, however, every CPA firm should have quality control procedures applicable to *every aspect of its practice.* In the broad sense, the concept of "quality control" means that CPA firms should establish controls to provide assurance that they meet their responsibilities to their clients and to the public.

Figure 2.6 indicates the five areas in which the AICPA has indicated that quality control procedures are appropriate. In addition, the table explains the basic objective to be achieved in each area and provides an example procedure that a CPA firm might implement as a step toward achieving the objective. The PCAOB also has adopted the AICPA quality control standards as its interim quality control standards, making them applicable to public company practice.

FIGURE 2.6   Elements of Quality Control

Element of Quality Control	Basic Objective to Provide Reasonable Assurance That:	Example Procedures
Independence, integrity, and objectivity	Personnel maintain independence (in fact and in appearance) in all required circumstances, perform all professional services with integrity, and maintain objectivity in discharging professional responsibilities.	An investigation is made to determine the firm's independence before accepting a new audit client.
Personnel management	1. Individuals supervising audit and attestation engagements and signing reports must have the competencies appropriate to the engagement. 2. Those hired possess appropriate characteristics to perform competently. 3. Work is assigned to those with appropriate technical training and proficiency. 4. Personnel participate in appropriate continuing education and other professional development activities. 5. Personnel selected for advancement have the necessary qualifications.	Prospective employees are interviewed by both the personnel partner and a technical partner in the area in which they will work.
Acceptance and continuance of clients and engagements	The likelihood of association with a client whose management lacks integrity is minimized.	Background information is gathered on all prospective audit clients and is discussed at a partners' meeting before accepting the client.
Engagement performance	Work performed meets applicable professional standards, regulatory requirements, and the firm's standards of quality. If applicable, SEC Practice Section requirements for a concurring partner review should be followed.	Working papers are reviewed by the manager, and any deficiencies are discussed with the preparer. Working papers for SEC engagements must be reviewed by a concurring partner.
Monitoring	Policies and procedures established for each of other elements are suitably designed and effectively applied.	A quality control partner periodically tests the application of quality control procedures.

Regulation of Accounting Firms

In the United States public accounting firms are regulated by a number of organizations, including the Public Company Accounting Oversight Board, the American Institute of Certified Public Accountants, the Securities and Exchange Commission, the various courts, and the state boards of accountancy.

Public Company Accounting Oversight Board

As described in Chapter 1, the **Public Company Accounting Oversight Board (PCAOB)** was established in 2002[4] with the following functions:

- Register public accounting firms that prepare audit reports for financial statement issuers.

[4] Until 2002, the *Public Oversight Board* (POB) served as a part of the profession's system of self-regulation. It was an autonomous board made up of five prominent individuals with a broad spectrum of business, professional, regulatory, and legislative experience. The POB oversaw the activities of the AICPA's SEC Practice Section (including its peer review activities), made inquiries into alleged audit failures, and periodically reported to the SEC and Congress. The POB was disbanded in 2002, with its responsibilities subsequently taken over by the Public Company Accounting Oversight Board.

- Establish or adopt auditing, quality control, ethics, independence, and other standards relating to audit reports for issuers.
- Conduct inspections of registered public accounting firms.
- Perform other duties or functions to promote high professional standards for audits, and enforce compliance with the Sarbanes-Oxley Act of 2002 (discussed in Chapter 1).

The PCAOB is composed of five members—only two are CPAs—selected from among prominent individuals who have demonstrated a commitment to the interests of investors and the public and an understanding of the issues faced by the PCAOB. Members are appointed by the Securities and Exchange Commission and may serve no more than two five-year terms.

All accounting firms that audit SEC registrants must register with the PCAOB. As part of that registration process, each firm pledges to cooperate with any inquiry made by the PCAOB. The PCAOB may impose monetary damages and may suspend firms and accountants from working on engagements for publicly traded companies. It may also make referrals to the Justice Department to consider criminal cases.

The PCAOB performs inspections of the public audit practices of **registered public accounting firms** for compliance with the Sarbanes-Oxley Act, PCAOB and SEC requirements, and professional standards. CPA firms that audit more than 100 public companies are inspected annually, and firms that audit 100 or fewer public companies are ~~audited~~ [→ inspected] at least every three years.

Peer Review and Inspections

Members of the AICPA who are in public practice and have financial reporting responsibilities must have a sample of their work reviewed by an independent party. To meet this requirement, many CPA firms undergo a peer review performed directly by another CPA firm or a team of CPAs. A **peer review** involves a study of the adequacy of the firm's established quality control policies and tests to determine the extent of the firm's compliance with those policies. In large part, the tests consist of a review of working paper files and reports for selected engagements. The engagements are evaluated for compliance with established quality control policies and professional standards, including promotions of employees, continuing education of firm personnel, staffing of engagements, client acceptance, and the employment of professional personnel.

Based on the peer reviewers' study and tests of the quality controls, they issue a report that includes an opinion as to the adequacy of the reviewed firm's quality control system. Suggestions for improvement to the system are outlined in a "letter of comments" issued by the peer reviewers to the reviewed firm. Peer reviews are educational in that firms are encouraged to develop and implement strong systems of quality control. In addition, if a firm fails to take appropriate corrective action various sanctions may be imposed (e.g., additional continuing education requirements, admonishments, suspension from membership).

Inspections performed by the PCAOB staff meet the AICPA's practice review requirement for the public auditing practices of those firms. The Sarbanes-Oxley Act provides that an **inspection** shall include at least the following three general components:

1. An inspection and review of selected audit and review engagements.
2. An evaluation of the sufficiency of the quality control system of the firm and the manner of the documentation and communication of the system.
3. Performance of such other testing of the audit, supervisory, and quality control procedures as are considered necessary.

Inspections by the PCAOB staff differ from peer reviews conducted by CPA firms. Generally, the PCAOB staff focuses on selected quality control issues only and may also consider other aspects of practice management, such as the determinates of partner compensation. In addition, while peer reviews focus on evaluating and testing compliance with the firm's quality control system, a PCAOB inspection focuses primarily on evaluating performance of a sample of individual audit and review engagements. In selecting the engagements for inspection, the PCAOB staff uses a risk assessment process to identify engagements that have a higher risk of lack of compliance with professional standards. As an example, an engagement may be selected primarily because it is in a high-risk industry. Once an audit is selected, the inspection focuses on the high-risk aspects of that engagement, such as the audit work on revenue recognition and accounting estimates. When a lack of compliance with professional standards is found, the PCAOB staff attempts to ascertain the cause of the lack of compliance, which may lead to the identification of a defect in the firm's quality control system.

Each inspection results in a written report transmitted to the SEC and appropriate regulatory authorities. Also included is the letter of comments by the PCAOB inspectors, and any responses by the CPA firm. While the content of most of the reports are made available to the public, discussions of potential defects in a firm's quality control system are not made public unless the firm does not address the issue within 12 months.

International Accounting and Auditing Standards

Learning Objective 8

Auditing standards are currently determined on a country-by-country basis. However, as securities markets around the world have become more multinational, a need has developed for common auditing and accounting standards. The **International Federation of Accountants (IFAC)** is a worldwide organization of national accounting bodies (e.g., the AICPA) of approximately 114 countries, established to help foster a coordinated worldwide accounting profession with harmonized standards. One of its committees, the **International Auditing and Assurance Standards Board (IAASB)** issues *International Standards on Auditing* that provide procedural and reporting guidance to auditors.

The pronouncements of the IAASB do not override the national auditing standards of its members. Rather they are meant to foster the development of consistent worldwide professional standards. Members from countries that do not have such standards are encouraged to adopt IAASB standards; members from countries that already have standards are encouraged to compare them to IAASB standards and to seek to eliminate any material inconsistencies.

The international auditing standards-setting process is progressing at a rapid pace. It is likely that within the next five years an audit in conformity with IAASB standards will be acceptable for multinational securities offerings in virtually all countries.

The International Audit Report

The reporting guidance of the IAASB is similar to that included in U.S. standards, but the report differs in content, as illustrated below.[5]

[5] The AICPA Auditing Standards Board is considering a proposal to change the U.S. audit report for nonpublic companies to conform to the international audit report.

Independent Auditors' Report

To the Shareholders of ABC Company:

We have audited the accompanying financial statements of ABC Company, which comprise the balance sheet as of December 31, 20X1, and the income statement, statement of changes in equity, and cash flow statement for the year then ended, and a summary of significant accounting policies and other explanatory notes.

Management's Responsibility for the Financial Statements

Management is responsible for the preparation and fair presentation of these financial statements in accordance with International Financial Reporting Standards. This responsibility includes: designing, implementing, and maintaining internal control relevant to the preparation and fair presentation of financial statements that are free from material misstatement, whether due to fraud or error; selecting and applying appropriate accounting policies; and making accounting estimates that are reasonable in the circumstances.

Auditor's Responsibility

Our responsibility is to express an opinion on these financial statements based on our audit. We conducted our audit in accordance with International Standards on Auditing. Those standards require that we comply with ethical requirements and plan and perform the audit to obtain reasonable assurance whether the financial statements are free from material misstatement.

An audit involves performing procedures to obtain audit evidence about the amounts and disclosures in the financial statements. The procedures selected depend on the auditor's judgment, including the assessment of the risks of material misstatement of the financial statements, whether due to fraud or error. In making those risk assessments, the auditor considers internal control relevant to the entity's preparation and fair presentation of the financial statements in order to design audit procedures that are appropriate in the circumstances, but not for the purpose of expressing an opinion on the effectiveness of the entity's internal control. An audit also includes evaluating the appropriateness of accounting policies used and the reasonableness of accounting estimates made by management, as well as evaluating the overall presentation of the financial statements.

We believe that the audit evidence we have obtained is sufficient and appropriate to provide a basis for our audit opinion.

Opinion

In our opinion, the financial statements present fairly in all material respects, the financial position of ABC Company as of December 31, 20X1, and of its financial performance and its cash flows for the year then ended in accordance with International Financial Reporting Standards.

February 17, 20X2
Los Angeles, California, USA

Robert Blue
Blue, Smith & Company

The international audit report has an expanded description of management's responsibility for the financial statements and internal controls. It also contains an enhanced explanation of the audit process, which includes a description of the auditors' responsibility for internal control. The auditors also have certain reporting options. As an example, instead of indicating that the financial statements "present fairly, in all material respects," the auditors may substitute the phrase "give a true and fair view," as required of auditors in the United Kingdom. Also, the report may indicate that the financial statements comply with the provisions of the country's relevant statutes or laws. The report may be signed using the personal name of the auditor, the firm, or both—as is done in the above illustration. Inclusion of the city of the CPA firm office that performed the audit is a required part of the international report.

In some countries auditors have other reporting responsibilities, such as a responsibility to report certain matters that come to the auditors' attention. If those matters are addressed in the international audit report on the financial statements, they should be included in a separate section of the report after the opinion paragraph.

Chapter Summary

This chapter described the nature of generally accepted auditing standards, attestation standards, and quality control standards. To summarize:

1. The passage of the Sarbanes-Oxley Act of 2002 has significantly altered the regulatory environment of auditors and audit firms. Previously, the AICPA played a primary role in the development of auditing, attestation, and quality control standards and in the self-regulation of individual auditors and CPA firms. Now, the AICPA issues standards applicable only to nonpublic accounting and auditing engagements. The PCAOB issues standards for public company audits and regulates the public company practices of auditors and registered audit firms.

2. The AICPA 10 generally accepted auditing standards were adopted by the AICPA to provide a measure of quality for audits. These standards are divided into three types: general standards, standards of fieldwork, and standards of reporting. All audits must be performed in accordance with generally accepted auditing standards and any other applicable standards.

3. An audit provides reasonable assurance of detecting material misstatements of the financial statements (both errors and fraud) and illegal acts that have a direct and material effect on the determination of financial statement amounts. Although an audit does not provide reasonable assurance of detecting illegal acts that have only an indirect effect on the financial statements, the auditors remain alert for such acts. If illegal acts are discovered, regardless of their type, the auditors must carefully evaluate their effects on the financial statements.

4. The AICPA attestation standards were adopted to provide a general framework for the attest function and to set boundaries for these types of engagements. Similar to the generally accepted auditing standards, the 11 attestation standards are structured as general standards, standards of fieldwork, and standards of reporting.

5. CPA firms establish quality control systems to ensure that all professional engagements are performed in accordance with applicable professional standards. The AICPA's Quality Control Standards provide guidance in developing these systems. CPA firms with SEC reporting clients undergo inspections of their public company audit practice by the Public Company Accounting Oversight Board. In addition, CPA firms arrange to have their practices peer reviewed by other CPAs. Obtaining such practice reviews is a requirement for membership in the AICPA.

6. International financial markets would be facilitated if auditing and accounting standards were more uniform. Currently, the International Auditing and Assurance Standards Board issues pronouncements designed to foster the development of consistent worldwide auditing standards.

Key Terms Introduced or Emphasized in Chapter 2

Adequate disclosure   All essential information as required by generally accepted accounting principles (or some other appropriate basis of accounting) is included in the financial statements.

Adverse opinion   An opinion issued by the auditors that the financial statements they have audited *do not present fairly* the financial position, results of operation, or cash flows in conformity with accounting principles generally accepted in the United States of America.

Audit risk   The risk that the auditors may unknowingly fail to appropriately modify their opinion on financial statements that are materially misstated.

Auditors' report   A very precise document designed to communicate exactly the character and limitations of the responsibility being assumed by the auditors; in standard form, the report consists of an introductory paragraph, a scope paragraph, and an opinion paragraph.

Consistency   The concept of using the same accounting principles from year to year so that the successive financial statements issued by a business entity will be comparable.

Disclaimer of opinion   A form of report in which the auditors state that they do not express an opinion on the financial statements; it should include a separate paragraph stating the auditors' reasons for disclaiming an opinion and also disclosing any reservations they may have concerning the financial statements.

Error   An unintentional misstatement of financial statements or omission of an amount or a disclosure.

Fraud   For financial statement audits, "fraud" includes two types of intentional misstatements of financial statements—misstatements arising from fraudulent financial reporting and misstatements arising from misappropriation of assets. Legally, fraud is the misrepresentation by a person of a material fact, known by that person to be untrue or made with reckless indifference as to whether the fact is true, with intent to deceive and with the result that another party is injured.

Generally accepted auditing standards (GAAS)   A set of 10 standards adopted by the AICPA and binding on its members—designed to ensure the quality of the auditors' work.

Illegal acts   Violations of laws or governmental regulations.

Independence   A most important auditing standard, which prohibits CPAs from expressing an opinion on financial statements of an enterprise unless they are independent with respect to such enterprise; independence is impaired by a direct financial interest, service as an officer or trustee, certain loans to or from the enterprise, and various other relationships.

Inspection   (conducted by the Public Company Accounting Oversight Board)   A process that leads to an assessment of the degree of compliance of each registered public accounting firm and associated persons of that firm with the Sarbanes-Oxley Act of 2002 and the board's requirements in connection with its performance of audits, issuance of audit reports, and related matters.

Internal control   A process, effected by the entity's board of directors, management, and other personnel, designed to provide reasonable assurance regarding the achievement of objectives in the following categories: (1) reliability of financial reporting; (2) effectiveness and efficiency of operations; and (3) compliance with applicable laws and regulations.

International Auditing and Assurance Standards Board (IAASB)   A committee of the International Federation of Accountants, established to issue standards on auditing and reporting practices to improve the degree of uniformity of auditing practices and related services throughout the world.

International Federation of Accountants (IFAC)   A worldwide organization of national accounting bodies to help foster a coordinated worldwide accounting profession with harmonized standards.

Peer review   The study and evaluation of a CPA firm's quality control policies and procedures by another CPA firm or a team of qualified CPAs.

Public Company Accounting Oversight Board (PCAOB)   A board established by the Sarbanes-Oxley Act of 2002 to provide oversight of accounting firms that audit public companies by (1) establishing or adopting professional and ethical standards, (2) conducting inspections of CPA firms, and (3) enforcing compliance with professional and ethical standards. The board is composed of five individuals appointed by the SEC.

Qualified opinion   The appropriate form of audit report when there is a limitation in the scope of the audit or when the financial statements depart from GAAP significantly enough to require mention in the auditors' report, but not so significantly as to necessitate disclaiming an opinion or expressing an adverse opinion.

Quality control standards   AICPA standards for establishing quality control policies and procedures that provide reasonable assurance that all of a CPA firm's engagements are conducted in accordance with applicable professional standards.

Registered public accounting firm   A public accounting firm registered with the Public Company Accounting Oversight Board in accordance with the Sarbanes-Oxley Act of 2002. Any CPA firm auditing SEC reporting companies must be registered.

Standard unqualified opinion   The form of audit report issued when the examination was adequate in scope and the auditors believe that the financial statements present fairly the financial position, operating results, and cash flows in conformity with generally accepted accounting principles.

Review Questions

2–1. Contrast the roles of the AICPA and the PCAOB in the development of auditing standards.

2–2. What is the difference between generally accepted accounting principles (GAAP) and AICPA generally accepted auditing standards (GAAS)? Give an example of a generally accepted accounting principle and an example of a generally accepted auditing standard falling under the subhead of *general standards*.

2–3. The generally accepted auditing standards established by the AICPA list first the requirement that "the examination is to be performed by a person or persons having adequate technical training and proficiency as an auditor." What would be the usual avenues for an individual to meet these personal qualifications?

2–4. What relationship exists between AICPA generally accepted auditing standards (GAAS) and the Statements on Auditing Standards (SASs)?

2–5. The first SAS issued was substantially larger and different in coverage from all the following ones. What explains this difference?

2–6. Explain briefly the auditors' responsibility for detecting illegal acts by clients.

2–7. You are to evaluate the following quotation: "If a CPA firm completes a nonpublic company audit of Adam Company's financial statements following AICPA generally accepted auditing standards and is satisfied with the results of the audit, an *unqualified* audit report may be issued. On the other hand, if no audit is performed of the current year's financial statements, but the CPA firm has performed satisfactory audits in prior years, has confidence in the management of the company, and makes a quick review of the current year's financial statements, a qualified report may be issued."

    Do you agree? Give reasons to support your answer.

2–8. Pike Company has had an annual audit performed by the same firm of certified public accountants for many years. The financial statements and copies of the audit report are distributed to stockholders each year shortly after completion of the audit. Who is primarily responsible for the fairness of these financial statements? Explain.

2–9. Draft the standard form of audit report commonly issued after a satisfactory audit of a nonpublic client's financial statements.

2–10. Davis & Co., Certified Public Accountants, after completing an audit of Samson Company, decided that it would be unable to issue an unqualified opinion. What circumstances might explain this decision?

2–11. State the principal assertions made by the auditors in the opinion paragraph of the AICPA auditors' standard report.

2–12. Alan Weston, CPA, completed an audit of Kirsten Manufacturing Company and issued an unqualified audit report. What does this tell us about the extent of the auditing procedures included in the audit?

2–13. When a CPA firm completes an audit of a nonpublic business and issues a report, does it express an opinion on the client's accounting records, financial statements, or both? Give reasons.

2–14. A CPA firm does not guarantee the financial soundness of a client when it renders an opinion on financial statements, nor does the CPA firm guarantee the absolute accuracy of the statements. Yet the CPA firm's opinion is respected and accepted. What is expected of the CPA firm in order to merit such confidence?

2–15. If a CPA firm has performed a thorough professional audit of a client's financial statements, should it not be able to issue a report dealing with facts rather than the mere expression of an opinion? Explain.

2–16. What is a "material" amount from the perspective of auditors? Give an example of how that amount may differ based on the nature of the item.

2–17. List the five categories of generally accepted accounting principles. Explain how the auditors determine the appropriate principle when there is a conflict between sources in two of the categories.

2–18. Do the AICPA attestation standards supersede any of the AICPA generally accepted auditing standards? Explain.

2–19. What is the meaning of *quality control* and *peer review* as these terms relate to the operation of a CPA firm? Is peer review mandatory? Explain.

2–20. Explain the basic objective of establishing quality control procedures in the following areas.

    a. Engagement performance.

    b. Acceptance and continuation of clients and engagements.

    c. Monitoring.

2–21. Do the AICPA's *Statements of Quality Control Standards* require every CPA firm to implement similar quality control procedures? Explain.

2–22. What are the duties and responsibilities of the Public Company Accounting Oversight Board?

2–23. Your CPA firm has been requested to perform a peer review of the firm of William & Stafford. What is involved in the performance of such an engagement? Discuss.

2–24. What is the International Auditing and Assurance Board? What is the purpose of its pronouncements? Do these pronouncements establish standards that override a member nation's auditing standards?

2–25. Briefly describe four differences between an international audit report and one based on the U.S. reporting standards.

Questions Requiring Analysis

Required:

2–26. Various organizations develop standards for audits and regulate CPA firms. Compare and contrast the roles of the AICPA, the PCAOB, and the state boards of accountancy along the following dimensions:

    a. Standard setting.

    b. Regulation of CPA firms.

    c. Source of authority.

2–27. An attitude of independence is a most essential element of an audit by a firm of certified public accountants. Describe several situations in which the CPA firm might find it somewhat difficult to maintain this independent point of view.

2–28. Jane Lee, a director of a nonpublic corporation with a number of stockholders and lines of credit with several banks, suggested that the corporation appoint as controller John Madison, a certified public accountant on the staff of the auditing firm that had made annual audits of the corporation for many years. Lee expressed the opinion that this move would effect a considerable savings in professional fees because annual audits would no longer be needed. She proposed to give the controller, if appointed, an internal auditing staff to carry on such continuing investigations of accounting data as appeared necessary. Evaluate this proposal.

2–29. Reed, CPA, accepted an engagement to audit the financial statements of Smith Company. Reed's discussions with Smith's new management and the predecessor auditor indicated the possibility that Smith's financial statements may be misstated due to the possible occurrence of errors, fraud, and illegal acts.

Required:

    a. Identify and describe Reed's responsibilities to detect Smith's errors and fraud. Do *not* identify specific audit procedures.

    b. Describe Reed's responsibilities to detect Smith's material illegal acts. Do *not* identify specific audit procedures.

    c. Identify and describe Reed's responsibilities to report Smith's illegal acts.
    (AICPA, adapted)

2–30. While the AICPA administers a peer review program for CPA firms, the PCAOB staff performs practice inspections.

Required:
    a. Describe a peer review.
    b. On what part of a firm's practice does the PCAOB staff focus its inspections?
    c. Describe a PCAOB inspection.

Multiple Choice Questions

2–31. Select the best answer for each of the following items and give reasons for your choice.

    a. Which of the following organizations can revoke the right of an individual to practice as a CPA?

      (1) The Public Company Accounting Oversight Board.

      (2) The American Institute of Certified Public Accountants.

      (3) The Securities and Exchange Commission.

      (4) The applicable state board of accountancy.

    b. The AICPA over time has played an important role in standards setting. Which of the following standards are currently established by the AICPA?

      (1) Accounting standards applicable to nonpublic companies.

      (2) Auditing standards applicable to audits of nonpublic companies.

      (3) Quality control standards applicable to audits of public companies.

      (4) Standards for reviews of the interim financial information issued by public companies.

    c. Which of the following are not interpretive publications under the AICPA's hierarchy of generally accepted auditing standards?

      (1) Statements on Auditing Standards.

      (2) Appendices to Statements on Auditing Standards.

      (3) Auditing guidance in AICPA Audit and Accounting Guides.

      (4) AICPA Auditing Statements of Position.

    d. The three AICPA generally accepted auditing standards classified as standards of fieldwork may be summarized as:

      (1) The need to maintain an independence in mental attitude throughout the audit.

      (2) The criteria for audit planning and evidence gathering.

      (3) The criteria for the content of the auditors' report on financial statements.

      (4) The competence, independence, and professional care to be exerted while performing the audit.

    e. A basic objective of a CPA firm is to provide professional services that conform with professional standards. Reasonable assurance of achieving this basic objective is provided through:

      (1) Compliance with generally accepted reporting standards.

      (2) A system of quality control.

      (3) A system of peer review.

      (4) Continuing professional education.

    f. Which of the following is *not* explicitly included in an unqualified standard audit report for a nonpublic company?

      (1) The CPA's opinion that the financial statements comply with generally accepted accounting principles.

      (2) That generally accepted auditing standards were followed during the audit.

      (3) That internal control of the client was satisfactory.

      (4) The subjects of the audit.

    g. The general group of the AICPA generally accepted auditing standards requires that:

      (1) The auditors maintain an independent mental attitude.

(2) The audit be conducted in conformity with generally accepted accounting principles.

(3) Assistants, if any, be properly supervised.

(4) The auditors obtain an understanding of internal control.

h. Which AICPA quality control standard would *most* likely be satisfied when a CPA firm maintains records indicating which partners or employees of the firm were previously employed by the CPA firm's clients?

(1) Professional relationship.

(2) Personnel management.

(3) Independence, integrity, and objectivity.

(4) Monitoring.

i. An audit provides reasonable assurance of detecting material:

	Fraudulent Financial Reporting	Misappropriation of Assets
(1)	Yes	Yes
(2)	Yes	No
(3)	No	Yes
(4)	No	No

j. Which of the following is not included in an integrated audit report on the financial statements of a public company?

(1) The report states that the audit was performed in accordance with AICPA standards.

(2) The report indicates that the financial statements are the responsibility of management.

(3) The report indicates that the auditors have also audited the effectiveness of the company's internal control.

(4) The report is signed in the name of the CPA firm.

k. Audit firms that are subject to inspections by the PCAOB staff include:

(1) All audit firms.

(2) Audit firms that are registered with the SEC.

(3) Audit firms that are registered with the PCAOB.

(4) Audit firms that are registered with a state board of accountancy.

l. Which of the following is not a difference noted when comparing the AICPA audit report to the international audit report?

(1) The international audit report has an expanded discussion of management's responsibility for the financial statements and internal controls.

(2) The international audit report may be signed using the personal name of the audit partner, the audit firm, or both.

(3) The international audit report contains an enhanced description of the nature of an audit.

(4) The international audit report includes an opinion on internal control.

(AICPA, adapted)

Problems

2–32. John Clinton, owner of Clinton Company, applied for a bank loan and was informed by the banker that audited financial statements of the business must be submitted before the bank could consider the loan application. Clinton then retained Arthur Jones, CPA, to perform an audit. Clinton informed Jones that audited financial statements were required by the bank and that the audit must be completed within three weeks. Clinton also promised to pay Jones a fixed fee plus a bonus if the bank approved the loan. Jones agreed and accepted the engagement.

The first step taken by Jones was to hire two accounting students to conduct the audit. He spent several hours telling them exactly what to do. Jones told the students not to spend time reviewing controls but instead to concentrate on proving the mathematical accuracy of the ledger accounts and summarizing the data in the accounting records that support Clinton Company's financial statements. The students followed Jones's instructions and after two weeks gave Jones the financial statements that did not include any notes. Jones reviewed the statements and prepared an unqualified audit report. The report, however, did not refer to generally accepted accounting principles.

Required: List on the left side of the sheet of paper the generally accepted auditing standards that were violated by Jones, and indicate how the actions of Jones resulted in a failure to comply with each standard. Organize your answer as follows:

Generally Accepted Auditing Standards	*Actions by Jones Resulting in Failure to Comply with Generally Accepted Auditing Standards*
General standards	
(1) The audit is to be performed by a person or persons having adequate technical training and proficiency as an auditor.	(1)

2–33.   Joe Rezzo, a college student majoring in accounting, helped finance his education with a part-time job maintaining all accounting records for a small business, White Company, located near the campus. Upon graduation, Rezzo passed the CPA examination and joined the audit staff of a national CPA firm. However, he continued to perform all accounting work for White Company during his "leisure time." Two years later, Rezzo received his CPA certificate and decided to give up his part-time work with White Company. He notified White that he would no longer be available after preparing the year-end financial statements.

On January 7, Rezzo delivered the annual financial statements as his final act for White Company. The owner then made the following request: "Joe, I am applying for a substantial bank loan, and the bank loan officer insists upon getting audited financial statements to support my loan application. You are now a CPA, and you know everything that's happened in this company and everything that's included in these financial statements, and you know they give a fair picture. I would appreciate it if you would write out the standard audit report and attach it to the financial statements. Then I'll be able to get some fast action on my loan application."

Required: *a.* Would Rezzo be justified in complying with White's request for an auditor's opinion? Explain.

b. If you think Rezzo should issue the audit report, do you think he should first perform an audit of the company despite his detailed knowledge of the company's affairs? Explain.

c. If White had requested an audit by the national CPA firm for which Rezzo worked, would it have been reasonable for that firm to accept and to assign Rezzo to perform the audit? Explain.

2–34.   The following report for the audit of a nonpublic company is deficient in several respects.

To Whom It May Concern:

We have examined the accounting records of Garland Corporation for the year ended June 30, 20X1. We counted the cash and marketable securities, studied the accounting methods in use (which were consistently followed throughout the year), and made tests of the ledger accounts for assets and liabilities. The internal control contained no weaknesses.

In our opinion the accompanying balance sheet and related income statement present correctly the financial condition of the Corporation at June 30, 20X1.

The accounting records of Garland Corporation are maintained in accordance with accounting principles generally observed throughout the industry. Our examination was made in accordance with generally accepted auditing standards, and we certify the records and financial statements without qualification.

Required: Evaluate the report systematically from beginning to end, considering each sentence in turn. Use a separate paragraph with an identifying heading for each point, as for example, Paragraph 1, Sentence 1. You may also wish to make comments on the overall contents of each paragraph and upon any omissions. Give reasons to support your views. After completing this critical review of the report, draft a revised report, on the assumption that your audit was adequate in all respects and disclosed no significant deficiencies.

2–35.   The business activities of Casa Royale, Inc., consist of the administration and maintenance of approximately 400 condominiums and common property owned by individuals in a suburban residential development. Revenue consists of monthly fees collected from each condominium owner, plus some miscellaneous revenue. The principal expenses are property taxes and maintenance of all the buildings, shrubbery, swimming pools, lakes, parking lots, and other facilities. The furniture, fixtures, and equipment owned by the corporation and used to perform its maintenance functions represent about 25 percent of its total assets of $400,000.

The corporation retained Howard Smith, CPA, to perform an audit of its financial statements for the current year and received from him the following audit report.

Independent Auditors' Report
Board of Governors
Casa Royale, Inc.

I have audited the accompanying balance sheet of Casa Royale, Inc., as of December 31, 20X1, and the related statements of income, retained earnings, and cash flows for the year then ended. These financial statements are the responsibility of the Company's management. My responsibility is to express an opinion on these financial statements based on my audit.

I conducted my audit in accordance with auditing standards generally accepted in the United States of America. Those standards require that I plan and perform the audit to obtain reasonable assurance about whether the financial statements are free of material misstatement. An audit includes examining, on a test basis, evidence supporting the amounts and disclosures in the financial statements. An audit also includes assessing the accounting principles used and significant estimates made by management, as well as evaluating the overall financial statement presentation. I believe that my audit provides a reasonable basis for my opinion.

As further amplified in Note 3 to the financial statements, my engagement did not include an examination of records relating to furniture, fixtures, equipment, or other assets indicated on the balance sheet.

In my opinion, except for the effect of such adjustments, if any, as might have been determined to be necessary had I been able to examine evidence regarding plant assets, the financial statements referred to above present fairly, in all material respects, the financial position of Casa Royale, Inc., as of December 31, 20X1, and the results of its operations and its cash flows for the year then ended in conformity with accounting principles generally accepted in the United States of America.

Howard Smith, CPA

The note to the financial statements referred to in the audit report read as follows: "The equipment necessary for administration and maintenance was acquired in various years going back as far as the origin of the Corporation 10 years ago. Therefore, the records do not lend themselves readily to application of standard auditing procedures and are not included in our engagement of independent auditors. The equipment is being depreciated using the straight-line method over various estimated useful lives."

Required:

    a. What type of audit report did the CPA issue? Was this the appropriate type of report under the circumstances? Explain.

    b. What contradiction, if any, exists between the scope paragraph of the audit report and the note to the financial statements? Do you consider the note to be a reasonable statement? Why or why not?

    c. Did the omission of the examination of plant assets from the audit engagement have any bearing on the evidence needed by the auditor in order to express an opinion on the income statement? Explain fully.

2–36.   Bart James, a partner in the CPA firm of James and Day, received the following memorandum from John Gray, president of Gray Manufacturing Corporation, an audit client of many years.

Dear Bart:

I have a new type of engagement for you. You are familiar with how much time and money we have been spending in installing equipment to eliminate the air and water pollution caused by our manufacturing plant. We have changed our production process to reduce discharge of gases; we have changed to more expensive fuel sources with less pollution potential; and we have discontinued some products because we couldn't produce them without causing considerable pollution.

I don't think the stockholders and the public are aware of the efforts we have made, and I want to inform them of our accomplishments in avoiding danger to the environment. We will devote a major part of our annual report to this topic, stressing that our company is the leader of the entire industry in combating pollution. To make this publicity more convincing, I would like to retain your firm to study what we have done and to attest as independent accountants that our operations are the best in the industry as far as preventing pollution is concerned.

To justify your statement, you are welcome to investigate every aspect of our operations as fully as you wish. We will pay for your services at your regular audit rates and will publish your "pollution opinion" in our annual report to stockholders immediately following some pictures and discussion of our special equipment and processes for preventing industrial pollution. We may put this section of the annual report in a separate cover and distribute it free to the public. Please let me know at once if this engagement is acceptable to you.

Required: Put yourself in Bart James's position and write a reply to this client's request. Indicate clearly whether you are willing to accept the engagement and explain your attitude toward this proposed extension of the auditor's attest function.

In-Class Team Case

2–37.   Hide-It (HI), a family-owned business based in Tombstone, Arizona, builds custom homes with special features, such as hidden rooms and hidden wall safes. Hide-It has been an audit client for three years.

You are about to sign off on a "clean" opinion on HI's current annual financial statements when Art Hyde, the VP-Finance, calls to tell you that the Arizona Department of Revenue has seized control of a Hide-It bank account that includes about $450,000 of company funds; the account is not currently recorded in the accounting system and you had been unaware of it. In response to your questions about the origin of the funds, Art assures you that the funds, though not recorded as revenue, had been obtained legitimately. He explains that all of the money came from separately billed but unrecorded change orders to items in contracts completed before you became HI's auditor, and before he or any members of current management became involved with the company. You subsequently determine that there is insufficient evidence to allow you to reconstruct the nature of these cash transactions, although the following analysis is available from the Arizona Department of Revenue:

Deposits 1/17/X2–12/3/X4	$455,000
Interest earned 1/2/X2–12/31/X8	95,000
Withdrawals 2/12/X3–4/7/X7	(100,000)
Balance 12/31/X8	$450,000

Art also informs you that HI has agreed to pay a combined tax and penalty of 12 percent on the total funds deposited within 120 days as required by a recently enacted rule that provides amnesty for tax evaders. Furthermore, he states that negotiations with the Internal Revenue Service are in process.

Required:

a. The professional standards define errors as unintentional misstatements or omissions of amounts or disclosures in the financial statements. Is the situation described an error?

b. The professional standards state that fraud relates to intentional misstatements or omissions of amounts or disclosures in the financial statements. Misstatements due to fraud may occur due to either (*a*) fraudulent financial reporting or (*b*) misappropriation of assets. Does the situation appear to be fraud? If so, is it fraudulent financial reporting, misappropriation of assets, or both?

c. The professional standards outline certain responsibilities relating to illegal acts, and distinguish between "direct effect" and "indirect effect" illegal acts. Is the situation described herein an illegal act as discussed within the auditing standards? If so, is it "direct" or "indirect"?

d. Should the CPA firm resign in this situation? If the decision is not clear-cut, what additional information would you desire before deciding?

Research and Discussion Case

2–38.   Enormo Corporation is a large multinational audit client of your CPA firm. One of Enormo's subsidiaries, Ultro, Ltd., is a successful electronics assembly company that operates in a small Caribbean country. The country in which Ultro operates has very strict laws governing the transfer of funds to other countries. Violations of these laws may result in fines or the expropriation of the assets of the company.

During the current year, you discover that $50,000 worth of foreign currency was smuggled out of the Caribbean country by one of Ultro's employees and deposited in one of Enormo's bank accounts. Ultro's management generated the funds by selling company automobiles, which were fully depreciated on Ultro's books, to company employees.

You are concerned about this illegal act committed by Ultro's management and decide to discuss the matter with Enormo's management and the company's legal counsel. Enormo's management and board of directors seemed to be unconcerned with the matter and expressed the opinion that you were making far too much of a situation involving an immaterial dollar amount. They also believe that it is unnecessary to take any steps to prevent Ultro's management from engaging in illegal activities in the future. Enormo's legal counsel indicated that the probability was remote that such an illegal act would ever be discovered, and that if discovery occurred, it would probably result in a fine that would not be material to the client's consolidated financial statements.

Your CPA firm is ready to issue the integrated audit report on Enormo's financial statements and internal control for the current year, and you are trying to decide on the appropriate course of action regarding the illegal act.

Required:

    a. Discuss the implications of this illegal act by Ultro's management.

    b. Describe the courses of action that are available to your CPA firm regarding this matter.

    c. State your opinion as to the course of action that is appropriate. Explain.

Suggested References

AICPA, *Professional Standards,* Volume 2, Commerce Clearing House, *Statements on Quality Control Standards,* Section QC 10.

AICPA, *Statement on Auditing Standards No. 99,* "Consideration of Fraud in a Financial Statement Audit" (New York, 1996) AU 316.

AICPA, *Statement on Auditing Standards No. 54,* "Illegal Acts by Clients" (New York, 1988) AU 317.

FASB Statement No. 5, "Accounting for Contingencies," paragraphs 8–12.

Chapter 3

Professional Ethics

Chapter learning objectives

After studying this chapter, you should be able to:

LO1. Describe the nature of ethics and ethical dilemmas.

LO2. Describe a profession's reasons for establishing professional ethics.

LO3. Discuss the Principles section of the American Institute of Certified Public Accountants (AICPA) *Code of Professional Conduct.*

LO4. Describe each of the Rules contained in the AICPA *Code of Professional Conduct.*

LO5. Explain the concept of independence and identify circumstances in which independence is impaired.

LO6. Contrast the independence rules for audits of public companies with those for audits of nonpublic companies.

LO7. Discuss The Institute of Internal Auditor's *Code of Ethics.*

All recognized professions have recognized the importance of ethical behavior and have developed codes of professional ethics. Our purpose in this chapter is to discuss the nature of professional ethics as well as to present and discuss the AICPA *Code of Professional Conduct,* the additional requirements for auditors of public companies, and The Institute of Internal Auditors *Code of Ethics.*

The Nature of Ethics

Ethics has been defined as the study of moral principles and values that govern the actions and decisions of an individual or groups. While personal ethics vary from individual to individual at any point in time, most people within a society are able to agree as to what is considered ethical and unethical behavior. In fact, a society passes laws that define what its citizens consider to be the more extreme forms of unethical behavior.

Much of what is considered unethical in a particular society is not specifically prohibited—so, how do we know whether we are acting ethically? Who decides what standards of conduct are appropriate? Is any type of behavior "ethical" as long as it does not violate a law or a rule of one's profession?

A good starting point for considering ethics is to examine the context in which most ethical questions arise—relationships among people. Any relationship between two or more individuals carries with it sets of expectations by each of the individuals involved. Certainly, the relationship between a certified public accountant (CPA) and a client offers a number of interesting challenges. For example: Is it ethical for a senior auditor to underreport the number of hours worked on an audit engagement? Is it ethical to accept tickets to a baseball game from an audit client? May a CPA ethically allow a client to pay for a business lunch and still maintain independence? Are there ethical issues involved in a situation in which a staff auditor wishes to date the controller of one of his firm's audit clients? Does it matter whether the staff auditor works on that engagement?

What Are Ethical Dilemmas?

An ethical dilemma is a situation that an individual faces involving a decision about appropriate behavior. A simple example of an ethical dilemma is presented below.

> Assume that a student at your college finds an expensive wristwatch in one of the restrooms. What actions, if any, does the student take to find the original owner?

An ethical dilemma generally involves a situation in which the welfare of one or more other individuals is affected by the results of the decision. In the dilemma presented above, the welfare of the wristwatch's original owner is affected by the student's decision.

Ethical dilemmas faced by auditors often have an effect on the welfare of a large number of individuals or groups. As an example, if an auditor makes an unethical decision about the content of an audit report, the wealth of thousands of investors and creditors may be affected.

A Framework for Ethical Decisions

How do we make decisions about an appropriate course of action when faced with an ethical dilemma? As a starting point, let's consider how people make decisions in general. Certainly, many decisions require little conscious thought. The untied shoelace is quickly retied. The disposable pen that skips is quickly discarded and replaced. However, when the results of the decision have more significant consequences, a formal decision process is generally used. The steps involved in making any decision generally include:

1. Identify the problem.
2. Identify possible courses of action.
3. Identify any constraints relating to the decision.
4. Analyze the likely effects of the possible courses of action.
5. Select the best course of action.

Various frameworks have been proposed for addressing ethical dilemmas.[1] However, since almost every decision faced by a CPA has an ethical dimension, it would appear to be appropriate to analyze ethical dilemmas using the general decision-making framework presented on the prior page. Let's illustrate the use of this framework in the following situation.

Making Ethical Decisions—A Professional Example

Assume that you have worked for a public accounting firm for approximately six months, and you were recently assigned to the audit of a small manufacturing company. The senior auditor on the job assigned you the task of extracting financial information about comparable companies from several financial databases on the Internet. She indicated that the work must be completed by Monday morning. While you had hoped to complete the assignment on Friday, things didn't work out and you had to come to work on Saturday.

On Saturday, your expectation that it would take only a couple hours to complete the task faded and you didn't finish until 4 P.M., after eight hours of work. You believe that part of the problem was that you were out late Friday night at a Dave Matthews Band concert and you just weren't all that efficient. Although you completed the task, you exceeded the budgeted hours for the task by six hours. Because of the circumstances (inefficient work and the blown budget) you are tempted to underreport the number of hours that you actually worked. While your firm has an informal policy that encourages employees to report all hours worked, you are aware that the policy is often ignored by other staff auditors. In addition, you are aware that your evaluation on this audit will be based not only on the quality of your work, but also on your ability to meet time budgets. You have been criticized on your evaluations on previous engagements for taking too long to perform certain tasks.

Since you are paid a straight monthly salary and a year-end bonus based on performance, your pay will not be directly affected by underreporting the hours worked. You could even argue that not reporting the hours might improve your evaluation and lead to a bigger bonus.

Now let's analyze this ethical dilemma using the decision-making framework previously presented.

1. *Identify the problem.* The problem in this case is that you have exceeded the time budget for your assigned task.

2. *Identify possible courses of action.* Although there are any number of options for reporting the number of hours worked, for simplicity's sake let's assume that you are considering only two: (1) reporting only two of the eight hours worked on Saturday to exactly meet the budget, or (2) reporting all eight hours.

3. *Identify any constraints relating to the decision.* Ethical dilemmas such as this one frequently involve both internal and external standards that serve as constraints. Internal standards may be the result of your religious or other beliefs about the manner in which you should behave and make decisions. These standards involve such concepts as truthfulness, fairness, loyalty, and caring for others. Perhaps you believe that one must be absolutely truthful in every situation; alternatively, you might believe that in certain circumstances absolute truthfulness is not necessary. As an example, some people might believe that caring for others is sometimes more important than telling the truth. They might decide that it is not proper to tell a patient with heart failure that he is unlikely to survive the night, even if he asks. Some peoples' concepts of loyalty and fairness might also prevent them from being completely truthful in all cases.

   External standards are those that are imposed upon an individual by society, peers, organizations, employers, or his or her profession. In this circumstance the relevant external standards include the informal firm policy about reporting time and the AICPA *Code of Professional Conduct* which requires "integrity" on the part of CPAs.

4. *Analyze the likely effects of the possible courses of action.* Since ethical dilemmas ordinarily affect individuals who are not involved in the decision-making process, this step

---

[1] For a description of models that have been suggested for use to resolve ethical dilemmas faced by professionals, see *Ethical Decisions in Medicine* by Howard Brody (Boston: Little, Brown and Company, 1981), second edition.

involves considering the implications of the various courses of action on both the individual involved and anyone else that is affected by the decision. Also, it is important to consider both the short-term and the long-term effects. The following table presents these considerations as they apply to the two alternative courses of action in this situation.

5. *Select the best course of action.* You are the only one who can determine how to respond in situations such as this. The individual whose utmost consideration is career advancement may believe that underreporting the time is the solution. However, that individual should realize that in the long run he or she may be "caught" and the negative reaction by the firm could be extreme. Alternatively, the individual with the simple rule "tell the truth" has the obvious solution of reporting all the hours.

Alternative 1: Report Only Two Hours

Effect on:	Positive Effects:	Negative Effects:
You	• Performance evaluation may be improved. • Bonus may be positively affected.	• Is inconsistent with AICPA *Code of Professional Conduct.* • Is not consistent with informal firm policy. • Action is dishonest.
The CPA firm		• Informal policy is violated. • Possible underbilling of the client. • May encourage the development of unrealistic budgets in the future that may affect the morale of employees and could lead to substandard performance of audits. • Underreporting of time on a large scale may adversely affect firm's ability to attract and retain employees.
Other staff	• The senior auditor may be positively evaluated by completing the job on budget.	• May lead to the development of unrealistic budgets that adversely affect morale and lead to improper performance evaluations or force staff to underreport time.
The client	• May lead to a lower total audit fee (particularly if combined with other underreporting of time).	• May cause substandard audits in the future if staff members struggle to meet unrealistic budgets.

Alternative 2: Report All Eight Hours

Effect on:	Positive Effects:	Negative Effects:
You	• Action is truthful. • Consistent with informal firm policy. • Consistent with AICPA *Code of Professional Conduct.*	• Performance evaluation may be negatively affected. • Bonus may be negatively affected.
The CPA firm	• Results in proper billing of client. • More realistic budgets may be developed in the future.	
Other staff	• More realistic budgets may lead to higher morale.	• Senior auditor may be negatively evaluated due to budget overrun.
The client	• May lead to better audits as staff auditors will be given more realistic budgets in the future.	• May lead to a higher (though more accurate) audit fee.

Discussion

This ethical dilemma is constructed to illustrate the steps involved in making a professional decision. It is simplified in that the CPA could realistically decide to report any number of hours between zero and eight. Notice that one might attempt to "rationalize" underreporting some time by focusing on the inefficiency of the work and the inappropriateness of charging the client for this inefficiency. Another solution to this dilemma would be to charge the hours, but make it clear in a note to the senior auditor that you do not believe it fair to charge the client for some of the hours because of your inefficiency.

While this dilemma had a "correct" answer of eight hours, many other decisions involve "gray areas," where there are no obvious answers. For example, consider the case in which the auditors are engaged by management of a company to evaluate the appropriateness of an accounting method that is being used to account for certain transactions. Presumably, if the auditors agree with management's accounting method, they will be engaged to audit the company. In researching the issue, the auditors find that no accounting standards specifically apply. While the auditors believe that there is some justification for management's method of accounting, they believe that another method is more acceptable. This is clearly an ethical dilemma in which there is no definitive answer. Nonetheless, auditors who do not carefully consider whether management's method can be justified, or who sacrifice their principles to obtain the audit engagement, are not playing a very valuable role in society.

The above examples show that an individual's self-interest may be inconsistent with acting in accordance with his or her ethical beliefs. This is often the case in many of the ethical dilemmas that are faced by individuals as well as professional accountants.

The purpose of the remainder of this chapter is to discuss the requirements of the AICPA *Code of Professional Conduct* and The Institute of Internal Auditors *Code of Ethics*. In addition, we will describe the additional requirements for auditors of public companies. These requirements attempt to provide auditors with a minimum set of standards for making ethical decisions. They cannot, however, address all situations, and the auditors often are called on to use professional judgment to make decisions in ethically perplexing situations.

The Need for Professional Ethics

Learning Objective 2

To understand the importance of a code of ethics to public accountants and other professionals, one must understand the nature of a profession as opposed to other vocations. There is no universally accepted definition of what constitutes a profession; yet, for generations, certain types of activities have been recognized as professions while others have not. Medicine, law, engineering, architecture, and theology are examples of disciplines long accorded professional status. Public accounting is a relative newcomer to the ranks of the professions, but it has achieved widespread recognition in recent decades.

All the recognized **professions** have several common characteristics. The most important of these characteristics are (1) a responsibility to serve the public, (2) a complex body of knowledge, (3) standards of admission to the profession, and (4) a need for public confidence. Let us briefly discuss these characteristics as they apply to public accounting.

Responsibility to Serve the Public

The certified public accountant is a representative of the public—creditors, stockholders, consumers, employees, and others—in the financial reporting process. The role of the independent attester is to ensure that information is *fair to all parties* and not biased to benefit one group at the expense of another. This responsibility to serve the public interest must be a basic motivation for the professional. Public accountants must maintain a high degree of independence from their clients if they are to be of service to the larger community. Independence is perhaps the most important concept embodied in public accounting's *Code of Professional Conduct.*

Complex Body of Knowledge

Any practitioner or student of accounting has only to look at the abundance of authoritative pronouncements governing financial reports to realize that accounting is a complex body of knowledge. One reason such pronouncements continue to proliferate is that accounting must reflect what is taking place in an increasingly complex environment. As the environment changes—such as the trend toward business reorganizations beginning in the 1980s through today—accounting principles and auditing practices must adapt. The continual growth in the "common body of knowledge" for practicing accountants has led the AICPA and other professional and regulatory bodies to enact continuing education requirements for CPAs. The need for technical competence and familiarity with current standards of practice is embodied in the *Code of Professional Conduct.*

Standards of Admission to the Profession

Attaining a license to practice as a certified public accountant requires an individual to meet minimum standards for education and experience. The individual must also pass the uniform CPA examination showing mastery of the body of knowledge described above. Once licensed, certified public accountants must adhere to the ethics of the profession or risk disciplinary action.

Need for Public Confidence

Physicians, lawyers, certified public accountants, and all other professionals must have the confidence of the public to be successful. To the CPA, however, public confidence is of special significance. The CPA's product is credibility. Without public confidence in the attestor, the attest function serves no useful purpose.

Professional ethics in public accounting as in other professions have developed gradually and are still in a process of change as the practice of public accounting itself changes. Often new concepts are added as a result of unfortunate incidents which, though they reflect unfavorably upon the profession, may not specifically violate existing standards.

Professional Ethics in Public Accounting

Careless work or lack of integrity on the part of any CPA may lead the public to a negative view toward the entire profession. Consequently, the members of the public accounting profession acted in unison through the AICPA to devise a code of conduct. This code provides practical guidance to the individual member in maintaining a professional attitude. In addition, this code is designed to provide assurance to clients and to the public that the profession intends to maintain high standards and to enforce compliance by individual members.

Concerns about the credibility of audits, as discussed in Chapter 1, caused Congress to question the AICPA's ethical rules and enforcement processes. As a result, the Public Company Accounting Oversight Board (PCAOB) was given the authority to develop and enforce ethical rules for audits of public companies. As with other professional standards, the PCAOB adopted the AICPA ethical standards existing at April 16, 2003, as interim standards until it could develop its own. Therefore, the ethical standards of the PCAOB do not currently differ significantly from those of the AICPA, with the exception of the rules relating to the types of nonattest services that may be performed for audit clients. In this chapter, we will focus on the AICPA standards, pointing out where ethical rules for audits of public companies differ.

The AICPA *Code of Professional Conduct*

Learning Objective 3

The AICPA *Code of Professional Conduct* is designed to provide a framework for expanding professional services and responding to other changes in the profession, such as the increasingly competitive environment. It consists of two sections. The first section, the **Principles,** is a goal-oriented, positively stated discussion of the profession's responsibilities to the public, clients, and fellow practitioners. The Principles provide the framework for the Rules, the second section of the Code. The **Rules** are enforceable applications of the Principles. They define acceptable behavior and identify sources of authority for performance standards.

To provide guidelines for the scope and application of the Rules, the AICPA issues **Interpretations.** Senior Technical Committees of the AICPA, such as the Auditing Standards Board, interpret the Rules applying to their area of responsibility; the Professional Ethics Executive Committee issues interpretations that apply to all professional activities. The AICPA also issues **Ethics Rulings** that explain the application of the Rules and Interpretations to specific factual circumstances involving professional ethics. Figure 3.1 summarizes the relationships among the Principles, Rules, Interpretations, and Ethics Rulings.

FIGURE 3.1
AICPA Professional Ethics

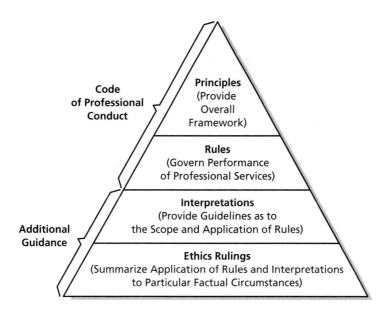

A portion of the Principles section of the *Code of Professional Conduct* is quoted below, followed by a presentation and analysis of the section of the Code that includes the Rules.

Section I—Principles[2]

Preamble

Membership in the American Institute of Certified Public Accountants is voluntary. By accepting membership, a certified public accountant assumes an obligation of self-discipline above and beyond the requirements of laws and regulations.

These Principles of the *Code of Professional Conduct* of the American Institute of Certified Public Accountants express the profession's recognition of its responsibilities to the public, to clients, and to colleagues. They guide members in the performance of their professional responsibilities and express the basic tenets of ethical and professional conduct. The Principles call for an unswerving commitment to honorable behavior, even at the sacrifice of personal advantage.

Article I—Responsibilities

In carrying out their responsibilities as professionals, members should exercise sensitive professional and moral judgments in all their activities.

As professionals, certified public accountants perform an essential role in society. Consistent with that role, members of the American Institute of Certified Public Accountants have responsibilities to all those who use their professional services. Members also have a continuing responsibility to cooperate with each other to improve the art of accounting, maintain the public's confidence, and carry out the profession's special responsibilities for self-governance. The collective efforts of all members are required to maintain and enhance the traditions of the profession.

Article II—The Public Interest

Members should accept the obligation to act in a way that will serve the public interest, honor the public trust, and demonstrate commitment to professionalism.

A distinguishing mark of a profession is acceptance of its responsibility to the public. The accounting profession's public consists of clients, credit grantors, governments, employers, investors, the business and financial community, and others who rely on the objectivity and integrity of certified public accountants to maintain the orderly functioning of commerce. This reliance imposes a public interest responsibility on certified public accountants. The public interest is defined as the collective well-being of the community of people and institutions the profession serves.

In discharging their professional responsibilities, members may encounter conflicting pressures from among each of those groups. In resolving those conflicts, members should act with integrity, guided by the precept that when members fulfill their responsibility to the public, clients' and employers' interests are best served.

Those who rely on certified public accountants expect them to discharge their responsibilities with integrity, objectivity, due professional care, and a genuine interest in serving the public. They are expected to provide quality services, enter into fee arrangements, and offer a range of services—all in a manner that demonstrates a level of professionalism consistent with these Principles of the *Code of Professional Conduct.*

All who accept membership in the American Institute of Certified Public Accountants commit themselves to honor the public trust. In return for the faith that the public reposes in them, members should seek continually to demonstrate their dedication to professional excellence.

Article III—Integrity

To maintain and broaden public confidence, members should perform all professional responsibilities with the highest sense of integrity.

Article IV—Objectivity and Independence

A member should maintain objectivity and be free of conflicts of interest in discharging professional responsibilities. A member in public practice should be independent in fact and appearance when providing auditing and other attestation services.

Article V—Due Care

A member should observe the profession's technical and ethical standards, strive continually to improve competence and the quality of services, and discharge professional responsibility to the best of the member's ability.

Article VI—Scope and Nature of Services

A member in public practice should observe the Principles of the Code of Professional Conduct *in determining the scope and nature of services to be provided.*

Each of these Principles should be considered by members in determining whether or not to provide specific services in individual circumstances. In some instances, they may represent an overall constraint on the nonattest services that might be offered to a specific client. No hard-and-fast rules can be developed to help members reach these judgments, but they must be satisfied that they are meeting the spirit of the Principles in this regard.

In order to accomplish this, members should—

- Practice in firms that have in place internal quality-control procedures to ensure that services are competently delivered and adequately supervised.
- Determine, in their individual judgments, whether the scope and nature of other services provided to an audit client would create a conflict of interest in the performance of the audit function for that client.
- Assess, in their individual judgments, whether an activity is consistent with their role as professionals.

Section II—Rules

Applicability

The bylaws of the American Institute of Certified Public Accountants require that members adhere to the Rules of the Code of Professional Conduct. *Members must be prepared to justify departures from these Rules.*

Figure 3.2 is a complete listing of the Rules, which are presented and analyzed below.

Rule 101—Independence

A member in public practice shall be independent in the performance of professional services as required by standards promulgated by bodies designated by Council.

Interpretation 101–1 of the Code contains examples of transactions, interests, and relationships that impair independence. Specifically, the interpretation indicates that public accounting firm independence will be considered to be impaired if:

A. During the period of a professional engagement a covered member:

1. Had or was committed to acquire any direct or material indirect financial interest in the client.

2. Was a trustee of any trust or executor or administrator of any estate if such trust or estate had or was committed to acquire any direct or material indirect financial interest in the client and

    (i) The covered member had the authority to make investment decisions for the trust or estate; or

FIGURE 3.2
The Rules of the AICPA
Code of Professional
Conduct

Rule	Title
101	Independence
102	Integrity and Objectivity
201	General Standards
202	Compliance with Standards
203	Accounting Principles
301	Confidential Client Information
302	Contingent Fees
501	Acts Discreditable
502	Advertising and Other Forms of Solicitation
503	Commissions and Referral Fees
504	(Deleted)
505	Form of Organization and Name

 (ii) The trust or estate owned more than 10 percent of the client's outstanding equity securities or other ownership interests or the value of the trust's or estate's holdings in the client exceeded 10 percent of the total assets of the trust or estate.

 3. Had a **joint closely held investment** that was material to the covered member.

 4. Except as specifically permitted in Interpretation 101–5, had any loan to or from the client, any officer or director of the client, or any individual owning 10 percent or more of the client's outstanding equity securities or other ownership interests.[3]

B. During the period of the professional engagement, a partner or professional employee of the firm, his or her immediate family, or any group of such persons acting together owned more than 5 percent of a client's outstanding equity securities or other ownership interests.

C. During the period covered by the financial statements or during the period of the professional engagement, a partner or professional employee of the firm was simultaneously associated with the client as a:

 1. Director, officer, or employee, or in any capacity equivalent to that of a member of management;

 2. Promoter, underwriter, or voting trustee; or

 3. Trustee for any pension or profit-sharing trust of the enterprise.

Analysis of Independence

Learning Objective 5

The first Rule of Conduct is concerned with the vital issue of CPA **independence.** Two distinct ideas are involved in the concept of independence. First, CPAs must in fact be independent of any enterprises for which they provide attestation services. *Independence in fact* refers to the CPAs' ability to maintain an objective and impartial mental attitude throughout the engagement. Second, the relationships between CPAs and their clients must be such that the accountants will *appear independent* to third parties. If the attest function is to lend credibility to information, it is essential that users of the information *perceive* that CPAs are objective and impartial.

---

[3] Interpretation 101–5 allows certain loans from financial institution clients, including (1) automobile loans and leases collateralized by the automobile, (2) loans of the surrender value under the terms of an insurance policy, (3) borrowings fully collateralized by cash deposits at the same financial institution (e.g., "passbook loans"), and (4) credit cards and cash advances on checking accounts up to $5,000. In addition, certain "grandfathered loans," outstanding when the interpretation was issued, are allowed (e.g., a home mortgage with a financial institution that subsequently becomes an audit client); these loans must be current as to all terms and may not be renegotiated.

Applicability of the Independence Rule

The independence rule does not apply to all services performed by public accountants. CPAs perform a host of services in which the client is the major beneficiary and which do not require independence, such as management consulting, tax, and accounting services. In performing these services, the CPAs are not providing assurance on information for third parties, and *observance of the independence rule is not required* as long as no attestation services are also being provided to the client.

The independence rule applies to auditing, but it also applies to all other attestation services, such as reviews of financial statements, examinations of financial forecasts, and the application of agreed-upon procedures to information. Our comments below regarding independence apply to CPAs when they perform any attestation service for a client.

Independence Terminology

It is important to recognize that independence concerns exist both at the individual CPA level and at the public accounting firm level; one, both, or neither may be considered independent with respect to a client or potential client. A public accounting firm does not necessarily lose independence with respect to an engagement when one (or more) of its employees or partners are not independent. For example, if a professional employee of a public accounting firm owns stock in a company he or she is not independent. The public accounting firm may or may not be considered independent based on a consideration of additional factors. Interpretation 101–1 sets forth the general rules in this area.

Of primary importance to understanding Section A of Interpretation 101–1 is an understanding of the terms (1) "covered member," (2) "direct and indirect financial interests," and (3) "office in which the lead attest engagement partner primarily practices."

The first phrase, **covered member,** refers to an individual, firm, or entity that is capable of influencing an attest engagement and includes:

- An individual on the **attest engagement team.**
- An **individual in a position to influence the attest engagement** (e.g., a partner who directly supervises the partner who is in charge of the attest engagement).
- A partner in the office in which the partner in charge of the attest engagement primarily practices in connection with the attest engagement.
- Certain partners or **managers** who provide nonattest services to the client.
- The public accounting firm, including its employee benefit plan.
- Any entity controlled by one or more of the above.

A covered member must comply with the highest level of independence restrictions on financial, business, and other relationships with a client. A careful reading of Interpretation 101–1 reveals that the individuals within the firm affected under the three sections differ as follows:

> Section A—Applies only to *covered members.*
>
> Sections B and C—Apply to all *partners* and all *professional employees.*

Second, Section A of Interpretation 101–1 uses the terms "direct" and "indirect" financial interests. These terms are important because for an individual CPA *any* **direct financial interest** in an attest client impairs independence, while only a *material* **indirect financial interest** impairs independence. A direct financial interest includes an investment in the client, such as owning capital stock or providing loans to the client. An indirect financial interest generally involves an intermediary of some sort; for example, a CPA may invest in companies or in mutual funds, which in turn may hold financial interests in attest clients.

Finally, the *office in which the lead attest engagement partner primarily practices* in connection with the attest engagement is important because other partners in that office are treated as covered members under the requirements of Section A of Interpretation 101–1. Rather than use this rather bulky phrase in subsequent discussion, we will refer to the office as the "engagement office." Figure 3.3 summarizes public accounting firm independence as it is affected by a lack of independence by various individuals in the firm.

Illustrative Case
Indirect Financial Interests

John Bates, a partner and covered member in the public accounting firm of Reynolds and Co., owns shares in a regulated mutual investment fund, which in turn holds shares of stock in audit clients of Reynolds and Co. The public accounting firm inquired of the AICPA Professional Ethics Division whether this financial interest by Bates affected his independence with respect to the clients.

The response was that this indirect interest would not normally impair the independence of the CPA, because investment decisions are made only by the mutual fund's management. However, if the portfolio of the mutual fund were heavily invested in securities of a client of Reynolds and Co., the indirect interest could become material to Bates and thereby impair his independence. Since Bates was found to be independent, his firm is independent.

FIGURE 3.3   **The Effects of Partner and Professional Staff Relationships on Firm Independence**

Section of Interpretation 101–1:	Partners			Professional Employees		
	Serving on the Attest Engagement	In the Engagement Office	In Other Offices	Serving on the Attest Engagement	In the Engagement Office	In Other Offices
A. Has direct or material indirect financial interest, loan, or joint business investment; or serves as trustee or administrator of estate or trust that has direct or material indirect interest.	Firm not independent	Firm not independent	Firm independent (*unless the individual is a covered member*)	Firm not independent	Firm independent (*unless the individual is a covered member*)	Firm independent (*unless the individual is a covered member*)
B. Owns 5 percent or more of client's out-standing equity or other ownership interest, or C. Is simultaneously associated with client as director, officer, employees, promoter, trustee, etc.	Firm not independent	Firm not independent	Firm not independent	Firm not independent	Firm not independent	Firm not independent

Financial Interests in Attest Clients

The restrictions in financial interests included in Section A of Interpretation 101–1 apply only to covered members. When a public accounting firm acquires a new attest client,[4] those who will become covered members must free themselves from any financial or other interest described in Section A of Interpretation 101–1. By disposing of such interests, the CPAs avoid a challenge to their independence in dealing with the new client. To illustrate, assume that a professional

---

[4] The period for which independence is required is the **period of the professional engagement**, which begins when a CPA either signs an initial engagement letter (or other agreement), or begins to perform an attest engagement, whichever is earlier. It ends with the termination of the professional relationship. The period *does not* end with the issuance of a report and recommence with the beginning of the following year's attest engagement.

employee (e.g., a senior) has a direct financial interest in a prospective client and is going to be placed on the engagement team. That individual is not independent because of the financial interest. Figure 3.3 shows that the public accounting firm also is not independent if that employee retains the investment and serves on the attest engagement. The solution here is to make certain that the employee either disposes of the investment or does not become a covered member (i.e., does not work on the engagement). Thus, the independence of a large public accounting firm is not necessarily impaired merely because one employee has a financial interest in the client. Many problems may be resolved easily by assigning a nonindependent professional employee to other engagements.

Part B of the interpretation sets forth the general provision that the CPA firm is not independent if any firm partners or professional employees, or their immediate families, own more than 5 percent of the equity of the client.

Past Employment with the Client

A lack of independence arising from a financial interest described in Sections A or B of Interpretation 101–1 can be remedied simply by disposing of the financial interest before the engagement commences. This is not true of employment relationships considered in Section C of Interpretation 101–1. CPAs who previously were employed by the client in a management capacity must disassociate themselves from that client and must not participate in audits of any periods during which they were employed by the client. The firm remains independent of the client (even if the individual is a partner), but the individual CPA is not independent.

Future Employment with the Client

Partners and covered members must report to the public accounting firm any specific offer or the intention to seek employment with an audit client. After such communication, the public accounting firm should remove that CPA from all engagements for that client until the offer has been rejected or employment is no longer being sought. The firm should also consider whether additional procedures are necessary to provide reasonable assurance that all work of that CPA was performed with objectivity and integrity.

When a public accounting firm professional accepts employment with the audit client, the engagement team should consider the need to modify the engagement procedures to adjust for the risk that audit effectiveness could be reduced due to the professional's knowledge of the audit plan. When the professional will have significant interaction with the engagement team, the firm should assess whether the existing team members have the appropriate experience and status to deal effectively with the former firm professional. Particular care should be taken in reviewing the audit when the former firm professional joins an attest client in a **key position**—one in which he or she has primary responsibility for, or influence over, accounting or financial statement reporting decisions.

For auditors of public companies, the restrictions are more stringent. The Sarbanes-Oxley Act of 2002 requires that one year pass before a member of the audit team may accept employment by SEC registrant in certain designated positions (e.g., chief executive officer, controller, chief financial or accounting officer).

Interests of a CPA's Relatives

Another question that often arises in discussions of independence may be stated as follows: How is independence affected by a financial interest or business position held by a relative of a CPA? The answer depends on the *closeness* of the family relationship and on whether the CPA works in the engagement office.

Interests of a Covered Member's Immediate Family The independence rules generally assume that the interests of covered members and their immediate families are indistinguishable from each other. Thus, as a general rule, a covered member's **immediate family members** (spouses, spousal equivalents, or dependents) are subject to the independence requirements. Accordingly, for example, if a covered member's spouse owns even one share of a client's stock, the situation is evaluated as if the covered member held the stock and independence is impaired.

Illustrative Case
Employment with Clients

The situation in which audit clients hire audit firm personnel is difficult. On the one hand, it provides great professional opportunities for individuals who enter the public accounting profession. On the other, independence concerns have led to the restrictions presented in this section.

Questions were raised about the number of ex–Arthur Andersen employees hired by Enron Corporation prior to its collapse (see Chapter 1). Although both firms refused to disclose details, the positions and numbers of ex–Arthur Andersen employees hired by Enron seem significant. *The Wall Street Journal* reported that Enron executives who had previously worked with Arthur Andersen in auditing included its chief accounting officer, its chief financial officer, and the vice president of corporate development. The *Washington Post* indicated that, over the years Arthur

Andersen served as auditor, 86 employees left the firm and accepted positions at Enron.

In addition, questions arose as to the nature of the relationship between continuing Arthur Andersen employees and those of Enron. Again, *The Wall Street Journal* reported that Arthur Andersen auditors and consultants "shared in office birthdays, frequented lunch-time parties in a nearby park and participated in weekend fundraisers for charities. They even went on Enron employees' ski trips to Beaver Creek, Colorado." One Enron employee suggested that "People just thought they were Enron employees . . . they walked and talked the same way." Consistently, the *Washington Post* reported that the chief accounting officer was the Arthur Andersen partner's "regular golfing buddy," and that people at Enron referred to Andersen as "Enron Prep."

A public accounting firm may retain its independence with respect to the engagement only by making certain that the CPA is not a covered member for that particular client.

There are two exceptions to the general rule that the interests of covered members and their immediate families are considered indistinguishable from one another. A family member may be employed with the attest client if the family member is not in a position to influence the client's financial statements. More specifically, the family member must not be employed in a key position. The second exception allows, in certain instances, the immediate family of covered members to hold a financial interest through an employer's benefit plan. This exception does not, however, apply to the immediate family of partners or professionals on the attest engagement team or of those who can influence the engagement team.

Interests of Close Relatives   Independence may also be impaired by financial interests or business relationships of close relatives (parents, siblings, or nondependent children). The independence standard for **close relatives** applies to (1) members of the attest engagement team, (2) individuals in a position to influence the attest engagement, and (3) any partner in the engagement office. For these three groups, public accounting firm independence is impaired if a close relative holds:

- A key position with the client, or
- A financial interest in the client that either (1) is material to the close relative, or (2) enables the close relative to exercise **significant influence** over the client.

Other Considerations for All Relatives and Friends   The ethics standards do not attempt to enumerate every circumstance in which the appearance of independence might be questioned. In addition to the above guidance, a CPA should consider whether personal or business relationships would lead a reasonable person, aware of all the relevant factors, to conclude that there is an unacceptable threat to independence. Figure 3.4 provides a brief summary of the complex independence requirements that apply to a CPA's relatives. Professional employees with potential problems should consult their firm's policies, as well as Interpretation 101–1 on family relationships.

Other Situations That May Impair Independence

It is impossible to describe all the situations that impair the appearance of independence. Interpretations and Ethics Rulings are issued regularly describing the application of Rule 101 to new situations. For example, rulings have been issued regarding past-due fees, gifts from clients, and client-CPA litigation.

FIGURE 3.4   Effects of Interests of Family Members, Relatives, and Friends

Relative	General Rule	Major Exceptions
Immediate family of a covered member (spouse, spousal equivalent, or dependent)	A covered member's immediate family is subject to Rule 101 and its Interpretation and Rulings.	Independence **not** impaired when: 1. A covered member's immediate family member is employed by the client in other than a key position; or 2. A family member of a partner in the engagement office (or partner or manager who provides nonattest services) participates in a retirement, savings, compensation, or similar plan sponsored by the client or that invests in the client.
Close relatives of attest engagement team members, individuals in a position to influence the attest engagement, and partners in the engagement office (parent, sibling, or nondependent child)	Independence is impaired if (1) a member on the attest engagement, (2) an individual with position to influence the attest engagement, or (3) a partner in the engagement office has a close relative who has a key position with the client or a material financial interest of which the individual is aware.	
Other considerations for all other relatives and friends	Normally no effect on independence.	Independence may be impaired when a reasonable person aware of all relevant facts would conclude that there is an unacceptable threat to independence.

If fees owed by a client to a public accounting firm become long overdue, it may appear that the CPAs' prospects for collection depend upon the nature of their report on the current financial statements. Thus, the public accounting firm's independence is considered impaired if fees for professional services rendered in prior years have not been collected before issuance of the CPAs' report for the current year.

An outsider may question the independence of a public accounting firm in situations in which a partner or employee accepts an expensive gift from a client. It would appear that special considerations might be tied to the acceptance of the gift, and the CPA might not act with complete impartiality. To avoid this implication of a lack of independence, CPAs should decline all but token gifts from attest clients.

Litigation involving the public accounting firm and the client may also affect the independence of CPAs. The relationship between the CPAs and client management must be characterized by complete candor and full disclosure. A relationship with these characteristics may not exist when litigation places the CPAs and client management in an adversarial position. CPAs in litigation, or potential litigation, with a client must evaluate the situation to determine whether the significance of the litigation affects the client's confidence in the CPAs or the CPAs' objectivity.

Providing Nonattest Services for Attest Clients

An ethical issue that has been at the forefront of the profession in recent years is the possible threat to the CPAs' independence when they perform attest services and nonattest services for the same client. What restrictions exist on providing nonattest services for a client?

The AICPA's Interpretation 101–3 requires that while the CPAs should not perform management functions or make management decisions for the attest client, they may provide

Illustrative Case
Independence and Nonattest Work

A number of highly publicized cases were highlighted by the SEC and Congress as examples of situations in which performing nonattest services for a client may have affected auditor independence. As an example, Global Crossing Ltd. reported it paid Arthur Andersen $2.3 million in audit fees in 2000, but the company paid Arthur Andersen more than $12 million in fees for nonattest work.

advice, research materials, and recommendations to assist the client. Accordingly, the client must agree to:

- Make all management decisions and perform all management functions.
- Designate a competent employee, preferably within senior management, to oversee the services.
- Evaluate the adequacy and results of the services performed.
- Accept responsibility for the results of the services.
- Establish and maintain internal control, including monitoring ongoing activities.

Before performing nonattest services, the CPAs must establish and document in writing the understanding with the client, including objectives of the engagement, services to be performed, the client's acceptance of its responsibilities, the CPAs' responsibilities, and any limitations of the engagement. Interpretation 101–3 provides the following examples of general activities that would impair a CPA's independence:

- Authorizing, executing, or consummating a transaction.
- Preparing source documents (e.g., purchase orders, payroll time records, and customer orders).
- Having custody of client assets.
- Supervising client employees in their normal recurring activities.
- Determining which recommendations should be implemented.
- Reporting to the board of directors on behalf of management.
- Serving as a client's stock transfer or escrow agent, registrar, or general counsel.

The above examples make it clear that a CPA who becomes a part-time controller for a client and assumes a *decision-making role* in the client's affairs is not in a position to make an independent audit of the financial statements. However, a CPA who provides bookkeeping or accounting services for the client can maintain independence under the AICPA rules. As long as the client takes responsibility for the financial statements and the auditors perform their engagement in accordance with generally accepted auditing standards, independence is not impaired. Of course, the accounting services provided cannot include executing transactions or performing other management functions. If the AICPA ruled that independence is impaired whenever the auditors perform accounting services, such a ruling would adversely affect many small public accounting firms with practices including considerable financial statement write-up work and occasional audits for small nonpublic clients. As we will describe in the next section, the rules for auditors of public companies prohibit them from performing any accounting or bookkeeping services for the client, along with a host of other services.

The AICPA maintains that public accounting firms have long been rendering consulting services to management while continuing to perform audits in an independent manner that serves the public interest. The AICPA and public accounting firms believe that the additional knowledge of the client that comes from performing these services actually enhances the audit. It also allows public accounting firms to have associates with more expertise, especially in the area of information technology. However, this is not the view of many critics of the profession, including some individuals from the Securities and Exchange Commission (SEC) and

Congress. These concerns led to the provisions of the Sarbanes-Oxley Act of 2002 that prohibit the performance of a wide range of nonattest services for public company audit clients.

Independence—Requirements for Audits of Public Companies

Learning Objective 6

Independence standards for public companies are currently a combination of pronouncements by the AICPA and the SEC and the legal requirements of the Sarbanes-Oxley Act of 2002, as enforced and modified by the PCAOB. Historically, the AICPA has issued, and continues to issue, independence standards which apply to its members. The SEC also has established independence standards for audits of public companies that supplement those of the AICPA.

With passage of the Sarbanes-Oxley Act of 2002, the PCAOB is now responsible for adopting or establishing the ethical and independence standards for audits of public companies, with the authority and oversight of the SEC. The Sarbanes-Oxley Act of 2002 makes it unlawful for a registered public accounting firm that audits a public company to provide a variety of nonattest services to that client. Figure 3.5 summarizes those services as well as the AICPA's guidance. Bear in mind that the AICPA's guidance is relevant for nonpublic clients only.

FIGURE 3.5 **Comparison of Sarbanes-Oxley and AICPA Requirements Regarding Providing Nonattest Services to Audit Clients**

Service Not Allowed by Sarbanes-Oxley	AICPA *Code of Professional Conduct* Requirements
Bookkeeping or other services related to the accounting records or financial statements	Allowed, providing the auditors do not: • Determine or change journal entries without client approval. • Authorize or approve transactions. • Prepare source documents. • Make changes to source documents without client approval.
Financial information systems design and implementation	Auditors are allowed to: • Implement system not developed by auditor (e.g., off-the-shelf accounting packages). • Assist in setting up chart of accounts and financial statement format. • Design, develop, install, or integrate an information system unrelated to the financial statements or accounting records. • Provide training to client employees on the information and control system.
Appraisal, valuation and actuarial services	Allowed, providing services do not: • Relate to a material portion of the financial statements, *and* • Involve a significant degree of subjectivity.
Internal audit outsourcing services	Allowed, providing the client understands its responsibility for internal control and: • Designates competent individual(s) within company to be responsible for internal audit. • Determines scope, risk, and frequency of internal audit activities. • Evaluates findings and results. • Evaluates adequacy of audit procedures performed.
Management functions or human resources	Auditors may provide various types of advice but may not perform management functions.
Various investment services	Certain services are allowed, including: • Assisting in developing corporate finance strategies. • Recommending allocation of funds to investments.
Legal services and expert services unrelated to auditing	Legal services are not directly addressed; various other services are allowed if auditors do not make management decisions.
Certain tax services, such as tax planning for potentially abusive tax transactions and providing individual tax services to client officers who play a significant role in financial reporting	No specific restrictions.

Illustrative Case
Tax Services and Independence

The issue of independence and tax services was vividly illustrated in the Sprint Corp. case. Sprint had a policy of allowing its audit firm, Ernst & Young LLP, to perform tax planning services for its top executives. The chief executive officer and the president of Sprint adopted a tax shelter strategy recommended by Ernst & Young. When the shelter was determined to be ineffective, the executives were faced with potential liabilities of millions of dollars in back taxes, which created a conflict of interest between them and Ernst & Young. Rather than discharge the auditors, the board of directors of Sprint elected to force out the two executives. The Sprint case and similar cases resulted in the PCAOB standards restricting the performance of tax services for the executives of audit clients.

In addition, CPAs generally may provide allowed nonattest services only if they are approved in advance by the audit committee of the client's board of directors. Also, clients must disclose in their annual report fees paid for (1) audit services, (2) audit-related services, (3) tax services, and (4) other services.

Independence Requirements of Government Auditing Standards   The Government Accountability Office (GAO)—formerly called the General Accounting Office—develops additional requirements for audits of entities that receive federal financial assistance. These requirements are included in *Government Auditing Standards* as discussed in Chapter 21. With regard to auditor independence, *Government Auditing Standards* also are more restrictive than those of the AICPA. As an example, a public accounting firm cannot allow personnel working on nonattest engagements to also work on the audit. In addition, *Government Auditing Standards* place restrictions on the nature of the nonattest services that may be provided to an audit client. Nonattest services must be deemed not to be significant or material to the subject matter of the audit. Under the GAO's interpretation of this requirement, restrictions are placed on the nature of bookkeeping, payroll, valuation, information technology, human resources, and internal audit services.

Independence—A Matter of Degree

The concept of independence is not absolute; no CPAs can claim *complete* independence of a client. Rather, independence is relative—a matter of degree. As long as the CPAs work closely with client management and are paid fees by their clients, complete independence can be considered merely an ideal. CPAs must strive for the greatest degree of independence consistent with this business environment.

Recent regulations by the SEC and stock exchanges have served to increase the CPAs' independence in dealings with management and to improve the quality of financial reporting by public companies. The New York Stock Exchange, the American Stock Exchange, and NASDAQ have established requirements for independent **audit committees** by all listed companies. According to these requirements, audit committees must consist of at least three independent and financially literate individuals, and the chairman must have accounting or financial management expertise. In addition, the Sarbanes-Oxley Act of 2002 makes the audit committee directly responsible for appointing, compensating, and overseeing the public accounting firm. The SEC regulations require public companies to file a copy of the audit committee's charter every three years and disclose whether its members are independent of management. All of these requirements increase the auditors' ability to deal independently with management.

Rule 102—Integrity and Objectivity

In the performance of any professional service, a member shall maintain objectivity and integrity, shall be free of conflicts of interest, and shall not knowingly misrepresent facts or subordinate his or her judgment to others.

Analysis of Integrity and Objectivity

Rule 102 applies to all members of the AICPA and all services provided by CPAs. It recognizes that clients, employers, or others may at times attempt to influence the judgment of CPAs on professional matters. To maintain the confidence and respect of the public, CPAs must never subordinate their professional judgments to others. Interpretation 102–1 states that a CPA will be found to have knowingly misrepresented facts in violation of Rule 102 when he or she knowingly:

- Makes, or permits or directs another to make, materially incorrect entries in a client's financial statements or records.
- Fails to correct financial statements that are materially false or misleading when the member has such authority.
- Signs, or permits or directs another to sign, a document containing materially false and misleading information.

It is often difficult to determine if an individual has "knowingly misrepresented facts." Thus in evaluating whether a CPA has violated that Section of Rule 102, we must look to whether, based on the circumstances, the CPA *should have* known of the misrepresentation. A ruling that a CPA violated Rule 102 is most commonly based upon evidence that the CPAs should have been knowledgeable about the facts.

Rule 201—General Standards

A member shall comply with the following standards and with any interpretations thereof by bodies designated by Council.

A. Professional Competence. Undertake only those professional services that the member or the member's firm can reasonably expect to be completed with professional competence.

B. Due Professional Care. Exercise due professional care in the performance of professional services.

C. Planning and Supervision. Adequately plan and supervise the performance of professional services.

D. Sufficient Relevant Data. Obtain sufficient relevant data to afford a reasonable basis for conclusions or recommendations in relation to any professional services performed.

Analysis of General Standards

In addition to performing audits and other attestation services, CPAs also provide accounting, review, tax, and consulting services. Clients and the general public expect these services to be performed with competence and professional care. Therefore, the general standards of Rule 201 apply to *all CPA services.*

Rule 202—Compliance with Standards

A member who performs auditing, review, compilation, management consulting, tax, or other professional services shall comply with standards promulgated by bodies designated by Council.

Analysis of Compliance with Standards

Rule 202 requires CPAs to adhere to professional standards issued by other technical bodies. To date, the Council of the AICPA has recognized six bodies and given them authority for the performance standards summarized in Figure 3.6. CPAs must become familiar with such statements and apply them to their engagements. To violate standards prescribed by these bodies is to violate Rule 202 of the Code.

Professional Standards for Consulting Services

As indicated above, the AICPA's Management Consulting Services Executive Committee is authorized to issue *Statements on Standards for Consulting Services* to provide practitioners with authoritative guidance on providing consulting services to their clients. Consulting services are broadly defined by these standards to include virtually all services other than auditing and attestation services, accounting and review services, and tax services. To the general standards

FIGURE 3.6 Technical Bodies and Their Authority

Technical Body	Authority	Performance Standards[†]
Auditing Standards Board (ASB)	Prescribes auditing standards and responsibilities with respect to supplementary information outside the financial statements	*Statements on Auditing Standards*
Management Consulting Services Executive Committee (MCSEC)	Prescribes standards for management advisory services	*Statements on Standards for Consulting Services*
Accounting and Review Services Committee (ARSC)	Prescribes standards for unaudited financial information services for nonpublic companies	*Statements on Standards for Accounting and Review Services*
ASB, MCSEC, and ARSC	Prescribe attestation standards in their areas	*Statements on Standards for Attestation Engagements*
Financial Accounting Standards Board, Governmental Accounting Standards Board, and Federal Accounting Standards Advisory Board*	Prescribe disclosure standards for supplementary information outside the financial statements	*Statements of Financial Accounting Standards, Statements of Governmental Accounting Standards, Statements of Federal Financial Accounting Standards,* and related *Interpretations*

*Rule 203 gives these bodies authority for accounting standards.
[†]The list includes only the highest level standards. The bodies also issue various forms of interpretive guidance.

contained in Rule 201, these standards add the following additional requirements for these types of engagements:

1. *Client interest.* The practitioner should strive to meet the objectives of the client while maintaining integrity and objectivity.
2. *Understanding with client.* The practitioner should establish a written or oral understanding with the client about the nature, scope, and limitations of the consulting engagement.
3. *Communication with client.* The practitioner should inform the client of (a) any conflicts of interest that may occur with respect to the engagement, (b) any significant reservations about the scope or benefits of the engagement, and (c) all significant findings or events.

Rule 203—Accounting Principles

A member shall not (1) express an opinion or state affirmatively that the financial statements or other financial data of any entity are presented in conformity with generally accepted accounting principles or (2) state that he or she is not aware of any material modifications that should be made to such statements or data in order for them to be in conformity with generally accepted accounting principles, if such statements or data contain any departure from an accounting principle promulgated by bodies designated by Council to establish such principles that has a material effect on the statements or data taken as a whole. If, however, the statements or data contain such a departure and the member can demonstrate that due to unusual circumstances the financial statements or data would otherwise have been misleading, the member can comply with the rule by describing the departure, its approximate effects, if practicable, and the reasons why compliance with the principle would result in a misleading statement.

Analysis of Accounting Principles

Rule 203 recognizes the authority of certain designated bodies to issue accounting principles. Under this rule, the AICPA has designated the *Statements* and *Interpretations* of the Financial Accounting Standards Board (FASB), the Governmental Accounting Standards Board (GASB), and the Federal Accounting Standards Advisory Board (FASAB) as primary sources of generally accepted accounting principles. CPAs should not issue an unqualified opinion on a set of financial statements that materially depart from one of these pronouncements, except in the situation in which application of the pronouncement would result in misleading financial statements.

Rule 301—Confidential Client Information

A member in public practice shall not disclose any confidential client information without the specific consent of the client.

This rule shall not be construed (1) to relieve a member of the member's professional obligations under rules 202 and 203, (2) to affect in any way the member's obligation to comply with a validly issued and enforceable subpoena or summons, (3) to prohibit review of a member's professional practice under AICPA or state CPA society authorization, or (4) to preclude a member from initiating a complaint with or responding to any inquiry made by a recognized investigative or disciplinary body.

Members of a recognized investigative or disciplinary body and professional practice reviewers shall not use to their own advantage or disclose any member's confidential client information that comes to their attention in carrying out their official responsibilities. However, this prohibition shall not restrict the exchange of information with a recognized investigative or disciplinary body or affect, in any way, compliance with a validly issued and enforceable subpoena or summons.

Analysis of Confidential Client Information

Rule 301 stresses the confidential nature of information obtained by CPAs from their clients. The nature of accountants' work makes it necessary for them to have access to their clients' most confidential financial affairs. Independent accountants may thus gain insider knowledge of impending business combinations, proposed financing, prospective stock splits or dividend changes, contracts being negotiated, and other confidential information that, if disclosed or otherwise improperly used, could bring the accountants quick monetary profits. Of course, the client could be financially injured, as well as embarrassed, if the CPAs were to "leak" such information. Any loose talk by independent public accountants concerning the affairs of their clients would immediately brand them as lacking in professional ethics. On the other hand, the confidential relationship between the CPA and the client is not a justification for the CPA to cooperate in any deceitful act. The personal integrity of the CPA is essential to the performance of the attest function.

Reporting Illegal Acts

Should auditors be required to report illegal acts by clients to regulatory agencies? Rule 301 of the Code of Conduct prohibits CPAs from directly disclosing such information to outside parties, unless the auditors have a legal duty to do so. An amendment of the Securities Exchange Act of 1934, the *Private Securities Reform Act of 1995,* includes a requirement for fraud reporting, or *whistleblowing* by the auditors. The requirements of this law apply when the client has committed an illegal act and (a) it has a material effect on the financial statements, (b) senior management and the board of directors have not taken appropriate remedial action, and (c) the failure to take remedial action is reasonably expected to warrant a departure from a standard audit report, or resignation by the auditors. In these circumstances, the auditors must, *as soon as practicable,* communicate their conclusions directly to the client's board of directors. Within one day, the management of the client must send a notification to the Securities and Exchange Commission of having received such a communication from the auditors, and a copy of the notification should be sent to the auditors. If the auditors do not receive the copy within the one-day period, they have one day to *directly communicate* the matter to the SEC.

Auditors also are required to communicate illegal acts in other situations. When illegal activities cause the auditors of a public company to lose faith in the integrity of senior management, they will resign and a Form 8–K, which discloses the reasons for the auditors' resignation, will be filed with the SEC by management. The auditors must file a response to the filing indicating whether or not they agree with management's reasons, and providing the details when they disagree. In addition, when the auditors are performing an audit in accordance with the Single Audit Act, they may be required to disclose illegal acts by the client to an agency that provides federal financial assistance to the client. Single audits are described in detail in Chapter 21.

Confidentiality versus Privileged Communications

The communications between CPAs and their clients are confidential, but they are not *privileged* under common law, as are communications with attorneys, clergymen, or physicians. The difference is that disclosure of legally privileged communications cannot be required by a subpoena or court order. Thus, CPAs may be compelled to disclose their communications with clients in certain types of court proceedings. Some individual states, however, have adopted statutes providing that public accountants cannot be required by the state courts to give evidence gained in confidence from clients. Such state laws, however, do not apply to federal courts where there are not privileged communications.

Rule 302—Contingent Fees

A member in public practice shall not:

1. *Perform for a contingent fee any professional services for, or receive such a fee from a client for whom the member or the member's firm performs:*

   a. *An audit or review of a financial statement; or*

   b. *A compilation of a financial statement when the member expects, or reasonably might expect, that a third party will use the financial statement and the member's compilation report does not disclose a lack of independence; or*

   c. *An examination of prospective financial information; or*

2. *Prepare an original or amended tax return or claim for a tax refund for a contingent fee for any client.*

   The prohibition in (1) above applies during the period in which the member or the member's firm is engaged to perform any of the services listed above and the period covered by any historical financial statements involved in any such listed services.

   Except as stated in the next sentence, a contingent fee is a fee established for the performance of any service pursuant to an arrangement in which no fee will be charged unless a specified finding or result is attained, or in which the amount of the fee is otherwise dependent upon the finding or result of such service. Solely for purposes of this rule, fees are not regarded as being contingent if fixed by courts or other public authorities, or, in tax matters, if determined based on the results of judicial proceedings or the findings of governmental agencies.

   A member's fees may vary depending, for example, on the complexity of services rendered.

Analysis of Contingent Fees

An accountant is prohibited by Rule 302 from providing services on a contingent fee basis in certain circumstances. A CPA may not receive a contingent fee for the preparation of original or amended tax returns or claims for tax refunds. Preparation of a tax return includes giving advice on how particular items should be handled on the return. Also, no contingent fee engagements are allowed for services performed for a client that also engages that public accounting firm to perform audits, reviews, certain compilations of financial statements, or examinations of **prospective financial information.** For example, consulting services may not be performed for a contingent fee for an audit client of the public accounting firm.

The CPAs may perform services for contingent fees for other clients. Consider a public accounting firm with a prospective new client whose management requests assistance in redesigning its cash disbursements system. In such circumstances, if none of the services described in part 1 of the rule are provided for that client, the CPAs may perform the service for a contingent fee. For example, the CPAs may redesign the disbursements system and receive a fee that is contingent on the amount of cost savings realized by the client in processing future cash disbursements. The CPAs' fee might be, for example, 25 percent of the next four years' cost savings.

The PCAOB rules contain an additional restriction with respect to contingent fees. The auditors of public companies are prohibited from accepting engagements for tax services that are determined based on the results of judicial proceedings or the findings of government agencies.

Rule 501—Acts Discreditable

A member shall not commit an act discreditable to the profession.

Analysis of Acts Discreditable

Rule 501 gives the AICPA the authority to discipline those members who act in a manner damaging to the reputation of the profession. The three circumstances outlined in Interpretation 102–1 (page 76) related to misleading entries and financial statements are considered discreditable. Beyond these illustrations, the rule is not specific as to what constitutes a discreditable act; it is subject to interpretation. In the past, such acts as signing a false or misleading opinion or statement, committing a felony, and engaging in discrimination or harassment in employment practices have been interpreted to be violations of Rule 501.

One interesting practice that has been interpreted to be discreditable is failure to return client records. These situations generally arise when the CPAs have been discharged and not paid for their services. To refuse to return a client's ledger is clearly wrong, but what if the CPAs retain working papers needed by the client? To enforce collection of a fee, some CPAs have refused to allow the client or the successor CPAs access to their working papers. Since the working papers are the CPAs' property, this is a legitimate business practice, not a violation of Rule 501. However, CPAs should be aware that when working papers provide the only support for entries in the client's financial records, those working papers should be made available to the client after the CPAs' fees have been paid.

Rule 502—Advertising and Other Forms of Solicitation

A member in public practice shall not seek to obtain clients by advertising or other forms of solicitations in a manner that is false, misleading, or deceptive. Solicitation by the use of coercion, overreaching, or harassing conduct is prohibited.

Analysis of Advertising and Other Forms of Solicitation

For many years advertising by CPAs was strictly forbidden by the AICPA Rules. Most certified public accountants considered advertising in any form to be unprofessional. However, this prohibition was dropped because it was deemed a possible violation of federal antitrust laws. Members of the public accounting profession may advertise their services so long as the advertising is not false, misleading, or deceptive. Unethical advertising includes that which creates unjustified expectations of favorable results or indicates an ability to influence a court or other official body.

Acceptable advertising is that which is informative and based upon verifiable fact. Indications of the types of services offered, certificates and degrees of members of the firm, and fees for services are all acceptable forms of advertising.

Rule 503—Commissions and Referral Fees

1. *Prohibited commissions. A member in public practice shall not for a commission recommend or refer to a client any product or service, or for a commission recommend or refer any product or service to be supplied by a client, or receive a commission, when the member or the member's firm also performs for that client:*

   a. *An audit or review of a financial statement.*

   b. *A compilation of a financial statement when the member expects, or reasonably might expect, that a third party will use the financial statement and the member's compilation report does not disclose a lack of independence.*

   c. *An examination of prospective financial information.*

   This prohibition applies during the period in which the member is engaged to perform any of the services listed above and the period covered by any historical financial statements involved in such listed services.

2. *Disclosure of permitted commissions. A member in public practice who is not prohibited by this rule from performing services for or receiving a commission and who is paid or expects to be paid a commission shall disclose that fact to any person or entity to whom the member recommends or refers a product or service to which the commission relates.*

3. *Referral fees. Any member who accepts a referral fee for recommending or referring any service of a CPA to any person or entity or who pays a referral fee to obtain a client shall disclose such acceptance or payment to the client.*

Analysis of Commissions and Referral Fees

Clients look to their CPAs for objective advice on the purchase of products and services, including services from other CPAs. Historically, CPAs have been prohibited from accepting a commission from the providers of such products and services. The consent agreement between the AICPA and the Federal Trade Commission, mentioned under Rule 302, also caused a change in this rule to allow the collection of commissions from certain clients. As an example, CPAs that do not perform financial statement audits, reviews, certain compilations, or examinations of prospective information for a client may receive commissions for purchasing and selling securities for that client, provided they disclose the existence of the commissions to the client.

Rule 505—Form of Organization and Name

A member may practice public accounting only in a form of organization permitted by state law or regulation, whose characteristics conform to resolutions of Council.

A member shall not practice public accounting under a firm name that is misleading. Names of one or more past owners may be included in the firm name of a successor organization.

A firm may not designate itself as "Members of the American Institute of Certified Public Accountants" unless all of its owners are members of the Institute.

Analysis of Form of Organization and Name

The *Code of Professional Conduct* allows CPAs to practice in any legal business form. This includes the ability to practice as professional corporations, limited liability partnerships (companies), partnerships, or sole practitioners.

Many state laws, as well as the *Code of Professional Conduct,* allow CPAs to form professional corporations. Professional corporations have certain tax advantages not available to partnerships, such as tax deductibility of pension and profit-sharing plans. The shareholders of professional corporations retain liability for acts of the corporation, regardless of whether they participated in the engagement resulting in the liability. Besides providing for financial liability, the organization must be established such that two-thirds ownership, voting rights, and control over professional matters must rest with individuals authorized to practice public accounting.

Currently, most states allow CPAs to practice in the form of a limited liability partnership (company). Although similar to professional corporations in many ways, limited liability forms of organization protect the personal assets of any partner or shareholder not directly involved in providing services on engagements resulting in liability.

Previous versions of Rule 505 prohibited public accountants from practicing under a name that was fictitious or indicated a specialization. Because this prohibition was sensitive to antitrust attack, the revised Rule 505 allows fictitious names so long as they are not false, misleading, or deceptive.

Alternative Practice Structures

As indicated in Chapter 1, public accounting firms are entering into what is referred to as "alternative practice structures" in which publicly traded companies (e.g., American Express Co., Century Business Services, and H&R Block) purchase public accounting firms. A typical alternative practice arrangement may be as follows:

- Public Company buys the nonattest portion of a public accounting firm's practice from the public accounting firm's partners for cash, stock, or a combination of both.
- Public Company has subsidiaries such as a bank, an insurance company, a broker-dealer, and a professional services subsidiary that offer clients the nonattest public accounting services.
- Public accounting firm partners and employees become employees of Public Company performing nonattest public accounting work under the Public Company name.
- The attest practice of the public accounting firm remains intact with the "shell" of the public accounting firm and continues to be owned by the original partners of the public accounting firm (who are now also employees of Public Company).
- The public accounting firm leases staff from Public Company to perform the attest services.

Figure 3.7 summarizes the typical structures of these types of firms.

Illustrative Case
The Impact of Liability

Large malpractice lawsuits and economic conditions resulted in the 1990 bankruptcy of Leventhol & Horwath, the seventh largest public accounting firm in the United States. Not only did the partners lose their investment in the firm, they found themselves personally liable for a portion of the partnership liabilities.

In 2002, Arthur Andersen, a limited liability partnership (LLP), suffered serious financial losses and dissolution due to

legal liability. Partners not involved with engagements resulting in legal liability have to this point been able to limit their liability to loss of their capital accounts in accord with the provisions of an LLP. However, attorneys of plaintiffs with losses are expected to attempt to broaden partner liability by legally testing the liability limitations of the LLP form of organization.

Alternative practice structures present a number of questions and potential threats to independence. For example, because the partners of the attest firm are employees of Public Company, these partners may have a difficult time maintaining independence when auditing a client that is important to Public Company. To illustrate, pressure may be exerted by Public Company management to issue a standard unqualified report when there is substantial doubt concerning going-concern status relating to a client that has a significant debt to Public Company. Or, perhaps Public Company may provide attest clients with services that place personnel in a position equivalent to that of client management.

The CPA as Tax Advisor—Ethical Problems

What is the responsibility of the CPA in serving as tax advisor? The CPA has a primary responsibility to the client; that is, to see that the client pays the proper amount of tax and no more. In the role of tax advisor, the certified public accountant may properly resolve questionable issues in favor of the client; the CPA is not obliged to maintain the posture of independence required in attestation work. However, CPAs must adhere to the same standards of objectivity and integrity in tax work as in all other professional activities.

A second responsibility of CPAs on tax engagements is to the public, whose interests are represented by the government—more specifically by the Internal Revenue Service (IRS). To meet this responsibility, CPAs must observe the preparer's declaration on the tax returns they prepare. The declaration requires the preparer to state that the return is "true, correct, and complete . . . based on all information of which the preparer has any knowledge." To comply with this declaration, what steps must the public accounting firm take to acquire knowledge relating to the tax return? The firm is not required to make an audit; knowledge of the return may be limited to information supplied to the firm by the client. However, if this information

FIGURE 3.7   **Illustration of an Alternative Practice Structure**

	Public Company	**CPA Firm**
Structure	Publicly traded corporation owned by stockholders.	Partnership or other form of organization authorized to perform audit and attest services owned by the partners.
Services performed	Nonattest services.	Audit and attest services.
Staffing of engagements	Partners and staff who are now employees of the public company.	Partners and staff time are leased from the public company.
Management of the practice	Practice is managed by officers of the public company.	Practice is managed by partners of the CPA firm.

appears unreasonable or contradictory, the CPAs are obligated to make sufficient investigation to resolve these issues. Information that appears plausible to a layman might appear unreasonable to CPAs, since they are experts in evaluating financial data. CPAs are not obligated to investigate any and all information provided by the taxpayer, but they cannot ignore clues that cast doubt on the accuracy of these data.

In addition to being guided by the declaration on the tax return, CPAs should look to a series of pronouncements issued by the AICPA, entitled *Statements on Responsibilities in Tax Practice.* These statements address such questions as: Under what circumstances should a CPA sign the preparer's declaration on a tax return? What is the CPA's responsibility for errors in previously filed returns? Should CPAs disclose the taking of positions that differ from IRS interpretations of the tax code? The purpose of this series is to provide guidance to CPAs, and the statements are not directly enforceable under the *Code of Professional Conduct.*

Enforcement of Professional Ethics

The AICPA and the state societies of CPAs have established a joint ethics enforcement plan. Under the plan, complaints about a CPA's conduct are first referred to the Professional Ethics Division of the AICPA for investigation. If the Professional Ethics Division finds the complaint to be valid, it may take several courses of action. For minor violations, the Division may take direct remedial action, such as requiring the member to get additional continuing education. More serious violations are turned over to the joint trial board for a hearing. If found guilty, the offending member may be censured, suspended from membership for up to two years, or expelled permanently from the AICPA. Although expulsion from the AICPA would not in itself cause the loss of a CPA's license, the damage to the CPA's professional reputation would be substantial.

The provisions of the AICPA Rules have been used as a model by the boards of accountancy throughout the country to develop the ethical standards in their states. Thus, revocation of the CPA's license to practice also is a possible consequence of violation of the AICPA ethical standards.

Finally, ethical violations by auditors of public companies also are investigated and enforced by the SEC and the Public Company Accounting Oversight Board. Severe violations may result in suspension of the CPA's or the public accounting firm's right to practice as an auditor of public companies. Lesser penalties may involve monetary fines or remedial measures, such as the required implementation of new quality control procedures.

Ethics for Internal Auditors

Internal auditors, acting through their national organization, The Institute of Internal Auditors, have developed their own code of professional ethics. The Institute of Internal Auditors *Code of Ethics* is organized with an Introduction, Fundamental Principles, and a Code of Conduct. The Code of Conduct primarily addresses internal auditors' obligations to their employers, but it also includes provisions that prescribe integrity, objectivity, and competency in the practice of the internal auditing profession. Violation of the articles of the Code could result in revocation of the auditor's membership in The Institute of Internal Auditors or forfeiture of the auditor's "Certified Internal Auditor" designation. The Institute of Internal Auditors *Code of Ethics* is reproduced below.

Learning Objective 7

The Institute of Internal Auditors
Code of Ethics

Introduction

The purpose of The Institute's *Code of Ethics* is to promote an ethical culture in the profession of internal auditing.

Internal auditing is an independent, objective assurance and consulting activity designed to add value and improve an organization's operations. It helps an organization accomplish its objectives by bringing a systematic, disciplined approach to evaluate and improve the effectiveness of risk management, control, and governance processes.

A code of ethics is necessary and appropriate for the profession of internal auditing, founded as it is on the trust placed in its objective assurance about risk management, control, and governance. The Institute's *Code of Ethics* extends beyond the definition of internal auditing to include two essential components:

1. Principles that are relevant to the profession and practice of internal auditing;
2. Rules of Conduct that describe behavior norms expected of internal auditors. These rules are an aid to interpreting the Principles into practical applications and are intended to guide the ethical conduct of internal auditors.

The *Code of Ethics* together with The Institute's *Professional Practices Framework* and other relevant Institute pronouncements provide guidance to internal auditors serving others. "Internal auditors" refers to Institute members, recipients of or candidates for IIA professional certifications, and those who provide internal auditing services within the definition of internal auditing.

Applicability and Enforcement

This *Code of Ethics* applies to both individuals and entities that provide internal auditing services. For Institute members and recipients of or candidates for IIA professional certifications, breaches of the *Code of Ethics* will be evaluated and administered according to The Institute's Bylaws and Administrative Guidelines. The fact that a particular conduct is not mentioned in the Rules of Conduct does not prevent it from being unacceptable or discreditable, and therefore, the member, certification holder, or candidate can be liable for disciplinary action.

Principles

Internal auditors are expected to apply and uphold the following principles:

Integrity

The integrity of internal auditors establishes trust and thus provides the basis for reliance on their judgment.

Objectivity

Internal auditors exhibit the highest level of professional objectivity in gathering, evaluating, and communicating information about the activity or process being examined. Internal auditors make a balanced assessment of all the relevant circumstances and are not unduly influenced by their own interests or by others in forming judgments.

Confidentiality

Internal auditors respect the value and ownership of information they receive and do not disclose information without appropriate authority unless there is a legal or professional obligation to do so.

Competency

Internal auditors apply the knowledge, skills, and experience needed in the performance of internal auditing services.

Rules of Conduct

1. Integrity

Internal auditors:

1.1. Shall perform their work with honesty, diligence, and responsibility.
1.2. Shall observe the law and make disclosures expected by the law and the profession.
1.3. Shall not knowingly be a party to any illegal activity, or engage in acts that are discreditable to the profession of internal auditing or to the organization.
1.4. Shall respect and contribute to the legitimate and ethical objectives of the organization.

2. Objectivity

Internal auditors:

2.1. Shall not participate in any activity or relationship that may impair or be presumed to impair their unbiased assessment. This participation includes those activities or relationships that may be in conflict with the interests of the organization.

2.2. Shall not accept anything that may impair or be presumed to impair their professional judgment.

2.3. Shall disclose all material facts known to them that, if not disclosed, may distort the reporting of activities under review.

3. Confidentiality

Internal auditors:

3.1. Shall be prudent in the use and protection of information acquired in the course of their duties.

3.2. Shall not use information for any personal gain or in any manner that would be contrary to the law or detrimental to the legitimate and ethical objectives of the organization.

4. Competency

Internal auditors:

4.1. Shall engage only in those services for which they have the necessary knowledge, skills, and experience.

4.2. Shall perform internal auditing services in accordance with the *Standards for the Professional Practice of Internal Auditing.*

4.3. Shall continually improve their proficiency and the effectiveness and quality of their services.

Chapter Summary

This chapter explained the need for professionals to adhere to high standards of professional conduct, and described the details of the codes of ethics that apply to both external and internal auditors. To summarize:

1. Ethics are the moral principles and values that govern the behavior of individuals and groups. An *ethical dilemma* is a situation that involves a decision about appropriate behavior. A key aspect of an ethical dilemma is that it generally affects parties that are not involved in the decision. For example, if management of a corporation decides to pollute the environment, it affects all of the members of society. Professional accountants are faced with difficult personal and professional ethical dilemmas on a daily basis.

2. Among the characteristics common to recognized professions are (a) acknowledgment of a responsibility to serve the public, (b) existence of a complex body of knowledge, (c) standards of admission to the profession, and (d) a need for public confidence.

3. The membership of the AICPA has adopted the *Code of Professional Conduct,* consisting of two sections—Principles and Rules. In addition, the AICPA issues Interpretations and Ethics Rulings to provide further guidance on appropriate ethical conduct.

4. Independence is required when CPAs perform audits and other types of attest engagements. Interpretation 101–1 provides guidance on various financial and business relationships that may impair a CPA's independence. That standard prohibits all direct financial interests in a client, as well as material indirect financial interests. Certain independence rules apply only to covered members and others apply to all partners and professional employees. In the audit of a public company, the auditors must also adhere to the ethics and independence requirements of the SEC, the Sarbanes-Oxley Act of 2002, and the Public Company Accounting Oversight Board.

5. The Rules of the AICPA *Code of Professional Conduct* set forth the professional standards that must be followed by CPAs when performing various types of professional services. For example, Rule 202 requires auditors to adhere to *Statements on Auditing Standards.* Accounting standards of the FASB, the GASB, and the FASAB are enforced by Rule 203.

6. In performing an audit, the auditors have access to the details of the client's most confidential information. If the auditors disclosed this information, they might damage their clients' businesses. Therefore, CPAs are required to maintain a strict confidentiality relationship with their clients.

7. CPAs generally may accept engagements for contingent fees and receive commissions for referrals, but only if they do not also provide certain attestation or compilation services for the client.

8. A public accounting firm may practice public accounting in any form of organization permitted by law or regulation, including as a sole practitioner, partnership, professional corporation, or limited liability partnership (company).

9. The *Code of Ethics* of The Institute of Internal Auditors primarily addresses internal auditors' obligations to their employers, but it also includes provisions requiring integrity, objectivity, and competency in the practice of internal auditing.

Key Terms Introduced or Emphasized in Chapter 3

Attest engagement team   Consists of individuals participating in the attest engagement, including those who perform concurring and second partner reviews. The attest engagement team includes all employees and contractors retained by the firm who participate in the attest engagement, irrespective of their functional classification (for example, audit, tax, or management consulting services), except specialists as discussed in *SAS No. 73,* "Using the Work of a Specialist," and individuals who perform only routine clerical functions, such as word processing and photocopying.

Audit committee   A committee of a corporation's board of directors that engages, compensates, and oversees the work of the independent auditors, monitors activities of the internal auditing staff, and intervenes in any disputes between management and the independent auditors. Members of the audit committee must be independent directors, that is, members of the board of directors who do not also serve as corporate officers, or have other relationships that might impair independence.

Close relative   A parent, sibling, or nondependent child.

Covered member   A covered member may be: (*a*) an individual on the attest engagement team; (*b*) an individual in a position to influence the attest engagement; (*c*) a partner or manager who provides nonattest services to the attest client beginning once he or she provides 10 hours of nonattest services to the client within any fiscal year and ending on the later of the date (1) the firm signs the report on the financial statements for the fiscal year during which those services were provided, or (2) he or she no longer expects to provide 10 or more hours of nonattest services to the attest client on a recurring basis; (*d*) a partner in the office in which the lead attest engagement partner primarily practices in connection with the attest engagement; (*e*) the firm, including the firm's employee benefit plans; or (*f*) an entity whose operating, financial, or accounting policies can be controlled by any of the individuals or entities described in (*a*) through (*e*) or by two or more such individuals or entities if they act together.

Direct financial interest   A personal investment under the direct control of the investor. The *Code of Professional Conduct* prohibits CPAs from having any direct financial interests in their attest clients. Investments made by a CPA's spouse or dependents also are regarded as direct financial interests of the CPA.

Ethics Rulings   Pronouncements of the AICPA that explain the application of Rules and Interpretations of the *Code of Professional Conduct* to specific factual circumstances involving professional ethics.

Immediate family member   A spouse, spousal equivalent, or dependent (whether or not related).

Independence   An important Rule of Conduct that prohibits CPAs from performing attestation services for an enterprise unless they are independent with respect to such enterprise; independence is impaired by a financial interest, service as an officer or trustee, loans to or from the enterprise, and various other relationships.

Individual in a position to influence the attest engagement   An individual who: (*a*) evaluates the performance or recommends the compensation of the attest engagement partner; (*b*) directly supervises or manages the attest engagement partner, including all successively senior levels above that individual through the firm's chief executive; (*c*) consults with the attest engagement team regarding technical or industry-specific issues related to the attest engagement; or (*d*) participates in or oversees at all successively senior levels, quality control activities, including internal monitoring, with respect to the specific attest engagement.

Indirect financial interest   An investment in which the specific investment decisions are not under the direct control of the investor. An example is an investment in a professionally managed mutual fund. The *Code of Professional Conduct* allows CPAs to have indirect financial interests in attest clients, as long as the investment is not material in relation to the CPA's net worth.

Interpretations   Guidelines issued by the AICPA for the scope and application of the Rules of Conduct.

Joint closely held investment   An investment in an entity or property by the member and the client (or the client's officers or directors, or any owner who has the ability to exercise significant influence over the client) that enables them to control (as defined by GAAP for consolidation purposes) the entity or property.

Key position   A position in which an individual has: (*a*) primary responsibility for significant accounting functions that support material components of the financial statements; (*b*) primary responsibility for the preparation of the financial statements; or (*c*) the ability to exercise influence over the contents of the financial statements, including when the individual is a member of the board of directors, or similar governing body, chief executive officer, president, chief financial officer, chief operating officer, general counsel, chief accounting officer, controller, director of internal audit, director of financial reporting, treasurer, or any equivalent position.

Manager   A professional employee of the public accounting firm who either has continuing responsibility for the overall planning and supervision of engagements or has the authority to determine that an engagement is complete subject to final partner approval, if required.

Period of the professional engagement   A period that begins when a member either signs an initial engagement letter or other agreement to perform attest services or begins to perform an attest engagement for a client, whichever is earlier. The period lasts for the entire duration of the professional relationship (which could cover many periods) and ends with the formal or informal notification, either by the member or the client, of the termination of the professional relationship or by the issuance of a report, whichever is later. Accordingly, the period does not end with the issuance of a report and recommence with the beginning of the following year's attest engagement.

Principles   The part of the AICPA *Code of Professional Conduct* that expresses the profession's responsibilities to the public, clients, and colleagues and provides a framework for the Rules.

Profession   An activity that involves a responsibility to serve the public, has a complex body of knowledge, has standards for admission, and has a need for public confidence.

Prospective financial information   Presentations of future financial position, results of operations, or cash flows. Such presentations are often referred to as financial forecasts or projections.

Rules   A group of enforceable ethical standards included in the AICPA *Code of Professional Conduct*.

Significant influence   One who meets the criteria established in *Accounting Principles Board Opinion No. 18*, "The Equity Method of Accounting for Investments in Common Stock," and its interpretations (AC section 18) to determine the ability of an investor to exercise significant influence over another entity. In general, these criteria include an ownership interest of 20 percent or more of the entity.

Review Questions

3–1.   What is meant by the term *ethical dilemma?* Describe an ethical dilemma that you have faced.

3–2.   What are the two major types of constraints on decisions that involve ethical issues? Provide examples of each type.

3–3.   What is the basic purpose of a code of ethics for a profession?

3–4.   Briefly describe the two parts of the AICPA *Code of Professional Conduct.*

3–5.   In Chapter 2, the 10 generally accepted auditing standards were discussed. How does the AICPA *Code of Professional Conduct* relate, if at all, to these 10 generally accepted auditing standards?

3–6.   Explain how a CPA might have an indirect financial interest in an audit client. Does the AICPA *Code of Professional Conduct* prohibit such interests?

3–7.   Bill Scott works as a manager in the Phoenix office of an international public accounting firm. His father has just taken a position as a purchasing agent for one of the public accounting firm's Phoenix clients. Has Bill's independence been impaired with respect to this audit client? Has the public accounting firm's independence been impaired if Bill does not work on the audit?

3–8.   Three months ago, a national public accounting firm hired Greg Scott to work as a staff auditor in its New York office. Yesterday, Scott's father was hired to be the chief financial officer of one of the public accounting firm's New York office clients. Has the independence of the public accounting firm with respect to this client been impaired?

3–9.   Sara Kole, CPA, has been requested by the president of Noyes Company, a closely held corporation and audit client, to cosign Noyes Company checks with the Noyes treasurer when the president is away on business trips. Would Kole violate the AICPA *Code of Professional Conduct* if she accepted this request? Explain.

3–10.   With respect to ethics, what are the responsibilities of the Public Company Accounting Oversight Board? What is the source of the Board's authority?

3–11.   Describe what is meant by the term "covered member." Which part (or parts) of AICPA *Code of Professional Conduct* Standard 101 on independence relies on the concept of a covered member?

3–12.   How do the rules for the audit of public versus nonpublic companies differ with respect to the independence of a CPA who performs routine accounting services for a client?

3–13.   What bodies are given authority to issue performance standards under Rule 202 of the AICPA *Code of Professional Conduct?* What authoritative standards does each body issue?

3–14.   Comment on the following: In performing a consulting engagement for a client, a CPA may perform any services that the client requests.

3–15.   Identify the circumstances under which a CPA may *not* perform professional services on a contingent fee basis.

3–16. Jian Zhang is a CPA who often serves as an expert witness in court cases. Is it proper for Zhang to receive compensation in a damage suit based on the amount awarded to the plaintiff? Discuss.

3–17. Sandy Schultz, CPA, has performed a consulting services job in which she made recommendations which ultimately resulted in one of her audit clients purchasing a computer manufactured by the AMZ Computer Corporation. Shortly thereafter, Ms. Schultz was surprised when she received a $1,000 unsolicited commission from AMZ Computer Corporation. Would acceptance of this commission violate the AICPA *Code of Professional Conduct?* Explain.

3–18. Laura Clark, wife of Jon Clark, CPA, is a life insurance agent. May Jon Clark refer audit clients needing officer life insurance to Laura Clark or to another life insurance agent who will share a commission with Laura Clark? Explain.

3–19. In what organizational forms may CPAs practice public accounting?

3–20. Must a CPA maintain independence and an impartial mental attitude when preparing a client's income tax return? Explain.

3–21. In preparing a client's income tax return, a CPA feels that certain expenses are unreasonably high and probably are overstated. Explain the CPA's responsibilities in this situation.

3–22. "Since internal auditors are employees, they have no ethical responsibilities to others beyond their employers." Comment on this statement.

Questions Requiring Analysis

Required:

3–23. Sally Adams is an audit manager for the firm of Jones & Smith, CPAs, and is assigned to the audit of Libra Fashions, Inc. Near the middle of the audit, Sally was offered the job of Libra's chief financial officer.

   a. Discuss the implications of this offer assuming Libra is a nonpublic corporation.

   b. Discuss the implications of this offer assuming Libra is a public company.

3–24. Jenko Corp. is an audit client of the Phoenix office of Williams and Co., CPAs. Williams and Co. has offices in Arizona, including ones in Phoenix, Tucson, and Tombstone. For purposes of independence, the AICPA requires that no "covered member" may have a direct or a material indirect financial interest in an audit client such as Jenko. Determine whether each of the following individuals is a covered member.

   a. Bill Jones is a partner in the Tucson office of Williams. He does not work on the Jenko audit.

   b. Mary Adams is a first-year staff assistant who works on the Jenko audit.

   c. Mary Anderson is a partner in the Phoenix office of Williams. She does not work on the Jenko audit.

   d. Bill Jepson, a staff auditor, is also the treasurer of Jenko Corp.

   e. Ken Sanders, a Tombstone office partner, provides no services for the Jenko audit other than serving as a consultant to the attest team regarding industry-related issues specific to Jenko.

3–25. Tracy Smith, CPA, is in charge of the audit of Olympic Fashions, Inc. Seven young members of the public accounting firm's professional staff are working with Smith on this engagement, and several of the young auditors are avid skiers. Olympic Fashions owns two condominiums in Aspen, Colorado, which it uses primarily to entertain clients. The controller of Olympic Fashions has told Smith that she and any of her audit staff are welcome to use the condominiums at no charge any time that they are not already in use. How should Smith respond to this offer? Explain.

3–26. Harris Fell, CPA and member of the AICPA, was engaged to audit the financial statements of Wilson Corporation. Fell had half-completed the audit when he had a dispute with the management of Wilson Corporation and was discharged. Hal Compton, CPA, was promptly engaged to replace Fell. Wilson Corporation did not compensate Fell for his work to date; therefore, Fell refused to allow Wilson Corporation's management to examine his working papers. Certain of the working papers consisted of adjusting journal entries and supporting analysis. Wilson Corporation's management had no other source of this information. Did Fell violate the AICPA *Code of Professional Conduct?* Explain fully.

3–27. Wilson and Wiener, CPAs, are performing the audit of Griffin Incorporated, a public company. The CEO of Griffin has asked the partner in charge of the audit to perform the following nonattest engagements:

   a. Internal audit outsourcing.

   b. Preparation of the corporate tax return.

   c. Tax planning for the corporate executives of Griffin.

   d. Implementation of a new financial reporting control system.

For each of the above, state whether Wilson and Wiener is permitted to perform the proposed engagement. If Wilson and Wiener is permitted to perform the service, indicate any steps required for Wilson and Wiener to accept the engagement.

3–28.   Ron Barber, CPA, is auditing the financial statements of DGF, Inc., a publicly held company. During the course of the audit, Barber discovered that DGF has been making illegal bribes to foreign government officials to obtain business, and he reported the matter to senior management and the board of directors of DGF.

Required:

a. If management and the board of directors take appropriate remedial action, should Barber be required to report the matter outside the company?

b. Describe Barber's appropriate response if management and the board of directors fail to take appropriate remedial action.

Multiple Choice Questions

3–29.   Select the best answer for each of the following. Explain the reasons for your selection.

a. Which of the following is not a covered member for an attest engagement under Rule 101 of the AICPA Code of Professional Conduct?

(1) An individual assigned to the attest engagement.

(2) A partner in the office of the partner in charge of the attest engagement.

(3) A manager who is in charge of providing tax services to the attest client.

(4) A partner in the national office of the firm that performs marketing services.

b. Which of the following is not prohibited by the AICPA Code of Professional Conduct?

(1) Advertising in newspapers.

(2) Payment of commission to obtain an audit client.

(3) Acceptance of a fee for a review of financial statements that is contingent.

(4) Engaging in discriminatory employment practices.

c. In which of the following situations would a public accounting firm have violated the AICPA *Code of Professional Conduct* in determining its fee?

(1) A fee is based on whether or not the public accounting firm's audit report leads to the approval of the client's application for bank financing.

(2) A fee is to be established at a later date by the Bankruptcy Court.

(3) A fee is based upon the nature of the engagement rather than upon the actual time spent on the engagement.

(4) A fee is based on the fee charged by the client's former auditors.

d. A public accounting firm would *least* likely be considered in violation of the AICPA independence rules in which of the following instances?

(1) A partner's checking account, which is fully insured by the Federal Deposit Insurance Corporation, is held at a financial institution for which the public accounting firm performs attest services.

(2) A manager of the firm donates services as vice president of a charitable organization that is an audit client of the firm.

(3) An attest client owes the firm fees for this and last year's annual engagements.

(4) A covered member's dependent son owns stock in an attest client.

e. Which of the following is implied when a CPA signs the preparer's declaration on a federal income tax return?

(1) The return is not misleading based on all information of which the CPA has knowledge.

(2) The return is prepared in accordance with generally accepted accounting principles.

(3) The CPA has audited the return.

(4) The CPA maintained an impartial mental attitude while preparing the return.

f. The AICPA *Code of Professional Conduct* states that a CPA shall not disclose any confidential information obtained in the course of a professional engagement except with the consent of the client. This rule may preclude a CPA from responding to an inquiry made by:

(1) An investigative body of a state CPA society.

(2) The trial board of the AICPA.

(3) A CPA-shareholder of the client corporation.

(4) An AICPA quality review body.

g. Which of the following is most likely to be a violation of the AICPA rules of conduct by Bill Jones, a sole practitioner with no other employees?

(1) Jones performs consulting services for a percentage of the client's savings; these are the only services provided for the client.

(2) Jones names his firm Jones and Smith, CPAs.

(3) Jones advertises the services he provides in an Internet set of telephone "yellow pages."

(4) Jones, without client consent, makes available working papers for purposes of a peer review of his practice.

h. Bill Adams, CPA, accepted the audit engagement of Kelly Company. During the audit, Adams became aware of his lack of competence required for the engagement. What should Adams do?

(1) Disclaim an opinion.

(2) Issue an adverse opinion.

(3) Suggest that Kelly Company engage another CPA to perform the audit.

(4) Rely on the competence of client personnel.

i. Which of the following nonattest services may be performed by the auditors of a public company?

(1) Internal audit outsourcing.

(2) Tax planning for all company officers.

(3) Bookkeeping services.

(4) Preparation of the company's tax return.

j. In providing nonattest services to an attest client, a CPA is allowed to perform which of the following functions?

(1) Maintaining custody of the client's securities.

(2) Training client employees.

(3) Supervising client employees.

(4) Acting as the third approver of large client expenditures.

k. Rule 202—Compliance with Standards, requires CPAs to adhere to all of the following applicable standards, except:

(1) Statements on Standards for Consulting Services.

(2) Statements on Auditing Standards.

(3) Statements on Standards for Attestation Engagements.

(4) Statements on Responsibilities in Tax Practice.

l. Which of the following provisions is not included in The Institute of Internal Auditors Code of Ethics?

(1) Performance of work with honesty, diligence, and responsibility.

(2) Prudence in the use and protection of information acquired in the course of their duties.

(3) Use of appropriate sampling methods to select areas for audit.

(4) Continually improve their proficiency and effectiveness and the quality of services.

(AICPA, adapted)

Problems

3–30.   Gary Watson, a graduating business student at a small college, is currently interviewing for a job. Gary was invited by both Tilly Manufacturing Co. and Watson Supply Company to travel to a nearby city for an interview. Both companies have offered to pay Gary's expenses. His total expenses for the trip were $96 for mileage on his car and $45 for meals. As he prepares the letters requesting reimbursement, he is considering asking for the total amount of the expenses from both employers. His rationale is that if he had taken separate trips, each employer would have had to pay that amount.

a. Who are the parties that are directly affected by this ethical dilemma?

b. Are the other students at the college potentially affected by Gary's decision? Explain.

    c. Are the professors at the college potentially affected by Gary's decision? Explain.

    d. What would you do in this situation?

    e. What would you do if both companies mailed you $141 for your expenses with no action on your part?

3–31. The firm of McGraw and West, CPAs, has two offices, one in Phoenix and one in San Diego. The firm has audited the Cameron Corporation out of its Phoenix office for the past five years. For each of the following independent cases, which occurred during the year under audit, indicate whether the independence of either (*a*) the CPA involved or (*b*) the firm would be impaired.

    a. Mary McGraw, a partner in the San Diego office, fell wildly in love with Bill Smith, the treasurer for Cameron Corporation. They were married in Las Vegas. During the week McGraw still lives in San Diego and works in that office, while Bill Smith lives in Phoenix, working for Cameron. On weekends they commute to their home in Yuma. Mary does not participate in the engagement.

    b. Jim West is the father of Will West, a Phoenix partner. Jim West has a material investment in Cameron. Will West is unaware of his father's investment, but does participate in the engagement.

    c. Bill Johnson, a senior in the San Diego office, has a material investment in the capital stock of Cameron. He does not participate in the engagement.

    d. Sandra Steversen, a staff assistant in the Phoenix office, works on the Cameron audit. Her uncle works as the chief accounting officer for Cameron.

3–32. James Daleiden, CPA, is interested in expanding his practice through acquisition of new clients. For each of the following independent cases, indicate whether Daleiden would violate the AICPA *Code of Professional Conduct* by engaging in the suggested practice and explain why. If more information is needed to arrive at a final determination, indicate the nature of such information.

    a. Daleiden wishes to form a professional corporation and use the name "AAAAAAAA the CPAs," so as to obtain the first ad in the yellow pages of the telephone book.

    b. Daleiden wishes to prepare a one-page flyer which he will have his son stuff on the windshields of each car at the Pleasant Valley shopping mall. The flyer will outline the services provided by Daleiden's firm and will include a $50-off coupon for services provided on the first visit.

    c. Daleiden has a thorough knowledge of the tax law. He has a number of acquaintances who prepare their own tax returns. He proposes to offer to review these returns before they are filed with the Internal Revenue Service. For this review, he will charge no fee unless he is able to identify legal tax savings opportunities. He proposes to charge each individual one-third of the tax savings he is able to identify.

    d. Daleiden and his associates audit a number of municipalities. He proposes to contact other CPAs and inform them of his interest in obtaining more of these types of audits. He offers a $500 "finder's fee" to CPAs who forward business to him.

3–33. The firm of Bell & Greer, CPAs, has been asked to perform attest services for Trek Corporation for the year ended December 31, Year 5. Bell & Greer has two offices: one in Los Angeles and the other in Newport Beach. Trek Corporation would be audited by the Los Angeles office. For each of the following independent cases, indicate whether Bell & Greer would be independent with respect to Trek Corporation and explain why.

    a. A partner in the Los Angeles office of Bell & Greer has been a long-time personal friend of the chief executive officer of Trek Corporation.

    b. The former controller of Trek Corporation became a partner in the Newport Beach office of Bell & Greer on March 15, Year 5, resigning from Trek Corporation on that date.

    c. A manager in the Newport Beach office of Bell & Greer is the son of the treasurer of Trek Corporation.

    d. A partner in the Newport office of Bell & Greer jointly owns a cattle ranch in Montana with one of the directors of Trek Corporation. The value of the investment is material to both parties.

    e. Trek Corporation has not yet paid Bell & Greer for professional services rendered in Year 4. This fee is substantial in amount and is now 15 months past due.

3–34. Auditors must not only appear to be independent; they must also be independent in fact.

Required:

    a. Explain the concept of an "auditor's independence" as it applies to third-party reliance upon financial statements.

     b. (1) What determines whether or not an auditor is independent in fact?

        (2) What determines whether or not an auditor appears to be independent?

     c. Explain how an auditor may be independent in fact but not appear to be independent.

     d. Would Joe Marks, a CPA, be considered independent for an audit of the financial statements of:

        (1) A church for which he is serving as treasurer without compensation? Explain.

        (2) A women's club for which his wife is serving as treasurer-accountant if he is not to receive a fee for the audit? Explain.

3–35. Donald Westerman is president of Westerman Corporation, a manufacturer of kitchen cabinets. He has been approached by Darlene Zabish, a partner with Zabish and Co., CPAs, who suggests that her firm can design a payroll system for Westerman that will either save his corporation money, or be free. More specifically, Ms. Zabish proposes to design a payroll system for Westerman on a contingent fee basis. She suggests that her firm's fee will be 25 percent of the savings in payroll for each of the next four years. After four years Westerman will be able to keep all future savings. Westerman Corporation's payroll system costs currently are approximately $200,000 annually, and the corporation has not previously been a client of Zabish.

Westerman discussed this offer with his current CPA, Bill Zabrinski, whose firm annually audits Westerman Corporation's financial statements. Zabrinski states that this is a relatively simple task, and that he would be willing to provide the service for $30,000.

Required:

     a. Would either Zabish or Zabrinski violate the AICPA *Code of Professional Conduct* by offering to provide these services? Explain.

     b. Now assume that Westerman has indicated to Zabrinski that he was leaning toward accepting Zabish's offer. Zabrinski then offered to provide the service for 15 percent of Westerman's savings for the next three years. Would performing the engagement in accordance with the terms of this offer violate the AICPA *Code of Professional Conduct?* Explain.

3–36. Roland Company, a retail store, has utilized your services as independent auditor for several years. During the current year, the company opened a new store, and in the course of your annual audit, you verify the cost of the fixtures installed in the new store by examining purchase orders, invoices, and other documents. This audit brings to light an understated invoice nearly a year old in which a clerical error by the supplier, Western Showcase, Inc., caused the total of the invoice to read $28,893.62 when it should have read $82,893.62. The invoice was paid immediately upon receipt without any notice of the error, and subsequent statements and correspondence from Western Showcase, Inc., showed that the account with Roland Company had been paid in full. Assume that the amount in question is material in relation to the financial position of both companies.

Required:

     a. What action should you take in this situation?

     b. If the client should decline to take any action in the matter, would you insist that the unpaid amount of $54,000 be included in the liabilities shown on the balance sheet as a condition necessary to your issuance of an unqualified audit report?

     c. Assuming that you were later retained to make an audit of Western Showcase, Inc., would you utilize the information gained in your audit of Roland Company to initiate a reopening of the account with that company?

3–37. A nonpublic audit client, March Corporation, requested that John Day, CPA, conduct a feasibility study to advise management of the best way the corporation can use electronic data processing equipment and which computer, if any, best meets the corporation's requirements. Day is technically competent in this area and accepts the engagement. Upon completion of Day's study the corporation accepts his suggestions and installs the computer and related equipment that he recommended.

Required:

     a. Discuss the effect that acceptance of this consulting services engagement would have upon John Day's independence in expressing an opinion on the financial statements of March Corporation.

     b. A local company printing data processing forms customarily offers a commission for recommending it as a supplier. The client is aware of the commission offer and suggests that Day accept it. Would it be proper for Day to accept the commission with the client's approval? Discuss.

3–38. Thomas Gilbert and Susan Bradley formed a professional corporation called "Financial Services Inc.—A Professional Corporation," each taking 50 percent of the authorized common stock. Gilbert is a CPA and a member of the AICPA. Bradley is a CPCU (Chartered Property Casualty Underwriter). The corporation performs auditing and tax services under Gilbert's direction and insurance services under Bradley's supervision.

One of the corporation's first audit clients was Grandtime Company. Grandtime had total assets of $600,000 and total liabilities of $270,000. In the course of his examination, Gilbert found that Grandtime's building with a carrying value of $240,000 was pledged as collateral for a 10-year-term note in the amount of $200,000. The client's financial statements did not mention that the building was pledged as collateral for the 10-year-term note. However, as the failure to disclose the lien did not affect either the value of the assets or the amount of the liabilities, and his examination was satisfactory in all other respects, Gilbert rendered an unqualified opinion on Grandtime's financial statements. About two months after the date of his opinion, Gilbert learned that an insurance company was planning to loan Grandtime $150,000 in the form of a first-mortgage note on the building. Realizing that the insurance company was unaware of the existing lien on the building, Gilbert had Bradley notify the insurance company of the fact that Grandtime's building was pledged as collateral for a term note.

Shortly after the events described above, Gilbert was charged with several violations of professional ethics.

Required: Identify and discuss at least four ethical implications of those acts by Gilbert that were in violation of the AICPA *Code of Professional Conduct*.

3–39. Gloria and Deloria, CPAs, have recently started their public accounting firm and intend to provide attestation and a variety of consulting services for their clients, which are all nonpublic. Both Ms. Gloria and Mr. Deloria have particular expertise in designing payroll and other disbursement systems. Ms. Gloria is concerned about whether any of the following services would impair their audit independence.

a. For each of the services in the accompanying table provide a judgment as to whether providing the service would impair attest independence. In all 12 situations assume that management has designated a management-level individual to be responsible for overseeing the CPA's services and has established appropriate internal control. Also assume that the client is privately held and does not report to the SEC.

b. Now assume that the 12 services are being contemplated for nonattest clients. Which of the services does the AICPA *Code of Professional Conduct* prohibit under this assumption?

Situation Number	Service Description	Independence Impaired (Yes, No, Indeterminate)	Additional Information Needed for "Indeterminate" Replies
1	Customize and implement a prepackaged payroll system.	No /No	
2	Manage the portion of a client's local area network system related to payroll.	Yes/No	
3	Using payroll time records approved by management, generate unsigned payroll checks on a continuing basis for the client; the client signs the checks.	No/No	
4	Prepare the payroll tax return form and sign it on behalf of management.	Yes/No	
5	Approve employee time cards.	Yes/No	
6	Accept responsibility to sign checks, but only in emergency situations.	Yes/No	
7	Monitor employee time cards and make changes when errors are detected.	Yes/No	
8	Post client-approved entries to client's trial balance.	No/No	
9	Provide all the initial training and instruction to client employees on a newly implemented payroll information and control system.	No/No	

(*Table continued on next page*)

Situation Number	Service Description	Independence Impaired (Yes, No, Indeterminate)	Additional Information Needed for "Indeterminate" Replies
10	Screen candidates and recommend the most highly qualified candidate to serve as treasurer for the client.	Yes / No	
11	Supervise client personnel in the daily operation of the payroll system.	Yes / No	
12	Present payroll business risk considerations to the board of directors on behalf of management.	Yes / No	

3–40. The firm of Schilling & Co., CPAs, has offices in Chicago and Green Bay, Wisconsin. Gillington Company, which has one million shares of outstanding stock, is audited by the Chicago office of Schilling; Welco of the Chicago office is the partner in charge of the audit. For each of the following circumstances, indicate whether the public accounting firm's independence is impaired with respect to Gillington Company.

a. Johnson, a partner of the Chicago office, owns 100 shares of the stock of Gillington. He has no responsibilities with respect to the Gillington audit.

b. Gizmo, a partner in the Green Bay office, owns 600 shares of the stock of Gillington. He has no responsibilities with respect to the Gillington audit.

c. Masterson is a staff assistant in the Green Bay office and owns 10 percent of Gillington's outstanding common stock. Masterson provides no services to Gillington and is not able to influence the engagement.

d. Schilling, the partner in charge of the entire firm, works in the Green Bay office. He owns 100 shares of Gillington stock (market value $2 per share), but provides no services on the engagement.

e. Gorman is a staff assistant on the audit. Gorman's mother owns shares of Gillington that are material to her net worth and of which Gorman has knowledge.

In-Class Team Cases

3–41. The issue of whether the performance of nonattest (consulting) services for audit clients impairs independence of the auditors has been widely debated within the public accounting profession. Restrictions on the performance of consulting is a major aspect of the Sarbanes-Oxley Act of 2002.

Required:

a. Describe the restrictions that are placed on the performance of nonattest services for audit clients by the Sarbanes-Oxley Act of 2002.

b. List arguments for restricting nonattest services for audit clients.

c. List arguments against restricting nonattest services for audit clients.

d. Present your opinion and support it with one or more of the arguments listed above.

3–42. You are the Partner-in-Charge of a large metropolitan office of a regional public accounting firm. Two members of your professional staff have come to you to discuss problems that may affect the firm's independence. Neither of these situations has been specifically answered by the AICPA Professional Ethics Division. Therefore, you must reach your own conclusions as to what to advise your staff members, and what actions, if any, are to be taken by the firm.

Case 1: Don Moore, a partner in the firm, has recently moved into a condominium which he shares with his girlfriend, Joan Scott. Moore owns the condominium and pays all the expenses relating to its maintenance. Otherwise, the two are self-supporting. Scott is a stockbroker, and recently she has started acquiring shares in one of the audit clients of this office of the public accounting firm. The shares are held in Scott's name. At present, the shares are not material in relation to her net worth.

Case 2: Mary Reed, a new staff auditor with the firm, has recently separated from her husband. Mary has filed for divorce, but the divorce cannot become final for at least five months. The property settlement is being bitterly contested. Mary's husband has always resented her professional career and has just used community property to acquire one share of common stock in each of the publicly owned companies audited by the office in which Mary works.

Required: For each case, you are to:

a. Set forth arguments indicating that the firm's independence has *not* been impaired.

b. Set forth arguments indicating that the firm's independence *has* been impaired.

c. Express your personal opinion. Identify those arguments from part (*a*) or part (*b*) that you found most persuasive. If you believe that the firm's independence has been impaired, make suggestions about how the problem might be resolved.

Research and Discussion Case

3–43. The International Bank of Commerce (IBC) is an audit client of your public accounting firm. IBC is a multinational financial institution that operates in 23 countries. During the current year's audit, you have discovered the following problems:

a. Improper loans were made to stockholders and other related parties, and

b. Loans were recorded on the books that appear to be either false or deceitful.

You are especially concerned about these findings because it appears that members of senior management were aware of, and participated, in these illegal activities. In accordance with *SAS No. 54,* "Illegal Acts by Clients," you have communicated these illegal acts to IBC's audit committee of the board of directors. However, you are not satisfied with the committee's reaction to the situation. The chairman of the audit committee thanked you cordially, but the committee took no action to investigate the activities or prevent their occurrence in the future.

Required:

a. Describe the consequences if you immediately communicated the matters directly to the SEC.

b. Describe your appropriate course of action in this situation.

c. Present arguments for and against requiring auditors to report illegal acts directly to regulatory agencies.

Suggested References

AICPA, *Professional Standards,* Volume 2, Commerce Clearing House, Section ET 101. (*Code of Professional Conduct,* Rule 101).

AICPA, *Professional Standards,* Volume 2, Commerce Clearing House, Section ET 301. (*Code of Professional Conduct,* Rule 301).

AICPA, *Statement on Auditing Standards No. 54,* "Illegal Acts by Clients" (New York, 1988) AU 317.

Chapter 4

Legal Liability of CPAs

Chapter learning objectives

After studying this chapter, you should be able to:

LO1. Describe the types of CPA liability.

LO2. Distinguish between CPAs' liability under common law and under statutory law.

LO3. Explain the proof requirements for clients and third parties seeking recovery from CPAs under common law and the defenses available to CPAs.

LO4. Explain the proof requirements for plaintiffs under statutory law and the defenses available to the auditors.

LO5. Compare the requirements for CPA liability under the Securities Act of 1933 with those under the Securities Exchange Act of 1934.

LO6. Describe CPA legal liability for accounting and review services.

In this era of litigation, investors and creditors who suffer financial losses and experience market downturns are likely to find certified public accountants (CPAs), as well as attorneys and corporate directors, tempting targets for recovery through suits that allege professional "malpractice." Because of this situation, CPAs should approach every engagement with the prospect that they may be required to defend their work in court. Even if the court finds in favor of the CPAs, the costs of defending a legal action can be astronomical. As a result of the numbers of lawsuits and the cost of defending them, the price of professional liability insurance is high.

Costs are not the only concern in this area; lawsuits damage a professional's reputation. In extreme cases, the CPAs may even be tried criminally for certain types of conduct or omissions during an audit. Everyone who is considering a career in public accounting should be aware of the potential legal liability inherent in the practice of accounting.

The Scope of CPA Liability

Learning Objective 1

The sheer number of parties suffering significant losses due at least partially to using information on which CPAs have reported creates a situation in which potential liability may exceed that of other professionals such as physicians. If a physician or an attorney is negligent, the injured party is usually limited to the professional's patient or client. If CPAs are negligent in expressing an opinion on financial statements, millions of investors as well as firm creditors may sustain losses.

Amounts in excess of $300 million have been awarded to parties as a result of litigation against public accounting firms. Although public accounting firms often maintain professional liability insurance for such losses, the amounts awarded to plaintiffs have sometimes exceeded the limits of the public accounting firms' professional liability insurance.

Litigation Placed in Perspective

As we discuss CPAs' liability for negligence, gross negligence, and fraud, there may be a tendency to conclude that CPAs are often careless in rendering professional services. This is simply not the case. The overwhelming majority of engagements are completed successfully without any allegations of improper conduct. However, in any endeavor as complex as auditing and attestation, it is inevitable that some mistakes will be made. Also, as discussed in Chapter 2, a properly conducted examination provides *reasonable assurance,* not absolute assurance, of detecting material misstatements.

Any large public accounting firm that performs thousands of audits will, at one time or another, find that it has issued an unqualified report on financial statements that appear in hindsight, in some respect, misleading. In some circumstances, CPA liability may be relatively obvious. In others, it will not be obvious whether the situation is due to inadequate performance, or due to other factors. To illustrate, consider the audit of the financial statements of a computer manufacturer and, more specifically, the allowance for estimated warranty costs included therein. The estimate made in February, when the financial statements are issued, may seriously understate the subsequent actual costs incurred if a large number of computers are returned because of a manufacturing defect. Investors who have sustained large losses will attempt to recover those losses, regardless of whether they believe the CPAs are at fault. Thus, if the cost of bringing suit against a company's CPAs is relatively low and offers even a chance of recovery, the injured parties may initiate legal action.

CPAs must recognize occasional allegations of misconduct as a fact of life. Some of the lawsuits brought against CPAs will be frivolous—often simple attempts by **plaintiffs** to recover their losses. Others will have some basis in fact—perhaps judgmental errors were made by the CPAs during the engagement. No matter how careful CPAs are, any public accounting firm may find itself a **defendant** in litigation.

Sources of CPA Liability

Learning Objective 2

In the United States, CPAs have both **common law** liability and **statutory law** liability. Common law liability develops through case decisions generally arising due to breach of contract, negligence, and fraud. Statutory liability develops when a governmental unit (e.g., a state or the federal government) passes laws and regulations that either implicitly or explicitly impose potential liability upon CPAs.

Illustrative Case
Litigation

Sources at the Accountants' Coalition, a Washington lobbying group, have confirmed that during some recent years CPAs have spent approximately 20 percent of their revenues from audit and accounting services on litigation costs and settlements. A vice president of a major insurance company stated in the *Wall Street Journal* that his company is no longer willing to insure accounting firms for liability. The company continues to insure engineers, architects, attorneys, physicians, and surgeons. "The risks aren't as great," the vice president observed. Even when a claim is litigated successfully, the costs can be high. The chair of an international public accounting firm described a lawsuit against his firm for an audit with fees of approximately $20,000. Although the firm successfully defended itself in the case that went to trial, the cost of the firm's defense was approximately $6 million.

The standards for recovery as well as individuals afforded remedies varies by source or "theory" of liability. These theories are explained briefly in the following overview and then discussed in detail in the remaining sections of the chapter.

1. *Contract.* CPAs enter into a contract with their client (ordinarily through the engagement letter) and agree to provide services. The potential for liability occurs when there is a **breach of contract** and when damages result due to a failure of one or both parties to a contract to perform in accordance with the contract's provisions.[1] A public accounting firm might be sued by the client for breach of contract, for example, if the firm has failed to perform the engagement in accordance with the engagement letter and the client has suffered resulting damages.

2. *Negligence.* Both clients and third parties sue CPAs for the **tort**[2] of negligence. **Negligence,** also referred to as ordinary or simple negligence, is a violation of a legal duty to exercise a degree of care that an ordinary prudent person would exercise under similar circumstances. For the CPA, negligence is failure to perform a duty in accordance with applicable standards. For practical purposes, negligence may be viewed as "failure to exercise due professional care."

   Gross negligence is the lack of even slight care, indicative of a *reckless disregard* for one's professional responsibilities. Substantial failures on the part of an auditor to comply with generally accepted auditing standards might be interpreted as gross negligence. As discussed in detail later in this chapter, the question of whether third parties must prove a CPA guilty of gross negligence (rather than ordinary negligence) to recover losses revolves in part around jurisdictional differences in interpretation of the common law.

3. *Fraud.* **Fraud** is defined as misrepresentation by a person of a material fact, known by that person to be untrue or made with reckless indifference to whether the fact is true, with the intention of deceiving the other party and with the result that the other party is injured. Rule 102 of the AICPA's *Code of Professional Conduct* (discussed in Chapter 3) states that a member of the AICPA shall not knowingly misrepresent facts. The CPAs found to have violated this provision of Rule 102 might be sued for fraud by the client or another injured party.

   Constructive fraud differs from fraud as defined above in that constructive fraud does not involve a misrepresentation with intent to deceive. Gross negligence on the part of an auditor has been interpreted by the courts as constructive fraud.

4. *Statutory liability.* CPAs have statutory liability under both the federal securities laws and state securities laws, often called "blue sky" laws. The Securities Act of 1933, which

---

[1] Breach of contract liability is based on failure to carry out a duty created in the contract. For further information see *Duties and Liabilities of Public Accountants,* by D. Y. Causey, Jr., and S. A. Causey (Accountant's Press), seventh edition, 2002.

[2] Legally, a tort is a wrongful act, injury, or damage (not involving breach of contract) for which a civil action can be brought.

applies to initial stock offerings, imposes liability to investors on CPAs for their audit work relating to financial statements used to register the securities for sale. The Securities Exchange Act of 1934 imposes liability on CPAs for their work on the financial statements included with a company's ongoing reports to the Securities and Exchange Commission. The standards for liability differ under these statutes, but each provides a means for recovery against the CPAs by investors.

Sources of liability for CPAs also include criminal statutes and the Racketeer Influenced Corrupt Organizations (RICO) Act (discussed later in the chapter).

An injured party, the plaintiff, may elect to bring suit against CPAs under common law, any applicable statute law, or both. As one might expect, plaintiffs usually select the theory or theories that have the best prospects for success. Since the federal securities acts allow class-action lawsuits in which an entire class of investors becomes the plaintiff in a single legal action, and hold CPAs auditing financial statements to very strict standards, most lawsuits against auditors by stockholders or bondholders of publicly owned corporations allege violations of these federal statutes.

CPA liability may arise from improper performance on any type of engagement—audit, other attest, tax, accounting services, or consulting services. However, CPAs are not liable to any party if they can prove that they performed their services with *due professional care*. Exercising due professional care is a *complete defense* against any charge of improper conduct. However, CPAs do face the disadvantage that investors, juries, and judges view their conduct knowing the outcome of the investment and the company's fate—hindsight may work against the CPAs. Often the issue comes down to the simple question of whether the CPAs should have known or seen the problems that were evolving.

CPAs' Liability to Their Clients under Common Law

Learning Objective 3

When CPAs take on any type of engagement, they are obliged by their contract with the client—generally the engagement letter—to exercise due professional care. This obligation exists whether or not it is specifically set forth in the contract with the client. The "client" is ordinarily the company itself,[3] as contrasted to the shareholders. But the contract obligations are important because they may provide the client and third parties additional recovery rights. If the CPAs fail to perform according to the terms of the contract, the CPAs have liability to clients through the common law theory of breach of contract.

If, however, the work is completed according to the terms of the contract, but the work has errors or falls short of professional standards, the CPAs' client would have tort action for negligence against the CPAs. In many cases the client would have both types of recovery theories available for use against the CPAs.

Although legal differences exist between breach of contract and tort actions, in general, to establish CPA liability, a client must prove the following elements:

1. *Duty*—The CPAs accepted a duty of due professional care to exercise skill, prudence, and diligence.[4]
2. *Breach of duty*—The CPAs breached their duty of due professional care through negligent performance.
3. *Losses (damages)*—The client suffered losses.
4. *Causation (proximate cause)*—The damages were caused by the CPAs' negligent performance.

---

[3] The client's rights in some circumstances may be assigned to others. The *right of subrogation* allows insurers who pay the insured for a loss any right of action that the insured had. For example, if a fidelity bonding company pays the CPAs' client for a loss due to employee theft, the fidelity bonding company would have the same recovery rights against the CPAs as did the client. Also, a bankruptcy trustee or receiver of a company that has failed will ordinarily have the client's rights.

[4] This element is often relatively easy to prove since by accepting an engagement the CPAs assume a responsibility to exercise due care.

Illustrative Case
Liability for Nonattest Engagements

Liability for negligent performance is not limited to the area of auditing. Several large international public accounting firms have been sued by clients for allegedly performing negligent consulting services related to the installation of sophisticated enterprise-wide computer systems for those clients. Untimely installation may be considered to be a breach of contract terms, and failure to perform adequate testing of the systems may constitute a failure to comply with professional standards.

The Elements of Duty and Breach of Duty

The auditors' duty is defined by generally accepted auditing standards, the engagement letter, and legal considerations. In a breach of contract action, the client establishes that the CPAs' duty was breached by showing either that the auditors did not perform the obligations listed in the engagement letter or that the performance did not meet professional standards. For example, the CPAs may be sued for not performing the contractual obligations when, through no fault of the client, the audit was not completed by some agreed-upon time. Alternatively, a lawsuit arguing that the audit did not meet professional standards may be based upon the CPAs' failure to detect a fraud perpetrated by a client employee. In this second example, the key factor in determining whether the CPAs are liable is not just whether the CPAs failed to uncover fraud, but whether this failure stems from the CPAs' negligence.

Regardless of the type of engagement involved, the CPAs must perform the contract according to its terms and the performance of the work under the contract must meet applicable professional standards.

In Chapter 2 we discussed the auditor's responsibility for detecting misstatements due to **errors** and **fraud.** Auditors must design their audits to provide *reasonable assurance* of detecting misstatements due to errors and fraud that are material to the financial statements. In doing so, they must exercise due care and professional skepticism in planning, performing, and evaluating the results of audit procedures.

These requirements *do not imply* that auditors were negligent whenever misstatements due to errors or fraud are later found to exist in audited financial statements. An audit has certain limitations; it does not involve a complete and detailed examination of all records and transactions. To do so would entail a prohibitive cost, which would certainly not be warranted under ordinary business conditions. There can never be absolute assurance that errors or fraud do not exist among the transactions not included in the CPAs' tests. Also, the possibility exists that the documents have been so skillfully forged, or other fraud so expertly concealed, that the application of normal auditing techniques would not reveal the fraud. When a public accounting firm's audit *has been made in accordance with generally accepted auditing standards,* the firm has not breached its duty and *should not be held liable* for failure to detect the existence of errors or fraud.

The Element of Losses (Damages)

A plaintiff's losses, or damages, are dependent upon the nature of the engagement performed by the CPAs. On a financial statement audit they may include losses by the client from embezzlement. On a tax engagement, they may include tax penalties or extra taxes paid.

The Element of Causation (Proximate Cause)

Causation exists when damage to another is directly attributable to a wrongdoer's act. Even though a public accounting firm might have been negligent in rendering services, it will not be liable for the *plaintiff's* loss if its negligence was not the cause of the loss. The auditors' primary defense to litigation brought for breach of contract or negligence is ordinarily to show that the audit was performed with due professional care and that there was no negligence in the performance of the contract and professional duties.

An additional possible defense for the auditors is that the loss is due to other causes. The auditors might be able to show that, regardless of whether negligence was involved, the negligence alleged by the client was not the **proximate cause** of the client's loss. Demonstrating **contributory negligence** by the client is one means of showing that the auditors' negligence was not the cause (or sole cause) of the client's loss. In jurisdictions (e.g., states) that

Illustrative Case
Who Is the Client?

In *Cenco, Inc. v. Seidman & Seidman* (1982) the court clarified the auditors' liability to the corporation when prior management has been engaged in improper activities.

Several former top managers of Cenco had engaged in a massive fraudulent scheme to inflate the corporation's inventories. However, seven of nine members of the board of directors were not involved in the fraud, although there was evidence that they were negligent in allowing the fraud to go undetected.

When the fraud was discovered, the stockholders sued the corporation, its corrupt managers, and Seidman & Seidman,

the corporation's auditors. The corporation then filed a cross-complaint against Seidman, and Seidman responded with a contributory negligence defense. Seidman settled the class-action suit by the stockholders before it went to the jury. In the cross-complaint by the corporation, the jury found that Seidman was not liable for breach of contract, negligence, or fraud. In upholding the decision, the U.S. Court of Appeals for the Seventh Circuit indicated it was appropriate to impute the actions of corrupt management to the corporation. Thus the corporation was a party to the fraud and not entitled to recover losses from the auditors.

follow pure contributory negligence doctrines, the auditors may entirely eliminate their liability to the client by establishing the defense of contributory negligence by the client. However, very few states follow the doctrine of contributory negligence.

Many states rely on the concept of **comparative negligence.** Comparative negligence permits juries to examine the issue of causation and assess a percentage figure of fault to the CPAs, any other defendants, and the client. This system permits the allocation of damages among the parties based on the extent to which each is at fault. For example, a jury might determine that the CPAs were 50 percent at fault for the losses resulting from a failure to detect an employee embezzlement scheme, that management consultants were 30 percent responsible, and that client management was 20 percent responsible. The client will be able to recover from the CPAs and the management consultants 50 percent and 30 percent, respectively, of the losses. This allocation of damages is also referred to as **proportionate liability.**

Joint and several liability represents another approach to liability that in general benefits a plaintiff's litigation against multiple defendants. Under joint and several liability the defendants are liable for their pro rata share of any damages awarded (as is the case with proportionate liability), but they also may be held liable for damages of other defendants who prove to be unable to pay their share of the damages. Using our earlier example in which the CPAs were found to be 50 percent responsible for losses, if the management consultants did not have the ability to pay all of the losses attributed to them, the auditors as joint defendants would be required to make up the difference.

Auditors' Common Law Liability to Third Parties

Clients have recourse against auditors for damages caused by an improper audit through both breach of contract and tort actions against the auditors. But what about the many third parties who rely upon audited financial statements? How may these parties recover their losses from auditors who have performed an improper audit?

As is the case for clients, third parties must establish that losses resulted from the CPAs' performance and that the CPAs breached a duty of due professional care. In a typical case, a third party seeking damages from a public accounting firm seeks to establish that it sustained a loss caused by relying upon misleading financial statements which included an audit report that was the product of an inadequate audit. The auditors named as defendants in a common law action are in the position of having to refute the charges brought by the plaintiffs.

A plaintiff who can establish gross negligence or fraud on the part of the auditors (as well as breach of duty and losses) will be able to establish liability against the auditors. Also, in certain situations, the plaintiff need only establish ordinary negligence to establish liability against the auditors. Auditors' liability to third parties for ordinary negligence under common law varies from one jurisdiction to another. Three general approaches may be used to summarize auditors' liability to third-party financial statement users under common law in the various state courts—the *Ultramares (Known User) Approach,* the *Restatement (Foreseen User) Approach,* and the *Rosenblum (Foreseeable User) Approach.*

Ultramares (Known User) Approach[5]

The most widely cited common law **precedent** stems from the landmark case **Ultramares v. Touche & Co.** (1931). In this case, the defendant CPAs issued an unqualified opinion on the balance sheet of a company engaged in the importation and sale of rubber. On the basis of the CPAs' opinion, Ultramares, a factor, made several loans to the company. Shortly thereafter, the company was declared bankrupt, and Ultramares sued the CPAs for ordinary negligence. The New York Court of Appeals (the state's highest court) ruled that the CPAs should be held liable for *ordinary negligence* only to their client and any third party (beneficiary) specifically identified as a user of the CPAs' report. The court went on to indicate that the auditors should be held liable to *unidentified* third-party users of the audit report for *gross negligence or fraud.* In the *Ultramares* case, the audit was performed "primarily for the benefit" of the client; Ultramares was not specifically identified as a user of the audit report. Therefore, to recover its losses, Ultramares would have been required to prove that the CPAs were grossly negligent in performing their audit. The case eventually was settled out of court, with no determination of whether the auditors had been grossly negligent.

The *Ultramares* precedent has been reaffirmed and interpreted in many subsequent cases. These cases have clarified the conditions necessary for parties to be considered to be **third-party beneficiaries** of the audit. For example, the New York Court of Appeals upheld and interpreted the *Ultramares* precedent in the case of **Credit Alliance Corp. v. Arthur Andersen & Co.** (1985). The court stated that before auditors may be held liable for ordinary negligence to a third party, they must have *been aware* that the financial statements were to be used for a particular purpose by a *known party or parties,* and must have taken *some action* to indicate that knowledge.

Restatement of Torts (Foreseen User) Approach

The principle of auditor liability for ordinary negligence to a limited class of foreseen third parties is supported by the American Law Institute's (ALI's) **Second Restatement of the Law of Torts** (*Restatement*). *Restatements of law* are compilations of the majority view of the common law of the states on various topics such as contracts and torts and are meant to serve as guides for judges when they are issuing opinions in which there are common law issues. The *Restatement* approach to third-party liability, also referred to as the foreseen third-party approach, expands the auditors' liability for ordinary negligence to include third parties who are foreseen users of the audited financial statements. *The specific identity of foreseen users need not be known to the CPAs.*

The courts in many states have followed the *Restatement* principle, including a court in Rhode Island in the leading case of *Rusch Factors, Inc. v. Levin* (1968). In that case, the CPAs were found liable for ordinary negligence to a third party that subsequently provided financing to the audit client. The third party had *not* been specifically identified to the CPAs, although they were aware that the financial statements were to be used to help obtain the financing. In *Williams Controls v. Parente, Randolph, Orlando & Associates,* 39 F. Supp. 2d 517 (1999), a more recent example, the court held the auditors liable to a purchaser of a client's business even though that purchaser was not the one originally identified when the audit began. The court noted that when the audit engagement letter was signed the auditors knew that their work would be used for purposes of completing a sale of one of the client's divisions. Who the buyer would be was irrelevant for purposes of auditor liability under the *Restatement* principle. The courts of many states follow this principle of liability to third parties.[6]

---

[5] This approach is referred to by numerous other titles, including the *third-party beneficiary approach,* the *primary benefit approach,* and the *privity (or near privity) approach.*

[6] Some courts have applied a type of modified rule in which they have limited the liability of the auditors to the intended user and not any subsequent users who are substituted such as a second bank or another buyer. One of the reasons for this limitation to the primary intended party is that circumstances change with each departing user of the financial statements and the auditors should have the benefit of full information before liability is imposed.

Illustrative Case
Liability to Third Parties

Dianne Holiday, CPA, performed the audit of Lyman Corporation for the year ended December 31. Holiday was aware that Lyman intended to use the audit report to obtain a bank loan. However, no specific bank was identified to Holiday. After the report was issued, Lyman obtained loans from the First National Bank and Dime Box State Bank. Also, Wallace Manufacturing Co. relied on Holiday's opinion in providing trade credit to Lyman. If the court applied the known user principles of the *Restatement* (foreseen user)

approach, Holiday could be held liable to First National and Dime Box if she was found guilty of ordinary negligence in the performance of her audit. The banks form a limited class of third parties who could be foreseen to rely on the audit report. Wallace Manufacturing Co., on the other hand, would have to prove *gross negligence* on the part of Holiday to recover its losses. The audit was not performed for the use of trade creditors; therefore, Wallace would not be considered a part of a limited class of foreseen users.

Rosenblum (Foreseeable User) Approach

This approach was based originally on the 1983 New Jersey **Rosenblum v. Adler** Supreme Court case, which rejected the approaches arising out of *Ultramares* and the *Second Restatement of Torts* and established a very different standard. In this case, the defendant CPAs issued an unqualified report on the financial statements of Giant Stores Corporation, which showed the corporation to be profitable. In reliance upon these statements, Rosenblum sold a catalog showroom business to Giant in exchange for shares of Giant's stock. Shortly afterward, Giant filed for bankruptcy and the stock became worthless. Rosenblum sued Giant's CPAs, alleging ordinary negligence. The case was dismissed by the trial court, on the premise that the CPAs were not liable to unidentified third parties for ordinary negligence. However, the New Jersey Supreme Court reversed the lower court, finding that CPAs *can be held liable for ordinary negligence* to any third party the auditors could "reasonably foresee" as recipients of the statements for routine business purposes. This approach has the potential effect of expanding CPA liability to third parties whose purposes are totally unknown to the CPAs. At this point, however, few states have elected to follow the *Rosenblum* approach.

Summary of Third-Party Liability Approaches

Common law cases are decided, in large part, by reference to established precedents—that is, past decisions. The *Ultramares* (known user), *Restatement* (foreseen user), and *Rosenblum* (foreseeable user) approaches create conflicting precedents as to which third parties can hold the auditors liable for ordinary negligence. Variants of each of these approaches exist in the various states. Figure 4.1 summarizes differences in third-party ability to recover damages for CPAs' ordinary negligence liability under the three basic approaches.

FIGURE 4.1
Summary of Third-Party Common Law Liability for Ordinary Negligence

Approach	Requirements for a Third Party to Recover Losses Due to CPA's Ordinary Negligence
Ultramares approach (known user approach)	The auditors knew that the audited financial statements were for use for a *particular purpose by a known user* (third-party beneficiary).
Restatement approach (foreseen user approach)	The auditors knew the audited financial statements were for use for a *particular purpose,* but the auditors *did not necessarily know the specific user* (e.g., the financial statements were known to be for use in helping to sell the business to an unidentified purchaser).
Rosenblum approach (foreseeable user approach)	The auditors should have realized that it was *reasonably foreseeable* that the financial statements would be used by this user.

Liability to Third Parties under Statutory Law

Statutory law is written law, created by state or federal legislative bodies. Most states have "blue sky" laws, which regulate the issuance and trading of securities within the state. The two most important federal laws relating to auditors' liability are the **Securities Act of 1933** (the 1933 Act) and the **Securities Exchange Act of 1934** (the 1934 Act). CPAs must also be concerned with the application of the Racketeer Influenced and Corrupt Organizations Act (RICO). Even though our discussion of statutory law will be limited to these three federal acts, CPAs should be familiar with other federal laws along with the blue sky laws in those states in which their clients sell securities.

Litigation against auditors that is based on statutory provisions does not enjoy the latitude available under common law. While common law can vary from state to state and can evolve with differing factual circumstances and changing conditions, statutorily based litigation is constrained to a greater extent by the underlying law.

Securities Act of 1933

The 1933 Act requires a company intending to offer its securities for sale to the public to first file a **registration statement** with the SEC.[7] This registration statement includes audited financial statements, and numerous other disclosures. Under the 1933 Act, both the company filing the registration statement and its auditors may be held liable to purchasers of the securities in the event that the registration statement is found to contain material misstatements or omissions.[8] The wording of Section 11(a) of the Act provides as follows:

> In case any part of the registration statement, when such part became effective, contained an untrue statement of a material fact or omitted to state a material fact required to be stated therein or necessary to make the statements therein not misleading, any person acquiring such security (unless it is proved that at the time of such acquisition he knew of such untruth or omission) may . . . sue.

Plaintiffs' Rights under the 1933 Act

The 1933 Act offers protection to only a limited group of investors—those who initially purchase a security offered for sale under the registration statement.[9] For those investors, however, the 1933 Act shifts much of the burden of proof from the plaintiff to the defendant. The plaintiffs (security purchasers) need only prove that (1) they sustained a loss and (2) the registration statement was misleading. They *need not* prove[10] that they relied upon the registration or that the auditors were negligent.

Auditors' Defenses under the 1933 Act

If auditors are to avoid liability for the plaintiffs' losses, they generally must affirmatively prove that (1) they conducted the audit with **due diligence,** (2) the plaintiffs' losses were not caused by misstated financial statements, (3) the plaintiff knew of the financial statement misstatement when the securities were purchased, or (4) the statute of limitations—one year after the discovery of the misstatement, but no more than three years after the security was first offered to the public—had expired.

---

[7] The 1933 Act requires registration statements to be filed by any company that will offer securities for sale to the public through the mails or interstate commerce. There are certain exceptions, for example, for charitable institutions and other not-for-profit organizations, and for offerings of small dollar amounts.

[8] The auditors are liable for misstatements or omissions in only those portions of the registration statement covered by their audit and report.

[9] Secondary purchasers who bought securities within the first year of the registration statement also may bring suit against the company and the auditors under the Securities Act of 1933.

[10] An exception exists in that Section 11 requires reliance when the plaintiff purchases the security after the issuance of an earnings statement covering a period of at least 12 months following the effective date of the registration statement.

As a practical matter, it is the due diligence defense that auditors often raise. Section 11 of the act states that the auditors are not liable if they:

> had, after reasonable investigation, reasonable ground to believe and did believe, at the time . . . the registration statement became effective, that the statements therein were true and that there was no omission to state a material fact.

The due diligence standard of the 1933 Act establishes a high level of auditors' responsibility for justifying their performance. Not only are auditors liable for losses caused by acts of ordinary negligence, but they must *prove their innocence* rather than merely refute the accusations of the plaintiffs. Establishing the due diligence defense has proved difficult for auditors, and the standing precedent on interpretation of due diligence is *Escott v. BarChris Construction Corporation,* 283 F. Supp. 643 (1968). The case was an action under Section 11 of the Securities Act of 1933 by purchasers of BarChris's registered debentures against the directors, underwriters, and independent auditors of BarChris. Subsequent to issuance of the debentures, BarChris, a builder of bowling alleys, went bankrupt. The plaintiffs claimed that the registration statement for the debentures contained materially false statements and material omissions; the defendants all countered with the due diligence defense. The court found that the registration statement (Form S-1) was false and misleading and that with a few exceptions none of the defendants had established their due diligence defense. The court also found that the public accounting firm had failed to comply with generally accepted auditing standards. The court was especially critical of the public accounting firm's conduct of the S-1 review, so called because it is an investigation carried out by the public accounting firm some time after completion of the audit, but just prior to the effective date of the registration statement filed with the SEC. In an S-1 review, the CPAs look for any evidence arising since their audit that indicates that the registration statement is misleading as filed. The court criticized the public accounting firm for performing too limited a review and for being "too easily satisfied with glib answers by management" to inquiries.

While the *BarChris* case was decided over 35 years ago, it remains the standing precedent for auditor liability. In fact, its interpretation of Section 11, in terms of the auditors' defenses, was so stringent that there are relatively few additional cases related to Section 11 liability because of defendants' unwillingness to litigate cases fully when there is such a strict standard of auditor liability.

Securities Exchange Act of 1934

The 1934 Act requires all companies under SEC jurisdiction to file annual audited and quarterly reviewed financial statements with the SEC.[11] The act also creates potential liability for the filing company and its auditors to anyone who buys or sells the company's securities in the event that these annual statements are found to be misleading. While the 1933 Act creates liability only to those investors involved in the initial distribution of a public offering, the 1934 Act expands that liability to subsequent purchasers and sellers of the stock. The two primary liability sections of the act are Sections 10 and 18.

Section 10, with Rule 10b-5 promulgated by the SEC under Section 10(b) of the act, reads as follows:

> It shall be unlawful for any person, directly or indirectly, by the use of any means or instrumentality of interstate commerce or of the mails, or of any national securities exchange . . .
>
> (1) to employ any device, scheme, or artifice to defraud,
> (2) to make any untrue statement of a material fact or to omit to state a material fact necessary in order to make the statements . . . not misleading, or
> (3) to engage in any act, practice, or course of business which operates or would operate as a fraud or deceit upon any person, in connection with the purchase or sale of any security.

[11] Companies under SEC jurisdiction include those (1) whose securities are listed on a national stock exchange or (2) with equity securities traded on the over-the-counter market, and total assets exceeding $5 million and 500 or more stockholders.

Section 18(a) of the 1934 Act, which relates to misstated financial statements, provides for liability to [emphasis added]:

> any person (not knowing that such statement was false or misleading) who, in reliance upon such statement, shall have purchased or sold a security at a price which was affected by such statement, for damages by such reliance, *unless the person sued shall prove that he acted in good faith* and had no knowledge that such statement was false or misleading.

Plaintiffs' Rights under the 1934 Act

The 1934 Act offers protection to both original and subsequent purchasers and sellers of securities. Under both Section 10 and Section 18 the plaintiffs (security purchasers and sellers) must prove that (1) they sustained losses, (2) the financial statements were misleading, and (3) they relied upon the financial statements. Section 10(b) and Rule 10b-5, as interpreted by the landmark **Ernst & Ernst v. Hochfelder** case, require that the plaintiffs prove **scienter** (intent to deceive, manipulate, or defraud) on the part of the auditors.

Ernst & Ernst v. Hochfelder was brought by a group of investors against the public accounting firm that for 21 years had audited the financial statements of First Securities Company of Chicago, a small brokerage firm. The president of First Securities, who was also its majority stockholder, committed suicide, leaving a note stating that the firm was insolvent and disclosing a fraud that he had perpetrated upon several investors. The president had persuaded the investors to mail him their personal checks, the funds from which he was to invest in escrow accounts yielding high returns to the investors. There were no such escrow accounts in the accounting records of First Securities Company; instead, the president was engaged in a **ponzi scheme** in which he diverted the investors' checks to his own use immediately upon receipt.

The investors filed suit under SEC Rule 10b-5 (and the related Securities Exchange Act of 1934 Section 10[b]) against the public accounting firm, charging it with *ordinary negligence,* and thus with responsibility for the investors' losses in the fraud. The plaintiffs *did not accuse the public accounting firm of fraud or intentional misconduct.* That is, they did not attempt to prove scienter.

The basis for the plaintiffs' charge of negligence was that the public accounting firm failed to discover a weakness in First Securities Company's control that enabled the company's president to carry on the fraud. The control weakness, called the "mail rule," was the president's policy that *only he* could open mail addressed to him at First Securities, or addressed to First Securities to his attention. It is common practice at financial institutions for *all* incoming mail to be opened in the mailroom, in part to avoid the possibility of employees' perpetrating some type of fraud.

The case was ultimately resolved by the U.S. Supreme Court, which ruled that an action for damages under Section 10(b) of the 1934 Act and the related SEC Rule 10b-5 was not warranted in the absence of scienter on the auditors' part. The court held that auditors are liable under section 10(b) only upon proof of intent to deceive, manipulate, or defraud.[12] In summary, the auditors' primary defense under Section 10 is that there is no scienter. That is, auditors show that they did not perform the audit with the intent to deceive, manipulate, or defraud.

Auditors' Defenses under the 1934 Act

Under Section 18, the auditors may avoid liability by proving "good faith," which they will normally be able to establish unless they have been guilty of gross negligence or fraud. In addition, to avoid liability for the plaintiffs' losses under either Section 10 or 18, the auditors may rely on causation—that the losses experienced by the plaintiffs were caused by factors other than the auditors' behavior.

Proportionate Liability under the 1934 Act

Historically, defendants in actions under the 1934 Act were jointly and severally liable for all the plaintiffs' losses. However, the *Private Securities Litigation Reform Act of 1995* amended

---

[12] The Court did not rule on whether the existence of reckless behavior would be sufficient to establish scienter and thereby impose liability.

Illustrative Case
Joint and Several Liability

Assume that $50 million of damages is awarded to a plaintiff, and the auditors' percentage of responsibility is established at 10 percent. If all other defendants are able to pay their share of the award, the auditors' share will be $5 million (10% × $50,000,000).

On the other hand, if some defendants are unable to pay their share, the auditors' liability may be increased, with the auditors having:

1. Joint and several liability to small investors with a net worth of less than $200,000 and recoverable damages that exceed 10 percent of their net worth.

2. Joint and several liability to other investors with a limit of 50 percent of the auditors' proportionate share, in this case an additional $2,500,000 ($5,000,000 × 50%).

If the CPAs were found to be knowingly involved in violations of the law, they may be found liable for the entire $50 million of losses.

the 1934 Act to place limits on the amount of the auditors' liability. In general the amendment establishes proportionate liability. If one or more of the defendants are not able to pay their share of the losses, the auditors will have unlimited joint and several liability only to certain small investors. To other investors, the auditors' liability for losses caused by other parties is limited to an amount not to exceed 50 percent of the auditors' proportionate share of the losses. If the auditors were knowingly involved in violations of the law, complete joint and several liability may be imposed.

In addition to the 1995 reforms, Congress passed the Securities Litigation Uniform Standards Act in 1998 to establish uniform standards for bringing class-action securities suits in both state and federal courts. Under these standards, plaintiffs and their lawyers must follow certain certification procedures and there are consolidation rules with regard to the trial of these cases.

Comparison of the 1933 and 1934 Acts

Learning Objective 5

The 1933 and 1934 Acts differ in investors protected and the burden of proof required. The 1933 Act offers recourse only to individuals acquiring the initial distribution of securities, whereas the 1934 Act offers recourse to *any* person buying or selling the securities at a later date.

In comparison to common law, both of the federal securities acts shift significant burdens of proof from the plaintiffs to the defendants. However, some differences exist between the defendant's burden under the 1933 Act and the 1934 Act. Under the 1933 Act, plaintiffs *need not prove reliance* upon the audited financial statements. The 1934 Act, however, generally requires plaintiffs to prove that they relied upon the misleading statements.

Next, both acts place the burden of proving adequate performance on the defendants. The 1933 Act requires the auditors to prove "due diligence"; if they were ordinarily negligent they will not be able to establish this defense. The 1934 Act is more lenient in that Section 10 requires the existence of scienter, while Section 18 requires auditors to prove that they acted in good faith. Because it requires the existence of gross negligence or fraud, the "good faith" defense is considerably easier to establish than is "due diligence." Figure 4.2 summarizes important similarities and differences between the two acts.

Racketeer Influenced and Corrupt Organizations Act

In 1970, Congress enacted the Racketeer Influenced and Corrupt Organizations Act (RICO) as a weapon against mobsters and racketeers who were influencing legitimate business. A discussion of RICO would appear to be out of place in a discussion of legal liability of auditors. However, the act broadly defines the term *racketeering activities* to include crimes such as mail fraud and fraud in the sale of securities. Prior to 1993, these provisions were used successfully in a small number of cases against CPAs in which it could be shown that the CPAs knew, or perhaps should have known, of material misstatements of financial statements when the problems

FIGURE 4.2 Summary of Auditor Civil Liability under the 1933 Securities Act (Section 11) and the 1934 Securities Exchange Act (Sections 10 and 18)

Act	What Must Be Proved by the Third Party?			Basic Standard of Liability
	A Loss?	Misleading Financial Statements?	Reliance on Financial Statements?	
1933 Securities Act— Section 11	Yes	Yes	No	Auditor must prove due diligence
1934 Securities Exchange Act—Section 10	Yes	Yes	Yes	Third party must prove existence of scienter (auditors' intent to deceive, manipulate, or defraud)
1934 Securities Exchange Act—Section 18	Yes	Yes	Yes	Auditor must prove good faith

were indicative of a pattern of improper activity. A primary concern with the RICO Act is the provision that allows triple damages in civil cases brought under the act.

In 1993, a favorable ruling by the U.S. Supreme Court, in the case of *Reves v. Ernst & Young,* relieved much of the concern about auditors' liability under the RICO Act. The court decided that the accountants cannot be held liable under the RICO Act unless they actually participated in the operation or management of the organization. Subsequently, the *Private Securities Litigation Reform Act of 1995* eliminated securities fraud as an offense in a civil RICO action unless there is a prior conviction. However, a number of states continue to have their own versions of RICO.

Auditors' Criminal Liability under the Securities Acts

Both the Securities Act of 1933 and the Securities Exchange Act of 1934 include provisions for *criminal charges* against CPAs who willfully (knowingly) allow misstatements in SEC filings, as do other statutes. Most directly relevant are Section 24 of the Securities Act of 1933 and Section 32(a) of the Securities Exchange Act of 1934. In addition, in extreme cases CPAs can be prosecuted under the criminal provisions of RICO, where it can be shown that the CPAs actually participated in the management or operation of a company that is indicted under RICO.

The *Continental Vending Machine Corporation* case was accompanied by a celebrated criminal case involving three members of the public accounting firm that audited Continental's financial statements. The criminal charges rocked the profession, because there was no intent to defraud on the part of the CPAs; they were convicted of criminal fraud on the basis of gross negligence. The verdict of guilty was affirmed by a U.S. Court of Appeals, and the U.S. Supreme Court refused to review the case. The three CPAs were later pardoned by the president of the United States.

In the *Continental Vending* case (*United States v. Simon,* 425 F.2d 796 [1969]), the U.S. government brought charges of fraud against three CPAs. The charges hinged upon a note to Continental's audited financial statements, which read:

> The amount receivable from Valley Commercial Corp. (an affiliated company of which . . . [Continental's president] is an officer, director, and stockholder) bears interest at 12 percent a year. Such amount, less the balance of the notes payable to that company, is secured by the assignment to the Company of Valley's equity in certain marketable securities. As of . . . [the date of the auditors' report] . . . the amount of such equity at current market quotations exceeded the net amount receivable.

The note did not disclose—and the auditors were aware—that the affiliated company had loaned approximately that same amount to Continental's president. The president was unable to repay the affiliate, which was unable to repay Continental. In addition, most of the collateral furnished by the president was stock and convertible debentures of Continental itself.

The auditors' defense in this case was that the note complied with existing generally accepted accounting principles. Eight "leaders of the profession" testified as expert witnesses that the note was consistent with generally accepted accounting principles and the audit was performed in accordance with generally accepted auditing standards. However, the judge rejected this argument and instructed the jury to evaluate whether the financial statements were "fairly presented" without reference to generally accepted accounting principles. The finding by the jury that the balance sheet did not present fairly Continental's financial position led to conviction of the three CPAs.

Because the *Continental Vending* case involved both criminal and civil proceedings, it has significant implications for the public accounting profession. Not only is civil liability an ever-present hazard for CPAs, but criminal charges may also be involved.

Criminal Liability under Other Statutes

In addition to the securities laws, CPAs and public accounting firms may be subject to prosecution under a host of other criminal statutes. This fact became all too apparent to the profession when, in June 2002, Arthur Andersen became the first major accounting firm ever convicted of a felony. The indictment, which named only the firm and not any employees or partners, accused Arthur Andersen of the "wholesale destruction of documents" relating to the Enron Corporation collapse. Representatives of Arthur Andersen stated that the firm was merely applying its document retention policy in destroying the documents. While prosecutors emphasized the great volume of documents destroyed, the jury, in finding Arthur Andersen guilty, based its verdict primarily on an e-mail message written by an Arthur Andersen attorney. In that e-mail message the attorney advised an Arthur Andersen partner to revise a memo to omit certain information, including a comment that an Enron press release that included an earnings announcement was misleading. Arthur Andersen representatives acknowledged that the conviction effectively put the firm out of business. The case is particularly relevant to the profession in that it illustrates how the actions of a relatively small number of employees can lead to disastrous results for the firm. Ultimately, the conviction was overturned by the U.S. Supreme Court based on the fact that the jury was given inappropriate instructions.

SEC and Public Company Accounting Oversight Board Regulation

The SEC has issued rules for the appearance and practice of CPAs, attorneys, and others before the Commission under the statutes it administers. Rule of Practice 2(e), giving the SEC the power of suspension and disbarment, has the following wording:

> The Commission may deny, temporarily or permanently, the privilege of appearing or practicing before it in any way to any person who is found by the Commission . . . (1) not to possess the requisite qualifications to represent others, or (2) to be lacking in character or integrity or to have engaged in unethical or improper professional conduct.

On occasion, the Commission has taken punitive action against public accounting firms when it has found the audit work deficient with regard to financial statements filed with the Commission. These actions against public accounting firms usually arise when a listed corporation encounters financial difficulties and it later appears that misleading financial statements had served to conceal for a time the losses being incurred by the company. In recent years, the SEC has taken action against public accounting firms by the use of consent decrees in which the CPAs have agreed to certain penalties or restrictions. For example, a public accounting firm may settle charges brought by the SEC through a consent decree in which it agrees not to accept new SEC clients during a specified period and to permit a review of its practice.

The *Private Securities Litigation Reform Act of 1995* (discussed earlier in this chapter) requires auditors to play a more active disclosure role with respect to their clients. Under these changes to the 1934 Act, auditors who discover illegal acts by a client are required to report them to the board of directors of their clients, and, in some cases, the auditors are required to report those activities to the SEC. Auditors are relieved of any SEC sanctions if they timely report required information about clients to the SEC. The failure to take the necessary statutory steps for disclosure and reporting can result in additional liability for the auditor, including the possibility that such failure rises to the level of fraud or collusion with the client.

As discussed in Chapter 2, the Public Company Accounting Oversight Board also may conduct investigations and disciplinary proceedings on both registered public accounting firms and professional employees (including owners). Board sanctions may include monetary damages, suspension of firms and accountants from working on engagements for publicly traded companies, and referral of criminal cases to the Justice Department.

CPAs' Liability for Accounting and Review Services

Learning Objective 6

Up to this point, we have emphasized the liability of public accounting firms when they are associated with audited financial statements. In addition, CPAs are subject to legal liability when they perform accounting services, such as write-up work and *compilations* of unaudited financial statements. These services differ from audits in that the CPAs neither perform the verification procedures involved in an audit nor do they issue an auditors' opinion as to the fairness of the financial information.

The term **compilation of financial statements** refers to the *preparation* of financial statements based upon information provided to the CPAs by the client (or the client's representatives). A compilation is *not intended to lend any assurance* to any party that the CPAs have determined the information to be reliable. A **review of financial statements** consists of *limited* verification procedures, *substantially less in scope than an audit,* designed to provide users of the unaudited financial statements with a *limited* degree of assurance as to the statements' reliability. Compilations and reviews are described in Chapter 19.

Do CPAs associated with unaudited financial statements have any potential legal liability? The answer is *yes.* The CPAs, acting as *accountants* rather than as *auditors,* still have a liability to their client to exercise due professional care. In addition, they still may be liable for losses to third parties.

When CPAs are associated with unaudited financial statements, a possibility exists that the client or third parties may misinterpret the extent of their services and believe that the accountants are acting as auditors. The risks to public accounting firms engaged in the preparation of unaudited financial statements were brought sharply into focus by the *1136 Tenants' Corporation v. Rothenberg* case. In this case, an incorporated apartment cooperative, which was owned by its shareholder-tenants and managed by a separate realty agent, orally retained a public accounting firm for a period of 17 months to perform certain services, including the preparation of financial statements for the cooperative. The public accounting firm's fee was to be only $600 per year.

The public accounting firm submitted financial statements of the corporation for one full year and the first six months of the following year. The financial statements bore the notation "subject to comments in letter of transmittal." The referenced letter of transmittal read in part:

> Pursuant to our engagement, we have reviewed and summarized the statements of your managing agent and other data submitted to us by . . . [the agent], pertaining to 1136 Tenants' Corporation. . . .
>
> The following statements were prepared from the books and records of the Corporation. No independent verifications were undertaken thereon.

The client corporation later sued the public accounting firm for damages totaling $174,000 for the CPAs' alleged failure to discover defalcations of the corporation's funds committed by the managing agent. The client contended that the CPAs had been retained to render all necessary accounting and *auditing* services for it. The CPAs maintained they had been engaged to do write-up work only, although a working paper they had prepared supporting accrued expenses payable in the balance sheet included an entry for "audit expense."

The New York state trial court ruled in favor of the plaintiff on a decision affirmed by the Appellate Court of New York. The latter found that the CPAs' working papers indicated that the CPAs had examined the client's bank statements, invoices, and bills, and had made notations in their working papers concerning "missing invoices."

In summary, the court held the CPAs liable because it found that they had led their client to believe that they were performing an audit. Consequently, the courts held the CPAs responsible for performing their work in accordance with generally accepted auditing standards, which they clearly had not done. More important, however, the court also concluded that the CPAs had a duty to follow up on significant problems (the missing invoices) uncovered during their engagement. Thus, it is probable that the public accounting firm would have been held liable to its client *even if the court had recognized that the firm was not performing an audit.* Whenever CPAs encounter evidence that their client may be sustaining a loss through embezzlement or other fraud, they should warn the client immediately.

There are several lessons for public accounting firms in the *1136 Tenants' Corporation* case:

1. CPAs who prepare unaudited financial statements should adhere closely to Rules of Conduct 102 and 202 of the AICPA's *Code of Professional Conduct.* Rule 102 states that a CPA shall not knowingly misrepresent facts, and Rule 202 requires a public accounting firm to comply with professional standards, including standards for accounting and review services. The actions of the public accounting firm described in the preceding paragraph might be construed as violating both rules.

2. **Engagement letters** are as essential for accounting and review services as they are for independent audits. Oral arrangements for accounting and review services are of scant assistance when there is a dispute as to the nature of the services to be rendered by the public accounting firm to the client.

3. The CPAs engaged to perform *accounting or review* services should be alert for, and follow up on, such unusual items as missing invoices. As professionals, CPAs are bound to exercise *due professional care,* even though their engagements do not include independent audits of the client's financial statements.

4. CPAs should report on financial statements clearly and concisely, using, to the extent possible, the standardized language set forth in *Statements on Auditing Standards* and *Statements on Standards for Accounting and Review Services.* Reports should indicate the nature of the services rendered and the degree of responsibility being assumed by the public accounting firm.

CPAs' Posture in the Age of Litigation

In addition to the preceding court cases, numerous other actions against CPAs, under both common law and the Securities Acts, are pending trial. It is apparent that lawsuits will continue to plague the public accounting profession, as they have the legal and medical professions. The question thus is: What should be CPAs' reaction to this age of litigation?

In the opinion of the authors, positive actions helpful to CPAs in withstanding threats of possible lawsuits include the following:

1. Greater emphasis upon compliance with the public accounting profession's generally accepted auditing standards and ethical requirements. Close analysis of the court cases and other actions described in this chapter discloses numerous instances in which the auditors appear not to have complied fully with one or more auditing and ethical standards.

2. Retaining legal counsel that is familiar with CPAs' legal liability. The CPAs should thoroughly discuss all potentially dangerous situations with their legal counsel and should carefully consider their counsel's advice.

3. Maintenance of adequate liability insurance coverage. Although liability insurance coverage should not be considered a substitute for the CPAs' compliance with the preceding recommendations, public accountants must protect themselves against possible financial losses from lawsuits. Adequate liability insurance is essential.

4. Thorough investigation of prospective clients. As indicated in preceding sections of this chapter, many court cases involving CPAs have been accompanied by criminal charges against top management of the CPAs' clients. CPAs should use great care in screening prospective clients to avoid the risks involved in professional relationships with the criminally inclined.

5. Obtaining a thorough knowledge of the client's business. One of the major causes of audit failures has been a lack of understanding by auditors of the client's business and of industry practices.

6. Use of engagement letters for all professional services. Controversies over what services were performed by the CPAs can be minimized by a clearly written contract describing the agreed-upon services. CPAs also may insert various types of clauses to limit liability in engagement letters. For example, a clause may be included in the letter that indemnifies and holds harmless the CPAs from all liability and costs resulting from knowing misrepresentations by management. Engagement letters are discussed in Chapter 6.

7. In planning engagements, carefully assessing the risk of errors and fraud in the client's financial statements. The CPAs should exercise special care when the client has material weaknesses in internal control.

8. Exercising extreme care in audits of clients in financial difficulties or with a high degree of business risk. Creditors and shareholders of companies that are insolvent or in bankruptcy are likely to seek recovery of their losses. As the court cases described in this chapter demonstrate, litigation involving CPAs tends to center around auditing of clients who later become bankrupt. Other litigation-sensitive audit engagements include rapid-growth entities, entities that have recently completed or are contemplating initial public offerings, and entities with material related-party transactions.

9. Making certain that working papers have been professionally and completely assembled. Chapter 5 provides details on working paper preparation and assembly.

Chapter Summary

This chapter described the legal environment of auditors, emphasizing legal liability under both common law and statutory law. To summarize:

1. Under common law, CPAs are liable to their clients for failure to exercise due professional care. Accordingly, ordinary negligence is a sufficient degree of misconduct to hold CPAs liable for damages caused to their clients.

2. Auditors' liability to third parties under common law varies from state to state. One way to summarize these differences is to consider three general approaches—(a) *Ultramares* (known user) approach, (b) *Restatement* (foreseen user) approach, and (c) *Rosenblum* (foreseeable user) approach. Under the *Ultramares* (known user) approach, CPAs are held liable for ordinary negligence only to third-party beneficiaries for whose benefit the audit was performed. Other third parties must prove gross negligence on the part of the auditors. Under the *Restatement* (foreseen user) approach, liability for ordinary negligence to third parties is extended to include any limited class of parties that could be foreseen to rely upon the financial statements. The *Rosenblum* (foreseeable user) approach extends the auditors' liability for ordinary negligence even further to include any third party the auditors could reasonably foresee as recipients of the financial statements.

3. Auditors may also be held liable to third parties under the federal securities laws, which allow class action lawsuits by purchasers or sellers of a company's securities. The Securities Act of 1933 is unique in that most of the burden of proof in litigation is shifted to the auditors, with the primary defenses available to the auditor consisting of (1) knowledge of the plaintiffs of the errors or omissions or (2) due diligence by the auditors. Due diligence is a difficult defense to establish.

4. CPAs are also subject to criminal prosecution for violation of various statutes, including criminal fraud in which their conduct was intentional or involved collusion with the client.

5. To protect themselves from the liability crisis of today, auditors strive to adhere to a high level of professional performance. They also attempt to avoid engagements that have a very high risk of litigation.

Key Terms Introduced or Emphasized in Chapter 4

Breach of contract   Failure of one or both parties to a contract to perform in accordance with the contract's provisions. A public accounting firm might be sued for breach of contract, for example, if the firm failed to perform the engagement in accordance with the engagement letter. Negligence on the part of the CPAs also constitutes breach of contract.

Common law   Unwritten law that has developed through court decisions; it represents judicial interpretation of a society's concept of fairness. For example, the right to sue a person for fraud is a common law right.

Compilation of financial statements   The preparation of financial statements by CPAs based on representations of management, with the expression of no assurance concerning the statements' compliance with generally accepted accounting principles.

Constructive fraud   Performing duties with such recklessness that persons believing the duties to have been completed carefully are being misled. It differs from fraud in that constructive fraud does not involve knowledge of misrepresentations within the financial statements.

Comparative negligence   A concept used by certain courts to allocate damages between negligent parties based on the degree to which each party is at fault. The allocation of damages is referred to as *proportionate liability*.

Contributory negligence   Negligence on the part of the plaintiff that has contributed to his or her having incurred a loss. Contributory negligence may be used as a defense, because the court may limit or bar recovery by a plaintiff whose own negligence contributed to the loss.

Credit Alliance Corp. v. Arthur Andersen & Co.   A common law decision by the New York Court of Appeals (New York's highest court) stating that auditors must demonstrate knowledge of reliance on the financial statements by a third party for a particular purpose to be held liable for ordinary negligence to that party. Basically, this case upheld the *Ultramares v. Touche & Co.* rule.

Defendant   The party against which damages and suit are brought against by the defendant.

Due diligence   A public accounting firm's contention that its audit work was adequate to support its opinion on financial statements included in a registration statement filed with the SEC under the Securities Act of 1933.

Engagement letter   A written contract summarizing the contractual relationship between the CPAs and the client. The engagement letter typically specifies the scope of professional services to be rendered, expected completion dates, and the basis for determination of the CPAs' fee. Engagement letters are discussed more fully in Chapter 6.

Ernst & Ernst v. Hochfelder   A landmark case in which the U.S. Supreme Court decided that auditors could not be held liable under the Securities Exchange Act of 1934 for ordinary negligence.

Error   An unintentional misstatement of financial statements or omission of an amount or a disclosure.

Fraud   Misrepresentation by a person of a material fact, known by that person to be untrue or made with reckless indifference as to whether the fact is true, with intent to deceive and with the result that another party is injured.

Gross negligence   Lack of even slight care, indicative of a reckless disregard for one's professional responsibilities. Substantial failures on the part of an auditor to comply with generally accepted auditing standards might be interpreted as gross negligence.

Joint and several liability   A legal concept that holds a class of defendants jointly responsible for losses attributed to the class as well as liable for any share of losses that cannot be collected from those unable to pay their share. Thus, a financially responsible defendant may be required to pay losses attributed to defendants that do not have the ability to pay.

Negligence   Violation of a legal duty to exercise a degree of care that an ordinarily prudent person would exercise under similar circumstances. Also referred to as ordinary or simple negligence.

Plaintiff   The party claiming damages and bringing suit against the defendant.

Ponzi scheme   A swindle in which a quick return on an initial investment is paid out of funds of new investors to lure the victims into bigger risks. This is named for Charles Ponzi who in 1919 convinced people he could make them 50 percent profit in 45 days by an international trading scam. Old investors were paid off with cash from new investors. Ultimately such schemes collapse and the newest investors lose their investment as there is no actual appreciation of assets involved.

Precedent   A legal principle that evolves from a common law court decision and then serves as a standard for future decisions in similar cases.

Proportionate liability   A method of allocating damages to each group that is liable according to that group's pro rata share of any damages recovered by the plaintiff. For example, if the plaintiff was awarded a total of $1,000,000 and the CPAs were found to bear 40 percent of the responsibility for the damages, the CPAs would be assessed $400,000.

Proximate cause   Damage to another is directly attributable to a wrongdoer's act. The issue of proximate cause may be raised as a defense in litigation. Even though a public accounting firm might have been negligent in rendering services, it will not be liable for the plaintiff's loss if its negligence was not the proximate cause of the loss.

Registration statement   A document including audited financial statements that must be filed with the SEC by any company in order to sell its securities to the public through the mails or interstate commerce. The Securities Act of 1933 provides liability to security purchasers for material misrepresentations in registration statements.

Review of financial statements   The performance of limited investigative procedures that are substantially less in scope than an audit made in accordance with generally accepted auditing standards. The procedures provide the CPAs with a basis to provide *limited assurance* that the financial statements are in accordance with generally accepted accounting principles.

Rosenblum v. Adler   A common law decision by the New Jersey Supreme Court that holds CPAs liable for acts of ordinary negligence to "reasonably foreseeable third parties" not in privity of contract. Conflicts with the precedents established in both the *Ultramares* and the *Restatement of Law of Torts* approaches to liability.

Scienter   Intent to deceive, manipulate, or defraud. The U.S. Supreme Court held in the *Hochfelder* case that scienter must be proved for the auditors to be held liable under the Securities Exchange Act of 1934.

Second Restatement of the Law of Torts   A summary of tort liability, which when applied to auditor common law liability, expands auditors' liability for ordinary negligence to include third parties of a limited class of known or intended users of the audited financial statements. Conflicts with the precedents established by the *Ultramares* and the *Rosenblum* approaches to liability.

Securities Act of 1933   A federal securities statute covering registration statements for securities to be sold to the public. The act requires auditors to exercise "due diligence," and creates both civil and criminal penalties for misrepresentation.

Securities Exchange Act of 1934   A federal securities statute requiring public companies to file annual audited financial statements with the SEC. The act requires auditors to "act in good faith," and creates civil and criminal penalties for misrepresentation.

Statutory law   Written law created by state or federal legislative bodies. CPAs must concern themselves particularly with the federal securities acts and state blue sky laws. These laws regulate the issuance and trading of securities.

Third-party beneficiary   A person, not the auditors or their client, who is named in a contract (or known to the contracting parties) with the intention that such person should have definite rights and benefits under the contract.

Tort   A civil wrong. For financial statements audits, the primary tort involved is that of performing the engagement negligently.

Ultramares v. Touche & Co.   A common law decision by the New York Court of Appeals (New York's highest court) stating that auditors are liable to third parties not in privity of contract for acts of fraud or gross negligence, but not for ordinary negligence. Conflicts with precedents established by the *Restatement of Torts* and *Rosenblum* approaches to liability.

Review Questions

4–1.   Explain why the potential liability of auditors for professional "malpractice" exceeds that of physicians or other professionals.

4–2.   Distinguish between ordinary negligence and gross negligence within the context of the CPAs' work.

4–3.   What is meant by the term *privity?* How does privity affect the auditor's liability under common law?

4–4.   Define the term *third-party beneficiary.*

4–5.   Distinguish between common law and statutory law.

4–6.   Briefly describe the differences in liability to third parties under the known user, foreseen user, and foreseeable user approaches to CPA liability.

4–7.   Briefly describe the different common law precedents set by the *Ultramares v. Touche* case and the *Rosenblum v. Adler* case.

4–8.   What landmark case was embraced by the court in the case of *Credit Alliance Corp. v. Arthur Andersen & Co.?* Identify the two factors that the court stated must be proved for the auditors to be held liable for ordinary negligence to a third party.

4–9. Compare auditors' common law liability to clients and third-party beneficiaries with their common law liability to other third parties.

4–10. Contrast *joint and several liability* with *proportionate liability.*

4–11. Compare the rights of plaintiffs under common law with the rights of persons who purchase securities registered under the Securities Act of 1933 and sustain losses. In your answer emphasize the issue of who must bear the burden of proof.

4–12. State briefly a major distinction between the Securities Act of 1933 and the Securities Exchange Act of 1934 with respect to the type of transactions regulated.

4–13. Why was the *Ernst & Ernst v. Hochfelder* decision considered a "victory" for the accounting profession?

4–14. How was the *Continental Vending* case unusual with respect to penalties levied against auditors?

4–15. Why did Congress enact the Racketeer Influenced and Corrupt Organizations Act? Why has it been of concern to auditors? What recent developments have reduced this concern?

4–16. How does the SEC regulate auditors who appear and practice before the commission?

4–17. In the *1136 Tenants' Corporation* case, what was the essential difference in the way the client and the CPAs viewed the work to be done in the engagement?

4–18. Comment on the following statement: While engagement letters are useful for audit engagements, they are not necessary for compilation and review engagements.

4–19. Rogers and Green, CPAs, admit they failed substantially to follow generally accepted auditing standards in their audit of Martin Corporation. "We were overworked and understaffed and never should have accepted the engagement," said Rogers. Does this situation constitute fraud on the part of the public accounting firm? Explain.

4–20. Assume that in a particular audit the CPAs were negligent but not grossly negligent. Indicate whether they would be "liable" or "not liable" for the following losses proximately caused by their negligence and determine that liability under the various theories discussed and followed by different states:

   a. Loss sustained by client; suit brought under common law.

   b. Loss sustained by trade creditor, not in privity of contract; suit brought in a state court that adheres to the *Ultramares v. Touche* precedent.

   c. Loss sustained by a bank known to the auditors to be relying on the financial statements for a loan; suit brought in a state court that adheres to the *Credit Alliance v. Arthur Andersen* precedent.

   d. Losses to stockholders purchasing shares at a public offering; suit brought under Securities Act of 1933.

   e. Loss sustained by a bank named as a third-party beneficiary in the engagement letter; suit brought under common law.

   f. Loss sustained by a lender not in privity of contract; suit brought in a state court that adheres to the *Rosenblum v. Adler* precedent.

   g. Losses sustained by stockholders; suit brought under Sections 18(a) and 10(b) of the Securities Exchange Act of 1934.

Questions Requiring Analysis

4–21. Glover, Inc., engaged Herd & Irwin, CPAs, to assist in the installation of a new computerized production system. Because the firm did not have experienced staff available for the engagement, Herd & Irwin assigned several newly hired staff assistants without sufficient supervision. As a result, Glover, Inc., incurred significant losses when the production system crashed causing significant backlogs and lost product sales.

Required: Describe the implications of this situation for Herd & Irwin.

4–22. Jensen, Inc., filed suit against a public accounting firm, alleging that the auditors' negligence was responsible for failure to disclose a large defalcation that had been in process for several years. The public accounting firm responded that it may have been negligent, but that Jensen, Inc., was really to blame because it had completely ignored the public accounting firm's repeated recommendations for improvements in internal control.

Required: If the public accounting firm was negligent, is it responsible for the loss sustained by the client? Does the failure by Jensen, Inc., to follow the auditors' recommendation for better internal control have any bearing on the question of liability? Explain.

4–23. The public accounting firm of Hanson and Brown was expanding very rapidly. Consequently, it hired several staff assistants, including James Small. Subsequently, the partners of the firm became dissatisfied with Small's production and warned him that they would be forced to discharge him unless his output increased significantly.

At that time, Small was engaged in audits of several clients. He decided that to avoid being fired, he would reduce or omit entirely some of the required auditing procedures listed in audit programs prepared by the partners. One of the public accounting firm's non-SEC clients, Newell Corporation, was in serious financial difficulty and had adjusted several of its accounts being examined by Small to appear financially sound. Small prepared fictitious working papers in his home at night to support purported completion of auditing procedures assigned to him, although he in fact did not examine the Newell adjusting entries. The public accounting firm rendered an unqualified opinion on Newell's financial statements, which were grossly misstated. Several creditors, relying upon the audited financial statements, subsequently extended large sums of money to Newell Corporation.

Required: Would the public accounting firm be liable to the creditors who extended the money in reliance on the erroneous financial statements if Newell Corporation should fail to pay its creditors? Explain.

4–24. Wanda Young, doing business as Wanda Young Fashions, engaged the CPA partnership of Scott & Green to audit her financial statements. During the audit, Scott & Green discovered certain irregularities that would have indicated to a reasonably prudent auditor that James Smith, the chief accountant, might be engaged in a fraud. However, Scott & Green, not having been engaged to discover defalcations, submitted an unqualified opinion in its report and did not mention the potential defalcation problem.

Required: What are the legal implications of the above facts as they relate to the relationship between Scott & Green and Wanda Young? Explain.

4–25. Susan Harris is a new assistant auditor with the public accounting firm of Sparks, Watts, and Wilcox, CPAs. On her third audit assignment, Harris examined the documentation underlying 60 disbursements as a test of controls over purchasing, receiving, vouchers payable, and cash disbursement procedures. In the process, she found five disbursements for the purchase of materials with no receiving reports in the documentation. She noted the exceptions in her working papers and called them to the attention of the senior auditor. Relying on prior experience with the client, the senior auditor disregarded Harris's comments, and nothing further was done about the exceptions.

Subsequently, it was learned that one of the client's purchasing agents and a member of its accounting department were engaged in a fraudulent scheme whereby they diverted the receipt of materials to a public warehouse while sending the invoices to the client. When the client discovered the fraud, the conspirators had obtained approximately $700,000—$500,000 of which was obtained after the completion of the audit.

Required: Discuss the legal implications and liabilities to Sparks, Watts, and Wilcox as a result of the above facts.

(AICPA, adapted)

4–26. Sawyer and Sawyer, CPAs, audited the financial statements of Rattler Corporation that were included in Rattler's Form 10-K which was filed with the SEC. Subsequently, Rattler Corporation went bankrupt and the stockholders of the corporation brought a class-action lawsuit against management, Sawyer and Sawyer, and the corporation's board of directors and attorneys for misstatements of the financial statements.

Assume that the jury in the case decides that responsibility for $5 million in losses should be allocated as follows:

Management	70%
Board of directors	20
Auditors	5
Attorneys	5
	100%

Required:
a. Under what securities act would the stockholders initiate this lawsuit?
b. Assuming that all the defendants in the case are financially able to pay their share of the losses, calculate the amount of losses that would be allocated to Sawyer and Sawyer.
c. Assuming that the attorneys had no financial resources, describe how Sawyer and Sawyer's share of the losses might be increased.

4–27.   The international CPA firm of Arthur Andersen faced significant liability in conjunction with its audits of Enron Corporation.

Required:

    a. From a legal liability perspective, describe the unique features of this audit case.

    b. Describe the important implications of this audit case for a firm of public accountants.

4–28.   Dandy Container Corporation engaged the accounting firm of Adams and Adams to audit financial statements to be used in connection with an interstate public offering of securities. The audit was completed, and an unqualified opinion was expressed on the financial statements that were submitted to the Securities and Exchange Commission along with the registration statement. Two hundred thousand shares of Dandy Container common stock were offered to the public at $11 a share. Eight months later the stock fell to $2 a share when it was disclosed that several large loans to two "paper" corporations owned by one of the directors were worthless. The loans were secured by the stock of the borrowing corporations, which was owned by the director. These facts were not disclosed in the financial statements. The director involved and the two corporations are insolvent.

Required:

State whether each of the following statements is true or false, and explain why.

    a. The Securities Act of 1933 applies to the above-described public offering of securities.

    b. The accounting firm has potential liability to any person who acquired the stock.

    c. An insider who had knowledge of all the facts regarding the loans to the two paper corporations could nevertheless recover from the accounting firm.

    d. In court, investors who bought shares in Dandy Container need only show that they sustained a loss and that failure to explain the nature of the loans in question constituted a false statement or misleading omission in the financial statements.

    e. The accountants could avoid liability if they could show they were not negligent.

    f. The accountants could avoid or reduce the damages asserted against them if they could establish that the drop in the stock's market price was due in whole or in part to other causes.

    g. The Securities and Exchange Commission would defend any action brought against the accountants in that the SEC examined and approved the registration statement.

4–29.   Gordon & Moore, CPAs, were the auditors of Fox & Company, a brokerage firm. Gordon & Moore examined and reported on the financial statements of Fox, which were filed with the Securities and Exchange Commission.

Several of Fox's customers were swindled by a fraudulent scheme perpetrated by two key officers of the company. The facts establish that Gordon & Moore were negligent, but not reckless or grossly negligent, in the conduct of the audit, and neither participated in the fraudulent scheme nor knew of its existence.

The customers are suing Gordon & Moore under the antifraud provisions of Section 10(b) and Rule 10b-5 of the Securities Exchange Act of 1934 for aiding and abetting the fraudulent scheme of the officers. The customers' suit for fraud is predicated exclusively on the negligence of the auditors in failing to conduct a proper audit, thereby failing to discover the fraudulent scheme.

Required:

Answer the following, setting forth reasons for any conclusions stated.

    a. What is the probable outcome of the lawsuit? Explain.

    b. What other theory of liability might the customers have asserted?

(AICPA, adapted)

4–30.   Match the important cases listed below with the appropriate legal precedent or implication.

Case:

    a. Hochfelder v. Ernst

    b. Escott v. BarChris Construction Corp.

    c. Credit Alliance v. Arthur Andersen & Co.

    d. Ultramares v. Touche & Co.

    e. Rosenblum v. Adler

    f. Rusch Factors, Inc. v. Levin

    g. United States v. Simon (Continental Vending)

Legal precedent or implication:

    1. A landmark case establishing that auditors should be held liable to third parties not in privity of contract for gross negligence, but not for ordinary negligence.

    2. A case in which the court used the guidance of the *Second Restatement of the Law of Torts* to decide the auditors' liability to third parties under common law.

    3. A landmark case in which the auditors were held liable under Section 11 of the Securities Act of 1933.

4. A case in which auditors were held liable for criminal negligence.

5. A case that established that auditors should not be held liable under the Securities Exchange Act of 1934 unless there was intent to deceive.

6. A case that established the precedent that auditors should be held liable under common law for ordinary negligence to all foreseeable third parties.

7. A common law case in which the court held that auditors should be held liable for ordinary negligence only to third parties they know will use the financial statements for a particular purpose.

Multiple Choice Questions

4–31. Select the best answer for each of the following questions and explain the reasons for your choice.

a. If a CPA performs an audit recklessly, the CPA will be liable to third parties who were unknown and not foreseeable to the CPA for:

(1) Strict liability for all damages incurred.

(2) Gross negligence.

(3) Either ordinary or gross negligence.

(4) Breach of contract.

b. Which of the following approaches to auditors' liability is least desirable from the CPA's perspective?

(1) The Ultramares approach.

(2) The Rosenblum approach.

(3) The Restatement of Torts approach.

(4) The Forseen User approach.

c. In cases of breach of contract plaintiffs generally have to prove all of the following, except:

(1) The CPAs had a duty.

(2) The CPAs made a false statement.

(3) The client incurred losses related to the CPAs' performance.

(4) The CPAs breached their duty.

d. If the CPAs provided negligent tax advice to a public company, the client would bring suit under:

(1) The Securities Act of 1933.

(2) The Securities Exchange Act of 1934.

(3) The Federal Income Tax Law.

(4) Common Law.

e. Which of the following cases reaffirmed the principles in the Ultramares case?

(1) Credit Alliance Corp. v. Arthur Andersen & Co.

(2) Rosenblum v. Adler.

(3) Ernst & Ernst v. Hochfelder.

(4) Escott v. BarChris Construction Corporation.

f. Under common law the CPAs who were negligent may mitigate some damages to a client by proving:

(1) Contributory negligence.

(2) The CPAs' fee was not material.

(3) The CPAs were not competent to accept the engagement.

(4) The CPAs' negligence was caused by the fact that they had too much work.

g. Under the Securities and Exchange Act of 1934, auditors and other defendants are faced with:

(1) Joint liability.

(2) Joint and several liability.

(3) Proportionate liability.

(4) Limited liability.

h. A CPA issued an unqualified opinion on the financial statements of a company that sold common stock in a public offering subject to the Securities Act of 1933. Based on a misstatement in the financial statements, the CPA is being sued by an investor who purchased shares of this public offering. Which of the following represents a viable defense?

(1) The investor has *not* proved fraud or negligence by the CPA.

(2) The investor did *not* actually rely upon the false statement.

(3) The CPA detected the false statement after the audit date.

(4) The false statement is immaterial in the overall context of the financial statements.

i. Which of the following elements is most frequently necessary to hold a CPA liable to a client?

(1) Acted with scienter or guilty knowledge.

(2) Was not independent of the client.

(3) Failed to exercise due care.

(4) Did not use an engagement letter.

j. Which statement best expresses the factors that purchasers of securities registered under the Securities Act of 1933 need prove to recover losses from the auditors?

(1) The purchasers of securities must prove ordinary negligence by the auditors and reliance on the audited financial statements.

(2) The purchasers of securities must prove that the financial statements were misleading and that they relied on them to purchase the securities.

(3) The purchasers of securities must prove that the financial statements were misleading; then, the burden of proof is shifted to the auditors to show that the audit was performed with "due diligence."

(4) The purchasers of securities must prove that the financial statements were misleading and the auditors were negligent.

k. The most significant result of the *Continental Vending* case was that it:

(1) Created a more general awareness of the possibility of auditor criminal prosecution.

(2) Extended the auditor's responsibility to all information included in registration statements.

(3) Defined the CPA's responsibilities for unaudited financial statements.

(4) Established a precedent for auditors being held liable to third parties under common law for ordinary negligence.

l. The *1136 Tenants'* case was important because of its emphasis upon the legal liability of the CPA when associated with:

(1) A review of annual statements.

(2) Unaudited financial statements.

(3) An audit resulting in a disclaimer of opinion.

(4) Letters for underwriters.

(AICPA, adapted)

Problems

4–32.   Risk Capital Limited, a publicly held Delaware corporation, was considering the purchase of a substantial amount of the treasury stock held by Florida Sunshine Corporation, a closely held corporation. Initial discussions with the Florida Sunshine Corporation began late in 200X.

Wilson and Wyatt, CPAs, Florida Sunshine's public accountants, regularly prepared quarterly and annual unaudited financial statements. The most recently prepared unaudited financial statements were for the fiscal year ended September 30, 200X.

On November 15, 200X, after protracted negotiations, Risk Capital agreed to purchase 100,000 shares of no-par, Class A treasury stock of Florida Sunshine at $12.50 per share. However, Risk Capital insisted upon audited statements for the calendar year 200X. The contract specifically provided: "Risk Capital shall have the right to rescind the purchase of said stock if the audited financial statements of Florida Sunshine for calendar year 200X show a material adverse change in the financial position of the Corporation."

At the request of Florida Sunshine, Wilson and Wyatt audited the company's financial statements for the year ended December 31, 200X. The December 31, 200X, audited financial statements furnished to Florida Sunshine by Wilson and Wyatt showed no material adverse change from the September 30, 200X, unaudited statements. Risk Capital relied upon the audited statements and purchased the treasury stock of Florida Sunshine. It was subsequently discovered that, as of the balance sheet date, the audited statements contained several misstatements and that in fact there had been a material adverse change in the financial position of the corporation. Florida Sunshine has become insolvent, and Risk Capital will lose virtually its entire investment.

Risk Capital seeks recovery against Wilson and Wyatt.

Required: a. Discuss each of the theories of liability that Risk Capital will probably assert as its basis for recovery.

b. Assuming that only ordinary negligence by Wilson and Wyatt is proved, will Risk Capital prevail? State yes or no and explain.

4–33. Meglow Corporation, a closely held manufacturer of dresses and blouses, sought a loan from Busch Factors. Busch had previously extended $50,000 credit to Meglow but refused to lend any additional money without obtaining copies of Meglow's audited financial statements.

Meglow contacted the public accounting firm of Seavers & Dean to perform the audit. In arranging for the audit, Meglow clearly indicated that its purpose was to satisfy Busch Factors as to the corporation's sound financial condition and to obtain an additional loan of $100,000. Seavers & Dean accepted the engagement, performed the audit in a negligent manner, and rendered an unqualified opinion. If an adequate audit had been performed, the financial statements would have been found to be misleading.

Meglow submitted the audited financial statements to Busch Factors and obtained an additional loan of $70,000. Busch refused to lend more than that amount. After several other factors also refused, Meglow finally was able to persuade Maxwell Department Stores, one of its customers, to lend the additional $30,000. Maxwell relied upon the financial statements audited by Seavers & Dean.

Meglow is now in bankruptcy, and Busch seeks to collect from Seavers & Dean the $120,000 it loaned Meglow. Maxwell seeks to recover from Seavers & Dean the $30,000 it loaned Meglow.

Required: a. Will Busch recover? Explain.

b. Will Maxwell recover? Explain.

4–34. After Commuter Airlines was forced into bankruptcy, the company's stockholders brought suit against Thomas & Ross, the company's independent auditors. Three independent assumptions concerning this litigation are listed below:

a. Commuter Airlines is not under SEC jurisdiction. The plaintiff's suit is brought under common law in a state court that adheres to the *Ultramares* doctrine of auditors' liability.

b. Commuter Airlines had recently issued its publicly held securities. The stockholders' suit is brought in federal court under the Securities Act of 1933.

c. Commuter Airlines is under SEC jurisdiction. The stockholders' suit is brought in federal court alleging violations of Sections 18(a) and 10(b) of the Securities Exchange Act of 1934.

Required: Under each of the independent assumptions, separately explain (1) the allegations that must be proved in court by the plaintiffs, and (2) any defenses for which the auditors must bear the burden of proof if they are to avoid or reduce their liability.

4–35. Charles Worthington, the founding and senior partner of a successful and respected public accounting firm, was a highly competent practitioner who always emphasized high professional standards. One of the policies of the firm was that all reports by members or staff be submitted to Worthington for review.

Recently, Arthur Craft, a junior partner in the firm, received a phone call from Herbert Flack, a close personal friend. Flack informed Craft that he, his family, and some friends were planning to create a corporation to engage in various land development ventures; that various members of the family are presently in a partnership (Flack Ventures), which holds some land and other assets; and that the partnership would contribute all its assets to the new corporation and the corporation would assume the liabilities of the partnership.

Flack asked Craft to prepare a balance sheet of the partnership that he could show to members of his family, who were in the partnership, and to friends, to determine whether they might have an interest in joining in the formation and financing of the new corporation. Flack said he had the partnership general ledger in front of him and proceeded to read to Craft the names of the accounts and their balances at the end of the latest month. Craft took the notes he made during the telephone conversation with Flack, classified and organized the data into a conventional balance sheet, and had his secretary type the balance sheet and an accompanying letter on firm stationery. He did not consult Worthington on this matter or submit this work to him for review.

The transmittal letter stated: "We have reviewed the books and records of Flack Ventures, a partnership, and have prepared the attached balance sheet at March 31, 200X. We did not perform an audit in conformity with generally accepted auditing standards, and therefore do not express an opinion on the accompanying balance sheet." The balance sheet was prominently marked "unaudited." Craft signed the letter and instructed his secretary to send it to Flack.

Required: What legal problems are suggested by these facts? Explain.

4–36.   The limitations on professional responsibilities of CPAs when they are associated with unaudited financial statements are often misunderstood. These misunderstandings can be reduced substantially if CPAs carefully follow professional pronouncements in the course of their work and take other appropriate measures.

Required: The following list describes four situations CPAs may encounter in their association with and preparation of unaudited financial statements. Briefly discuss the extent of the CPAs' responsibilities and, if appropriate, the actions to be taken to minimize misunderstandings. Identify your answers to correspond with the letters in the following list.

a. A CPA was engaged by telephone to perform accounting work, including the compilation of financial statements. His client believes that the CPA has been engaged to audit the financial statements and examine the records accordingly.

b. A group of business executives who own a farm managed by an independent agent engage Linda Lopez, a CPA, to compile quarterly unaudited financial statements for them. The CPA compiles the financial statements from information given to her by the independent agent. Subsequently, the business executives find the statements were inaccurate because their independent agent was embezzling funds. The executives refuse to pay the CPA's fee and blame her for allowing the situation to go undetected, contending that she should not have relied on representations from the independent agent.

c. In comparing the trial balance with the general ledger, a CPA finds an account labeled "Audit Fees" in which the client has accumulated the CPA's quarterly billings for accounting services including the compilation of quarterly unaudited financial statements.

d. To determine appropriate account classification, John Day, CPA, reviewed a number of the client's invoices. He noted in his working papers that some invoices were missing but did nothing further because he thought they did not affect the unaudited financial statements he was compiling. When the client subsequently discovered that invoices were missing, he contended that the CPA should not have ignored the missing invoices when compiling the financial statements and had a responsibility to at least inform him that they were missing.

4–37.   Mark Williams, CPA, was engaged by Jackson Financial Development Company to audit the financial statements of Apex Construction Company, a small closely held corporation. Williams was told when he was engaged that Jackson Financial needed reliable financial statements that would be used to determine whether to purchase a substantial amount of Apex Construction's convertible debentures at the price asked by the estate of one of Apex's former directors.

Williams performed his audit in a negligent manner. As a result of his negligence, he failed to discover substantial defalcations by Carl Brown, the Apex controller. Jackson Financial purchased the debentures, but it would not have done so if the defalcations had been discovered. After discovery of the fraud, Jackson Financial promptly sold them for the highest price offered in the market at a $70,000 loss.

Required: *a.* What liability does Williams have to Jackson Financial? Explain.

b. If Apex Construction also sues Williams for negligence, what are the probable legal defenses Williams's attorney would raise? Explain.

c. Will the negligence of Mark Williams, CPA, prevent him from recovering on a liability insurance policy covering the practice of his profession? Explain.

4–38.   Cragsmore & Company, a medium-sized partnership of CPAs, was engaged by Marlowe Manufacturing, Inc., a closely held corporation, to audit its financial statements for the year ended December 31, 200X.

Before preparing the audit report, William Cragsmore, a partner, and Joan Willmore, a staff senior, reviewed the disclosures necessary in the notes to the financial statements. One note involved the terms, costs, and obligations of a lease between Marlowe and Acme Leasing Company.

Willmore suggested that the note disclose the following: "Acme Leasing Company is owned by persons who have a 35 percent interest in the capital stock and who are officers of Marlowe Manufacturing, Inc."

On Cragsmore's recommendation, this was revised by substituting "minority shareholders" for "persons who have a 35 percent interest in the capital stock and who are officers."

The audit report and financial statements were forwarded to Marlowe Manufacturing for review. The officer-shareholders of Marlowe who also owned Acme Leasing objected to the revised wording and insisted that the note be changed to describe the relationship between Acme and Marlowe as merely one of affiliation. Cragsmore acceded to this request.

The audit report was issued on this basis with an unqualified opinion. But the working papers included the drafts that showed the changes in the wording of the note.

Subsequent to delivery of the audit report, Marlowe suffered a substantial uninsured fire loss and was forced into bankruptcy. The failure of Marlowe to carry any fire insurance coverage was not noted in the financial statements.

Required: What legal problems for Cragsmore & Company are suggested by these facts? Discuss.

(AICPA, adapted)

4–39. Items (*a*) through (*f*) relate to what a plaintiff who purchased securities must prove in a civil liability suit against a CPA. For each item, determine whether it must be proved assuming application of the following acts:

1. Only applies to Section 11 of the 1933 Securities Act.
2. Only applies to Section 10(b) of the Securities Exchange Act.
3. Applies to both acts.
4. Applies to neither of the acts.

The plaintiff security purchaser must allege or prove:

a. Material misstatements were included in a filed document.
b. A monetary loss occurred.
c. Lack of due diligence by the CPA.
d. Privity with the CPA.
e. Reliance on the document.
f. The CPA had scienter.

(AICPA, adapted)

In-Class Team Case

4–40. The following appeared in a brief article in a major business newspaper: A local court is in the process of ruling on whether the public accounting firm of James Willis and Co., CPAs, PC, should be required to pay all or part of $16 million in damages relating to Geiger Co. for failing to detect a scheme to defraud the company, a former audit client.

Geiger Co., an SEC registrant, charges that Willis was negligent in failing to discover fraud committed by the company's controller and wants Willis to foot the bill for all $16 million in claims by and against the company. The company claims that if it had known about the fraud, it could have stopped it and recovered financially. The bank involved claims that it granted the loan based on misstated financial statements. The shareholders involved claim that they purchased the stock on the American Stock Exchange at an inflated price due to the misstated financial statements. They acknowledged that while stock had been outstanding and traded for many years (10) prior to the fraud, they made their investment decisions relying upon the misstated financial statements.

Willis's general counsel said, "We anxiously await a decision that will show that CPAs are not guarantors for everything that goes on in the company." Geiger Co.'s lawyer said that she anxiously awaited a decision because it will "clearly show that CPAs are liable for finding fraud."

Assume that Willis performed that audit with ordinary negligence and this ordinary negligence is the reason that the defalcation was not discovered and recovered. Further, assume that the $16,000,000 of loss is properly allocated as follows:

Company itself	$8,000,000
Bank that gave a commercial loan	5,000,000
Shareholders	3,000,000

Reply from the perspective that the only issues involved here are whether the plaintiffs involved may recover from a CPA that has performed the engagement with this degree of negligence. Assume the situation described above, and assume that other elements of proof (e.g., loss, proximate cause) are not at issue.

Required: *a.* Assume that the case is brought under common law, and that the state in which Geiger Co. is headquartered follows the *known user* approach for third-party legal liability.

1. Should Willis be found liable to the company, Geiger Co., itself? Explain.
2. Should Willis be found liable if sued by a bank that used the financial statements as a basis for providing a loan and, due to the misstatement, lost $5 million on the loan? Explain.
3. Should Willis be found liable if sued by shareholders who invested in the stock of the company? Assume these investors invested relying upon the misstated financial statements and as a result thereof lost $3 million. Explain.

4. Which of answers 1, 2, and 3 might change if the jurisdiction involved followed the *Restatement of Torts* approach? Explain.

b. Assume that the case is brought under the Securities Act of 1933. Answer the following from the perspective of CPA liability under that act.

1. Should Willis be found liable to the company, Geiger Co., itself? Explain.

2. Should Willis be found liable if sued by a bank that used the financial statements as a basis for providing a loan and, due to the misstatement, lost $5 million on the loan? Explain.

3. Should Willis be found liable if sued by shareholders who invested in the stock of the company? Assume these investors invested relying upon the misstated financial statements and as a result thereof lost $3 million. Explain.

4. Which, if any, of answers 1, 2, and 3 might change if the stock involved had been issued to the public for the first time and the financial statements involved had been included in a registration statement for the securities? Explain.

c. Assume that the case is brought under the Securities Exchange Act of 1934. Answer the following from the perspective of CPA liability under that act.

1. Should Willis be found liable to the company, Geiger Co., itself? Explain.

2. Should Willis be found liable if sued by a bank that used the financial statements as a basis for providing a loan and, due to the misstatement, lost $5 million on the loan? Explain.

3. Should Willis be found liable if sued by shareholders who invested in the stock of the company? Assume these investors invested relying upon the misstated financial statements and as a result thereof lost $3 million. Explain.

Research and Discussion Case

4–41. You are a partner in the Denver office of a national public accounting firm. During the audit of Mountain Resources, you learn that this audit client is negotiating to sell some of its unproved oil and gas properties to SuperFund, a large investment company. SuperFund is an audit client of your New York office.

Mountain Resources acquired these properties several years ago at a cost of $15 million. The company drilled several exploratory wells but found no developable resources. Last year, you and Mountain Resources agreed that the value of these unproved properties had been "impaired" as defined in paragraph 28 of *FASB 19*. The company wrote the carrying value of the properties down to an estimated realizable value of $9 million and recognized a $6 million loss. You concurred with this treatment and issued an unqualified auditors' report on the company's financial statements.

You are now amazed to learn that the sales price for these properties being discussed by Mountain Resources and SuperFund is $42 million. You cannot understand why SuperFund would pay such a high price and you wonder what representations Mountain Resources may have made to SuperFund concerning these properties. The management of Mountain Resources declines to discuss the details of the negotiations with you, calling them "quite delicate" and correctly pointing out that the future sale of these properties will not affect the financial statements currently under audit.

Required:

a. Summarize the arguments for advising SuperFund (through your New York office) that you consider the properties grossly overpriced at $42 million.

b. Summarize the arguments for remaining silent and not offering any advice to SuperFund on this matter.

c. Express your personal opinion as to the course of action you should take. Indicate which arguments from part (*a*) or part (*b*) most influenced your decision.

Suggested References

AICPA, *Professional Standards,* Volume 2, Commerce Clearing House, Section ET 301 (*Code of Professional Conduct,* Rule 301).

AICPA, *Statement on Auditing Standards No. 99,* "Consideration of Fraud in a Financial Statement Audit" (New York, 2003) AU 316.

AICPA, *Statement on Auditing Standards No. 54,* "Illegal Acts by Clients" (New York, 1988) AU 317.

FASB Statement No. 19, "Financial Accounting and Reporting by Oil and Gas Producing Companies," paragraphs 15, 28, and 208.

Chapter 5

Audit Evidence and Documentation

Chapter learning objectives

After studying this chapter, you should be able to:

LO1. Explain the relationship between audit evidence and audit risk.

LO2. Identify and explain the components of audit risk.

LO3. Distinguish between the concepts of competence and sufficiency as they apply to audit evidence.

LO4. List and describe types of audit evidence.

LO5. Describe the purposes of audit documentation.

LO6. Discuss the factors that affect the auditors' judgment as to the nature and extent of audit documentation.

LO7. Identify matters that must be included in audit working papers.

LO8. Describe the types of working papers and the way they are organized.

During financial statement audits, the auditors gather and evaluate *audit evidence,* also referred to as *evidence* or *evidential matter,* to form an opinion about whether the financial statements follow the appropriate criteria, usually generally accepted accounting principles. The auditors must gather sufficient competent audit evidence to provide an adequate basis for their opinion on the financial statements.

The Relationship of Audit Risk to Audit Evidence

Learning Objective 1

As discussed in Chapter 2, the term **audit risk** refers to the possibility that the auditors may unknowingly fail to appropriately modify their opinion on financial statements that are materially misstated. In other words, it is the risk that the auditors will issue an unqualified opinion on financial statements that contain a material departure from generally accepted accounting principles. Audit risk is reduced by gathering audit evidence—the more competent evidence that is gathered, the less audit risk assumed. Auditors must gather sufficient audit evidence to reduce audit risk to a low level in every audit. One obvious way to gather additional evidence is to increase the extent of the audit procedures. However, additional evidence may also be obtained by selecting more effective audit procedures, or by performing the procedures closer to (or after) the balance sheet date. The requirement to obtain sufficient competent evidence is reflected in the third standard of fieldwork, which states:

> *Sufficient competent evidential matter* is to be obtained through inspection, observation, inquiries, and confirmations to afford a reasonable basis for an opinion regarding the financial statements under audit. [emphasis added]

Financial Statement Assertions

Audit procedures are designed to obtain evidence about management's assertions that are embodied in the financial statements. When the auditors have gathered sufficient audit evidence about each material financial statement assertion, they have sufficient evidence to support their opinion. The financial statement assertions, as summarized in *SAS 31* (AU 326), "Evidential Matter," include:

1. *Existence or occurrence*—assets, liabilities, and owners' equity reflected in the financial statements exist; the recorded transactions have occurred.
2. *Completeness*—all transactions, assets, liabilities, and owners' equity that should be presented in the financial statements are included.
3. *Rights and obligations*—the client has rights to assets and obligations to pay liabilities that are included in the financial statements.
4. *Valuation or allocation*—assets, liabilities, owners' equity, revenues, and expenses are presented at amounts that are determined in accordance with generally accepted accounting principles.
5. *Presentation and disclosure*—accounts are described and classified in the financial statements in accordance with generally accepted accounting principles, and disclosures are materially correct, complete, and clearly communicated.

The auditors use the above assertions in assessing risks by considering the different types of potential misstatements that might occur and thereby designing appropriate audit procedures. In combination, the assertions address the fair presentation of:

- Financial statement *account balances.*
- *Transactions and events* occurring during the period under audit.
- *Presentations and disclosures.*

FIGURE 5.1   **International Auditing and Assurance Standards Board Presentation of Financial Statement Assertions***

Assertions about Account Balances	Assertions about Transactions and Events	Assertions about Presentation and Disclosure
Existence—Assets, liabilities, and equity interests exist.	*Occurrence*—Transactions and events that have been recorded have occurred and pertain to the entity.	*Occurrence*—Disclosed events and transactions have occurred.
Rights and obligations—The entity holds or controls the rights to assets, and liabilities are the obligations of the entity.		*Rights and obligations*—Disclosed events pertain to the entity.
Completeness—All assets, liabilities, and equity interests have been recorded.	*Completeness*—All transactions and events have been recorded.	*Completeness*—All disclosures that should have been included have been included.
Valuation and allocation—Assets, liabilities, and equity interests are included at appropriate amounts.	*Accuracy*—Amounts and other data relating to recorded transactions have been recorded appropriately.	*Accuracy and valuation*—Information is disclosed fairly and at appropriate amounts.
	Cutoff—Transactions and events have been recorded in the correct accounting period.	
	Classification—Transactions and events have been recorded in the proper accounts.	*Classification and understandability*—Information is presented and described clearly.

*International Standards on Auditing, Section 500 (revised), *Audit Evidence.*

Chapter 6 presents more information on the nature of these assertions, which are emphasized throughout this text.

An alternate approach to considering financial statement assertions is to derive specific financial statement assertions for each of the three financial statement components described above—balances, transactions, and disclosures. This is the approach taken in international auditing standards issued by the International Auditing and Assurance Standards Board; these assertions are presented in Figure 5.1. While these expanded assertions are consistent with the five assertions presented in *SAS 31*, they provide additional details.

Audit Risk at the Assertion Level

Learning Objective 2

Since an audit involves gathering evidence about each material financial statement assertion, audit risk can be evaluated at the assertion level. For each financial statement account, *audit risk* consists of the (1) risk that a material misstatement in an assertion about the account has occurred, and (2) risk that the auditors do not detect the misstatement. The first risk, the risk of material misstatement, may be separated into two components—inherent risk and control risk. The risk that auditors will not detect the misstatement is called detection risk.

Inherent Risk

The possibility of a material misstatement of an assertion before considering the client's internal control is referred to as **inherent risk.** Factors that affect inherent risk relate to either the nature of the client and its industry, or to the nature of the particular financial statement account.

Business characteristics of the client and its industry affect the inherent risk of the audit as a whole. Therefore, these characteristics affect the assertions about a number of financial statement accounts. For example, business characteristics such as the following are indicative of high inherent risk:

- Inconsistent profitability of the client relative to other firms in the industry.
- Operating results that are highly sensitive to economic factors.
- Going concern problems.
- Large known and likely misstatements detected in prior audits.
- Substantial turnover, questionable reputation, or inadequate accounting skills of management.

Since these factors increase the overall risk of the audit, they are important to the auditors' decisions about whether to accept the engagement.

Inherent risk also varies by the nature of the account. Assume that in a given business the balance of the Inventory account amounts to only one-fifth that of the Property and Equipment account. Does this relationship indicate that the auditors should spend only one-fifth as much time in the audit of inventory as in the audit of plant and equipment? The answer to this question is no. Inventory is much more susceptible to error or theft than are plant and equipment, and the great number of inventory transactions affords an opportunity for misstatements to be well hidden. Inherent risk also varies by the assertion about a particular account. As an example, valuation of assets is often a more difficult assertion to audit than is existence of the assets. In general, assertions with high inherent risk involve:

- Difficult-to-audit transactions or balances.
- Complex calculations.
- Difficult accounting issues.
- Significant judgment by management.
- Valuations that vary significantly based on economic factors.

In assessing inherent risk, it is often useful to segregate transactions into three types—routine, nonroutine, and estimation. **Routine transactions** involve recurring financial statement activities recorded in the accounting records in the normal course of business. Examples of routine transactions are sales, purchases, cash disbursements, cash receipts, and payroll transactions. The routine nature of these transactions restricts inherent risk, although controls certainly must be implemented to assure proper recording.

Nonroutine transactions involve activities that occur only periodically, such as the taking of physical inventories, calculating depreciation expense, and adjusting financial statements for foreign currency gains and losses. Inherent risk may be high for nonroutine transactions because they are not part of the normal flow of transactions and specialized skills may be needed to perform the activity.

Generally, the transactions with the highest level of inherent risk are **estimation transactions** which are the activities that create accounting estimates. These activities have high inherent risk because they involve management judgments or assumptions. Examples of estimation transactions include estimating the allowance for uncollectible accounts, establishing warranty reserves, and assessing assets for impairment.

The auditors use their knowledge of the client's industry and the nature of its operations, including information obtained in prior year audits, to assess inherent risk for the financial statement assertions.

Control Risk

The risk that a material misstatement will not be prevented or detected on a timely basis by the client's internal control is referred to as **control risk.** This risk is entirely based on the effectiveness of the client's internal control.

To assess control risk, auditors consider the client's controls, emphasizing those controls that affect the reliability of financial reporting. Well-designed controls that operate effectively increase the reliability of accounting data. Errors are prevented or brought to light on a timely basis by the built-in proofs and cross-checks that are in the system.

To obtain an understanding of the client's internal control and to determine whether it is designed and operating effectively, the auditors use a combination of inquiry, inspection, observation, and reperformance procedures. If the auditors find that the client has designed effective internal control for a particular account and that the prescribed practices operate effectively in day-to-day operations, they will assess control risk for the related assertions to be low, and thereby accept a higher level of detection risk. Thus, the effectiveness of the client's internal control is a major factor in determining how much evidence the auditors will gather to restrict detection risk. Detailed descriptions of the auditors' consideration of internal control are included in Chapter 7.

Detection Risk

The risk that the auditors will fail to detect the misstatement with their audit procedures is called **detection risk.** In other words, detection risk is the possibility that the auditors' procedures will lead them to conclude that a material misstatement does *not* exist in an account or assertion when in fact such misstatement does exist. Detection risk is restricted by performing **substantive tests.** For each account, the scope of the auditors' substantive tests, including their nature, timing, and extent, determines the level of detection risk. The specific substantive tests for various accounts and transactions are described in Chapters 10 through 16.

Audit Risk Illustrated

Figure 5.2 describes the interrelationships between the three components of audit risk. The bag of sand in the figure represents *inherent risk,* the susceptibility of an account balance to material misstatements. The sieves represent the ways by which the client and the auditors attempt to remove the misstatements from the financial statements. The first sieve represents the client's internal control, and the risk that it will fail to detect or prevent a misstatement is *control risk.* The auditors' audit procedures are represented by the second sieve, and the risk that it will fail to detect a misstatement is *detection risk.* The risk that the misstatements will get through both sieves is *audit risk.*

Measuring Audit Risk

In practice the various components of audit risk are not typically quantified. Instead, the auditors usually use qualitative categories, such as low risk, moderate risk, and maximum risk. Also, auditors may either consider the risk of material misstatement directly, or they may separately consider its components of inherent risk and control risk. For purposes of considering the relationships among the risks, we here provide a separate assessment approach. The professional standards allow either a quantified or a nonquantitative approach, but they include the

FIGURE 5.2
An Illustration of Audit Risk

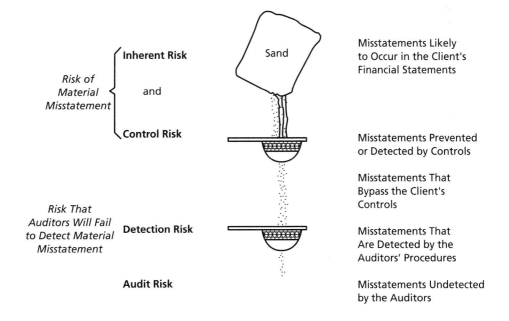

Inherent Risk	Misstatements Likely to Occur in the Client's Financial Statements
Risk of Material Misstatement { and	
Control Risk	Misstatements Prevented or Detected by Controls
	Misstatements That Bypass the Client's Controls
Risk That Auditors Will Fail to Detect Material Misstatement — Detection Risk	Misstatements That Are Detected by the Auditors' Procedures
Audit Risk	Misstatements Undetected by the Auditors

following formula to illustrate the relationships among audit risk, inherent risk, control risk, and detection risk:

$$AR = IR \times CR \times DR$$

where:

AR = Audit risk
IR = Inherent risk
CR = Control risk
DR = Detection risk

To illustrate how audit risk may be quantified, assume that the auditors have assessed inherent risk for a particular assertion at 50 percent and control risk at 40 percent. In addition, they have performed audit procedures that they believe have a 20 percent risk of failing to detect a material misstatement in the assertion. The audit risk for the assertion may be computed as follows:

$$AR = IR \times CR \times DR$$
$$= .50 \times .40 \times .20$$
$$= .04$$

Thus, the auditors face a 4 percent audit risk that material misstatement has occurred and evaded both the client's controls and the auditors' procedures. Realize, however, that the model expresses general relationships and is not necessarily intended to be a mathematical model to precisely consider the factors that influence audit risk in actual audit situations.

It is important to realize that while auditors gather evidence to *assess* inherent risk and control risk, they gather evidence to *restrict* detection risk to the appropriate level. Inherent risk and control risk are a function of the client and its operating environment. Regardless of how much evidence the auditors gather, they cannot change these risks. Therefore, evidence gathered by the auditors is used to assess the levels of inherent and control risk.

Detection risk, on the other hand, is a function of the effectiveness of the audit procedures performed. If the auditors wish to reduce the level of detection risk, they simply obtain additional competent evidence. As a result, detection risk is the only risk that is completely a function of the sufficiency of the procedures performed by the auditors.

Audit Evidence

Learning Objective 3

Audit evidence is all of the information used by an auditor in arriving at conclusions on which the audit opinion is based. This information includes both the accounting records underlying the financial statements and a variety of types of other information.

What constitutes **sufficient** competent audit evidence? This question arises repeatedly when planning and performing every audit. When CPAs are accused of negligence in the performance of an audit, the answer to this question will often determine their innocence or guilt. To provide auditors with guidelines for answering this question, the Auditing Standards Board has issued *SAS 31* (AU 326).

To be **competent,** evidence must be both *relevant* and *valid*. For evidence to be relevant it must relate to the assertion being considered. For example, an auditor may analyze the aging of the accounts receivable and the subsequent collection of receivables to obtain audit evidence of the *valuation* assertion for the allowance for doubtful accounts.

The validity (reliability) of evidence is dependent on the circumstances in which it is obtained. While this makes generalizations difficult and subject to exceptions, audit evidence is *ordinarily* more valid when it is:

1. Obtained from independent sources *outside the client company.*
2. Generated internally through a system with *effective controls.*
3. Obtained *directly* by the auditor (e.g., observation of application of a control), rather than indirectly or by inference (e.g., inquiry about application of a control).

4. *Documentary* in form (paper, electronic media, or other media) rather than an oral representation.

5. Provided by *original documents* rather than photocopies or facsimiles.

In addition to the above, audit evidence that arises from two or more different sources provides auditors more total assurance than the items would provide if considered individually. For example, an auditor may observe an employee opening the mail and processing cash receipts to evaluate the operating effectiveness of controls over cash receipts. But, because that observation is only at the point in time it is made, the auditor also may make inquiries of client personnel and inspect documentation of the operation of such controls to obtain a combination of audit evidence that is considered very reliable. Conversely, if inconsistencies arise between the sources of audit evidence, the auditor may derive little assurance with respect to the effective operation of the control.

The term *sufficient* relates to the quantity of evidence that the auditors should obtain. The quantity of audit evidence needed is affected by the risk of misstatements (the greater the risk, the more audit evidence required) and also the reliability of the evidence. In the great majority of cases the auditor finds it necessary to rely on evidence that is persuasive rather than conclusive. Auditors are seldom convinced beyond *all* doubt that all aspects of the statements are properly stated.

Types of Audit Evidence

Learning Objective 4

The auditors gather a combination of many types of audit evidence to adequately restrict audit risk. The *major types* of audit evidence may be summarized as follows:

1. Accounting information system
2. Documentary evidence
3. Third-party representations
4. Physical evidence
5. Computations
6. Data interrelationships
7. Client representations

1. Accounting Information System

An accounting information system consists of the methods and records established to record, process, summarize, and report the company's transactions and to maintain accountability over related assets, liability, and equity. This includes the initial entries which are often a part of integrated information systems. Ordinarily included here are the ledgers and journals (or equivalent electronic tables that capture those data).

Since the financial statements are prepared based upon the accounting records, auditors are required to document in their working papers how the accounting records agree or reconcile with the financial statements. They are also required to understand the financial reporting process, including how:

• Transactions are entered into the general ledger (or equivalent record).

• Journal entries (including adjustments) are initiated, recorded, and processed in the general ledger.

The records themselves and their support provide the auditors with some evidence when they test record accuracy through procedures such as analysis, reperforming procedures followed in the financial reporting process, and reconciling related types of information. As an example, consider the procedure of verifying an amount in the financial statements by tracing it back through the accounting records. The auditors will ordinarily carry this process through the ledgers to the journals and compare the item to such basic documentary evidence as a paid check, invoice, or other source documents. The consistency of processing among the various records in and of itself provides a certain amount of audit evidence.

The dependability of ledgers and journals as evidence is indicated by the extent of internal control over their preparation. Whenever possible, subsidiary ledgers for receivables, payables, and plant equipment should be maintained by persons not responsible for the general ledger. All general journal entries should be approved in writing by the controller or other official. If ledgers and journals are produced by a computer system, various computer controls should be in effect. When controls of this type exist and the records appear to be well maintained, the auditors may regard the ledgers and journals as affording some support for the financial statements.

2. Documentary Evidence

Documentary evidence includes a variety of records in support of the company's business and accounting information system, including checks, invoices, contracts, and minutes of meetings. The competence of documentary evidence depends in part on whether it was created within the company (e.g., a sales invoice) or outside the company (e.g., a vendor's invoice). Some documents created within the company (e.g., checks) are sent outside the organization for endorsement and processing; because of this critical review by outsiders, these documents are regarded as more reliable than other documents created by client personnel.

In appraising the reliability of documentary evidence, the auditors should consider whether the document is of a type that could easily be forged or created in its entirety by a dishonest employee. A stock certificate evidencing an investment in marketable securities is usually elaborately engraved and would be difficult to falsify. On the other hand, a note receivable may be created by anyone in a moment either merely by filling in the blank spaces in one of the standard note forms available at any office supply store or by filling data into a template included in computer software.

Documentary Evidence Created Outside the Client Organization and Transmitted Directly to the Auditors   A few documents are prepared outside the client organization and transmitted directly to the auditors. An example is the *cutoff bank statement,* which is a bank statement covering a specified number of business days (usually 7 to 10) after the client's balance sheet date. Auditors use this statement to determine that reconciling items shown on the year-end bank statement are complete and have cleared the bank within a reasonable time. Cutoff bank statements are discussed in more detail in Chapter 10.

Documentary Evidence Created Outside the Client Organization and Held by the Client   Many externally created documents examined by the auditors will be in the client's possession. Examples include bank statements, vendors' invoices and statements, property tax bills, notes payable, contracts, customers' purchase orders, and stock and bond certificates. In deciding how much reliance to place upon this type of evidence, the auditors should consider whether the document is of a type that could be easily created or altered by someone in the client's employ. The auditors should be particularly cautious in accepting as audit evidence photo or fax copies of documents, or documents that appear to have been altered in any way. Both photo and fax copies may easily be altered in a manner that makes detection difficult. Alterations to a document may have been made deliberately to misstate the facts and to mislead auditors or others who rely upon the document.

In pointing out the possibility that externally created documents in the client's possession might have been forged or altered, it is not intended to discredit this type of evidence. Externally created documents in the possession of the client are used extensively by auditors and are considered, in general, as a stronger type of evidence than documents created by the client.

Documentary Evidence Created and Held within the Client Organization   No doubt the most dependable single piece of *documentary evidence* created within the client's organization is a paid check. The check bears the endorsement of the payee and a perforation or stamp indicating payment by the bank. Because of this review and processing of a check by outsiders, the auditors will usually look upon a paid check as a strong type of evidence. The paid check may be viewed as evidence that an asset was acquired at a given cost, or as proof that a liability was paid or an expense incurred.

Most documents created within the client organization represent a lower quality of evidence than a paid check because they circulate only within the company and do not receive the critical review of an outsider. Examples of internally created documents that do not leave the client's possession are sales invoices, shipping notices, purchase orders, receiving reports, and credit memoranda. Of course, the original copy of a sales invoice or purchase order is sent to the customer or supplier, but the copy available for the auditor's inspection has not left the client's possession.

The degree of reliance to be placed on documents created and used only within the organization depends on the effectiveness of the internal control. If the control procedures are so designed that a document prepared by one person must be critically reviewed by another, and if all documents are serially numbered and all numbers in the series accounted for, these documents may represent reasonably good evidence. Adequate internal control will also provide for extensive segregation of duties so that no one employee handles a transaction from beginning to end. An employee who maintains records or creates documents, such as credit memoranda, should not have access to cash. Under these conditions there is no incentive for an employee to falsify a document, since the employee creating documents does not have custody of assets.

On the other hand, if internal control is weak, the auditors cannot place as much reliance on documentary evidence created within the organization and not reviewed by outsiders. If an employee is authorized to create documents such as sales invoices and credit memoranda and also has access to cash, an incentive exists to falsify documents to conceal a theft. If documents are not controlled by serial numbers, the possibility arises that the auditors are not being given access to all documents or that duplicates are being used to support fictitious transactions. Not only is there the danger of fictitious documents being created to cover theft by an employee, but also there is the possibility that management is purposely presenting misleading financial statements and has prepared false supporting documents for the purpose of deceiving the auditors.

"Electronic Documents" Much of the "hard-copy" documentation described above is not maintained when the client has a sophisticated computerized accounting system. When an **electronic data interchange (EDI)** system is used, source documents such as invoices, purchase orders, checks, and bills of lading are replaced with "electronic documents." A purchase transaction may be automatically initiated by a client's computer by sending an electronic message directly to a supplier's computer system. This electronic message replaces the traditional purchase order. The other documentation of the purchase transaction may consist of an invoice and a bill of lading generated in electronic form by the supplier's computer system. To determine the degree of reliance that may be placed upon such electronic documents, the auditors will test the controls over the computer system. Chapter 8 describes the controls that are used in computerized information systems in detail and Chapters 10 through 16 include illustrations of such systems.

3. Third-Party Representations

Auditors obtain a variety of representations from a number of outside parties, such as the client's customers, vendors, financial institutions, and attorneys. In addition, evidence may be obtained from specialists in some audits.

Confirmations Confirmation requests are used in the audit of a number of accounts, including cash, accounts and notes receivable, debt accounts, and capital stock accounts. As an example, in the audit of accounts receivable, customers are requested by the client to send a reply directly to the auditors that confirms the amount owed to the client.

As indicated in *SAS 67* (AU 330), "The Confirmation Process," confirmation requests to third parties (e.g., customers, vendors, financial institutions) can be used to address any of the assertions about a particular financial statement amount. However, they do not address all assertions equally well. Confirmations generally are effective at providing evidence about the assertion of *existence* of accounts, but they are less effective at addressing *completeness* and the appropriate *valuation.* For example, while a returned account receivable confirmation provides reliable evidence about the existence of an obligation, it does not address whether the debtor can actually pay the obligation. The account may actually be worthless.

To ensure the reliability of the confirmation process, the auditors should carefully design the confirmation requests to seek the appropriate information and make it easy for the recipient to respond. The auditors also should consider whether it is necessary to specifically address the confirmation request to an individual in the outside organization that has easy access to the information being confirmed. As an example, information about the terms of a debt agreement at a financial institution might best be sent to the client's loan officer.

To make sure that the confirmation reply comes directly to the auditors and not to the client, the auditors will enclose with the confirmation request a return envelope addressed to the auditors' office. If the replies were addressed to the auditors at the client's place of business, an opportunity would exist for someone in the client's organization to intercept a returned confirmation and alter the information reported, or even destroy the letter. The envelope containing the confirmation should bear the auditors' return address. In that way if the address is fictitious, the confirmation may be returned by the post office directly to the auditors.

Lawyers' Letters   The primary source of information about litigation that is pending against the client is obtained from *lawyers' letters*. To obtain these letters, the auditors ask the client to request their attorneys to furnish directly to the auditors their assessments of the outcomes of litigation being handled for the client. Lawyers' letters are discussed in Chapter 16.

Reports of Specialists   Auditors may not be experts in performing such technical tasks as judging the value of highly specialized inventory or making actuarial computations to verify liabilities for postretirement benefits. Audit evidence about such matters is best obtained from qualified specialists. Other examples of audit tasks that may require the use of a specialist include valuations of works of art or restricted securities, and legal interpretations of regulations or contracts.

In *SAS 73* (AU 336), "Using the Work of a Specialist," the Auditing Standards Board recognized the necessity for auditors to consult with experts, when appropriate, as a means of gathering competent audit evidence. *SAS 73* defines a **specialist** as a person possessing special skill or knowledge in a field other than accounting and auditing, giving as examples actuaries, appraisers, attorneys, engineers, environmental consultants, and geologists. Regardless of whether the specialist is hired by the client or by the auditors, the provisions of *SAS 73* must be followed.

The auditors are responsible for performing procedures to evaluate the adequacy of the professional qualifications and reputation of the specialist. This usually involves making inquiries about the specialist's credentials and experience. Auditors cannot accept a specialist's findings blindly; they must obtain an understanding of the methods or assumptions used to determine whether the findings are suitable for corroborating the financial statements. They should also test any data furnished to the specialist by the client. The auditors should not refer to the specialist in their audit report unless the specialist's findings do not support the representations in the financial statements, thus causing the auditors to modify their report.

While it is desirable for the specialist to be unrelated to the client, it is acceptable for the specialist to have a relationship with the client. The specialist may even be employed by the client. However, the auditors should assess the risk that the specialist's objectivity might be impaired because of this relationship. If the auditors believe that the specialist's objectivity might be impaired, they should perform additional procedures or hire an independent specialist.

4. Physical Evidence

Audit evidence that the auditors can actually see is referred to as **physical evidence.** As an example, the best evidence of the existence of certain assets is the auditors' examination of the assets themselves. The existence of property and equipment, such as automobiles, buildings, office equipment, and factory machinery, may be conclusively established by physical examination. Similarly, evidence about the existence of cash may be obtained by counting, and the client's inventory may be observed as it is counted by client personnel. The auditors also can determine whether a control procedure is being performed by observing the employees performing the procedure.

At first thought, it might seem that physical examination of an asset would conclusively verify all assertions relating to the account; but this is often not true. As an example, the observation of the client's count of inventory may leave some important questions unanswered. The quality and condition of merchandise or of goods in process are vital in determining their

Illustrative Case
Inventory Observation

During the observation of the physical inventory of a company manufacturing semiconductors—small chips of photographically etched silicon that channel electricity along microscopic pathways—one of the auditors counted semiconductors purportedly worth several hundred thousand dollars. He then asked why apparently identical appearing semiconductors on another wall were not being counted. The client informed him that those semiconductors were defective and could not be sold. To the auditor, the defective semiconductors were identical in appearance with those included in the count. Shortly thereafter the auditor entered academics.

salability. If the goods counted by the auditors contain hidden defects or are obsolete, a mere counting of units does not substantiate their balance sheet valuation. Therefore, CPAs are alert to any clues that raise doubt as to the quality or condition of inventories. Occasionally, the auditors may need to arrange for specialists, such as engineers and chemists, to provide information about the quality or condition of inventories.

The auditors' physical examination also does not provide proof of ownership of assets. A fleet of automobiles used by salespeople and company executives, for example, might be leased rather than owned. In addition, physical examination does not substantiate the cost of the assets.

In summary, physical examination or observation provides high-quality evidence as to the *existence* of certain assets, but generally it needs to be supplemented by other types of evidence to determine the ownership, proper valuation, and condition of these assets. For some types of assets, such as accounts receivable or intangible assets, even the existence of the assets cannot be verified through physical evidence.

5. Computations

Another type of audit evidence consists of the results of computations made independently by the auditors to prove the arithmetical accuracy of the client's analyses and records. In its simplest form, an auditor's computation might consist of footing a column of figures in a sales journal or in a ledger account to provide that column total. Independent computations may be used to prove the accuracy of such client calculations as earnings per share, depreciation expense, allowance for uncollectible accounts, revenue recognized on a percentage-of-completion basis, and provisions for federal and state income taxes. Specialists may become involved in certain computations. For example, because the computation of a client's liability for postretirement benefits involves actuarial assumptions and computations beyond the auditor's area of expertise, auditors usually rely on the services of an actuary to compute this liability.

6. Data Interrelationships

Data interrelationships involve the comparison of relationships among financial and, sometimes, nonfinancial data. Data interrelationships differ from computations. As indicated in the preceding section, computations verify mathematical processes. Data interrelationships rely upon plausible relationships among both financial and nonfinancial data. For example, a plausible relationship may exist in an industry between annual square footage of sales space and retail sales. Analytical procedures, the primary means used by auditors to analyze data interrelationships, are described later in this chapter.

7. Oral and Written Client Representations

Throughout an audit the auditors ask a great many questions of the officers and employees of the client's organization. Oral inquiries are made on an endless range of topics—the location of records and documents, the reasons underlying an unusual accounting procedure, the probabilities of collecting a long past-due account receivable. In making inquiries, auditors should consider the knowledge, objectivity, experience, responsibility, and qualifications of the individual being questioned and should use carefully structured questions to address relevant issues. Client replies should be carefully evaluated and, as appropriate, followed up with additional questions.

Illustrative Case
Reliance on Management Representations

The income statement of the National Student Marketing Corporation (NSMC) included total gains of $370,000 from the sale of two subsidiary companies to employees of the subsidiaries. Consideration for the sale was notes receivable collateralized by 7,700 shares of NSMC stock. Because both subsidiaries had been operating at substantial losses, NSMC's independent auditors obtained written representations from three officers of NSMC that there were no indemnification or repurchase commitments given to the purchasers.

The SEC criticized the auditors for relying too heavily on management representations regarding the sales. The SEC considered the sales to be sham transactions that would have been brought to light had the auditors sufficiently extended their audit procedures. NSMC had executed various side agreements to assume all risks of ownership after the "sale" of one subsidiary and had agreed to make cash contributions and guarantee a bank line of credit of the other subsidiary after the "sale." Further, the NSMC stock collateralizing the notes receivable had been given to the subsidiaries' "purchasers" by officers of NSMC.

Generally, oral client representations are not sufficient in themselves, but they may be useful in disclosing situations that require investigation or in corroborating other forms of evidence. For example, after making a careful analysis of all past-due accounts receivable, an auditor will normally discuss with the credit manager the prospects of collecting specific accounts. If the opinions of the credit manager are in accordance with the estimates of uncollectible accounts that have been made independently by the auditor, this oral evidence will constitute support for the conclusions reached. In repeat audits of a business, the auditor will be in a better position to evaluate the opinions of the credit manager based on the manager's estimates in prior years.

Auditors also obtain written representations from clients. At the conclusion of the audit, the CPAs obtain from the client a written **representation letter** summarizing the most important oral representations made by management during the engagement. Many specific items are included in this representation letter. For example, management usually represents that all liabilities known to exist are reflected in the financial statements. The representations generally fall into the following broad categories:

1. All accounting records, financial data, and minutes of directors' meetings have been made available to the auditors.
2. The financial statements are complete and were prepared in conformity with generally accepted accounting principles.
3. Management believes that the adjusting entries brought to its attention by the auditors and not recorded are not material, individually or in the aggregate.
4. Management acknowledges its responsibility to design and implement programs and controls to prevent and detect fraud and to disclose information to the auditors on allegation of fraud or suspected fraud.
5. All items requiring disclosure (such as loss contingencies, illegal acts, and related party transactions) have been properly disclosed.

SAS 85 (AU 333), "Management Representations," requires auditors to obtain a representation letter on every engagement and provides suggestions as to its form and content. These letters are dated as of the date of the auditors' report (ordinarily the last day of fieldwork) and usually are signed by both the client's chief executive officer and chief financial officer.

A client representation letter *should never be used as a substitute for performing other audit procedures.* The financial statements already constitute written representation by the client; hence, a representation letter does little more than assert that the original representations were correct.

Although representation letters are not a substitute for other necessary audit procedures, they do serve several important audit purposes. One purpose is to remind the client officers of their primary and personal responsibility for the financial statements. Another purpose is to document in the audit working papers the client's responses to the significant questions asked by the auditors during the engagement. Also, a representation by management may be the only evidence available with respect to management's *future intentions.* For example, whether maturing debt is classified as a current or a long-term liability may depend upon whether management has both the ability and the *intent* to refinance the debt.

Audit Procedures

Auditors perform audit procedures to obtain audit evidence that will allow them to draw reasonable conclusions as to whether the client's financial statements follow generally accepted accounting principles. Those audit procedures allow the auditors to address the risk of material misstatement (composed of inherent risk and control risk) in four ways:

1. Obtain an understanding of the client and its environment to assess the risks of material misstatement (inherent risk).
2. Obtain an understanding of the clients' internal control.
3. Design and perform tests of controls to test the operating effectiveness of controls in preventing, or detecting, material misstatements.
4. Design and perform substantive procedures to test supporting financial statement assertions or detect material misstatements. Substantive procedures include (*a*) analytical procedures, (*b*) direct tests of transactions occurring during the period, and (*c*) direct tests of ending financial statement balances.

Chapters 6 and 7 provide basic guidance on obtaining an understanding of the client and its internal control—points 1, 2, and 3. The following section emphasizes the nature, timing, or extent of substantive procedures performed—point 4.

Nature of Substantive Audit Procedures

Substantive procedures include (1) analytical procedures (discussed in detail later in this chapter), (2) direct tests of transactions occurring during the period, and (3) direct tests of ending financial statement balances. Substantive procedures that are *direct tests of transactions* occurring during the period address whether particular types of transactions have been properly accounted for during the period (e.g., purchases and retirements of equipment). Substantive procedures that are *direct tests of ending financial statement balances* directly address whether there are misstatements in the ending balance of an account (e.g., confirmation of ending accounts receivable balances).

The nature of the substantive tests used on an audit will be responsive to the assessed risks of misstatement, with the objective of efficiently obtaining sufficient competent audit evidence to achieve the planned level of assurance for each audit area.

One way for the auditors to address a high risk area is to select a more effective audit procedure. For example, if the auditors want to increase the assurance obtained relating to the existence of accounts receivable, they could decide to directly test the ending balance by confirming the accounts rather than relying upon the inspection of internal documents. While the details of audit procedures for various accounts and transaction cycles will be discussed in Chapters 10 through 16, Figure 5.3 summarizes the most common types of audit procedures that the auditors may decide to use and provides examples of each.

Timing of Substantive Audit Procedures

Audit procedures may be performed before the client's year-end (i.e., at interim dates) or subsequent to year-end. The auditors may obtain more assurance by shifting audit procedures from an interim date to year-end. Performing procedures at an interim date increases audit risk, because material misstatements may arise in the remaining period, between the date of the tests and year-end. This incremental audit risk must be controlled by performing additional audit procedures that cover the remaining period, or by the fact that the auditors are confident that the client's controls are operating effectively to prevent material misstatements. The timing of audit procedures is discussed in more detail in Chapter 6.

FIGURE 5.3 Audit Procedures

Audit Procedure	Example
Accounting Information System	
Comparison—Agreeing amounts from different internal records.	Comparing the total of the accounts receivable control account with the total of the accounts receivable subsidiary ledger.
Documentary Evidence	
Tracing—Establishing the *completeness* of transaction processing by following a transaction forward through the accounting records.	Comparing information on selected receiving reports to the purchases journal.
Vouching—Establishing the *existence* or *occurrence* of recorded transactions by following a transaction back to supporting documents from a subsequent processing step (also referred to as "tracing back").	Comparing recorded purchase transactions in the purchases journal to supporting evidence such as invoices, paid checks, and receiving reports.
Inspection—Reading or point-by-point review of a document or record (the terms *examine, review, read,* and *scan* are used to describe the inspection technique).	Reading a loan agreement to verify terms.
Reconciliation—Establishing agreement between two sets of independently maintained but related records.	Reconciling the general ledger account Cash in Bank with the bank statement.
Third-Party Representations	
Confirmation—Obtaining and evaluating a response from a debtor, creditor, or other party in reply to a request for information about a particular item affecting the financial statements.	Confirming accounts receivable.
Physical Evidence	
Physical examination—Viewing physical evidence of an asset.	Physically examining plant and equipment.
Observation—Viewing a client activity.	Observing the client's inventory-taking procedures.
Computations	
Reperformance—Repeating a client activity. This may include operations such as footing (proving the total of a vertical column of figures); cross footing (proving the total of a horizontal row of figures); and extending (recomputing by multiplication).	Recalculating depreciation expense.
Data Interrelationships	
Analytical procedures—Evaluations of financial information made by a study of expected relationships among financial and nonfinancial data.	Comparing financial ratios for the year under audit with those of prior years.
Client Representations	
Inquiries—Questions directed toward appropriate client personnel.	Questioning the client's controller about the segregation of duties for cash receipt transactions.

Extent of Substantive Audit Procedures

Holding other factors such as the nature and timing of procedures constant, the greater the risk of material misstatement, the greater the needed extent of substantive procedures. The major way in which the auditors increase the extent of substantive tests of transactions and balances is to examine more items. To be cost effective, audits must involve the use of samples, but the sample sizes must be sufficient to restrict audit risk to a low level. The considerations used in determining appropriate sample sizes are described in Chapter 9.

Cost of Audit Procedures

CPAs can no more disregard the cost of alternative audit procedures than a store manager can disregard a difference in the cost of competing brands of merchandise. While cost is not the primary factor influencing auditors in deciding what evidence should be obtained, it is always an important consideration. Also, the greater the risk of material misstatement of the item to be verified, the stronger the evidence required by the auditors, and the greater the cost they are willing to incur in obtaining it. As we have indicated, sufficient competent audit evidence is obtained when audit risk is reduced to an acceptable level. Therefore, the most efficient set of audit procedures is that which achieves the required low level of audit risk at the minimum audit cost.

Analytical Procedures

Analytical procedures involve evaluations of financial statement information by a study of relationships among financial and nonfinancial data. A basic premise underlying the application of analytical procedures is that plausible relationships among data may reasonably be expected to exist and continue in the absence of known conditions to the contrary. Therefore, the auditors can use these relationships to obtain evidence about the reasonableness of financial statement amounts. *SAS 56* (AU 329), "Analytical Procedures," provides guidance on the nature of these procedures and examples of how they are applied.

Nature of Analytical Procedures

Techniques used in performing analytical procedures range in sophistication from straightforward analysis of trends and ratios to complex mathematical models involving many relationships and data from many previous years. A simple analytical procedure is to compare revenue and expense amounts for the current year to those of prior periods, noting significant differences. A more sophisticated analytical procedure might involve the development of a multiple regression model to estimate the amount of sales for the year using economic and industry data. Analytical procedures also may involve computations of percentage relationships of various items in the financial statements, such as gross profit percentages. In all these approaches, the auditors attempt to identify unexpected differences or the absence of expected differences. Such differences may indicate misstatements in the financial statements that should be investigated fully by the auditors.

Essentially, the process of performing analytical procedures consists of four steps:

1. Develop an expectation of an account (or ratio) balance.
2. Determine the amount of difference from the expectation that can be accepted without investigation.
3. Compare the company's account (ratio) balance with the expectation.
4. Investigate and evaluate significant differences from the expectation.

Developing an Expectation

A variety of types of information are available to the auditors to develop expectations for analytical procedures, including:

1. Financial information for comparable prior periods.
2. Anticipated results, such as budgets and forecasts.
3. Relationships among elements of financial information within a period.
4. Information derived from similar firms in the same industry, such as industry averages.
5. Relationships between financial information and relevant nonfinancial data.

Every audit client generates internal financial information that may be used in performing analytical procedures. Financial reports of prior years, forecasts, production reports, and monthly performance reports are but a few data sources that may be expected to bear predictable relationships to financial statement amounts. In establishing these relationships, auditors may use dollar amounts, physical quantities, ratios, or percentages. To increase the precision of the procedures, separate relationships may be computed for each division or product line.

Industry averages are available through such sources as Dun & Bradstreet's *Key Business Ratios* and Robert Morris Associates's *Annual Statement Studies.* These averages provide a potentially rich source of information for developing expectations for analytical procedures. Comparisons with industry statistics may alert auditors to classification errors, improper applications of accounting principles, or other misstatements in specific items in the client's financial statements. In addition, these comparisons may highlight the client's strengths and weaknesses relative to similar companies, thus providing the auditors with a basis for making constructive recommendations to the client.

Certain problems may be encountered in using industry averages for analytical procedures because of a lack of comparability among companies and the inability to obtain current industry data. Other companies in the same industry may be larger or smaller, engage in other lines of business that affect their ratios, or use different accounting methods than does the auditors' client. In addition, the time required to assemble industry averages creates a situation in which the most recent averages are always a year or so old. Thus, auditors should carefully consider the comparability and timeliness of the data before drawing conclusions based upon comparisons with industry averages.

Types of Expectations   Auditors develop expectations using a number of different techniques, including trend analysis, ratio analysis, regression analysis, and reasonableness tests. *Trend analysis* involves the review of changes in an account balance over time. For example, a review of the client's sales for the past three years might reveal a consistent growth rate of about 7 percent. This information would assist the auditors in developing an expectation about what sales should be for the current year.

Ratio analysis involves comparisons of relationships between two or more financial statement accounts, or comparisons of account balances to nonfinancial data (e.g., revenue per sales order). Traditional financial ratios typically are classified into four categories:

1. Liquidity ratios, such as the current ratio and the quick ratio.
2. Leverage ratios, such as the debt to equity ratio and the long-term debt to equity ratio.
3. Profitability ratios, such as gross profit percentage and return on total assets.
4. Activity ratios, such as inventory turnover and accounts receivable turnover.

Because ratio analysis involves examination of the relationships between two or more variables and may involve industry data, it is often a richer form of analysis than is trend analysis.

There are two basic approaches to ratio analysis, horizontal analysis and cross-sectional analysis. While **horizontal analysis** involves a review of the client's ratios and trends over time, **cross-sectional analysis** involves comparisons of the ratios of similar firms at a point in time—that is, cross-sectional analysis involves comparing the client's ratios to industry averages.

Figure 5.4 provides an illustration of horizontal (trend) and cross-sectional analysis of a client's income statement. The figure also illustrates a *common-size* income statement, in which all revenues and expenses are presented as a percentage of net sales. A common-size income statement is particularly useful because many expenses, such as cost of goods sold, would be expected to bear a predictable relationship to net sales. A common-size balance sheet presents all assets, liabilities, and owners' equity amounts as a percentage of total assets. The development of common-size financial statements is also known as **vertical analysis.**

If the auditors decide to use a more sophisticated analysis it will often take the form of regression analysis. *Regression analysis* involves the use of statistical models to quantify the auditors' expectation about a financial statement amount or ratio. As an example, the auditors could develop an expectation about the client's sales for this year with a model that uses the amount spent on advertising, the square footage of selling space, and personal disposable income. Regression analysis has advantages over other forms of analysis in that more variables may be used to predict the financial statement balance, and the reliability and precision of the expectation may be precisely measured.

Another method that is used to develop a more precise expectation of a financial statement balance is a reasonableness test. A *reasonableness test* is similar to regression analysis in that

FIGURE 5.4 Techniques for Analytical Procedures

Brody Corporation Income Statement

	Dollars (000s Omitted)					Common-Size Statements			Industry Averages
	20X6 (Audited)	20X7 (Audited)	Percent Change	20X8 (Unaudited)	Percent Change	20X6 (Audited)	20X7 (Audited)	20X8 (Unaudited)	20X7
Gross sales	78,428	82,212	4.8	88,236	7.3	103%	105%	103%	104%
Less: Returns and allowances	2,284	4,235	85.4	2,644	-37.6	3%	5%	3%	4%
Net sales	76,144	77,977	2.4	85,592	9.8	100%	100%	100%	100%
Cost of goods sold	46,213	46,478	0.6	51,234	10.2	61%	60%	60%	58%
Gross profit	29,931	31,499	5.2	34,358	9.1	39%	40%	40%	42%
Selling & administrative expenses	20,105	22,487	11.8	21,834	-2.9	26%	29%	26%	28%
Income from operations	9,826	9,012	-8.3	12,524	39.0	13%	12%	15%	14%
Interest expense	1,930	1,584	-17.9	3,189	101.3	3%	2%	4%	3%
Net income before taxes	7,896	7,428	-5.9	9,335	25.7	10%	10%	11%	11%
Income taxes	3,807	6,189	62.6	7,761	25.4	5%	8%	9%	4%
Net income	4,089	1,239	-69.7	1,574	27.0	5%	2%	2%	7%
EPS	0.78	0.24	-69.2	0.30	25.0				

Ratios									
Current	1.7	1.9		1.9					2.1
Quick	1.0	1.1		1.1					1.3
Receivables turnover	5.3	5.6		4.7					5.1
Days' sales in ending receivables	68.1	64.3		76.6					65.6
Inventory turnover	4.7	3.2		1.7					3.5
Days' sales in ending inventory	76.0	75.0		112.5					74.4
Interest expense/ outstanding debt	0.11	0.08		0.08					0.09

Horizontal (Trend) Analysis   Vertical Analysis   Cross-Sectional Analysis an explicit expectation is computed for the financial statement amount using financial or nonfinancial data. As an example, the auditors might use the average occupancy rate and the average room rates of a hotel to develop an estimate of the hotel's revenues for the period. A reasonableness test differs from regression analysis in that it is less formal and is not based on a statistical model.

Determine Amount of Difference That Can Be Accepted

The amount of difference between the expectation and the financial statement balance or ratio that can be accepted without investigation is determined primarily by the amount that is considered to be a material misstatement. However, this amount must be consistent with the degree of assurance desired from the procedure. If regression analysis is used, the items that should be investigated will be specifically identified by the statistical model based on the degree of precision and reliability specified by the auditors. When trend or ratio analysis is used the auditors typically use professional judgment to specify an absolute amount of difference, or a percentage difference that will result in investigation.

Compare the Account (Ratio) Balance with the Expected Balance

Once the auditors have determined the expectation and the amount of difference that can be accepted, they can make the actual comparisons to determine where the significant differences lie.

Investigate and Evaluate Significant Differences

The auditors must investigate any significant differences between their expectations and the client's financial statement amounts or ratios to determine whether they represent misstatements. This may involve reconsidering the methods and factors used in developing the expectation. Inquiry of management may be of assistance in this regard. Management's explanations, however, must ordinarily be corroborated with other audit evidence. If the auditors are unable to corroborate management's explanation or management has no explanation, they will often be required to expand their tests of the related financial statement amounts to determine whether or not they are materially misstated. Figure 5.5 provides some of the misstatements or problems that may be discovered when the auditors investigate significant differences uncovered by various analytical procedures.

Timing of Analytical Procedures

Auditing standards require the application of analytical procedures at the *planning* and *overall final review* stages of audits. The auditors also may decide to use them during the audit as *substantive tests* to provide evidence as to the reasonableness of the specific account balances.

Analytical procedures performed in planning the audit are used to assist the auditors in determining the nature, timing, and extent of audit procedures that will be used to obtain

FIGURE 5.5 **Potential Misstatements Disclosed by Analytical Procedures**

Analytical Procedure	Potential Misstatements
1. Comparison of inventory levels for the current year to that of prior years.	Misstatement of inventory; inventory obsolescence problem.
2. Comparison of research and development expense to the budgeted amount.	Misclassification of research and development expenses.
3. Comparison of accounts receivable turnover for the current year to that of prior years.	Misstatement of sales or accounts receivable; misstatement of the allowance for uncollectible accounts.
4. Comparison of the client's gross profit percentage to published industry averages.	Misstatement of sales and accounts receivable; misstatement of cost of goods sold and inventory.
5. Comparison of production records in units to sales.	Misstatement of sales; misstatement of inventory.
6. Comparison of interest expense to the average outstanding balance of interest-bearing debt.	Understatement of liabilities; misstatement of interest expense.

evidence about specific accounts. At the planning stage, the objective of analytical procedures is to help the auditors identify unusual transactions, events, or amounts that might affect the fairness of the financial statements. Planning analytical procedures also are used to increase the auditors' understanding of the client's business. During planning analytical procedures, *SAS 99* (AU 316), "Consideration of Fraud in a Financial Statement Audit," requires auditors to perform analytical procedures relating to revenue to identify any unusual or unexpected relationships involving revenue accounts that may be indicative of fraud. For example, one procedure might be to compare revenue recorded by month during the current year with comparable prior years' revenue.

Analytical procedures may be used as substantive tests to provide evidence about one or more financial statement assertions. While the auditors are not required to use analytical procedures as substantive tests, they are usually the most efficient test of certain assertions. For example, performing analytical procedures often is the most efficient way to evaluate the completeness of various revenue and expense accounts. Chapters 10 through 16 illustrate the use of analytical procedures as substantive tests for various types of financial statement accounts.

Finally, analytical procedures must be used as a part of the overall review stage of an audit to assist the auditor in assessing the adequacy of the evidence that has been collected and the validity of the conclusions reached. At the final review stage of an audit these procedures generally include reviewing the financial statements and notes and recomputing ratios (if necessary) to identify any unusual or unexpected balances or relationships that have not been previously identified and explained.

Extent of Analytical Procedures

Auditors must consider the cost and likely effectiveness of analytical procedures in determining how much they will be used for a particular audit. While the cost is often low due to the availability of computers to perform computations and the simplicity of many procedures performed manually, the effectiveness of analytical procedures will vary from one audit to the next.

A primary measure of the effectiveness of an analytical procedure is its *precision*. Precision depends on a number of factors, including the predictability of the relationships, the technique used to develop the expectation, and the reliability of the underlying data used. If much "noise" exists in relationships between variables (e.g., sales and cost of goods sold), material differences might exist and not be identified by analytical procedures. Generally, precision can be improved by performing a more detailed analysis. For example, precision may be improved by performing analytical procedures with monthly rather than annual data.

The reliability of the underlying data that are used for analytical procedures may be evaluated by considering the source of the data. If the client generated the data, the auditors will consider the controls that are applied to their development. In some cases, the auditor may have to apply audit procedures to the data to test their reliability before they are used in the analytical procedure.

Audit Evidence for Subjective Areas

Gathering evidence in the areas of accounting estimates, fair market values, and related party transactions merits special attention due to the required judgments that need to be made by both management and the auditors.

Evidence on Accounting Estimates

The auditors must be especially careful in considering financial statement accounts that are affected by estimates made by management (often referred to as accounting estimates), particularly those for which a wide range of accounting methods are considered acceptable. As discussed previously, accounting estimates are usually created by *estimation transactions*. Examples of accounting estimates include allowances for loan losses and obsolete inventory and estimates of warranty liabilities. Making accounting estimates is management's responsibility, and such estimates are generally more susceptible to material misstatement than other financial statement amounts that are more certain in amount. *SAS 57* (AU 342), "Auditing

Illustrative Case
Risks Related to Accounting Estimates

The financial difficulty of the savings and loan industry during the late 1980s and early 1990s provides a good example of the potential risk to CPAs presented by accounting estimates. A number of savings and loan institutions ran into financial difficulties due in large part to making loans that subsequently proved to be uncollectible.

One savings and loan institution that made over $1 billion in real estate loans during the late 1980s originally estimated its required loan loss reserve to be $11 million. Subsequently, the Federal Deposit Insurance Corporation (FDIC) alleged that those loans resulted in losses of $450 million. Shortly thereafter, the FDIC filed a lawsuit against the CPA firm that had audited the institution.

Accounting Estimates," requires the auditors to determine that (*a*) all necessary estimates have been developed, (*b*) accounting estimates are reasonable, and (*c*) accounting estimates are properly accounted for and disclosed.

Determining whether all necessary estimates have been developed and accounted for properly (steps [*a*] and [*c*]) requires knowledge of the client's business and the applicable generally accepted accounting principles. When evaluating the reasonableness of accounting estimates (step [*b*]), the auditors obtain an understanding of how management developed the estimates, and then use one or more of these three basic approaches:

1. Review and test management's process of developing the estimates; this will often involve evaluating the reasonableness of the steps performed by management.
2. Independently develop an estimate of the amount to compare to management's estimate.
3. Review subsequent events or transactions bearing on the estimate, such as actual payments of an estimated amount made subsequent to year-end.

As discussed in Chapter 2, *SAS 99* (AU 316) requires the auditors to perform a retrospective analysis of significant accounting estimates for evidence of bias on the part of management. If the auditors find that prior estimates appear biased, they will consider this factor in evaluating management estimates for the current year audit.

The wide range of potential accounting methods complicates the auditing of transactions involving accounting estimates. Pensions, leases, and long-term construction contracts are just a few examples of transactions with complex accounting methods that vary depending on the nature of the agreements and the specific circumstances. It is the auditors' responsibility to evaluate whether the accounting rules followed are appropriate in the given circumstances.

Evidence on Fair Market Values

In recent years changes in generally accepted accounting principles have required companies to significantly increase the use of fair values for measuring, presenting, and disclosing various assets, liabilities, and components of equity. For example, fair values are used for various investments, intangible assets, impaired assets, and derivatives. *SAS 101* (AU 328), "Auditing Fair Value Measurements and Disclosures," provides guidance on auditing fair value measurements and disclosures.

Fair value is generally considered to be the amount at which an asset (or liability) could be bought or sold in a current transaction between willing parties. Its determination is easiest when there are published price quotations in an active market (e.g., a stock exchange). Determining fair value becomes more difficult when an active market does not exist, for example, in cases involving certain real estate investment properties and complex derivative financial instruments. In valuing these assets, fair value may be determined by analogizing to another existing market, or through the use of a valuation model (e.g., a model based on forecasts and discounting of future cash flows). The approach to auditing fair values is similar to that of other estimates in that one or more of three approaches is used: (1) review and test management's process, (2) independently develop an estimate, or (3) review subsequent events.

When following the approach of reviewing management's process, the auditors consider whether the assumptions used by management are reasonable, whether the valuation model seems appropriate, and whether management has used all relevant information that is reasonably available. The second approach involves developing one's own estimate and offers the advantage of allowing the auditors to compare that estimate with that developed by management. Often auditors will use a combination of these two approaches, and also may decide to employ the assistance of a valuation specialist.

The third approach allows the auditors to use information obtained subsequent to year-end to help evaluate the reasonableness of management's estimate. For example, the sale of an investment property shortly after the period end may provide evidence on its value as of year-end. Yet, even in this type of situation auditors must carefully consider the audit evidence since the sale might be impacted by circumstances that changed subsequent to year-end. For example, the prices of actively traded marketable securities that change after the period end may not constitute competent evidence of values that existed at the period end. Also, regardless of the approach or approaches followed, the auditors should evaluate whether the disclosures of fair values required by GAAP have been properly presented.

Evidence on Related Party Transactions

How should auditors react if a corporation buys a parcel of real estate from one of its executive officers at an obviously excessive price? This situation illustrates the type of problem that may arise for auditors when the client company enters into **related party transactions**. The term *related parties* refers to individuals or entities who may have dealings with the client in which one party is significantly influenced by the other such that it may not pursue its separate interests. Examples of related parties include officers, directors, principal owners, and members of their immediate families; and affiliated companies, such as subsidiaries. A related party transaction is any transaction between the company and these parties, other than normal compensation arrangements, expense allowances, and similar transactions arising in the ordinary course of business. Since transactions with related parties are not conducted at "arm's length," the auditors should be aware that the *economic substance* of these transactions might differ from their form. Related party transactions have often been used to facilitate fraudulent financial reporting. Accordingly, auditors should determine the business purpose of any significant and unusual related party transactions that they encounter.

Even if the transactions are recorded appropriately, the auditors also must be concerned that material related party transactions are *adequately disclosed* in the client's financial statements or the related notes.[1]

Disclosure of related party transactions should include: the nature of the relationship; a description of the transactions, including dollar amounts; and amounts due to and from related parties, together with the terms and manner of settlement.

The primary challenge for the auditors is identifying any related party transactions that management has not disclosed, because they may be recorded in the accounting records with all other transactions. *SAS 45* (AU 334), "Omnibus Statement on Auditing Standards," suggests guidelines for first determining related parties and, then, identifying related party transactions. Common methods of determining related parties include making inquiries of management and reviewing SEC filings, stockholders' listings, and *conflict-of-interest statements* obtained by the client from its executives. A list of all known related parties should be prepared at the beginning of the audit so that the audit staff may be alert for related party transactions throughout the engagement. This list is retained in the auditors' permanent file for reference and updating in successive engagements. As they perform the audit, the auditors will be alert for transactions with these parties and for any transactions with unusual terms that might be indicative of related party negotiations.

Audit Documentation

Learning Objective 5

Audit documentation, also known as **working papers** or workpapers, is the record of the audit procedures performed, relevant audit evidence obtained, and the conclusions the auditors reach. The professional standards, require that audit documentation provide the principal support for (1) the representation that the auditors performed the audit in accordance with

---

[1] FASB *Statement 57,* "Related Party Disclosures," contains requirements for disclosure of related party transactions.

generally accepted auditing standards, and (2) the opinion expressed on the financial information. In addition to these primary objectives, audit documentation also serves the following functions:

- Assists both continuing audit team members and auditors new to the engagement in planning and performing the audit, as such it also serves as a record of matters of continuing significance for future audits.
- Assists audit team members responsible for supervision in reviewing the quality of the work performed.
- Demonstrates the accountability of the various audit team members for the work performed.
- Assists (1) internal firm quality control reviewers, (2) inspection or peer review individuals, and (3) successor auditors with performing their roles.

Audit working papers take the form of bank reconciliations or analyses of ledger accounts; others may consist of photocopies of **minutes** of directors' meetings; still others might be organization charts or flowcharts of the client's internal control. Working trial balances, audit programs, correspondence (including e-mail) concerning significant matters, internal control questionnaires, letters or representations obtained from the client and from the client's legal counsel, and returned confirmation forms—all of these schedules, lists, notes, and documents—are part of the auditors' audit documentation.

Learning Objective 6

How detailed must documentation be? This depends on several factors, such as the nature of the auditing procedure being performed, the risk of misstatement involved in the area being tested, the significance of the evidence to the overall audit, the extent of judgment involved in performing the work, and the nature of the findings or results. At a minimum, the auditors should document all audit findings that they believe to be significant. Audit documentation should be sufficient to allow an **experienced auditor** to understand the audit work performed, the evidence obtained, and the significant conclusions reached. In this context, an experienced auditor is one that possesses the competencies and skills to perform an audit of the client, but who has had no previous experience with the client. The working papers should also demonstrate that the accounting records agree or reconcile to the financial statements being audited.

Learning Objective 7

It is very important for the auditors to document audit findings or issues that are significant and the actions taken to address them, including matters such as the selection of appropriate accounting principles, accounting for complex and unusual transactions, and issues related to accounting estimates. They also should document test results that indicate that the financial statements may be materially misstated, any significant difficulties encountered in applying auditing procedures, proposed audit adjustments, and findings that could result in a modification of the audit report. Finally, the audit documentation should identify those who performed and reviewed the work and the related dates of performance.

Confidential Nature of Working Papers

To conduct a satisfactory audit, the auditors must be given unrestricted access to all information about the client's business. Much of this information is confidential, such as the profit margins on individual products, tentative plans for business combinations with other companies, and the salaries of officers and key employees. Officers of the client company would not be willing to make available to the auditors information that is restricted from competitors, employees, and others unless they could rely on the auditors maintaining a professional silence on these matters.

Much of the information gained in confidence by the auditors is recorded in their working papers; consequently, the working papers are confidential in nature. The AICPA *Code of Professional Conduct* includes a rule that generally prohibits a member in public practice from disclosing confidential information.

Under normal circumstances, auditors think of confidential information as being information that must not be divulged *outside* the client organization. But the confidential nature of information in the auditors' working papers has another dimension: Often it must not be divulged *within* the client organization. If, for example, the client does not want certain employees to know the levels of executive salaries, the auditors obviously should not defeat this policy by exposing their working papers to unauthorized client personnel. Also, the working papers may identify particular accounts, branches, or time periods to be tested by the auditors; to permit the client's employees to learn of these in advance would weaken the significance of the tests.

Since audit working papers are highly confidential, they must be safeguarded at all times. Safeguarding working papers usually means keeping them locked in a file cabinet or an audit case during lunch and after working hours.

Ownership of Audit Working Papers

Audit working papers are the *property of the auditors,* not of the client. At no time does the client have the right to demand access to the auditors' working papers. After the audit, the working papers are retained by the auditors.

Clients may sometimes find it helpful to refer to information from the auditors' working papers from prior years. Auditors usually are willing to provide this information, but their working papers should not be regarded as a substitute for the client's own accounting records.

Working Papers and Auditors' Liability

The **audit file** includes the working papers for a particular engagement and is the principal record of the work performed during the audit. If the auditors are subsequently charged with negligence, the working papers included in the audit file will be a major factor in refuting or substantiating the charge. Although properly prepared audit documentation will help the auditors should litigation become involved, improperly prepared documentation will work against them.

If a lawsuit is brought against the auditors, the plaintiffs will subpoena the audit documentation and analyze it in great detail, looking for contradictions, omissions, or any evidence of carelessness or fraud. This possibility suggests the need for public accounting firms to make their own critical review of the documentation at the end of each engagement. During this review, the auditors should bear in mind that any unexplained contradictory statements may be used at a later date to support a charge of improper auditing.

How long should audit documentation be retained? The professional standards require a period of not less than five years, while the Sarbanes-Oxley Act of 2002 requires that auditors maintain documentation for seven years. Thus, for public clients, auditors must retain working papers for seven years, but they may destroy them after 5 years if the client is a nonpublic company.

Changing Audit Documentation after the Date of the Audit Report

Auditors are given 60 days after the audit **report date** to complete the audit file by assembling a complete and final set of audit documentation.[2] During this period they are able to perform routine file-assembling procedures such as deleting or discarding superseded documentation and sorting, collating, and cross-referencing final working papers. In addition they may sign off various checklists and add information received subsequent to the date of the auditors' report (e.g., an original confirmation that was previously faxed). The updated or revised audit documentation should contain all of the information, evidence, and conclusions that were in any superseded documentation. However, if certain information is no longer relevant or valid, it may be discarded during this 60-day period.[3] After the close of this 60-day period, referred to as the **documentation completion date**, no information may be discarded from audit working papers.

If new information is added to the working papers after the issuance of the audit report—either before or after the documentation completion date—documentation should include (1) when and by whom changes were made and reviewed, (2) specific reasons for the changes, and (3) the effect, if any, of the changes on the auditors' conclusions.

Differences of Opinion

On occasion inconsistencies will arise in the working papers because different members of the audit staff—say, a senior and the engagement partner—will reach different conclusions on

[2] Public Company Accounting Oversight Board Standard No. 2, "Audit Documentation," allows only a 45-day period for publicly traded clients.

[3] See Chapter 16's Section on, "Post-Audit Responsibilities," for additional auditor responsibilities when it is discovered that an important audit procedure was omitted or that facts existing at the date of the balance sheet were not appropriately considered.

some complex auditing or accounting issue. In such cases, the disagreeing auditors should discuss the matter to see if they can reach agreement. If they are able to do so, the working papers should be revised to reflect their common opinion. If they are not able to reach agreement, the opinion of the partner-in-charge of the engagement will prevail with respect to the content of the auditors' report. However, all other members of the audit team have the right to document in the working papers *their disagreement* with the ultimate decision. In the event that a staff person elects to document his or her disagreement, the partner-in-charge obviously should be extremely thorough in documenting the rationale underlying the firm's ultimate decision in a carefully written memorandum. The SEC interprets the Sarbanes-Oxley Act of 2002 as requiring that working papers be retained regardless of whether they support or are inconsistent with the auditors' final conclusion relating to significant matters. However, the act does not require retention of preliminary views when those preliminary views are based on incomplete information or data.

Types of Working Papers

Learning Objective 8

Since the audit working papers document a variety of information gathered by the auditors, there are numerous types of papers. However, there are certain general categories into which most working papers may be grouped; these are: (1) audit administrative working papers; (2) working trial balance and lead schedules; (3) adjusting journal entries and reclassification entries; (4) supporting schedules, analyses, reconciliations, and computational working papers; and (5) corroborating documents.

Audit Administrative Working Papers

Auditing is a sophisticated activity requiring planning, supervision, control, and coordination. Certain working papers are specifically designed to aid the auditors in the planning and administration of engagements. These working papers include audit plans and programs, internal control questionnaires and flowcharts, engagement letters, and time budgets. Memoranda of the planning process and significant discussions with client management are also considered **administrative working papers.**

Working Trial Balance

The **working trial balance** is a schedule listing the balances of the accounts in the general ledger for the current and previous year, and also providing columns for the auditors' proposed adjustments and reclassifications and for the final amounts that will appear in the financial statements. A working trial balance is the "backbone" of the entire set of audit working papers; it is the key schedule that controls and summarizes all supporting papers. A portion of a working trial balance is shown in Figure 5.6.

Figure 5.6 **Working Trial Balance Abstract**

Process Company, Inc.
Working Trial Balance
For the Period Ended December 31, 20X5

Prepared by ATT

Reviewed by RBS

Page 1

Account #	Account Name	Prior Period Balance 12/31/X4	Unadjusted Trial Balance DR	(CR)	Ref #	Adjustments DR	(CR)	Balance Sheet DR	CR
1001.01	Cash	398,743	481,413.00					481,413	
1010.01	Short-Term Investments		167,890.00					167,890	
1040.01	Accounts Receivable	2,053,914	2,298,722.00					2,298,722	
1045.01	Allowance for Doubtful Accounts	(45,325)		(56,984.00)	AJE-11		(10,456.00)		67,440
1050.01	Inventories	2,567,665	2,701,814.00		AJE-12		(129,799.00)	2,572,015	

In many audits, the client furnishes the auditors with a working trial balance after all normal end-of-period journal entries have been posted. Before accepting the trial balance for their working papers, the auditors should compare the amounts to the general ledger to determine that the trial balance is prepared accurately.

Lead Schedules

Separate **lead schedules** (also called *grouping sheets* or *summary schedules*) are set up to combine similar general ledger accounts, the total of which appears on the working trial balance as a single amount. For example, a lead schedule for Cash might combine the following general ledger accounts: Petty Cash, $500; General bank account, $196,240; Factory Payroll bank account, $500; and Dividend bank account, $1,000. Similar lead schedules would be set up for Accounts Receivable, Inventories, Stockholders' Equity, Net Sales, and other balance sheet or income statement captions.

Adjusting Journal Entries and Reclassification Entries

During the course of an audit engagement, the auditors may discover various types of misstatements in the client's financial statements and accounting records. These misstatements may be large or small in amount; they may arise from the omission of transactions or from the use of incorrect amounts; or they may result from improper classification or **cutoff,** or from misinterpretation of transactions. Generally, these misstatements are accidental errors; however, the auditors may discover fraud in the accounting records.

To correct **material** errors or fraud discovered in the financial statements and accounting records, the auditors draft **adjusting journal entries (AJEs),** which they recommend for entry in the client's accounting records. In addition, the auditors develop **reclassification journal entries (RJEs)** for items that, although correctly recorded in the accounting records, must be reclassified for fair presentation in the client's financial statements. For example, accounts receivable with large credit balances should be *reclassified* as a liability in the balance sheet. Reclassification entries affect only the financial statement presentation; therefore, they are *not recorded* in the client's accounting records. Reclassification entries appear only on accounting worksheets.

Supporting Schedules

Although all types of working papers may loosely be called schedules, auditors prefer to use this term to describe a listing of the elements or details comprising the balance in an asset or liability account at a specific date. Thus, a list of amounts owed to vendors making up the balance of the Trade Accounts Payable account is properly described as a *schedule.*

Analysis of a Ledger Account

An **analysis** of a ledger account is another common type of audit working paper. The purpose of an analysis is to show *all changes* in an asset, liability, equity, revenue, or expense account during the period covered by the audit. If a number of the changes are individually immaterial, they may be recorded as a single item in the analysis working paper. Account analyses are most useful in substantiating those accounts affected by relatively few transactions during the year. Examples include plant asset accounts, long-term debt accounts, capital stock accounts, and retained earnings.

To analyze a ledger account, the auditors first list the beginning balance and indicate the nature of the items comprising this balance. Next, the auditors list and investigate the nature of all debits and credits to the account during the period. These entries, when combined with the beginning balance, produce a figure representing the balance in the account as of the audit date. If any misstatements or omissions of importance are detected during this analysis of the account, the necessary adjusting journal entry approved by the client is entered on the working paper to produce the adjusted balance required for the financial statements.

Reconciliations

Frequently, auditors wish to prove the relationship between amounts obtained from different sources. When they do so, they obtain or prepare working papers known as reconciliations.

These reconciliations provide evidence as to the accuracy of one or both of the amounts and are important to the audit of many accounts, including cash, accounts receivable, and inventories.

Computational Working Papers

Another type of supporting working paper is the computational working paper. The auditors' approach to verifying certain types of accounts and other figures is to make an independent computation and compare their results with the amounts shown by the client's records. Examples of amounts that might be verified by computation are interest expense, depreciation, payroll taxes, income taxes, pension liabilities, and earnings per share.

Corroborating Documents

Auditing is not limited to the examination of financial records, and working papers are not confined to schedules and analyses. During the course of an audit, the auditors may gather much purely expository material to substantiate their report. One common example is copies of minutes of directors' and stockholders' meetings. Other examples of **corroborating documents** include copies of articles of incorporation and bylaws; copies of important contracts, bond indentures, and mortgages; memoranda pertaining to examination of records; audit confirmations; and representation letters from the client and from the client's legal counsel.

Organization of Working Papers

The auditors usually maintain two files of working papers for each client: (1) current files for every completed audit and (2) a permanent file of relatively unchanging data. The current file (as for the 2005 audit) pertains solely to that year's audit; the permanent file contains such things as copies of the articles of incorporation, which are of continuing audit interest.

The Current Files

The auditors' report for a particular year is supported by the working papers contained in the current files. Many CPA firms have found it useful to organize the current files around the arrangement of the accounts in the client's financial statements. The administrative working papers usually begin the current files, including a draft of the financial statements and the auditors' report. These working papers are followed by the working trial balance and the adjusting and reclassification entries. The remaining portion of the current files consists of working papers supporting the balances and other representations in the client's financial statements. It begins with working papers for each asset account and continues with papers for liabilities, owners' equity accounts, and revenue and expense accounts.

Each working paper in a file is assigned an index number, and information is tied together through a system of cross-referencing. In this way, a reviewer may trace back amounts on the working trial balance to the supporting working papers. Figure 5.7 illustrates a system of cross-referencing and a typical arrangement of the current files after the administrative working papers.

The Permanent File

The **permanent file** serves three purposes: (1) to refresh the auditors' memories on items applicable over a period of many years; (2) to provide new staff members with a quick summary of the policies and organization of the client; and (3) to preserve working papers on items that show relatively few or no changes, thus eliminating the necessity for their preparation year after year.

Much of the information contained in the permanent file is gathered during the course of the first audit of a client's records. A considerable portion of the time spent on a first audit is devoted to gathering and appraising background information, such as copies of articles of incorporation and bylaws, leases, patent agreements, pension plans, labor contracts, long-term construction contracts, known related parties, charts of accounts, and prior years' tax returns.

Analyses of accounts that show few changes over a period of years are also included in the permanent file. These accounts may include land, buildings, accumulated depreciation, long-term investments, long-term liabilities, capital stock, and other owners' equity accounts. The initial investigation of these accounts must often include the transactions of many years. Once these historical analyses have been brought up to date, the work required in subsequent examinations

FIGURE 5.7 **Organization of the Current Files**

will be limited to a review of the current year's transactions in these accounts. In this respect, the permanent file is a timesaving device because current changes in such accounts need only be added to the permanent papers without reappearing in the current working papers. Adequate cross-referencing in the working papers, of course, should be provided to show where in the permanent file such information is to be found.

Guidelines for Preparation of Working Papers

We will now summarize in a few short paragraphs our basic guidelines for preparing working papers that will meet current professional standards.

A separate, properly identified working paper should be prepared for each topic. Proper identification of a working paper is accomplished by a heading that includes the name of the client company, a clear description of the information presented, and the applicable date or the period covered. If the working paper was prepared by the client's staff, it should be labeled "PBC" (prepared by client) and appropriately tested.

Complete and specific identification of documents examined, employees interviewed, and sites visited is essential for good working paper practice. The preparer of a working paper should date and sign or initial the working paper; the signatures or initials of the senior, manager, or partner who reviewed the working paper should also appear on the paper.

Working papers should be appropriately referenced and cross-referenced to the working trial balance or relevant lead schedule. Where reference is necessary between working papers, there must be adequate cross-referencing.

The nature of verification work performed by the auditors should be clearly indicated on each working paper. A review of paid purchase invoices, for example, might be supplemented by inspection of the related purchase orders and receiving documents to substantiate the authenticity of the invoices examined; a description of this verification procedure should be included on the working paper. As audit working papers are prepared, the auditors will use several different symbols to identify specific steps in the work performed. These symbols, or **tick marks,** provide a very concise means of indicating the audit procedures applied to particular amounts. Whenever tick marks are employed, they must be accompanied by a legend explaining their meaning.

The working papers should include comments by the auditors indicating their conclusions on each aspect of the work. In other words, the auditors should clearly express the opinion they have formed as a result of having performed the audit procedures summarized in the working paper. Figure 5.8 illustrates such a conclusion related to the audit of the allowance for uncollectible accounts, along with other aspects of a properly prepared working paper.

Computer-Generated Working Papers

Traditionally working papers have been prepared in pencil on columnar paper. Today, many working papers are prepared on laptop computers carried by the auditors to the work site. When an adjustment is entered on computer-based working papers, it appears instantly on the appropriate lead schedules, the adjustments schedule, and the working trial balance. The necessary cross-references are automatically entered on each schedule. If the adjustment affects taxable income, the income tax expense account and the tax liability are automatically adjusted using the client's marginal tax rate. In addition, all the subtotals, column totals, and cross-footings in the working papers are instantly adjusted.

When working papers are maintained manually, all of these entries and changes must be made by hand with a pencil, an eraser, and a calculator. With a computer, an adjustment that might take a half hour or more to "push through" manual working papers can be entered in a few seconds. Thus, computers have taken much of the "pencil pushing" and the "number crunching" out of working paper preparation.

Many CPA firms are making full use of the document scanning, data linking, networking, and telecommunications capabilities of personal computers. These firms can produce numerous electronic working papers, creating a nearly "paperless audit."

Review of Audit Working Papers

Working papers are reviewed at every supervisory level of a CPA firm. Senior auditors review the working papers of staff assistants; managers review all working papers prepared by staff assistants and by senior auditors; the partner in charge of the engagement reviews the entire set of working papers. Many CPA firms also require a review by a second partner.

What Do Reviewers Look For?

All reviewers look to see that the working papers properly document the audit. However, there are differences in the nature of the reviews. The senior's review is the most technical, and it generally is performed promptly after the completion of the individual working paper. Seniors look primarily to see that the staff assistant has performed the audit procedures properly and that the assistant's findings and conclusions are clearly expressed.

The reviews by managers and partners are often performed near the *end* of the engagement, when the reviewer may examine at one time the entire set of working papers. These reviewers are primarily interested in determining that the audit was performed in accordance with generally accepted auditing standards and that the working papers properly support the auditors' report that will be issued on the financial statements. There are several advantages to reviewing all of the working papers at once. The reviewer can determine that the working papers

FIGURE 5.8 **Preparation of a Working Paper**

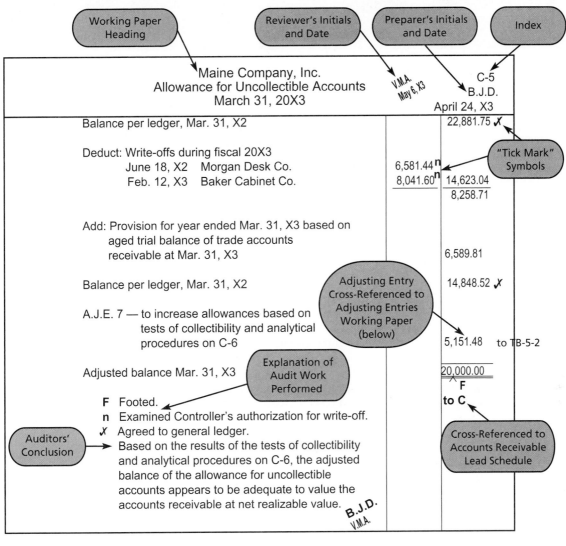

"tie together"—that is, that amounts are properly carried forward from one working paper to another. As we mentioned earlier in the chapter, these reviewers should look critically for any inconsistencies, omissions, or "loose ends" that might later support a plaintiff's allegations of improper auditing. In addition, the reviewer should consider whether the various immaterial discrepancies that were passed without adjustment might *cumulatively* have a material effect upon the financial statements.

Illustrative Case
Audit Documentation Issues

An AICPA *Audit Risk Alert* summarized recurring peer review comments on working papers and made the following suggestions concerning the preparation and review of working papers.

- Auditors should evaluate with professional skepticism the evidence obtained in relation to their accumulated knowledge of the client and the industries in which it operates. Professional skepticism is especially important when management is pressured for results and is also

called for when the financial statements before they are audited show unusually favorable results.

- Auditors should not leave open points in the working papers, whether in the form of open questions, marginal notes, or "to do" lists. An adversary will look for and find all the things the auditors said they should do but did not.
- Auditors should destroy superseded drafts of schedules, memoranda, financial statements, and reports in both hard copy and computer format.

The purposes of a *second partner review* are to provide assurance that all the CPA firm's in-house *quality control policies* have been complied with, as well as to provide a "second opinion" that the audit was performed in accordance with generally accepted auditing standards. The second partner review, sometimes called a *cold review,* usually is performed by a partner with no personal or professional ties to the audit client. Multioffice CPA firms sometimes bring in a partner from another office to perform the second partner review. Not until all these reviewers have "signed off" on the audit working papers is the CPA firm's name signed to the auditors' report.

Chapter Summary

This chapter focuses on the concept of sufficient competent audit evidence and the manner in which this evidence is documented in the audit working papers. To summarize:

1. The third standard of fieldwork requires the auditors to obtain sufficient competent audit evidence to support their audit opinion. To be competent, evidence must be both relevant and valid. In general, evidence is considered more valid when it is (*a*) obtained from independent sources outside the client organization; (*b*) generated from an accounting system that has effective internal control; or (*c*) obtained directly by the auditors, rather than from a secondary source. The auditors use professional judgment to determine the amount of evidence that is sufficient to support their opinion.

2. Evidence is gathered by the auditors to reduce audit risk—the risk of failing to modify their opinion on financial statements that are materially misstated. Since financial statements consist of a series of assertions by management, the auditors must obtain sufficient competent audit evidence about each material financial statement assertion.

3. At the individual account balance level, audit risk consists of (*a*) the risk that a material misstatement in an assertion has occurred (composed of inherent risk and control risk), and (*b*) the risk that the auditors do not detect the misstatement (detection risk). Audit evidence is gathered by the auditors to assess both inherent and control risk, and to restrict detection risk.

4. Auditors must be especially careful in considering financial statement accounts that are affected by estimates made by management, such as the allowance for doubtful accounts. The inherent risk of these types of accounts is generally much greater than for other financial statement accounts.

5. Audit documentation is the connecting link between the client's accounting records and the auditors' report. Such documentation is the property of the auditors and is primarily used to illustrate the auditors' compliance with professional standards and to support the auditors' opinion. Other functions of audit documentation include providing assistance in planning and performing the audit; facilitating supervision and review of audit work; providing a record of matters relevant to future audits; enabling other auditors to conduct peer reviews and inspections; and assisting successor auditors.

Key Terms Introduced or Emphasized in Chapter 5

Note: Figure 5.3 defines a number of audit procedures. Those terms are not repeated in this glossary.

Adjusting journal entries (AJEs)   Journal entries designed to correct misstatements found in a client's records.

Administrative working papers   Working papers specifically designed to help the auditors in the planning and administration of the engagement, such as audit programs, internal control questionnaires and flowcharts, time budgets, and engagement memoranda.

Analysis   A working paper showing all changes in an asset, liability, equity, revenue, or expense account during the period covered by the audit.

Audit evidence   Any information that corroborates or refutes the auditors' premise that the financial statements present fairly the client's financial position and operating results.

Audit file   The unit of storage for a specific audit engagement. The audit documentation for each year's audit of a company is included in its audit file.

Audit risk   The risk that the auditors may unknowingly fail to appropriately modify their opinion on financial statements that are materially misstated.

Common-size financial statements   Financial statements that present each amount as a percentage of some financial statement base. As an example, a common-size income statement presents all revenues and expenses as a percentage of net sales. See *vertical analysis.*

Competent   The competence of audit evidence relates to its quality. To be competent, evidence must be both reliable (valid) and relevant.

Control risk   The risk that a material misstatement that could occur in an account will not be prevented or detected on a timely basis by internal control.

Corroborating documents   Documents and memoranda included in the working papers that substantiate representations contained in the client's financial statements. These working papers include audit confirmations, lawyers' letters, copies of contracts, copies of minutes of directors' and stockholders' meetings, and representation letters from the client's management.

Cross-sectional analysis   A technique that involves comparing the client's ratios for the current year with those of similar firms in the same industry.

Cutoff   The process of determining that transactions occurring near the balance sheet date are assigned to the proper accounting period.

Detection risk   The risk that the auditors' procedures will lead them to conclude that a financial statement assertion is not materially misstated when in fact such misstatement does exist.

Documentation completion date   The date on which documentation should be completed. This is within 60 days of the delivery date.

Electronic data interchange (EDI)   A system in which data are exchanged electronically between the computers of different companies. In an EDI system source documents are replaced with electronic transactions created in a standard format.

Estimation transaction   A transaction involving management's judgments or assumptions, such as determining the allowance for doubtful accounts, establishing warranty reserves, and assessing assets for impairment.

Experienced auditor   For purposes of audit documentation, an individual (whether internal or external to the CPA firm) who possesses the competencies and skills enabling him or her to perform an audit and who has a reasonable understanding of the audit processes and of auditing and financial reporting issues relevant to the industry in which the client operates.

Horizontal analysis   A technique that involves comparing financial statement amounts and ratios for a particular company from year to year.

Inherent risk   The risk of material misstatement of a financial statement assertion, assuming there were no related controls.

Lead schedule   A working paper with columnar headings similar to those in a working trial balance, set up to combine similar ledger accounts the total of which appears in the working trial balance as a single amount.

Material   Of substantial importance. Significant enough to affect evaluations or decisions by users of financial statements. Information that should be disclosed in order that financial statements constitute a fair presentation. Involves both qualitative and quantitative considerations.

Minutes   A formal record of the issues discussed and actions taken in meetings of stockholders or the board of directors.

Nonroutine transaction   A transaction that occurs only periodically, such as counting and pricing inventory, calculating depreciation expense, or determining prepaid expenses.

Permanent file   A file of working papers containing relatively unchanging data, such as copies of articles of incorporation and bylaws; copies of minutes of directors', stockholders', and committee meetings; and analyses of such ledger accounts as land and retained earnings.

Physical evidence   Evidence derived by the auditors from physical examination.

Reclassification journal entry (RJE)   A working paper entry drafted by the auditors to assure fair presentation of the client's financial statements, such as an entry to transfer accounts receivable credit balances to the current liabilities section of the client's balance sheet. Since reclassification entries do not correct misstatements in the client company's accounting records, they are not posted to the client's ledger accounts.

Related party transaction   A transaction in which one party has the ability to influence significantly the management or operating policies of the other party, to the extent that one of the transacting parties might be prevented from pursuing fully its own separate interests.

Report date (audit report date)   The date on which the auditor has obtained sufficient competent audit evidence to support the opinion on the financial statements or other financial information being reported upon. The audit report is ordinarily dated as of this date.

Representation letter   A single letter or separate letters prepared by officers of the client company at the auditors' request setting forth certain representations about the company's financial position or operations.

Routine transaction   A transaction for a recurring financial activity recorded in the accounting records in the normal course of business, such as sales, purchases, cash receipts, cash disbursements, and payroll.

Specialist   A person or firm possessing special skill or knowledge in a field other than accounting or auditing, such as an actuary.

Substantive tests   Tests of account balances and transactions designed to detect any material misstatements in the financial statements. Substantive tests directly affect detection risk.

Sufficient   Sufficient audit evidence is a measure of the quantity of the evidence required.

Tick mark   A symbol used in working papers by the auditor to indicate a specific step in the work performed. Whenever tick marks are used, they must be accompanied by a legend explaining their meaning.

Vertical analysis   A form of analysis that presents financial statement amounts for a period as a percentage of some financial statement base. This analysis involves the preparation of *common-size financial statements.*

Working papers   Papers that document the evidence gathered by auditors to show the work they have done, the methods and procedures they have followed, and the conclusions they have developed in an audit of financial statements or other type of engagement.

Working trial balance   A working paper that lists the balances of accounts in the general ledger for the current and the previous year and also provides columns for the auditors' adjustments and reclassifications and for the final amounts that will appear in the financial statements.

Review Questions

5–1.   Describe the relationship between detection risk and audit risk.

5–2.   Define inherent risk. Can the auditors reduce inherent risk by performing audit procedures?

5–3.   Distinguish among routine, nonroutine, and estimation transactions. Include an example of each.

5–4.   Distinguish between the components of audit risk that the auditors gather evidence to assess versus the component of audit risk that they collect evidence to restrict.

5–5.   In a conversation with you, Mark Rogers, CPA, claims that both the *sufficiency* and the *competence* of audit evidence are a matter of judgment in every audit. Do you agree? Explain.

5–6.   "The best means of verification of cash, inventory, office equipment, and nearly all other assets is a physical count of the units; only a physical count gives the auditors complete assurance as to the accuracy of the amounts listed on the balance sheet." Evaluate this statement.

5–7.   As part of the verification of accounts receivable as of the balance sheet date, the auditors might inspect copies of sales invoices. Similarly, as part of the verification of accounts payable, the auditors might inspect purchase invoices. Which of these two types of invoices do you think represents the stronger type of evidence? Why?

5–8.   In verifying the asset accounts Notes Receivable and Marketable Securities, the auditors examined notes receivable and stock certificates. Which of these documents represents the stronger type of evidence? Why?

5–9.   When in the course of an audit might the auditor find it useful to apply analytical procedures?

5–10.   Give at least four examples of *specialists* whose findings might provide competent evidence for the independent auditors.

5–11.   What are the major purposes of obtaining representation letters from audit clients?

5–12.   The cost of an audit might be significantly reduced if the auditors relied upon a representation letter from the client instead of observing the physical counting of inventory. Would this use of a representation letter be an acceptable means of reducing the cost of an audit?

5–13.   List and briefly describe the three approaches to auditing accounting estimates that are included in a client's financial statements.

5–14.   "In deciding upon the type of evidence to be gathered in support of a given item on the financial statements, the auditors should not be influenced by the differences in cost of obtaining alternative forms of evidence." Do you agree? Explain.

5–15.   What are *related party transactions?*

5–16.   What disclosures should be made in the financial statements regarding material related party transactions?

5–17.   Evaluate the following statement: "Identifying related parties and obtaining a client representation letter are two required audit procedures normally performed on the last day of fieldwork."

5–18.   What are the major functions of audit working papers?

5–19.   Why are the prior year's audit working papers a useful reference to staff assistants during the current audit?

5–20.   List the major types of audit working papers and give a brief explanation of each. For example, one type of audit working paper is an account analysis. This working paper shows the changes that occurred in a given account during the period under audit. By analyzing an account, the auditors determine its nature and content.

5–21.   "Audit working papers are the property of the auditors, who may destroy the papers, sell them, or give them away." Criticize this quotation.

5–22.   Describe a situation in which a set of audit working papers might be used by third parties to support a charge of gross negligence against the auditors.

5–23.   Should the working trial balance prepared by the auditors include revenue and expense accounts if the balances of these accounts for the audit year have been closed into retained earnings prior to the auditors' arrival? Explain.

5–24.   Why are the final figures from the prior year's audit included in a working trial balance or lead schedule?

5–25.   Should the auditors prepare adjusting journal entries to correct all errors they discover in the accounting records for the year under audit? Explain.

5–26.   Explain the meaning of the term *permanent file* as used in connection with audit working papers. What kinds of information are usually included in the permanent file?

5–27.   List several rules to be observed in the preparation of working papers that will reflect current professional practice.

5–28.   "I have finished my testing of footings of the cash journals," said the assistant auditor to the senior auditor. "Shall I state in the working papers the periods for which I verified footings, or should I just list the totals of the receipts and disbursements I have proved to be correct?" Prepare an answer to the assistant's question, stressing the reasoning involved.

5–29.   What is the purpose of a "second partner review"? What should be the extent of the second partner's association with the engagement being reviewed?

5–30.   In their review of audit working papers, what do managers and partners look for?

Questions Requiring Analysis

5–31.   Financial statements contain five broad assertions about the accounts included in the statements.

   a. Identify who makes these assertions.

   b. List and describe each of the assertions.

5–32.   Auditors gather a number of different types of evidence in the course of an audit, including physical evidence, third-party representations, documentary evidence, computations, data interrelationships, client representations, and accounting records. Listed below are 10 audit procedures that are typically performed in an audit:

   1. Observe the client's inventory-taking procedures.

2. Obtain a report on the valuation of inventory by a specialist.

3. Examine an invoice in support of a sales transaction.

4. Examine an invoice in support of a purchase transaction.

5. Test the extensions on an inventory schedule.

6. Inspect the client's bank statement.

7. Examine equipment in the client's plant.

8. Obtain a confirmation of an account payable directly from the vendor.

9. Review the client's general ledger.

10. Perform analytical procedures to test the completeness of sales transactions.

Required:

    a. For each audit procedure identify the type of evidence that the procedure gathers. If the procedure gathers documentary evidence, state whether the evidence is received directly by the auditors, created externally and held by the client, or created internally by the client.

    b. Comment on the relative reliability of the three forms of documentary evidence.

5–33.   Marion Watson & Co., CPAs, is planning its audit procedures for its tests of the valuation of inventories of East Coast Manufacturing Co. The auditors on the engagement have assessed inherent risk and control risk for valuation of inventories at 100 percent and 50 percent, respectively.

Required:

    a. Calculate the appropriate level of detection risk for the audit of this assertion, given that the auditors wish to restrict audit risk for the assertion to 3 percent.

    b. Calculate the appropriate level of detection risk for the audit of this assertion, given that the auditors wish to restrict audit risk for the assertion to 5 percent.

5–34.   In an audit of financial statements, the auditors gather various types of audit evidence. List seven major types of evidence and provide a procedural example of each.

5–35.   Comment on the competence of each of the following examples of audit evidence. Arrange your answer in the form of a separate paragraph for each item. Explain fully the reasoning employed in judging the competence of each item.

    a. Copies of client's sales invoices.

    b. Auditors' independent computation of earnings per share.

    c. Paid checks returned with a bank statement.

    d. Response from customer of client addressed to auditors' office confirming amount owed to client at balance sheet date.

    e. Representation letter signed by controller of client company stating that all liabilities of which she has knowledge are reflected in the company's accounts.

5–36.   Analytical procedures are extremely useful throughout the audit.

Required:

    a. Explain how analytical procedures are useful in:

        (1) The planning stage of the audit.

        (2) The substantive testing stage of the audit.

        (3) The overall review stage of the audit.

    b. List the five sources of information that are available to the auditors in developing expectations for analytical procedures.

    c. List and describe four techniques that may be used by the auditors in developing expectations for analytical procedures.

5–37.   When analytical procedures disclose unexpected changes in financial relationships relative to prior years, the auditors consider the possible reasons for the changes. Give several possible reasons for the following significant changes in relationships:

    a. The rate of inventory turnover (ratio of cost of goods sold to average inventory) has declined from the prior year's rate.

    b. The number of days' sales in accounts receivable has increased over the prior year.

5–38.   One of the assets of Vista Corporation is 6,000 acres of land in a remote area of the Arizona desert. The land is held as a long-term investment and is carried in the accounting records at a cost of $200 per acre. A recent topographical map prepared by the U.S. Soil Conservation Service shows the land to be nearly flat with no standing bodies of water. The land is accessible only by aircraft or four-wheel-drive vehicles. Evaluate the merits of the auditors personally (physically) examining this land as a means of obtaining audit evidence.

5–39. Auditors are required on every engagement to obtain a representation letter from the client.

Required:
    a. What are the objectives of the client's representation letter?

    b. Who should prepare and sign the client's representation letter?

    c. When should the client's representation letter be obtained?

5–40. What would you accept as satisfactory documentary evidence in support of entries in the following?

    a. Sales journal.

    b. Sales returns journal.

    c. Voucher or invoice register.

    d. Payroll journal.

    e. Check register.

5–41. An important part of every audit of financial statements is the preparation of audit working papers.

Required:
    a. Discuss the relationship of audit working papers to each of the standards of fieldwork.

    b. You are instructing an inexperienced staff assistant on her first auditing assignment. She is to examine an account. An analysis of the account has been prepared by the client for inclusion in the audit working papers. Prepare a list of the comments, commentaries, and notations that the staff assistant should make or have made on the account analysis to provide an adequate working paper as evidence of her examination. (Do not include a description of audit procedures applicable to the account.)

(AICPA, adapted)

5–42. The preparation of working papers is an integral part of the CPAs' audit of financial statements. On a recurring engagement the CPAs review the working papers from their prior audit while planning the current examination to determine the papers' usefulness for the current engagement.

Required:
    a. (1) What are the purposes or functions of audit working papers?

       (2) What records of the auditors may be included in audit working papers?

    b. Describe what professional standards state about the sufficiency of audit documentation in audit working papers.

    c. To comply with generally accepted auditing standards, the auditors include certain evidence in their working papers, for example, "evidence that the engagement was planned and work of assistants was supervised and reviewed." What other evidence should the auditors include in audit working papers to comply with generally accepted auditing standards?

(AICPA, adapted)

5–43. The partnership of Smith, Frank & Clark, a CPA firm, has been the auditor of Greenleaf, Inc., for many years. During the annual audit of the financial statements for the year ended December 31, 20X2, a dispute developed over whether certain disclosures should be made in the financial statements. The dispute resulted in Smith, Frank & Clark being dismissed and Greenleaf engaging another CPA firm. Greenleaf demanded that Smith, Frank & Clark turn over all working papers applicable to the Greenleaf audits or face a lawsuit. Smith, Frank & Clark refused. Greenleaf has instituted a suit against Smith, Frank & Clark to obtain the working papers.

Required:
    a. Will Greenleaf succeed in its suit? Explain.

    b. Discuss the rationale underlying the rule of law applicable to the ownership of audit working papers.

(AICPA, adapted)

5–44. "Working papers should contain facts and nothing but facts," said student A. "Not at all," replied student B. "The audit working papers may also include expressions of opinion. Facts are not always available to settle all issues." "In my opinion," said student C, "a mixture of facts and opinions in the audit working papers would be most confusing if the papers were produced as a means of supporting the auditors' position when their report has been challenged." Evaluate the issues underlying these arguments.

5–45. At 12 o'clock, when the plant whistle sounded, George Green, an assistant auditor, had his desk completely covered with various types of working papers. Green stopped work immediately, but not wanting to leave the desk with such a disorderly appearance he took a few minutes to sort the papers into proper order, place them in a neat pile, and weight them down with a heavy ashtray. He then departed for lunch. The auditor-in-charge, who had been observing what was going on, was critical of the assistant's actions. What do you think was the basis for criticism by the auditor-in-charge?

Multiple Choice Questions

5–46.   Select the best answer for each of the following questions. Explain the reasons for your selection.

a. Which of the following is not a financial statement assertion made by management?

(1) Existence of recorded assets and liabilities.

(2) Completeness of recorded assets and liabilities.

(3) Valuation of assets and liabilities.

(4) Effectiveness of internal control.

b. Which of the following business characteristics is not indicative of high inherent risk?

(1) Operating results that are highly sensitive to economic factors.

(2) Large likely misstatements detected in prior audits.

(3) Substantial turnover of management.

(4) A large amount of assets.

c. As part of their audit, auditors obtain a representation letter from their client. Which of the following is *not* a valid purpose of such a letter?

(1) To increase the efficiency of the audit by eliminating the need for other audit procedures.

(2) To remind the client's management of its primary responsibility for the financial statements.

(3) To document in the audit working papers the client's responses to certain verbal inquiries made by the auditors during the engagement.

(4) To provide evidence in those areas dependent upon management's future intentions.

d. Which of the following statements best describes why auditors investigate related party transactions?

(1) Related party transactions generally are illegal acts.

(2) The substance of related party transactions may differ from their form.

(3) All related party transactions must be eliminated as a step in preparing consolidated financial statements.

(4) Related party transactions are a form of management fraud.

e. Of the following, which is the *least* persuasive type of audit evidence?

(1) Confirmations mailed by outsiders to the auditors.

(2) Correspondence between the auditors and suppliers.

(3) Copies of sales invoices inspected by the auditors.

(4) Canceled checks returned in the year-end bank statement directly to the client.

f. Analytical procedures are most likely to detect:

(1) Weaknesses of a material nature in internal control.

(2) Unusual transactions.

(3) Noncompliance with prescribed control activities.

(4) Improper separation of accounting and other financial duties.

g. Which of the following is not a primary approach to auditing an accounting estimate?

(1) Review and test management's process for developing the estimate.

(2) Review subsequent transactions.

(3) Confirm the amounts.

(4) Develop an independent estimate.

h. A primary purpose of the audit working papers is to:

(1) Aid the auditors by providing a list of required procedures.

(2) Provide a point of reference for future audit engagements.

(3) Support the underlying concepts included in the preparation of the basic financial statements.

(4) Support the auditors' opinion.

i. In what section of the audit working papers would a long-term lease agreement be filed?

(1) Current working paper file.

(2) Permanent working paper file.

(3) Lead schedule file.

(4) Corroborating documents file.

j. Which of the following is not a function of audit working papers?

(1) Assist management in illustrating the financial statements are in accordance with generally accepted accounting principles.

(2) Assist audit team members responsible for supervision in reviewing the work.

(3) Assist auditors in planning future engagements.

(4) Assist peer reviewers and inspectors in performing their roles.

k. In using the work of a specialist, the auditors referred to the specialist's findings in their report. This would be an appropriate reporting practice if the:

(1) Client is not familiar with the professional certification, personal reputation, or particular competence of the specialist.

(2) Auditors, as a result of the specialist's findings, give a qualified opinion on the financial statements.

(3) Client understands the auditors' corroborative use of the specialist's findings in relation to the representations in the financial statements.

(4) Auditors, as a result of the specialist's findings, decide to indicate a division of responsibility with the specialist.

l. A difference of opinion concerning accounting and auditing matters relative to a particular phase of the audit arises between an assistant auditor and the auditor responsible for the engagement. After appropriate consultation, the assistant auditor asks to be disassociated from the resolution of the matter. The working papers would probably:

(1) Remain silent on the matter since it is an internal matter of the auditing firm.

(2) Note that the assistant auditor is completely dissociated from responsibility for the auditors' opinion.

(3) Document the additional work required, since all disagreements of this type will require expanded substantive testing.

(4) Document the assistant auditor's position and how the difference of opinion was resolved.

Problems

5–47. Audit risk should be considered when planning and performing an audit of financial statements in accordance with generally accepted auditing standards.

Required:

a. Define audit risk.

b. Describe its components of inherent risk, control risk, and detection risk.

c. Explain the interrelationship among these components.

d. Which (if any) of these components is completely a function of the sufficiency of the evidence gathered by the auditors' procedures? Explain your answer.

e. Comment on the following: "Since cash is often less than 1 percent of total assets, inherent and control risk for that account must be low. Accordingly, detection risk should be established at a high level."

(AICPA, adapted)

5–48. Assume that the auditors find serious weaknesses in the internal control of Oak Canyon, Inc., a producer and distributor of fine wines. Would these internal control weaknesses cause the auditors to rely more or less upon each of the following types of evidence during their audit of Oak Canyon?

a. Documents created and used only within the organization.

      b. Physical evidence.

      c. Evidence provided by specialists.

      d. Analytical procedures.

      e. Accounting records.

Required: For each of the above five items, state your conclusion and explain fully the underlying reasoning.

5–49. The financial statements of Wayne Company indicate that large amounts of notes payable to banks were retired during the period under audit. Evaluate the reliability of each of the following types of evidence supporting these transactions:

      a. Debit entries in the Notes Payable account.

      b. Entries in the check register.

      c. Paid checks.

      d. Notes payable bearing bank perforation stamp PAID and the date of payment.

      e. Statement by client's treasurer that notes had been paid at maturity.

      f. Letter received by auditors directly from bank stating that no client indebtedness existed as of the balance sheet date.

5–50. During your examination of the accounts receivable of Hope Ranch, a new client, you notice that one account is much larger than the rest, and you therefore decide to examine the evidence supporting this customer's account. Comment on the relative reliability and adequacy of the following types of evidence:

      a. Computer printout from accounts receivable subsidiary ledger.

      b. Copies of sales invoices in amount of the receivable.

      c. Purchase orders received from customer.

      d. Shipping documents describing the articles sold.

      e. Letter received by client from customer acknowledging the correctness of the receivable in the amount shown on client's accounting records.

      f. Letter received by auditors directly from customer acknowledging the correctness of the amount shown as receivable on client's accounting records.

5–51. Trend analysis, common-size financial statements, and ratios are presented for the Brody Corporation in Figure 5.4. Assume that you are auditing Brody's financial statements for the year ended 12/31/X8. You have performed tests of controls over the recording of gross sales and believe that the system is operating effectively and that 7 percent represents an accurate estimate of the increase in gross sales for 20X8 over the amount for 20X7. You should also assume that the financial statements for 20X6 and 20X7 are not misstated.

Required:
      a. Analyze Figure 5.4 and identify any accounts that appear to represent significant variations from what one might expect. For each of the accounts identify another account that might also be out of line due to the manner in which the double-entry bookkeeping system records transactions.

      b. Identify any ratios that appear to represent significant variations from what one might expect. For each ratio identify the financial statement account or accounts that may be misstated.

5–52. Included in the financial statements are a variety of accounting estimates (e.g., allowance for doubtful accounts, obsolete inventory, warranty liability). Audit procedures must be designed to obtain evidence about the assertions of management related to all accounts, including those based on accounting estimates.

Required:
      a. List three approaches to auditing accounting estimates. Provide an example of how an auditor might apply each of the three approaches in auditing the allowance for doubtful accounts, which management has established at 1 percent of credit sales.

      b. Discuss the meaning of the valuation or allocation assertion as it relates to the allowance for doubtful accounts.

      c. Discuss factors that bear on whether the allowance for doubtful accounts is likely to be an account with high inherent risk.

5–53. Criticize the following working paper that you are reviewing as senior auditor on the December 31 audit of Pratt Company.

Pratt Company
Cash

Per bank		$44,874.50√
Deposit in transit		5,843.10①
Bank charges		(2.80)②
Outstanding checks		
	1,246.40√	
	3,412.72√	
	840.00√	
	1,013.60③	
	1,200.00③	
	967.50Y	8,680.22
Per ledger	*f*	$42,034.58√

f Footed column

√ Verified

①The client saved a copy of the deposit slip that is filled out. Per discussion with client, this represents cash sales on 12/31/0X. I agreed totals to the Cash Receipts Journal on 12/31/0X. Properly posted on bank statement as having been received by bank on 1/9/0Y.

②Represents December bank service charge. Agreed charge to December bank statement in which bank charged client $2.80. Recorded as cash disbursement in January of 200Y.

③Per client, check written (to pay account receivable) before year-end, but not mailed until 1/2/0Y because on 12/31/0X the last office mail was picked up at 3 PM due to year-end party of mail room employees.

J.M.W.

1-15-0Y

5–54. One of the practical problems confronting the auditors is that of determining whether adjusting journal entries or other corrective actions are warranted for misstatements, omissions, and inconsistencies. The following items were noted by the auditors during their year-end audit of a small manufacturing partnership having net sales of approximately $1.6 million; net income of approximately $40,000; total assets of nearly $2 million; and total partners' capital of $300,000.

(1) Proceeds of $250 from the sale of fully depreciated office equipment were credited to Miscellaneous Revenue rather than to Gain and Loss on Sales of Equipment, a ledger account that had not been used for several years.

(2) The Trade Accounts Receivable control account showed a balance of $79,600. The individual accounts composing this balance included three with credit balances of $320, $19, and $250, respectively.

(3) Several debits and credits to general ledger accounts had been made directly without use of journal entries. The amounts involved did not exceed $500.

(4) Credit memoranda were not serially numbered or signed, but a file of duplicates was maintained.

(5) General journal entries did not include explanations for any but unusual transactions.

(6) Posting references were occasionally omitted from entries in general ledger accounts.

(7) An expenditure of $200 for automobile repairs was recorded as a December expense, although it was shown by the invoice to be a November charge.

(8) The auditors' count of petty cash disclosed a shortage of $20.

(9) Expenditures for advertising amounting to $8,000 were charged to the Advertising Expense account; other advertising expenses amounting to $3,000 had been charged to Miscellaneous Expense.

(10) On September 12, the client borrowed $288,000 from First Bank by signing a 120-day note payable in the face amount of $300,000. The note matures on January 10. The client's accountant had charged the entire $12,000 interest included in the face amount of the note to the interest expense of the current year. He stated that he did not consider deferring part of the interest to the following year to be warranted by the dollar amounts involved.

Required: State clearly the position the auditors should take with respect to each of the above items during the course of an annual audit. If adjusting journal entries are necessary, include them in your solution.

5–55. Marilyn Terrill is the senior auditor for the audit of Uden Supply Company for the year ended December 31, 20X4. In planning the audit, Marilyn is attempting to develop expectations for planning analytical procedures based on the financial information for prior years and her knowledge of the business and the industry, including:

1. Based on economic conditions, she believes that the increase in sales for the current year should approximate the historical trend.
2. Based on her knowledge of industry trends, she believes that the gross profit for 20X4 should be about 2 percent less than the percentage for 20X3.
3. Based on her knowledge of regulations, she is aware that the effective tax rate for the company for 20X4 has been reduced by 5 percent from that in 20X3.
4. Based on a review of the general ledger, she determined that average depreciable assets have increased by 10 percent.
5. Based on her knowledge of economic conditions, she is aware that the effective interest rate on the company's line of credit for 20X4 was approximately 12 percent. The average outstanding balance of the line of credit was $2,300,000. This line of credit is the company's only interest-bearing debt.
6. Based on her discussions with management and her knowledge of the industry, she believes that the amount of other expenses should be consistent with the trends from prior years.

Comparative income statement information for Uden Supply Company is presented in the accompanying table.

UDEN SUPPLY COMPANY
Comparative Income Statements
Years Ended December 20X1, 20X2, and 20X3
(Thousands)

	20X1 Audited	20X2 Audited	20X3 Audited	20X4 Expected
Sales	8,700	9,400	10,100	_____
Cost of goods sold	6,000	6,500	7,000	_____
Gross profit	2,700	2,900	3,100	_____
Sales commissions	610	660	710	_____
Advertising	175	190	202	_____
Salaries	1,061	1,082	1,103	_____
Payroll taxes	184	192	199	_____
Employee benefits	167	174	181	_____
Rent	60	61	62	_____
Depreciation	60	63	66	_____
Supplies	26	28	30	_____
Utilities	21	22	23	_____
Legal and accounting	34	37	40	_____
Miscellaneous	12	13	14	_____
Interest expense	210	228	240	_____
Net income before taxes	80	150	230	_____
Income taxes	18	33	50	_____
Net income	62	117	180	_____

Required:

a. Describe the purpose of analytical procedures performed in the planning stage of the audit.

b. Develop the expected amounts for 20X4 for each of the income statement items.

c. Uden's unaudited financial statements for the current year show a 31 percent gross profit rate. Assuming that this represents a misstatement from the amount that you developed as an expectation, calculate the estimated effect of this misstatement on net income before taxes for 20X4.

d. Indicate whether you believe that the difference calculated in part (*c*) is material. Explain your answer.

In-Class Team Case

5–56. Houseco, an audit client of Jones, CPA, for the past five years, is a manufacturer of various household products. Approximately four years ago Houseco developed a better toaster than had been available and sales took off, especially during the most recent two years, 20X7 and 20X8. Currently, the company controls approximately 25 percent of the toaster market in the United States. In addition, the company manufactures other products, including vacuum cleaners, floor polishers, and electric fondue pots.

Much of the increased sales performance is due to Donald Skaldon, who became the chief executive officer in 20X4. Donald and several other officers were able to accomplish a leveraged stock buyout in 20X6. This seems to have worked out very well since Donald suggests that his net worth grew from less than $300,000 to well over $5 million due to increases in the value of the common stock he holds in the company. He is also excited since the company's unaudited results show earnings per share of $1.21, one cent more than the most optimistic analysts had projected. He points out to Jones that sales are up over 38 percent compared to the previous year and net income has increased by 54 percent. All is well.

Jones is beginning the planning analytical procedures for the 20X8 audit to obtain information to help plan the nature, timing, and extent of other audit procedures. More specifically he wants to identify areas that may represent specific risks relevant to this year's audit.

Required: Use the balance sheet on page 166 and income statement on page 167 to identify accounts that may represent specific risks relevant to this year's audit. For each area briefly note why you think it represents a risk.

Research and Discussion Cases

5–57. You are the partner on the audit of Datasave, Inc., a small publicly held corporation that manufactures high-speed tape drives for the computer industry. The audit of Datasave had been progressing satisfactorily until you were about a month away from issuing your opinion. Suddenly, and quite mysteriously, Carl Wagner, the financial vice president, resigned. John Ross, who had been a manager with a large CPA firm, was quickly hired to replace Wagner. Although the change in Datasave's chief financial officer caused some disruption, the audit was completed on a timely basis.

As the last step in the audit process, you have prepared the representation letter for signing. You wanted the letter to be signed by William Cox, the president; Robert Star, the controller; and Wagner, who occasionally came to the company's offices to resolve matters regarding his past compensation. The signatures of Cox and Star were obtained, and you approached Wagner for his signature. In response to your request, Wagner replied, "I no longer am employed with this crazy company. Why should I take any responsibility for the financial statements?" Despite your attempts to persuade him, Wagner refused to sign the letter. Wagner also refused to discuss the reasons for his resignation, other than to say the reasons were personal.

When you discussed the problem of Wagner's refusal to sign with Cox, he indicated that there was no problem because Ross would sign the letter. You see this as a possible solution, but you are aware that Ross knows very little about the financial statements for the year under audit. Also, you are still somewhat concerned about the reasons for Wagner's resignation.

Required:
a. Describe fully the alternatives that are available to you in this situation.
b. Express your personal opinion as to the appropriate course of action and provide reasoning to support your opinion.

5–58. Marshall and Wyatt, CPAs, has been the independent auditor of Interstate Land Development Corporation for several years. During these years, Interstate prepared and filed its own annual income tax returns.

During 20X6, Interstate requested Marshall and Wyatt to audit all the necessary financial statements of the corporation to be submitted to the Securities and Exchange Commission (SEC) in connection with a multistate public offering of 1 million shares of Interstate common stock. This public offering came under the provisions of the Securities Act of 1933. The audit was performed carefully and the financial statements were fairly presented for the respective periods. These financial statements were included in the registration statement filed with the SEC.

While the registration statement was being processed by the SEC, but before the effective date, the Internal Revenue Service (IRS) obtained a federal court subpoena directing Marshall and Wyatt to turn over all its working papers relating to Interstate for the years 20X2–20X5. Marshall and Wyatt initially refused to comply for two reasons. First, Marshall and Wyatt did

Houseco Balance Sheet

	Dollars (000s omitted)			Vertical Analysis			Horizontal Analysis	
	12/31/X6 (Audited)	12/31/X7 (Audited)	12/31/X8 (Unaudited)	12/31/X6 (Audited)	12/31/X7 (Audited)	12/31/X8 (Unaudited)	(X7−X6)/X6 (Audited)	(X8−X7)/X7 (Unaudited)
Assets								
Cash	63	514	885	0%	1%	1%	716%	72%
Accounts receivable	14,402	27,801	51,076	33%	43%	43%	93%	84%
Inventories—RM	2,682	9,182	18,049	6%	14%	15%	242%	97%
Inventories—WIP	491	638	4,151	1%	1%	4%	30%	551%
Inventories—FG	6,589	9,757	16,935	15%	15%	14%	48%	74%
Total inventories	9,762	19,577	39,153	23%	30%	33%	101%	100%
Other current assets	708	1,449	3,015	2%	2%	3%	105%	108%
Total current assets	24,935	49,341	94,111	58%	76%	80%	98%	91%
Fixed assets (net)	18,267	15,900	24,029	42%	24%	20%	(13%)	51%
Total assets	43,202	65,241	118,140	100%	100%	100%	51%	81%
Liability and Equity								
Accounts payable	7,344	15,072	13,288	17%	23%	11%	105%	(12%)
Accrued liabilities	3,127	5,468	4,710	7%	8%	4%	75%	(14%)
Current portion L/T debt	2,707	900	1,250	6%	1%	1%	(67%)	39%
Income taxes payable	1,554	2,619	3,782	4%	4%	3%	69%	44%
Total current liabilities	14,732	24,059	23,030	34%	37%	19%	63%	(4%)
Bank debt	14,800	19,841	62,057	34%	30%	53%	34%	213%
Deferred income taxes	685	1,254	1,881	2%	2%	2%	83%	50%
Total liabilities	30,217	45,154	86,968	70%	69%	74%	49%	93%
Common stock	7,775	7,775	7,903	18%	12%	7%	0%	2%
Retained earnings	5,210	12,312	23,269	12%	19%	20%	136%	89%
Total liabilities and equity	43,202	65,241	118,140	100%	100%	100%	51%	81%

Houseco Income Statement

	Dollars (000s omitted)			Vertical Analysis			Horizontal Analysis	
	12/31/X6 (Audited)	12/31/X7 (Audited)	12/31/X8 (Unaudited)	12/31/X6 (Audited)	12/31/X7 (Audited)	12/31/X8 (Unaudited)	(X7−X6)/X6 (Audited)	(X8−X7)/X7 (Unaudited)
Gross sales	78,428	133,504	183,767	103%	104%	101%	70%	38%
—Returns & allow.	2,284	5,270	2,644	3%	4%	1%	131%	(50%)
Net sales	76,144	128,234	181,123	100%	100%	100%	68%	41%
Cost of goods sold	46,213	70,756	94,934	61%	55%	52%	53%	34%
Gross margin	29,931	57,478	86,189	39%	45%	48%	92%	50%
Sell, advertising, R&D expenses	20,105	42,600	64,285	26%	33%	35%	112%	51%
Income from operations	9,826	14,878	21,904	13%	12%	12%	51%	47%
Interest expense	1,930	1,584	3,189	3%	1%	2%	(18%)	101%
Income before taxes	7,896	13,294	18,715	10%	10%	10%	68%	41%
Income taxes	3,807	6,189	7,761	5%	5%	4%	63%	25%
Net income	4,089	7,105	10,954	5%	6%	6%	74%	54%
EPS	.46	.78	1.21					

Ratios

Current	1.7	2.1	4.1
Quick	1.0	1.2	2.3
Receivable turnover	5.3	6.3	4.7
Days' sales in ending receivables	68.1	57.1	76.6
Inventory turnover	4.7	4.8	3.2
Days' sales in ending inventory	76.0	75.0	112.5
Interest expense/Debt	0.11	0.08	0.05

not prepare Interstate's tax returns. Second, Marshall and Wyatt claimed that the working papers were confidential matters subject to the privileged communications rule. Subsequently, however, Marshall and Wyatt did relinquish the subpoenaed working papers.

Upon receiving the subpoena, Wyatt called Dunkirk, the chair of Interstate's board of directors, and asked him about the IRS investigation. Dunkirk responded, "I'm sure that the IRS people are on a fishing expedition and that they will not find any material deficiencies."

A few days later Dunkirk received a written memorandum from the IRS stating that it was contending Interstate had underpaid its taxes during the period under review. The memorandum revealed that Interstate was being assessed $800,000, including penalties and interest for the three years. Dunkirk forwarded a copy of this memorandum to Marshall and Wyatt.

This $800,000 assessment was material relative to the financial statements as of December 31, 20X6. The amount for each year individually, exclusive of penalty and interest, was not material relative to each respective year.

Required:

a. In general terms, discuss the extent to which a CPA firm's potential liability to third parties is increased in an SEC registration audit.

b. Discuss the implications of the IRS investigation, if any, relative to Marshall and Wyatt's examination of Interstate's 20X6 financial statements. Discuss any additional investigative procedures that the auditors should undertake or any audit judgments that should be made as a result of this investigation.

c. Can Marshall and Wyatt validly refuse to surrender the subpoenaed working papers to the IRS? Explain.

(AICPA, adapted)

Suggested References

Part a:

This textbook, pages 105–108.

AICPA, *Statement on Auditing Standards No. 19,* "Client Representations" (New York, 1977) AU 333.

Part b:

An intermediate accounting text.

AICPA, *Professional Standards, Volume 1,* Commerce Clearing House, *Statement on Auditing Standards 1,* Section 560.

FASB Statement 5, "Accounting for Contingencies."

Part c:

This textbook, pages 147–148.

AICPA, *Statement on Auditing Standards No. 58,* "Reports on Audited Financial Statements" (New York, 1988) AU 508.

Chapter 6

Planning the Audit; Linking Audit Procedures to Risk

Chapter learning objectives

After studying this chapter, you should be able to:

LO1. Identify the factors considered by auditors in accepting new clients.

LO2. Explain a CPA's responsibilities when planning an audit.

LO3. Explain how the auditors assess a client's business risk and use these risks to determine inherent risks.

LO4. Describe the manner in which an audit is affected by the auditors' assessment of audit risk and materiality.

LO5. Describe how the auditors address fraud risk.

LO6. Explain how risks of material misstatement are linked to the nature, timing, and extent of audit procedures.

LO7. Distinguish between the systems portion of the audit program and the substantive test portion.

LO8. Describe the major steps in the audit process.

How do auditors determine whether a prospective client is reputable and should be accepted as a client? After accepting an audit client, how do auditors go about planning the engagement and preparing the initial audit program? When one considers the potential legal liability involved, it becomes obvious that auditors do not merely accept a new audit client and then arrive at the client's premises to "start auditing." The first standard of fieldwork states:

> The work is to be *adequately planned*, and assistants, if any, are to be *properly supervised*. [emphasis added]

The concept of adequate planning includes investigating a prospective client before deciding whether to accept the engagement; obtaining an understanding of the client's business operations and its environment; assessing audit risk and materiality; developing an overall strategy to organize, staff, coordinate, and schedule the audit activities; and linking risks to audit procedures. Although much planning is done before beginning the actual audit fieldwork, the planning process continues throughout the engagement. Whenever a problem is encountered during the audit, the auditors must plan their response to the situation. This chapter describes the dynamic process of planning the audit, beginning with obtaining a client and proceeding through the design of the audit program. It also provides an overview of the entire audit.

Obtaining Clients

Learning Objective 1

Public accounting is a competitive profession, and most CPA firms are anxious to obtain new clients. Some new engagements are easily obtained through business transactions such as the acquisition of a company by an existing client and the client's desire to have the entire audit performed by one CPA firm. Others are obtained competitively through a partner's business or social contacts which lead to a request that the CPA firm submit a proposal for performing the company's annual audit. Such prospective clients may range from start up companies seeking a first audit to long-established companies considering replacing their current auditor. What risks are involved with a prospective new client? How does a CPA firm evaluate the risk associated with a prospective client? What other professional responsibilities exist relating to acquiring a new client?

As a starting point, it is essential for a CPA firm to maintain its integrity, objectivity, and reputation for providing high quality services. No auditor can afford to be regularly associated with clients who are engaging in management fraud or other misleading practices. The continuing wave of litigation involving auditors underscores the need for CPA firms to develop quality control policies for thoroughly investigating prospective clients *before accepting an engagement.* The CPAs should investigate the history of the prospective client, including such matters as the identities and reputations of the directors, officers, and major stockholders.

Even if the auditors perform an audit in accordance with generally accepted auditing standards, they may be sued by stockholders or creditors that sustain a loss. Therefore, auditors will consider the reputation of management and the financial strength and credit rating of a prospective client to help assess the overall risk of association with the particular business. This overall risk is often referred to as the **engagement risk.**

To help assess engagement risk, the auditors generally obtain management's permission to make inquiries of other third parties about a prospective audit client. For example, the client's banker can provide information regarding the client's financial history and credit rating. The

Illustrative Case
Fraud at ZZZZ Best Co.

ZZZZ Best Co. was a carpet cleaning company started in 1981 by Barry Minkow, a 15-year-old high school student. Although the company experienced significant growth during the mid-1980s, it was not fast enough for Minkow. He hired several officers with criminal records and conceived a plan to restore damaged buildings for insurance companies. A number of multimillion-dollar restoration contracts were supposedly undertaken that later were found to be completely fictitious. Minkow attempted to cover up the scheme by spending several million dollars to lease a building and make it appear to be a legitimate restoration project when the CPAs insisted upon visiting the site. Prior to the time the fraud was uncovered, the company's stock had a market value in excess of $211 million. Shortly thereafter, the stock was worthless. This case clearly illustrates the risks involved in accepting young companies with rapid growth, the need to investigate the background of key officers of a company, and the need to have a thorough understanding of the client's operations and industry.

client's legal counsel can provide information about the client's legal environment, including such matters as pending litigation and disputes with regulatory agencies.

Engagement risk is increased when the client company is in a weak financial position or is greatly in need of additional capital. When an audit client goes bankrupt, the auditors often are named as defendants in lengthy and costly lawsuits, with possible damage to their professional reputation. For that reason, some CPAs choose to avoid engagements entailing a relatively high engagement risk; others may accept such engagements, recognizing the need to expand audit procedures to compensate for the unusually high levels of risk.

In addition to evaluating engagement risk, the auditors should consider whether they can complete the audit in accordance with generally accepted auditing standards. As discussed in Chapter 3, the CPA firm must be independent of the client to perform an audit. Therefore, the auditors must determine whether there are any conditions that would prevent them from performing an *independent* audit of the client. Consideration also will be given to whether the partners and staff have appropriate training and experience to competently complete the engagement. If the auditors have no experience in a particularly complex industry, they may decide that a competent audit of a prospective client in that industry cannot be performed unless the CPA firm hires appropriately experienced personnel.

Submitting a Proposal

To obtain the audit, the auditors may be asked to submit a competitive proposal that will include information on the nature of services that the firm offers, the qualifications of the firm's personnel, anticipated fees, and other information to convince the prospective client to select the firm. The CPA firm also may be asked to make an oral presentation to the prospective client's audit committee and management to provide a basis for the selection. As is discussed in further detail later in this chapter, when the auditors replace other auditors, they must attempt to communicate with the predecessor auditors before finally accepting the new engagement.

Audit Committees

Arrangements for the audit should be made through contact with the company's **audit committee.** Public companies must establish such a committee within the board of directors to take an active role in overseeing the company's accounting and financial reporting policies and practices. Audit committees are required by the New York Stock Exchange, the American Stock Exchange, and NASDAQ.

An audit committee must be composed of at least three *independent directors*—that is, those *outside directors* (neither officers nor employees) who have no other relationship that might impair their independence. Although audit committee members are paid for serving on the board of directors, the Sarbanes-Oxley Act of 2002 provides that audit committee members should not receive any consulting, advisory, or other compensatory fee from the company, or be in any way affiliated with the company. Also, the members of the audit committee must be financially literate. Finally, the audit committee must be responsible for appointment, compensation, and oversight of the auditors.

During the course of the audit the auditors will discuss with the audit committee matters such as weaknesses in internal control, proposed audit adjustments, disagreements with management as to accounting principles, the quality of accounting principles used by the company, and indications of management fraud or other illegal acts by corporate officers. Since these communications assist the audit committee in its oversight of the financial reporting process of the company, they are required by generally accepted auditing standards. Chapters 7 and 16 present a detailed discussion of the required communications to audit committees.

Not all entities have audit committees. For example, the concept of an audit committee does not apply to businesses organized as sole proprietorships, partnerships, and small, closely held corporations. Arrangements for an audit of these businesses often are made with the owners, a partner, or an executive, such as the president or the controller.

Fee Arrangements

When the business engages the services of independent public accountants, it will usually ask for an estimate of the cost of the audit. Staff time is the basic unit of measurement for audit fees. Each public accounting firm develops a per hour or per diem fee schedule for each category of audit staff, based on direct salaries and such related costs as payroll taxes and benefits. The direct rate is then increased for overhead costs and a profit element. In addition to standard per diem or per hour fees, clients are charged for direct costs incurred by the public accounting firm for staff travel, report processing, and other out-of-pocket expenditures.

Estimating a fee for an audit involves the application of the CPA firm's daily or hourly rates to the estimated time required. Since the exact number of hours cannot be determined in advance, the auditors may merely give a rough estimate of the fee. Or they may multiply the rates by the estimated time and quote a range or bracket of amounts within which the total fee will fall. In a competitive situation, a fixed fee may be quoted that is "discounted" from the standard to meet the competition.

Communication with Predecessor Auditors

SAS 84 (AU 315), "Communications between Predecessor and Successor Auditors," requires the successor auditors to attempt to communicate with the predecessor *before accepting the engagement.* Because the **predecessor auditors** are an excellent source of information about a prospective client, in many circumstances this communication will occur before a formal proposal is presented to a prospective client. In other situations (e.g., the prospective client's request or other reasons), the communication will occur subsequent to presentation of a formal proposal.

Because auditors are ethically prohibited from disclosing confidential client information without the client's consent, the **successor auditors** must ask management of the prospective client to authorize the predecessor auditors to respond fully to the successor's inquiries. If a prospective client is reluctant to authorize communications with the predecessor auditors, the successor auditors should seriously consider the implications in deciding whether to accept the engagement.

When permission has been granted, the successor auditors' inquiries will include questions about disagreements with management over accounting principles, the predecessor's understanding of the reason for the change in auditors, and other matters that will assist the successor auditors in deciding whether to accept the engagement. This communication with the predecessor auditors is extremely important as it aids the successor auditors in evaluating the *integrity of management.* A review of cases involving management fraud reveals that a significant number of the companies involved had recently changed their auditors, often because of disagreements over accounting principles.

For public companies there is another source of information about the reason for a change in auditors. Regulations of the SEC require companies subject to its jurisdiction to file a Form 8-K reporting changes in independent auditors, and the reasons therefore. The companies also must report the details of any significant disagreements between management and the auditors occurring over the prior three years. The auditors that have resigned or been discharged must provide a response indicating whether they agree with the company's form and providing any necessary details. This requirement discourages management from the practice of **shopping for accounting principles,** in which management changes auditors to a CPA firm that is more likely to sanction a disputed accounting principle. A company's management might, for example, search for auditors who would accept a questionable revenue recognition method as being in accordance with generally accepted accounting principles. Concern about shopping also led to the issuance of *SAS 97* (AU 625), "Reports on the Application of Accounting Principles," which provides guidance to public accountants when they get a request for a *written or oral* report on the accounting treatment of a prospective or completed transaction from a company that is audited by another CPA firm.

Before providing a report on accounting principles, *SAS 97* requires the accountants to take steps to make sure they have a complete understanding of the form and substance of the transaction, including consulting with the company's current auditors. They also should review existing accounting principles, and consult appropriate references and experts to provide an adequate basis for their conclusions. Although cases in which management actually shops for accounting principles are not common, it is clear that if management is allowed to change auditors casually, undue pressure is placed on auditors' independence.

Shopping for accounting principles is also discouraged by the provision of the Sarbanes-Oxley Act of 2002 requiring that the audit committee of a public company be responsible for the appointment, compensation, and oversight of the auditors.

First-Year Procedures

A new client should be informed as to the extent of investigation of the beginning balances of such accounts as plant and equipment and inventories. To determine the propriety of depreciation expense for the current year and the proper balances in plant and equipment accounts at the balance sheet date, the auditors must investigate the validity of the property accounts at the beginning of the current period. Similarly, if the auditors are unable to obtain satisfactory evidence as to the balance of *beginning inventories,* they will not have sufficient evidence about cost of goods sold, and it will be necessary to disclaim an opinion on the income statement.

When satisfactory prior-year audits of the business have been performed by a predecessor auditor, as discussed in the preceeding section, the successor auditor will ordinarily have communicated with the predecessor on matters such as management integrity, disagreements that the predecessor may have had with management communications with the audit committee, and the predecessors' understanding of the reasons for the change in auditors. *SAS 84* (AU 315) recommends a second communication with the predecessor subsequent to acceptance of the new client. This second communication relates primarily to the review of working papers related to opening balances and the consistency of application of accounting principles. Ordinarily the successor auditors will be able to accept the opening balances of the current year with a minimum of verification work. In cases in which no satisfactory recent audit has been made, an extensive analysis of transactions of prior years will be necessary to establish account balances as of the beginning of the current year. In these latter situations, where appropriate, the client should be informed that the scope and cost of the initial audit may exceed that of repeat engagements, which will not require extensive analysis of prior years' transactions.

Use of the Client's Staff

The auditors should obtain an understanding with the client as to the extent to which the client's staff, including the internal auditors, can help prepare for the audit. The client's staff should have the accounting records up to date when the auditors arrive. In addition, many audit working papers can be prepared for the auditors by the client's staff, thus reducing the cost of the audit and freeing the auditors from routine work. The auditors may set up the columnar headings or spreadsheet templates for such working papers and give instructions to the client's staff as to the information to be gathered. These working papers should bear the label *Prepared by Client,* or *PBC,* and also an indication of the auditor who verified the work performed by the client's staff. Working papers prepared by the client should never be accepted at face value; such papers must be reviewed and tested by the auditors.

Among the tasks that may be assigned to the client's employees are preparation of a trial balance of the general ledger, preparation of an aged trial balance of accounts receivable, analyses of accounts receivable written off, lists of property additions and retirements during the year, and analyses of various revenue and expense accounts. Many of these "working papers" may be in the form of computer spreadsheets and other computerized data files.

Other CPAs

When a portion of the client (e.g., a subsidiary in a distant city) is audited by another CPA firm, efforts must be coordinated. For example, if the accounts of the subsidiary are to be consolidated with the overall enterprise, and if that subsidiary is audited by another CPA firm, the auditors must coordinate the timing of necessary reports and procedures to be performed. Use of the work of other auditors is discussed in Chapter 17.

Arranging for Specialists

CPAs may lack the qualifications necessary to perform certain technical tasks relating to the audit. For example, judging the valuation of a diamond inventory may require employing a specialist in gem appraisal, or evaluating the reasonableness of the fair value of a complex financial derivative instrument may require the use of a securities valuation expert. Effective planning involves arranging for the appropriate use of specialists both inside and outside of the client organization. This should include consideration of the need for specialized skills in assessing the effects on the audit of the client's use of information technology. Using the work of specialists was discussed in detail in Chapter 5.

Engagement Letters

The auditors should establish an understanding with the client regarding the services to be performed, including the objectives of the engagement, management's responsibilities, the auditor's responsibilities, and limitations of the engagement. Although this understanding may be obtained through oral communications and documented in the working papers, it is ordinarily preferable from a good business perspective to establish the understanding in writing, generally through an **engagement letter.** When the engagement letter is accepted by the authorized client official, it represents an *executory contract* between the auditor and the client. Engagement letters do not follow any standard form; a typical engagement letter is presented in Figure 6.1.

The use of engagement letters is not limited to audit engagements. Professional standards for accounting and review services also require that the accountant have an understanding with the client as to the nature of the services to be performed. This "understanding" *preferably should be in writing* and signed by the client and the CPA.

Audit Planning

Learning Objective 2

Learning Objective 3

Once the client has been obtained, the planning process intensifies as the auditors concentrate their efforts on performing procedures to obtain a detailed understanding of the client and its environment, develop an overall audit strategy, and assess the risks of material misstatement of the financial statements. Most CPA firms have adopted the approach of obtaining a broad understanding of the client and its environment to identify the client's significant business risks. **Business risks** are threats to achieving management's objectives. As examples, a major competitor may represent a threat to management's achieving its sales goals, scarcity of raw materials may threaten management's ability to achieve the budgeted levels of production, or government regulation may threaten the very viability of the client. Significant business risks are important because many of them create related risks of material misstatement that the auditors should address in designing their audit procedures. Recall from Chapter 5 that these risks of material misstatement, before considering the client's internal control, are referred to as *inherent risks*.

FIGURE 6.1
Engagement Letter for Financial Statement Audit

Adams, Barnes & Co.

Certified Public Accountants

Mr. Loren Steele, Controller   September 1, 20X5
Keystone Computers & Networks, Inc.
14645 40th Street
Phoenix, Arizona 85280

Dear Mr. Steele:

This letter is to confirm our arrangements for our audit of the financial statements of Keystone Computers & Networks, Inc., for the year ended December 31, 20X5.

We will audit the Corporation's balance sheet as of December 31, 20X5, and the related statements of income, retained earnings, and cash flows for the year then ended. The objective of our audit is the expression of an opinion on the financial statements. We will also issue a report on compliance with various debt covenants as required by your debt agreement with Western Financial Services.

We will conduct our audit in accordance with generally accepted auditing standards. Those standards require that we obtain reasonable, rather than absolute, assurance about whether the financial statements are free of material misstatement, whether caused by error or fraud. Accordingly, an audit cannot be relied upon to identify all material errors, fraud, or illegal acts that may exist. Also an audit is not designed to detect error or fraud that is immaterial to the financial statements.

Our audit will include such tests of the company records as we consider necessary. Important among our audit planning procedures will be steps taken to understand your company's business and its risks. Also, in order to comply with professional obligations to identify misrepresentations, we may include retrospective, surprise, and nonstandard procedures in our audit plan. If, for any reason, we are unable to complete the audit, we may decline to express an opinion or issue a report as a result of the engagement.

While an audit includes obtaining an understanding of internal control sufficient to plan the audit and to determine the nature, timing, and extent of audit procedures to be performed, it is not designed to provide assurance on internal control or to identify reportable conditions. However, we will communicate any reportable conditions of which we become aware and make any other communications required by generally accepted auditing standards.

The financial statements are the responsibility of the Company's management. Management is also responsible for (1) establishing and maintaining effective internal control over financial reporting, (2) establishing systems and procedures for the prevention and detection of fraud, (3) identifying and ensuring that the Company complies with the laws and regulations applicable to its activities, (4) making all financial records and related information available to us, and (5) at the conclusion of the engagement, providing us with a letter that confirms certain representations made during the audit, including that the effects of any uncorrected misstatements that we bring to your attention are immaterial to the financial statements taken as a whole.

Our audit is scheduled for performance and completion as follows:

Begin fieldwork	November 10, 20X5
Completion of fieldwork	February 20, 20X6
Delivery of audit report	March 5, 20X6

Our fees for this audit will be based on the time spent by various members of our staff at our regular rates, plus direct expenses. We will notify you immediately of any circumstances we encounter that could significantly affect our initial fee estimate of $60,000.

In order for us to work as efficiently as possible, it is understood that your accounting staff will provide us with a year-end trial balance by January 15, 20X6, and also with the schedules and account analyses described on the separate attachment.

If these arrangements are in accordance with your understanding, please sign this letter in the space provided and return a copy to us at your earliest convenience.

Very truly yours,

Charles Adams

Charles Adams, CPA

Accepted by: _____
Date: _____

Obtaining an Understanding of the Client's Business and Its Environment

When should a health club recognize its revenue from the sale of lifetime memberships? Is a company organized to produce a single motion picture a going concern? What basis should be used to record a barter of goods over the **Internet?** What is a reasonable depreciable life for today's most advanced information systems? We will not attempt to answer these questions in this textbook; we raise them simply to demonstrate that the auditors must obtain a good working knowledge of an audit client's business and its environment if they are to design effective audit procedures. An understanding of the client and its environment encompasses:

- The nature of the client, including the client's application of accounting policies.
- The industry, regulatory, and other external factors affecting the client.
- The client's objectives and strategies and related business risks.
- Methods used by the client to measure and review performance.
- The client's internal control.

Performing procedures to obtain an understanding of the entity and its environment is an essential part of planning and performing an audit. Specifically, the understanding establishes a frame of reference for the auditors to use in: (1) considering the appropriateness of the accounting policies applied by the client, (2) identifying areas where special audit consideration may be necessary (specialized risks), (3) establishing appropriate materiality, (4) developing expectations for analytical procedures, (5) designing and performing audit procedures, and (6) evaluating audit evidence.

The Nature of the Client

"What is the client's business model?" "Who are its major customers and suppliers?" "What types of transactions does the client engage in?" "How are they accounted for?" These are the types of questions that the auditors attempt to answer to obtain an understanding of the nature of the client. The auditors' understanding of the nature of the client will include the client's competitive position, organizational structure, governance processes, accounting policies and procedures, ownership, capital structure, and product lines. Then the auditors turn their attention to the client's critical business processes and obtain an understanding of how these processes create value for the client's customers. Using a manufacturing company as an example, the auditors will obtain an understanding of:

- The processes used to procure, store, and manage raw materials.
- The processes used to machine, assemble, package, and test products.
- The processes used to create demand for products and services and to manage relations with customers.
- The processes used to establish contract terms and to bill and collect receivables.
- The processes used to take orders and deliver goods.
- The activities performed after the goods and services have been delivered (e.g., installation, training, warranty, and customer service).
- The processes used to acquire and maintain human resources and technology, including research and development.

Industry, Regulatory, and Other External Factors

The factors envisioned here include industry conditions, such as the competitive environment, supplier and customer relationships, and technological developments. They also include the regulatory, legal, and political environment and general economic conditions. These factors may subject the client to specialized risks that may in turn affect the audit. Many firms—including the Big 4 firms to varying degrees—have adopted a financial model to evaluate the client's industry that considers the attractiveness and other characteristics of the industry. Concerning the *overall attractiveness of the industry,* they consider such factors as:

- Barriers to entry.
- Strength of competitors.
- Bargaining power of suppliers of raw materials and labor.
- Bargaining power of customers.

The other *characteristics of the client's industry* that are considered include factors such as economic conditions and financial trends, governmental regulations, changes in technology, and widely used accounting methods.

Objectives and Strategies and Related Business Risks

The client's objectives are the overall plans of the entity as defined by management. Management attempts to achieve these objectives by developing strategies, or operational actions.

However, achieving management's objectives is always subject to business risks. As described above, these are the conditions that threaten management's ability to execute strategies and achieve its objectives. The auditors obtain an understanding of the client's operating and financing strategies and attempt to identify significant business risks faced by the client. Significant risks that may be identified for a particular client might include risks related to competition, changes in government regulations, changes in technology, volatility of raw material prices, interruption of supplies of critical raw materials, changes in major markets, or increases in interest rates. In obtaining their understanding of these matters, the auditors are particularly interested in management's risk assessment process. Well-operated companies use formal processes for identifying business risks and devising ways to mitigate them. An understanding of this process can assist the auditors in identifying significant business risks and evaluating their audit significance. Many of these business risks may create risks of material misstatement of the financial statements.

Methods of Measuring and Reviewing Performance

Management may use a variety of techniques to measure and review performance, such as budgets, key performance indicators, variance analysis, and segment performance reports. Many firms have developed a *balanced scorecard* that uses a combination of financial and non-financial performance measures to assess the financial, customer, internal business process, and learning and growth perspectives of the organization. These measurement systems assist management in gauging progress toward meeting its objectives. External parties also may measure and review the client's performance. Examples include bond rating agencies, credit agencies, and financial analysts. The methods of measuring and reviewing performance are important to the auditors in determining the incentives of management and other employees because their compensation is often tied to the measures. These incentives may create pressure on management or employees to misstate the financial statements or otherwise engage in fraud. In addition, the auditors may use these measures in designing analytical procedures to provide evidence about the fairness of the financial statements.

Internal Control

Internal control is designed to provide reasonable assurance of achieving objectives related to reliable financial reporting, efficiency and effectiveness of operations, and compliance with applicable laws and regulations. The nature and extent of the audit work to be performed on a particular engagement depend largely upon the effectiveness of the client's internal control in preventing or detecting material misstatements in the financial statements. Before auditors can evaluate the effectiveness of internal control, they need a knowledge and understanding of how it works: what controls exist and who performs them, how various types of transactions are processed and recorded, and what accounting records and supporting documentation exist. The auditors must have a sufficient understanding of the design and implementation of internal control to plan the audit. Chapter 7 focuses on the auditors' consideration of internal control.

Sources of Information

Much information about the nature of the client may be obtained through inquiries of management and other personnel. For example, the auditors may use inquiry to determine the major types of sales transactions and the nature of the client's customers. The auditors may combine inquiry and inspection to determine the content of sales contracts and the accounting policies used for recognizing revenues under the contracts. They also make inquiries of other personnel within the organization. As an example, production personnel can provide the auditors with a more detailed understanding of production processes. In addition, informal discussions between the auditors and key officers of the client can provide information about the history, size, operations, accounting records, and internal control of the enterprise. Finally, the auditors may make numerous inquiries to identify and assess fraud risks as described later in this chapter.

Many other sources of information on clients are available to the auditors. AICPA *Audit and Accounting Guides* and *Industry Risk Alerts,* trade publications, and governmental agency

Illustrative Case
Understanding the Client's Business

The importance of an understanding of the client's business was dramatically illustrated by the Volkswagen AG case. In this case, the company reported that "criminal manipulation" of its foreign-exchange positions had cost the firm as much as $259 million. The fraud prompted the resignation of the company's chief financial officer and the firing of its foreign-exchange manager. The auditors did not detect the fraud until fraudulent contracts came due and were rejected by banks. An insider suggested that auditors often don't know enough about complicated currency instruments to detect such problems.

publications are useful in obtaining an orientation to the client's industry. Previous audit reports, annual reports to stockholders, SEC filings, and prior years' tax returns are excellent sources of financial background information.

Electronic Research

A number of *computerized research tools* are available to allow the auditors to efficiently obtain information for use in their audits. Some examples include:

1. Accounting and auditing professional standards may be searched and retrieved on the FASB's *Financial Accounting Research System* and the AICPA's *reSOURCE ONLINE Accounting and Auditing Literature.* In addition, the FASB provides its standards on its Web site, www.fasb.org. The *Financial Accounting Research System* provides, on a CD-ROM, Statements on Financial Accounting Standards, Emerging Issues Task Force Abstracts, and FASB Implementation Guides. The AICPA's *reSOURCE ONLINE Accounting and Auditing Literature* provides access to all AICPA professional standards, audit and accounting guides, and technical practice aids over the Internet.

2. Financial information about companies in the client's industry may be obtained from a number of sources, including *Compustat* and *Disclosure SEC Database (Disclosure).* Subscribers to *Disclosure* may search and retrieve financial data that have been extracted from SEC filings and annual reports of public companies. Auditors also may obtain the SEC filings of certain public companies, including their financial statements, on *EDGAR* (Electronic Data Gathering and Retrieval System), which may be accessed on the Internet.

3. Current developments for companies and their industries may be obtained from the Internet. The Internet provides online access to newspaper and journal articles. In addition, many companies and industry associations have World Wide Web *home pages* that describe current developments and statistics. Appendix A to the chapter includes several Internet addresses that may be useful in performing accounting and auditing research.

Tour of Plant and Offices

Another useful preliminary step for the auditors is to arrange an inspection tour of the plant and offices of a prospective client. This tour will give the auditors some understanding of the plant layout, manufacturing process, principal products, and physical safeguards surrounding inventories. During the tour, the auditors should be alert for signs of potential problems. Rust on equipment may indicate that plant assets have been idle; excessive dust on raw materials or finished goods may indicate a problem of obsolescence. A knowledge of the physical facilities will assist the auditors in planning how many audit staff members will be needed to participate in observing the physical inventory.

The tour affords the auditors an opportunity to observe firsthand what types of information technology and internal documentation are used to record such activities as receiving raw materials, transferring materials into production, and shipping finished goods to customers. An understanding of these computer applications and documentation is essential to the auditors' consideration of internal control. Inquiries of personnel in various departments may provide the auditors with critical information about the client's operations and may serve to confirm information obtained from financial management.

In visiting the offices, the auditors will learn the location of various computer terminals and accounting records. The auditors can ascertain the practical extent of segregation of duties within the client organization by observing the number of office employees. In addition, the tour will afford an opportunity to meet the key personnel whose names appear on the organization chart. The auditors will record the background information about the client in a *permanent file* available for reference in future engagements.

Analytical Procedures

As described in Chapter 5, **analytical procedures** involve comparisons of financial statement balances and ratios for the period under audit with auditor expectations developed from sources such as the client's prior years' financial statements, published industry statistics, and budgets. When used for planning purposes, analytical procedures assist the auditors in planning the nature, timing, and extent of audit procedures that will be used for the specific accounts. The approach used is one of obtaining an understanding of the client's business and transactions and identifying areas that may represent higher risks. The auditors will then plan a more thorough investigation of these potential problem areas. *SAS 56* (AU 329), "Analytical Procedures," requires the auditors to perform analytical procedures as a part of the planning process for *every* audit.

An example of the use of an analytical procedure for planning purposes is the comparison of the client's inventory turnover for the current year with comparable statistics from prior years. A significant decrease in inventory turnover might lead the auditors to consider the possibility that the client has excessive amounts of inventory. As a result, the auditors would plan more extensive procedures to search for inventory items that may be obsolete.

Developing an Overall Audit Strategy

Learning Objective 4

After obtaining a knowledge of the client and its environment, the auditors should formulate an overall audit strategy for the upcoming engagement. The best audit strategy is the approach that results in the most *efficient* audit—that is, an effective audit performed at the least possible cost. *SAS 47* (AU 312), "Audit Risk and Materiality in Conducting an Audit," states that in planning the audit, the auditors must consider the appropriate levels of *materiality* and *audit risk*.

Materiality

The concept of materiality recognizes that some matters are important to the fair presentation of financial statements, while others are not important. The materiality concept is basic to the audit, because the audit report states that an audit is performed to obtain reasonable assurance about whether the financial statements are free of *material* misstatement.

Materiality judgments require the use of professional judgment and are based on management and auditor perceptions of the needs of a reasonable person who will rely on the financial statements. In making such a judgment the auditors often use *FASB Statement of Financial Accounting Concepts No. 2,* "Qualitative Characteristics of Accounting Concepts," which defines materiality as:

> . . . the magnitude of an omission or misstatement of accounting information that, in the light of surrounding circumstances, makes it probable that the judgment of a reasonable person relying on the information would have been changed or influenced by the omission or misstatements.

It is important to realize that this definition involves a consideration of both quantitative and qualitative factors—particularly when evaluating a misstatement that has been identified. Under certain circumstances, a misstatement that would ordinarily be considered immaterial in quantitative terms may be material because of its nature. As an example, an illegal payment of an otherwise immaterial amount could be material if there is a reasonable possibility that it could lead to a material contingent liability or a material loss of revenue.

Auditors consider materiality both in planning the audit and in evaluating audit findings. In *planning* the audit, auditors use materiality in determining the proper scope of audit procedures. The audit must be planned to obtain reasonable assurance of detecting material misstatements of the financial statements. In *evaluating* audit findings, the auditors use materiality to evaluate whether actual or likely misstatements that have been found are material to the financial statements. This is a critical decision because a material misstatement should result in audit report modification, while an immaterial misstatement should not. Because this chapter emphasizes planning, we will emphasize the planning concept of materiality, but we also will provide a brief discussion of materiality for evaluation purposes. Materiality for evaluation purposes is also addressed in Chapter 16.

Planning Materiality

The auditors' purpose in considering materiality at the planning stage of the audit is to determine the appropriate scope of their audit procedures. Audit procedures should be designed to detect material misstatements, but not so as to waste time searching for immaterial misstatements that cannot affect the auditors' report. As described in Chapter 5, the scope of the auditors' procedures for an account is directly related to the risk of material misstatement of that account. The auditors will perform extensive procedures on an account with a high risk of material misstatement. No audit procedures will be performed on an account that is quantitatively immaterial unless, based on qualitative considerations, the account is significant. For example, an Accounts Receivable from Officers account might be considered material regardless of its size.

While planning the audit, the auditors also may become aware of a number of accounting expediencies followed by the client which may result in immaterial misstatements. The concept of materiality often allows auditors to "pass over" certain conceptual accounting errors, such as charging low-cost items such as small tools or business machines directly to expense accounts. But even in these situations, the auditors need to carefully consider the possibility that the effect of such accounting expediencies may differ materially from results obtained following generally accepted accounting principles. Accounting expediencies are not acceptable simply because the client's management says the amounts involved are immaterial or because the amounts involved were considered immaterial in the past.

Quantifying Planning Materiality at the Overall Financial Statement Level   Auditing standards require auditors to consider materiality when planning the audit, but they are not required to quantify the amount. Many CPA firms, however, have found it beneficial to quantify planning materiality to make sure that all of the professional staff on an audit view materiality for the audit in the same way.

Auditors use various approaches in determining a materiality measure for planning purposes. Some auditors rely upon judgment to estimate the amount that would materially distort the individual financial statements. The auditors may, for example, estimate that a $100,000 misstatement of net income on the income statement is material, while a $200,000 misstatement of total assets on the balance sheet is material. Since most misstatements affect both net income and total assets, the auditors would then design their audit to detect the smallest misstatement that would be material to any one of the financial statements, in this case $100,000. Auditors also may use *rules of thumb* related to a financial statement base, such as net income, total revenues, or total assets, to develop these estimates of overall materiality. Rules of thumb that are commonly used in practice include:

- 5 percent to 10 percent of net income before taxes.
- ½ percent to 1 percent of total assets.
- ½ percent to 1 percent of total revenues.
- 1 percent of total equity.

The appropriate financial statement base for computing materiality will vary based on the nature of the client's business. For example, total revenues for a financial institution are often too small to use as the base, in conjunction with the percentages presented above. In addition, if a company is in a near-breakeven position, net income for the year will be much

Illustrative Case
Materiality Guidelines

One of the Big 4 CPA firms has developed the following table to assist its audit staff in determining planning materiality based on the greater of total assets or total sales.

If the Greater of Total Assets or Total Revenues Is:		Materiality Is:	
Over	But Not Over	Times	The Excess Over
$ 0	$ 30,000	0 + .05900	$ 0
30,000	100,000	1,780 + .03100	30,000
100,000	300,000	3,970 + .02140	100,000
300,000	1,000,000	8,300 + .01450	300,000
1,000,000	3,000,000	18,400 + .01000	1,000,000
3,000,000	10,000,000	38,300 + .00670	3,000,000
10,000,000	30,000,000	85,500 + .00460	10,000,000
30,000,000	100,000,000	178,000 + .00313	30,000,000
100,000,000	300,000,000	397,000 + .00214	100,000,000
300,000,000	1,000,000,000	826,000 + .00145	300,000,000
1,000,000,000	3,000,000,000	1,840,000 + .00100	1,000,000,000
3,000,000,000	10,000,000,000	3,830,000 + .00067	3,000,000,000
10,000,000,000	30,000,000,000	8,550,000 + .00046	10,000,000,000
30,000,000,000	100,000,000,000	17,800,000 + .00031	30,000,000,000
100,000,000,000	300,000,000,000	39,700,000 + .00021	100,000,000,000
300,000,000,000	—	82,600,000 + .00015	300,000,000,000

To illustrate application of the table, assume that a company has $12,670,000 of total assets and $20,520,000 of total revenue. Planning materiality would be calculated as described below:

$85,500 + .00460 ($20,520,000 − $10,000,000) = $133,892.

too small to be used as the financial statement base. In that situation, the auditors will often choose another financial statement base or use an average of net income over a number of prior years.

Auditors typically use a "sliding scale" for calculating overall materiality. For example, they might use 1 percent of total sales for materiality on the audit of a small business and ½ percent of total sales on the audit of a large corporation. This is because the absolute amount of materiality is also important. Consider a small business with $2,000,000 in revenue. If ½ percent of total revenue was used as a rule of thumb, $10,000 would be calculated as overall materiality. However, it is unlikely that $10,000 would affect a user's decision about the financial position and results of operations of any such company. In addition, it would be impractical to audit the company to that level of precision.

Allocating Overall Materiality to Individual Accounts Once the auditors have determined planning materiality for the overall financial statements, they may decide to allocate materiality to individual financial statement accounts. Such an allocation is most frequently made to help establish the scope of substantive tests when audit sampling is being used for one or more accounts. When materiality is allocated to a particular account, it is referred to as the amount of tolerable misstatement of the account. Chapter 9 illustrates how tolerable misstatement is used in conjunction with substantive tests using audit sampling.

When considering the allocation of materiality to individual accounts, it is important to understand that simply allocating materiality to all accounts dollar for dollar, so that the total amount of all the tolerable misstatements is equal to overall planning materiality, is far too conservative. This is because misstatements of various accounts often counterbalance each other.

That is, the overstatement of one asset may be offset by the understatement of another. Another reason that materiality should not be allocated dollar for dollar is the double-entry bookkeeping system, which allows detection of misstatements in an account by auditing a related account. For example, if at year-end a purchase of inventory on credit is recorded at an improper amount, the misstatement may be detected by the tests of inventories, accounts payable, or cost of goods sold.

A number of techniques are used to allocate materiality to individual accounts in practice—we will describe two. In using the first technique, the auditors multiply the amount of overall planning materiality by some factor, usually from 1.5 to 2. This amount is then allocated to the various balance sheet accounts.

The second technique involves allocating materiality only to those accounts that are to be tested with audit sampling. In using this approach, the auditors typically reduce overall materiality by an estimate of the aggregate amount of misstatement that will go undetected. Undetected misstatement is expected because the auditors design their tests to detect only material misstatement—smaller amounts often go undetected. The amount of overall materiality, reduced by this estimate of undetected misstatement, is then used as tolerable misstatement for every account that is being tested with audit sampling. Since estimating the amount of undetected misstatement is very difficult, many CPA firms have developed rules of thumb; 25 to 50 percent of overall materiality is often used as an estimate of the amount of undetected misstatement.

Evaluation Materiality

As indicated previously, the use of evaluation materiality typically involves circumstances in which one or more misstatements have been identified, and the auditors must evaluate whether the amounts involved are material. The auditors' approach is to first consider whether the misstatements identified are quantitatively material. Here the auditors must consider not only the known amount of misstatement but also any likely or projected misstatement. As an example, if the auditors test 10 percent of a population and find a $10,000 misstatement, they would expect the entire population to include a misstatement of about $100,000 ($10,000 ÷ 10%)[1]. Rules-of-thumb materiality amounts applied for planning purposes are often used in this quantitative analysis. If the auditors believe that the amount is not quantitatively material, they must still consider whether qualitative factors make the item material.

Qualitative Considerations of Materiality   Qualitative factors are particularly significant to evaluation materiality. As an example, related party transactions of relatively small amounts might be considered material to the company's financial statements. Examples of other factors that may make an item qualitatively material include the following:

- A misstatement of the financial statements that would affect a company's compliance with a contractual agreement might be material regardless of its amount. As an illustration, assume that a company's long-term debt agreement requires the company to maintain working capital of at least $500,000; otherwise, the total debt becomes payable upon demand. If the company's working capital on the balance sheet is only slightly more than $500,000, a small misstatement might disguise a violation of the debt agreement. Since the violation would mean that the company's long-term debt should be reclassified as a current liability, the small misstatement becomes material to the financial statements.
- A misstatement that would cause a company not to make the consensus earnings-per-share estimate of financial analysts might be considered material even though it is somewhat less than what would normally be considered material.

Planning materiality and the overall process of evaluating audit procedures are described in greater detail in Chapter 16.

---

[1] The topics of projection of misstatements and evaluating overall audit findings are discussed in Chapters 9 and 16.

Illustrative Case
The Allocation of Materiality

To illustrate the allocation of materiality to individual accounts, assume that the auditors have determined that overall materiality for the entire financial statements is $100,000. Using the first technique described above with a factor of 2, the auditors would allocate a total of $200,000 ($100,000 × 2) to the various balance sheet accounts. For audit efficiency, the auditors should allocate more of this amount to those accounts that are more time-consuming to audit, and little or none of this amount to those that are easy to audit. For example, cash can usually be audited to the penny at a low cost; therefore, no amount of materiality may be allocated to that account. The auditors will allocate the majority of the $200,000 to accounts that are difficult to audit, such as accounts receivable and inventories.

Assume that the auditors have decided to use the second technique to allocate materiality and are planning to use audit sampling in the substantive tests of two accounts—inventories and accounts receivable. If the auditors use 40 percent of overall materiality as an estimate of the amount of undetected misstatement, they will use $60,000 [$100,000 − (40% × $100,000)] as tolerable misstatement for each of the two accounts.*

* This allocation method relies on an assumption that the auditors will use probability-proportional-to-size (PPS) sampling or a nonstatistical sampling approach that is based on PPS theory. These sampling techniques are described in Chapter 9.

The Relationship between Planning and Evaluation Materiality   Should planning materiality equal evaluation materiality? The professional standards suggest that, theoretically, if the auditors' judgment about materiality at the planning stage was based on the same information available at the evaluation stage, materiality for planning and evaluation purposes would be the same. However, since it is ordinarily impossible for the auditor to anticipate all circumstances that may arise, the auditors' preliminary judgment about materiality ordinarily will differ from the judgment about materiality used in evaluating the audit findings.[2]

Audit Risk

As discussed in Chapter 5, the term **audit risk** refers to the possibility that the auditors may unknowingly fail to appropriately modify their opinion on financial statements that are materially misstated. At the overall financial statement level, audit risk is the chance that a material misstatement exists in the financial statements and the auditors do not detect the misstatement with their audit procedures. Auditors are aware that few audits involve material misstatements of financial statements, but when such misstatements do exist, they can result in millions of dollars of potential liability to the auditors. Experience has shown that many undetected misstatements of financial statements are intentional fraud, rather than unintentional errors.

The auditors must plan and perform the audit to obtain reasonable assurance that material misstatements, whether caused by *errors* or *fraud,* are detected. Accordingly, in developing an audit plan, the auditors must identify and assess inherent risks of material misstatement of the

[2] We question the premise that theoretically the planning and evaluation amounts should equal one another. Recall our example of the misstatement in the audit of a company that is very close to violating a loan covenant. Assume that, historically, audits of the company have been planned and performed using a materiality measure of approximately $150,000. Further, assume that this year, for the first time, the company is within $10,000 of violating the loan covenant. The professional standards would seem to suggest that this year's audit would be performed with a materiality measure of $10,000, since we know during the audit planning stage how close the company is to violating the covenants. Yet, it seems that changes in the scope of the audit to accommodate this $10,000 planning materiality level might well cost prohibitive. Thus, we would argue that the incorporation of many qualitative factors will occur at the evaluation stage only, and that the evaluation concept might normally be expected to be less than planning materiality. Extension of this line of reasoning would suggest that the planning materiality level be based primarily on overall, general circumstances for many companies, while evaluation materiality be based on the circumstances of the engagement.

Illustrative Case
Litigation and Management Fraud

An analysis of 456 court cases filed against CPAs indicates that management fraud was present approximately 44 percent of the time. Other employee defalcations were believed to be present 2 percent of the time. An assortment of accounting and auditing errors was alleged in the remaining cases.

financial statements. Inherent risks are identified based on the procedures that the auditors perform to obtain an understanding of the client and its environment. Then, the auditors use judgment to assess the effects of the risks on the audit.

Assessing Inherent Risks

In assessing inherent risks of material misstatements of the financial statements, the auditors will consider their significance and the likelihood that they could result in a material misstatement of the financial statements. They also will attempt to consider each risk in relation to **management assertions** about accounts and classes of transactions in the financial statements. Recall that these assertions are:

1. Existence or occurrence
2. Completeness
3. Rights and obligations
4. Valuation or allocation
5. Presentation and disclosure

In other words, the auditors try to relate each identified risk to "what can go wrong" at the assertion level. As an example, if the auditors identify a significant risk of inventory obsolescence, this means there is a risk that the valuation assertion regarding inventory could be misstated. Next, the auditors consider the controls established by management to mitigate this risk. Then, the auditors consider whether the risk is of a magnitude that could result in a material misstatement of the financial statements and, finally, they consider the likelihood that the risk will result in a material misstatement. This assessment is then used to adjust the overall approach to the audit or modify the nature, timing, and extent of the audit procedures. Because of the significance and unique nature of fraud, the Auditing Standards Board recently issued *SAS No. 99* (AU 316) to provide guidance for the auditors in assessing the risks of material misstatement of the financial statements due to *fraud*.

Addressing the Risks of Material Misstatement Due to Fraud

Learning Objective 5

The auditors' consideration of risks of material misstatement from fraud recognizes that there are two distinct types: (1) misstatements arising from **fraudulent financial reporting (management fraud),** and (2) misstatements arising from **misappropiation of assets (defalcations).** The auditors' fraud risk assessment involves identifying risks of material misstatement of the financial statements due to fraud and determining the appropriate audit response. To identify fraud risks the auditors perform a number of procedures including having discussion among engagement personnel, making inquiries of management and others within the organization, performing analytical procedures, and considering fraud risk factors.

Discussion among Engagement Personnel

In identifying fraud risks and developing an appropriate response, *SAS No. 99* requires the auditors to have a discussion among the audit team members about fraud risk. Specifically, the discussion should be designed to allow the more experienced team members to share insights and exchange ideas about how and where the entity's financial statements might be susceptible to material misstatement due to fraud and to emphasize the importance of maintaining the proper degree of professional skepticism regarding the possibility of fraud. The discussion also will review errors that are expected to occur based on the results of prior audits. The discussion should involve the engagement partner and should focus on incentives and opportunities that make fraud possible, including consideration of the possibility of management override of internal control.

Making Inquiries Related to Fraud

Inquiries of management and other personnel assist the auditors in identifying fraud risks. Therefore, the auditors are required to inquire of members of management about their knowledge of fraud and alleged fraud, their understanding of the risks of fraud, and programs or controls that have been implemented to mitigate those risks. The auditors also inquire about how management monitors operating units or business segments in other locations, and how management communicates its views about ethical behavior to employees. The auditors should obtain management's perspective regarding the effectiveness of internal control in detecting fraud and whether this perspective has been reported to the audit committee.

Inquiries are directed to internal auditors and members of the audit committee to get their views about fraud risks and determine whether these individuals have knowledge of fraud or suspected fraud. To get a more complete perspective and collaborate management's responses, auditors should also make inquiries of other employees, such as operating personnel not directly involved in financial reporting; employees involved in initiating, recording, or processing complex or unusual transactions; and in-house legal counsel. These inquiries are important because fraud often is uncovered through information received in response to inquiries.

Performing Planning Analytical Procedures to Identify Fraud Risks

Planning analytical procedures also may provide the auditors with indications of fraud risks. When the results of analytical procedures reveal an unusual or unexpected relationship, this may provide an indication that the financial statements may be misstated due to fraud. Because revenue manipulation is one of the most common techniques used in fraudulent financial reporting, *SAS No. 99* requires the auditor to perform planning analytical procedures related to revenue. For example, the auditors might compare monthly revenue for the current year with comparable prior years for an indication that revenue may be misstated.

Considering Fraud Risk Factors

In identifying fraud risks, the auditors also consider various fraud risk factors that may be indicative of fraud. *SAS No. 99* provides lists of such factors organized around the three fundamental conditions necessary for the commission of fraud: (1) some type of incentive or pressure, (2) an opportunity to commit the fraud, and (3) an attitude that allows the individual to rationalize the act. As an illustration, an accounts receivable clerk who is having financial difficulty may feel pressured to commit fraud, and a weakness in internal control may provide that individual with the opportunity to steal cash receipts. Finally, the employee may be able to rationalize the theft based on a belief that he or she is underpaid. Appendix 6B provides listings of fraud risk factors for misstatements arising from both fraudulent financial reporting and misappropriation of assets.

Identifying Fraud Risks

After holding the engagement team discussion, performing the inquiries and planning analytical procedures, and considering the presence of fraud risk factors and other information that might be relevant, the auditors are ready to identify fraud risks that may require an audit response. In identifying the risks that require an audit response, the auditors consider a number of factors, including the type and significance of the risk, the likelihood that the risk will result in a material misstatement, and its pervasiveness. Since material misstatements due to fraudulent financial reporting often involve management override of internal controls resulting in overstatement of revenue, auditors ordinarily determine that there is a fraud risk related

Illustrative Case
Fraud at WorldCom

WorldCom, Inc., became the largest company to file for bankruptcy in corporate history. The bankruptcy was precipitated by the discovery of one of the largest accounting frauds, with profits fraudulently inflated by more than $11 billion. Company internal memos indicate that senior WorldCom executives overrode internal controls and ordered subordinates to alter the company's books.

to revenue recognition. For all fraud risks identified by the auditors, they should obtain an understanding of the programs and controls enacted by management to mitigate the risks. This information about controls will assist the auditors in determining the significance of the risk and in designing an effective audit approach to address the risks.

Even if specific risks of material misstatement due to fraud are not identified by the auditors, there is always a possibility of management override of internal control. Therefore, *SAS No. 99* requires the auditors to address this risk apart from whether they identify other fraud risks.

Responding to Fraud Risks

How do the auditors respond to fraud risks? They respond in the following three ways: (1) a modification in approach having an overall effect on how the audit is conducted, (2) an alteration in the nature, timing, and extent of the procedures performed, and (3) performance of procedures to further address the risk of management override of internal control.

Overall Response   In response to fraud risks, the auditors may modify their overall approach to the audit in one or more of the following ways:

- *Professional skepticism and audit evidence.* The auditors may respond by designing procedures to obtain more reliable evidence in support of specific financial statement items, or by obtaining additional corroboration of management's explanations or representations concerning material matters, such as through third-party confirmation, the use of a specialist, or examination of documentation from independent sources.
- *Assigning personnel and supervision.* The auditors may respond by assigning additional staff with specialized skill and knowledge or by assigning more experienced staff to the engagement. In addition, the extent of the supervision of the audit staff should be adjusted to reflect the fraud risks identified.
- *Accounting principles.* The auditors may decide to further consider management's selection and application of significant accounting principles, particularly those related to subjective measurements and complex transactions.
- *Predictability of auditing procedures.* The auditors may incorporate an added element of unpredictability in the selection of auditing procedures. As examples, they may use differing sampling techniques, adjust the timing of testing from what otherwise would be expected, or perform procedures at locations on an unannounced basis.

Alterations in Audit Procedures   Alterations of the nature, timing, or extent of audit procedures to address a fraud risk may involve applying procedures that provide more reliable evidence, shifting tests from the interim period to near year-end, or increasing the sample size for a particular substantive test. As an example, the auditors might decide to interview personnel involved in activities in areas where a fraud risk has been identified to obtain their insights about the risk and how controls address that risk. Linking audit procedures to risks is described in more detail later in this chapter.

Response to the Possibility of Management Override As indicated previously, *SAS No. 99* requires the auditors, on every audit, to design procedures to further address the risk of management override of controls. Specifically, these procedures include:

- *Examining journal entries and other adjustments for evidence of material misstatement due to fraud.* Material misstatements of financial statements due to fraud often involve the manipulation of the financial reporting process by recording inappropriate journal entries or adjustments. Therefore, the auditors should review such entries and adjustments for suspicious characteristics, such as entries made to unrelated, unusual, or seldom-used accounts; entries recorded at the end of the period or as post-closing entries that have little or no explanation or description; or entries made either before or during the preparation of the financial statements that do not have account numbers.
- *Reviewing accounting estimates for biases.* Fraudulent financial reporting often is accomplished through intentional misstatement of accounting estimates, such as the allowance for uncollectible accounts. Thus, auditors should perform a retrospective review of significant accounting estimates reflected in the financial statements of the prior year to determine whether management judgments and assumptions relating to the estimates indicate a possible bias on the part of management. For example, in performing a retrospective review of the allowance for uncollectible accounts, the auditors might compare management's estimate used in the prior financial statements with the amounts eventually determined to be uncollectible. Evidence of bias in the prior year should be considered in auditing the current year accounting estimates.
- *Evaluating the business rationale for significant unusual transactions.* During the course of the audit, if the auditors encounter significant transactions that are outside the normal course of business for the client or otherwise appear unusual, they should gain an understanding of their business rationale. The auditors should be especially alert for significant unusual transactions with related parties.

Evaluating the Results of Audit Tests The auditors' concern about fraud does not stop at the planning phase of the audit. Throughout the engagement, the auditors should be alert for conditions that may indicate that a fraud was committed, such as those presented in Figure 6.2. In addition, analytical procedures performed during the course of the audit may reveal unusual or unexpected relationships that may indicate the occurrence of fraud. As an example, an unexpected relationship between sales volume as determined from the accounting records and sales volume determined from production statistics maintained by operations personnel may indicate a fraudulent misstatement of sales.

At or near completion of the audit, the auditors should evaluate whether the accumulated results of audit procedures and other observations affect the assessment of the risks of material misstatement due to fraud made earlier in the audit.

Discovery of Fraud What do the auditors do if they obtain evidence of fraud? They should evaluate the implications for the audit and communicate their suspicions to an appropriate level of management, at least one level above the level involved. If the fraud involves senior management or material misstatement of the financial statements, the matter should be reported to the audit committee of the board of directors. In very serious situations, the auditors may decide to withdraw from the engagement.

Responding to Risks of Material Misstatement

To summarize, the auditors may respond to risks of material misstatement by modifying the overall approach to the audit, or by adjusting the nature, timing, and extent of the audit procedures. Adjustments to the overall approach may involve applying a heightened degree of skepticism to the engagement, assigning to the engagement more experienced staff or individuals with specialized skills, providing more supervision for the engagement, or incorporating additional elements of unpredictability in the selection of audit procedures. The way in which auditors link the nature, timing, and extent of audit procedures to risks will be described later in this chapter.

FIGURE 6.2 Conditions Indicative of Fraud

Discrepancies in the Accounting Records	Conflicting or Missing Evidential Matter	Problematic or Unusual Relationships between the Auditors and Client
• Transactions that are not recorded in a complete or timely manner or are improperly recorded as to amount, accounting period, classification, or entity policy. • Unsupported or unauthorized balances or transactions. • Last-minute adjustments that significantly affect financial results. • Evidence of employees' access to systems and records inconsistent with that necessary to perform their authorized duties.	• Missing documents. • Unavailability of other than photocopied or electronically transmitted documents when documents in original form are expected to exist. • Significant unexplained items on reconciliations. • Inconsistent, vague, or implausible responses from management or employees arising from inquiries or analytical procedures. • Unusual discrepancies between the entity's records and confirmation replies. • Missing inventory or physical assets of significant magnitude. • Unavailable or missing electronic evidence, inconsistent with the entity's record-retention practices or policies. • Inability to produce evidence of key systems development and program-change testing and implementation activities for current-year system changes and deployments.	• Denial of access to records, facilities, certain employees, customers, vendors, or others from whom audit evidence might be sought. • Undue time pressures imposed by management to resolve complex or contentious issues. • Complaints by management about the conduct of the audit or management intimidation of audit team members, particularly in connection with the auditors' critical assessment of audit evidence or in the resolution of potential disagreements with management. • Unusual delays by the entity in providing requested information. • Tips or complaints to the auditors about fraud. • Unwillingness to facilitate auditor access to key electronic files for testing through the use of computer assisted audit techniques. • Denial of access to key information technology operations staff and facilities including security, operations, and systems development personnel.

Documenting the Audit Planning Process and Risk Assessments

The planning and risk assessment process is documented in the audit working papers through the preparation of *audit plans, time budgets,* and *audit programs.* These "planning and supervision" working papers serve a dual purpose. First, they provide documentary evidence of the CPA firm's compliance with the requirements of the first standard of fieldwork. Second, these working papers provide the auditor-in-charge with a means of coordinating, scheduling, and supervising the activities of the audit staff members involved in the engagement.

Audit Plan

An **audit plan** is an overview of the engagement that outlines the nature and characteristics of the client and its environment and the overall audit strategy. Although audit plans differ in form and content among public accounting firms, a typical plan includes details on the following:

1. Objectives of the audit (e.g., audit for stockholders, special-purpose audit, SEC filings).

2. Nature and extent of other services, such as preparation of tax returns, to be performed for the client.

3. Timing and scheduling of the audit work, including determining which procedures may be performed before the balance sheet date, what must be done on or after the balance sheet date, and setting dates for such critical procedures as cash counts, accounts receivable confirmations, and inventory observation.

4. Description of the client company and its environment.

5. Work to be done by the client's staff.

6. Staffing requirements during the engagement.

7. Target dates for completing major segments of the engagement, such as the consideration of internal control, tax returns, the audit report, and SEC filings.

8. Discussions among the engagement team about significant risks.

9. Significant risks of material misstatement due to error or fraud and the auditors' response to those risks.

10. Preliminary judgments about materiality levels for the engagement.

With respect to the auditors' consideration of fraud, they must document in the audit plan or in other sections of the working papers (1) the discussion among engagement team personnel about fraud risks held during planning, (2) the procedures performed to identify fraud risks, (3) the fraud risks identified and the response to those risks, (4) any other conditions that caused the auditors to perform additional fraud-related procedures, and (5) the nature of any communications made to management, the audit committee, or others about fraud.

The audit plan is normally drafted before starting work at the client's offices. However, the plan may be modified throughout the engagement as special problems are encountered and as the auditors' consideration of internal control leads to identification of areas requiring more or less audit work. An audit plan is included as a part of the illustrative audit case in Appendix 6C at the end of this chapter.

Time Budgets for Audit Engagements

Public accounting firms usually charge clients on a time basis, and detailed time budgets can assist the auditors in estimating the audit fee. A **time budget** for an audit is constructed by estimating the time required for each step in the audit program for each of the various levels of auditors and totaling these estimated amounts. Time budgets serve other functions in addition to providing a basis for estimating fees. The time budget communicates to the audit staff those areas the manager or partner believe are of high risk and require more time. It also is an important tool of the audit senior—it is used to measure the efficiency of the staff and to determine at each stage of the engagement whether the work is progressing at a satisfactory rate.

There is always pressure to complete an audit within the estimated time. The staff assistant who takes more than the normal time for a task is not likely to be popular with supervisors or to win rapid advancement. Ability to do satisfactory work when given abundant time is not a sufficient qualification, *for time is never abundant in public accounting.*

The development of time budgets is facilitated in repeat engagements by reference to the preceding year's detailed time records. Sometimes time budgets prove quite unattainable because the client's records are not in satisfactory condition, or because of other special circumstances that arise. Even when time estimates are exceeded, there can be no compromise with qualitative standards in the performance of the fieldwork. The CPA firm's professional reputation and its legal liability to clients and third parties do not permit any short-cutting or omission of audit procedures to meet a predetermined time estimate.

Audit Program

An **audit program** is a detailed list of the audit procedures to be performed in the course of the audit. A tentative audit program is developed based on the auditors' initial risk assessments. This tentative program, however, may require frequent modification as the audit progresses. For example, the nature, timing, and extent of substantive test procedures are influenced by the auditors' final assessment of control risk. Thus, not until tests of controls have been completed can a final version of the audit program be completed. Even this version may require modification if the auditors revise their preliminary estimates of materiality or risk for the engagement, or if the substantive tests disclose unexpected problems such as an additional fraud risk.

Linking Audit Procedures to Risks

Learning Objective 6

As indicated previously, substantive audit procedures are determined based on the auditors' assessment of inherent and control risks of various assertions about accounts and classes of transactions. This is a very difficult but critical area of audit judgment. It is important for the auditors to design substantive tests that are clearly focused on the risks. As an example, assume that a software company sells expensive software systems and maintenance using standard contracts. Also assume that the auditors have identified as a significant business risk and inherent risk that sales personnel, informally or through written side agreements, may be modifying the terms of contracts with customers which may affect the amount of revenue that should be recognized. The auditors must design tests that are focused on determining whether such modifications of terms have been made, perhaps by obtaining tailored confirmations from customers about the existence of such side agreements.

The Audit Trail

In developing audit procedures, the auditors are assisted by the organized manner in which accounting systems record, classify, and summarize data. The flow of accounting data begins with the recording of thousands of individual transactions on such documents as invoices and checks. The information recorded on these original "source" documents is summarized in journals and the amounts in the journals are posted to ledger accounts. At the end of the year, the balances in the ledger accounts are arranged in the form of financial statements.

In thinking of the accounting records as a whole, we may say that a continuous trail of evidence exists—a trail of evidence that links the thousands of individual transactions composing a year's business activity with the summary figures in the financial statements. In a manual accounting system, this *audit trail* consists of source documents, journal entries, and ledger entries. An audit trail also exists within a computer-based accounting system, although it may have a substantially different form; this is discussed in Chapter 8.

Just as a hiker may walk in either direction along a mountain path, an auditor may follow the audit trail in either of two directions. Figure 6.3 illustrates these concepts relating to the *direction of testing*. For example, the auditor may follow specific transactions from their origin (the source documents) forward to their inclusion in the financial statement summary figures. This approach provides the auditor with assurance that all transactions have been properly interpreted and processed; it is a test of the *completeness assertion*. If a transaction was never recorded, the omission can be detected only by tracing in the direction from the source documents to the journals and ledgers. Note, however, that transactions that are not supported *can never* be found by tracing forward from source documents to the journal entries (left to right).

If the auditors' objective is to detect unsupported financial statement amounts, they should follow the stream of evidence back to its source. This type of test involves tracing back amounts in the financial statements to ledgers and journals and, finally, *vouching* them to the original source documents, such as invoices and receiving reports. By vouching from right to left in Figure 6.3, the auditors may identify journal entries that are not supported and, possibly, not valid. This process of vouching, working backward from the financial statement figures to the detailed documents, provides evidence that financial statement figures are based upon valid transactions; it tests the *existence or occurrence assertion*.

FIGURE 6.3
Direction of Tests

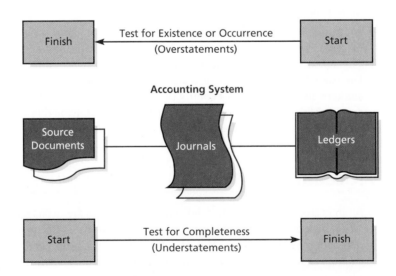

Although the technique of working along the audit trail is a useful one, bear in mind that the auditors also must acquire evidence from sources other than the client's accounting records.

Transaction Cycles (Classes of Transactions)

A **transaction cycle,** or class of transactions, is the sequence of procedures applied by the client in processing a particular type of recurring transaction. The term *cycle* conveys the idea that the same sequence of procedures is applied to each transaction in that cycle. Because of their importance to financial reporting, the auditors' consideration of internal control often is organized around the client's major transaction cycles. While they differ from company to company, typical cycles include: (1) the revenue (sales and collections) cycle; (2) the acquisition (purchases and disbursements) cycle; (3) the conversion (production) cycle; (4) the payroll cycle; (5) the investing cycle; and (6) the financing cycle.

To illustrate a specific transaction cycle, consider a company's processes for sales and collections of receivables. The activities performed to process sales transactions might include receiving a customer's purchase order, approving credit, shipping merchandise, preparing the sales invoice, recording the sale, recording the accounts receivable, billing the customer, and handling and recording the cash remitted by the customer. Ultimately, both a sales entry (recorded in the sales journal) and a cash receipts entry (recorded in the cash receipts journal) capture the essential information for financial reporting purposes. That information is then recorded in the appropriate ledger accounts (e.g., accounts receivable, sales, and cash). Figure 6.4 shows the accounts receivable general ledger account and how the sales and collections cycle affects that account. The figure also illustrates how sales returns and allowances and write-offs of uncollectible accounts affect the Accounts Receivable account.

Organization of the Audit Program

The audit program may be viewed as including two major sections. The first section deals with the procedures to assess the effectiveness of the client's internal control (the "systems portion"), and the second section deals with financial statement account balances (the "substantive test portion").

Learning Objective 7

The Systems (Internal Control) Portion of the Program

As indicated above, the systems portion of the audit program is generally organized around the major transaction cycles of the client's accounting system. Audit procedures in the systems portion of the program typically include obtaining an understanding of the controls for each transaction cycle, preparing a flowchart for each cycle, testing the significant controls, and assessing control risk for the related financial statement assertions.

Figure 6.4 is helpful in illustrating the relationship between tests of controls over transactions and substantive procedures. Note that while the auditors' overall objective is to determine whether the ending financial statement balance is correct, two approaches are possible: (1) testing controls over transactions that occurred during the year, or (2) testing the ending

FIGURE 6.4
Transactions Affecting Accounts Receivable

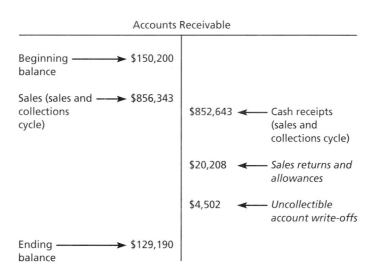

account balance directly. That is, if the controls over the transactions that are recorded into the account are effective, assurance is obtained regarding the ending balance. Alternatively, auditors may directly test the ending balance of the account. As a practical matter, auditors use a combination of these two approaches. Indeed, even if controls are considered extremely strong, some substantive tests must be performed for all significant financial statement accounts.

The systems portion of the audit program includes tests of controls over transactions. The evidence obtained from these tests may be of two types—evidence about the effectiveness of controls and evidence that substantiates the recorded amount of the transactions. For example, a test of a control may involve selecting a sample of sales transactions to test whether recorded transactions were properly approved. This procedure provides evidence to help assess control risk (or the combination of inherent risk and control risk). It does *not* provide evidence to restrict detection risk, since no evidence substantiating the transactions and related balances has been collected (for example, a sale may be approved but may be recorded at an erroneous amount). However, if the auditors simply extend the test to include a determination of whether the transactions were properly recorded, evidence is collected to substantiate sales transactions and the accounts receivable balance.

Accordingly, some tests of controls provide substantive evidence about an account or class of transactions. These procedures are referred to as **dual purpose procedures (tests)** since they serve as both a test of controls and a substantive test of the details of the transactions that occurred during the year. It should be emphasized, however, that the systems portion of the audit program primarily addresses tests of internal control and assessing control risk.

As a result of their consideration of internal control, the auditors will make appropriate modifications in the substantive test portion of the audit program. For example, because of weaknesses in internal control over the proper recording of sales, the auditors may assess control risk (or combined inherent and control risk) for the assertion of existence of accounts receivable as high and decide to send additional accounts receivable confirmations. Alternatively, strong controls may lead the auditors to decide to perform less extensive substantive tests than would be the case if controls did not function effectively.

The Substantive Test Portion of the Program

The portion of the audit program aimed at substantiating financial statement amounts is organized in terms of major financial statement accounts and classes or transactions, such as cash, accounts receivable, sales, inventories, and plant and equipment. Substantive procedures are used to restrict detection risk for these accounts. As an example, consider the financial statement account, accounts receivable. Examples of audit procedures for accounts receivable include: confirm with debtors their balance due, review the year-end cutoff of sales transactions, and analyze subsequent collections of year-end receivables. These procedures all help substantiate the year-end accounts receivable balance.

Most audit firms organize much of the substantive portion of their audit programs around the balance sheet accounts. Then, they complete the programs with any additional procedures needed to substantiate income statement accounts and information in financial statement footnotes. An advantage of this balance sheet approach is that highly competent evidence generally is available to substantiate assets and liabilities. For example, the ending balance of accounts receivable as presented in Figure 6.5 is usually subject to direct verification by such procedures as inspection of externally created documentary evidence, confirmation, and review of subsequent cash collections. Other assets such as inventory may be physically examined. Liabilities can be verified by examination of externally created documents, confirmation, and inspection of canceled checks after the liability has been paid.

In contrast, consider the nature of revenues and expenses in double-entry accounting. The entry to record revenues or expenses has two parts: (1) the recognition of the revenue or expense, and (2) the corresponding change in an asset or liability account. Revenues and expenses have no tangible form; they exist only as entries in the client's accounting records, representing changes in owners' equity. Consequently, the best evidence supporting the existence of revenues or expenses is often the verifiable change in the related asset or liability account. As a result, many income statement accounts may be verified indirectly by auditing the related balance sheet accounts.

FIGURE 6.5   The Auditors' Approach to Auditing Financial Statement Accounts

	Income Statement Items		Cash Transactions		Balance Sheet Items		
Financial Statement Relationships	Revenue	=	Cash receipts from customers	−	Beginning balance of Accounts Receivable	+	Ending balance of Accounts Receivable
	Cost of goods sold	=	Cash payments for merchandise	−	Beginning balance of Accounts Payable	+	Ending balance of Accounts Payable
				+	Beginning balance of Inventory	−	Ending balance of Inventory
	Expenses	=	Cash payments for expenses	−	Beginning balances of Accrued Expenses	+	Ending balances of Accrued Expenses
				+	Beginning balances of Prepaid Expenses	−	Ending balances of Prepaid Expenses
	↑		↑		↑		↑
Auditors' Approach to Substantiation	Verify indirectly by substantiating right hand side of equation; also use analytical procedures, direct computations, and tests of transactions.		Substantiate by testing transactions; also by performing reconciliations of cash accounts.		Substantiate by reference to last year's audit working papers.		Substantiate by substantive tests in current year.

Indirect Verification of Income Statement Accounts   Figure 6.5 shows the relationship between income statement accounts and the related changes in cash or other balance sheet items. By substantiating the changes in the asset and liability accounts, the auditors indirectly verify revenue, cost of goods sold, and expenses. As an example, most revenue transactions involve a debit to either Cash or Accounts Receivable. If the auditors are able to satisfy themselves that all cash receipts and all changes in accounts receivable during the year have been properly recorded, they have indirect evidence that revenue transactions have been accounted for properly.

Direct Verification of Income Statement Accounts   Not all of the audit evidence pertaining to income statement accounts is indirect. The verification of a major balance sheet item often involves several closely related income statement accounts that can be verified through computation or other direct evidence. For example, in substantiating the marketable securities owned by the client, it is a simple matter to compute the related interest revenue, dividends revenue, and gains or losses on sales of securities. In substantiating the balance sheet items of plant assets and accumulated depreciation, the auditors make computations that also substantiate depreciation expense. Uncollectible accounts expense is substantiated in conjunction with the balance sheet item Allowance for Doubtful Accounts. In addition to these computations, the auditors' *analytical procedures* provide direct evidence as to the reasonableness of various revenues and expenses.

Certain income statement accounts, such as revenues, are of such significance that the auditors virtually always obtain direct evidence about the fairness of the amounts, typically by performing tests of details of a sample of transactions or substantive analytical procedures.

Summary of the Relationship between Tests of Controls and Substantive Tests

Tests of controls provide auditors with evidence as to whether prescribed controls are in use and operating effectively. The results of these tests assist the auditors in evaluating the *likelihood* that material misstatements have occurred. Substantive tests, on the other hand, are designed to *detect* material misstatements if they exist in the financial statements. The amount of substantive testing done by the auditors is greatly influenced by their assessment of the likelihood that material misstatements exist.

To illustrate, assume that a client's procedures manual indicates that the finished goods warehouse is to be locked at all times and accessible only to authorized personnel. Through tests of controls consisting of inquiry and observation, the auditors learn that the warehouse often is unlocked and that several employees who are not authorized to be in the warehouse regularly eat lunch there. As the client's internal control procedure is not operating properly, the auditors should recognize that the *risk* of inventory shortages is increased. However, the tests of controls have *not* determined that an inventory shortage does, in fact, exist.

The principal substantive test to detect shortages of inventories is the auditors' observation of a physical inventory taken by the client. As part of this observation, the auditors make test counts of various items. In the case of the unlocked warehouse, the auditors' test has shown that internal control cannot be relied upon to prevent shortages. Therefore, the auditors should increase the number of test counts in an effort to verify the existence of inventory.

Objectives of Audit Programs

The audit procedures contained in the audit program are designed to be responsive to potential material misstatements of the financial statements. To make sure that the program addresses all potential misstatements, auditors often develop audit objectives for each significant account balance and class of transactions. These objectives follow directly from management assertions that are contained in the client's financial statements. From these assertions, general objectives may be developed for each major type of balance sheet account, including assets, liabilities, and owners' equity, and the related income statement accounts. Figure 6.6 presents the relationships between financial statements, management's account balance assertions (discussed in Chapter 5), and audit objectives.

General Objectives of Audit Programs for Assets

The audit program for each financial statement account must be tailored to address potential misstatements of that account. The potential misstatements for cash are not identical to the potential misstatements for accounts receivable. For example, questions about proper net realizable value cause valuation to be a bigger risk for accounts receivable. However, it is

FIGURE 6.6
Relationship of Financial Statement Assertions to the Audit

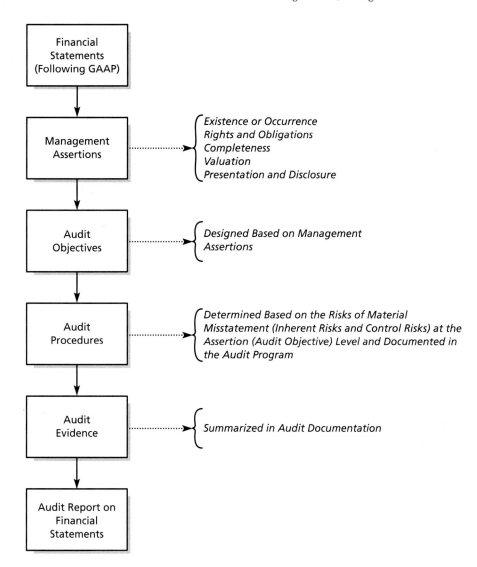

useful to realize that each audit program follows basically the same general approach to verifying the balance sheet items and related income statement amounts. To varying degrees based on the auditors' assessments of risk, the substantive audit program for each asset account will need to include procedures to address the following general objectives:

> **Substantive Audit Program for Asset Accounts Stated in Terms of General Objectives**
> A. Establish the *existence* of assets.
> B. Establish that the company has *rights* to the assets.
> C. Establish *completeness* of recorded assets.
> D. Determine the appropriate *valuation* of the assets.
> E. Determine the appropriate financial statement *presentation and disclosure* of the assets.

Changes in these audit objectives, with respect to audit programs for liability and owners' equity accounts, will be discussed in later chapters.

Substantiation of Account Balances

The central purpose of the auditors' risk assessment process, including their assessment of control risk, is to determine the nature, timing, and extent of the audit work necessary to substantiate the account. In subsequent chapters, considerable attention will be given to the auditors' inherent and control risk assessments; let us now discuss the objectives of the auditors' substantive procedures.

Existence of Assets

The first step in substantiating an asset is to verify the existence of the item. For assets such as cash on hand, marketable securities, and inventories, existence of the asset usually may be verified by physical observation or inspection, and by *vouching* from the recorded entry to the documents created when the assets were acquired.

When assets are in the custody of others, such as cash in banks and inventory on consignment, the appropriate audit procedure may be direct confirmation with the outside party. The existence of accounts receivable normally is verified by confirming with customers the amounts receivable. To verify the existence of intangibles, the auditors must gather evidence that costs have been incurred and that these costs represent probable future economic benefits.

Rights to the Assets

Usually, the same procedures that verify existence also establish the company's rights to the asset. For example, confirming cash balances in bank accounts establishes existence of the cash and the company's ownership rights to that cash. Similarly, inspecting marketable securities verifies both existence and ownership because the registered owner's name usually appears on the face of the security certificate.

With other assets, such as plant and equipment, physical examination establishes existence *but not ownership.* Plant and equipment may be rented or leased rather than owned. To verify the client's rights to plant assets, the auditors must inspect documentary evidence such as property tax bills, purchase documents, and deeds.

The client may not hold legal title to all assets that are appropriately included in the financial statements. Instead, the client may own *rights* to use the assets conveyed by contracts, such as leases. The ownership of these rights may be established by reviewing the underlying contracts.

Establishing Completeness

Effective internal control provides assurance that acquisitions are recorded and helps the auditors to establish the completeness of recorded assets. When such controls are found to be ineffective, the scope of substantive tests must be increased, but this is often a difficult task. When the auditors are testing the completeness of assets, they are looking for assets that have been acquired but not recorded in the accounting records. Therefore, analyzing recorded entries in the asset accounts will not be effective for this purpose; the auditors must take a different approach.

Many tests for unrecorded assets involve *tracing* from the "source documents" created when the assets were acquired to entries recording the assets in the accounting records. To test for unrecorded accounts receivable, for example, the auditors might select a sample of shipping documents issued during the year and trace the details to recorded sales transactions.

Observation and physical examination are important to testing the completeness of recorded physical assets. To illustrate, during the observation of the client's physical inventory, the auditors are alert for inventory items that are not counted or included in the inventory summary. Physically examining equipment may reveal purchases that have not been properly capitalized.

Analytical procedures also may be used to bring conditions to light that indicate that all assets may not be recorded. For example, a low gross profit percentage for the current year in comparison to prior years may indicate that the client has a substantial amount of unrecorded inventory.

Verifying the Cutoff of Transactions   As a part of the auditors' procedures for establishing completeness as well as existence of recorded assets, the auditors will verify the client's *cutoff* of transactions included in the period. The financial statements should reflect all transactions occurring through the end of the period and none that occur subsequently. The term *cutoff* refers to the process of determining that transactions occurring near the balance sheet date are assigned to the proper accounting period.

The impact of cutoff errors upon the financial statements varies with the nature of the error. For example, a cutoff error in recording acquisitions of plant assets affects the balance sheet but probably does not affect the income statement, since depreciation usually is not recorded on assets acquired within a few days of year-end. On the other hand, a cutoff error in recording shipments of merchandise to customers affects both inventory and the cost of sales. In order to improve their financial picture, some clients may "hold their records open" to include in the current year cash receipts and revenue from the first part of the next period.

To verify the client's cutoff of transactions, the auditors should review transactions recorded shortly before and after the balance sheet date to ascertain that these transactions are assigned to the proper period. When such documents as checks, receiving reports, and shipping documents are serially numbered, noting the last serial number issued during the period will assist the auditors in determining that a proper cutoff has been made in recording transactions.

Valuation of Assets

Determining the proper valuation of assets requires a thorough knowledge of generally accepted accounting principles. The auditors must establish not only that the accounting method used to value a particular asset is generally accepted; they must also determine that the method of valuation is appropriate and properly applied in the circumstances. Once the auditors are satisfied as to the appropriateness of the method, the auditors will perform procedures to test the accuracy of the client's application of the method of valuation to the asset.

A number of assets are valued at cost. Therefore, a common audit procedure is to vouch the acquisition cost of assets to paid checks and other documentary evidence. If the acquisition cost is subject to depreciation or amortization, the auditors must evaluate the reasonableness of the cost allocation program and verify the computation of the remaining unallocated cost. Increasingly generally accepted accounting principles require assets to be valued at fair values. Assets valued at fair value or the lower of cost or market, and those whose carrying value must be compared to fair value to determine whether their values are impaired, necessitate an examination of their fair values. Fair values are audited by comparison to prices on existing markets or by examination of valuation models used to develop the values.

Finally, the amount appearing as an asset on a financial statement is almost always the accumulation of many smaller items. For example, the amount of inventory on a financial statement might consist of the cost of thousands or, perhaps, hundreds of thousands of individual products. The auditors must test the clerical accuracy of the underlying records to determine that they accumulate to the total appearing in the general ledger and, therefore, the amount in the financial statements. The auditors often use their audit software to perform these tests of clerical accuracy of the records.

Financial Statement Presentation and Disclosure

Even after all dollar amounts have been substantiated, the auditors must perform procedures to ensure that the financial statement presentation conforms to the requirements of authoritative accounting pronouncements and the general principle of adequate disclosure. Procedures falling into this category include the review of subsequent events; search for related party transactions; investigation of loss contingencies; review of disclosure of such items as accounting policies, leases, compensating balances, and pledged assets; and consideration of the classification and description of items in the financial statements.

An Illustration of Audit Program Design

The above general objectives apply to all types of assets. Audit procedures for a particular asset account must be designed to accomplish the *specific audit objectives and risks* related to that asset. These specific objectives and risks vary with the nature of the asset and the generally accepted accounting principles that govern its valuation and presentation.

In designing an audit program for a specific account, the auditors start by listing the specific objectives related to the account. Then, they identify the inherent risks related to each of these specific audit objectives. You can think of these risks as declarations of "what could go

FIGURE 6.7   Relationship among Audit Objectives, Risks of Material Misstatement, and Audit Procedures

General Audit Objectives for Assets	Specific Audit Objectives for Accounts Receivable	Risks of Material Misstatement: "What Can Go Wrong"	Example Audit Procedures
Existence of assets	All recorded receivables exist.	Receivables may have been recorded that do not exist.	Confirm a sample of receivables by direct communication with debtors.
		Management may have fraudulently overstated revenue and receivables by making inappropriate adjusting journal entries.	Review monthly adjusting entries for suspicious items.
Rights to assets	The client has rights to the receivables.	Accounting personnel may erroneously be treating a sale of receivables as a liability.	Review confirmations of liabilities to determine if receivables have been sold or factored.
Completeness of assets	All receivables are recorded.	Management may have shipped items before the end of the period but not recorded the sales and related receivables until the subsequent period.	Select a sample of sales invoices in the subsequent period and examine the related shipping document for date of shipment.
Valuation of assets	Receivables are presented at net realizable value.	Allowance for uncollectible accounts may be misestimated by management.	Investigate the credit ratings for delinquent and large receivables.
		Allowance for sales returns and allowances may be misestimated by management.	Compare the amount of credits given to customers in the subsequent period to the amount estimated by management.
		Software routine to develop aged trial balance of receivables may have been erroneously programmed.	Obtain an aged trial balance of receivables, test its clerical accuracy, and reconcile to the ledgers.
Financial statement presentation of assets	Receivables are properly presented in the balance sheet, with appropriate disclosures.	Accounting personnel may have failed to identify related party transactions.	Provide a list of related parties to all members of the audit team to assist in identification of the transactions.

wrong resulting in a material misstatement of the account." Figure 6.7 provides a description of the relationships among audit objectives, risks of material misstatement, and audit procedures.

Figure 6.7 includes examples of identified risks related to each audit objective and only one procedure to address each risk. Usually, a greater number of risks are related to each objective and several procedures may have to be performed to address a particular risk. For example, the audit objective of determining that receivables are properly presented in the balance sheet is not achieved solely by performing procedures focusing on the risk of inadequate disclosure of related party transactions. The audit program must include procedures that focus on other risks related to presentation and disclosure, such as procedures that focus on the risk that the financial statements fail to disclose that receivables are pledged as collateral for debt. In addition, the complete audit program will include tests of the client's internal control that provide support for the auditors' assessments of control risk.

Chapters 10 through 16 consider the manner in which auditors design tests of controls and substantive procedures for various financial statement accounts. Specific audit objectives and sample audit procedures are presented for various accounts to provide a framework for our discussion. It is important to remember that the audit programs presented in the textbook merely illustrate *typical* procedures. In actual practice, audit programs must be tailored to each client's risks and internal control. The audit procedures comprising audit programs may vary substantially from one engagement to the next.

Audit Process

Although specific audit procedures vary from one engagement to the next, the fundamental steps are essentially the same in almost every engagement:

Learning Objective 8

1. Obtain an understanding of the client and its environment.
2. Identify and assess inherent risks of material misstatement, including risks of fraud.
3. Obtain a sufficient understanding of internal control to plan the audit.
4. Determine the planned assessed level of control risk and design additional tests of controls and planned substantive tests.
5. Perform additional tests of controls.
6. Reassess control risk and modify planned substantive tests.
7. Perform substantive tests and complete the audit.
8. Form an opinion and issue the audit report.

1. Obtain an Understanding of the Client and Its Environment

The understanding of the client and its environment enables the auditors to identify inherent risks that may result in material misstatements of the financial statements and evaluate the reasonableness of audit evidence gathered.

2. Identify and Assess Inherent Risks of Material Misstatement, Including Risks of Fraud

As indicated previously, the auditors' understanding of the client and its environment provides a basis for the auditors' assessment of **inherent risks** of material misstatement for significant assertions in the financial statements. Many inherent risks arise because of business risks faced by management. Of particular concern to the auditors are risks of material misstatement due to fraud.

3. Obtain a Sufficient Understanding of Internal Control to Plan the Audit

The nature and extent of the audit work to be performed on a particular engagement depend largely upon the effectiveness of the client's internal control in preventing or detecting material misstatements in the financial statements. Before auditors can evaluate the effectiveness of internal control, they need a knowledge and understanding of how it works: what controls exist and who performs them, how various types of transactions are processed and recorded, and what accounting records and supporting documentation exist. Thus, obtaining an understanding of the client's internal control is a required step in every audit.

Information about the client's internal control comes from interviews with client personnel, audit working papers from prior years' engagements, plant tours, and the client's manuals. In gathering information about internal control, it is often useful to study the sequence of activities used in processing major categories of transaction cycles. In the process of obtaining an understanding of internal control, the auditors will often obtain some evidence about the operating effectiveness of certain control activities.

A working knowledge of the client's internal control system is needed throughout the audit; consequently, the auditors prepare working papers fully describing their understanding of the system. Frequent reference to these working papers will be made to aid in designing audit procedures, ascertaining where documents are filed, familiarizing new audit staff with internal control, and as a refresher in beginning next year's engagement.

The description of internal control is usually prepared in the form of systems flowcharts. As an alternative to flowcharts, parts of internal control may be described by written narratives or by the completion of specially designed questionnaires. All of these working papers are illustrated and discussed in Chapter 7.

4. Determine the Planned Assessed Level of Control Risk and Design Additional Tests of Controls and Planned Substantive Tests

After analyzing the design of internal control, the auditors must decide whether the system, as designed, seems strong enough to prevent or detect and correct material misstatements. In terms of the audit risk model, the auditors determine the planned assessed level of **control risk** for each significant assertion. If they assess internal control to be weak (control risk is high), they will rely primarily on substantive tests to reduce audit risk for the assertion to an acceptable level. On the other hand, if the system is capable of preventing or detecting and correcting misstatements, the auditor will decide which additional controls, if any, can efficiently be tested. These considerations will be used to design additional tests of controls and planned substantive tests.

5. Perform Additional Tests of Controls

Tests of controls are performed to determine whether key controls have been *properly designed and are operating effectively.* To illustrate a *test of a control,* consider the control activity in which the accounting department accounts for the serial sequence of all shipping documents before preparing the related journal entries. The purpose of this control is to ensure that each shipment of merchandise is recorded in the accounting records (i.e., to ensure the completeness of recorded sales and accounts receivable). To test the operating effectiveness of the control, the auditors might review evidence of the client's accounting for the sequence of shipping documents and select a sample of shipping documents prepared at various times throughout the year to inspect the related journal entries.

Notice that a test of a control measures the effectiveness of a particular control; it *does not* substantiate the dollar amount of an account balance. Also, a particular control may affect several financial statement amounts. If, for example, the tests described above indicate that the accounting department does not effectively account for the serial sequence of shipping documents, the auditors should be alert to the possibility of material misstatements in sales revenue, accounts receivable, cost of goods sold, and inventories.

6. Reassess Control Risk and Modify Planned Substantive Tests

After completing their tests of controls, the auditors are in a position to reassess control risk based on the results of the tests and determine whether it is necessary to modify their planned substantive tests. **Substantive tests** are procedures designed to substantiate the fairness of specific financial statement assertions. As indicated previously, substantive tests are determined by the levels of inherent risk and control risk. Auditors should make an intensive investigation of account balances in areas for which the combination of inherent risk and control risk is high; however, they are justified in performing less extensive testing of financial statement assertions for which they have determined that inherent and control risk are low. This process of deciding upon the matters to be emphasized during the audit, based upon the assessment of inherent and control risks, means that the auditors will modify their audit program by expanding substantive tests in some areas and by reducing them in others.

7. Perform Substantive Tests and Complete the Audit

Some procedures for verifying account balances may be performed early in the audit. However, only after having completed their assessment of inherent and control risks are the auditors in a position to complete the procedures necessary to substantiate account balances.

8. Form an Opinion and Issue the Audit Report

The audit report is dated when the auditors have accumulated sufficient competent evidence to support their opinion. This date is often the *last day of field work,* which is the date on which the last audit procedures are completed at the client's office. However, the report is not actually issued on that date. Since the audit report represents an acceptance of considerable responsibility by the CPA firm, a partner will make a final review of the working papers from the engagement to determine that a thorough audit has been completed. In addition, other required procedures are performed, such as the second partner review. The process usually results in audit report issuance a week or more after the last day of fieldwork.

Timing of Audit Work

The value of audited financial statements is enhanced if the statements are available on a timely basis after the year-end. To facilitate an early release of the audit report, auditors normally begin the audit well before the balance sheet date. The period before the balance sheet date is termed the **interim period.** Audit work that can always be started during the interim period includes the consideration of internal control, issuance of the management letter, and substantive tests of transactions that have occurred to the interim date.

As discussed in Chapter 5, interim tests of certain financial statement balances, such as accounts receivable, may also be performed, but this results in additional risk that must be controlled by the auditors. Significant misstatements due to error or fraud could arise in these accounts during the *remaining period* between the time that the interim test was performed and the balance sheet date. Thus, to rely on the interim test of a significant account balance, the auditors must perform additional tests of the account during the remaining period.

Performing audit work during the interim period has numerous advantages, in addition to facilitating the timely release of the audited financial statements. The independent auditors may be able to assess internal control more effectively by observing and testing controls at various times throughout the year. Also, they can give early consideration to accounting problems. Another advantage is that interim auditing creates a more uniform work load for CPA firms. With a large client, such as General Motors, the auditors may have office space within the client's buildings and perform audit procedures throughout the entire year.

Chapter Summary

This chapter explained the manner in which auditors plan an audit and design audit programs. To summarize:

1. Investigating a potential audit client is essential because auditors want to avoid accepting clients that have unscrupulous management. As a part of their investigation, the auditors are required to communicate with the predecessor auditors. Arrangements for the engagement are set forth in the engagement letter, which makes clear the nature of the engagement, any limitations on the work, and the responsibilities of the client.

2. Once the client has been accepted, the auditors will perform procedures to obtain a more detailed understanding of the client and its environment, and they will develop an overall audit strategy which considers both materiality and audit risk. The auditors must plan their audit to provide reasonable assurance that the financial statements are free from material misstatement, whether caused by error or fraud. The auditors' understanding of the client and its environment and planning analytical procedures will provide a basis for their identification and assessment of risks of material misstatement of the financial statements.

3. Auditors are particularly concerned about fraud—both fraudulent financial reporting and misappropriation of assets. To identify fraud risks, the auditors have an audit team discussion of potential fraud, make inquires and perform analytical procedures, and consider the presence of fraud risk factors. The auditors react to fraud risks as they do to other risks of material misstatements, with an overall response or a modification of the nature, timing, and extent of audit procedures. However, the auditors are required in all audits to perform procedures to address the risk of management override of internal control.

4. The planning process is documented with audit plans, time budgets, and audit programs. Audit programs generally include both a systems portion that focuses on the client's internal control and a substantive testing portion. The audit procedures that are contained in the audit program are designed around the assertions of management, which are embodied in the financial statements, and the auditors' assessments of risks and controls.

5. Audit procedures should be responsive to the auditors' assessments of inherent risks of material misstatement of the financial statements. Inherent risks specify "what could go wrong" to cause a material misstatement of the financial statements, and audit procedures must be designed to detect the misstatement if it actually occurred.

6. Subsequent to inherent risk assessment, the audit process consists of considering and testing the client's internal control, performing substantive tests, forming an opinion on the financial statements, and issuing the audit report.

Key Terms Introduced or Emphasized in Chapter 6

Analytical procedures   Tests that involve comparisons of financial data for the current year to that of prior years, budgets, nonfinancial data, or industry averages. From a planning standpoint, analytical procedures help the auditors obtain an understanding of the client's business, identify financial statement amounts that appear to be affected by errors or fraud, or identify other potential problems.

Audit committee   A committee composed of outside directors (members of the board of directors who are neither officers nor employees) charged with responsibility for appointing, compensating, and overseeing the auditors.

Audit plan   A broad overview of an audit engagement prepared in the planning stage of the engagement. Audit plans usually include such matters as the objectives of the engagement, the nature of the work to be performed, significant audit and fraud risks, a time schedule for major audit work and completion of the engagement, and staffing requirements.

Audit program   A detailed listing of the specific audit procedures to be performed in the course of an audit engagement. Audit programs provide a basis for assigning and scheduling audit work and for determining what work remains to be done. Audit programs are specially tailored to the risks and internal controls of each engagement.

Audit risk   At the overall engagement level, this is the risk that the auditors may unknowingly fail to appropriately modify their opinion on financial statements that are materially misstated. At the financial statement assertion level, it is the risk that a particular assertion about an account balance is materially misstated.

Business risks   Risks that threaten management's ability to achieve the organization's objectives.

Control risk   The risk that a material misstatement that could occur in an account will not be prevented or detected on a timely basis by internal control.

Dual-purpose procedure (test)   An audit procedure that serves as a test of controls and as a substantive test. For example, a test of controls over equipment acquisitions may address authorization (providing evidence on control effectiveness) and whether the transaction tested has been properly recorded in the year's acquisitions (providing substantive evidence on the dollar amounts). As another example, a substantive test may reveal a misstatement and be extended to determine the nature of the control that did not operate effectively, thereby providing evidence on operating effectiveness.

Engagement letter   A formal letter sent by the auditors to the client at the beginning of an engagement summarizing the nature of the engagement, any limitations on the scope of audit work, work to be done by the client's staff, and the basis for the audit fee. The purpose of engagement letters is to avoid misunderstandings; they are essential on nonaudit engagements as well as audits.

Engagement risk   The risk of loss or injury to the auditors' reputation by association with a client that goes bankrupt or one whose management lacks integrity.

Fraudulent financial reporting (management fraud)   Material misstatement of financial statements by management with the intent to mislead financial statement users.

Inherent risk   The risk of material misstatement of an assertion about an account without considering internal control.

Interim period   The time interval from the beginning of audit work to the balance sheet date. Many audit procedures can be performed during the interim period to facilitate early issuance of the audit report.

Internet   An international network of independently owned computers that operates as a giant computing network. Data on the Internet are stored on "Web servers," which are computers scattered throughout the world.

Management assertions   Representations of management that are communicated, explicitly or implicitly, by the financial statements.

Misappropriation of assets (defalcations)   Theft of client assets by an employee or officer of the organization.

Predecessor auditors   A CPA firm that formerly served as auditor but has resigned from the engagement or has been notified that its services have been terminated.

Shopping for accounting principles   Conduct by some enterprises that discharge one independent auditing firm after seeking out another firm that will sanction a disputed accounting principle or financial statement presentation.

Substantive tests   Tests of account balances and transactions designed to detect any material misstatements in the financial statements. The nature, timing, and extent of substantive testing are determined by the auditors' assessment of risks and their consideration of the client's internal control.

Successor auditors   The auditors who have accepted an engagement or who have been invited to make a proposal for an engagement to replace the CPA firm that formerly served as auditors.

Time budget   An estimate of the time required to perform each step in the audit.

Transaction cycle   The sequence of procedures applied by the client in processing a particular type of recurring transaction. The term *cycle* reflects the idea that the same sequence of procedures is applied to each similar transaction. The auditors' consideration of internal control often is organized around the client's major transaction cycles.

Review Questions

6–1.   What information should a CPA firm seek in its investigation of a prospective client?

6–2.   Describe the requirements for composition of the audit committee of a board of directors of a public company.

6–3.   State the purpose and nature of an engagement letter.

6–4.   Discuss what is meant by the phrase "shopping for accounting principles." What mechanisms have served to prevent this practice by management?

6–5.   Criticize the following statement: "Throughout this audit, for all purposes, we will define a 'material amount' as $500,000."

6–6.   Describe the two types of misstatements due to fraud. Which one generally is of more concern to the auditors?

6–7.   Many CPA firms are taking a business risk approach to audits. Define what is meant by business risk. Provide an example of a business risk that could result in a risk of material misstatement of the financial statements.

6–8.   Define and differentiate between an *audit plan* and an *audit program.*

6–9.   Should a separate audit program be prepared for each audit engagement, or can a standard program be used for most engagements?

6–10.   "An audit program is desirable when new staff members are assigned to an engagement, but an experienced auditor should be able to conduct an audit without reference to an audit program." Do you agree? Discuss.

6–11.   Suggest some factors that might cause an audit engagement to exceed the original time estimate. Would the extra time be charged to the client?

6–12.   What problems are created for a CPA firm when audit staff members underreport the amount of time spent in performing specific audit procedures?

6–13.   Why is audit work usually organized around balance sheet accounts rather than income statement accounts?

6–14.   Identify the general objectives of the auditors' substantive procedures with respect to any major asset category.

6–15.   What is meant by making a proper year-end *cutoff*? Explain the effects of errors in the cutoff of sales transactions in both the income statement and the balance sheet.

6–16.   What are the purposes of the audit procedures of (*a*) tracing a sample of journal entries forward to the ledgers and (*b*) vouching a sample of ledger entries back to the journals?

6–17.   Charles Halstead, CPA, has a number of clients who desire audits at the end of the calendar year. In an effort to spread his work load more uniformly throughout the year, he is preparing a list of audit procedures that could be performed satisfactorily before the year-end balance sheet date. What audit work, if any, might be done in advance of the balance sheet date?

6–18.   Define and differentiate between a test of controls and a substantive test.

6–19.   The audit plan, the audit program, and the time budget are three important working papers prepared early in an audit. What functions do these working papers serve in the auditors' compliance with generally accepted auditing standards? Discuss.

6–20.   Auditing standards require the auditors to have a team meeting regarding the risk of fraud for the engagement. What is the purpose of this meeting?

6–21.   How can a CPA make use of the preceding year's audit working papers in a recurring audit?

6–22.   When planning an audit, the auditors must assess the levels of risk and materiality for the engagement. Explain how the auditors' judgments about these two factors affect the auditors' planned audit procedures.

Questions Requiring Analysis

6–23.   Morgan, CPA, is approached by a prospective audit client who wants to engage Morgan to perform an audit for the current year. In prior years, this prospective client was audited by another CPA. Identify the specific procedures that Morgan should follow in deciding whether to accept this client.

6–24.   Mary Deming has been asked to accept an engagement to audit a small financial institution. Deming has not previously audited a financial institution.

Required:

    a. Describe the types of knowledge about the prospective client and its environment that Deming must obtain to plan the engagement.

    b. Explain how Deming may obtain this knowledge.

    c. Discuss how this knowledge of the client and its environment will help Deming in planning and performing an audit in accordance with generally accepted auditing standards.

6–25.   Arthur Samuels, CPA, agreed to perform an audit of a new client engaged in the manufacture of power tools. After some preliminary discussion of the purposes of the audit and the basis for determination of the audit fee, Samuels asked to be taken on a comprehensive guided tour of the client's plant facilities. Explain specific ways that the knowledge gained by Samuels during the plant tour may help in planning and conducting the audit.

6–26.   A CPA has been asked to audit the financial statements of a publicly held company for the first time. All preliminary discussions have been completed between the CPA, the company, the predecessor auditors, and all other necessary parties. The CPA is now preparing an engagement letter. List the items that should be included in the engagement letter.

6–27.   Auditors must plan and perform their audits to provide reasonable assurance of detecting material misstatements in financial statements, including those resulting from fraud.

Required:

    a. Distinguish between fraudulent financial reporting and misappropriation of assets.

    b. Describe the three fundamental conditions necessary for the commission of fraud. Provide an illustration of these three conditions for a case of fraudulent financial reporting.

    c. Describe the three ways in which the auditors may respond to fraud risks in an audit.

6–28.   In planning every audit, the auditors are required to consider materiality for audit purposes. Described below are financial statement data from two separate companies:

	Franklin Co.	Tyler Co.
Total assets	$34,900,000	$2,700,000
Total revenue	29,600,000	4,500,000
Equity	13,800,000	1,000,000
Net income before taxes	1,600,000	90,000

Required:

    a. Develop an estimate of the appropriate amount of planning materiality for Franklin Co., and describe how you arrived at the estimate.

    b. Develop an estimate of the appropriate amount of planning materiality for Tyler Co., and describe how you arrived at the estimate.

    c. Describe five characteristics of a small misstatement that might render it qualitatively material.

6–29.   The auditors sometimes decide to allocate the amount of planning materiality to various financial statement accounts.

Required:

    a. Explain why auditors typically decide to allocate planning materiality to individual financial statement accounts.

    b. Describe why the total amount of planning materiality allocated to individual accounts may exceed overall materiality.

6–30.   John Wells, CPA, is planning the audit of CVG Services, Inc. As a result of his planning procedures, Wells has identified several fraud risks.

Required:

    a. Explain in detail how Wells might respond to risks of material misstatement of the financial statements due to fraud.

    b. Describe the auditors' communication responsibilities in situations in which the auditors believe fraud has occurred.

6–31.   Listed below are several of the auditors' general objectives in performing substantive tests of an asset account:

    1. Establish the existence of assets.

2. Establish that the company has rights to the assets.

3. Establish the completeness of recorded assets.

4. Determine the appropriate valuation of the assets.

5. Establish the clerical accuracy of the underlying records.

6. Determine the appropriate financial statement presentation and disclosure of the assets.

Required: Indicate the general objective (or objectives) of each of the following audit procedures:

a. Observe the client's physical inventory.

b. Locate on the client's premises a sample of the equipment items listed in the subsidiary plant and equipment ledger.

c. Obtain a listing of inventory and reconcile the total to the general ledger.

d. Trace a sample of shipping documents to recorded sales transactions.

e. Identify related parties.

f. Vouch selected purchases of securities to brokers' advices.

6–32. Richard Foster, an assistant auditor, was assigned to the year-end audit work of Sipher Corporation. Sipher is a small manufacturer of language translation equipment. As his first assignment, Foster was instructed to test the cutoff of year-end sales transactions. Since Sipher uses a calendar year-end for its financial statements, Foster began by obtaining the computer-generated sales ledgers and journals for December and January. He then traced ledger postings for a few days before and after December 31 to the sales journals, noting the dates of the journal entries. Foster noted no journal entries that were posted to the ledger in the wrong accounting period. Thus, he concluded that the client's cutoff of sales transactions was effective.

Required: Comment on the validity of Foster's conclusion. Explain fully.

6–33. SEC filings of certain public companies can be accessed from EDGAR (Electronic Data Gathering and Retrieval System), which has the following Internet address:

www.sec.gov/edgar.shtml.

Required: *a.* Use EDGAR to locate a company in the software industry.

b. Access the latest Form 10-K for the company and read "Management's Discussion and Analysis" from Form 10-K.

c. Describe four significant business risks of the company as described in "Management's Discussion and Analysis."

6–34. In every audit engagement, the auditors must identify fraud risks that may require an audit response. Described below are four circumstances or factors that may create an increased risk of material misstatement of the financial statements due to fraud.

1. The compensation of management of a subsidiary of the client is heavily dependent on the net income of the subsidiary and controls over subsidiary management are weak.

2. The compensation of management of a telecommunications firm is significantly tied to revenue, and analytical procedures indicate that revenue may be overstated. The company engages in complex sales agreements.

3. Futures traders in an energy company are compensated based on the performance of their purchases and sales of energy futures contracts. The markets for these contracts have few participants, resulting in the need to value contracts on hand at year-end based on complex valuation models applied by the traders.

4. A chain of discount markets has inconsistent profit margins across stores as indicated by analytical procedures.

Required: *a.* For each of the four circumstances, indicate the fraud risk that the auditors should consider.

b. For each of the four circumstances, indicate a possible appropriate response by the auditors.

6–35. The text of the Securities Exchange Act of 1934 may be accessed on the Internet, using the following address:

www.law.uc.edu/CCL/34Act/index.html.

Required: *a.* Use the Internet to access the text of the Securities Exchange Act of 1934.

b. Read and summarize the internal control requirements of Section 13(b)(2) of the act.

Multiple Choice Questions

6–36. Select the best answer for each of the following. Explain the reasons for your selection.

a. In planning and performing an audit, auditors are concerned about risk factors for two distinct types of fraud: fraudulent financial reporting and misappropriation of assets. Which of the following is a risk factor for misappropriation of assets?

(1) Generous performance-based compensation systems.

(2) Management preoccupation with increased financial performance.

(3) An unreliable accounting system.

(4) Strained relationships between management and the auditors.

b. The audit committee of a company must be made up of:

(1) Representatives from the client's management, investors, suppliers, and customers.

(2) The audit partner, the chief financial officer, the legal counsel, and at least one outsider.

(3) Representatives of the major equity interests, such as preferred and common stockholders.

(4) Members of the board of directors who are not officers or employees.

c. Which of the following should not normally be included in the engagement letter for an audit?

(1) A description of the responsibilities of client personnel to provide assistance.

(2) An indication of the amount of the audit fee.

(3) A description of the limitations of an audit.

(4) A listing of the client's branch offices selected for testing.

d. Which portion of an audit may *not* be completed before the balance sheet date?

(1) Tests of controls.

(2) Issuance of a management letter.

(3) Substantive testing.

(4) Assessment of control risk.

e. Which of the following should the auditors obtain from the predecessor auditors before accepting an audit engagement?

(1) Analysis of balance sheet accounts.

(2) Analysis of income statement accounts.

(3) All matters of continuing accounting significance.

(4) Facts that might bear on the integrity of management.

f. As one step in testing sales transactions, a CPA traces a random sample of sales journal entries to debits in the accounts receivable subsidiary ledger. This test provides evidence as to whether:

(1) Each recorded sale represents a bona fide transaction.

(2) All sales have been recorded in the sales journal.

(3) All debit entries in the accounts receivable subsidiary ledger are properly supported by sales journal entries.

(4) Recorded sales have been properly posted to customer accounts.

g. The primary objective of tests of details of transactions performed as substantive tests is to:

(1) Comply with generally accepted auditing standards.

(2) Attain assurance about the reliability of the accounting system.

(3) Detect material misstatements in the financial statements.

(4) Evaluate whether management's policies and procedures operated effectively.

h. The risk that the auditors will conclude, based on substantive tests, that a material misstatement does not exist in an account balance when, in fact, such misstatement does exist is referred to as

(1) Business risk.

(2) Engagement risk.

(3) Control risk.

(4) Detection risk.

     i. Which of the following elements underlies the application of generally accepted auditing standards, particularly the standards of fieldwork and reporting?

        (1) Adequate disclosure.

        (2) Quality control.

        (3) Materiality and audit risk.

        (4) Client acceptance.

     j. Which of the following best describes what is meant by the term "fraud risk factor"?

        (1) Factors whose presence indicates that the risk of fraud is high.

        (2) Factors whose presence often have been observed in circumstances where frauds have occurred.

        (3) Factors whose presence requires modification of planned audit procedures.

        (4) Reportable conditions identified during an audit.

     k. Three conditions generally are present when fraud occurs. Select the one below that is not one of those conditions.

        (1) Incentive or pressure.

        (2) Opportunity.

        (3) Supervisory position.

        (4) Attitude.

     l. Which of the following is most likely to be an overall response to fraud risks identified in an audit?

        (1) Supervise members of the audit team less closely and rely more upon judgment.

        (2) Use less predictable audit procedures.

        (3) Only use certified public accountants on the engagement.

        (4) Place increased emphasis on the audit of objective transactions rather than subjective transactions.

(AICPA, adapted)

Problems

6–37. You are invited by John Bray, the president of Cheviot Corporation, to discuss with him the possibility of your conducting an audit of the company. The corporation is a small, closely held manufacturing organization that appears to be expanding. No previous audit has been performed by independent certified public accountants. Your discussions with Bray include an analysis of the recent monthly financial statements, inspection of the accounting records, and discussion of policies with the chief accountant. You also are taken on a guided tour of the plant by the president. He then makes the following statement:

> Before making definite arrangements for an audit, I would like to know about how long it will take and about how much it will cost. I want quality work and expect to pay a fair price, but since this is our first experience with independent auditors, I would like a full explanation as to how the cost of the audit is determined. Will you please send me a memorandum covering these points?

Write the memorandum requested by John Bray.

6–38. Valley Finance Company opened four personal loan offices in neighboring cities on January 2. Small cash loans are made to borrowers who repay the principal with interest in monthly installments over a period not exceeding two years. Ralph Norris, president of the company, uses one of the offices as a central office and visits the other offices periodically for supervision and internal auditing purposes.

Required: Assume that you agreed to audit Valley Finance Company's financial statements for the year ended December 31. No scope limitations were imposed.

     a. How would you determine the scope necessary to complete your audit satisfactorily? Discuss.

     b. Would you be responsible for the discovery of fraud in this audit? Discuss.

6–39. You are a new staff assistant with the Houston office of a national public accounting firm. Yesterday you read an article in *The Wall Street Journal* in which the managing partner of your firm's New York office discussed the problems caused for the public accounting profession by auditors underreporting the number of hours worked on audits.

You found this article interesting because of the experience you are having on the audit of Regal Industries, one of your office's largest clients. The fieldwork at Regal is being run by Mark Thomas, a very hard-working senior who is highly regarded within your office. Thomas made senior in record time and has established a reputation for bringing jobs in on schedule. Four staff assistants, including yourself, are working under Thomas. At the end of the engagement, Thomas will write a performance report on each assistant, which will be placed in the assistant's personnel file. The manager on the engagement also writes a performance evaluation on each assistant and on Thomas. You have heard, however, that managers usually agree with whatever the senior has said about an assistant's performance.

The budgeted time estimates for almost every audit procedure being performed at Regal seem too short. No one is able to finish anything on schedule. Last week, Thomas approached all the staff assistants about working Saturday to "catch up." He said that he was going to work a short day on Saturday and would not report the hours on his time sheet. He said that if you would do the same, he would buy lunch after you finished up on Saturday. You and two other assistants agreed. The fourth assistant, Dave Scott, declined, saying that he was going to a baseball game on Saturday.

The work on Saturday ran smoothly, and it was nice to wear jeans instead of dress clothes. You did quit a little early, although it was about 3:30, not noon. Afterward, Thomas bought everyone lunch at a popular restaurant.

During the following workweek, you noticed that Thomas seemed quite friendly toward you and the other two assistants who had worked on Saturday. He also was complimentary of your work. He was not complimentary of Scott's work; in fact, you heard him comment to the engagement manager that he thought Scott would be a "short-timer," a phrase used to describe staff assistants who do not last long in public accounting. You were not too sympathetic to Scott's plight, however, as you and the other staff assistants also feel that Scott's work on the engagement has been substandard.

It is now Thursday afternoon, and Thomas has just asked the three of you who worked last Saturday if you will do the same thing again this week. He did not ask Scott. Again, Thomas offered to buy lunch if you would leave the hours off your time sheets. You suspect that Thomas has read the article in *The Wall Street Journal,* because he seemed a little defensive about asking you to underreport your time. He pointed out that you are not paid by the hour anyway, so leaving the extra hours off of your time sheet "doesn't really cost you anything."

Required:
a. Briefly explain why the managing partner of an office would probably oppose the practice of underreporting hours worked by the audit staff.

b. Briefly explain why a senior might *not* oppose the practice.

c. Explain how you think the other two staff assistants asked to work Saturday will probably respond. If you would respond differently, explain.

d. Suggest quality control procedures that you think could be implemented by a CPA firm to discourage the underreporting of time by audit staff members.

6–40. Precision Industries, Inc., is a manufacturer of electronic components. When a purchase order is received from a customer, a sales clerk prepares a serially numbered sales order and sends copies to the shipping and accounting departments. When the merchandise is shipped to the customer, the shipping department prepares a serially numbered shipping advice and sends a copy to the accounting department. Upon receipt of the appropriate documents, the accounting department records the sale in the accounting records. All shipments are *FOB shipping point.*

Required:
a. How can the auditors determine whether Precision Industries, Inc., has made a proper year-end cutoff of sales transactions?

b. Assume that all shipments for the first five days of the following year were recorded as occurring in the current year. If not corrected, what effect will this cutoff error have upon the financial statements for the current year?

6–41. Michael Green, CPA, is considering audit risk at the financial statement level in planning the audit of National Federal Bank (NFB) Company's financial statements for the year ended December 31, 20X1. Audit risk at the financial statement level is influenced by the risks of material misstatements (including fraud risks), which may be indicated by a combination of factors related to management, the environment, and the entity. In assessing such factors Green has gathered the following information concerning NFB's environment.

Company Profile: NFB is a federally insured bank that has been consistently more profitable than the industry average by marketing mortgages on properties in a prosperous rural area that has experienced considerable growth in recent years. NFB packages its mortgages and sells them to large mortgage investment trusts. Despite recent volatility of interest rates, NFB has been able to continue selling its mortgages as a source of new lendable funds.

NFB's board of directors is controlled by Smith, the majority stockholder, who also acts as the chief executive officer. Management at the bank's branch offices has authority for directing and controlling NFB's operations and is compensated based on branch profitability. The internal auditor reports directly to Harris, a minority shareholder, who also acts as chairman of the board's audit committee.

The accounting department has experienced little turnover in personnel during the five years Green has audited NFB. NFB's formula consistently underestimates the allowance for loan losses, but its controller has always been receptive to Green's suggestions to increase the allowance during each engagement.

Recent Developments: During 20X1, NFB opened a branch office in a suburban town 30 miles from its principal place of business. Although this branch is not yet profitable due to competition from several well-established regional banks, management believes that the branch will be profitable by 20X3.

Also during 20X1, NFB increased the efficiency of its accounting operations by installing a new, sophisticated computer system.

Required: Based only on the information above, describe the factors that most likely would have an effect on the risks of material misstatement of the financial statements. Indicate whether each factor increases or decreases the risk. In addition, indicate whether the factor indicates increased risk of fraud. Use the format illustrated below.

Factor	Effect on Risks of Material Misstatement	Creates a Risk of Fraud?
Branch management has authority for directing and controlling operations	Increase	Yes

(AICPA, adapted)

Ethics Case

6–42. Tammy Potter, a new partner with the regional CPA firm of Tower & Tower, was recently appointed to the board of directors of a local civic organization. The chairman of the board of the civic organization is Lewis Edmond, who is also the owner of a real estate development firm, Tierra Corporation.

Potter was quite excited when Edmond indicated that his corporation needed an audit, and he wished to discuss the matter with her. During the discussion, Potter was told that Tierra Corporation needed the audit to obtain a substantial amount of additional financing to acquire another company. Presently, Tierra Corporation is successful, profitable, and committed to growth. The audit fee for the engagement should be substantial.

Since Tierra Corporation appeared to be a good client prospect, Potter tentatively indicated that Tower & Tower wanted to do the work. Potter then mentioned that Tower & Tower's quality control policies require an investigation of new clients and approval by the managing partner, Lee Tower.

Potter obtained the authorization of Edmond to make the necessary inquiries for the new client investigation. Edmond was found to be a highly respected member of the community. Also, Tierra Corporation was highly regarded by its banker and its attorney, and the Dun & Bradstreet report on the corporation reflected nothing negative.

As a final part of the investigation process, Potter contacted Edmond's former tax accountant, Bill Turner. Potter was surprised to discover that Turner did not share the others' high opinion of Edmond. Turner related that on an IRS audit 10 years ago, Edmond was questioned about the details of a large capital loss reported on the sale of a tract of land to a trust. Edmond told the IRS agent that he had lost all the supporting documentation for the transaction, and that he had no way of finding out the names of the principals of the trust. A search by an IRS auditor revealed that the land was recorded in the name of Edmond's married daughter and that Edmond himself was listed as the trustee. The IRS disallowed the loss and Edmond was assessed a civil fraud penalty. Potter was concerned about these findings, but eventually concluded that Edmond had probably matured to a point where he would not engage in such activities.

Required:
a. Present arguments supporting a decision to accept Tierra Corporation as an audit client.

b. Present arguments supporting a decision *not* to accept Tierra Corporation as an audit client.

c. Assuming that you are Lee Tower, set forth your decision regarding acceptance of the client, identifying those arguments from part (*a*) or part (*b*) that you found most persuasive.

Appendix **6A**

Selected Internet Addresses

Accounting and Auditing Web Sites

AICPA—www.aicpa.org

IIA—www.theiia.org

Various accounting—http://taxsites.com

Large Accounting Firms

BDO Seidman—www.bdo.com/

Deloitte & Touche LLP—www.deloitte.com/

Ernst & Young LLP—www.ey.com/

Grant Thornton LLP—www.gt.com/

KPMG LLP—www.us.kpmg.com/

McGladrey & Pullen, LLP—www.rsmmcgladrey.com

PricewaterhouseCoopers LLP—www.pwcglobal.com/

Securities and Exchange Commission

Home page—www.sec.gov/

EDGAR page—www.sec.gov/edgarhp.htm

Securities Act of 1933—www.law.uc.edu/CCL/33Act/index.html

Securities Exchange Act of 1934—www.law.uc.edu/CCL/34Act/index.html

Public Company Accounting Oversight Board

PCAOB—www.pcaobus.org

Appendix **6B**

Examples of Fraud Risk Factors

Risk Factors Relating to Misstatements Arising from Fraudulent Financial Reporting

INCENTIVES AND PRESSURES

1. Financial stability or profitability is threatened by economic, industry, or entity operating conditions, such as (or as indicated by):
   a. High degree of competition or market saturation, accompanied by declining margins.
   b. High vulnerability to rapid changes, such as changes in technology, product obsolescence, or interest rates.
   c. Significant declines in customer demand and increasing business failures in either the industry or overall economy.
   d. Operating losses making the threat of bankruptcy, foreclosure, or hostile takeover imminent.
   e. Recurring negative cash flows from operations or an inability to generate cash flows from operations while reporting earnings and earnings growth.
   f. Rapid growth or unusual profitability, especially compared to that of other companies in the same industry.
   g. New accounting, statutory, or regulatory requirements.

2. Excessive pressure exists for management to meet the requirements or expectations of third parties due to the following:

   a. Profitability or trend level expectations of investment analysts, institutional investors, significant creditors, or other external parties (particularly expectations that are unduly aggressive or unrealistic), including expectations created by management in, for example, overly optimistic press releases or annual report messages.

   b. Need to obtain additional debt or equity financing to stay competitive—including financing of major research and development or capital expenditures.

   c. Marginal ability to meet exchange listing requirements or debt repayment or other debt covenant requirements.

   d. Perceived or real adverse effects of reporting poor financial results on significant pending transactions, such as business combinations or contract awards.

3. Information available indicates that management or the board of directors' personal financial situation is threatened by the entity's financial performance arising from the following:

   a. Significant financial interests in the entity.

   b. Significant portions of their compensation (for example, bonuses, stock options, and earn-out arrangements) being contingent upon achieving aggressive targets for stock price, operating results, financial position, or cash flow.

   c. Personal guarantees of debts of the entity.

4. There is excessive pressure on management or operating personnel to meet financial targets set up by the board of directors or management, including sales or profitability incentive goals.

OPPORTUNITIES

1. The nature of the industry or the entity's operations provides opportunities to engage in fraudulent financial reporting that can arise from the following:

   a. Significant related party transactions not in the ordinary course of business or with related entities not audited or audited by another firm.

   b. A strong financial presence or ability to dominate a certain industry sector that allows the entity to dictate terms or conditions to suppliers or customers that may result in inappropriate or non-arm's-length transactions.

   c. Assets, liabilities, revenues, or expenses based on significant estimates that involve subjective judgments or uncertainties that are difficult to corroborate.

   d. Significant, unusual, or highly complex transactions, especially those close to period end that pose difficult "substance over form" questions.

   e. Significant operations located or conducted across international borders in jurisdictions where differing business environments and cultures exist.

   f. Significant bank accounts or subsidiary or branch operations in tax-haven jurisdictions for which there appears to be no clear business justification.

2. There is ineffective monitoring of management as a result of the following:

   a. Domination of management by a single person or small group (in a non-owner-managed business) without compensating controls.

   b. Ineffective board of directors or audit committee oversight over the financial reporting process and internal control.

3. There is a complex or unstable organizational structure, as evidenced by the following:

   a. Difficulty in determining the organization or individuals that have controlling interest in the entity.

   b. Overly complex organizational structure involving unusual legal entities or managerial lines of authority.

   c. High turnover of senior management, counsel, or board members.

4. Internal control components are deficient as a result of the following:

   a. Inadequate monitoring of controls, including automated controls and controls over interim financial reporting (where external reporting is required).

   b. High turnover rates or employment of ineffective accounting, internal audit, or information technology staff.

   c. Ineffective accounting and information systems, including situations involving reportable conditions.

ATTITUDES AND RATIONALIZATIONS

Risk factors reflective of attitudes and/or rationalizations by board members, management, or employees, that allow them to engage in and/or justify fraudulent financial reporting, may not be susceptible to observation by the auditor. Nevertheless, the auditor who becomes aware of the existence of such information should consider it in identifying the risks of material misstatement arising from fraudulent financial reporting. For example, auditors may become aware of the following information that may indicate a risk factor:

1. Ineffective communication, implementation, support, or enforcement of the entity's values or ethical standards by management or the communication of inappropriate values or ethical standards.

2. Nonfinancial management's excessive participation in or preoccupation with the selection of accounting principles or the determination of significant estimates.

3. Known history of violations of securities laws or other laws and regulations, or claims against the entity, its senior management, or board members alleging fraud or violations of laws and regulations.

4. Excessive interest by management in maintaining or increasing the entity's stock price or earnings trend.

5. A practice by management of committing to analysts, creditors, and other third parties to achieve aggressive or unrealistic forecasts.

6. Management failing to correct known significant deficiencies (reportable conditions) on a timely basis.

7. An interest by management in employing inappropriate means to minimize reported earnings for tax-motivated reasons.

8. Recurring attempts by management to justify marginal or inappropriate accounting on the basis of materiality.

9. A strained relationship between management and the current or predecessor auditor, as exhibited by the following:

   a. Frequent disputes with the current or predecessor auditor on accounting, auditing, or reporting matters.

   b. Unreasonable demands on the auditor, such as unreasonable time constraints regarding the completion of the audit or the issuance of the auditor's report.

   c. Formal or informal restrictions on the auditor that inappropriately limit access to people or information or the ability to communicate effectively with the board of directors or audit committee.

   d. Domineering management behavior in dealing with the auditor, especially involving attempts to influence the scope of the auditor's work or the selection or continuance of personnel assigned to or consulted on the audit engagement.

Risk Factors Relating to Misstatements Arising from Misappropriation of Assets

INCENTIVES AND PRESSURES

1. Personal financial obligations may create pressure on management or employees with access to cash or other assets susceptible to theft to misappropriate those assets.

2. Adverse relationships between the entity and employees with access to cash or other assets susceptible to theft may motivate those employees to misappropriate those assets. For example, adverse relationships may be created by the following:

   a. Known or anticipated future employee layoffs.

   b. Recent or anticipated changes to employee compensation or benefit plans.

   c. Promotions, compensation, or other rewards inconsistent with expectations.

OPPORTUNITIES

1. Certain characteristics or circumstances may increase the susceptibility of assets to misappropriation. For example, opportunities to misappropriate assets increase when there are the following:

   a. Large amounts of cash on hand or processed.

   b. Inventory items that are small in size, of high value, or in high demand.

   c. Easily convertible assets, such as bearer bonds, diamonds, or computer chips.

   d. Fixed assets that are small in size, marketable, or lacking observable identification of ownership.

2. Inadequate internal control over assets may increase the susceptibility of misappropriation of those assets. For example, misappropriation of assets may occur because there is the following:

    a. Inadequate segregation of duties or independent checks.

    b. Inadequate management oversight of employees responsible for assets, for example, inadequate supervision or monitoring of remote locations.

    c. Inadequate job applicant screening of employees with access to assets.

    d. Inadequate recordkeeping with respect to assets.

    e. Inadequate system of authorization and approval of transactions (for example, in purchasing).

    f. Inadequate physical safeguards over cash, investments, inventory, or fixed assets.

    g. Lack of complete and timely reconciliations of assets.

    h. Lack of timely and appropriate documentation of transactions, for example, credits for merchandise returns.

    i. Lack of mandatory vacations for employees performing key control functions.

    j. Inadequate management understanding of information technology, which enables information technology employees to perpetrate a misappropriation.

    k. Inadequate access controls over automated records, including controls over and review of computer systems event logs.

ATTITUDES AND RATIONALIZATIONS

Risk factors reflective of employee attitudes and/or rationalizations that allow them to justify misappropriations of assets are generally not susceptible to observation by the auditor. Nevertheless, the auditor who becomes aware of the existence of such information should consider it in identifying the risks of material misstatement arising from misappropriation of assets. For example, auditors may become aware of the following attitudes or behavior of employees who have access to assets susceptible to misappropriation:

1. Disregard for the need for monitoring or reducing risks related to misappropriation of assets.

2. Disregard for internal control over misappropriation of assets by overriding existing controls or by failing to correct known internal control deficiencies.

3. Behavior indicating displeasure or dissatisfaction with the company or its treatment of the employee.

4. Changes in behavior or lifestyle that may indicate assets have been misappropriated.

Appendix 6C

Illustrative Audit Case: Keystone Computers & Networks, Inc.

Part I: Audit Planning

The Keystone Computers & Networks, Inc. (KCN) case is used throughout the text to illustrate audit procedures and methodology. KCN is a company that sells and installs microcomputers and networking software to business customers. The CPA firm of Adams, Barnes & Co. has audited the financial statements of KCN for the past three years. This part of the case illustrates selective audit planning working papers prepared by the staff of Adams, Barnes & Co. for this year's audit. You should read through the information to obtain an understanding of the nature of the information that is important to planning an audit engagement. The working papers include:

- The balance sheet and income statement for the company for the prior year, 20X4.

- A trial balance for 12/31/X5, with comparative amounts for 12/31/X4.

- The analytical ratios working paper that is partially completed. (The ratios for 20X5 have been left off.)

- The audit plan for the audit of the financial statements for the year ended 12/31/X5.

- A fraud risk assessment.

- The engagement letter for the audit presented on page 175 of this chapter.

KEYSTONE COMPUTERS & NETWORKS, INC.
Balance Sheet
December 31, 20X4

Assets

Current Assets

Cash	$ 27,089
Trade receivables, less allowance for doubtful accounts of $9,600	843,852
Accounts receivable—officers	57,643
Inventory	694,744
Prepaid expenses	40,640
Total current assets	$1,663,968

Equipment and leasehold improvements, at cost

Office equipment and furniture	$ 280,881
Leasehold improvements	17,645
	$ 298,526
Less accumulated depreciation	125,976
Total fixed assets	$ 172,550
	$1,836,518

Liabilities and Stockholders' Equity

Current Liabilities

Line of credit	$ 309,346
Accounts payable	504,641
Current maturities of capital lease obligations	20,183
Accrued expenses	115,332
Total current liabilities	$ 949,502

Capital lease obligations, less current maturities	$ 135,465
Total liabilities	$1,084,967

Stockholders' equity

Common stock, $1 par value; 100,000 shares authorized; 20,000 shares issued and outstanding	$ 20,000
Additional paid-in capital	41,647
Retained earnings	689,904
	$ 751,551
	$1,836,518

KEYSTONE COMPUTERS & NETWORKS, INC.

Statements of Income and Retained Earnings
Year Ended December 31, 20X4

Net sales			$10,227,474
Cost of goods sold			6,867,473
Gross profit			$ 3,360,001
Selling expenses:			
Salaries	$513,040		
Payroll benefits and taxes	97,478		
Advertising and promotion	81,644		
Travel and entertainment	37,628		
Miscellaneous	16,322		
		$ 746,112	
Operating and administration expenses:			
Operating salaries	$802,988		
Administrative salaries	437,889		
Payroll benefits and taxes	223,433		
Rent	124,344		
Utilities	92,455		
Insurance	109,723		
Legal and accounting	73,544		
Bad debt	34,545		
Supplies	93,844		
Depreciation	25,644		
Software development	83,341		
Miscellaneous	37,644		
		$2,139,394	
Total selling, operating, and administrative expenses			$ 2,885,506
Operating income			$ 474,495
Interest expense			68,743
Income before income taxes			$ 405,752
Income taxes:			
Current		$ 71,342	
Deferred		3,245	
			74,587
Net income			$ 331,165
Retained earnings, January 1, 20X4			$ 358,739
Retained earnings, December 31, 20X4			$ 689,904

Keystone Computers & Networks, Inc.
Working Trial Balance
For the Period Ended December 31, 20X5

Prepared by _____ *WL* _____
Reviewed by _____
Page 1

Account #	Account Name	Prior Period Balance 12/31/X4	Unadjusted Trial Balance Dr (Cr)	Ref #	Adjustments Dr (Cr)	Balance Sheet Dr (Cr)
1000.10	Cash—First Natl. Bank	26,489	46,753			
1000.30	Cash in register	600	600			
1050.10	Accounts receivable—trade	853,452	1,023,545			
1050.40	Accounts receivable—officers	57,643	84,670			
1050.90	Allowance for bad debts	(9,600)	(10,400)			
1100.10	Inventories	694,744	903,766			
1300.10	Prepaid expenses	40,640	42,555			
2050.10	Furniture & fixtures	35,432	41,633			
2050.30	Office equipment	245,449	305,450			
2050.80	Leasehold improvements	17,645	17,645			
2050.90	Accumulated depreciation	(125,976)	(154,732)			
2100.00	Software development cost		58,674			
3050.10	Accounts payable—trade	(504,641)	(586,699)			
3100.00	Capital lease obligations—current	(20,183)	(21,050)			
3200.10	Accrued liabilities	(115,332)	(130,040)			
3300.30	Unearned service revenue		(22,100)			
3400.50	Line of credit	(309,346)	(365,867)			
4400.10	Capital lease obligations—noncurrent	(135,465)	(114,415)			
5050.10	Capital stock	(20,000)	(20,000)			
5100.10	Paid-in capital	(41,647)	(41,647)			
5700.10	Retained earnings	(689,904)	(689,904)			
5900.00	Dividends		90,000			
		0	458,437			
		0	(458,437)			
		0	0			

Keystone Computers & Networks, Inc.
Working Trial Balance
For the Period Ended December 31, 20X5

Account #	Account Name	Prior Period Balance 12/31/X4	Unadjusted Trial Balance Dr (Cr)	Ref #	Adjustments Dr (Cr)	Balance Sheet Dr (Cr)
6000.10	Sales of computers	(9,044,432)	(10,156,898)			
6010.10	Service revenue	(187,423)	(210,845)			
6020.10	Consulting revenue	(995,619)	(1,234,763)			
7020.10	Cost of sales	6,867,473	7,397,368			
7070.10	Salaries—sales	513,040	583,438			
7070.50	Payroll benefits—sales	97,478	125,354			
7075.10	Advertising & promotion	81,644	92,645			
7080.10	Travel & entertainment	37,628	44,655			
7080.30	Miscellaneous exp.—sales	16,322	21,455			
7090.10	Salaries—operations	802,988	983,455			
7090.30	Salaries—administrative	437,889	596,060			
7090.50	Payroll benefits—admin.	223,433	319,876			
7100.10	Rent	124,344	166,988			
7140.10	Utilities	92,455	110,876			
7200.10	Insurance	109,723	93,454			
7260.30	Legal & accounting	73,544	91,787			
7320.10	Bad debt expense	34,545	56,477			
7410.10	Supplies	93,844	119,967			
7600.10	Depreciation	25,644	28,756			
7650.10	Software development	83,341	63,222			
7700.10	Miscellaneous exp.—administrative	37,644	45,333			
7800.10	Interest expense	68,743	77,434			
7900.10	Current income taxes	71,342	122,467			
7900.70	Deferred income taxes	3,245	3,002			
9000.00	P & L Summary	331,165	(458,437)			
		0	458,437			
		0	0			

Keystone Computers & Networks, Inc.
Analytical Review Ratios
For the Period Ended December 31, 20X5

Prepared by _____ _WL_
Reviewed by _____

Ratio	Ending 12/31/X5	Ending 12/31/X4	Industry
Current ratio		1.752	1.300
Days' sales in accounts receivable, computed with average accounts receivable		33.224	37.000
Allowance for doubtful accounts/accounts receivable		.011	—
Bad debt expense/net sales		.003	—
Inventory turnover computed with average inventory		10.397	10.000
Days' inventory on hand computed with average inventory		35.222	36.000
Total liabilities/net worth		1.444	2.900
Return on total assets		.180	.090
Return on net worth		.441	.290
Return on net sales		.032	.023
Gross profit/net sales		.329	.240
Selling, operating, and administrative expense/net sales		.282	.239
Times interest earned		6.902	5.500

Keystone Computers & Networks, Inc.
Audit Plan
December 31, 20X5

		Date
Prepared by:	Warren Love (Senior)	August 14, 20X5
Reviewed by:	Karen West (Manager)	August 28, 20X5
Reviewed by:	Charles Adams (Partner)	September 5, 20X5

OBJECTIVES OF THE ENGAGEMENT

Audit of the financial statements of Keystone Computers & Networks, Inc. (KCN) for the year ended December 31, 20X5. Also, the company's debt agreement with Western Financial Services requires the company to furnish the lender a report by our firm on KCN's compliance with various restrictive debt covenants.

BUSINESS AND INDUSTRY CONDITIONS

KCN sells and installs microcomputers and networking hardware and software to business customers. The company provides repair, maintenance, training, and software customization services. KCN has also begun developing its own computer networking software to be sold as a product to its customers. The company's primary competitive strategy is to maintain a high level of technical expertise and a broad range of services.

The market for microcomputers and related products is extremely competitive. KCN competes with large retailers of microcomputers, such as Dell, CompUSA, and Microage. The company also competes with other value-added resellers who provide microcomputers and software products directly to customers. To effectively compete, the company must be able to obtain inventories of state-of-the-art equipment on a timely basis. Because the company does not have the buying power of some of its other competitors, it generally must charge a higher price for its products. Its customers are willing to pay the higher price because of the high level of expertise and service that the company provides.

The market for microcomputer products is also very sensitive to economic conditions.

PLANNING MEETINGS

On July 20, Karen West and I met with Loren Steele, controller, and Sam Best, president, of KCN to discuss the planning of the audit for the current year. On August 2, a planning meeting was held in our office with all members of the engagement team assigned to the audit.

AUDIT APPROACH

The company has had no significant changes in its internal control from the prior year. Therefore, consistent with the approach used in last year's audit, we plan to perform tests of controls to assess control risk at less than the maximum for most financial statement assertions.

RISKS

Several factors affect the risk of this engagement, including:

- As described above, KCN is in a very competitive business that is sensitive to economic conditions.
- KCN is a closely held company owned by five stockholders, Terry Keystone, Mark Keystone, John Keystone, Keith Young, and Rita Young. Terry and Mark Keystone are active members of the company's board of directors. None of the other owners take an active part in management of the business.
- Audited financial statements are required by Western Financial Services as a part of the company's line of credit agreement.
- The officers receive significant bonuses based on quarterly results. (see G-10 on page 220 for implications of this risk.)

  These factors indicate that the engagement to audit KCN has high risk.

SIGNIFICANT ACCOUNTING AND AUDITING MATTERS

The company began offering for sale extended warranties on computers during the current year. We need to review the method of revenue recognition to determine whether it complies with the requirements of FASB Technical Bulletin 90-1.

In the prior year, KCN began developing networking software products for sale. This year the company has started capitalizing certain costs of development. We need to review the method of accounting for the cost of software development to determine whether it complies with the requirements of FASB Statement No. 86.

PLANNING MATERIALITY

Because the firm has experienced steady growth in sales and earnings over the last three years, we believe that operating results are the most appropriate basis for estimating planning materiality as described below:

Comparison of Bases		Computation of Planning Materiality			
Financial Statement Base	Annualized for 12/31/X5	Base	Amount	Percentage	Materiality Estimate
Sales	$11,000,000	Sales	$11,000,000	1%	$110,000
Total assets	2,000,000	Total assets	2,000,000	1	20,000
Pretax net income	525,000	Pretax net income	525,000	10	52,500

The range for planning materiality is from $20,000 to $110,000. Based on the company's steady growth in sales and earnings and the fact that the company is not a public company, we have selected $70,000 as a reasonable materiality amount for planning purposes.

SCHEDULING AND STAFFING PLAN

Based on discussions with Ms. Steele, the following are tentative dates of importance for the audit:

Begin interim audit work	November 10, 20X5
Complete interim audit work	by November 15, 20X5
Issue management letter on interim work	by November 30, 20X5
Observe physical inventory	December 31, 20X5
Begin year-end audit work	February 12, 20X6
Complete fieldwork	by February 20, 20X6
Closing conference	February 25, 20X6
Issue audit report	by March 5, 20X6
Issue letter required by financing agreement	by March 5, 20X6
Issue updated management letter	by March 10, 20X6

Staffing time requirements for the engagement are described below:

	Assistant	Senior	Manager	Partner	Total
Interim	40	40	10	8	98
Final	40	30	15	12	97
	80	70	25	20	195

Fraud Risk Assessment		G-10
		CA
		8/14/X5

Client: *Keystone Computers & Networks, Inc.*

Financial Statement Date: *12/31/X5*

Procedure	Performed by	Comments
1. Consider the results of the discussion among engagement personnel about the risk of material misstatement due to fraud.	*CA*	*See G-21 for the agenda.*
2. Consider results of inquiries of management about the risks of fraud and how they are addressed.	*CA*	
3. Consider the results of planning analytical procedures.	*CA*	
4. Consider the existence of fraud risk factors listed on G-30 through G-35.	*CA*	
5. Consider any other information that might be relevant to the risk of material misstatement due to fraud.	*CA*	

Risks of Material Misstatement Due to Fraud

Management may be motivated to misstate financial results due to performance bonuses.
Specifically, management may attempt to:

1. Provide inappropriate incentives to sign sales contracts near quarter-and year-end.
2. Overstate revenue at quarter-and year-end.
3. Overstate inventories, quantities, or pricing.

Overall Responses

Risks were considered in staffing the engagement and determining the appropriate level of supervision.

Alterations of the Nature, Timing, and Extent of Procedures

Risks were considered in designing audit procedures for sales and accounts receivable and inventories. (See R-6 and R-9.)

Procedures were performed to address the risk of management override of internal controls. (See G-23–G-24.)

Appendix 6C
Problems

6C–1. The audit plan for the audit of Keystone Computers & Networks, Inc., appears on pages 218 through 221. Review each major section of the audit plan and briefly describe the purpose and content of the section. Organize your solution in the following manner:

Section	Purpose	Content
Objectives of the Engagement	To describe the services that are to be rendered to the client.	The objectives are (1) audit of KCN's financial statements for the year ended 12/31/X5, and (2) issuance of a letter on compliance with covenants of the client's letter of credit agreement.

6C–2. In the audit plan for the audit of Keystone Computers & Networks, Inc., on page 219 there is a section on significant accounting and auditing matters. The first of the matters described in this section involves the appropriate accounting for the sale of extended warranty contracts. Research this accounting issue and write a brief memorandum for the working papers describing the issue and summarizing the appropriate method of accounting for the revenue received from these contracts.

6C–3. In the audit plan for the audit of Keystone Computers & Networks, Inc., on page 219 there is a section on significant accounting and auditing matters. The second matter described involves capitalizing the costs of developing a software program for sale.

Required:
    a. Research this issue and write a brief memorandum for the working papers describing the issue and summarizing the appropriate method of accounting for the development costs.
    b. Based on your research, describe the major audit issue that you believe will be involved in auditing the software development costs.

6C–4. A partially completed analytical ratios working paper for Keystone Computers & Networks, Inc., is presented on page 218.

Required:

    a. Complete the working paper by computing the financial ratios for 20X5.
    b. After completing part (*a*), review the ratios and identify financial statement accounts that should be investigated because the related ratios are not comparable to prior-year ratios and industry averages.
    c. For each account identified in part (*b*), list potential reasons for the unexpected account balances and related ratios.

Chapter 7

Internal Control

Chapter learning objectives

After studying this chapter, you should be able to:

LO1. Define what is meant by internal control.

LO2. Distinguish among the major components of a client's internal control: the control environment, risk assessment, the accounting information system, control activities, and monitoring of controls.

LO3. Describe the auditors' consideration of internal control.

LO4. Discuss the techniques used by auditors to obtain an understanding of internal control.

LO5. Explain how the auditors assess control risk.

LO6. Describe the major types of tests of controls.

LO7. Describe the auditors' responsibility for communicating internal control-related matters.

LO8. Describe the nature of the audits performed under Section 404(b) of the Sarbanes-Oxley Act of 2002.

Our discussion of internal control in this chapter has four major objectives: first, to explain the meaning and significance of internal control; second, to discuss the major components of a client's internal control; third, to show how auditors go about considering internal control to meet the requirements of the second standard of fieldwork; and fourth, to provide an overview of audits of internal control performed under Section 404(b) of the Sarbanes-Oxley Act. No attempt is made in this chapter to present in detail the controls applicable to particular account balances and classes of transactions. Detailed information along those lines will be found in succeeding chapters as each phase of the audit is presented.

As discussed in Chapter 1, internal control has attained greatest significance in large-scale business organizations. Accordingly, the major part of the discussion in this chapter is presented in terms of the large corporation. A separate section is presented at the end of the chapter, however, dealing with the problem of achieving internal control in a small business.

The Meaning of Internal Control

Learning Objective 1

Differences of opinion have long existed about the meaning and objectives of internal control. Many people interpreted the term **internal control** as the steps taken by a business to prevent fraud—both misappropriation of assets and fraudulent financial reporting. Others, while acknowledging the importance of internal control for fraud prevention, believed that internal control has an equal role in assuring control over manufacturing and other processes. Such differences in interpretation also existed in the professional publications issued by the American Institute of Certified Public Accountants; the Institute of Internal Auditors, Inc.; and the Research Foundation of the Financial Executives Institute. It was not until the early 1990s that the various professional organizations worked together to develop a consensus on the nature and scope of internal control.

As a result of a number of instances of fraudulent financial reporting in the 1970s and early 1980s, the major accounting organizations[1] sponsored the National Commission on Fraudulent Financial Reporting (the Treadway Commission) to study the causal factors that are associated with fraudulent reporting and to make recommendations to reduce the incidence of fraudulent reporting. The commission made a number of recommendations that directly addressed internal control. For example, it emphasized the importance of a competent and involved audit committee and an active and objective internal audit function in preventing fraudulent practices. It also called on the sponsoring organizations to work together to integrate the various internal control concepts and definitions so as to develop common criteria to evaluate internal control. Accordingly, the Committee of Sponsoring Organizations (COSO) commissioned a study to:

- Establish a common definition of internal control to serve the needs of different parties.
- Provide a standard against which business and other entities can assess their control systems and determine how to improve them.

The study, titled *Internal Control—Integrated Framework,* defines internal control as:

> A *process,* effected by the entity's board of directors, management, and other personnel, designed to provide *reasonable assurance* regarding the achievement of *objectives* in the following categories:
>
> - Reliability of financial reporting.
> - Effectiveness and efficiency of operations.
> - Compliance with applicable laws and regulations. [emphasis added]

---

[1] The sponsoring organizations included the American Institute of Certified Public Accountants; the American Accounting Association; the Financial Executives Institute; the Institute of Internal Auditors, Inc.; and the Institute of Management Accountants.

COSO's definition of internal control emphasizes that internal control is a *process,* or a means to an end, and not an end in and of itself. The process is effected by individuals, not merely policy manuals, documents, and forms. By including the concept of *reasonable assurance,* the definition recognizes that internal control cannot realistically provide absolute assurance that an organization's objectives will be achieved. Reasonable assurance recognizes that the cost of an organization's internal control should not exceed the benefits expected to be obtained.

Finally, the definition of internal control is comprehensive in that it addresses the achievement of *objectives* in the areas of financial reporting, operations, and compliance with laws and regulations. It encompasses the methods by which top management delegates authority and assigns responsibility for such functions as selling, purchasing, accounting, and production. Internal control also includes the program for preparing, verifying, and distributing to various levels of management those current reports and analyses that enable executives to maintain control over the variety of activities and functions that are performed in a large organization. The use of budgetary techniques, production standards, inspection laboratories, time and motion studies, and employee training programs involves engineers and many others far removed from accounting and financial activities; yet all of these programs and activities are a part of internal control.

In the three areas of internal control—financial reporting, operations, and compliance—COSO states that a series of control objectives and subobjectives exists. To illustrate this concept, consider internal control over financial reporting. At the top level, the overall objective is to prepare and issue reliable financial information. At the very detailed level, as applied to accounts receivable, COSO illustrates the following control objectives (subobjectives):

1. All goods shipped are accurately billed in the proper period.
2. Invoices are accurately recorded for all authorized shipments and only for such shipments.
3. Authorized and only authorized sales returns and allowances are accurately recorded.
4. The continued completeness and accuracy of accounts receivable is ensured.
5. Accounts receivable records are safeguarded.

These control objectives are similar to the management assertions that were discussed in the preceding two chapters (See, for example, Figure 5.1). This is obviously the case because the overall objective of internal control over financial reporting is to prepare financial statements in accordance with generally accepted accounting principles. Specifically, COSO says that supporting the control objectives is a series of assertions that underlie the financial statements. However, there is one major difference between control objectives and assertions; the control objectives are broader in that they relate not only to financial reporting, but also to operations and compliance.

Which controls are most relevant to the audit of financial statements? Generally, the controls that are relevant to an audit are those that pertain to the reliability of financial reporting—that is, those that affect the preparation of financial information for external reporting purposes. However, other controls may be relevant if they affect the reliability of data that the auditors use to perform auditing procedures. For example, controls applicable to nonfinancial data (e.g., production statistics) that the auditors use in performing analytical procedures may be relevant to an audit.

Controls designed to safeguard the organization's assets are relevant to an audit if they affect reliability of financial reporting. For example, controls that limit access to the company's inventories may be relevant to a financial statement audit, while controls to prevent the excess use of materials in production generally are not. As long as the financial statements reflect the cost of the materials used, the auditors are not directly concerned with the inefficiencies of production.

The Foreign Corrupt Practices Act of 1977

The importance of establishing and maintaining effective internal control is also illustrated by the passage of the **Foreign Corrupt Practices Act.** In the mid-1970s, hundreds of American corporations acknowledged having made payments (bribes and kickbacks) to officials in foreign countries to obtain business. In most cases the payments were legal under the laws of the countries in which they were made, but they were not in accordance with American standards of business ethics. In some instances these questionable payments were made without the authorization or knowledge of top executives of the corporations involved. By passing the Foreign Corrupt Practices Act of 1977, Congress ordered an end to this practice. Payments to foreign officials for the purpose of securing business are specifically prohibited for *all American businesses* by the antibribery provisions of the act. To prevent top management from asserting that they were not aware of the payments, internal control provisions also were included in the act. These provisions require *all corporations under the jurisdiction of the SEC* (regardless of whether the corporation has international operations) to maintain a system of internal control that will provide reasonable assurance that:

1. Transactions are executed with the knowledge and authorization of management.
2. Transactions are recorded as necessary to permit the preparation of reliable financial statements and maintain accountability for assets.
3. Access to assets is limited to authorized individuals.
4. Accounting records of assets are compared to existing assets at reasonable intervals and appropriate action is taken with respect to any differences.

Violations of the Foreign Corrupt Practices Act can result in fines up to $1 million and imprisonment of the members of management that are responsible. Thus, an effective system of internal control, long viewed as essential to the operation of a large organization, is required by federal law.

Means of Achieving Internal Control

Learning Objective 2

Internal control varies significantly from one organization to the next, depending on such factors as organization size, nature of operations, and objectives. Yet certain features are essential to satisfactory internal control in almost any organization. In all systems, a variety of controls must be designed to accomplish the control objectives. Controls over financial reporting controls are often classified as preventive, detective, or corrective.

Preventive controls are aimed at avoiding the occurrence of misstatements in the financial statements. Examples of preventive controls include segregation of duties and requiring approval of period-ending journal entries. **Detective controls** discover misstatements after they have occurred. A policy requiring the preparation of monthly bank reconciliations is an example of a control that could detect misstatements of cash receipts or disbursements. When detective controls discover a misstatement, a **corrective control** is ordinarily needed to remedy the situation. Maintaining backup copies of key transactions and master files to allow the correction of data entry errors is a common example of a corrective control. It is important to realize that preventive controls often operate at the individual transaction level, while detective controls may operate at the transaction level or at a higher level.

The various controls designed to achieve a control objective often overlap. That is, the controls are **complementary** in that they function together to achieve the same control objective. To illustrate, consider the control that requires all cash disbursements to be authorized and the complementary control of requiring reconciliations of bank statements. These controls work together to help ensure that unauthorized transactions are prevented or detected. Controls are referred to as **redundant** if they address the same financial statement assertion or control objective. Finally, a **compensating control** reduces the risk that an existing or potential control weakness will result in a misstatement. As an example, a small business may not have enough personnel to allow for the adequate segregation of duties, but the owner-manager of the business may carefully review accounting records and reports to compensate for the weakness.

Internal control of an organization may be viewed as including five components: (1) the control environment, (2) the risk assessment process, (3) the information system relevant to financial reporting and communication (hereafter, the accounting information system), (4) control activities, and (5) the monitoring of controls.

The Control Environment

The control environment sets the tone of an organization by influencing the control consciousness of people. It may be viewed as the foundation for the other components of internal control. Control environment factors include integrity and ethical values, commitment to competence, board of directors or audit committee, management's philosophy and operating style, organizational structure, assignment of authority and responsibility, and human resource policies and practices.

Integrity and Ethical Values

The effectiveness of internal control depends directly upon the communication and enforcement of integrity and ethical values of the personnel who are responsible for creating, administrating, and monitoring controls. Management should establish behavioral and ethical standards that discourage employees from engaging in acts that would be considered dishonest, unethical, or illegal. To be effective, these standards must be effectively communicated by appropriate means, including by official policies, codes of conduct, and example.

Another way to reduce the incidence of improper behavior is to remove or reduce the incentives and temptations to engage in such behavior. For example, fraudulent financial reporting has often resulted from situations in which employees were placed under undue pressure to meet unrealistic performance goals. Inappropriate actions have been found to be more likely when management's compensation is heavily tied to the company's reported income. Increased temptation to commit improper acts may result from inadequate or ineffective controls, such as a lack of segregation of duties, or a board of directors that does not provide objective oversight of top management. Appendix A to this chapter provides examples of programs and controls that management can implement to prevent, deter, and detect fraud, summarized from an appendix to *SAS No. 99* (AU 316) "Consideration of Fraud in a Financial Statement Audit."

Commitment to Competence

Employees should possess the skills and knowledge essential to the performance of their job. If employees are lacking in skills or knowledge, they may be ineffective in performing their assigned duties. This is especially critical when the employees are involved in performing controls. Ideally, management should be committed to hiring employees with appropriate levels of education and experience and providing them with adequate supervision and training.

Board of Directors or Audit Committee

The control environment of an organization is significantly influenced by the effectiveness of its board of directors or its audit committee. The board of directors and audit committee are responsible for overseeing the actions of management. Factors that bear on the effectiveness of the board or audit committee include the extent of its independence from management, the experience and stature of its members, the extent to which it raises and pursues difficult questions with management, and its interaction with the internal and external auditors. In audits of SEC registrants, the Sarbanes-Oxley Act of 2002 requires that the audit committee be directly responsible for the appointment, compensation, and oversight of the work of the CPA firm (including resolution of any disagreements between management and the CPA firm).

As described in Chapter 6, the audit committee of the board of directors should be composed of independent directors who are not officers or employees of the organization and do not have other relationships that impair independence. This enables the audit committee to be effective at overseeing the quality of the organization's financial reports, and at acting as a deterrent to management override of controls and to management fraud.

Management Philosophy and Operating Style

Managements differ in both their philosophies toward financial reporting and their attitudes toward taking business risks. Some managements are extremely aggressive in financial reporting and place great emphasis on meeting or exceeding earnings projections. They may be willing to undertake activities of high risk with the prospect of high return. Other management teams are extremely conservative and risk averse. These differing philosophies and operating styles may have an impact on the overall reliability of the financial statements.

Illustrative Case
Importance of Organizational Structure

During an audit of a nonpublic company, the auditors' study of organizational lines of authority and their use of an internal control questionnaire disclosed that the receiving department personnel were under the direction of the purchasing agent. Accounts payable department employees had also been instructed to accept informal memoranda from the purchasing agent as evidence of receipt of merchandise and propriety of invoices.

Because of this deficiency in internal control, the auditors made a very thorough examination of purchase invoices and came across a number of large December invoices from one supplier bearing the notation: "Subject to adjustment at time of delivery of merchandise." Investigation of these transactions disclosed that the merchandise had not yet been delivered, but the invoices had been paid. The purchasing agent explained that he had requested the advance billing in an effort to reduce taxable income for the year under audit, during which profits had been higher than usual. Further investigation revealed that the purchasing agent held a substantial personal interest in the supplier making the advance billings, and that top management of the client company was not aware of this conflict of interest.

Management's philosophy and operating style also are reflected in the way the organization is managed. Controls in an informal organization are often implemented by face-to-face contact between employees and management. A more formal organization will establish written policies, performance reports, and exception reports to control its various activities.

Organizational Structure

Another control environment factor is the entity's **organizational structure.** A well-designed organizational structure provides a basis for planning, directing, and controlling operations. It divides authority, responsibilities, and duties among members of an organization by dealing with such issues as centralized versus decentralized decision making and appropriate segregation of duties among the various departments. When management decision making is centralized and dominated by one individual, that individual's abilities and moral character are extremely important to the auditors. When a decentralized style is used, procedures to monitor the decision making of the many managers involved become equally important.

The organizational structure of an entity should separate responsibilities for (1) *authorization* of transactions, (2) *recordkeeping* for transactions, and (3) *custody* of assets. In addition, to the extent possible, execution of the transaction should be segregated from these other responsibilities. The effectiveness of such structure is usually obtained by having designated department heads who are evaluated on the basis of the performance of their respective departments. The top executives of the major departments should be of equal rank and should report directly to the president or to an executive vice president. The partial organization chart in Figure 7.1 illustrates such an arrangement. If, for example, the controller were a line subordinate to the vice president of production, the organizational independence of the accounting department would be greatly impaired.

Responsibilities of Finance and Accounting Departments

Finance and accounting are the two departments most directly involved in the financial affairs of a business enterprise. The division of responsibilities between these departments illustrates the separation of the accounting function from operations and also from the custody of assets. Under the direction of the *treasurer,* the finance department is responsible for financial operations and custody of liquid assets. Activities of this department include planning future cash requirements, establishing customer credit policies, and arranging to meet the short- and long-term financing needs of the business. In addition, the finance department has custody of bank accounts and other liquid assets, invests idle cash, handles cash receipts, and makes cash disbursements. In short, it is the finance department that conducts financial activities.

The accounting department, under the authority of the *controller,* is responsible for all accounting functions and the design and implementation of internal control. With respect to financial activity, the accounting department records financial transactions but does not handle financial assets. Accounting records establish accountability over assets and provide the

FIGURE 7.1
Partial Organization Chart

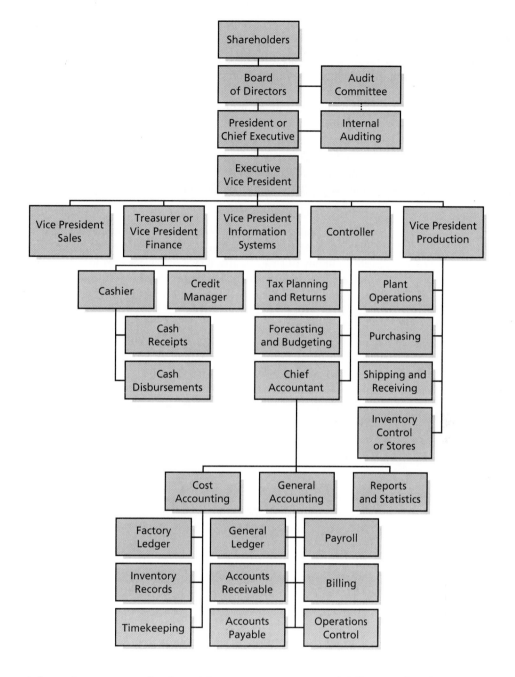

information necessary for financial reports, tax returns, and daily operating decisions. With respect to internal control, the accounting department maintains the independent records with which quantities of assets and operating results are compared. Often, this reconciliation function is performed by the *operations control group* or some other subdepartment within accounting.

Many of the subdepartments often found within accounting are illustrated in Figure 7.1. It is important for many of these subdepartments to be relatively independent of one another. For example, if the operations control group reconciles assets on hand to the accounting records, it is essential that the operations control personnel not maintain those records.

Assignment of Authority and Responsibility

Personnel within an organization need to have a clear understanding of their responsibilities and the rules and regulations that govern their actions. Therefore, to enhance the control environment, management develops employee job descriptions and clearly defines authority and responsibility within the organization. Policies also may be established describing appropriate business practices, knowledge and experience of key personnel, and the use of resources.

Human Resource Policies and Procedures

Ultimately, the effectiveness of internal control is affected by the characteristics of the organization's personnel. Thus, management's policies and practices for hiring, providing orientation for, training, evaluating, counseling, promoting, and compensating employees have a significant effect on the effectiveness of the control environment. As an example, standards for hiring the most qualified individuals with an emphasis on education, experience, and evidence of integrity and ethical behavior illustrate the organization's commitment to hiring competent and trustworthy people. Effective human resource policies often can mitigate other weaknesses in the control environment.

Fidelity Bonds

Effective human resource management is not a guarantee against losses from dishonest employees. It is often the most trusted employees who engineer large embezzlements. That they are so highly trusted explains why they have access to cash, securities, and company records and are in a position that makes embezzlement possible.

Most organizations purchase fidelity bonds to cover employees handling cash or other negotiable assets. **Fidelity bonds** are a form of insurance in which a bonding company agrees to reimburse an employer, within limits, for losses attributable to theft or embezzlement by bonded employees. Companies with only a few employees at risk may obtain individual fidelity bonds; larger concerns may prefer to obtain a blanket fidelity bond covering a number of employees. Before issuing fidelity bonds, underwriters investigate thoroughly the past records of the employees to be bonded. This service offers added protection by preventing the employment of persons with dubious records in positions of trust. Bonding companies are much more likely to prosecute fraud cases vigorously than are employers; general awareness of this fact is another deterrent against dishonesty on the part of bonded employees.

Risk Assessment

Risk assessment is used to describe management's process for identifying and responding to business risks faced by the organization and the results of that process. As discussed in Chapter 6, business risks include all threats to achieving management's objectives. Management's process of risk assessment is similar to the auditor's assessment of audit risk, as described in Chapters 5 and 6. However, the scope is more comprehensive in that it involves considering threats to the organization's objectives in the areas of operations, financial reporting, and compliance with laws and regulations. The process of risk assessment includes identifying the relevant risks, estimating the significance of those risks, and then deciding on actions to manage them.

The auditors are primarily concerned with the risks associated with the objective of reliable financial reporting—the threats to preparing financial statements in accordance with generally accepted accounting principles. The following factors might be indicative of increased financial reporting risk for a client:

- Changes in the organization's regulatory or operating environment.
- Changes in personnel.
- New or revamped information systems.
- Rapid growth of the organization.
- Changes in technology affecting production processes or information systems.
- New business models, products, or activities.
- Corporate restructurings.
- Expansion or acquisition of foreign operations.
- Adoption of new accounting principles or changing accounting principles.

The Accounting Information System[2]

Information is needed at all levels of an organization to assist management in meeting the organization's objectives. Of major concern to the auditors is the accounting information system, and the way in which responsibilities for internal control over financial reporting are communicated throughout the organization.

An organization's accounting information system consists of the methods and records established to record, process, summarize, and report an entity's transactions and to maintain accountability for the related assets, liabilities, and equity. Accordingly, an accounting information system should:

1. Identify and record all valid transactions.
2. Describe on a timely basis the transactions in sufficient detail to permit proper classification of transactions for financial reporting.
3. Measure the value of transactions in a manner that permits recording their proper monetary value in the financial statements.
4. Determine the time period in which transactions occurred to permit recording of transactions in the proper accounting period.
5. Present properly the transactions and related disclosures in the financial statements.

In addition to the typical system of journals, ledgers, and other recordkeeping devices, an *accounting information system* should include a chart of accounts and a manual of accounting policies and procedures as aids for communicating policies. A *chart of accounts* is a classified listing of all accounts in use, accompanied by a detailed description of the purpose and content of each. A *manual of accounting policies and procedures* states clearly in writing the methods of treating transactions. In combination, the chart of accounts and manual of accounting policies and procedures should provide clear guidance that will allow proper and uniform handling of transactions.

Proper communication involves providing employees with an understanding of their individual roles and responsibilities relating to financial reporting. Open communication channels are essential to proper functioning of an information system. Personnel that process information should understand how their activities relate to the work of others and the importance of reporting exceptions and other unusual items to an appropriate level of management.

Control Activities

Control activities are policies and procedures that help ensure that management's directives are carried out. These policies and procedures promote actions that address the risks that face the organization. While there are many different types of control activities performed in an organization, only the following types are generally relevant to an audit of the organization's financial statements:

- Performance reviews.
- Information processing controls.
- Physical controls.
- Segregation of duties.

Performance Reviews

These controls include reviews of actual performance as compared to budgets, forecasts, and prior period performance; relating different sets of data to one another; and performing overall reviews of performance. Performance reviews provide management with an overall indication of whether personnel at various levels are effectively pursuing the objectives of the organization.

---

[2] *Internal Control—Integrated Framework* refers to this component as the information system and communication. However, the accounting information system is of primary importance to an audit of financial statements.

By investigating the reasons for unexpected performance, management may make timely changes in strategies and plans or take other appropriate corrective action.

Information Processing Controls

A variety of control activities are performed to check the accuracy, completeness, and authorization of transactions. The two broad categories of information processing controls include *general control activities,* which apply to all information processing procedures, and *application control activities,* which apply only to one particular activity. Examples of general control activities would include those that help ensure the reliability of all information processing activities.

To understand the nature of application control activities, consider the controls over payroll that help to ensure that (1) only authorized payroll transactions are processed, and (2) authorized payroll transactions are processed completely and accurately. These application control activities would only affect the reliability of payroll processing. Chapter 8 provides a complete description of general and application control activities in a computer environment.

An important aspect of information processing controls is the proper authorization of all types of transactions. Authorization of transactions may be either general or specific. *General authorization* occurs when management establishes criteria for acceptance of a certain type of transaction. For example, top management may establish general price lists and credit policies for new customers. Transactions with customers that meet these criteria can then be approved by the credit department. *Specific authorization* occurs when transactions are authorized on an individual basis. For example, top management may consider individually and authorize specifically any sales transaction in excess of a specified amount, say $100,000.

Another control over information processing is a system of well-designed forms and documents. To illustrate, consider the processing of a credit sales transaction. The accounting department receives copies of internal documents prepared by the sales, credit, and shipping departments to properly record the transaction. The documents inform the accounting department that the sale was authorized and approved, and goods were shipped to the customer.

A control of wide applicability is the use of serial numbers on documents. Serial numbers provide control over the number of documents issued. Checks, tickets, sales invoices, purchase orders, stock certificates, and many other business papers can be controlled in this manner. For some documents, such as checks, it may be desirable to account for the sequence used by a monthly or weekly inspection of the documents issued. For other documents, as in the case of serially numbered admission tickets, control may be achieved by noting the last serial number issued each day, and thereby computing the total value of tickets issued during the day. In computerized accounting systems, the computer may assign numbers to the transactions and documents.

Physical Controls

These controls include those that provide physical security over both records and other assets. Activities that safeguard records may include maintaining control at all times over unissued prenumbered documents, as well as other journals and ledgers, and restricting access to computer programs and data files.

Only authorized individuals should be allowed access to the company's valuable assets. Direct physical access to assets may be controlled through the use of safes, locks, fences, and guards. Improper indirect access to assets, generally accomplished by falsifying financial records, must also be prevented. This may be accomplished by safeguarding the financial records, as described above.

Periodic comparisons should be made between accounting records and the physical assets on hand. Investigation as to the cause of any discrepancies will uncover weakness either in procedures for safeguarding assets or in maintaining the related accounting records. Without these comparisons waste, loss, or theft of the related assets may go undetected.

Figure 7.2 illustrates the use of an independently maintained record to establish accountability for assets. It is *not* essential that all three parties in the diagram (A, B, and C) be employees of the company; one or more may be an outside party or an electronic device. For example, if A is a bank with custody of cash on deposit, B would be the company employees maintaining records of cash receipts and disbursements, and C might be a computer program that

Illustrative Case
Importance of Custody Controls

A manufacturer of golf clubs operated a large storeroom containing thousands of sets of golf clubs ready for shipment. Detailed perpetual inventory records were maintained by the employee in charge of the storeroom. A shortage of several sets of clubs developed as a result of theft by another employee who had acquired an unauthorized key to the storeroom. The employee responsible for the storeroom discovered the discrepancy between the clubs in stock and the quantities of clubs as shown by the records. Fearing criticism of his recordkeeping, he changed the inventory records to agree with the quantities on hand. The thefts continued, and large losses were sustained before the shortages were discovered. If the inventory records had been maintained by someone not responsible for physical custody of the merchandise, there would have been no incentive to conceal a shortage by falsifying the records.

FIGURE 7.2
Establishing Accountability for Assets

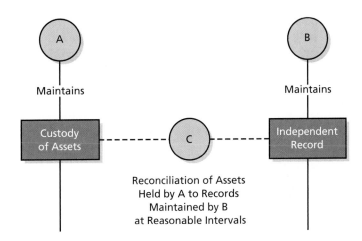

performs periodic bank reconciliations. Or, if A is a salesclerk with custody of cash receipts from sales, B could be a cash register with a locked-in tape, and C could be the departmental supervisor. Regardless of the nature of the parties involved, the principle remains the same: Accounting records should be maintained independently of custody of the related assets and should be compared at reasonable intervals to asset quantities on hand.

Segregation of Duties

A fundamental concept of internal control is that no one department or person should handle all aspects of a transaction from beginning to end. We have already discussed the segregation of responsibilities among departments. In a similar manner, no one individual should perform more than one of the functions of *authorizing* transactions, *recording* transactions, and *maintaining custody* over assets. Also, to the extent possible, individuals executing the specific transaction should be segregated from these functions. The goal is to not allow an individual to have **incompatible duties** that would allow him or her to both perpetrate and conceal errors or fraud in the normal course of his or her duties.

A credit sales transaction may be used to illustrate appropriate authorization and segregation procedures. Top management may have generally authorized the sale of merchandise at specified credit terms to customers who meet certain requirements. The credit department may approve the sales transactions by ascertaining that the extension of credit and terms of sale are in compliance with company policies. Once the sale is approved, the shipping department executes the transaction by obtaining custody of the merchandise from the inventory stores department and shipping it to the customer. The accounting department uses copies of the documentation created by the sales, credit, and shipping departments as a basis for recording the transaction and billing the customer. With this segregation of duties, no one department or individual can initiate and execute an unauthorized transaction.

Monitoring of Controls

Monitoring of controls, the last component of internal control, is a process to assess the quality of internal control performance over time. It is important to monitor internal control to determine whether it is operating as intended and whether any modifications are necessary. Monitoring can be achieved by performing ongoing activities or by separate evaluations. *Ongoing monitoring activities* include regularly performed supervisory and management activities, such as continuous monitoring of customer complaints, or reviewing the reasonableness of management reports. *Separate evaluations* are monitoring activities that are performed on a nonroutine basis, such as periodic audits by the internal auditors.

The Internal Audit Function

An important aspect of the organization's monitoring system is the internal audit function. Internal auditors investigate and appraise internal control and the efficiency with which the various units of the organization are performing their assigned functions, and they report their findings and recommendations to top management. As representatives of top management, the internal auditors are interested in determining whether each branch or department has a clear understanding of its assignment; is adequately staffed; maintains good records; properly safeguards cash, inventories, and other assets; and cooperates harmoniously with other departments. In addition, many internal audit departments perform internal consulting activities within their organizations. The manner in which the CPAs use the work of internal auditors is discussed later in this chapter; the internal auditing profession is discussed in detail in Chapter 21.

Limitations of Internal Control

Internal control can do much to protect against both errors and fraud and to ensure the reliability of accounting data. Still, it is important to recognize the existence of inherent limitations of internal control. Mistakes may be made in the performance of controls as a result of misunderstanding of instructions, mistakes of judgment, carelessness, distraction, or fatigue. Errors may also occur in designing, maintaining, or monitoring automated controls. Control activities—whether manual or automated—dependent upon separation of duties may be circumvented by collusion among two or more people or inappropriate management override of internal control. Management, for example, may enter into side agreements with customers that alter the terms and conditions of the company's standard contract in ways that would preclude revenue recognition, or management may improperly modify the accounting records.

The extent of the controls adopted by a business also is limited by cost considerations. It is not feasible from a cost standpoint to establish controls that provide absolute protection from fraud and waste; reasonable assurance in this regard is generally the best that can be achieved.

Enterprise Risk Management

In 2004, the Committee of Sponsoring Organizations (COSO) issued *Enterprise Risk Management—Integrated Framework.* This framework goes beyond internal control to focus on how organizations can maximize value for their stakeholders by effectively managing risks and opportunities. The enterprise risk management framework encompasses:

- Aligning the organization's risk appetite and its strategy.
- Enhancing risk response decisions by focusing on the best techniques for managing risk—risk avoidance, reduction, sharing, and acceptance.

Illustrative Case
Management Override

Management override is often as simple as posting improper adjusting journal entries to modify financial results. In a complaint filed by the Securities and Exchange Commission against WorldCom, Inc., the SEC accused senior management of disguising the true performance of the company by using undisclosed and improper accounting that overstated income by capitalizing various costs that should have been treated as expenses. The *New York Times* reported that the company's ex-controller admitted to investigators that he was aware of the expense shifts, but that financial pressures being faced by the company left him with little choice. The ability of management to override internal control is difficult to prevent. Companies must rely upon active participation by the audit committee and an effective internal audit department.

- Reducing operational surprises and losses.
- Identifying and managing multiple and cross-enterprise risks.
- Seizing opportunities.
- Improving the deployment of capital.

It is not necessary for a company to implement an enterprise risk management system that meets these criteria in order to have effective internal control. However, management of firms that implement these systems should do a much better job of managing business risks.

The Auditors' Consideration of Internal Control

The second standard of fieldwork states:

Learning Objective 3

> A sufficient understanding of internal control is to be obtained to plan the audit and to determine the nature, timing, and extent of the tests to be performed.

The auditors' understanding of the client's internal control provides a basis both to (1) *plan the audit,* and (2) *assess control risk.*

In planning an audit it is essential that the auditors have a sufficient understanding of the client's internal control. This encompasses both an understanding of the *design* of the policies, procedures, and records, and a knowledge of whether they have been *placed in operation* (implemented) by the client. It is difficult to imagine designing tests of financial statement balances without an understanding of internal control. For example, auditors who do not understand the client's controls over the execution and recording of credit sales would have a difficult time substantiating the balances of accounts receivable and sales.

The auditors' consideration of internal control also provides a basis for their assessment of **control risk**—the risk that material misstatements will not be prevented or detected by the client's internal control. If the auditors determine that the client's internal control is effective at preventing or detecting misstatements, they will assess control risk as low. They can then accept a higher level of detection risk, and substantive testing can be decreased. Conversely, if controls are weak, control risk is high and the auditors must increase the scope of their substantive tests to limit the level of detection risk. Therefore, the auditors' understanding of internal control is a major factor in determining the nature, timing, and extent of substantive testing necessary to verify the financial statement assertions.

A question arises as to what action the auditors should take when internal control is found to be seriously deficient. Can they complete a satisfactory audit and properly express an opinion on the fairness of financial statements of a company in which control risk is considered to be extremely high? The answer to this question depends on whether the auditors believe that inherent risk is at a satisfactory level so that substantive tests can be designed that will reduce audit risk to an acceptable level. For example, the auditors of a small business with a limited segregation of duties often apply an approach of restricting detection risk through extensive substantive tests of financial statement assertions, rather than performing tests of internal control.

Obtaining an Understanding of Internal Control to Plan the Audit

Learning Objective 4

As noted before, auditing standards require the auditors to obtain an understanding of internal control sufficient to plan the audit. This understanding should include knowledge about the *design* of relevant controls and whether they have been *placed in operation* by the entity. In planning the audit, that knowledge is used to:

1. Identify types of potential misstatements.
2. Consider factors that affect the risk of material misstatement.
3. Design tests of controls, when applicable.
4. Design substantive tests.

In making a judgment about the extent of the understanding of internal control that is necessary, the auditors consider knowledge related to the above four factors that has been obtained through other sources, such as previous audits and their understanding of the industry in which the client operates. As is discussed in further detail in Chapter 8, the auditors must consider whether specialized skills are needed relating to the client's use of information technology. For example, a professional with particular information technology skills may be needed on the audit team due to the complexity of the client's systems.

The auditors also consider their assessment of inherent risk, judgments about materiality, and the nature of the entity's operations. In all audits, the auditors' understanding of internal control must encompass the control environment, risk assessment, the accounting information and communication system, control activities, and monitoring.

The Control Environment

The auditors must obtain sufficient knowledge to understand management's attitudes, awareness, and actions concerning the control environment. It is important that the auditors concentrate on the substance of controls, rather than their form. For example, an organization may have, but not enforce, a *code of conduct* prohibiting unethical activities.

Risk Assessment

The auditors must obtain an understanding of the client's process for identifying and responding to business risks. This understanding includes how management identifies these risks, estimates their significance, and decides upon actions to manage them. If the client has implemented an enterprise risk management system, the auditors will obtain an understanding of the processes and controls that are implemented in the system. An understanding of the risk assessment process assists the auditors in identifying risks of material misstatement, because many risks of material misstatement arise as a result of business risks faced by management.

The client's risk assessment process differs from the auditors' consideration of audit risk in an audit. The purpose of the client's risk assessment process is to identify, analyze, and manage risks that affect the entity's ability to achieve management objectives. In an audit, the auditors assess risks to evaluate the likelihood of material misstatements in the financial statements.

The Accounting Information System

To understand the accounting information system, the auditors must become familiar with the:

- Types of transactions significant to the financial statements.
- Procedures, both automated and manual, by which transactions are initiated, recorded, processed, and reported, from their occurrence to their inclusion in the financial statements.

- Related accounting records and supporting accounts.
- Manner in which the information system captures other events and conditions that are significant to the financial statements.
- Financial reporting process used to prepare the financial statements, including significant accounting estimates and disclosures.

In obtaining an understanding of the client's accounting information system and the related control activities, auditors generally find it useful to divide the overall system into its major transaction cycles. The term **transaction cycle** refers to the policies and the sequence of procedures for processing a particular type of transaction. For example, the accounting system in a manufacturing business might be subdivided into the following major transaction cycles:

1. *Revenue (or sales and collections) cycle*—including processes, procedures, and policies for obtaining orders from customers, approving credit, shipping merchandise, preparing sales invoices (billing), recording revenue and accounts receivable, and handling and recording cash receipts.

2. *Acquisition (or purchases and disbursements) cycle*—including processes, procedures, and policies for initiating purchases of inventory, other assets, and services; placing purchase orders, inspecting goods upon receipt, and preparing receiving reports; recording liabilities to vendors; authorizing payment; and making and recording cash disbursements.

3. *Conversion (production) cycle*—including processes, procedures, and policies for storing materials, placing materials into production, assigning production costs to inventories, and accounting for the cost of goods sold.

4. *Payroll cycle*—including processes, procedures, and policies for hiring, terminating, and determining pay rates; timekeeping; computing gross payroll, payroll taxes, and amounts withheld from gross pay; maintaining payroll records; and preparing and distributing paychecks.

5. *Financing cycle*—including processes, procedures, and policies for authorizing, executing, and recording transactions involving bank loans, leases, bonds payable, and capital stock.

6. *Investing cycle*—including processes, procedures, and policies for authorizing, executing, and recording transactions involving investments in fixed assets and securities.

The transaction cycles for a particular company depend upon the nature of the company's business activities. A bank, for example, has no production cycle, but has both a lending cycle and a demand deposits cycle. Also, different auditors may elect to define a given company's transaction cycles in different ways. For example, the sales and collections cycle may alternatively be defined as two separate transaction cycles for (1) the processing and recording of credit sales, and (2) the handling and recording of cash receipts. The important point to recognize is that dividing internal control into transaction cycles enables the auditor to focus upon the controls that affect the reliability of assertions about specific accounts in the financial statements.

Control Activities

While obtaining an understanding of the other internal control components (the control environment, risk assessment, the accounting information system, and monitoring), auditors generally obtain some knowledge about the client's control activities. For example, while obtaining an understanding of documents relating to cash transactions, it is likely that the auditors will discover whether the bank accounts are reconciled. Whether it is necessary for the auditors to devote additional attention to obtaining an understanding of the other control activities depends on the circumstances of the engagement.

The auditors may find it necessary to understand and test certain control activities to audit a particular assertion. For example, when auditing a charitable organization that receives significant cash donations, the auditors may be unable to effectively plan the audit for the completeness assertion for cash contributions without understanding and testing controls related to cash receipts. In other circumstances the auditors may conclude that it would be too costly to audit a particular assertion using only substantive procedures; the most efficient course of action is to increase their understanding and testing of the client's internal control.

Monitoring of Controls

Finally, the auditors should obtain a sufficient understanding of the entity's monitoring methods relating to financial reporting to understand how those procedures are used to initiate actions to address inadequate performance. The auditors will also consider how the work of the internal auditors contributes to internal control. The auditors' consideration of the work of internal auditors is described later in this chapter.

Sources of Information about Internal Control

How do auditors gain an understanding of a client's internal control? Auditors obtain information about internal control by *inquiry* of appropriate client personnel, *inspecting* various entity documents and records, and *observing* control activities and operations as they are performed. In repeat engagements their investigation for the current year will stress areas shown as having questionable controls in prior years. It is imperative, however, that auditors recognize that the pattern of operations is an ever-changing one—controls that were adequate last year may now be ineffective.

Auditors may determine the duties and responsibilities of client personnel by inspecting organization charts and job descriptions and interviewing client personnel. Many clients have procedures manuals and flowcharts describing the approved practices to be followed in all phases of operations. Another excellent source of information is in the reports, working papers, and audit programs of the client's internal auditing staff.

The auditors' understanding of internal control encompasses not only the design of controls, but also whether they have been placed in operation. *Placed in operation* means that the control actually exists and is in use; that is, it does not just exist in theory or on paper.

While obtaining an understanding of internal control, the auditors may also obtain evidence about the *operating effectiveness* of various controls. The distinction between knowing that a control has been *placed in operation* and obtaining evidence on its *operating effectiveness* is important. To properly perform an audit, auditors are required to determine that the major controls have been placed in operation; they are *not* required to evaluate their operating effectiveness. However, if the auditors wish to assess control risk at a level below maximum, they must obtain evidence of the operating effectiveness of those controls. This evidence is obtained by performing tests of controls, which are discussed later in this chapter.

Documenting the Understanding of Internal Control

As the independent auditors obtain a working knowledge of internal control, they must document the information in their working papers. The form and extent of this documentation is affected by the size and complexity of the client, as well as the nature of the client's internal control. The documentation usually takes the form of internal control questionnaires, written narratives, or flowcharts.

Internal Control Questionnaire

The traditional method of describing internal control is to fill in a standardized **internal control questionnaire.** Many public accounting firms have developed their own questionnaires for this purpose. The questionnaire usually contains a separate section for each major transaction cycle, enabling the work of completing the questionnaire to be divided conveniently among several audit staff members.

Most internal control questionnaires are designed so that a "no" answer to a question indicates a weakness in internal control, but they ordinarily require the auditors to identify types of potential misstatements arising therefrom. In addition, questionnaires may provide for a distinction between major and minor control weaknesses, an indication of the sources of information used in answering questions, and explanatory comments regarding control deficiencies. A disadvantage of standardized internal control questionnaires is their lack of flexibility. They often contain many questions that are "not applicable" to specific systems, particularly systems for small companies. Also, the situation in which an internal control strength compensates for a weakness may not be obvious from examining a completed questionnaire. An internal control questionnaire relating to cash receipts is illustrated in Figure 7.3.

An internal control questionnaire is intended as a means for the auditors to document their understanding of internal control. If completion of the questionnaire is regarded as an end in

FIGURE 7.3
Internal Control Questionnaire

Internal Control Questionnaire
Cash Receipts—Sales Cycle

Client _Bennington Co., Inc._   Audit Date _December 31, 200X_

Names and Positions of Client Personnel Interviewed:
Lorraine Martin—Cashier; Helen Ellis—Head Bookkeeper; Wm. Dale—Manager

Question	Not Appl.	Yes	No	Weakness Major	Weakness Minor	Remarks
1. Are all persons receiving or disbursing cash bonded?		✓				
2. Is all incoming mail opened by a responsible employee who does not have access to accounting records?			✓	✓		H. Ellis is head bookkeeper
3. Does the employee assigned to the opening of incoming mail prepare a list of all checks and money received?			✓		✓	See mitigating control in #13
4. a) Is a copy of the listing of mail receipts forwarded to the accounts receivable department for comparison with the credits to customers' accounts?	✓					
b) Is a copy of this list turned over to an employee other than the cashier for comparison with the cash receipts records?	✓					
5. Are receipts from cash sales and other over-the-counter collections recorded by sales registers or point-of-sale terminals?	✓					
6. Are the daily totals of cash registers or other mechanical devices verified by an employee not having access to cash?	✓					
7. Are physical facilities and mechanical equipment for receiving and recording cash adequate and conducive to good control?		✓				
8. Is revenue from investments, rent, concessions, and similar sources scheduled in advance so that nonreceipt on due date would be promptly investigated?	✓					
9. Do procedures for sale of scrap materials provide for direct reporting to accounting department concurrently with transfer of receipts to cashier?	✓					
10. Are securities and other negotiable assets in the custody of someone other than the cashier?	✓					
11. Are collections by branch offices deposited daily in a bank account subject to withdrawal only by home office executives?	✓					
12. Are each day's receipts deposited intact and without delay by an employee other than the accounts receivable bookkeeper?		✓				
13. Are the duplicate deposit tickets returned by the bank and compared with the cash receipts record and mailroom list of receipts by an employee other than the cashier or accounts receivable bookkeeper?		✓				W. Dale Manager
14. Are the duplicate deposit tickets properly filed and available for inspection by auditors?		✓				Chronological sequence
15. Are NSF checks or other items returned by the bank delivered directly to an employee other than the cashier and promptly investigated?		✓				W. Dale Manager
16. Is the physical arrangement of offices and accounting records designed to prevent employees who handle cash from having access to accounting records?			✓		✓	Small company doesn't permit this

Prepared by _V.M. Harris_   Date _Sept. 6, 0X_   Manager Review _____   Date _____

Senior Review _____   Date _____   Partner Review _____   Date _____

itself, there may be a tendency for the auditors to fill in the "yes" and "no" answers in a mechanical manner, without any real understanding or study of the transaction cycle. For this reason, some public accounting firms prefer to use written narratives or flowcharts in lieu of, or in conjunction with, questionnaires.

Written Narrative of Internal Control

Written narratives of internal control are memoranda that describe the flow of transaction cycles, identifying the employees performing various tasks, documents prepared, records maintained, and the division of duties. Figure 7.4 is a written narrative, describing internal control over cash receipts.

Flowcharts of Internal Control

Many CPA firms consider systems flowcharts to be more effective than questionnaires or narrative descriptions in documenting their understanding of a client's accounting information

Bennington Co., Inc.
Cash Receipts Procedures
December 31, 200X

All cash receipts are received by mail in the form of checks. Lorraine Martin, cashier, picks up the mail every morning at the post office and delivers it unopened to Helen Ellis, the head bookkeeper.

Ellis opens and distributes the mail. Customers' checks are given to Martin, who records the remittance in the cash receipts journal, prepares duplicate deposit slips, and mails the day's receipts intact to First National Bank. The bank returns the validated duplicate deposit slips by mail, and Ellis files them in chronological order. Ellis posts the accounts receivable subsidiary ledger from the cash receipts journal on a daily basis.

Any customers' checks charged back by the bank are given by Ellis to the manager, William Dale, who follows up and redeposits the checks. Ellis also forwards monthly bank statements unopened to Dale. Dale reconciles the monthly bank statement, compares the dates and amounts of deposits with the entries in the cash receipts journal, and reviews the propriety of sales discounts recorded in the cash receipts journal.

Martin, Ellis, and Dale are all bonded.

Val Martin Hawkins
September 6, 200X

system and the related control activities. A **systems flowchart** is a diagram—a symbolic representation of a system or a series of procedures with each procedure shown in sequence. To the experienced reader, a flowchart conveys a clear image of the system, showing the nature and sequence of procedures, division of responsibilities, sources and distribution of documents, and types and location of accounting records and files. The standard symbols used in systems flowcharting are illustrated in Figure 7.5; however, the symbols used and the flowcharting technique vary somewhat among different public accounting firms.

Separate systems flowcharts are prepared for each major transaction cycle. Each flowchart is divided into vertical columns representing the various departments (or employees) involved in processing the transactions. Departmental responsibility for procedures, documents, and records is shown by reviewing the related flowcharting symbol beneath the appropriate departmental heading. Flowcharts usually begin in the upper left-hand corner; directional flowlines then indicate the sequence of activity. The normal flow of activity is from top to bottom and from left to right. These basic concepts of systems flowcharting are illustrated in Figure 7.6.

The advantage of a flowchart over a questionnaire or a narrative is that a flowchart provides a clearer, more specific portrayal of the client's system. There is less opportunity for misunderstanding, blank spots, or ambiguous statements when one uses lines and symbols rather than words to describe internal control. Furthermore, in each successive annual audit, updating a flowchart is a simple process requiring only that the auditor add or change a few lines and symbols.

A possible disadvantage of flowcharts is that internal control weaknesses are not identified as prominently as in questionnaires. A "no" answer in an internal control questionnaire is a conspicuous red flag calling attention to a dangerous situation. A flowchart may not provide so clear a signal that a particular control is absent or is not being properly enforced. For that reason, some CPA firms use both flowcharts and questionnaires to describe internal control. The flowchart clearly depicts internal control, while the questionnaire serves to remind the auditors of controls that should be present.

The Walk-Through

After describing internal control in their working papers, the auditors will generally verify that it has been placed in operation by performing a walk-through of each transaction cycle. The term **walk-through** refers to tracing several transactions (perhaps only one or two)

FIGURE 7.5
Widely Used
Flowcharting Symbols

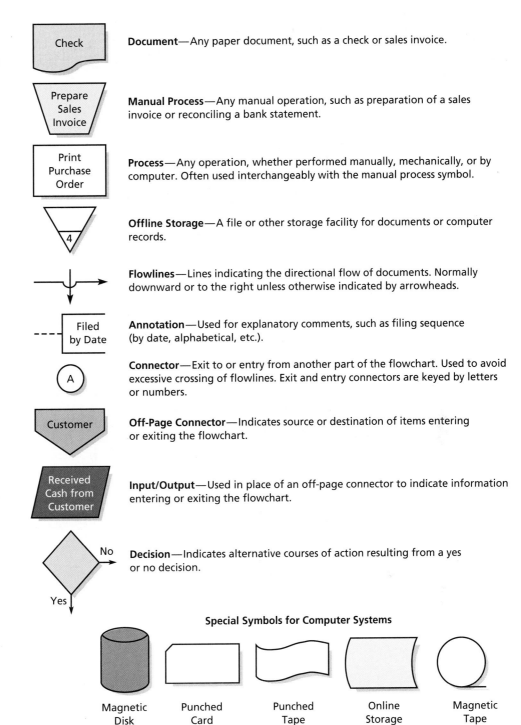

Document—Any paper document, such as a check or sales invoice.

Manual Process—Any manual operation, such as preparation of a sales invoice or reconciling a bank statement.

Process—Any operation, whether performed manually, mechanically, or by computer. Often used interchangeably with the manual process symbol.

Offline Storage—A file or other storage facility for documents or computer records.

Flowlines—Lines indicating the directional flow of documents. Normally downward or to the right unless otherwise indicated by arrowheads.

Annotation—Used for explanatory comments, such as filing sequence (by date, alphabetical, etc.).

Connector—Exit to or entry from another part of the flowchart. Used to avoid excessive crossing of flowlines. Exit and entry connectors are keyed by letters or numbers.

Off-Page Connector—Indicates source or destination of items entering or exiting the flowchart.

Input/Output—Used in place of an off-page connector to indicate information entering or exiting the flowchart.

Decision—Indicates alternative courses of action resulting from a yes or no decision.

Special Symbols for Computer Systems

Magnetic Disk Punched Card Punched Tape Online Storage Magnetic Tape

through each step in the cycle. To perform a walk-through of the sales and collections cycle, for example, the auditors might begin by selecting several sales orders and following the related transactions through the client's sequence of procedures. The auditors would determine whether such procedures as credit approval, shipment of merchandise, preparation of sales invoices, recording of the accounts receivable, and processing of the customers' remittances were performed by appropriate client personnel and in the sequence indicated in the audit working papers. If the auditors find that internal control functions differently from the working paper description, they will modify the working papers to describe the actual process.

FIGURE 7.6 Cash Receipts Flowchart

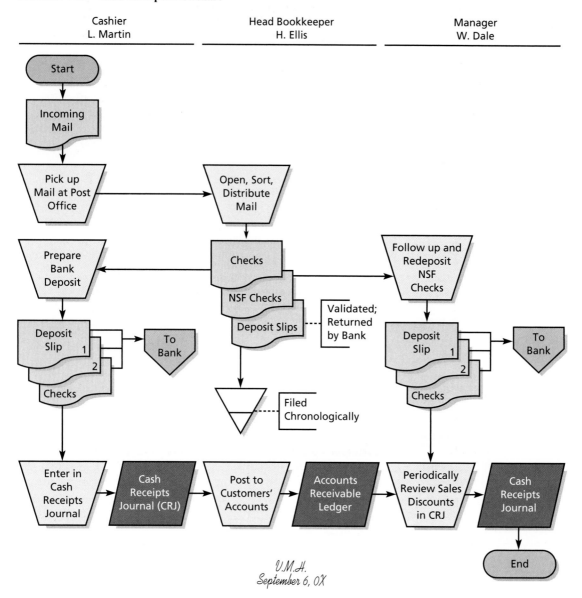

V.M.H.
September 6, 0X

Assessing Control Risk

Assessing control risk involves evaluating the effectiveness of a client's internal control in preventing or detecting material misstatements in the financial statements. When a client's internal control is tested and found to be effective in preventing or detecting material misstatements, the auditors will be able to reduce the nature, timing, or extent of their substantive audit procedures.

Learning Objective 5

Recall from Chapter 5 that most of the independent auditors' work involves gathering and evaluating evidence about the major financial statement assertions—existence or occurrence, completeness, rights and obligations, valuation or allocation, and presentation and disclosure. Therefore, the auditors assess control risk in terms of these five assertions. Assessing control risk is an iterative process that is refined as the auditors obtain increasing amounts of evidence about the effectiveness of various controls. It may be summarized as the following steps: (1) determine the planned assessed level of control risk and design additional tests of controls and the planned substantive tests, (2) perform additional tests of controls, (3) reassess control risk and modify planned substantive tests, and (4) document the assessed level of control risk.

Determining the Planned Assessed Level of Control Risk and Designing Additional Tests of Controls and the Planned Substantive Tests

After documenting their understanding of controls, the auditors will determine a **planned assessed level of control risk** for the various financial statement assertions. For assertions with weak controls, the auditors may simply plan to assess control risk at the maximum level and no tests of the related controls need to be performed.

For financial statement assertions that *appear* to have effective controls, the auditors must determine whether it is efficient to obtain the necessary evidence to justify an assessment of control risk at a lower level. To assess control risk at less than the maximum level for a particular assertion, the auditors must:

1. Identify those controls that are likely to prevent or detect material misstatements of the assertion.
2. Perform tests of controls to evaluate their effectiveness.

The auditors' planned assessed level of control risk and their assessments of inherent risk are used to develop the initial audit program of substantive testing. For assertions with a high planned assessed level of control risk, the auditors will plan substantial substantive procedures. Planned substantive procedures can be restricted or in some circumstances eliminated for assertions with a low planned assessed level of control risk. However, the lower the planned assessed level of control risk, the more evidence that must be obtained about the operating effectiveness of the controls.

Therefore, in making decisions about the planned assessed levels of control risk, the auditors must consider the trade-off between tests of controls and substantive testing. **Tests of controls** provide evidence that internal controls are operating effectively, allowing the auditors to assess control risk at a lower level, which, in turn, allows them to reduce the time spent performing substantive procedures. When controls *appear* to be effective, the auditors must ask themselves, "Is the time required to perform tests of controls to justify an assessment of a lower level of control risk justified in terms of its resulting decrease in the scope of substantive testing?" Control risk may be assessed at a level below the maximum only when the auditors have evidence on the operating effectiveness obtained by performing tests of controls.

The auditors' approach also may be dictated by the nature of the client's information system. For example, when the client has a sophisticated information technology system, the auditors may conclude that substantive procedures by themselves cannot in and of themselves provide sufficient audit evidence. When this is the case there may be no other option than relying upon a combination of tests of controls and substantive procedures.

As indicated previously, the auditors may have gathered some evidence about the effectiveness of certain controls when they performed procedures to obtain an understanding of controls. For example, in evaluating the design of the control environment, the auditors may have made inquiries about management's use of budgets, observed management comparing monthly budgeted and actual expenses, and inspected reports pertaining to the investigation of variances. For efficiency purposes, the auditors may have decided to perform virtually all the tests of controls during the process of obtaining an understanding of internal control. However, for many audits the auditors will design additional tests of controls at this point to support their assessed level of control risk.

Performing Additional Tests of Controls

Learning Objective 6

Tests of controls address: (1) how controls are applied, (2) the consistency with which they are applied, and (3) by whom or by what means (e.g., electronically) the controls are applied.

Nature of Tests of Controls

The audit procedures used to test the effectiveness of internal control include:

1. *Inquiries* of appropriate client personnel.
2. *Inspection* of documents and reports.
3. *Observation* of the application of controls.
4. *Reperformance* of the controls.

It is important to recognize that tests of controls focus on the operation of controls rather than on the accuracy of financial statement amounts. To illustrate this distinction, assume that the client has implemented the control of requiring a second person to review the quantities, prices, extensions, and footing of each sales invoice. The purpose of this control is to prevent material errors in the billing of customers and the recording of sales transactions.

To test the operating effectiveness of this control of requiring a second-person review, the auditors may make inquiries of client personnel and observe application of the procedure. They might also select a sample of, say, 30 sales invoices prepared throughout the year. They would inspect the invoice copy for the initials of the reviewer, and reperform the procedure by comparing the quantities to those listed on the related shipping documents, comparing unit prices to the client's price lists, and verifying the extensions and footings. The results of this test provide the auditors with evidence as to the existence and valuation of the recorded sales and accounts receivable. If numerous deviations from the control are found, the auditors will expand their substantive procedures with respect to existence and valuation of accounts receivable and sales transactions. For example, a substantive test of financial statement amounts might involve selecting a sample of recorded sales transactions to determine that they have been properly recorded and included in the year's total sales.

The control described above leaves documentary evidence of performance, the reviewer's initials, that allow it to be tested by sampling. Controls that do not leave documentary evidence of performance must be tested entirely through observation by the auditors and inquiry of client personnel. Segregation of duties, for example, is tested by observing the client's employees as they perform their duties and inquiring as to who performed those duties throughout the period under audit. The auditors also should determine whether employees performed *incompatible duties* when other employees were absent from work on sick leave or vacation.

Timing of Tests of Controls

Timing of the performance of tests of controls depends upon the auditors' objectives. If the auditors test the operation of controls at a particular time, their audit evidence relates only to that time (e.g., tests of counting procedures over the annual physical inventory counting at period end); but, if the auditors test controls throughout a period, they obtain evidence on the effectiveness of the operation of controls for the period (e.g., tests of general controls pertaining to modifying and using a computer program). For many controls, the auditors will want evidence on operating effectiveness throughout the period.

Extent of Tests of Controls

Generally, the auditors increase the extent of their tests of controls as they reduce the planned assessed level of control risk. However, this may not be the case for automated controls. The inherent consistency of such controls make extensive testing unnecessary; if they operate effectively at one time and are not changed, they will continue to operate effectively. Chapter 9 discusses required sample sizes for tests of controls.

Evidence from Tests of Controls Performed in Prior Audits

When the client has been audited in prior years, the auditors may have obtained evidence about the operating effectiveness of controls from tests performed in those audits. If the auditors plan to use this evidence, they should obtain evidence about whether changes in specific controls have occurred subsequent to the prior year's audit. If there have been changes, the new controls must be tested in the current audit to provide a basis for reducing control risk. If the auditors determine that the controls have not changed, they may rely on evidence of operating effectiveness obtained from prior year audits.[3] Even in situations when there are no changes in controls, tests of the controls must be reperformed periodically.

Reassessing Control Risk and Modifying Planned Substantive Tests

After the auditors have completed the tests of controls, they are in a position to reassess control risk based on the results of the tests. The results of the tests of controls may reveal that the level of control risk is actually higher than the planned level. If this is the case, modifications must be made in the nature, timing, and extent of the planned substantive tests in the audit program. For example, the auditors may decide to increase the extent of their substantive testing or perform certain substantive tests at year-end rather than at an interim date.

[3] The Public Company Accounting Oversight Board (PCAOB) standards for audits of internal control do not allow the auditors to rely on tests of controls performed in prior years.

FIGURE 7.7
Summary of Internal Control Documentation Requirements

	Control Risk Assessed at Maximum Level	Control Risk Assessed below Maximum Level
Understanding of Internal Control	In all cases document the understanding through techniques such as questionnaires, narratives, and flowcharts.	
Control Risk	1. State that control risk is assessed at the maximum.	1. State that control risk is assessed below the maximum. The level itself (e.g., moderate, low) need *not* be documented.
	2. The basis for assessing at the maximum need *not* be documented.	2. The basis for assessing below the maximum (i.e., tests of controls that were performed) *must* be documented.

Documenting Information on the Assessed Level of Control Risk

The auditors' **assessed level of control risk** will have identified the financial statement assertions with maximum control risk and those assertions for which control risk is considered to be less than the maximum level. The auditors must document these conclusions in their working papers. They must also describe the basis for all assessments that are at less than the maximum level. Figure 7.7 summarizes auditor internal control documentation requirements relating to both obtaining an understanding of internal control and control risk assessment.

A working paper, such as Figure 7.8, is often used to summarize the auditors' assessments of control risk and the resulting modifications in substantive tests. Notice that the extensions and limitations of audit procedures are described in detail to facilitate completion of the final version of the audit program.

The auditors' consideration of internal control is very complex. Figure 7.9 is a flowchart that highlights the major steps in the auditors' consideration of internal control.

Decision Aids for Audit Program Modification

Modifying audit programs for various levels of control risk, while considering other factors such as levels of materiality and inherent risk, involves complex judgments. How many additional items should the auditors test to compensate for high control risk? Is the risk of material misstatement for a particular assertion low enough to make it feasible to test the assertion at an interim date rather than at year-end? Without guidance from the CPA firm, different auditors within that firm might arrive at different answers to these questions. In fact, research on these types of audit judgments has revealed just that; there is a good deal of variance in auditors' program decisions.

CPA firms initially reacted to this problem by developing policies that place limits on individual auditors' decisions. The establishment of minimum audit sample sizes for particular types of tests is an example of such a policy. More recently, CPA firms have attempted to add even more structure to auditors' program decisions through the use of decision aids or guides. An **audit decision aid** is a checklist, standard form, or computer program that helps the auditors make a particular decision by ensuring that they consider all relevant information or by assisting them in combining the information to make the decision. By reducing the variance in auditors' program judgments, decision aids promote the performance of audits that meet firm and professional requirements.

Consideration of the Work of Internal Auditors

Many of the audit procedures performed by **internal auditors** are similar in nature to those employed by independent auditors. This raises the question of how the work of the internal auditors affects the independent auditors' work. The Auditing Standards Board has addressed this issue in *SAS 65* (AU 322), "The Auditor's Consideration of the Internal Audit Function in an Audit of Financial Statements."

Because the internal audit function is an important aspect of the client's monitoring component of internal control, the independent auditors consider the existence and quality of the function in their assessment of control risk. Through its contribution to internal control, the

FIGURE 7.8 **Working Paper for Summarizing Assessment of Control Risk**

WP Index   <u>CR-1</u>

Understanding of Internal Control,
Control Risk Assessment, and Impact on Substantive Procedures

Client: _Arntco, Inc._   Balance Sheet Date: _12/31/X3_

Completed by: _R.W._   Date: _9/15/X3_   Reviewed by: _K.J._   Date: _10/28/X3_

We obtained sufficient knowledge of the design of the control environment, risk assessment, the accounting information and communication system, control activities, and monitoring to plan the audit, and determined that the policies and procedures have been placed in operation.

Workpapers related to our understanding of the control structure are included at _Perm. Files ICS-1 through ICS-7._ Except as noted below, and on the reference workpapers, we have assessed control risk to be at the maximum and have designed our substantive audit procedures accordingly.

For those significant assertions related to the account balances indicated below, we have assessed control risk at less than the maximum, and the effects of such assessment have been reflected in our audit program. For assertions for each account balance or class of transactions where control risk has been assessed at less than the maximum, tests of controls have been performed to provide evidential matter sufficient to evaluate the effectiveness of the policies and procedures relevant to the various assertions.

CASH   WORKPAPER REF _____

_____

_____

_____

_____

ACCOUNTS RECEIVABLE   WORKPAPER REF ___C-2___

Control risk is assessed as slightly below the maximum for the following assertions: existence and valuation (other than for net realizable value, which risk is assessed at the maximum). Control risk for completeness is assessed as moderate. Accordingly, primary audit evidence for existence, ownership, and valuation (other than net realizable value) will be obtained by year-end confirmation of all key items (over $100,000), a nonstatistical representative sample of the remaining population (see workpaper C-5) and cutoff tests at year-end. Evidence about the net realizable value objective will be obtained by procedures set forth in the audit program, which consider: subsequent cash collection, the aged trial balance, analytical procedures, and review of specific accounts with the owner-manager. Audit evidence for completeness will be obtained by application of (1) year-end cutoff tests and (2) analytical procedures applied to sales (see workpaper C-6).

INVENTORY   WORKPAPER REF ___D-5___

Prior experience and tests of controls indicate good controls over physical counts and pricing of material items in inventory. These tests of controls provide sufficient evidence to support a low control risk assessment for the existence and valuation assertions.

EXPENSE ACCOUNTS   WORKPAPER REF _____

Source: Adapted AICPA. _Audit Guide: Consideration of Internal Control in a Financial Statement Audit_ (New York, 1996).

work of the internal auditors may reduce the amount of audit testing performed by the independent auditors.

The independent auditors begin by obtaining an understanding of the work of the internal auditors to determine its relevance to the audit. They make inquiries about such matters as the internal auditors' activities and audit plans. If the independent auditors conclude that the internal auditors' work is relevant and that it would be efficient to consider it, they assess the _competence_ and _objectivity_ of the internal audit staff and evaluate the quality of their work.

In evaluating the competence of the internal auditors, the independent auditors consider the educational level, professional experience, and professional certifications of the internal audit staff.

Fidelity bonds   A form of insurance in which a bonding company agrees to reimburse an employer for losses attributable to theft or embezzlement by bonded employees.

Foreign Corrupt Practices Act   Federal legislation prohibiting payments to foreign officials for the purpose of securing business. The act also requires all companies under SEC jurisdiction to maintain a system of internal control providing reasonable assurance that transactions are executed only with the knowledge and authorization of management.

Incompatible duties   Assigned duties that place an individual in a position to both perpetrate and conceal errors or fraud in the normal course of job performance.

Inherent risk   The risk of material misstatement of a financial statement assertion, assuming there are no related controls.

Integrated audit   Public Company Accounting Oversight Board *Standard No. 2* requires that public companies undergo both (1) an audit of internal control over financial reporting, and (2) an audit of the financial statements. The overall audit approach is referred to as an integrated audit because each audit provides the auditor with evidence relevant to the other audit.

Internal auditors   Corporation employees who design and execute audit programs to test the effectiveness and efficiency of all aspects of internal control. The primary objective of internal auditors is to evaluate and improve the effectiveness and efficiency of the various operating units of an organization rather than to express an opinion as to the fairness of financial statements.

Internal control   A process, effected by the entity's board of directors, management, and other personnel, designed to provide reasonable assurance regarding the achievement of objectives in the categories of (1) effectiveness and efficiency of operations, (2) reliability of financial reporting, and (3) compliance with applicable laws and regulations. Prior to 1996, the AICPA's *Professional Standards* referred to an entity's internal control as its internal control structure.

Internal control questionnaire   One of several methods of describing internal control in audit working papers. Questionnaires are usually designed so that "no" answers prominently identify weaknesses in internal control.

Management letter   A report to management containing the auditors' recommendations for correcting any deficiencies disclosed by the auditors' consideration of internal control. In addition to providing management with useful information, a management letter may also help limit the auditors' liability in the event a control weakness subsequently results in a loss by the client.

Material weakness   A significant deficiency, or combination of significant deficiencies, that results in more than a remote likelihood that a material misstatement of the annual or interim financial statements will not be prevented or detected.

Organizational structure   The division of authority, responsibility, and duties among members of an organization.

Planned assessed level of control risk   The level of control risk the auditor uses in developing a preliminary audit strategy, which includes an appropriate combination of tests of controls and substantive procedures.

Preventive controls   Controls that deter control problems before they occur.

Redundant controls   Duplicate controls that achieve a control objective.

Significant deficiency   A control deficiency (or a combination of control deficiencies) that adversely affects the company's ability to initiate, authorize, record, process, or report external financial data reliably in accordance with generally accepted accounting principles, such that there is more than a remote likelihood that a misstatement of the company's annual or interim financial statements which is more than inconsequential will not be prevented or detected.

Suitable criteria   Criteria are the standards or benchmarks used to measure and present the subject matter and against which the CPA evaluates the subject matter. Suitable criteria are established or developed by groups composed of experts that follow due process procedures, including exposure of the proposed criteria for public comment. Suitable criteria must have each of the following attributes: objectivity, measurability, completeness, and relevance.

Systems flowchart   A symbolic representation of a system or series of procedures with each procedure shown in sequence. Systems flowcharts are a widely used method of describing internal control in audit working papers.

Tests of controls   Tests directed toward the design or operation of a control to assess its effectiveness in preventing or detecting material misstatements of financial statement assertions.

Transaction cycle   The sequence of procedures applied by the client in processing a particular type of recurring transaction. The auditors' working paper description of internal control often is organized around the client's major transaction cycles.

Walk-through   A test of the accuracy and completeness of the auditors' working paper description of internal control. A walk-through is performed by tracing several transactions through each step of the related transaction cycle, noting whether the sequence of procedures actually performed corresponds to that described in the audit working papers.

Written narrative of internal control   A written summary of internal control for inclusion in audit working papers. Written narratives are more flexible than questionnaires, but by themselves are practical only for describing relatively small, simple systems.

Review Questions

7–1.   What is internal control?

7–2.   Identify the five components of an organization's internal control.

7–3.   List the factors that make up an organization's *control environment.*

7–4.   How does separation of the recordkeeping function from custody of assets contribute to internal control?

7–5.   Name three factors you consider of greatest importance in protecting a business against losses through embezzlement.

7–6.   Describe what is meant by the *risk assessment* component of internal control and how it contributes to internal control.

7–7.   Describe the two types of *monitoring* and provide an example of each.

7–8.   Identify the four types of *control activities* and describe how each type contributes to effective internal control.

7–9.   One basic concept of internal control is that no one employee should handle all aspects of a transaction. Assuming that a general category of transactions has been authorized by top management, how many employees (or departments) should participate in each transaction, as a minimum, to achieve strong internal control? Explain in general terms the function of each of these employees.

7–10.   Compare the objectives of the internal auditors with those of the independent auditors.

7–11.   What consideration, if any, may independent auditors give to the work of a client's internal audit staff?

7–12.   What are the purposes of the consideration of internal control required by generally accepted auditing standards?

7–13.   A prospective client informs you that all officers and employees of the company are bonded, and he requests that under these circumstances you forgo a consideration of internal control in order to reduce the cost of an audit. Construct a logical reply to this request.

7–14.   Suggest a number of sources from which you might obtain the information needed to prepare a description of internal control in the audit working papers.

7–15.   "All experienced auditors would design exactly the same audit program for a particular audit engagement." Do you agree? Explain.

7–16.   Under what circumstances are tests of controls *efficient* audit procedures?

7–17.   How is the auditors' understanding of the client's internal control documented in the audit working papers?

7–18.   What is a management letter? What is the letter's significance?

7–19.   In view of the consideration afforded internal control by the auditors, how do you account for the fact that the auditors' standard report makes no reference to internal control in describing the scope of the audit?

7–20.   You have discussed with the president of Vista Corporation several material weaknesses in internal control that have come to your attention during your audit. At the conclusion of this discussion, the president states that he will personally take steps to remedy these problems and that there is no reason for you to bring these matters to the attention of the board of directors. He explains that he believes the board should deal with major policy decisions and not be burdened with day-to-day management problems. How would you respond to this suggestion? Explain fully.

7–21.   Distinguish between the two subsections of Section 404 of the Sarbanes-Oxley Act of 2002.

7–22.   List the six stages of the auditors' overall approach in an audit of internal control performed in accordance with PCAOB requirements.

Questions Requiring Analysis

7–23. Management is responsible for designing and maintaining its organization's internal control. In designing internal control, management must consider controls related to each of the five major internal control components, including the control environment; risk assessment; the accounting information system; control activities; and monitoring.

Required:

a. Management is considering controls for the following three *control environment* factors. For each, describe how the factor contributes to effective internal control.

(1) Integrity and ethical values.

(2) Commitment to competence.

(3) Board of directors or audit committee.

b. Explain how *risk assessment* contributes to effective internal control, and identify four factors that result in increased financial reporting risk.

c. Identify the five major objectives of an *accounting information system.*

d. Describe the purpose of the following two types of *control activities.*

(1) Performance reviews.

(2) Information processing.

e. Explain the two types of *monitoring,* and provide an example of each.

7–24. The definition of internal control as contained in the *Internal Control—Integrated Framework* (COSO) and professional standards is quite broad and comprehensive.

Required:

a. Define *internal control* and its purpose.

b. Explain the major concepts that are included in the definition of internal control.

c. List and describe the five components of internal control.

d. Identify the major limitations of internal control.

7–25. Listed below are controls that have been developed by the management of Cirus Manufacturing Co.

1. Management surveys customers about their satisfaction with the company's service.

2. The human resources department investigates the educational background of prospective employees.

3. Invoices are reviewed for accuracy before they are mailed to customers.

4. Management periodically evaluates the threats to preparing reliable financial statements.

5. The internal auditors periodically evaluate the controls in the various departments of the company.

6. Management has developed and distributed a *code of conduct.*

7. Budgets and forecasts are used by the production departments to control expenses.

8. The accounting department uses a manual of accounting policies and procedures.

9. Entry into the warehouse is strictly controlled by security personnel.

10. Management has prepared and distributed an organizational chart.

Required:

For each of the controls, identify the internal control component and, if applicable, the subcomponent or factor to which it relates.

7–26. As a part of obtaining an understanding of the client and its environment, the auditors must obtain an understanding of each of the components of an entity's internal control. In addition, they assess control risk for the assertions embodied in the account balance, transaction type, and disclosure components of the financial statements.

Required:

a. Identify the components of an entity's internal control.

b. For what purposes should an auditor's understanding of the internal control components be used in planning an audit?

c. Explain why an auditor might decide to assess control risk at the maximum level for one or more financial statement assertions.

d. What must an auditor do to support assessing control risk at less than the maximum level when the auditor has determined that controls have been placed in operation?

7–27. Auditors may restrict substantive procedures based on the results of tests of controls.

Required:

a. Discuss and contrast the concepts of the planned assessment of control risk and the revised assessment of the risk after tests of controls have been performed.

b. Using internal control for the existence assertion for accounts receivable, provide an example that distinguishes among the concepts discussed in part (*a*) above.

7–28. The auditors' consideration of internal control begins with obtaining an understanding of the internal control.

Required:

a. Describe the remaining stages of the auditors' consideration.

b. Provide examples of audit procedures that are performed at each stage (including the stage of obtaining an understanding).

7–29. Henry Bailey, CPA, is planning the audit of The Neighborhood Store, a local grocery cooperative. Because The Neighborhood Store is a small business operated entirely by part-time volunteer personnel, internal control is weak. Bailey has decided that he will assess control risk at the highest level for all assertions and not restrict audit procedures in any area. Under these circumstances, may Bailey omit the consideration of internal control in this engagement? Explain.

7–30. Adherence to generally accepted auditing standards requires, among other things, a proper understanding of the existing internal control. The most common approaches to documenting the understanding of internal control include the use of a questionnaire, preparation of a written narrative, preparation of a flowchart, and combinations of these methods.

Required:

a. Discuss the advantages to CPAs of documenting internal control by using:

(1) An internal control questionnaire.

(2) A written narrative.

(3) A flowchart.

b. If they are satisfied that no material weaknesses in internal control exist after completing their description of internal control, is it necessary for the CPAs to conduct tests of controls? Explain.

7–31. Management is responsible for establishing effective internal control for its organization, including measures to prevent, deter, and detect fraud. Appendix 7A on pages 266–268 describes antifraud programs and measures.

Required:

a. What are the three major categories of antifraud measures and the measures that should be established under each category?

b. Under the measure of "create a positive workplace environment" provide:

(1) Two examples of antifraud controls.

(2) Two examples of factors that detract from a positive workplace environment.

(AICPA, adapted)

7–32. During your first audit of a medium-size manufacturing company, the owner, John Bell, explains that in order to establish clear-cut lines of responsibility for various aspects of the business, he has made one employee responsible for the purchasing, receiving, and storing of merchandise. A second employee has full responsibility for maintenance of accounts receivable records and collections from customers. A third employee is responsible for personnel records, timekeeping, preparation of payrolls, and distribution of payroll checks. Bell asks your opinion concerning this plan of organization. Explain fully the reasons supporting your opinion.

7–33. Internal auditing is a staff function found in virtually every large corporation. The internal audit function is also performed in many smaller companies as a part-time activity of individuals who may or may not be called internal auditors. The differences between the audits by independent auditors and the work of internal auditors are more basic than is generally recognized.

Required:

a. Briefly discuss the auditing work performed by the independent public accountant and the internal auditor with regard to:

(1) Auditing objectives.

(2) General nature of auditing work.

b. In conducting their audit, the independent auditors may consider the work of the internal auditors. Discuss briefly the reason for this consideration.

7–34. During your first audit of a manufacturing company with approximately 100 production employees, you find that all aspects of factory payroll are handled by one employee and that none of the usual controls over payroll are observed. What action will you take?

7–35. You are performing an audit of Systex Corporation and evaluating various internal controls. Classify the following controls as being preventive (P), detective (D), or corrective (C). Explain your answers.

    a. Annual physical inventory.

    b. Monthly reconciliation of bank accounts.

    c. Segregation of duties over purchasing.

    d. Supervisory approval of time cards.

    e. Dual signatures for checks.

    f. Adjustment of perpetual inventory records to physical counts.

    g. Management review budget/actual information.

    h. Internal audits of payroll.

7–36.   Randall, Inc., is a private company that manufactures heavy machinery. The company has an active audit committee and board of directors. The audit committee consists of two outside directors and Howard Kress, the company chief financial officer. The audit committee meets quarterly to provide oversight of financial reporting. The committee reviews new accounting policies and unusual transactions. Howard Kress personally reviews and approves any related party transactions. Internal audits of operating units are performed by the internal auditor, who reports directly to Laura Howe, the chief operating officer.

       The company has a written code of conduct, and employees agree to adhere to the code when they are hired. The company also has a hotline for confidential reporting of unethical behavior that is staffed by the corporate controller. The audit committee reviews summaries of all incidents and investigations performed.

Required: Identify the strengths in Randall's system of corporate governance and provide suggestions for improvement in the system. Organize your answer as follows:

Weakness	Recommended Improvement

Multiple Choice Questions

7–37.   Select the best answer for each of the following questions. Explain the reason for your selection.

    a. Which of the following would be least likely to be considered an objective of internal control?

       (1) Checking the accuracy and reliability of accounting data.

       (2) Detecting management fraud.

       (3) Encouraging adherence to managerial policies.

       (4) Safeguarding assets.

    b. An entity's ongoing monitoring activities often include:

       (1) Periodic audits by internal audit.

       (2) The audit of the annual financial statements.

       (3) Approval of cash disbursements.

       (4) Management review of weekly performance reports.

    c. A primary objective of procedures performed to obtain an understanding of internal control is to provide the auditors with:

       (1) Knowledge necessary to plan the audit.

       (2) Evidential matter to use in reducing detection risk.

       (3) A basis for modifying tests of controls.

       (4) An evaluation of the consistency of application of management policies.

    d. An auditor may compensate for a weakness in internal control by increasing the:

       (1) Extent of tests of controls.

       (2) Extent of detection risk.

       (3) Extent of substantive tests of details.

       (4) Extent of inherent risk.

    e. Controls over financial reporting are often classified as preventative, detective, or corrective. Which of the following is an example of a detective control?

       (1) Segregation of duties over cash disbursements.

    (2) Requiring approval of purchase transactions.

    (3) Preparing bank reconciliations.

    (4) Maintaining backup copies of key transactions.

f. Which of the following symbols indicate that a file has been consulted?

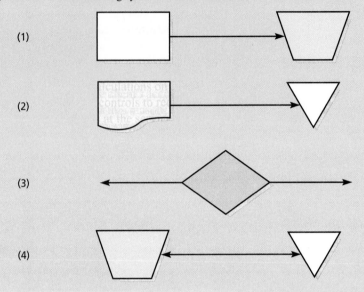

    (1)

    (2)

    (3)

    (4)

g. When a CPA decides that the work performed by internal auditors may have an effect on the nature, timing, and extent of the CPA's procedures, the CPA should consider the competence and objectivity of the internal auditors. Relative to objectivity, the CPA should:

    (1) Consider the organizational level to which the internal auditors report the results of their work.

    (2) Review the internal auditors' work.

    (3) Consider the qualifications of the internal audit staff.

    (4) Review the training program in effect for the internal audit staff.

h. Effective internal control in a small company that has an insufficient number of employees to permit proper separation of responsibilities can be improved by:

    (1) Employment of temporary personnel to aid in the separation of duties.

    (2) Direct participation by the owner in key recordkeeping and control activities of the business.

    (3) Engaging a CPA to perform monthly write-up work.

    (4) Delegation to each employee of full, clear-cut responsibility for a separate major transaction cycle.

i. Of the following statements about internal control, which one is *not* valid?

    (1) No one person should be responsible for the custody and the recording of an asset.

    (2) Transactions must be properly authorized before such transactions are processed.

    (3) Because of the cost/benefit relationship, a client may apply controls on a test basis.

    (4) Controls reasonably ensure that collusion among employees *cannot* occur.

j. Proper segregation of functional responsibilities calls for separation of the:

    (1) Authorization, recordkeeping, and custodial functions.

    (2) Authorization, execution, and payment functions.

    (3) Receiving, shipping, and custodial functions.

    (4) Authorization, approval, and execution functions.

k. To have an adequate basis to issue a management report on internal control under Section 404(a) of the Sarbanes-Oxley Act, management must do all of the following, except:

    (1) Establish internal control with no material weakness.

    (2) Accept responsibility for the effectiveness of internal control.

(3) Evaluate the effectiveness of internal control using suitable control criteria.

(4) Support the evaluation with sufficient evidence.

l. When the auditors are performing a first-time internal control audit in accordance with the Sarbanes-Oxley Act and PCAOB standards, they must:

(1) Modify their report for any significant deficiencies identified.

(2) Test all controls.

(3) Perform walkthroughs for each major class of transactions.

(4) Perform a separate assessment of controls over operations.

Problems

7–38. Orange Corp., a high-technology company, utilizes the following procedures for recording materials and transferring them to work in process.

(1) Upon receipt of raw materials by stores, the storekeeper prepares a stock-in report with part number and quantities, files the original by date, and sends a copy to accounting.

(2) The inventory accounting clerk uses the stock-in report to post the perpetual inventory records using standard costs and files the stock-in report by date.

(3) Raw materials requisitions, which show part number and quantity, are prepared by the manufacturing clerk and approved by the supervisor of manufacturing. A copy of the requisition is sent to accounting, and the original is filed by job order.

(4) The inventory accounting clerk reviews the requisitions for completeness, transfers the cost from raw materials to work in process, and files the requisitions by date.

Required:

Prepare a flowchart that describes the client's system of recording raw materials and transferring them to work in process.

7–39. At the Main Street Theatre, the cashier, located in a box office at the entrance, receives cash from customers and operates a machine that ejects serially numbered tickets. To gain admission to the theater, a customer hands the ticket to a door attendant stationed some 50 feet from the box office at the entrance to the theater lobby. The attendant tears the ticket in half, opens the door for the customer, and returns the stub to the customer. The other half of the ticket is dropped by the door attendant into a locked box.

Required:

a. What controls are present in this phase of handling cash receipts?

b. What steps should be taken regularly by the manager or other supervisor to give maximum effectiveness to these controls?

c. Assume that the cashier and the door attendant decided to collaborate in an effort to abstract cash receipts. What action might they take?

d. Continuing the assumption made in (*c*) of collusion between the cashier and the door attendant, what features of the controls would be likely to disclose the embezzlement?

7–40. Island Trading Co., a client of your CPA firm, has requested your advice on the following problem. It has three clerical employees who must perform the following functions:

(1) Maintain general ledger.

(2) Maintain accounts payable ledger.

(3) Maintain accounts receivable ledger.

(4) Maintain cash disbursements journal and prepare checks for signature.

(5) Issue credit memos on sales returns and allowances.

(6) Reconcile the bank account.

(7) Handle and deposit cash receipts.

Required:

Assuming that there is no problem as to the ability of any of the employees, the company requests your advice on assigning the above functions to the three employees in such a manner as to achieve the highest degree of internal control. It may be assumed that these employees will perform no other accounting functions than the ones listed and that any accounting functions not listed will be performed by persons other than these three employees.

a. List four possible unsatisfactory combinations of the above-listed functions.

b. State how you would recommend distributing the above functions among the three employees. Assume that, with the exception of the nominal jobs of the bank reconciliation and the issuance of credits on returns and allowances, all functions require an equal amount of time.

7–41.   Prospect Corporation, your new audit client, processes its sales and cash receipts in the following manner:

(1) *Sales.* Salesclerks prepare sales invoices in triplicate. The original and second copy are presented to the cashier, and the third copy is retained by the sales clerk in the sales book. When the sale is for cash, the customer pays the sales clerk, who presents the money to the cashier with the invoice copies.

A credit sale is approved by the cashier from an approved credit list. After receiving the cash or approving the invoice, the cashier validates the original copy of the sales invoice and gives it to the customer. At the end of each day, the cashier recaps the sales and cash received, files the recap by date, and forwards the cash and second copy of all sales invoices to the accounts receivable clerk.

The accounts receivable clerk balances the cash received with cash sales invoices and prepares a daily sales summary. Cash sales are posted by the accounts receivable clerk to the cash receipts journal, and the daily sales summary is filed by date. Cash from cash sales is included in the daily bank deposit (preparation of the bank deposit is described with cash receipts in the following section). The accounts receivable clerk posts credit sales invoices to the accounts receivable ledger and then sends all invoices to the inventory control clerk in the sales department.

The inventory clerk posts to the inventory control cards and files the sales invoices numerically.

(2) *Cash receipts.* The mail is opened each morning by a mail clerk in the sales department. The mail clerk prepares a remittance advice (showing customer and amount paid) for each check and forwards the checks and remittance advices to the sales department supervisor. The supervisor reviews the remittance advices and forwards the checks and advices to the accounting department supervisor.

The accounting department supervisor, who also functions as credit manager in approving new credit and all credit limits, reviews all checks for payments on past-due accounts and then gives the checks and remittance advices to the accounts receivable clerk, who arranges the advices in alphabetical order. The remittance advices are posted directly to the accounts receivable ledger cards. The checks are endorsed by stamp and totaled. The total is posted to the cash receipts journal. The remittance advices are filed chronologically.

After receiving the cash from the previous day's cash sales from the cashier, the accounts receivable clerk prepares the daily deposit slip in triplicate. The original and second copy of the deposit slip accompany the bank deposit, and the third copy is filed by date. The bank deposit is sent directly to National Bank.

Required:

a. Prepare a systems flowchart of internal control over sales transactions as described in part 1 above.

b. Prepare a systems flowchart of internal control over cash receipts as described in part 2 above.

7–42.   You have been asked by the board of trustees of a local church to review its accounting procedures. As part of this review you have prepared the following comments relating to the collections made at weekly services and recordkeeping for members' pledges and contributions:

(1) The church's board of trustees has delegated responsibility for financial management and of the financial records to the finance committee. This group prepares the annual forecast and approves major disbursements, but is not involved in collections or recordkeeping. No internal or independent audit has been considered necessary in recent years because the same trusted employee has kept church records and served as financial secretary for 15 years.

(2) The offering at the weekly service is taken by a team of ushers. The head usher counts the offering in the church office following each service. He then places the offering and a notation of the amount counted in the church safe. The next morning the financial secretary opens the safe and recounts the offering. He withholds about $100 to meet cash expenditures during the coming week and deposits the remainder of the offering intact. In order to facilitate the deposit, members who contribute by check are asked to draw their checks to cash.

(3) At their request a few members are furnished prenumbered, predated envelopes in which to insert their weekly contributions. The head usher removes the cash from the envelopes to be counted with the loose cash included in the offering and discards the envelopes. No record is maintained of issuance or return of the envelopes, and the envelope system is not encouraged.

(4) Each member is asked to prepare a contribution pledge card annually. The pledge is regarded as a moral commitment by the member to contribute a stated weekly amount. Based upon the amounts shown on the pledge cards, the financial secretary furnishes a letter requesting members to support the tax deductibility of their contributions.

Required: Describe the weaknesses and recommend improvements in procedures for:

a. Offerings given at weekly services.

b. Recordkeeping for members' pledges and contributions.

Organize your answer sheets as follows:

Weakness	Recommended Improvement

(AICPA, adapted)

7–43. Auditors must have an understanding of the various terms that relate to their consideration of internal control of an organization.

Required: For each term presented below, select the category that most clearly defines or includes the term. The categories may be selected once, more than once, or not at all.

Term	Category
1. Accounting information system	a. Generally of no concern to auditors
2. Control environment	
3. Flowchart	b. Control condition
4. Controls over operating effectiveness	c. Component of internal control
5. Significant deficiency in internal control design	
6. Monitoring	d. Documentation
7. Questionnaire	e. Placed in operation
8. Walk-through	f. Material weakness
9. Very significant deficiency in internal control design	g. Test of control
10. Reasonable assurance	h. Reportable condition
	i. Relationship of costs and benefits

7–44. A CPA's audit working papers include the narrative description below of the cash receipts and billing portions of the internal control of Parktown Medical Center, Inc. Parktown is a small health care provider owned by a publicly held corporation. It employs seven salaried physicians, 10 nurses, three support staff in a common laboratory, and three clerical workers. The clerical workers perform such tasks as reception, correspondence, cash receipts, billing, and appointment scheduling and are adequately bonded. They are referred to in the narrative as "office manager," "clerk 1," and "clerk 2."

Narrative: Most patients pay for services by cash or check at the time services are rendered. Credit is not approved by the clerical staff. The physician who is to perform the respective services approves credit based on an interview. When credit is approved, the physician files a memo with the billing clerk (clerk 2) to set up the receivable from data generated by the physician.

The servicing physician prepares a charge slip that is given to clerk 1 for pricing and preparation of the patient's bill. Clerk 1 transmits a copy of the bill to clerk 2 for preparation of the revenue summary and for posting in the accounts receivable subsidiary ledger.

The cash receipts functions are performed by clerk 1, who receives cash and checks directly from patients and gives each patient a prenumbered cash receipt. Clerk 1 opens the mail, immediately stamps all checks "for deposit only," and lists cash and checks for deposit. The cash and checks are deposited daily by the office manager. The list of cash and checks together with the related remittance advices are forwarded by clerk 1 to clerk 2. Clerk 1 also serves as receptionist and performs general correspondence duties.

Clerk 2 prepares and sends monthly statements to patients with unpaid balances. Clerk 2 also prepares the cash receipts journal and is responsible for the accounts receivable subsidiary ledger. No other clerical employee is permitted access to the accounts receivable subsidiary ledger. Uncollectible accounts are written off by clerk 2 only after the physician who performed the respective services believes the account to be uncollectible and communicates the write-off approval to the office manager. The office manager then issues a write-off memo that clerk 2 processes.

The office manager supervises the clerks, issues write-off memos, schedules appointments for the doctors, makes bank deposits, reconciles bank statements, and performs general correspondence duties.

Additional services are performed monthly by a local accountant who posts summaries prepared by the clerks to the general ledger, prepares income statements, and files the appropriate payroll forms and tax returns. The accountant reports directly to the parent corporation.

Required: Based only on the information in the narrative, describe the reportable conditions and one resulting misstatement that could occur and not be prevented or detected by Parktown's internal control over the cash receipts and billing function. Do *not* describe how to correct the reportable conditions and potential misstatements. Use the format illustrated below.

Reportable Condition	Potential Misstatement
There is no control to verify that fees are recorded and billed at authorized rates and terms.	Accounts receivable could be overstated and uncollectible accounts understated because of the lack of controls.

(AICPA, adapted)

7–45.   North, CPA, is planning an audit of the financial statements of General Co. In determining the nature, timing, and extent of the auditing procedures, North is considering General's internal audit function, which is staffed by Tyler.

Required: a. In what ways may Tyler's work be relevant to North, the independent auditor?

b. What factors should North consider and what inquiries should North make in deciding whether to use Tyler's work?

(AICPA, adapted)

In-Class Team Case

7–46.   Assume that you have been hired by Willington, CPA, as a new staff assistant. He informs you that his approach to audits has always been to assess control risk at the maximum and perform all the substantive tests he considers necessary. However, he has recently read an article in *The Journal of Accountancy* that indicates that a more efficient audit may sometimes be achieved by performing some tests of controls and thereby assessing control risk at a lower level. Willington shows you the following table that came from the article:

	Assessed Level of Control Risk		
Inherent Risk	**Low**	**Moderate**	**Maximum**
Low	Highest allowable detection risk (*lowest allowable scope of substantive procedures*)	High detection risk (*low scope of substantive procedures*)	Moderate detection risk (*moderate scope of substantive procedures*)
Moderate	High detection risk (*low scope of substantive procedures*)	Moderate detection risk (*moderate scope of substantive procedures*)	Low detection risk (*very high scope of substantive*
Maximum	Moderate detection risk (*moderate scope of substantive procedures*)	Low detection risk (*very high scope of substantive procedures*)	Lowest detection risk (*highest scope of substantive procedures*)

He understands that the table is only for illustrative purposes and that other "in between" levels of the various risks are possible, but he wants you to use the ones in the table to help him understand the trade-offs between tests of controls and substantive tests. He understands that while these risks would be assessed at the assertion level for the various accounts, he simply wants to better understand how the various tests performed in an audit "tie together." To keep things simple, he says to assume that inherent risk is at the maximum level in all cases.

He has roughed out a table that he wants you to complete for the following three cases:

Case A: Controls, as described by management, appear strong, and Willington wishes to test them to the extent possible. In this case he realizes that the results of the tests of controls may reveal that the controls are not operating effectively. Accordingly, Case A has three subcases:

A(1) Controls are found to be strong and operate effectively.

A(2) Controls are found to operate moderately effectively.

A(3) Controls, despite management's description, are found to be ineffective.

Case B: Controls, as described by management, appear strong, but Willington wishes to use his old approach of not testing them.

Case C: Controls, as described by management, appear weak.

Required: Fill out the chart on the following page using the following reply options.

Question	Reply Options	
1. At what level is the planned assessed level of control risk?	*Low* *Moderate* *Maximum*	
2. Describe the scope of tests of control that will be performed.	*None* *Tests Performed*	
3. At what level is the assessed level of control risk?	*Low* *Moderate* *Maximum*	
4. What must be documented in the working papers concerning internal control (select one or more)?	*Understanding* of internal control *Assessed level* of control risk *Basis* for assessing control risk *below* the maximum *Basis* for assessing control risk *at* the maximum	
	a. Acceptable Level of Detection Risk	**b. Scope of Substantive Tests**
5. What is the (a) acceptable level of detection risk and (b) the resulting scope of substantive tests?	*Lowest*	*Highest scope—Heavy emphasis on externally generated evidence, performed at year-end, and/or using larger samples.*
	Low	*High scope—Emphasis on externally generated evidence, performed at year-end, and/or using larger samples.*
	Moderate	*Moderate*
	High	*Low scope—Emphasis on internally generated evidence, performed at interim dates, and/or using smaller samples.*
	Highest	*Lowest scope—Heavy emphasis on internally generated evidence, performed at interim dates, and/or using smaller samples.*

	Case A—Controls Appear Strong; Auditor Decides to Test Controls to Extent Possible			Case B—Controls Appear Strong but Auditor Does Not Test	Case C—Controls Appear Weak
1. At what level is the planned assessed level of control risk?* (*low; moderate; maximum*)					
2. Describe the scope of tests of controls that will be performed. (*none; tests performed*)					
Results of Tests of Controls 3. At what level is the assessed level of control risk? (*low; moderate; maximum*)	*A(1)—Controls Strong (Operating Effectively)*	*A(2)—Controls Operating Moderately Effectively*	*A(3)—Controls Operating Ineffectively*		
4. What must be documented in the working papers concerning internal control? (*understanding; assessed level; basis*)					
5. (a) What is the acceptable level of detection risk? (*lowest; low; moderate; high; highest*)					
5. (b) Describe the scope (nature, timing, and extent) of substantive tests. (*highest; high; moderate; low; lowest*)					

*Inherent risk is assessed at the maximum level; evaluation of controls is based on management's description.

Appendix 7A

Antifraud Programs and Control Measures

SAS No. 99 (AU 316), "Consideration of Fraud in a Financial Statement Audit," includes an appendix that provides examples of programs and controls that management can implement to prevent, deter, and detect fraud—referred to as "measures." It suggests three categories of measures:

1. Create and maintain a culture of honesty and high ethics.
2. Evaluate the risks of fraud and implement processes, procedures, and controls to mitigate those risks.
3. Develop an appropriate oversight process.

Figure 7.13 summarizes the measures and provides examples.

FIGURE 7.13   **Antifraud Measures**

1. Create and Maintain a Culture of Honesty and High Ethics	
Measure	**Examples of Measure**

Set tone at the top.	• Establish, communicate, and enforce a corporate code of conduct with employee involvement.
	• Management's activities should show employees that dishonest or unethical behavior will not be tolerated.
	• Examples of factors that *detract* from a positive tone:
	   ▪ Statement by management of an absolute need to meet operating and financial targets.
	   ▪ Establishment of unachievable goals.

Create a positive workplace environment.	• Encourage and empower employees to help create a positive workplace.
	• Allow employees to participate in developing and updating the code of conduct.
	• Encourage employees and give them the means to communicate concerns about potential violations of the code of conduct without fear of retribution.
	• Examples of factors that *detract* from a positive workplace environment:
	   ▪ Top management that does not seem to care about or reward appropriate behavior.
	   ▪ Negative feedback and lack of recognition for job performance.
	   ▪ Perceived inequities in the organization.
	   ▪ Autocratic rather than participative management.
	   ▪ Low organizational loyalty or feelings of ownership.
	   ▪ Unreasonable budget expectations or other financial targets.
	   ▪ Fear of delivering "bad news" to supervisors and/or management.
	   ▪ Less than competitive compensation.
	   ▪ Poor training and promotion opportunities.
	   ▪ Lack of clear organizational responsibilities.
	   ▪ Poor communication practices or methods within the organization.

Hire and promote appropriate employees.	• Conduct background investigations on individuals being considered for employment or for promotion to a position of trust. • Thoroughly check a candidate's education, employment history, and personal references. • Train new employees about the entity's values and code of conduct. • Incorporate into regular performance reviews an evaluation of how each individual has contributed to creating an appropriate workplace environment in line with the entity's values and code of conduct. • Periodically objectively evaluate compliance with the entity's values and code of conduct.
Properly train employees.	• Training should include information on the company's values and its code of conduct. • Training should include information on the need to communicate certain matters and the manner in which it should be done. • Conduct refresher training. • Require periodic confirmation by employees of their responsibilities.

Discipline.	• Expectations about the consequences of committing fraud should be clearly communicated throughout the company.
	• Appropriate actions should be taken in response to alleged fraud, including:
	   ▪ A thorough investigation of the incident.
	   ▪ Appropriate and consistent actions against violators.
	   ▪ Relevant controls should be assessed and improved.
	   ▪ Communications and training should reinforce the entity's values, code of conduct, and expectations.

(Continued)

FIGURE 7.13 *Concluded*

2. Evaluate the Risks of Fraud and Implement Processes, Procedures, and Controls to Mitigate Those Risks	
Measure	**Examples of Measure**
Identify and measure fraud risks.	• Consider vulnerability of company to fraudulent financial reporting, misappropriation of assets, and corruption (bribery and other such illegal acts). • Consider organizational, industry, and country-specific characteristics that influence the risk of fraud.
Mitigate fraud risks.	• Change certain activities (e.g., cease doing business in certain locations). • Change certain processes (e.g., implement lockbox system at a bank instead of receiving payments at the company's various locations).
Implement and monitor controls and other measures.	• Evaluate whether controls have been implemented in areas of high risk of fraud. • Implement appropriate oversight measure by board of directors or audit committee to control for risk of management override of controls.

3. Develop an Appropriate Oversight Process	
Measure	**Examples of Measure**
Management.	• Oversee activities of employees by implementing and monitoring processes and controls.
Audit committee (or board of directors where no audit committee exists).	• Evaluate management's identification of fraud risks, implementation of antifraud measures, and creation of an appropriate "tone at the top." • Consider likelihood of management override. • Consider communicating with management one or two levels below senior management. • Have an open and candid dialogue with independent auditors on management's risk assessment process and internal control.
Internal auditors.	• Determine whether fraud has been committed. • Evaluate fraud risks. • Deter fraud.
Independent auditors.	• Assist management and audit committee in assessment of company's process for identifying, assessing, and responding to fraud risks.

Chapter **8**

Consideration of Internal Control in an Information Technology Environment

Chapter learning objectives

After studying this chapter, you should be able to:

LO1. Contrast the characteristics of an information technology–based system with those of a less sophisticated system.

LO2. Describe the nature of various types of information technology–based systems.

LO3. Describe the appropriate organizational structure in an information technology environment.

LO4. Distinguish among general control activities, application control activities, and user control activities in an information technology–based system.

LO5. Explain the manner in which the auditors obtain an understanding of internal control in an information technology environment.

LO6. Discuss the ways in which the auditors may test controls in an information technology environment.

LO7. Describe the nature of generalized audit software programs and the ways that they are used by the auditors.

The rapid increase in technology-based processing by business continues to have a dramatic effect on public accounting. No longer is the challenge of auditing information technology (IT) activities limited to large clients only. With the advent of inexpensive microcomputer systems, even the smallest audit clients use information technology for most accounting functions.

In a traditional IT environment, information is processed on a large mainframe computer by a separate information systems department, often using software developed by employees of that department. The other departments of the company, referred to as *user departments,* send their data to the information systems department and receive computer-generated reports when processing is complete. However, in recent years, commercially available software packages are replacing client-developed software and many information processing activities have been decentralized.

Commercially available computer software varies from applications costing less than $100 that are in essence electronic checkbooks (e.g., *Quicken, Money*) or basic general ledger systems (e.g., *Quickbooks*) to enterprise resource planning (ERP) systems costing into the tens, and even hundreds of millions of dollars (e.g., systems by J.D. Edwards, BAAN, Oracle, Peoplesoft, and SAP).

Computer applications are frequently implemented by personnel within user departments, using **off-the-shelf software** packages. This eliminates the need for the client to employ computer programmers for those applications. A typical small business uses a microcomputer to run an off-the-shelf general ledger package that provides the basis for its accounting system. Often, the computing power of a single microcomputer is sufficient to meet all the accounting needs of a small business.

A typical large business has a **client/server** IT architecture in which a number of "client" microcomputers are connected to either the corporate mainframe system or to another "server" computer. Data are entered and reports are generated at the various locations by user department personnel; the nature of the application determines whether processing is performed on the microcomputer or the server.

While large companies have historically written a variety of programs to meet their accounting and other information needs, more recently they are purchasing off-the-shelf transaction processing programs that are configured to varying degrees to meet their specific needs. As an example, a company may install an enterprise resource planning program that provides an enterprisewide structure for meeting the needs of all users in the organization. These systems collect and report a far wider variety of information than traditional accounting information systems. As these examples illustrate, auditors must be prepared to work in an ever-changing environment in which the client's accounting records are maintained on anything from an inexpensive bookkeeping system to a multimillion-dollar enterprise-wide system.

In addition to the above changes, the development of **electronic commerce** (e-commerce) continues to have a profound effect on accounting information systems. Electronic commerce involves the electronic processing and transmission of data between customer and client. A variety of activities may be involved including electronic trading of goods and services, online delivery of digital products, and electronic funds transfer (discussed later in this chapter).

Although IT has created some challenging problems for professional accountants, it has also broadened the horizons of these professionals and expanded the range and value of the services they offer. Technology is more than a tool for performing routine accounting tasks with unprecedented speed and accuracy. It makes possible the development of information that could not have been gathered in the past because of time and cost limitations. When a client maintains accounting records with a complex and sophisticated IT-based system, auditors often find it helpful, and even necessary, to utilize technology in performing many auditing procedures.

This chapter will consider some of the most significant ways in which auditing work is affected by IT, but it cannot impart extensive technical knowledge. Independent auditors will find additional familiarity with IT to be of ever-increasing value in the accounting profession.

Nature of IT-Based Systems

Learning Objective 1

Before considering the impact of IT on the work of the certified public accountant, some understanding of the nature of IT and its capabilities is needed. An IT-based system usually consists of a digital computer and peripheral equipment known as *hardware* and equally essential *software,* consisting of various programs and routines for operating the system.

Hardware

The principal hardware component of a digital computer is the *central processing unit* (CPU). The CPU processes programs of instructions for manipulating (moving and changing) data. The data may be numbers, characters, images (in digital form), sound (in digital form), or anything else that can be represented by a set of on/off characters (bits).

Digital computer circuitry has two states in that any given circuit may be *on* or *off.* Using an internal code, or machine language, capable of representing with two symbols any kind of data, all data may be expressed internally by the computer by a combination of on and off circuits. An example of a machine language is the *binary* number system.

Peripheral to the central processing unit are devices for recording input and devices for secondary storage, output, and communications. Peripheral devices in direct communication with the CPU are said to be **online,** in contrast to **offline** equipment not in direct communication with the CPU.

A first step in IT processing is to convert the data to machine-readable form. This is the role of recording and input devices, such as optical scanners, electronic cash registers, and bar code readers.

Secondary storage devices are used to augment the capacity of the storage unit of the CPU. Examples of secondary storage devices are magnetic tape, magnetic disk, and optical compact disk drives. Magnetic and optical compact disk drives have the advantage of **direct (random) access,** which allows for faster location and retrieval of data. Magnetic tapes and magnetic cartridges allow for only **sequential access;** data are retrieved by a linear search.

Machines must also be used to translate the output of the computer back into a recognizable code or language. Output equipment includes printers and display terminals.

Software

Information technology–based systems use two major types of software: system software and application software. **System software** consists of programs that control and coordinate hardware components and provide other support to application software. The system software known as the **operating system** is important to the control of IT operations because it may be used to control access to programs and stored data and to maintain a log of all system activities. Other system software includes *utility programs,* for recurring tasks such as sorting, sequencing, and merging of data, and *specialized security (access control) software.*

Programs designed to perform a specific data processing task, such as payroll processing, are known as **application software.** Early application programs were laboriously written in machine language, but today programming languages such as *COBOL* (common business-oriented language), **C++,** and **JAVA** are much like English. Programming in C++ and other *source languages* is made possible by another type of software, the *compiler,* which is a computer program used to translate a *source-language program* into machine language. The machine-language version of a program is called an *object program.*

Characteristics of Various Types of IT-Based Systems

In some ways IT-based systems enhance the reliability of financial information. Information technology processes transactions uniformly and eliminates the human errors that may occur in a manual system. On the other hand, defects in programs can result in processing all transactions incorrectly. Also, errors or fraudulent items that do occur in IT processing may not be detected by the client's personnel because few people are involved with information processing. Thus, IT precision does not ensure that the output will be reliable.

Information technology–based systems differ as to their characteristics. A system, regardless of its size, may possess one or more of the following elements:

1. Batch processing.
2. Online capabilities.
3. Database storage.
4. IT networks.
5. End user computing.

Batch Processing

When **batch processing** is used, input data are gathered and processed periodically in discrete groups. An example of batch processing is accumulating all of a day's sales transactions and processing them as a "batch" at the end of that day. While batch IT-based systems do not provide up-to-the-minute information, they are often more efficient than other types of systems.

Online Capabilities

Online systems allow users to have direct (online) access to the data stored in the system. Online systems may be divided into two types: (1) online transaction processing (OLTP) and (2) online analytical processing (OLAP) systems.

Online transaction processing (OLTP) systems are used to process various types of accounting and other transactions. When an online system is in use, individual transactions may be entered directly from the originators at remote locations. The transactions may be held in a transaction file and later posted to the records as a batch, or real-time processing may be used. In *online, real-time* (OLRT) systems, transactions are processed immediately and all accounting records are updated instantaneously. These systems are frequently found in banks and other financial institutions. Online, real-time systems allow a teller at any branch to update a customer's account immediately by recording deposits or withdrawals on a computer terminal. Similarly, customers are able to transact business directly with the system by inserting an identification card in an automatic teller machine (ATM).

The use of an online, real-time system results in significant changes in internal control. Original source documents may not be available to support input into the system and the overall amount of the hard copy (printed) audit trail may be substantially reduced. In these systems, essential controls should be programmed into the software. For example, the validity of data should be checked by the computer as transactions and data are entered into the system.

Online analytical processing (OLAP) involves the use of software technology that enables a user to query the system and conduct various analyses, ordinarily directly from the user's desktop computer. For example, management of an airline may download its online transaction processing reservation database into a **data warehouse**—another database that allows more efficient detailed statistical and graphical analysis of the reservation information. Management may then use the statistical reports and analyses generated by the OLAP system to make various operating decisions. The data also may be used in conjunction with decision support systems or expert systems. **Decision support systems** combine models and data in an attempt to solve unstructured problems with extensive user involvement. Alternatively, an **expert system** guides decision processes in a well-defined area and allows decisions comparable to those of an expert. As an example, banks may use expert systems to assess credit risk related to potential loan customers.

Database Storage

In a traditional IT-based system, each computer application has its own *application data files.* For example, the **master file** of accounts receivable is an application data file, maintained by the accounts receivable department, that contains customer account activity for a period of time and information about each customer. Much of the information in this file is also included in the customer master file maintained by the sales department. This data redundancy is expensive in terms of storage cost. Also, data inconsistencies may arise because the information may not be up-to-date in all files.

In a **database system,** separate application files are replaced with integrated database files that are shared by many users and application programs. A database system eliminates much data redundancy, and since the database is normally stored on a direct access device, the system responds quickly to users' requests for information. Both batch or online, real-time systems can use database storage.

From a control standpoint, it is essential that the database be secured against improper access or alteration. Organizations that use database systems often create a **database administrator** function, with responsibility for implementing and maintaining central databases and controlling access to the data.

IT Networks

The advent of **telecommunications**—the electronic transmission of information by radio, wire, **fiber optics, microwave,** laser, and other electromagnetic systems—has made it possible to transfer information between computers. **Networks** of computers linked together through telecommunication links enable companies to communicate information back and forth between geographically dispersed business locations. Indeed, this has led to the creation and development of electronic commerce.

Networks that span a large geographical area are called **wide area networks (WANs).** In contrast, a **local area network (LAN)** is a communications network that allows resources, data, and program sharing within a limited geographical area. An example is a network that connects computers and printers within a single building.

Many companies take advantage of **Internet** technology in establishing their networks. Some companies use the Internet to facilitate the exchange of information through remote locations or for electronic commerce involving buying or selling products over the Internet. Other companies have adopted Internet software for use in their closed networks, which are referred to as **Intranets.** When these Intranets include external business partners they are often referred to as **Extranets.**

Networking enables companies to implement **distributed data processing,** in which information and programs are shared by a large number of users. The network may provide company executives with online access to the vast amount of data stored in a number of the company's computers. Users may selectively retrieve data and process it to their personal specifications with microcomputers located in their departments.

Because data in an IT network may potentially be altered at any location that can access the system, weak controls at a single location can jeopardize the reliability of the entire networked system. Accordingly, security controls should be established at each location to ensure that data can be changed and accessed only by authorized personnel.

End User Computing

When a company implements **end user computing,** the user departments are responsible for the development and execution of certain IT applications. A user department both generates and uses its own information. For these applications, the information systems department is generally not involved, although certain files may be kept for user departments in mainframe storage. End user computing is possible because of the processing power now available with microcomputers. The end user IT system is the opposite of the traditional data processing environment, in which all information needed by users is provided by programs that are purchased or written and tested by the information systems department.

Controls over end user computing are only as good as those instituted by the user departments. For example, if user departments do not adequately test new programs, the reliability of all information in a system may be compromised. As is the case with IT networks, security controls must be established at each location to prevent unauthorized access to the company's data.

Impact of IT on the Audit Trail

Information technology may affect the fundamental manner in which transactions are initiated, recorded, processed, and reported. In a manual or mechanical data processing system, an audit trail (transaction trail) of hard-copy paper documentation links individual transactions with the summary figures in the financial statements. For example, individuals may manually record sales orders on paper forms, authorize credit, prepare shipping reports and invoices, record sales in a sales journal, and maintain accounts receivable records. The controls an auditor may test in such a system are also manual, and may include such procedures as approvals and reviews of activities and reconciliations and follow-up on reconciling items. Alternatively, in an electronic commerce environment, the information systems may use automated procedures to initiate, record, process, and report transactions. Records in electronic format may replace such paper documents as sales orders, invoices, shipping documents, and related accounting records. Two areas of high risk in such systems are unauthorized access and equipment failure. Control in such systems consists of a combination of automated controls and manual controls. In many applications, IT is able to electronically create, update, and delete data in computer-based records without any visible evidence of a change being made. In addition, the development of telecommunications has created an environment in which data may be altered not only within a specific computer, but by various computers both within and outside the client's organization.

During the early development of IT-based systems, the electronic transfer of information led to some concern among accountants that computerized processing would obscure or even eliminate the audit trail. Although it is technically possible to design an information system that would leave no audit trail, such a system would be neither practical nor desirable. An adequate audit trail is necessary to enable management to direct and control the operations of the business, to permit file reconstruction in the event of transmission and processing errors or computer failure, and to accommodate the needs of independent auditors and governmental agencies.

An audit difficulty with advanced IT-based systems is that while an audit trail may exist, it may not exist in printed form; it may be available only in machine-readable form. Because it can be quite voluminous, audit trail information may be kept online for only a short period of time, then transferred to a low-cost storage medium, such as magnetic tape. Electronic commerce conducted over the Internet provides a good example as often no printed output may exist related to initiating and processing transactions. After processing, the details of the transactions are often stored on a long-term basis on magnetic tape.

A related development that has significantly affected the audit trail is the advent of **electronic data interchange (EDI)** systems in which a company and its customers or suppliers use telecommunication links to exchange business data electronically over a private line of communication, as contrasted to the Internet. Source documents, such as invoices, purchase orders, checks, and bills of lading, are replaced with electronic transactions. For example, in an EDI system a purchase transaction may be automatically initiated by the client's IT-based system by sending an electronic message (purchase order) directly to a supplier's system. Invoicing and payment for the purchase may also be processed electronically. When EDI is being used, the auditors should consider client data retention and processing policies in planning the nature and timing of their audit procedures. For example, the auditors might identify transactions to be tested at the time they are processed so that information about the transactions can be obtained before it is purged from the IT-based system. Also, emphasis should be placed on coordinating the efforts of external and internal auditors to ensure adequate audit coverage.

The client's methods of processing transactions and policies for retaining audit trail information may even affect the auditors' overall approach to auditing certain assertions. To illustrate, when EDI transaction data are retained for a limited period, the auditors may find that the lack of hard-copy records makes performance of a primarily substantive audit for certain assertions difficult or impossible. Accordingly, for those assertions, the auditors may switch to a systems approach that includes tests of controls performed throughout the period to reflect the client's record retention policies. Thus, when significant information is initiated, recorded, processed, or reported electronically, the auditor may determine that it is not possible to design effective substantive procedures that by themselves would provide sufficient competent audit evidence.

During the design of an IT-based system, management will normally consult with both its internal and its external auditors to ensure that an adequate audit trail is built into the system and retained. In an IT-based system, of course, the audit trail may consist of computer printouts, computer logs, and documents stored in machine-readable form, rather than the more traditional handwritten source documents, journals, and ledgers. Portions of the audit trail, such as the date and time of the last change in a record, and the person making the change, are often stored as part of the online records.

Internal Control in an IT Environment

The discussion of internal control in Chapter 7 stressed the need for a proper division of duties. In a manual information system, no one employee should have complete responsibility for a transaction, and the work of one person should be verified by the work of another handling other aspects of the same transaction. The division of duties in such a manner ensures accurate records and reports and protects the company against losses from fraud or carelessness.

In an IT-based system, work normally divided among many employees may be performed electronically. Consolidation of activities and integration of functions are to be expected, since technology can conveniently handle many related aspects of a transaction. For example, a computerized payroll system could maintain personnel files with information on seniority, insurance, and the like; calculate employee pay; distribute labor costs; and prepare payroll checks and payroll records.

Despite the integration of several functions in an IT-based system, the importance of internal control is not in the least diminished. The essential factors described in Chapter 7 for satisfactory internal control remain relevant. Separation of duties and clearly defined responsibilities continue to be key factors. These traditional control concepts are augmented, however, by controls written into the computer programs and controls built into the computer hardware. Our discussion of controls in an IT-based environment will include a description of the organizational structure of the information system function, internal auditing of an IT-based system, and control activities.

Organizational Structure of the Information System Function

Because of the ability of the IT-based system to process data efficiently, there is a tendency to combine the performance of many data processing functions. In a manual or mechanical system, these combinations of functions may be considered incompatible from the standpoint of achieving strong internal control. For example, in a manual system, the function of recording cash receipts is generally segregated from responsibility for posting entries to the subsidiary accounts receivable. Because one of these procedures serves as a check upon the other, assigning both functions to one employee would enable the employee to conceal his or her own errors. A properly programmed computer, however, has no tendency or motivation to conceal its errors and may record these transactions simultaneously. Therefore, what appears to be an incompatible combination of functions may be combined in an IT-based system without weakening internal control.

When apparently incompatible functions are combined in the IT-based system, compensating controls are necessary to prevent improper human intervention with processing. A person with the opportunity to make unauthorized changes in programs or data files is in a position to exploit the concentration of data processing functions in an IT-based system. For example, an IT-based system used to process accounts payable may be designed to approve a vendor's invoice for payment only when that invoice is supported by a purchase order and receiving report. An employee able to make unauthorized changes to data or programs in that system could cause unsubstantiated payments to be made to specific vendors.

Computer programs and data files cannot be changed without the use of IT equipment. When changes are made, however, there may be no visible evidence of the alteration. Thus, the organization of the information systems department should prevent its personnel from having inappropriate access to equipment, programs, or data files. This is accomplished by providing definite lines of authority and responsibility, segregation of functions, and clear definition of duties for each employee in the department. The organization of the information systems department varies from one company to another in terms of reporting responsibility, relationships with other departments, and responsibilities within the department. As illustrated by

FIGURE 8.1
Organization of
Information Systems
Department

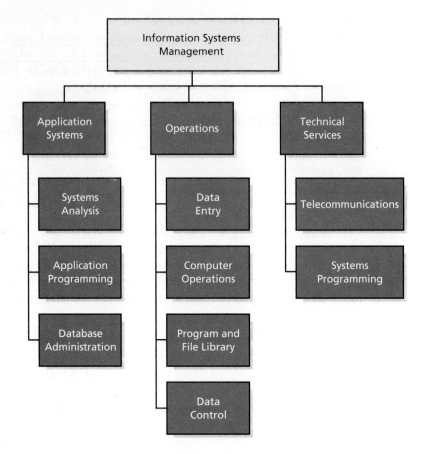

Figure 8.1, the organizational structure of a well-staffed information systems department should include the separation of responsibilities discussed next.

Information Systems Management

The information systems manager (director) should supervise the operation of the department and may report to the vice president of finance or administrative services or to the controller. When the head of information systems reports to the controller, the controller should not have direct involvement with IT operations. Alternatively, the position may be elevated to the vice president level, with reporting responsibility directly to the president. In many companies this high-level person is called the *chief information officer* (CIO).

Systems Analysis

Systems analysts are responsible for designing the information system. After considering the objectives of the business and the IT processing needs of the various user departments, they determine the goals of the system and the means of achieving them. Using system flowcharts and other tools, they outline the IT-based system.

Application Programming

Guided by the specifications provided by the systems analysts, the *application programmers* design flowcharts of the computer programs required by the system. They then code the required programs in computer language, generally making use of specialized programming languages, such as C++, and software tools, such as assemblers, compilers, and utility programs. They test the programs with *test data* composed of genuine or dummy records and transactions and perform the necessary debugging. Finally, the application programmers prepare the necessary application documentation, such as the computer operator instructions.

Database Administration

The database administrator has the responsibility for planning and administering the company's database. The primary objectives of this individual are to design the database and to control its use.

Data Entry

Personnel involved with this function prepare and verify input data for processing. Central data entry operators have largely been replaced with new technology. Today, data may be input via terminals or microcomputers in user departments, scanned directly from source documents or via EDI. Data changes for online, real-time systems are normally entered directly into the system by users through telecommunication links so that computer files can be updated immediately.

IT Operations

IT operators run and monitor central computers in accordance with standard instructions. On occasion, the IT operators may need to intervene through the console during a run in order to correct an indicated error. The IT's operating system should be programmed to maintain a detailed log of all operator intervention. The separation of IT operations from programming is an important one from the standpoint of achieving effective internal control. An employee performing both functions has more opportunity to make unauthorized changes in programs.

Program and File Library

The purpose of the file library is to protect computer programs, master files, transaction (detail) tapes, and other records from loss, damage, and unauthorized use or alteration. To ensure adequate control, the librarian maintains a formal checkout system for making files and programs available to authorized users.

In many systems, a portion of the library function is performed by the computers. The computer operators or the users enter special code numbers or passwords to gain access to programs and files stored within the system. The system automatically maintains a log showing when these programs and files are used and by whom.

Data Control

The data control group of an information systems department reviews and tests all input procedures, monitors processing, reviews exception reports, handles the reprocessing of exceptions detected by the system, and reviews and distributes all IT output. This group also reviews the log of operator interventions and the library log of program usage.

Telecommunications

Telecommunications specialists are responsible for maintaining and enhancing IT networks and network connections in a company. They monitor the network for indications of problems, including attempts to improperly access IT-based systems via the network.

Systems Programming

Systems programmers are responsible for troubleshooting the operating system or systems in use, upgrading it when new software releases are provided by the vendor, and working with application system programs when the applications interact with the operating system in a nonstandard or problematical way. Systems programmers are normally responsible for the proper functioning of the security features built into or added to operating systems.

Other Organizational Controls

Besides segregating functions, the information systems department should cross-train programmers, rotate operator assignments, require mandatory vacations, and obtain adequate fidelity bonds for information systems employees. At least two information systems employees should be present whenever the IT facility is in use. Careful screening policies in hiring information systems personnel are also important to achieve effective internal control.

Computer-Based Fraud

The history of computer-based fraud shows that the person responsible for frauds in many situations set up the system and controlled its modifications.

The number of personnel and the organizational structure will of course determine the extent to which segregation of duties is possible. At a minimum, the function of programming should be separated from the function of controlling data entry, and the function of the computer operator should be segregated from the functions having detailed knowledge or custody

Illustrative Case
Fraud by Programmers

A programmer for a large bank wrote a program for identifying and listing all overdrawn accounts. Later, he was able to insert a patch in the program to cause the computer to ignore overdrafts in his own account. The programmer was then able to overdraw his bank account at will, without the overdraft coming to management's attention. The fraud was not discovered until there were computer problems and the listing of overdrawn accounts had to be prepared manually.

of the programs. If one person is permitted to perform duties in several of these functions, internal control is weakened, and the opportunity exists for fraudulent data to be inserted in the system.

Whenever the responsibilities for recordkeeping and custody of the related assets are combined, the opportunities for an employee to conceal the abstraction of assets are increased. Since recordkeeping is an essential part of the information system's function, it is highly desirable to limit the access of information systems personnel to company assets. These employees can be considered to have direct access to cash if the information systems department prepares signed checks. They also have indirect access to assets if, for example, the computer is used to generate shipping orders authorizing the release of inventory.

This combination of recordkeeping with access to assets seriously weakens internal control unless adequate *compensating controls* are present. One type of compensating control is the use of predetermined *batch totals,* such as document counts and totals of significant data fields, prepared in departments independent of information systems. For example, if the information systems department performs the function of printing checks, another department should be responsible for authorizing the preparation of the checks. The authorizing department should maintain a record of the total number and dollar amount of checks authorized. These independently prepared batch totals should then be compared with the IT output before the checks are released.

Organizational controls are reasonably effective in preventing an individual employee from perpetrating a fraud, but they do not work as well at preventing fraud involving collusion. If key employees or company officers conspire in an effort to commit fraud, controls that rely upon separation of duties can be rendered inoperative.

Internal Auditing in an IT Environment

While the information systems department is primarily responsible for day-to-day maintenance of the controls for IT processing, the internal auditors are interested in evaluating the overall efficiency and effectiveness of information systems operations and the related controls throughout the company.

The internal auditors should participate in the design of the IT-based system to ensure that the system provides a proper audit trail and includes adequate controls. Once the system becomes operative, internal auditors review all aspects of the system on a test basis to determine whether prescribed controls are operating as planned. Among other things, the internal auditors perform tests to determine that no changes are made in the system without proper authorization, programming personnel are functionally separate from IT operating personnel, adequate documentation is maintained, control activities are functioning effectively, and the data control group is performing its assigned functions.

Control Activities in an IT System

Learning Objective 4

Information technology control activities often are classified as general control activities, application control activities, and user control activities. Whereas **general control activities** apply to a number of or to all IT applications, application control activities and user control activities relate to only a specific application, such as the preparation of payroll. **Application control activities** include both *programmed control activities,* which are written into the

Illustrative Case
Fraud at Equity Funding

Equity Funding Corporation of America went into bankruptcy after it was discovered that the company's financial statements had been grossly and fraudulently misleading for a period of years. A subsidiary of the company had been manufacturing bogus insurance policies on fictitious persons and then selling these policies to other insurance companies. When the fraud was discovered, Equity Funding's balance sheet included more than $120 million in fictitious assets, far exceeding the $75 million net income reported over the 13-year life of the company.

Perhaps the most startling revelation of the Equity Funding scandal was that numerous officers and employees of the company had worked together for years to perpetrate and conceal the fraud. The fictitious transactions had been carefully integrated into the company's computer-based

accounting system. A wide variety of fraudulent supporting documents had been prepared for the sole purpose of deceiving auditors and governmental regulatory agencies. Upon disclosure of the activities, several members of top management were convicted of criminal charges.

The Equity Funding scandal is often described as a computer-based fraud. It was not the use of computers, however, that enabled the company to deceive auditors and government investigators. Rather, the fraudulent activities were successfully concealed for a number of years because of the unprecedented willingness of a large number of company officers and employees to participate in the scheme. Collusion of the magnitude existing at Equity Funding renders internal control ineffective.

FIGURE 8.2
IT Control Activities

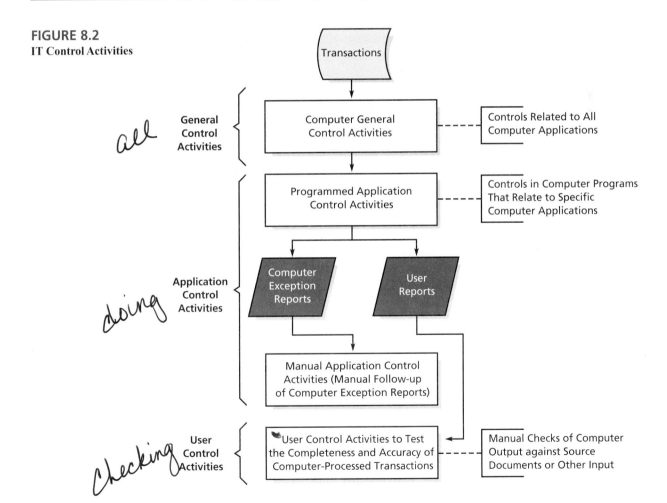

computer programs, and *manual follow-up activities* performed on the exception reports that are generated by the system. **User control activities** are those performed by users to test the accuracy and completeness of IT reports. Figure 8.2 illustrates the relationship among these three types of IT control activities.

General Control Activities

[handwritten margin note: General: developing changing access operations]

General control activities support many applications. General control activities include activities to control: (*a*) developing and customizing new programs and systems; (*b*) changing existing programs and systems; (*c*) access to programs and data; and (*d*) IT operations.

Developing and Customizing New Programs and Systems

These controls ensure that the systems and programs that are developed or customized by the information systems department meet users' needs, are free from errors, and include adequate controls and documentation. Examples include policies requiring user involvement in purchase and development processes and appropriate testing of systems and programs before they are implemented. By requiring the information systems department to obtain technical assistance from personnel in other departments, such as the internal auditors, assurance is provided that the hardware and system software being purchased or developed will include appropriate controls.

Another important consideration in developing or customizing new IT-based systems and applications is the preparation of adequate *system documentation.* The purpose of system documentation is to provide an overall description of the IT-based system in the form of system flowcharts and descriptions of the nature of input, operations, and output. It also establishes responsibilities for entering data, performing control tasks, and correcting and reprocessing erroneous data. Documentation describing each application program, as a minimum, should include:

1. A description of the purpose of the program.
2. Program approval and change sheets showing authorization for the initial program and subsequent changes.
3. Information on the organization of data used by the program.
4. A users' manual containing instructions for inputting data and applying user control activities.
5. **Program flowcharts** showing the major steps and logic of the computer program.
6. Program listing in source language.
7. A list and explanation of processing controls associated with the program.
8. Examples of computer output, including exception reports.
9. An **operations manual** containing instructions for running the program.
10. Information on testing and results, and test data used in testing and debugging the programs.

Changing Existing Programs and Systems

Frequently, changes in programs are suggested by users who have noted various difficulties associated with a processing system. These suggestions are generally documented in a **change request log,** which is used to initiate various program changes.

The process of changing programs and systems must be carefully controlled. There should be appropriate reviews of all changes, and the modified program should be thoroughly tested before it is implemented. In addition, all changes should be adequately documented, showing what was changed and why.

Access to Programs and Data

Every IT-based system should have adequate security controls to safeguard equipment, files, and programs against loss, damage, and access by unauthorized personnel. When programs or files can be accessed from microcomputers or online terminals, users should be required to enter a user identification (user ID) name and password in order to gain access to the system. These passwords should be changed periodically and the list of authorized user IDs should be updated frequently to reflect changes in personnel. The computer's operating system also should be programmed to maintain a log of all failed access attempts and should produce a warning if repeated attempts are made to gain access. The importance of these controls has been dramatically illustrated by several highly publicized incidents of "hackers" using home computers to gain entry to both military and commercial IT systems.

When data are transmitted over telecommunications facilities, *data transmission controls* should be established to prevent unauthorized access or changes to information when it is being transmitted. From the auditors' perspective, significant data transmission controls include:

1. *Parity check.* Data are processed and transmitted by the system in arrays of *bits.* In addition to the bits necessary to represent the numeric or alphabetic characters, redundant *parity* bits may be added that may be used to verify the integrity of the information as it is processed or transmitted.

2. *Data encryption.* Data are stored and transmitted in code to make it difficult for unauthorized individuals to read the information.

3. *Message acknowledgment techniques.* Techniques to help ensure that the receiving device receives a complete message. One common form of message acknowledgment technique is *echo check,* in which the receiving device sends a message that verifies a transmission back to the sending device.

4. *Private lines.* Data are transmitted over telephone lines that are owned or leased by the organization and, therefore, may be secured.

Access to programs and data within the information systems department should also be carefully controlled. Programmers should not have access to input data or application programs that are currently in use; computer operators should have access to only the application programs currently being used. Generally, only the database administrator should have access to all data files, especially the files of authorized users. Passwords should be encrypted so that only a user knows his or her password.

Physical controls are necessary to protect IT equipment against sabotage, fire, and water damage. The best way to prevent deliberate damage is to limit access to authorized personnel only. Visitors to a centralized information systems facility should be accompanied by authorized personnel. Information systems personnel should be carefully screened before being hired, and management should always be alert to the possibility of damage by a disgruntled employee. Frequently, the IT facility is kept in an inconspicuous location. The facility should have no windows and few doors; entrances should be controlled by guards or badge-activated locks. In addition, the computer room should have a fire-suppression system, air conditioning, and emergency power, and it should be above likely flood levels.

IT Operations Controls

To minimize the opportunity for unauthorized changes in programs, the computer operators should have access only to the *operations manual* that contains the instructions for processing programs, and not detailed program documentation. The operations manual should be sufficient to allow operators to solve routine operational problems and to train new operators.

Careful job scheduling and monitoring helps control the possibility of inappropriate program modification. The data control group should monitor the computer operator's activities by reviewing the operations log, which records a description of each run, the elapsed time for the run, operator console interventions, machine halts, and files used.

Magnetic tapes or disks can be damaged by exposure to magnetic fields or excessive heat. Also, it is possible that a program or a file will accidentally be erased while it is being processed by the system. As a precaution against such accidents, duplicate copies should be made of all files and programs, and databases should be transferred to backup disks or tapes at regular intervals. These backup copies should be stored at a separate location from the originals.

In a batch IT-based system, multiple generations of master files should be retained to enable reproduction of files lost or destroyed. Under this *grandfather-father-son* principle of file retention, the current updated master file is the *son,* the master file utilized in the updating run that produced the son is the *father,* and the previous father is the *grandfather.* Records of transactions for the current and the prior period also should be retained to facilitate updating the older master files in the event that the current master file is accidentally destroyed. If multiple generations are stored in separate locations, risk of losing all copies is minimized.

Application Control Activities

Application control activities apply to the processing of individual applications. They relate to the use of IT to initiate, record, process, and report transactions or other financial data. These controls begin with requirements for proper authorization of the transactions to be processed. When transaction data are originally recorded on **hard-copy** source documents, such as sales orders, authorization may be indicated by the appropriate person initialing the document. In online systems, transaction data may be entered directly into the system from the departments initiating the transactions. Authorization of transactions may be accomplished by assigning to authorized terminal users an identification name that must be entered before the system will accept any data. Also, the operating system should maintain a log of activity at each terminal to be reviewed by the system's control group for evidence of unauthorized use.

As indicated by Figure 8.2, application control activities may be classified as programmed control activities or manual follow-up activities.

Programmed Control Activities

Programmed control activities are those written into computer programs that help ensure the accuracy of IT input and processing. A major aspect of programmed control activities are *input validation (edit) checks* that are performed on the data being entered. Examples of these controls include:

1. *Limit test.* A test of the reasonableness of a field of data, using a predetermined upper and/or lower limit.
2. *Validity test.* A comparison of data (for example, employee, vendor, and other codes) against a master file or table for accuracy.
3. *Self-checking number.* A self-checking number contains redundant information, such as the last two digits being a mathematical combination of the others, permitting a check for accuracy.

Input validation checks increase the accuracy of input data by rejecting any data that fail to meet an edit check and by informing the user that revised information is needed. The data can also be tested for completeness. For example, the program can determine whether all required fields in an on-screen form are completed.

Input controls in batch IT systems are used to determine that no data are lost or added to the batch. The sequence of serial numbers or source documents composing each batch should be accounted for. In addition, the following controls help ensure the accuracy and completeness of batch processing:

1. *Item (or record) count.* A count of the number of items or transactions being input in a given batch.
2. *Control total.* A control total is the total of one field of information for all items in a batch. An example would be total sales for a batch of sales orders.
3. *Hash total.* A hash total is a total of one field of information for all items in a batch, used in the same manner as a control total. The difference between a hash total and a control total is that a hash total has no intrinsic meaning. An example of a hash total would be the sum of the employee Social Security numbers being input for payroll processing.

Comparison of totals may be performed either by the hardware or manually by the control group.

Processing controls are designed to ensure the reliability and accuracy of IT processing activities. A number of the input controls described above are programmed as processing controls, including limit tests, validity tests, self-checking numbers, item counts, and control and hash totals. In addition, *file labels,* such as **header labels,** may be used to ensure that the proper transaction file or master file is being used on a specific run. For magnetic tapes, *internal labels* that are machine-readable are used in conjunction with gummed-paper external labels to prevent operators from accidentally processing the wrong file.

Manual Follow-Up Activities

Most manual follow-up activities consist of review and analysis of outputs that have been generated in the form of *exception reports.* For example, a report might be produced that lists transactions where information was missing, was inconsistent with other information, or appeared to be invalid for some other reason.

The effectiveness of manual follow-up activities depends upon the effectiveness of the programmed control activities that produce the exception reports. Thus, if a program does not generate an exception for an improper transaction, no manual follow-up is likely since the transaction is not included on the exception report. In addition, problems will persist if user departments do not take actions to correct transactions listed on exception reports, or if they fail to analyze the underlying causes for the exceptions.

User Control Activities

User control activities are designed to test the completeness and accuracy of IT-processed transactions. These controls are generally designed to ensure the reliability of IT output (summary reports and transaction data). Reconciliation of control totals generated by the system to the totals developed at the input phase is an important aspect of user control activities. In some systems, user departments may appraise the reliability of output from the information systems department by extensive review and testing. For example, sales invoices generated by the IT-based system may be tested for clerical accuracy and pricing by an accounting clerk. Although these user control activities can be very effective, it is generally more efficient to implement effective application control activities and have users merely test the overall reasonableness of the output.

Control in Microcomputer Systems

Although technology is reducing the extent of the differences between microcomputers and large mainframe computers, microcomputers have a smaller capacity and are slower at processing data than mainframe computers. However, microcomputers have the advantage of giving office personnel and salespeople direct access to a computer system without the constraints of a centralized system. For that reason, even audit clients with sophisticated centralized computer systems are likely to use microcomputers for a variety of on-site recordkeeping functions.

In a microcomputer environment, computers are located in user departments and operated by user personnel who have little or no computer training. Processing usually is performed with commercial off-the-shelf packages. For secondary storage when the computer is operating, microcomputers use hard-disk drives where programs are stored. Magnetic tapes or high-volume compact disks are used as backup for the hard disk.

Internal control over microcomputers is enhanced when computer processing procedures are documented and users are well trained. To ensure that the client can reconstruct financial records, backup disks or tapes of files should be made frequently and stored away from the originals in a secure location. Since microcomputers are located in user departments, there is a greater risk of use by unauthorized personnel. Therefore, microcomputers should be programmed to require the user to enter an authorization code to gain access to application menus that control specific programs and files. In addition, management should consider installing hardware controls such as a locking on/off switch on the microcomputer to prevent unauthorized use of the machine after business hours, or keeping critical programs on removable hard drives that can be locked up when not in use. The auditors are concerned with these and other controls over microcomputers when the information processed by them may affect the reliability of the information in the client's financial statements.

A significant risk in the use of microcomputers is the possibility of software viruses. A **software virus** is a program that has the ability to attach itself to a legitimate program and modify other programs and systems. Viruses can cause loss of data and programs. Controls that help to prevent computer viruses include:

1. Obtain software only from reputable sources.
2. Prohibit the use of unauthorized programs.
3. Prohibit the downloading of programs from sources such as computer bulletin boards.
4. Use computer virus–detection software.

The Auditors' Consideration
of Internal Control in an IT Environment

Learning Objective 5

Regardless of how the client's financial statements are produced, the auditors must obtain a sufficient understanding of internal control to plan the audit. This understanding provides the auditors with a basis for assessing control risk, which affects the nature, timing, and extent of the work necessary to complete the audit. In discussing the auditors' consideration of internal control in an IT environment, we will describe how the auditors obtain an understanding of internal control, document this understanding, and assess control risk.

Obtaining an Understanding of IT-Based System Controls

Specialized skills may be needed to understand internal control or to design effective audit tests for clients with IT-based systems. Therefore, training and education about IT systems and controls are an important part of the professional development programs of many CPA firms. Some CPA firms have trained *IT specialists* who act as consultants to the firm's other auditors on audits that involve particularly complex IT systems. Other CPA firms rely on outside consultants to provide this assistance on complex engagements. In either case, the auditor in charge of the engagement should have sufficient IT-related knowledge to review the adequacy of the procedures performed by the specialist. The results of the specialist's procedures must be considered when planning the nature, timing, and extent of other audit procedures.

Documenting IT-Based System Controls

The auditors' documentation of the client's IT-based system varies depending on the complexity of the system. For a client with simple internal control a *written narrative* might be adequate. However, IT-based systems are usually documented by the use of systems flowcharts or specially designed internal control questionnaires.

Systems Flowcharts

As explained in Chapter 7, *systems flowcharts* are a commonly used technique for documenting internal control in audit working papers. An advantage of using systems flowcharts is that the information systems department should have them available as part of the standard documentation.

An illustration of a systems flowchart for sales, accounts receivable, and cash receipts appears in Figure 8.3. The following description of the illustrated procedures and IT systems should be helpful in studying the illustrated flowchart.

1. Orders are received from sales representatives, and sales invoices are printed. A computer file of sales transactions is generated as a by-product of order processing and sales invoice preparation. Two copies of the invoices are mailed to the customer, one copy is sent to the shipping department, and one copy is filed offline.
2. Individual cash remittances from customers are received from the mailroom and verified to a batch total, which is also received from the mailroom. These remittances are entered via terminals to a computer file of cash receipts transactions, with the total input being compared to the batch total. After comparison of batch totals, any necessary corrections are made to the transactions file.
3. The accounts receivable master file is updated by processing both the sales transactions file and the cash receipts transactions file. A by-product of the updating of the accounts receivable master file is an exception report for the run and a printout (on an online terminal) of any job messages.

The client's documentation of IT processing activities usually includes program flowcharts as well as systems flowcharts. Program flowcharts illustrate the detailed logic of specific computer programs. In some circumstances auditors may use program flowcharts to obtain an understanding of the program controls contained in specific IT applications. This, however, involves careful consideration of the detailed logic of the program, is extremely time-consuming, and generally exceeds the level of knowledge required to plan the audit.

FIGURE 8.3
Systems Flowchart

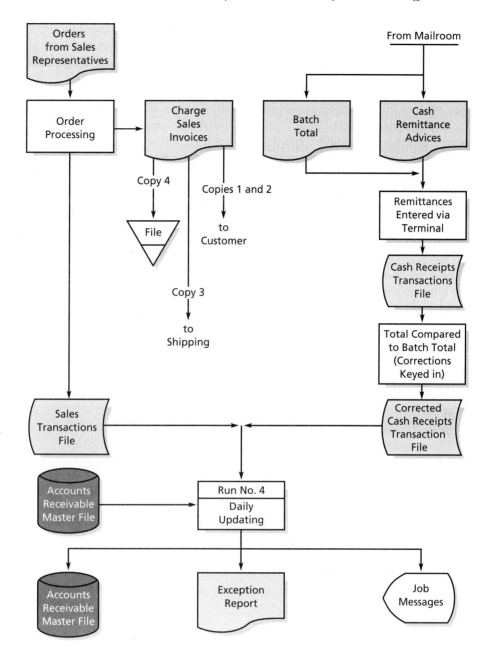

Internal Control Questionnaires for IT-Based Systems

As an alternative or supplement to systems flowcharts, the auditor may decide to document an IT-based system with specialized questionnaires. A specialized IT internal control questionnaire for the general control activities over access to the IT-based system is illustrated in Figure 8.4.

Assessing Control Risk—Testing IT-Based System Controls

Learning Objective 6

Assessing control risk involves evaluating the effectiveness of a client's automated and manual controls in preventing or detecting material misstatements in the financial statements. This process was described in detail in Chapter 7. In this section we focus on tests of controls pertaining to IT-based systems.

Determining the Approach to the Audit

After obtaining an understanding of the client's internal control, the auditors are in a position to determine an effective and efficient approach to the audit. When the client's IT-based system is relatively simple and produces hard-copy documents and records, the auditors may decide

FIGURE 8.4 **Internal Control Questionnaire**

Access to IT System Resources		KP 8/15/X1
	Yes, No, N/A	Comments
1. Does the company have documented policies and procedures for IT security?	No	*No written policies.*
2. Are there adequate physical controls to restrict access to the IT Facilities to authorized individuals?	Yes	*Card key access. Visitors are accompanied by authorized personnel.*
3. Are programmers restricted from access to application programs, job control language, and live data files?	Yes	*The operating system security program restricts access to other programs and data.*
4. Has a test library procedure been established so that programming is not performed using live data files and applicable programs?	Yes	*Test data files are used for testing programs.*
5. Are operators restricted from access to source programs?	Yes	*Source programs cannot be accessed by operators.*
6. Are utility programs that can alter data without any audit trail adequately controlled and their use logged for subsequent management reviews?	Yes	*Access to utility programs is restricted by the security program.*
7. Is there terminal access control software that restricts who can access the system, what programs can be used, and what files the user and/or program can access?	Yes	*Access restricted by use of passwords.*
8. Does terminal access control rely on passwords or other identification/validation process to control access to the system?	Yes	*Unattended terminals log off automatically after 10 minutes of inactivity.*
9. Are passwords controlled to ensure that they are confidential, unique, and updated to reflect needed changes on a timely basis?	Yes	*Policies restrict access to passwords.*
10. Are all significant events (security violations, use of critical software, or system commands, etc.) logged and promptly investigated by appropriate management personnel?	Yes	*Reviewed by security manager.*

Source: Adapted from the AICPA Audit Guide, *Consideration of Internal Control in a Financial Statement Audit* (New York, 1996).

that it is efficient to assess control risk at a high level and bypass the IT processing. Using this approach, the auditors will test transactions manually. If the results of these tests are satisfactory, the auditors will assume that the client's system is processing data properly. This technique is called *auditing around the computer* because the auditors bypass the computer rather than performing tests of the IT controls. While auditing around the computer can be an effective approach in certain circumstances, it is unacceptable if the reason for its use is merely the auditors' lack of understanding of the client's IT processing activities. The approach of auditing around the computer often relies upon substantive tests to reduce detection risk to an acceptable level. Such an approach is only appropriate when an auditor is satisfied that such substantive tests will be effective in reducing detection risk to an acceptable level. When a significant amount of information supporting the financial statements is in electronic form, an auditor may determine that it is not possible to design effective substantive tests that by themselves provide sufficient evidence that the financial statements are not materially misstated. Examples of such situations include the following:

- A client conducts business using information technology to initiate orders for goods using predetermined decision rules and pays for the related payables using system-generated information regarding the receipt of goods.

- A client provides electronic services to its customers (for example, an Internet service provider or a telephone company) and uses the computer to log services provided to users, initiate billing, process billing, and record such amounts.

In both of the above situations an auditor will normally decide that it is necessary to test controls, in addition to performing substantive tests.

Tests of Controls

The purpose of tests of controls is to provide reasonable assurance that the controls described in the audit working papers are actually operating as planned. Regardless of the nature of the client's system, auditors must conduct tests of those controls they intend to consider in their assessment of control risk. The nature of the IT-based system may, however, affect the specific procedures employed by the auditors in testing the controls.

Procedures to Test General Control Activities

The auditors will usually begin their consideration of IT control activities by testing general control activities. This is an efficient approach since the effectiveness of specific application control activities is dependent on the existence of effective general control activities over all IT activities. The auditors, for example, would get little audit evidence from testing programmed control activities in a payroll program in an environment where programmers can easily make unauthorized changes in any program. In the absence of controls over program modification, the auditors have no evidence that the program being tested is identical to the one used to process data during the year. Such weaknesses would limit the auditors' ability to rely on application control activities to reduce their assessment of control risk.

Tests of the effectiveness of controls for development of new programs and systems may include making inquiries of personnel, reviewing the minutes of meetings of users and the IT staff, and inspecting the documentation of the tests performed on the systems before they were implemented. The auditors may have discussions with users to determine that they understand the systems and to obtain their assessments of the operation of the system.

To test controls over program changes, the auditors may review the documentation of any changes made and compare them to the log of manager approvals. Manuals being used by users and operators may be inspected to determine that they are the most recent versions.

Controls over access to programs and data may be tested through inquiry of client personnel and observation of the segregation of duties and physical controls over equipment. The IT-generated log of access violations may be inspected for evidence of review and follow-up by control group personnel.

Operations controls may be tested through inquiry of computer operators about adherence to policies and follow-up on exceptions and other problems. The auditor may also review reports summarizing appropriate corrective actions taken on operations problems by computer operators, vendors, programmers, the database administrator, and users.

Procedures to Test Application Control Activities

Tests of application control activities vary significantly, depending upon the nature of the system and application. For example, in a batch system, input controls may be tested by accounting for the serial sequence of source documents in selected batches, reviewing and verifying reconciliations of batch control totals, and comparing control totals to IT output. In an online, real-time system, on the other hand, control totals are normally not used, and the auditors will design tests that ensure that only authorized data are accepted as input, and that input validation checks are applied to ensure the accuracy of the data.

A primary approach to assessing application control activities is to test the manual follow-up activities by inspecting the exception reports generated by the system and reviewing the way in which the exceptions were handled. Analysis of exception reports may be especially effective when commercial off-the-shelf software is being used, but only if the auditors are confident that the software has not been modified. The controls that were configured into the system upon installation may have been "turned off" if the client has ineffective general controls over changes to existing systems. In such circumstances the auditor may be familiar with the nature, strengths, and limitations of these software programs and have knowledge of the original control configuration. Thus, testing the operation of the system itself may be of lesser importance than in circumstances in which the client has developed its own software.

When the auditors are unsure of the software's operation, testing using computer-assisted audit techniques (CAAT) becomes especially helpful. These techniques include the use of *test data, integrated test facilities, controlled programs, program analysis techniques, tagging and tracing,* and *generalized audit software programs.* Computer-assisted audit techniques are used by both external and internal auditors.

Test Data

In the audit of a manual accounting system, the auditors trace sample transactions through the *records* from their inception to their final disposition. In the audit of an IT-based system, a comparable approach is the use of **test data.** The test data developed by the client's programmers may be used by the independent auditors once they have satisfied themselves by study of flowcharts and printouts that the tests are valid. As an alternative, the auditors may develop their own test data, but this approach is often too time-consuming to be practicable.

To test programmed control activities, the test data should include significant exceptions that would affect the auditors' assessment of control risk. Among these would be transactions with missing data, erroneous transactions, illogical transactions, out-of-balance batches, and out-of-sequence records. The auditors will carefully appraise the programmed control activities that relate to financial statement assertions for which they wish to assess control risk at a level below the maximum. Dummy transactions and records used in test data can be specially coded to avoid contamination of the client's genuine records and files. If the client's IT-based system includes an integrated test facility, the auditors may use this facility to prevent their test data from contaminating the client's files.

Integrated Test Facility

One method used by internal and external auditors to test and monitor controls in data processing applications is an **integrated test facility.** An integrated test facility is a subsystem of dummy records and files built into the regular IT-based system. These dummy files permit test data to be processed simultaneously with regular (live) input without adversely affecting the live data files or output. The test data, which include transactions and exceptions pertaining to controls to be tested, affect only the dummy files and dummy output. For this reason, an integrated test facility is often called the *minicompany approach* to testing the system. Integrated test facilities may be built into both batch and online, real-time IT systems.

The auditors monitor the processing of test data, studying the effects upon the dummy files, exception reports, and other output produced. An integrated test facility for payroll applications, for example, could be set up by including a fictitious department and records for fictitious employees in the payroll master file. Input data for the dummy department would be included with input data from actual departments. The auditors would monitor all output relating to the dummy department, including payroll records, exception reports, and payroll checks. In this situation, strict control would be necessary to prevent misuse of the dummy payroll checks.

A problem with integrated test facilities is the risk that someone may manipulate the real data files by transferring data to or from the dummy files. Controls should exist to prevent unauthorized access to the dummy files, and the auditors should monitor all activity in these files. Also, the test facility must be carefully designed to ensure that real files are not inadvertently contaminated with the fictitious test data.

Controlled Programs

As an alternative or supplement to the test data approach, the auditors may monitor the processing of current data by using a duplicate program that is held under their control. They then compare their output to that developed by the client's copy of the program. They may also reprocess historical data with their controlled program for comparison with the original output. Reprocessing historical data may alert the auditors to undocumented changes in the client's programs.

Controlled programs are advantageous because the auditor may test the client's program with both genuine (live) and test data. Through controlled programs, auditors may test programmed control activities without risk of contaminating the client's files. Also, the testing may be conducted at an independent IT facility without using the client's computer or information systems personnel.

Program Analysis Techniques

Program analysis techniques have been developed that can generate computer-made flowcharts of other programs. A trained auditor can examine the flowcharts to test the logic of application programs and to ensure that the client's program documentation describes the program that is actually being used.

Tagging and Tracing Transactions

This technique involves *tagging* transactions with an indicator when they are entered into the system. The computer provides the auditors with a printout of the details of the steps in processing tagged transactions. This printout is examined for evidence of unauthorized program steps. **Tagging and tracing** is possible only when the appropriate logic has been built into the IT-based system.

Generalized Audit Software

Many large CPA firms use **generalized audit software** (computer programs) that can be used to test the reliability of the client's programs as well as to perform many specific auditing functions. This audit software is suited for use on a wide variety of IT-based systems.

One application of computer audit software is to verify the reliability of the client's programs through a process termed *parallel simulation.* The generalized audit software may be set up to perform processing functions essentially equivalent to those of the client's programs. If the client's program is operating properly, the output of the client's processing of a group of transactions should be equivalent to the output from the generalized audit software package.

A significant value of generalized audit software lies in the fact that the auditors are able to conduct independent processing of live data. Often, the verification of the client's output would be too large a task to be undertaken manually, but it can be done efficiently using generalized audit software. Even when manual verification is possible, the use of generalized audit software allows the auditors to expand greatly the size of the sample of transactions to be tested. An extensive examination of the client's files may become a feasible and economic undertaking. It is not necessary, however, to duplicate all the client's IT processing. Testing should be performed only to the extent necessary to support the auditors' assessment of control risk.

Procedures to Test User Control Activities

Tests of user control activities will vary significantly with the nature of the control. However, the primary objective is to obtain assurance that users are, at a minimum, testing IT output for reasonableness. Therefore, typical tests involve inquiries of users about test procedures performed and inspection of any documentation that exists.

Substantive Testing with Computers

Learning Objective 7

To use the computer to test the records, the auditors must first find a way to access the records. In many situations this is not particularly difficult. As an example, if a client uses a microcomputer, the auditors may obtain a copy of the client's records that can be analyzed and processed on the auditors' microcomputer. In other situations, the auditors may decide to "download" the client's data using a computer link between the client's computer and the auditors' microcomputer. Finally, the auditors' generalized audit software may be run on the client's IT-based system to directly access the client's computer records.

Once the auditor has accessed the client's records, substantive tests of the records can be performed using generalized audit software. Audit software may be used to rearrange the data in a format more useful to the auditors, compare the data to other files, make computations, and select random samples. Applications of this nature include:

1. *Examining the client's records for overall quality, completeness, and valid conditions.* In auditing a manual system, the auditors become aware of the general quality, accuracy, and

validity of the client's records through visual observation. Since the auditors do not have the same physical contact with computer-based records, the audit software may be used to scan the client's files for various improprieties. For example, the accounts receivable file may be scanned for account balances in excess of credit limits, and the depreciation expense may be recomputed for each item in the plant assets file. The great speed of the computer often makes it possible to perform such calculations for each item in the population, rather than having to rely upon a sample-based test.

2. *Rearranging data and performing analyses.* The audit software may be used to rearrange the data in the client's files into a format more useful to the auditors. For example, the accounts receivable file may be reorganized into the format of an aged trial balance. Data from the client's files may be printed out in the format of the auditors' working papers. In addition, the audit software can make analytical computations, such as computing turnover ratios to identify slow-moving inventory.

3. *Selecting audit samples.* Audit samples may be selected from the client's files on a random basis or using any other criteria specified by the auditors. Examples include selection of the inventory items to be test counted and the accounts receivable to be confirmed. An additional time savings may result if the audit software is used to print out the actual confirmation requests.

4. *Comparing data on separate files.* When similar data are contained in two or more files, the audit software can compare the files and identify any discrepancies. For example, the changes in accounts receivable over a period of time may be compared to the details of the cash receipts and credit sales transactions files. Also, actual operating results may be compared to budgets or forecasts.

5. *Comparing the results of audit procedures with the client's records.* Data obtained by the auditors may be converted to machine-readable form and compared to the data in computer-based files. For example, the results of the auditors' inventory test counts can be compared to the perpetual inventory file.

Using Audit Software: An Illustration	To illustrate some of the possible uses of generalized audit software, let us consider a specific example. Assume that an auditor is planning to observe a client's physical count of inventories at a specific date. All inventory is stored either in the client's distribution center or at a public warehouse. The client maintains computer-based perpetual inventory records, which are updated daily. This inventory file contains the following information:

Part number.	Location.
Cost per unit.	Date of last sale.
Description of item.	Quantity on hand.
Date of last purchase.	Quantity sold during the year.

The client has provided the auditor with a computerized copy of the inventory file as of the date of the physical count.

The left-hand column in Figure 8.5 indicates typical inventory audit procedures the CPA might perform. The right-hand column indicates how generalized audit software might be helpful in performing these procedures.

Auditors do not need extensive technical IT knowledge in order to make use of generalized audit software. In fact, many CPA firms have found that they can train auditors to effectively use generalized audit software within a few days. Because of the simplified procedures that have been developed, auditors can, after limited training, use generalized audit software independently—that is, without assistance from the client's information systems personnel.

Computer Service Centers and Outsourced Computer Processing

Computer service centers provide processing services to customers who decide not to invest in their own computer facilities, generally because of their small size. *Outsourcing companies* run computer centers and provide a range of computer processing services to companies that

FIGURE 8.5

Illustration of the Uses of Generalized Audit Software

Source: AICPA, adapted from Uniform CPA Examination.

Basic Inventory Audit Procedure	How Generalized Audit Software Might Be Used
1. Observe the physical count, making appropriate test counts.	1. Determine which items are to be test counted by selecting from the inventory file a sample of items that provides the desired dollar coverage.
2. Test the mathematical accuracy of the inventory extensions and footings.	2. For each item in the inventory file, multiply the quantity on hand by the cost per unit and add the extended amounts.
3. Compare the auditors' test counts to the inventory records.	3. Organize the auditors' test counts and compare them to inventory records.
4. Compare the client's physical count data to the inventory records.	4. Compare the quantity of each item counted to the quantity on hand in the inventory file.
5. Perform a lower-of-cost-or-market test by obtaining a list of current costs per item from vendors.	5. Compare the current costs per unit to the cost per unit in the inventory file; print out the extended value for each item, using the lower of the two unit costs, and add extended amounts.
6. Test purchase and sales cutoff.	6. List a sample of items on the inventory file for which the date of last purchase or last sale is on, or immediately before, the date of the physical count.
7. Confirm the existence of items located in public warehouses.	7. List items located in public warehouses and print confirmations.
8. Analyze inventory for evidence of obsolescence or slow-moving items.	8. List items from the inventory file for which the turnover ratio (quantity sold divided by quantity on hand) is low or for which the date of last sale indicates a lack of recent transactions.

have decided to concentrate on core business operations. Often very large companies have outsourced much or all of their central computer processing. In addition, many companies are entering into arrangements with outsourcing companies to handle the electronic business that they conduct over the Internet. These situations create similar requirements for the auditors. For simplicity, the term *service organization* will be used to refer to both a computer service center and an outsourcing company.

The auditors must be concerned about controls at the service organization when the services provided are *part of the client's information system.* A service organization's services are part of the client's information system if they affect any of the following:

- How the client's transactions are initiated.
- The accounting records, supporting information, and specific accounts in the financial statements involved in the processing and reporting of the client's transactions.
- The accounting processes involved from the initiation of the transactions to their inclusion in the financial statements, including electronic means used to transmit, process, maintain, and access information.
- The financial reporting process used to prepare the client's financial statements, including significant estimates and disclosures.

When a service organization is part of the client's information system, the service organization's controls interact with the client's internal control. Accordingly, the auditors' understanding of internal control must be based, in part, on an understanding of processing activities at the service organization. A visit to the service organization may be necessary to obtain this understanding. In addition, if the auditors plan to reduce their assessed level of control risk based on certain controls, they must obtain evidence of their operating effectiveness regardless of whether those controls are applied by the client or by the service organization.

When there is a low degree of interaction between the client's controls and those at the service organization, the auditors may find that controls applied by the client are adequate to ensure that errors or fraud in transactions are detected. For example, the client's personnel may develop input control totals and compare them to the service organization's output. They may also reperform computer calculations on a test basis. When such controls are adequate, the auditors need test only client controls to reduce their assessment of control risk; there is no need to perform tests of controls at the service organization.

In other situations, there is a high degree of interaction and the controls performed at the service organization are necessary to achieve the client's control objectives. This means that the auditors' assessment of control risk cannot be significantly reduced without evidence that controls at the service organization are operating effectively. To obtain this evidence, the auditors may have to perform tests at the service organization.

Reports of Service Auditors

Most service organizations perform similar processing services for numerous clients. If the auditors of each client (called *user auditors*) were to visit the service organization for the purpose of reviewing controls, they would ask similar questions and perform similar tests of controls. It may be advantageous for the service organization to engage its own auditors (called *service auditors*) to study their internal control and issue a **service auditors' report.** The user auditors may then elect to rely on this report as an alternative to visiting the service organization themselves.

SAS 70 (AU 324), "Reports on the Processing of Transactions by Service Organizations," presents two types of reports that service auditors may provide: (1) reports on controls placed in operation, and (2) reports on controls placed in operation and tests of operating effectiveness. A report on controls placed in operation provides a detailed description of the service organization's internal control; it provides the user auditors with an understanding of the system, but it does not provide a basis for reliance on the operating effectiveness of control activities at the service organization.

To consider the service organization's controls in their assessments of control risk, the user auditors must have evidence that those controls are operating effectively. This evidence can be obtained only from tests performed directly by the user auditors, or a report on controls placed in operation and tests of operating effectiveness by the service auditors. If the service auditors' report provides an adequate basis for the user auditors' assessment of control risk, usually there is no need for the user auditors to perform their own tests at the organization. They may decide to rely solely on the results of the service auditors' tests. However, the user auditors should take steps to satisfy themselves as to the professional reputation of the service auditors.

Chapter Summary

This chapter describes the auditors' consideration of internal control in an IT environment. To summarize:

1. Auditors encounter IT-based recordkeeping in virtually every audit engagement. Even the smallest of audit clients can be expected to use a microcomputer at least to process its accounting records.

2. The use of an IT system by a client does not change the need to establish effective internal control; however, it does change the nature of the controls. More advanced IT features, such as online capabilities, database storage, IT networks, and end user computing, present special control risks. Therefore, specialized controls are needed, including passwords, validity tests, and computer logs.

3. The use of an IT may significantly affect the control system of the organization. From an organizational standpoint, it is essential to segregate the function of programming from the function of controlling input to the computer programs, and the function of the computer operator from those having detailed knowledge or custody of the computer programs.

4. IT controls are often classified as general control activities, application control activities, and user control activities. General control activities apply to all IT applications, and application control activities and user control activities relate only to a specific application. The auditors often consider general control activities first, because application and user control activities cannot be assumed to be effective if the general control activities are weak.

5. To test application control activities, the auditors will often use computer-assisted audit techniques, such as test data, integrated test facilities, controlled programs, program analysis techniques, and tagging and tracing transactions.

6. While generalized audit software also may be used to test application controls, it is more often used by the auditors to perform substantive tests of computerized records. Generalized audit software may be used to perform such functions as testing the clerical accuracy of records, making comparisons of related data, and selecting random samples.

Key Terms Introduced or Emphasized in Chapter 8

Application control activities   Controls relating to a specific IT task, such as preparation of payroll.

Application software   Software designed to perform a specific task, for example, preparation of the general ledger.

Batch processing   A system in which like transactions are processed periodically as a group.

C++   A programming language that is widely used because of its portability across various types of hardware.

Change request log   A log which consists of suggestions for changes in programs. These changes have often been initiated by users who have noted problems or possible enhancements for a program.

Client/server   (IT architecture) A network system in which several computers (clients) share the memory and other capabilities of a larger computer (the server), or that of printers, databases, and so on.

Controlled programs   Duplicate client application programs that are maintained under the auditors' control in order to test the programmed control activities.

Data warehouse   A subject-oriented, integrated collection of data used to support management decision-making processes.

Database administrator   The administrative function of maintaining and safeguarding databases.

Database system   A system that eliminates data redundancy and enforces data integrity by storing data separately from (outside) programs, and contains data for two or more IT applications.

Decision support systems   IT information systems that combine models and data in an attempt to solve nonstructured problems with extensive user involvement.

Direct (random) access   A storage technique in which each piece of data is assigned an address and may be retrieved without searching through other stored data. A magnetic disk drive is a direct access device.

Distributed data processing   An IT system that uses communication links to share data and programs among various users in remote locations throughout the organization. The users may process the data in their own departments.

Electronic commerce   Involves the electronic processing and transmission of data between customer and client. A variety of activities may be included, including electronic trading of goods and services, online delivery of digital products, and electronic funds transfer.

Electronic data interchange (EDI)   A system in which data are exchanged electronically between the computers of different companies. In an EDI system source documents are replaced with electronic transactions created in a standard format.

End user computing   An environment in which a user department is responsible for developing or purchasing, and running, an IT system (application) with minimal or no support from the central information systems department.

Expert system   A computerized information system that guides decision processes within a well-defined area and allows the making of decisions comparable to those of an expert.

Extranet   Private corporate IT networks that use Internet software to link employees and business partners.

Fiber optic transmission   Transmission using a glass or plastic filament cable used to communicate signals in the form of light waves.

File   An organized collection of related records, such as a customer file.

General control activities   Control activities applicable to all or many IT systems in an organization. General control activities include controls over the development of programs and systems, controls over changes to programs and systems, controls over IT operations, and controls over access to programs and data.

Generalized audit software   Computer programs used by auditors to locate and process data contained in a client's IT-based records. The programs perform such functions as rearranging the data in a format more useful to the auditors, comparing records, selecting samples, and making computations. This software is compatible with a wide variety of different IT systems.

Hard copy   IT output in printed form, such as printed listings, reports, and summaries.

Header label   A machine-readable record at the beginning of a file that identifies the file.

Integrated test facility   A set of dummy records and files included in an IT system enabling test data to be processed simultaneously with live input.

Internet   An international network of independently owned computers that operates as a giant computing network. Data on the Internet are stored on "Web servers," computers scattered throughout the world.

Intranet   Internal networks to a company that allow employees to use Internet capabilities, such as browsers, search engines, and e-mail.

JAVA   An object-oriented computer language that operates on many different platforms.

Local area network (LAN)   A communications network that interconnects computers within a limited area, typically a building or a small cluster of buildings.

Master file   A file of relatively permanent data or information that is updated periodically.

Microwave transmission   Transmission using electromagnetic waves of certain radio frequencies.

Networks (of computers)   A group of interconnected computers, allowing transfers of data between them.

Offline   Pertaining to peripheral devices or equipment not in direct communication with the central processing unit of the computer.

Off-the-shelf software   Commercially available software created for a variety of users in the same industry or with the same application.

Online   Pertaining to peripheral devices or equipment in direct communication with the central processing unit of the computer.

Online analytical processing (OLAP)   An information system that allows the user to query the system, conduct an analysis, etc., while the user is at a computer. The database for an OLAP system is often generated from the transactions-based database used for online transaction processing.

Online transaction processing (OLTP)   A processing method in which the IT system processes data immediately after it is captured and provides updated information to the user on a timely basis. OLTP examples include airlines reservation systems and banking systems.

Operating system   Software that coordinates and controls hardware components. For example, authorization procedures may be programmed into the operating system to restrict access to files and programs to authorized personnel only.

Operations manual   A manual that contains the instructions for processing a program. The manual should include sufficient information to allow operators to effectively operate programs, but should not include detailed program documentation.

Patch   A new section of coding added in a rough or expedient way to modify a program.

Program analysis techniques   Techniques for testing programmed control activities that involve the examination of computer-generated flowcharts of application programs.

Program flowchart   A graphic representation of the major steps and logic of a computer program.

Sequential access   A storage technique in which data are read and written in linear (i.e., account number) sequence. A magnetic tape drive is a sequential storage device.

Service auditors' report   A report issued by the auditor of a service organization to provide information about the internal control of the organization. User auditors make use of these reports in considering internal control over data processing performed for their clients by the service organization.

Software virus   A program that can attach itself to a legitimate program and modify other programs and systems. A virus may cause the loss of data or programs on a system.

System software   Programs that control and coordinate hardware components and provide other support to application software.

Tagging and tracing   A technique for testing programmed control activities in which selected transactions are tagged when they are entered for processing. A computer program provides a printout of the steps in processing the tagged transactions that may be reviewed by the auditors.

Telecommunications The electronic transmission of information by radio, wire, fiber optics, microwave, laser, and other electromagnetic systems.

Test data A set of dummy records and transactions developed to test the adequacy of a computer program or system.

User control activities Controls performed by users of IT information to test its accuracy and completeness.

Wide area network (WAN) A communications network that interconnects computers within a large geographical area.

Review Questions

8–1.   An IT system uses two types of software: system software and application software. Explain the difference between these two types of software.

8–2.   Distinguish between end user computing and a distributed data processing network.

8–3.   What is meant by a local area network?

8–4.   Distinguish between user control activities and manual application control activities.

8–5.   What are internal and external file labels? Why are they used?

8–6.   Distinguish general control activities from application control activities and give examples of the types of controls included in each of these broad categories.

8–7.   An information systems department usually performs numerous IT processing functions that would be separated in a manual system. Does this imply that separation of duties is not a practical means of achieving internal control in a computerized system? Explain.

8–8.   Explain briefly what is meant by an "online, real-time system."

8–9.   Explain the meaning of the term *documentation* as it pertains to computers and an information systems department. How might a client's documentation be used by the auditors?

8–10. The number of personnel in an information systems department may limit the extent to which segregation of duties is feasible. What is the minimum amount of segregation of duties that will permit satisfactory internal control?

8–11. Compare the responsibilities and objectives of the data control group in an information systems department to those of the internal auditors with respect to IT processing activities.

8–12. Define and give the purpose of each of the following controls:

   a. Record counts

   b. Limit test

   c. Validity test

   d. Hash totals

8–13. Differentiate between a system flowchart and a program flowchart.

8–14. Auditors should be familiar with the terminology employed in IT processing. The following statements contain some of the terminology so employed. Indicate whether each statement is true or false.

   a. A recent improvement in computer hardware is the ability to automatically produce error listings. Previously, this was possible only when provisions for such a report were included in the program.

   b. The control of input and output to and from the information systems department should be performed by an independent *data control group.*

   c. An internal-audit computer program that continuously monitors IT processing is a feasible approach for improving internal control in *OLRT systems.*

   d. An *internal label* is one of the controls built into magnetic tape drive hardware by the hardware manufacturers.

   e. A limit test in a computer program is comparable to a decision that an individual makes in a manual system to judge a transaction's reasonableness.

   f. A principal advantage of using magnetic tape files is that data need not be recorded *sequentially.*

   g. A major advantage of disk files is the ability to gain random access to data on the disk.

   h. The term *grandfather-father-son* refers to a method of protecting computer records rather than to generations in the evolution of computer hardware.

   i. When they are not in use, tape and disk files should be stored apart from the computer room under the control of a librarian.

8–15. List and define three types of *data transmission controls.*

8–16. Describe briefly the controls that should be established over the operation of a microcomputer to prevent use by unauthorized personnel.

8–17. What is meant by the term *telecommunications*?

8–18. Explain briefly what is meant by a *distributed data processing system.*

8–19. Explain briefly what is meant by *electronic data interchange* (EDI). How does EDI affect a company's audit trail?

8–20. Is it probable that the use of IT will eventually eliminate the audit trail, making it impossible to trace individual transactions from their origin to the summary totals in the financial statements? Explain.

8–21. Do auditors usually begin their consideration of internal control over IT activities with a review of general or application control activities? Explain.

8–22. Describe the audit technique known as *tagging and tracing.* What is the purpose of the technique?

8–23. What is a computer service center? Are the auditors of a client that uses a service center concerned about the controls applied at the organization? Explain.

Questions Requiring Analysis

8–24. A primary requirement of effective internal control is a satisfactory plan of organization. Explain the characteristics of a satisfactory plan of organization for an information systems department, including the relationship between the department and the rest of the organization.

8–25. Distinguish between batch processing and online, real-time (OLRT) processing. In which of these systems is strong internal control over input most easily attained? Explain.

8–26. Auditors encounter the use of microcomputers on almost every audit engagement.

　　a. How do microcomputers differ from large computers?

　　b. When are the auditors concerned with internal control over the use of microcomputers?

8–27. The use of test data is one method of performing tests of processing controls in an IT-based system. Identify and discuss several other methods by which auditors may test internal processing controls over IT activity.

8–28. Discuss how generalized audit software can be used to aid the auditors in examining accounts receivable in a fully IT-based system.

8–29. An integrated test facility (ITF) is a method used by both internal and external auditors for testing IT-based system controls. Discuss the advantages and disadvantages of implementing an ITF.

(CIA, adapted)

8–30. Many companies have part or all of their IT processing done by computer service centers.

　　a. What controls should the company maintain to ensure the accuracy of processing done by a service center?

　　b. How do auditors assess internal control over applications processed for an audit client by a service center?

　　c. What is a service auditors' report on the processing of transactions by a service organization?

　　d. What two types of reports are provided by service auditors?

　　e. How do user auditors use each type of report?

Multiple Choice Questions

8–31. Select the best answer for each of the following questions. Explain the reasons for your selection.

　　a. LAN is the abbreviation for:

　　　　(1) Large Area Network.

　　　　(2) Local Area Network.

　　　　(3) Longitudinal Analogue Network.

　　　　(4) Low Analytical Nets.

　　b. End-user computing is most likely to occur on which of the following types of computers?

　　　　(1) Mainframe.

　　　　(2) Minicomputers.

       (3) Personal computers.

       (4) Personal reference assistants.

  c. When erroneous data are detected by computer program controls, data may be excluded from processing and printed on an exception report. The exception report should probably be reviewed and followed up on by the:

       (1) Data control group.

       (2) System analyst.

       (3) Supervisor of IT operations.

       (4) Computer programmer.

  d. An accounts payable program posted a payable to a vendor not included in the online vendor master file. A control which would prevent this error is a:

       (1) Validity check.

       (2) Range check.

       (3) Limit test.

       (4) Control total.

  e. When an online, real-time (OLRT) IT processing system is in use, internal control can be strengthened by:

       (1) Providing for the separation of duties between data input and error handling operations.

       (2) Attaching plastic file protection rings to reels of magnetic tape before new data can be entered on the file.

       (3) Making a validity check of an identification number before a user can obtain access to the computer files.

       (4) Preparing batch totals to provide assurance that file updates are made for the entire input.

  f. The auditors would most likely be concerned with which of the following controls in a distributed data processing system?

       (1) Hardware controls.

       (2) Systems documentation controls.

       (3) Access controls.

       (4) Disaster recovery controls.

  g. The auditors would least likely use software to:

       (1) Access client data files.

       (2) Prepare spreadsheets.

       (3) Assess computer control risk.

       (4) Construct parallel simulations.

  h. Auditors often make use of computer programs that perform routine processing functions such as sorting and merging. These programs are made available by IT companies and others and are referred to as:

       (1) Compiler programs.

       (2) Utility programs.

       (3) User programs.

       (4) Supervisory programs.

  i. Which of the following is least likely to be considered by the auditors considering engagement of an information technology specialist on an audit?

       (1) Complexity of the client's systems and IT controls.

       (2) Number of financial institutions at which the client has accounts.

       (3) Client's use of emerging technologies.

       (4) Extent of entity's participation in electronic commerce.

  j. Which of the following is an advantage of generalized audit software packages?

       (1) They are all written in one identical computer language.

       (2) They can be used for audits of clients that use differing computing equipment and file formats.

        (3) They have reduced the need for the auditor to study input controls for computer-related procedures.

        (4) Their use can be substituted for a relatively large part of the required tests of controls.

    k. The increased presence of the microcomputer in the workplace has resulted in an increasing number of persons having access to the system. A control that is often used to prevent unauthorized access to sensitive programs is:

        (1) Backup copies of data, on diskettes.

        (2) User identification names and passwords.

        (3) Input validation checks.

        (4) Record counts of the number of input transactions in a batch being processed.

    l. An auditor will use the computer test data method in order to gain assurances with respect to the:

        (1) Security of data in a system.

        (2) IT system capacity.

        (3) Controls contained within a program.

        (4) Degree of data entry accuracy for batch input data.

(CIA, adapted)

Problems

8–32. The Ultimate Life Insurance Company has a database system that stores policy and payment information. The company is now planning to provide its branch offices with terminals that have online access to the central IT facility.

Required:

    a. Define a *database.*

    b. Give one fundamental advantage of a database.

    c. Describe three security measures to safeguard the database system from improper access through the terminals.

(CIA, adapted)

8–33. CPAs may audit around or through computers in the audit of the financial statements of clients who use IT to process accounting data.

Required:

    a. Describe the auditing approach referred to as "auditing around the computer."

    b. Under what conditions do CPAs decide to audit through the computer instead of around the computer?

    c. In auditing through the computer, CPAs may use test data.

        (1) What is test data?

        (2) Why do CPAs use test data?

    d. How can the CPAs be satisfied that the computer programs presented to them for testing are actually those used by the client for processing accounting data?

(AICPA, adapted)

8–34. Johnson, CPA, was engaged to audit the financial statements of Horizon Incorporated, which has its own IT installation. While obtaining an understanding of internal control, Johnson found that Horizon lacked proper segregation of the programming and operating functions. As a result, Johnson intensified the consideration of internal control surrounding the system and concluded that the existing compensating general control activities provided reasonable assurance that the objectives of internal control were being met.

Required:

    a. In a properly functioning IT environment, how is the separation of the programming and operating functions achieved?

    b. What are the compensating general control activities that Johnson most likely found?

(AICPA, adapted)

8–35. As you are planning the annual audit of Norton Corporation, you note that the company has a number of microcomputers in use in various locations. One of the machines has been installed in the stores department which has the responsibility for disbursing stock items and for maintaining stores records. In your audit, you find that an employee receives the requisitions for stores, disburses the stock, maintains the records, operates the computer, and authorizes adjustments to the total amounts of stock recorded by the computer.

When you discuss the applicable controls with the department manager, you are told that the microcomputer is assigned exclusively to that department. Therefore, the manager contends that it does not require the same types of controls applicable to large IT systems.

Required:

a. Comment on the manager's contention.

b. Discuss five types of control that would apply to this microcomputer application.

(CIA, adapted)

8-36. A CPA's client, The Outsider, Inc., is a medium-sized manufacturer of products for the leisure time activities market (camping equipment, scuba gear, bows and arrows, and so on). During the past year, an IT-based system was installed, and inventory records of finished goods and parts were converted to computer processing. Each record of the inventory master file contains the following information:

Item or part number.	Total value of inventory on hand at cost.
Description.	Date of last sale or usage.
Size.	Quantity sold or used this year.
Unit of measure code.	Economic order quantity.
Quantity on hand.	Code number of major vendor.
Cost per unit.	Code number of secondary vendor.

In preparation for year-end inventory, the client has created two sets of preprinted inventory count cards. One set is for the client's inventory counts and the other is for the CPA's use to make audit test counts. The following information has been printed on the cards:

Item or part number.
Description.
Size.
Unit of measure code.

The item or part number has been bar-coded on the cards. The client's cards have been printed in inventory location sequence, and the CPA's set of cards have been printed in item/part number sequence.

In taking the year-end inventory, the client's personnel will write the actual counted quantity on the face of each card in their set. When all counts are complete, the counted quantity will be keyed and the item or part number bar code will be read by a bar code scanner. The count data will then be stored as a separate file and processed against the inventory master file. The quantity-on-hand figures in the inventory master file will be adjusted to reflect the actual count. A computer listing will be prepared to show any missing inventory count cards and all quantity adjustments of more than $100 in value. These items will be investigated by client personnel, and all required adjustments will be made. When adjustments have been completed, the final year-end balances will be computed and posted to the general ledger.

The CPA has available generalized audit software that can read and process the data files involved. Also, the CPA has access to a bar code reading system.

Required:

a. In general and without regard to the facts above, discuss the nature of generalized audit software and list the various types of uses of such software.

b. List and describe at least five ways generalized audit software can be used to assist in the audit of inventory of The Outsider, Inc. (For example, the software can be used to read the inventory master file and list items of high unit cost or total value. Such items can be included in the CPA's test counts to increase the dollar coverage of the audit.)

(AICPA, adapted)

8-37. You are auditing for the first time the financial statements of Central Savings and Loan Association for the year ending December 31, 20X3. The CPA firm that audited the association's financial statements for the prior year issued an unqualified audit report.

The association uses an online, real-time IT-based system. Each teller in the association's main office and seven branch offices has an online terminal. Customers' mortgage payments and savings account deposits and withdrawals are recorded in the accounts by the computer from data input by the teller at the time of the transaction. The teller keys the proper account by account number and enters the information in the terminal to record the transaction. The IT facility is housed at the main office.

Required:

You would expect the association to have certain controls in effect because an online, real-time IT-based system is used. List the controls that should be in effect solely because this type of system is used, classifying them as:

a. Those controls pertaining to input of information.

b. All other types of IT controls.

8–38.   Lee Wong, CPA, is auditing the financial statements of the Alexandria Corporation, which has a batch-processing IT-based system for shipping and invoicing that it purchased from a software vendor. The following comments have been extracted from Wong's notes on IT operations and the processing and control of shipping notices and customer invoices.

Each type of computer run is assigned to a specific employee, who is responsible for making program changes, running the program, and answering questions. This procedure has the advantage of eliminating the need for records of IT operations because each employee is responsible for his or her own computer runs. At least one IT department employee remains in the computer room during office hours, and only IT department employees have keys to the computer room.

System documentation consists of those materials furnished by the software vendor—a set of record formats and program listings. These and the tape library are kept in a corner of the IT department.

The corporation considered the desirability of program controls, but decided to retain the manual controls in place prior to the conversion to software vendor's system.

Company products are shipped directly from public warehouses, which forward shipping notices to general accounting. There a billing clerk enters the price of the item and accounts for the numerical sequence of shipping notices from each warehouse. The billing clerk also prepares daily adding machine tapes (control tapes) of the units shipped and the unit prices.

Shipping notices and adding machine control tapes are forwarded to the IT department for inputting and processing. Extensions are made on the computer. Output consists of invoices (in six copies) and a daily sales register. The daily sales register shows the aggregate totals of units shipped and unit prices, which the computer operator compares to the control tapes.

All copies of the invoice are returned to the billing clerk. The clerk mails three copies to the customer, forwards one copy to the warehouse, maintains one copy in a numerical file, and retains one copy in an open invoice file that serves as a detailed accounts receivable record.

Required: Describe weaknesses in internal control over information and data flows and the procedures for processing shipping notices and customer invoices, and recommend improvements in these controls and processing procedures. Organize your answer sheets as follows:

Weakness	Recommended Improvement

(AICPA, adapted)

In-Class Team Case

8–39.   The accompanying flowchart summarizes Jenz Corporation's processing of sales. Some of the flowchart symbols are labeled to indicate controls and records. For each symbol numbered 1 through 13, select one response from either the list of operations and controls (A through O) or the list of documents, journals, ledgers, and files (P through Z).

Operations and Controls	Documents, Journals, Ledgers, and Files
A. Enter shipping data	P. Shipping document
B. Verify agreement of sales order and shipping document	Q. General ledger master file
C. Write-off accounts receivable	R. General journal
D. To warehouse and shipping department	S. Master price file
E. Authorize accounts receivable write-off	T. Sales journal
F. Prepare aged trial balance	U. Sales invoice
G. To sales department	V. Cash receipts journal
H. Release goods for shipment	W. Uncollectible accounts file
I. To accounts receivable department	X. Shipping file
J. Enter price data	Y. Aged trial balance
K. Determine that customer exists	Z. Open order file
L. Match customer purchase order with sales order	
M. Perform customer credit check	
N. Prepare sales journal	
O. Prepare sales invoice	

(AICPA, adapted)

Jenz Corporation

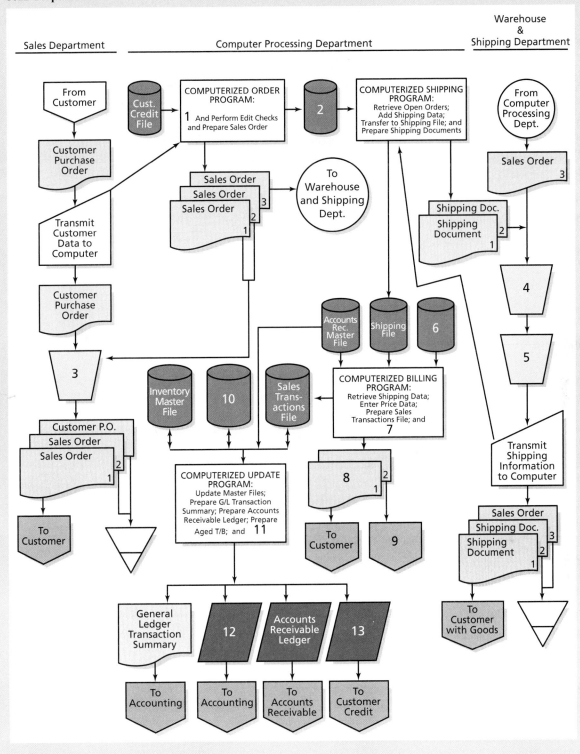

Chapter 9

Audit Sampling

Chapter learning objectives

After studying this chapter, you should be able to:

LO1. Distinguish between statistical and nonstatistical sampling.

LO2. Describe the methods of selecting a representative sample.

LO3. Understand the different types of sampling plans used in auditing.

LO4. Explain the effects of changes in various population characteristics and changes in sampling risk on required sample size.

LO5. Plan, perform, and evaluate samples for tests of controls, using statistical and nonstatistical methods.

LO6. Plan, perform, and evaluate samples for substantive tests, using mean-per-unit sampling.

LO7. Describe the difference and ratio methods of estimation.

LO8. Plan, perform, and evaluate samples for substantive tests using nonstatistical methods.

In Chapter 5 we discussed the need for sufficient, competent evidential matter as the basis for audit reports. As business entities have evolved in size, auditors increasingly have had to rely upon sampling procedures as the only practical means of obtaining this evidence. This reliance upon sampling procedures is one of the basic reasons that audit reports are regarded as expressions of opinion, rather than absolute certifications of the fairness of financial statements.

Audit sampling, whether statistical or nonstatistical, is the process of selecting a group of items (called the sample) from a large group of items (called the **population** or field) and using the characteristics of the sample to draw inferences about the characteristics of the entire population of items. The underlying assumption is that the sample will allow the auditors to make accurate inferences about the population. Basic to audit sampling is **sampling risk**— the risk that the auditors' conclusion based on a sample might be different from the conclusion they would reach if they examined every item in the entire population.

Sampling risk is *reduced* by increasing the size of the sample. At the extreme, when an entire population is examined there is no sampling risk. But auditing large samples or the entire population is costly. A key element in efficient sampling is to balance the sampling risk against the cost of using larger samples.

Auditors may also draw erroneous conclusions because of *nonsampling errors*—those due to factors not directly caused by sampling. For example, the auditors may fail to apply appropriate audit procedures, or they may fail to recognize errors in the documents or transactions that are examined. The risk pertaining to nonsampling errors is referred to as **nonsampling risk.** Nonsampling risk can generally be reduced to low levels through effective planning and supervision of audit engagements and implementation of appropriately designed quality control procedures by the CPA firm. The procedures discussed throughout this text help control nonsampling risk. In the remainder of this chapter we will emphasize sampling risk.

Comparison of Statistical and Nonstatistical Sampling

Learning Objective 1

A sample is said to be *nonstatistical* (or judgmental) when the auditors estimate sampling risk by using *professional judgment* rather than statistical techniques. This is not to say that nonstatistical samples are carelessly selected samples. Indeed, both nonstatistical and statistical audit samples should be selected in a way that they may be expected to allow the auditor to draw valid inferences about the population. In addition, the misstatements found in either a nonstatistical or a statistical sample should be used to estimate the total amount of misstatement in the population (called the **projected misstatement**). However, nonstatistical sampling provides no means of quantifying sampling risk. Thus, the auditors may find themselves taking larger and more costly samples than are necessary, or unknowingly accepting a higher than acceptable degree of sampling risk.

The use of *statistical sampling does not eliminate professional judgment* from the sampling process. It does, however, allow the auditors to measure and control sampling risk. Through *statistical sampling* techniques, the auditors may specify in advance the sampling risk that they want in their sample results and then compute a sample size that controls sampling risk at the desired level. Since statistical sampling techniques are based upon the laws of probability, the auditors are able to control the extent of the sampling risk in relying upon sample results. Thus, statistical sampling may assist auditors in (1) designing efficient samples, (2) measuring the sufficiency of the evidence obtained, and (3) objectively evaluating sample results. However, these advantages are not obtained without additional costs of training the audit staff, designing sampling plans, and selecting items for examination. For these reasons, nonstatistical samples are widely used by auditors, especially for tests of relatively small populations. Both statistical and nonstatistical sampling can provide auditors with sufficient competent evidential matter.[1]

---

[1] *SAS 39* (AU 350), "Audit Sampling," and the AICPA Auditing Practice Release, *Audit Sampling,* provide auditors with guidelines for planning, performing, and evaluating both statistical and nonstatistical samples.

Selecting a Random Sample

Learning Objective 2

A common mistake is to equate statistical sampling with random sampling. *Random sampling* is simply a method of selecting items for inclusion in a sample; it can be used in conjunction with either statistical or nonstatistical sampling. To emphasize this distinction, we will use the term **random selection** rather than "random sampling" to refer to the procedure of selecting the items for inclusion in a sample.

The principle involved in unrestricted random selection is that every item in the population has an *equal chance* of being selected for inclusion in the sample. Although random selection results in an unbiased sample, it is not necessarily a **representative sample.** Sampling risk still exists that purely by chance a sample will be selected that does not possess essentially the same characteristics as the population. However, since the *risk of a nonrepresentative* random sample stems from the laws of probability, this risk may be measured by statistical formulas.

The sample also may not be representative of the actual population because the population being sampled differs from the actual population. The auditors select an audit sample from a **physical representation of the population.** For example, a sample of accounts payable may be selected from a computer listing (the physical representation) of recorded accounts payable. Any conclusions based on this sample relate only to the population on the computer listing. The auditors' conclusions do not consider the possibility that certain creditors (with balances due) are completely omitted from the listing. Stated in terms of the financial statement assertions, existence is addressed to a greater extent than is completeness. Therefore, it is essential that the auditors consider whether the physical representation reflects the proper population.

The concept of a random sample requires that the person selecting the sample will *not influence or bias* the selection either consciously or unconsciously. Thus, some type of impartial selection process is necessary to obtain a truly random sample. Techniques often used for selecting random samples include *random number tables, random number generators,* and *systematic selection.*

Random Number Tables

One of the easiest methods of selecting items at random is the use of a *random number table.* A portion of a random number table is illustrated in Figure 9.1. The random numbers appearing in Figure 9.1 are arranged into columns of five digits. Except that the columnar arrangement permits the reader of the table to select numbers easily, the columns are *purely arbitrary* and otherwise meaningless. Each digit on the table is a random digit; the table does not merely represent a listing of random five-digit numbers.

In using a random number table, the first step is to establish correspondence between the digits in the table and the items in the population. This is most easily done when the items in the population are consecutively numbered. On occasion, however, auditors may find it necessary to renumber the population to obtain correspondence. For example, if transactions are numbered A–001, B–001, and so on, the auditors may assign numbers to replace the alphabetic characters. Next, the auditors must select a starting point and a systematic route to be used in reading the random number table. Any route is permissible, as long as it is followed consistently.

FIGURE 9.1
Table of Random Numbers

Row	Columns (1)	(2)	(3)	(4)	(5)
1	04734	39426	91035	54839	76873
2	10417	19688	83404	42038	48226
3	07514	48374	35658	38971	53779
4	52305	86925	16223	25946	90222
5	96357	11486	30102	82679	57983
6	92870	05921	65698	27993	86406
7	00500	75924	38803	05386	10072
8	34862	93784	52709	15370	96727
9	25809	21860	36790	76883	20435
10	77487	38419	20631	48694	12638

To illustrate the use of a random number table, assume that a client's accounts receivable are numbered from 1 to 5,000 and that the auditors want to select a random sample of 110 accounts for confirmation. Using the table in Figure 9.1, the auditors decide to start at the top of column 2 and to proceed from top to bottom. Reading only the first four digits of the numbers in column 2, the auditors would select 3942, 1968, and 4837 as three of the account numbers to be included in their sample. The next number, 8692, would be ignored, since there is no account with that number. The next numbers to be included in the sample would be 1148, 592, 2186, and so on.

In using a random number table, it is possible that the auditors will draw the same number more than once. If they ignore the number the second time it is selected and go on to the next number, they are *sampling without replacement.* This term means that an item once selected is not replaced in the population of eligible items, and consequently it cannot be drawn for inclusion in the sample a second time.

The alternative to sampling without replacement is sampling with replacement. *Sampling with replacement* means that once an item has been selected, it is immediately replaced into the population of eligible items and may be selected a second time. When applied to a random number table, the procedure is to include the number in the analysis as frequently as it occurs in the sample.

Statistical formulas can be used to compute sample size either with or without replacement. Most frequently auditors use sampling without replacement. This results in a *slightly smaller* required sample size and eliminates questions about the propriety of including items more than once in evaluating the sample results.

Random Number Generators

Even when items are assigned consecutive numbers, the selection of a large sample from a random number table may be a very time-consuming process. Computer programs called *random number generators* may be used to provide any length list of random numbers applicable to a given population. Random number generators may be programmed to select random numbers with specific characteristics, so that the list of random numbers provided to the auditors includes only numbers present in the population. A random number generator is a standard program in all generalized audit software and spreadsheet packages (e.g., ACL, IDEA, and Excel).

Systematic Selection

An approach that is less time-consuming than selecting a random number for each item to be included in the sample is **systematic selection.** This technique involves selecting *every nth item* in the population following one or more random starting points.

To illustrate systematic selection, assume that auditors wish to examine 200 paid checks from a population of 10,000 checks. If only one random starting point were used, the auditors would select every 50th check (10,000 ÷ 200) in the population. As a starting point, the auditors would select at random one of the first 50 checks. If the random starting point is check No. 37, check Nos. 37, 87 (37 + 50), and 137 (87 + 50) would be included in the sample, as well as every 50th check number after 137.

If the auditors had elected to use five random starting points, 40 checks (200 ÷ 5) would have to be selected from each random start. Thus, the auditors would select every 250th check number (10,000 ÷ 40) after each of the five random starting points between 1 and 250.

Selecting every *n*th item in the population may *not* result in a random sample when positions in the population are assigned in other than a random order. For example, if expensive inventory parts are always assigned an identification number ending in 9, systematic selection could result in a *highly biased sample* that would include too many expensive items or too many inexpensive items.

To prevent drawing a nonrandom or biased sample when systematic selection is used, the auditors should first attempt to determine whether the population is arranged in random order. If the population is not in random order, the auditors should use multiple random starting points for their systematic selection process.

The systematic selection technique has the advantage of enabling the auditors to obtain a sample from a population of unnumbered documents or transactions. If the documents to be examined are unnumbered, there is no necessity under this method to number them either physically or mentally, as required under the random number table selection technique. Rather, the auditors merely count off the sampling interval to select the documents or use a ruler to measure the interval. *Generalized audit software packages* include routines for systematic selection of audit samples from computer-based files.

Other Methods of Sample Selection

Two other selection techniques that are used by auditors include *haphazard selection* and *block selection.* Neither of these two methods applies probabilistic methods to selecting the items for the sample. For that reason, they should not generally be used in conjunction with statistical sampling plans.

Haphazard Selection

When haphazard sample selection is used, the auditors select the items from the population on an *arbitrary basis,* but without any conscious bias. For example, a haphazard sample of **vouchers** contained in a file drawer might be selected by pulling vouchers from the drawer without regard for the voucher's size, shape, or location in the drawer. If used, a haphazard sample should not consist of items selected in a careless manner; the sample should be expected to be representative of the population.

Block Selection

A block sample consists of all items in a selected time period, numerical sequence, or alphabetical sequence. For example, in testing internal control over cash disbursements, the auditors might decide to vouch all disbursements made during the months of April and December. In this case, the sampling unit is months rather than individual transactions. Thus, the sample consists of two blocks selected from a population of 12. Due to *the relatively large number of blocks needed to form a reasonable audit conclusion,* block sampling cannot generally be relied upon to efficiently produce a representative sample.

Stratification

Auditors often stratify a population before computing the required sample size and selecting the sample. **Stratification** is the technique of dividing a population into relatively homogeneous ~~alike~~ subgroups called *strata.* These strata then may be sampled separately; the sample results may be evaluated separately, or combined, to provide an estimate of the characteristics of the total population. Whenever items of extremely high or low values or other unusual characteristics are segregated in this manner, each stratum becomes more homogeneous. The effect is to *require a smaller number of sample items* to evaluate the several strata separately than to evaluate the total population without the use of stratification.

Besides increasing the efficiency of sampling procedures, stratification enables auditors to relate sample selection to the materiality or other characteristics of items and, possibly, to apply different audit procedures to each stratum. For example, in selecting accounts receivable for confirmation (discussed in detail in Chapter 11), auditors might stratify and test the population as follows:

Stratum	Composition of Stratum	Number of Accounts (Method of Selection Used)
1	Accounts of $10,000 and over	All accounts
2	Accounts of $5,000 to $9,999.99	50 accounts (random number generator)
3	Accounts of less than $5,000	30 accounts (random number generator)

When the auditors are using audit sampling for substantive testing, stratification is almost always applied. For example, the auditors generally will not accept sampling risk for any item that by itself could materially misstate the population. For that reason, the auditors will test every item with a book balance of more than the tolerable misstatement. They will then select samples from each of the other strata.

Types of Statistical Sampling Plans

Learning Objective 3

The sampling procedures used to accomplish specific audit objectives are called *sampling plans.* Statistical sampling plans may be used to estimate many different characteristics of a population, but every estimate is either of (1) *an occurrence rate* or (2) *a numerical quantity.* The sampling terms corresponding to occurrence rates and numerical quantities are *attributes* and *variables,* respectively. Specifically, the major types of statistical sampling plans used for audit sampling include the following:

1. *Attributes sampling.* This sampling plan enables the auditors to estimate the rate of occurrence of certain characteristics in the population (e.g., deviations from performance of a prescribed control). **Attributes sampling** frequently is used in performing tests of controls. For example, the auditor might use attributes sampling to estimate the percentage of the cash disbursements processed during the year that were not approved.

2. *Discovery sampling.* This form of attributes sampling is designed to locate at least one deviation (exception) in the population. **Discovery sampling** often is used in situations in which the auditors expect a very low rate of occurrence of some critical deviation. As an example, the auditors might use discovery sampling to attempt to locate a fraudulent cash disbursement.

3. *Classical variables sampling.* These sampling applications provide the auditors with an estimate of a numerical quantity, such as the dollar balance of an account. As would be expected, this technique is primarily used by auditors to perform substantive tests. For example, variables sampling might be used to plan, perform, and evaluate a sample of accounts receivable selected for confirmation. Frequently used variables sampling plans include **mean-per-unit estimation, ratio estimation,** and **difference estimation.**

4. *Probability-proportional-to-size sampling (PPS).* This technique, which is also referred to as *dollar-unit sampling,* applies attributes sampling theory to develop an estimate of the total dollar amount of misstatement in a population. **Probability-proportional-to-size sampling** is used as an alternative to classical variables sampling methods for performing substantive tests of transactions or balances. Unlike classical variables sampling techniques that define the sampling unit as each transaction or account balance in the population, PPS sampling defines the sampling unit as each individual dollar making up the book value of the population. A transaction or account is selected for audit if a dollar from that transaction or account is selected from the population. Therefore, each transaction or account has a probability proportional to its size of being selected for inclusion in the sample.

Sometimes one sampling plan may be used for the *dual purposes* of (1) testing a control and (2) substantiating the dollar amount of an account balance. For example, a **dual-purpose test** might be used to evaluate the effectiveness of a control over recording sales transactions and to estimate the total overstatement or understatement of the sales account.[2]

Allowance for Sampling Risk (Precision)

Learning Objective 4

Whether the auditors' objective is estimating attributes or variables, the sample results may lead to inaccurate inferences about the population. Some degree of **sampling error**—the difference between the actual rate or amount in the population and that indicated by the sample—is usually present. In utilizing statistical sampling techniques, auditors are able to measure and control the risk of material sampling error by deciding on the appropriate levels of sampling risk and the allowance for sampling risk.

The **allowance for sampling risk** is the amount used to create a range, set by + or − limits from the sample results, within which the true value of the population characteristic being measured is likely to lie. For example, assume a sample is taken to determine the occurrence rate of a certain type of deviation from the performance of a control. The sample indicates a deviation rate of 2.1 percent. We have little assurance that the deviation rate in the population is exactly 2.1 percent, but we know that the sample result probably approximates

---

[2] The size of a sample used for a dual purpose test should be the larger of the two samples that would have been required for the two separate purposes.

the population deviation rate. Therefore, using statistical sampling techniques, we may set an interval around the sample result within which we expect the population deviation rate to be. An allowance for sampling risk of ±1 percent would indicate that we expect the true population deviation rate to lie between 1.1 and 3.1 percent.

The wider the interval we allow, the more confident we may be that the true population characteristic is within it. In the preceding example, an allowance for sampling risk of ±2 percent would mean that we assume the population deviation rate to be between 0.1 percent and 4.1 percent. While being more confident that the true population characteristic falls within an interval is desirable, the increased size of the interval leads to a less precise conclusion.

The allowance for sampling risk may also be used to construct a dollar interval. For example, we may attempt to establish the total dollar value of receivables within an interval of ±$10,000. As is discussed later in this chapter, the allowance for sampling risk required by auditors usually is determined in light of the amount of a tolerable misstatement. **Tolerable misstatement** is an estimate of the maximum monetary misstatement that may exist in an account that, when combined with the misstatement in other accounts, will not cause the financial statements to be materially misstated.

Sample Size

The size of the sample has a significant effect upon both the allowance for sampling risk and sampling risk. With a very small sample, we cannot have low sampling risk unless we allow a very large allowance for sampling risk (**precision**). As the sample size increases, both sampling risk and the allowance for sampling risk decrease. In other words, the smaller the allowance for sampling risk or the sampling risk desired by the auditors, the larger the required sample.

Sample size is also affected by certain characteristics of the population being tested. As the population increases in size, the sample size necessary to estimate the population with specified sampling risk and allowance for sampling risk will increase; however, if the population size is above approximately 500, an increase in its size has only a very small effect on the required sample size. In attributes sampling, sample size also increases as the **expected population deviation rate** increases. Finally, in classical variables sampling, greater variability among the item values in the population (a larger standard deviation) increases the required sample size.

Audit Sampling for Tests of Controls

Learning Objective 5

Tests of controls are used to determine whether the client's internal control is operating in a way that would prevent or detect material misstatements in the financial statements. As discussed in Chapter 7, audit sampling cannot be used to test the operating effectiveness of all controls. In general, sampling can be used only when performance of the control leaves some *evidence of performance,* such as a completed document or the initials of the person performing the procedure. This evidence of performance allows the auditors to determine whether the control was applied to each item included in the sample. The results of tests of controls are most frequently presented in terms of the *rate of deviation* from performance of the prescribed control—also called the **deviation rate.**

A deviation from performance of a control does not necessarily indicate a misstatement of the financial statements. To illustrate the distinction between deviations and financial statement misstatements, assume that the auditors have selected a sample of 50 large cash disbursement vouchers to test for approval by the assistant controller. If the auditors find that 5 of the 50 vouchers were not properly approved, the deviation rate in the sample is 10 percent (5 deviations ÷ 50 vouchers), but the financial statements may not be misstated. All five vouchers may represent valid cash disbursements that were properly recorded. However, the auditors may conclude from the results of this test that there is a relatively high risk of invalid cash disbursements, because the sample results indicate that the assistant controller fails to approve about 10 percent of the vouchers processed. The auditors will use this evidence to increase the assessed level of control risk for the financial statement accounts that are affected by the cash disbursements cycle. Also, existence of the weakness will ordinarily be

FIGURE 9.2 Sampling Risk for Tests of Controls

The Test of Controls Sample Indicates:	Actual Extent of Operating Effectiveness of the Control Procedure Is:	
	Adequate for Planned Assessed Level of Control Risk	**Inadequate for Planned Assessed Level of Control Risk**
Extent of Operating Effectiveness Is Adequate	Correct decision	Incorrect decision (risk of assessing control risk too low)
Extent of Operating Effectiveness Is Inadequate	Incorrect decision (risk of assessing control risk too high)	Correct decision

communicated to management and, if appropriate, to the audit committee. The communication of control-related matters is discussed in Chapter 7.

Sampling Risk for Tests of Controls

When performing tests of controls, the auditors are concerned with two aspects of sampling risk:

1. *The risk of assessing control risk too high.* This risk is the possibility that the sample results will cause the auditors to assess control risk at a higher level than is warranted based on the actual operating effectiveness of the control.
2. *The risk of assessing control risk too low.* This more important risk is the possibility that the sample results will cause the auditors to assess control risk at a lower level than is warranted based on the actual operating effectiveness of the control. Figure 9.2 illustrates these two aspects of sampling risk for tests of controls.

The **risk of assessing control risk too high** relates to the *efficiency* of the audit process. When the sample results cause the auditors to assess control risk at a higher level than it actually is, the auditors will perform more substantive testing than is necessary in the circumstance. This unnecessary testing reduces the efficiency of the audit, but it does not lessen the *effectiveness* of the audit as a means of detecting material misstatements in the client's financial statements. For that reason, the auditors usually do not attempt to directly control the risk of assessing control risk too high.

The **risk of assessing control risk too low** is of utmost concern. If the auditors assess control risk to be lower than it actually is, they will inappropriately reduce the extent of their substantive tests. This unwarranted reduction in substantive testing lessens the overall effectiveness of the audit as a means of detecting material misstatements in the client's financial statements. Therefore, the auditors carefully control the risk of assessing control risk too low when performing tests of controls.

Attributes Sampling

As indicated previously, attributes sampling is widely used for tests of controls when auditors are estimating the rate of deviations from prescribed controls. For example, if an attributes sample indicates a deviation rate of 5 percent with an allowance for sampling risk of ±3 percent, the auditors could infer that between 2 and 8 percent of the items in the population contain deviations. In this example, 2 percent is the *lower deviation rate* (lower precision limit) and 8 percent is the *upper deviation rate* (upper precision limit) for the sample estimate. Tests of controls are designed to provide the auditors with assurance that deviation rates do not exceed acceptable levels. Therefore, the auditors are concerned only with the upper deviation rate for the sample estimate. The relevant question from the above example is whether the auditors can accept a deviation rate as high as 8 percent, not whether they can accept a deviation rate as low as 2 percent. The lower deviation rate is not pertinent to the objective of the test. For this reason, auditors generally use one-sided tests in attributes sampling; they consider only the upper deviation rate that will permit them to assess control risk at the planned level. In tests of controls the upper deviation rate is called the **tolerable deviation rate.**

Attributes sampling for tests of controls generally involves the following 10 steps:

1. Determine the objective of the test.
2. Define the attributes and deviation conditions.
3. Define the population to be sampled.
4. Specify the risk of assessing control risk too low and the tolerable deviation rate.
5. Estimate the expected population deviation rate.
6. Determine the sample size.
7. Select the sample.
8. Test the sample items.
9. Evaluate the sample results.
10. Document the sampling procedure.

Determine the Objective of the Test

The objective of tests of controls is to provide evidence about the design or operating effectiveness of internal control. The auditors perform tests of controls to support their planned assessed level of control risk. Accordingly, an attributes sample will be selected and tested to provide evidence that a particular internal control is operating adequately to support the auditors' planned assessed level of control risk.

Define the Attributes and "Deviation" Conditions

The auditors use professional judgment to define the attributes and deviation conditions for a particular test of controls. Attributes are characteristics that provide evidence that a control was actually performed. An example is the existence of the initials of the individual performing the control on the appropriate document. When a sample item does not have one or more of the attributes, it is classified as a deviation. As an example, assume that the auditors are performing a test of controls for the valuation of sales transactions. One of the controls that they decide to test is the review of sales invoices that is performed by an accounting clerk. The clerk's review includes: (1) comparing quantities on each invoice to shipping documents, (2) comparing prices on each invoice to authorized price lists, (3) testing the clerical accuracy of each invoice, and (4) initialing a copy of the invoice to indicate that the procedure was performed. In performing the test of this control, the auditors will classify a transaction as a deviation if any one or more of the following deviation conditions exists.

1. The quantities on the invoice do not agree with the shipping documents.
2. The prices on the invoice do not agree with authorized price lists.
3. The invoice has a clerical inaccuracy.
4. The invoice copy is not initialed by the accounting clerk.

It is important that the attributes and deviation conditions be precisely defined before the test of control is performed; otherwise, a staff accountant may not make the appropriate decision about which sample items represent deviations.

If a document selected for testing cannot be located, the auditors generally will not be able to apply alternate procedures to determine whether the control was applied. Simply selecting another item is not appropriate. In such circumstances, at a minimum, the misplaced document should be treated as a deviation for evaluation purposes and documented. Also, because the disappearance of documents is consistent with many possible explanations, ranging from unintentional misfiling to material fraud, the auditors should carefully consider the overall implications of the situation.

Define the Population

The auditors should determine that the population from which the sample is to be selected is appropriate for the specific audit objective. For example, if the auditors wish to test the operating effectiveness of a control designed to ensure that all shipments have been recorded as sales, they will not select a sample from the sales journal—that population is created by recorded sales and could not be expected to contain shipments that were not recorded. The appropriate population for detecting such deviations would be a population that contains all of the items shipped (e.g., the file of shipping documents).

Specify the Risk of Assessing Control Risk Too Low and the Tolerable Deviation Rate

How do auditors determine the appropriate risk of assessing control risk too low and the tolerable deviation rate for a test of a control? The answer, in short, is professional judgment. The risk of assessing control risk too low—that is, the risk that the actual deviation rate exceeds the tolerable deviation rate—is a critical risk in tests of controls. As discussed previously, this risk impacts the effectiveness of the audit. Since the results of tests of controls play a major role in determining the nature, timing, and extent of other audit procedures, auditors usually specify a low level of risk—5 or 10 percent is often used.[3]

Auditors specify the tolerable deviation rate based on (1) their planned assessed level of control risk, and (2) the degree of assurance desired from the evidential matter in the sample. The lower the planned assessed level of control risk (or more assurance desired from the sample), the lower the tolerable deviation rate.

The AICPA's *Auditing Practice Release* includes the following overlapping ranges to illustrate the relationship between the planned assessed level of control risk and the tolerable deviation rate:

Planned Assessed Level of Control Risk	Tolerable Deviation Rate
Low	2–7%
Moderate	6–12%
Slightly below the maximum	11–20%
Maximum	Omit test

Estimate the Expected Population Deviation Rate

In addition to the tolerable deviation rate and the risk of assessing control risk too low, the **expected population deviation rate** also affects the sample size in attributes sampling. This expected deviation rate is significant because it represents the rate that the auditors expect to discover in their sample from the population.

In estimating the expected population deviation rate, the auditors often use the sample results from prior years, as documented in their working papers. The auditors may also estimate the rate based on their experience with similar tests on other audit engagements or by examining a small pilot sample.

Determine the Sample Size

As indicated above, the three major factors that determine the sample size for a test of a control are the risk of assessing control risk too low, the tolerable deviation rate, and the expected population deviation rate. The population size also has an effect on sample size, but only when the population is very small. Figure 9.3 summarizes the effects of these factors on the required sample size for a test of controls.

Tables to Determine Sample Size

To enable auditors to use attributes sampling without resorting to complex mathematical formulas, tables such as the one in Figure 9.4 have been developed.

Figure 9.4 may be used to determine required sample sizes at 5 percent risk of assessing control risk too low. Similar tables are available for other levels or risk, such as 1 percent and 10 percent. The horizontal axis of the table is the tolerable deviation rate specified by the auditors. The vertical axis is the expected deviation rate estimated by the auditors to exist within the population. The numbers in the body of the table indicate the required sample sizes. The number in parentheses shown after the required sample size is the allowable number of deviations

---

[3] Some sources use the term *confidence level* to represent the complement of the risk of assessing control risk too low. Thus, a 95 percent confidence level is identical to a 5 percent risk of assessing control risk too low (100 percent − 5 percent).

FIGURE 9.3
Factors Affecting
Sample Size for Tests
of Controls

Factor	Change in Factor	Effect upon Required Sample Size
Auditors' Requirements:		
Risk of assessing control risk too low	Increase	Decrease
Tolerable deviation rate	Increase	Decrease
Population Characteristics:		
Population deviation rate (expected)	Increase	Increase
Population size	Increase	Increase (if population is small)

FIGURE 9.4 **Statistical Sample Sizes for Tests of Controls at 5 Percent Risk of Assessing Control Risk Too Low (with allowable number of deviations in parentheses)**

Expected Population Deviation Rate (as percentages)	Tolerable Deviation Rate										
	2%	3%	4%	5%	6%	7%	8%	9%	10%	15%	20%
0.00%	149(0)	99(0)	74(0)	59(0)	49(0)	42(0)	36(0)	32(0)	29(0)	19(0)	14(0)
0.25	236(1)	157(1)	117(1)	93(1)	78(1)	66(1)	58(1)	51(1)	46(1)	30(1)	22(1)
0.50	*	157(1)	117(1)	93(1)	78(1)	66(1)	58(1)	51(1)	46(1)	30(1)	22(1)
0.75	*	208(2)	117(1)	93(1)	78(1)	66(1)	58(1)	51(1)	46(1)	30(1)	22(1)
1.00	*	*	156(2)	93(1)	78(1)	66(1)	58(1)	51(1)	46(1)	30(1)	22(1)
1.25	*	*	156(2)	124(2)	78(1)	66(1)	58(1)	51(1)	46(1)	30(1)	22(1)
1.50	*	*	192(3)	124(2)	103(2)	66(1)	58(1)	51(1)	46(1)	30(1)	22(1)
1.75	*	*	227(4)	153(3)	103(2)	88(2)	77(2)	51(1)	46(1)	30(1)	22(1)
2.00	*	*	*	181(4)	127(3)	88(2)	77(2)	68(2)	46(1)	30(1)	22(1)
2.25	*	*	*	208(5)	127(3)	88(2)	77(2)	68(2)	61(2)	30(1)	22(1)
2.50	*	*	*	*	150(4)	109(3)	77(2)	68(2)	61(2)	30(1)	22(1)
2.75	*	*	*	*	173(5)	109(3)	95(3)	68(2)	61(2)	30(1)	22(1)
3.00	*	*	*	*	195(6)	129(4)	95(3)	84(3)	61(2)	30(1)	22(1)
3.25	*	*	*	*	*	148(5)	112(4)	84(3)	61(2)	30(1)	22(1)
3.50	*	*	*	*	*	167(6)	112(4)	84(3)	76(3)	40(2)	22(1)
3.75	*	*	*	*	*	185(7)	129(5)	100(4)	76(3)	40(2)	22(1)
4.00	*	*	*	*	*	*	146(6)	100(4)	89(4)	40(2)	22(1)
5.00	*	*	*	*	*	*	*	158(8)	116(6)	40(2)	30(2)
6.00	*	*	*	*	*	*	*	*	179(11)	50(3)	30(2)
7.00	*	*	*	*	*	*	*	*	*	68(5)	37(3)

Note: This table assumes a large population.
*Sample size is too large to be cost effective for most audit applications.
Source: AICPA, *Auditing Practice Release, Audit Sampling* (New York, 1999).

that may be observed in the sample for the results to support the auditors' planned assessed level of control risk.[4]

To use Figure 9.4, the auditors stipulate the expected deviation rate in the population and the tolerable deviation rate.[5] Then, the auditors read the sample size from the table at the intersection of the stipulated tolerable deviation rate and the expected population deviation rate. For example, assume the auditors expect the deviation rate in the population to be 1 percent

[4] The number of deviations allowable in a sample sometimes exceeds the expected deviation rate multiplied by the sample size. This is because the allowable number of deviations is always rounded to the nearest whole number as it is not possible to observe a partial deviation in a sample item. The sample sizes have been adjusted to reflect this rounding.

[5] Some tables require the auditors to specify population size. Figures 9.4 and 9.5 assume an infinite population. When populations are small, required sample sizes are only slightly smaller.

and specify a 9 percent tolerable deviation rate to justify their planned assessed level of control risk related to this control. Figure 9.4 shows that these specifications result in a sample size of 51 items, which must contain no more than 1 control deviation if the auditors' planned control risk assessment is to be supported by the test.

Select the Sample

When the auditors are using attributes sampling, it is essential that the sample items be selected in a manner so as to achieve a random sample. Random samples may be selected using random number tables, random number generators, or systematic sampling. When selecting the sample items, the auditors often select extra items to be substituted for any voided, unused, or inapplicable items. An inapplicable item is one that would not be expected to have a particular attribute. For example, assume the auditors are testing a sample of cash disbursement transactions to determine that they are all supported with receiving reports. If a rent payment is selected, the item would be inapplicable, because it would not be expected to be supported with a receiving report.

Test the Sample Items

When testing the sample items, an auditor examines each sample item for the attributes of interest. Each item will be classified as to whether it contains a deviation from the prescribed control. The auditor performing the test should also be alert for evidence of any unusual matters, such as evidence of fraud or related party transactions.

Evaluate the Sample Results

After testing the sample items and summarizing the deviations from a prescribed control, the auditors evaluate the sample results. In evaluating the results the auditors must consider not only the actual number of deviations observed, but also the nature of the deviations. The auditors' evaluation will include the following four steps:

1. *Determine the deviation rate.* Calculating the deviation rate in the sample involves dividing the number of observed deviations by the sample size.
2. *Determine the achieved upper deviation rate.* The auditors will use computer software or a table to determine the achieved upper deviation rate (also referred to as the achieved upper precision limit). This deviation rate represents the maximum population deviation rate that the auditors can expect based on the results of the sample.
3. *Consider the qualitative aspects of the deviations.* In addition to considering the deviation rate in the sample, the auditors will consider the nature of the deviations and any implications for other phases of the audit. Deviations that result from intentional acts (fraud) are of much more concern than those that are due to a misunderstanding of instructions or carelessness.
4. *Reach an overall conclusion.* The auditors will combine the sample evidence with the results of other relevant tests of controls to determine if the combined results support the auditors' planned assessed level of control risk. If not, the auditors will increase the assessed level of control risk, which will result in an increase in the extent of the planned substantive tests.

Tables to Evaluate Sample Results

The tables presented in this chapter may be used to evaluate sample results in two different, but related, ways. The first approach is to use Figure 9.4. When the number of deviations found in the sample does not exceed the allowable number of deviations (the parenthetical number in Figure 9.4), the auditors conclude that the population's deviation rate does not exceed the tolerable deviation rate. Therefore, the results support the auditors' planned assessed level of control risk. On the other hand, when the number of deviations found in the sample exceeds the allowable number of deviations, the auditors conclude that the population's deviation rate exceeds the tolerable deviation rate and therefore must generally increase their assessed level of control risk.

The second approach for evaluating sample results is to use Figure 9.5. This approach allows auditors to obtain a more precise conclusion; one which includes determining the achieved upper deviation rate. The achieved upper deviation rate is the maximum deviation

FIGURE 9.5 Statistical Sampling Results Evaluation Table for Tests of Controls: Achieved Upper Deviation Rate at 5 Percent Risk of Assessing Control Risk Too Low

Sample Size	Actual Number of Deviations Found										
	0	1	2	3	4	5	6	7	8	9	10
25	11.3	17.6	*	*	*	*	*	*	* *	*	*
30	9.5	14.9	19.6	*	*	*	*	*	*	*	*
35	8.3	12.9	17.0	*	*	*	*	*	*	*	*
40	7.3	11.4	15.0	18.3	*	*	*	*	*	*	*
45	6.5	10.2	13.4	16.4	19.2	*	*	*	*	*	*
50	5.9	9.2	12.1	14.8	17.4	19.9	*	*	*	*	*
55	5.4	8.4	11.1	13.5	15.9	18.2	*	*	*	*	*
60	4.9	7.7	10.2	12.5	14.7	16.8	18.8	*	*	*	*
65	4.6	7.1	9.4	11.5	13.6	15.5	17.4	19.3	*	*	*
70	4.2	6.6	8.8	10.8	12.6	14.5	16.3	18.0	19.7	*	*
75	4.0	6.2	8.2	10.1	11.8	13.6	15.2	16.9	18.5	20.0	*
80	3.7	5.8	7.7	9.5	11.1	12.7	14.3	15.9	17.4	18.9	*
90	3.3	5.2	6.9	8.4	9.9	11.4	12.8	14.2	15.5	16.8	18.2
100	3.0	4.7	6.2	7.6	9.0	10.3	11.5	12.8	14.0	15.2	16.4
125	2.4	3.8	5.0	6.1	7.2	8.3	9.3	10.3	11.3	12.3	13.2
150	2.0	3.2	4.2	5.1	6.0	6.9	7.8	8.6	9.5	10.3	11.1
200	1.5	2.4	3.2	3.9	4.6	5.2	5.9	6.5	7.2	7.8	8.4

Note: This table presents upper limits as percentages. This table assumes a large population.
*Over 20 percent.
Source: AICPA, *Auditing Practice Release, Audit Sampling* (New York, 1999).

rate that is supported by the sample results. When the achieved upper deviation rate is more than the tolerable deviation rate, the planned assessed level of control risk relating to the control is not supported.

To illustrate the second approach for evaluation of a sample, assume that two deviations are found in the sample of 51. As indicated previously, the auditors selected this sample with a specified risk of assessing control risk too low of 5 percent, a tolerable deviation rate of 9 percent, and an expected population deviation rate of 1 percent. A maximum of 1 deviation was allowable. Referring to Figure 9.5, we find that the exact sample size of 51 does not appear. When this happens, the auditors may interpolate; use more detailed tables, sometimes generated by a computer program; or use the largest sample size listed on the table that does not exceed the sample size actually selected. Using the latter approach, the auditors evaluate the results using a slightly smaller size of 50. Figure 9.5 indicates that when 2 deviations are found in a sample size of 50, the achieved upper deviation rate is 12.1 percent. This tells the auditors that, statistically, there is a 5 percent chance that the actual deviation rate is higher than 12.1 percent; but this exceeds the 9 percent tolerable deviation rate. The most likely effect of this sample result will be an increase in the assessed level of control risk, with a corresponding increase in the scope of substantive testing for the related financial statement assertions. Only when the upper deviation rate found in Figure 9.5 is less than or equal to the tolerable deviation rate would the sample results support the auditors' planned assessed level of control risk.

Document the Sampling Procedure

Finally, the auditors will document the significant aspects of the prior nine steps in the working papers. This documentation should include an identification of the items tested for tests of operating effectiveness that involve the inspection of documents.

Detailed Illustration of Attributes Sampling

The following procedures for applying attributes sampling are based upon the use of the tables in Figures 9.4 and 9.5; however, only slight modifications of the approach are necessary if other tables are used.

1. *Determine the objective of the test.* Assume that the auditors wish to test the effectiveness of the client's control of matching receiving reports with purchase invoices as a step in authorizing payments for purchases of materials. They are interested in the clerical accuracy of the matching process and in determining whether the control that requires the matching of purchase invoices and receiving reports is operating effectively.

2. *Define the attributes and deviation conditions.* The auditors define the deviation conditions as any one or more of the following with respect to each invoice and the related receiving report:

   a. Any invoice not supported by a receiving document.

   b. Any invoice supported by a receiving document that is applicable to another invoice.

   c. Any difference between the invoice and the receiving document as to quantities received.

   For this test, the only procedure required is inspection of the documents and matching of the receiving reports with invoices.

3. *Define the population to be sampled.* The client prepares a serially numbered voucher for every purchase of materials. The receiving report and purchase invoice are attached to each voucher. Therefore, the sampling unit for the test is an individual voucher. Since the test of controls is being performed during the interim period, the population to be tested consists of 3,653 vouchers for purchases of material during the first 10 months of the year under audit. If at any point the auditor determines that the physical representation of the population (the 3,653 vouchers) has omitted vouchers that should be included in the first 10 months, the auditors should also test those vouchers.

4. *Specify the risk of assessing control risk too low and the tolerable deviation rate.* The auditors realize that errors in matching receiving reports with purchase orders can affect the financial statements through overpayments to vendors and misstatements of purchases and accounts payable. They also plan to assess control risk at a low level for the assertions of existence, occurrence, and valuation of purchases, inventories, and accounts payable. Based on these considerations, the auditors decide upon a tolerable deviation rate of 7 percent, with a 5 percent risk of assessing control risk too low.

5. *Estimate the expected population deviation rate.* In the audits of the previous three years, the auditors observed that exceptions for the type described above produced deviation rates of 1.2 percent, 1.3 percent, and 1.1 percent. Therefore, the auditors conservatively select an expected deviation rate of 1.5 percent.

6. *Determine the sample size.* Since the stipulated risk of assessing control risk too low is 5 percent, Figure 9.4 is applicable. At the intersection of the column for a tolerable deviation rate of 7 percent and the row for a 1.5 percent expected deviation rate, the sample size is found to be 66 items. The allowable number of deviations in the sample is 1.

7. *Select the sample.* Since the vouchers are serially numbered, the auditors decide to use a generalized audit software program to generate a list of random numbers to select the sample for testing.

8. *Test the sample items.* The auditors proceed to examine the vouchers and supporting documents for each of the types of deviations previously defined. As they perform the test, the auditors will be alert for any unusual matters, such as evidence of fraud.

9. *Evaluate the sample results.* In evaluating the sample results, the auditors consider not only the actual number of deviations observed, but also the nature of the deviations. We will discuss three possible sets of circumstances: (*a*) the actual number of deviations is equal to or less than the allowable number; (*b*) the actual number of deviations is more than the allowable number; and (*c*) one or more deviations observed contain evidence of a deliberate manipulation or circumvention of internal control.

   First, assume that no deviation is identified. Recall that the allowable number of deviations from Figure 9.4 is 1. Because the number of deviations (here, none) does not exceed the allowable number, the auditors may conclude that there is less than a 5 percent risk that the population deviation rate is greater than 7 percent, the tolerable rate. In this case, the sample results support the auditors' planned assessed level of control risk. Alternatively, using the second approach and referring to Figure 9.5, for a sample size of 65 (the highest number still less than the actual sample size), the auditors find that when zero deviations are observed the achieved upper deviation rate is 4.6 percent. This rate supports the auditors' planned assessed level of control risk.

Next, assume that the number of deviations observed in the sample is 3, and none of the observed deviations indicate deliberate manipulation or circumvention of internal control. Using the first approach for evaluating results presented earlier, because this exceeds the allowable 1 deviation, the auditors simply conclude that the achieved upper deviation rate is greater than 7 percent. Or, if they wish to use the second approach for evaluating results, they may use Figure 9.5 to find that the achieved upper deviation rate is 11.5 percent. In light of these results, the auditors should increase the assessed level of control risk in this area and increase the extent of their substantive testing procedures (i.e., decrease detection risk). As a preliminary step to any modification of their audit program, the auditors should investigate the cause of the unexpectedly high deviation rate.

Finally, assume that one or more of the deviations discovered by the auditors indicates a deliberate circumvention of controls indicative of possible fraud. In such a circumstance other auditing procedures become necessary. The auditors must evaluate the effect of the deviation on the financial statements and adopt auditing procedures that are specifically designed to detect the type of deviation observed. Indeed, the nature of the deviation may be more important than its rate of occurrence.

10. *Document the sampling procedures.* Finally, each of the nine prior steps, as well as the basis for overall conclusions, should be documented in the auditors' working papers. Figure 9.6 is an illustrative working paper that documents the results of this test of controls, as well as tests of other controls for the purchasing cycle.

Other Statistical Attributes Sampling Approaches

Discovery Sampling

Discovery sampling is actually a modified case of attributes sampling. The purpose of a discovery sample is to detect at least one deviation, with a predetermined risk of assessing control risk too low, if the deviation rate in the population is greater than the specified tolerable deviation rate. One important use of discovery sampling is to locate examples of a suspected fraud.

Although discovery sampling is designed to locate relatively rare items, it cannot locate a needle in a haystack. If an extremely small number of deviations exist within a population (e.g., 0.1 percent or less), no sample of reasonable size can provide adequate assurance that an example of the deviation will be encountered. Still, discovery sampling can (with a very high degree of confidence) ensure detection of deviations occurring at a rate as low as 0.3 to 1 percent.

Discovery sampling is used primarily to search for critical deviations. When a deviation is critical, such as evidence of fraud, any deviation rate may be intolerable. Consequently, if such deviation is discovered, the auditors may abandon their sampling procedures and undertake a thorough examination of the population. If no deviations are found in discovery sampling, the auditors may conclude (with the specified risk of assessing control risk too low) that the critical deviation does not occur to the extent of the tolerable deviation rate.

To use discovery sampling, the auditors must specify their desired risk of assessing control risk too low and the tolerable deviation rate for the test. The required sample size then may be determined by referring to an appropriate attributes sampling table, with the assumption that the expected deviation rate in the population is 0 percent.

To illustrate discovery sampling, assume that auditors have reason to suspect that someone has been preparing fraudulent purchase orders, receiving reports, and purchase invoices in order to generate cash disbursements for fictitious purchase transactions. In order to determine whether this has occurred, it is necessary to locate only one set of the fraudulent documents in the client's file of paid vouchers.

Assume the auditors desire a 5 percent risk that their sample will not bring to light a fraudulent voucher if the population contains 2 percent or more fraudulent items. Referring to Figure 9.4, the auditors find that a sample size of 149 is required for an expected population deviation rate of 0 percent and a tolerable deviation rate of 2 percent. Assuming that the

FIGURE 9.6 Documentation of the Results of Tests of Controls

Scantech, Inc.					R-22
Attributes Sampling Summary—Purchase Transactions					WEB
December 31, 20X2					11/23/X2

Objectives of test:	(1) To test the operating effectiveness of the procedures for matching receiving reports with purchase invoices; (2) To test the operating effectiveness of the procedures for matching purchase orders with purchase invoices; (3) To test the operating effectiveness of the procedures for testing the clerical accuracy of purchase invoices.

Population: Voucher register entries for the first 10 months of the year.	**Size:** 3,653

Sampling unit: Individual vouchers.

Random selection procedure: Random number generator.

Risk of assessing control risk too low: 5 percent.

Attributes Tested:	Planning Parameters:			Sample Results:	
	Tolerable Deviation Rate	Expected Deviation Rate	Sample Size	Number of Deviations	Achieved Maximum Rate
1. Quantity and other data on receiving report agree with purchase invoice.	7%	1.5%	66	1	7.1%
2. Prices and other data on purchase order agree with purchase invoice.	10%	1%	46	0	6.5%
3. Clerical accuracy of purchase invoice has been verified.	7%	0%	42	0	7.3%

Conclusion:	The results support the assessment of a low level of control risk for existence and valuation of purchases, inventory, and accounts payable.

auditors select and examine the 149 vouchers and no fraudulent vouchers are found, they may conclude that there is only a 5 percent risk that there are more than 2 percent fraudulent vouchers in the population.

Sequential (Stop-or-Go) Sampling

Another approach used in practice is **sequential (stop-or-go) sampling.** Under a sequential sampling plan, the audit sample is taken in several stages. The auditors start by examining a small sample. Then, based on the results of this initial sample, they decide whether to (1) assess control risk at the planned level, (2) assess control risk at a higher level than planned, or (3) examine additional sample items to get more information. If the sample results do not provide enough information to make a clear-cut decision about internal control, the auditors examine additional items and repeat the decision process until the tables being used indicate that a decision as to the assessed level of control risk can be made.

The primary advantage of a sequential approach is that for very low population deviation rates smaller sample sizes may be required as compared to the fixed-sized sample plans. Disadvantages of sequential approaches include the fact that sample sizes may be larger for populations with moderate deviation rates and the process of drawing samples at several stages may not be as efficient.

Nonstatistical Attributes Sampling

The major differences between statistical and nonstatistical sampling in attributes sampling are the steps for determining sample size and evaluating sample results. As is the case with statistical sampling, auditors who use nonstatistical sampling need to consider the risk of assessing control risk too low and the tolerable deviation rate when determining the required sample size. But these factors need not be quantified. In evaluating results, the auditors should compare the deviation rate of the sample to the tolerable deviation rate. If the sample size was appropriate and the sample deviation rate is somewhat lower than the tolerable deviation rate, the auditors can generally conclude that the risk of assessing control risk too low is at an acceptable level. As the sample deviation rate gets closer to the tolerable deviation rate, it becomes less and less likely that the population's deviation rate is lower than the tolerable level. The auditors must use their professional judgment to determine the point at which the assessed level of control risk should be increased above the planned level.

Audit Sampling for Substantive Tests

Learning Objective 6

Substantive tests are designed to detect misstatements, both due to errors and fraud, that may exist in the financial statements. Accordingly, the sampling plans that are used for substantive tests are designed to estimate the dollar amount of misstatement in a particular account balance. Based on the sample results, the auditors then conclude whether there is an unacceptably high risk of material misstatement in the balance. The actual steps involved may be summarized as:

1. Determine the objective of the test.
2. Define the population and sampling unit.
3. Choose an audit sampling technique.
4. Determine the sample size.
5. Select the sample.
6. Test the sample items.
7. Evaluate the sample results.
8. Document the sampling procedure.

Statistical procedures that typically are used for substantive tests include classical variables and probability-proportional-to-size sampling plans. This chapter emphasizes classical variables plans, especially the mean-per-unit estimation method. Appendix 9A presents an overview of the probability-proportional-to-size method.

Sampling Risk for Substantive Tests

Similar to sampling risk for tests of controls, there are two aspects of sampling risk for substantive tests, including:

1. *The risk of incorrect rejection (alpha risk) of an account.* This is the possibility that sample results will indicate that an account balance is materially misstated when, in fact, it is not misstated.
2. *The risk of incorrect acceptance (beta risk) of an account.* This is the possibility that sample results will indicate that an account balance is not materially misstated when, in fact, it is materially misstated.

The nature of these risks parallels the sampling risks of tests of controls. If the auditors make the first type of error and incorrectly reject an account balance, their audit will lack efficiency since they will perform additional audit procedures that will eventually reveal that

FIGURE 9.7

Sampling Risk for Substantive Tests

	The Population Actually Is:	
The Substantive Test Sample Indicates:	**Not Materially Misstated**	**Material Misstated**
The Population Is Not Materially Misstated	Correct decision	Incorrect decision (risk of incorrect acceptance)
The Population Is Material Misstated	Incorrect decision (risk of incorrect rejection)	Correct decision

the account is not materially misstated. Thus, the risk of incorrect rejection does not relate to the effectiveness of the audit.[6]

If the auditors make the second type of error, incorrect acceptance, the effectiveness of the audit is compromised. Therefore, the risk of incorrect acceptance is of primary concern to auditors; failure to detect a material misstatement may lead to accusations of negligence and to extensive legal liability. Figure 9.7 illustrates both aspects of sampling risk for substantive tests.

Classical Variables Sampling

Classical **variables sampling** plans enable auditors to estimate a numerical quantity, such as the dollar amount of an account balance. This makes these techniques particularly useful for performing substantive tests. Classical variables sampling methods include *mean-per-unit estimation, ratio estimation,* and *difference estimation.*

Mean-per-Unit Estimation

Mean-per-unit estimation enables auditors to estimate the mean audited value of the items in a population, with specified sampling risk and allowance for sampling risk (precision), by determining the mean audited value of the items in a sample. An estimate of the total audited value of the population is obtained by multiplying the sample **mean** (the average audited value in the sample) times the number of items in the population. The *projected misstatement* (the most likely amount of misstatement in the population) may then be calculated as the difference between this estimated total audited value and the client's book value. The assumption underlying mean-per-unit estimation is that a sample's mean audited value will, for a certain sampling risk and allowance for sampling risk, represent the true audited mean of the population.

Controlling Sampling Risk

The risks of incorrect acceptance and incorrect rejection may be controlled independently of one another. For example, auditors may design a sample that limits both risks to 10 percent, or they may hold the **risk of incorrect acceptance** to 5 percent while allowing the **risk of incorrect rejection** to rise to 40 percent or more. In establishing the planned level of the risk of incorrect acceptance, auditors must consider the extent of the evidence that must be obtained from the substantive test. This is determined by the auditors' assessments of inherent risk and control risk for the assertions being tested, and the extent of the evidence obtained from any other substantive tests of those assertions. Appendix 9B of this chapter describes the process in greater detail.

The risk of incorrect rejection also must be established. In stipulating this risk the auditors should consider the time and other costs involved in performing additional audit procedures when the sample results erroneously indicate that a correct book balance is materially misstated.

In mean-per-unit estimation, as was the case with attributes sampling, the allowance for sampling risk is used to control sampling risk. The appropriate planned allowance for sampling

---

[6] Audit effectiveness will be affected only if incorrect rejection leads to client recording of an improper journal entry to adjust the account to the misstated amount suggested by the auditors' substantive tests.

FIGURE 9.8
Risk Coefficients

Acceptable Level of Risk	Incorrect Acceptance Coefficient	Incorrect Rejection Coefficient
1.0%	2.33	2.58
4.6	1.68	2.00
5.0	1.64	1.96
10.0	1.28	1.64
15.0	1.04	1.44
20.0	0.84	1.28
25.0	0.67	1.15
30.0	0.52	1.04
40.0	0.25	0.84
50.0	0.00	0.67

risk may be determined from the following formula.

$$\text{Planned allowance for sampling risk} = \frac{\text{Tolerable misstatement}}{1 + \dfrac{\text{Incorrect acceptance coefficient}}{\text{Incorrect rejection coefficient}}}$$

The *tolerable misstatement* is the maximum monetary misstatement that may exist in the account without causing the financial statements to be materially misstated. Risk coefficients from a table such as Figure 9.8, not the risks themselves, are inserted into the formula. Notice that the risks and coefficients vary inversely—that is, a *decreased* risk is consistent with an *increased* coefficient.

Determination of Sample Size

The factors directly included in the sample size formula for mean-per-unit estimation are (1) the population size, (2) the planned risk of incorrect rejection, (3) the estimated variability (**standard deviation**) among item values in the population, and (4) the planned allowance for sampling risk. The relationship of these factors to the required sample size is expressed by the following formula:[7]

$$\text{Sample size} = \left(\frac{\text{Population size} \times \text{Incorrect rejection coefficient} \times \text{Estimated standard deviation}}{\text{Planned allowance for sampling risk}}\right)^2$$

We have already described how most of the factors in this formula are determined. The estimate of the population's standard deviation of audited values may obtain this estimate by calculating the standard deviation of the book values of the population, or by using the standard deviation of the audited values obtained in the previous year's audit. Alternatively, auditors may obtain an estimate of the standard deviation of the audited values by taking a pilot sample of approximately 50 items.[8] Generalized audit software packages include routines

---

[7] This formula is based upon an infinite population. The effect on sample size when the population is finite but of significant size is small. Symbolically, this formula may be stated as:

$$n = \left(\frac{N \times U_r \times SD}{A}\right)^2$$

where n = sample size, N = population size, U_r = incorrect rejection coefficient, SD = estimated standard deviation, and A = planned allowance for sampling risk.

[8] An estimate of the standard deviation may be made from a sample by taking the square root of the following quotient: the sum of the squares of the deviation of each sample item value from the sample mean, divided by one less than the number of items in the sample. Symbolically, the formula for estimating the standard deviation is:

$$\sqrt{\frac{\Sigma(x - \bar{X})^2}{n - 1}}$$

FIGURE 9.9   Factors Affecting Sample Size for Substantive Tests

Factor	Change in Factor	Effect on Required Sample Size
Auditors' Requirements:		
Risk of incorrect rejection	Increase	Decrease
Risk of incorrect acceptance	Increase	Decrease
Tolerable misstatement	Increase	Decrease
Population Characteristics:		
Population size	Increase	Increase (if population is small)
Standard deviation (if classical variables sampling is used)	Increase	Increase
Expected misstatement (if probability-proportional-to-size sampling is used)	Increase	Increase

designed to estimate the standard deviation of the book values of a population either from a pilot sample or from the population book values. Figure 9.9 summarizes the effect of the standard deviation as well as the other factors on the required sample size.

Evaluation of Sample Results

Recall that the auditors determined sample size based on the planned sampling risks and on an estimate of the standard deviation of the population. When the auditors' estimate of the population's standard deviation is exactly the same as that found in the sample, the planned allowance for sampling risk may be used for evaluation purposes. However, this is seldom the case. The auditors' estimate of the population standard deviation usually differs from that of the subsequent sample. When this occurs, the sample taken does not control both risks at their planned levels because the auditors have underestimated or overestimated the variability of the population in computing the required sample size. Although there are various ways of adjusting the allowance for sampling risk, one that maintains the risk of incorrect acceptance at its planned level is described below:

$$\text{Adjusted allowance for sampling risk} = \text{Tolerable misstatement} - \frac{(\text{Population size} \times \text{Incorrect acceptance coefficient} \times \text{Sample standard deviation})}{\sqrt{\text{Sample size}}}$$

Once the auditors calculate the adjusted allowance for sampling risk, the client's book value is accepted or rejected based on whether it falls within the interval constructed by the audited sample mean $\pm$ the adjusted allowance for sampling risk. If the book value falls within the interval, the sample results support the conclusion that the account balance is materially correct. On the other hand, if the client's book value does not fall within the interval, the sample results indicate that there is too great a risk that the account balance is materially misstated. In this situation, the auditors will either convince the client to adjust the book value to an acceptable amount or perform additional tests of the population to determine more definitively whether it is actually materially misstated.

Illustration of Mean-per-Unit Estimation

1. *Determine the objective of the test.* Assume that the auditors wish to test the existence and gross valuation of recorded accounts receivable of a small public utility client. They wish to test the book value of accounts receivable by confirming a sample of the accounts through direct correspondence with the customers.

2. *Define the population and sampling unit.* The client's records have 100,000 accounts recorded at a total book value of $6,250,000. The auditors believe that the customers will be able to confirm the total outstanding account balance. Therefore, the account balance is used as the sampling unit instead of the individual transactions making up the balance. Figure 9.10 summarizes the accounts.

FIGURE 9.10
Population of Accounts Receivable

ABC COMPANY		
Accounts Receivable		
December 31, 20X3		
Account Number	**Account Name**	**Book Value**
000,001	Aaron, William	$ 65.55
000,002	Adams, James	66.44
000,003	Adams, Susan	82.42
000,004	Ahohn, Jennifer	55.14
000,005	Ahrons, Kenneth	44.96
⋮	⋮	⋮
003,000	Carhon, Sandra	65.00
⋮	⋮	⋮
099,999	Zenit, Darlene	82.50
100,000	Zyen, Chem	99.20
Total book value		$6,250,000.00
Mean account value*		$62.50

*$6,250,000/100,000.

3. *Choose an audit sampling technique.* The auditors have decided to use the mean-per-unit technique.

4. *Determine the sample size.* To calculate the required sample size the auditors must determine (*a*) the tolerable misstatement for accounts receivable, (*b*) the planned levels of sampling risk (the risks of incorrect acceptance and rejection), (*c*) the estimate of the population standard deviation, and (*d*) the population size.

Based on their consideration of internal control, the auditors believe that all accounts are included in the 100,000 accounts in the client's subsidiary ledger (the physical representation of the population). In view of the materiality of the dollar amounts involved, the auditors assess the tolerable misstatement to be $364,000. Since internal control over existence and valuation of accounts receivable is very weak, the auditors assess control risk at the maximum level, that is, 100 percent. In addition, they assess inherent risk at 100 percent and plan to perform only very limited other substantive tests of these assertions. Therefore, the auditors decide on a 5 percent risk of incorrect acceptance. Based on a consideration of the costs of performing additional procedures when an account is improperly rejected, a 4.6 percent risk of incorrect rejection is planned by the auditors. From this information and by using risk coefficients obtained from Figure 9.8, the planned allowance for sampling risk may be calculated as follows:

$$\text{Planned allowance for sampling risk} = \frac{\text{Tolerable misstatement}}{1 + \dfrac{\text{Incorrect acceptance coefficient}}{\text{Incorrect rejection coefficient}}}$$

$$= \frac{\$364,000}{1 + \dfrac{1.64}{2.00}}$$

$$= \$200,000$$

To estimate the standard deviation of the population, the auditors use a generalized audit software program to calculate the standard deviation of the recorded book values of the individual customers' accounts. The result is $15.

Using the sample-size formula, the required sample size may now be computed as follows:

$$\text{Sample size} = \left(\frac{\text{Population size} \times \text{Incorrect rejection coefficient} \times \text{Estimated standard deviation}}{\text{Planned allowance for sampling risk}}\right)^2$$

$$= \left(\frac{100,000 \times 2.00 \times \$15}{\$200,000}\right)^2 = \left(\frac{\$3,000,000}{\$200,000}\right)^2$$

$$= 225 \text{ accounts}$$

5. *Select the sample.* The client's accounts receivable are from residential customers and do not vary greatly in size. For this reason, the auditors decide to use a random number table to select an unstratified random sample.

6. *Test the sample items.* The auditors send the confirmations and perform additional procedures as appropriate.

7. *Evaluate the sample results.* Confirmation of the 225 accounts, as summarized in Figure 9.11, results in a sample with a mean audited value of $61 per account. Figure 9.11 also indicates that the mean book value of the 225 accounts in the sample was $63. Notice that this $63 mean sample book value differs somewhat from the mean book value of the entire population, $62.50, in Figure 9.10. This difference of $0.50 per account is due to chance and is not directly used in the mean-per-unit analysis.

As a first case, assume that the confirmation results also indicate a standard deviation of the sample's audited values of $15. Since the sample's standard deviation equals that used in planning, the adjusted allowance for sampling risk equals the planned allowance of $200,000. In this case, the auditors' estimate of the total value of the population is $6,100,000, and the acceptance interval for the sample result is that amount plus or minus the allowance for sampling risk of $200,000, calculated as follows:

$$\text{Estimated total audited value} = \text{Mean audited value} \times \text{Number of accounts}$$
$$= \$61 \times 100,000 \text{ accounts} = \$6,100,000$$

$$\text{Acceptance interval} = \text{Estimated total audited value} \pm \text{Allowance for sampling risk}$$
$$= \$6,100,000 \pm \$200,000$$
$$= [\$5,900,000 \text{ to } \$6,300,000]$$

FIGURE 9.11

Auditors' Sample of Accounts Receivable

ABC COMPANY
Sample of Accounts Receivable
December 31, 20X3

Sample Item Number	Account Number	Account Name	Book Value	Audited Value	Difference
001	000,002	Adams, James	$ 66.44	$ 66.44	$ 0.00
002	000,005	Ahrons, Kenneth	44.96	43.00	1.96
003	001,100	Banner, Jane	92.16	92.16	0.00
004	002,200	Boynton, Willis	72.12	68.50	3.62
005	003,000	Carhon, Sandra	65.00	65.00	0.00
⋮	⋮	⋮	⋮	⋮	⋮
⋮	⋮	⋮	⋮	⋮	⋮
224	093,212	Yelbow, Sharlene	82.50	82.50	0.00
225	100,000	Zyen, Chem	99.20	92.00	7.20
Total value (sample)			$14,175.00	$13,725.00	$450.00
Mean values (total value/225)			$63.00	$61.00	$2.00

FIGURE 9.12
Acceptance Interval for Substantive Test

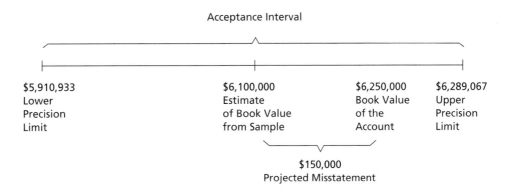

Because the client's book value of $6,250,000 falls within this acceptance interval, the sample results indicate that the client's valuation of accounts receivable is not materially misstated. However, the sample results indicate a *projected misstatement* of $150,000, calculated as follows:

$$\text{Projected misstatement} = \text{Estimated total audited value} - \text{Book value of population}$$
$$= \$6,100,000 - \$6,250,000$$
$$= \$150,000 \text{ overstatement}$$

This projected misstatement will be considered when the auditors are analyzing the total amount of potential misstatement in the financial statements. Also, the auditors may suggest that the client correct the accounts that their test revealed to be misstated, even though the misstatements are less than the tolerable misstatement amount.

How do the auditors evaluate the results if the sample's standard deviation differs from the estimate? They may use the formula discussed above to calculate an adjusted allowance for sampling risk. For example, if the standard deviation of the sample's audited values had instead been equal to $16, the adjusted allowance for sampling risk may be calculated as follows:

$$\begin{aligned}\text{Adjusted allowance for sampling risk} &= \text{Tolerable misstatement} - \frac{(\text{Population size} \times \text{Incorrect acceptance coefficient} \times \text{Sample standard deviation})}{\sqrt{\text{Sample size}}}\end{aligned}$$

$$= \$364,000 - \frac{(100,000 \times 1.64 \times \$16)}{\sqrt{225}}$$

$$= \$189,067$$

Thus, the acceptance interval would be constructed as $6,100,000 ± $189,067 ($5,910,933 to $6,289,067). As illustrated by Figure 9.12, the client's book value ($6,250,000) also falls within this interval. Therefore, the sample results still indicate that the account does not contain a material misstatement.

As in other types of sampling, the auditors should consider the qualitative aspects of any misstatements found in their sample. "What caused the misstatements?" "Do any of the misstatements indicate fraud?" and "What are the implications of the misstatements for other audit areas?" are questions the auditors would attempt to answer in their qualitative evaluation of the results.

8. *Document the sampling procedures.* Each of the prior seven steps, as well as the basis for overall conclusions, should be documented in the auditors' working papers. This documentation should include an identification of the items tested.

Difference and Ratio Estimation

Learning Objective 7

Mean-per-unit estimation uses the mean audited value of the sample as the basis for estimating the projected misstatement and total audited value of a population. Two other options are difference and ratio estimation. Although closely related, difference estimation and ratio estimation are two distinct sampling plans; each is appropriate under slightly different circumstances.

In applying **difference estimation,** the auditors use a sample to estimate the average difference between the audited value and book value of items in a population. The average difference is estimated by dividing the net misstatement in the sample by the number of items in the sample.[9] The projected misstatement is determined by multiplying the estimated average difference by the number of items in the population. This may be viewed as:

$$\text{Projected misstatement} = \left[\frac{\text{Sample net misstatement}}{\text{Sample items}}\right] \times \text{Population items}$$

The estimated total audited value is equal to the book value of the account plus or minus the projected misstatement, depending upon whether the misstatement is an understatement or an overstatement.

In **ratio estimation,** the auditors use a sample to estimate the ratio of the misstatement in a sample to its book value and project it to the entire population.[10] The ratio of misstatements is simply the sample net misstatement divided by the book value of the items in the sample. An estimate of the projected misstatement is obtained by multiplying this estimated ratio by the total population book value, as illustrated below:

$$\text{Projected misstatement} = \left[\frac{\text{Sample net misstatement}}{\text{Book value of sample}}\right] \times \text{Population book value}$$

Alternatively, identical results are obtained by using the average misstatement in the sample, divided by the average book value in the sample, and multiplying times the total population book value, as illustrated below:

$$\text{Projected misstatement} = \left[\frac{\text{Sample average misstatement}}{\text{Sample average book value}}\right] \times \text{Population book value}$$

The estimated total audited value equals the book value of the account plus or minus the projected misstatement, depending upon whether the misstatement is an understatement or an overstatement.

Use of Difference and Ratio Estimation

The use of difference or ratio estimation techniques requires that (1) each population item has a book value, (2) an audited value may be determined for each sample item, and (3) differences between audited and book values (misstatements) are relatively frequent. If the occurrence rate of misstatements is very low, a prohibitively large sample is required to disclose a representative number of misstatements. When these requirements are met, ratio estimation or difference estimation is often more efficient than mean-per-unit estimation.

Difference estimation is most appropriate when the size of misstatements does not vary significantly in comparison to book value. This might be the case when errors are occurring randomly, independently of account size.

---

[9] Symbolically, the estimated average difference is computed as follows:

$$\hat{d} = \frac{1}{n}\sum_{j=1}^{n}(a_j - b_j)$$

[10] Symbolically, this process is expressed:

$$\hat{R} = \frac{\sum(a_j - b_j)}{\sum b_j}$$

where $\hat{R}$ (pronounced R caret) represents the estimated ratio of misstatement to book value, a_j represents the audited value of each sample item, and b_j represents the book value of each sample item.

Ratio estimation is preferred when the size of misstatements is nearly proportional to the book values of the items. That is, it is appropriate when larger accounts have large misstatements and smaller accounts have small misstatements. For example, this might often be the case for receivables—small accounts might be expected to have small misstatements in dollar terms and large accounts to have large misstatements in dollar terms.

Illustration of Difference and Ratio Estimation

The information presented in Figures 9.10 and 9.11 may be used to illustrate the use of difference and ratio estimation techniques. Recall that the population consists of 100,000 accounts with an aggregate book value of $6,250,000; Figure 9.11 indicates that the total book and audited values of the sample are, respectively, $14,175 and $13,725. The auditors calculate the required sample size, randomly select the accounts to be sampled, and apply auditing procedures to determine the correct account balances. In actuality, differences in the sample size formulas[11] would cause the sample size to differ from that obtained using the mean-per-unit method, but in this illustration we will continue to assume a sample size of 225, as summarized in Figure 9.11.

Difference Estimation

If difference estimation is used, the auditors would estimate the average difference per item to be a $2 overstatement ($450 ÷ 225 items). Multiplying the $2 by the 100,000 accounts in the population indicates that the projected misstatement for accounts receivable is a $200,000 overstatement, as calculated below:

$$\text{Projected misstatement} = \left[\frac{\text{Sample net misstatement}}{\text{Sample items}} \right] \times \text{Population items}$$

$$= \frac{\$450}{225} \times 100,000$$

$$= \$2 \times 100,000$$

$$= \$200,000$$

The estimated total audited value of the account is calculated as follows:

$$\text{Estimated total audited value} = \text{Population book value} - \text{Projected overstatement}$$

$$= \$6,250,000 - 200,000$$

$$= \$6,050,000$$

Ratio Estimation

For ratio estimation, the auditors would estimate the projected misstatement using the following formula:

$$\text{Projected misstatement} = \left[\frac{\text{Sample net misstatement}}{\text{Book value of sample}} \right] \times \text{Population book value}$$

$$= \left[\frac{\$450}{\$14,175} \right] \times \$6,250,000 = \$198,413$$

Alternatively, averages may be used as follows:

$$\text{Projected misstatement} = \left[\frac{\text{Sample average misstatement}}{\text{Sample average book value}} \right] \times \text{Population book value}$$

$$= \left[\frac{\$2}{\$63} \right] \times 6,250,000 = \$198,413$$

[11] The major differences in the formulas are that the standard deviations used would be those for the ratios and differences.

Because the projected misstatement indicates an overstatement, this difference is subtracted from the book value to obtain the estimated total audited value as follows:

$$\text{Estimated total audited value} = \text{Population book value} - \text{Projected overstatement}$$
$$= \$6{,}250{,}000 - \$198{,}413$$
$$= \$6{,}051{,}587$$

If the projected misstatement had been an understatement, the amount would have been added to the population book value.

Formulas are available for both difference and ratio estimation to calculate an adjusted allowance for sampling risk to control sampling risk in a manner similar to the mean-per-unit method. Since we do not present them, we do not take the analysis further than the calculation of projected misstatement and the estimated total audited value.

Nonstatistical Sampling for Substantive Tests

Learning Objective 8

The major differences between statistical and nonstatistical sampling in substantive testing are in the procedures used to determine the sample size and evaluate the sample results. In using nonstatistical sampling the auditors may decide not to quantify the factors used to arrive at the sample size, although they will consider the relationships that are summarized in Figure 9.9. In evaluating the sample results, the auditors also project the misstatements found in the sample to the population and consider sampling risk, but the level of risk is not quantified. While the auditors may use unassisted judgment for determining the sample size and for evaluating the sample results, many CPA firms have adopted structured approaches to nonstatistical sampling that are based on statistical methods. This increases the consistency of sampling judgments that are made by various auditors throughout the firm.

Illustration of Nonstatistical Sampling

The following example illustrates the use of a structured nonstatistical sampling plan.

1. *Determine the objective of the test.* Assume that the auditors are performing a test of the valuation of inventory by testing the pricing of a sample of inventory items by reference to vendors' invoices. The inventory consists of 2,000 items with a book value of $3,000,000.

2. *Define the population and sampling unit.* The physical representation of the population consists of a listing of the inventory items on hand at year-end, and the auditors have determined that the sampling unit will be each individual product.

3. *Choose the audit sampling technique.* The auditors have decided to use a structured approach to nonstatistical sampling.

4. *Determine the sample size.* To determine the required sample size the auditors will use the following formula:

$$\text{Sample size} = \left[\frac{\text{Population book value} \times \text{Reliability factor}}{\text{Tolerable misstatement}} \right]$$

The **reliability** factor for the formula is selected from a table such as the one that is illustrated by Figure 9.13. It is based on the auditors' combined assessment of inherent and control risk and the auditors' assessment of the risk that other substantive procedures will fail to detect a material misstatement of the assertions. Both risks are assessed on qualitative scales from maximum risk (100 percent) to low risk.

In our example, assume that the auditors have assessed the combination of inherent and control risk at slightly below the maximum. They have also performed analytical procedures on the inventory account that the auditors believe have a moderate risk of not detecting a material misstatement in the valuation of the inventory account. Using these assessments of risk, the auditors obtain a reliability factor of 2.0 using Figure 9.13. If the

FIGURE 9.13
Reliability Factors for Nonstatistical Sampling Plan

Combined Assessment of Inherent and Control Risk	Risk That Other Substantive Procedures (e.g., analytical procedures) Will Fail to Detect a Material Misstatement		
	Maximum	Moderate	Low
Maximum	3.0	2.3	1.9
Slightly below maximum	2.7	2.0	1.6
Moderate	2.3	1.6	1.2
Low	1.9	1.2	1.0

Note: This table is applicable when the auditors expect few misstatements in the population.

auditors have decided that $100,000 is the amount of tolerable misstatement for the inventory account, the sample size would be calculated as follows:

$$\text{Sample size} = \left[\frac{\text{Population book value} \times \text{Reliability factor}}{\text{Tolerable misstatement}} \right]$$

$$= \left[\frac{\$3,000,000 \times 2.0}{\$100,000} \right]$$

$$= 60 \text{ items}$$

5. *Select the sample.* Even though nonstatistical sampling is being used, the auditors generally select the sample on a stratified basis.

6. *Test the sample items.* The auditors examine vendors' invoices supporting the price of each product selected for testing. Assume that the auditors find two products that were priced at improper prices, resulting in a total overstatement of the account of $6,600. In addition, the total book value of the sample is calculated to be $1,100,000.

7. *Evaluate the sample results.* In evaluating the sample results, the auditors will begin by projecting the misstatements found in the sample to the population. A number of methods may be used. However, the auditors typically use the ratio or difference method illustrated on pages 325 through 328. In this example, the auditors decide to use the ratio method of projecting the misstatement, as illustrated below:

$$\text{Projected misstatement} = \left[\frac{\text{Sample net misstatement}}{\text{Book value of sample}} \right] \times \text{Population book value}$$

$$= \left[\frac{\$6,600}{\$1,100,000} \right] \times \$3,000,000$$

$$= \$18,000$$

After calculating the projected amount of misstatement in the population, the auditors will then compare that amount with the amount of tolerable misstatement. In this situation, the auditors compare $18,000 with $100,000, and use professional judgment to evaluate whether there is a sufficiently low risk of material misstatement of the account. Since the projected misstatement is only 18 percent ($18,000 ÷ $100,000) of tolerable misstatement, the auditors would likely conclude that the account balance is acceptable. As the amount of projected misstatement gets closer to the amount of tolerable misstatement for the account, the auditors are more likely to conclude that the risk of material misstatement is too high.[12] When the auditors conclude that the risk of misstatement is high they will not accept the client's book balance as being materially correct and will either convince the client to adjust the book value or perform additional audit tests on the population.

[12] Some references suggest that when the projected misstatement exceeds one-third of the tolerable misstatement the sampling risk is becoming "too high."

The auditors will also perform a qualitative evaluation of the misstatements found in the population to determine if there are implications for other aspects of the audit. Intentional misstatements would generally have greater implications for the audit than clerical errors.

8. *Document the sampling procedures.* The nonstatistical sampling procedures described on page 329 would be documented in a manner similar to that used for statistical sampling plans.

Chapter Summary

This chapter presented the concepts and techniques used by auditors to perform audit sampling. To summarize:

1. Audit sampling is defined as applying an audit procedure to less than 100 percent of the items in a population to make some conclusion about that population.

2. Auditors may use statistical or nonstatistical sampling to perform tests of controls or substantive tests. Statistical sampling allows the auditors to measure and control sampling risk. Sampling risk is the risk that the auditors will make an incorrect conclusion from the sample results because the sample is not representative of the population.

3. The major type of statistical sampling plan for tests of controls is attributes sampling, which can provide the auditors with an estimate of the extent of the deviations from a prescribed internal control policy or procedure.

4. The two aspects of sampling risk for tests of controls include the risk of assessing control risk too high, which relates to the efficiency of the audit, and the risk of assessing control risk too low, which is critical because it relates to the effectiveness of the audit.

5. The major factors that affect the required sample size for an attributes sample are the risk of assessing control risk too low, the tolerable deviation rate, and the expected deviation rate in the population.

6. The two aspects of sampling risk for substantive tests include the risk of incorrect rejection and the risk of incorrect acceptance. The risk of incorrect acceptance is the critical risk, because if the auditors accept a materially misstated account balance, they may issue an inappropriate audit opinion.

7. When a classical variables sampling plan is used, the required sample size is determined by the risk of incorrect acceptance, the risk of incorrect rejection, the amount of tolerable misstatement for the account, and the standard deviation of the items in the account.

8. Classical variables sampling methods include mean-per-unit estimation, difference estimation, and ratio estimation.

9. In evaluating the results of a classical variables sampling plan, the auditors compute an acceptance interval; if the client's book value falls within the interval, it is accepted as being materially correct. Otherwise, the auditors generally must perform additional testing to determine whether the client's balance is actually misstated or the sample was not representative.

10. Many CPA firms use structured approaches to nonstatistical sampling for substantive tests. Such approaches increase the consistency of sampling decisions by various staff members within the firms.

Key Terms Introduced or Emphasized in Chapter 9

Allowance for sampling risk (ASR, precision)   An interval around the sample results in which the true population characteristic is expected to lie.

Attributes sampling   A sampling plan enabling the auditors to estimate the rate of deviation (occurrence) in a population.

Deviation rate   A defined rate of departure from prescribed controls. Also referred to as *occurrence rate* or *exception rate*.

Difference estimation   A sampling plan that uses the difference between the audited (correct) values and book values of items in a sample to calculate the estimated total audited value of the population. Difference estimation is used in lieu of ratio estimation when the differences are not nearly proportional to book values.

Discovery sampling   A sampling plan for locating at least 1 deviation, providing that the deviation occurs in the population with a specified frequency.

Dual-purpose test   A test designed to test a control and to substantiate the dollar amount of an account using the same sample.

Estimated total audited value   Based on the variables sampling method used (e.g., mean-per-unit, ratio, difference) and the sample selected, the most likely point estimate of the account audited value.

Expected population deviation rate   An advance estimate of a deviation rate. This estimate is necessary for determining the required sample size in an attributes sampling plan.

Mean   The average item value, computed by dividing total value by the number of items composing total value.

Mean-per-unit estimation   A classical variables sampling plan enabling the auditors to estimate the average dollar value (or other variable) of items in a population by determining the average value of items in a sample.

Nonsampling risk   The aspects of audit risk not due to sampling. This risk normally relates to "human" rather than "statistical" errors.

Physical representation of the population   The population from which the auditors sample. The physical representation of the population differs from the actual population when it does not include items that exist in the actual population. For example, the auditors sample from a trial balance of receivables which may or may not include all actual receivables.

Population   The entire field of items from which a sample might be drawn.

Precision   See *allowance for sampling risk.*

Probability-proportional-to-size sampling   A variables estimation procedure that uses attributes theory to express a conclusion in monetary (dollar) amounts.

Projected misstatement   An estimate of the most likely amount of monetary misstatement in a population.

Random selection   Selecting items from a population in a manner in which every item has an equal chance of being included in the sample.

Ratio estimation   A sampling plan that uses the ratio of audited (correct) values to book values of items in the sample to calculate the estimated total audited value of the population. Ratio estimation is used in lieu of difference estimation when the differences are nearly proportional to book values.

Reliability   The complement of the risk of incorrect acceptance.

Representative sample   A sample possessing essentially the same characteristics as the population from which it was drawn.

Risk of assessing control risk too high   This risk is the possibility that the assessed level of control risk based on the sample is greater than the true operating effectiveness of the control.

Risk of assessing control risk too low   This most important risk is the possibility that the assessed level of control risk based on the sample is less than the true operating effectiveness of the controls.

Risk of incorrect acceptance   The risk that sample results will indicate that a population is not materially misstated when, in fact, it is materially misstated.

Risk of incorrect rejection   The risk that sample results will indicate that a population is materially misstated when, in fact, it is not.

Sampling error   The difference between the actual rate or amount in the population and that of the sample. For example, if an actual (but unknown) deviation rate of 3 percent exists in the population, and the sample's deviation rate is 2 percent, the sampling error is 1 percent.

Sampling risk   The risk that the auditors' conclusion based on a sample might be different from the conclusion they would reach if the test were applied to the entire population. For tests of controls, sampling risks include the risks of assessing control risk too high and too low; for substantive testing, sampling risks include the risks of incorrect acceptance and rejection.

Sequential (stop-or-go) sampling   A sampling plan in which the sample is selected in stages, with the need for each subsequent stage being conditional on the results of the previous stage.

Standard deviation   A measure of the variability or dispersion of item values within a population; in a normal distribution, 68.3 percent of all item values fall within ± 1 standard deviation of the mean, 95.4 percent fall within ± 2 standard deviations, and 99.7 percent fall within ± 3 standard deviations.

Stratification   Dividing a population into two or more relatively homogeneous subgroups (strata). Stratification increases the efficiency of most sampling plans by reducing the variability of items in each stratum. The sample size necessary to evaluate the strata separately is smaller than would be needed to evaluate the total population.

Systematic selection   The technique of selecting a sample by drawing every nth item in the population, following one or more random starting points.

Tolerable deviation rate   The maximum population rate of deviations from a prescribed control that the auditor will tolerate without modifying the planned assessment of control risk.

Tolerable misstatement   An estimate of the maximum monetary misstatement that may exist in an account balance without causing the financial statements to be materially misstated.

Variables sampling   Sampling plans designed to estimate a numerical measurement of a population, such as a dollar value.

Voucher   A document authorizing a cash disbursement. A voucher usually provides space for the initials of employees performing various approval functions. The term *voucher* may also be applied to the group of supporting documents used as a basis for recording liabilities or for making cash disbursements.

Review Questions

9–1.   Define, and differentiate between, nonstatistical (judgmental) sampling and statistical sampling.

9–2.   Describe the difference between sampling risk and nonsampling risk.

9–3.   Explain what is meant by the following statement: "When sampling, the auditors must determine that the physical representation of the actual population is complete."

9–4.   In selecting items for examination, an auditor considered three alternatives: (*a*) random number table selection, (*b*) systematic selection, and (*c*) random number generator selection. Which, if any, of these methods would lead to a random sample if properly applied?

9–5.   Explain briefly the term *systematic selection* as used in auditing and indicate the precautions to be taken if a random sample is to be obtained. Is systematic selection applicable to unnumbered documents? Explain.

9–6.   Explain the meaning of sampling without replacement and sampling with replacement.

9–7.   Which technique results in a smaller sample size, sampling with or without replacement?

9–8.   An auditor is sampling with replacement and, by chance, a particular account has been selected twice. Should it be included two times in the sample?

9–9.   What are the three major factors that determine the sample size for an attributes sampling plan?

9–10.   When using attributes sampling the auditors must estimate the expected population deviation rate. What sources are used to make this estimate?

9–11.   When performing attributes sampling, may auditors include several types of attributes in their definition of a deviation? Explain.

9–12.   What effects will an auditor's belief that the population's actual deviation rate exceeds the tolerable deviation rate have on the test of controls sample size?

9–13.   What is a dual-purpose test?

9–14.   When performing a dual-purpose test, how does the auditor arrive at the required sample size?

9–15.   If a sample of 100 items indicates a deviation rate of 3 percent, should the auditors conclude that the entire population also has approximately a 3 percent deviation rate?

9–16.   What relationship exists between the expected population deviation rate and sample size?

9–17.   What would be the difference between an attributes sampling plan and a variables sampling plan in a test of inventory extensions?

9–18.   Describe what is meant by a sequential sampling plan.

9–19.   The 10 following statements apply to unrestricted random sampling without replacement. Indicate whether each statement is true or false. Briefly discuss each false statement.

    a.   When sampling from the population of accounts receivable for certain objectives, the auditor might sample only active accounts with balances.

    b.   To be random, every item in the population must have an equal chance of being selected for inclusion in the sample.

    c.   In general, all items in excess of a material misstatement need to be examined and sampling of them is inappropriate.

    d.   It is likely that five different random samples from the same population could produce five different estimates of the true population mean.

    e.   A 100 percent sample would have to be taken to eliminate sampling risk.

    f.   The effect of the inclusion by chance of a very large or very small item in a random sample can be lessened by increasing the size of the sample.

    g.   The standard deviation is a measure of the variability of items in a population.

    h.   The larger the standard deviation of a population, the smaller the required sample size.

    i.   Unrestricted random sampling with replacement may result in a larger sample size than unrestricted random sampling without replacement.

    j.   Unrestricted random sampling normally results in a smaller sample size than does stratified sampling.

9–20. In performing a substantive test of the book value of a population, auditors must be concerned with two aspects of sampling risk. What are these two aspects of sampling risk, and which aspect is of greater importance to auditors? Explain.

9–21. Explain how the auditors may obtain an estimate of a population's standard deviation to determine an appropriate sample size.

9–22. For what purposes is the planned allowance for sampling risk used in mean-per-unit sampling?

9–23. Using the approach presented in this chapter for mean-per-unit sampling, when is it necessary to calculate an adjusted allowance for sampling risk?

9–24. The mean of the audited values in a sample is $20. The accounts in that sample have a mean book value of $21, and the entire population of 10,000 accounts has an average book value of $19. Using mean-per-unit sampling, calculate the estimated total audited value of the account.

9–25. What conditions are necessary for the auditors to use either the ratio or difference estimation techniques?

9–26. What options are available to an auditor when the client's book value falls outside the acceptance interval calculated using the estimate of the total value of the population (the adjusted allowance for sampling risk)?

9–27. Explain how, in using the mean-per-unit method to evaluate results, the auditors use the differences between the audited values and the book values of the individual items in their sample.

9–28. Is it correct to say that when using nonstatistical variables sampling, one is unable to project the misstatements identified to the entire population? Explain why this is or is not the case.

9–29. When using nonstatistical sampling, what relationship must exist between the projected misstatement and tolerable misstatement in order for the auditors to conclude that an account balance is acceptable?

Questions Requiring Analysis

9–30. CPAs may decide to apply nonstatistical or statistical techniques to audit testing.

Required:

    a. List and explain the advantages of applying statistical sampling techniques to audit testing.

    b. List and discuss the decisions involving professional judgment that must be made by the CPAs in applying statistical sampling techniques to tests of controls.

    c. You have applied attributes sampling to the client's pricing of the inventory and discovered from your sampling that the sample deviation rate exceeds your tolerable rate. Discuss the courses of action you take.

9–31. One of the generally accepted auditing standards states that sufficient competent evidential matter is to be obtained through inspection, observation, inquiries, and confirmation to afford a reasonable basis for an opinion regarding the financial statements under audit. Some degree of uncertainty is implicit in the concept of "a reasonable basis for an opinion," because the concept of sampling is well established in auditing practice.

Required:

    a. Explain the auditor's justification for accepting the uncertainties that are inherent in the sampling process.

    b. Discuss the nature of sampling risk and nonsampling risk. Include the effect of sampling risk on substantive tests of details and on tests of internal control.

(AICPA, adapted)

9–32. In performing a test of controls for sales order approvals, the CPAs stipulate a tolerable deviation rate of 8 percent with a risk of assessing control risk too low of 5 percent. They anticipate a deviation rate of 2 percent.

Required:

    a. What type of sampling plan should the auditors use for this test?

    b. Using the appropriate table or formula from this chapter, compute the required sample size for the test.

    c. Assume that the sample indicates four deviations. May the CPAs conclude with a 5 percent risk of assessing control risk too low that the population deviation rate does not exceed the tolerable rate of 8 percent?

9–33. An auditor has reason to suspect that fraud has occurred through forgery of the treasurer's signature on company checks. The population under consideration consists of 3,000 checks. Can discovery sampling rule out the possibility that any forged checks exist?

9–34.   Robert Rotter, CPA, is considering the use of a mean-per-unit estimation sampling plan. Explain the factors that Rotter would consider in determining:

a. The acceptable risk of incorrect rejection.

b. The tolerable misstatement in the population.

c. The acceptable risk of incorrect acceptance.

9–35.   The professional development department of a large CPA firm has prepared the following illustration to familiarize the audit staff with the relationships of sample size to population size and variability and the auditors' specifications as to the tolerable misstatement and the risk of incorrect acceptance.

	Characteristics of Population 1 Relative to Population 2		Audit Specifications as to a Sample from Population 1 Relative to a Sample from Population 2	
	Size	Variability	Tolerable Misstatement	Planned Risk of Incorrect Acceptance
Case 1	Larger	Equal	Equal	Equal
Case 2	Equal	Larger	Larger	Equal
Case 3	Larger	Equal	Smaller	Equal
Case 4	Smaller	Smaller	Equal	Lower
Case 5	Smaller	Equal	Larger	Higher

Required:

For each of the five cases in the above illustration, indicate the relationship of the sample size to be selected from population 1 relative to the sample from population 2. Select your answer from the following numbered responses and state the reasoning behind your choice. The required sample size from population 1 is:

(1) Larger than the required sample size from population 2.

(2) Equal to the required sample size from population 2.

(3) Smaller than the required sample size from population 2.

(4) Indeterminate relative to the required sample size from population 2.

9–36.   An auditor used a nonstatistical sampling plan to audit the inventory of an auto supply company. The auditor tested the recorded cost of a sample of inventory items by reference to vendors' invoices. In performing the test, the auditor verified all the items on two pages selected at random from the client's 257-page inventory listing. The sampling plan resulted in a test of $50,000 of the total book value of $5,000,000, and the auditor found a total of $5,000 in overstatements in the sample. Since the senior indicated that a material misstatement in the inventory account was $100,000, the auditor concluded that the recorded inventory value was materially correct.

Required:

Evaluate the auditor's sampling plan and the manner in which the results were evaluated.

9–37.   Cathy Williams is auditing the financial statements of Westerman Industries. In the performance of mean-per-unit estimation of credit sales, Williams has decided to limit the risk of incorrect rejection to 25 percent and the risk of incorrect acceptance to 10 percent. Williams considers the tolerable misstatement in this revenue account to be ±$500,000. Calculate the planned allowance for sampling risk.

9–38.   Ratio estimation and difference estimation are two widely used variables sampling plans.

Required:

a. Under what conditions are ratio estimation or difference estimation appropriate sampling plans for estimating the total dollar value of a population?

b. What relationship determines which of these two plans will be most efficient in a particular situation?

9–39.   Bill Jones wishes to use nonstatistical sampling to select a sample of his client's 3,000 accounts receivable, which total $330,000. He believes that $30,000 represents a reasonable tolerable misstatement. He also has assessed both the combination of inherent and control risk at the maximum level, and the risk that other substantive procedures will fail to detect a material misstatement at the maximum. He wishes to use a structured approach. Use the formula presented in the text to calculate the required sample size.

9–40.   During an audit of Potter Company, an auditor needs to estimate the total value of the 5,000 invoices processed during June. The auditor estimates the standard deviation of the population to be $30. Determine the size sample the auditor would select to achieve an allowance for sampling risk (precision) of ±$25,000 with 4.6 percent risk of incorrect rejection.

(AICPA, adapted)

Multiple Choice Questions

9–41. Select the best answer for each of the following questions. Explain the reasons for your selection.

a. Which of the following is an element of sampling risk?

(1) Choosing an audit procedure that is inconsistent with the audit objective.

(2) Concluding that no material misstatement exists in a materially misstated population based on taking a sample that includes no misstatement.

(3) Failing to detect an error on a document that has been inspected by an auditor.

(4) Failing to perform audit procedures that are required by the sampling plan.

b. In assessing sampling risk, the risk of incorrect rejection and the risk of assessing control risk too high relate to the:

(1) Efficiency of the audit.

(2) Effectiveness of the audit.

(3) Selection of the sample.

(4) Audit quality controls.

c. Which of the following statistical sampling techniques is least desirable for use by the auditors?

(1) Random number table selection.

(2) Block selection.

(3) Systematic selection.

(4) Random number generator selection.

d. The auditors primary objective in selecting a sample of items from an audit population is to obtain:

(1) A random sample.

(2) A stratified sample.

(3) A representative sample.

(4) A large sample.

e. Discovery sampling is particularly effective when:

(1) There are a large number of errors in the population.

(2) The auditors are looking for critical deviations that are not expected to be frequent in number.

(3) The auditors know where deviations are likely to occur.

(4) The population is large in size.

f. The auditors are using unstratified mean-per-unit sampling to audit accounts receivable as they did in the prior year. Which of the following changes in characteristics or specifications would result in a larger required sample size this year than that required in the prior year?

(1) Larger variance in the dollar value of accounts.

(2) Smaller population size.

(3) Larger tolerable misstatement.

(4) Higher risk of incorrect acceptance.

g. Which of the following sampling techniques is typically used for tests of controls?

(1) Mean-per-unit sampling.

(2) Difference sampling.

(3) Attribute sampling.

(4) Probability-proportional-to-size sampling.

h. Which of the following is accurate regarding tolerable misstatement?

(1) Tolerable misstatement is directly related to materiality.

   (2) Tolerable misstatement cannot be determined until the sample results are evaluated.

   (3) Tolerable misstatement does not affect sample size.

   (4) Tolerable misstatement is a measure of reliability of the sample.

i. In which of the following circumstances is it least likely that tests of controls will be performed?

   (1) The expected deviation rate exceeds the tolerable deviation rate.

   (2) The planned assessed level of control risk is at a level slightly below the maximum.

   (3) The risk of assessing control risk too low is less than the expected deviation rate.

   (4) The tolerable deviation rate exceeds the risk of assessing control risk too low.

j. An auditor needs to estimate the average highway weight of tractor-trailer trucks using a state's highway system. Which estimation method is most appropriate?

   (1) Mean per unit.

   (2) Difference.

   (3) Ratio.

   (4) Probability proportional to size.

k. The auditors have sampled 50 accounts from a population of 1,000 accounts receivable. The sample items have a mean book value of $200, and a mean audited value of $203. The book value in the population is $198,000. What is the estimated audited value of the population using the mean-per-unit method?

   (1) $198,000

   (2) $200,000

   (3) $201,000

   (4) $203,000

l. Using the same facts as in (e) above, what is the estimated total audited value of the population using the difference method?

   (1) $198,000

   (2) $200,000

   (3) $201,000

   (4) $203,000

Problems

9–42. The use of statistical sampling techniques in an audit of financial statements does not eliminate judgmental decisions.

Required:

a. Identify and explain four areas in which judgment may be exercised by CPAs in planning a statistical test of controls.

b. Assume that the auditors' sample shows an unacceptable deviation rate. Discuss the various actions that they may take based upon this finding.

c. A nonstratified sample of 80 accounts payable vouchers is to be selected from a population of 3,200. The vouchers are numbered consecutively from 1 to 3,200 and are listed, 40 to a page, in the voucher register. Describe four different techniques for selecting a random sample of vouchers for inspection.

(AICPA, adapted)

9–43. Sampling for attributes is often used to allow an auditor to reach a conclusion concerning a rate of occurrence in a population. A common use in auditing is to test the rate of deviation from a prescribed control to determine whether the planned assessed level of control risk is appropriate.

Required:

a. When an auditor samples for attributes, identify the factors that should influence the auditors' judgment concerning the determination of:

   (1) Acceptable level of risk of assessing control risk too low.

   (2) Tolerable deviation rate.

   (3) Expected population deviation rate.

b. State the effect on sample size of an increase in each of the following factors, assuming all other factors are held constant:

   (1) Acceptable level of the risk of assessing control risk too low.

(2) Tolerable deviation rate.

(3) Expected population deviation rate.

c. Evaluate the sample results of a test for attributes if authorizations are found to be missing on 7 check requests out of a sample of 100 tested. The population consists of 2,500 check requests, the tolerable deviation rate is 8 percent, and the acceptable level of risk of assessing control risk too low is 5 percent.

d. How may the use of statistical sampling assist the auditors in evaluating the sample results described in (*c*), above?

(AICPA, adapted)

9–44. As part of your audit of the Abba Company accounts payable function, your audit program includes a test of controls addressing the company policy requiring that all vouchers be properly approved. You estimate the population deviation rate to be 3 percent.

Required:

a. In addition to an estimate of population deviation rate, what factors affect the size of the sample needed?

b. What bases could be used to provide an estimate of the population deviation rate?

c. Assume that a sample of 100 has been drawn, audit tests performed, and a sample deviation rate of 4 percent computed. Furthermore, you have selected a 5 percent risk of assessing control risk too low as appropriate. Use the appropriate table to determine the achieved upper deviation rate.

d. What actions can be taken to deal with a situation in which the achieved upper deviation rate exceeds the tolerable rate?

9–45. You have been asked to test the effectiveness of Ingo Corporation's control of manually approving all purchases over $25,000. During the year, Ingo Corporation has made 1,000,000 purchases, of which 3,000 were over $25,000. Jian Zhang, CIA, your supervisor, has asked you to use a tolerable deviation rate of 4 percent (although she expects the rate to be only approximately 0.25 percent) and a 5 percent risk of assessing control risk too low.

a. What is the planned assessed level of control risk (use the table on page 312 of the text)?

b. Determine the appropriate sample size using Figure 9.4.

c. Use Figure 9.5 to determine the achieved upper deviation rate if no deviations were included in the sample. What is the assessed level of control risk?

d. What is the achieved upper deviation rate if 2 deviations were found in the sample? What is the assessed level of control risk?

e. What is the achieved upper deviation rate if 8 deviations were found in the sample? What is the assessed level of control risk?

 Scott Duffney, CPA, has randomly selected and audited a sample of 100 of Will-Mart's accounts receivable. Will-Mart has 3,000 accounts receivable accounts with a total book value of $3,000,000. Duffney has determined that the account's tolerable misstatement is $250,000.

His sample results are as follows:

Average audited value $990
Average book value   998

Required:

Calculate the accounts receivable estimated audited value and projected misstatement using the:

(*a*) Mean-per-unit method.

(*b*) Ratio method.

(*c*) Difference method.

9–47. The auditors wish to use mean-per-unit sampling to evaluate the reasonableness of the book value of the accounts receivable of Smith, Inc. Smith has 10,000 accounts receivable accounts with a total book value of $1,500,000. The auditors estimate the population's standard deviation to be equal to $25. After examining the overall audit plan, the auditors believe that the account's tolerable misstatement is $60,000, and that a risk of incorrect rejection of 5 percent and a risk of incorrect acceptance of 10 percent are appropriate.

Required:

a. Calculate the required sample size.

b. Assuming the following results:

Average audited value $146
Standard deviation of sample   28

Use the mean-per-unit method to:

(1) Calculate the point estimate of the account's audited value.

(2) Calculate the projected misstatement for the population.

(3) Calculate the adjusted allowance for sampling risk.

(4) State the auditors' conclusion in this situation.

9–48. You are the auditor of Jexel, an auto air conditioner service and repair company, and you have decided to use the mean-per-unit method to test the existence and gross valuation of recorded accounts receivable. The client's records include 10,000 accounts with a total book value of $1,250,000. You decide to use tolerable misstatement of $182,000, an incorrect acceptance risk of 5 percent, and an incorrect rejection risk of 4.6 percent. Using generalized audit software you estimated the standard deviation of the population as $25.

    a. Determine the sample size.

    b. Assume you tested the sample and got the following results: the mean audited value of the 25 accounts was $122. Assuming that the standard deviation of the sample's audited value is also $25, will you accept the account as not being materially misstated? What is the projected misstatement for the population?

    c. Assuming that the standard deviation of the sample's audited value is $20, will you accept the account as not being materially misstated? Show your calculations. What is the projected misstatement for the population?

9–49. In the audit of Potomac Mills, the auditors wish to test the costs assigned to manufactured goods. During the year, the company has produced 2,000 production lots with a total recorded cost of $5.9 million. The auditors select a sample of 200 production lots with an aggregate book value of $600,000 and vouch the assigned costs to the supporting documentation. Their audit discloses misstatements in the cost of 52 of the 200 production lots; after adjustment for these misstatements, the audited value of the sample is $582,000.

Required:

    a. Show how the auditors would compute an estimate of the total cost of production lots manufactured during the year using each of the following sampling plans. (Do not compute the allowance for sampling risk or the risk of incorrect acceptance of the estimates.)

       (1) Mean-per-unit estimation.

       (2) Ratio estimation.

       (3) Difference estimation.

    b. Explain why mean-per-unit estimation results in a higher estimate of the population value than does ratio estimation in this particular instance.

9–50. To test the pricing and mathematical accuracy of sales invoices, the auditors selected a sample of 200 sales invoices from a total of 41,600 invoices that were issued during the year under audit. The 200 invoices represented total recorded sales of $22,800. Total sales for the year amounted to $5 million. The test disclosed that of the 200 invoices audited, five were not properly priced or contained errors in extensions and footings. The five incorrect invoices represented $720 of the total recorded sales, and the errors found resulted in a net understatement of these invoices by $300.

Required:

Explain what conclusions the auditors may draw from the above information, assuming the sample was selected:

    a. Using nonstatistical sampling.

    b. As part of a difference estimation plan for estimating the total population value.

    c. As part of an attributes sampling plan using a stipulated tolerable deviation rate of 5 percent and a risk of assessing control risk too low of 5 percent.

9–51. The auditors of Landi Corporation wish to use a structured approach to nonstatistical sampling to evaluate the reasonableness of the accounts receivable. Landi has 15,000 receivable accounts with a total book value of $2,500,000. The auditors have assessed the combined level of inherent and control risk at a moderate level and believe that their other substantive procedures are so limited as to require a "maximum" risk assessment. After considering the overall audit plan, the auditors believe that the account's tolerable misstatement is $57,500.

Required:

    a. Calculate the required sample size.

    b. Assuming the following results:

Number of items in sample	100
Total audited value of sample items	$16,200
Total book value of sample items	$17,000

(1) Use the ratio estimation method to calculate the projected misstatement of the population.

(2) Use the difference estimation method to calculate the projected misstatement of the population.

c. Use the results obtained in (*b*) to arrive at a conclusion as to whether to "accept" or "reject" the population.

9–52. The auditors wish to test the valuation of accounts receivable in the audit of Kaplan Corporation. The client has $1,000,000 of total recorded receivables, composed of 2,000 accounts. The auditors have decided to use structured nonstatistical sampling and have determined the following:

Tolerable misstatement	$50,000
Assessment of inherent and control risk	Moderate
Risk related to other substantive procedures	Moderate

Required:

a. Calculate the required sample size.

b. Assume that the auditors have tested the sample and discovered three misstatements:

Book Value	Audited Value
$100	$ 90
512	600
900	520

The remainder of the sample had an average value (book and audited) of $501.00. Use the ratio estimation method to calculate the projected misstatement of the population.

Use the results obtained in (*b*) to come to a conclusion about whether to "accept" or "reject" the population.

In-Class Team Case

9–53. Baker, CPA, was engaged to audit Mill Company's financial statements for the year ended December 31, 200X. After obtaining an understanding of Mill's internal control, Baker decided to obtain evidential matter about the effectiveness of both the design and operation of the controls that may support a low assessed level of control risk concerning Mill's shipping and billing functions. During the prior years' audits Baker had used nonstatistical sampling, but for the current year Baker decided to use a statistical sample in the tests of controls to eliminate the need for judgment.

Baker wanted to assess control risk at a low level, so a tolerable rate of deviation of 20 percent was established. To estimate the population deviation rate and the achieved upper deviation rate, Baker decided to apply the discovery sampling method with an expected population deviation rate of 3 percent for the 8,000 shipping documents, and decided to defer consideration of the risk of assessing control risk too low until evaluating the sample results. Baker used the tolerable rate, the population size, and the expected population deviation rate to determine that a sample size of 80 would be sufficient. When it was subsequently determined that the actual population was about 10,000 shipping documents, Baker increased the sample size to 100.

Baker's objective was to ascertain whether Mill's shipments had been properly billed. Baker took a sample of 100 invoices by selecting the first 25 invoices from the first month of each quarter. Baker then compared the invoices to the corresponding prenumbered shipping documents.

When Baker tested the sample, 8 deviations were discovered. Additionally, one shipment that should have been billed at $10,443 was actually billed at $10,434. Baker considered this $9 to be immaterial and did not count it as a deviation.

In evaluating the sample results Baker made the initial determination that a reliability level of 95 percent (risk of assessing control risk too low of 5 percent) was desired and, using the appropriate statistical sampling table, determined that for 8 observed deviations from a sample size of 100, the achieved upper deviation rate was 14 percent. Baker then calculated the allowance for sampling risk to be 5 percent, the difference between the actual sample deviation rate (8 percent) and the expected deviation rate (3 percent). Baker reasoned that the actual sample deviation rate (8 percent) plus the allowance for sampling risk (5 percent) was less than the achieved upper deviation rate (14 percent); therefore, the sample supported a low level of control risk.

Required: Describe each incorrect assumption, statement, and inappropriate application of attributes sampling in Baker's procedures.

(AICPA, adapted)

Probability-Proportional-to-Size (PPS) Sampling

Probability-proportional-to-size (PPS) sampling[13] is a technique that applies the theory of attributes sampling to estimate the total dollar amount of misstatement in a population. It has gained popularity because of its ease of use and because it often results in smaller samples than classical variables approaches.

Whereas classical variables sampling plans define the population as a group of accounts or transactions, PPS sampling defines the population as the individual dollars comprising the population's book value. Thus, a population of 5,000 accounts receivable with a total dollar value of $2,875,000 is viewed as a population of 2,875,000 items (dollars), rather than 5,000 items (accounts).

Determination of Sample Size

The factors affecting sample size in PPS sampling are (1) the population book value, (2) the reliability factor, (3) the tolerable misstatement, (4) the expected misstatement in the account, and (5) the expansion factor. Specifically, the sample size for PPS may be computed as follows:

$$\text{Sample size} = \frac{\text{Population book value} \times \text{Reliability factor}}{\text{Tolerable misstatement} - (\text{Expected misstatement} \times \text{Expansion factor})}$$

Several of the factors in the PPS formula need very little additional explanation. The population book value is the recorded amount of the population being audited. The tolerable misstatement is the maximum monetary misstatement that may exist in the population without causing the financial statements to be materially misstated. The expected misstatement is the auditors' estimate of the dollar amount of misstatement in the population. The auditors estimate the expected misstatement using professional judgment based on prior experience and knowledge of the client. The other factors used to calculate sample size are based on the auditors' desired risk of incorrect acceptance and are obtained from tables, such as the one in Figure 9.14. The "zero misstatements" row of Figure 9.14 is always used for obtaining the

FIGURE 9.14 **Reliability Factors for Misstatements of Overstatement**

Number of Overstatement Misstatements	Risk of Incorrect Acceptance								
	1%	5%	10%	15%	20%	25%	30%	37%	50%
0*	4.61	3.00	2.31	1.90	1.61	1.39	1.21	1.00	0.70
1	6.64	4.75	3.89	3.38	3.00	2.70	2.44	2.14	1.68
2	8.41	6.30	5.33	4.72	4.28	3.93	3.62	3.25	2.68
3	10.05	7.76	6.69	6.02	5.52	5.11	4.77	4.34	3.68
4	11.61	9.16	8.00	7.27	6.73	6.28	5.90	5.43	4.68
5	13.11	10.52	9.28	8.50	7.91	7.43	7.01	6.49	5.68
6	14.57	11.85	10.54	9.71	9.08	8.56	8.12	7.56	6.67
7	16.00	13.15	11.78	10.90	10.24	9.69	9.21	8.63	7.67
8	17.41	14.44	13.00	12.08	11.38	10.81	10.31	9.68	8.67
9	18.79	15.71	14.21	13.25	12.52	11.92	11.39	10.74	9.67
10	20.15	16.97	15.41	14.42	13.66	13.02	12.47	11.79	10.67

*The 0 row is always used for the reliability factor in the sample size formula and for basic precision.
Source: AICPA, *Auditing Practice Release, Audit Sampling* (New York, 1999).

[13] Variations of this sampling technique are called *dollar-unit sampling* and *monetary-unit sampling*.

FIGURE 9.15
Expansion Factors for Expected Misstatement

Source: AICPA, *Auditing Practice Release, Audit Sampling* (New York, 1999).

				Risk of Incorrect Acceptance					
	1%	5%	10%	15%	20%	25%	30%	37%	50%
Factor	1.9	1.6	1.5	1.4	1.3	1.25	1.2	1.15	1.0

reliability factor for determining sample size. Thus, if a 10 percent risk of incorrect acceptance is desired, the auditors use a reliability factor of 2.31. The expansion factor comes directly from Figure 9.15. For a 10 percent risk of incorrect acceptance, the factor is 1.5.

Controlling Sampling Risk

As is the case with classical variables approaches, the auditors decide on an appropriate level of risk of incorrect acceptance based on the extent of the evidence required from the sample. This level of risk is then used to obtain the appropriate factors to calculate sample size. The risk of incorrect rejection is indirectly controlled by the auditors' estimate of expected misstatement that is used to calculate the PPS sample size. To reduce the risk of incorrect rejection, the auditors increase their estimate of expected misstatement. If the auditors underestimate the expected misstatement, the sample size will not be large enough and additional testing may be necessary in order to accept the account balance as being materially correct.

Method of Sample Selection

Auditors generally use a *systematic selection* approach when using PPS. However, since the sampling unit is based on dollars, not individual accounts, the sampling interval is also based on dollars. The sampling interval is calculated as follows:

$$\text{Sample interval} = \frac{\text{Population book value}}{\text{Sample size}}$$

To illustrate, assume that the auditors are sampling 200 items from a population of accounts receivable totaling $300,000; the sampling interval is calculated to be $1,500 ($300,000 ÷ 200). A random starting point is selected between $1 and $1,500, say, $412. The account with the 412th dollar will be the first sample item. Then, the sample will include the accounts receivable that contain every $1,500 from the starting point, as illustrated in Figure 9.16. The accounts included in Figure 9.16 are considered "logical units" because when applying PPS the auditors generally cannot audit only the dollar selected but must audit the entire account, invoice, or voucher. Consider the confirmation of accounts receivable. Sending a confirmation of a specific dollar in a selected balance is not generally feasible; the auditors must confirm the entire account balance or transaction from the account balance. Also note that, in using a systematic sampling plan, every account with a book value as large or larger than the sampling interval will be included in the sample. In our example, since every 1,500th dollar is being selected in Figure 9.16, account 0003 for $1,700 will always be included.

FIGURE 9.16
PPS Selection Process

Account Number	Book Value	Cumulative Total	Dollar Selected	Sample Item Book Value
0001	$1,000	$ 1,000	$ 412	$1,000
0002	42	1,042		
0003	1,700	2,742	1,912	1,700
0004	666	3,408		
0005	50	3,458	3,412	50
.	.	.	.	.
.	.	.	.	.
.	.	.	.	.
4217	17	300,000		

Evaluation of Sample Results

After the sample has been selected and procedures applied to arrive at audited values for the individual accounts, the PPS sample is evaluated. The PPS evaluation procedure involves calculating an **upper limit on misstatement,** which is an estimate of the maximum amount of misstatement in the account. The upper limit on misstatement has two already familiar components—the **projected misstatement** and the *allowance for sampling risk.* However, in PPS sampling, the allowance for sampling risk is made up of two other components, the **basic precision** and the **incremental allowance.** Mathematically, these relationships may be described as follows:

$$\begin{array}{lcl}\text{Upper limit} & = & \text{Projected} & + & \text{Allowance for} \\ \text{on misstatement} & & \text{misstatement} & & \text{sampling risk} \end{array}$$

$$\begin{array}{lcl}\text{Allowance for} & = & \text{Basic} & + & \text{Incremental} \\ \text{sampling risk} & & \text{precision} & & \text{allowance} \end{array}$$

Therefore:

$$\begin{array}{lcl}\text{Upper limit} & = & \text{Projected} & + & \text{Basic} & + & \text{Incremental} \\ \text{on misstatement} & & \text{misstatement} & & \text{Precision} & & \text{allowance} \end{array}$$

As is the case with the classical approaches, the projected misstatement may be viewed as the auditors' "best estimate" of the most likely misstatement in the population. The projected misstatement in the population is determined by summing the projected misstatement for each account, or other logical unit, in the sample. Thus, when the sample includes no misstatements, the projected misstatement is zero. If misstatements do exist in the sample, the method used to project the misstatements in a particular account depends on whether the book value of the account found to be in error is less than the sampling interval. For accounts with book values that are less than the amount of the sampling interval, the projected misstatement is calculated by multiplying the percentage of misstatement in the account, known as the **tainting,** times the sampling interval. Thus, if an account with a book value of $100 is found to have an audited value of $60, the misstatement in the account is $40 ($100 − $60) and the tainting is 40 percent ($40 ÷ $100). The tainting of 40 percent would then be multiplied by the sampling interval to get the projected misstatement for that account. Accounts with balances less than the sampling interval are used to represent other unselected items in that interval. Thus, for accounts with book values that are less than the sampling interval, *the account's tainting percentage is projected to the entire interval from which it was selected.*

For accounts with book values equal to or greater than the sampling interval, *the actual misstatement in the account is used as the projected misstatement.* The reason for the difference in the methods of calculation of the projected misstatement is that every account with a book value equal to or greater than the sampling interval will be included in the sample. These items do not represent other unselected items in that sampling interval; therefore, the actual misstatement in the account is equal to the projected misstatement.

The next step in determining the upper limit on misstatements involves calculating the two components of the allowance for sampling risk—the basic precision and the incremental allowance. The basic precision is always found by multiplying the reliability factor for zero misstatements from Figure 9.14 by the sampling interval.

When misstatements are discovered in the sample, the incremental allowance is found by (1) ranking the projected misstatements for the accounts with book values less than the sampling interval from largest projected misstatement to smallest projected misstatement, (2) multiplying each projected misstatement by an incremental factor calculated from the reliability factors in Figure 9.14, and (3) summing the resulting amounts. When no misstatements of accounts with book values less than the sampling interval are found in the sample, the incremental allowance is zero.

To complete the quantitative evaluation of the sample results, the auditors compute the upper limit on misstatements. When misstatements are found, the upper limit is computed by adding together the projected misstatement, the basic precision, and the incremental allowance. Of course, if no misstatements are found in the sample, the upper limit on misstatements consists only of the basic precision.

After the upper limit on misstatements is calculated, the auditors compare it to the tolerable misstatement for the account. If the upper limit on misstatements is less than or equal to tolerable misstatement, the sample results support the conclusion that the population is not misstated by more than tolerable misstatement at the specified level of sampling risk. On the other hand, if the upper limit on misstatements exceeds the amount of tolerable misstatement, the sample results do not provide the auditors with enough assurance that the misstatement in the population is less than the tolerable misstatement.

Illustration of PPS Sampling

The case used to illustrate mean-per-unit sampling on pages 322 through 325 is used to illustrate PPS sampling. The population, in that case, had a book value of $6,250,000 and the auditors decided on a tolerable misstatement for the account of $364,000 and a 5 percent risk of incorrect acceptance. Additionally, assume that based on prior audits, the auditors expect $50,000 of misstatement in the population.

Since the auditors are using a risk of incorrect acceptance of 5 percent, the reliability factor from Figure 9.14 is 3.00, and the expansion factor from Figure 9.15 is 1.6. Remember for calculating sample size that the zero misstatement row of Figure 9.14 is always used. Using this information, the sample size and sampling interval may be calculated as follows:

$$\text{Sample size} = \frac{\text{Population book value} \times \text{Reliability factor}}{\text{Tolerable misstatement} - (\text{Expected misstatement} \times \text{Expansion factor})}$$

$$= \frac{\$6,250,000 \times 3.00}{\$364,000 \times (\$50,000 \times 1.6)} = 66$$

$$\text{Sampling interval} = \frac{\text{Population book value}}{\text{Sample size}}$$

$$= \frac{\$6,250,000}{66} = \$95,000 \text{ (approximately)}$$

Using the PPS selection method, the auditors select the accounts, perform confirmation procedures, and find the following three misstatements:

Book Value	Audited Value
$ 100	$ 90
2,000	1,900
102,000	102

Based on the above results, the projected misstatement, basic precision, and the incremental allowance are calculated in Figure 9.17.

FIGURE 9.17 **PPS Illustration of Calculation of Upper Limit on Misstatement**

Projected Misstatement:

Book Value	Audited Value	Misstatement	Tainting Percentage	Sampling Interval	Projected Misstatement	Upper Limit on Misstatements
$ 100	$ 90	$ 0	10%	$95,000	$ 9,500	
2,000	1,900	100	5	95,000	4,750	
102,000	102	101,898	NA	NA	101,898	
$104,100	$2,092	$102,008			———	$116,148

Basic Precision: = Reliability factor × Sampling interval
              = 3.0 × $95,000 = $285,000

Incremental Allowance:

Reliability Factor	Increment	(Increment − 1)	Projected Misstatement	Incremental Allowance	
3.00		—	—	—	
4.75	1.75	0.75	$9,500	$7,125	
6.30	1.55	0.55	4,750	2,613	9,738
Upper Limit on Misstatement:					$410,886

The calculation of projected misstatement is straightforward, and no table values are required. Note that the tainting percentages for the first two misstatements are computed by dividing the misstatement amount by the book value of the account. Then, the tainting percentages are multiplied by the sampling interval to calculate the projected misstatement. Because the book value of the account containing the third misstatement is greater than the sampling interval of $95,000, the projected misstatement for that account is equal to the amount of the misstatement.

The second element of the upper limit on misstatement, basic precision, is simply the reliability factor for zero misstatements and a risk of incorrect acceptance of 5 percent (from Figure 9.14) multiplied by the sampling interval.

The calculation of the incremental allowance uses the projected misstatements of the accounts with book values less than the sampling interval. These projected misstatements are ranked by size from largest projected misstatement to smallest and multiplied by the increment in the reliability factors, reduced by 1. These incremental reliability factors are derived from the factors in Figure 9.14. Because a 5 percent risk of incorrect acceptance was selected and two misstatements were found in accounts with balances less than the sampling interval, the factors of 3.00, 4.75, and 6.30 are taken from Figure 9.14. An incremental factor is calculated as the difference between successive factors. For example, the incremental factor for the first error is 4.75 − 3.00, or 1.75. Then 1 is subtracted from the incremental factor to arrive at the factor that is multiplied by the first projected misstatement, in this case 0.75. This process is repeated for each additional projected misstatement.

Because the upper limit ($410,886) is in excess of the tolerable misstatement ($364,000), the auditors would not accept the population as being materially correct. Thus, adjustment of the account, expansion of the test, or audit report modification would be appropriate.[14] In this situation, the most logical approach would be to persuade the client to adjust for the $102,008 in actual misstatements found in the sample. This would reduce the upper limit on misstatements to $308,878 ($410,886 − $102,008) and enable the auditors to accept the account as being materially correct.

Focus on Generalized Audit Software

ACL Services Ltd. is a leading provider of generalized audit software. That software can, among many other things, perform probability-proportional-to-size sampling (referred to as monetary unit sampling). The following is a printout of results using ACL for the problem we have presented in this appendix:

Confidence: 95%, Interval 95,000

Item	Error	Most Likely Error	Upper Error Limit
Basic Precision			285,000
100.00	10.00	9,500.00	16,625.00
2,000.00	100.00	4,750.00	7,363.00
102,000.00	101,898.00	101,898.00	101,898.00
Totals		116,148.00	410,886.00

Some of the terminology used differs as follows:

ACL	Text
Confidence	1 − Risk of incorrect acceptance (see footnote 3 earlier in this chapter)
Most likely error	Projected misstatement
Upper error limit	Upper limit on misstatement

Notice that ACL doesn't separately present the incremental allowance. To obtain the "incremental allowance" one may subtract both the basic precision and the most likely error from the total ($410,886.00 − $116,148.00 − $285,000.00 = $9,738.00).

Considerations in Using PPS Sampling

Although the formulas for PPS sampling at first seem difficult, once a user becomes familiar with them, they are easier to apply in practice than the classical variables sampling methods. An estimate of the standard deviation of the population need not be made, and the PPS selection method automatically results

---

[14] In many circumstances such as this, the client requests that the auditors expand the test to either identify the specific misstatements or to determine that the account is not materially misstated.

FIGURE 9.18
Relative Advantages and Disadvantages of Classical Variables Sampling and Probability–Proportional-to-Size Sampling

Classical Variables Sampling	
Advantages	**Disadvantages**
1. When there are many misstatements in the population, variables sampling techniques will result in a smaller sample size. 2. Items with zero and negative balances do not require any special treatment. 3. Sample size may be somewhat easier to expand if that becomes necessary.	1. To determine the sample size, the standard deviation of the population must be estimated. 2. To evaluate results, the sample's standard deviation must be calculated. 3. Variables sampling (especially mean-per-unit) usually must be stratified, requiring the use of a computer to perform the computations.

Probability-Proportional-to-Size (PPS) Sampling	
Advantages	**Disadvantages**
1. The technique is generally easier to use. 2. No estimate of the standard deviation of the population is needed. 3. Automatically stratifies the population because items are selected based on their dollar amount. 4. When there are few misstatements, the technique will generally result in a smaller sample size. 5. Sample selection can begin before the entire population is available.	1. Special considerations are required to handle understated accounts and negative balances. 2. Each item in the population must have a book value. 3. When misstatements are found, the technique might overstate the allowance for sampling risk. 4. For accounts with a moderate number of misstatements, the sample size may exceed that of the classical techniques.

in an efficient stratification of the sample. The method also provides smaller sample sizes when few misstatements are expected in the sample.

The advantages of PPS sampling do not come without cost. If there are a moderate number of differences between recorded and audited amounts, classical variables sampling methods will result in a smaller sample size. Also, when using PPS sampling special consideration must be given to (1) accounts with zero balances, (2) accounts with negative balances, and (3) accounts that are understated. CPA firms use various methods to overcome these limitations. Figure 9.18 summarizes advantages and disadvantages of the classical and PPS approaches.

Appendix 9B

Audit Risk

What level of risk of incorrect acceptance is acceptable for a substantive test? Based on the discussion in Chapter 5, we know that the extent of substantive tests is determined by the levels of inherent and control risk for the assertions being tested. This relationship was illustrated by the formula for **audit risk** that follows:

$$AR = IR \times CR \times DR$$

where

   AR = The allowable audit risk that a material misstatement might remain undetected for the account balance and related assertions.

   IR = **Inherent risk,** the risk of a material misstatement in an assertion, assuming there were no related controls.

   CR = **Control risk,** the risk that a material misstatement that could occur in an assertion will not be prevented or detected on a timely basis by internal control.

   DR = **Detection risk,** the risk that the auditors' procedures will fail to detect a material misstatement if it exists.

Since substantive procedures may consist of both tests of details using sampling and other types of substantive tests, such as analytical procedures, one modification of this formula is necessary to calculate the risk of incorrect acceptance for a substantive test. Detection risk must be separated into two components:

AP = The risk that analytical procedures and any other substantive procedures not using audit sampling will fail to detect a material misstatement.

TD = The allowable risk of incorrect acceptance for the substantive test of details.

With this modification, the revised formula is presented below:

$$AR = IR \times CR \times AP \times TD$$

Mathematically we may rearrange the terms in the formula as follows to solve for the appropriate risk of incorrect acceptance for the substantive test of details:

$$TD = \frac{AR}{IR \times CR \times AP}$$

To illustrate, assume that the auditors are willing to accept a 5 percent audit risk of material misstatement in the assertion of existence of the client's accounts receivable. They believe that the inherent risk of that assertion is 100 percent. After considering internal control over the revenue cycle, they assess control risk at a level of 50 percent, and they believe that the analytical procedures performed to test the assertion have a 40 percent risk of failing to detect a material misstatement. The appropriate level of risk of incorrect acceptance may be calculated as follows:

$$TD = \frac{AR}{IR \times CR \times AP}$$

$$= \frac{.05}{(1.00) \times (0.50) \times (0.40)}$$

$$= 0.25$$

Thus, the auditors must plan an audit sample for the substantive test of details with a risk of incorrect acceptance of 25 percent.

Implementing this formula in practice is quite difficult—it is not easy to precisely quantify the various levels of risks. For this reason, most CPA firms have implemented approaches that are less mathematical. However, the formula is useful in illustrating the relationships between the various types of risk. We know from the formula that in circumstances in which the auditors assess inherent risk and control risk as high and do not perform other effective tests of the assertion, the risk of incorrect acceptance must be set at a very low level. Decreases in inherent risk, control risk, or the risk that other procedures will fail to detect a material misstatement allow the auditors to accept a higher risk of incorrect acceptance for the substantive test of details.

Key Terms Introduced or Emphasized in Chapter 9 Appendixes

Audit risk   The risk that the auditors may unknowingly fail to appropriately modify their opinion on financial statements that are materially misstated.

Basic precision   In probability-proportional-to-size sampling, the reliability factor (for zero misstatements at the planned risk of incorrect acceptance) times the sampling interval.

Control risk   The risk of a material misstatement occurring in an assertion and not being detected on a timely basis by internal control.

Detection risk   The risk that the auditors' procedures will lead them to conclude that an assertion is not materially misstated, when in fact such misstatement does exist.

Dollar-unit sampling   See probability-proportional-to-size sampling.

Incremental allowance   In probability-proportional-to-size sampling, an amount determined by ranking the misstatements for logical units that are less than the sampling interval and considering incremental changes in reliability factors.

Inherent risk   The risk of material misstatement in an account, assuming there were no related controls.

Probability-proportional-to-size (PPS) sampling A variables sampling procedure that uses attributes theory to express a conclusion in monetary (dollar) amounts.

Projected misstatement In probability-proportional-to-size sampling, an amount calculated for logical units less than the size of the sampling interval by multiplying the percentage of misstatement (the "tainting") times the sampling interval.

Tainting In probability-proportional-to-size sampling, the percentage of misstatement of an item (misstatement amount divided by book value).

Upper limit on misstatement In probability-proportional-to-size sampling, the sum of projected misstatement, basic precision, and the incremental allowance. This total is used to evaluate sample results.

Questions and Problems for Chapter 9 Appendixes

9A–1. List the factors affecting sample size in a PPS sample.

9A–2. "When using a systematic sample selection technique with PPS sampling, every account larger than the sampling interval will automatically be included in the sample." Do you agree? Explain.

9A–3. When using PPS sampling, do auditors select sample items based on individual dollars, audit individual dollars, or both?

9A–4. A company has an inventory with a book value of $4,583,231, which includes 116 product lines and a total of 326,432 units. How many items compose this population for purposes of applying a probability-proportional-to-size sampling plan? Explain.

9A–5. "When no misstatements are found in a PPS sample, the upper limit on misstatement is equal to zero." Is this statement correct? Explain.

9A–6. A PPS sample with a sampling interval of $2,000 includes an item with an audited value of $90. This value was $30 lower than the account's book value. Calculate the tainting percentage for this account.

9A–7. The reliability factor table provides factors for as many as three computations when planning and evaluating the results of a PPS sample. Describe in general terms each of these computations.

9A–8. In a probability-proportional-to-size sample with a sampling interval of $20,000, an auditor discovered that a selected account receivable with a recorded amount of $10,000 had an audit amount of $2,000. Calculate the projected misstatement for this one item.

9A–9. Chris York, CPA, is considering the use of probability-proportional-to-size sampling in examining the sales transactions and accounts receivable of Carter Wholesale Company.

Required:

    a. How does the definition of the items in an accounts receivable population vary between probability-proportional-to-size sampling and mean-per-unit sampling?

    b. Should a population of accounts receivable be stratified by dollar value before applying probability-proportional-to-size sampling procedures? Discuss.

9A–10. The auditors of Dunbar Electronics want to limit the risk of material misstatement in the valuation of inventories to 2 percent. They believe that there exists a 50 percent risk that a material misstatement could have bypassed the client's internal control and that the inherent risk of the account is 80 percent. They also believe that the analytical procedures performed to test the assertion have a 40 percent risk of failing to detect a material misstatement.

Required:

    a. Briefly discuss what is meant by audit risk, inherent risk, control risk, and the risk that analytical procedures might fail to detect a material misstatement.

    b. Calculate the maximum allowable risk of incorrect acceptance for the substantive test of details.

    c. What level of detection risk is implicit in this problem?

9A–11. The auditors wish to test the valuation of accounts receivable in the audit of Desert Enterprises of Bullhead City. The client has $500,000 of total recorded receivables, composed of 850 accounts. The auditors have determined the following:

Tolerable misstatement	$25,000
Risk of incorrect acceptance	5%
Expected misstatement	$ 2,000

The auditors have decided to use probability-proportional-to-size sampling.

Required:
a. For planning the sample, calculate:
   (1) Required sample size.
   (2) Sampling interval.

b. Assume that the auditors have tested the sample and discovered three misstatements:

Book Value	Audited Value
$ 50	$ 47
800	760
8,500	8,100

   (1) Projected misstatement.
   (2) Basic precision.
   (3) Incremental allowance.
   (4) Upper limit on misstatement.

c. Explain how the auditors would consider the results calculated in (*b*).

In-Class Team Case for Chapter 9 Appendixes

9A–12. Edwards has decided to use probability-proportional-to-size (PPS) sampling, sometimes called dollar-unit sampling, in the audit of a client's accounts receivable balance. Few, if any, misstatements of the account balance are expected.

Edwards plans to use the following PPS sampling table:

Number of Overstatement Misstatements	Risk of Incorrect Acceptance				
	1%	5%	10%	15%	20%
0	4.61	3.00	2.31	1.90	1.61
1	6.64	4.75	3.89	3.38	3.00
2	8.41	6.30	5.33	4.72	4.28
3	10.05	7.76	6.69	6.02	5.52
4	11.61	9.16	8.00	7.27	6.73

Required:
a. Identify the advantages of using PPS sampling over classical variables sampling.

b. Calculate the sampling interval and the sample size Edwards should use given the following information:

Tolerable misstatement	$15,000
Risk of incorrect acceptance	5%
Estimated misstatement	$0
Recorded amount of accounts receivable	$300,000

Note: Requirements (*c*) through (*f*) are not related to (*a*) and (*b*).

c. Assuming a sampling interval of $5,000, calculate the total projected misstatement if the following three errors were discovered in a PPS sample:

Misstatement	Book Value	Audited Value
1	$ 400	$ 320
2	500	0
5	6,000	2,500

d. Calculate basic precision and incremental allowance.

e. Calculate the upper limit on misstatements.

f. Will you accept or reject the account as materially correct? Explain.

(AICPA, adapted)

9A–13. Assume that the table below is a computer printout generated by audit software using PPS sampling.

Population book value = $2,400,000

Tolerable misstatement = $280,000

Projected Misstatement:

Book Value	Audited Value	Misstatement	Tainting Percentage	Sampling Interval	Projected Misstatement
$ 1,000	$ 0	$ 1,000	100%	$ 80,000	$ 1,000
750	600	150	20	80,000	16,000
85,000	60,000	25,000	NA	NA	25,000
					$ 42,000

Basic Precision: $= 3.0 \times \$80,000 =$ $240,000

Incremental Allowance:

Reliability Factor	Increment	(Increment − 1)	Projected Misstatement	Incremental Allowance
3.00				
4.75	1.75	.75	$16,000	$12,000
6.30	1.55	.55	1,000	550
				$12,550

Answer the following questions:

Required:

  a. What was the planned sample size?

  b. Describe a circumstance that could cause the actual sample size to deviate from the planned sample size.

  c. What is the most likely misstatement in the population?

  d. What risk of incorrect acceptance is being accepted in this sample? Explain.

  e. Calculate the upper limit on misstatement.

  f. Would one "accept" or "reject" the population as being materially correct? Explain.

Integrating Problem for Chapter 9 and the Appendixes

9A–14. Bill Pei, CPA, is about to begin his audit of the accuracy of his client's accounts receivable. Based on experience, he expects that approximately 1 percent of the client's 40,000 accounts have errors. The total book value of receivables is $5 million. Pei has established $390,000 as the amount of tolerable misstatement, 5 percent for the risk of incorrect acceptance, and 10 percent for the risk of incorrect rejection. The auditors estimate the standard deviation of the accounts to be $45.

Required:

  a. Using mean-per-unit sampling, calculate the required sample size.

  b. Now ignore part (*a*). Assume that as part of an attributes sampling plan using a stipulated tolerable rate of 5 percent and a risk of assessing control risk too low of 5 percent, the auditors wish to test the receivables valuation—that is, each account will either be considered as correct, or a deviation. What sample size would be required for this test?

Additional information for parts (c) through (g):

Now ignore your (*a*) and (*b*) answers, and assume that the auditor selected a random sample of 208 accounts (square root = 14.4), representing a total book value of receivables of $40,800. He found five errors, representing a $20,300 overstatement as follows:

Misstatement	Book Value	Audited Value
1	$26,000	$5,950
2	1,000	900
3	220	200
4	180	120
5	100	30
	$27,500	$7,200

The standard deviation of the book value of the sample was $50, while the standard deviation of the audited values of the sample was $55. For part (*g*) assume a sampling interval of $24,038 ($5,000,000/208).

c. Using mean-per-unit estimation, what is the projected misstatement for the population?

d. Using mean-per-unit sampling, calculate the adjusted allowance for sampling risk and use it to calculate the appropriate interval for use in deciding whether to "accept" or "reject" the population.

e. Using difference estimation, calculate the projected misstatement for the population.

f. Given the five misstatements presented above, what statistical conclusion may be made using attributes sampling (recall part [*b*] above)?

g. Using PPS sampling, calculate:

(1) Projected misstatement.

(2) Basic precision.

(3) Incremental allowance for sampling risk.

Chapter 10

Cash and Financial Investments

Chapter learning objectives

After studying this chapter, you should be able to:

LO1. Describe the sources and nature of cash.

LO2. Identify the auditors' objectives for the audit of cash.

LO3. Explain the nature of the cash receipts and disbursements cycles, and describe the fundamental controls over the business processes related to cash.

LO4. Assess inherent and fraud risks for cash.

LO5. Assess control risk and design typical tests of controls used by auditors to support the assessed levels of control risk for cash.

LO6. Explain how the auditors design substantive audit procedures and address the risks of material misstatement of cash.

LO7. Describe the risks involved in auditing financial investments, including why the auditors might need specialized skills.

LO8. Identify the auditors' objectives in the audit of financial investments.

LO9. Describe typical internal controls over the business processes related to financial investments.

LO10. Describe tests of controls and substantive procedures used to audit financial investments.

This chapter describes the approach to the audit of cash and financial investments. Our discussion of these two types of assets is combined because of the interrelationship between them. Cash and many financial investments are liquid in nature, and transfers between the two accounts occur frequently.

Cash

Sources and Nature of Cash

Cash normally includes general, payroll, petty cash, and, less frequently, savings accounts. General accounts are checking accounts similar in nature to those maintained by individuals. Cash sales, collections of receivables, and investment of additional capital typically increase the account; business expenditures decrease it. Under the terms of a bank loan agreement, the cash in a company's general account sometimes must be maintained at a specified minimum balance, referred to as a *compensating balance.*

Payroll and petty cash accounts are "imprest" at a low balance. When payroll is paid, a check from the general account is drawn to deposit funds into the payroll account. Petty cash, used for very small expenditures, is replenished as necessary.

Cash equivalents are often combined with cash items to create the current asset classification called "cash and cash equivalents." *Cash equivalents* include money market funds, certificates of deposit, savings certificates, and other similar types of deposits. Any item that cannot be converted to cash on short notice should be classified as an investment, a receivable, or a prepaid expense, rather than as a cash equivalent.

Normal internal control activities (e.g., reconciliation of bank accounts) detect most errors that occur in these accounts. On the other hand, the liquid nature of cash increases the risk of undetected fraud.

The Auditors' Objectives in the Audit of Cash

The auditors' *objectives* in the audit of cash are to:

1. Consider the *inherent risks* related to cash, including fraud risks.
2. Consider *internal control* over cash transactions.
3. Substantiate the *existence* of recorded cash.
4. Establish the *completeness* of recorded cash.
5. Determine that the client has *rights* to recorded cash.
6. Determine that the *presentation* and *disclosure* of cash, including restricted funds (such as compensating balances and bond sinking funds), are appropriate.

In addition to the above, the auditors might add a valuation objective that relates to procedures for reconciling underlying records to the general ledger results and, if appropriate, proper valuation of foreign currency translation. We omit a separate valuation objective in the above list due to the ordinarily very limited valuation issues relating to cash (e.g., there is no need to consider valuation issues such as *net realizable value,* as with receivables, or the *lower of cost or market,* as with inventories).

How Much Audit Time for Cash?

The consideration of materiality applies to audit work on cash as well as to other aspects of the audit. The counting of a small petty cash fund, which is inconsequential in relation to the company's overall financial position, accomplishes little in achieving the auditors' objective of expressing an opinion on the financial statements. Nevertheless, auditors do devote a larger proportion of the total audit hours to cash than might be suggested by the relatively small amount of cash shown on the balance sheet.

Several reasons exist to explain the auditors' traditional emphasis on cash transactions. Liabilities, revenue, expenses, and most other assets flow through the Cash account; that is, these items either arise from or result in cash transactions. Thus, the examination of cash transactions assists the auditors in the substantiation of many other items in the financial statements.

Another reason contributing to extensive auditing of cash is that cash is the most liquid of assets and offers the greatest temptation for theft, embezzlement, and misappropriation. Inherent risk is high for liquid assets, and auditors tend to respond to high-risk situations with more intensive investigation. However, the detection of fraud is relevant to overall fairness of the client's financial statements only if such fraud is material in amount.

On occasion, auditors may encounter evidence of small-scale employee fraud. After determining that such fraud could *not* have a material effect upon the financial statements, the auditors should review the situation with the management and the audit committee of the board of directors before investigating the matter further. This discussion will alert the client to the situation, protect the auditors from charges of negligence, and avoid wasting audit time on matters that are not material to the financial statements and that may better be pursued by client personnel.

Internal Control over Cash Transactions

Learning Objective 3

Most of the processes relating to cash handling are the responsibility of the finance department, under the direction of the treasurer. These processes include handling and depositing cash receipts; signing checks; investing idle cash; and maintaining custody of cash, marketable securities, and other negotiable assets. In addition, the finance department must forecast cash requirements and make both short-term and long-term financing arrangements.

Ideally, the functions of the finance department and the accounting department should be integrated in a manner that provides assurance that:

1. All cash that should have been received *was* in fact received, recorded accurately, and deposited promptly.
2. Cash disbursements have been made for authorized purposes only and have been properly recorded.
3. Cash balances are maintained at adequate, but not excessive, levels by forecasting expected cash receipts and payments related to normal operations. The need for obtaining loans or for investing excess cash is thus made known on a timely basis.

A detailed study of the business processes of the client is necessary in developing the most efficient control procedures, but there are some general guidelines to good cash-handling practices in all types of business. These guidelines for achieving internal control over cash may be summarized as follows:

1. Do not permit any one employee to handle a transaction from beginning to end.
2. Separate cash handling from recordkeeping.
3. Centralize receiving of cash to the extent practical.
4. Record cash receipts on a timely basis.
5. Encourage customers to obtain receipts and observe cash register totals.
6. Deposit cash receipts daily.
7. Make all disbursements by check or electronic funds transfer, with the exception of small expenditures from petty cash.
8. Have monthly bank reconciliations prepared by employees not responsible for the issuance of checks or custody of cash. The completed reconciliation should be reviewed promptly by an appropriate official.
9. Forecast expected cash receipts and disbursements and investigate variances from forecasted amounts.

Internal Control over Cash Receipts

Cash Sales

Control over cash sales is strongest when two or more employees (usually a salesclerk and a cashier) participate in each transaction with a customer. Restaurants and cafeterias often use a centrally located cashier who receives cash from the customer along with a sales ticket prepared by another employee. Theaters generally have a cashier selling prenumbered tickets, which are collected by a door attendant when the customer is admitted. If tickets or sales checks are serially numbered and all numbers accounted for, this separation of responsibility for the transaction is an effective means of preventing fraud.

In many retail establishments, the nature of the business is such that one employee must make over-the-counter sales, deliver the merchandise, receive cash, and record the transaction.

In this situation, dishonesty may be discouraged by proper use of cash registers or electronic point-of-sale systems. The protective features of cash registers include (1) visual display of the amount of the sale in full view of the customer; (2) a printed receipt, which the customer is urged to take with the merchandise; and (3) accumulation of a locked-in total of the day's sales.

Electronic Point-of-Sale Systems

Many retail stores use various types of electronic cash registers, including online computer terminals. Often, an electronic scanner reads the *universal product code* on the product. The salesperson need only scan the code for the register to record the sale at the product's price, which is stored in the computer. Thus, the risk of a salesperson recording sales at erroneous prices is substantially reduced.

Besides providing strong control over cash sales, electronic point-of-sale systems often may be programmed to perform numerous other control functions. For example, online registers may verify the credit status of charge account customers, update accounts receivable and perpetual inventory records, and provide special printouts accumulating sales data by product line, salesperson, department, and type of sale.

Collections from Credit Customers

In many manufacturing and wholesale companies, cash receipts include many checks received through the mail. This situation poses little threat of defalcation unless one employee is permitted to receive and deposit these checks and also to record the credits to the customers' accounts. Typical internal control over cash received through the mail is described below.

Incoming mail usually is opened in the mailroom, where an employee endorses the checks "for deposit only" to the company's account and prepares a *control listing* of the incoming cash receipts. This listing shows the amount received from each customer and identifies the customer by name or account number. A copy of the control listing is forwarded to the controller. Another copy of the control listing and the cash receipts are forwarded to the cashier. The remittance advices and a copy of the control (shown below) listing are forwarded to the employee responsible for the customers' accounts.

Which controls tend to prevent the mailroom employee from abstracting the receipts from several customers, destroying the remittance advices, and omitting these receipts from the control listing? First, incoming cash receipts consist primarily of checks made payable to the company. Second, if customers' accounts are not credited for payments made, the customers will complain to the company. If these customers can produce paid checks supporting their claims of payment and these checks do not appear on the mailroom control listings, responsibility for the abstraction is quickly focused upon the mailroom employee.

The checks are transferred to the cashier (with a copy of the control listing), who deposits the day's receipts intact in the bank. Control is exercised over the cashier by periodic

Check

Pilot Stores	987604
1425 G St.	
Irvine, CA 92345	Date: Dec. 5, 20XX
Pay to the	
order of Wood Supply Co.	$8085.00
Eight thousand eighty-five and no/100	
First National Bank	Pilot Stores
California	*Jackie Cohen*

Remittance Advice	
Wood Supply Co.	
Inv. #7462537	$8085.00

CONTROL LISTING		
Payer	Cust. No.	Amount
Xxxxxxxxx	######	$$$$$.$$
Xxxxxxxxx	######	$$$$$.$$
Xxxxxxxxx	######	$$$$$.$$
Pilot Stores	12654	$8085.00
Xxxxxxxxx	######	$$$$$.$$
Xxxxxxxxx	######	$$$$$.$$
		$$$$$.$$

reconciliation of the operations control copies of the mailroom control listings with the cash receipts journal and the details of the validated deposit slips received from the bank.

Businesses receiving a large volume of cash through the mail often use a lockbox system to strengthen internal control and hasten the depositing of cash receipts. The **lockbox** is actually a post office box controlled by the company's bank. The bank picks up mail at the post office box several times a day, credits the company's checking account for cash received, and sends the remittance advices to the company. Internal control is strengthened by the fact that the bank has no access to the company's accounting records.

The employee responsible for the customers' accounts ledger enters the details of cash receipts into the computer in batches. The cash receipts program creates a file of cash receipt transactions that is used to update the general ledger and the master file of accounts receivable. This computer program creates control totals and exception reports that detail any invalid customer account numbers or unusual payment amounts. The manual follow-up procedures on exceptions reports and the reconciliations of control totals are performed by the operations control group.

The division of responsibilities, sequence of procedures, and controls over cash sales and collections from customers are illustrated in the systems flowchart in Figure 10.1, on pages 356 and 357.

Electronic Funds Transfer

Financial institutions have developed **electronic funds transfer (EFT) systems** that process funds-related transactions for customers as an alternative to paying by checks. Increasingly, **electronic data interchange (EDI)** systems, which allow the interchange of data from one company's computer to another's, are electronically transferring funds between companies' bank accounts. These systems have advantages over checking systems in that they reduce paper flow and may reduce processing costs and delays. They do, however, require an extensive set of computer network controls relating to system access and data entry, as well as backup controls for situations in which a system breakdown occurs.

Internal Control over Cash Disbursements

Ideally, cash disbursements should be made by check, electronic funds transfer, or, for minor items, from petty cash funds.

Checking Account Disbursements

A principal advantage of requiring disbursement by check is obtaining evidence of receipt from the payee in the form of an endorsement on the check. Other advantages include (1) the centralization of disbursement authority in the hands of a few designated officials—only persons authorized to sign checks; (2) a permanent record of disbursements; and (3) a reduction in the amount of cash kept on hand.

To secure in full the internal control benefits implicit in the use of checks, it is essential that all checks be prenumbered and all numbers in the series be accounted for. Unissued prenumbered checks should be adequately safeguarded against theft or misuse. Voided checks should be defaced to eliminate any possibility of further use and filed in the regular sequence of paid checks. Dollar amounts should be printed on all checks by the computer or a check-protecting machine. This practice makes it difficult for anyone to alter a check by raising its amount.

Officials authorized to sign checks should review the documents supporting the payment and perforate (deface) these documents at the time of signing the check to prevent them from being submitted a second time. The official signing checks should maintain control of the checks until they are placed in the mail. Typically, the check comes to the official complete except for signature. To make a variety of fraudulent schemes involving falsified documents less likely, the signed checks should not be returned to the accounting department, which prepared them for signature.

Most companies issuing a large volume of checks use computers or check-signing machines. The authorized signature (usually that of the treasurer) may be printed automatically on each check as it is processed. If the computer generates signed checks, item counts, control totals, and cash totals (reconciled by finance department personnel) may be used to make certain that checks are issued only for authorized cash disbursements. When a check-signing

FIGURE 10.1 **Cash Receipts Cycle**

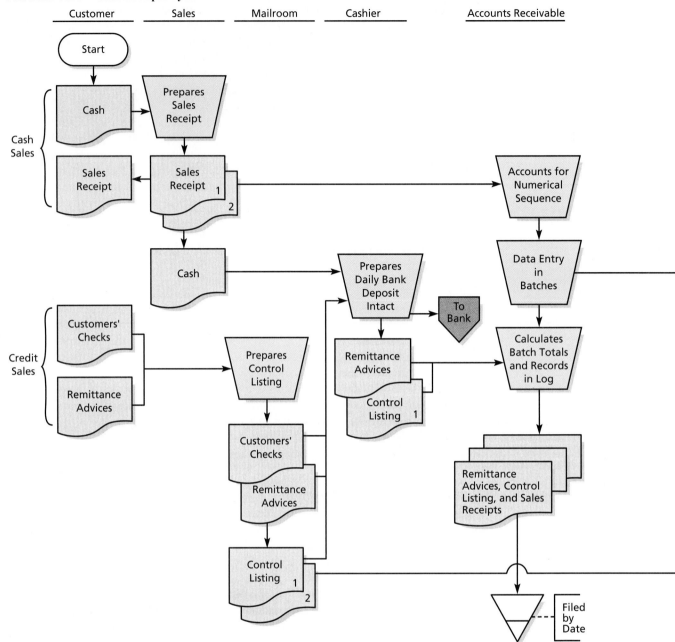

machine is used, a key should be required to retrieve the signed checks, and the facsimile signature plate should be removed from the machine and safeguarded when the machine is not in use. A second, manual signature may also be required on checks signed by a computer or a check-signing machine for large disbursements, say over $10,000.

Reconciliation of monthly bank statements is essential to adequate internal control over cash receipts and disbursements. An employee having no part in authorizing or accounting for cash transactions or in handling cash should reconcile bank statements. Statements from the bank should come unopened to this employee. Each month the completed bank reconciliation should be reviewed by a responsible company official and approved in writing.

A voucher system is one method of achieving strong internal control over cash disbursements by providing assurance that all disbursements are properly authorized and reviewed before a check is issued. In a typical voucher system, the accounting department is responsible for assembling the appropriate documentation to support every cash disbursement. For

Data Processing	Operations Control	Bank

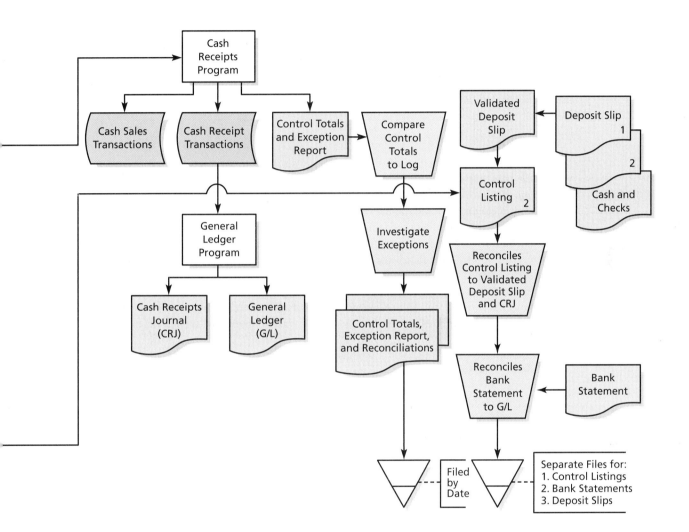

example, before authorizing payment for merchandise purchased, the accounting department assembles copies of the purchase order, receiving report, and vendor's invoice and determines that these documents are in agreement. After determining that the transaction is properly supported, an accounting employee prepares a voucher, which is filed in a tickler file according to the date upon which payment will be made.

A **voucher,** in this usage, is an authorization sheet that provides space for the initials of the employees performing various authorization functions. Authorization functions include such procedures as extending and footing the vendor's invoice; determining the agreement of the invoice, purchase order, and receiving report; and recording the transaction in the accounts. Transactions are recorded in a **voucher register** (which normally replaces a purchases journal) by an entry debiting the appropriate asset, liability, or expense account and crediting Vouchers Payable. The separation of the function of invoice verification and approval from

Illustrative Case
Importance of Cash Controls

One large construction company ignored basic controls over cash disbursements. Unissued checks were stored in an unlocked supply closet, along with Styrofoam coffee cups. The company check-signing machine deposited signed checks into a box that was equipped with a lock. Despite warnings from their independent auditors, company officials found it "too inconvenient" to keep the box locked or to pay attention to the check-counter built into the machine. The company maintained very large bank balances and did not bother to reconcile bank statements promptly.

A three-week-old bank statement and a group of paid checks were given to an employee with instructions to prepare a bank reconciliation. The employee noticed that the group of paid checks accompanying the bank statement was not complete. No paid checks could be found to support over $700,000 in charges on the bank statement. Further investigation revealed that more than $1 million in unauthorized and unrecorded checks had been paid from various company bank accounts. The checks had been issued out of sequence and had been signed by the company check-signing machine. The company was unable to determine who was responsible for the theft, and the money was never recovered.

the function of cash disbursement is another step that tends to prevent errors and fraud. On the payment date, the voucher and supporting documents are removed from the tickler file and the check is prepared *but not signed.* The voucher, supporting papers, and the check (complete except for signature) are forwarded to the finance department for signature.

In a computerized purchasing system, vendor invoice information will be entered by the accounting department and it may be matched by the computer with purchase order and receiving information that was entered by the other departments. If the information matches, the computer will approve the payment and automatically record the voucher as a payable. Transactions with inconsistencies will not be processed, but will be listed on an exception report for review and follow-up by the operations control group. Just prior to its due date, the computer will generate a check in payment of the invoice. If the checks are signed by the computer, they need not be sent to the vouchers payable department for mailing.

Another control the auditors may expect to find in a well-managed accounts payable department is the monthly balancing of the detailed records of accounts payable (or vouchers) to the general ledger control account. These reconciliations are saved as evidence of the performance of this procedure and as an aid in locating any subsequent errors or fraud.

Vendors' statements, received monthly, should be reconciled promptly with the accounts payable ledger or list of open vouchers, and any discrepancies should be fully investigated. In some industries, it is common practice to make advances to vendors, which are recovered by making percentage deductions from invoices. When advances are made, the auditors should ascertain that procedures are being followed to ensure that deductions from the invoices are being made in accordance with the terms of the agreement.

The operation of a voucher system is illustrated in the flowchart in Figure 10.2.

Internal Control Aspects of Petty Cash Funds

Internal control over payments from an imprest petty cash fund is achieved when the custodian of the petty cash fund reviews support from employees seeking reimbursement for their small expenditures on behalf of the company. Further control exists when the custodian requests replenishment of the fund and another individual reviews the support for completeness and authenticity and subsequently defaces that support to prevent reuse.

Audit tests of petty cash emphasize transactions rather than the year-end balance. The auditors may test one or more replenishment transactions by examining petty cash vouchers and verifying their numerical sequence.

Petty cash funds are sometimes kept in the form of separate bank accounts. The bank should be instructed in writing not to accept for deposit in such an account any checks payable to the company. The deposits will be limited to checks to replenish the fund and drawn payable to the bank or to the custodian of the fund. The prohibition against deposit of checks payable to the company

FIGURE 10.2 **Flowchart of a Cash Disbursements Cycle (Voucher System)**

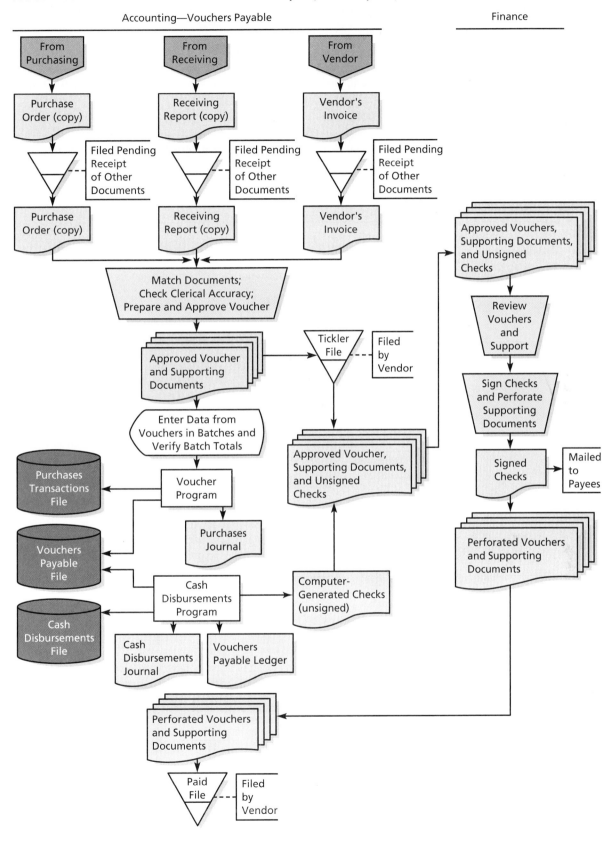

is designed to prevent the routing of cash receipts into petty cash, since this would violate the basic assumption of limited disbursements and review at the time of replenishing the fund.

Audit Documentation for Cash

Auditors' working papers for cash typically include a flowchart or a written description of controls. An internal control questionnaire is also often used, especially in larger companies. A related working paper will summarize tests of controls for cash transactions and the assessments of risk for the financial statement assertions about cash.

Additional cash working papers include an audit program, a lead schedule, cash count sheets, bank confirmations, bank reconciliations, lists of outstanding checks, lists of checks being investigated, recommendations to the client for improving internal control, and notes concerning proper presentation and disclosure of cash in the client's balance sheet.

Audit of Cash

The following steps indicate the general pattern of work performed by the auditors in the verification of cash. Selection of the most appropriate procedures for a particular audit will be guided, of course, by the nature of the controls in force and by other circumstances of the engagement.

A. Consider inherent risks, including fraud risks.
B. Consider internal control over cash.
　1. *Obtain an understanding of internal control* over cash.
　2. *Assess control risk* and *design additional tests of controls and substantive tests* for cash.
　3. *Perform additional tests of controls* for those controls which the auditors plan to consider to support their planned assessed levels of control risk, such as:
　　a. Test the accounting records and reconciliations by reperformance.
　　b. Compare the details of a sample of cash receipts listings to the cash receipts journal, accounts receivable postings, and authenticated deposit slips.
　　c. Compare the details of a sample of recorded disbursements in the cash payments journal to accounts payable postings, purchase orders, receiving reports, invoices, and paid checks.
　4. *Reassess control risk* and *modify substantive tests* for cash.
C. Perform substantive tests of cash transactions and balances.
　1. Obtain analyses of cash balances and reconcile them to the general ledger.
　2. Send standard confirmation forms to financial institutions to verify amounts on deposit.
　3. Obtain or prepare reconciliations of bank (financial institution) accounts as of the balance sheet date and consider need to reconcile bank activity for additional months.
　4. Obtain a cutoff bank statement containing transactions of at least seven business days subsequent to balance sheet date.
　5. Count and list cash on hand.
　6. Verify the client's cutoff of cash receipts and cash disbursements.
　7. Analyze bank transfers for last week of audit year and first week of following year.
　8. Investigate any checks representing large or unusual payments to related parties.
　9. Evaluate proper financial statement presentation and disclosure of cash.

Figure 10.3 relates these substantive tests to the primary audit objectives.

Learning Objective 4

A. Consider the Inherent Risks of Cash, Including Fraud Risks.

Risks of material misstatement arise jointly from inherent risk and control risk. Most inherent risks relate to business risks faced by the client's management. In the area of cash and financial investments, management is particularly concerned with business risks related to the possible theft of these liquid assets. This is also a significant concern of the auditors as most misstatements of assets involve overstatement.

In addition to concerns about the overstatement of cash, auditors are aware that cash may have been improperly abstracted during the period, even though the year-end cash may be properly stated. To distinguish between the situations, assume that the client's balance sheet

FIGURE 10.3
Objectives of Major Substantive Tests of Cash Transactions and Balances

Substantive Tests	Primary Audit Objectives
Obtain analyses of cash balances and reconcile them to general ledger.	*Valuation*
Send standard confirmation forms to financial institutions. Obtain reconciliations of bank balances and consider reconciling bank activity. Obtain bank cutoff statement. Count cash on hand.	*Existence and rights*
Verify the client's cutoff of cash transactions. Analyze bank transfers occurring around year-end.	*Existence and rights* *Completeness*
Investigate payments to related parties. Evaluate financial statement presentation and disclosure.	*Presentation and disclosure*

shows "Cash $250,000." For most clients, the primary risks are that errors or fraud either (1) create a situation in which $250,000 overstates actual cash, or (2) have improperly reduced the balance to $250,000.

Concerning the first risk (overstated cash), a shortage may have been concealed merely by the insertion of a fictitious check in the cash on hand at year-end, or by the omission of an outstanding check from the year-end bank reconciliation. Note that the omission of an outstanding check may be indicative of either an error or fraud. For example, poor internal control may result in a situation in which human error resulted in the check not being recorded in disbursements. On the other hand, although recorded in cash disbursements, the check may have been omitted from the outstanding check list to allow the individual who has embezzled that amount of cash to hide fraud.

Concerning the second risk—the year-end cash is correct, but should be higher—the auditors' problem is not misstated cash, but fraud and its effect on other accounts. Consequently, the auditors have in mind such basic questions as: (1) Do the client's records reflect all cash transactions that took place during the year? and (2) Were all cash payments properly authorized and for a legitimate business purpose? Examples of fraud that may be disclosed in searching for answers to these questions are:

1. Interception of cash receipts before any record is made.
2. Payment for materials not received.
3. Duplicate payments.
4. Overpayments to employees or payments to fictitious employees.
5. Payments for personal expenditures of officers or related parties.

Based on their knowledge of the client and its business, the auditors may identify other business risks that result in risks of material misstatements. In some engagements, the auditors may be particularly concerned with the risk of the completeness of recorded cash. As an example, management of a privately held company may be motivated to understate assets (including cash) to minimize income taxes. Also, for a particular client there may be a significant risk that management maintains bank accounts not recorded on the books for such purposes as making illegal bribes. Thus, in such situations, there is a heightened risk that not all cash may be recorded in the financial records. In other cases, the manner in which the client collects cash may present significant business and inherent risks. For example, a charitable organization may receive a large amount of funds from cash donations, creating a significant inherent risk that not all cash donations may be received and recorded.

The auditors also may identify fraud risks related to cash transactions. In such cases, the auditors should obtain an understanding of the programs and controls used by management to mitigate these risks and determine whether the controls have been placed in operation. Strengths and weaknesses in the client's internal control serve to mitigate or increase the effects of these fraud risks.

B. Consider Internal Control Over Cash.

1. Obtain an Understanding of Internal Control.

In the audit of a small business, the auditors may prepare a written description of controls, based upon the questioning of owners and employees and upon firsthand observation. For larger companies, a flowchart or internal control questionnaire is usually employed to describe internal control. An internal control questionnaire for cash receipts was illustrated in Chapter 7. Among the questions included in a questionnaire for cash disbursements are whether all disbursements (except those from petty cash) are made by prenumbered checks and whether voided checks are marked "void" and saved. The existence of these controls permits the auditors to determine that all disbursements have been recorded by accounting for the sequence of checks issued or voided during the period.

Other points to be made clear by the questionnaire include: (1) whether check-signing authority is restricted to selected executives not having access to accounting records or to vouchers and other documents supporting checks submitted for signature, and (2) whether checks are mailed directly to the payees after being signed. The internal control questionnaire will also cover cash disbursements for payroll and for dividends, as well as bank reconciliation procedures.

After the auditors have prepared a flowchart (or other description) of internal control, they often will conduct a walk-through of the system. The term *walk-through* means to trace a few transactions through each step of the system to determine that transactions actually are being processed in the manner indicated by the flowchart. The walk-through allows the auditors to determine that internal control as described in the working papers has actually been *placed in operation.*

As the auditors verify their understanding of the cash receipts and disbursements cycles, they will observe whether there is appropriate segregation of duties and inquire about who performed various functions throughout the year. They will also inspect the various documents and reconciliations that are important to the client's internal control over cash receipts and disbursements. Cash forecasts or budgets also will be inspected and the auditors will review the evidence of the follow-up on variances from forecasted amounts of receipts and disbursements. These tests of controls may provide the auditors with sufficient evidence to assess control risk for certain financial statement assertions at less than the maximum.

2. Assess Control Risk and Design Additional Tests of Controls and Substantive Tests for Cash.

After obtaining an understanding of the client's internal control over cash receipts and disbursements, the auditors determine their planned assessed levels of control risk for the assertions about the cash account. If additional evidence of effectiveness of the controls is needed to support these assessed levels, the auditors will design additional tests of control. In designing these tests, the auditors must decide which ones will result in sufficient reductions in substantive tests to justify the time spent performing them.

By considering these assessments of control risk in conjunction with their assessments of inherent risk, the auditors are able to identify "what could go wrong" to cause the cash accounts to be materially misstated. Figures 10.4 and 10.5 provide examples of possible material misstatements of cash that may be identified by the auditors based on the client's operations and environment, and on weaknesses in its internal control over cash receipts and cash disbursements. Once these risks of material misstatement have been identified and assessed, the auditors can plan appropriate substantive tests that address them.

3. Perform Additional Tests of Controls for Those Controls That the Auditors Plan to Consider in Their Assessment of Control Risk.

Tests directed toward the effectiveness of controls help to evaluate the client's internal control and determine whether the auditors' assessed levels of control risk can be supported. Certain tests of controls are performed as the auditors obtain an understanding of the client's internal control; these tests were described in our discussion of that process. The following are examples of typical additional tests of controls.

FIGURE 10.4 **Potential Misstatements—Cash Receipts**

Description of Misstatement	Examples	Internal Control Weaknesses or Factors That Increase the Risk of the Misstatement
Recording fictitious cash receipts	**Fraud:** • Overstating cash receipts on the books by transferring cash between bank accounts without appropriate recording of the transfer to cover up an embezzlement of cash.	• Lack of segregation of duties of the functions of access to cash and recordkeeping; no effective review of bank reconciliations.
Failure to record receipts from cash sales	**Fraud:** • A cashier fails to ring up and record cash sales and embezzles the cash. **Error:** • A bookkeeper accidentally omits the recording of the receipts from one cash register for the day.	• Inadequate supervision of cashiers; failure to encourage customers to obtain cash receipts. • Inadequate controls for reconciling cash register tapes and accounting records; inadequate controls for reconciling bank accounts.
Failure to record cash from collection of accounts receivable	**Fraud:** • A cashier embezzles cash payments by customers on receivables, without recording the receipts in the customers' accounts. • A bookkeeper who has access to cash receipts embezzles cash collected from customers and writes off the related receivables. **Error:** • A bookkeeper accidentally fails to record payment on a receivable.	• Lack of segregation of duties between personnel who have access to cash receipts and those who make entries into the accounts receivable records. • Lack of segregation of duties between personnel who have access to cash receipts and those who make entries into the accounts receivable records. • Inadequate reconciliations of subsidiary records of accounts receivable with the general ledger control account.
Early (late) recognition of cash receipts—"cutoff problems"	**Fraud:** • Holding the cash receipts journal open to record next year's cash receipts as having occurred in this year. **Error:** • Recording cash receipts based on bad information about date of receipt.	• Ineffective board of directors, audit committee, or internal audit function; "tone at the top" not conducive to ethical conduct; undue pressure to show improved financial position. • Failure to list and deposit cash receipts on a timely basis.

a. Test the Accounting Records and Reconciliations by Reperformance.

To determine that the client's accounting procedures are operating effectively, the auditors perform tests of the accuracy of the client's journals and ledgers. In a computer-based system, journal and ledger entries may be created simultaneously from the same source documents, and the auditors might choose to use generalized audit software to test the accuracy of the accounting records.

In a manual system, information on source documents is entered first in a journal; at a later date the information is summarized and posted from journals to ledgers. The auditors must manually determine that documents are accurately entered to the journals, the journals are accurately

FIGURE 10.5 Potential Misstatements—Cash Disbursements

Description of Misstatement	Examples	Internal Control Weaknesses or Factors That Increase the Risk of the Misstatement
Inaccurate recording of a purchase or disbursement	**Fraud:** • A bookkeeper prepares a check to himself and records it as having been issued to a major supplier. **Errors:** • A disbursement is made to pay an invoice for goods that have not been received. • Disbursements for travel and entertainment are improperly included with merchandise purchases.	• Inadequate segregation of duties of recordkeeping and preparing cash disbursements, or check signer does not review and cancel supporting documents. • Ineffective controls for matching invoices with receiving documents before disbursements are authorized. • Ineffective accounting coding procedures may result from incompetent accounting personnel, inadequate chart of accounts, or no controls over the posting process.
Duplicate recording and payment of purchases	**Error:** • A purchase is recorded when an invoice is received from a vendor and recorded again when a duplicate invoice is sent by the vendor.	• Ineffective controls for review and cancellation of supporting documents by the check signer.
Unrecorded disbursements	**Fraud:** • In conjunction with unrecorded (but deposited) cash receipts, an employee writes and cashes an unrecorded check for the identical amount.	• Ineffective control over recordkeeping for and access to cash.

footed, and the data properly posted to the ledgers. The auditors also may decide to test the client's procedures for reconciling bank (financial institution) accounts. They may select a sample of the reconciliations performed during the year, noting who performed them, and *reperform* the reconciliation process by reference to accounting records, bank statements, and canceled checks.

b. Compare the Details of a Sample of Cash Receipts Listings to the Cash Receipts Journal, Accounts Receivable Postings, and Authenticated Deposit Slips.

Satisfactory internal control over cash receipts demands that each day's collections be deposited intact no later than the next banking day. To provide assurance that cash receipts have been deposited intact, the auditors should compare the detail of the original cash receipts listings (mailroom listings and register tapes) to the detail of the daily deposit tickets. The *detail* of cash receipts refers to a listing of the amount of each individual check and the total amount of currency composing the day's receipts.

Comparison of the daily entries in the cash receipts journal with bank deposits may disclose a type of fraud known as *lapping*. Lapping is the concealment of a cash shortage by delaying the recording of cash receipts. The table on page 365 provides an illustration.

If cash collected from customer A is withheld by the cashier, a subsequent collection from customer B may be entered as a credit to A's account. B's account will not be shown as paid until a collection from customer C is recorded as a credit to B. Unless the money abstracted by the cashier is replaced, the accounts receivable as a group remain overstated; but judicious shifting of the overstatement from one account receivable to another may avert protests from customers receiving monthly statements. The following schedule makes clear how a lapping activity may be carried on. In companies in which the cashier has access to the general accounting records, shortages created in this manner have sometimes been transferred to inventory accounts or elsewhere in the records for temporary concealment.

Lapping is most easily carried on when an employee who receives collections from customers is responsible for the posting of customers' accounts. Familiarity with customers' accounts makes it relatively easy to lodge a shortage in an account that will not be currently questioned.

Date	Actually Received From	Actual Cash Receipts	Recorded as Received From	Receipts Recorded and Deposited	Receipts Withheld
Dec. 1	Abbott	$ 750			$ 750
	Crane	1,035	Crane	$1,035	
2	Barstow	750	Abbott	750	
	White	130	White	130	
3	Crawford	1,575	Barstow	750	825
	Miller	400	Miller	400	
		$4,640		$ 3,065	$ 1,575

c. Compare the Details of a Sample of Recorded Disbursements in the Cash Disbursements Journal to Accounts Payable Postings, Purchase Orders, Receiving Reports, Invoices, and Paid Checks.

Satisfactory internal control over cash disbursements requires that controls exist to provide assurance that disbursements are properly authorized. Testing cash disbursements involves tracing selected items back through the cash payments journal to original source documents, including vouchers, purchase orders, receiving reports, invoices, and paid checks. While examining these documents, the auditors have an opportunity to test many of the controls over cash disbursements. For example, they will notice whether all paid vouchers and supporting documents have been perforated or canceled. Also, they will determine whether agreement exists among the supporting documents and note the presence of all required authorization signatures. The auditors also may review the file of paid checks to test the client's procedures for accounting for the numerical sequence of checks.

4. Reassess Control Risk and Modify Substantive Tests for Cash.

When the auditors have completed the procedures described in the preceding sections, they should reassess the level of control risk for each financial statement assertion regarding cash. The auditors then decide what modifications, if any, are necessary to the planned audit program of substantive tests of cash transactions and balances.

Learning Objective 6

C. Perform Substantive Tests of Cash Transactions and Balances.

1. Obtain Analyses of Cash Balances and Reconcile to the General Ledger.

Primary Audit Objective:	
Valuation	☑

The auditors will prepare or obtain a schedule that lists all of the client's cash accounts. For cash in bank accounts, this schedule will typically list the bank, the account number, the account type, and the year-end balance per books. The auditors will trace and reconcile all accounts to the general ledger as necessary.

2. Send Standard Confirmation Forms to Financial Institutions to Verify Amounts on Deposit.

Primary Audit Objectives:	
Existence	☑
Rights	☑

One of the objectives of the auditors' work on cash is to substantiate the existence of the amount of cash shown on the balance sheet. A direct approach to this objective is to confirm amounts on deposit and obtain or prepare reconciliations between bank statements and the accounting records.

FIGURE 10.6 Confirmation Form

STANDARD FORM TO CONFIRM ACCOUNT
BALANCE INFORMATION WITH FINANCIAL INSTITUTIONS

The Fairview Corporation
CUSTOMER NAME

ORIGINAL
To be mailed to accountant

We have provided to our accountants the following information as of

the close of business on ___December 31___, 20 _X3_,
regarding our deposit and loan balances. Please confirm the accuracy
of the information, noting any exceptions to the information provided.
If the balances have been left blank, please complete this form by furnishing
the balance in the appropriate space below.* Although we do not request
or expect you to conduct a comprehensive, detailed search of your records,
if during the process of completing this confirmation additional information
about other deposit and loan accounts we may have with you comes to your
attention, please include such information below. Please use the enclosed
envelope to return the form directly to our accountants.

Financial
Institution's
Name and
Address

Security National Bank
1000 Wilshire Boulevard
Los Angeles, California 90017-3562

1. At the close of business on the date listed above, our records indicated the following deposit balance(s):

ACCOUNT NAME	ACCOUNT NO.	INTEREST RATE	BALANCE*
General Account	133-7825	None	$89,548.92
Payroll Account	133-8765	None	8,212.05

2. We were directly liable to the financial institution for loans at the close of business on the date listed above as follows:

ACCOUNT NO./ DESCRIPTION	BALANCE*	DATE DUE	INTEREST RATE	DATE THROUGH WHICH INTEREST IS PAID	DESCRIPTION OF COLLATERAL
55-8965T	$324,877	6/15/X7	$12\frac{1}{2}\%$	12/15/X3	Furniture & Fixtures
Credit Line	$200,000	3/31/X4	$13\frac{1}{4}\%$	12/31/X3	Unsecured

Judith Fareri   January 16, 20X4
(Customer's Authorized Signature)   (Date)

The information presented above by the customer is in agreement with our records. Although we have not conducted a comprehensive, detailed search
of our records, no other deposit or loan accounts have come to our attention except as noted below.

Jeanne M. Mebus   January 31, 20X4
(Financial Institution Authorized Signature)   (Date)

Audit Inquiry Clerk
(Title)

EXCEPTIONS AND/OR COMMENTS

Please return this form directly to our accountants:

Douglas & Troon, CPAs
800 Hill Street
Los Angeles, CA 90014-7865

*Ordinarily, balances are intentionally left blank if they are not
available at the time the form is prepared.

Approved 1990 by American Bankers Association, American Institute of Certified Public Accountants, and Bank Administration
Institute. Additional forms available from: AICPA – Order Department, P.O. Box 1003, NY, NY 10108 – 1003

0451 5951

Confirmation of amounts on deposit by direct communication with financial institution officials is obtained in most audits. Account balances are confirmed with a standard form as illustrated by Figure 10.6. This revised **standard confirmation form,** agreed to by the AICPA, the American Bankers Association, and the Bank Administration Institute, addresses *only* the client's deposit and loan balances. Information identifying accounts and loans and their balances is normally included on the form to assist the financial institution in completing it. Thus, the form is primarily used to *corroborate* the existence of recorded information. However, the confirmation may also lead to the *discovery* of additional accounts or loans and, therefore, it provides limited evidence about the *completeness* of recorded amounts. Although the personnel

Illustrative Case
Controlling Confirmation Requests

The need to control the confirmation process is illustrated in the Parmalat fraud case. In that case, an *SEC Litigation Release* reports that the auditors received a bank confirmation confirming that a subsidiary of Parmalat held the equivalent of $4.8 billion (denominated in euros) in cash and marketable securities in a Bank of America account in New York City. The bank account and marketable securities did not exist.

It is believed that the auditors used Parmalat's internal mail to request financial information, and the confirmation was intercepted by a member of management. According to *The Wall Street Journal,* prosecutors believed that the reply information on the fraudulent confirmation was created in Parmalat's main offices by scanning a Bank of America's logo into a computer, printing it out, and then passing the sheet of paper several times through a fax machine to make it look more authentic.

at the financial institution will not conduct a detailed search of the records, they will include information about additional deposits and loans that they note while completing the confirmation.

The details of other financial arrangements are also confirmed with financial institutions, using separate confirmation letters sent to the individual at the financial institution that is responsible for the client's financial arrangements or knowledgeable about those arrangements. For example, the auditors may send a separate confirmation form to corroborate compensating balance arrangements or authorized check signers. These confirmation forms are described in detail in Chapter 15.

Primary Audit Objectives:	
Existence	☑
Rights	☑

3. Obtain or Prepare Reconciliations of Bank (Financial Institution) Accounts as of the Balance Sheet Date and Consider the Need to Reconcile Bank Activity for Additional Months.

Determining a company's cash position at the close of the period requires a reconciliation of the balance per the bank statement at that date with the balance per the company's accounting records. Even though the auditors may not be able to begin their fieldwork for some time after the close of the year, they will prepare a bank reconciliation as of the balance sheet date or test the one prepared by the client.

If the client has made the year-end reconciliation, there is no need for duplicating the work. However, the auditors should examine the reconciliation in detail to satisfy themselves that it has been properly prepared. Inspection of a reconciliation prepared by the client will include verifying the arithmetical accuracy, comparing balances to the bank statement and ledger account, and investigating the reconciling items. The importance of a careful review of the client's reconciliation is indicated by the fact that a cash shortage may be concealed merely by omitting a check from the outstanding check list or by purposely making an error in addition on the reconciliation.

There are many satisfactory forms of bank reconciliations. The form most frequently used by auditors begins with balance per bank and ends with unadjusted balance per the accounting records. The format permits the auditors to post adjusting entries affecting cash directly to the bank reconciliation working paper so that the final adjusted balance can be cross-referenced to the cash lead schedule or to the working trial balance.

The mechanics of balancing the ledger account with the bank statement by no means completes the auditors' verification of cash on deposit. The authenticity of the individual items making up the reconciliation must be established by reference to their respective sources. The balance per the bank statement, for example, is not accepted at face value but is verified by direct confirmation with the bank, as described in the preceding pages. Other verification procedures associated with the reconciliation of the bank statement will now be discussed.

The auditors should investigate any checks outstanding for a year or more. If checks remain outstanding for long periods, internal control over cash disbursements is weakened. Employees who become aware that certain checks have long been outstanding and may never be presented have an opportunity to conceal a cash shortage merely by omitting the old outstanding check from the bank reconciliation. Such omissions will serve to increase the apparent balance of cash on deposit and may thus induce an employee to abstract a corresponding amount of cash on hand. It is good practice for the client to eliminate long-outstanding checks of this nature by an entry debiting the Cash account and crediting Unclaimed Wages or another special liability account. This will reduce the work required in bank reconciliations, as well as lessen the opportunity for fraud.

When internal control over the recording of cash receipts and disbursements is considered weak, the auditors may use additional reconciliation procedures. For example, a **proof of cash** may be prepared, which in addition to reconciling the account balance, reconciles cash transactions occurring during a specified period. Specifically, the technique is used to identify:

- Cash receipts and disbursements recorded in the accounting records, but not on the bank statement.
- Cash deposits and disbursements recorded on the bank statement, but not on the accounting records.
- Cash receipts and disbursements recorded at different amounts by the bank than in the accounting records.

A proof of cash is essentially a fraud detection procedure that may be used for any months during the year.

A proof of cash for the test period of September is illustrated in Figure 10.7. Notice that this working paper is so organized that the first and last columns reconcile the cash balance per bank and the balance per accounting records at the beginning of the test period (Column 1) and at the end of this period (Column 4). These outside columns are equivalent to typical monthly bank reconciliations. The two middle columns reconcile the bank's record of deposits with the client's record of cash receipts (Column 2) and the bank's record of paid checks with the client's record of cash disbursements (Column 3).

Next, consider the source of the figures used in this reconciliation. The amounts "per bank statement" are taken from the September 30 bank statement. The subsequent rows of deposits, checks, and other items are taken from the August and September bank reconciliations, and the amounts "per books" are taken from the client's Cash general ledger account and cash receipts and disbursements journals.

4. Obtain a Cutoff Bank Statement Containing Transactions of at Least Seven Business Days Subsequent to Balance Sheet Date.

Primary Audit Objectives:	
Existence	☑
Rights	☑

A **cutoff bank statement** is a statement covering a specified number of *business days* (usually 7 to 10) following the end of the client's fiscal year. The client will request the bank to prepare such a statement and mail it directly to the auditors. This statement is used to test the accuracy of the year-end reconciliation of the company's bank accounts. It allows the auditors to examine firsthand the checks listed as outstanding and the details of deposits in transit on the company's reconciliation.

With respect to checks that were shown as outstanding at year-end, the auditors should determine the dates on which the bank paid these checks. By noting the dates of payment of these checks, the auditors can determine whether the time intervals between the dates of the check and the time of payment by the bank were unreasonably long. Unreasonable delay in the presentation of these checks for payment constitutes a strong implication that the checks were not mailed by the client until some time after the close of the year. The appropriate adjusting entry in such cases consists of a debit to Cash and a credit to a liability account.

In examining the cutoff bank statement, the auditors will also watch for any paid checks issued on or before the balance sheet date but not listed as outstanding on the client's year-end bank reconciliation. Thus, the cutoff bank statement provides assurance that the amount of cash shown on the balance sheet was not overstated by omission of one or more checks from the list of checks outstanding.

Check 21 Act

Historically, checks have taken days to clear in large part because they have literally been flown about the country in the clearing process. Under the **Check Clearing for the 21st Century Act ("Check 21 Act")** checks may be processed electronically. Electronic processing

FIGURE 10.7 **Proof of Cash**

THE FAIRVIEW CORPORATION
Account No. 101
Proof of Cash for September 200X
December 31, 200X

A-6
SM
11/15/0X

	Balance 8/31/0X	Deposits	Checks and Charges	Balance 9/30/0X
Per Bank Statement	$39,236.40 ✗	$46,001.00 ✗	$40,362.90 ✗	$44,874.50 ✗
Deposits in Transit				
at 8/31/0X	600.00 ✗	(600.00)		
at 9/30/0X		837.50		837.50
Outstanding Checks				
at 8/31/0X	(1241.00) ⊮		(1241.00)	
at 9/30/0X			3402.00	(3402.00) ⊬
Bank Service Charge				
August	4.60 ✓		4.60	
September			(2.80)	2.80 ✗
Check of customer A.D.				
Speeler charged back by Bank				
9/12/0X, redeposited 9/12/0X		(900.00)	(900.00)	
Per Books	$38,600.00	$45,338.50	$41,625.70	$42,312.80
	∕∕	∕∕	∕∕	∕∕

✓ *Traced to client's 8/31/0X bank statement.*

✗ *Traced to client's 9/30/0X bank statement.*

⊮ *Per adding machine tape at A-4-2.*

⊬ *Per adding machine tape at A-4-3.*

∕∕ *Traced to general ledger.*

Footed cash receipts journal and check register for 9/0X. Accounted for numerical sequence of all checks issued
September 200X (26610–6792). No exceptions noted.

K.W. 10/16/0X

involves creating a "substitute check," an electronic image of the original that is processed in hours rather than days. The substitute check is the legal equivalent of the original check for all purposes. Under the Check 21 Act, any financial institution in the check clearing process may *truncate* (destroy) paper checks and create a substitute check for processing. This new form of check processing has several audit implications. First, if the client's checks are processed electronically, the auditors who wish to see evidence of the check itself must rely upon the substitute check because the original check will no longer be available. Second, it becomes virtually impossible for a client to kite checks (manipulate bank balances so that temporarily overstated cash balances conceal a cash shortage, as discussed later in this chapter) if its financial institutions use this form of processing. However, the auditors should realize that while processing will be much faster, they should still expect reconciliations to include outstanding checks, because some checks drawn near the end of the year may be sent through the mail, and some checks will not be promptly presented for payment by payees.

5. Count and List Cash on Hand.

Primary Audit Objectives:	
Existence	☑
Rights	☑

Cash on hand ordinarily consists of undeposited cash receipts, petty cash funds, and change funds. The petty cash funds and change funds may be counted at any time before or after the balance sheet date; many auditors prefer to make a surprise count of these funds.

The count of cash on hand is of special importance in the audit of banks and other financial institutions. Whenever auditors make a cash count, they should insist that the *custodian of the funds be present throughout the count.* At the completion of the count, the auditors should obtain from the custodian a signed and dated acknowledgment that the funds were counted in the custodian's presence and were returned intact by the auditors. Such procedures avoid the possibility of an employee trying to explain a cash shortage by claiming that the funds were intact when turned over to the auditors.

A first step in the verification of cash on hand is to establish control over all negotiable assets, such as cash funds, securities and other investments, notes receivable, and warehouse receipts. Unless all negotiable assets are verified at one time, an opportunity exists for a dishonest officer or employee to conceal a shortage by transferring it from one asset category to another.

It is not uncommon to find included in cash on hand some personal checks cashed for the convenience of officers, employees, and customers. Such checks, of course, should not be entered in the cash receipts journal because they are merely substitutes for currency previously on hand. The auditors should determine that these checks are valid and collectible, thus qualifying for inclusion in the balance sheet figure for cash. This may be accomplished by the auditors' examination of the last bank deposit for the period and determination that it includes all checks received through year-end. The auditors will retain a validated deposit slip from this deposit for comparison to any checks subsequently charged back by the bank.

6. Verify the Client's Cutoff of Cash Receipts and Cash Disbursements.

Primary Audit Objectives:

Existence ☑
Rights ☑
Completeness ☑

An accurate cutoff of cash receipts (and of cash disbursements) at year-end is essential to a proper statement of cash on the balance sheet. The balance sheet figure for cash should include all cash received on the final day of the year and none received subsequently. If the auditors can arrange to be present at the client's office at the close of business on the last day of the fiscal year, they will be able to verify the cutoff by counting the undeposited cash receipts. It will then be impossible for the client to include in the records any cash received after this cutoff point without the auditor being aware of such actions.

Of course, the auditors cannot visit every client's place of business on the last day of the fiscal year, nor is their presence at this time normally essential to a satisfactory verification of cash. As an alternative to a count on the balance sheet date, auditors can verify the cutoff of cash receipts by determining that deposits in transit as shown on the year-end bank reconciliation appear as credits on the bank statement on the first business day of the new year. Results of the auditors' consideration of internal control will dictate the necessary scope of these procedures.

The auditors should be aware of possible **window dressing** related to cash transactions. For example, if the cash receipts are not deposited daily, cash received for a few days after the close of the year may be included in a deposit dated as of year-end, thus overstating the cash balance at the balance sheet date.

Other approaches to window dressing improve but do not outright misrepresent the cash position. For example, a corporate officer who has borrowed money from the corporation may repay the loan just before the end of the year and then promptly obtain the loan again after year-end; in such a situation disclosure in the notes to the financial statements may be appropriate.

Other forms of window dressing do not require action by the auditors. Many companies make strenuous efforts at year-end to achieve an improved financial picture by rushing shipments to customers, pressing for collection of receivables, and sometimes paying liabilities down to an unusually low level. Such efforts to improve the financial picture to be reported are not improper. Before giving approval to the balance sheet presentation of cash, the auditors must exercise their professional judgment to determine whether the client has engaged in window dressing of a nature that causes the financial statements to be misleading.

7. Analyze Bank Transfers for the Last Week of the Audit Year and the First Week of the Following Year.

Primary Audit Objectives:

Existence ☑
Rights ☑
Completeness ☑

The purpose of analyzing bank transfers is to disclose overstatements of cash balances resulting from **kiting.** Many businesses maintain checking accounts with a number of banks and often find it necessary to transfer funds from one bank to another. When a check drawn on one bank is deposited in another, several days (called the float period) usually pass before the check clears the bank on which it is drawn. During this period, the amount of the check is included in the balance on deposit at both banks. *Kiting* refers to manipulations that utilize such temporarily overstated bank balances to conceal a cash shortage or meet short-term cash needs.

Auditors can detect manipulations of this type by preparing a schedule of bank transfers for a few days before and after the balance sheet date. This working paper lists all bank transfers and shows the dates that the receipt and disbursement of cash were recorded in the cash journals and on the bank statements. A partial illustration of a schedule of bank transfers is shown below.

	Bank Accounts			Date of Disbursement		Date of Receipt	
Check No.	From	To	Amount	Books	Bank	Books	Bank
5897	General	Payroll	$30,620	12/28	1/3	12/28	12/28
6006	General	Branch 4	24,018	1/2	1/4	12/30	12/30
6029	Branch 2	General	10,000	1/3	1/5	1/3	12/31

Disclosure of Kiting

By comparing the dates on the schedule of bank transfers, auditors can determine whether any manipulation of the cash balance has taken place. The increase in one bank account and decrease in the other bank account should be recorded in the cash journals in the same accounting period. Notice that Check No. 6006 in the transfer schedule was recorded in the cash journals as a receipt on December 30 and a disbursement of January 2. As a result of recording the debit and credit parts of the transaction in different accounting periods, cash is overstated on December 31. For the cash receipts journal to remain in balance, some account must have been credited on December 30 to offset the debit to Cash. If a revenue account was credited, the results of operations were overstated along with cash.

Kiting may also be used to conceal a cash shortage. Assume, for example, that a financial executive misappropriates $10,000 from a company's general checking account. To conceal the shortage on December 31, the executive draws a check transferring $10,000 from the company's branch bank account to the general account. The executive deposits the transfer check in the general account on December 31, but records the transfer in the accounting records as occurring early in January. As of December 31, the shortage in the general account has been replaced, no reduction has yet been recorded in the branch account, and no shortage is apparent. Of course, the shortage will reappear in a few days when the transfer check is paid from the branch account.

A bank transfer schedule should disclose this type of kiting because the transfer deposit appears on the general account bank statement in December, while the transaction was not recorded in the cash journals until January. Check No. 6029 in the transfer schedule illustrates this discrepancy. These illustrations suggest the following rules for determining when it is likely that a cash transfer has misstated the cash balance:

1. The dates of recording the transfer *per the books* (from the cash disbursements and cash receipts journals, respectively) are from different financial statement periods, *or*
2. The date the check was recorded *by the bank* (either the disbursement or the receipt, but not both) is from the financial statement period prior to when it is recorded on the books.

A third type of kiting uses the float period to meet short-term cash needs. For example, assume that a business does not have sufficient cash to meet the month-end payroll. The company might draw a check on its general account in one bank, deposit it in a payroll account in another bank, and rely upon subsequent deposits being made to the general account before the transfer check is presented for payment. If the transfer is properly recorded in the accounting records, this form of kiting will not cause a misstatement of the cash balance for financial reporting purposes. However, banks attempt to detect this practice and may not allow the customer to draw against the deposit until the check has cleared the other account. In some deliberate schemes to defraud banks, this type of kiting has been used to create and conceal overdrafts of millions of dollars.

Primary Audit Objective:
Presentation ☑

8. Investigate Any Checks Representing Large or Unusual Payments to Related Parties.

Any large or unusual checks payable to directors, officers, employees, affiliated companies, or cash should be carefully reviewed by the auditors to determine whether the transactions (1) were properly authorized and recorded and (2) are adequately disclosed in the financial statements.

To provide assurance that cash disbursements to related parties were authorized transactions and were properly recorded, the auditors should determine that each such transaction has been charged to the proper account, is supported by adequate vouchers or other documents, and was specifically approved in advance by an officer other than the one receiving the funds.

The need for financial statement disclosure of transactions with related parties was discussed in Chapter 5. To determine that such transactions are adequately disclosed, the auditors must obtain evidence concerning the relationship between the parties, the substance of each transaction (which may differ from its form), and the effect of each transaction upon the financial statements. Disclosure of related party transactions should include the nature of the relationships, description of the transactions, and the dollar amounts involved.

Primary Audit Objective:
Presentation ☑

9. Evaluate Proper Financial Statement Presentation and Disclosure of Cash.

The balance sheet figure for cash should include only those amounts that are available for use in current operations. A bank deposit that is restricted in use (for example, cash deposited with a trustee for payments on long-term debt) should not be included in cash. Agreements to maintain *compensating balances* should be disclosed. The auditors must also make sure that the caption, cash or cash and equivalents, on the client's balance sheet corresponds to that used in the statement of cash flows.

Interim Audit Work on Cash

To avoid a concentration of audit work shortly after the year-end, CPA firms try to complete as many auditing procedures as possible on an interim basis during the year. The consideration of internal control over cash, for example, can be performed in advance of the client's year-end. The audit work on cash at year-end can then be limited to such substantive tests as a review of the client's bank reconciliations, confirmation of year-end bank balances, investigation of the year-end cutoff, and a general review of cash transactions during the interval between the interim work on cash and the end of the period.

Financial Investments

Learning Objective 7

The most important group of financial investments, from the viewpoint of the auditors, consists of marketable stocks and bonds because they are found more frequently and usually are of greater dollar value than other kinds of investment holdings. Other types of investments often encountered include commercial paper issued by corporations, mortgages and trust deeds, and the cash surrender value of life insurance policies. The auditors also must be concerned with derivatives that are used to hedge various financial and operational risks or for speculation. Derivatives are financial instruments that "derive" their value from other financial instruments, underlying assets, or indexes. For example, a simple derivative would involve a commitment by a company to purchase a commodity at a certain price at some point in the future. Other derivatives are much more complex, involving, for example, relationships between fluctuations in European interest rates and the price of copper.

The Need for Specialized Knowledge

The audit of financial investments can be very complex, requiring specialized skill or knowledge in performing audit tasks such as:

- Identifying controls at service organizations that provide financial services and are part of the client's information system.
- Obtaining an understanding of information systems for securities and derivatives that are highly dependent on computer technology.

Illustrative Case
Auditing Derivative Transactions

Enron used derivative contracts in its energy trading division as one way of significantly overstating its reported net income. The company purchased and sold long-term futures contracts for commodities, such as gas, for which there were no active markets and therefore no reliable prices to value the contracts for financial statements. Company employees, who benefited directly from the profits made from the trading activities, priced the contracts using discretionary valuation models based on their own assumptions and methods. Unrealized trading "gains" accounted for slightly more than half of the company's $1.41 billion reported pretax profit for 2000 and about one-third of its reported pretax profit for 1999.

- Applying complex accounting principles to various types of financial investments.
- Understanding the methods used to determine the fair values of financial investments, especially those that must be valued using complex valuation models.
- Assessing inherent and control risk for assertions about derivatives used in hedging activities.

Therefore, the auditors may decide that the assistance of specialists either within or outside the firm is needed to assist in the audit of complex financial investments.

The Auditors' Objectives in Examination of Financial Investments

Learning Objective 8

The auditors' *objectives* in the examination of financial investments are to:

1. Consider *inherent risks,* including fraud risks.
2. Consider *internal control* over financial investments.
3. Determine the *existence* of recorded financial investments and whether the client has *rights* to the investments.
4. Establish the *completeness* of recorded financial investments.
5. Determine that the *valuation* of financial investments is appropriate; that is, determine that such valuation is in accordance with the cost, fair value, or equity method of accounting and that any unrealized appreciation or depreciation in value is appropriately recorded.
6. Determine that the *presentation* and *disclosure* of financial investments and realized and unrealized gains and losses are appropriate.

In conjunction with their audit of financial investments, the auditors will also verify the related accounts of interest income and dividends, accrued interest revenue, and realized and unrealized gains and losses on investments.

The liquid nature of financial investments that are marketable makes the potential for fraud high. Auditors must coordinate their cash and marketable securities audit procedures to detect any possible fraud involving unauthorized substitution (e.g., sale of securities to hide a cash shortage) between the accounts.

Internal Control over Financial Investments

Learning Objective 9

The major elements of adequate internal control over financial investments include the following:

1. Formal investment policies that limit the nature of investments in securities and other financial instruments.
2. An investment committee of the board of directors that authorizes and reviews financial investment activities for compliance with investment policies.
3. Separation of duties between the *executive authorizing purchases and sales* of securities and derivative instruments, the *custodian of the securities,* and the *person maintaining the records* of investments.
4. Complete detailed records of all securities and derivative instruments owned and the related provisions and terms.
5. Registration of securities in the name of the company.

6. Periodic physical inspection of securities on hand by an internal auditor or an official having no responsibility for the authorization, custody, or recordkeeping of investments.

7. Determination of appropriate accounting for complex financial instruments by competent personnel.

In many concerns, segregation of the functions of custody and recordkeeping is achieved by the use of an independent safekeeping agent, such as a stockbroker, bank, or trust company. Since the independent agent has no direct contact with the employee responsible for maintaining accounting records of the investments in securities, the possibilities of concealing fraud through falsification of the accounts are greatly reduced. If securities are not placed in the custody of an independent agent, they should be kept in a bank safe-deposit box under the joint control of two or more of the company's officials. *Joint control* means that neither of the two custodians may have access to the securities except in the presence of the other. A list of securities in the box should be maintained in the box, and the deposit or withdrawal of securities should be recorded on this list along with the date and signatures of all persons present. The safe-deposit box rental should be in the name of the company, not in the name of an officer having custody of securities.

Complete detailed records of all securities and derivative instruments owned are essential to satisfactory control. These records frequently consist of a subsidiary record for each security and derivative instrument, with such identifying data as the exact name, face amount or par value, certificate number, number of shares, date of acquisition, name of broker, cost, terms, and any interest or dividend payments received. Actual interest and dividends should be compared to budgeted amounts, and significant variances should be investigated. The purchase and sale of investments often is entrusted to a responsible financial executive, subject to frequent review by an investment committee of the board of directors.

An internal auditor or other responsible employee should, at frequent intervals, inspect the securities on hand, compare the serial numbers and other identifying data of the securities examined with the accounting records, and reconcile the subsidiary record for securities with the control account. If the entity engages in derivative transactions, the individual should also review the terms of derivative instruments for compliance with investment policies and proper financial accounting and disclosure.

In some situations, the auditors may need to consider controls at a service organization because it provides services that are part of the client's information system. Such services include those that affect the initiation of transactions, accounting processing or accounting records, or financial statement reporting. As an example, the auditors must be concerned about the controls of a stockbroker that initiates purchases and sales of investments and reports the results to the client. As described in Chapter 8, the auditors may obtain information about the controls at a service organization by reviewing user manuals or other systems documentation, reviewing service contracts, obtaining an *SAS No. 70* report from another auditor, or personally visiting the service organization.

Internal Control Questionnaire

A questionnaire used by the auditors in assessing controls relating to financial investments will include such questions as the following: Does the client have investment policies that reflect appropriate risk management? Are securities and similar instruments under the joint control of responsible officials? Are all persons having access to securities properly bonded? Is an independent safekeeping agent retained? Are competent personnel involved in reviewing and accounting for derivative instruments? Are all purchases and sales of securities and derivatives authorized by a financial executive and reviewed by an investment committee of the board of directors?

Audit Program for Financial Investments

Learning Objective 10

Listed below are procedures typically performed by auditors to achieve the objectives described earlier.

A. Consider inherent risks, including fraud risks.

B. Consider internal control over financial investments.

    1. *Obtain an understanding of internal control* over financial investments.

    2. *Assess control risk* and *design additional tests of controls and substantive tests* for financial investments.

    3. *Perform additional tests of controls* for those controls the auditors plan to consider to support their planned assessed levels of control risk, such as:

        a. Trace several transactions for purchases and sales of investments through the accounting system.

        b. Review reports of investment activity prepared for the investment committee.

        c. Inspect reports by internal auditors on their periodic inspection and review of securities and derivative instruments.

        d. Inspect monthly reports on securities owned, purchased, and sold and amounts of revenue earned and budgeted.

    4. *Reassess control risk* and *modify substantive tests* for financial investments.

C. Perform substantive tests of financial investment transactions and year-end balances.

    1. Obtain or prepare analyses of the investment accounts and related revenue, gain, and loss accounts and reconcile them to the general ledger.

    2. Inspect securities on hand and review agreements underlying derivatives.

    3. Confirm securities and derivative instruments with holders and counterparties.

    4. Vouch selected purchases and sales of financial investments during the year and verify the client's cutoff of investment transactions.

    5. Review investment committee minutes and reports.

    6. Perform analytical procedures.

    7. Make independent computations of revenue from securities.

    8. Inspect documentation of management's intent to classify derivative transactions as hedging activities.

    9. Evaluate the method of accounting for investments.

    10. Test the valuation of financial investments.

    11. Evaluate financial statement presentation and disclosure of financial investments.

Inherent Risks of Financial Investments

As discussed above, the fact that securities are often very liquid significantly increases the risk of fraud. In addition, the accounting for financial investments can be very complex, increasing the risk that the investments will not be valued appropriately. If the client personnel engage in speculation, they may be motivated to use various improper techniques to hide or delay reporting losses. The use of derivatives almost always increases the risk of material misstatement of the financial statements. Auditors must obtain a thorough understanding of the various professional standards for accounting for these types of financial instruments, including those of the Financial Accounting Standards Board, the Emerging Issues Task Force, and the Securities and Exchange Commission.

Figure 10.8 provides illustrations of typical errors and fraud that the auditors might identify and assess in the audit of financial investments. Such misstatements may arise due to improper valuation, unauthorized transactions, or inadequate disclosure of such matters as derivative trading activities.

Substantive Tests for Financial Investments

SAS 92, "Auditing Derivative Instruments, Hedging Activities, and Investments in Securities," provides guidance on auditing financial investments, including the types of substantive procedures that are typically performed. Figure 10.9 presents these substantive procedures, which are described in the next section.

Primary Audit Objective:
Valuation ☑

1. Obtain or Prepare Analyses of the Investment Accounts and Related Revenue, Gain, and Loss Accounts and Reconcile Them to the General Ledger.

The analysis of financial investments will show the beginning and ending balances for the year, purchases and sales of investments during the year, interest and dividends earned, and realized

FIGURE 10.8 Potential Misstatements—Financial Investments

Description of Misstatement	Examples	Internal Control Weaknesses or Factors That Increase the Risk of the Misstatement
Misstatement of recorded value of investments	**Error:** • Failure to record changes in market values of investments. **Fraud:** • Misstatement of the value of closely held investment. • Recording fictitious securities.	• Inadequate accounting manual; incompetent accounting personnel. • Ineffective board of directors, audit committee, or internal audit function; "tone at the top" not conducive to ethical conduct; undue pressure to meet earnings targets.
Unauthorized investment transactions	**Fraud:** • An employee with access to securities converts them for personal use.	• Inadequate segregation of duties of recordkeeping for and custody of securities.
Incomplete recording of investments	**Error:** • Failure to record derivative agreements which are imbedded in other agreements.	• Inadequate accounting manual; incompetent accounting personnel. • Inadequate monitoring by internal auditors.

FIGURE 10.9

Objectives of Major Substantive Tests of Financial Investments

Substantive Tests	Primary Audit Objectives
Obtain analysis of investments and related accounts and reconcile to ledger.	*Valuation*
Inspect securities on hand and review agreements underlying derivatives.	*Existence and rights Completeness*
Confirm securities and derivative instruments with holders and counterparties.	*Valuation*
Vouch selected purchases and sales of investments during the year.	
Verify the client's cutoff of investment transactions.	
Review investment committee minutes and reports.	*Completeness*
Perform analytical procedures.	*Existence and rights*
Make independent computations of revenue from securities.	*Completeness*
Inspect documentation of management's intent to classify derivative transactions as hedges.	*Valuation Presentation and disclosure*
Evaluate the method of accounting for investments.	
Test the valuation of financial investments.	
Evaluate financial statement presentation and disclosure of financial investments.	*Presentation and disclosure*

and unrealized gains and losses. The auditors may verify the beginning balances of investments by reference to the prior year's audit working papers. If numerous purchases and sales of investments have occurred during the year, separate schedules of those transactions may support an overall summary schedule of investments. The auditors will make certain that totals on the schedules agree with totals recorded in the general ledger.

<table>
<tr><td>

Primary Audit Objectives:

Existence	☑
Rights	☑
Completeness	☑
Valuation	☑

</td></tr>
</table>

2. Inspect Securities on Hand and Review Agreements Underlying Derivatives.

The auditors will count securities held by the client at year-end, verify that the securities are registered in the company's name, and record in the working papers a description of the securities, including the serial numbers. When the client's records indicate that a particular security has been held since the last audit, the auditors may compare the serial number of the certificate with that shown in the prior year's working papers. This will allow the auditors to detect securities that have been sold without authorization during the year and replaced before this year's audit.

While the count of securities ideally is made at the balance sheet date, concurrently with the count of cash and other negotiable instruments, this is not always possible. When not possible, if the securities are kept in a bank safe-deposit box, the client may instruct the bank in writing on the balance sheet date that no one is to have access to the box unless accompanied by the auditors. This arrangement makes it possible to count the securities at a more convenient time after the balance sheet date. Also, banks maintain records of access to safe-deposit boxes that can be examined by the auditors to determine who has had access to the box and at what dates. A representative of the client should be present when the auditors count the securities, and that individual should acknowledge in writing that the securities were returned intact.

The auditors will also review and analyze the **derivative** instruments and other agreements that may contain embedded derivatives. For example, a loan agreement might contain a provision to swap a fixed interest rate for a variable interest rate under certain circumstances. This analysis is designed to determine that all derivatives are properly recorded and valued in the financial statements.

Primary Audit Objectives:

Existence	☑
Rights	☑
Completeness	☑
Valuation	☑

3. Confirm Securities and Derivative Instruments with Holders and Counterparties.

Client-owned securities and other financial instruments will often be in the hands of brokers or banks for safekeeping. In such cases the auditors send a confirmation request, signed by the client, to the holders of the investments to determine existence and ownership. If the broker or bank initiates investment transactions and maintains the related accountability for them, or records investment transactions and processes the related data, the auditors should consider obtaining a service auditor's report on the processing of transactions, as described in Chapter 8. The auditors also often confirm the terms of derivative instruments with the counterparties—the other parties obligated under the agreements.

Primary Audit Objectives:

Existence	☑
Rights	☑
Completeness	☑
Valuation	☑

4. Vouch Selected Purchases and Sales of Financial Investments During the Year and Verify the Client's Cutoff of Investment Transactions.

To determine that investments purchased and sold during the period are recorded properly, the auditors vouch a sample of transactions by reference to **brokers' advices** and cash records. In addition, they review transactions for one or two weeks after the balance sheet date to ensure a correct cutoff of transactions. Sometimes sales occur shortly before the balance sheet date but go unrecorded until the securities are delivered to the broker early in the next period. Also, inspection and confirmation procedures will help ensure a proper cutoff of securities transactions.

Primary Audit Objective:

Completeness	☑

5. Review Investment Committee Minutes and Reports.

Review of investment committee minutes and reports may disclose unrecorded purchases and sales of securities or other financial instruments. This procedure is especially important if the client uses derivatives because transactions giving rise to derivatives may not involve the payment or receipt of cash. For example, if a client engages in a foreign exchange forward contract, there may be no exchange of cash at the time the contract is executed. In addition, derivatives may be embedded in other financial instruments such as a loan agreement.

Primary Audit Objectives:

Existence	☑
Rights	☑
Completeness	☑

6. Perform Analytical Procedures or Make Independent Computations.

The auditors can use analytical procedures to test the reasonableness of the amounts of recorded dividend and interest income, or they can verify the amounts by independent computation. Dividends that should have been received and recorded can be computed by referring to **dividend record books** published by investment advisory services. These books show dividend declarations, amounts, and payment dates for all listed stocks. Interest earned on bonds and notes also can be computed independently by the auditors and compared with recorded amounts in the client's records. This provides evidence that investment income has not been embezzled, the client actually owns the securities recorded in the accounting records, and there are no unrecorded derivative instruments.

7. Inspect Documentation of Management's Intent to Classify Derivative Transactions as Hedging Activities.

Primary Audit Objectives:

Valuation ☑
Presentation ☑

To account for a derivative instrument as a hedge of an asset, liability, or future transaction, management must establish at inception the intent to hedge, the method to be used to assess its effectiveness as a hedge, and the measurement approach for determining the ineffective portion of the hedge. Therefore, review of the documentation of management's intent is essential to the audit of the client's accounting for derivative instruments.

8. Evaluate the Accounting Methods Used and Test the Valuation.

Primary Audit Objectives:

Valuation ☑
Presentation ☑

The method of valuation and presentation of many types of financial investments is guided by *FASB No. 115,* "Accounting for Certain Investments in Debt and Equity Securities." *FASB No. 115* divides securities into three portfolios—trading securities, available-for-sale securities, and held-to-maturity securities. Securities in both the *trading* and *available-for-sale* portfolios are valued at their current market values. Any unrealized gains and losses on securities in the trading portfolio are recorded in the income statement; unrealized gains and losses on securities classified as available-for-sale are excluded from net income and reported in a separate component of stockholders' equity until they are realized.

Accounting for derivative instruments is guided by *FASB No. 133,* "Accounting for Derivative Instruments and Hedging Activities." All derivative instruments are valued at their fair values, but the unrealized gains or losses are accounted for differently depending on whether or not the instruments are classified as hedges. Unrealized gains or losses on the effective portions of hedges of recorded assets or liabilities are offset by related increases and decreases in the hedged assets or liabilities. Unrealized gains or losses on the effective portions of hedges of future transactions are recorded as part of other comprehensive income in the client's financial statements. Such gains or losses become adjustments to the recording of the hedged transactions when they occur. Finally, unrealized gains or losses on the ineffective portions of hedge derivatives and nonhedge derivatives are recorded as a part of net earnings in the client's financial statements.

To audit the fair values of marketable securities or derivatives, current market prices can be obtained by reference to quotes in financial publications, such as *The Wall Street Journal* or various sources on the Internet, or by obtaining representations from securities brokers. If a security or derivative has no active market, management may obtain an appraisal of fair value from a securities appraiser. In such cases, the auditors should refer to *SAS 73,* "Using the Work of a Specialist," which requires that they consider the professional qualifications and independence of the appraiser and obtain an understanding of the methods and assumptions used. When a valuation model, such as an option-pricing model, is used, the auditors should assess the reasonableness and appropriateness of the model and evaluate the reasonableness of the underlying assumptions. The auditors should determine that the model considers all aspects of risk, such as counterparty credit risk, risk of adverse changes in market factors, and risk of losses from legal or regulatory action.

For derivatives classified as hedges, the auditors must satisfy themselves as to the continued effectiveness of the derivative as a hedge and determine that the gains and losses from the effective and ineffective portions of the hedge are appropriately classified.

If the company has the positive intent and ability to hold marketable debt securities to maturity, they may be classified as *held-to-maturity* and valued at cost, net of any unamortized discount or premium. Nonmarketable securities also are usually valued at cost. When the cost method is used, the auditors determine the value by vouching the original purchase and recomputing any unamortized discount or premium. To determine that there is no permanent decline in value of the investment, the auditors will obtain information about its current market value.

Investments in common stock that give the investor company the ability to exercise significant influence over operating and financial policies of the investee require use of the equity method of accounting. Ownership of 20 percent of the voting stock of an investee is used as a general indication of ability to exert influence in the absence of evidence to the contrary. Such factors as investor representation on the investee's board of directors and material intercompany transactions also suggest an ability to exercise influence.

When auditing an investment accounted for by the equity method, the auditors must verify that the investment was recorded properly initially. They also must obtain evidence regarding subsequent amounts of income from the investment and of other adjustments to the investment account. This evidence is usually obtained from *audited* financial statements of the investee.

If the audited financial statements of an investee are not available for the period covered by the independent auditors' report on the investor, the auditors should perform a sufficient investigation of the investee's financial statements to determine the fairness of amounts recorded by the investor. In some cases this might involve performing audit procedures at the investee's place of business.

If the auditors find evidence of impairment of the value of any investment, it should be written down to its net realizable value.

9. Evaluate Financial Statement Presentation and Disclosure of Investments.

> Primary Audit
> Objective:
>
> Presentation ☑

The auditors must determine that investments are properly separated into short-term and long-term portfolios. In addition, generally accepted accounting principles require the disclosure of the method of accounting for the securities and aggregate market values of the various portfolios. Disclosure must also be provided about the amount of realized and unrealized gains and losses, as well as the allowance for market decline of both the current and long-term portfolios. In addition, the financial statements should disclose the details about debt and equity securities and derivative instruments held at year-end.

Chapter Summary

This chapter described the fundamental controls over cash receipts and disbursements and financial investments. It also explained how the auditors design tests of controls for cash and financial investments and substantive tests for these accounts. To summarize:

1. Since cash generally has a high degree of inherent risk, more audit time is devoted to the audit of the account than is indicated by its dollar amount.

2. Internal control over cash receipts should provide assurance that all cash received is recorded promptly and accurately. Control over cash sales is strongest when two or more employees participate in each transaction, or when a cash register or an electronic point-of-sale system controls collections. When cash receipts consist of checks received through the mail, the receipts should be listed and controlled by personnel who do not maintain cash or accounts receivable records. The control listing should be reconciled to the entries in the cash receipts journal and deposit records from the financial institution.

3. Internal control over cash disbursements is best achieved when all payments are made by check or well-controlled electronic funds transfers, except for payment of minor items from petty cash funds. Separation of the functions of preparation of the payments from that of signing checks tends to prevent errors and fraud in cash disbursements.

4. The principal objectives for the substantive tests of cash are to (*a*) substantiate the existence of recorded cash, (*b*) establish the completeness of recorded cash, (*c*) determine that the client has rights to recorded cash, and (*d*) evaluate the adequacy of the presentation and disclosure of the cash accounts. A primary substantive test of cash is confirmation of the balances of the company's accounts with financial institutions.

5. The high value and liquid nature of many financial investments makes the separation of the authorization, custody, and recordkeeping functions especially important. In addition, securities should be registered in the name of the company; complete, detailed records of securities should be maintained; and securities should be physically inspected periodically. Derivative instruments are financial investments that present particular risks because of the complex accounting and valuation principles that are applicable.

6. Auditors often vouch investment transactions during the year and inspect securities on hand at year-end. The liquid nature of many investments in securities makes cutoff tests especially important. Appropriate accounting for securities and derivatives is very complex and depends on the nature of the instrument and management's intent. Therefore, in auditing the valuation of certain financial investments, the auditors may use the work of a specialist, such as a security appraiser.

Key Terms Introduced or Emphasized in Chapter 10

Brokers' advice   A notification sent by a stockbrokerage firm to a customer reporting the terms of a purchase or sale of securities.

Check Clearing for the 21st Century Act ("Check 21 Act")   This act allows financial institutions to create and process electronic "substitute checks" in place of customer written hardcopy checks. The purpose of this act is to decrease the time for check clearing.

Cutoff bank statement   A bank statement covering a specified number of business days (usually 7 to 10) after the client's balance sheet date. Auditors use this statement to determine that checks issued on or before the balance sheet date and paid during the cutoff period were listed as outstanding on the year-end bank reconciliation. Another use is to determine that reconciling items shown on the year-end bank reconciliation have cleared the bank within a reasonable amount of time.

Derivatives   Financial instruments that "derive" their value from other financial instruments, underlying assets, or indexes. Examples are options, forward contracts, and futures contracts.

Dividend record book   A reference book published monthly by investment advisory services reporting detailed information concerning all listed and many unlisted securities; includes dividend dates and amounts, current prices of securities, and other condensed financial data.

Electronic data interchange (EDI)   A computer network between companies that allows the interchange of data from one company's computer to the other's (e.g., allows purchases and sales between two firms to be processed electronically).

Electronic funds transfer (EFT) system   A computer system that transmits and processes funds-related cash disbursement and receipt transactions. Increasingly, companies are electronically transferring funds between bank accounts rather than issuing checks. See also *electronic data interchange.*

Kiting   Manipulations causing an amount of cash to be included simultaneously in the balance of two or more bank accounts. Kiting schemes are based on the float period—the time necessary for a check deposited in one bank to clear the bank on which it was drawn.

Lockbox   A post office box controlled by a company's bank at which cash remittances from customers are received. The bank picks up the remittances, immediately credits the cash to the company's bank account, and forwards the remittance advices to the company.

Proof of cash   An audit procedure that reconciles the bank's record of cash activity with the client's accounting records for a test period. The working paper used for the proof of cash is a four-column bank reconciliation.

Standard confirmation form   A confirmation form, agreed to by the AICPA, the American Bankers Association, and the Bank Administration Institute, that is designed to provide corroborating evidence about the client's account balances and outstanding loans.

Voucher   A document authorizing a cash disbursement. A voucher usually provides space for employees to initial after they have performed approval functions. (The term *voucher* may also be applied to the group of documents that support a cash disbursement.)

Voucher register   A special journal used to record the liabilities for payment originating in a voucher system. The debit entries are the cost distribution of the transaction, and the credits are Vouchers Payable. Every transaction recorded in a voucher register corresponds to a voucher authorizing future payment of cash.

Window dressing   Action taken by the client shortly before the balance sheet date to improve the financial picture presented in the financial statements.

Review Questions

10–1.   Describe circumstances that might cause the auditors to identify understatement of assets as a significant audit risk.

10–2.   Give two reasons audit work on cash is likely to be more extensive than might appear to be justified by the relative amount of the balance sheet figure for cash.

10–3.   "If the auditors discover any evidence of employee fraud during their work on cash, they should extend their investigation as far as necessary to develop a complete set of facts, regardless of whether the amounts involved are or are not material." Do you agree with the quoted statement? Explain.

10–4.   It is sometimes said that audit work on cash is facilitated by the existence of two independent records of the client's cash transactions, which are available for comparison by the auditors. Identify these two independent records.

10–5.   Explain how a lockbox system contributes to internal control over cash receipts.

10–6. The auditors' work on cash may include preparing a description of controls and performing tests of controls. Which of these two steps should be performed first? What is the purpose of tests of controls?

10–7. State one broad general objective of internal control over each of the following: cash receipts, cash disbursements, and cash balances.

10–8. Among the departments of J-R Company are a purchasing department, receiving department, accounting department, and finance department. If you were preparing a flowchart of a voucher system to be installed by the company, in which department would you show:

    a. The assembling of the purchase order, receiving report, and vendor's invoice to determine that these documents are in agreement?

    b. The preparation of a check?

    c. The signing of a check?

    d. The mailing of a check to the payee?

    e. The perforation of the voucher and supporting documents?

10–9. Describe the audit implications of the Check Clearing for the 21st Century Act.

10–10. During your audit of a small manufacturing firm, you find numerous checks for large amounts drawn payable to the treasurer and charged to the Miscellaneous Expense account. Does this require any action by the auditor? Explain.

10–11. Prepare an example of lapping of cash receipts, showing actual transactions and the cash receipts journal entries.

10–12. During your reconciliation of bank accounts in an audit, you find that a number of checks for small amounts have been outstanding for more than a year. Does this situation call for any action by the auditor? Explain.

10–13. What information do CPAs request from a financial institution on the standard confirmation form?

10–14. How can the auditors corroborate compensating balance arrangements?

10–15. What action should be taken by the auditors when the count of cash on hand discloses a shortage?

10–16. Explain the objectives of each of the following audit procedures for cash:

    a. Obtain a cutoff bank statement subsequent to the balance sheet date.

    b. Compare paid checks returned with bank statement to list of outstanding checks in previous reconciliation.

    c. Trace all bank transfers during the last week of the audit year and the first week of the following year.

    d. Investigate any checks representing large or unusual payments to related parties.

10–17. Explain two procedures by which auditors may verify the client's cutoff of cash receipts.

10–18. What is the meaning of the term *window dressing* when used in connection with year-end financial statements? How might the term be related to the making of loans by a corporation to one or more of its executives?

10–19. An audit client that has never before invested in securities recently acquired more than a million dollars in cash from the sale of real estate no longer used in operations. The president intends to invest this money in marketable securities until such time as the opportunity arises for advantageous acquisition of a new plant site. He asks you to enumerate the principal factors you would recommend to create strong internal control over marketable securities.

10–20. A well-financed audit client of your CPA firm invests large amounts in marketable securities. As part of its internal control, the company uses a monthly report of securities transactions. The report is prepared by the controller and presented to the investment committee of the board of directors. What information should this report contain?

10–21. What information should be noted by the auditors during their inspection of securities on hand?

10–22. Salvador Corporation made an investment in Letter.com, Inc. in exchange for 100,000 options to purchase Letter.com's stock at $20 per share. Since the stock options are not marketable, Salvador's management has this derivative valued by a security appraiser. The appraiser uses an option-pricing model to determine the fair value of the derivative for the financial statements. Describe how you would audit the valuation of the stock options.

10–23.   In what ways can the audit of financial investments present special risks requiring specialized skill and knowledge?

10–24.   How can the auditors determine that all dividends applicable to marketable securities owned by the client have been received and recorded?

10–25.   If a security or derivative is not marketable, how do the auditors typically obtain evidence about the fair value of the instrument?

Questions Requiring Analysis

10–26.   Fluid Controls, Inc., a manufacturing company, has retained you to perform an audit for the year ended December 31. Prior to the year-end, you begin to obtain an understanding of the new client's controls over business processes related to the cash account.

You find that nearly all the company's cash receipts are in the form of checks received through the mail, but there is no prelisting of cash receipts before they are recorded in the accounts. Also the incoming mail is opened either by the cashier or by the employee maintaining the accounts receivable subsidiary ledger, depending on which employee has time available. The controller stresses the necessity of flexibility in assignment of duties to the 20 employees comprising the office staff, in order to keep all employees busy and achieve maximum economy of operation.

Required: *a.* Explain how prelisting of cash receipts strengthens internal control.

b. List specific duties that should not be performed by an employee assigned to prelist the cash receipts in order to avoid any opportunity for that employee to conceal embezzlement of cash receipts.

(AICPA, adapted)

10–27.   Henry Mills is responsible for preparing checks, recording cash disbursements, and preparing bank reconciliations for Signet Corporation. While reconciling the October bank statement, Mills noticed that several checks totaling $937 had been outstanding for more than one year. Concluding that these checks would never be presented for payments, Mills prepared a check for $937 payable to himself, forged the treasurer's signature, and cashed the check. Mills made no entry in the accounts for this disbursement and attempted to conceal the theft by destroying the forged check and omitting the long-outstanding checks from subsequent bank reconciliations.

Required: *a.* Identify the weaknesses in Signet Corporation's internal control.

b. Explain several audit procedures that might disclose the fraudulent disbursement.

10–28.   During the first few months of the year, John Smith, the cashier in a small company, was engaged in lapping operations. However, he was able to restore the amount of cash "borrowed" by March 31, and he refrained from any fraudulent acts after that date. Will the year-end audit probably lead to the discovery of his lapping activities? Explain.

10–29.   An assistant auditor received the following instructions from her supervisor: "Here is a cutoff bank statement covering the first seven business days of January. Compare the paid checks returned with the statement and dated December 31 or earlier with the list of checks outstanding at December 31." What type of fraud might this audit procedure bring to light? Explain.

10–30.   "When auditors are verifying a client's bank reconciliation, they are particularly concerned with the possibility that the list of outstanding checks may include a nonexistent or fictitious check, and they also are concerned with the possibility of omission from the reconciliation of a deposit in transit." Criticize the above quotation and revise it into an accurate statement.

10–31.   In the audit of a client with a fiscal year ending June 30, the CPAs obtain a July 10 bank statement directly from the bank. Explain how this cutoff bank statement will be used:

a. In the review of the June 30 bank reconciliation.

b. To obtain other audit information.

(AICPA, adapted)

10–32.   In the audit of Wheat, Inc., for the year ended December 31, you discover that the client had been drawing checks as creditors' invoices became due but had not been mailing the checks immediately. Because of a working capital shortage, some checks have been held for two or three weeks.

The client's controller informs you that unmailed checks totaling $48,500 were on hand at December 31 of the current year. He states that these December-dated checks had been entered in the cash disbursements journal and charged to the respective creditors' accounts in December because the checks were prenumbered. However, these checks were not actually mailed until early January. The controller wants to adjust the cash balance and accounts payable at December 31 by $48,500 because the Cash account had a credit balance. He objects to submitting to his bank your audit report showing an overdraft of cash.

Discuss the propriety of adjusting the cash balance and accounts payable by the indicated amount of outstanding checks.

10–33. Explain how each of the following items would appear in a four-column proof of cash for the month of November. Assume the format of the proof of cash begins with bank balances and ends with the unadjusted balances per the accounting records.

   a. Outstanding checks at November 30.

   b. Deposits-in-transit at October 31.

   c. Check issued and paid in November, drawn payable to Cash.

   d. The bank returned $1,800 in NSF checks deposited by the client in November; the client redeposited $1,450 of these checks in November and $350 in December, making no additional entries in the accounting records.

10–34. During the current year, the management of Hanover, Inc., entered into a futures contract to hedge the price of silver that will be needed for next year's production. The contract, which is held by the Hanover's commodity broker, is marketable and exchanged on the Chicago Board of Trade.

Required:

   a. Describe the types of controls that should be established by a company that engages in derivative trading.

   b. List the substantive procedures that the auditors would use to audit this derivative.

10–35. During your audit of Miles Company, you prepared the following bank transfer schedule:

MILES COMPANY
Bank Transfer Schedule
December 31, 200X

Check Number	Bank Accounts		Amount	Date Disbursed		Date Deposited	
	From	To		Books	Bank	Books	Bank
2020	1st Natl.	Suburban	$32,000	1/4	1/5	12/31	1/3
2021	1st Natl.	Capital	21,000	12/31	1/4	12/31	1/3
3271	2nd State	Suburban	6,700	1/3	1/5	1/3	12/30
0659	Midtown	Suburban	5,500	12/30	1/5	12/30	1/3

Required:

   a. Describe the purpose of a bank transfer schedule.

   b. Identify those transfers that should be investigated and explain the reason.

(AICPA, adapted)

10–36. Your are the auditor in charge of the audit of Steffens Corporation. In the audit of investments, you have just been given the following list of securities held by Steffens Corporation at December 31, 20X3.

STEFFENS CORPORATION
Schedule of Marketable Securities
December 31, 20X3

	Market Value December 31
10,000 shares of Microsoft Corp.	$521,000
6,000 shares of General Motors Corp.	194,000
8,000 shares of Beta Corporation	(not publicly traded)
400 Hilton 5% Convertible Bonds	361,000

Required: *a.* Identify the potential audit problems that may be indicated by the schedule.

b. To value the shares of Beta Corporation, management has employed a securities valuation firm. Explain the audit considerations involved in auditing the value developed by the valuation firm.

Multiple Choice Questions

10–37.   Select the best answer for each of the following situations and give reasons for your choice.

a. Which of the following controls most likely would reduce the risk of diversion of customer receipts by a client's employees?

(1) A bank lockbox system.

(2) Prenumbered remittance advices.

(3) Monthly bank reconciliations.

(4) Daily deposit of cash receipts.

b. To provide assurance that each voucher is submitted and paid only once, the auditors most likely would examine a sample of paid vouchers and determine whether each voucher is:

(1) Supported by a vendor's invoice.

(2) Stamp "paid" by the check signer.

(3) Prenumbered and accounted for.

(4) Approved for authorized purchases.

c. In testing controls over cash disbursements, the auditors most likely would determine that the person who signs checks also:

(1) Reviews the monthly bank reconciliation.

(2) Returns the checks to accounts payable.

(3) Is denied access to the supporting documents.

(4) Is responsible for mailing the checks.

d. To gather evidence regarding the balance per bank in a bank reconciliation, the auditors would examine any of the following except:

(1) Cutoff bank statement.

(2) Year-end bank statement.

(3) Bank confirmation.

(4) General ledger.

e. You have been assigned to the year-end audit of a financial institution and are planning the timing of audit procedures relating to cash. You decide that it would be preferable to:

(1) Count the cash in advance of the balance sheet date in order to disclose any kiting operations at year-end.

(2) Coordinate the count of cash with the cutoff of accounts payable.

(3) Coordinate the count of cash with the count of marketable securities and other negotiable assets.

(4) Count the cash immediately upon the return of the confirmation letters from the financial institution.

f. Which of the following procedures would the auditors most likely perform to test controls relating to management's assertion about the completeness of cash receipts for cash sales at a retail outlet?

(1) Observe the consistency of the employee's use of cash registers and tapes.

(2) Inquire about employees' access to recorded but undeposited cash.

(3) Trace deposits in the cash receipts journal to the cash balance in the general ledger.

(4) Compare the cash balance in the general ledger with the bank confirmation request.

g. Reconciliation of the bank account should not be performed by an individual who also:

(1) Processes cash disbursements.

(2) Has custody of securities.

(3) Prepares the cash budget.

(4) Reviews inventory reports.

h. The auditors suspect that a client's cashier is misappropriating cash receipts for personal use by lapping customer checks received in the mail. In attempting to uncover this embezzlement scheme, the auditors most likely would compare the:

(1) Details of bank deposit slips with details of credits to customer accounts.

(2) Daily cash summaries with the sums of the cash receipts journal entries.

(3) Individual bank deposit slips with the details of the monthly bank statements.

(4) Dates uncollectible accounts are authorized to be written off with the dates the write-offs are actually recorded.

i. In order to guard against the misappropriation of company-owned marketable securities, which of the following is the *best* course of action that can be taken by a company with a large portfolio of marketable securities?

(1) Require that one trustworthy and bonded employee be responsible for access to the safekeeping area where securities are kept.

(2) Require that employees who enter and leave the safekeeping area sign and record in a log the exact reason for their access.

(3) Require that employees involved in the safekeeping function maintain a subsidiary control ledger for securities on a current basis.

(4) Require that the safekeeping function for securities be assigned to a bank or stockbroker that will act as a custodial agent.

j. Hall Company had large amounts of funds to invest on a temporary basis. The board of directors decided to purchase securities and derivatives and assigned the future purchase and sale decisions to a responsible financial executive. The best person or persons to make periodic reviews of the investment activity would be:

(1) An investment committee of the board of directors.

(2) The chief operating officer.

(3) The corporate controller.

(4) The treasurer.

k. The auditors who physically examine securities should insist that a client representative be present in order to:

(1) Detect fraudulent securities.

(2) Lend authority to the auditors' directives.

(3) Acknowledge the receipt of securities returned.

(4) Coordinate the return of securities to the proper locations.

l. The best way to verify the amounts of dividend revenue received during the year is:

(1) Recomputation.

(2) Verification by reference to dividend record books.

(3) Confirmation with dividend paying companies.

(4) Examining cash disbursements records.

Problems

10–38. The Art Appreciation Society operates a museum for the benefit and enjoyment of the community. During hours when the museum is open to the public, two clerks who are positioned at the entrance collect a $5 admission fee from each nonmember patron. Members of the Art Appreciation Society are permitted to enter free of charge upon presentation of their membership cards.

At the end of each day, one of the clerks delivers the proceeds to the treasurer. The treasurer counts the cash in the presence of the clerk and places it in a safe. Each Friday afternoon the treasurer and one of the clerks deliver all cash held in the safe to the bank and receive an authenticated deposit slip that provides the basis for the weekly entry in the cash receipts journal.

The board of directors of the Art Appreciation Society has identified a need to improve its internal control over cash admission fees. The board has determined that the cost of installing turnstiles, sales booths, or otherwise altering the physical layout of the museum will greatly exceed any benefits which may be derived. However, the board has agreed that the sale of admission tickets must be an integral part of its improvement efforts.

Smith has been asked by the board of directors of the Art Appreciation Society to review the internal control over cash admission fees and provide suggestions for improvement.

Required: Indicate weaknesses in the existing internal control over cash admission fees that Smith should identify, and recommend one improvement for each of the weaknesses identified.

Organize the answer as indicated in the following illustrative example:

Weakness	Recommendation
1. There is no documentation to establish the number of paying patrons.	1. Prenumbered admission tickets should be issued upon payment of the admission fee.

(AICPA, adapted)

10–39.   The cashier of Mission Corporation intercepted customer A's check, payable to the company in the amount of $500, and deposited it in a bank account that was part of the company petty cash fund, of which he was custodian. He then drew a $500 check on the petty cash fund bank account payable to himself, signed it, and cashed it. At the end of the month, while processing the monthly statements to customers, he was able to change the statement to customer A to show that A had received credit for the $500 check that had been intercepted. Ten days later he made an entry in the cash receipts journal that purported to record receipt of a remittance of $500 from customer A, thus restoring A's account to its proper balance but overstating cash in the bank. He covered the overstatement by omitting from the list of outstanding checks in the bank reconciliation two checks, the aggregate amount of which was $500.

Required: Discuss briefly what you regard as the more important deficiencies in internal control in the above situation and, in addition, include what you consider a proper remedy for each deficiency.

(AICPA, adapted)

10–40.   John Harris, CPA, has been engaged to audit the financial statements of the Spartan Drug Store, Inc. Spartan is a medium-sized retail outlet that sells a wide variety of consumer goods. All sales are for cash or check. Cashiers utilize cash registers to process these transactions. There are no receipts by mail and there are no credit card or charge sales.

Required: Construct the "Processing Cash Collections" segment of the internal control questionnaire on "Cash Receipts" to be used in the evaluation of internal control over the Spartan Drug Store, Inc. Each question should elicit either a yes or a no response. Do *not* discuss the controls over cash sales.

(AICPA, adapted)

10–41.   Following are typical questions that might appear on an internal control questionnaire for investments in marketable securities.

1. Is custody of investment securities maintained by an employee who does not maintain the detailed records of the securities?

2. Are securities registered in the company name?

3. Are investment activities reviewed by an investment committee of the board of directors?

Required: a. Describe the purpose of each of the above controls.

b. Describe the manner in which each of the above procedures might be tested.

c. Assuming that the operating effectiveness of each of the above procedures is found to be inadequate, describe how the auditors might alter their substantive tests to compensate for the increased level of control risk.

10–42.   You are the senior auditor-in-charge of the July 31, 200X, audit of Reliable Auto Parts, Inc. Your newly hired staff assistant reports to you that she is unable to complete the four-column proof of cash for the month of April 200X, which you instructed her to do as part of the consideration of internal control over cash.

Your assistant shows you the working paper below that she has prepared. Your review of your assistant's work reveals that the dollar amounts of all of the items in her working paper are correct. You learn that the accountant for Reliable Auto Parts, Inc., makes no journal entries for bank service charges or note collections until the month following the bank's recording of the item. In addition, Reliable's accountant makes no journal entries whatsoever for NSF checks that are redeposited and cleared.

RELIABLE AUTO PARTS, INC.
Proof of Cash for April 200X
July 31, 200X

	Balance 3/31/0X	Deposits	Checks	Balance 4/30/0X
Per bank statement	$ 71,682.84	$61,488.19	$ 68,119.40	$ 65,051.63
Deposits in transit:				
At 3/31/0X	2,118.18			(2,118.18)
At 4/30/0X		4,918.16		4,918.16
Outstanding checks:				
At 3/31/0X	(14,888.16)		14,888.16	
At 4/30/0X			(22,914.70)	22,914.70
Bank service charges:				
March 200X	(22.18)		22.18	
April 200X			(19.14)	19.14
Note receivable collected by bank 4/30/0X		18,180.00		18,180.00
NSF check of customer L. G. Waite, charged back by bank 3/31/0X, redeposited and cleared 4/3/0X	(418.19)	418.19		
Balances as computed	58,472.49	85,004.54	60,095.90	108,964.45
Balances per book	59,353.23	45,689.98	76,148.98	28,894.23
Unlocated difference	$ (880.74)	$39,314.56	$(16,053.08)	$ 80,071.22

Required: Prepare a corrected four-column proof of cash in good form for Reliable Auto Parts, Inc., for the month of April 200X.

10–43. The following client-prepared bank reconciliation is being examined by Kautz, CPA, during an examination of the financial statements of Cynthia Company:

CYNTHIA COMPANY
Bank Reconciliation
Village Bank Account 2
December 31, 200X

Balance per bank (a)		$ 18,375.91
Deposits in transit (b)		
12/30	$1,471.10	
12/31	2,840.69	4,311.79
Subtotal		22,687.70
Outstanding checks (c)		
837	6,000.00	
1941	671.80	
1966	320.00	
1984	1,855.42	
1985	3,621.22	
1987	2,576.89	
1991	4,420.88	(19,466.21)
Subtotal		3,221.49
NSF check returned 12/29 (d)		200.00
Bank charges		5.50
Error Check No. 1932		148.10
Customer note collected by the bank ($2,750 plus $275 interest) (e)		(3,025.00)
Balance per books (f)		$ 550.09

Required: Indicate one or more audit procedures that should be performed by Kautz in gathering evidence in support of each of items *a* through *f* above.

(AICPA, adapted)

10–44.   During the audit of Sunset Building Supply, you are given the following year-end bank reconciliation prepared by the client:

SUNSET BUILDING SUPPLY
Bank Reconciliation
December 31

Balance per 12/31 bank statement	$48,734
Add: Deposits in transit	4,467
	$53,201
Less: Checks outstanding	20,758
Balance per ledger, 12/31	$32,443

According to the client's accounting records, checks totaling $31,482 were issued between January 1 and January 14 of the following year. You have obtained a cutoff bank statement dated January 14 containing paid checks amounting to $50,440. Of the checks outstanding at December 31, checks totaling $3,600 were not returned in the cutoff statement, and of those issued per the accounting records in January, checks totaling $8,200 were not returned.

Required: *a.* Prepare a working paper comparing (1) the total of all checks returned by the bank or still outstanding with (2) the total per the client's records of checks outstanding at December 31 plus checks issued from January 1–14.

b. Suggest four possible explanations for the situation disclosed in your working paper. State what action you would take in each case, including any adjusting entry you would propose.

10–45.   MLG Company's auditor received confirmations and cutoff statements with related checks and deposit tickets for MLG's three general-purpose bank accounts directly from the banks. The auditor has assessed control risk for the assertions about cash as low. The proper cutoff of external cash receipts and disbursements was established. No bank accounts were opened or closed during the year.

Required: Prepare the audit program of substantive procedures to verify MLG's bank balances. Ignore any other cash accounts.

(AICPA, adapted)

10–46.   You are in charge of the audit of the financial statements of Hawk Corporation for the year ended December 31. The corporation has a policy of investing its surplus cash in marketable securities. Its stock and bond certificates are kept in a safe-deposit box in a local bank. Only the president or the treasurer of the corporation has access to the box.

You were unable to obtain access to the safe-deposit box on December 31 because neither the president nor the treasurer was available. Arrangements were made for your staff assistant to accompany the treasurer to the bank on January 11 to examine the securities. Your assistant has never examined securities that were being kept in a safe-deposit box and requires instructions. To inspect all the securities on hand should not require more than one hour.

Required: *a.* List the instructions that you would give to your assistant regarding the examination of the stock and bond certificates kept in the safe-deposit box. Include in your instructions the details of the securities to be examined and the reasons for examining these details.

b. Upon returning from the bank, your assistant reported that the treasurer had entered the box on January 4. The treasurer stated that the purpose of the January 4 visit to the safe-deposit box had been to remove an old photograph of the corporation's original building. The photograph was reportedly loaned to the local chamber of commerce for display purposes. List the additional audit procedures that are required because of the treasurer's action.

(AICPA, adapted)

In-Class Team Case

10–47. Listed below are eight interbank cash transfers for Steven Smith Co., indicated by the letters *a* through *h*, of a client for late December 200X and early January 200Y.

	Disbursing Bank (Month/Day)		Receiving Bank (Month/Day)		
	Per Bank	Per Books	Per Bank	Per Books	Amount
a.	12/29	12/29	12/29	12/29	$52,000
b.	1/02	12/30	12/31	12/30	16,000
c.	1/04	12/31	1/02	1/02	24,000
d.	1/04	12/31	1/02	12/31	44,000
e.	1/04	1/01	1/03	1/01	15,600
f.	1/02	1/01	12/31	12/31	76,000
g.	1/03	1/02	12/31	1/02	42,000
h.	12/31	1/03	12/30	1/03	10,000

For each of transfers *a* through *h:* (1) indicate whether cash is *understated, overstated,* or *correct* as a result of the transfer, and (2) provide a brief example of what could cause the situation. Answer in a form such as the one illustrated below.

Transfer	Understated, Overstated, or Correct	Example
a.	Correct	*Book entries:* The transfer was recorded in the accounting records as a check written on the disbursing bank on December 29 and a corresponding cash receipt recorded to receiving bank on that date. *Bank entries:* The check was taken to the receiving bank on December 29 and deposited. The accounts are both in the same bank, and accordingly the transaction was recorded in both accounts as of that date.
b.		
⋮		
h.		

Research and Discussion Case

10–48. On October 21, Rand & Brink, a CPA firm, was retained by Suncraft Appliance Corporation to perform an audit for the year ended December 31. A month later, James Minor, president of the corporation, invited the CPA firm's partners, George Rand and Alice Brink, to attend a meeting of all officers of the corporation. Mr. Minor opened the meeting with the following statement:

"All of you know that we are not in a very liquid position, and our October 31 balance sheet shows it. We need to raise some outside capital in January, and our December 31 financial statements (both balance sheet and income statement) must look reasonably good if we're going to make a favorable impression upon lenders or investors. I want every officer of this company to do everything possible during the next month to ensure that, at December 31, our financial statements look as strong as possible, especially our current position and our earnings.

"I have invited our auditors to attend this meeting so they will understand the reason for some year-end transactions that might be a little unusual. It is essential that our financial statements carry the auditors' approval, or we'll never be able to get the financing we need. Now, what suggestions can you offer?"

The vice president for sales was first to offer suggestions: "I can talk some of our large customers into placing some orders in December that they wouldn't ordinarily place until the first part of next year. If we get those extra orders shipped, it will increase this year's earnings and also increase our current assets."

The vice president in charge of production commented: "We can ship every order we have now and every order we get during December before the close of business on December 31. We'll have to pay some overtime in our shipping department, but we'll try not to have a single unshipped order on hand at year-end. Also, we could overship some orders, and the customers wouldn't make returns until January."

The controller spoke next: "If there are late December orders from customers that we can't actually ship, we can just label the merchandise as sold and bill the customers with December 31 sales invoices. Also, there are always some checks from customers dated December 31 that don't reach us until January—some as late as January 10. We can record all those customers' checks bearing dates of late December as part of our December 31 cash balance."

The treasurer offered the following suggestions: "I owe the company $50,000 on a call note I issued to buy some of our stock. I can borrow $50,000 from my mother-in-law about Christmas time and repay my note to the company. However, I'll have to borrow the money from the company again early in January, because my mother-in-law is buying an apartment building and will need the $50,000 back by January 15.

"Another thing we can do to improve our current ratio is to write checks on December 31 to pay most of our current liabilities. We might even wait to mail the checks for a few days or mail them to the wrong addresses. That will give time for the January cash receipts to cover the December 31 checks."

The vice president of production made two final suggestions: "Some of our inventory, which we had tentatively identified as obsolete, does not represent an open-and-shut case of being unsalable. We could defer any write-down until next year. Another item is some machinery we have ordered for delivery in December. We could instruct the manufacturer not to ship the machines and not to bill us before January."

After listening to these suggestions, the president, James Minor, spoke directly to Rand and Brink, the auditors. "You can see I'm doing my best to give you full information and cooperation. If any of these suggested actions would prevent you from giving a clean bill of health to our year-end statements, I want to know about it now so we can avoid doing anything that would keep you from issuing an unqualified audit report. I know you'll be doing a lot of preliminary work here before December 31, but I'd like for you not to bill us before January. Will you please give us your reactions to what has been said in this meeting?"

Required:

a. Put yourself in the role of Rand & Brink, CPAs, and evaluate *separately* each suggestion made in the meeting. What general term is applicable to most of the suggested actions?

b. Could you assure the client that an unqualified audit report would be issued if your recommendations were followed on all the matters discussed? Explain.

c. Would the discussion in this meeting cause you to withdraw from the engagement?

Ethics Case

10–49.   Today you had lunch with your friend Sarah Teasdale. Sarah has worked with Zaird & Associates, CPAs, for about two years. You've been with Zaird for only nine months. You discussed with her your difficulties in getting jobs done in the budgeted number of hours. Sarah said, "Ya, that's a problem. You'll get quicker with experience, but—don't tell anyone I told you this— some of those programs are pretty awful and include some pretty outdated and even some stupid procedures. Sometimes I just sign the program, but skip doing the procedure. I don't do this often, but sometimes the procedure isn't capable of detecting anything." You said little to her after this, but are now thinking about whether you need to become more "practical" about how you perform your work.

Required:

a. Identify your problem here.

b. Identify your possible courses of action. For each of these courses identify any constraints relating to the decision (e.g., personal standards, societal norms, professional ethical standards, other professional standards), and analyze the course of action's likely effects.

c. Select the best course of action.

The Auditing & Attestation section of the Uniform CPA Exam includes simulations much like the following. Although the exam itself is computerized, the simulation is presented in the text for your convenience. The course's website includes additional simulations in a computerized format.

CPA Simulation 10–50. The following simulation has three parts:

- Company profile
- Industry information
- Financial statements
- Questions

The company profile, industry information, and financial statements are also used as the basis for the simulations in Chapters 11, 12, and 14. Each of those chapters has a different set of questions.

Company profile:

In 20X1, Gary Sherwood founded Sherwood Stone Company (SSC). In the middle of its second year of existence, the company completed development of a large extraction pit area and constructed an aggregate processing plant which is equipped to crush, screen, and wash aggregate products. By 20X4 the sand and gravel operation was profitable and growing market conditions justified modifications and expansion. Currently, SSC produces a wide range of sand and stone products from its pit near Bisbee, Arizona. The materials it develops are composed of sand and stone materials for commercial construction and highway projects.

SSC sells to a wide variety of commercial and governmental customers, with only one of its numerous customers—Wingo Corporation—accounting for more than 5 percent of total sales. In total, Wingo has represented approximately 30 percent of sales (and receivables) for the past few years. Wingo Corporation is by far Arizona's largest street and road contractor and seems solid financially. Virtually all of SSC's sales are on credit, although all but the smallest contracts require "progress" billings that result in payment being received by SSC on a pro rata basis with delivery of materials to the customer. Payments from customers are made directly to the company's lockbox system with SSC's local bank. All transactions occur in U.S. dollars, and SSC maintains both a general checking account and a payroll account.

SSC has worked closely with Wingo Corporation developing a superior road paving product ("QuietRide"). Not only is the car ride relatively quiet on QuietRide roads, it is also relatively cool (thus lengthening the life of automobile tires) and less likely to lead to cars sliding in rainy conditions. While Wingo Corporation holds the overall patent, SSC has patented a critical component that is used in the product (the component is "QSand"). The product now accounts for approximately 25 percent of the company's sales (all to Wingo Corporation), and 33 percent of its profits.

The success of QSand has led SSC to start developing another product, QDeck. QDeck will be a final finishing coat over the pool deck—the concrete walking and lounging area that surrounds a swimming pool. QDeck is intended to address two problems: (1) individuals slipping and falling on pool decks while walking with wet feet, and (2) individuals burning their feet on the deck on particularly hot days. Gary indicates that the current compound seems to allow good traction and does remain much cooler than products of other companies. The problem being addressed at this point is that the current compound seems to crack easily and has a relatively short useful life. Indeed, in one test of the product on the deck at Gary's home, Gary's wife Madonna cut her foot on one of the cracks and required several stitches to close the wound. Gary laughed and said that at least she didn't slip or burn her feet on that hot day when it happened. More seriously, he suggested that this deficiency is currently being worked on and must be solved before the product goes to market. The product is being independently developed and is intended for both residential and commercial markets.

In 20X8 the company experienced a level of profitability just slightly above that of 20X7—but this was well below the net incomes of the preceding few years. Gary suggested to you that, surprisingly, intense price competition from several smaller competitors in the Bisbee area caused the somewhat low level of profitability. But, he added, he didn't expect the problem to last for long because he doubted that those companies could continue to operate selling at those lower prices. Gary had hoped for a more profitable year in 20X8, as a significant amount of the company's long-term debt is payable in 20X9. SSC is currently involved in discussions with the bank on refinancing.

SSC added significant additional crushing and washing plant and equipment during 20X8 to increase production in the future by more than 100 percent while expanding capabilities to produce custom specification materials.

No dividends have been paid during the past two years, although previously most of the earnings were distributed through dividends to SSC's five shareholders—CEO and Chair of the Board of Directors Gary Sherwood, his wife Madonna Sherwood, CFO Jane Zhan, and two college friends of Gary's who invested in the company, Cindy Stone and Kelly Higgins. These five individuals make up the company's board of directors.

The Bank of Arizona is the financial institution with which SSC maintains its two cash accounts (a general and payroll cash account) and obtains a significant portion of its financing; the inventories are pledged on the Bank of Arizona loan. This year, in reaction to pressure from the bank, SSC established an audit committee composed of Madonna Sherwood, Cindy Stone, and Kelly Higgins.

You are working on your firm's fifth audit of SSC. The previous audits have all resulted in standard unqualified audit reports.

Industry information: The industry activities consist extraction and preparation of sand and rock products. These activities include the cleaning, separating, and sorting quarried sand and the process of crushing rocks. The products are in the form of sand used in making concrete; sand used in laying bricks (which contains little soil); sand used for fill (which contains a large amount of soil), and quartz sand. It excludes the products of gravel quarrying (sandstone, gravel stone, and iron sand).

While sales within the industry are relatively unaffected by changes in technology or obsolescence, industry sales rely heavily upon both the residential and commercial construction markets as well as government spending. During the past five years construction has performed well and that trend is expected to continue for at least the coming several years. Sand and gravel production has increased at approximately 4 percent per year during this time period, as has construction within the central Arizona area.

The sand and gravel market in southern and central Arizona has been particularly healthy due in large part to the growth of the Phoenix and Tucson metropolitan areas. The most significant question facing the industry is whether the strong construction will continue as expected.

SHERWOOD STONE COMPANY
Balance Sheet
December 31, 20X8 and 20X7

	20X8	20X7
Assets		
Current Assets		
Cash and cash equivalents	$ 7,077	$ 5,351
Accounts receivable	4,717,959	3,336,277
Inventory	2,398,365	2,534,505
Other current assets	23,997	14,280
Total current assets	7,147,398	5,890,413
Fixed assets, net	556,849	104,677
Total assets	$7,704,247	$5,995,090
Liabilities and Shareholders' Equity		
Current Liabilities		
Accounts payable	$ 477,393	$ 442,630
Current maturities of notes payable	1,767,331	583,250
Accrued expenses	262,066	291,844
Other current liabilities	222,044	279,481
Total current liabilities	2,728,834	1,597,205
Long-term debt, less current maturity	4,549,908	4,142,880
Total liabilities	$7,278,742	$5,740,085
Shareholders' Equity		
Common stock	$ 80,265	$ 80,265
Retained Earnings	345,240	174,740
Total shareholders' equity	425,505	255,005
Total liabilities plus shareholders' equity	$7,704,247	$5,995,090

SHERWOOD STONE COMPANY
Income Statement
Two Years Ended December 31, 20X8 and 20X7

	20X8	20X7
Revenue	$29,837,731	$24,166,764
Cost of goods sold	25,241,773	20,156,994
Gross profit	$ 4,595,958	$ 4,009,770
Operating expenses	$ 3,810,648	$ 3,189,759
Repairs and maintanence	125,835	54,916
Depreciation	44,342	42,137
Interest expense	371,557	440,187
Total expenses	$ 4,352,382	$ 3,726,999
Net income before taxes	$ 243,576	$ 282,771
Provision for income taxes	73,076	113,109
Net income	$ 170,500	$ 169,662

SHERWOOD STONE COMPANY
Statement of Cash Flows
Year Ended December 31, 20X8

Cash Flows from Operations	
Net income	$ 170,500
Adjustments to net income	
Depreciation	44,342
Increase in receivables	(1,381,682)
Decrease in inventory	136,140
Increase in other current assets	(9,716)
Increase in accounts payable	34,763
Decrease in accrued expenses	(29,778)
Decrease in other current liabilities	(57,437)
Net cash provided (used) by operations	$ (1,092,868)
Cash Flows from Investing Activities	
Purchase of property and equipment	$ (480,578)
Cash Flows from Financing Activities	
New debt	$ 2,355,732
Debt payments	(780,560)
Net cash provided (used) by financing activities	$ 1,575,172
Net Increase in Cash and Cash Equivalents	$ 1,726
Cash and equivalents at beginning of year	$ 5,351
Cash and equivalents at end of year	$ 7,077

During the past two years the economy of the United States has been in a recovery period, yet unemployment remains high as compared to previous periods of recovery. Thus, there are questions concerning continuing construction demand.

Requirements

Risks:

a. Which of the following represents a correct statement concerning the risk of misappropriation of cash for SSC?

(1) This is not a major concern on this audit due to the relatively low amount of cash and cash equivalents.

(2) Deposit of cash into a lockbox system decreases the risk of misappropriation.

(3) The level of net cash provided by financing activities, minus the cash increase, represents a measure of the maximum possible misappropriation.

(4) A large increase in the current maturities of notes payable, as is the case in this problem, is generally considered a risk factor indicating that it is likely that a misappropriation of assets has occurred.

b. Which of the following correctly identifies a risk facing SSC that might adversely affect cash receipts during the coming years?

(1) Establishment of the audit committee.

(2) Increase in the popularity of home swimming pools.

(3) Sales to many different customers.

(4) Sales to Wingo Corporation.

Audit findings:

Ratio	20X8
Percentage increase in cash	32.2%
Net cash provided (used) by operations	(1,092,868)

The above table presents information relating to the current financial statements. Select an audit finding that is consistent with these metrics. The finding need not correspond to the exact number of dollars involved. But, of the replies listed, it should potentially lead to the most significant change in the direction indicated by the change in the ratio.

c. Which statement is most accurate relating to SSC's cash position as of year-end 20X8:

(1) The combination of the income for the year and the level of cash makes it relatively clear that a significant embezzlement has occurred.

(2) The low level of cash at year-end makes the valuation assertion for cash particularly important to this audit.

(3) The shorter times involved in clearing checks written by the company under the Check 21 Act has led to an increase in cash.

(4) Proceeds from the new debt were largely used, but did have the effect of increasing cash.

d. The net cash provided by (used) operations

(1) Indicates that SSC is under an extreme risk of bankruptcy due to its limited cash and high level of accounts payable.

(2) Indicates a misstatement, given the increase in cash during the year.

(3) Is negative primarily due to the increase in accounts receivable.

(4) Is negative due to large debt payments during the year.

Audit procedures:

The auditor performs a number of procedures relating to cash—some unique, some not unique. For each substantive procedure, identify its primary objective related to the SSC audit, or indicate that the procedure serves no purpose, given the situation described for the SSC audit (reply 8 in the list that follows). Replies should *not* be used more than once.

Substantive Procedure:

e. Prepare a bank transfer schedule.

f. Prepare a four-column proof of cash.

g. Use a standard confirmation form to confirm account balance information with SSC's financial institution.

h. Obtain a bank cutoff statement.

Replies: A Primary Objective of the Procedure is to:

(1) Detect kiting.

(2) Detect lapping.

(3) Determine that receivables are being collected and converted to cash in a reasonable amount of time.

(4) Establish the valuation of cash to reflect currency translation losses and gains.

(5) Reconcile cash receipt and disbursement totals between company records and bank records.

(6) Verify reconciling items on the year-end bank reconciliation.

(7) Verify year-end cash and liability balance information.

(8) None. This procedure serves no purpose since SSC maintains only two bank accounts.

Communications:

i. Your firm has performed the audit of SSC for the past five years. The "company profile" section of this problem describes the company's board of directors. Recent emphasis on corporate governance has caused your firm to increasingly document its understanding of the nature of the board of directors. In a memorandum to the audit team, explain your view on the likely effectiveness of the board of directors as an oversight mechanism for SSC.

Remember: Your response will be graded for both technical relevance and writing skills. For writing skills, you should demonstrate an ability to develop, organize, and express your ideas clearly. Do not convey information in the form of a table, bullet-point list, or other abbreviated presentation.

Memorandum

TO: Audit Team

Subject: SSC Board of Directors

Research:

Note: It is possible to work through this section in a meaningful way only if you have the professional standards available—preferably in electronic form.

j. Your partner on the audit has asked you to research the assertions that are addressed by confirmations. Using the professional standards, find the assertions addressed by confirmations, as per the AICPA *Statements on Auditing Standards*. Do this by copying and pasting the report to a workspace. You should *not* edit the report in any way.

Suggested References

Appropriate chapters from any intermediate accounting textbook.

Chapter 11

Accounts Receivable, Notes Receivable, and Revenue

Chapter learning objectives

After studying this chapter, you should be able to:

LO1. Describe the nature of receivables.

LO2. Describe the auditors' objectives for the audit of receivables and revenue.

LO3. Describe the documents, records, and accounts that compose the revenue (sales) transactions cycle and the fundamental controls over receivables and revenue.

LO4. Assess the risks of material misstatement (inherent and control risks) of receivables and revenue.

LO5. Design typical tests of controls used by auditors to support the assessed levels of control risk for the financial statement assertions related to receivables and revenue.

LO6. Explain how the auditors design substantive audit procedures to address the risks of material misstatement of receivables and revenue.

This chapter describes the audit of receivables and revenue, both products of the revenue cycle. In broad terms, this cycle includes receiving orders from customers, providing and billing merchandise or services to customers, and recording and collecting accounts receivable. Receivables from customers include both accounts receivable and various types of notes receivable.

Receivables

Sources and Nature of Accounts Receivable

Learning Objective 1

Accounts receivable include not only claims against customers arising from the sale of goods or services, but also a variety of miscellaneous claims such as loans to officers or employees, loans to subsidiaries, claims against various other firms, claims for tax refunds, and advances to suppliers.

Trade notes and accounts receivable usually are relatively large in amount and should appear as separate items in the current assets section of the balance sheet at their net realizable value. Auditors are especially concerned with the presentation and disclosure of loans to officers, directors, and affiliated companies. These related party transactions are commonly made for the convenience of the borrower rather than to benefit the lending company. Consequently, such loans are often collected only at the convenience of the borrower. It is a basic tenet of financial statement presentation that transactions not characterized by arm's-length bargaining should be fully disclosed.

Sources and Nature of Notes Receivable

Notes receivable are written promises to pay certain amounts at future dates. Typically, notes receivable are used for handling transactions of substantial amount; these negotiable documents are widely used by both industrial and commercial concerns. In banks and other financial institutions, notes receivable usually constitute the single most important asset.

An installment note or contract may be used in an exchange that grants possession of goods to a purchaser but permits the seller to retain a lien on the goods until the final installment under the note has been received. Installment notes are widely used in the sale of industrial machinery, farm equipment, and automobiles. Other transactions that may lead to the acquisition of notes receivable include the disposal of items of plant and equipment; the sale of divisions of a company; the issuance of capital stock; and the making of loans to officers, employees, and affiliated companies.

The Auditors' Objectives in Auditing Receivables and Revenue

Learning Objective 2

The auditors' *objectives* in the audit of receivables and revenues are to:

1. Consider *inherent risks,* including fraud risks.
2. Consider *internal control* over receivables and revenue.
3. Substantiate the *existence* of receivables and the *occurrence* of revenue transactions.
4. Establish the *completeness* of receivables and revenue transactions.
5. Determine that the client has *rights* to the recorded receivables.
6. Determine that the *valuation* of receivables and revenue is at appropriate net realizable values.
7. Determine that the *presentation* and *disclosure* of receivables and revenue are adequate, including the separation of receivables into appropriate categories, adequate reporting of any receivables pledged as collateral, and disclosure of related party sales and receivables.

Because of the close relationship between revenue and accounts receivable, the two can best be considered jointly. The determination of the amount of revenue to be recognized for a particular period is integrally related to a number of financial statement accounts, including sales and accounts receivable, adjustments to sales and accounts receivable, service revenue, deferred revenues, and cash. In addition, it is a major determinant of the amount of net income that the company reports for a particular period. Therefore, the audit of revenue and receivables is an area of significant risk to auditors.

Illustrative Case
Fraudulent Revenue Recognition

The National Commission of Fraudulent Financial Reporting sponsored a study of incidences of fraudulent financial reporting, as reported in SEC Accounting and Auditing Enforcement Releases from 1985 through 1997. The researchers found inappropriate revenue recognition in 50 percent of the cases.

Internal Control of Accounts Receivable and Revenue	To understand internal control over accounts receivable and revenue, the auditors must consider the various components, including the control environment, risk assessment, monitoring, (accounting) information and communication system, and control activities.

Control Environment

Because of the risk of intentional misstatement of revenues, the control environment is very important to effective internal control over revenue and receivables. Of particular importance is an independent audit committee of the board of directors that monitors management's judgments about revenue recognition principles and estimates, as well as an effective internal audit function. Management should establish a *tone at the top* of the organization that encourages integrity and ethical financial reporting. These ethical standards should be communicated and observed throughout the organization. Also, incentives for dishonest reporting, such as undue emphasis on meeting unrealistic sales or earnings targets, should be eliminated.

Appropriate revenue recognition may involve complex accounting principles, estimates, and computations. As a result, management should make a *commitment to competence*, especially as it relates to key financial and accounting personnel. Increased control is indicated when management effectively identifies the skills and training needed to perform key functions and implements effective procedures to ensure that these functions are performed by competent personnel.

Management's philosophy and operating style, as indicated by its attitude toward financial reporting, are also important to control of revenue and receivables. The relevant questions include: Is management aggressive or conservative in selecting methods of revenue recognition? Are estimates of uncollectible accounts developed in a conscientious manner?

With regard to the client's *human resource policies and practices,* management should make appropriate background checks of prospective employees and obtain fidelity bonds on employees in positions of trust. Internal control is also improved when individuals who maintain accounting records or cash are required to take vacations and when their assigned duties are rotated periodically.

Risk Assessment

As discussed in Chapter 6, risk assessment involves identification, analysis, and management of risks relevant to the preparation of financial statements. In relation to the revenue cycle, management should develop a formal process of monitoring external factors, such as changes in economic conditions, competition, customer demand, and regulations that may affect the risk of achieving the company's sales objectives. In addition, management should evaluate the effects of internal factors, such as changes in accounting principles, the introduction of new products and services, and the use of new types of sales transactions. These factors may create new risks for the company, indicating a need to implement new types of controls to prevent the misstatement of revenue.

Monitoring

Ongoing monitoring activities by management primarily involve reviewing various types of reports, including sales by product line, by major customer, by geographic area, and by salesperson. In addition, management often will carefully review the aging of accounts receivable and may solicit feedback from customers about the accuracy of billings.

Internal auditors also contribute to the monitoring process. As a part of their audit activities, they may periodically take over the mailing of monthly statements to customers, or send confirmations and investigate discrepancies reported. They also may perform extensive reviews of shipping reports, invoices, cash receipts, credit memoranda, and the aged trial balances of accounts receivable to determine whether prescribed control activities are being carried out consistently. (In addition, reports of regulatory agencies should be considered in making improvements in internal control.) These periodic evaluations also can be used to improve the operating effectiveness of control activities.

Revenue Cycle— Accounting System and Control Activities

Learning Objective 3

For many companies the primary source of revenue is from the sale of goods or services to customers on credit. Ineffective controls over credit sales and receivables can be costly to a business. When control activities over sales on account are inadequate, large credit losses are almost inevitable. For example, merchandise may be shipped to customers whose credit standing has not been approved. Shipments may be made to customers without notice being given to the billing department; consequently, no sales invoice is prepared. Sales invoices may contain errors in prices and quantities; and if sales invoices are not controlled by serial numbers, some may be lost and never recorded as accounts receivable. To avoid such difficulties, strong controls over credit sales are necessary. Usually, internal control over credit sales is strengthened by a division of duties so that different departments or individuals are responsible for (1) preparation of the sales order, (2) credit approval, (3) issuance of merchandise from stock, (4) shipment, (5) billing, (6) invoice verification, (7) maintenance of control accounts, (8) maintenance of customers' ledgers, (9) approval of sales returns and allowances, and (10) authorization of write-offs of uncollectible accounts. When this degree of subdivision of duties is feasible, accidental errors are likely to be detected quickly through the comparison of documents and amounts emerging from independent units of the company, and the opportunity for fraud is reduced to a minimum. While our discussion of the accounting system and control activities will be developed primarily in terms of the sales processes of manufacturing companies, most of the principles also apply to service organizations.

Controlling Customers' Orders

The controlling and processing of orders received from customers require carefully designed operating procedures and numerous controls if costly errors are to be avoided. Important initial steps include registering the customer's *purchase order,* reviewing items and quantities to determine whether the order can be filled within a reasonable time, and preparing a *sales order* (examples shown below). The sales order is a translation of the terms of the customer's

			78644
	PURCHASE ORDER		
	Pilot Stores		
	1425 G St.		
	Irvine, CA 92345		

To: Wood Supply Co.   Date: Nov. 10, 200X
21 Main St.   Ship via: Jon Trucking
Suisun, CA 95483   Terms: 2/10, n/40

Enter our order for

Qty.	Description	Price	Total
20 doz	Q Clamps #26537489	$235.00	$4700.00
10	120 hp Generators #45983748	355.00	3550.00
		Wood Supply Co. By *Bill Jones*	

			476538
	SALES ORDER		
	Wood Supply Co.		
	21 Main St.		
	Suisun, CA 95483		

To: Pilot Stores   Date: Nov. 23, 200X
1425 G St.
Irvine, CA 92345   Credit Approval: *MS*

Cust. No.: 12654

Description	Part No.	Quantity
Q Clamps	26537489	20 doz.
120 hp Generators	45983748	10

order into a set of specific instructions for the guidance of various divisions, including the credit, finished goods stores, shipping, billing, and accounts receivable units. The action to be taken by the factory upon receipt of a sales order will depend upon whether the goods are standard products carried in stock or are to be produced to specifications set by the customer.

Credit Approval

Before sales orders are processed, the credit department must determine whether goods may be shipped to the customer on open account. This department is supervised by a credit manager who reports to the treasurer or the vice president of finance. The credit department implements management's credit policies and uses them to evaluate prospective and continuing customers by studying the customer's financial statements and by referring to reports of credit agencies, such as Dun & Bradstreet, Inc. Once a new customer has been granted a line of credit, approval of a particular sales transaction involves a simple determination of whether the customer has sufficient unused credit. This process is often performed by the IT system. If the sales transaction will cause the customer's credit limit to be exceeded, the computer will print out the details for the credit department, which will initiate the process of determining whether to increase the customer's line of credit. When credit is not approved, the customer is notified and an effort is made to negotiate some other terms, such as cash on delivery.

Issuing Merchandise

Companies that carry standard products in stock maintain a finished goods storeroom supervised by a storekeeper. The storekeeper issues the goods covered by a sales order to the shipping department only after the sales order has been approved by the credit department. Perpetual inventory records of finished goods should be maintained by the accounting department, not by the storekeeper.

The Shipping Function

When the goods are transmitted by the finished goods storeroom to the shipping department, this group must arrange for space in railroad cars, aircraft, or motor freight carriers. Shipping documents, such as *bills of lading* (see the next page), are created at the time of loading the goods into cars or trucks. The shipping documents are numerically controlled and are entered in a shipping register before being forwarded to the billing department. When shipments are made by truck, some type of gate control is also needed to ensure that all goods leaving the plant have been recorded as shipments. This may require the surrender to the gatekeeper of copies of shipping documents.

The Billing Function

The term *billing* means notifying the customer of the amount due for goods or services delivered. This notification is accomplished by preparing and mailing a *sales invoice* (see the next page). A department not under the control of sales executives should perform billing. The function is generally assigned to a separate section within the accounting, data processing, or finance department. The billing section has the responsibility of (1) accounting for the serially numbered shipping documents, (2) comparing shipping documents with sales orders and customers' purchase orders and change notices, (3) entering pertinent data from these documents on the sales invoice, (4) applying prices and discounts from price lists to the invoice, (5) making the necessary extensions and footings, and (6) accumulating the total amounts billed. When a formal contract exists, as is often the case when dealing with governmental entities, that contract usually specifies prices, delivery procedures, inspection and acceptance routines, method of liquidating advances, and numerous other details. Accordingly, the contract is an extremely important source of information for preparation of the sales invoice.

Sales invoices are often generated by the IT system based upon information that has already been entered into the system. Shipping department personnel input information about the quantities of goods shipped, and prices to be charged have either been entered by personnel in

```
                                    10026574                                         7462537
            BILL OF LADING                                       INVOICE
Wood Supply Co.                                              Wood Supply Co.
21 Main St.                                                    21 Main St.
Suisun, CA 95483        Date: Nov. 25, 200X                 Suisun, CA 95483

Cosigned to:            Order No: 476538        Sold to: Pilot Stores      Date: Nov. 27, 200X
                                                         1425 G St.
  Pilot Stores                                           Irvine, CA 92345  Your order no. 78644
  1425 G St.
                        Shipper: Jon Trucking                              Shipped: Nov. 25, 200X
  Irving, CA 92345
                                                                          Shipped via: Jon Trucking
                                                                          Terms: 2/10, n/40
```

Quantity	Description	Weight
5 Boxes	20 doz. Q Clamps #26537489	142
10 Crates	10-Generators #45983748	2560
		2702
Shipper's Acceptance: Bill Warren		

Qty.	Description	Price	Total
20 doz.	Q Clamps	$235.00	$ 4700.00
10	120 hp Generators	355.00	3550.00
			$ 8250.00

the sales department when the sales order was generated or are contained in a master file of sales prices. As the sales invoices are printed, the IT system also creates an electronic sales transactions file that is used in conjunction with the cash receipts transactions file to update the master file of accounts receivable. Periodically, the IT system updates the general ledger and prints the sales journal and the subsidiary ledger of accounts receivable. The computer also generates monthly statements for mailing to customers.

Controls should be established to ensure the accuracy of the invoices before they are mailed to customers. When a manual accounting system is in use, these might consist of a second-person review of the accuracy of prices, credit terms, transportation charges, extensions, and footings. When an IT-based billing system is in use, this objective is generally achieved by implementing input validation (edit) checks and various batch processing controls.

Collection of Receivables

Most receivables held by companies are collected by receipt of customers' checks and remittance advices through the mails. The cashier will control and deposit checks. The remittance advices or a listing of the receipts will then be forwarded to the accounts receivable section or the data processing department, which will record them in the appropriate accounts in the customers' ledger. The total reduction in accounts receivable will be posted periodically to the general ledger control account from the total of the accounts receivable column in the cash receipts journal. Internal control over collections from customers is shown in the cash receipt flowchart in Figure 10.1 of Chapter 10.

An *aged trial balance* of customers' accounts should be prepared at regular intervals for use by the credit department in carrying out its collection program.

Adjustments to Sales and Receivables

All adjustments to sales for allowances, returns, and write-offs of accounts receivable should be supported by serially numbered *credit memoranda* (at the top of page 403) signed by an officer or responsible employee having no duties relating to cash handling or to the maintenance of customers' ledgers. Good internal control over credits for returned merchandise usually includes a requirement that the goods be received and examined before credit is given. The credit memoranda should then bear the serial number of the receiving report on the returned shipment.

The credit manager should initiate the process of uncollectible receivable write-off, with subsequent authorization by the treasurer. Receivables that are written off should then either be turned over to a collection agency or retained and transferred to a separate ledger and

```
                                              No. 4584
                  CREDIT MEMORANDUM
                     Wood Supply Co.
                       21 Main St.
                    Suisun, CA 95483

Customer: Howe Carpet Co.          Date: Dec. 15, 200X
          894 Reed St.
          Orange, CA 92786

Customer No.: 687960               Invoice No. 7598597
Receiving Report No.: N/A
```

Description	Amount
Allowance for substandard goods	$550.00

Authorized by: *Janis Morris*

control account. The records may be of a memorandum nature rather than part of the regular accounting system. Also, when possible—generally when the debtor is still in existence—statements requesting payment should continue to be mailed. Otherwise, any subsequent collections may be embezzled by employees without the necessity of falsifying records to conceal the theft.

The division of responsibility, sequence of procedures, and basic documentation of the handling of credit sales transactions are illustrated in the systems flowchart in Figure 11.1 on pages 404–405.

Internal Control over Notes Receivable

As previously stated, a basic characteristic of effective control consists of the subdivision of duties. As applied to notes receivable, this principle requires that:

1. The custodian of notes receivable not have access to cash or to the general accounting records.
2. The acceptance and renewal of notes be authorized in writing by a responsible official who does not have custody of the notes.
3. The write-off of defaulted notes be approved in writing by responsible officials and effective procedures adopted for subsequent follow-up of such defaulted notes.

These rules are obviously corollaries of the general proposition that the authorization, recording, and custodial functions should be separate, especially for cash and receivables.

If the acceptance of a note from a customer requires written approval of a responsible official, the likelihood of fictitious notes being created to offset a theft of cash is significantly reduced. The same review and approval should be required for renewal of a note; otherwise, an opportunity is created for the diversion of cash when a note is collected and the concealment of the shortage by fictitious renewal of the paid note. The protection given by this procedure for executive approval of notes will be stronger if the internal auditing department periodically confirms notes directly with the makers.

The abstraction of cash receipts is sometimes concealed by failing to make an entry to record receipt of a partial payment on a note. Satisfactory control over the recording of partial payments requires that the date and amount of the payment and the new unpaid balance should be recorded and maintained by the accounting system. Notes written off as uncollectible should be kept under accounting control because occasionally debtors may attempt to reestablish their credit in later years by paying old dishonored notes. Any credit memoranda or journal

FIGURE 11.1   **Dixieline Industries Ltd.: Credit Sales Systems Flowchart, December 31, 200X**

DIXIELINE INDUSTRIES LTD.
CREDIT SALES SYSTEMS FLOWCHART
DECEMBER 31, 200X

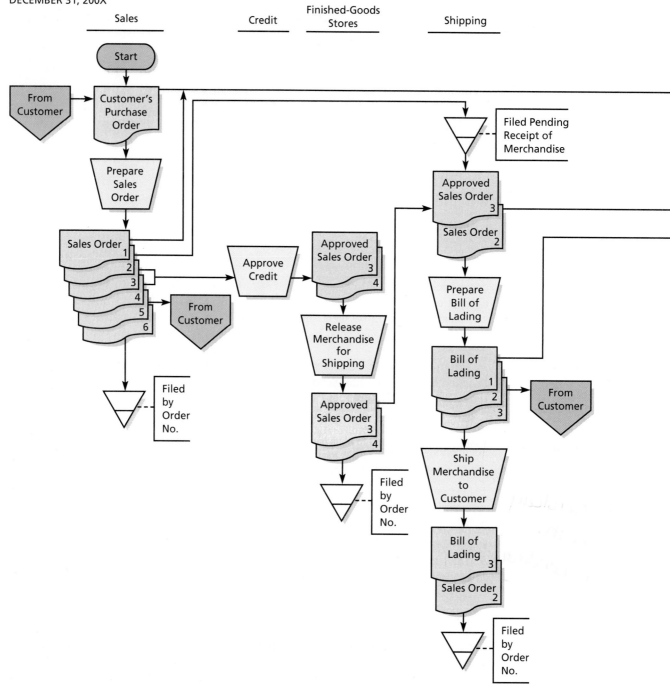

vouchers for partial payments, write-offs, or adjustment of disputed notes should be authorized by proper officials and kept under numerical control.

Adequate controls over notes receivable secured by mortgages and trust deeds must include follow-up procedures that assure prompt action on delinquent property taxes and insurance premiums, as well as nonpayment of interest and principal installments.

In many companies, internal control is strengthened by the preparation of monthly reports summarizing notes receivable transactions during the month and the details of notes owned at

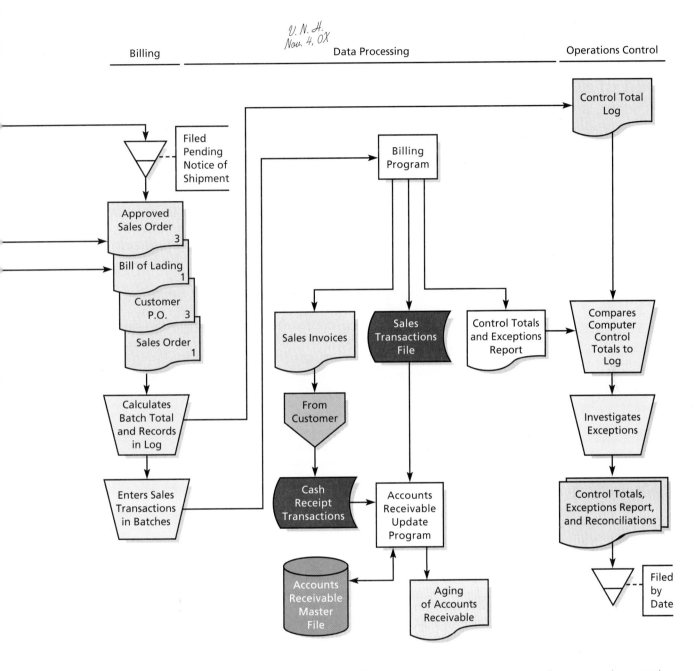

Billing • Data Processing • Operations Control

V. N. H.
Nov. 4, 0X

the end of the reporting period. These reports are often designed to focus executive attention immediately upon any delinquent notes and to require advance approval for renewals of maturing notes. In addition, a monthly report on notes receivable ordinarily will show the amounts collected during the month, the new notes accepted, notes discounted, and interest earned. The person responsible for reporting on note transactions should be someone other than the custodian of the notes.

Audit Documentation for Receivables and Revenue

Besides preparing lead schedules for receivables and net revenue, the auditors obtain or prepare the following working papers:

1. Aged trial balance of trade accounts receivable (often a computer printout).
2. Analyses of other accounts receivable.

3. Analysis of notes receivable and related interest.
4. Analysis of allowance for uncollectible accounts and notes.
5. Comparative analyses of revenue by month, by product, or by territory, or by relating forecasted revenue to actual revenue.

Audit of Receivables and Revenue

The following audit steps are typical of the work done in the verification of notes, accounts receivable, and revenue.

A. Consider inherent risks, including fraud risks.
B. Consider internal control over receivables and revenue.
   1. *Obtain an understanding of internal control* over receivables and revenue.
   2. *Assess control risk and design additional tests of controls and substantive tests* for receivables and revenue.
   3. *Perform additional tests of controls* for those controls which the auditors plan to consider to support their planned assessed level of control risk, such as:
      a. Examine significant aspects of a sample of sales transactions.
      b. Compare a sample of shipping documents to related sales invoices.
      c. Review the use and authorization of credit memoranda.
      d. Reconcile selected cash register tapes and sales tickets with sales journals.
      e. Test IT application controls.
      f. Examine evidence of review and approval of revenue estimates.
   4. *Reassess control risk* and *modify substantive tests* for receivables and revenue.
C. Perform substantive tests of receivables and revenue.
   1. Obtain an **aged trial balance** of trade accounts receivable and analyses of other accounts receivable and reconcile to ledgers.
   2. Obtain analyses of notes receivable and related interest.
   3. Inspect notes on hand and confirm those with holders.
   4. Confirm receivables with debtors.
   5. Review the year-end cutoff of sales transactions.
   6. Perform analytical procedures for accounts receivable, notes receivable, and revenue.
   7. Review significant year-end sales contracts for unusual terms.
   8. Verify interest earned on notes and accrued interest receivable.
   9. Evaluate the propriety of the client's accounting methods for receivables and revenue.
   10. Evaluate accounting estimates related to revenue recognition.
   11. Determine adequacy of allowance for uncollectible accounts.
   12. Ascertain whether any receivables have been pledged.
   13. Investigate any transactions with or receivables from related parties.
   14. Evaluate the business purpose of significant and unusual sales transactions.
   15. Evaluate financial statement presentation and disclosure of receivables and revenue.

Figure 11.2 relates these major substantive tests of receivables and revenue to their primary audit objectives.

As discussed in Chapter 6, it is essential for the auditors to have a thorough understanding of the client's business and the industry in which it operates. Regarding revenue and receivables, this understanding includes matters such as:

• The types of products and services sold.
• The classes and categories of the client's customers.
• Whether the business is affected by seasonal or cyclical demand.
• Typical marketing policies for the client and its industry.
• Policies regarding pricing, sales returns, discounts, extension of credit, and normal delivery and payment terms.

FIGURE 11.2 **Objectives of Major Substantive Tests of Receivables and Revenue**

Substantive Tests	Primary Audit Objectives
Obtain aged listing of receivables and reconcile to ledgers. Obtain analyses of notes receivable and related interest.	*Valuation*
Inspect notes on hand and confirm those not on hand.	*Existence, occurrence, and rights*
Confirm receivables with debtors.	*Existence, occurrence, and rights Valuation*
Review the year-end cutoff of sales transactions.	*Existence, occurrence, and rights Completeness*
Perform analytical procedures. Review significant year-end sales contracts.	*Existence, occurrence, and rights Completeness Valuation*
Verify interest earned on notes receivable.	*Existence, occurrence, and rights Completeness*
Evaluate the propriety of client's accounting for transactions. Evaluate accounting estimates related to revenues. Determine adequacy of allowance for uncollectible accounts.	*Valuation*
Ascertain the existence of pledged receivables. Investigate receivables from related parties.	*Presentation and disclosure*
Evaluate the business purpose of significant and unusual sales transactions.	*Existence, occurrence, and rights Valuation Presentation and disclosure*
Evaluate financial statement presentation and disclosure.	*Presentation and disclosure*

- Compensation arrangements that are based on recorded revenue.
- Typical revenue recognition principles used in the industry and their methods of application.

An understanding of these matters helps ensure that the auditors effectively execute the audit program for receivables and revenue.

A. Consider Inherent Risks, Including Fraud Risks.

The auditors face a number of potential inherent risks related to receivables and revenues. Many of these risks are derived from business risks that are faced by management, such as:

- Restrictions placed on sales by laws and regulations.
- Decline in sales due to economic declines, product obsolescence, increased competition, or shifts in product or service demand.
- Inability to collect receivables.

Risk of material misstatement also arises from the possibility of fraud. Improper revenue recognition has been the most common technique used by management to engage in fraudulent financial reporting. Therefore, the audit of revenue and receivables is often an area of significant risk to auditors. This is so much so that *SAS 99,* "Consideration of Fraud in a Financial Statement Audit," indicates that the auditors should ordinarily presume that there is a risk of material misstatement due to fraud relating to revenue recognition.

If the auditors identify a fraud risk related to receivables and revenue, they will make sure that they understand the controls established by management to control the risk. They will also determine that the controls have been implemented. Finally, the auditors will design their responses

Illustrative Case
Typical Cases of Fraudulent Revenue Recognition

CASE 1

The case of California Micro Devices Corp. is typical of the situations involving management misstatement of revenue. In this case, management had no revenue recognition policies and significantly overstated revenue using a number of techniques, including:

- Recording revenue on products that were not yet shipped or even ordered.
- Failing to decrease revenue for returned products.
- Paying distributors "handling fees" to accept shipments of products for which they had unlimited rights of return and booking the shipments as sales.

It was reported that at the peak of the fraud, as much as 70 percent of total sales was in the "fake" category.

CASE 2

According to an SEC release, civil fraud charges were filed against certain members of management of Peregrine Systems, Inc., a software development company. Peregrine's financial results were restated for its 2000, 2001, and 2002 fiscal years, reducing aggregate revenue during those years by $507 million.

According to the complaint, members of top management determined near the end of each quarter in that period how much additional revenue was needed to meet or exceed analysts' expectations. To meet the numbers, management entered into sham deals with resellers of the company's software. When the related uncollectible receivables began to build, management obtained loans collateralized by the receivables, which were treated as sales of the receivables. Eventually, some of the receivables were written off as a part of the write-off of assets acquired in an unrelated acquisition.

to the risks. As discussed in Chapter 6, the auditors' responses may take one or more of the following forms:

1. A response that has an overall effect on how the audit is conducted. For example, the auditors might assign personnel with significant experience in the client's industry to evaluate the accounting principles used to recognize revenue.

2. A response involving the design of audit procedures. For example, the auditors might require the confirmation of accounts receivable to be performed at year-end as opposed to an interim date.

3. A response involving performing procedures to further address the risk of material misstatement due to management's override of internal control. For example, the auditors will evaluate particularly carefully the business purpose of any unusual and significant sales transactions that they encounter, and they will evaluate the allowance for uncollectible accounts for evidence of management bias.

B. Consider Internal Control Over Receivables and Revenue.

1. Obtain an Understanding of Internal Control.

Learning Objective 5

The auditors' consideration of controls over receivables and revenue may begin with the preparation of a written description or flowchart and the completion of an internal control questionnaire. Typical of the questions comprising an internal control questionnaire for revenue and receivables are the following: Are orders from customers initiated and reviewed by the sales department? Are sales invoices prenumbered and all numbers accounted for? Are all sales approved by the credit department before shipment? Are estimates of revenue performed by competent personnel using appropriate methods?

After the auditors have prepared a description of the controls, they will determine whether the client is actually using the policies and procedures—that is, whether they have been *placed in operation*. As the auditors confirm their understanding of the revenue cycle, they will observe whether there is an appropriate segregation of duties and inquire as to who performed various functions throughout the year. They will also review revenue budgets and the follow-up on the variances; perform a walk-through of the cycle; inspect various documents, such as bills of lading, sales invoices, and customer statements; and review document files to determine that the client is appropriately accounting for the sequence of prenumbered documents. Figure 11.3 (on pages 410–411) illustrates these documents and the primary accounts involved in the revenue cycle. As the auditors obtain their understanding of internal control, they may gain evidence that provides a basis to assess control risk for certain financial statement assertions about receivables and revenue at less than the maximum.

2. Assess Control Risk and Design Additional Tests of Controls and Substantive Tests.

Based on their understanding of the client's internal control over receivables and revenue, the auditors develop their planned assessed levels of control risk for the various financial statement assertions. To support these planned levels, the auditors may need to obtain additional evidence about the operating effectiveness of the client's controls by designing additional tests of controls. In designing these tests, the auditors must decide which ones will result in sufficient reductions in substantive tests to justify the time spent performing them.

The auditors will also design the planned substantive tests based upon their assessments of inherent risks and control risks. In doing so, it is useful to consider the types of misstatements that could occur based on these assessments. Figure 11.4 (on pages 412–413) provides examples of potential misstatements of revenue and receivables and weaknesses in internal control that would make them more likely to occur.

3. Perform Additional Tests of Controls.

Tests directed toward the effectiveness of controls help to evaluate the client's internal control and determine whether the auditors' planned assessed levels of control risk can be supported. Certain tests of controls are performed as the auditors obtain an understanding of the client's internal control; these were described in our earlier discussion of that process. The following are examples of typical additional tests:

a. Examine Significant Aspects of a Sample of Sales Transactions.

To determine that the controls portrayed in the flowchart are effectively functioning in everyday operations, the auditors will examine significant aspects of a sample of sales transactions. The size of the sample and the transactions included therein may be determined by either statistical or nonstatistical sampling techniques. The auditors often use generalized computer audit programs to select the transactions to be tested.

In manufacturing companies, the audit procedure for verification of a sales transaction that has been selected for testing may begin with a comparison of the customer's purchase order, the client's sales order, and the duplicate copy of the sales invoice. The descriptions and quantities of items are compared on these three documents and traced to the duplicate copy of the related shipping document. The credit manager's signature denoting approval of the customer's credit should appear on the sales order.

The extensions and footings on each invoice in the sample should be proved to be arithmetically correct. In addition, the date of each invoice should be compared with two other dates: (1) the date on the related shipping document and (2) the date of entry in the accounts receivable subsidiary ledger.

Consistent pricing and sales discount policies are a necessary element of good internal control over sales transactions. After discussing the policies with management, the auditors can verify the prices and discounts on the invoices selected for testing by comparison with authorized price lists, catalogs, or contracts with customers. After proving the accuracy of selected individual invoices, the auditors next trace the invoices to the sales journal and to postings in the accounts receivable subsidiary ledger.

When performing tests of sales transactions, the auditors should be alert for indications of consigned shipments treated as sales. Some companies that dispose of only a small portion of their total output by consignment fail to make any distinction between consignment shipments and regular sales.

If the subsidiary records for receivables include some accounts with large debit entries and more numerous small credit entries, this should suggest to the auditors that goods have been shipped on consignment and that payments are being received only as the consignee makes sales. Notations such as "Consignment shipment" or "On approval" are sometimes found in

FIGURE 11.3   Overview of the Revenue and Cash Receipts Cycle—Documents and Accounts

Sales

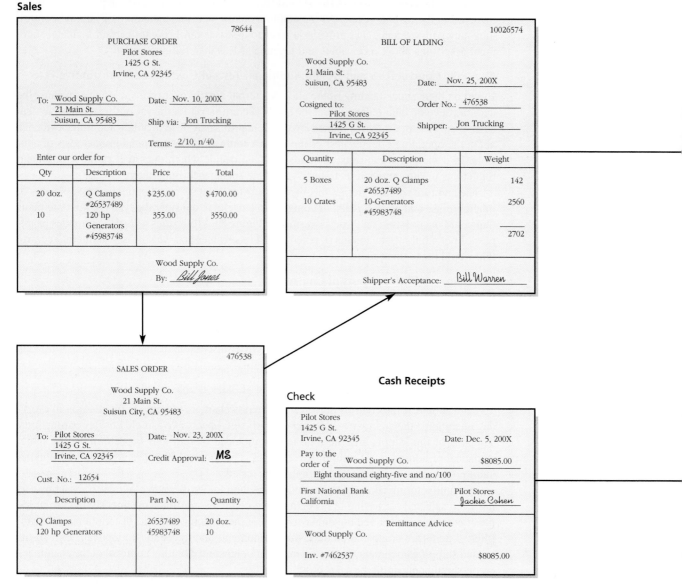

subsidiary ledgers or on the duplicate copies of sales invoices. Numerous large returns of merchandise are also suggestive of consignment shipments.

The auditors should also investigate the controls for sales to related parties. Effective control over intercompany or interbranch transfers of merchandise often requires the same kind of formal procedures for billing, shipping, and collection functions as for sales to outsiders; hence, these movements of merchandise are often invoiced and recorded as sales. When the operations of the several organizational units are combined or consolidated into one income statement, however, it is apparent that any transactions not representing sales to outsiders should be eliminated from consolidated sales. In the audit of a client that operates subsidiaries or branches, the auditors should investigate the procedures for recording movements of merchandise among the various units of the company.

b. Compare a Sample of Shipping Documents to Related Sales Invoices.

The preceding step in the audit program called for an examination of selected sales transactions and a comparison of the invoices with sales records and shipping documents. That

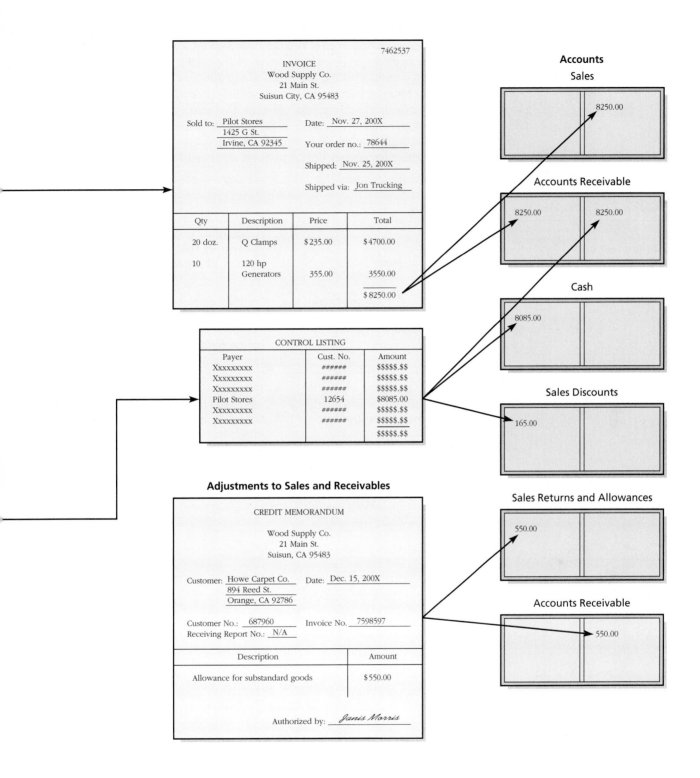

procedure would not, however, disclose orders that had been shipped but not billed. To assure that all shipments are billed, the auditors may obtain a sample of shipping documents issued during the year and compare these to sales invoices. In making this test, particular emphasis should be placed upon accounting for all shipping documents by serial number. Any voided shipping documents should have been mutilated and retained in the files. The purposeful or accidental destruction of shipping documents before the creation of a sales invoice might go undetected if this type of test were not made.

c. Review the Use and Authorization of Credit Memoranda.

All allowances to customers for returned or defective merchandise should be supported by serially numbered credit memoranda signed by an officer or responsible employee having no duties relating to handling cash or to the maintenance of customers' ledgers. Good internal control over credits for returned merchandise usually includes a requirement that the returned goods be received and examined before credit is granted. The memoranda should then bear the date and serial number of the receiving report on the return shipment.

In addition to establishing that credit memoranda were properly authorized, the auditors should make tests of these documents similar to those suggested for sales invoices. Prices,

FIGURE 11.4   Potential Misstatements—Revenue

Description of Misstatement	Examples	Internal Control Weaknesses or Factors That Increase the Risk of the Misstatement
Recording unearned revenue	**Fraud:** • Recording fictitious sales without receiving a customer order or shipping the goods. • Intentional overshipment of goods.	• Ineffective board of directors, audit committee, or internal audit function; "tone at the top" not conducive to ethical conduct; undue pressure to meet sales targets.
	Errors: • Recording sales based on the receipt of orders from customers rather than on the shipment of goods. • Inaccurate billing and recording of sales. • Recording cash that represents a liability (e.g., receipt of a customer's deposit) as revenue.	• Ineffective billing process in which billing is not tied to shipping information. • Ineffective controls for testing invoices, or ineffective input validation checks and computer reconciliations to ensure the accuracy of databases. • Inadequate accounting manual; incompetent accounting personnel.
Early (late) recognition of revenue—"cutoff problems"	**Fraud:** • Holding the sales journal open to record next year's sales as having occurred in the current year.	• Ineffective board of directors, audit committee, or internal audit function; "tone at the top" not conducive to ethical conduct; undue pressure to meet sales targets.
	Error: • Recording sales in the wrong period based on incorrect shipping information.	• Ineffective cutoff procedures in the shipping department.
Recording revenues when significant uncertainties exist	**Fraud:** • Recording sales when the customer is likely to return the goods.	• Ineffective board of directors, audit committee, or internal audit function; "tone at the top" not conducive to ethical conduct; undue pressure to meet sales targets.
	Error: • Recording sales when the customer's payment is contingent upon the customer receiving financing or selling the goods to another party (e.g., consignment sales).	• Aggressive attitude of management toward financial reporting; incompetent chief accounting officer.

FIGURE 11.4 Concluded

Description of Misstatement	Examples	Internal Control Weaknesses or Factors That Increase the Risk of the Misstatement
Recording revenues when significant services must still be performed by seller	**Fraud:** • Recording franchise revenues when the franchises are sold even though an obligation to perform significant services still exists.	• Ineffective board of directors, audit committee, or internal audit function; "tone at the top" not conducive to ethical conduct; undue pressure to meet sales targets.
	Error: • Amount of revenue earned on franchises is miscalculated.	• Aggressive attitude of management toward financial reporting; incompetent chief accounting officer.
Overestimation of the amount of revenue earned	**Fraud:** • Misstating the percentage of completion of several projects by a construction company using the percentage-of-completion method of revenue recognition. • Overestimating the percentage of completion on projects by a construction company using the percentage-of-completion method of revenue recognition.	• Ineffective board of directors, audit committee, or internal audit function; "tone at the top" not conducive to ethical conduct; incompetent individuals involved in the estimation process. • Aggressive attitude of management toward financial reporting; incompetent personnel involved in the estimation/accounting process.

extensions, and footings should be verified, and postings traced from the sales return journal or other accounting record to the customers' accounts in the subsidiary receivable ledgers.

d. Reconcile Selected Cash Register Tapes and Sales Tickets with Sales Journals.

In the audit of clients that make a substantial amount of sales for cash, the auditors may compare selected daily totals in the sales journal with cash register readings or tapes. The serial numbers of all sales tickets used during the selected periods should be accounted for and the individual tickets examined for accuracy of calculations and traced to the sales summary or journal.

e. Test IT Application Controls.

If the client has established effective IT application controls for sales transactions, the auditors might decide to test these controls directly instead of testing a sample of sales transactions. Tests of application controls might involve inspecting evidence of the operations control group's reconciliation of batch control totals for sales transactions, and the follow-up on any transactions that are listed on exception reports. The auditors might also observe the application of input validity tests as sales transactions are entered. They may even enter test data to obtain additional evidence about performance of application controls.

Focus on the Airline Industry

Electronic ticketing has become basic to the airline industry. Under these systems a passenger may book a flight over the telephone or by computer and be assigned a reservation number rather than being issued a physical ticket. Since no ticket is created until the passenger checks in for the flight, the auditor is limited in the extent to which he or she can examine "paper" support for transactions. Accordingly, audit procedures must be developed relating to the associated revenues and receivables. Auditors often choose to test the computer controls in such situations.

4. Reassess Control Risk and Modify Substantive Tests.

When the auditors have completed the procedures described in the preceding sections, they should reassess the extent of control risk for each financial statement assertion regarding receivables and sales transactions. These assessments will determine whether the auditors should modify their planned substantive tests for the financial statement assertions about receivables and sales. Figure 11.5 summarizes the relationship between these assertions, the controls, and typical tests of controls. This figure illustrates which controls affect the auditors' assessments of control risk for the various assertions.

FIGURE 11.5   Assessing Control Risk for Receivables and Revenue

Control	Typical Tests of the Control	Existence or Occurrence	Completeness	Rights and Obligations	Valuation or Allocation	Presentation & Disclosure
Segregate duties over sales and collections of receivables	Observe and make inquiries about the performance of various functions.	X	X	X	X	
Match sales invoices with shipping documents, purchase orders, and sales orders	Select a sample of sales invoices and compare details to shipping documents, purchase orders, and sales orders.	X		X	X	
Review of the clerical accuracy of sales invoices by a second person	Select a sample of sales invoices and examine them for evidence of second-person review.				X	
Obtain credit approval of sales prior to shipment	Make inquiries about credit policies; select a sample of sales transactions and examine evidence of credit approval.	X			X	
Mail monthly statements to customers and follow up on errors reported	Observe and make inquiries about the mailing of statements and review evidence of follow-up.	X	X	X	X	
Reconcile bank (financial institution) accounts monthly	Review a sample of bank reconciliations performed during the year.	X		X	X	
Use control listing to control cash collections	Observe, make inquiries about the process, and reconcile selected listings to the bank and accounting records.	X	X	X	X	
Use budgets and analyze variances from actual amounts	Examine budgets and evidence of follow-up on variances.	X	X	X	X	
Use prenumbered shipping and billing documents and account for the sequence	Observe and make inquiries about the use of prenumbered documents and inspect evidence of accounting for the sequence.		X			
Use credit memoranda for authorization of adjustments to sales and receivables	Select a sample of credits to customers' accounts and inspect credit memoranda and other supporting documents.		X		X	
Use a chart of accounts and an independent review of account classifications	Inspect the chart of accounts and evidence of the review of account classifications.					X

FIGURE 11.6   **Computerized Aging of Accounts Receivable**

B. Perform Substantive Tests of Receivables and Revenue.

<table>
<tr><td>Primary Audit
Objective:</td></tr>
<tr><td>Valuation ☑</td></tr>
</table>

Learning Objective 6

1. Obtain an Aged Trial Balance of Trade Accounts Receivable and Analyses of Other Accounts Receivable and Reconcile to Ledgers.

An *aged trial balance* of trade accounts receivable at the audit date is commonly prepared by employees of the client for the auditors, often in the form of a computer printout. The client-prepared schedule illustrated in Figure 11.6 has a multipurpose format designed to display the aging of customers' accounts, the estimate of probable credit losses, and the confirmation control information. The summary of so many phases of the examination of receivables in a single working paper is practicable only for small concerns with a limited number of customers. If the client has any accounts receivable other than trade accounts, the auditors also should obtain similar analyses of those accounts.

When trial balances or analyses of accounts receivable are furnished to the auditors by the client's employees, some independent verification of the listing is essential. Determination of the proper extent of testing should be made in relation to the adequacy of the controls over receivables. The auditors should test footings, crossfootings, and agings. In testing agings, it is important to test some accounts classified as current, as well as those shown as past due. These selected accounts should be traced to the subsidiary ledgers. The totals of schedules prepared by client personnel should also be compared with related controlling accounts. In addition, the balances of the subsidiary ledger records should be verified by footing the debit and credit columns on a test basis. Generalized computer audit programs may be used to perform these tests when the client's accounts receivable are processed by an IT system.

Primary Audit Objective:
Valuation ☑

2. Obtain Analyses of Notes Receivable and Related Interest and Reconcile to the General Ledger.

An analysis of notes receivable supporting the general ledger control account may be prepared for the auditors by the client's staff. The information to be included in the analysis normally will include the name of the maker, date, maturity, amount, and interest rate. In addition to verifying the accuracy of the analysis prepared by the client, the auditors should trace selected items to the accounting records and to the notes themselves.

Primary Audit Objectives:
Existence ☑
Rights ☑

3. Inspect Notes on Hand and Confirm Those with Holders.

The inspection of notes receivable on hand should be performed concurrently with the count of cash and securities to prevent the concealment of a shortage by substitution of cash for misappropriated negotiable instruments, or vice versa. Any securities held by the client as collateral for notes receivable should be inspected and listed at the same time. The auditors should maintain complete control over all negotiable instruments until the count and inspection are completed.

Notes receivable owned by the client may be held by others at the time of the examination. Confirmation in writing from the *holder* of the note is considered an acceptable alternative to inspection; it does not, however, eliminate the need for securing confirmation from the *maker* of the note. The confirmation letter sent to a bank, collection agency, secured creditor, or other holder should contain a request for verification of the name of the maker, the balance of the note, the interest rate, and the due date.

Printed note forms are readily available at any bank and may be easily prepared using commercially available software; an unscrupulous officer or employee of the client company desiring to create a fictitious note could do so by obtaining a bank note form and filling in the amount, date, maturity, and signature. The relative ease of creating a forged or fictitious note suggests that physical inspection by the auditors represents a less significant and conclusive audit procedure in verification of notes receivable than for cash or securities.

Primary Audit Objectives:
Existence ☑
Rights ☑
Valuation ☑

4. Confirm Receivables with Debtors.

The term **confirmation** was defined in Chapter 5 as a type of documentary evidence secured from outside the client organization and transmitted directly to the auditors. Direct communication with debtors is the most essential and conclusive step in the verification of accounts and notes receivable. By confirming an account receivable, the auditors prove that the receivable and the customer *exist.* Written acknowledgment of the debt by the debtor serves the purposes of (*a*) establishing the existence and gross valuation of the asset, and (*b*) providing some assurance that no lapping or other manipulation affecting receivables is being carried on at the balance sheet date. However, the confirmation of a receivable provides only limited evidence about the completeness and valuation assertions because only recorded amounts are confirmed, and debtors may acknowledge debts even though they are not able to pay them.

A better understanding of the emphasis placed on confirmation of receivables can be gained by a brief review of auditing history. Audit objectives and procedures were drastically revised in the late 1940s. Before that time the usual audit did not include procedures to assure that the receivables were genuine claims against existing companies or that inventories actually existed and had been accurately counted. Requiring the auditors to confirm receivables (or to observe the taking of physical inventory) was considered too expensive and not particularly important. Auditors generally relied in that early era upon a written statement by management concerning the validity of receivables and the existence of inventories. This approach was drastically revised after some spectacular fraud cases involving millions of dollars in fictitious receivables and inventories showed the need for stronger audit evidence.

SAS 67, "The Confirmation Process," summarizes the current requirements regarding confirmations. It indicates that there is a presumption that the auditor will confirm accounts receivable, unless (*a*) accounts receivable are immaterial, (*b*) the use of confirmations would be ineffective, or (*c*) the auditor's combined assessment of inherent risk and control risk is low, and that assessment, in conjunction with other substantive tests, is sufficient to reduce audit risk for the applicable assertions to an acceptably low level.

Illustrative Case
Equity Funding Fraud

In the Equity Funding Corporation of America fraud, fictitious receivables selected for confirmation by the auditors bore addresses of employees who were conspirators in the fraud. The fictitious confirmation requests were thus signed and returned to the auditors by the recipients.

All requests for confirmation of notes and accounts receivable should be mailed in envelopes bearing the CPA firm's return address. A stamped or business reply envelope addressed to the office of the auditors should be enclosed with the request. Confirmation requests should be deposited personally by the auditors at the post office or in a government mailbox. These procedures are designed to prevent the client's employees from having any opportunity to alter or intercept a confirmation request or the customer's reply thereto. The entire process of confirming receivables will obviously contribute nothing toward the detection of overstated or fictitious accounts if the confirmation requests or replies from customers pass through the hands of the client. Requests returned as undeliverable by the post office may be of prime significance to the auditors and hence should be returned directly to their office.

An important part of confirming notes and accounts receivable is considering the validity of the debtors' addresses. The auditors should investigate thoroughly any suspicious circumstances, such as an excessive number of *individual* debtors with addresses that are post office boxes; the boxes may have been rented under fictitious debtors' names by employees of the client company who are engaged in accounts receivable fraud.

To improve the rate of responses to confirmation requests, the auditors should carefully design the form to make sure that the person receiving the confirmation is likely to have easy access to the information requested. For example, customers that use a voucher system for cash disbursements may be better able to confirm unpaid transactions, rather than total receivable balances. The auditors should also try to include on the form the details of the transactions, such as customers' purchase order numbers.

In some cases, the confirmation process may result in oral or facsimile (fax) responses. Oral responses, generally obtained through telephone conversations in which the auditor is assured as to the identity of the respondent, should be documented in the working papers. In addition, the auditor should consider asking the customer to return a written confirmation.

The auditors should carefully consider replies received via fax, as it is possible to program a fax machine with an incorrect transmitting number and name, thus leaving the recipient with missing information about the source of the document. Accordingly, a dishonest individual can send a falsified fax reply that appears to be from the debtor's offices. This problem may be controlled to a certain extent by using a fax machine that has a "pulling function," or by calling the purported sender to ensure the confirmation received is valid.

Positive and Negative Confirmation Requests

There are two methods of confirming receivables by direct communication with the debtor. In each type of communication, the *client* makes the formal request for confirmation, although the auditors control the entire confirmation process.

The use of **positive confirmations,** as illustrated by Figure 11.7, consists of a request addressed to the debtor asking for a reply. Most positive forms ask the debtor to confirm directly to the auditors the accuracy of the dollar amount shown on the confirmation request. Other positive forms, referred to as *blank forms,* do not state the amount on the request, but ask the debtor company to fill in the balance.

The use of **negative confirmations** consists of a communication addressed to the debtor company asking it to advise the auditors *only* if the balance shown is incorrect. A negative confirmation request may be in the form of a letter or it may be made merely by applying a

FIGURE 11.7
**Positive Form of
Accounts Receivable
Confirmation Request
(with Customer Reply)**

SMITH & CO. _____

1416 Eighteenth Street • Los Angeles • California • 90035

December 31, 20X1

Martin, Inc.
6700 Holmes Street
Kansas City, Missouri 64735

Dear Sirs:

Please confirm directly to our auditors

Adams, Barnes & Co.
Certified Public Accountants
1800 Avenue of the Stars
Los Angeles, California 90067

the correctness of the balance of your account payable to us as shown below
and on the enclosed statement at December 31, 20X1. If the amount is not in
agreement with your records at that date, please provide any information which
will aid our auditors in reconciling the difference.

Your prompt return of this form in the enclosed stamped envelope is
essential to the completion of the audit of our financial statements and will
be appreciated.

Smith & Co.

By _____M.J. Crowley_____
(Controller)

THIS IS NOT A REQUEST FOR PAYMENT, BUT MERELY FOR
CONFIRMATION OF YOUR ACCOUNT.

- -

The statement of our account showing a balance of $24,689.00 due Smith &
Co. at December 31, 20X1 is correct except as noted below.

Martin, Inc.

Date: _January 16, 20X2_   By _____Howard Martin_____

Exceptions: _None_

---

rubber stamp to the customer's regular monthly statement, or by attaching a gummed label
bearing the words shown in Figure 11.8.

The positive form generally provides more assurance than the negative form because the
auditors are alerted to the need for further investigation if a reply is not received. However,
when positive confirmations ask recipients to confirm the accuracy of information provided on
the request, there is a risk that the recipient may simply sign and return it without verifying the
information. Blank forms control for this possibility by requiring the recipient to provide the
information. But negative confirmations generally result in lower response rates and, therefore,
require more follow-up procedures.

When the negative form of confirmation request is used, the lack of a reply from a given
customer is interpreted as satisfactory evidence, when in fact the customer may simply have
ignored the confirmation request. Since the auditors need not follow up on nonreplies, the

FIGURE 11.8
Negative Form of Accounts Receivable Confirmation Request

Please examine this statement carefully. If it does not agree with your records, please report any differences to our auditors.

Adams, Barnes & Co.
Certified Public Accountants
1800 Avenue of the Stars
Los Angeles, California 90067

A business reply envelope requiring no postage is enclosed for your convenience.

THIS IS NOT A REQUEST FOR PAYMENT

expense of using negative confirmation requests is less than for the positive form; thus, more customers can be contacted for the same cost.

Although positive confirmation requests may be used in any circumstance, the use of solely negative requests should be reserved for situations in which (*a*) the combined assessed level of inherent and control risk is low, (*b*) a large number of small balances is involved, and (*c*) the auditors have no reason to believe that the recipients of the requests are not likely to give them consideration. When the auditors use negative requests, they should consider supplementing the confirmation process with other substantive procedures. In many situations a combination of positive and negative confirmation requests is used, with the positive form used for large balances and the negative form for small balances.

Size of Sample

In the audit of most companies, the confirmation process for accounts receivable is limited to a sample. The sample should always be large enough to warrant the drawing of valid inferences about the entire population of receivables. Generally, auditors are able to stratify the population in a manner so as to allow confirmation of a majority of the dollar amount of receivables.

As discussed in Chapter 9, the size of the sample will vary with the levels of sampling risk accepted (the risk of incorrect rejection and acceptance), the tolerable misstatement, and certain characteristics of the population. The results of confirmation tests in prior years serve as another guide to the auditors in setting sample size; significant exceptions in prior years' confirmation results signal the need for extensive confirmation of the current year's receivables. Finally, the choice between the positive and negative forms of confirmation requests influences the size of the sample. The number of confirmations mailed is usually increased when the negative form is used.

In selecting the individual accounts to be confirmed, it is customary to include all customers with balances above a selected dollar amount and to select a sample of accounts from the remaining receivables. Generalized computer audit programs are useful in stratifying computer-processed accounts receivable to facilitate the selection of a representative sample.

Discrepancies in Customers' Replies

The auditors should resolve differences reported by customers. The majority of such reported discrepancies arise because of normal lags in the recording of cash receipts or sales transactions, or because of misunderstanding on the part of the customer company as to the date of the balance it is asked to confirm. Some replies may state that the balance listed is incorrect because it does not reflect recent cash payments; in such instances, the auditors normally trace the reported payments to the cash records.

Alternative Audit Procedures for Nonrespondents

The percentage of replies to positive confirmation requests that can be expected will vary greatly according to the type of debtor. When using positive confirmation requests, the auditors should generally follow up with a second and sometimes a third request to produce replies. When replies are still not received, the auditors should apply alternative procedures to the accounts, unless (1) the amount of the nonresponses is not significant when projected as a 100 percent misstatement to the total balance of receivables, and (2) there are no unusual characteristics related to the nonresponses. The best *alternative auditing procedure* is examination

Illustrative Case
Importance of Follow-up on Nonrespondents

During the first audit of a small manufacturing company, the auditors sent confirmation requests to all customers whose accounts showed balances in excess of $1,000. Satisfactory replies were received from all but one account, which had a balance of approximately $30,000. A second confirmation request sent to this customer produced no response; but before the auditors could investigate further, they were informed by the cashier-accountant that the account had been paid in full. The auditors asked to examine the customer's check and the accompanying remittance advice, but they were told that the check had been deposited and the remittance advice destroyed. Further questioning concerning transactions with this customer evoked such vague responses that the auditors decided to discuss the account with the officers of the company. At this point the cashier-accountant confessed that the account in question was a fictitious one created to conceal a shortage and that to satisfy the auditors he had "collected" the account receivable by diverting current collections from other customers whose accounts had already been confirmed.

of subsequent cash receipts in payment of the receivable. However, in order to make certain that the payment is for a receivable that existed at year-end, the auditors also may need to examine shipping documents, customer purchase orders, or sales invoices for the sales transactions making up the receivable. Examination of these sales documents is also the alternative procedure used for receivables that are not paid during the subsequent period.

The Confirmation Process in Perspective

A summary should be prepared outlining the extent and nature of the confirmations sent and the overall results obtained. Such a summary is a highly important part of the audit working papers.

The auditors face more than one type of risk in relying upon the confirmation process to form an opinion about the fairness of the accounts receivable as a whole. We have already recognized the risk that some accounts with erroneous balances may not be included in the sample confirmed, and also the risk that replies may not be received from some customers having erroneous balances. Finally, there is the risk that customers may routinely return confirmation requests without actually comparing the balance with their records. Such responses would give the auditors a false sense of security. Despite these risks, however, the confirming of accounts receivable provides valuable evidence and represents an important part of the auditors' work.

It has sometimes been said that the best proof available to the auditors as to the existence of an account receivable is its collection during the course of their audit. But this statement requires qualification, as indicated by the situation described in the above "Illustrative Case."

Reviewing and Confirming Accounts and Notes Written off as Uncollectible

If any accounts or notes receivable of significant amount were written off as uncollectible during the year, the auditors should determine that these write-offs were properly authorized. In the absence of proper authorization procedures, a dishonest employee could conceal permanently a theft of cash merely by a charge to accounts or notes receivable followed by a write-off of that asset.

A systematic review of the notes and accounts written off can conveniently be made by obtaining or preparing an analysis of the allowance for doubtful accounts and notes. Debits to the allowance may be traced to the authorizing documents and to the control record of accounts and notes written off; confirmation requests may be mailed to some of the debtors to determine that the account or note was genuine when it was first recorded in the accounts. Credit entries should be compared with the charges to uncollectible accounts and notes expense. Any write-off that appears unreasonable should be fully investigated. Charge-off of a note or account receivable from an officer, stockholder, or director is unreasonable on its face and warrants the most searching investigation by the auditors. The computation of percentages relating the year's write-offs to net credit sales, to uncollectible accounts expense, and to the allowance for doubtful accounts and notes may be useful in bringing to light any abnormal write-offs.

Primary Audit
Objectives:

Existence ☑
Rights ☑
Completeness ☑

5. Review the Year-end Cutoff of Sales Transactions.

One of the more common methods of falsifying accounting records is to inflate the sales for the year by holding open the sales journal beyond the balance sheet date. Shipments made in the first part of January may be covered by sales invoices bearing a December date and included in December sales. The purpose of such misleading entries is to present a more favorable financial picture than actually exists. Since sales are frequently used as the base for computation of bonuses and commissions, an additional incentive for padding the Sales account is often present. A related abuse affecting accounts receivable is the practice of holding the cash journals open beyond the balance sheet date; auditing procedures designed to detect this practice were described in connection with the audit of cash transactions in Chapter 10.

To guard against errors in the cutoff of sales records (whether accidental or intentional), the auditors should compare the sales recorded for several days before and after the balance sheet date with the duplicate sales invoices and shipping documents. The effectiveness of this step is largely dependent upon the degree of segregation of duties between the shipping, receiving, and billing functions. If warehousing, shipping, billing, and receiving are independently controlled, it is most unlikely that records in all these departments will be manipulated to disguise shipments of one period as sales of the preceding period. On the other hand, one individual with control over both shipping records and billing documents could manipulate both sets of records if overstatement of the year's sales was attempted.

Fictitious sales are occasionally recorded at year-end as a means of overstating financial results. Therefore, auditors should be aware of, and investigate:

a. Unusually large increases in year-end sales to a single customer or a few. This might be indicative of *bill and hold transactions,* in which sales are billed but goods are not shipped. Bill and hold transactions must meet stringent requirements to qualify as a sale as set forth in SEC *Staff Accounting Bulletin No. 104.*

b. Large increases in revenue and receivables along with increases in gross profit margins that are inconsistent with the client's experience or industry averages.

c. Inappropriate changes in accounting principles that result in an increase in recorded revenue.

d. Substantial sales returns following the balance sheet date that might indicate merchandise shipped to customers without a customer order for those goods or **channel stuffing,** in which sales are boosted by inducing customers to buy substantially more inventory than they can promptly resell.

As discussed in Chapter 10, the term **window dressing** refers to actions taken around the balance sheet date to improve the financial picture presented in the financial statements. A number of window dressing practices represent proper and appropriate business practices, such as a special year-end promotion to boost sales and making diligent efforts to ship out all orders. However, window dressing practices such as those listed above result in fraudulent misstatements of the financial statements. To guard against such manipulations, the auditors should review carefully all substantial sales returns following the balance sheet date that may apply to receivables originating in the year under audit. Consideration should be given to reflecting these returns in the current year's business by means of adjusting entries. Confirmation of accounts receivable, if made at the balance sheet date, should also serve to bring any large unauthorized shipments to the attention of the auditors.

Primary Audit
Objectives:

Existence ☑
Rights ☑
Completeness ☑
Valuation ☑

6. Perform Analytical Procedures for Accounts Receivable, Notes Receivable, and Revenue.

In planning the audit, *SAS No. 99,* "Consideration of Fraud in a Financial Statement Audit," requires the auditors to perform analytical procedures with the objective of identifying potential misstatements of revenue. Several ratios and relationships can be computed to indicate the overall reasonableness of the amounts shown for accounts receivable, revenue, and notes receivable. Examples include: (*a*) the gross profit rate (by product line, store, or region), (*b*) the ratio of sales in the last month or week to total sales for the quarter or year, (*c*) revenue in relation to productive capacity, (*d*) units shipped in relation to revenues and production records,

Illustrative Case
What Do You Do with Stale Doughnuts?

Former company and franchise employees stated that by mid-2003 Krispie Kreme Doughnuts, Inc., was double-shipping wholesale orders to some grocers at the end of quarterly reporting periods in order to temporarily boost sales and earnings, even though executives knew many of the doughnuts would be returned for credit later. It was reported that it was commonplace for management to inappropriately channel stuff in order to meet analysts' expectations. This was inappropriate because Krispie Kreme's management did not take into consideration the additional amounts of sales returns involved.

(*e*) accounts receivable turnover, (*f*) the ratio of accounts receivable to the year's net credit sales, (*g*) the ratio of accounts written off during the year to the ending balance of accounts receivable, (*h*) the ratio of returns and allowances to sales, (*i*) the ratio of interest revenue to notes receivable, and (*j*) the ratio of uncollectible account expense to credit sales. These ratios and relationships are compared with corresponding data for the preceding years, and with budgets, performance statistics, or comparable industry averages.

Focus on the Casino Industry

Casinos have few documents to support their revenue transactions. This makes it difficult for auditors to apply tests of details to the revenues of these types of organizations. An AICPA *Audit Risk Alert* on the casino industry emphasizes the use of analytical procedures to audit revenues. In developing expectations about the amounts of revenues, the auditors should consider:

- Demographic data of casino clientele.
- Betting limits established by regulatory agencies.
- Effects of adverse weather conditions or special events, such as conventions, on casino attendance.
- Seasonality of casino operations.
- General economic conditions.
- Effects of intense competition.
- Impact of promotional programs.
- Probable win ratios.

Auditors are warned that while, in the long term, fluctuations may be likely to conform to expected patterns, the element of chance—a fundamental characteristic of casino operations—makes short-term fluctuations common.

Primary Audit Objectives:	
Existence	☑
Rights	☑
Completeness	☑
Valuation	☑

7. Review Significant Year-end Sales Contracts for Unusual Terms.

To boost the level of sales for a period, management may be inclined to modify the terms of sales contracts near year-end. These modifications may affect the collectibility of the related accounts receivable, the customers' return rights, and even whether the sales meet the criteria to be recognized in the current period. Therefore, the auditors should carefully review any significant year-end sales contracts for unusual pricing, billing, delivery, return, exchange, or acceptance clauses.

Primary Audit Objectives:	
Existence	☑
Rights	☑
Completeness	☑

8. Verify Interest Earned on Notes and Accrued Interest Receivable.

The most effective verification of the Interest Earned account consists of an *independent computation* by the auditors of the interest earned during the year on notes receivable. The working paper used to analyze notes receivable should show the interest rate and date of issuance of each note. The interest section of this working paper consists of four columns, which show for each note receivable owned during the year the following information:

a. Accrued interest receivable at the beginning of the year (taken from the preceding year's audit working papers).

b. Interest earned during the year (computed from the terms of the notes).

c. Interest collected during the year (traced to cash receipts records).

d. Accrued interest receivable at the end of the year (computed by the auditors).

These four columns compose a self-balancing set. The beginning balance of accrued interest receivable (first column) plus the interest earned during the year (second column) and minus the interest collected (third column) should equal the accrued interest receivable at the end of the year (fourth column). The totals of the four columns should be cross-footed to ensure that they are in balance; in addition, the individual column totals should be traced to the balances in the general ledger.

If the interest earned for the year as computed by the auditors does not agree with interest earned as shown in the accounting records, the next step is an analysis of the ledger account. Any unaccounted-for credits in the Interest Earned account deserve particular attention because these credits may represent interest received on notes that have never been recorded.

For financial institutions or other clients having numerous notes receivable, the auditors may verify interest computations on only a sample of the notes. In addition, they should test the reasonableness of total interest earned for the year by applying a weighted average rate of interest to the average balance of the Notes Receivable ledger account during the year.

Primary Audit Objectives:

Existence	☑
Rights	☑
Valuation	☑

9. Evaluate the Propriety of the Client's Accounting Methods for Receivables and Revenue.

As indicated earlier in this chapter, many instances of misstatements in financial statements have involved the inappropriate recognition of revenue and related receivables—often through the premature recording of revenues or the recording of fictitious revenues. Previous steps in this audit program have addressed this risk through consideration of a proper year-end cutoff of sales transactions (step 5), performance of analytical procedures for accounts receivable, notes receivable, and revenue (step 6), and the review of significant year-end sales contracts for unusual terms (step 7). In step 9 we directly address the propriety of the accounting methods relating to receivables and revenue.

From a conceptual standpoint, "revenues are considered to have been earned when the entity has substantially accomplished what it must do to be entitled to the benefits represented by the revenues."[1] The SEC, in *Staff Accounting Bulletin No. 104,* provides the following criteria that ordinarily should exist for revenue to be recognized:

- Persuasive evidence of an arrangement exists.
- Delivery has occurred or services have been rendered.
- The seller's price to the buyer is fixed or determinable.
- Collectibility is reasonably assured.

The auditors must carefully evaluate the propriety of the client's treatment of certain transactions to determine that they meet these criteria, not only in form but also in substance. Problems that the auditors might discover include:

a. An allowance for sales returns may not be set up for goods shipped to customers with the right to return the goods under certain circumstances.

b. Management or client personnel may have established, formally or informally, **side agreements** that significantly alter the terms of sale.

c. Cash receipts from franchise fees may be inappropriately recognized when services have not been rendered to the franchisees.

d. **Bill and hold transactions** may be recorded when they do not meet the requirements for revenue recognition.

e. Notes receivable may not bear reasonable interest rates at the time they are accepted, resulting in a need to discount the notes to present values.

f. Management might use the percentage-of-completion method of revenue recognition in inappropriate circumstances or might overestimate the amount of revenue earned.

g. Management of a software company might recognize excessive amounts of revenue on a multiple element agreement that involves providing software and postcontract customer support.

[1] Statement of Financial Accounting Concepts No. 5, para. 83b.

> ### Focus on the Construction Industry
>
> Construction contractors often use the percentage-of-completion method to recognize income on long-term contracts. Under this method, a contractor computes the extent of progress toward completion of each contract in progress. For example, if a contract is 70 percent complete at year-end and on target cost-wise, the contractor will recognize 70 percent of the contract's revenues, costs, and gross profit. Although the method is well established in the construction industry, auditors must carefully consider whether the contractor's estimates of costs to complete the contracts are reasonable, and whether it is probable that losses may be incurred on contracts. When making this determination auditors should consider:
>
> - The controls over the contractors' estimation process, including the competence of the personnel making the estimates.
> - Explanations for apparent disparities between estimates and past performance on contracts.
> - Information gained in other areas of the audit.
> - Industry and economic conditions, and expected future trends.
>
> When slow economic growth is expected, and intense competition exists, there may be an increased risk that a construction contractor may be inclined to compensate for low revenue growth by underestimating the costs to complete projects. Although overestimating the percentage of completion is one way of underestimating costs, another is to project a lower than reasonable level of inflation on future costs.

The above illustration focusing on the construction industry makes it clear that auditors must have a thorough understanding of generally accepted accounting principles and the *substance,* as well as the form, of the client's revenue transactions. The auditors carefully examine the various documents pertaining to the transactions to determine that proper accounting principles have been followed. If they believe that there is a risk that the terms of contracts may have been modified, they should consider confirming the terms with the customer.

10. Evaluate Accounting Estimates Related to Revenue Recognition.

Primary Audit Objective:
Valuation ☑

The auditors are responsible for evaluating the reasonableness of accounting estimates related to receivables and the recognition of revenue. Examples of these accounting estimates include sales returns, revenues accounted for by the percentage-of-completion method, and the allowance for uncollectible accounts. In accordance with *SAS No. 57,* "Auditing Accounting Estimates," the auditors audit accounting estimates by reviewing and testing management's method of developing the estimates, by developing their own estimates, or by reviewing subsequent transactions and other events that provide evidence about the accuracy of the estimates.

Because fraudulent financial reporting often is accomplished through the intentional misstatement of accounting estimates, the auditors are required to perform a retrospective review of the prior year's significant accounting estimates to determine whether they indicate bias on the part of management. As an example, the auditors of a construction contractor could compare prior-year estimates of cost to completed projects with the actual costs incurred. If these comparisons indicate a bias on the part of management, the auditors will use this information in auditing the current year accounting estimates.

11. Determine Adequacy of Allowance for Uncollectible Accounts.

Primary Audit Objective:
Valuation ☑

The allowance for uncollectible accounts represents a particularly significant accounting estimate for most organizations. Accordingly, we will provide a detailed explanation of the audit procedures applied to this account. As a starting point, the retrospective analysis of accounting estimates described in the preceding section provides overall information about the quality of management's prior estimates. This information will almost certainly influence the auditors' approach to auditing the allowance account, which may primarily involve evaluating management's process of developing the estimate, reviewing subsequent transactions, or developing the auditors' own estimate.

If the auditors elect to use the overall approach of evaluating management's process, they will consider both the reasonableness of the process and the competence of the personnel involved. If the process is well designed and controlled, the auditors may decide to focus on tests of controls to obtain much or all of the evidence about the reasonableness of the allowance.

Since the best evidence of the *collectibility* of accounts receivable is payment by the debtors subsequent to the balance sheet date, the approach of analyzing subsequent transactions is also an appropriate overall audit approach. In the audit working papers, the auditors should document the subsequent payments inspected; the illustrated trial balance of trade accounts receivable (Figure 11.6, page 415) includes a special column for this purpose.

The auditors also may decide to independently develop their own estimate of the amount of uncollectible receivables to compare to management's estimate. The following procedures may be used by the auditors both in developing an estimate and in evaluating the reasonableness of management's estimate:

a. Compare the details of the aging of accounts receivable to prior years' aging. Examine the past-due accounts receivable listed in the aging schedule that have not been paid subsequent to the balance sheet date, noting such factors as the size and recentness of payments, settlement of old balances, and whether recent sales are on a cash or a credit basis. The client's customer correspondence file may contain much of this information.

b. Investigate the credit ratings for delinquent and unusually large accounts. This is particularly efficient when receivables from one or a few customers represent a major portion of the total. Financial statements and credit data should be available in the client's credit files.

c. Review confirmation exceptions for an indication of amounts in dispute or other clues as to possible uncollectible accounts.

d. Summarize in a working paper those accounts whose collectibility is doubtful based on the preceding procedures. List customer names, doubtful amounts, and reasons for considering these accounts doubtful.

e. Review with the credit manager the current status of significant doubtful accounts, ascertaining the collection action taken and the opinion of the credit manager as to ultimate collectibility. Indicate in the working papers the credit manager's opinion as to the collectible portion of each account listed, and use this information to assist in evaluating the collectibility of specific accounts.

f. Compute relationships, such as the number-of-days'-sales in accounts receivable and the relationship of the valuation allowance to (1) accounts receivable and (2) net credit sales. Compare the ratios to comparable ratios for prior years and industry averages, and investigate any unexpected results.

After completion of procedures such as the above, the auditors will determine the reasonableness of management's estimate of the allowance for uncollectible accounts.

Receipt of a Note in Settlement of a Past-due Receivable

A client may receive a note receivable from a customer in settlement of a past-due account receivable—thereby creating an interest-bearing asset. When this occurs, may the auditors conclude that the collectibility of the account does not need to be considered? The answer here is "no," as collectibility issues may very well exist with respect to the note. First, the decision to accept a note in payment as opposed to a cash payment leads one to question the financial stability of the note maker. A provision for loss becomes more probable when notes have been repeatedly renewed, payments on installment notes have been late and/or irregular, notes have been defaulted upon, and the makers of the notes are companies known to be in financial difficulties. To appraise the collectibility of notes receivable, the auditors may investigate the credit standing of the makers. Reports from credit-rating agencies and financial statements from the makers of the notes should be available for this purpose in the client's credit department.

Evaluation of any collateral supplied by makers of notes is another step in determining the collectibility of notes receivable. The auditors should determine the current market value of securities held as collateral by the client, either by reference to market quotations or by inquiry of brokers.

12. Ascertain Whether Any Receivables Have Been Pledged.

The auditors should inquire directly as to whether any notes or accounts receivable have been pledged or assigned. Evidence of the **pledging of receivables** may also be disclosed through the medium of financial institution confirmation requests, which specifically call for a description of the collateral securing bank loans. Analysis of the interest expense accounts may reflect charges from the pledging of receivables to finance companies.

Accounts receivable that have been pledged should be plainly identified through coding in the accounts receivable records. Accounts labeled in this manner would be identified by the auditors in their initial review of receivables and confirmed by direct correspondence with the bank to which they were pledged. The auditors cannot, however, proceed on the assumption that all pledged receivables have been labeled to that effect, and they must be alert to detect any suggestions of an unrecorded pledging of accounts receivable.

13. Investigate Any Transactions with or Receivables from Related Parties.

Transactions between the corporation and its officers, directors, stockholders, or affiliates require particular attention from the auditors because these related party transactions are not the result of arm's-length bargaining by parties of opposing interests. Furthermore, such transactions may be prohibited by federal or state law or by the corporation's bylaws. The independent auditors have an obligation to stockholders, creditors, and others who rely upon audited statements to require adequate disclosure of any significant related party transactions.

To identify related party transactions, the auditors should review (1) proxy and other filings with the SEC or other regulatory agencies, (2) conflict-of-interest statements obtained by the company from its management, (3) transactions with customers or suppliers that have unusual terms, and (4) accounting records for unusual balances or transactions, particularly those occurring near year-end. If related party transactions are discovered, the auditors should obtain an understanding of the transactions, determine whether the transactions have been approved by the board of directors or other appropriate officials, confirm the terms of the transactions with the related parties, evaluate the collectibility of any receivables outstanding, and evaluate the adequacy of disclosure of the details of the transactions in the notes to the financial statements.

14. Evaluate the Business Purpose of Significant and Unusual Sales Transactions.

Auditors are required by *SAS No. 99,* "Consideration of Fraud in a Financial Statement Audit," to evaluate the business purpose of any transaction that comes to their attention that is significant and unusual. Such transactions may be indicative of fraudulent financial reporting.

15. Evaluate Financial Statement Presentation and Disclosure of Receivables and Revenue.

The auditors must ascertain that the financial presentation of accounts and notes receivable and the related disclosures are in accordance with generally accepted accounting principles. Related party receivables should be shown separately with disclosure of the nature of the relationships and the amounts of the transactions. Any unusual terms of notes receivable should be disclosed in the notes. Also, the amounts of allowances for uncollectible receivables should be shown as deductions from the related receivables. Finally, significant concentrations of credit risk arising from trade accounts receivable should be disclosed in accordance with *FASB Statement No. 105,* "Disclosure of Information about Financial Instruments with Off-Balance Sheet Risk and Financial Instruments with Concentrations of Credit Risk."

Interim Audit Work on Receivables and Revenue

Much of the audit work on receivables and revenue can be performed one or two months before the balance sheet date. The **interim audit work** may consist of the consideration of controls and, in some cases, the confirmation of accounts receivable as well. A decision to carry out the confirmation of receivables at an interim date rather than at year-end is justified only if control risk for existence of accounts receivable is low.

If interim audit work has been done on receivables and revenue, the year-end audit work may be modified considerably. For example, if the confirmation of accounts receivable was performed at October 31, the year-end audit program would include preparation of a summary analysis of postings to the Accounts Receivable controlling account for the period from November 1 through December 31. This analysis would list the postings by month, showing the journal source of each. These postings would be traced to the respective journals, such as the sales journal and cash receipts journal. The amounts of the postings would be compared with the amounts in preceding months and with the corresponding months in prior years. The purpose of this work is to bring to light any significant variations in receivables during the months between the interim audit work and the balance sheet date.

In addition to this analysis of the entries to the receivable accounts for the intervening period, the audit work at year-end would include obtaining the aging of the accounts receivable at December 31, confirmation of any large accounts in the year-end trial balance that are new or delinquent, and the usual investigation of the year-end cutoff of sales and cash receipts.

Chapter Summary

In this chapter we described the details of controls over receivables and revenue, the auditors' consideration of these controls, and substantive tests of the receivables and revenue accounts. To summarize:

1. The audit of receivables and revenue represents significant audit risk because (*a*) many incidences of financial statement fraud have involved the overstatement of receivables and revenue, (*b*) revenue recognition may be based on complex accounting rules, and (*c*) receivables and revenue are usually subject to valuation using significant accounting estimates. Companies should establish effective high-level controls over the financial reporting of these accounts, including (*a*) an audit committee to oversee the reliability of reporting of revenue, (*b*) an internal audit department to monitor compliance with other revenue cycle controls, (*c*) human resource policies and practices to ensure that competent personnel are involved in determining revenue and receivables estimates, and (*d*) effective monitoring policies and procedures. In addition, a sound accounting system and effective control activities should be established for the revenue cycle.

2. The revenue cycle includes the receiving of orders from customers, the delivery and billing of goods and services, and the recording and collection of accounts receivable. Effective internal control over sales transactions is best achieved by having separate departments responsible for preparing sales orders, approving credit, shipping merchandise, billing customers, maintaining the accounts receivable subsidiary ledger, and authorizing adjustments to sales and accounts receivable.

3. The auditors' consideration of internal control over revenue and cash receipts provides them with a basis for assessing control risk for the related financial statement assertions. To assess control risk at less than the maximum for a particular assertion, the auditors must perform tests of the operating effectiveness of the controls. The auditors' assessments of inherent and control risks then are used to determine the nature, timing, and extent of the substantive tests of receivables and revenue.

4. The primary objectives for the auditors' substantive tests of receivables and revenue are to (*a*) substantiate the existence of receivables and the occurrence of revenue transactions, (*b*) establish the completeness of receivables and revenue, (*c*) determine that the client has rights to the recorded receivables, (*d*) determine that the valuation of receivables and revenue is at an appropriate net realizable value, and (*e*) establish that the presentation and disclosure of receivables and revenue are appropriate.

5. The most time-consuming and critical audit procedures for receivables and revenue are those designed to test the assertions of existence, occurrence, and valuation. Among the procedures designed to achieve these objectives is confirmation of accounts receivable, which is generally required in all audits. Acknowledgment of the debt provides evidence of existence of receivables and occurrence of sales, as well as the gross valuation of the amounts. An important part of obtaining evidence about the proper valuation of accounts receivable is the auditors' evaluation of the adequacy of the allowance for uncollectible accounts. Since this account is a management estimate, it is typically audited by a combination of inquiry of management, analytical procedures, and inspection of various documents.

6. Other significant aspects of the audit include evaluation of the appropriateness of the client's methods of revenue recognition, and procedures directed at identifying and evaluating the disclosure of related party transactions and receivables.

Key Terms Introduced or Emphasized in Chapter 11

Aged trial balance   A listing of individual customers' accounts classified by the number of days subsequent to billing, that is, by age. A preliminary step in estimating the collectibility of accounts receivable.

Bill and hold transactions   Transactions in which sales of merchandise are billed to customers prior to delivery, with the goods being held by the seller. These transactions may overstate revenues and net income if they do not meet specific requirements for recognition as sales.

Channel stuffing   A marketing practice that suppliers sometimes use to boost sales by inducing customers to buy substantially more inventory than they can promptly resell. Channel stuffing without appropriate provision for sales returns is an example of booking tomorrow's revenue today in order to window dress the financial statements.

Confirmation   The process of obtaining evidence by written communication with the debtor or other party to a transaction.

Interim audit work   Those audit procedures that can be performed before the balance sheet date. The purpose is to facilitate earlier issuance of the audit report and to spread the auditors' work more uniformly over the year.

Negative confirmation   A confirmation request addressed to the debtor requesting a reply only if the balance shown on the confirmation is incorrect.

Pledging of receivables   To assign to a bank, factor, finance company, or other lender an exclusive claim against accounts receivable as security for a debt.

Positive confirmation   A confirmation request sent to the debtor asking it to confirm directly to the auditors the accuracy of the dollar amount shown on the request. Calls for a reply regardless of whether the amount is correct or incorrect.

Side agreements   Formal or informal modifications of normal terms and conditions of sales transactions to entice customers to accept delivery of goods or services.

Window dressing   Action taken by the client shortly before the balance sheet date to improve the financial picture presented in the financial statements.

Review Questions

11–1.   Explain the difference between a *customer's order* and a *sales order,* as these terms might be used by a manufacturing company making sales on credit.

11–2.   Explain why the audit of revenue and receivables presents the auditors with significant audit risk.

11–3.   An inexperienced clerk assigned to the preparation of sales invoices in a manufacturing company became confused as to the nature of certain articles being shipped, with the result that the prices used on the invoices were far less than called for in the company's price lists. What controls could be established to guard against such errors?

11–4.   State briefly the objective of the billing process. What important document is created by the billing department?

11–5.   Criticize the following quotation: "A credit memorandum should be issued only when an account receivable is determined to be uncollectible."

11–6.   The controller of a new client operating a medium-size manufacturing business complains to you that he believes the company has sustained significant losses on several occasions because certain sales invoices were misplaced and never recorded as accounts receivable. What control can you suggest to guard against such problems?

11–7.   Comment on the following: "Any voided prenumbered shipping documents should be properly canceled and disposed of to eliminate any possibility of improper shipment of goods."

11–8.   The accounts receivable section of the accounting department in Wind Power, Inc., maintains subsidiary ledgers that are posted from copies of the sales invoices transmitted daily from the billing department. How may the accounts receivable section be sure that it receives promptly a copy of each sales invoice prepared?

11–9.   Among specific procedures that contribute to good internal control over the business processes related to accounts receivable are (*a*) the approval of uncollectible account write-offs and credit memoranda by an executive and (*b*) the sending of monthly statements to all customers. State three other procedures conducive to strong internal control.

11–10.   In the audit of an automobile agency, you find that installment notes received from the purchasers of automobiles are promptly discounted with a bank. Would you consider it necessary to confirm these notes by a communication with the bank? With the makers? Explain.

11–11. Your review of notes receivable from officers, directors, stockholders, and affiliated companies discloses that several notes of small amounts were written off to the allowance for uncollectible notes during the year. Have these transactions any special significance? Explain.

11–12. What auditing procedures, if any, are necessary for notes receivable but not required for accounts receivable?

11–13. The confirmation of accounts receivable is an important auditing procedure. Should the formal request for confirmation be made by the client or by the auditors? Should the return envelope be addressed to the client, to the auditors in care of the client, or to the auditors' office? Explain.

11–14. State briefly the *audit objectives* that are addressed by the following audit procedure: "Confirm accounts receivable and notes receivable by direct communication with debtors."

11–15. In selecting accounts receivable for confirmation, the auditors discover that the client company's records show the addresses of many individual customers to be post office boxes. What should be the auditors' reaction to this situation?

11–16. Several accounts receivable confirmations have been returned with the notation "verification of vendors' statements are no longer possible because of our data processing system." What alternative auditing procedures could be used to verify these accounts receivable?

11–17. What alternative auditing procedures may be undertaken in connection with the confirmation of accounts receivable where customers having substantial balances fail to reply after second request forms have been mailed directly to them?

11–18. A CPA firm wishes to test the client's sales cutoff at June 30, 200X. Describe the steps that the auditors should include in this test.

11–19. In your first audit of Hydro Manufacturing Company, a manufacturer of outboard motors, you discover that an unusually large number of sales transactions were recorded just before the end of the fiscal year. What significance would you attach to this unusual volume?

11–20. In connection with an audit, what are the purposes of a review of sales returns and allowances subsequent to the balance sheet date?

11–21. In the examination of credit memoranda covering allowances to customers for goods returned, how can the auditors ascertain whether the customer actually did return merchandise in each case in which accounts receivable were reduced?

11–22. Cite various procedures auditors employ that might lead to the detection of an inadequate allowance for doubtful accounts receivable.

11–23. Give an example of a type of receivable originating without arm's-length bargaining. Comment on the presentation of such receivables in the balance sheet.

11–24. Describe a retrospective review of an accounting estimate. With respect to the audit of revenue, what is the purpose of performing this review?

Questions Requiring Analysis

11–25. You have been assigned to the audit of Processing Solutions, Inc., a privately held corporation that develops and sells computer systems. The systems are sold under one-to-five-year contracts that provide for a fixed price for licensing, delivery, and setup of the systems and maintenance and technical support for the life of the contract. Your review of the working papers reveals that premature revenue recognition is a risk that must be addressed in the audit.

Required:
a. Describe the criteria from SEC *Staff Accounting Bulletin No. 104* that must be met to recognize revenue under generally accepted accounting principles.

b. Describe two techniques that management of Processing Solutions might use to overstate revenue.

c. For the two techniques identified in (*b*), describe an auditing procedure that might be employed by the auditors to detect the overstatement of revenue.

11–26. Listed below are audit situations that may affect the audit of receivables and revenue.

a. The audit of a machinery manufacturing company that engages in bill and hold transactions.

b. The audit of a software company that engages in multiple element agreements that involve a fixed fee for software, updates, and customer support.

c. The audit of a construction company that uses the percentage-of-completion method of accounting for contracts.

d. The audit of a manufacturing company that uses complex sales agreements that allow product returns under certain circumstances.

e. The audit of a software company whose salespeople often modify the terms of sales contracts with various side agreements.

Required: For each circumstance provide an indication of its audit significance and any special audit procedures that would result.

11–27. If you were preparing a credit sales system flowchart, what document would you show as:

a. The source for posting debits to a customer's account in the accounts receivable ledger?

b. Authorization to the finished goods stores to release merchandise to the shipping department?

c. The source for preparing a sales order?

d. The source for preparing a bill of lading?

e. The source for an entry in the sales journal?

11–28. Elizabeth Cole, the senior auditor-in-charge of the audit of Thorne Company, a small manufacturer, was busy writing the audit report for another engagement. Accordingly, she sent Martin Joseph, a recently hired staff assistant of the CPA firm, to begin the audit of Thorne Company, with the suggestion that Joseph start with the accounts receivable. Using the preceding year's audit working papers for Thorne Company as a guide, Joseph prepared a trial balance of Thorne's trade accounts receivable, aged them, prepared and mailed positive confirmation requests, examined underlying documents plus other support for charges and credits to the Accounts Receivable ledger account, and performed such other work as he deemed necessary to assure the validity and collectibility of the accounts receivable. At the conclusion of Joseph's work, Cole traveled to Thorne Company to review Joseph's working papers. Cole found that Joseph had carefully followed the prior year's audit working papers.

Required: State how the three generally accepted auditing standards of fieldwork were fulfilled, or were not fulfilled, in the audit of the accounts receivable of Thorne Company.

(AICPA, adapted)

11–29. In their work on accounts receivable and elsewhere in an audit, the independent auditors often make use of confirmation requests.

a. What is an audit confirmation request?

b. What characteristics should an audit confirmation response possess if a CPA firm is to consider it to be valid evidence?

c. Distinguish between a positive confirmation request and a negative confirmation request in the auditors' examination of accounts receivable.

d. In confirming a client's accounts receivable, what characteristics should be present in the accounts if the CPA firm is to use negative confirmations?

11–30. During preliminary conversations with a new staff assistant you instruct her to send out confirmation requests for both accounts receivable and notes receivable. She asks whether the confirmation requests should go to the makers of the notes or to the holders of the notes, in the case of notes that have been discounted. Provide an answer to her question and give reasons for your answer.

11–31. Tom Jones, CPA, is auditing the financial statements of a manufacturing company with a significant amount of trade accounts receivable. Jones is satisfied that the accounts are properly summarized and classified and are valued in accordance with generally accepted accounting principles. Jones plans to use accounts receivable confirmation requests to satisfy the third standard of fieldwork as to trade accounts receivable.

Required:
a. Identify and describe the two forms of accounts receivable confirmation requests and indicate what factors Jones should consider in determining when to use each.

b. Assume Jones has received a satisfactory response to the confirmation requests. Describe how Jones could evaluate collectibility of the trade accounts receivable.

(AICPA, adapted)

11–32. Lakeside Company has retained you to conduct an audit so that it will be able to support its application for a bank loan with audited financial statements. The president of Lakeside states that you will have unlimited access to all records of the company and may carry out any audit procedures you consider necessary, except that you are not to communicate with customers. The president feels that contacts with customers might lead them to believe that Lakeside is in financial difficulty. Under these circumstances, will it be possible for you to issue the auditors' standard unqualified audit report? Explain.

11–33. During the audit of Solar Technologies, Inc., the auditors sent confirmation requests to customers whose accounts had been written off as uncollectible during the year under audit. An executive of Solar protested, saying, "You people should be verifying that the receivables on the books are collectible. We know the ones we wrote off are no good."

Required:
   a. What purpose, if any, is served by this audit procedure?

   b. Does the Solar executive's statement suggest some misunderstanding of audit objectives? Explain.

11–34. Your regular annual audit of Palisades, Inc., included the confirmation of accounts receivable. You decided to use the positive form of confirmation request. Satisfactory replies were received from all but one of the large accounts. You sent a second and a third request to this customer but received no reply. At this point an employee of the client company informed you that a check had been received for the full amount of the receivable. Would you regard this as a satisfactory disposition of the matter? Explain.

11–35. Many CPAs are sharing information over the Internet. Auditnet is an Internet site that contains audit programs donated by various CPAs. Auditnet's address is www.auditnet.org. You can get to the audit programs by selecting the "audit programs" category.

   a. Select the accounts receivable audit program, and summarize the items that the program indicates should be considered in determining the adequacy of the allowance for doubtful accounts.

   b. Describe the procedure for testing completeness of sales.

11–36. Walter Conn, CPA, is engaged to audit the financial statements of Matthews Wholesaling for the year ended December 31, 200X. Conn obtained and documented an understanding of the client and its environment, including internal control over the business processes relating to accounts receivable. He assessed the risks of material misstatement for all of the assertions about accounts receivable at a moderate level. Conn requested and obtained from Matthews an aged accounts receivable schedule listing the total amount owed by each customer as of December 31, 200X, and sent positive confirmation requests to a sample of the customers.

Required:
What additional substantive audit procedures should Conn consider applying in auditing the accounts receivable?

(AICPA, adapted)

11–37. An assistant auditor was instructed to "test the aging of accounts receivable as shown on the trial balance prepared by the client." In making this test, the assistant traced all past-due accounts shown on the trial balance to the ledger cards in the accounts receivable subsidiary ledger and computed the aging of these accounts. The assistant found no discrepancies and reported to the senior auditor that the aging work performed by the client was satisfactory.

Comment on the logic and adequacy of this test of the aging of accounts receivable.

11–38. You have been assigned to the audit of Utopia Industries, Inc., for the year ended December 31, 20X1. The company makes components for communications and defense applications. To obtain an understanding of the methods of revenue recognition used by such businesses and the risks involved, you decide to review the SEC filings of other companies in the same industry.

Required:
   a. Use the Internet to search the SEC's EDGAR (Electronic Data Gathering and Retrieval System) for the 10-Ks of two companies that are in Utopia's industry (Standard Industrial Classification Code—3812—Search, Detection, Navigational, Guidance, Aeronautical Systems). The URL for EDGAR is www.sec.gov/edgarhp.htm. You can obtain a list of these companies by searching for the number 3812.

   b. Review the notes to the financial statements of the two companies and summarize their methods of revenue recognition.

   c. Describe the special audit risks that are inherent in the methods of revenue recognition used by the companies.

Multiple Choice Questions

11–39. Select the best answer for each of the following and explain fully the reason for your selection.

   a. Which of the following is *least* likely to be considered an inherent risk relating to receivables and revenues?

     (1) Restrictions placed on sales by laws and regulations.

     (2) Decline in sales due to economic declines.

(3) Decline in sales due to product obsolescence.

(4) Over-recorded sales due to a lack of control over the sales entry function.

b. Which of the following would provide the most assurance concerning the valuation of accounts receivable?

(1) Trace amounts in the accounts receivable subsidiary ledger to details on shipping documents.

(2) Compare receivable turnover ratios to industry statistics for reasonableness.

(3) Inquire about receivables pledged under loan agreements.

(4) Assess the allowance for uncollectible accounts for reasonableness.

c. Which of the following is an example of fraudulent financial reporting relating to sales?

(1) Inaccurate billing due to a lack of controls.

(2) Lapping of accounts receivable.

(3) Misbilling a client due to a data input error.

(4) Recording sales when the customer is likely to return the goods.

d. Which of the following is an example of misappropriation of assets relating to sales?

(1) Accidentally recording cash that represents a liability as revenue.

(2) Holding the sales journal open to record next year's sales as having occurred in the current year.

(3) Intentionally recording cash received from a new debt agreement as revenue.

(4) Theft of cash register sales.

e. There is a presumption that auditors will confirm accounts receivable *unless* the auditors' combined assessment of inherent risk and control risk is low.

(1) And accounts receivable are immaterial, or the use of confirmations would be ineffective.

(2) And accounts receivable are composed of large accounts.

(3) And the effectiveness of confirmations is absolutely determined.

(4) Or accounts receivable are from extremely reputable customers.

f. Which of the following is not among the criteria that ordinarily exist for revenue to be recognized?

(1) Collectibility is reasonably assured.

(2) Delivery has occurred or is scheduled to occur in the near future.

(3) Persuasive evidence of an arrangement exists.

(4) The seller's price to the buyer is fixed or determinable.

g. To determine that all sales have been recorded, the auditors would select a sample of transactions *from* the:

(1) Shipping documents file.

(2) Sales journal.

(3) Accounts receivable subsidiary ledger.

(4) Remittance advices.

h. Which of the following would most likely be detected by an auditors' review of the client's sales cutoff?

(1) Excessive goods returned for credit.

(2) Unrecorded sales discounts.

(3) Lapping of year-end accounts receivable.

(4) Inflated sales for the year.

i. To test the existence assertion for recorded receivables, the auditors would select a sample *from* the:

(1) Sales orders file.

(2) Customer purchase orders.

(3) Accounts receivable subsidiary ledger.

(4) Shipping documents (bills of lading) file.

j. Which assertion relating to sales is most directly addressed when the auditors compare a sample of shipping documents to related sales invoices?

    (1) Existence or occurrence.

    (2) Completeness.

    (3) Rights and obligations.

    (4) Presentation and disclosure.

k. Cooper, CPA, is auditing the financial statements of a small rural municipality. The receivable balances represent residents' delinquent real estate taxes. Internal control at the municipality is weak. To determine the existence of the accounts receivable balances at the balance sheet date, Cooper would most likely:

    (1) Send positive confirmation requests.

    (2) Send negative confirmation requests.

    (3) Examine evidence of subsequent cash receipts.

    (4) Inspect the internal records, such as copies of the tax invoices that were mailed to the residents.

l. Identify the control that is most likely to prevent the concealment of a cash shortage resulting from the improper write-off of a trade account receivable:

    (1) Write-offs must be approved by a responsible official after review of credit department recommendations and supporting evidence.

    (2) Write-offs must be approved by the accounts receivable department.

    (3) Write-offs must be authorized by the shipping department.

    (4) Write-offs must be supported by an aging schedule showing that only receivables overdue by several months have been written off.

Problems

11–40. Halston Toy Manufacturing Co. introduced a number of new products in the last quarter of the year. The company has a liberal return policy allowing retail customers to return products within 120 days of purchase.

Required:

a. Describe the audit problem indicated by this scenario.

b. List audit procedures that could be used to audit the allowance for sales returns.

11–41. The following are typical questions that might appear on an internal control questionnaire for accounts receivable:

1. Are sales invoices checked for proper pricing, terms, and clerical accuracy?

2. Are shipping documents prenumbered and all numbers accounted for?

3. Is customer credit approval obtained from the credit department prior to shipment of goods?

Required:

a. Describe the purpose of each of the above controls.

b. Describe the manner in which the operating effectiveness of each of the above procedures might be tested.

c. Assuming that the operating effectiveness of each of the above procedures is found to be inadequate, describe how the auditors might alter their substantive tests to compensate for the increased level of control risk.

11–42. A CPA's audit working papers include the narrative description below of the cash receipts and billing portions of internal control of Parktown Medical Center, Inc. Parktown is a small health care provider that is owned by a publicly held corporation. It employs seven salaried physicians, 10 nurses, three support staff in a common laboratory, and three clerical workers. The clerical workers perform such tasks as reception, correspondence, cash receipts, billing, and appointment scheduling and are adequately bonded. They are referred to in the narrative as "office manager," "clerk 1," and "clerk 2."

Narrative:

Most patients pay for services by cash or check at the time services are rendered. Credit is not approved by the clerical staff. The physician who is to perform the respective services approves credit based on an interview. When credit is approved, the physician files a memo with the billing clerk (clerk 2) to set up the receivable from data generated by the physician.

    The servicing physician prepares a charge slip that is given to clerk 1 for pricing and preparation of the patient's bill. Clerk 1 transmits a copy of the bill to clerk 2 for preparation of the revenue summary and for posting in the accounts receivable subsidiary ledger.

    The cash receipts process is performed by clerk 1, who receives cash and checks directly from patients and gives each patient a prenumbered cash receipt. Clerk 1 opens the mail and immediately stamps all checks "for deposit only" and lists cash and checks for deposit. The cash and checks are deposited daily by the office manager. The list of cash and checks together with the related remittance advices are forwarded by clerk 1 to clerk 2. Clerk 1 also serves as receptionist and performs general correspondence duties.

Clerk 2 prepares and sends monthly statements to patients with unpaid balances. Clerk 2 also prepares the cash receipts journal and is responsible for the accounts receivable subsidiary ledger. No other clerical employee is permitted access to the accounts receivable subsidiary ledger. Uncollectible accounts are written off by clerk 2 only after the physician who performed the respective services believes the account to be uncollectible and communicates the write-off approval to the office manager. The office manager then issues a write-off memo that clerk 2 processes.

The office manager supervises the clerks, issues write-off memos, schedules appointments for the doctors, makes bank deposits, reconciles bank statements, and performs general correspondence duties.

Additional services are performed monthly by a local accountant who posts summaries prepared by the clerks to the general ledger, prepares income statements, and files the appropriate payroll forms and tax returns. The accountant reports directly to the parent corporation.

Required:

Based only on the information in the narrative, describe the internal control weaknesses and one resulting misstatement that could occur and not be prevented or detected by Parktown's internal control concerning the cash receipts and billing processes. Do *not* describe how to correct the weaknesses and potential misstatements. Use the format illustrated below.

Internal Control Weakness	Potential Misstatement
There is no control to verify that fees are recorded and billed at authorized rates and terms.	Accounts receivable could be overstated and uncollectible accounts understated because of the lack of controls.

(AICPA, adapted)

11–43. During your examination of the financial statements of Martin Mfg. Co., a new client, for the year ended March 31, 200X, you note the following entry in the general journal dated March 31, 200X:

Notes Receivable	550,000	
Land		500,000
Gain on sale of land		50,000

To record sale of excess plant-site land to Ardmore Corp. for 8 percent note due five years from date. No interest payment required until maturity of note.

Your review of the contract for sale between Martin and Ardmore, your inquiries of Martin executives, and your study of the minutes of Martin's directors' meetings uncover the following facts:

(1) The land has been carried in your client's accounting records at its cost of $500,000.

(2) Ardmore Corp. is a land developer and plans to subdivide and resell the land acquired from Martin Mfg. Co.

(3) Martin had originally negotiated with Ardmore on the basis of a 12 percent interest rate on the note. This interest rate was established by Martin after a careful analysis of Ardmore's credit standing and current money market conditions.

(4) Ardmore had rejected the 12 percent interest rate because the total outlay on a 12 percent note for $550,000 would amount to $880,000 at the end of five years, and Ardmore thought a total outlay of this amount would leave it with an inadequate return on the subdivision. Ardmore held out for a total cash outlay of $770,000, and Martin Mfg. Co. finally agreed to this position. During the discussions, it was pointed out that the present value of $1 due five years hence at an annual interest rate of 12 percent is approximately $0.567.

Required:

Ignoring income tax considerations, is the journal entry recording Martin's sale of the land to Ardmore acceptable? Explain fully and draft an adjusting entry if you consider one to be necessary.

11–44. Lawrence Company maintains its accounts on the basis of a fiscal year ending October 31. Assume that you were retained by the company in August to perform an audit for the fiscal year ending October 31, 200X. You decide to perform certain auditing procedures in advance of the balance sheet date. Among these interim procedures is the confirmation of accounts receivable, which you perform at September 30.

The accounts receivable at September 30 consisted of approximately 200 accounts with balances totaling $956,750. Seventy-five of these accounts with balances totaling $650,725 were selected for confirmation. All but 20 of the confirmation requests have been returned; 30 were signed without comments, 14 had minor differences that have been cleared satisfactorily, and 11 confirmations had the following comments:

1. We are sorry, but we cannot answer your request for confirmation of our account because Moss Company uses a computerized accounts payable voucher system.

2. The balance of $1,050 was paid on September 23, 200X.

3. The above balance of $7,750 was paid on October 5, 200X.

4. The above balance has been paid.

5. We do not owe you anything at September 30, 200X, since the goods represented by your invoice dated September 30, 200X, Number 25,050, in the amount of $11,550, were received on October 5, 200X, on FOB destination terms.

6. An advance payment of $2,500 made by us in August 200X should cover the two invoices totaling $1,350 shown on the statement attached.

7. We never received these goods.

8. We are contesting the propriety of the $12,525 charge. We think the charge is excessive.

9. Amount okay. As the goods have been shipped to us on consignment, we will remit payment upon selling the goods.

10. The $10,000, representing a deposit under a lease, will be applied against the rent due to us during 200X, the last year of the lease.

11. Your credit in the amount of $440, dated September 5, 200X, cancels the above balance.

Required: What steps would you take to clear satisfactorily each of the above 11 comments?

(AICPA, adapted)

11–45.   Milton Chambers, CPA, was retained by Hall Corporation to perform an audit of its financial statements for the year ending December 31. In a preliminary meeting with company officials, Chambers learned that the corporation customarily accepted numerous notes receivable from its customers. At December 31, the client company's controller provided Chambers with a list of the individual notes receivable owned at that date. The list showed for each note the date of the note, amount, interest rate, maturity date, and name and address of the maker. After a careful consideration of the internal control relating to notes receivable, Chambers turned his attention to the list of notes receivable provided to him by the controller.

Chambers proved the footing of the list and determined that the total agreed with the general ledger control account for notes receivable and also with the amount shown in the balance sheet. Next he selected 20 of the larger amounts on the list of notes receivable for detailed investigation. This investigation consisted of confirming the amount, date, maturity, interest rate, and collateral, if any, by direct communication with the makers of the notes. By selection of the larger amounts, Chambers was able to verify 75 percent of the dollar amount of notes receivable by confirming only 20 percent of the notes. However, he also selected a random sample of another 20 percent of the smaller notes on the list for confirmation with the makers. Satisfactory replies were received to all confirmation requests.

The president of Hall Corporation informed Chambers that the company never required any collateral in support of the notes receivable; the replies to confirmation requests indicated no collateral had been pledged.

No notes were past due at the balance sheet date, and the credit manager stated that no losses were anticipated. Chambers verified the credit status of the makers of all the notes he had confirmed by reference to the audited financial statements of the makers and Dun & Bradstreet, Inc., credit ratings.

By independent computation of the interest accrued on the notes receivable at the balance sheet date, Chambers determined that the accrued interest receivable as shown on the balance sheet was correct.

Since Chambers found no deficiencies in any part of his audit, he issued an unqualified audit report. Some months later, Hall Corporation became insolvent and the president fled the country. Chambers was sued by creditors of the company, who charged that his audit was inadequate and failed to meet minimum professional standards. You are to comment on the audit program followed by Chambers with respect to notes receivable *only*.

11–46.   As part of his audit of the financial statements of Marlborough Corporation for the year ended March 31, 200X, Mark Wayne, CPA, is reviewing the balance sheet presentation of a $1,200,000 advance to Franklin Olds, Marlborough's president. The advance, which represents 50 percent of current assets and 10 percent of total assets, was made during the year ended March 31, 200X. It has been described in the balance sheet as "miscellaneous accounts receivable" and classified as a current asset.

Olds informs the CPA that he has used the proceeds of the advance to purchase 35,000 shares of Marlborough's common stock, in order to forestall a takeover raid on the company. He is reluctant to have his association with the advance described in the financial statements because he does not have voting control and fears that this will "just give the raiders ammunition."

Olds offers the following four-point program as an alternative to further disclosure:

(1)   Have the advance approved by the board of directors. (This can be done expeditiously because a majority of the board members are officers of the company.)

(2)   Prepare a demand note payable to the company with interest of 12 percent (the average bank rate paid by the company).

(3)   Furnish an endorsement of the stock to the company as collateral for the loan. (During the year under audit, despite the fact that earnings did not increase, the market price of Marlborough common rose from $20 to $40 per share. The stock has maintained its $40 per share market price subsequent to year-end.)

(4)   Obtain a written opinion from the company attorney supporting the legality of the company's advance and the use of the proceeds.

Required:

a.   Discuss the proper balance sheet classification of the advance to Olds and other appropriate disclosures in the financial statements and notes. (Ignore SEC regulations and requirements, tax effects, creditors' restrictions on stock repurchases, and the presentation of common stock dividends and interest revenue.)

b.   Discuss each point of Olds's four-point program as to whether it is desirable and as to whether it is an alternative to further disclosure.

c.   If Olds refuses to permit further disclosure, what action should the CPA take? Discuss.

d.   In his discussion with the CPA, Olds warns that the raiders, if successful, probably will appoint new auditors. What consideration should the CPA give to this factor? Explain.

(AICPA, adapted)

11–47.   You are conducting an annual audit of Granite Corporation, which has total assets of approximately $1 million and operates a wholesale merchandising business. The corporation is in good financial condition and maintains an adequate accounting system. Granite Corporation owns about 25 percent of the capital stock of Desert Sun, Inc., which operates a dude ranch. This investment is regarded as a permanent one and is accounted for by the equity method.

During your audit of accounts and notes receivable, you uncover the information shown below concerning three short-term notes receivable due in the near future. All three of these notes receivable were discounted by Granite Corporation with its bank shortly before the balance sheet date.

1.   A 13 percent, 60-day note for $50,000 received from a customer of unquestioned financial standing.

2.   A 15 percent, six-month note for $60,000 received from the affiliated company, Desert Sun, Inc. The affiliated company is operating profitably, but is presently in a weak cash position because of recent additions to buildings and equipment. The president of Granite Corporation intends to make an $80,000 advance with a five-year maturity to Desert Sun, Inc. The proposed advance will enable Desert Sun, Inc., to pay the existing 15 percent, $60,000 note at maturity and to meet certain other obligations.

3.   A 14 percent, $20,000 note from a former key executive of Granite Corporation whose employment had been terminated because of chronic alcoholism and excessive gambling. The maker of the note is presently unemployed and without personal resources.

Required:

Describe the proper balance sheet presentation with respect to these discounted notes receivable. Use a separate paragraph for each of the three notes, and state any assumptions you consider necessary.

11–48.   The July 31, 200X, general ledger trial balance of Aerospace Contractors, Inc., reflects the following accounts associated with receivables. Balances of the accounts are after all adjusting journal entries proposed by the auditors and accepted by the client.

Accounts receivable—commercial	$ 595,000
Accounts receivable—U.S. government	3,182,000
Allowance for uncollectible accounts and notes	75,000 cr.
Claims receivable—public carriers	7,000
Claims receivable—U.S. government terminated contracts	320,000
Due from Harwood Co., investee	480,000
Notes receivable—trade	15,000

Remember that two or more ledger accounts are often combined into one amount in the financial statements in order to achieve a concise presentation. The need for brevity also often warrants the disclosure of some information parenthetically, as for example, the amount of the allowance for doubtful accounts.

Required:

a. Draft a partial balance sheet for Aerospace Contractors at July 31, 200X. In deciding which items deserve separate listing, consider materiality as well as the nature of the accounts.

b. Write an explanation of the reasoning employed in your balance sheet presentation of these accounts.

In-Class Team Case

11–49.

Ming, CPA, is engaged to audit the financial statements of Wellington Sales, Inc., for the year ended December 31, 200X. Ming obtained and documented an understanding of the client's business and environment, including internal control over business processes relating to accounts receivable. She assessed the risks of material misstatement for the assertions of existence, rights, and valuation of accounts receivable at a high level. Ming requested and obtained from Wellington an aged accounts receivable schedule listing the total amount owed by each customer as of December 31, 200X, and sent positive confirmation requests (signed by Sam Blocker, the controller of Wellington). Ming has asked Zimber, the staff assistant assigned to the engagement, to follow up on the eight returned confirmations that appear on the following two pages. Assume that each confirmation is material if the potential misstatement is projected to the population. Also, assume that in all cases the debit balance is the result of a credit to "Sales." In several circumstances a "Note to files" is included with additional information relating to the confirmation.

Required:

Describe the procedure or procedures, if any, that Zimber should perform to resolve each of the nine confirmations (below) with exceptions that were returned and, if possible, provide the audited value of the account. Assume that all amounts involved are considered material.

Confirmation #5

The statement of our account showing a balance of $20,000 due Wellington Sales, Inc., at December 31, 200X, is correct except as noted below:

Abbington Co.

By *Alfred Martin*

Date: 1/16/0Y

Exceptions: *Yes, we ordered $20,000 worth of merchandise from Wellington in November. However, we mailed Wellington a check for $20,000 on 12/18/0X.*

Note to files: Blocker indicates that the check was received and deposited on 12/28/0X, but posted to the wrong customer's account.

Confirmation #22

The statement of our account showing a balance of $12,222 due Wellington Sales, Inc., at December 31, 200X, is correct except as noted below:

Wilson Dilco

By *Kent Parry*

Date: 2/2/0Y

Exceptions: ***No way. Forget it. Wellington said we'd have these goods in 10 days on December 2. When we didn't receive them, I canceled the order on December 12th. Wiggo Smiggo Corporation shipped us similar goods overnite. We'll never deal with Wellington again as long as I am around.***

Confirmation #47

The statement of our account showing a balance of $22,000 due Wellington Sales, Inc., at December 31, 200X, is correct except as noted below:

The Big Edge
By *Bert Quinton*

Date: 1/22/0Y

Exceptions: ***We use a voucher system by individual invoice. We cannot verify the balance, but Wellington is one of our regular suppliers. We probably owe them something.***

Confirmation #51

The statement of our account showing a balance of $75,000 due Wellington Sales, Inc., at December 31, 200X, is correct except as noted below:

Farkele Corporation of America and the World
By *Robby Boertson*

Date: 1/9/0Y

Exceptions: ***Our records show that we sent them a check for the amount due on 12/29/0X.***

Confirmation #62

The statement of our account showing a balance of $2,500 due Wellington Sales, Inc., at December 31, 200X, is correct except as noted below:

Pibson Gonker Corporation
By *Sam Sheffield*

Date: 1/30/0Y

Exceptions:

Note to files: This confirmation was returned by the postal service as "return to sender, address unknown."

Confirmation #68

The statement of our account showing a balance of $66,000 due Wellington Sales, Inc., at December 31, 200X, is correct except as noted below:

Yanrarian Ruckus Company
By *Tom Turken*

Date: 2/7/0Y

Exceptions: ***We mailed that check for the full amount on 1/3/0Y. The merchandise was not received until 12/23/0X.***

Confirmation #72

The statement of our account showing a balance of $22,000 due Wellington Sales, Inc., at December 31, 200X, is correct except as noted below:

Yeg Co.
By *Alfred Martin*

Date: 1/30/0Y

Exceptions: ***Yes, I guess we owe this amount, but Wellington made clear to us that we could return any of the items we did not sell. But, so far, sales are good, and we've sold most of the items.***

Confirmation #77

The statement of our account showing a balance of $32,000 due Wellington Sales, Inc., at December 31, 200X, is correct except as noted below:

Zell Incorporated
By *John Nolan*

Date: 1/19/0Y

Exceptions: ***We received $24,000 worth of goods on consignment from Wellington on 2/10/0X, but they are not sold yet.***

Confirmation #79

The statement of our account showing a balance of $42,000 due Wellington Sales, Inc., at December 31, 200X, is correct except as noted below:

Zentigton Corporation
By *Wallace Olson*

Date: 1/22/0Y

Exceptions: *Yes, we ordered $42,000 of merchandise on October 15, but Wellington was out of stock until recently. They seem to always be out of stock. We finally received the goods on January 4, 200Y.*

Ethics Cases

11–50.   You are an assistant auditor with Zaird & Associates, CPAs. Universal Air (UA), your fifth audit client in your eight months with Zaird, is a national airline based in your home town. UA has continued to grow while remaining healthy financially over the eight years of its existence. Indeed, as you start the audit you notice that (unaudited) sales are up 30 percent this year (20X1), with earnings up 40 percent. Your firm Zaird & Associates has been UA's only auditor.

During the audit you noticed that UA records sales when tickets are sold—debit receivable (or cash), credit sales. In performing substantive tests relating to receivables you also found that some of the "sales" are for 20X2 flights—generally in January and early February. You brought up this matter to your in-charge senior and she indicated that she also wondered about this last year when she worked on the audit. She suggested that she concluded that this isn't likely to be a problem for at least three reasons (any one of which would be sufficient to allow the current method):

1. The company has been using this approach since its inception eight years ago. Thus, any overstatement of this year's sales at year-end is likely to be "averaged out" by an understatement at the beginning of the year, since the company followed the same policy last year (and the years before).

2. Valid reasons exist for including the sales when "booked." The small airline's earning process is probably best considered about complete when the sale is made because this is the toughest part of the revenue generation process. The planes are scheduled to fly for the first six months of next year, and will fly, regardless of whether these relatively few passengers who paid before year-end for next year's flights are on them; there are virtually no variable costs incurred for these passengers, except for a few very small bags of peanuts and a few 2-liter bottles of soda.

3. Imagine what a nightmare it would be to have to record an entry when a passenger buys a ticket, and then another one when the flight occurs.

She says she is willing to discuss this with you if you disagree, but at this point she thinks it isn't a problem.

Required: *a.* Discuss whether you agree or disagree with each of her reasons.

Now assume that you potentially agree with her first justification. You think that maybe a journal entry could be made at year-end to estimate the liability for next-year flights. Yet, this wouldn't be necessary if everything does "average out" and any year-end liability is immaterial.

b. Given this situation, would you expect the procedure to "average out" over the year?

c. How might one determine whether it does "average out" over the year?

11–51.   You have worked with Zaird & Associates, CPAs, for a little more than a year and are beginning your second audit of Universal Air (UA). This year you even have an assistant reporting to you—Jane McClain.

Jane has come to you with a concern. She noticed that when sales are "booked" over the Internet an entry is made debiting a receivable account (from the credit card) and crediting sales. When a ticket is canceled the only entry made is to a database that maintains specific flight information on seat availability. Jane has discovered that customers are e-mailed a "Canceled Reservation" form when this occurs. But no accounting journal entry is recorded, and no refund occurs until the customer requests (in writing) a refund. If the customer never requests the refund, the receivable is billed to the credit card and collected; when billed to the credit card many customers complain and are given a refund, with an accompanying journal entry being made for the cancellation.

After analyzing the "Canceled Reservation" form you note that it says nothing about requiring a written cancellation for a refund. UA's controller responded to your inquiry about the policy of requiring a written request for a refund by indicating that the policy is presented on the Web site's "business policies and procedures" section. Furthermore the controller says that in total about two-thirds of the customers ask for and receive refunds, while one-third do not. She then states to you that, "The other 1/3 must not be aware of the policy, or simply don't care. What the heck, *caveat emptor!*"

At this point you discussed the situation with Bill Radman, partner-in-charge of the audit. Subsequently, he made an inquiry of Zaird's attorneys about the legality of the policy, and received a reply that while it is probably a questionable policy, they are unable to say it is illegal—in fact, it probably is not. Upon further investigation you find that this policy has been in existence for three years (since your first year on the audit) and neither you nor anyone else in your firm has identified it previously.

Required:

a. Is this a reportable condition? Should it be reported to the audit committee?

b. Should it be reported elsewhere? Where? How?

c. What impact should this policy have on the audit?

CPA Simulation

11–52. *See Chapter 10, pages 391 through 393 for the background information (company profile, industry information, and financial statements) relating to this simulation case.*

Questions

Risks:

a. Which of the following is most likely to decrease the risk of SSC's receivables being valued significantly above their net realizable value?

(1) Customers are located in Arizona.

(2) SSC's audit committee is independent of management.

(3) SSC uses "progress billings" for large contracts.

(4) The QuietRide product is superior to its competition.

b. Which of the following correctly identifies a risk facing SSC that might adversely affect sales during the coming years?

(1) A general slowdown in the economy.

(2) Sales to many smaller customers other than Wingo Corporation.

(3) Increased attention to developing new products.

(4) A board of directors dominated by management.

Audit findings:

Ratio	20X8	20X7
Gross profit percentage (Gross profit/Revenue)	0.154	0.166
Receivable turnover (Revenue/Accounts receivable)	6.324	7.244

The above table presents two ratios that were identified as significant in the current and prior years' audits of SSC. Compare the values of each ratio. Then select an audit finding that is consistent with these metrics. The finding need not explain the entire change. But, of the replies listed, it should potentially lead to the most significant change in the direction indicated by the change in the ratio.

Ratios:

c. An audit finding most consistent with the change in the gross profit percentage:

d. An audit finding most consistent with the change in the receivable turnover:

Audit Findings:

(1) Increases in costs of purchases were not completely passed on to customers through higher selling prices.

(2) Decreases in accounts receivable as of the 20X8 year-end.

(3) Owners' equity increased due to retention of profits.

(4) A larger percentage of sales occurred during the last month of 20X8, as compared to 20X7.

(5) Interest expense decreased during 20X8.

(6) The percentage tax included in the provision for income taxes for 20X8 was less than the percentage in 20X7.

(7) A significant amount of long-term debt became current.

(8) Several large sales on December 31, 20X7, were not recorded until January 1, 20X8.

Audit procedures:

The auditor determines that each of the following objectives will be part of SSC's audit. For each audit objective, select a substantive procedure that would help to achieve that objective. Each of the procedures may be used once, more than once, or not at all.

Audit Objective:

e. Establish the completeness of receivables transactions.

f. Determine that the valuation of receivables is at appropriate net realizable values.

g. Determine that the presentation and disclosure of receivables is adequate.

h. Establish that the client has rights to the recorded receivables.

Substantive Procedures:

(1) Analyze the relationship of accounts receivable and purchases and compare it with relationships for preceding periods.

(2) Vouch sales recorded in January of 20X9.

(3) Vouch sales recorded in December of 20X8.

(4) Review the aged trial balance for significant past due accounts.

(5) Obtain an understanding of the business purpose of transactions that resulted in accounts receivable balances.

(6) Review board of director minutes for approval of all customers' credit limits.

(7) Review financial statement drafts of financial statements.

Communication:

i. This is your firm's fifth audit of SSC. This year the company has formed an audit committee—composed of Madonna Sherwood, Cindy Stone, and Kelly Higgins. In a memorandum to the audit team (below) explain the likely effect of this change on audit risk. Madonna is chairperson of the audit committee.

Remember: Your response will be graded for both technical relevance and writing skills. For writing skills you should demonstrate an ability to develop, organize, and express your ideas clearly. Do not convey information in the form of a table, bullet-point list, or other abbreviated presentation.

Memorandum

TO: Audit Team

Subject: SSC Audit Committee

Reporting:

Note: This section is possible to work in a meaningful way only if you have the professional standards available—preferably in electronic form.

j. You are now considering the confirmation of accounts receivable. Using the professional standards, provide circumstances in which such confirmation is not required on an audit. Do this by copying and pasting the information to a workspace. You should *not* edit the excerpt in any way.

Appendix 11A

Illustrative Audit Case: Keystone Computers & Networks, Inc.

Part II: Consideration of Internal Control

This second part of the audit case of Keystone Computers & Networks, Inc. (KCN) illustrates the manner in which auditors obtain an understanding of internal control, perform tests of controls, and assess control risk. The process is illustrated with the revenue and cash receipts cycle, and includes the following working papers:

- A questionnaire to evaluate the control environment, risk assessment, and monitoring components of the company's internal control. Since this questionnaire is designed for nonpublic companies, it does not address factors that are generally found only in public companies, such as an audit committee of the board of directors.

- An organizational chart for the company. This working paper helps the auditors evaluate the overall segregation of functions within the company.

- A flowchart description of the revenue and cash receipts cycle of the company and the related controls prepared by the staff of Adams, Barnes & Co. (ABC), CPAs.

- ABC's working paper for assessment of control risk for accounts receivable and revenue as it would appear before any tests of controls are performed. This working paper identifies the controls and weaknesses for the revenue and cash receipts cycle. It also relates the controls and weaknesses to the various financial statement assertions about revenue and accounts receivable.

- The audit program for tests of controls for the revenue and cash receipts cycle. This working paper describes the various tests of controls that were performed by the staff of ABC to obtain evidence about the operating effectiveness of the controls. These tests provide the support for the auditors' assessed level of control risk.

- ABC's working paper documenting the results of tests of controls that were performed using audit sampling.

- ABC's working paper for assessment of control risk for accounts receivable and revenue as it would appear after all tests of controls are performed. Notice that the auditors have checked the boxes indicating that the controls are operating effectively. This allows ABC's staff to arrive at the final assessed level of control risk as indicated at the bottom of the working paper.

You should read through the information to obtain an understanding of the way in which auditors document their understanding of internal control and the assessment of control risk for a transaction cycle. You may also wish to review the planning documentation presented on pages 213 through 220 of Chapter 6 to refresh your knowledge about the nature of the company's business.

OBTAINING AND DOCUMENTING AN UNDERSTANDING OF THE REVENUE AND CASH RECEIPTS CYCLE

ABC's consideration of the controls relating to the revenue cycle began by updating various working papers, including the following:

- Control Environment, Risk Assessment, and Monitoring Questionnaire—IC-3 and IC-4.
- Organizational Chart of KCN—IC-5.
- Revenue and Cash Receipts Cycle Flowchart—IC-8.
- Assessment of Control Risk Worksheet (before tests of controls are performed)—IC-20.[1]

The Control Environment, Risk Assessment, and Monitoring Questionnaire (IC-3 and IC-4), the Organizational Chart (IC-5), and the Revenue and Cash Receipts Cycle Flowchart (IC-8) required only limited updating as there were few changes in internal control during the year, and key personnel are the same as in the preceding year. After completing the description of internal control the audit staff of ABC observed operation of the system and found that the controls had been placed in operation.

The staff of ABC then used the documentation of internal control to identify controls and weaknesses on Schedule IC-20. This schedule includes check boxes in the appropriate columns to designate the financial statement assertions that are addressed by the internal control policy or procedure. For the weaknesses, an "X" is included in the appropriate columns. Before tests of controls are performed, the check boxes are blank because the auditors do not know whether the controls are operating effectively.

---

[1] This schedule is included twice (incomplete and complete) for illustrative purposes. In an actual audit, only the completed schedule would be included.

Control Environment, Risk Assessment, and Monitoring Questionnaire—Nonpublic Companies

IC-3
WL
11/10/X5

Client: *Keystone Computers & Networks, Inc.*

Financial Statement Date: *12/31/X5*

Control Environment	Yes	No	N/A	Comments

Management Philosophy and Operating Style

1. Does management adequately consider the potential effects of taking large or unusual business risks prior to doing so? — ✔

2. Are business risks adequately monitored? — ✔

3. Is management not overly aggressive with respect to financial reporting? — ✔

4. Are financial statement estimates developed in a conscientious manner? — ✔

Organizational Structure

5. Is the organization of the entity clearly defined in terms of lines of authority and responsibility? — ✔

6. Does the entity have a current organizational chart and related materials such as job descriptions? — ✔

7. Are policies and procedures for authorization of transactions established at an adequately high level? — ✔

8. Are such policies and procedures adequately adhered to? — ✔

Methods of Assigning Authority and Responsibility

9. Are authority and responsibility to deal with organizational goals and objectives, operating functions, and regulatory requirements adequately delegated? — ✔

10. Has management established and communicated policies about appropriate business practices and conduct and conflicts of interest? — ✔

11. Has the entity developed an IT systems documentation that indicates the procedures for authorizing transactions and approving systems changes? — ✔

Board of Directors, Integrity and Ethical Values, Commitment to Competence

12. Is the level of experience, status, and independence of the members of the board of directors appropriate for the organization? — ✔

13. Are there regular meetings of the board of directors to set policies and objectives, review the entity's performance, and take appropriate action and are minutes of such meetings prepared and signed on a timely basis? — ✔

(continued)

Control Environment, Risk Assessment, and Monitoring Questionnaire—Nonpublic Companies

Client: *Keystone Computers & Networks, Inc.*

Financial Statement Date: *12/31/X5*

Control Environment	Yes	No	N/A	Comments

Board of Directors, Integrity and Ethical Values, Commitment to Competence

14. Has management taken adequate actions to reduce incentives and temptations that might prompt employees to engage in dishonest, illegal, and unethical acts? ✔

15. Does management exhibit an adequate commitment to competence in the performance of essential jobs within the organization? ✔

Human Resource Policies and Procedures

16. Does the entity employ sound hiring practices, including background investigations, where appropriate? ✔

17. Are employees adequately trained to meet their job responsibilities? ✔

18. Is employee performance evaluated at regular intervals? ✔

19. Are employees in positions of trust bonded? ✔

20. Are employees in positions of trust required to take vacations and are their duties rotated while they are on vacation? ✔

Risk Assessment

21. Is the chief executive officer attuned to external and internal factors that affect the risk of achieving the entity's objectives? ✔

Monitoring

22. Are key management personnel sufficiently involved with operations to monitor the effectiveness of internal controls? ✔

23. Does management have a formal process for considering reportable conditions from external auditors? ✔

Conclusion: *The control environment, risk assessment process, and monitoring procedures appear to be adequate to provide an atmosphere conducive to the effective operation of other controls.*

KEYSTONE COMPUTERS & NETWORKS, INC.
Organizational Chart
12/31/X5

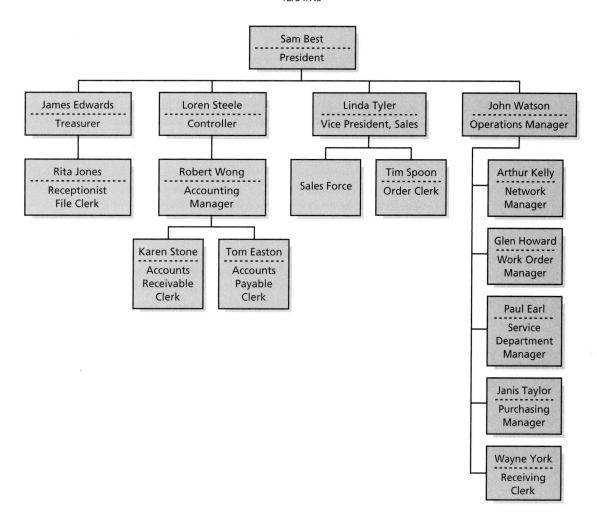

TESTING CONTROLS AND ASSESSING CONTROL RISK

When obtaining an understanding of the overall internal control, ABC's audit staff first considered the elements of control environment, risk assessment, and monitoring as documented with the questionnaire at IC-3 and IC-4. As indicated on the questionnaire, they found these components to be strong for a nonpublic company and to reflect an atmosphere conducive to the effective operation of the accounting information system and control activities.

Based on their understanding of internal control, ABC's staff planned assessed levels of control risk at a low level for completeness and at a moderate level for existence or occurrence, rights, and valuation. As with most small businesses, the auditors found that KCN had no effective controls to address the presentation and disclosure assertion. Based on the planned assessed levels, the audit staff of ABC designed a program (IC-12 and IC-13) to test the controls. Schedule IC-15 illustrates how they determined sample size and evaluated the results of tests of controls that involved audit sampling.

The completed Schedule IC-20 on pages 448–449 includes check marks to indicate that the tests of controls demonstrated that the related controls were operating effectively. Based on these results, the auditors' assessed levels of control risk—indicated in the last row of Schedule IC-20—were supported at their planned levels. These assessments will be used in conjunction with the inherent risk assessments to determine the nature, timing, and extent of substantive tests of revenue and accounts receivable. These tests are illustrated in Part III of the case in Appendix 11B.

KEYSTONE COMPUTERS & NETWORKS, INC.
Internal Control Structure—Sales and Collections Cycle
12/31/X5

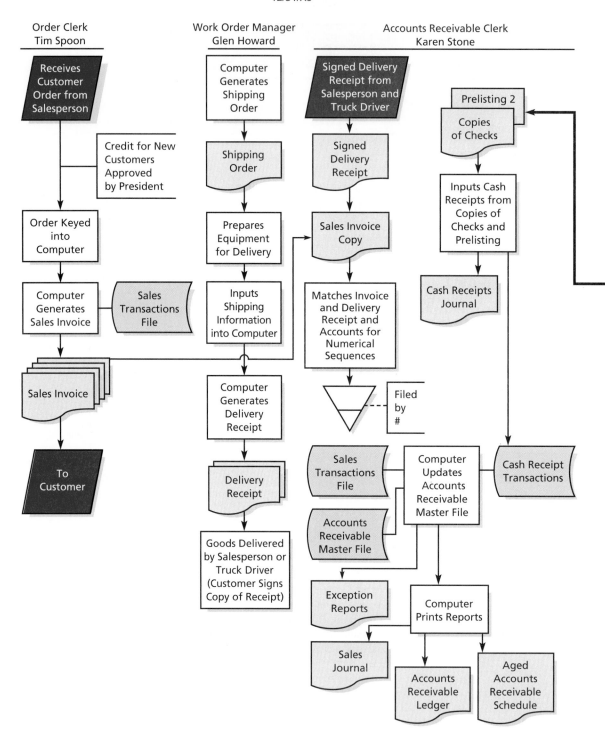

Order Clerk
Tim Spoon

Receives Customer Order from Salesperson

Credit for New Customers Approved by President

Order Keyed into Computer

Computer Generates Sales Invoice

Sales Transactions File

Sales Invoice

To Customer

Work Order Manager
Glen Howard

Computer Generates Shipping Order

Shipping Order

Prepares Equipment for Delivery

Inputs Shipping Information into Computer

Computer Generates Delivery Receipt

Delivery Receipt

Goods Delivered by Salesperson or Truck Driver (Customer Signs Copy of Receipt)

Accounts Receivable Clerk
Karen Stone

Signed Delivery Receipt from Salesperson and Truck Driver

Signed Delivery Receipt

Sales Invoice Copy

Matches Invoice and Delivery Receipt and Accounts for Numerical Sequences

Filed by #

Prelisting 2
Copies of Checks

Inputs Cash Receipts from Copies of Checks and Prelisting

Cash Receipts Journal

Sales Transactions File

Computer Updates Accounts Receivable Master File

Cash Receipt Transactions

Accounts Receivable Master File

Exception Reports

Computer Prints Reports

Sales Journal

Accounts Receivable Ledger

Aged Accounts Receivable Schedule

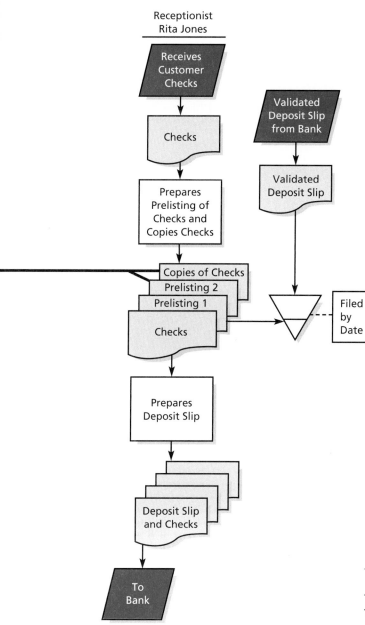

Receptionist
Rita Jones

Receives Customer Checks

Checks

Prepares Prelisting of Checks and Copies Checks

Copies of Checks
Prelisting 2
Prelisting 1
Checks

Validated Deposit Slip from Bank

Validated Deposit Slip

Filed by Date

Prepares Deposit Slip

Deposit Slip and Checks

To Bank

Notes:

1. The company uses Great Plains ACCPAC, a commercial accounting software package that has not been modified.

2. The company has a local area network, with computer terminals in the purchasing, work order, and accounting departments.

3. Sales orders are entered on an online terminal that applies the following application controls:
   - The order clerk's password is verified before transactions are accepted.
   - Customer numbers are agreed to customer master file information.
   - Computer determines whether the customer has sufficient credit limit remaining to make the purchase. If rejected, the customer's credit limit must be increased by the president or the terms must be changed to cash on delivery.
   - Computer will require override of the transaction by the order clerk any time the sales price of an item is less than its cost.
   - Computer assigns number to sales invoice.

4. Shipping information is entered on an online terminal that applies the following controls:
   - The work order manager's password is verified before shipping data are accepted.
   - The shipping data are agreed to details of the sales transactions that were entered by the sales order clerk. If the name of the customer or the quantities shipped do not agree the system will reject the data. Override will be accepted by the system only from the vice president of sales by password.
   - Computer assigns number to delivery receipt.

5. Cash receipts are entered to an online terminal that applies the following controls:
   - The accounts receivable clerk's password is verified before transactions are accepted.
   - When the customer number is entered the company name is presented on screen for comparison by clerk.

6. As the computer updates the accounts receivable master file, it produces an exception report that contains any items with invalid customer numbers and any unusually large cash payments in relation to the customer's account balance. The accounting manager reviews and follows up on exceptions and any corrections are made the same day.

7. The accounting manager reconciles the master file of accounts receivable to the general ledger on a monthly basis.

8. Monthly statements are mailed to customers.

9. The receptionist endorses incoming checks "for deposit only" to the company's account.

10. Cash sales are minor in amount and the cash is accepted by the receptionist who maintains the company's cash fund.

11. Cash deposits are made daily.

12. Computer summaries of cash collections of accounts receivable and cash sales are reconciled to validated bank deposit slips and the prelisting of cash receipts by the accounting manager.

13. Sales returns and allowances are approved by the vice president of sales.

14. Write-offs of accounts receivable are approved by the president after initiation by the controller, but not on a regular basis.

15. Accounting manager reconciles bank account on a monthly basis.

KEYSTONE COMPUTERS & NETWORKS, INC.

Assessment of Control Risk—Revenue Cycle
12/31/X5

IC-20

WL

11/13/X5

Controls	Existence or Occurrence	Completeness	Rights	Valuation	Presentation and Disclosure
Sales					
1. Separation of duties for authorization, credit approval, shipping, and accounting for sales transactions.	☐	☐	☐	☐	
2. Company uses an unmodified commercial software package.	☐	☐	☐	☐	
3. Credit lines are approved by the president.				☐	
4. Computer verifies the order clerk's password before sales data can be entered.	☐		☐	☐	
5. Application controls (input validation checks) are applied to ensure the accuracy of the billing process.				☐	
6. Computer assigns numbers to sales invoices.		☐			
7. Computer verifies the work order manager's password before shipping data can be entered.	☐		☐	☐	
8. Input validation checks are applied to shipping data as they are entered.				☐	
9. Computer assigns numbers to delivery receipts.		☐			
10. Accounts receivable clerk matches invoices with delivery receipts and accounts for numerical sequences.		☐			
11. Accounting manager reconciles the accounts receivable master file to the general ledger monthly.	☐	☐	☐	☐	
12. Monthly statements are mailed to customers.	☐	☐	☐	☐	
13. Sales returns and allowances are approved by the vice president of sales.				☐	

KEYSTONE COMPUTERS & NETWORKS, INC.

Assessment of Control Risk—Revenue Cycle

12/31/X5

IC-20

WL

11/13/X5

Controls	Existence or Occurrence	Completeness	Rights	Valuation	Presentation and Disclosure
Sales					
14. Separation of duties of custody of cash from records of cash receipts and accounts receivable.	☐		☐	☐	
15. Checks are prelisted and stamped with restrictive endorsement when received.	☐		☐	☐	
16. Application controls (input validation checks) are applied to ensure the accuracy of the recording of cash receipts.				☐	
17. Control totals are reconciled by the accounting manager.	☐	☐	☐	☐	
18. Exception reports are reviewed and followed up on by the accounting manager.				☐	
19. Computer summaries of cash collections and cash sales are reconciled to bank deposits and prelisting of cash receipts by accounting manager.	☐	☐	☐	☐	
20. Accounting manager reconciles bank account on a monthly basis.	☐	☐	☐	☐	
Internal Control Weaknesses					
1. Sales invoices are prepared and mailed prior to delivery of goods.	X		X	X	
2. Accounts receivable are not written off on a regular basis.				X	
Planned Assessed Level of Control Risk	*Moderate*	*Low*	*Moderate*	*Moderate*	*Maximum*

Audit Program—Tests of Controls—Revenue Cycle

IC-12
WL
11/12/X5

Client: *Keystone Computers & Networks, Inc.*

Financial Statement Date: *12/31/X5*

Procedure	Performed by	
	Initials	Date

Sales Transactions

1. Observe and inquire about the segregation of duties for sales transactions. — *WL* — *11/15/X5*

2. Inspect documentation of the Great Plains ACCPAC software package. — *WL* — *11/15/X5*

3. Inquire about the president's procedures for approving credit limits. — *WL* — *11/15/X5*

4. Observe the order clerk when entering customer orders and enter several test transactions to determine that:

   a. Password must be entered to enter customer orders. — *MP* — *11/14/X5*

   b. The system performs a validity check for the customer's number. — *MP* — *11/14/X5*

   c. The system determines that the customer's credit limit is not exceeded. — *MP* — *11/14/X5*

   d. The system compares sales price to cost of product and requires override when cost exceeds sales price. — *MP* — *11/14/X5*

5. Observe that the computer assigns numbers to sales invoices. — *MP* — *11/14/X5*

6. Review the sales invoice file with delivery reports attached to obtain evidence that all numbers are accounted for and all invoices have an attached delivery report. — *MP* — *11/14/X5*

7. Inquire about the accounting manager's procedures for reconciling the accounts receivable master file to the general ledger. — *WL* — *11/15/X5*

8. Observe the mailing of monthly statements. — *MP* — *1/6/X6*

9. Inquire about the procedures for approval of sales returns and allowances by the vice president—sales. — *WL* — *11/15/X5*

Audit Program—Tests of Controls—Revenue Cycle

(Concluded)

Client: *Keystone Computers & Networks, Inc.*

Financial Statement Date: *12/31/X5*

Procedure	Performed by	
	Initials	Date
Cash Receipts		
10. Observe and inquire about the segregation of duties for cash receipts.	*WL*	*11/15/X5*
11. Observe the prelisting and endorsement of checks by the receptionist.	*MP*	*11/13/X5*
12. Observe the accounts receivable clerk entering cash receipts to determine that:		
a. Password must be entered to enter cash receipts.	*MP*	*11/14/X5*
b. Customer's name is shown on screen when customer number is entered.	*MP*	*11/14/X5*
13. Test the procedures for reconciling control totals from the accounts receivable program as follows:		
a. Inquire about the procedures.	*WL*	*11/14/X5*
b. Select a sample of printouts of the control totals and inspect them for evidence of reconciliation. Use the following parameters:		
(1) Risk of assessing control risk too low—10%.		
(2) Tolerable deviation rate—7%.		
(3) Expected deviation rate—1%.	*WL*	*11/14/X5*
14. Test the procedures for review and follow up on the exception reports from the accounts receivable program as follows:		
a. Inquire about the procedures.	*WL*	*11/14/X5*
b. Select a sample of exceptions reports and inspect them for evidence of follow-up on the exceptions. Use the following parameters:		
(1) Risk of assessing control risk too low—10%.		
(2) Tolerable deviation rate—10%.		
(3) Expected deviation rate—0%.	*WL*	*11/14/X5*
15. Test the procedures for reconciling the computer summary of cash collections and cash sales to the deposit slips and prelisting of cash receipts as follows:		
a. Inquire about the procedures.	*WL*	*11/14/X5*
b. Select a sample of the computer summaries and inspect them for evidence of reconciliation. Use the following parameters:		
(1) Risk of assessing control risk too low—10%.		
(2) Tolerable deviation rate—10%.		
(3) Expected deviation rate—1%.	*WL*	*11/14/X5*
16. Inquire about the procedures for reconciliation of bank accounts.	*WL*	*11/14/X5*
17. Inspect four bank reconciliations performed during the year.	*WL*	*11/14/X5*

KEYSTONE COMPUTERS & NETWORKS, INC.

Attributes Sampling Summary—Revenue Cycle

December 31, 19X5

Objectives of test: *(1) To test the operating effectiveness of the procedures for reconciling control totals of computer run for updating accounts receivable; (2) To test the operating effectiveness of the procedures for review and follow-up on the exception reports from the computer run for updating accounts receivable; (3) To test the operating effectiveness of the procedures for reconciling the computer summary of cash collections and cash sales to the deposit slips and prelisting of cash receipts.*

Test	Population	Size
1	Control total reports	234
2	Exception reports	234
3	Computer summaries of collections and cash sales	234

Sampling unit: *Individual reports*

Random selection procedure: *Random number table*

Risk of assessing control risk too low: *10 percent*

	Planning Parameters			Sample Results	
Attributes Tested:	**Tolerable Deviation Rate**	**Expected Deviation Rate**	**Sample Size**	**Number of Deviations**	**Achieved Maximum Rate**
1. Existence of a reconciliation of control totals initialed by the accounting manager.	*7%*	*1%*	*55*	*1*	*7%*
2. Indication of disposition of exceptions initialed by the accounting manager.	*10%*	*0%*	*22*	*0*	*10%*
3. Existence of a reconciliation of cash collections and cash sales to prelisting and deposit slips initialed by the accounting clerk.	*10%*	*1%*	*38*	*0*	*6.4%*

Conclusion: *The results support the assessment of control risk for completeness at a low level, and for existence, occurrence, rights, and valuation at a moderate level.*

KEYSTONE COMPUTERS & NETWORKS, INC.

Assessment of Control Risk—Revenue Cycle

12/31/X5

IC-20

WL

11/13/X5

Controls	Existence or Occurrence	Completeness	Rights	Valuation	Presentation and Disclosure
Sales					
1. Separation of duties for authorization, credit approval, shipping, and accounting for sales transactions.	☑	☑	☑	☑	
2. Company uses an unmodified commercial software package.	☑	☑	☑	☑	
3. Credit lines are approved by the president.				☑	
4. Computer verifies the order clerk's password before sales data can be entered.	☑		☑	☑	
5. Application controls (input validation checks) are applied to ensure the accuracy of the billing process.				☑	
6. Computer assigns numbers to sales invoices.		☑			
7. Computer verifies the work order manager's password before shipping data can be entered.	☑		☑	☑	
8. Input validation checks are applied to shipping data as they are entered.				☑	
9. Computer assigns numbers to delivery receipts.		☑			
10. Accounts receivable clerk matches invoices with delivery receipts and accounts for numerical sequences.		☑			
11. Accounting manager reconciles the accounts receivable master file to the general ledger monthly.	☑	☑	☑	☑	
12. Monthly statements are mailed to customers.	☑	☑	☑	☑	
13. Sales returns and allowances are approved by the vice president of sales.				☑	

(continued)

KEYSTONE COMPUTERS & NETWORKS, INC.   IC-20

Assessment of Control Risk—Revenue Cycle   *WL*

12/31/X5   *11/13/X5*

(Concluded)

Controls	Existence or Occurrence	Completeness	Rights	Valuation	Presentation and Disclosure
Sales					
14. Separation of duties of custody of cash from records of cash receipts and accounts receivable.	☑		☑	☑	
15. Checks are prelisted and stamped with restrictive endorsement when received.	☑		☑	☑	
16. Application controls (input validation checks) are applied to ensure the accuracy of the recording of cash receipts.				☑	
17. Control totals are reconciled by the accounting manager.	☑	☑	☑	☑	
18. Exception reports are reviewed and followed up on by the accounting manager.				☑	
19. Computer summaries of cash collections and cash sales are reconciled to bank deposits and prelisting of cash receipts by accounting manager.	☑	☑	☑	☑	
20. Accounting manager reconciles bank account on a monthly basis.	☑	☑	☑	☑	
Internal Control Weaknesses					
1. Sales invoices are prepared and mailed prior to delivery of goods.	X		X	X	
2. Accounts receivable are not written off on a regular basis.				X	
Assessed Level of Control Risk	*Moderate*	*Low*	*Moderate*	*Moderate*	*Maximum*

Appendix 11A Problems

11A–1. A summary of the controls for the revenue and cash receipts cycle of Keystone Computers & Networks, Inc., appears on pages 442–454.

Required:

a. For the following three controls over sales indicate one type of error or fraud that the control serves to prevent or detect. Organize your solution as follows:

Control	Error or Fraud Controlled
1. Application controls are applied when customer orders are entered by the sales order clerk.	
2. The computer assigns numbers to sales invoices when they are prepared.	
3. Monthly statements are mailed to customers.	

b. For the following three controls over cash receipts indicate one type of error or fraud that the control serves to prevent or detect. Organize your solution as follows:

Control	Error or Fraud Controlled
1. Cash receipts are prelisted by the receptionist.	
2. The accounting manager reconciles control totals generated by the accounts receivable computer program.	
3. The computer summaries of cash collections and cash sales are reconciled to prelistings of cash receipts and cash deposits by the accounting manager.	

11A–2. As indicated on the control risk assessment working paper on page 454, the auditors identified two weaknesses in internal control over the revenue cycle of KCN. Describe the implications of each of the two weaknesses in terms of the type of errors or fraud that could result.

11A–3. As indicated on the working paper on page 452, the auditors decided to apply audit sampling to three controls for the revenue and cash receipts cycle.

Required:

a. Describe the characteristic that a control must possess in order to be tested with audit sampling.

b. Assume that the auditors decided to use audit sampling to test the operating effectiveness of the procedures for matching sales invoices with delivery receipts. Determine the required sample size, using the following parameters.
- Risk of assessing control risk too low—5 percent
- Tolerable deviation rate—15 percent
- Expected deviation rate—1 percent

c. Prepare a working paper similar to the one on page 452 documenting the planned audit procedure described in part (*b*).

Appendix 11B

Illustrative Audit Case: Keystone Computers & Networks, Inc.

Part III: Substantive Tests—Accounts Receivable and Revenue

This part of the audit case illustrates the manner in which the auditors design substantive tests of balances. The substantive tests are illustrated for two accounts—receivables and revenue. This aspect of the audit is illustrated with the following audit documentation:

- ABC's risk assessment working paper that combines the auditors' assessments of inherent and control risks into an overall risk of material misstatement for the assertions.
- The substantive audit program of accounts receivable and revenue.
- The audit sampling plan for the confirmation of accounts receivable.

Adams, Barnes & Cos. assessment of control risk is described in Part II of the audit case on pages 441 through 454. To refresh your knowledge of the case, review that part as well as Part I on pages 213 through 220 of Chapter 6.

Risk Assessment—Revenue Cycle			RA-8

WL
11/24/X5

Client: *Keystone Computers & Networks, Inc.*

Financial Statement Date: *12/31/X5*

Assertion	Inherent Risk	Control Risk	Overall Risk of Material Misstatement
Existence of receivables and occurrence of revenue transactions	*Fraud risk*	*Moderate*	*High*
Completeness of receivables and revenue	*Moderate*	*Low*	*Low*
Rights to receivables	*High*	*Moderate*	*Moderate/High*
Valuation of receivables	*Fraud risk*	*Moderate*	*High*
Presentation and disclosure	*Moderate*	*Maximum*	*Moderate*

Fraud Risks:
Description: *Management may be motivated to overstate revenue and receivables to improve financial results due to impending sale of business.*
Controls: *Because Keystone is a nonpublic company without an independent board or audit committee, there are no significant internal controls to prevent management from overstating results.*
Audit Response: *The nature, timing, and extent of audit procedures will be modified as described below:*
a. *Accounts receivable will be confirmed at year-end using a 5 percent risk of incorrect acceptance.*
b. *A review of the monthly sales reports by salesperson will be performed to identify any unusual individual sales or sales volume.*
c. *Credit files of customers with large receivables (over $25,000) will be reviewed for indications of fictitious customers.*

		B-6
Audit Program—Substantive Tests—Accounts Receivable and Revenues		*WL*
		11/13/X5

Client: *Keystone Computers & Networks, Inc.*

Financial Statement Date: *12/31/X5*

	Performed by	
Procedure	**Initials**	**Date**
Sales Transactions		
1. Obtain an aged trial balance of accounts receivable as of 12/31/X5.	*MP*	*1/6/X6*
2. Select a sample of customers' accounts at 12/31/X5 for positive confirmation using probability-proportional-to-size sampling based on the following parameters:		
a. Risk of incorrect acceptance of 5%.		
b. Tolerable misstatement of $35,000.		
c. Expected misstatement of $10,000.	*MP*	*1/7/X6*
3. Use generalized audit software to:		
a. Foot the master file of accounts receivable at 12/31/X5.	*MP*	*2/12/X6*
b. Test the client-prepared aging of accounts receivable.	*MP*	*1/7/X6*
c. Select the specific accounts for confirmation.	*MP*	*1/7/X6*
4. Mail accounts receivable confirmation requests.	*MP*	*1/8/X6*
5. Send second requests for all unanswered confirmation requests.	*MP*	*1/25/X6*
6. For confirmation requests to which no reply is received perform the following alternative procedures:		
a. Test items subsequently paid to remittance advices which identify the specific invoices paid. If necessary, reconcile the amounts paid to sales invoices and delivery receipts.	*MP*	*2/16/X6*
b. For items not paid, inspect the invoices and delivery receipts for the sales transactions making up the account balance.	*MP*	*2/16/X6*
7. Resolve exceptions noted on confirmation requests.	*MP*	*2/16/X6*
8. Review credit files for customers with accounts receivable above $25,000 at 12/31/X5. Investigate any indications of fictitious accounts.	*MP*	*2/16/X6*
9. Summarize the results of the confirmation procedures.	*MP*	*2/16/X6*

(continued)

Audit Program—Substantive Tests—Accounts Receivable and Revenues

B-6
WL
11/13/X5

(Concluded)

Client: *Keystone Computers & Networks, Inc.*

Financial Statement Date: *12/31/X5*

Procedure	Performed by Initials	Date
10. Review the adequacy of the allowance for uncollectible accounts by performing the following procedures:		
a. Review the aged trial balance of accounts receivable with the president.	*WL*	*2/13/X6*
b. Review confirmation exceptions for indications of disputed amounts.	*WL*	*2/13/X6*
c. Analyze and review trends in the following relationships:		
(1) Accounts receivable to net sales.	*WL*	*2/15/X6*
(2) Allowance for bad debts to accounts receivable.	*WL*	*2/15/X6*
(3) Bad debt expense to net sales.	*WL*	*2/15/X6*
11. At year-end, review the file of sales invoices that are waiting to be matched with delivery receipts for any sales transactions that were not executed and, therefore, should be recorded in the subsequent period.	*MP*	*12/31/X5*
12. For all sales recorded in the last week of the year inspect the related delivery receipt to determine that the sale occurred before 12/31/X5.	*MP*	*2/12/X6*
13. Review credit memoranda for sales returns and allowances through the last day of fieldwork to determine if an adjustment is needed to record the items as of year-end.	*MP*	*2/16/X6*
14. Perform analytical procedures for sales and accounts receivable including comparison of the following to prior years and/or industry data:	*WL*	*2/12/X6*
a. Gross profit percentage by month.	*WL*	*2/12/X6*
b. Sales by month by salesperson.	*WL*	*2/16/X6*
c. Accounts receivable turnover.	*WL*	*2/16/X6*
d. Advertising expense as a percentage of sales.	*WL*	*2/16/X6*
e. Net receivables as a percentage of total current assets.	*WL*	*2/16/X6*
15. Ascertain whether any accounts have been assigned, pledged, or discounted by review of agreements and confirmation with banks.	*WL*	*2/13/X6*
16. Ascertain by inquiry whether any accounts are owed by employees or related parties such as officers, directors, or shareholders, and:		
a. Obtain an understanding of the business purpose for the transactions that resulted in the balances.	*WL*	*2/16/X6*
b. Ascertain the amounts involved.	*WL*	*2/16/X6*
c. Confirm the balances.	*WL*	*1/25/X6*

Keystone Computers & Networks, Inc.
Audit Sample Plan for Confirmation of Accounts Receivable
12/31/X5

Objective: *Establish the existence and gross valuation of accounts receivable and occurrence and accuracy of sales by confirmation.*

Population: *The trial balance of 433 accounts receivable at 12/31/X5, with a total book value of $1,023,545.*

Definition of Misstatement: *Any amount that is determined not to be a valid account receivable.*

Sampling Technique: *Probability-proportional-to-size.*

Sampling Parameters:

1. **Tolerable misstatement:**

Total materiality as indicated in the audit plan	$70,000
Less: Estimate of undetected misstatement (50% of overall materiality)	35,000
Tolerable misstatement for this test	$35,000

2. **Risk of incorrect acceptance:**

   Because we have assessed the risk of material misstatement as high, the risk of incorrect acceptance will be set at 5 percent.

3. **Expected misstatement:**

   Based on prior-year audits, the expected misstatement for the account is $10,000.

Calculation of Sample Size and Sampling Interval:

$$\text{Sample size} = \frac{\text{Book value of population} \times \text{Reliability factor}}{\text{Tolerable misstatement} - (\text{Expected misstatement} \times \text{Expansion factor})}$$

$$= \frac{\$1,023,545 \times 3.00}{\$35,000 - (\$10,000 \times 1.6)}$$

$$= 162$$

$$\text{Sampling interval} = \frac{\text{Book value of population}}{\text{Sample size}} = \frac{\$1,023,545}{162} = \$6,300 \ (\text{rounded})$$

Actual sample size was only 94 because a number of accounts were more than twice the sampling interval.

KEYSTONE COMPUTERS & NETWORKS
Monthly Sales Report
For the Three Years Ended 12/31/X5

	Sales of Computers			Consulting Revenue			Service Revenue		
	20X3	20X4	20X5	20X3	20X4	20X5	20X3	20X4	20X5
January	$ 587,000	$ 701,000	$ 784,000	$ 63,000	$ 75,000	$ 86,000	$ 12,000	$ 14,000	$ 15,000
February	590,000	744,000	862,000	72,000	75,000	90,000	13,000	16,000	17,000
March	643,000	762,000	907,000	67,000	82,000	102,000	13,000	15,000	17,000
April	656,000	733,000	762,000	66,000	81,000	92,000	12,000	16,000	19,000
May	668,000	731,000	806,000	68,000	79,000	95,000	14,000	15,000	17,000
June	657,000	765,000	894,000	66,000	84,000	111,000	13,000	17,000	18,000
July	681,000	702,000	796,000	73,000	79,000	96,000	14,000	16,000	18,000
August	679,000	754,000	856,000	69,000	87,000	102,000	13,000	15,000	17,000
September	675,000	802,000	932,000	68,000	84,000	116,000	13,000	16,000	19,000
October	701,000	764,000	758,000	75,000	87,000	105,000	15,000	16,000	18,000
November	734,000	774,000	849,000	73,000	91,000	113,000	14,000	16,000	18,000
December	737,000	812,000	951,000	72,000	92,000	127,000	14,000	15,000	18,000
Total	$8,008,000	$9,044,000	$10,157,000	$832,000	$996,000	$1,235,000	$160,000	$187,000	$211,000

Note: Amounts were generated by ACL program from Keystone's general ledger.

Appendix 11B Problems

11B–1. In Part II (Appendix 11A) of the audit case, the audit staff of Adams, Barnes & Co. identified the following two internal control weaknesses:

a. Sales invoices are prepared and mailed prior to delivery of goods.

b. Accounts receivable are not written off on a regular basis.

Required: Review the audit program on pages 457 through 458 and identify the substantive audit procedures that were designed specifically to address the misstatements that are made more probable due to these weaknesses.

11B–2. Assume that you have been assigned to the audit of Keystone after audit planning has occurred. Review the planning information on pages 213 through 220 and the audit program for the accounts receivable and revenue (B-6 on pages 457–458). The manager on the engagement has given you the task of reviewing the monthly revenue report on page 460 (B-11).

a. Based on your review of the report, describe any unusual relationships that might indicate a risk of misstatement of revenues based on your knowledge of the company derived from a review of the information on pages 213 through 220.

b. Identify any procedures on the audit program for receivables and revenue that might address the risk(s) identified in (*a*).

c. Design two other procedures that would address the risk(s) identified in (*a*).

11B–3. Keystone Computers & Networks, Inc. (KCN), has 433 accounts receivable, with a total book value of $1,023,545. From that population, Adams, Barnes & Co. (ABC), CPAs, selected a sample of 94 accounts for confirmation for the year ended December 31, 20X5, as illustrated by the working paper on page 459. First and second confirmation requests resulted in replies for all but 10 of those accounts. ABC performed alternative procedures on those 10 accounts and noted no exceptions. Of the 84 replies, 5 had exceptions as described below (with ABC follow-up):

1. "The balance of $1,200 is incorrect because we paid that amount in full on December 31, 20X5." *Follow-up: An analysis of the cash receipts journal revealed that the check had been received in the mail on January 9, 20X6.*

2. "Of the balance of $30,000, $330 is incorrect because on December 19 we returned a printer to Keystone when we found that we didn't need it. We ordered it in the middle of November when we had anticipated a need for it. When we received the printer we realized it was unnecessary and returned it unopened." *Follow-up: An analysis of the transaction revealed that it was received by Keystone on December 31, 20X5, and that the adjustment to the account had been processed on January 2, 20X6.*

3. "The balance of $300 is correct, and we paid it on January 5, 19X6." *Follow-up: An analysis of the cash receipts journal revealed that the check had been received on January 10, 20X6.*

4. "Of the balance of $13,000, $1,000 is incorrect because it represents goods that we didn't receive until January 5, 20X6." *Follow-up: Inspection of shipping records reveals that the item was shipped on January 3, 20X6.*

5. "Of the account's $1,800 balance, we paid $1,746 and the $54 (3 percent of the total) remains unpaid because the Keystone salesperson told us that she would be able to obtain a 'special' discount beyond the normal." *Follow-up: While inspection of the sales agreement indicated no such discount arrangement, discussions with Loren Steele (controller) and Sam Best (president) indicated that the salesperson had inappropriately granted such a discount to the client. On January 15 of 20X6 they processed the discount and credited the account for $54.*

Required: *a.* For each of the five exceptions, determine the account's proper "audited value."

b. Use the probability-proportional-to-size method with your analysis from part (*a*) to evaluate your sample's results. The risk of incorrect acceptance is 5 percent.

Chapter 12

Inventories and Cost of Goods Sold

Chapter learning objectives

After studying this chapter, you should be able to:

LO1. Describe the nature of inventories and cost of goods sold.

LO2. Describe the auditors' objectives for the audit of inventories and cost of goods sold.

LO3. Describe the documents, records, and accounts that are involved in the purchases and production (conversion) cycles and the fundamental controls over inventories, purchasing, and production.

LO4. Assess the risks of material misstatement (inherent and control risks) of inventories, purchases, and cost of goods sold.

LO5. Design typical tests of controls used by auditors to support the assessed risks of material misstatement (inherent and control risks) for the financial statement assertions related to inventories and cost of goods sold.

LO6. Explain how the auditors design substantive audit procedures to address the risks of material misstatement of inventories and cost of goods sold.

Learning Objective 1

The interrelationship of inventories and cost of goods sold makes it logical for the two topics to be considered together. The controls that assure the fair valuation of inventories are found in the purchases (or acquisition) cycle. These controls include procedures for selecting vendors, ordering merchandise or materials, inspecting goods received, recording the liability to the vendor, and authorizing and making cash disbursements. In a manufacturing business, the valuation of inventories also is affected by the production (or conversion) cycle, in which various manufacturing costs are assigned to inventories, and the cost of inventories is then transferred to the cost of goods sold.

The selection of an accounting method and consistency in its application also affect the valuation of both inventories and cost of goods sold. During periods of inflation, limitations of historical cost affect the relevance of cost of goods sold as much as they affect inventories. Thus, it is not surprising that the Financial Accounting Standards Board (FASB) experimented with requiring supplemental disclosure of current replacement cost of inventories.[1] Although companies are no longer required to disclose this information, many companies include a discussion of the effects of inflation in "Management's Discussion and Analysis of Financial Condition," which is a required section of a company's annual Form 10-K filed with the SEC.

Sources and Nature of Inventories and Cost of Goods Sold

The term *inventories* is used in this chapter to include (1) goods on hand ready for sale, whether the merchandise of a trading concern or the finished goods of a manufacturer; (2) goods in the process of production; and (3) goods to be consumed directly or indirectly in production: raw materials, purchased parts, and supplies.

The Auditors' Approach to Auditing Inventories and Cost of Goods Sold

Learning Objective 2

The auditors' *objectives* in the audit of inventories and cost of goods sold are to:

1. Consider *inherent risks,* including fraud risks.
2. Consider *internal control* over inventories and cost of goods sold.
3. Determine the *existence* of inventories and the occurrence of transactions affecting cost of goods sold.
4. Establish the *completeness* of inventories.
5. Establish that the client has *rights* to the recorded inventories.
6. Determine that the *valuation* of inventories and cost of goods sold is arrived at by appropriate methods.
7. Determine that the *presentation and disclosure* of inventories and cost of goods sold is adequate, including disclosure of classifications of inventories, accounting methods, and any inventories pledged as collateral for loans.

In conjunction with the audit of inventories and cost of goods sold, the auditors will also obtain evidence about the related purchases, sales, purchase returns, and sales returns accounts.

The responsibilities of independent auditors with respect to the validity of inventories can best be understood by considering the spectacular *McKesson & Robbins* fraud case. The hearings conducted by the SEC in 1939 disclosed that the audited financial statements of McKesson & Robbins, Inc., a drug company listed on the New York Stock Exchange, contained $19 million of fictitious assets, about one-fourth of the total assets shown on the balance sheet. The fictitious assets included $10 million of nonexistent inventories. How was it possible for the independent auditors to have conducted an audit and to have issued an unqualified report without discovering this gigantic fraud? The audit program followed for inventories in this case was in accordance with customary auditing practice of the 1930s. The significant point is that in that period it was customary to limit the audit work on inventories to an examination of records only; the standards of that era did not require any observation, physical count, or other actual contact with the inventories.

Up to the time of the *McKesson & Robbins* case, auditors had avoided taking responsibility for verifying the accuracy of inventory quantities and the physical existence of the goods. With questionable logic, many auditors had argued that they were experts in handling figures and

---

[1] The requirement for mandatory disclosure of current cost information was rescinded by *FASB Statement No. 89,* "Financial Reporting and Changing Prices."

analyzing accounting records but were not qualified to identify and measure the great variety of raw materials and manufactured goods found in the factories, warehouses, and store buildings of their clients.

The *McKesson & Robbins* case brought a quick end to such limited views of the auditors' responsibilities. In 1939, Statements on Auditing Procedures 1 and 2, the first formal auditing standards issued by the AICPA, affirmed the importance of the auditors' observation of physical inventories, but authorized the substitution of other auditing procedures under certain circumstances. *SAS 1* (AU 331.09-.11) continues to distinguish between companies that determine inventory quantities solely by an annual physical count (**periodic inventory system**) and companies with well-kept perpetual inventory records. The latter companies often have strong internal control over inventories and may employ sampling techniques to verify the records by occasional test counts throughout the year rather than by a complete annual count of the entire inventory. For those clients the auditors' observation of physical inventory may be limited to such counts as they consider appropriate, and these counts may occur during or after the end of the period being audited.

The auditors' approach to the verification of inventories and cost of goods sold should be one of awareness of the possibility of fraud, as well as of the prevalence of accidental error in the determination of inventory quantities and amounts. Fraudulent misstatement of inventories has often been employed to evade income taxes, to conceal shortages arising from various illegal schemes, and to mislead stockholders or other inactive owners as to a company's profits and financial position.

Internal Control over Inventories and Cost of Goods Sold

The importance of adequate internal control over inventories and cost of goods sold from the viewpoint of both management and the auditors can scarcely be overemphasized. In some companies, management stresses controls over cash and securities but pays little attention to control over inventories. Since many types of inventories are composed of items not particularly susceptible to theft, management may consider controls to be unnecessary in this area. Such thinking ignores the fact that controls for inventories affect nearly all the functions involved in producing and disposing of the company's products.

Control Environment

As described in Chapter 7, the control environment reflects the overall attitude, awareness, and actions of management and the board of directors concerning the importance of control and the way it is used in the entity. The aspects of the control environment that are particularly relevant to the auditors' consideration of the inventories and cost of goods sold include:

1. **Commitment to competence and human resource policies and practices.** These policies and practices help ensure that appropriately qualified and trained personnel are assigned the responsibilities for purchasing goods and services and receiving and storing the goods. A *commitment to competence* with respect to plant personnel is important to ensuring that the manufacturing process is efficient and effective and that prescribed control activities are being performed.

2. **Integrity and ethical values.** Purchasing and cash disbursement activities provide ample opportunity for fraud by employees, as well as by management. Communication of management's integrity and ethical values helps ensure that disbursements are for authorized and legitimate goods that were actually received and that the accounting for the purchases is appropriate. The importance of competence and integrity may be illustrated by considering the company's purchasing agents who negotiate the terms of purchases with the company's various suppliers. If these individuals are incompetent, they may commit the company to large purchases at unfavorable terms. If purchasing agents accept "kickbacks," the company will not only lose the amounts accepted, but may make purchases of substandard goods or pay excessive prices.

3. **Organizational structure and assignment of authority and responsibility.** Internal control is improved when the client's organizational structure is appropriate and when levels of authority and responsibility for purchasing and production activities are clearly communicated. It is especially important for personnel involved in purchasing, receiving, and production to understand their responsibilities for the application of controls.

Illustrative Case
Bid Rigging at Sheraton

The need for proper control over the purchasing function is dramatically illustrated by a case in which two buyers for the Sheraton hotels allegedly rigged the bidding for produce products by providing one supplier with competitive bid information. With this information, the supplier obtained a number of contracts by placing the lowest bid. In exchange, the buyers allegedly received hundreds of thousands of dollars in kickback payments, received monthly from the supplier in the form of cash slid under the door of the buyers' offices.

The "off the books" nature of kickbacks makes them particularly difficult for auditors to detect. In this case the two buyers were arrested as a part of a federal investigation of corruption at city produce markets. Factors that might indicate the existence of kickbacks include:

- A purchasing employee who appears to be living beyond his or her means.
- An improper or questionable basis for selecting suppliers.
- Selection of a supplier with high prices, or at prices that have increased significantly since the supplier was first selected.
- Purchasing records that indicate that one company consistently "wins contracts" as the lowest bidder, often by a relatively small amount.
- Continued purchases from a supplier providing products of questionable quality.
- Tips from other employees.

Risk Assessment

The risk of material misstatement of the financial statements is reduced when management evaluates and manages the risks related to purchasing and producing goods and services. Aspects of concern to the auditors include management's assessment of risks related to (1) the availability of a supply of goods, services, and skilled labor; (2) the stability of prices and labor rates; (3) the generation of sufficient cash flow to pay for purchases; (4) changes in technology that affect manufacturing processes; and (5) the obsolescence of inventory.

Monitoring

Relevant monitoring controls for the purchases cycle include management review of reports of purchases from suppliers, inventory on hand, and accounts payable balances. Management also may establish a process of obtaining feedback from suppliers, including complaints about delays in payments. Monitoring controls for the production cycle include observations by production supervisors of the performance of various activities and functions and quality and performance reviews. Management should also have a formal process for considering recommendations by the internal auditors for improvements in the purchasing and production functions and the related control activities.

Purchases and Production Cycles—Accounting Systems and Control Activities

Learning Objective 3

Purchasing, receiving, storing, issuing, processing, and shipping are the physical functions directly connected with inventories; the cost accounting system and the perpetual inventory records compose the recording functions. Since the auditors are interested in the final products of the recording functions, it is necessary for them to understand and evaluate the cost accounting system and the perpetual inventory records, as well as the various control activities and original documents underlying the preparation of financial data.

The Purchasing Function

Strong internal control over purchases ordinarily involves an organizational structure that delegates to a separate department of the company exclusive authority to make all purchases of materials and services. The purchasing, receiving, and recording functions should be clearly separated and lodged in separate departments. In small companies, this type of departmentalized operation may not be possible; but even in very small enterprises, it is usually feasible to make one properly supervised person responsible for all purchase transactions.

A purchase transaction begins with the issuance of a properly approved *purchase requisition* (next page top) by the stores department or another department needing the goods or services. A copy of the requisition is sent to the purchasing department to provide a basis for preparing the serially numbered *purchase order* (next page top). The requisition should include a precise description of the type and quantity of the goods or services desired.

	67467500
Perfect Manufacturing Co. Purchase Requisition	

Department: Raw Materials Stores	Date: <u>May 10, 20XX</u> Date Required: <u>June 5, 20XX</u>

Quantity	Description
9,000 sheets	2×8, 1/2" steel sheets #278473

	Approved By: *Casey Rowe*

	AA09847
PURCHASE ORDER Perfect Manufacturing Co. 1212 Belaire Blvd. Houston, TX 77062	

To: <u>Carson Steel Co.</u>   Date: <u>May 12, 20XX</u>
<u>1671 21st St.</u>
<u>Houston, TX 77021</u>   Ship via: <u>SOS Delivery</u>

Terms: <u>2/10, n/30</u>

Enter our order for:

Qty.	Description	Price	Total
9,000 sheets	2×8, 1/2" steel #278473	$21.00	$189,000

Perfect Manufacturing Co.
By: *Linda Jones*

Copies of the purchase order should be forwarded to the accounting and receiving departments. The copy sent to receiving should have the quantities blacked out to increase the likelihood that receiving personnel will make independent counts of the merchandise received. Even though the buyer may actually place an order by telephone, the formal purchase order should be prepared and forwarded. In many large organizations, purchase orders are issued only after compliance with extensive procedures for (1) determining the need for the item, (2) obtaining competitive bids, and (3) obtaining approval of the financial aspect of the commitment.

The Receiving Function

All goods received by the company—without exception—should be cleared through a receiving department that is independent of the purchasing, storing, and shipping departments. The receiving department is responsible for (1) the determination of quantities of goods received, (2) the detection of damaged or defective merchandise, (3) the preparation of a *receiving report* (below), and (4) the prompt transmittal of goods received to the stores department.

	5874983
Perfect Manufacturing Co. Receiving Report	

Received From: <u>Carson Steel Co.</u> <u>1671 21st St.</u> <u>Houston, TX 77021</u>	Date: <u>June 5, 20XX</u> Order No: <u>AA09847</u> Carrier: <u>SOS Delivery</u>

Quantity	Description
9,000 sheets	2×8, 1/2" steel #278473

	Received By: *Don Warren*

	4503945
Perfect Manufacturing Co. Materials Requisition	

Production Order: 8576409

Department: Milling #23	Date: <u>June 10, 20XX</u> Date Required: <u>June 10, 20XX</u>

Quantity	Description	Unit Cost	Total Cost
350 sheets	2×8, 1/2" steel	$32.40	$11,340.00

		Approved By: *John West*

The Storing Function

As goods are delivered to stores, they are counted, inspected, and receipted for. The stores department then notifies the accounting department of the amount received and placed in stock. In performing these functions, the stores department makes an important contribution to overall control of inventories. By signing for the goods, it fixes its own responsibility, and by notifying the accounting department of actual goods stored, it provides verification of the receiving department's work.

The Issuing Function

The stores department, being responsible for all goods under its control, has reason to insist that a prenumbered requisition (on the previous page, bottom right) be issued for all items passing out of its hands to serve as a signed receipt from the department accepting the goods. Requisitions are usually prepared in triplicate. The department making the request retains one copy; another serves as the stores department's receipt; and the third is a notice to the accounting department for cost distribution. To prevent the indiscriminate writing of requisitions for questionable purposes, some organizations establish policies requiring that requisitions be drawn only upon the authority of a bill of materials, an engineering order, or a sales order. In wholesale and retail concerns, shipping orders, rather than factory requisitions, serve to authorize withdrawals from stores.

The Production (Conversion) Function

Overall production should be controlled with a **master production schedule** that presents the gross production needs for a particular period. Because the schedule is developed based on forecasts of demand for the company's products, it helps to ensure that the company will meet its customers' needs, while not overstocking particular products. The master production schedule also ensures that materials and labor are available, on a timely basis, to meet the production demands for the period. Once the required resources are determined to be available, **production orders** are prepared to authorize the production of specific products.

Responsibility for the goods in production must be fixed, usually on factory supervisors or superintendents. *Materials requisitions* and *move tickets* document the flow of the goods and related responsibility as they progress through the production process. Thus, from the time materials are delivered to the factory until they are completed and routed to a finished goods storeroom, a designated supervisor should be in control and be prepared to answer for their location and disposition.

Job time tickets (at the top of next page) are prepared to document the labor or machine hours devoted to a particular production job. Each job time ticket should be reviewed and approved by the department supervisor before it is entered into the cost accounting system.

The controls for goods in production usually include regular inspection procedures to reveal defective work. This aids in disclosing inefficiencies in the productive system and also tends to prevent inflation of the goods in process inventory by the accumulation of cost of goods that will eventually be scrapped. If scrapped materials have substantial salvage value, the materials should be segregated, controlled, and inventoried.

The Shipping Function

Shipments of goods should be made only after proper authorization has been received. This authorization will normally be a sales order approved by the credit department, although the shipping function also includes the returning of defective goods to suppliers. In this latter case, the authorization may take the form of a shipping authorization from a purchasing department executive.

The shipping department will prepare, or the computer system will generate, a prenumbered *shipping document* (next page top right) indicating the goods shipped. One copy of the shipping document should be retained by the shipping department as evidence of shipment; a second copy should be sent to the billing department where it will be used—with the customer's purchase order and the sales order—as the basis for invoicing the customer; and a third copy should be enclosed as a packing slip with the goods when they are shipped. The control aspect of this procedure is strengthened by the fact that an outsider, the customer, will

Perfect Manufacturing Co. Job Time Ticket Production Order: 8576409			
Date: 06/18/XX Dept. No. 23 Dept. Milling			
Employee		Hourly Rate	Operation
No. 2954	Name Larry Cobb	$22.50	Cut to shape
Start Time 6:00 A.M.	End Time 11:30 A.M.	Total Hours 5.5	Total Labor Dollars $123.75
Quantity Completed: 350 Valve Bases			
		Approved By: *Chee Chow*	

	54654566
SHIPPING DOCUMENT Perfect Manufacturing Co. 1212 Belaire Blvd. Houston, TX 77062	
Consigned to: Flour Valve Co. 5485 First St. Kansas City, MO 66220	Date: Oct. 21, 20XX Order No. 6779938 Shipper: Union Pacific

Quantity	Description	Weight
150	9' Outflow valves #2988388	7845
Packed by: *Leon Jones*		Received by: *John Carr*

generally inspect the packing slip and notify the company of any discrepancy between this list, the goods ordered, and the goods actually received.

When the goods are shipped using a common carrier, a fourth copy of the shipping document, required in this case to be a **bill of lading,** is provided to the carrier. In addition, the copy forwarded to billing will include additional evidence of shipment in the form of trucking bills, carriers' receipts, or freight bills. Subsequent audit is facilitated by grouping together the documents showing that shipments were properly authorized and carried out.

Established shipping routines should be followed for all types of shipments, including the sale of scrap, return of defective goods, and forwarding of materials and parts to subcontractors.

The Cost Accounting System

An adequate cost accounting system is necessary to account for the usage of raw materials and supplies, to determine the content and value of goods in process inventories, and to compute the finished goods inventory. This system comprises all the records, orders, and requisitions needed for proper accounting for the disposition of materials as they enter the flow of production and as they continue through the factory in the process of becoming finished goods. The cost accounting system also serves to accumulate labor costs and indirect costs that contribute to the goods in process and the finished goods inventories. The cost accounting system thus forms an integral part of the internal control over inventories.

The figures produced by the cost accounting system should be controlled by general ledger accounts. The costs of direct materials and labor are recorded in individual goods (work) in process accounts for each job order or process. Periodically, manufacturing overhead is applied to the jobs or processes and recorded in the accounts.

Underlying this upper level of control between the factory records and the general ledger is a system of production orders, material requisitions, job tickets or other labor distributions, and factory overhead distributions. Control is affected by various procedures that verify the accuracy of production records. Allocations of direct materials and labor costs are recomputed and reconciled to material and payroll records. Manufacturing overhead costs that are applied using predetermined rates are adjusted to actual costs at the end of the period.

Many companies have established standard cost systems that help identify the causes of ineffectiveness and waste through a study of variances between actual and standard costs. These systems provide for the prompt pricing of inventories and for control over operations. All the various types of cost accounting systems are alike in that they are designed to contribute to effective internal control by tracing the execution of managerial directives in the factory, providing reliable inventory figures and safeguarding company assets.

The Perpetual Inventory System

Perpetual inventory records constitute an extremely important part of internal control. These records, by showing at all times the quantity of goods on hand, provide information essential to intelligent purchasing, sales, and production-planning policies. With such a record it is possible to guide procurement by establishing points of minimum and maximum quantities for each standard item stocked.

The use of a **perpetual inventory system** allows companies to control the high costs of holding excessive inventory, while minimizing the risk of running out of stock. The company can control inventories through reorder points and economic order quantities, including *just-in-time* ordering systems in which inventory levels are kept to a minimum.

If perpetual inventory records are to produce the control implicit in their nature, it is desirable that the subsidiary records be maintained both in quantities and dollars for all stock, that the subsidiary records be controlled by the general ledger, and that trial balances be prepared at reasonable intervals. In addition, both the detailed records and the general ledger control accounts should be adjusted to agree with physical counts whenever taken.

Perpetual inventory records discourage inventory theft and waste, since storekeepers and other employees are aware of the accountability over goods established by this continuous record of goods received, issued, and on hand. The records, however, must be periodically verified through the physical counting of goods.

IT Systems

An IT-based inventory system makes it much easier for the client to maintain control over inventories, purchasing, and the manufacturing process. The IT system can automatically generate purchase requisitions and orders when inventory levels reach predetermined reorder points. The client's purchasing system may even be linked to the system of its suppliers, allowing **electronic data interchange (EDI)** to completely coordinate production and purchasing. The IT system also maintains records of responsibility for goods as they are routed through the production process. Details of direct labor and material usage are entered, and the computer allocates these direct costs to jobs or processes, applies manufacturing overhead costs based on predetermined rates, and maintains perpetual records of the costs of goods in process, finished, and sold. The system also generates various financial reports, including *responsibility accounting reports* that indicate actual costs, standard costs, and the related variances.

Good internal control in IT systems requires the normal segregation of the purchasing, receiving, storing, processing, and shipping functions. In addition, the client should establish appropriate IT controls that promote the accuracy of data as they are entered into the system and maintain their integrity after they are entered.

Audit Documentation for Inventories and Cost of Goods Sold

The auditors may prepare a great variety of working papers in their verification of inventories and cost of goods sold. These papers will range in form from written comments on the manner in which the physical inventory was taken to elaborate analyses of production costs of finished goods and goods in process. Selected working papers will be illustrated in connection with the audit procedures to be described in later sections of this chapter.

Audit of Inventories and Cost of Goods Sold

The following steps for the verification of inventories and cost of goods sold will be discussed in detail in the succeeding pages. The program is appropriate for a manufacturing company that takes a complete physical inventory to verify the perpetual inventories at the close of each fiscal year.

A. Consider inherent risks, including fraud risks.
B. Consider internal control over inventories and cost of goods sold.
　1. *Obtain an understanding of internal control* over inventories and cost of goods sold.
　2. *Assess control risk and design additional tests of controls and substantive tests* for inventories and cost of goods sold.

3. *Perform additional tests of controls* for those controls which the auditors plan to consider to support their planned assessed levels of control risk, such as:
    a. Examine significant aspects of a sample of purchase transactions.
    b. Test of the cost accounting system.
4. *Reassess control risk* and *modify substantive tests* for inventories and cost of goods sold.

C. Perform substantive tests of inventories and cost of goods sold transactions.
1. Obtain listings of inventory and reconcile to ledgers.
2. Evaluate the client's planning of physical inventory.
3. Observe the taking of physical inventory and make test counts.
4. Review the year-end cutoff of purchases and sales transactions.
5. Obtain a copy of the completed physical inventory, test its clerical accuracy, and trace test counts.
6. Evaluate the bases and methods of inventory pricing.
7. Test the pricing of inventories.
8. Perform analytical procedures.
9. Determine whether any inventories have been pledged and review purchase and sales commitments.
10. Evaluate financial statement presentation of inventories and cost of goods sold, including the adequacy of disclosure.

Figure 12.1 relates the objectives of the major substantive tests of inventories and cost of goods sold to the primary audit objectives.

A. Consider Inherent Risks, Including Fraud Risks.

Generally, inventories represent an asset with significant inherent risks. Some of these risks arise from business risks faced by management, such as the risks of losses due to poor product quality, obsolescence, or theft. Other factors that affect the risks of material misstatement of inventories include:

1. Inventories often constitute a large current asset of an enterprise and are very susceptible to major errors and fraud.
2. The accounting profession allows numerous alternative methods for valuation of inventories, and different methods may be used for various classes of inventories.

FIGURE 12.1
Objectives of Major Substantive Tests of Inventories and Cost of Goods Sold

Substantive Tests	Primary Audit Objectives
Obtain listings of inventory and reconcile to ledgers.	*Valuation*
Evaluate the client's planning of physical inventory.	*Existence and rights* *Completeness*
Observe the taking of the physical inventory. Review the year-end cutoff of purchase and sales transactions. Obtain a copy of the completed physical inventory and test its accuracy.	*Valuation*
Evaluate the bases and methods of inventory pricing. Test the pricing of inventories.	*Valuation*
Perform analytical procedures.	*Existence and rights* *Completeness* *Valuation*
Determine whether any inventories have been pledged and review commitments.	*Valuation* *Presentation and disclosure*
Evaluate financial statement presentation and disclosure.	*Presentation and disclosure*

3. The determination of inventory value directly affects the cost of goods sold and has a major impact on net income for the year. Therefore, if management is inclined to engage in fraudulent financial reporting, the fraud will likely involve overstatement of inventory.

4. The determination of inventory quality, condition, and value is inherently a more complex and difficult task than is the case with most other elements of financial position. Many items, such as precious gems, sophisticated electronic parts, and construction in progress, present significant problems of identification and valuation.

If auditors identify a fraud risk with respect to inventories, they will make sure that they understand the programs and controls established by management to control the risk. They will also determine that the controls have been implemented. Finally, the auditors will design appropriate procedures to respond to that risk.

B. Consider Internal Control over Inventories and Cost of Goods Sold.

1. Obtain an Understanding of Internal Control.

As previously indicated, the consideration of controls may involve the filling out of a questionnaire, the writing of descriptive memoranda, or the preparation of flowcharts depicting the organizational structure and the flow of materials and documents. In obtaining an understanding of internal control over inventory, the auditors should become thoroughly familiar with the procedures for purchasing, receiving, storing, and issuing goods and for controlling production, and they should obtain an understanding of the cost accounting system and the perpetual inventory records.

The auditors should also give consideration to the physical protection of inventories. Any deficiencies in storage facilities, in guard service, or in physical handling that may lead to losses from weather, fire, flood, or theft may appropriately be called to the attention of management.

The matters to be investigated in the auditors' consideration of controls over inventory and cost of sales are fairly well indicated by the following questions: Are perpetual inventory records maintained for each class of inventory? Are perpetual inventory records verified by physical inventories at least once each year? Do the procedures for physical inventories include the use of prenumbered tags, with all tag numbers accounted for? Are differences between physical inventory counts and perpetual inventory records investigated before the perpetual records are adjusted? Is a separate purchasing department responsible for purchasing all materials, supplies, and equipment? Does a separate receiving department process all incoming shipments? Are materials and supplies held in the custody of a stores department and issued only upon receipt of properly approved requisitions?

After the auditors have prepared a flowchart (or other description) of internal control, they should determine that the client is using those procedures, that is, they should determine whether the controls have been *placed in operation.* This information may be obtained through

---

Focus on the Agribusiness Industry

Accounting for the inventory of an agricultural producer provides a good example of the need for industry expertise when obtaining an understanding of a client's internal control over inventory. Auditors of agricultural producers that are involved in raising animals must pay special attention to the effectiveness of the agricultural producer's internal control, including whether:

- The controls provide accurate quantity and cost data for the raised animals.
- The payroll records are sophisticated enough to allow labor cost to be allocated to the appropriate animal component of inventory.
- Direct and indirect costs of developing animals raised for a productive function are accurately accumulated until the animals reach maturity, at which point the costs are depreciated over the animals' estimated productive life.
- Direct and indirect costs of developing animals raised for sale are accumulated to ensure the accuracy of inventory and cost of animals sold.

inquiries of entity personnel, inspection of documents, and observation of activities. As the auditors obtain their understanding of the controls, they will observe whether there is an appropriate segregation of duties and inquire as to who performed various functions throughout the year. They will also inspect various documents, such as purchase requisitions, purchase orders, material requisitions, move tickets, time tickets, and shipping advices, and review document files to determine that the client is appropriately accounting for the sequence of prenumbered documents. Inventory, production, and responsibility accounting reports will be examined, and the auditors will review the evidence of follow-up on variances from standard costs. These procedures may provide the auditors with sufficient evidence to assess control risk for certain financial statement assertions about inventories and cost of goods sold as being at less than the maximum.

2. Assess Control Risk and Design Additional Tests of Controls.

Based on their understanding of internal control, the auditors determine the planned assessed levels of control risk for the various financial statement assertions. To support these assessments, the auditors may need to obtain additional evidence of the operating effectiveness of the client's controls by designing additional tests of controls. In designing these tests, the auditors must decide which ones will result in sufficient reductions in substantive tests to justify the time spent performing them.

The auditors' assessments of control risk and inherent risk will be used to plan the nature, timing, and extent of substantive tests for inventories. In designing planned substantive tests, the auditors often find it useful to consider the types of misstatements that might occur along with the weaknesses in internal control and other factors that make the misstatements more likely to occur. Figure 12.2 provides examples of such misstatements. You should also refer back to Figure 11.4 on pages 412 and 413, which presents a number of misstatements of revenues that may also involve misstatements of inventory.

3. Perform Additional Tests of Controls.

Learning Objective 5

Tests directed toward the effectiveness of controls help to evaluate the client's internal control and determine whether the auditors can support their planned assessed levels of control risk for the assertions about the inventory and cost of goods sold accounts. Certain tests of controls are performed as the auditors obtain an understanding of the client's internal control; these tests were described in our discussion of that process. The following are examples of typical additional tests.

a. Examine Significant Aspects of a Sample of Purchase Transactions.

The proper recording of purchase transactions and cash disbursements is essential to reliable accounting records. Therefore, the auditors test the key control procedures in the client's purchasing transaction cycle. Tests of this cycle may include the following steps:

1. Select a sample of purchase transactions.
2. Examine the purchase requisition or other authorization for each purchase transaction in the sample.
3. Examine the related vendor's invoice, receiving report, and paid check for each purchase order in the sample. Trace transactions to the voucher register and check register.
4. Inspect vendors' invoices for approval of prices, freight and credit terms, and account distribution, and recompute extensions and footings.
5. Compare quantities and prices in the invoice, purchase order, and receiving report.
6. Trace postings from voucher register to general ledger and any applicable subsidiary ledgers.

b. Test the Cost Accounting System.

For a client in the manufacturing field, the auditors must become familiar with the client's cost accounting system. A wide variety of practices will be encountered for the costing of finished units. The cost accounting records may be controlled by general ledger accounts or operated independently of the general accounting system. In the latter case, the cost of

FIGURE 12.2   Potential Misstatements—Inventory*

Description of Misstatement	Examples	Internal Control Weaknesses or Factors That Increase the Risk of the Misstatement
Misstatement of inventory costs	**Fraud:** • Intentional misstatement of production costs assigned to inventory. • Intentional misstatement of inventory prices.	• Ineffective board of directors, audit committee, or internal audit function; "tone at the top" not conducive to ethical conduct; undue pressure to meet earnings targets.
	Errors: • The assignment of direct labor costs, direct material costs, or factory overhead to inventory items is inaccurate. • Erroneous pricing of inventory.	• Ineffective cost accounting system; failure to update standard costs on a timely basis. • Ineffective input validation controls on the database of inventory costs; ineffective supervision of the personnel that enter the costs on the final inventory schedule.
Misstatement of inventory quantities	**Fraud** • Items are stolen with no journal entry reflecting the theft. • Inventory quantities in locations not visited by auditors are systematically overstated.	• Ineffective physical controls over inventories. • Ineffective board of directors, audit committee, or internal audit function; "tone at the top" not conducive to ethical conduct; undue pressure to meet earnings targets.
	Error: • Miscounting of inventory by personnel involved in physical inventory.	• Ineffective controls or supervision of physical inventory.
Early (late) recognition of purchases—"cutoff problems"	**Fraud:** • Intentional recording of purchases in the subsequent period.	• Ineffective board of directors, audit committee, or internal audit function; "tone at the top" not conducive to ethical conduct; undue pressure to meet earnings targets.
	Error: • Recording purchases of the current period in the subsequent period.	• Ineffective accounting procedures that do not tie recorded purchases to receiving data.

*See also Figure 11.4, Potential Misstatements—Revenue, since many types of revenue misstatements involve misstatement of inventory.

completed units may be difficult or impossible to verify and may represent nothing more than a well-reasoned guess. Because cost accounting methods vary so widely, even among manufacturing concerns in the same industry, audit procedures for a cost accounting system must be designed to fit the specific circumstances encountered in each case.

In any cost accounting system, the three elements of manufacturing cost are direct materials costs, direct labor costs, and manufacturing overhead. Cost accounting systems may accumulate either actual costs or standard costs according to *processes* or *jobs*. The auditors' tests of the client's cost accounting system are designed to determine that costs allocated to specific jobs or processes are appropriately compiled.

To achieve this objective, the auditors test the propriety of direct materials quantities and unit costs, direct labor-hours and hourly rates, and overhead rates and allocation bases. Quantities of direct materials charged to jobs or processes are vouched to materials requisitions, and unit materials costs are traced to the raw materials perpetual inventory records or purchase invoices. The auditors examine job time tickets or time summaries supporting direct labor-hours accumulations and trace direct labor hourly rates to union contracts or individual employee personnel files.

The auditors must recognize that a variety of methods are generally accepted for the application of manufacturing overhead to inventories. A predetermined rate of factory overhead applied on the basis of machine-hours, direct labor dollars, direct labor-hours, or some similar basis is used by many manufacturing companies. *FASB No 151,* "Inventory Costs–an Amendment to ARB No. 43, Chapter 4," clarifies that variable manufacturing costs should be allocated to products on the basis of the actual level of activity. Fixed manufacturing overhead, on the other hand, should be allocated based on the normal capacity of the production facility.

A distinction between factory overhead, on the one hand, and overhead costs pertaining to selling or general administration of the business, on the other, must be made under generally accepted accounting principles because selling expenses and general and administrative expenses are written off in the period incurred. The difference in the accounting treatment accorded to factory overhead and to nonmanufacturing overhead implies a fundamental difference between these two types of cost. Nevertheless, as a practical matter it is often impossible to say with finality what proportion of a particular expenditure, such as the salary of a vice president in charge of production, should be classified as factory overhead and as general and administrative expense. Despite this difficulty, a vital procedure in the audit of cost of goods sold for a manufacturing concern is determining that factory overhead costs are reasonably allocated in the accounts. Failure to distribute factory costs to the correct accounts can cause significant distortions in the client's predetermined overhead rate and in over- or underapplied factory overhead. The auditors may find it necessary to obtain or prepare analyses of a number of the factory overhead subsidiary ledger accounts and to verify the propriety of the charges thereto. Then, the auditors must determine the propriety of the total machine-hours, direct labor-hours, or other aggregate allocation base used by the client company to predetermine the factory overhead rate.

If standard costs are in use, it is desirable to compare them with actual costs for representative items and to ascertain whether the standards reflect current materials and labor usage and unit costs. The composition of factory overhead, the basis for its distribution by department and product, and the effect of any change in basis during the year should be reviewed. The standard costs of selected products should be verified by testing computations, extensions, and footings and by tracing charges for labor, material, and overhead to original sources.

The auditors' study of a manufacturing company's cost accounting system should give special attention to any changes in cost methods made during the year and the effect of such changes on the cost of sales. Close attention should also be given to the methods of summarizing costs of completed products and to the procedures for recording the cost of partial shipments.

If the client company has supply contracts with U.S. government agencies, the auditors should determine whether standards issued by the Cost Accounting Standards Board were complied with. Cost accounting standards issued to date have dealt with such matters as consistency in estimating, accumulating, allocating, and reporting costs, and depreciation of plant assets.

4. Reassess Control Risk and Design Substantive Tests.

Learning Objective 6

The description and tests of controls of the client's internal control over inventories and cost of goods sold provide the auditors with evidence as to weaknesses and strengths of the system. Based on this information, the auditors reassess control risk for the financial statement assertions about inventories and cost of goods sold. Figure 12.3 illustrates the relationship between the assertions and the various controls. It also shows how these policies and procedures are typically tested. The auditors' assessments of control risk and inherent risk are then used to design the substantive tests for these accounts.

C. Perform Substantive Tests of Inventories and Cost of Goods Sold Transactions.

1. Obtain Listings of Inventories and Reconcile to Ledgers.

Primary Audit Objective:

Valuation ☑

The auditor will obtain a schedule of listings of inventories that will be reconciled to both the general ledger and appropriate subsidiary ledgers. The nature of the listings will vary depending upon whether the client engages in manufacturing or simply sells products at retail. The auditors'

FIGURE 12.3 Assessing Control Risk for Inventories, Production, and Purchases

Internal Control Policy or Procedure	Typical Tests of the Control Policy or Procedure	Existence or Occurrence	Completeness	Rights and Obligations	Valuation or Allocation	Presentation & Disclosure
Segregate duties over purchases and custody of inventories	Observe and make inquiries about the performance of various functions.	X	X	X	X	
Use prenumbered requisitions, purchase orders, and receiving reports and account for the sequence of documents	Observe and make inquiries about the use of prenumbered documents and inspect evidence of accounting for the sequence.		X			
Establish procedures for authorizing purchase transactions, reconciling purchase invoices to purchase orders and receiving reports, and verifying the clerical accuracy of purchase invoices	Observe and make inquiries about purchase procedures, and test a sample of purchase transactions by inspecting evidence of authorizations and reconciliations, comparing the details to authorized purchase orders and receiving reports, and recomputing the invoice amounts.	X		X	X	
Establish general ledger control of inventories of raw materials, goods in process, and finished goods, and periodically reconcile to production records	Inspect accounting and production records and selected reconciliations.	X		X	X	X
Establish controls for the cost accounting system that accumulates appropriate inventory costs on a job order or process cost basis, such as independent review of cost accumulations	Inspect evidence of independent reviews of cost accumulations, recompute material costs by reference to requisitions and purchase invoices, and recompute direct labor costs by reference to time and payroll records and overhead application rates.				X	
Analyze and follow up on variances from standard costs	Inspect inventory reports and examine evidence of follow-up on variances.	X	X		X	
Use perpetual records to control inventories	Inquire about the perpetual inventory procedures, and test the records by reference to purchase invoices, receiving reports, and production records.	X	X		X	X
Use appropriate procedures for taking the physical inventory	Review the inventory instructions and observe the inventory-taking process.	X	X	X	X	
Establish appropriate physical controls over inventories	Observe and inquire about the physical control policies and procedures.	X		X		

goal in performing this step is to make sure the inventory records agree with what is recorded in the financial statements.

2. Evaluate the Client's Planning of Physical Inventory.

Efficient and effective inventory taking requires careful advance planning. Cooperation between the auditors and client personnel in formulating the procedures to be followed will prevent unnecessary confusion and will aid in securing a complete and well-controlled count. A first step is the designation by the client management of an individual employee, often a

Primary Audit Objectives:	
Existence	☑
Completeness	☑
Rights	☑
Valuation	☑

Illustrative Case
Fraud at Phar-Mor

Several years ago, it was reported that audits of Phar-Mor, Inc., a discount drugstore chain, did not detect a $50 million overstatement of inventory. The allegedly fraudulent overstatements occurred at stores at which the client knew in advance the CPAs did not intend to observe inventory counts. The client refrained from making fraudulent adjustments at the stores where it knew that the CPAs would observe the inventories. In another case, auditors are reported to have permitted company officials to follow them and record where test counts of inventory were taken; the managers subsequently falsified counts for inventory items that weren't test counted by the auditors.

representative of the controller, to assume responsibility for the physical inventory. This responsibility will begin with the drafting of procedures and will carry through to the final determination of the dollar value of all inventories.

In planning the physical inventory, the client should consider many factors, such as (*a*) selecting the best date or dates, (*b*) suspending production in certain departments of the plant, (*c*) segregating obsolete and defective goods, (*d*) establishing control over the counting process through the use of inventory tags or sheets, (*e*) achieving proper cutoff of sales and purchase transactions, and (*f*) arranging for services of engineers or other specialists to determine the quantity or quality of certain goods or materials.

Once the plan has been developed, it must be documented and communicated in the form of written instructions to the personnel taking the physical inventory. These instructions normally will be drafted by the client and reviewed by the auditors, who will judge their adequacy. A set of instructions prepared by the controller of a large clothing store for use by supervisors is shown in Figure 12.4. In evaluating the adequacy of the instructions, the auditors should consider the nature and materiality of the inventories, as well as the existing internal control. Normally, the auditors will insist that the inventory be taken at or near the balance sheet date. However, if the client has effective internal control, including perpetual records, the auditors may be satisfied to observe inventory counts performed during the year. If the client plans to use a statistical sampling technique to estimate the quantities of inventories, the auditors will evaluate the statistical validity of the sampling method and the propriety of the sampling risk and the allowance for sampling risk.

Advance planning by the senior auditor-in-charge is also necessary to ensure efficient use of audit staff members during the inventory taking. The auditor-in-charge should determine the dates of the counts, the extent of the test counts, the need for client assistance, the number of auditors needed at each location, and the estimated time required. When multiple locations are involved, the auditors must determine whether the assessed levels of inherent and control risk may justify omission of observation at certain locations. When only certain locations are to be observed, the auditors should consider not informing the client of the specific locations in advance. In addition, the observation should be planned in a manner so as to ensure that client employees are not aware of the exact nature of all items that are test-counted by the auditors.

Advance planning may also reveal to the auditors a need to rely upon the advice of a **specialist** for discharging their responsibility for testing inventory. For example, the auditors of a retail jeweler might engage an independent expert in gems to assist in identifying the precious stones and metals included in the client's inventory. Similarly, the auditors of a chemical producer might rely upon the expert opinion of an independent chemist as to the identity of components of the client's inventories. Guidelines for using the work of a specialist are presented in Chapter 5.

When written instructions are prepared by the auditing firm for the use of its staff in a particular engagement, these instructions are not made available to the client. Their purpose

FIGURE 12.4

GLEN HAVEN DEPARTMENT STORES, INC.

Instructions for Physical Inventory,
August 5, 200X

TO ALL SUPERVISORS:

A complete physical inventory of all departments in each store will be taken Sunday, August 5, 200X, beginning at 8:30 a.m. and continuing until completed. Employees are to report at 8:15 a.m. to receive their final briefing on their instructions, which are appended hereto.

Within one week prior to August 5, supervisors should make sure that merchandise in departments is well organized. All merchandise with the same stock number should be located together. Merchandise that is damaged should be segregated for separate listing on inventory sheets.

Each count team should be formed and started by a supervisor, and should be periodically observed by that supervisor to assure that instructions are being complied with in the counting and listing processes.

A block of sequential prenumbered inventory sheets will be issued to each supervisor at 8:00 a.m. August 5, for later issuance to count teams. Each supervisor is to account for all sheets—used, unused, or voided. In addition, each supervisor will be furnished at that time with a listing of count teams under his or her supervision.

When a count team reports completion of a department, that team's supervisor should accompany a representative of the independent auditors, McDonald & Company, in performing test counts. A space is provided on each inventory sheet for the supervisor's signature as reviewer. When the independent auditors have "cleared" a department, the supervisor responsible should take possession of the count sheets. All completed count sheets are to be placed in numerical sequence and turned over to me when the entire inventory has been completed.

Before supervisors and employees leave the stores Saturday evening, August 4, they are to make certain that "housekeeping" is in order in each department, and that all merchandise bears a price ticket.

If you have any questions about these instructions or any other aspect of the physical inventory, please see me.

J. R. Adams

J. R. Adams
Controller
July 24, 200X

---

is to help ensure that all auditors understand their assignments and can therefore work efficiently during the physical inventory. Figure 12.5 provides an example of such instructions.

3. Observe the Taking of Physical Inventory and Make Test Counts.

It is not the auditors' function to *take* the inventory or to control or supervise the taking; this is the responsibility of management. The auditors' responsibility is to *observe* the inventory taking. However, to observe the inventory taking implies a much more active role than that of a mere spectator. **Observation** by the auditors includes determining that all usable inventory owned by the client is included in the count and that the client's employees comply with the written inventory instructions. As part of the process of observing the physical inventory, the auditors will be alert to the possibility of inclusion of any obsolete or damaged merchandise in inventory. Excessive dust or rust on raw materials inventory items may be indicative of obsolescence or infrequent sale. Such merchandise should be segregated by the client and written down to its net realizable value.

The auditors will also *record the serial number of the final receiving and shipping documents issued before the taking of inventory* so that the accuracy of the cutoff can be determined at a

Primary Audit Objectives:	
Existence	☑
Completeness	☑
Rights	☑
Valuation	☑

FIGURE 12.5

MCDONALD & COMPANY
Certified Public Accountants

Glen Haven Department Stores, Inc.
Inventory Observation—Instructions for Audit Staff
August 1, 200X

We will observe physical inventory taking at the following stores of Glen Haven Department Stores, Inc., on August 5, 200X.

Store	Store Manager	Our Staff
Wilshire	J. M. Baker	John Rodgers, Faye Arnold
Crenshaw	Roberta Bryan	Weldon Simpkins
Valley	Hugh Remington	Roger Dawson

Report to assigned stores promptly at 8:00 a.m. Attached are copies of the company's detailed instructions to employees who are to take the physical inventories and to supervisors who are to be in charge. These instructions appear to be complete and adequate; we should satisfy ourselves by observation that the instructions are being followed.

All merchandise counted will be listed on prenumbered inventory sheets. We should make test counts of approximately 5 percent of the stock items to ascertain the accuracy of the physical counts. A majority of the counts should be performed on the high-value stock, as described on the enclosed listing. Test counts are to be recorded in working papers, with the following information included:
    Department number
    Inventory sheet number
    Stock number
    Description of item
    Quantity
    Selling price per price tag

We should ascertain that adequate control is maintained over the prenumbered inventory sheets issued. Also, we should prepare a listing of the last numbers used for transfers, markdowns, and markups in the various departments and stores. Inventory sheets are not to be removed from the departments until we have "cleared" them; we should not delay this operation.

Each staff member's working papers should include an opinion on the adequacy of the inventory taking. The papers should also include a summary of time incurred in the observation.

No cash or other cutoff procedures are to be performed as an adjunct to the inventory observation.

---

later date. Shipments or receipts of goods taking place during the counting process should be closely observed and any necessary reconciliations made. Observation of the physical inventory by the auditors also stresses determining that the client is controlling the inventory tags or sheets properly. These should be prenumbered so that all tags or sheets can be accounted for.

During the inventory observation, the auditors will make test counts of selected inventory items. The extent of the test counts will vary widely, depending upon levels of inherent risk and control risk and the materiality of the client's inventory. A representative number of test counts should be recorded in the audit working papers for subsequent comparison with the completed inventory listing.

Serially numbered (or computer-generated) inventory count tags are usually attached to each lot of goods during the taking of a physical inventory. The design of the tag and the procedures for using it are intended to guard against two common pitfalls: (*a*) accidental omission of goods from the count and (*b*) double counting of goods.

Illustrative Case
Fraudulent Misstatement of Inventories

Unscrupulous management has used a variety of methods to misstate inventories. One method involved recording fictitious inventory, sometimes in such quantities that the resulting total recorded inventory was in excess of the company's storage capacity. Another method involved placing scrap materials in product boxes to be counted as inventory. Two other methods involved retaining items in inventory, even though they had been recorded as sales (**bill and hold** schemes), and recording inventory that had been shipped between the company's warehouses in the inventory totals of more than one warehouse.

The ways in which management has circumvented the auditors' tests have also varied. In one instance, fictitious count sheets were created. In another situation, client personnel obtained knowledge of the items tested by the auditors and increased the recorded quantities of items not tested. Finally, client personnel have actually gained access to the auditors' working papers and altered them to support the fictitious inventory.

These cases illustrate the need for extreme care by the auditors in planning and performing inventory procedures.

Many companies use two-employee teams to count the inventories. Each team is provided with a sequence of the serially numbered tags and is required to return to the physical inventory supervisor any voided or unused tags.

The actual counting, the filling in of inventory tags, and the pulling of these tags are done by the client's employees. While the inventory tags are still attached to the goods, the auditors may make such test counts as they deem appropriate in the circumstances. The auditors will list in their working papers the tag numbers for which test counts were made. The client employees will not ordinarily collect (pull) the inventory tags until the auditors indicate that they are satisfied with the accuracy of the count.

In comparing their test counts to the inventory tags, the auditors are alert for errors not only in quantities but also in part numbers, descriptions, units of measure, and all other aspects of the inventory item. For test counts of goods in process inventory, the auditors must determine that the percentage or stage of completion indicated on the inventory tag is appropriate.

If the test counts made by the auditors indicate discrepancies, the goods are recounted at once by the client's employees and the error corrected. If an excessive number of errors is found, the inventories for the entire department or even for the entire company should be recounted.

The client often transfers the information listed on the inventory tags to serially numbered inventory sheets. These sheets are used in pricing the inventory and in summarizing the dollar amounts involved. After the inventory tags have been collected, the client employee supervising the inventory determines that all tags are accounted for by serial number. The auditors should ascertain that numerical control is maintained over both inventory tags and inventory sheets.

Clients using electronic equipment may facilitate inventory counting and summarizing through machine-readable inventory tags. Prior to the physical inventory, the tags may be encoded with tag numbers, part numbers, descriptions, and unit prices. After the physical inventory, the information from the tags is scanned into the computer, which extends quantity times unit price for each inventory item and prints out a complete inventory summary.

The test counts and tag numbers listed by the auditors in their working papers will be traced later to the client's inventory summary sheets. A discrepancy will be regarded not as an error in counting but as a mistake in copying data from the tags, a purposeful alteration of a tag, or the creation of a fictitious tag.

During the observation of physical inventories, the auditors should make inquiries to determine whether any of the materials or goods on hand are the property of others, such as goods held on **consignment** or customer-owned materials sent in for machine work or other processing.

Audit procedures applicable to goods held by the client on consignment may include a comparison of the physical inventory with the client's records of consigned goods on hand, review of contracts and correspondence with consignors, and direct written communication with the consignors to confirm the quantity and value of goods held at the balance sheet date and to disclose any client liability for unremitted sales proceeds or from inability to collect consignment accounts receivable.

Each auditor participating in the observation of the inventory will prepare working papers. These papers should indicate the extent of test counts, describe any deficiencies noted, and express a conclusion as to whether the physical inventory appeared to have been properly taken in accordance with the client's instructions. The auditor-in-charge should prepare a concise summary memorandum indicating the overall extent of observation and the percentage of inventory value covered by quantity tests. The memorandum may also include comments on the consideration given to the factors of quality and condition of stock, the treatment of consigned goods on hand, and the control of shipments and receipts during the counting process. Figure 12.6 illustrates this type of memorandum.

FIGURE 12.6

THE WILSHIRE CORPORATION
Comments on Observation of Physical Inventory   D-9

December 31, 200X

1. Advance Planning of Physical Inventory.

    A physical inventory was taken by the client on December 31, 200X. Two weeks in advance of this date we reviewed the written inventory instructions prepared by L. D. Frome, Controller. These instructions appeared entirely adequate and reflected the experience gained during the counts of previous years. The plan called for a complete closing down of the factory on December 31, since the preceding year's count had been handicapped by movements of productive material during the counting process. Training meetings were conducted by Frome for all employees assigned to participate in the inventory; at these meetings the written instructions were explained and discussed.

2. Observation of Physical Inventory.

    We were present throughout the taking of physical inventory on December 31, 200X. Prior to the count, all materials had been neatly arranged, labeled, and separated by type. Two-employee inventory teams were used: one employee counting and calling quantities and descriptions; the other employee filling in data on the serially numbered inventory tags. As the goods were counted, the counting team tore off the "first count" portion of the inventory tag. A second count was made later by another team working independently of the first; this second team recorded the quantity of its count on the "second count" portion of the tag.

    We made test counts of numerous items, covering approximately 60 percent of the total inventory value. These counts were recorded on our working papers and used as noted below. Our observation throughout the plant indicated that both the first and second counts required by the inventory instructions were being performed in a systematic and conscientious manner. The careful and alert attitude of employees indicated that the training meetings preceding the count had been quite effective in creating an understanding of the importance of an accurate count. Before the "second count" portions of the tags were removed, we visited all departments in the company with Frome and satisfied ourselves that all goods had been tagged and counted.

    No goods were shipped on December 31. We ascertained that receiving reports were prepared on all goods taken into the receiving department on this day. We recorded the serial numbers of the last receiving report and the last shipping advice for the year 200X. (See D-9-1.) We compared the quantities per the count with perpetual inventory records and found no significant discrepancies.

3. Quality and Condition of Materials.

    Certain obsolete parts had been removed from stock prior to the count and reduced to a scrap carrying value. On the basis of our personal observation and questions addressed to supervisors, we have no reason to believe that any obsolete or defective materials remained in inventory. During the course of inventory observation, we tested the reasonableness of quantities of 10 items, representing 40 percent of the value of the inventory, by comparing the quantity on hand with the quantity used in recent months; in no case did we find that the quantity in inventory exceeded three months' normal usage.

                                                                        V.M.H.
                                                                        Jan. 3, 0Y

Inventories in Public Warehouses and on Consignment

Companies that store inventories in public warehouses ordinarily receive receipts for those goods. Examination of these receipts is not sufficient verification of goods stored in public warehouses. The AICPA has recommended direct confirmation in writing from outside custodians of inventories and supplementary procedures when the amounts involved represent a significant proportion of the current assets or of the total assets of a concern. These supplementary procedures include review of the client's procedures for investigating prospective warehouses and evaluating the performance of warehouses having custody of the client's goods. The auditors should also consider obtaining accountants' reports on the warehouses' controls relevant to custody of stored goods. If the amounts are quite material, or if any reason for doubt exists, the auditors may decide to visit the warehouses and observe a physical inventory of the client's merchandise stored at the warehouses.

A starting point for the verification of goods in the hands of consignees is to obtain from the client a list of all consignees and copies of the consignment contracts. Contract provisions concerning the payment of freight and other handling charges, the extension of credit, computation of commissions, and frequency of reports and remittances require close attention. After review of the contracts and the client's records of consignment shipments and collections, the auditors should communicate directly with the consignees and obtain full written information on consigned inventory, receivables, unremitted proceeds, and accrued expenses and commissions as of the balance sheet date.

Often, the client may own raw materials that are processed by a subcontractor before being used in the client's production process. The auditors should request the subcontractor to confirm quantities and descriptions of client-owned materials in the subcontractor's possession.

Inventory Verification When Auditors Are Engaged After the End of the Year

A company desiring an independent audit should engage the auditors well before the end of the year so they can participate in advance planning of the physical inventory and be prepared to observe the actual counting process. Occasionally, however, auditors are not engaged until after the end of the year and therefore find it impossible to observe the taking of inventory at the close of the year. For example, the illness or death of a company's individual practitioner CPA near the year-end might lead to the engagement of new auditors shortly after the balance sheet date.

Under these circumstances, the auditors may conclude that sufficient competent evidence cannot be obtained concerning inventories to permit them to express an opinion on the overall fairness of the financial statements. On the other hand, under other circumstances, the auditors may be able to obtain satisfaction concerning the inventories by alternative auditing procedures. These favorable circumstances might include the existence of strong internal control, perpetual inventory records, availability of instructions and other records showing that the client had carried out a well-planned physical inventory at or near the year-end, and the making of test counts by the newly appointed auditors. If the auditors are to express an unqualified opinion, their investigation of inventories must include some physical contact with items of inventory and must be thorough enough to compensate for the fact that they were not present when the physical inventory was taken. Whether such alternative auditing procedures will be feasible and will enable the auditors to satisfy themselves depends upon the circumstances of the particular engagement.

4. Review the Year-End Cutoff of Purchases and Sales Transactions.

Primary Audit Objectives:	
Existence	☑
Completeness	☑
Rights	☑
Valuation	☑

An accurate cutoff of purchases is one of the most important factors in verifying the existence and completeness of the year-end inventory. Assume that a shipment of goods costing $10,000 is received from a supplier on December 31, but the purchase invoice does not arrive until January 2 and is entered as a January transaction. If the goods are included in the December 31 physical inventory but there is no December entry to record the purchase and the liability, the result will be an overstatement of both net income for the year and retained earnings and an understatement of accounts payable, each error being in the full amount of $10,000 (ignoring income taxes).

An opposite situation may arise if a purchase invoice is received and recorded on December 31, but the merchandise covered by the invoice is not received until several days later and is not included in the physical inventory taken at the year-end. The effect on the financial statements of recording a purchase without including the goods in the inventory is to understate net income, retained earnings, and inventory.

How can the auditors determine that the liability to suppliers has been recorded for all goods included in inventory? Their approach is to *examine on a test basis the purchase invoices and receiving reports for several days before and after the inventory date.* Each purchase invoice in the files should have a receiving report attached; if an invoice recorded in late December is accompanied by a receiving report dated December 31 or earlier, the goods must have been on hand and included in the year-end physical inventory. However, if the receiving report carried a January date, the goods were not included in the physical count made on December 31.

A supplementary approach to the matching of purchase invoices and receiving reports is to examine the records of the receiving department. For each shipment received near the year-end, the auditors should determine that the related purchase invoice was recorded in the same period.

The effect on the financial statements of failing to include a year-end in-transit purchase as part of physical inventory is often not a serious one, *provided* the related liability is not recorded until the following period. In other words, a primary point in effecting an accurate cutoff of purchases is that both sides of a purchase transaction must be reflected in the same accounting period. If a given shipment is included in the year-end physical inventory of the purchaser, the entry debiting Inventories and crediting Accounts Payable must be made. If the shipment is not included in the purchaser's year-end physical inventory, the purchase invoice must not be recorded until the following period.

Adjustments to achieve an accurate cutoff of purchases should, of course, be made by the client's staff; the function of the auditors should be to review the cutoff and determine that the necessary adjustments have been made.

Chapter 11 includes a discussion of the audit procedures for determining the accuracy of the sales cutoff. The sales cutoff is mentioned again at this point to emphasize its importance in determining the fairness of the client's inventory and cost of goods sold as well as accounts receivable and sales.

5. Obtain a Copy of the Completed Physical Inventory, Test Its Clerical Accuracy, and Trace Test Counts.

Primary Audit Objectives:

Existence ☑
Completeness ☑
Rights ☑
Valuation ☑

The testing of extensions and footings on the final inventory listing may disclose misstatements of physical inventories. Often this test consists of "sight-footing" to the nearest hundred dollars or thousand dollars of the inventory listings. Generalized audit software may also be used to test extensions and footings.

In testing extensions, the auditors should be alert for two sources of substantial errors—misplaced decimal points and incorrect extension of *count* units by *price* units. For example, an inventory listing that extends 1,000 units times $1C (per hundred) as $1,000 will be overstated by $990. An inventory extension of 1,000 sheets of steel times $1 per pound will be substantially understated if each sheet of steel weighs more than one pound.

The auditors also should trace to the completed physical inventory their test counts made during the observation of physical inventory. During this tracing, the auditors should be alert for any indications that inventory tags have been altered or that fictitious inventory tags have been created. The auditors also reconcile inventory tag number sequences in the physical inventory listing to tag numbers noted in their audit working papers for the inventory observation. This procedure is designed to determine that the client has not omitted inventory items from the listing or included additional items that were not present during the physical inventory.

Another test of the clerical accuracy of the completed physical inventory is the reconciliation of the physical counts to inventory records. Both the quantities and the values of the items should be compared to the company's perpetual records. The totals of various sections of inventory should also be compared with the corresponding control accounts. All substantial discrepancies should be investigated fully. The number, type, and cause of the discrepancies revealed by such comparisons are highly significant in assessing control risk for inventories.

Illustrative Case
Fraudulent Financial Reporting at U.S. Foodservices

An alleged fraud at U.S. Foodservices (USF) provides an illustration of the often complex nature of inventory valuation. In a typical promotional allowance arrangement, USF would pay the full wholesale price for a product and then receive rebates of a portion of the price from the supplier if certain purchase volume and other conditions were met.

To meet earnings targets, federal prosecutors charged that nine former USF employees overstated the promotional allowances (and earnings) by more than $800,000,000. To hide the fraud, USF convinced suppliers to return confirmations to auditors confirming the fraudulent amounts.

Participation by the suppliers makes this sort of fraud extremely difficult—and perhaps, impossible—for auditors to detect. It is possible that industry knowledge would lead the auditors to question the large amount of allowances. Also, if details of the computation of allowances are included in sales agreements, the auditors could calculate the proper amounts and compare them with the recorded amounts. However, if the allowances are based on unwritten side agreements between the parties, examining agreements will not be effective in detecting the misstatements. Certainly, subsequent years' results will reveal the misstatements.

Primary Audit Objective:

Valuation ☑

6. Evaluate the Bases and Methods of Inventory Pricing.

The auditors are responsible for determining that the bases and methods of pricing inventory are in accordance with generally accepted accounting principles. The investigation of inventory pricing often will emphasize the following three questions:

1. What method of pricing does the client use?
2. Is the method of pricing the same as that used in prior years?
3. Has the method selected by the client been applied consistently and accurately in practice?

For the first question—the method of pricing—a long list of alternatives is possible, including such methods as cost; cost or market, whichever is lower; the retail method; and quoted market price (as for metals and staple commodities traded on organized exchanges). The cost method, of course, includes many diverse systems, such as last-in, first-out (LIFO); first-in, first-out (FIFO); specific identification; weighted average; and standard cost.

The second question raised in this section concerns a change in method of pricing inventory from one year to the next. For example, let us say that the client has changed from the FIFO method to the LIFO method. The nature and justification of the change in method of valuing inventory and its effect on income should be disclosed in accordance with the provisions of *APB Opinion No. 20,* "Accounting Changes." In addition, the auditors must insert in the audit report an explanatory paragraph concerning the lack of consistency between the two years.

The third question posed deals with consistent accurate application in practice of the method of valuation adopted by the client. To answer this question the auditors must test the pricing of a representative number of inventory items.

Primary Audit Objective:

Valuation ☑

7. Test the Pricing of Inventories.

The testing of prices applied to inventories of raw materials, purchased parts, and supplies by a manufacturing company is similar to the testing of prices of merchandise in a trading business. In both cases the cost of inventory items, whether LIFO, FIFO, weighted average, or specific identification, is readily verified by reference to purchase invoices. An illustration of a computerized working paper prepared by an auditor in making price tests of an inventory of raw materials and purchased parts is presented in Figure 12.7.

Audit procedures for verification of the inventory values assigned to goods in process and finished goods are not so simple and conclusive as in the case of raw materials or merchandise for which purchase invoices are readily available. To determine whether the inventory valuation method used by the client has been properly applied, the auditors must make tests of the pricing of selected items of finished goods and goods in process. The pricing of these items must be tested by reference to the client's cost accounting records of accumulated direct

FIGURE 12.7 Test of Inventory Pricing

The Wilshire Corporation
Test of Pricing—Raw Materials and Purchased Parts
December 31, 200X   D-5

Part No.	Description	Per Inventory Quantity/Price	Per Vendor's Invoice				
			Vendor	Date	No.	Quantity @ Price	
8Z 182	Aluminum 48 x 144 x .025	910 sheets @ 10.10	Hardy & Co.	Dec. 18, 0X	5415	1000 @ 10.10	✓
8Z 195	Aluminum 45/72 x .032	804 sheets @ 9.01	Watson Mfg. Co.	Nov. 28, 0X	3201	500 @ 9.01	✓
				Dec. 22, 0X	3456	400 @ 9.01	✓
K1125	Stainless steel .025 x 23	80,625 lbs @ .80	Ajax Steel Co.	Dec. 3, 0X	K182	100,000 @ .80	✓
K1382	Stainless steel .031 x 17	65,212 lbs @ .82	Ajax Steel Co.	Dec. 3, 0X	K182	75,000 @ .82	✓
XL3925	10 H.P. Electronic Motor	50 units @ 400.00	Cronyn Mfg. Co.	Nov. 18, 0X	D2532	100 @ 400.00	✓
XJ3824	3/4 H.P. Electronic Motor	645 units @ 30.50	Long & Co.	Dec. 29, 0X	E9215	650 @ 30.50	✓

Inventory value of raw materials and purchased parts selected for price testing—$301,825.56.

Percent of total raw materials and purchased parts selected for price testing—$301,825.56/$503,615.10 = 60%.

See audit program B-4 for method of selecting raw materials and purchased parts for price testing.

✓ = Agreed to prices on the vendor's invoice.

Conclusion:

Based on our tests, the pricing of raw materials and purchased parts appears to be materially correct.

CMB
1/4/0Y

material, direct labor, and manufacturing overhead costs. Items of large total value will be selected for testing so that the tests will encompass a significant portion of the dollar amount of inventories.

Lower-of-Cost-or-Market Test

As a general rule, inventories should not be carried at an amount in excess of net realizable value. The lower-of-cost-or-market rule is a common means of measuring any loss of utility in the inventories. A lower-of-cost-or-market test generally involves comparing the recorded cost of a sample of inventory items with the items' net realizable values.

8. Perform Analytical Procedures.

Material misstatements of inventory may be disclosed by analytical procedures designed to establish the general reasonableness of inventory figures. As an example, major increases or decreases in the amounts of various types of inventory as compared to prior-year amounts may be identified and investigated.

In certain lines of business, particularly retail and wholesale companies, gross profit margins may be quite uniform from year to year. Any major difference between the ending inventory estimated by the gross profit percentage method and the count of inventory at year-end should be investigated fully. If the client has inventory in a number of stores, some of which were not visited by the auditors, comparing gross profit by store may reveal overstatements in those not visited.

Another useful test is the computation of rates of inventory turnover (preferably by individual product) based on the relationship between the cost of goods sold for the year and the average inventory as shown on the monthly financial statements. These turnover rates may be compared with rates prevailing in prior years. A decreasing rate of turnover suggests the

Primary Audit Objectives:	
Existence	☑
Completeness	☑
Rights	☑
Valuation	☑

possibility of obsolescence or of unnecessarily large amounts of inventories. Scanning perpetual inventory records may also reveal obsolete items.

> ### Focus on the Computer Hardware and Software Industry
> Given the pace of technological advances and the highly competitive nature of the computer hardware and software industry, rapid inventory obsolescence is common. Product life cycles are typically short and competitive products with superior price and performance can quickly enter the marketplace. Analytical procedures may be used to determine whether inventory amounts and trends appear proper. However, simply making comparisons of the current year's amounts and ratios to those of prior years is not effective. The auditors must consider what is expected to happen in the industry. In developing expected amounts for analytical procedures, consideration must be given to expected future demand for the client's products and anticipated technological advances that render existing inventories obsolete. The auditors may find analyses of management's sales forecasts useful for this purpose.

The auditors' analytical procedures for inventory transactions will often include a comparison of the volume of purchase transactions from period to period. Comparisons of transactions, classified by vendor and type of product, may reveal unusual variations of quantities purchased or unusual concentrations of purchases with particular vendors, indicating possible conflicts of interest.

The auditors also should scan all general ledger accounts relating to cost of goods sold to make certain that they contain no apparent misstatements. For example, the auditors may discover that miscellaneous revenue and expenses were erroneously closed into cost of goods sold.

The auditors of a manufacturer should obtain from the client or prepare an analysis of costs of goods sold by month, broken down into raw materials, direct labor, and factory overhead elements. The analysis should also include a description of all unusual and nonrecurring charges or credits to cost of goods sold.

Using Nonfinancial Information

Using nonfinancial information for developing expectations for analytical procedures can be especially effective for inventories. For example, when the client has inventory stored in a number of warehouses, the auditor may compare the amount of inventory stored in each warehouse with its size in square feet. Comparisons can also be made between inventory in dollars and in units, and for a manufacturing firm, inventory and cost of goods sold amounts may be compared to various production statistics, such as direct labor-hours and machine-hours.

Primary Audit Objectives:	
Valuation	☑
Presentation	☑

9. Determine Whether Any Inventories Have Been Pledged and Review Purchase and Sales Commitments.

The verification of inventories includes a determination by the auditors as to whether any goods have been pledged or subjected to a lien of any kind. Pledging of inventories to secure bank loans may be brought to light when bank balances and indebtedness are confirmed.

A record of outstanding **purchase commitments** is usually readily available, since this information is essential to management in maintaining day-to-day control of the company's inventory position and cash flow.

In some lines of business, it is customary to enter into firm contracts for the purchase of merchandise or materials well in advance of the scheduled delivery dates. Comparison by the auditors of the prices quoted in such commitments with the vendors' prices prevailing at the balance sheet date may indicate substantial losses if firm purchase commitments are not protected by firm sales contracts. Such losses should be reflected in the financial statements.

The quantities of purchase commitments should be reviewed in the light of current and prospective demand, as indicated by past operations, the backlog of sales orders, and current conditions within the industry. If quantities on order appear excessive by these standards, the auditors should seek full information on this phase of operations. Purchase commitments may need to be disclosed in the financial statements.

Sales commitments are indicated by the client's *backlog* of unfilled sales orders. Losses inherent in firm sales commitments are generally recognized in the lower-of-cost-or-market valuation of inventories, with *market* being defined as the net realizable value of the goods in process or finished goods inventories applicable to the sales commitments. In addition, the backlog may include sales orders for which no production has been started as of the balance sheet date. The auditors must review the client's cost estimates for these sales orders. If estimated total costs to produce the goods ordered exceed fixed sales prices, the indicated loss and a related liability should be recorded in the client's financial statements for the current period.

Primary Audit Objective:
Presentation ☑

10. Evaluate Financial Statement Presentation of Inventories and Cost of Goods Sold, Including the Adequacy of Disclosure.

One of the most important factors in proper presentation of inventories in the financial statements is disclosure of the inventory pricing method or methods in use. Other important disclosures include the following:

1. Changes in methods of valuing inventory, with the dollar effect and justification for the change reported, in accordance with *APB Opinion No. 20.*
2. The various classifications of inventory, such as finished goods, work in process, and raw materials.
3. The details of any arrangements relating to any pledged inventory.
4. Deduction of valuation allowance for inventory losses.
5. Existence and terms of inventory purchase commitments.

The auditors will review the client's disclosures of such matters to determine whether they comply with generally accepted accounting principles.

Problems Associated with Inventory of First-Year Audit Clients

The need for the auditors to be present to observe the taking of the ending inventory has been strongly emphasized in auditing literature. However, the figure for beginning inventory is equally significant in determining the cost of goods sold and the net income for the year. In the initial audit of a client, the auditors may not have been present to observe the taking of inventory at the beginning of the year. What procedures can they follow to obtain evidence that the beginning inventories are fairly stated?

The first factor to consider is whether another CPA firm audited the client for the preceding year. If a review of the predecessor firm's working papers indicates compliance with generally accepted auditing standards, the new auditors can accept the beginning inventories with a minimum of investigation. That minimum might include the following steps: (1) study of the inventory valuation methods used, (2) review of the inventory records, (3) review of the inventory sheets used in taking the preceding year's physical inventory, and (4) comparison of the beginning and ending inventories, broken down by product classification.

If there was no satisfactory audit for the preceding year, the investigation of the beginning inventories would include not only the procedures mentioned above but also the following steps: (1) discussion with the person in the client's organization who supervised the physical inventory at the preceding balance sheet date, (2) study of the written instructions used in planning the inventory, (3) tracing of numerous items from the inventory tags or count sheets to the final summary sheets, (4) tests of the perpetual inventory records for the preceding period by reference to supporting documents for receipts and withdrawals, and (5) tests of the overall reasonableness of the beginning inventories in relation to sales, gross profit, and rate of inventory turnover. An investigation along these lines will sometimes give the auditors assurance that the beginning inventory was carefully compiled and reasonable in amount; in other cases, these procedures may raise serious doubts as to the validity of the beginning inventory figure. In these latter cases, the auditors will not be able to issue an unqualified opinion as to *statements of income and cash flows.* They may be able, however, to give an unqualified opinion on the *balance sheet,* since this financial statement does not reflect the beginning inventories.

Chapter Summary

This chapter described details of the controls over inventories and cost of goods sold, the auditors' consideration of these controls, and substantive tests of inventories and cost of goods sold. To summarize:

1. The audit of inventories presents the auditors with significant risk because: (*a*) they often represent a very substantial portion of current assets, (*b*) numerous valuation methods are used for inventories, (*c*) the valuation of inventories directly affects cost of goods sold, and (*d*) the determination of inventory quality, condition, and value is inherently complex.

2. Effective internal control over inventories requires appropriate controls over purchasing, receiving, and issuing, supplies and materials, producing and shipping products, and cost accounting. A perpetual inventory system is also important.

3. The auditors' objectives in the audit of inventories and cost of goods sold are to: (*a*) consider inherent risks; (*b*) consider relevant controls; (*c*) establish the existence of, and the client's rights to, inventories; (*d*) establish the completeness of inventories; (*e*) determine that inventories and cost of goods sold are valued in accordance with GAAP; and (*f*) determine that presentation and disclosures of inventory accounts are appropriate.

4. The auditors' consideration of inherent risks and the controls over inventories, purchases, and production will allow them to design appropriate substantive tests of inventory and cost of goods sold accounts.

5. In the audit of inventories, auditors are primarily concerned about the existence assertion, that is, the possibility of overstatement of year-end balances. Therefore, a primary substantive test for inventory accounts is observation of the client's physical inventory. Other substantive procedures include price tests of the valuation of inventory items, cutoff tests, analytical procedures, and tests of the financial statement presentation and disclosure.

Key Terms Introduced or Emphasized in Chapter 12

Bill and hold transactions   Transactions in which sales of merchandise are billed to customers prior to delivery, with the goods being held by the seller. These transactions may overstate revenues and net income if they do not meet specific requirements for recognition as sales.

Bill of lading   A document issued by a common carrier acknowledging the receipt of goods and setting forth the provisions of the transportation agreement.

Consignment   A transfer of goods from the owner to another person who acts as the sales agent of the owner.

Cost Accounting Standards Board   A five-member board established by Congress to narrow the options in cost accounting that are available under generally accepted accounting principles. Companies having significant supply contracts with certain U.S. government agencies are subject to the cost accounting standards established by the board.

Electronic data interchange (EDI)   A system in which data are exchanged electronically between the computers of different companies. In an EDI system source documents are replaced with electronic transactions created in a standard format.

Job time tickets   A document designed to accumulate the labor and machine time devoted to a particular production order.

Master production schedule   A schedule that is used to plan overall production for a period of time. The schedule illustrates the gross production of each of the company's products.

Observation   The auditors' evidence-gathering technique of viewing a client activity to obtain physical evidence of performance.

Periodic inventory system   A method of accounting in which inventories are determined solely by means of a physical inventory at the end of the accounting period.

Perpetual inventory system   A method of accounting for inventories in which controlling accounts and subsidiary ledgers are maintained to record receipts and issuances of goods, both in quantities and in dollar amounts. The accuracy of perpetual inventory records is tested periodically by physical inventories.

Production order   A document that authorizes the production of a specific quantity of a product.

Purchase commitment   A contractual obligation to purchase goods at fixed prices, entered into well in advance of scheduled delivery dates.

Sales commitment   A contractual obligation to sell goods at fixed prices, entered into well in advance of scheduled delivery dates.

Specialist   A person possessing special skill or knowledge in a field other than accounting or auditing, such as a real estate appraiser.

Review Questions

12–1. Many auditors consider the substantiation of the figure for inventory to be a more difficult and challenging task than the verification of most other items on the balance sheet. List several specific factors that support this view.

12–2. Explain the significance of the purchase order to adequate internal control over purchase transactions.

12–3. What segregation of duties would you recommend to attain maximum internal control over purchasing activities in a manufacturing concern?

12–4. Do you believe that the normal review of purchase transactions by the auditors should include examination of receiving reports? Explain.

12–5. The client's cost accounting system is often an important part of the CPAs' audit of the financial statements of a manufacturing company. For what purposes do the auditors consider the cost accounting system?

12–6. What part, if any, do the independent auditors play in the planning for a client's physical inventory?

12–7. What are the purposes of the auditors' observation of the taking of the physical inventory? (Do not discuss the procedures or techniques involved in making the observation.)

12–8. For what purposes do the auditors make and record test counts of inventory quantities during their observation of the taking of the physical inventory? Discuss.

12–9. Once the auditors have completed their test counts of the physical inventory, will they have any reason to make later reference to the inventory tags used by the client's employees in the counting process? Explain.

12–10. When perpetual inventory records are maintained, is it necessary for a physical inventory to be taken at the balance sheet date? Explain.

12–11. What is meant by a "bill and hold" scheme?

12–12. What charges and credits may be disclosed in the auditors' analysis of the Cost of Goods Sold account of a manufacturing concern?

12–13. A client company wishes to conduct its physical inventory on a sampling basis. Many items will not be counted. Under what general conditions will this method of taking inventory be acceptable to the auditors?

12–14. Hana Ranch Company, which has never been audited, is asked on October 1 by its bank to arrange for a year-end audit. The company retains you to make this audit and asks what measures, if any, it should take to ensure a satisfactory year-end physical inventory. Perpetual inventories are not maintained. How would you answer this inquiry?

12–15. "A well-prepared balance sheet usually includes a statement that the inventories are valued at cost." Evaluate this quotation.

12–16. Darnell Equipment Company uses the LIFO method of valuation for part of its inventories and weighted-average cost for another portion. Would you be willing to issue an unqualified opinion under these circumstances? Explain.

12–17. "If the auditors can determine that all goods in the physical inventory have been accurately counted and properly priced, they will have discharged fully their responsibility with respect to inventory." Evaluate this statement.

12–18. How do the independent auditors use the client's backlog of unfilled sales orders in the examination of inventories?

12–19. The controller of a new client company informs you that most of the inventories are stored in bonded public warehouses. He presents warehouse receipts to account for the inventories. Will careful examination of these warehouse receipts constitute adequate verification of these inventories? Explain.

12–20. Enumerate specific steps to be taken by the auditors to ascertain that a client's inventories have not been pledged or subjected to a lien of any kind.

Questions Requiring Analysis

12–21. Nolan Manufacturing Company retains you on April 1 to perform an audit for the fiscal year ending June 30. During the month of May, you make extensive studies of internal control over inventories.

All goods purchased pass through a receiving department under the direction of the chief purchasing agent. The duties of the receiving department are to unpack, count, and inspect the goods. The quantity received is compared with the quantity shown on the receiving department's copy of the purchase order. If there is no discrepancy, the purchase order is stamped "OK—Receiving Dept." and forwarded to the accounts payable section of the accounting department. Any discrepancies in quantity or variations from specifications are called to the attention of the buyer by returning the purchase order to him with an explanation of the circumstances. No records are maintained in the receiving department, and no reports originate there.

As soon as goods have been inspected and counted in the receiving department, they are sent to the factory production area and stored alongside the machines in which they are to be processed. Finished goods are moved from the assembly line to a storeroom in the custody of a stock clerk, who maintains a perpetual inventory record in terms of physical units, but not in dollars.

What weaknesses, if any, do you see in the internal control over inventories?

12–22. At the beginning of your annual audit of Crestview Manufacturing Company's financial statements for the year ended December 31, 200X, the company president confides in you that Henry Ward, an employee, is living on a scale in excess of that which his salary would support.

The employee has been a buyer in the purchasing department for six years and has charge of purchasing all general materials and supplies. He is authorized to sign purchase orders for amounts up to $500. Purchase orders in excess of $500 require the countersignature of the general purchasing agent.

The president understands that the usual audit of financial statements is not designed, and cannot be relied upon, to provide absolute assurance that fraud and conflicts of interest will be discovered, although their discovery may result. The president authorizes you, however, to expand your regular audit procedures and to apply additional audit procedures to determine whether there is any evidence that the buyer has been misappropriating company funds or has been engaged in activities that were conflicts of interest.

Required: List the audit procedures you would apply to the company records and documents in an attempt to discover evidence within the purchasing department of defalcations being committed by the buyer. Give the purpose of each audit procedure.

(AICPA, adapted)

12–23. A number of companies employ outside service companies that specialize in counting, pricing, extending, and footing inventories. These service companies usually furnish a certificate attesting to the value of the physical inventory.

Assuming that the service company took the client company's inventory on the balance sheet date:

a. How much reliance, if any, can the auditors place on the inventory certificate of outside specialists? Discuss.

b. What effect, if any, would the inventory certificate of outside specialists have upon the type of report the auditors would render? Discuss.

c. What reference, if any, would the auditors make to the certificate of outside specialists in their audit report?

(AICPA, adapted)

12–24. Ace Corporation does not conduct a complete annual physical count of purchased parts and supplies in its principal warehouse, but uses statistical sampling instead to estimate the year-end inventory. Ace maintains a perpetual inventory record of parts and supplies and believes that statistical sampling is highly effective in determining inventory values and is sufficiently reliable so as to make a physical count of each item of inventory unnecessary.

Required: *a.* Identify the audit procedures that should be used by the independent auditor that change or are in addition to normal required audit procedures when a client utilizes statistical sampling to determine inventory value and does not conduct a 100 percent annual physical count of inventory items.

b. List at least 10 normal audit procedures that should be performed to verify physical quantities whenever a client conducts a periodic physical count of all or part of its inventory.

(AICPA, adapted)

12–25. The observation of a client's physical inventory is a mandatory auditing procedure when possible for the auditors to carry out and when inventories are material.

Required:

   a. Why is the observation of physical inventory a mandatory auditing procedure? Explain.

   b. Under what circumstances is observation of physical inventory impossible?

   c. Why is the auditors' review of the client's control of inventory tags important during the observation of physical inventory? Explain.

12–26. During your observation of the November 30, 200X, physical inventory of Jay Company, you note the following unusual items:

   a. Electric motors in finished goods storeroom not tagged. Upon inquiry, you are informed that the motors are on consignment to Jay Company.

   b. A cutting machine (one of Jay's principal products) in the receiving department, with a large "REWORK" tag attached.

   c. A crated cutting machine in the shipping department, addressed to a nearby U.S. naval base, with a Department of Defense "Material Inspection and Receiving Report" attached, dated November 30, 200X, and signed by the Navy Source Inspector.

   d. A small, isolated storeroom with five types of dusty raw materials stored therein. Inventory tags are attached to all of the materials, and your test counts agree with the tags.

Required:

What additional procedures, if any, would you carry out for each of the above? Explain.

12–27. Santa Rosa Corporation is a closely held furniture manufacturing company employing approximately one thousand employees. On December 15, the corporation retained the firm of Warren and Wood, Certified Public Accountants, to perform a December 31 year-end audit. The president of the corporation explained that perpetual inventory records were maintained and that every attention was given to maintaining strong internal control. A complete count of inventories had been made at November 30 by the company's own employees; in addition, extensive test counts had been made in most departments at various intervals during the year. Although the company was not large, it employed an internal auditor and an assistant who had devoted their full time to analysis of internal control and appraisal of operations in the various organizational units of the company.

The certified public accountant who had audited Santa Rosa Corporation for several years had died during the current year, and the company had decided to forgo an annual audit. The physical inventory had therefore been taken at November 30 without being observed by an independent public accountant. Shortly thereafter, a major stockholder in the company had demanded that new auditors be retained. The president explained to Warren and Wood that the company was too far behind on its delivery schedules to take time out for another physical inventory, but that all the papers used in the recent count were available for their review. The auditors reviewed these papers, made a thorough analysis of the controls over inventory, and made test counts at December 31 of large items representing 10 percent of the total value of inventory. The items tested were traced to the perpetual inventory records, and no significant discrepancies were found. Inventories at December 31 amounted to $4 million out of total assets of $9 million.

Required:

Assume that the auditors find no shortcomings in any aspect of the audit apart from the area of inventories. You are to prepare:

   a. An argument setting forth the factors that indicate the issuance of an unqualified audit opinion.

   b. An opposing argument setting forth the factors that indicate the auditors should not issue an unqualified opinion.

12–28. One of the problems faced by the auditors in their verification of inventory is the possibility that slow-moving and obsolete items may be included in the goods on hand at the balance sheet date. In the event that such items are identified in the physical inventory, their carrying value should be written down to an estimated scrap value or other recoverable amount.

Prepare a list of the auditing procedures that the auditors should employ to determine whether slow-moving or obsolete items are included in the physical inventory.

12–29. You are engaged in the audit of Reed Company, a new client, at the end of its first fiscal year, June 30, 20X1. During your work on inventories, you discover that all of the merchandise remaining in stock on June 30, 20X1, had been acquired July 1, 20X0, from Andrew Reed, the sole shareholder and president of Reed Company, for an original selling price of $10,000 cash and a note payable due July 1, 20X3, with interest at 15 percent, in the amount of $90,000. The merchandise had been used by the president when he operated a similar business as a sole proprietor.

How can you verify the pricing of the June 30, 20X1, inventory of Reed Company? Explain.

12–30. Many CPAs are sharing information over the Internet. Auditnet is an Internet site that contains audit programs donated by various CPAs. Auditnet's address is www.auditnet.org. You can get to the audit programs by selecting the "audit programs" category.

a. Select the inventory program, and summarize the procedures for testing inventory cutoff.

b. Describe the inspection procedures done by the auditors when they arrive at an inventory location for their observation.

12–31. Grandview Manufacturing Company employs standard costs in its cost accounting system. List the audit procedures that you would apply to ascertain that Grandview's standard costs and related variance amounts are acceptable and have not distorted the financial statements. (Confine your audit procedures to those applicable to raw materials.)

Multiple Choice Questions

12–32. Select the best answer for each of the following and explain fully the reason for your selection.

a. Which of the following is *least* likely to be among the auditors' objectives in the audit of inventories and cost of goods sold?

(1) Determine that the valuation of inventories and cost of goods sold is arrived at by appropriate methods.

(2) Determine the existence of inventories and the occurrence of transactions affecting cost of goods sold.

(3) Establish that the client includes only inventory on hand at year-end in inventory totals.

(4) Establish the completeness of inventories.

b. The receiving department is *least* likely to be responsible for the:

(1) Determination of quantities of goods received.

(2) Detection of damaged or defective merchandise.

(3) Preparation of a shipping document.

(4) Transmittal of goods received to the store's department.

c. The document issued by a common carrier acknowledging the receipt of goods and setting forth the provisions of the transportation agreement is the:

(1) Bill of lading.

(2) Job time shipping.

(3) Production order.

(4) Production schedule.

d. Which of the following should be included as a part of inventory costs of a manufacturing company?

	Direct Labor	Raw Materials	Factory Overhead
(1)	Yes	Yes	Yes
(2)	Yes	No	No
(3)	No	Yes	No
(4)	No	No	No

e. The organization established by Congress to narrow the options in cost accounting that are available under generally accepted accounting principles is the

(1) Cost Accounting Standards Board.

(2) Financial Accounting Standards Board.

(3) Public Company Accounting Oversight Board.

(4) Securities and Exchange Commission.

f. When a primary risk related to an audit is possible overstated inventory, the assertion most directly related is:

(1) Existence.

(2) Completeness.

(3) Clarity.

(4) Presentation.

g. Instead of taking a physical inventory count on the balance-sheet date, the client may take physical counts prior to the year-end if internal control is adequate and:

(1) Computerized records of perpetual inventory are maintained.

(2) Inventory is slow-moving.

(3) Computer error reports are generated for missing prenumbered inventory tickets.

(4) Obsolete inventory items are segregated and excluded.

h. The auditor's analytical procedures will be facilitated if the client:

(1) Uses a standard cost system that produces variance reports.

(2) Segregates obsolete inventory before the physical inventory count.

(3) Corrects material weaknesses in internal control before the beginning of the audit.

(4) Reduces inventory balances to the lower of cost or market.

i. When perpetual inventory records are maintained in quantities and in dollars, and internal control over inventory is weak, the auditor would probably:

(1) Want the client to schedule the physical inventory count at the end of the year.

(2) Insist that the client perform physical counts of inventory items several times during the year.

(3) Increase the extent of tests for unrecorded liabilities at the end of the year.

(4) Have to disclaim an opinion on the income statement for that year.

j. Which of the following is the best audit procedure for the discovery of damaged merchandise in a client's ending inventory?

(1) Compare the physical quantities of slow-moving items with corresponding quantities in the prior year.

(2) Observe merchandise and raw materials during the client's physical inventory taking.

(3) Review the management's inventory representations letter for accuracy.

(4) Test overall fairness of inventory values by comparing the company's turnover ratio with the industry average.

k. McPherson Corp. does not make an annual physical count of year-end inventories, but instead makes weekly test counts on the basis of a statistical plan. During the year, Sara Mullins, CPA, observes such counts as she deems necessary and is able to satisfy herself as to the reliability of the client's procedures. In reporting on the results of her examination, Mullins:

(1) Can issue an unqualified opinion without disclosing that she did not observe year-end inventories.

(2) Must comment in the scope paragraph as to her inability to observe year-end inventories, but can nevertheless issue an unqualified opinion.

(3) Is required, if the inventories are material, to disclaim an opinion on the financial statements taken as a whole.

(4) Must, if the inventories are material, qualify her opinion.

l. The primary objective of a CPA's observation of a client's physical inventory count is to:

(1) Discover whether a client has counted a particular inventory item or group of items.

(2) Obtain direct knowledge that the inventory exists and has been properly counted.

(3) Provide an appraisal of the quality of the merchandise on hand on the day of the physical count.

(4) Allow the auditor to supervise the conduct of the count so as to obtain assurance that inventory quantities are reasonably accurate.

(AICPA, adapted)

Problems

12–33. Described below are potential financial statement misstatements that are encountered by auditors.

a. Inventory is understated because warehouse personnel overlooked several racks of parts in taking the physical inventory.

b. Inventory is overstated because warehouse personnel included inventory items received subsequent to year-end while recording the purchase in the subsequent year to hide inventory shortages.

c. Inventory is overstated because management instructed computer personnel to make changes in the file used to price inventories.

Required:

For each misstatement, identify whether the misstatement results from error or fraud, the type of controls that would serve to prevent or detect the misstatement, and the substantive tests that might be used by the auditors to detect the misstatement. Organize your answer as follows:

Misstatement	Error or Fraud	Control	Substantive Procedure
a.			

12–34. Williams Pharmaceutical Company produces a number of drugs that are regulated by various agencies, including in the United States the federal Food and Drug Administration (FDA). These agencies issue licenses that approve drugs for sale and establish specific regulations regarding production quality and inventory security, violations of which can result in fines or suspension of product licenses. All the drugs are protected under patents filed in various jurisdictions, and Williams markets the drugs in the United States as well as a number of other countries. The company faces significant competition from other pharmaceutical companies globally.

Required:

a. Identify three business risks that are faced by Williams with respect to production processes and inventories.

b. For each of the risks identified in part (*a*), state whether the business risk results in a current-period inherent risk of material misstatement of the financial statements (financial reporting risk). If the business risk results in a financial reporting risk, describe that risk in terms of the type of financial statement misstatement that could occur.

c. Provide examples of how Williams's management might mitigate the risks (e.g., specific controls) identified in part (*b*) as financial reporting risks.

d. For each risk identified in part (*b*) as a financial reporting risk, describe substantive auditing procedures that might be used by the auditors if management did not have controls to mitigate the risk.

12–35. You have been engaged by the management of Alden, Inc., to review its controls over the purchase, receipt, storage, and issue of raw materials. You have prepared the following comments, which describe Alden's procedures.

(1) Raw materials, which consist mainly of high-cost electronic components, are kept in a locked storeroom. Storeroom personnel include a supervisor and four clerks. All are well trained, competent, and adequately bonded. Raw materials are removed from the storeroom only upon written or oral authorization of one of the production supervisors.

(2) There are no perpetual-inventory records; hence, the storeroom clerks do not keep records of goods received or issued. To compensate for the lack of perpetual records, a physical-inventory count is taken monthly by the storeroom clerks, who are well supervised. Appropriate procedures are followed in making the inventory count.

(3) After the physical count, the storeroom supervisor matches quantities counted against a predetermined reorder level. If the count for a given part is below the reorder level, the supervisor enters the part number on a materials requisition list and sends this list to the accounts payable clerk. The accounts payable clerk prepares a purchase order for a predetermined reorder quantity for each part and mails the purchase order to the vendor from whom the part was last purchased.

(4) When ordered materials arrive at Alden, they are received by the storeroom clerks. The clerks count the merchandise and agree the counts to the carrier's bill of lading. All bills of lading are initialed, dated, and filed in the storeroom to serve as receiving reports.

Required:

Describe the weaknesses in internal control and recommend improvements in Alden's procedures for the purchase, receipt, storage, and issuance of raw materials. Organize your answer sheet as follows:

Weakness	Recommended Improvements

(AICPA, adapted)

12–36. Described at the top of the next page are potential financial statement misstatements that are encountered by auditors in the audit of inventory and cost of goods sold.

a. Management of a chain of discount department stores systematically overstates inventory quantities at selected locations.

b. Accounting personnel of a manufacturing company make computational errors that understate the production costs of certain inventory items.

c. Management of a computer reseller overstates inventory value by failing to recognize the loss in value of certain inventory items that are obsolete.

d. Production personnel for a high-tech manufacturing company include in inventory items that failed to meet essential quality standards.

Required: For each misstatement, describe the substantive auditing procedures that may be used by auditors to detect the misstatement. Organize your answer as shown below:

Misstatement	Audit Procedures
a.	

12–37.   Royal Meat Processing Company buys and processes livestock for sale to supermarkets. In connection with the audit of the company's financial statements, you have prepared the following notes based on your review of inventory procedures:

1. Each livestock buyer submits a daily report of his or her purchases to the plant superintendent. This report shows the dates of purchase and expected delivery, the vendor and the number, and weights and type of livestock purchased. As shipments are received, any available plant employee counts the number of each type received and places a check mark beside this quantity on the buyer's report. When all shipments listed on the report have been received, the report is returned to the buyer.

2. Vendors' invoices, after a clerical review, are sent to the appropriate buyer for approval and returned to the accounting department. A disbursement voucher and a check for the approved amount are prepared in the accounting department. Checks are forwarded to the treasurer for signature. The treasurer's office sends signed checks directly to the buyer for delivery to the vendor.

3. Livestock carcasses are processed by lots. Each lot is assigned a number. At the end of each day a tally sheet reporting the lots processed, the number and type of animals in each lot, and the carcass weight is sent to the accounting department, where a perpetual inventory record of processed carcasses and their weights is maintained.

4. Processed carcasses are stored in a refrigerated cooler located in a small building adjacent to the employee parking lot. The cooler is locked when the plant is not open, and a company guard is on duty when the employees report for work and leave at the end of their shifts. Supermarket truck drivers wishing to pick up their orders have been instructed to contact someone in the plant if no one is in the cooler.

5. Substantial quantities of by-products are produced and stored, either in the cooler or elsewhere in the plant. By-products are initially accounted for as they are sold. At this time the sales manager prepares a two-part form: One copy serves as authorization to transfer the goods to the customer, and the other becomes the basis for billing the customer.

Required: For each of notes 1 to 5 above, state the weaknesses, if any, in the present inventory procedures and your suggestions, if any, for improvement.

(AICPA, adapted)

12–38.   The following are typical questions that might appear on an internal control questionnaire for inventory:

1. Are written procedures prepared by the client for the taking of the physical inventory?

2. Do the client's inventory-taking procedures include a requirement to identify damaged inventory items?

3. Does the client maintain perpetual inventory records?

Required: a. Describe the purpose of each of the above controls.

b. Describe the manner in which each of the above procedures might be tested.

c. Assuming that the operating effectiveness of each of the above procedures is found to be inadequate, describe how the auditors might alter their substantive tests to compensate for the increased level of control risk.

12–39.   Late in December, your CPA firm accepted an audit engagement at Nash Jewelers, Inc., a corporation that deals largely in diamonds. The corporation has retail jewelry stores in several eastern cities and a diamond wholesale store in New York City. The wholesale store also sets the diamonds in rings and other quality jewelry.

The retail stores place orders for diamond jewelry with the wholesale store in New York City. A buyer employed by the wholesale store purchases diamonds in the New York diamond market; the wholesale store then fills orders from the retail stores and from independent customers and maintains a substantial inventory of diamonds. The corporation values its inventory by the specific identification cost method.

Required:

Assume that at the inventory date you are satisfied that Nash Jewelers, Inc., has no items left by customers for repair or sale on consignment and that no inventory owned by the corporation is in the possession of outsiders.

a. Discuss the problems the auditors should anticipate in planning for the observation of the physical inventory on this engagement because of the:

   (1) Different locations of inventories.

   (2) Nature of the inventory.

b. Assume that a shipment of diamond rings was in transit by corporation messenger from the wholesale store to a retail store on the inventory date. What additional audit steps would you take to satisfy yourself as to the gems that were in transit from the wholesale store on the inventory date?

(AICPA, adapted)

12–40. You are an audit manager of the rapidly growing CPA firm of Raye and Coye. You have been placed in charge of three new audit clients, which have the following inventory features:

1. Canyon Cattle Co., which maintains 15,000 head of cattle on a 1,000-square-mile ranch, mostly unfenced, near the south rim of the Grand Canyon in Arizona.

2. Rhoads Mfg. Co., which has raw materials inventories consisting principally of pig iron loaded on gondola freight cars on a siding at the company's plant.

3. Strawser Company, which is in production around the clock on three shifts, and which cannot shut down production during the physical inventory.

Required:

What problems do you anticipate in the observation of physical inventories of the three new clients, and how would you deal with the problems?

12–41. Smith is the partner in charge of the audit of Blue Distributing Corporation, a wholesaler that owns one warehouse containing 80 percent of its inventory. Smith is reviewing the working papers that were prepared to support the firm's opinion on Blue's financial statements, and Smith wants to be certain essential audit records are well documented.

Required:

What substantive tests should Smith expect to find in the working papers to document management's assertion about completeness as it relates to the inventory quantities at the end of the year?

(AICPA, adapted)

12–42. David Anderson, CPA, is engaged in the audit of the financial statements of Redondo Manufacturing Corporation for the year ended June 30, 200X. Redondo's inventories at year-end include finished merchandise on consignment with consignees and finished merchandise stored in public warehouses. The merchandise in public warehouses is pledged as collateral for outstanding debt.

Required:

Normal inventory and notes payable auditing procedures have been satisfactorily completed. Describe the specific additional auditing procedures that Anderson should undertake with respect to:

a. Consignments out.

b. Finished merchandise in public warehouses pledged as collateral for outstanding debt.

(AICPA, adapted)

12–43. Payne Press Company is engaged in the manufacture of large-size presses under specific contracts and in accordance with customers' specifications. Customers are required to advance 25 percent of the contract price. The company records sales on a shipment basis and accumulates costs by job orders. The normal profit margin over the past few years has been approximately 5 percent of sales, after provision for selling and administrative expenses of about 10 percent of sales. Inventories are valued at the lower of cost or market.

Among the jobs you are reviewing in the course of your annual audit of the company's December 31 financial statements is Job No. 2357, calling for delivery of a three-color press at a firm contract price of $50,000. Costs accumulated for the job at the year-end aggregated $30,250. The company's engineers estimated that the job was approximately 55 percent complete at December 31. Your audit procedures have been as follows:

1. Examined all contracts, noting pertinent provisions.
2. Observed physical inventory of jobs in process and reconciled details to job order accounts.
3. Tested controls over input of labor, material, and overhead charges into the various jobs to determine that such charges were authentic and had been posted correctly.
4. Confirmed customers' advances at year-end.
5. Reconciled goods in process job ledger with control account.

Required: With respect to Job No. 2357:

    a. State what additional audit procedures, if any, you would follow and explain the purpose of the procedures.

    b. Indicate the manner and the amount at which you would include Job No. 2357 in the balance sheet.

(AICPA, adapted)

In-Class Team Case

12–44. Hovington, CPA, knows that while audit objectives relating to inventories may be stated in terms of the assertions as presented in this chapter, they may also be subdivided and stated more specifically. He has chosen to do so and has prepared the second column of the following table.

Financial Statement Assertion	Specific Audit Objective	Audit Procedure
	1. The entity has legal title to inventories.	
	2. Recorded inventory quantities include all products on hand.	
	3. Inventories are reduced, when appropriate, to replacement cost or net realizable value.	
	4. Cost of inventories is properly calculated.	
	5. The major categories of inventories and their basis of valuation are adequately reported in the financial statements.	

Required: Assume that Hovington's client, a retail department store, does no production. For each specific inventory audit objective listed above, select the most closely related financial statement assertion and the most appropriate audit procedure from the following:

Financial Statement Assertion	Audit Procedure
A. Completeness	F. Examine current vendors' price lists.
B. Existence or occurrence	G. Review drafts of the financial statements.
C. Presentation and disclosure	H. Select a sample of items during the physical inventory count and determine that they have been included on count sheets.
D. Rights and obligations	I. Select a sample of recorded items and examine supporting vendors' invoices, and contracts.
E. Valuation or allocation	J. Select a sample of recorded items on count sheets during the physical inventory count and determine that items are on hand.
	K. Test reasonableness of direct labor rates.

Financial statement assertions and audit procedures may be selected once, more than once, or not at all.

Ethics Case

12–45.   You have been with Zaird & Associates for approximately three months and are completing your work on the BizCaz audit. BizCaz produces pullover knit shirts to address the business casual market both for men and women. Although your experience has been limited, an unexpected staff resignation has resulted in you working directly with the engagement's in-charge senior on inventory. This has been a learning experience for you, as you have helped perform various tests of controls which may be summarized as indicating that internal control over inventory (including the perpetual records) seems strong. It is your impression that those tests resulted in a decrease in substantive testing, thereby allowing a particularly efficient audit.

At the beginning of the audit, Jan Wheeler, the in-charge senior, told you that the management team of BizCaz has always been helpful and friendly. Throughout the audit you have found the situation to be as good as described. In fact, BizCaz allows each auditor to purchase up to three shirts at a particularly attractive price of $12 per shirt, the cost for which employees may purchase shirts. The shirts have a market value of around $50, although the direct labor and material costs of each shirt are only $10.

Near the conclusion of the audit, after you and the other three staff members paid the controller and told him your sizes, he walked to the warehouse, removed 12 shirts from the appropriate piles and brought them out. That evening you gave the situation some thought. On the one hand, the company didn't lose any money on your purchase of the shirts—but on the other hand, you would never have been able to purchase such high-quality clothes for such a low price.

Required:

1. Is it acceptable to purchase these shirts from the audit client in this manner?

2. Discuss the effect of any information presented in the case on the adequacy of the audit.

Research and Discussion Case

12–46.   Western Trading Company is a sole proprietorship engaged in the grain brokerage business. At December 31, 200X, the entire grain inventory of the company was stored in outside bonded warehouses. The company's procedure of pricing inventories in these warehouses includes comparing the actual cost of each commodity in inventory with the market price as reported for transactions on the commodity exchanges at December 31. A write-down is made on commodities in which cost is in excess of market. During the course of the 200X audit, the auditors verified the company's computations. In addition to this, they compared the book value of the inventory with market prices at February 15, 200Y, the last day of fieldwork. The auditors noted that the market prices of several of the commodities had declined sharply subsequent to year-end, until their market price was significantly below the commodities' book values.

The inventory was repriced by the auditors on the basis of the new market prices, and the book value of the inventory was found to be in excess of market value on February 15 by approximately $21,000. The auditors proposed that the inventories be written down by $17,000 to this new market value, net of gains on the subsequent sales. The management protested this suggestion, stating that in their opinion the market decline was only temporary and that prices would recover in the near future. They refused to allow the write-down to be made. Accordingly, the auditors qualified their audit opinion for a departure from generally accepted accounting principles.

Required:

a. Were the auditors justified in issuing a qualified opinion in this situation? Discuss fully, including alternative courses of action.

b. State your opinion as to the course of action that was appropriate in this situation.

Suggested References

AICPA, *Professional Standards,* AU section 560.01–.09.

FASB, *Professional Standards,* Current Text, sections I78.109–.118 and C59.112.

CPA Simulation

12–47.   *See Chapter 10, pages 391 through 393 for the background information (company profile, industry information, and financial statements) relating to this simulation case.*

Questions

a. Which of the following correctly identifies a risk facing SSC that might affect its ability to continue as a going concern over the long run?

1. Competition from several competitors.

2. Your CPA firm's decision to issue standard unqualified audit reports not mentioning going-concern status during the past five years.

3. Obsolescence of all products due to rapid changes in technology in the industry.

4. The nature of inventory items—small in size, high in value.

b. The most significant risk factor relating to the risk of misstatement arising from fraudulent financial reporting for SSC is that the company

1. Officers serve on the board of directors.

2. Must refinance a significant portion of its debt.

3. Operates in the Bisbee, Arizona, area.

4. Paid no dividend this year.

Ratio	20X8	20X7
Inventory turnover (Cost of goods sold/Inventory)	10.52	7.95
Net income	$170,500	$169,662

The above table presents a ratio and financial information that were identified as significant in the current and prior years' audits of SSC. Compare the values of each. Then select an audit finding that is consistent with these metrics. The finding need not explain the entire change. However, of the replies listed, it should potentially lead to the most significant change in the direction indicated by the change in the ratio.

Ratios and financial information:

c. An audit finding consistent with the change in inventory turnover for SSC.

d. An audit finding consistent with the increase in net income.

1. Increases in costs of purchases were more than completely passed on to customers through higher selling prices.

2. Increases in inventory.

3. Increases in debt outstanding.

4. A larger percentage of sales occurred during the last month of 20X8, as compared to 20X7.

5. Interest expense increased during 20X8 due to the new debt.

6. The percentage tax included in the provision for income taxes for 20X8 was less than the percentage tax in 20X7.

The auditor determines that each of the following objectives will be part of SSC's audit. For each audit objective, select a substantive procedure that would help to achieve that objective. Each of the procedures may be used once, more than once, or not at all.

Audit objective:

e. Determine that the presentation and disclosure of inventories and cost of goods sold are adequate.

f. Establish that the client has rights to the recorded inventories.

g. Establish the completeness of inventories.

h. Determine that appropriate items have been recorded at market values.

Substantive procedure:

1. Examine current vendors' price lists.

2. Obtain confirmation of inventories pledged under loan agreements.

3. Select a sample of items during the physical inventory count and determine that each has been included on count sheets.

4. Select a sample of recorded items on count sheets and examine supporting vendors' invoices and contracts.

5. Calculate turnover ratios for inventory items.

6. Select a sample of recorded items on count sheets during the physical inventory count and determine that these items are on hand.

7. Test the reasonableness of general and administrative labor rates.

Communication:

i. Jill Swizoo, the audit manager, has pointed out to you that while revenues have increased by over 20 percent, net income before taxes is lower, but net income is higher than in 20X7. Write a brief memo regarding any factors that are obviously creating each of these two circumstances—net income before taxes decreasing, and net income increasing.

Remember: Your response will be graded for both technical relevance and writing skills. For writing skills you should demonstrate an ability to develop, organize, and express your ideas clearly. Do not convey information in the form of a table, bullet-point list, or other abbreviated presentation.

Memorandum

TO: Jill Swizoo
Subject: SSC Net Income

Research:

Note: This section is possible to work in a meaningful way only if you have the professional standards available—preferably in electronic form.

j. Auditors ordinarily must observe the counting of inventories that are on hand. Using the professional standards, find this requirement and the related guidance. Do this by copying and pasting the report to a workspace. You should *not* edit the information in any way. Also, you may ignore information on inventories held in public warehouses as SSC has no such inventory.

Chapter 13

Property, Plant, and Equipment: Depreciation and Depletion

Chapter learning objectives

After studying this chapter, you should be able to:

LO1. Describe the nature of property, plant, and equipment and depreciation.

LO2. Identify the auditors' objectives for the audit of property, plant, and equipment.

LO3. Explain the fundamental controls over property, plant, and equipment.

LO4. Assess the risks of material misstatement (inherent and control risks) of property, plant, and equipment.

LO5. Design typical tests of controls used by auditors to support the assessed risks of material misstatement (inherent and control risks) for the financial statement assertions related to property, plant, and equipment.

LO6. Explain how the auditors design substantive audit procedures to address the risks of material misstatement of property, plant, and equipment.

LO7. Explain the auditors' approach to the audit of depreciation.

LO8. Describe how the auditors design audit procedures to audit intangible assets.

Learning Objective 1

The term *property, plant, and equipment* includes all tangible assets with a service life of more than one year that are used in the operation of the business and are not acquired for the purpose of resale. Three major subgroups of such assets are generally recognized:

1. *Land,* such as property used in the operation of the business, has the significant characteristic of not being subject to depreciation.
2. *Buildings, machinery, equipment, and land improvements,* such as fences and parking lots, have limited service lives and are subject to depreciation.
3. *Natural resources* (wasting assets), such as oil wells, coal mines, and tracts of timber, are subject to depletion as the natural resources are extracted or removed.

Acquisitions and disposals of property, plant, and equipment are usually large in dollar amount, but concentrated in only a few transactions. Individual items of plant and equipment may remain unchanged in the accounts for many years.

The Auditors' Approach to Auditing Property, Plant, and Equipment

Learning Objective 2

The auditors' *objectives* in the audit of property, plant, and equipment are to:

1. Consider *inherent risks,* including fraud risks.
2. Consider *internal control* over property, plant, and equipment.
3. Determine the *existence* of recorded property, plant, and equipment.
4. Establish the *completeness* of recorded property, plant, and equipment.
5. Establish that the client has *rights* to the recorded property, plant, and equipment.
6. Determine that the *valuation or allocation* of the cost of property, plant, and equipment is in accordance with generally accepted accounting principles.
7. Determine that the *presentation and disclosure* of property, plant, and equipment, including disclosure of depreciation methods, is appropriate and complete.

In conjunction with the audit of property, plant, and equipment, the auditors also obtain evidence about the related accounts of depreciation expense, accumulated depreciation, and repairs and maintenance expense.

Contrast with Audit of Current Assets

In many companies, the investment in plant and equipment amounts to 50 percent or more of the total assets. However, the audit work required to verify these properties is usually a much smaller proportion of the total audit time spent on the engagement. The verification of plant and equipment is facilitated by several factors not applicable to audit work on current assets.

First, a typical unit of property or equipment has a high dollar value, and relatively few transactions may lie behind a large balance sheet amount. Second, there is usually little change in the property accounts from year to year. The Land account often remains unchanged for a long span of years. The durable nature of buildings and equipment also tends to hold accounting activity to a minimum for these accounts. By way of contrast, such current assets as accounts receivable and inventory may have a complete turnover several times a year.

A third point of contrast between the audit of plant assets and the audit of current assets is the significance of the year-end cutoff of transactions on net income. For current assets, the year-end cutoff is a critical issue; for plant assets, it is generally not. For example, in our discussion of inventories in Chapter 12, we emphasized the importance of an accurate year-end cutoff of the transactions for purchases and sales of merchandise. An error in the cutoff of a $50,000 purchase or sales transaction may cause a $50,000 error in the year's pretax net income. The possibility of such errors is substantial because a large volume of merchandise transactions is normal at year-end. For plant assets, on the other hand, a year-end cutoff error in recording an acquisition or retirement ordinarily will not affect net income for the year. Moreover, for many companies, there may be no transactions in plant assets occurring at the year-end. Of course, a cutoff error relating to acquisition or retirement of plant assets could cause slight inaccuracies in depreciation or in the timing of gains or losses on disposals. The problem of year-end cutoff for plant assets, however, must be considered a minor one in contrast to the audit of current assets.

Internal Control over Plant and Equipment

Learning Objective 3

The amounts invested in plant and equipment represent a large portion of the total assets of many industrial concerns. Maintenance, rearrangement, and depreciation of these assets are major expenses in the income statement. The total expenditures for the assets and related expenses make strong internal control essential to the preparation of reliable financial statements. Errors in measurement of income may be material if assets are scrapped without their cost being removed from the accounts, or if the distinction between capital and revenue expenditures is not maintained consistently. The losses that inevitably arise from uncontrolled methods of acquiring, maintaining, and retiring plant and equipment are often greater than the losses from fraud in cash handling.

In large enterprises, the auditors may expect to find an annual plant budget used to forecast and to control acquisitions and retirements of plant and equipment. Many small companies also forecast expenditures for plant assets. Successful utilization of a plant budget presupposes the existence of reliable and detailed accounting records for plant and equipment. A detailed knowledge of the kinds, quantities, and condition of existing equipment is an essential basis for intelligent forecasting of the need for replacements and additions to the plant.

Other key controls applicable to plant and equipment are as follows:

1. A subsidiary ledger consisting of a separate record for each unit of property. An adequate plant and equipment ledger facilitates the auditors' work in analyzing additions and retirements, in verifying the depreciation provision and maintenance expenses, and in comparing authorizations with actual expenditures.

2. A system of authorizations requiring advance executive approval of all plant and equipment acquisitions, whether by purchase, lease, or construction. Serially numbered capital **work orders** are a convenient means of recording authorizations.

3. A reporting procedure assuring prompt disclosure and analysis of variances between authorized expenditures and actual costs.

4. An authoritative written statement of company policy distinguishing between **capital expenditures** and **revenue expenditures.** A dollar minimum ordinarily will be established for capitalization; any expenditures of a lesser amount automatically are classified as charges against current revenue.

5. A policy requiring all purchases of plant and equipment to be handled through the purchasing department and subjected to standard routines for receiving, inspection, and payment.

6. Periodic physical inventories designed to verify the existence, location, and condition of all property listed in the accounts and to disclose the existence of any unrecorded units.

7. A system of retirement procedures, including serially numbered *retirement work orders,* (below) stating reasons for retirement and bearing appropriate approvals.

	394837
Perfect Manufacturing Co. Retirement Work Order	
Department: Milling	Date: <u>October 10, 20XX</u>
Property ID No. 75666	Description Drill Press
Disposition: <u>Scrapped</u>	
	Approved By: *Austine Webb*

Audit Documentation

The key audit working paper for property, plant, and equipment is a summary analysis such as that illustrated in Figure 13.1. This working paper follows the approach we have previously described of *emphasizing changes during the year under audit.* The working paper shows the beginning balances for the various types of plant assets; these amounts are the ending balances shown in the prior year's working papers. Next, the working paper shows the additions and retirements during the year. These are the transactions upon which the auditors' attention will be focused. A final column shows the ending balances that must equal the beginning balances plus the additions and minus the retirements. A similar set of four columns is used to summarize the changes in the accounts for accumulated depreciation.

Among the other audit working papers for property, plant, and equipment are analyses of the year's additions and retirements, analyses of repairs and maintenance expense accounts, and tests of depreciation. The analyses of plant additions and retirements and the tests of depreciation are cross-indexed to the summary analysis, as illustrated in Figure 13.1. In the audit of larger companies, it is common practice for the client to prepare for the auditors both a listing of the year's additions and a schedule of the year's disposals.

Initial Audits and Repeat Engagements

The auditing procedures listed in subsequent pages are applicable to repeat engagements and therefore concern only transactions of the current year. In the auditors' first audit of a new client that has changed auditors, the beginning balances of plant and equipment may be substantiated by reference to the predecessor firm's working papers. If, in previous years, audits were performed by another reputable CPA firm, it is not customary in a first audit to go beyond a general review of the history of the plant and equipment as recorded in the accounts.

In a first audit of a company that has *not* previously been audited, the ideal approach is a complete historical analysis of the property accounts. By thorough review of all major charges and credits to the property accounts since their inception, the auditors can establish the validity of the beginning balances of property, plant, and equipment and accumulated depreciation.

If the client has been in business for many years, the review of transactions in earlier years necessarily must be performed on a test basis in order to stay within reasonable time limits. However, the importance of an analysis of transactions of prior years deserves emphasis. Only by this approach can the auditors be in a sound position to express an opinion as to the propriety of the current period's depreciation. If repair and maintenance expenses have been capitalized, or asset additions have been recorded as operating expenses, or retirements of property have gone unrecorded, the depreciation expense will be misstated regardless of the care taken in the selection of depreciation rates. The auditors should make clear to the client that the initial examination of plant and equipment requires procedures that need not be duplicated in subsequent engagements.

Audit of Property, Plant, and Equipment

The following steps are typical of the work required in many engagements for the verification of property, plant, and equipment. The procedures for accumulated depreciation are covered in a separate program on pages 513–515.

A. Consider inherent risks, including fraud risks.
B. Consider internal control over property, plant, and equipment.
  1. *Obtain an understanding of internal control* over property, plant, and equipment.
  2. *Assess control risk and design additional tests of controls and substantive tests* for the assertions about property, plant, and equipment.
  3. *Perform additional tests of controls* for those controls that the auditors plan to consider to support their planned assessed levels of control risk.
  4. *Reassess control risk* for each of the major financial statement assertions about property, plant, and equipment based on the results of tests of controls and, if necessary, *modify substantive tests.*

FIGURE 13.1 Analysis of Property, Plant, and Equipment

THE MANDVILLE CORPORATION
Summary of Property, Plant, and Equipment and Accumulated Depreciation
December 31, 20X2

K-1

Account Number	Description	Balance 12/31/X1	Additions	Retirements	Balance 12/31/X2	Method	Rate	Balance 12/31/X1	Provision	Retirements	Balance 12/31/X2
		Assets						Accumulated Depreciation			
151	Land	500,000 2/	151,000		651,000						
152-3	Land Improv.	135,000 2/	10,000		145,000 ✓	S.L.	5%	13,500 2/	7,000		20,500 ✓
154-5	Buildings	4,500,000 2/	495,000		4,995,000 ✓	S.L.	3%	292,000 2/	142,420		434,420 ✓
156-7	Equipment	800,000 2/	110,000	60,000	850,000 ✓	S.L.	10%	235,000 2/	70,600	50,600	255,000 ✓
	TOTALS	5,935,000	766,000	60,000	6,641,000			540,500	220,020	50,600	709,920
				K-1-1	K				K-1-2	K-1-1	K

2/ Agreed to prior year work papers.
✓ Footed plant and equipment subsidiary ledger cards. No exceptions.

Conclusion:
As a result of our audit procedures for property, plant, and equipment and related depreciation, it is our opinion that the 12/31/X2 balances are fairly stated.

WMH
1/17/X3

CMW
1/25/X3

C. Perform substantive tests of property, plant, and equipment and related revenue and expenses.

1. Obtain a summary analysis of changes in property owned and reconcile to ledgers.
2. Vouch additions to property, plant, and equipment during the year.
3. Make physical inspection of major acquisitions of plant and equipment.
4. Analyze repair and maintenance expense accounts.
5. Investigate the status of property, plant, and equipment not in current use.
6. Test the client's provision for depreciation.
7. Investigate potential impairments of property, plant, and equipment.
8. Investigate retirements of property, plant, and equipment during the year.
9. Examine evidence of legal ownership of property, plant, and equipment.
10. Review rental revenue from land, buildings, and equipment owned by the client but leased to others.
11. Examine lease agreements on property, plant, and equipment leased to and from others.
12. Perform analytical procedures for property, plant, and equipment.
13. Evaluate financial statement presentation and disclosure for plant assets and for related revenue and expenses.

These substantive audit procedures are summarized in Figure 13.2 along with the primary audit objectives.

A. Consider Inherent Risks, Including Fraud Risks.

Learning Objective 4

After they have obtained an understanding of the client and its business, the auditors will identify and assess inherent risks related to property, plant, and equipment.

If any of the inherent risks identified by the auditors involve the possibility of fraud, they will make sure that they understand the programs and controls established by management to control the risk. They will also determine that the controls have been implemented. Finally, the auditors will design an appropriate response to the risk.

B. Consider Internal Control over Property, Plant, and Equipment.

1. Obtain an Understanding of Internal Control.

In obtaining an understanding of internal control over property, plant, and equipment, the auditors may utilize a written description, flowcharts, or an internal control questionnaire. The

FIGURE 13.2
Objectives of Major Substantive Tests of Property, Plant, and Equipment and Depreciation

Substantive Tests	Primary Audit Objectives
Obtain a summary analysis of changes in property owned and reconcile to ledgers.	*Valuation*
Vouch additions during year. Make physical inspection of major acquisitions.	*Existence and rights* *Valuation or allocation*
Analyze repair and maintenance expense accounts.	*Valuation or allocation*
Investigate the status of property not in current use.	*Valuation or allocation* *Presentation and disclosure*
Test the client's provision for depreciation. Investigate potential impairments.	*Valuation and allocation*
Investigate retirements of property during the year. Examine evidence of legal ownership. Review rental revenue.	*Existence and rights*
Examine lease agreements. Perform analytical procedures.	*Existence and rights* *Completeness* *Valuation or allocation*
Evaluate financial statement presentation and disclosure.	*Presentation and disclosure*

following are typical of the questions included in a questionnaire: Are plant ledgers regularly reconciled with general ledger control accounts? Are periodic physical inventories of plant assets compared with the plant ledgers? Are variances between plant budgets and actual expenditures for plant assets subject to review and approval of executives? Does the sale, transfer, or dismantling of equipment require written executive approval on a serially numbered retirement work order? Is there a written policy for distinguishing between capital expenditures and revenue expenditures?

After preparing a description of internal control, the auditors will determine whether the controls as described to them have been *placed in operation.* To confirm their understanding of these policies and procedures, they will observe whether there is an appropriate segregation of duties over the acquisition of plant assets and inquire as to who performed various functions throughout the period. They will also inspect the subsidiary ledger of property, plant, and equipment; the serially numbered work orders; and the plant and equipment budget and examine evidence of the follow-up on variances from the budget. These procedures may provide the auditors with sufficient evidence to assess control risk for certain financial statement assertions about property, plant, and equipment as being at less than the maximum.

2. Assess Control Risk and Design Additional Tests of Controls and Substantive Tests.

Learning Objective 5

Based on their understanding of the client's internal control over property, plant, and equipment, the auditors develop their planned assessments of control risk for the various financial statement assertions. To support these assessments of control risk, the auditors may need to obtain additional evidence of the operating effectiveness of the client's controls by designing additional tests of controls. In designing these tests, the auditors must decide which ones will result in sufficient reductions in substantive tests to justify the time spent performing them.

The auditors' assessments of control risk along with their assessments of inherent risk will be used to plan the nature, timing, and extent of substantive tests. In designing planned substantive tests, the auditors will consider potential misstatements that may occur—and the weaknesses in control or other conditions that make the misstatements more likely to occur—as illustrated in Figure 13.3.

FIGURE 13.3 Potential Misstatements—Investments in Property, Plant, and Equipment

Description of Misstatement	Examples	Internal Control Weaknesses or Factors That Increase the Risk of the Misstatement
Misstatement of acquisitions of property, plant, and equipment	**Fraud:** • Expenditures for repairs and maintenance expenses recorded as property, plant, and equipment acquisitions to overstate income.	• Undue pressure to meet earning targets.
	Error: • Purchases of equipment erroneously reported in maintenance and repairs expense account.	• Inadequate accounting manual; incompetent accounting personnel.
Failure to record retirements of property, plant, and equipment	**Error:** • An asset that has been replaced is discarded due to its lack of value, without an accounting entry.	• Inadequate accounting policies, e.g., failure to use retirement work orders.
Improper reporting of unusual transactions	**Error:** • A "gain" recorded on an exchange of nonmonetary assets that lacks commercial substance.	• Inadequate accounting manual; incompetent accounting personnel.

3. Perform Additional Tests of Controls.

Tests directed toward the effectiveness of controls are used to evaluate the client's internal control and determine whether the auditors can justify their planned assessed levels of control risk for the assertions about property, plant, and equipment accounts. Certain tests of controls are performed as the auditors obtain an understanding of the client's internal control; these tests were described in our discussion of that process. Additional tests of controls, for example, might include selecting a sample of purchases of plant and equipment to test the controls related to authorization, receipt, and proper recording of the transactions. A sample of recorded retirements also may be tested for proper authorization and supporting retirement work orders. These tests often will be combined with the substantive tests of additions and retirements described below.

4. Reassess Control Risk and Modify Substantive Tests.

The final step in the auditors' consideration of internal control involves a reassessment of control risk based on the results of the tests of controls. The auditors then decide whether they should modify their planned program of substantive tests for the property, plant, and equipment assertions.

C. Perform Substantive Tests of Property, Plant, and Equipment and Related Revenue and Expenses.

1. Obtain a Summary Analysis of Changes in Property Owned and Reconcile to Ledgers.

The auditors may verify the beginning balances of plant and equipment assets by reference to the prior year's audit working papers. In addition to beginning balances, the summary analysis will show the additions and retirements of plant and equipment during the year under audit. As the audit progresses, the auditors will examine a sample of these additions and retirements. The detailed working papers showing this verification will support and be cross-indexed to the summary analysis worksheet.

Before making a detailed analysis of changes in property accounts during the year, the auditors will want to be sure that the amounts in the subsidiary ledgers agree in total with the balances in the controlling accounts. Reconciliation of the subsidiary ledgers with the controlling accounts can be performed very quickly with the use of generalized audit software.

2. Vouch Additions to Property, Plant, and Equipment During the Year.

The vouching of additions to the property, plant, and equipment accounts during the period under audit is one of the most important substantive tests. The extent of the vouching is dependent upon the auditors' assessment of control risk for the existence and valuation of plant and equipment. The vouching process utilizes a working paper analysis of the general ledger control accounts and includes the tracing of entries through the journals to original documents, such as contracts, deeds, construction work orders, invoices, canceled checks, and authorization by appropriate individuals.

The specific steps to be taken in investigating the year's additions usually will include the following:

a. Review changes during the year in construction in progress and examine supporting work orders, both incomplete and closed.

b. Trace transfers from the Construction in Progress account to the property accounts, observing propriety of classification. Determine that all completed items have been transferred out of the account.

c. On a test basis, vouch purchases of property, plant, and equipment to invoices, deeds, contracts, or other supporting documents. Recompute extensions, footings, and treatment of discounts. Make certain repairs and maintenance expenses were not improperly capitalized.

d. Investigate all instances in which the actual cost of acquisitions substantially exceeded authorized amounts. Determine whether such excess expenditures were analyzed and approved by appropriate officials.

e. Investigate fully any debits to property, plant, and equipment accounts not arising from acquisition of physical assets.

f. Determine that the total cost of any plant and equipment assets purchased on the installment plan is reflected in the asset accounts and that the unpaid installments are set up as liabilities.

The accounting for plant assets acquired in a nonmonetary exchange is specified by *APB Opinion No. 29* (as amended by *FASB No. 153*), "Accounting for Nonmonetary Transactions." Generally, these assets are recorded at fair value, unless fair value is not determinable, the exchange is to facilitate sales to customers, or the exchange lacks commercial substance.

Assets constructed by a company for its own use should be recorded at the cost of direct material, direct labor, and applicable overhead cost. However, auditors may apply the additional test of comparing the total cost of self-constructed equipment with bids or estimated purchase prices for similar equipment from outside suppliers; excess costs of self-constructed assets should be expensed in the period that construction is completed.

Related Party Transactions

Assets acquired from affiliated corporations, from promoters or stockholders, or by any other type of related party transaction not involving arm's-length bargaining between buyer and seller have sometimes been recorded at inflated amounts. The auditors should inquire into the methods by which the sales price was determined, the cost of the property to the vendor, length of ownership by the vendor, and any other available evidence that might indicate an arbitrarily determined valuation. Material related party transactions must be disclosed in the notes to the financial statements.

Primary Audit Objectives:	
Existence	☑
Rights	☑
Valuation	☑

3. Make a Physical Inspection of Major Acquisitions of Plant and Equipment.

The auditors usually make a physical inspection of major units of plant and equipment acquired during the year under audit. This step is helpful in maintaining a good working knowledge of the client's operations and also in interpreting the accounting entries for both additions and retirements.

The audit procedure of physical inspection may flow in either direction between the plant assets and the records of plant assets. By tracing items in the plant ledger to the physical assets, the auditors prove that the assets shown in the accounting records *actually* exist and are in current use. The alternative testing procedure is to inspect selected assets in the plant and trace these assets to the detailed records. This test provides evidence that existing assets are recorded.

The physical inspection of plant assets may be limited to major units acquired during the year or may be extended to include tests of older equipment as well. In a few situations (especially when control risk is very high), the auditors may conclude that the taking of a complete physical inventory is needed. Bear in mind, however, that a complete physical inventory of plant and equipment is a rare event. If such an inventory is required, the auditors' role is to *observe* the physical inventory.

Let us consider an example of a situation in which the auditors might conclude that a complete physical inventory of equipment is needed. Assume that a client is engaged in commercial construction work and that the client owns and operates a great many units of costly mobile equipment. Such equipment may often be scrapped or sold upon the authorization of a field supervisor. Under these circumstances, the auditors might regard a complete physical inventory of plant and equipment as essential. Similarly, in the audit of clients owning a large number of automobiles and trucks, the auditors may insist upon observing a physical count, as well as examining legal title.

Some large companies, as part of their internal control, perform occasional physical inventories of plant and equipment at certain locations or in selected departments. The *observation* of these limited counts is often carried out by the client's internal auditing staff rather than by the independent auditors.

Primary Audit Objective:	
Valuation	☑

4. Analyze Repair and Maintenance Expense Accounts.

The auditors' principal objective in analyzing repair and maintenance expense accounts is to discover items that should have been capitalized. Many companies have a written policy setting the minimum expenditure to be capitalized. For example, company policy may prescribe that no expenditure for less than $300 shall be capitalized regardless of the service life of the item purchased. In such cases, the auditors will analyze the repair and maintenance accounts with a view toward determining the consistency of application of this policy as well as compliance with generally accepted accounting principles. To determine that the accounts contain only proper repair and maintenance charges, the auditors will trace the larger expenditures to written authorizations for the transaction. The accuracy of the client's accounting for the expenditures may be verified by reference to vendors' invoices, material requisitions, and labor time records.

One useful means of identifying any capital expenditures that are included in the repair and maintenance accounts is to obtain or prepare an analysis of the monthly amounts of expense with corresponding amounts listed for the preceding year. Any significant variations from month to month or between corresponding months of the two years should be fully investigated. If maintenance expense is classified by the departments serviced, the variations are especially noticeable.

5. Investigate the Status of Property, Plant, and Equipment Not in Current Use.

Land, buildings, and equipment not in current use should be investigated thoroughly to determine the prospects for their future use in operations. Plant assets that are temporarily idle need not be reclassified, and depreciation may be continued at normal rates. On the other hand, idle equipment that has been dismantled, or that for any reason appears unsuitable for future operating use, should be written down to an estimated realizable value and excluded from the plant and equipment classification. In the case of standby equipment and other property not needed at present or prospective levels of operation, the auditors should consider whether the carrying value is recoverable through future use in operations.

6. Test the Client's Provision for Depreciation.

See the separate *depreciation* program following this audit program.

7. Investigate Potential Impairments of Property, Plant, and Equipment.

FASB No. 144, "Accounting for the Impairment or Disposal of Long-Lived Assets," requires that long-lived assets be reviewed for impairment whenever events or changes in circumstances indicate that the carrying amount of an asset may not be recoverable. In these circumstances, if the sum of the expected future cash flows from the asset is less than its carrying amount, an impairment loss is recognized. The impairment loss is equal to the difference between the book value and the fair market value of the asset.

Auditors must be alert for any changes in circumstances that may affect the recoverability of property, plant, and equipment as well as long-lived intangible assets. Examples of changes in circumstances that should result in a test of impairment include a significant decrease in the market value of the asset, a significant adverse change in the way the asset is used, or an adverse change in the physical condition of the asset. If specific assets appear to be impaired, the auditors should evaluate the reasonableness of management's determination of the impairment loss. In some cases, this may require the work of a valuation specialist.

8. Investigate Retirements of Property, Plant, and Equipment During the Year.

The principal purpose of this procedure is to determine whether any property has been replaced, sold, dismantled, or abandoned without such action being reflected in the accounting records. Nearly every thorough physical inventory of plant and equipment reveals missing units of property—units disposed of without a corresponding reduction of the accounts.

If a machine is sold for cash or traded in on a new machine, the transaction generally will involve the use of documents, such as a cash receipts form or a purchase order; the processing of these documents may bring the retirement to the attention of accounting personnel. However, plant assets may be scrapped rather than sold or traded in on new equipment; consequently, there may be no paperwork to evidence the disappearance of a machine. How is the accounting department expected to know when the asset has been retired?

One method of preventing unrecorded retirements is enforcement of a companywide policy that no plant asset shall be retired from use without prior approval on a special type of serially numbered retirement work order. A copy of the retirement work order is routed to the accounting department, thus providing some assurance that retirements will be reflected in the accounting records.

What specific steps should the auditors take to discover any unrecorded retirements? The following measures often are effective:

a. If major additions of plant and equipment have been made during the year, determine whether old equipment was traded in or replaced by the new units.

b. Analyze the Miscellaneous Revenue account to locate any cash proceeds from sale of plant assets.

c. If any of the company's products have been discontinued during the year, investigate the disposition of plant facilities formerly used in manufacturing such products.

d. Inquire of executives and supervisors whether any plant assets have been retired during the year.

e. Examine retirement work orders or other source documents for authorization by the appropriate official or committee.

f. Investigate any reduction of insurance coverage to determine whether this was caused by retirement of plant assets.

9. Examine Evidence of Legal Ownership of Property, Plant, and Equipment.

<table>
<tr><td colspan="2">Primary Audit
Objectives:</td></tr>
<tr><td>Existence</td><td>☑</td></tr>
<tr><td>Rights</td><td>☑</td></tr>
</table>

To determine that plant assets are the property of the client, the auditors look for such evidence as a deed, a title insurance policy, property tax bills, receipts for payments to mortgagee, and fire insurance policies. Additionally, the fact that rental payments are not being made is supporting evidence of ownership.

It is sometimes suggested that the auditors may verify ownership of real property and the absence of liens by examination of public records. This step is seldom taken. Inspection of the documentary evidence listed above usually provides adequate proof of ownership. If some doubt exists as to whether the client has clear title to property, the auditors should obtain the opinion of the client's legal counsel or request that a title search be performed by a title insurance company.

Possession of a deed is not proof of present ownership, because when real property is sold, a new deed is prepared and the seller retains the old one. This is true of title insurance policies as well. Better evidence of continuing ownership is found in property tax bills made out in the name of the client and in fire insurance policies, rent receipts from lessees, and regular payments of principal and interest to a mortgagee or trustee.

The disclosure of liens on property is considered during the examination of liabilities, but in the audit work on plant and equipment the auditors should be alert for evidence indicating the existence of liens. Purchase contracts examined in verifying the cost of property may reveal unpaid balances. Insurance policies may contain loss payable endorsements in favor of a secured party.

The auditors can readily ascertain the ownership of automobiles and trucks by reference to certificates of title and registration documents. The ease of transfer of title to automotive equipment, plus the fact that it is often used as collateral for loans, makes it important that the auditors examine the title to such property.

10. Review Rental Revenue from Land, Buildings, and Equipment Owned by the Client but Leased to Others.

<table>
<tr><td colspan="2">Primary Audit
Objectives:</td></tr>
<tr><td>Existence</td><td>☑</td></tr>
<tr><td>Rights</td><td>☑</td></tr>
</table>

In testing rental revenue from land and buildings, it is often desirable for the auditors to obtain or to sketch a map of the property and to make a physical inspection of each unit. This may disclose that premises reported as vacant are in fact occupied by lessees and are producing revenue not reflected in the accounting records. If the client's property includes an office or apartment building, the auditors should obtain a floor plan of the building as well as copies of all lease contracts. In this way, they can account for all available rental space as revenue-producing or vacant and can verify reported vacancies by physical inspection at the balance sheet date. If interim audit work is being performed, vacancies should also be verified by inspection and discussion with management during the year.

Examination of leases will indicate whether tenants are responsible for the cost of electricity, water, gas, and telephone service. These provisions should be reconciled with utility expense accounts. Rental revenue accounts should be analyzed in all cases and the amount compared with lease agreements and cash records.

Primary Audit Objectives:	
Existence	☑
Completeness	☑
Rights	☑
Valuation	☑

11. Examine Lease Agreements on Property, Plant, and Equipment Leased to and from Others.

The preceding step addressed rental revenue from leases. The auditors also must be aware that generally accepted accounting principles require differing accounting treatments for operating and capital leases. The auditors should carefully examine lease agreements to determine whether the accounting for the assets involved is proper. For example, the auditors must be alert for the client's possible use of improper accounting techniques, such as the following.

- Assets under a lease that are being improperly accounted for (e.g., leases that meet the criteria for capital treatment are treated as operating leases).
- Leasehold improvements to buildings under operating leases that are being depreciated over the estimated useful life of the improvements rather than the shorter term of the lease, when renewal of the lease is not reasonably assured.
- A lease that provides a rent holiday that is not properly accounted for. For example, if a lease provides for six months of free rent, this benefit should be amortized over the life of the lease.

Primary Audit Objectives:	
Existence	☑
Completeness	☑
Rights	☑
Valuation	☑

12. Perform Analytical Procedures for Property, Plant, and Equipment.

The specific trends and ratios used in judging the overall reasonableness of recorded amounts for plant and equipment will vary with the nature of the client's operations. Among the ratios and trends used by auditors for this purpose are the following:

a. Total cost of plant assets divided by annual output in dollars, pounds, or other units.

b. Total cost of plant assets divided by cost of goods sold.

c. Comparison of repairs and maintenance expense on a monthly basis and from year to year.

d. Comparison of acquisitions for the current year with prior years.

e. Comparison of retirements for the current year with prior years.

Acquisitions and retirements may vary widely from year to year; however, it is essential that the auditors be aware of these variations and judge their reasonableness in the light of trends in the client's past and present operations. Analytical procedures relating to depreciation are discussed later in this chapter as part of the audit program for depreciation.

Primary Audit Objective:	
Presentation	☑

13. Evaluate Financial Statement Presentation and Disclosure for Plant Assets and for Related Revenue and Expenses.

The balance sheet or accompanying notes should disclose balances of major classes of depreciable assets. Accumulated depreciation may be shown by major class or in total, and the method or methods of computing depreciation should be stated. The total amount of depreciation should be disclosed in the income statement or supporting notes.

In addition, adequate financial statement presentation and disclosure will ordinarily reflect the following principles:

a. The basis of valuation should be explicitly stated. At present, cost is the generally accepted basis of valuation for plant and equipment; property not in use should be valued at the lower of cost or estimated realizable value.

b. Property pledged to secure loans should be clearly identified.

c. Property not in current use should be segregated in the balance sheet.

Depreciation

The Auditors' Perspective toward Depreciation

Determining the annual depreciation expense involves two decisions by the client company: first, an estimate of the useful economic lives of various groups of assets, and second, a choice among several depreciation methods, each of which would lead to a different answer. The wide range of possible amounts for annual depreciation expense because of these decisions by the client suggests that the auditors should maintain a perspective of looking for assurance of overall reasonableness. Specifically, overall tests of the year's depreciation expense are of special importance.

Among the methods of computing depreciation expense most frequently encountered are the straight-line method and the declining-balance method. Far less common, although quite acceptable, are methods based on units of output or hours of service. The most widely adopted types of accelerated depreciation methods are fixed percentage of declining balance and sum-of-the-years' digits. The essential characteristic of these and other similar methods is that depreciation is greatest in the first year and becomes smaller in succeeding years.

CPAs often encounter clients maintaining their records using federal income tax rules, such as the modified accelerated cost recovery system (MACRS). Although such methods are considered a systematic method of depreciating the cost of an asset, the depreciable lives of the assets are often much shorter than their useful economic lives. If the recovery periods are not reasonable, depreciation expense may be materially misstated and the auditors will not be in a position to issue an unqualified opinion on the financial statements.

Learning Objective 7

The Auditors' Objectives in Auditing Depreciation

Depreciation is an accounting estimate. Recall from Chapter 5 that, in evaluating the reason ableness of accounting estimates, auditors first obtain an understanding of the client's processes and controls. Then, they use one or more of the following three basic approaches:

1. Review and test management's process of developing the estimate.
2. Review subsequent events or transactions bearing on the estimate.
3. Independently develop an estimate of the amount to compare to management's estimate.

For depreciation, while a combination of all of the above approaches may be used, the emphasis is ordinarily upon the first basic approach—reviewing and testing management's process for calculating depreciation.

As we discussed earlier, depreciation relates most directly to the *valuation or allocation* audit objective. To meet this objective, the auditors, in examining management's process for calculating depreciation, determine (1) that the methods in use are acceptable, (2) that the methods are being followed consistently, and (3) that the calculations required by the chosen methods are accurate. The audit program in the following section conveys a more detailed picture of the auditors' objectives.

Audit Program— Depreciation Expense and Accumulated Depreciation

The following outline of substantive tests to be performed by the auditors in reviewing depreciation is stated in sufficient detail to be largely self-explanatory. Consequently, no point-by-point discussion will be presented. Techniques for testing the client's provision for depreciation for the year are, however, discussed immediately following the audit program.

1. Review the depreciation policies set forth in company manuals or other management directives. Determine whether the methods in use are designed to allocate costs of plant and equipment assets systematically over their service lives.
   a. Inquire whether any extra working shifts or other conditions of accelerated production are present that might warrant adjustment of normal depreciation rates.
   b. Discuss with executives the possible need for recognition of obsolescence resulting from technological or economic developments. For example, assume that a new, improved model of computer has recently become available and that it would fit the company's needs more effectively. Should the remaining estimated useful life of an older computer

presently owned by the company be reevaluated in the light of this technological advance?

2. Obtain or prepare a summary analysis (see Figure 13.1) of accumulated depreciation for the major property classifications as shown by the general ledger control accounts, listing beginning balances, provisions for depreciation during the year, retirements, and ending balances.

   a. Compare beginning balances with the audited amounts in last year's working papers.

   b. Determine that the totals of accumulated depreciation recorded in the plant and equipment subsidiary records agree with the applicable general ledger controlling accounts.

3. Test the provisions for depreciation.

   a. Compare rates used in the current year with those employed in prior years and investigate any variances.

   b. Test computations of depreciation provisions for a representative number of units and trace to individual records in the property ledger. Be alert for excessive depreciation on fully depreciated assets. Generalized audit software can be used to test the depreciation calculations in the client's records if the client maintains computer-based records.

   c. Compare credits to accumulated depreciation accounts for the year's depreciation provisions with debit entries in related depreciation expense accounts.

4. Test deductions from accumulated depreciation for assets retired.

   a. Trace deductions to the working paper analyzing retirements of assets during the year.

   b. Test the accuracy of accumulated depreciation to date of retirement.

5. Perform analytical procedures for depreciation.

   a. Compute the ratio of depreciation expense to total cost of plant and compare with prior years.

   b. Compare the percentage relationships between accumulated depreciation and related property accounts with those prevailing in prior years. Discuss significant variations from the normal depreciation program with appropriate members of management.

Testing the Client's Provision for Depreciation

We have emphasized the importance of determining the overall reasonableness of the amount of depreciation expense, which is usually a material amount on the income statement. An *over-all* test of the annual provision for depreciation requires the auditors to perform the following steps:

1. List the balances in the various asset accounts at the beginning of the year.

2. Deduct any fully depreciated assets, since these items should no longer be subject to depreciation.

3. Add one-half of the asset additions for the year.

4. Deduct one-half of the asset retirements for the year (exclusive of any fully depreciated assets).

These four steps produce average amounts subject to depreciation at the regular rates in each of the major asset categories. By applying the appropriate rates to these amounts, the auditors determine on an overall average basis the amount of the provision for depreciation. The computed amount is then compared with the client's figures. Precise agreement is not to be expected, but any material difference between the depreciation expense computed in this manner and the amount set up by the client should be investigated fully.

Examination of Natural Resources

In the audit of companies operating properties subject to depletion (mines, oil and gas deposits, timberlands, and other natural resources), the auditors follow a pattern similar to that used in evaluating the provision for depreciation expense and accumulated depreciation. They determine whether depletion has been recorded consistently and in accordance with generally accepted accounting principles, and they test the mathematical accuracy of the client's computations.

The depletion of timberlands is usually based on physical quantities established by **cruising.** (The term *cruising* means the inspection of a tract of forestland for the purpose of estimating the total lumber yield.) The determination of physical quantities to use as a basis for depletion is more difficult in many mining ventures and for oil and gas deposits. The auditors often rely upon the opinions of such specialists as mining engineers and geologists about the reasonableness of the depletion rates being used for such resources. Under these circumstances, the auditors must comply with the provisions of *SAS 73,* "Using the Work of a Specialist," as discussed in Chapter 5.

If the number of tons of ore in a mining property could be accurately determined in advance, an exact depletion cost per ton could be computed by dividing the cost of the mine by the number of tons available for extraction. In reality, the contents of the mine can only be estimated, and the estimates may require significant revision as mining operations progress.

The auditors investigate the ownership and the cost of mining properties by examining deeds, leases, tax bills, vouchers, paid checks, and other records in the same manner that they verify the plant and equipment of a manufacturing or trading concern. The costs of exploration and development work in a mine customarily are capitalized until such time as commercial production begins. After that date additional development work generally is treated as an expense. The large oil companies capitalize the costs of drilling oil wells only if they are found to be productive. Under this "successful efforts" policy, the costs of drilling wells that prove not to be productive are immediately written off. However, some smaller companies follow an alternative "full-cost" policy, under which all drilling costs are capitalized and amortized over future years.

Examination of Intangible Assets

Learning Objective 8

The balance sheet caption "Intangible Assets" includes a variety of assets. All intangible assets are characterized by a lack of physical substance. Furthermore, they do not qualify as current assets, and they are nonmonetary—that is, they do not represent fixed claims to cash.

Among the more prominent intangible assets are goodwill, patents, trademarks, franchises, and leaseholds. Since intangible assets are lacking in physical substance, their value lies in the rights or economic advantages afforded in their ownership. Because of their intangible nature, these assets may be more difficult to identify than units of plant and equipment. When a client treats an expenditure as creating an intangible asset, the auditors must look for objective evidence that a genuine asset has come into existence.

The auditors' substantiation of intangible assets may begin with an analysis of the ledger accounts for these assets. Debits to the accounts should be traced to evidence of payment having been made and to documentary evidence of the rights or benefits acquired. Credits to the accounts should be reconciled with the client's program of amortization or traced to appropriate authorization for the write-off of the asset.

One intangible asset that may be large in amount yet of questionable future economic benefit is *goodwill.* Goodwill arises in accounting for business combinations in which the price paid to acquire another company exceeds the fair value of the identifiable net assets acquired. When business combinations result in the recording of goodwill, the auditors should review the allocation of the lump-sum acquisition cost among tangible assets, identifiable intangible assets, and goodwill. They must also determine whether goodwill is properly allocated to all the various reporting units acquired in the acquisition. Often, the auditors will have to use the services of a business valuation specialist to assist them in evaluating the reasonableness of the valuation and allocation.

Once goodwill is acquired it remains at its purchase price; it is not amortized. Instead, goodwill assigned to reporting units should be tested for impairment on an annual basis and between annual tests in certain circumstances. These tests involve determining the fair value of the reporting units for comparison to their carrying value. If the fair value of a reporting unit is less than its carrying value, an impairment loss is recognized for the difference. In auditing these impairment tests, the auditors may find it useful to use the services of a valuation specialist.

As part of an analysis of intangible assets with definite useful lives, the auditors should review the reasonableness of the client's amortization program. Amortization is ordinarily computed by the straight-line method over the assets' estimated useful lives. As with property, plant, and equipment, long-lived intangible assets must be continually reviewed for impairment when circumstances indicate that the carrying value of the asset may not be recoverable.

Examination of Plant, Equipment, and Intangibles in Advance of the Balance Sheet Date

Most of the audit work on plant, equipment, and intangibles can be done in advance of the balance sheet date. For the initial audit of a new client, the time-consuming task of reviewing the records of prior years and establishing the beginning balances in the accounts for the current period ordinarily will be completed before the year-end.

In repeat engagements, as well as in first audits, the consideration of internal control can be carried out at any convenient time during the year. Many auditing firms lighten their year-end work loads by performing interim work during October and November, including the analysis of the plant and equipment ledger accounts for the first 9 or 10 months of the year. After the balance sheet date, the work necessary on property accounts is then limited to examination of the transactions for the final two or three months.

Chapter Summary

In this chapter we presented the appropriate controls for property, plant, and equipment accounts, the auditors' consideration of these controls, and the substantive procedures for property, plant, and equipment. To summarize:

1. The financial statement capital "property, plant, and equipment" includes tangible assets with a useful life of more than one year that are used in operations. In the audit of property, plant, and equipment, the auditors' primary objectives are to (*a*) consider inherent risks, including fraud risks; (*b*) consider controls over these assets; (*c*) determine the existence of property, plant, and equipment; (*d*) establish the propriety of the valuation or allocation methods, including the reasonableness of the depreciation program; (*e*) establish the completeness of recorded property, plant, and equipment; and (*f*) evaluate the adequacy of presentation and disclosure for property, plant, and equipment.

2. Key controls over property, plant, and equipment should include proper authorization of acquisitions, adequate records for the various units of property, periodic physical inspection of property, and the use of serially numbered retirement work orders.

3. In the audit of property, plant, and equipment for a continuing client, the emphasis of the testing is on transactions that occurred during the year, as contrasted to an emphasis on ending balances. Depreciation expense is often tested by recomputation or through the use of analytical procedures.

4. The auditors' objectives for the audit of natural resources and intangible assets are similar to those for property, plant, and equipment. Often in auditing the depletion of natural resources, the auditors must rely upon specialists to estimate the quantity and quality of the resource. The audit of intangible assets typically involves vouching the cost of the assets and evaluating and testing the allocation methods used by the client.

5. A significant risk with respect to property, plant, and equipment and intangible assets is the risk of unrecognized impairment.

Key Terms Introduced or Emphasized in Chapter 13

Capital expenditure   An expenditure for property, plant, and equipment that is properly charged to an asset account.

Cruising   The inspection of a tract of forestland for the purpose of estimating the total lumber yield.

Revenue expenditure   An expenditure for property, plant, and equipment that is properly charged to an expense account.

Work order   A serially numbered accounting document authorizing the acquisition of plant assets. A separate series of retirement work orders may be used to authorize the retirement or disposal of plant assets, and a third variety consists of documents authorizing repair or maintenance of plant assets.

Review Questions

13–1.   The auditors' verification of plant and equipment is facilitated by several factors not applicable to audit work on current assets. What are these factors?

13–2.   K-J Corporation has current assets of $5 million and approximately the same amount of plant and equipment. Should the two groups of assets require about the same amount of audit time? Give reasons.

13–3. What are the objectives of establishing internal control over plant and equipment?

13–4. Identify at least three elements of strong internal control over property, plant, and equipment.

13–5. Explain the use of a system of authorizations for additions to plant and equipment.

13–6. Moultrie Company discovered recently that a number of its property and equipment assets had been retired from use several years ago without any entries being made in the accounting records. The company asks you to suggest procedures that will prevent unrecorded retirement of assets.

13–7. Does a failure to record the retirement of machinery affect net income? Explain.

13–8. The auditors' verification of current assets such as cash, securities, and inventories emphasizes observation, inspection, and confirmation to determine the physical existence of these assets. Should the auditors take a similar approach to establish the existence of the recorded plant assets? Explain fully.

13–9. You are making your first audit of Clarke Manufacturing Company. The Plant and Equipment account represents a very substantial portion of the total assets. What verification, if any, will you make of the balances of the ledger accounts for Plant and Equipment as of the beginning of the period under audit?

13–10. What documentary evidence is usually available to the auditors in the client's office to substantiate the legal ownership of property, plant, and equipment?

13–11. Should the auditors examine public records to determine the legal title of property apparently owned by the client?

13–12. In response to threats from a terrorist organization, Technology International installed protective measures consisting of chainlink fences, concrete road barriers, electronic gates, and underground parking at its manufacturing facilities. The costs of these installations were debited to the Land account. Indicate with reasons your approval or disapproval of this accounting treatment.

13–13. Should the independent auditors observe a physical inventory of property and equipment in every audit engagement? Discuss.

13–14. Hamlin Metals Company has sales representatives covering several states and provides automobiles for them and for its executives. Describe any substantive tests you would consider appropriate for the company's fleet of more than 100 automobiles, other than the verification procedures generally applicable to all property and equipment.

13–15. What is a principal objective of the auditors in analyzing a Maintenance and Repairs expense account?

13–16. Gibson Manufacturing Company acquired new factory machinery this year and ceased using the old machinery. The old equipment was retained, however, and is capable of being used if the demand for the company's products warrants additional production. How should the old machinery be handled in the accounting records and on the financial statements?

13–17. List three substantive tests the auditors could use to detect unrecorded retirements of property, plant, and equipment.

13–18. Do the auditors question the service lives adopted by the client for plant assets, or do they accept the service lives without investigation? Explain.

13–19. Explain why the auditors may need to use the work of a specialist in the audit of goodwill.

13–20. Explain how the existence of lease agreements may result in understated plant and equipment.

13–21. Suggest several comparisons to be made as part of the auditors' analytical procedures for:

    a. Plant and Equipment.

    b. Depreciation.

Questions Requiring Analysis

13–22. Give the purposes of each of the following procedures that may be included in an internal control, and explain how each procedure contributes to strong internal control:

    a. Forecasting of expenditures for property, plant, and equipment.

    b. Maintaining a plant ledger for property, plant, and equipment.

(AICPA, adapted)

13–23. An executive of a manufacturing company informs you that no formal procedures have been followed to control the retirement of machinery and equipment. A physical inventory of plant assets has just been completed. It revealed that 25 percent of the assets carried in the ledger were not on hand and had presumably been scrapped. The accounting records have been adjusted to agree with the physical inventory. Outline internal control practices to govern future retirements.

13–24.   Gruen Corporation is a large diversified company with a large amount of property, plant, and equipment and intangible assets, including goodwill. In the past year the company has experienced a significant decline in a number of its lines of business.

Required: *a.* What risk of material misstatement is indicated from the information provided?

             b. Describe how the auditors would generally obtain evidence about the value of goodwill.

13–25.   Kadex Corporation, a small manufacturing company, did not use the services of independent auditors during the first two years of its existence. Near the end of the third year, Kadex retained Jones & Scranton, CPAs, to perform an audit for the year ended December 31. Officials of the company requested that the CPA firm perform only the audit work necessary to provide an audit report on the financial statements for the current year.

             During the first two years of its operation, Kadex had erroneously treated some material acquisitions of plant and equipment as revenue expenditures. No such errors occurred in the third year.

             a. Under these circumstances, would Jones & Scranton, CPAs, be likely to learn of the transactions erroneously treated as revenue expenditures in years 1 and 2? Explain.

             b. Would the income statement and balance sheet prepared at the end of year 3 be affected by the above accounting errors made in years 1 and 2? If so, identify the specific items. Explain fully.

13–26.   Allen Fraser was president of three corporations: Missouri Metals Corporation, Kansas Metals Corporation, and Iowa Metals Corporation. Each of the three corporations owned land and buildings acquired for approximately $500,000. An appraiser retained by Fraser in 20X1 estimated the current value of the land and buildings in each corporation at approximately $3,000,000. The appraisals were recorded in the accounts. A new corporation, called Midwest Corporation, was then formed, and Fraser became its president. The new corporation purchased the assets of the three predecessor corporations, making payment in capital stock. The balance sheet of Midwest Corporation shows land and buildings "valued at cost" in the amount of $9,000,000, the carrying values to the vendor companies at the time of transfer to Midwest Corporation. Do you consider this treatment acceptable? Explain.

13–27.   Your new client, Ross Products, Inc., completed its first fiscal year March 31, 20X4. During the course of your audit you discover the following entry in the general journal, dated April 1, 20X3.

Building	2,400,000	
Mortgage Note Payable		1,400,000
Common Stock		1,000,000

To record (1) acquisition of building constructed by J. A. Ross Construction Co. (a sole proprietorship); (2) assumption of Ross Construction Co. mortgage loan for construction of the Building; and (3) issuance of entire authorized common stock (10,000 shares, $100 par value) to J. A. Ross.

Required: Under these circumstances, what steps should the auditors take to verify the $2,400,000 recorded cost of the building? Explain fully.

13–28.   Shortly after you were retained to audit the financial statements of Case Corporation, you learned from a preliminary discussion with management that the corporation had recently acquired a competing business, the Mall Company. In your study of the terms of the acquisition, you find that the total purchase price was paid in cash and that the transaction was authorized by the board of directors and fully described in the minutes of the directors' meetings. The only aspect of the acquisition of the Mall Company that raises any doubts in your mind is the allocation of the total purchase price among the several kinds of assets acquired. The allocation, which had been specifically approved by the board of directors of Case Corporation, placed very high values on the tangible assets acquired and allowed nothing for goodwill.

             You are inclined to believe that the allocation of the lump-sum price to the several types of assets was somewhat unreasonable because the total price for the business was as much as or more than the current replacement cost of the tangible assets acquired. However, as an auditor, you do not claim to be an expert in property values. Would you question the propriety of the directors' allocation of the lump-sum purchase price? Explain fully.

13–29. List and state the purpose of all audit procedures that might reasonably be applied by the auditors to determine that all property and equipment retirements have been recorded in the accounting records.

13–30. Girard Corporation has just completed the acquisition of Williams, Inc., at a purchase price significantly higher than the fair values of the identifiable assets. Describe the audit issues caused by the acquisition and how the auditors would likely resolve the issues.

Multiple Choice Questions

13–31. Select the best answer for each of the questions below and explain fully the reason for your selection.

a. To assure accountability for fixed asset retirements, management should implement an internal control that includes:

(1) Continuous analysis of miscellaneous revenue to locate any cash proceeds from the sale of plant assets.

(2) Periodic inquiry of plant executives by internal auditors as to whether any plant assets have been retired.

(3) Utilization of serially numbered retirement work orders.

(4) Periodic observation of plant assets by the internal auditors.

b. The auditors may conclude that depreciation charges are insufficient by noting:

(1) Insured values greatly in excess of book values.

(2) Large amounts of fully depreciated assets.

(3) Continuous trade-ins of relatively new assets.

(4) Excessive recurring losses on assets retired.

c. Which of the following is an internal control weakness related to factory equipment?

(1) Checks issued in payment of purchases of equipment are not signed by the controller.

(2) All purchases of factory equipment are required to be made by the department in need of the equipment.

(3) Factory equipment replacements are generally made when estimated useful lives, as indicated in depreciation schedules, have expired.

(4) Proceeds from sales of fully depreciated equipment are credited to other income.

d. Which of the following accounts should be reviewed by the auditors to gain reasonable assurance that additions to property, plant, and equipment are *not* understated?

(1) Depreciation.

(2) Accounts Payable.

(3) Cash.

(4) Repairs.

e. The auditors are most likely to seek information from the plant manager with respect to the

(1) Adequacy of the provision for uncollectible accounts.

(2) Appropriateness of physical inventory observation procedures.

(3) Existence of obsolete machinery.

(4) Deferral of procurement of certain necessary insurance coverage.

f. To strengthen internal control over the custody of heavy mobile equipment, the client would most likely institute a policy requiring a periodic:

(1) Increase in insurance coverage.

(2) Inspection of equipment and reconciliation with accounting records.

(3) Verification of liens, pledges, and collateralizations.

(4) Accounting for work orders.

g. Which of the following statements is *not* typical of property, plant and equipment as compared to most current asset accounts?

(1) A property, plant and equipment cutoff error near year-end has a more significant effect on net income.

(2) Relatively few transactions occur in property, plant and equipment during the year.

(3) The assets involved with property, plant and equipment ordinarily have relatively longer lives.

(4) Property, plant and equipment accounts typically have higher dollar value.

h. For the audit of a continuing nonpublic client, the emphasis of the testing for property accounts is on:

(1) All transactions resulting in the ending balance.

(2) Tests of controls over disposals.

(3) Transactions that occurred during the year.

(4) Performing analytical procedures on beginning balances of the accounts.

i. Audit of which of the following accounts is most likely to reveal evidence relating to recorded retirements of equipment?

(1) Accumulated depreciation.

(2) Cost of goods sold.

(3) Purchase returns and allowances.

(4) Purchase discounts.

j. An effective procedure for identifying unrecorded retirements of equipment is to:

(1) Foot related property records.

(2) Recalculate depreciation on the related equipment.

(3) Select items of equipment in the accounting records and then locate them in the plant.

(4) Select items of equipment and then locate them in the accounting records.

k. Which of the following is *not* an overall test of the annual provision for depreciation expense?

(1) Compare rates used in the current year with those used in prior years.

(2) Test computation of depreciation provisions for a representative number of units.

(3) Test deductions from accumulated depreciation for assets purchased during the year.

(4) Perform analytical procedures.

l. The audit of intangible asserts typically involves

	Vouching the Cost of Assets	Testing Allocation Methods
(1)	Yes	Yes
(2)	Yes	No
(3)	No	Yes
(4)	No	No

(AICPA, adapted)

Problems

13–32. The following are typical questions that might appear on an internal control questionnaire relating to plant and equipment:

1. Has a dollar minimum been established for expenditures to be capitalized?

2. Are subsidiary ledgers for plant and equipment regularly reconciled with general ledger controlling accounts?

Required:

a. State the purpose of each of the above controls.

b. Describe the manner in which each of the above procedures might be tested.

c. Assuming that the operating effectiveness of each of the above procedures is found to be inadequate, describe how the auditors might alter their substantive tests to compensate for the increased level of control risk.

13–33. J. Barnes, CPA, has been retained to audit a manufacturing company with a balance sheet that includes the caption Property, Plant, and Equipment. Barnes has been asked by the company's management if audit adjustments or reclassifications are required for the following material items that have been included or excluded from Property, Plant, and Equipment.

1. A tract of land was acquired during the year. The land is the future site of the client's new headquarters, which will be constructed in the following year. Commissions were paid to the real estate agent used to acquire the land, and expenditures were made to relocate the previous owner's equipment. These commissions and expenditures were expensed and are excluded from Property, Plant, and Equipment.

2. Clearing costs were incurred to make the land ready for construction. These costs were included in Property, Plant, and Equipment.

3. During the land-clearing process, timber and gravel were recovered and sold. The proceeds from the sale were recorded as other income and are excluded from Property, Plant, and Equipment.

4. A group of machines was purchased under a royalty agreement, which provides royalty payments based on units of production from the machines. The cost of the machines, freight costs, unloading charges, and royalty payments were capitalized and are included in Property, Plant, and Equipment.

Required:

a. Describe the general characteristics of assets, such as land, buildings, improvements, machinery, equipment, and fixtures, that should normally be classified as Property, Plant, and Equipment, and identify audit objectives (i.e., how an auditor can obtain audit satisfaction) in connection with the examination of Property, Plant, and Equipment. Do not discuss specific audit procedures.

b. Indicate whether each of items 1–4, above, requires one or more audit adjustments or reclassifications, and explain why such adjustments or reclassifications are required or not required. Organize your answer as follows:

Item Number	Is Audit Adjustment or Reclassification Required?	Reason(s) Audit Adjustment or Reclassification Is Required or Not Required
	Yes or No	

(AICPA, adapted)

13–34. Assume that you are auditing the financial statements of Agee Corporation. During the course of the audit, you discover the following circumstances.

1. Management of Agee has decided to discontinue the production of consumer electronics, which represents a moderately large line of business for the company.

2. In auditing facility rent expense, you note that the amount is significantly less than in the prior year. When you discuss the matter with management, you are informed that management entered into a new 10-year building lease agreement about nine months ago, which provided for no lease payments for the first year of the lease.

3. In vouching additions to plant assets, you find that management has capitalized the leasehold improvements made on the building acquired in (2), which are being depreciated over an estimated useful life of 12 years.

4. Management has provided you with the following information about a test of impairment of the company's clothing and apparel reporting unit and a large piece of equipment used in the consumer products division of the company. The Clothing and Apparel reporting unit has $1,200,000 in goodwill associated with it.

Clothing and Apparel Reporting Unit

Carrying value of the unit	$12,600,000
Discounted value of estimated future cash flows	12,200,000
Market value of the unit	11,500,000

Equipment

Carrying value of the equipment	$1,200,000
Undiscounted estimated future cash flows	1,250,000
Discounted value of estimated future cash flows	1,000,000
Market value of the equipment	975,000

Required: Describe the implications of each of these circumstances, including any additional information or evidence that the auditors might require to resolve the issues identified.

13–35.   Nova Land Development Corporation is a closely held corporation engaged in purchasing large tracts of land, subdividing the tracts, and installing paved streets and utilities. The corporation does not construct buildings for the buyers of the land and does not have any affiliated construction companies. Undeveloped land usually is leased for farming until the corporation is ready to begin developing it.

The corporation finances its land acquisitions by mortgages; the mortgagees require audited financial statements. This is your first audit of the company, and you have now begun the audit of the financial statements for the year ended December 31.

Required: The corporation has three tracts of land in various stages of development. List the audit procedures to be employed in the verification of the physical existence and title to the corporation's three landholdings.

(AICPA, adapted)

13–36.   You are engaged in the audit of the financial statements of Holman Corporation for the year ended December 31, 20X6. The accompanying analyses of the Property, Plant, and Equipment and related accumulated depreciation accounts have been prepared by the chief accountant of the client. You have traced the beginning balances to your prior year's audit working papers.

HOLMAN CORPORATION
Analysis of Property, Plant, and Equipment
and Related Accumulated Depreciation Accounts
Year Ended December 31, 20X6

Description	Final 12/31/X5	Assets Additions	Assets Retirements	Per Ledger 12/31/X6
Land	$422,500	$ 5,000		$427,500
Buildings	120,000	17,500		137,500
Machinery and equipment	385,000	40,400	$26,000	399,400
	$927,500	$62,900	$26,000	$964,400

Description	Final 12/31/X5	Accumulated Depreciation Additions*	Accumulated Depreciation Retirements	Per Ledger 12/31/X6
Buildings	$ 60,000	$ 5,150		$ 65,150
Machinery and equipment	173,250	39,220		212,470
	$233,250	$44,370		$277,620

*Depreciation expense for the year.

All plant assets are depreciated on the straight-line basis (no residual value taken into consideration) based on the following estimated service lives: building, 25 years; and all other items, 10 years. The company's policy is to take one half-year's depreciation on all asset additions and disposals during the year.

Your audit revealed the following information:

1. On April 1, the company entered into a 10-year lease contract for a die casting machine, with annual rentals of $5,000 payable in advance every April 1. The lease is cancelable by either party (60 days' written notice is required), and there is no option to renew the lease or buy the equipment at the end of the lease. The estimated service life of the machine is 10 years with no residual value. The company recorded the die casting machine in the Machinery and Equipment account at $40,400, the present value at the date of the lease, and $2,020 applicable to the machine has been included in depreciation expense for the year.

2. The company completed the construction of a wing on the plant building on June 30. The service life of the building was not extended by this addition. The lowest construction bid received was $17,500, the amount recorded in the Buildings account. Company personnel constructed the addition at a cost of $16,000 (materials, $7,500; labor, $5,500; and overhead, $3,000).

3. On August 18, $5,000 was paid for paving and fencing a portion of land owned by the company and used as a parking lot for employees. The expenditure was charged to the Land account.

4. The amount shown in the machinery and equipment asset retirement column represents cash received on September 5 upon disposal of a machine purchased in July 20X2 for $48,000. The chief accountant recorded depreciation expense of $3,500 on this machine in 20X6.

5. Harbor City donated land and a building appraised at $100,000 and $400,000, respectively, to Holman Corporation for a plant. On September 1, the company began operating the plant. Since no costs were involved, the chief accountant made no entry for the above transaction.

Required:

Prepare the adjusting journal entries that you would propose at December 31, 20X6, to adjust the accounts for the above transactions. Disregard income tax implications. The accounts have not been closed. Computations should be rounded off to the nearest dollar. Use a separate adjusting journal entry for each of the above five paragraphs.

(AICPA, adapted)

13–37. Chem-Lite, Inc., maintains its accounts on the basis of a fiscal year ending March 31. At March 31, 20X1, the Equipment account in the general ledger appeared as shown below. The company uses straight-line depreciation, 10-year life, and 10 percent salvage value for all its equipment. It is the company's policy to take a full year's depreciation on all additions to equipment occurring during the fiscal year, and you may treat this policy as a satisfactory one for the purpose of this problem. The company has recorded depreciation for the fiscal year ended March 31, 20X1.

Equipment	
4/1/X0 Bal. forward	100,000
12/1/X0	10,500
1/2/X1	1,015
2/1/X1	1,015
3/1/X1	1,015

Upon further investigation, you find the following contract dated December 1, 20X0, covering the acquisition of equipment:

List price	$30,000
5% sales tax	1,500
Total	$31,500
Down payment	10,500
Balance	21,000
8% interest, 24 months	3,360
Contract amount	$24,360

Required:

Prepare in good form, including full explanations, the adjusting entry (entries) you would propose as auditor of Chem-Lite, Inc., with respect to the equipment and related depreciation accounts at March 31, 20X1. (Assume that all amounts given are material.)

(AICPA, adapted)

13–38. You are the senior accountant in the audit of Granger Grain Corporation, whose business primarily involves the purchase, storage, and sale of grain products. The corporation owns several elevators located along navigable water routes and transports its grain by barge and rail. Your staff assistant submitted the following working paper analysis for your review:

Granger Grain Corporation Advances Paid on Barges Under Construction—a/c 210 December 31, 20X1	
Advances made:	
1/15/X1—Ck. No. 3463—Jones Barge Construction Co.	$100,000*
4/13/X1—Ck. No. 4129—Jones Barge Construction Co.	25,000*
6/19/X1—Ck. No. 5396—Jones Barge Construction Co.	63,000*
Total payments	188,000
Deduct cash received 9/1/X1 from City Life Insurance Co.	188,000†
Balance per general ledger—12/31/X1	$ —0—

*Examined approved check request and paid check and traced to cash disbursements journal.

†Traced to cash receipts journal and to duplicate deposit ticket.

Required:

a. In what respects is this brief analysis incomplete for audit purposes? (Do not include any discussion of specific auditing procedures.)

b. What two different types of contractual arrangements may be inferred from your assistant's analysis?

c. What additional auditing procedures would you suggest that your staff assistant perform before you accept the working paper as being complete?

(AICPA, adapted)

In-Class Team Case

13–39. You are reviewing the property, plant, and equipment working papers of Mandville Corporation, a company that publishes travel guides. The lead schedule for the account is included in the chapter as Figure 13.1. The following are among the findings relating to changes in the account:

1. *Land:* The addition represents the purchase of land adjacent to the company's existing plant and is financed as follows:

> Contract sales price—2,000 shares of Mandville Corporation Common Stock
> Liabilities assumed by Mandville
> > Accrued county taxes at settlement date   (4,600)
> > Unpaid sewer installation assessment   (6,400)

On June 17, the date on which the buyer and seller discussed the transaction, shares of Mandville Corporation stock were selling for $77.50. On June 30, the settlement date (day of the sale), Mandville stock was selling for $70.00 per share. The journal entry for the purchase was recorded as:

Land	$151,000	
Common Stock		$ 20,000
Paid-in capital in excess of par		120,000
Accrued taxes payable		4,600
Accrued sewer assessment payable		6,400

Examination of publicly available records has indicated that prices of comparable land in the area have been relatively constant, selling in a range from $140,000 to $160,000 during the past 18 months.

2. *Land improvements:* This account was increased by three journal entries (each recorded with a debit to land improvements and a credit to cash) during the year. Each of these improvements relates to the new land which was purchased in point (1) above.

Sidewalk to building	$2,500
Repaving of road to building	3,500
Chain link fence (replaces rusted chain link fence surrounding property)	4,000

3. *Building:* The building was constructed by an independent contractor; the contract was for $473,000. Progress payments were made during construction through use of proceeds of a bank loan, for which the building serves as collateral. The interest during construction was capitalized ($22,000) while the interest subsequent to construction but prior to year-end ($20,000) was expensed.

4. *Equipment:* The change in the equipment was a trade of old book "update printing equipment" for two new computer servers and associated software that will maintain electronic updates. Until recently, updates of outdated portions of guidebooks were printed and "shrink-wrapped" with the guidebook. Now the updates will be available on Mandville's Web site. The old equipment had a cost of $60,000 and accumulated depreciation of $50,600 and was worth approximately its book value of $9,400, although the salesperson suggested that he was providing the company a $19,400 trade-in value. Accordingly, the following entry was made to record the exchange:

Equipment—computer servers	$110,000	
Accumulated Depr. (old equipment)	50,600	
Cash		$90,600
Equipment—printing equipment		60,000
Gain on exchange of assets		10,000

5. *Depreciation provisions:* Mandville uses software to calculate depreciation to the exact day.

Required:

a. For additions (1) through (4) above, prepare any necessary adjusting entries. If in any case your adjusting entry relies upon an assumption, provide that assumption.

b. For item (5) prepare a calculation of the depreciation provisions and determine whether they appear reasonable. For this calculation assume that acquisitions, on average, occur at mid-year. If the provision does *not* appear reasonable, discuss follow-up procedures related to the provisions. Use the following table for your calculation:

Acct.	Rate	Depr. on Beg. Balance	Add: Depr. on Additions	Less: Depr. on Retirements	Est. Depr.	Book Depr.	Difference
152–3	5%						
154–5	3%						
156–7	10%						
Totals							

Chapter 14

Accounts Payable and Other Liabilities

Chapter learning objectives

After studying this chapter, you should be able to:

LO1. Describe the nature of accounts payable and other liabilities.

LO2. Describe the auditors' objectives for the audit of accounts payable.

LO3. Identify and explain the fundamental controls over payables.

LO4. Assess the risks of material misstatement (inherent and control risks) of accounts payable and other liabilities.

LO5. Design typical tests of controls used by auditors to support the assessed level of control risk for the financial statement assertions related to accounts payable.

LO6. Explain how the auditors design substantive audit procedures to address the risks of material misstatement of accounts payable.

Now that the chapters dealing with the audit of assets have been completed, we are ready to consider the audit of liability accounts. In this chapter we discuss accounts payable and other current liabilities. Chapter 15 includes material on long-term debt, equity capital, and loss contingencies.

Accounts Payable

Sources and Nature of Accounts Payable

Learning Objective 1

The term *accounts payable* (often referred to as *vouchers payable* for a voucher system) is used to describe short-term obligations arising from the purchase of goods and services in the ordinary course of business. Typical transactions creating accounts payable include the acquisition on credit of merchandise, raw materials, plant assets, and office supplies. Other sources of accounts payable include the receipt of services, such as legal and accounting services, advertising, repairs, and utilities. Interest-bearing obligations should not be included in accounts payable but shown separately as bonds, notes, mortgages, or installment contracts.

Invoices and statements from suppliers usually evidence accounts payable arising from the purchase of goods or services and most *other liabilities*. However, **accrued liabilities** (sometimes called *accrued expenses*) generally accumulate over time, and management must make accounting estimates of the year-end liability. Such estimates are often necessary for salaries, pensions, interest, rent, taxes, and similar items.

The Auditors' Approach to Auditing Accounts Payable

Learning Objective 2

The auditors' *objectives* in the audit of accounts payable are to:

1. Consider *inherent risks,* including fraud risks.
2. Consider *internal control* over accounts payable.
3. Determine the *existence* of recorded accounts payable and that the client has obligations to pay these liabilities.
4. Establish the *completeness* of recorded accounts payable.
5. Determine that the *valuation* of accounts payable is in accordance with generally accepted accounting principles.
6. Determine that the *presentation* and *disclosure* of accounts payable are appropriate.

Lawsuits against CPA firms typically allege that the auditors failed to detect an overstatement of earnings. Management, especially of publicly held firms, is often under some pressure to report increased earnings. In previous chapters, we discussed the auditors' concern about exaggeration of earnings that results from the overstatement of assets. In the audit of liabilities, the auditors are primarily concerned with the possibility of understatement, or omission, of liabilities. An *understatement of liabilities* will exaggerate the financial strength of a company and conceal fraud just as effectively as an *overstatement of assets.* Furthermore, the understatement of liabilities is usually accompanied by the understatement of expenses and an overstatement of net income. For example, delaying the recording of bills for December operating expenses until January overstates income while understating accounts payable. Therefore, audit procedures for liabilities should have as a primary objective the determination of the *completeness* of recorded payables.

Audit procedures for detecting understated liabilities differ from those used to detect overstated assets. Overstating an asset account usually requires an improper entry in the accounting records, as by the recording of a fictitious transaction. Such an improper entry can be detected by the auditors through verification of the individual entries making up the balance of an asset account. By way of contrast, understating a liability account is generally possible merely by *failing to make an entry* for a transaction creating a liability. The omission of an entry is less susceptible to detection than is a fictitious entry. If the omission is detected, it is much easier to pass it off as an accidental error. Auditors have long recognized that the most difficult type of fraud to detect is one based on the *nonrecording* of transactions.

When accounts payable entries have been recorded, the existence of a definite financial commitment makes accomplishment of the valuation audit objective less difficult than for assets (other than cash). The situation with accrued liabilities is different. As we suggested earlier, in many circumstances exact measurement of these accounts will be difficult; the auditors must audit management's accounting estimates.

Internal Control over Accounts Payable

In thinking about internal control over accounts payable, it is important to recognize that the accounts payable of one company are the accounts receivable of other companies. It follows that there is little danger of errors being overlooked permanently since the client's creditors will generally maintain complete records of their receivables and will inform the client if payment is not received. This feature also aids auditors in the discovery of fraud, since the perpetrator must be able to obtain and respond to the demands for payment. Some companies, therefore, may choose to minimize their recordkeeping of liabilities and to rely on creditors to call attention to any delay in making payment. This viewpoint is not an endorsement of inaccurate or incomplete records of accounts payable, but merely a recognition that the self-interest of creditors constitutes an effective control in accounting for payables that is not present in the case of accounts receivable.

Discussions of internal control applicable to accounts payable may logically be extended to the entire purchase or acquisition cycle. In an effective purchasing system, a stores or inventory control department will prepare and approve the issuance of a purchase requisition that will be sent to the purchasing department. A copy of the purchase requisition will be filed numerically and matched with the subsequently prepared purchase order and finally with a copy of the receiving report.

The purchasing department, upon receiving the purchase requisition, will (1) determine that the item should be ordered and (2) select the appropriate vendor, quality, and price. Then, a serially numbered purchase order is issued to order the goods. Copies of the purchase order should be sent to stores, receiving, and the accounts payable department. The copy sent to receiving is generally "blind" in that the quantities are not included so as to encourage counting of quantities by the receiving department. But the fact that a vendor's packing slip (with quantities) is almost always included when goods are received may decrease the effectiveness of this control.

The receiving department should be independent of the purchasing department. When goods are received, they should be counted and inspected. Receiving reports should be prepared for all goods received. These documents should be serially numbered and prepared in a sufficient number of copies to permit prompt notification of the receipt of goods to the stores department, the purchasing department, and the accounts payable department.

Within the accounts (vouchers) payable department, all forms should be stamped with the date received. **Vouchers** and other documents originating within the department can be controlled through the use of serial numbers. Each step in the verification of an invoice should be evidenced by entering a date and signature on the voucher. Comparison of the quantities listed on the invoice with those shown on the receiving report and purchase order prevents the payment of charges for goods in excess of those ordered and received. Comparison of the prices, discounts, and terms of shipment as shown on the purchase order and on the vendor's invoice provides a safeguard against the payment of excessive prices.

The separation of the function of invoice verification and approval from the function of cash disbursement is another step that tends to prevent errors and fraud. Before invoices are approved for payment, written evidence must be presented to show that all aspects of the transaction have been verified. The official who signs checks should stamp or perforate the voucher and supporting documents so that they cannot be presented to support payment a second time.

In an IT-based purchasing system, vendor invoice information is entered by the accounting department and may be matched by the IT system with other information. When goods are received, information may be keyed into the IT system with subsequent automated preparation of a receiving report and updating of inventory records. The IT system can match the information from purchase orders, receiving reports, and vendors' invoices and approve appropriate payments of accounts payable. As indicated in Chapter 10, electronic processing of both cash receipts and disbursements can provide management with a continually up-to-date cash record.

Illustrative Case
The Importance of Controls over Accounts Payable

The need for good IT system controls has become increasingly important as in recent years companies have downsized their accounts payable department. For example, *The Wall Street Journal* reports that General Electric Co., which processes in excess of 10 million invoices annually, reduced its accounts payable staff from approximately 400 employees to 180. Part of this reduction was made possible by a decision not to compare invoices with support prior to payment of vendors; payables were analyzed only after the money had been disbursed. The *Journal* reports that GE reduced payroll costs, but duplicate payments and overpayments to vendors increased.

Other companies have encountered similar situations. One corporate official suggests that unscrupulous vendors have become skilled in fooling computerized payables checking systems. He suggests that some vendors send two invoices with different numbers for the same item, and others add a letter to the end of an invoice number.

However, the information technology controls discussed in Chapter 8 must be implemented to ensure the accuracy of the IT system's input, processing, and output.

Another control that the auditors may expect to find in a well-managed accounts payable department is the monthly balancing of the detailed records of accounts payable (or vouchers) to the general ledger control account. These reconciliations should be preserved as evidence of the performance of this procedure and as an aid in locating any subsequent errors.

STATEMENT
Carson Supply Co.
1671 21st St.
Houston, TX 77021

Customer: Morris Construction Co.   June 30, 20XX
1212 Belaire Blvd.
Houston, TX 77062

Date		Amount	Balance
June 1	Beginning balance		$32,785.00
June 5	Invoice #3276485	$ 5,250.00	38,035.00
June 9	Payment	−23,300.00	14,734.00
June 12	Credit #49944	−235.00	14,500.00
June 15	Invoice #3276678	10,220.00	24,720.00
June 26	Payment	14,500.00	
June 30	Ending balance		$10,220.00

Vendors' statements (above), received monthly, should be reconciled promptly with the accounts payable ledger or list of open vouchers, and any discrepancies fully investigated. In some industries, it is common practice to make advances to vendors, which are recovered by making percentage deductions from invoices. When such advances are in use, the auditors should ascertain that procedures are followed to assure that deductions from the invoices are made in accordance with the agreement.

The operation of a purchase or acquisition transaction cycle is illustrated in Figure 14.1.

Audit Documentation for Accounts Payable

The principal working papers are a lead schedule for accounts payable, trial balances of the various types of accounts payable at the balance sheet date, and confirmation requests for accounts payable. The trial balances are often in the form of computer printouts. In addition, the auditors may prepare a listing of *unrecorded* accounts payable discovered during the course of the audit, as illustrated later, in Figure 14.6.

FIGURE 14.1   **Flowchart of a Purchases System**

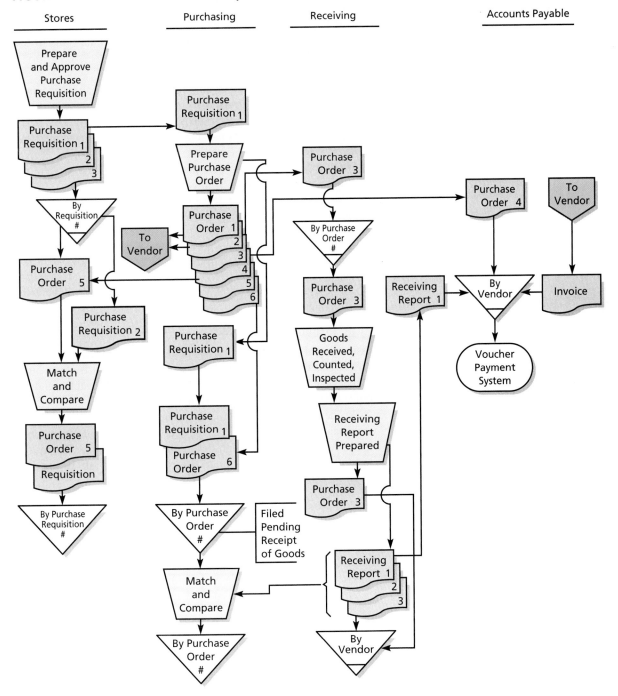

Audit Program

The following procedures are typical of the work required in many engagements for the audit of accounts payable.

A. Consider inherent risks, including fraud risks.

B. Consider internal control over accounts payable.

    1. *Obtain an understanding of internal control* over accounts payable.

    2. *Assess control risk* for each of the major financial statement assertions about accounts payable, *and design additional tests of controls* and substantive tests.

3. *Perform additional tests of controls* for those controls that the auditors plan to consider to support their planned assessed levels of control risk.
   a. Verify a sample of postings to the accounts payable control account.
   b. Vouch to supporting documents a sample of postings in selected accounts of the accounts payable subsidiary ledger.
   c. Test IT application controls.
4. *Reassess control risk* for each of the major financial statement assertions about accounts payable based on the results of tests of controls, *and modify substantive tests.*

C. Substantive tests of accounts payable transactions and balances.
   1. Obtain or prepare a trial balance of accounts payable as of the balance sheet date and reconcile with the general ledger.
   2. Vouch balances payable to selected creditors by inspection of supporting documents.
   3. Reconcile liabilities with monthly statements from creditors.
   4. Confirm accounts payable by direct correspondence with vendors.
   5. Perform analytical procedures for accounts payable and related accounts.
   6. Search for unrecorded accounts payable.
   7. Perform procedures to identify accounts payable to related parties.
   8. Evaluate proper balance sheet presentation and disclosure of accounts payable.

Figure 14.2 relates the objectives of the major substantive tests of payables to the primary audit objectives.

A. Consider Inherent Risks, Including Fraud Risks.

After they obtain an understanding of the client and its business, the auditors are in a position to identify and assess inherent risks of accounts payable. Many of these risks arise from business risks faced by management, such as the risk of payment of unauthorized payables, and the failure to capture all accounts payable for financial reporting purposes.

If any of the inherent risks identified by the auditors are related to fraud, the auditors will make certain that they understand the programs and controls established by management to control the risk. They will also determine that the controls have been implemented. Finally, the auditors will design appropriate responses to these fraud risks and all other risks of material misstatement.

B. Consider Internal Control over Accounts Payable.

1. Obtain an Understanding of Internal Control.

One approach used by auditors in becoming familiar with a client's internal control over accounts payable is to prepare a flowchart or to use flowcharts prepared by the client. In some engagements, the auditors may choose to prepare a narrative description covering such matters as the independence of the accounts payable department and the receiving department from the

---

FIGURE 14.2
Objectives of Major Substantive Tests of Accounts Payable

Substantive Tests	Primary Audit Objectives
Obtain trial balance of payables and reconcile with the ledgers.	*Valuation*
Vouch balances payable to selected creditors by inspecting supporting documents.	*Existence and obligations* *Valuation*
Reconcile liabilities with creditor's monthly statements. Confirm accounts payable. Perform analytical procedures.	*Completeness* *Existence and obligations* *Valuation*
Search for unrecorded accounts payable.	*Completeness*
Perform procedures to identify accounts payable to related parties. Evaluate financial statement presentation and disclosure.	*Presentation and disclosure*

purchasing department. The auditors might also use a questionnaire to obtain a description of accounts payable controls. Typical of the questions are the following: Is an accounts payable trial balance prepared monthly and reconciled to the general ledger controlling account? Are monthly statements from vendors reconciled with accounts payable ledgers or unpaid vouchers? Are advance payments to vendors recorded as receivables and controlled in a manner that assures that they will be recovered by offset against vendors' invoices? Are debit memos issued to vendors for discrepancies in invoice prices, quantities, or computations? Are debit balances in vendors' accounts brought to the attention of the credit and purchasing departments?

After the auditors have prepared a flowchart (or other description) of internal control, they determine whether the client is actually using the controls described to them; that is, they determine whether the controls have been *placed in operation*. The auditors will typically perform a walk-through of several purchase transactions and observe the implementation of the various controls. Figure 14.3, on pages 534–535, illustrates the documents and accounts that the auditors typically encounter in their consideration of controls over purchase transactions.

As the auditors verify their understanding of internal control, they will observe and inquire about the segregation of duties for purchases and cash disbursements. They will also inspect the various documents and reconciliations that are important to the client's internal control over accounts payable. For example, the reconciliations of monthly statements from vendors to the payables ledger will be inspected. Budgets for cash disbursements will be inspected and the auditors will review the evidence of the follow-up on variances from budgeted amounts of disbursements. These procedures may serve as tests of controls that provide the auditors with sufficient evidence to assess control risk for certain financial statement assertions about accounts payable as being at less than the maximum.

2. Assess Control Risk and Design Additional Tests of Controls and Substantive Tests.

Learning Objective 5

Based on their understanding of the client's internal control over accounts payable, the auditors develop their planned assessed levels of control risk for the assertions about accounts payable. To support these assessments, the auditors may need to obtain additional evidence of the operating effectiveness of various controls. This evidence is obtained by performing additional tests of controls. In designing these tests, the auditors must decide which ones will result in sufficient reductions in substantive tests to justify the time spent performing them.

The auditors' assessment of control risk, along with their assessment of inherent risk, will be used to plan the nature, timing, and extent of substantive tests for accounts payable. In designing planned substantive tests the auditors will consider potential misstatements that may occur and the weaknesses in control or other factors that make the misstatements more likely, as illustrated in Figure 14.4.

3. Perform Additional Tests of Controls.

Tests directed toward the effectiveness of controls help to evaluate the client's internal control and determine whether the auditors can support their planned assessed levels of control risk for the assertions about the accounts payable. A number of tests of controls relating to accounts payable have already been discussed in Chapters 10 and 12. In this chapter we briefly recap several significant tests.

a. Verify a Sample of Postings to the Accounts Payable Control Account.

The validity of the amount in the general ledger control account for accounts payable is established by tracing postings to the **voucher register** and cash disbursements journal. This work is performed before the balance sheet date as part of a general test of postings to all records. At the same time, the auditors should scrutinize all entries to the control account for the entire period under audit and should investigate any unusual entries.

b. Vouch to Supporting Documents a Sample of Postings in Selected Accounts of the Accounts Payable Subsidiary Ledger.

Testing the voucher register or the accounts payable ledgers by tracing specific items back through the cash payments journal, purchases journal, and other journals to original documents (such as purchase orders, receiving reports, invoices, and paid checks) is necessary to

FIGURE 14.3 Overview of the Purchases Cycle—Documents and Accounts

Purchases

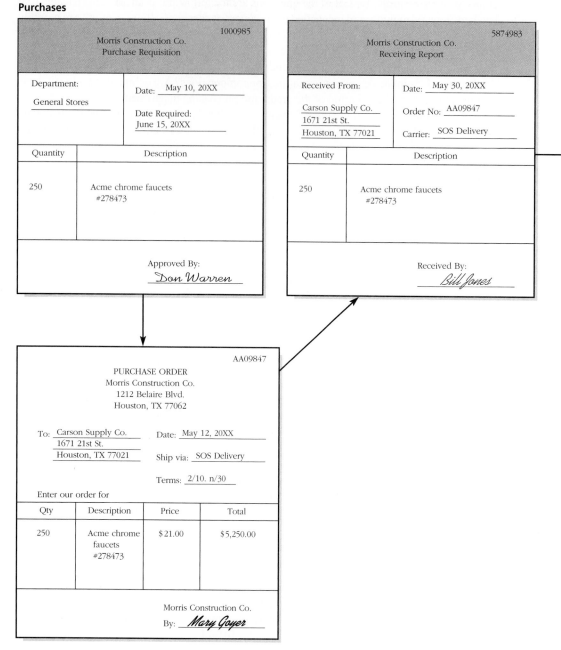

determine the operating effectiveness of certain controls. If the functions of purchasing, receiving, invoice verification, and cash disbursement are delegated to separate departments and controls appear adequate, the tracing of individual items from the ledgers to the original records may provide the auditors with sufficient evidence to assess control risk for certain assertions related to accounts payable as being at a low level.

The auditors may also perform tests by following the audit trail in the opposite direction. By tracing a representative sample of entries from the source documents to the accounts payable ledger, the auditors can verify that accounts payable are completely and accurately recorded on a timely basis.

c. Test IT Application Controls.

When the client has established effective IT application controls for purchase transactions, the auditors may find it more efficient to test these controls rather than to test a sample of purchase

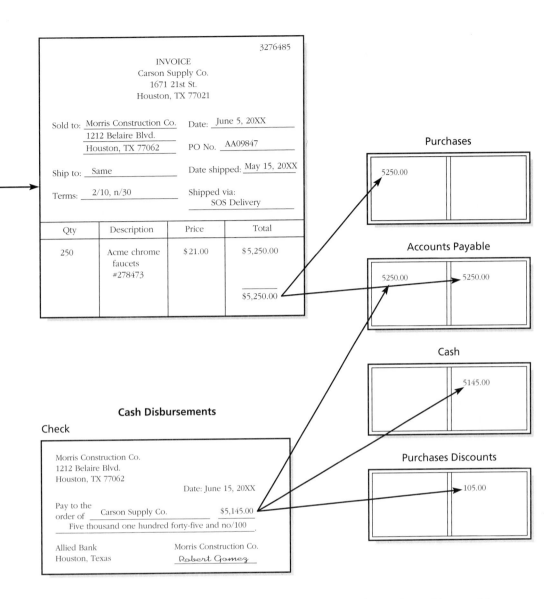

transactions. Batch processing controls might be tested by inspecting evidence of the reconciliations of batch control totals by the control group. In addition, a sample of the exception reports printed by the computer when the vendors' invoices do not match purchasing and receiving information might be inspected, as well as evidence of follow-up on these exceptions.

4. Reassess Control Risk and Modify Substantive Tests.

Learning Objective 6

Completion of the above audit procedures enables the auditors to perform a final assessment of control risk for each of the major financial statement assertions about accounts payable. The auditors use this reassessment of control risk to determine whether it is necessary to modify their planned program of substantive procedures.

An assessment of low control risk for accounts payable often means that the auditors have found that serially numbered receiving reports are prepared promptly by the client for all goods received, that serially numbered vouchers are prepared and recorded in the voucher register, and that payments are made promptly on the due dates and immediately recorded in the cash payments journal and accounts payable subsidiary ledger. Finally, at the end of each month, an employee who does not participate in processing accounts payable compares the individual accounts in the accounts payable subsidiary ledger with vendors' statements and also compares the total of the subsidiary record with the general ledger control account. This strong internal control would enable the auditors to minimize substantive testing of accounts payable.

FIGURE 14.4 Potential Misstatements—Accounts Payable

Description of Misstatement	Examples	Internal Control Weaknesses or Factors That Increase the Risk of the Misstatement
Inaccurate recording of a purchase or disbursement	**Fraud:** • A bookkeeper prepares a check to himself and records it as having been issued to a major supplier. **Error:** • A disbursement is made to pay an invoice for goods that have not been received.	• Inadequate segregation of duties of recordkeeping and preparing cash disbursements, or check signer does not review and cancel supporting documents. • Ineffective controls for matching invoices with receiving documents before disbursements are authorized.
Misappropriation of purchases	**Fraud:** • Goods are ordered but delivered to an inappropriate address and stolen.	• Ineffective controls for matching invoices with receiving documents before disbursements are authorized.
Duplicate recording of purchases	**Error:** • A purchase is recorded when an invoice is received from a vendor and recorded again when a duplicate invoice is sent by the vendor.	• Ineffective controls for review and cancellation of supporting documents by the check signer.
Late (early) recording of cost of purchases—"cutoff problems"	**Fraud:** • Purchases journal "closed early" with this period's purchases recorded as having occurred in subsequent period.	• Ineffective board of directors, audit committee, or internal audit function; "tone at the top" not conducive to ethical conduct; undue pressure to meet earnings target.

On the other hand, an assessment of high control risk for accounts payable often means that the auditors have found that the subsidiary record of accounts payable is not in agreement with the general ledger control account, that receiving reports and vouchers are used haphazardly, that purchase transactions often are not recorded until payment is made, and that many accounts payable are long past due. In this situation, the auditors must undertake extensive substantive work if they are to determine that the balance sheet amount for accounts payable includes all liabilities in existence at the balance sheet date.

C. Substantive Tests of Accounts Payable Transactions and Balances.

1. Obtain or Prepare a Trial Balance of Accounts Payable as of the Balance Sheet Date and Reconcile with the General Ledger.

One purpose of this procedure is to determine that the liability figure appearing in the balance sheet is in agreement with the individual items comprising the detailed records. A second purpose is to provide a starting point for substantive testing. The auditors will use the list of vouchers or accounts payable to select a representative group of items for careful examination.

The client company usually furnishes the auditors with a year-end trial balance. The auditors should verify the footing and the accuracy of individual amounts in the trial balance. If the schedule of individual items does not agree in total with the control account, the cause of the discrepancy must be investigated. In most situations, the auditors will arrange for the client's staff to locate such errors and make the necessary adjustments. Agreement of the control account and the list of individual account balances is not absolute proof of the total indebtedness; invoices received near the close of the period may not be reflected in either the control account or the subsidiary records, and other similar errors may exist without causing the accounts to be out of balance.

Primary Audit Objective:

Valuation ☑

**Primary Audit
Objectives:**

Existence	☑
Obligations	☑
Valuation	☑

2. Vouch Balances Payable to Selected Creditors by Inspection of Supporting Documents.

The vouching of selected creditors' balances to supporting vouchers, invoices, purchase orders, and receiving reports is a substantive test of the existence and valuation of accounts payable. For companies that use a voucher system, the verification of the individual vouchers is made most conveniently at the balance sheet date, when the vouchers will be together in the unpaid voucher file. The content of the unpaid voucher file changes daily; as vouchers are paid, they are removed from the file and filed alphabetically by vendor. Consequently, it is important that the client maintain a list of year-end unpaid vouchers. This listing should show the names of vendors, voucher numbers, dates, and amounts.

3. Reconcile Liabilities with Monthly Statements from Creditors.

**Primary Audit
Objectives:**

Completeness	☑
Existence	☑
Obligations	☑
Valuation	☑

In some companies, it is a regular practice each month to reconcile vendors' statements with the detailed records of payables. If the auditors find that the client's staff regularly performs this reconciliation, they may limit their review of vendors' statements to determining that the reconciliation work has been satisfactory.

If the client's staff has not reconciled vendors' statements and accounts payable, the auditors may do so on a selected basis. When control risk for accounts payable is high, the auditors may control incoming mail to assure that all vendors' statements received by the client are made available to the auditors. Among the discrepancies often revealed by reconciliation of vendors' statements are charges by the vendor for shipments not yet received or recorded by the client. Although conceptually all goods on which title has passed should be included in inventory (thus items shipped FOB [free on board] shipping point as of year-end and not yet received should be included), normal accounting procedures often do not provide for recording invoices as liabilities until the merchandise has been received. In-transit shipments on which title has passed should be listed and a decision reached as to whether they are sufficiently material to warrant year-end adjustment.

4. Confirm Accounts Payable by Direct Correspondence with Vendors.

**Primary Audit
Objectives:**

Completeness	☑
Existence	☑
Obligations	☑
Valuation	☑

Although **confirmation** of accounts payable is a widely used procedure, it is generally considered less necessary than is the confirmation of accounts receivable. One reason is that for accounts payable the auditors will find in the client's possession externally created evidence such as vendors' invoices and statements that substantiate the accounts payable. No such external evidence is on hand to support accounts receivable.

Another reason for the difference in significance attached to confirmation of accounts payable is that the greatest risk in the audit of liabilities is the possibility of unrecorded amounts. While confirmation can provide evidence about completeness, it is a more effective procedure for establishing existence and valuation of an item. To make the confirmation procedure more effective at addressing the completeness of accounts payable, the auditors will often use a *blank form,* as illustrated by Figure 14.5. This form asks the vendor to fill in the amount of the liability rather than to confirm a recorded amount.

Also, accounts payable confirmation requests should be mailed to vendors from whom substantial purchases have been made during the year, regardless of the size of their accounts at the balance sheet date (even to suppliers whose accounts show *zero balances*). These substantial suppliers may be identified by reference to cash disbursement records or computer print-outs of purchase volume by individual supplier, inquiry of purchasing department personnel, and examination of the accounts payable subsidiary ledger. Other accounts that often are confirmed by the auditors include those for which monthly statements are not available, accounts reflecting unusual transactions, accounts with parent or subsidiary corporations, and accounts secured by pledged assets.

5. Perform Analytical Procedures for Accounts Payable and Related Accounts.

**Primary Audit
Objectives:**

Completeness	☑
Existence	☑
Obligations	☑
Valuation	☑

To gain assurance as to the overall reasonableness of accounts payable, the auditor may compute ratios such as purchases divided by accounts payable and accounts payable divided by total current liabilities. These ratios are compared with ratios for prior years to disclose trends that warrant investigation.

The list of amounts payable to individual vendors should be reviewed to identify any companies from which the client does not ordinarily acquire goods or services. The amounts owed

FIGURE 14.5
Accounts Payable Confirmation

PACKAGE   SYSTEMS,   INC.

9200 CHANNEL STREET
NEW ORLEANS, LOUISIANA 70128

January 2, 20X2

Grayline Container, Inc.
4800 Madison Street
Dallas, Texas 75221

Dear Sirs:

Our independent auditors, Nelson & Gray, CPAs, are performing an audit of our financial statements. For this reason, please inform them in the space provided below the amount, if any, owed to you by this company at December 31, 20X1.

Please attach an itemized statement supporting any balance owed, showing all unpaid items. Your reply should be sent directly to Nelson & Gray, CPAs, 6500 Lane Avenue, New Orleans, Louisiana 70128. A stamped, addressed envelope is enclosed for your reply. Thank you.

Sincerely,

Robert W. James

Robert W. James
Controller

- -

Nelson & Gray, CPAs

Our records show that the amount of $_____26,800_____ was owed to us by Package Systems, Inc., at December 31, 20X1, as shown by the itemized statement attached.

Date: __Jan. 6, 20X2__   Signature ___*Sharon Steele*___

Title ___*Controller*___

---

to individual creditors should also be compared with balances in prior years. By studying yearly variations in purchases and other accounts closely related to accounts payable, the auditors may become aware of errors in accounts payable. Finally, the portion of accounts payable that is past due at year-end should be compared with corresponding data for previous years.

The auditors may test purchase discounts by computing the ratio of cash discounts earned to total purchases during the period and comparing this ratio from period to period. Any significant decrease in the ratio might indicate a change in terms of purchases, failure to take discounts, or fraudulent manipulation.

6. Search for Unrecorded Accounts Payable.

Throughout the audit the auditors must be alert for any unrecorded payables. For example, the preceding three steps of this program—reconciliation, confirmation, and analytical procedures—may disclose unrecorded liabilities. In addition to normal trade payables that may

Primary Audit Objective:
Completeness ☑

be unrecorded, other examples include unrecorded liabilities related to customers' deposits recorded as credits to accounts receivable, obligation for securities purchased but not settled at the balance sheet date, unbilled contractor or architect fees for a building under construction at the audit date, and unpaid attorney or insurance broker fees.

In addition to the prior audit steps, when searching for unrecorded accounts payable the auditors will examine transactions that were recorded following year-end. A comparison of cash payments occurring after the balance sheet date with the accounts payable trial balance is generally the most effective means of disclosing unrecorded accounts payable. All liabilities must eventually be paid and will, therefore, be reflected in the accounts at least by the time they are paid. Regular monthly expenses, such as rent and utilities, are often posted to the ledger accounts directly from the cash disbursements journal without any account payable or other liability having been set up. Therefore, the auditors will often examine all cash disbursements over specific dollar amounts that are made by the client during the **subsequent period.**

The auditors should also consider potential sources of unrecorded payables such as the following:

a. Unmatched invoices and unbilled receiving reports. These documents are called *work in process* in a voucher system. The auditors should review such unprocessed documents at the balance sheet date to ascertain that the client has recorded an account payable where appropriate.

b. Vouchers payable entered in the voucher register subsequent to the balance sheet date. Inspection of these records may uncover an item that should have been recorded as of the balance sheet date.

c. Invoices received by the client after the balance sheet date. Not all vendors send invoices promptly when goods are shipped or services are rendered. Accordingly, the auditors' review of invoices received by the client in the subsequent period may disclose unrecorded accounts payable as of the balance sheet date.

d. **Consignments** in which the client acts as a consignee. The consignee assumes liability for consigned merchandise when those goods have been sold to third parties. Those sales, especially shortly before the year-end, may not have been set up as a liability to the consignor. While the auditors' overall knowledge about the accounting for such consigned items will dictate the appropriate procedures, those related to the revenue cycle such as tests of sales transactions around year-end may reveal such sales.

A form of audit working paper used to summarize unrecorded accounts payable discovered by the auditors is illustrated in Figure 14.6.

When the auditors discover unrecorded liabilities, the next question is whether the omissions are sufficiently material to warrant proposing an adjusting entry. Will the adjustment cause a sufficient change in the financial statements to give a different impression of the company's current position or of its earning power? As previously indicated in the discussion of the reconciliation of vendors' statements with accounts payable, auditors may choose not to propose adjustments for the purpose of adding shipments in transit to the year-end inventory unless the shipments are unusually large.

As a further illustration of the factors to be considered in deciding upon the *materiality* of an unrecorded transaction, let us use as an example the December 31 annual audit of a small manufacturing company in good financial condition with total assets of $3 million and preadjustment net income of $100,000. The auditors' procedures bring to light the following unrecorded liabilities:

a. An invoice of $1,400, dated December 30 and bearing terms of FOB shipping point. The goods were shipped on December 30 but were not received until January 4. The invoice was also received and recorded on January 4.

In considering the materiality of this omission, the first point is that net income is not affected. The adjusting entry, if made, would add equal amounts to current assets (inventories) and to current liabilities; hence it would not change the amount of working capital. The

FIGURE 14.6 **Search for Unrecorded Liabilities**

```
                        THE PALERNO COMPANY                      M-1-1
                     Unrecorded Accounts Payable
                         December 31, 20X3                        ℒK
                                                                 2/19/X4


            Invoice                                  Account
    Date    Number        Vendor and Description     Charged        Amount

  12/31/X3   2581   Hayes Mfg. Co.—invoice and shipment in transit  Inventories   $10,650.00

  12/31/X3   2428   Tax & Williams—unpaid legal fees—see M-4        Legal          1,000.00
                                                                    Expenses

  12/31/X3    –     Allen Enterprises—12/19 account sales for       Sales         25,680.00
                    consigned goods

     –        –     Hart & Co.—machinery repairs (paid 1/1/X4)      Repairs       12,600.00
                                                                    Expense

     –        –     Grant Co.—shipment received 12/31/X3 per        Cost of Sales 15,820.00
                    receiving report no. 2907; invoice not yet
                    received

     –        –     Arthur & Baker—earned but unpaid architects' fee Construction
                    for building under construction—see K5          in Progress   23,370.00

                                                                                 $89,120.00


  – – – – – – – – – – – – – – – – – – – – – – – – – – – – – – – – – – – – – – – – –

  A.J.E. #8    131 Inventories                 10,650.00
               501 Cost of Sales               15,820.00
               156 Construction in Progress    23,370.00
               401 Sales                       25,680.00
               518 Legal Expenses               1,000.00
               527 Repairs Expense             12,600.00
               203 Accounts Payable                         89,120.00

               To record unrecorded accounts payable at 12/31/X3


               The above payables were identified principally in the audit of accounts payable.
               See audit program B-4 for procedures employed. In my opinion the $89,120
               adjustment includes all material unrecorded accounts payable.
                                                                       ℒK
                                                                      2/23/X4
```

omission does affect the current ratio very slightly. The auditor would probably consider this transaction as not sufficiently material to warrant adjustment.

b. Another invoice for $4,000, dated December 30 and bearing terms of FOB shipping point. The goods arrived on December 31 and were included in the physical inventory taken that day. The invoice was not received until January 8 and was entered as a January transaction.

This error should be corrected because the inclusion of the goods in the physical inventory without recognition of the liability has caused an error of $4,000 in pretax income for the year. Since the current liabilities are understated, both the amount of working capital and the current ratio are overstated. The owners' equity is also overstated. These facts point to the materiality of the omission and constitute strong arguments for an adjusting entry.

c. An invoice for $1,500, dated December 31, for a new office safe. The safe was installed on December 31, but the invoice was not recorded until paid on January 15.

Since the transaction involves only asset and liability accounts, the omission of an entry does not affect net income. However, working capital and the current ratio are affected by the error since the debit affects a noncurrent asset and the credit affects a current liability. Most auditors would probably not propose an adjusting entry for this item.

d. An invoice for $3,000, dated December 31, for advertising services rendered during October, November, and December. The invoice was not recorded until paid on January 15.

The argument for treating this item as sufficiently material to warrant adjustment is based on the fact that net income is affected, as well as the amount of working capital and the current ratio. The adjusting entry should probably be recommended in these circumstances.

The preceding examples suggest that a decision as to the materiality of an unrecorded transaction hinges to an important extent on whether the transaction affects net income. Assuming that an omitted transaction does affect net income and there is doubt as to whether the dollar amount is large enough to warrant adjustment, the auditors should bear in mind that about one-third of the effect of the error on net income may be eliminated by corporate income taxes. In other words, an adjusting entry to record an omitted expense item of $10,000 may reduce after-tax income by only $6,500. If the adjusting entry is not made, the only ultimate effect is a shift of $6,500 between the net incomes of two successive years. Unless the client requests all adjusting entries, the auditors should avoid proposing adjusting entries for clearly inconsequential errors in the year-end cutoff of transactions. However, it should be borne in mind that a number of insignificant individual misstatements may be material in their *cumulative* effect on the financial statements. Therefore, the auditors will accumulate the effects of the adjusting entries not proposed (passed) to consider them with misstatements detected in other accounts, as discussed in Chapter 16.

7. Perform Procedures to Identify Accounts Payable to Related Parties.

Primary Audit Objective:
Presentation ☑

Payables to a corporation's officers, directors, stockholders, or affiliates require particular attention by the auditors since they are not the result of arm's-length bargaining by parties of opposing interests. Here the auditors should consider the possibility that these payables relate to purchases of inventory or other asset items for which there may be valuation questions.

The independent auditors must search for such payables. All material payables to related parties must be disclosed in the financial statements.

8. Evaluate Proper Balance Sheet Presentation and Disclosure of Accounts Payable.

Primary Audit Objective:
Presentation ☑

Proper balance sheet presentation of accounts payable requires that any material amounts payable to related parties (directors, principal stockholders, officers, and employees) be listed separately from amounts payable to trade creditors.

Debit balances of substantial amount sometimes occur in accounts payable because of such events as duplicate payments made in error, return of merchandise to vendors after payment has been made, and advances to suppliers. If these debit balances are material, a reclassification entry should be made in the audit working papers so that the debit balances will appear as assets in the balance sheet rather than being offset against other accounts payable with credit balances.

If the client company acts as a consignee of merchandise, it is possible that sales of consigned goods shortly before the year-end may not have been set up as a liability to the consignor. An accurate determination of any amounts owing to consignors at the balance sheet date is one step in proper balance sheet presentation of liabilities.

Accounts payable secured by pledged assets should be disclosed in the balance sheet (or a note thereto) and cross-referenced to the pledged assets.

Other Liabilities

Notes payable are discussed in the next chapter. In addition to the accounts payable previously considered, other items classified as current liabilities include:

1. Amounts withheld from employees' pay.
2. Sales taxes payable.
3. Unclaimed wages.
4. Customers' deposits.
5. Accrued liabilities.

Amounts Withheld from Employees' Pay

Payroll deductions are numerous; among the more important are Social Security taxes and individual income taxes. Although the federal and state governments do not specify the exact form of records to be maintained, they do require that records of amounts earned and withheld be adequate to permit a determination of compliance with tax laws.

Income taxes withheld from employees' pay and not remitted as of the balance sheet date constitute a liability to be verified by the auditors. Accrued employer payroll taxes may be audited at the same time. This verification usually consists of tracing the amounts withheld to the payroll summary sheets, testing computations of taxes withheld and accrued, determining that taxes have been deposited or paid in accordance with federal and state laws and regulations, and reviewing quarterly tax returns.

Payroll deductions also are often made for union dues, charitable contributions, retirement plans, insurance, savings bonds, and other purposes. Besides verifying the liability for any such amounts withheld from employees and not remitted as of the balance sheet date, the auditors should review the adequacy of the withholding procedures and determine that payroll deductions have been properly authorized and accurately computed.

Sales Taxes Payable

In most sections of the country, business concerns are required to collect sales taxes imposed by state and local governments on retail sales. These taxes do not represent an expense to the business; the retailer merely acts as a collecting agent. Until the amounts collected from customers are remitted to the taxing authority, they constitute current liabilities of the business. The auditors' verification of this liability includes a review of the client's periodic tax returns. The reasonableness of the liability also is tested by a computation applying the tax rate to total taxable sales. In addition, the auditors should examine a number of sales invoices to ascertain that customers are being charged the correct amount of tax. Debits to the liability account for remittances to the taxing authority should be traced to copies of the tax returns and vouched to the paid checks.

Unclaimed Wages

Unclaimed wages are, by their very nature, subject to misappropriation. The auditors, therefore, are concerned with the adequacy of internal control over this item. A list of unpaid wages should be prepared after each payroll distribution. The payroll checks should not be left for more than a few days in the payroll department. Prompt deposit in a special bank account provides much improved control. The auditors will analyze the Unclaimed Wages account for the purpose of determining that (1) the credits represent all unclaimed wages after each payroll distribution and (2) the debits represent only authorized payments to employees, remittances to the state under unclaimed property laws, or transfers back to general cash funds through approved procedures.

Customers' Deposits

Many companies require that customers make deposits on returnable containers. Public utilities and common carriers also may require deposits to guarantee payment of bills or to cover equipment on loan to the customer. A review of the procedures followed in accepting and returning deposits should be made by the auditors with a view to disclosing any shortcomings in internal control. In some instances, deposits shown by the records as refunded to customers may in fact have been abstracted by employees.

The verification should include obtaining a list of the individual deposits and a comparison of the total with the general ledger control account. If deposits are interest-bearing, the amount of accrued interest should also be tested for reasonableness. As a general rule, the auditors do not attempt to confirm deposits by direct communication with customers; however, this procedure is desirable if the amounts involved are substantial or controls are considered to be deficient.

Accrued Liabilities

Most accrued liabilities (expenses) represent obligations payable sometime during the succeeding period for services or privileges received before the balance sheet date. Examples include interest payable, accrued property taxes, accrued payrolls and payroll taxes, income taxes payable, and amounts accrued under service guarantees.

Accrued liabilities represent accounting estimates made by the client of amounts that will subsequently become payable. Recall from Chapter 5 that, in evaluating the reasonableness of accounting estimates, auditors use one or more of the following three basic approaches:

1. Review and test management's process of developing the estimate.
2. Review subsequent events or transactions bearing on the estimate.
3. Independently develop an estimate of the amount to compare to management's estimate.

For most accrued liabilities the audit approach will emphasize a review and test of management's process of developing the estimates (see particularly audit program steps 1 through 5 below).

Subjective (as well as objective) factors may make it difficult to establish control over accrued liabilities. As a result, these estimates may be particularly susceptible to misstatement, especially in circumstances in which management is under pressure to show increased earnings.

The basic auditing steps for accrued liabilities are:

1. Examine any contracts or other documents on hand that provide the basis for the accrual.
2. Appraise the accuracy of the detailed accounting records maintained for this category of liability.
3. Identify and evaluate the reasonableness of the assumptions made that underlie the computation of the liability.
4. Test the computations made by the client in setting up the accrual.
5. Determine that accrued liabilities have been treated consistently at the beginning and end of the period.
6. Consider the need for accrual of other accrued liabilities not presently considered (that is, test completeness).
7. For significant estimates, perform retrospective analysis of the prior year estimates for evidence of management bias.

The following sections describe the nature of the audit of various accrued liabilities.

Accrued Property Taxes

Property tax payments are usually few in number and substantial in amount. It is, therefore, feasible for the audit working papers to include an analysis showing all of the year's property tax transactions. Tax payments should be verified by inspection of the property tax bills issued by local government units and by reference to the related paid checks. If the tax accruals at the balance sheet date differ significantly from those of prior years, an explanation of the variation should be obtained. The auditors should verify that property tax bills have been received on all taxable property or that an estimated tax has been accrued.

Accrued Payrolls

The examination of payrolls from the standpoint of appraising the adequacy of controls and substantiating the expenditures for the period under audit is considered in Chapter 16. The present consideration of payrolls is limited to the procedures required for testing accrued payrolls at the balance sheet date.

Accrued gross salaries and wages appear on the balance sheets of virtually all concerns. The accuracy of the amount accrued may be significant in the determination of total liabilities and also in the proper matching of costs and revenue. The verification procedure consists principally of comparing the amounts accrued to the actual payroll of the subsequent period and reviewing the method of allocation at the balance sheet date. Payments made at the first payroll dates of the subsequent period are reviewed to determine that no significant *unrecorded* payroll liability existed as of the balance sheet date.

Pension Plan Accruals

Auditing procedures for the accrued liability for pension costs may begin with a review of the copy of the pension plan in the auditors' permanent file. Then consideration should be given to the provisions of the Employee Retirement Income Security Act (ERISA). The auditors must determine that the client's accrued pension liability is presented in accordance with *FASB No. 87,* "Employers' Accounting for Pensions," including consideration of service cost, interest cost, amortization of transition and service costs, and gains and losses on pension plan assets. In auditing these amounts the auditors will obtain representations from an actuary and confirm the activity in the plan with the trustee. In evaluating the evidence from the actuary, the auditors should comply with the requirements of *SAS 73,* "Using the Work of a Specialist," as discussed in Chapter 5.

Postemployment Benefits Other than Pensions

Under *FASB No. 106,* "Employer's Accounting for Postemployment Benefits Other than Pensions," companies must accrue, during the years that employees perform services, the expected cost of providing health and similar retirement benefits to the employees, their beneficiaries, and their dependents. Determining the amount of these liabilities is a very complex procedure, because assumptions must be made about matters such as employee work lives and increases in medical costs. Since actuaries and other specialists develop these assumptions, the auditors should evaluate the assumptions and the specialists' qualifications in accordance with *SAS 73,* "Using the Work of a Specialist."

Accrued Vacation Pay

Closely related to accrued salaries and wages is the liability that may exist for accrued vacation pay. This type of liability arises from two situations: (1) an employee entitled by contract to a vacation during the past year may have been prevented from taking it by an emergency work schedule, and (2) an employee may be entitled to a future vacation of which part of the cost must be accrued to achieve a proper matching of costs and revenue.

The auditors' verification of accrued vacation pay may begin with a review of the permanent file copy of the employment contract or agreement stipulating vacation terms. The computation of the accrual should then be verified both as to arithmetical accuracy and for agreement with the terms of the company's vacation policy.

Product Warranty Liabilities

The products of many companies are sold with a guarantee of free service or replacement during a rather extended warranty period. The costs of rendering such services should be recognized as expenses in the year the product is sold rather than in a later year in which the replacement is made or the repair service is performed. If this policy is followed, the company will make an annual charge to expense and credit to a liability account based on the amount of the year's sales and the estimated future service or replacement cost. As repairs and replacements take place, the costs will be charged to the liability account.

The auditors should review the client's annual provision for estimated future expenditures and compute the percentage relationship between the amount in the liability account and the amount of the year's sales. If this relationship varies sharply from year to year, the client should be asked for an explanation. The auditors should also review the charges to the liability account month by month and be alert for the improper recording of other expenses in this account. Sudden variations in the monthly charges to the liability account require investigation. In general, the auditors should determine that the balance in the liability account for service guarantees moves in reasonable relationship with the trend of sales. The auditors also should be alert for changes in the client's products or repair costs that might affect the amount of the warranty liability.

Current income tax laws prohibit the deduction of provisions for warranty liabilities; deductions are permitted only when actual expenditures are incurred. Accordingly, the auditors should ascertain that the client is properly allocating income taxes attributable to the nondeductible provisions.

Accrued Commissions and Bonuses

Accrued commissions to sales representatives and bonuses payable to managerial personnel also require verification. The essential step in this case is reference to the authority for the commission or bonus. The basic contracts should be examined and traced to minutes of directors'

> ### Focus on the Airline Industry
>
> The frequent flyer travel award programs in the airline industry are similar to product warranty liabilities in the sense that a free service is associated with the purchase of airline tickets. These programs provide an excellent example of the accounting and auditing difficulties involved with many accrued liabilities. In these programs, travelers earn frequent flier mileage for flying with the airline, which may be exchanged for flight awards.
>
> In accounting for these programs, estimates must be made of the percentage of the mileage that will ultimately be redeemed as well as the expected cost of providing the travel. Currently, airlines account for the awards by the incremental cost method, which calculates the airline's liability as the incremental cost associated with transporting a passenger in an otherwise empty seat. While auditors may easily test computations and determine that the liability has been treated consistently at the beginning and end of the period, determining the reasonableness of the estimates of redemption rates and future costs is more difficult. Generally, they must use analytical procedures that focus on the prior experience of the client and other airline companies.

meetings. If the bonus or commission is based on the total volume of sales or some other objective measure, the auditors should verify the computation of the accrual by applying the prescribed rate to the amount used as a base.

Income Taxes Payable

Federal, state, and foreign income taxes on corporations represent a material factor in determining both net income and financial position. The auditors cannot express an opinion on either the balance sheet or income statement of a corporation without first obtaining evidence that the provision for income taxes has been properly computed. In the audit of small and medium-size companies, it is customary for the audit engagement to include the preparation of the client's tax returns. If the client's staff or other persons have prepared the income tax returns, the auditors must nevertheless verify the reasonableness of the tax liability if they are to express an opinion on the fairness of the financial statements. In performing such a review of a tax return prepared by the client's staff or by others, the auditors may sometimes discover an opportunity for a tax saving that has been overlooked; obviously such a discovery tends to enhance the client's appreciation of the services rendered by the auditors.

The auditors should analyze the Income Taxes Payable account and vouch all amounts to income tax returns, paid checks, or other supporting documents. The final balance in the Income Taxes Payable account will ordinarily equal the computed federal, state, and foreign taxes on the current year's income tax returns, less any payments thereon.

The tax expected to be paid by a corporation often differs from the actual tax paid due to temporary differences between taxable income and pretax accounting income. These differences result in the need to establish deferred tax liabilities or assets. The auditors determine the amount of deferred tax liabilities using schedules referred to as "tax accrual" working papers, which usually are reviewed by one of the CPA firm's tax specialists.

Besides reviewing the computation of the income tax liability for the current year, the auditors should determine the date to which income tax returns for prior years have been examined by IRS agents, as well as the particulars of any disputes or additional assessments. Review of the reports of revenue agents is also an essential step. In the first audit of a new client, the auditors should review any prior years' income tax returns not yet examined by revenue agents to make sure that there has been no substantial underpayment of taxes that would warrant presentation as a liability.

Accrued Professional Fees

Fees of professional firms include charges for the services of attorneys, public accountants, consulting engineers, and other specialists who often render services of a continuing nature but present bills only at infrequent intervals. By inquiry of officers and by review of corporate minutes, the auditors may learn of professional services received for which no liability has yet been reflected in the accounts. Review of the expense account for legal fees is always essential because it may reveal damage suits, tax disputes, or other litigation warranting disclosure in the financial statements.

Balance Sheet Presentation

Accrued expenses—interest, taxes, rent, and wages—are included in the current liability section of the balance sheet and sometimes combined into one figure. Income taxes payable, however, may be sufficiently material to be listed as a separate item. Deferred federal income taxes resulting from tax allocations should be classified as current liabilities (or assets) if they relate to the next year. Otherwise, deferred federal income taxes are classified as noncurrent.

Deferred credits to revenue for such items as rent or interest collected in advance that will be included in earnings in the succeeding period are customarily included in current liabilities. Deposits on contracts and similar advances from customers also are accorded the status of current liabilities because the receipt of an advance increases the current assets total and because the goods to be used in liquidating the advance are generally included in current assets.

Time of Examination

The nature and amount of **trade accounts payable** may change greatly within a few weeks' time; consequently, the auditors' verification of these rapidly changing liabilities is most effective when performed immediately after the balance sheet date. As emphasized at the beginning of this chapter, failure to record a liability will cause an overstatement of financial position. Audit work on accounts payable performed before the balance sheet date is of little value if the client fails to record important liabilities coming into existence during the remaining weeks of the year under audit. For this reason, many auditors believe that most of the audit work on accounts payable should be performed *after the balance sheet date.* Certainly, the auditors' search for unrecorded liabilities must be made after the balance sheet date because this search is concentrated on the transactions occurring during the first few weeks of the new year.

Some current liability accounts other than accounts payable are more suitable for preliminary audit work. The documents relating to accrued property taxes, for example, may be available in advance of the balance sheet date. Amounts withheld from employees' pay can be reviewed before the end of the year. The propriety of amounts withheld and of amounts remitted to the tax authorities during the year can be verified before the pressure of year-end work begins. The working papers relating to such liability accounts then may be completed very quickly after the end of the accounting period.

Chapter Summary

This chapter explained the fundamental controls over accounts payable and purchase transactions. It also discussed the auditors' consideration of these controls and the substantive procedures for accounts payable and purchases. To summarize:

1. Accounts payable are short-term obligations arising from the purchase of goods and services in the ordinary course of the business.
2. The purchases cycle includes initiating and authorizing purchases, ordering goods and services, and recording and paying accounts payable. Effective internal control over purchase transactions is best achieved by having separate departments responsible for purchasing, receiving, and accounting for the transactions. In this manner, payments are made only for those purchases that are properly authorized and received.
3. The auditors' principal objectives for the substantive tests of accounts payable and purchases are to: (*a*) substantiate the existence of recorded accounts payable and the occurrence of purchase transactions, (*b*) establish the completeness of accounts payable and purchase transactions, (*c*) determine that the client has obligations to pay the recorded accounts payable, (*d*) determine the appropriate valuation of accounts payable, and (*e*) determine that the presentation and disclosure of accounts payable and purchases are appropriate.
4. In auditing accounts payable and other liabilities, it is important for the auditors to remember that an understatement of liabilities will exaggerate the financial strength of a company in the same way as an overstatement of assets. Therefore, the auditors' substantive procedures primarily focus on the objective of determining the completeness of recorded amounts. A number of these procedures involve inspecting documents related to transactions occurring during the subsequent period to determine whether these items should have been recorded as liabilities at year-end.
5. Accrued liabilities represent obligations payable for services received before the balance sheet date that will be paid in the subsequent period. Examples include accrued warranty liabilities, accrued payroll, and accrued pension liabilities. The substantive procedures to audit these liabilities generally include inspection of documents, recomputation, and analytical procedures.

Key Terms Introduced or Emphasized in Chapter 14

Accrued liabilities (accrued expenses)   Short-term obligations for services of a continuing nature that accumulate over time. Examples include interest, taxes, rent, salaries, and pensions. They generally are not evidenced by invoices or statements.

Confirmation   Direct communication with vendors or suppliers to determine the amount of an account payable. Represents high-quality evidence because it is a document created outside the client organization and transmitted directly to the auditors.

Consignment   A transfer of goods from the owner to another person who acts as the sales agent of the owner.

Subsequent period   The time extending from the balance sheet date to the date of the auditors' report.

Trade accounts payable   Current liabilities arising from the purchase of goods and services from trade creditors, generally evidenced by invoices or statements received from the creditors.

Vendor's statement   A monthly statement prepared by a vendor (supplier) showing the beginning balance, charges during the month for goods or services, amounts collected, and ending balance. This externally created document should correspond (except for timing differences) with an account in the client's accounts payable subsidiary ledger.

Voucher   A document authorizing a cash disbursement. A voucher usually provides space for the initials of employees performing various approval functions. The term *voucher* may also be applied to the group of supporting documents used as a basis for recording liabilities or for making cash disbursements.

Voucher register   A journal used in a voucher system to record liabilities requiring cash payment in the near future. Every liability recorded in a voucher register corresponds to a voucher authorizing future payment.

Review Questions

14–1.   If a corporation overstates its earnings, are its liabilities more likely to be overstated or understated? Explain.

14–2.   Lawsuits against CPA firms are most likely to allege that the auditors were negligent in not detecting which of the following? (*a*) overstatement of liabilities and earnings, (*b*) understatement of assets and earnings, or (*c*) overstatement of owners' equity. Explain the reasoning underlying your choice.

14–3.   Assume that a highly placed employee has stolen company assets and is now planning to conceal the fraud by failing to make an accounting entry for a large transaction. Would the omission probably be for a transaction creating an asset or a liability? Explain.

14–4.   Suggest two reasons why the adjustments proposed by independent auditors more often than not call for reducing recorded earnings.

14–5.   Compare the auditors' approach to the verification of liabilities with their approach to the verification of assets.

14–6.   The auditors usually find in the client's possession documentary evidence, such as invoices, supporting both accounts receivable and accounts payable. Is there any difference in the quality of such evidence for accounts receivable and for accounts payable? Explain.

14–7.   Describe briefly an internal control activity that would prevent a paid disbursement voucher from being presented for payment a second time.

14–8.   The operating procedures of a well-managed accounts payable department will provide for the verification of several specific points before a vendor's invoice is recorded as an approved liability. What are the points requiring verification?

14–9.   List the major responsibilities of an accounts payable department.

14–10.   In achieving adequate internal control over operations of the accounts payable department, a company should establish procedures that will ensure that extensions and footings are proved on all invoices and that the propriety of prices is reviewed. What is the most effective means of assuring consistent performance of these duties?

14–11.   Which do you consider the more significant step in establishing strong internal control over accounts payable transactions: the approval of an invoice for payment, or the issuance of a check in payment of an invoice? Explain.

14–12.   For which documents relating to the accounts payable operation would you recommend the use of serial numbers as an internal control activity?

14–13.   What internal control activity would you recommend to call attention to failure to pay invoices within the discount period?

14–14. During the verification of the individual invoices composing the total of accounts payable at the balance sheet date, the auditors discovered some receiving reports indicating that the merchandise covered by several of these invoices was not received until after the balance sheet date. What action should the auditors take?

14–15. As part of the investigation of accounts payable, auditors sometimes vouch entries in selected creditors' accounts back through the journals to original documents, such as purchase orders, receiving reports, invoices, and paid checks. What is the principal purpose of this procedure?

14–16. Outline a method by which the auditors may test the propriety of cash discounts taken on accounts payable.

14–17. Is the confirmation of accounts payable by direct communication with vendors as useful and important an audit procedure as is the confirmation of accounts receivable? Explain.

14–18. Whitehall Company records its liabilities in an accounts payable subsidiary ledger. The auditors have decided to select some of the accounts for confirmation by direct communication with vendors. The largest volume of purchases during the year had been made from Ranchero Company, but at the balance sheet date this account has a zero balance. Under these circumstances should the auditors send a confirmation request to Ranchero Company, or would they accomplish more by limiting their confirmation program to accounts with larger year-end balances?

14–19. Vendors' statements and accounts payable confirmations are both forms of documentary evidence created outside the client organization and useful in audit work on accounts payable. Which of these two represents higher quality evidence? Why?

14–20. Explain how the auditors coordinate the year-end cutoff of accounts payable with their observation of the year-end physical inventory.

14–21. Identify three audit procedures (other than "Search for unrecorded accounts payable") that are concerned directly or indirectly with disclosing unrecorded accounts payable.

14–22. What do you consider to be the most important single procedure in the auditors' search for unrecorded accounts payable? Explain.

14–23. What is the purpose of the auditors' review of cash payments subsequent to the balance sheet date?

14–24. Most auditors are interested in performing as many phases of an audit as possible in advance of the balance sheet date. The verification of accounts payable, however, generally is regarded as something to be done after the balance sheet date. What specific factors can you suggest that make the verification of accounts payable less suitable than many other accounts for interim work?

14–25. What documentary evidence created outside the client's organization is particularly important to the auditors in verifying accrued property taxes?

14–26. What differences should auditors expect to find in supporting evidence for accrued liabilities as contrasted with accounts payable?

Questions Requiring Analysis

14–27. Compare the confirmation of accounts receivable with the confirmation of accounts payable under the following headings:

a. Generally accepted auditing procedures. (Justify the differences revealed by your comparison.)

b. Selection of accounts to be confirmed.

(AICPA, adapted)

14–28. In the course of your initial audit of the financial statements of Sylvan Company, you determine that of the substantial amount of accounts payable outstanding at the close of the period, approximately 75 percent is owed to six creditors. You have requested that you be permitted to confirm the balances owing to these six creditors by communicating with the creditors, but the president of the company is unwilling to approve your request on the grounds that correspondence in regard to the balances—all of which contain some overdue items—might give rise to demands on the part of the creditors for immediate payment of the overdue items and thereby embarrass Sylvan Company.

Given these circumstances, what alternative procedure would you adopt in an effort to satisfy yourself that the accounting records show the correct amounts payable to these creditors?

(AICPA, adapted)

14–29. The subsequent period in an audit is the time extending from the balance sheet date to the date of the auditors' report.

Required: Discuss the importance of the subsequent period in the audit of trade accounts payable.

14–30. Early in your first audit of Star Corporation, you notice that sales and year-end inventory are almost unchanged from the prior year. However, cost of goods sold is less than in the preceding year, and accounts payable also are down substantially. Gross profit has increased, but this increase has not carried through to net income because of increased executive salaries. Management informs you that sales prices and purchase prices have not changed significantly during the past year, and there have been no changes in the product line. Star Corporation relies on the periodic inventory system. Your initial impression of internal control is that several weaknesses may exist.

Suggest a possible explanation for the trends described, especially the decrease in accounts payable while sales and inventory were constant and gross profit increased. Explain fully the relationships involved.

14–31. During the course of any audit, the auditors are always alert for unrecorded accounts payable or other unrecorded liabilities.

Required: For each of the following audit areas, (1) describe an unrecorded liability that might be discovered and (2) state what auditing procedure or procedures might bring it to light.

a. Construction in progress (property, plant, and equipment).

b. Prepaid insurance.

c. License authorizing the client to produce a product patented by another company.

d. Minutes of directors' meetings.

14–32. In connection with their audit of the financial statements of Davis Company, the auditors reviewed the Federal Income Taxes Payable account.

Required: *a.* Discuss reasons why the auditors should review the federal income tax returns for prior years and the reports of internal revenue agents.

b. What information will these reviews provide? (Do not discuss specific tax return items.)

(AICPA, adapted)

14–33. Describe the audit steps that generally would be followed in establishing the propriety of the recorded liability for federal income taxes of a corporation you are auditing for the first time. Consideration should be given to the status of (*a*) the liability for prior years and (*b*) the liability arising from the current year's taxable income.

Multiple Choice Questions

14–34. Select the best answer for each of the following and explain the reason for your selection.

a. Which of the following procedures is least likely to be completed before the balance sheet date?

(1) Confirmation of receivables.

(2) Search for unrecorded liabilities.

(3) Observation of inventory.

(4) Review of internal accounting control over cash disbursements.

b. An audit of the balance in the accounts payable account is ordinarily not designed to:

(1) Detect accounts payable that are substantially past due.

(2) Verify that accounts payable were properly authorized.

(3) Ascertain the reasonableness of recorded liabilities.

(4) Determine that all existing liabilities at the balance sheet date have been recorded.

c. Which of the following is the best audit procedure for determining the existence of unrecorded liabilities?

(1) Examine confirmation requests returned by creditors whose accounts appear on a subsidiary trial balance of accounts payable.

(2) Examine unusual relationships between monthly accounts payable balances and recorded purchases.

(3) Examine a sample of invoices a few days prior to and subsequent to year-end to ascertain whether they have been properly recorded.

(4) Examine selected cash disbursements in the period subsequent to year-end.

d. Auditor confirmation of accounts payable balances at the balance sheet date may be unnecessary because:

(1) This is a duplication of cutoff tests.

(2) Accounts payable balances at the balance sheet date may *not* be paid before the audit is completed.

(3) Correspondence with the audit client's attorney will reveal all legal action by vendors for nonpayment.

(4) There is likely to be other reliable external evidence available to support the balances.

e. A client erroneously recorded a large purchase twice. Which of the following internal control measures would be most likely to detect this error in a timely and efficient manner?

(1) Footing the purchases journal.

(2) Reconciling vendors' monthly statements with subsidiary payable ledger accounts.

(3) Tracing totals from the purchases journal to the ledger accounts.

(4) Sending written quarterly confirmation to all vendors.

f. For effective internal control, the accounts payable department should compare the information on each vendor's invoice with the:

(1) Receiving report and the purchase order.

(2) Receiving report and the voucher.

(3) Vendor's packing slip and the purchase order.

(4) Vendor's packing slip and the voucher.

g. When confirming accounts payable, the approach is most likely to be one of:

(1) Selecting the accounts with the largest balances at year-end, plus a sample of other accounts.

(2) Selecting accounts that the client has previously done the most business, plus a sample of other accounts.

(3) Selecting a random sample of accounts payable at year-end.

(4) Confirming all accounts.

h. In an audit, the valuation of year-end accounts payable is most likely addressed by:

(1) Confirmation.

(2) Examination of cash disbursements immediately prior to year-end.

(3) Examination of cash disbursements immediately subsequent to year-end.

(4) Analytical procedures applied to vouchers payable at year-end.

i. Ordinarily, the most significant assertion relating to accounts payable is:

(1) Completeness.

(2) Existence.

(3) Presentation.

(4) Valuation.

j. The *least* likely audit approach for a management's estimate relating to an accrued liability is to:

(1) Independently develop an estimate of the amount to compare to management's estimate.

(2) Review and test management's process of developing the estimate.

(3) Review subsequent events or transactions bearing on the estimate.

(4) Send confirmations relating to the estimate.

k. To determine that each voucher is submitted and paid only once, when a payment is approved, supporting documents should be cancelled by the:

(1) Authorized members of the audit committee.

(2) Accounting department.

(3) Individual who signs the checks.

(4) Chief executive officer.

    l. In performing a test of controls, the auditors vouch a sample of entries in the purchases journal to the supporting documents. Which assertion would this test of controls most likely test?

    (1) Completeness.

    (2) Existence.

    (3) Valuation.

    (4) Rights.

Problems

14–35. The following are typical questions that might appear on an internal control questionnaire for accounts payable.

    1. Are monthly statements from vendors reconciled with the accounts payable listing?

    2. Are vendors' invoices matched with receiving reports before they are approved for payment?

Required:

    a. Describe the purpose of each of the above internal control activities.

    b. Describe the manner in which each of the above procedures might be tested.

    c. Assuming that the operating effectiveness of each of the above procedures is found to be inadequate, describe how the auditors might alter their substantive tests to compensate for the increased level of control risk.

14–36. As part of your first audit of the financial statements of Marina del Rey, Inc., you have decided to confirm some of the accounts payable. You are now in the process of selecting the individual companies to whom you will send accounts payable confirmation requests. Among the accounts payable you are considering are the following:

Company	Amount Payable at Year-End	Total Purchases from Vendor During Year
Dayco, Inc.	$ —	$1,980,000
Gearbox, Inc.	22,650	46,100
Landon Co.	65,000	75,000
Western Supply	190,000	2,123,000

Required:

    a. Which two of the above four accounts payable would you select as the most important to confirm? Explain your choice in terms of the audit objectives in sending accounts payable confirmation requests.

    b. Assume that you are selecting accounts receivable to be confirmed. Assume also that the four companies listed above are customers of your client rather than suppliers and that the dollar amounts are accounts receivable balances and total sales for the year. Which two companies would you select as the most important to confirm? Explain your choice.

14–37. James Rowe, CPA, is the independent auditor of Raleigh Corporation. Rowe is considering the audit work to be performed in the accounts payable area for the current year's engagement.

    The prior year's working papers show that confirmation requests were mailed to 100 of Raleigh's 1,000 suppliers. The selected suppliers were based on Rowe's sample that was designed to select accounts with large dollar balances. A substantial number of hours were spent by Raleigh employees and by Rowe resolving relatively minor differences between the confirmation replies and Raleigh's accounting records. Alternative audit procedures were used for those suppliers that did not respond to the confirmation requests.

Required:

    a. Identify the accounts payable audit objectives that Rowe must consider in determining the audit procedures to be followed.

    b. Identify situations in which Rowe should use accounts payable confirmations and discuss whether Rowe is required to use them.

    c. Discuss why the use of large dollar balances as the basis for selecting accounts payable for confirmation might not be the most efficient approach, and indicate what more efficient procedures could be followed when selecting accounts payable for confirmation.

(AICPA, adapted)

14–38. Taylor, CPA, is engaged in the audit of Rex Wholesaling for the year ended December 31. Taylor obtained an understanding of internal control relating to the purchasing, receiving, trade accounts payable, and cash disbursement cycles and has decided not to proceed with tests of controls. Based upon analytical procedures, Taylor believes that the trade accounts payable on the balance sheet as of December 31 may be understated.

Taylor requested and obtained a client-prepared trade accounts payable schedule listing the total amount owed to each vendor.

Required:

What additional substantive audit procedures should Taylor apply in examining the trade accounts payable?

14–39. Nancy Howe, your staff assistant on the April 30, 20X2, audit of Wilcox Company, was transferred to another audit engagement before she could complete the audit of unrecorded accounts payable. Her working paper, which you have reviewed and are satisfied is complete, appears below.

Invoice Date	Vendor and Description	Wilcox Company Unrecorded Accounts Payable April 30, 20X2	M–1–1 Amount
	Hill & Harper—unpaid legal fees at Apr. 30, X2 (see lawyer's letter at M–4)		1000 y
Apr.1,X2	Drew Insurance Agency—unpaid premium on fire insurance for period Apr. 1, X2– Mar. 31, X5 (see insurance broker letter at J–1–1)		1800 y
Apr.30,X2	Mays and Sage, Stockbrokers—advice for 100 shares of Madison Ltd. common stock (settlement date May 7, X2)		2125 —y
	Lane Company—shipment received Apr. 30, X2 per receiver no. 3361 and included in Apr. 30, X2 physical inventory; invoice not yet received (amount is per purchase order)		5863 —y
			10788 —

y–Examined document described.

In my opinion, the $10,788 adjustment includes all material unrecorded accounts payable.

N.A.H
May 29, X2

Required:

Prepare a proposed adjusting journal entry for the unrecorded accounts payable of Wilcox Company at April 30, 20X2. The amounts are material. (Do not deal with income taxes.)

14–40. You were in the final stages of your audit of the financial statements of Scott Corporation for the year ended December 31, 20X0, when you were consulted by the corporation's president, who believes there is no point to your examining the 20X1 voucher register and testing data in support of 20X0 entries. He stated that (1) bills pertaining to 20X0 that were received too late to be included in the December voucher register were recorded as of the year-end by the corporation by journal entry, (2) the internal auditors made tests after the year-end, and (3) he would furnish you with a letter representing that there were no unrecorded liabilities.

Required:

a. Should the independent auditors' test for unrecorded liabilities be affected by the fact that the client made a journal entry to record 20X0 bills that were received late? Explain.

    b. Should the independent auditors' test for unrecorded liabilities be affected by the fact that a letter is obtained in which a responsible management official represents that to the best of his knowledge all liabilities have been recorded? Explain.

    c. Should the independent auditors' test for unrecorded liabilities be eliminated or reduced because of the internal audit tests? Explain.

    d. Assume that the client company, which handled some government contracts, had no internal auditors but that auditors for a federal agency spent three weeks auditing the records and were just completing their work at this time. How would the independent auditors' unrecorded liability test be affected by the work of the auditors for a federal agency?

    e. What sources in addition to the 20X1 voucher register should the independent auditors consider to locate possible unrecorded liabilities?

(AICPA, adapted)

14–41. During the current year, your audit client, Video Corporation, was licensed to manufacture a patented type of television tube. The licensing agreement called for royalty payments of 50 cents for each tube manufactured by Video Corporation. What procedures would you follow in connection with your regular annual audit at December 31 to obtain evidence that the liability for royalties is correctly stated?

(AICPA, adapted)

In-Class Team Case

14–42. You have just been assigned as a member of the audit team of Bozarkana Company (a new client) and are considering accounts payable. Bozarkana Company uses a computerized voucher system for payables. As a starting point you asked Bill Bozarkana, the controller, for a summary of payables and received the following schedule of more than 1,000 unpaid vouchers at year-end:

Voucher#	Vendor Number	Purchase Order#	Receiving Report#	Date Payment Due	Amount
2334555	2133	654444	106500	1/2/0Y	$ 2,020.21
2334558	1098	654579	106820	1/2/0Y	12,344.56
2334567	2133	654593	106920	1/2/0Y	322.43
⋮					
⋮					
⋮					
2335643	2231	655456	107654	1/28/0Y	2,346.62
TOTAL PAYABLE					$2,225,980.83

Bill Bozarkana has indicated that the schedule is a listing of the "vouchers payable" file as of year-end and that the total is the result of a separate question ("query") of that file asking for total payables. You have the schedule in electronic and "hardcopy" form. Vouchers are issued sequentially, and voucher number 2335643 was the last one issued prior to year-end. You also have obtained the information relating to the following other computer files, which are available to you in electronic form, as shown at the top of the following page.

The client has made copies of these files available so that you and the assistant perform the necessary steps on the files. Furthermore, you have compared these copies to the client's copies and find that they are identical. Finally, you may assume that tests of controls have been performed on the controls related to the dates on the files. The controls were found to be effective.

Required:

    a. Discuss how you would establish samples in the following situations:

      (1) Randomly select 30 vouchers as of year-end and obtain the necessary information to send confirmations.

      (2) Randomly select 30 accounts with balances payable (per vendor) as of December 31.

      (3) Select all accounts (per vendor) with which the company has disbursed more than $500,000 during the year, but whose balance at year-end is zero.

File Name	Information in Table	Comment
Purchase requisitions	Purchase requisition number Date requisitioned Item number Item description Quantity	The table includes one row for each purchase requisition—only one type of item per requisition may be requisitioned.
Purchase orders	Purchase order number Date ordered Purchase requisition number Vendor number Item number Quantity Cost	The table includes multiple rows for each purchase order—one for each item ordered.
Receiving reports	Receiving report number Date shipped Date received Item number Quantity	The table includes multiple rows for each receiving report—one for each item received.
Vendor master	Vendor number Vendor name Vendor address	Table includes one line for each vendor.
Cash disbursements	Disbursement number Vendor number Check number or electronic funds transfer number Voucher number Amount	Table includes one line for each check or funds transfer (electronic payments).

    b. Provide detailed guidance on the following:

        (1) All purchases are sent to Bozarkana Company "FOB shipping point." Identify a procedure for testing whether any items shipped to the client prior to year-end have been omitted from vouchers payable as of year-end.

        (2) Select all disbursements over $300,000 in the first two weeks of January, and, for those not included as liabilities as of December 31, determine whether title had passed as of year-end to the goods, resulting in an unrecorded liability.

CPA Simulation

14–43.　*See Chapter 10, pages 391 through 393 for the background information (company profile, industry information, and financial statements) relating to this simulation case.*

Questions

Risks:

    a. A risk factor relating to misstatements arising from fraudulent financial reporting is:

        (1) Earnings this year are lower than management had hoped.

        (2) Accounts payable are limited to commercial suppliers.

        (3) Sales are made to residential, commercial, and governmental purchasers.

        (4) The industry faces great technological changes in almost all of its products.

    b. Of the following replies, which represents the most significant business risk to SSC?

        (1) The increase in accounts payable has resulted in an increase in the net cash used by operations.

        (2) The company issued new debt during 20X8.

        (3) The company increased both its accounts receivable and its accounts payable—an event that is very unusual.

        (4) Wingo Corporation's overall patent for Quite Ride.

Audit findings:

Ratio	20X8	20X7
Quick ratio ([Cash + Accounts receivable]/Current liabilities)	1.73	2.09
Percent increase in accounts payable	7.9%	2.3%

The above table presents two ratios that were identified as significant in the current and prior years' audits of SSC. Compare the values of each ratio. Then select an audit finding that is consistent with these metrics. The explanation need not explain the exact amount of the change. However, of the replies listed, it should potentially lead to the most significant change in the direction indicated by the change in the ratio.

c. An audit finding consistent with the change in the quick ratio for SSC:

   (1) Although the inventory was counted and included in the 20X8 year-end total, numerous year-end inventory purchases (for credit) were not recorded.

   (2) Significant portions of long-term debt became current as of year-end.

   (3) The company erroneously expensed equipment acquisitions during the year.

   (4) The company collected more of its receivables and thereby increased its cash position.

   (5) The company's inventories may be physically deteriorating and becoming obsolete.

d. An audit finding consistent with the change in accounts payable for 20X8:

   (1) The company apparently issued treasury stock, for which the payments have not yet been processed.

   (2) The company generated a profit during the year and paid out no dividend.

   (3) The company has increased its sales and, accordingly, an increase in payables seems likely.

   (4) The 20X8 increase in inventory requires that accounts payable increase.

   (5) The company had significant portions of long-term debt become current as of year-end.

Audit procedures:

The auditor determines that each of the following objectives will be part of SSC's audit. For each audit objective, select a substantive procedure that would help to achieve that objective. Each of the procedures may be used once, more than once, or not at all.

Audit Objective:

e. Determine the existence of year-end recorded accounts payable and that the client has obligations to pay these liabilities.

f. Establish the completeness of recorded accounts payable.

g. Determine that the presentation and disclosure of accounts payable are appropriate.

h. Determine that the valuation of warranty loss reserves is in accordance with generally accepted accounting principles.

Substantive Procedure:

   (1) Obtain a trial balance of payables and reconcile with the accounts payable subsidiary ledger.

   (2) Vouch sales from throughout the year.

   (3) Vouch purchases recorded after year-end.

   (4) Vouch sales recorded shortly before year-end.

   (5) Vouch major warranty expenses paid during 20X8.

   (6) Inquire of management concerning the existence of related party transactions.

   (7) Test the computations made by the client to set up the accrual.

   (8) Test the reasonableness of general and administrative labor rates.

   (9) Confirm outstanding year-end balances of payables.

   (10) Confirm warranty expenses payable as of year-end.

Communication:

i. Jill Swizoo, the audit manager, has asked you about the risks that SSC faces related to its new product QDeck. Write a brief memo about these business risks.

Remember: Your response will be graded for both technical relevance and writing skills. For writing skills, you should demonstrate an ability to develop, organize, and express your ideas clearly. Do not convey information in the form of a table, bullet-point list, or other abbreviated presentation.

Memorandum

TO: Jill Swizoo

Subject: SSC Developmental Swimming Pool Product—QDeck

Research:

Note: This section is possible to work in a meaningful way only if you have the professional standards available—preferably in electronic form.

j. In a discussion with Gary Sherwood, he has suggested that he might like to begin implementing certain antifraud programs and controls. Find the exact reference in the professional standards for this guidance. You need not cut and paste the guidance itself. Just provide the reference.

Appendix 14A

Illustrative Audit Case: Keystone Computers & Networks, Inc.

Part IV: Consideration of Internal Control

This part of the audit case of Keystone Computers & Networks, Inc. (KCN) illustrates the nature of internal control over the acquisition cycle and the way in which auditors assess control risk for this cycle. The following working papers are included:

- A flowchart description of the acquisition cycle of the company and the related controls prepared by the staff of Adams, Barnes & Co. (ABC), CPAs. This flowchart focuses on the (accounting) information system and control activities.

- ABC's working paper for assessment of control risk for accounts payable and purchases as it would appear before any tests of controls are performed. This working paper identifies the prescribed controls and weaknesses for the revenue cycle. It also relates the controls and weaknesses to the various financial statement assertions about accounts payable and purchases.

- You should read through the information to obtain an understanding of typical controls for this cycle. You may also wish to review the planning documentation presented on pages 213–220 of Chapter 6 to refresh your knowledge about the nature of the company's business and its environment. The Control Environment, Risk Assessment, and Monitoring Questionnaire on pages 442–444, and the Organizational Chart of KCN on page 452 can be used to help refresh your memory about these components of internal control.

KEYSTONE COMPUTERS & NETWORKS, INC.
Assessment of Control Risk—Acquisition Cycle
12/31/X5

Internal Controls	Existence or Occurrence	Completeness	Rights and Obligations	Valuation	Presentation and Disclosure
Sales					
1. Separation of duties for authorization of purchases, receiving merchandise, approving payment to vendors, and signing checks.	☐	☐	☐	☐	
2. Computer assigns number to purchase orders, receiving reports, and checks.		☐			
3. Computer matches information from vendors' invoices with purchase orders and receiving data.	☐		☐		
4. Computer tests numerical accuracy of vendors' invoices.				☐	
5. Approval of vendors' invoices prior to payment.	☐		☐	☐	
6. Checks are mailed by the check signer.		☐		☐	
7. Monthly reconciliation of bank accounts by an employee who is independent of invoice processing, cash disbursements, cash receipts, petty cash, and general ledger functions.	☐	☐	☐	☐	
8. Comparison of actual disbursements to budgeted amounts and investigation of variances.	☐	☐		☐	☐
Internal Control Weakness					
1. Approved vendors are selected by purchasing manager who also purchases goods.				X	
2. Vendors' statements are not reconciled to the accounting records.	X	X		X	
Planned Assessed Level of Control Risk	*Low*	*Moderate*	*Low*	*Moderate*	*Maximum*

KEYSTONE COMPUTER & NETWORKS, INC.
Internal Control—Acquisition Cycle
12/31/X5

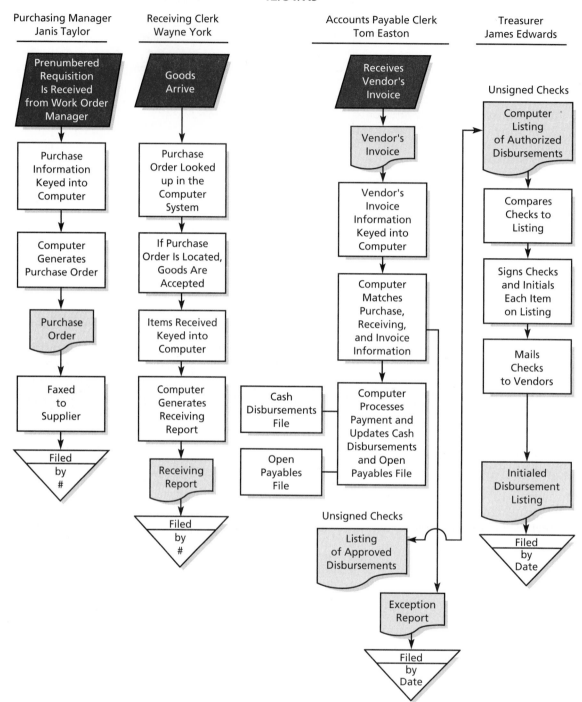

Notes:

1. The company uses Great Plains ACCPAC, a commercial accounting software package that has not been modified.

2. Approved vendors are selected by the purchasing manager.

3. The company has a local area network, with computer terminals in the sales, purchasing, work order, receiving, and accounting departments.

4. Purchase order data are entered on an online terminal that applies the following application controls:
   - The purchasing manager's password is verified before information is accepted.
   - Vendor numbers are agreed by computer to approved vendor master file list before purchase order is generated.
   - Computer assigns sequential numbers to purchase order.

5. Receiving information is entered on an online terminal that applies the following controls:
   - The receiving clerk's password is verified before information is accepted.
   - Computer assigns sequential numbers to purchase order.

6. Vendors' invoice information is entered on an online terminal that applies the following controls:
   - The accounts payable clerk's password is verified before information is accepted.
   - The computer recomputes the individual items and total amount of the invoice.

7. Computer agrees purchase order, receiving, and invoice data and produces an exception report for any situation in which the documents do not match. Accounts payable clerk follows up on exceptions and describes resolution on report.

8. Computer updates cash disbursements and open payables files.

9. The accounting manager reconciles the cash and open payables accounts to the general ledger on a monthly basis.

10. The accounting manager reconciles the bank account on a monthly basis.

11. Cash disbursements are budgeted and the controller analyzes and explains variances.

Appendix 14A Problems

Required:

14A–1. A summary of the controls for the acquisition cycle of Keystone Computers & Networks, Inc., appears on pages 441–452.

a. For the following three controls over the acquisition cycle indicate one type of error or fraud that the control serves to prevent or detect. Organize your solution as follows:

Control	Error or Fraud Controlled
1. Computer matches information from vendors' invoice with purchase order and receiving data.	
2. The computer assigns numbers to receiving reports.	
3. Checks are mailed by check signer.	

b. For each of the controls described above indicate how the auditors could test the control. Organize your answer as follows:

Control	Tests of Controls
1. Computer matches information from vendors' invoice with purchase order and receiving data.	
2. The computer assigns numbers to receiving reports.	
3. Checks are mailed by check signer.	

14A–2. As indicated on the risk assessment working paper on page 557, the auditors identified two weaknesses in internal control over the acquisition cycle of KCN. Describe the implications of each of the two weaknesses in terms of the type of errors or fraud that could result.

14A–3. The auditors' working paper that relates control strengths and weaknesses to the assertions about purchases and accounts payable is presented on page 557. This working paper also presents the auditors' planned assessed level of control risk for each of the assertions.

Prepare an audit program for tests of the controls over the acquisition cycle. (Note: You may want to use the tests of controls program for the revenue cycle, which is on pages 453–454, as a guide.)

Chapter 15

Debt and Equity Capital

Chapter learning objectives

After studying this chapter, you should be able to:

LO1. Describe the nature of interest-bearing debt.

LO2. Describe the auditors' objectives in auditing debt.

LO3. Assess the risks of material misstatement (inherent and control risks) of debt.

LO4. Identify and explain the fundamental controls over the financing cycle.

LO5. Design typical substantive tests used by auditors for the financial statement assertions related to debt.

LO6. Describe the nature of equity accounts.

LO7. Describe the auditors' objectives for the audit of equity accounts.

LO8. Describe the fundamental controls over capital stock and other types of equity accounts.

LO9. List the procedures for the audit of equity accounts.

Business corporations obtain substantial amounts of their financial resources by incurring interest-bearing debt and by issuing capital stock. The acquisition and repayment of capital is sometimes referred to as the *financing cycle*. This transaction cycle includes the sequence of procedures for authorizing, executing, and recording transactions that involve bank loans, mortgages, bonds payable, and capital stock as well as the payment of interest and dividends. In this chapter we present material on the auditors' approach to both debt and equity capital accounts.

Interest-Bearing Debt

Sources and Nature of Interest-Bearing Debt

Learning Objective 1

Long-term debt usually is substantial in amount and often extends for periods of 20 years or more. Debentures, secured bonds, and notes payable (sometimes secured by mortgages or trust deeds) are the principal types of long-term debt. **Debenture bonds** are backed only by the general credit of the issuing corporation and not by liens on specific assets. Since in most respects debentures have the characteristics of other corporate bonds, we shall use the term *bonds* to include both debentures and secured bonds payable.

The formal document creating bond indebtedness is called the *indenture* or **trust indenture.** When creditors supply capital on a long-term basis, they often insist upon placing certain restrictions on the borrowing company. For example, the indenture often includes a restrictive covenant that prohibits the company from declaring dividends unless the amount of working capital is maintained above a specified amount. The acquisition of plant and equipment, or the increasing of managerial salaries, may be permitted only if the current ratio is maintained at a specified level and if net income reaches a designated amount. Another device for protecting the long-term creditor is the requirement of a sinking fund or redemption fund to be held by a trustee. If these restrictions are violated, the indenture may provide that the entire debt is due on demand.

The Auditors' Approach to Auditing Interest-Bearing Debt

Learning Objective 2

The auditors' *objectives* in the audit of interest-bearing debt are to:

1. Consider *inherent risks,* including *fraud risks.*
2. Consider *internal control* over interest-bearing debt.
3. Determine the *existence* of recorded interest-bearing debt.
4. Establish the *completeness* of recorded interest-bearing debt.
5. Determine that the client has *obligations* to pay the recorded interest-bearing debt.
6. Determine that the *valuation* of interest-bearing debt is in accordance with generally accepted accounting principles.
7. Determine that the *presentation* and *disclosure* of interest-bearing debt are appropriate, including disclosure of the major provisions of loan agreements.

In conjunction with the audit of interest-bearing debt, the auditors will also obtain evidence about interest expense, interest payable, and bond discount and premium.

Many of the principles related to accounts payable also apply to the audit of interest-bearing debt. As is the case for accounts payable, the understatement of debt is considered to be a major potential audit problem. Related to disclosure of interest-bearing debt, the auditors must determine whether the company has met all requirements and restrictions imposed upon it by debt agreements.

Assessment of the Inherent Risks Related to Interest-Bearing Debt

Learning Objective 3

A major business risk related to interest-bearing debt is ensuring that the client obtains capital in the most effective and efficient manner. This risk is not indicative of a risk of material misstatement of the financial statements and, therefore, not of direct concern to the auditors. However, other business risks do equate to risks of material misstatement. As an example, management must be concerned with the business risk of noncompliance with debt covenants. This is also a concern of the auditors because noncompliance may affect the classification of debt and related disclosures. Many of the principles related to accounts payable also apply to the audit of interest-bearing debt. As is the case for accounts payable, the understatement of debt, whether due to error or fraud, is considered to be a major potential inherent risk.

Internal Control over Interest-Bearing Debt

Learning Objective 4

Authorization by the Board of Directors

Effective internal control over interest-bearing debt begins with the authorization to incur the debt. The bylaws of a corporation usually require that the board of directors approve borrowing. The treasurer of the corporation will prepare a report on any proposed financing, explaining the need for funds, the estimated effect of borrowing upon future earnings, the estimated financial position of the company in comparison with others in the industry both before and after the borrowing, and alternative methods of raising the funds. Authorization by the board of directors will include review and approval of such matters as the choice of a bank or trustee, the type of security, registration with the SEC, agreements with investment bankers, compliance with requirements of the state of incorporation, and listing of bonds on a securities exchange. After the issuance of long-term debt, the board of directors should receive a report stating the net amount received and its disposition, as, for example, acquisition of plant assets, addition to working capital, or other purposes.

Use of an Independent Trustee

Bond issues are always for large amounts—usually many millions of dollars. Therefore, only relatively large companies issue bonds; small companies obtain long-term capital through mortgage loans or other sources. Any company large enough to issue bonds and able to find a ready market for the securities will almost always utilize the services of a large bank as an independent trustee.

The trustee is charged with the protection of the creditors' interests and with monitoring the issuing company's compliance with the provisions of the indenture. The trustee also maintains detailed records of the names and addresses of the registered owners of the bonds, cancels old bond certificates and issues new ones when bonds change ownership, follows procedures to prevent overissuance of bond certificates, distributes interest payments, and distributes principal payments when the bonds mature. Use of an independent trustee largely solves the problem of internal control over bonds payable. Internal control is strengthened by the fact that the trustee does not have access to the issuing company's assets or accounting records and the fact that the trustee is a large financial institution with legal responsibility for its actions.

Interest Payments on Bonds and Notes Payable

Many corporations assign the entire task of paying interest to the trustee for either *bearer bonds* or *registered bonds*. Highly effective control is then achieved, since the company will issue a single check for the full amount of the semiannual interest payment on the entire bond issue. In the case of bearer bonds (coupon bonds), the trustee upon receipt of this check will make payment for coupons presented, cancel the coupons, and file them numerically. A second count of the coupons is made at a later date; the coupons then are destroyed and a cremation certificate is delivered to the issuing company. The trustee does not attempt to maintain a list of the holders of coupon bonds, since these securities are transferable by the mere act of delivery. If certain coupons are not presented for payment, the trustee will hold the funds corresponding to such coupons for the length of time prescribed by statute. In the case of registered bonds, the trustee will maintain a current list of holders and will remit interest checks to them in the same manner as dividend checks are distributed to stockholders.

For a note payable, there generally is only one recipient of interest. Companies control that disbursement in the same manner as other cash disbursements, without using a trustee.

Audit Documentation

A copy of the loan agreement or the indenture relating to a bond issue should be placed in the auditors' permanent file. A listing of the restrictions placed on the company is extracted from these documents to facilitate the auditors' tests of compliance with the debt provisions. Analyses of ledger accounts for notes and bonds payable, and the related accounts for interest and discount or premium, should be obtained for the current working papers file or the permanent file. A lead schedule is seldom required for short-term notes payable or for long-term debt.

Audit of Interest-Bearing Debt

Learning Objective 5

This audit program does not provide for the usual distinction between tests of controls and substantive testing. This is because individual transactions will generally be examined for all large debt agreements. To document internal control, the auditors will usually prepare a written description, as well as an internal control questionnaire. Questions included on a typical questionnaire are the following: (1) Are amounts of new interest-bearing debt authorized by appropriate management? (2) Is an independent trustee used for all bond issues? (3) Does a company official monitor compliance with debt provisions?

Because transactions are few in number but large in dollar amount, the auditors are generally able to substantiate the individual transactions. Therefore, testing of controls occurs through what actually amounts to dual-purpose transaction testing.

Audit procedures appropriate for the verification of interest-bearing debt include the following:

1. Obtain or prepare analyses of interest-bearing debt accounts and related interest, premium, and discount accounts.
2. Examine copies of notes payable and supporting documents.
3. Confirm interest-bearing debt with payees or appropriate third parties.
4. Vouch borrowing and repayment transactions to supporting documents.
5. Perform analytical procedures to test the overall reasonableness of interest-bearing debt and interest expense.
6. Test the computations of interest expense, interest payable, and amortization of discount and premium.
7. Evaluate whether debt provisions have been met.
8. Trace authority for issuance of interest-bearing debt to the corporate minutes.
9. Review notes payable paid or renewed after the balance sheet date.
10. Perform procedures to identify notes payable to related parties.
11. Send confirmation letters to financial institutions to obtain information about financing arrangements.
12. Evaluate proper financial statement presentation and disclosure of interest-bearing debt and related transactions.

Figure 15.1 relates these substantive tests to their primary audit objectives.

FIGURE 15.1
Objectives of Major Substantive Tests of Interest-Bearing Debt Transactions and Balances

Substantive Tests	Primary Audit Objectives
Obtain analyses of interest-bearing debt and related accounts.	Valuation
Examine copies of notes payable and supporting documents. Confirm interest-bearing debt. Vouch borrowing and repayment transactions.	Completeness Existence and obligations
Perform analytical procedures. Test computations of interest expense, interest payable, and amortization of discount and premium.	Completeness Existence and obligations Valuation
Evaluate whether debt provisions have been met. Trace authority for issuance of debt to corporate minutes. Review notes payable paid or renewed after the balance sheet date. Perform procedures to identify notes payable to related parties. Send confirmation letters about financing arrangements. Evaluate financial statement presentation and disclosure.	Presentation and disclosure

1. Obtain or Prepare Analyses of Interest-Bearing Debt Accounts and Related Interest, Premium, and Discount Accounts.

A notes payable analysis shows the beginning balance of each individual note, additional notes issued and payments on notes during the year, and the ending balance of each note. In addition, the beginning balances of interest payable or prepaid interest, interest expense, interest paid, and ending balances of interest payable or prepaid interest may be presented in the analysis working paper.

An analysis of the Notes Payable account will serve a number of purposes: (*a*) the payment or other disposition of notes listed as outstanding in the previous year's audit can be verified, (*b*) the propriety of individual debits and credits can be established, and (*c*) the amount of the year-end balance of the account is proved through the step-by-step examination of all changes in the account during the year.

In the first audit of a client, the auditors will analyze the ledger accounts for Bonds Payable, Bond Issue Costs, and Bond Discount (or Bond Premium) for the years since the bonds were issued. The working paper is placed in the auditors' permanent file; in later audits, any further entries in these accounts may be added to the analysis.

The accounts of the financing cycle are often relatively free of material misstatement. When misstatements occur they may be due to improper reporting of debt (e.g., a loan is recorded with a debit to cash and a credit to a revenue account), incomplete recording of debt (e.g., a loan is not recorded and the proceeds are maintained "off the books"), or improper amortization of loan-related discount and premium accounts. In some situations, note disclosures related to debt are incomplete.

The auditors must also be aware of clients with complex organizational structures involving numerous or unusual legal entities or contractual arrangements and transactions involving related parties. In these cases questions arise as to proper recording of the transactions. Also, the auditors should realize that a lack of compliance with the provisions of a debt agreement usually makes the debt involved entirely due and payable on demand.

2. Examine Copies of Notes Payable and Supporting Documents.

The auditors should examine the client's copies of notes payable and supporting documents such as mortgages and trust deeds. The original documents will be in the possession of the payees, but the auditors should make certain that the client has retained copies of the debt instruments and that their details correspond to the analyses described in the first procedure of this audit program.

3. Confirm Interest-Bearing Debt with Payees or Appropriate Third Parties.

Notes payable to financial institutions are confirmed as part of the confirmation of cash deposit balances. The standard confirmation form illustrated in Chapter 10 includes a request that the financial institution confirm all borrowings by the depositor.

Confirmation requests for notes payable to payees other than financial institutions should be drafted on the client's letterhead stationery, signed by the controller or other appropriate executive, and mailed by the auditors. Payees should be requested to confirm dates of origin, due dates, unpaid balances of notes, interest rates, dates to which interest has been paid, and collateral for the notes.

The auditors may also substantiate the existence and amount of a mortgage liability outstanding by direct confirmation with the mortgagee. The information received should be compared with the client's records and the audit working papers. When no change in the liability account has occurred in the period under audit, the only major procedure necessary will be this confirmation with the creditor. At the same time that the mortgagee is asked to confirm the debt, it may be asked for an indication of the company's compliance with the mortgage or trust deed agreement.

Bond transactions usually can be confirmed directly with the trustee. The trustee's reply should include an exact description of the bonds, including maturity dates and interest rates; bonds retired, purchased for the treasury, or converted into stock during the year; bonds outstanding at the balance sheet date; and **sinking fund** transactions and balances.

4. Vouch Borrowing and Repayment Transactions to Supporting Documents.

The auditors must obtain evidence that transactions in interest-bearing debt accounts were valid. To accomplish this objective, the auditors trace the cash received from the issuance of

---

Primary Audit
Objective:

Valuation	☑

Primary Audit
Objectives:

Existence	☑
Completeness	☑
Obligations	☑

Primary Audit
Objectives:

Existence	☑
Completeness	☑
Obligations	☑

Primary Audit
Objectives:

Existence	☑
Completeness	☑
Obligations	☑

notes, bonds, or mortgages to the validated copy of the bank deposit slip and to the bank statement. Any remittance advices supporting these cash receipts are also examined. The auditors can find further support for the net proceeds of a bond issue by referring to the underwriting contract and to the prospectus filed with the SEC.

Debits to a Notes Payable or a Mortgages Payable account generally represent payments in full or in installments. The auditors should examine these payments; in so doing, they also will account for payments of accrued interest. The propriety of installment payments should be verified by reference to the repayment schedule set forth in the note or mortgage copy in the client's possession.

A comparison of canceled notes payable with the debit entries in the Notes Payable account provides further assurance that notes indicated as paid during the year have, in fact, been retired. The auditors' inspection of these notes should include a comparison of the maturity date of the note with the date of cash disbursement. Failure to pay notes promptly at maturity is suggestive of financial weakness.

There is seldom any justification for a paid note to be missing from the files; a receipt for payment from the payee of the note is not a satisfactory substitute. If, for any reason, a paid note is not available for inspection, the auditors should review the request for a check or other vouchers supporting the disbursement and should discuss the transaction with an appropriate official.

In examining the canceled notes, the auditors should also trace the disposition of any collateral used to secure these notes. A convenient opportunity for diversion of pledged securities or other assets to an unauthorized use might be created at the time these assets are returned by a secured creditor.

5. Perform Analytical Procedures to Test the Overall Reasonableness of Interest-Bearing Debt and Interest Expense.

One of the most effective ways to determine the overall reasonableness of interest-bearing debt is to examine the relationship between recorded interest expense and the average principal amount of debt outstanding during the year. If the client is paying interest on debt that is not recorded, this relationship will not be in line with the interest rate at which the client company should be able to borrow. Therefore, the auditors can use these procedures as a test of the *completeness* of recorded interest-bearing debt.

The auditors also compare the year-end amount of interest-bearing debt with the amount in the prior year's balance sheet. A similar comparison is made of interest expense for the current year and the preceding year.

6. Test the Computations of Interest Expense, Interest Payable, and Amortization of Discount and Premium.

The auditors may test the accuracy of the client's computations of interest expense and interest payable. In addition, they may examine paid checks supporting interest payments and review the confirmations received from payees to verify the dates on which interest on each note or mortgage has been paid. A close study of interest payments is another means of bringing to light any unrecorded interest-bearing liabilities.

The total bond interest expense for the period usually reflects not only the interest actually paid and accrued, but also amortization of bond premium or discount. The auditors may also test the amounts amortized by independent computations.

7. Evaluate Whether Debt Provisions Have Been Met.

In the first audit of a client or upon the issuance of a new bond issue, the auditors will obtain a copy of the bond indenture for the permanent file. The indenture should be carefully studied, with particular attention to such points as the amount of bonds authorized, interest rates and dates, maturity dates, descriptions of property pledged as collateral, provisions for retirement or conversion, duties and responsibilities of the trustee, and any restrictions imposed on the borrowing company.

The indenture provisions may require maintenance of a sinking fund, maintenance of stipulated minimum levels of working capital, and insurance of pledged property. The indenture also may restrict dividends to a specified proportion of earnings, limit management compensation,

Illustrative Case
Violations of Debt Covenants

In the audit of a large construction company, the auditors found the client's working capital to be far below the minimum level stipulated in the indenture of long-term secured bonds payable. In addition, the client had allowed the required insurance coverage of pledged assets to lapse. These violations of the indenture were sufficient to cause the bond issue to become payable on demand.

Although the client agreed to reclassify the bond issue as a current liability and disclose the problem in the financial statements, the auditors were unable to satisfy themselves that the client could meet the obligation if the bondholders demanded payment. Also, if the bondholders foreclosed on the pledged assets, the ability of the client to continue as a going concern would be questionable. Thus, even after the liability was reclassified as current, the auditors had to add an explanatory paragraph to their report referring to the uncertainty regarding the company's ability to meet its obligations and remain a going concern.

and prohibit additional long-term borrowing, except under stipulated conditions. The auditors will perform tests to evaluate whether the company is in compliance with these provisions. For example, the auditors will examine evidence of insurance coverage, vouch payments to the sinking fund, and compare the amounts of management compensation and dividends paid to amounts allowed by the agreements.

If the company has not complied fully with the requirements, the auditors should inform both the client and the client's legal counsel of the violation. In some cases of violation, the entire bond issue may become due and payable on demand, and hence a current liability. When the client is in violation of an indenture provision and the penalty is to make the debt become payable upon demand, the client usually will be able to obtain a waiver of compliance with the provision. In other words, creditors often choose not to enforce contract terms fully. To enable the liability to be presented as long term, the waiver must waive compliance for a period of one year from the balance sheet date. Even if an appropriate waiver of compliance is obtained, the matter should be disclosed in the notes to the client's financial statements.

Auditors do not judge the legality of a bond issue; this is a problem for the client's attorneys. The auditors should be familiar, however, with the principal provisions of the federal Securities Act of 1933 and of the corporate blue sky laws of the client's state of incorporation. They should ascertain that the client has obtained an attorney's opinion on the legality of the bond issuance. In doubtful cases, they should obtain representations from the client's legal counsel.

Primary Audit Objective:
Presentation ☑

8. Trace Authority for Issuance of Interest-Bearing Debt to the Corporate Minutes.

The authority to issue interest-bearing debt generally lies with the board of directors. To determine that the bonds outstanding were properly authorized, the auditors should read the passages in the minutes of directors' (and stockholders') meetings concerning the issuance of debt. The minutes usually will cite the applicable sections of the corporate bylaws permitting the issuance of debt instruments and may also contain reference to the opinion of the company's counsel concerning the legality of the issue.

Primary Audit Objective:
Presentation ☑

9. Review Notes Payable Paid or Renewed After the Balance Sheet Date.

If any of the notes payable outstanding at the balance sheet date are paid before completion of the audit engagement, such cash payments will provide the auditors with additional evidence on the liability. Renewal of notes maturing shortly after the balance sheet date may alter the auditors' thinking as to the proper classification of these liabilities.

In the discussion of notes receivable in Chapter 11, emphasis was placed on the necessity of close scrutiny of loans to officers, directors, and affiliates because of the absence of arm's-length bargaining in these related party transactions. Similar emphasis should be placed on the examination of notes payable to insiders or affiliates, although the opportunities for self-dealing are more limited than with receivables. The auditors should scan the notes payable records for the period between the balance sheet date and the completion of the audit so that they may be aware of any unusual transactions, such as the re-establishment of an insider note that had been paid just prior to the balance sheet date.

Primary Audit Objective:
Presentation ☑

10. Perform Procedures to Identify Notes Payable to Related Parties.

As has been the case in other portions of the audit, the auditors must perform procedures to determine that any related party debt is properly disclosed. Note here that the lower number of transactions makes discovery of such transactions less difficult than in accounts with a large number of transactions such as accounts payable.

Primary Audit Objective:
Presentation ☑

11. Send Confirmation Letters to Financial Institutions to Obtain Information about Financing Arrangements.

Financing arrangements and transactions can be very complex, and the details of these arrangements and transactions must be adequately disclosed in the notes to the financial statements. If the auditors determine that additional evidence is needed to verify these details, they will send a *separate* confirmation letter to the financial institution. For example, confirmation letters may be used to obtain information about lines of credit, contingent liabilities, compensating balance arrangements, letters of credit, or futures contracts. These letters are signed by the client and specifically addressed to the client's loan officer or another official at the financial institution that is knowledgeable about the information. This expedites a response to the confirmation and enhances the quality of the evidence received. Figure 15.2 provides an example of a letter to confirm information about lines of credit.

Primary Audit Objective:
Presentation ☑

12. Evaluate Proper Financial Statement Presentation and Disclosure of Interest-Bearing Debt and Related Transactions.

Because of the interest of creditors in the current liability section of the balance sheet and the inferences that may be drawn from various uses of notes payable, adequate informative disclosure is extremely important. Classification of notes by types of payees, as well as by current or long-term maturity, is necessary. Notes payable to banks, notes payable to trade creditors, and notes payable to officers, directors, stockholders, and affiliates should be listed separately.

Secured liabilities and pledged assets should be cross-referenced to one another with an explanation in the notes to the financial statements. In the event of financial difficulties and dissolution, creditors expect to share in the assets in proportion to their respective claims; if certain assets, such as current receivables, have been pledged to one creditor, the risk to unsecured creditors is increased. Current liabilities should include not only those notes maturing within a period of 12 months (or a longer operating cycle) but also any installments currently payable on long-term obligations such as mortgages.

The essential point in balance sheet presentation of long-term liabilities is that they be adequately described, including details about the types of debt, amounts authorized and issued, interest rates, maturity dates, and any conversion or subordination features.

Long-Term Debt Payable in the Current Period

Long-term liabilities include all debts that will not be liquidated with the use of current assets. In other words, any bonds or notes falling due in the coming operating cycle that are to be paid from special funds or refinanced will be classified as long-term obligations regardless of maturity date. Before accepting a long-term classification for maturing obligations, auditors must satisfy themselves that the client has both the *intent* and the *ability* to refinance the obligation on a long-term basis. Intent and ability to refinance are demonstrated by the client through either (1) refinancing the obligation on a long-term basis before the issuance of the financial statements, or (2) entering into a financing agreement by that date, which clearly permits such refinancing. Any debt maturing currently and payable from current assets should be classified as a current liability.

Restrictions Imposed by Long-Term Debt Agreements

The major restrictions imposed on the company by long-term loan agreements are significant to the company's investors and creditors. Consequently, the nature of the restrictions should be clearly set forth in a note to the financial statements.

Unamortized Bond Premium or Discount

Unamortized premium should be added to the face amount of the bonds or debentures in the liability section of the balance sheet. Similarly, unamortized discount should be deducted from the face amount of the debt.

FIGURE 15.2
Illustrative Letter for Confirmation of Lines of Credit

Wallace Manufacturing, Inc.
1400 Main St.
Los Angeles, CA 90015

January 31, 20X5

Mr. Richard M. Smith
Senior Loan Officer
First United Bank
2330 Fourth Ave.
Los Angeles, CA 90010

Dear Mr. Smith:

In connection with an audit of the financial statements of Wallace Manufacturing, Inc., as of December 31, 20X4, and for the year then ended, we have advised our independent auditors of the information listed below, which we believe is a complete and accurate description of our line of credit from your financial institution as of the close of business on December 31, 20X4. Although we do not request or expect you to conduct a comprehensive, detailed search of your records, if during the process of completing this confirmation additional information about other lines of credit from your financial institution comes to your attention, please include such information below.

1. The company has available at your financial institution a line of credit totaling $47 million.
2. The current terms of the line of credit are contained in the letter dated May 11, 20X2.
3. The amount of unused line of credit, subject to the terms of the related letter, at December 31, 20X4, was $19 million.
4. The interest rate at the close of business on December 31, 20X4, was 9.2%.
5. There are no requirements for compensating balances in connection with this line of credit.

    Please confirm whether the information about the line of credit presented above is correct by signing below and returning this letter directly to our independent auditors, Warren & Clark, CPAs, 2100 Century Blvd., Los Angeles, CA 90053.

Sincerely,
Wallace Manufacturing, Inc.

By: *Robert Barr*
      Robert Barr
      Controller

— —

Dear Warren & Clark, CPAs:

The above information regarding the line of credit agrees with the records of this financial institution. Although we have not conducted a comprehensive, detailed search of our records, no information about other lines of credit came to our attention. [Note exceptions below or in an attached letter.]

_____
_____
_____
_____

First United Bank

By: *Richard Smith, Senior Loan Officer*   *2/20/X5*
      (Officer and Title)   (Date)

Time of Examination— Interest-Bearing Debt

Analysis of the ledger accounts for interest-bearing debt and interest expense takes very little time in most audits because of the small number of entries. Consequently, most auditors prefer to wait until the end of the year before analyzing these accounts.

Audit procedures intended to reveal any unrecorded liabilities cannot ordinarily be performed in advance of the balance sheet date. Such steps as the evaluation of compliance with debt provisions, tests of interest expense, and the investigation of notes paid or renewed shortly after the balance sheet date must necessarily await the close of the period being audited. The opportunities for performing audit work in advance of the balance sheet date are thus much more limited in the case of interest-bearing debt than for most of the asset groups previously discussed.

Equity Capital

Sources and Nature of Owners' Equity

Most of this section is concerned with the audit of stockholders' equity accounts of corporate clients; the audit of owners' equity in partnerships and sole proprietorships is discussed briefly near the end of the chapter.

Owners' equity for corporate clients consists of capital stock accounts (preferred and common) and retained earnings. Balances in the capital stock accounts change when the corporation issues or repurchases stock. Transfer of ownership of shares from one shareholder to another does not affect the account balances. Retained earnings are normally increased by earnings and decreased by dividend payments. Additionally, a few journal entries (e.g., prior period adjustments) may directly affect retained earnings. Transactions in the owners' equity accounts are generally few in number, but material in amount. No change may occur during the year in the capital stock accounts, and perhaps only one or two entries will be made to the retained earnings account.

The Auditors' Approach to Auditing Owners' Equity

The auditors' *objectives* in the audit of owners' equity are to:

1. Consider *inherent risks,* including fraud risks.
2. Consider *internal control* over owners' equity.
3. Determine the *existence* of recorded owners' equity.
4. Establish the *completeness* of recorded owners' equity.
5. Determine that the *valuation* of owners' equity is in accordance with generally accepted accounting principles.
6. Determine that the *presentation* and *disclosure* of owners' equity are appropriate.

In conjunction with the audit of owners' equity accounts, the auditors will also obtain evidence about the related accounts of dividends payable and capital stock discounts and premiums. Evidence is also gathered regarding the proper cutoff of cash receipts and disbursements relating to the equity accounts.

Internal Control over Owners' Equity

There are three principal elements of strong internal control over capital stock and dividends. These three elements are (1) the proper authorization of transactions by the board of directors and corporate officers, (2) the segregation of duties in handling these transactions (preferably the use of independent agents for stock registration and transfer and for dividend payments), and (3) the maintenance of adequate records.

Control of Capital Stock Transactions by the Board of Directors

All changes in capital stock accounts should receive formal advance approval by the board of directors. The board of directors must determine the number of shares to be issued and the price per share; if an installment plan of payment is to be used, the board must prescribe the terms. If plant and equipment, services, or any consideration other than cash is to be accepted in payment for shares, the board of directors must establish the valuation on the noncash assets received. Transfers from retained earnings to the Capital Stock and Paid-in Capital accounts, as in the case of stock dividends, are initiated by action of the board. In addition, stock splits and changes in par or stated value of shares require formal authorization by the board.

Authority for all dividend actions rests with the directors. The declaration of a dividend must specify not only the amount per share but also the date of record and the date of payment.

Independent Registrar and Stock Transfer Agent

In appraising internal control over capital stock, the first question that the auditors consider is whether the corporation employs the services of an independent stock registrar and a stock transfer agent or handles its own capital stock transactions. Internal control is far stronger when the services of an independent stock registrar and a stock transfer agent are utilized because the banks or trust companies acting in these capacities will have the experience, the specialized facilities, and the trained personnel to perform the work in an expert manner. Moreover, by placing the responsibility for handling capital stock certificates in separate and independent organizations, the corporation achieves to the fullest extent the internal control concept of separation of duties. The New York Stock Exchange and most other exchanges require that listed corporations utilize the services of an independent registrar.

The primary responsibility of the **stock registrar** is to avoid any overissuance of stock. The danger of overissuance is illustrated by the old story of a promoter who sold a 25 percent interest in a new corporation to each of 10 investors. To prevent such frauds, the registrar must verify that stock certificates are issued in accordance with the articles of incorporation and the formal authorization of the board of directors. The registrar obtains copies of the documents authorizing the total shares to be issued and maintains records of total shares issued and canceled. Each new certificate must be presented to the registrar for examination and registration before it is issued to a stockholder. The dangers of fraud and accidental error relating to improper issuance of stock certificates are greatly reduced when an independent registrar is employed.

Corporations with actively traded securities also employ independent **stock transfer agents.** Although the stock transfer agent maintains a record of the total shares outstanding, its primary responsibility is maintaining detailed stockholder records (name and address of each stockholder) and carrying out transfers of stock ownership.

The Stock Certificate Book and Stockholders Ledger

If the corporation does not utilize the services of an independent registrar and stock transfer agent, the board of directors usually assigns these functions to the secretary of the company. The board of directors should designate officers who are authorized to (1) sign stock certificates, (2) maintain records of stockholders, (3) maintain custody of unissued certificates, and (4) sign dividend checks. The stock certificates should be serially numbered by the printer, and from the time of delivery to the company until issuance, they should be in the exclusive custody of the designated officer. The signatures of two officers are generally required on stock certificates.

The certificates often are prepared in and torn from bound books called **stock certificate books,** with attached stubs similar to those in a checkbook. Each stub shows the certificate number and contains blank spaces for entering the number of shares represented by the certificate, the name of the stockholder, and the serial number of any previously issued certificate surrendered in exchange for the new one. Certificates should be issued in numerical sequence and not signed or countersigned until the time of issuance. When outstanding shares are transferred from one holder to another, the old certificate is surrendered to the company. The designated officer cancels the old certificate by perforating and attaching it to the corresponding stub in the certificate book.

The stock certificate book is not in itself an adequate record of the capital stock outstanding. The certificates appear in the book in serial number order, and a single stockholder may own several certificates listed at various places in the certificate book. A **stockholders ledger** provides a separate record for each stockholder, thus making it possible to determine at a glance the total number of shares owned by any one person. This record may be used in compiling the list of dividend checks or for any other communication with shareholders.

Internal Control over Dividends

The nature of internal control over the payment of dividends, as in the case of stock issuance, depends primarily upon whether the company performs the function of dividend payment itself or utilizes the services of an independent dividend-paying agent. If an independent dividend-paying agent is used, the corporation will provide the agent with a certified copy of the dividend declaration and with a check for the full amount of the dividend. The bank or trust company serving as stock transfer agent is usually appointed to distribute the dividend, since it maintains the detailed records of stockholders. The agent issues dividend checks to the individual stockholders and sends the corporation a list of the payments made. The use of an independent fiscal agent is to be recommended from the standpoint of internal control, for it materially reduces the possibility of fraud or error arising in connection with the distribution of dividends.

In a small corporation that does not use the services of a dividend-paying agent, the responsibility for payment of dividends is usually lodged with the treasurer and the secretary.

After declaration of a dividend by the board of directors, the secretary prepares a list of stockholders as of the date of record, the number of shares held by each, and the amount of the dividend each is to receive. The total of these individual amounts is proved by multiplying the dividend per share by the total number of outstanding shares.

Dividend checks controlled by serial numbers are drawn payable to individual stockholders in the amounts shown on the list described above. If the stockholders ledger is maintained on a computer master file, the dividend checks may be prepared by the computer directly from this record. The stockholder list and dividend checks are submitted to the treasurer for approval and signature. The checks should be reconciled by the treasurer with the total of shares outstanding and mailed without again coming under control of the officer who prepared them.

Cash in the amount of the total dividend is then transferred from the general bank account to a separate dividend bank account. As the individual dividend checks are paid from this account and returned by the bank, they should be matched with the check stubs or marked *paid* in the dividend check register. A list of outstanding checks should be prepared monthly from the open stubs or open items in the check register. This list should agree in total with the balance remaining in the dividend bank account. Companies with numerous stockholders prepare dividend checks in machine-readable form, so that the computer may perform the reconciliation of outstanding checks.

Audit Documentation for Owners' Equity

In addition to the lead schedule for owners' equity accounts, the auditors prepare an analysis of each equity account for the permanent file. A detailed analysis is essential for all aspects of a stock option plan: options authorized, issued, and outstanding. For a closely held corporation not served by a transfer agent, the auditors will often prepare for the permanent file a list of shareholders and the number of shares owned by each.

Audit Program—Capital Stock

The following procedures are typical of the work required in many engagements for the verification of capital stock:

Learning Objective 9

1. Obtain an understanding of internal control over capital stock transactions.
2. Examine articles of incorporation, bylaws, and minutes for provisions relating to capital stock.
3. Obtain or prepare analyses of the capital stock accounts.
4. Account for all proceeds from stock issues.
5. Confirm shares outstanding with the independent registrar and stock transfer agent.
6. For a corporation acting as its own stock registrar and transfer agent, reconcile the stockholder records with the general ledger.
7. Determine that appropriate accounting is applied to employee stock compensation plans.
8. Determine compliance with restrictions and preferences pertaining to capital stock and disclosures are appropriate.

Capital stock transactions are usually few in number; consequently, the auditors usually substantiate all transactions in audits of nonpublic companies. In public company integrated audits, the auditors will rely on internal controls because they must be tested to attest to internal controls. In addition to the preceding steps, the auditors must determine the appropriate financial statement presentation of capital stock. This topic is discussed later in this chapter, along with the financial statement presentation of other elements of owners' equity.

1. Obtain an Understanding of Internal Control over Capital Stock Transactions.

Even though the examination of capital stock consists primarily of substantive tests, the auditors, even in the audits of nonpublic companies, must acquire an understanding of the client's procedures for authorizing, executing, and recording capital stock transactions. This may be achieved by preparing a written description or flowchart of the system or by filling in an internal control questionnaire. If the questionnaire approach is employed, typical questions to be answered might include the following: Does the company utilize the services of an independent registrar and stock transfer agent? Are stockholders ledgers and transfer journals maintained? Are entries in owners' equity accounts reviewed periodically by an appropriate officer?

2. Examine Articles of Incorporation, Bylaws, and Minutes for Provisions Relating to Capital Stock.

In a first audit, copies of the articles of incorporation and bylaws obtained for the permanent file should be read carefully. The information required by the auditors for each issue of capital stock includes the number of shares authorized and issued; the par or stated value; dividend rates, if any; call and conversion provisions; stock splits; and stock options. The auditors will also review minutes of the meetings of directors and stockholders for authorizations of transactions related to the company's stock. By gathering evidence on these points, the auditors obtain assurance that capital stock transactions and dividend payments have been in accordance with legal requirements and specific authorizations by stockholders and directors. Also, they will be able to judge whether the balance sheet contains all necessary information to describe adequately the various stock issues and other elements of corporate capital.

3. Obtain or Prepare Analyses of the Capital Stock Accounts.

In an initial audit engagement, capital stock accounts should be analyzed from the beginning of the corporation to provide the auditors with a complete historical picture of corporate capital. Analysis of capital stock includes an appraisal of the nature of all changes and the vouching of these changes to the supporting documents and records. All changes in capital stock should bear the authorization of the board of directors.

The analyses of capital stock accounts may be prepared in a manner that permits additions during later audit engagements. After the initial audit, if the analyses are kept in the auditors' permanent file, all that will be necessary is to record the current period's increases and decreases and to vouch these transactions. The auditors then will have working papers showing all changes in capital stock from the inception of the corporation.

The auditors also should analyze the Treasury Stock account and prepare a list showing the number of shares of **treasury stock** on hand. All certificates on hand then may be inspected. If the certificates are not on hand, they should be confirmed directly with the custodian.

In their review of treasury stock transactions, the auditors should refer to permanent file copies of the minutes of directors' meetings to determine (*a*) that the acquisition or reissuance of treasury stock was authorized by directors and (*b*) that the price paid or received was in accordance with prices specified by the board.

4. Account for All Proceeds from Stock Issues.

Closely related to the analyses of Capital Stock accounts is the audit procedure of accounting for the receipt and proper disposition of all funds derived from the issuance of capital stock. The proceeds should be traced to the cash records and bank statements. SEC registration statements and contracts with underwriters may also be available as evidence of the amounts received from stock issues.

When assets other than cash are received as consideration for the issuance of capital stock, the entire transaction requires careful study. Generally the value of assets and services received in exchange for capital shares is established by action of the board of directors. The auditors must determine that these accounting estimates made by the client result in a reasonable valuation.

5. Confirm Shares Outstanding with the Independent Registrar and Stock Transfer Agent.

The number of shares issued and outstanding on the balance sheet date may be confirmed by direct communication with the independent registrar and stock transfer agent. The confirmation request should be written by the client on the client's letterhead, but it should be mailed by the auditors. Confirmation replies should be sent directly to the auditors, not to the client. All information contained in these replies should be traced to the corporate records. It is essential that the general ledger controlling accounts agree with the amount of stock issued as reported by the independent registrar and stock transfer agent. Because of the strong controls usually maintained over stock certificates, it is not customary to communicate with individual stockholders in establishing the number of shares outstanding.

Primary Audit Objectives:	
Existence	☑
Completeness	☑
Obligations	☑

Primary Audit Objective:	
Valuation	☑

Primary Audit Objectives:	
Existence	☑
Completeness	☑
Obligations	☑
Valuation	☑

Primary Audit Objectives:	
Existence	☑
Completeness	☑
Obligations	☑

6. For a Corporation Acting as Its Own Stock Registrar and Transfer Agent, Reconcile the Stockholder Records with the General Ledger.

When a corporation acts as its own transfer agent and registrar, the auditors must adopt alternative procedures to obtain evidence that is not available by direct confirmation with outside parties. These procedures include (*a*) accounting for stock certificate numbers, (*b*) examining canceled certificates, and (*c*) reconciling the stockholders ledger and stock certificate book with the general ledger.

The audit working papers should include a record of the last certificate number issued during the year. Reference to the working papers for the preceding audit, combined with the verification of certificate numbers issued during the current period, will enable the auditors to account for all certificates by serial number.

A working paper prepared during the auditors' examination of the stock certificate book of a small closely held corporation is designed to be utilized during several audits; it may be retained in the permanent file or forwarded to successive current files. Additionally, it is desirable for the auditors to inspect the unissued certificates to determine that all certificates purported to be unissued are actually on hand and blank.

Adequate internal control for corporations not utilizing the services of an independent registrar and stock transfer agent requires that all canceled stock certificates be perforated or marked in a manner precluding the possibility of further use. Canceled certificates should be attached to the corresponding stubs in the stock certificate book and permanently preserved. If reacquired certificates are not canceled properly, the danger exists that they may be reissued fraudulently by officers or employees. Auditors, therefore, will examine all canceled stock certificates on hand, noting in particular that they have been voided. The general ledger account for capital stock shows the total par value or stated value of all shares outstanding, plus any treasury shares. The stockholders ledger includes an account for each stockholder. The stock certificate book contains all canceled certificates and also open stubs for outstanding certificates. The auditors must reconcile these three records (general ledger control account, stockholders ledger, and stock certificate book) to establish the amount of outstanding stock and to rule out the possibility of an overissuance of shares. If this verification were not made, it would be possible for a dishonest official to issue unlimited amounts of stock and to withhold the proceeds from such sales.

A trial balance of the subsidiary stockholder records may be obtained from the client or prepared by the auditors and compared with the general ledger controlling account. In conjunction with this procedure, the total shares outstanding, as shown by the stock certificate book stubs, should also be reconciled with the control account and with the subsidiary trial balance. These procedures assure the auditors of the accuracy of the ledger account balances for capital stock.

7. Determine that Appropriate Accounting Is Applied to Employee Stock Compensation Plans.

Many corporations grant stock options or other similar instruments to officers and employees through incentive-type compensation plans. Accounting standards now require companies to recognize the compensation cost related to these awards. Specifically, the compensation cost is measured as the fair value of the options on the date they are granted to the employee. This cost is then recognized as compensation expense over the period in which the options vest.

The accounting for these instruments at fair value presents a particular challenge for the auditors. Because they are not traded on a market, the fair value of the instruments are determined using option pricing models. To determine that the fair value is reasonable, the auditors must evaluate the appropriateness of the model used and the reasonableness of the valuation assumptions. In addition, they must obtain evidence that the computations are accurate. *SAS 101,* as discussed on pages 144–145, provides guidance for auditing financial statement items that are measured at fair value. In this area, the auditors may decide to rely on the work of a specialist.

8. Determine Compliance with Restrictions and Preferences Pertaining to Capital Stock and Disclosures Are Appropriate.

When *stock options* are granted, the corporation must hold a portion of the authorized but unissued stock in reserve so that it will be in a position to fulfill the option agreements.

Similarly, corporations with convertible debentures or convertible preferred stocks outstanding must hold in reserve a sufficient number of common shares to meet the demands of preferred stockholders and debenture holders who may elect to convert their securities into common stock.

The auditors must become thoroughly familiar with the terms of any stock options and stock purchase plans and with the conversion features of debenture bonds and preferred stock, so that they can determine appropriate measurement and adequate disclosure of these agreements. The auditors must also verify the shares issued during the year through conversion or exercise of stock options and must ascertain that the number of shares held in reserve at the balance sheet date does not exceed the corporation's authorized but unissued stock.

Retained Earnings and Dividends

Audit work on retained earnings and dividends includes two major steps: (1) the analysis of retained earnings and any appropriations of retained earnings and (2) the review of dividend procedures for both cash and stock dividends.

On a first-year audit, the analysis of retained earnings and any appropriations of retained earnings should cover the entire history of these accounts. Such an analysis is prepared for the permanent file and is added to in each annual audit. Credits to the Retained Earnings account ordinarily represent amounts of net income transferred from the Income Summary account. Debits to the Retained Earnings account ordinarily include entries for net losses, cash and stock dividends, and for the creation or enlargement of appropriated reserves. Appropriations of retained earnings require specific authorization by the board of directors. The only verification necessary for these entries is to ascertain that the dates and amounts correspond to the actions of the board.

In the verification of cash dividends, the auditors usually will perform the following steps:

1. Determine the dates and amounts of dividends authorized.
2. Verify the amounts paid.
3. Determine the amount of any preferred dividends in arrears.
4. Review the treatment of unclaimed dividend checks.

The auditors' analysis of dividend declarations may reveal the existence of cash dividends declared but not paid. These dividends must be shown as liabilities in the balance sheet. The auditors also may review the procedures for handling unclaimed dividends and ascertain that these items are recognized as liabilities. The amount of any accumulated dividends in arrears on preferred stock should be computed. If a closely held company has irregular dividend declarations or none at all, the auditors should consider whether the federal penalty surtax on reasonably accumulated retained earnings might be assessed. In the verification of stock dividends, there is an additional responsibility of determining that the proper amounts have been transferred from retained earnings to capital stock and paid-in capital accounts for both large and small stock dividends.

In evaluating client disclosures, the auditors must be aware that changes in retained earnings during the year may be shown in a separate statement or combined with the income statement. A combined statement of income and retained earnings often is presented. In this form of presentation, the amount of retained earnings at the beginning of the year is added to the net income figure, dividends declared are subtracted from the subtotal, and the final figure represents the new balance of retained earnings.

One of the most significant points to consider in determining the presentation of retained earnings in the balance sheet is the existence of any restriction on the use of this retained income. Agreements with banks, bondholders, and other creditors commonly impose limitations on the payment of dividends. These restrictions must be fully disclosed in the notes to the financial statements.

Financial Statement Presentation of Stockholders' Equity

The presentation of capital stock in the balance sheet should include a complete description of each issue. Information to be disclosed includes the title of each issue; par or stated value; dividend rate, if any; dividend preference; conversion and call provisions; number of shares authorized, issued, and in treasury; dividends in arrears, if any; and shares reserved for stock options or for conversions.

Treasury stock preferably is shown in the stockholders' equity section, at cost, as a deduction from the combined total of paid-in capital and retained earnings. In many states, an amount of retained earnings equivalent to the cost of the treasury shares must be restricted. A note to the financial statements discloses this restriction.

Changes in retained earnings during the year may be shown in a separate statement or combined with the income statement. A combined statement of income and retained earnings often is presented. In this form of presentation, the amount of retained earnings at the beginning of the year is added to the net income figure, dividends paid are subtracted from the subtotal, and the final figure represents the new balance of retained earnings.

One of the most significant points to consider in determining the presentation of retained earnings in the balance sheet is the existence of any restriction on the use of this retained income. Agreements with banks, bondholders, and other creditors very commonly impose limitations on the payment of dividends. These restrictions must be fully disclosed in the notes to financial statements.

Time of Examination— Stockholders' Equity

The transactions involving stockholders' equity accounts generally are few in number, but material in amount. Because so few transactions occur, it usually is efficient to make the analysis after the close of the period. In the first audit of a new client, however, some preliminary work can be done advantageously in obtaining and reviewing copies of the articles of incorporation and bylaws and in analyzing the capital accounts.

For a continuing client, the auditors will often find that audit time required will be small in relation to the dollars in these accounts and much less than is required for assets, liabilities, revenue, or expense. Thus, while the capital stock account often has a larger balance than the cash account, the audit work required for capital stock is usually far less.

Audit of Partnerships and Sole Proprietorships

Perhaps the most common reason for a small business to arrange for an independent audit is the need for audited financial statements in order to obtain a bank loan. Often, a banker, when approached by the owners of a small business applying for a loan, will request audited financial statements as an aid to reaching a decision on the loan application.

Procedures for Audit of Partners' Accounts

A most significant document underlying the partnership form of organization is the partnership contract. The auditors are particularly interested in determining that the distribution of net income has been carried out in accordance with the profit-sharing provisions of the partnership contract. Maintenance of partners' capital accounts at prescribed levels and restriction of drawings by partners to specified amounts are other points often covered in the contract; compliance with these clauses should be verified by the auditors in determining the propriety of the year's entries in the capital accounts. Partners' loan accounts also require reference to the partnership contract to determine the treatment intended by the partners.

Occasionally, the auditors may find that a partnership is operating without any written agreement of partnership. This situation raises a question of whether profits have been divided in accordance with the understanding existing between the partners. For their own protection, the auditors may wish to obtain from each partner a written statement confirming the balance in his or her capital account and approval of the method used in dividing the year's earnings. They may also suggest that the firm develop a written partnership agreement.

Procedures for Audit of Sole Proprietorships

In general, the same principles described for the audit of corporate capital are applicable to the examination of the capital accounts and drawing accounts of a sole proprietorship or partnership. Analyses are made of all proprietorship accounts from the beginning of the business; the initial capital investment and any additions are traced to the cash and asset records; and the net income or loss for the period and any withdrawals are verified. In the case of a sole proprietorship, a common source of difficulty is the practice of intermingling business and personal transactions, making it necessary for the auditors to segregate personal net worth from business capital. Adjustments may also be required to transfer from expense accounts to the owner's drawing account any personal expenditures paid with company funds.

Chapter Summary

The details of the audit of long-term debt and equity accounts were discussed in this chapter. The chapter includes a description of the controls for these types of accounts, and the audit procedures that the auditors use to substantiate long-term debt and equity accounts. To summarize:

1. The financing cycle involves the activities of the company that are designed to obtain capital funds. It typically involves the issuance and repayment of debt and equity, as well as payment of interest and dividends. A primary concern for both of these types of transactions is proper authorization by the appropriate official in the company or by the board of directors.

2. Control over the issuance of bonds by a company is enhanced when an independent trustee represents the interest of the bondholders. The responsibilities of the trustee include monitoring the company's compliance with the requirements of the bond agreement and processing the payments of interest and principal to individual bondholders.

3. Capital stock transactions are best controlled by employing a registrar/transfer agent who monitors the issuance of the company's stock and handles transfers of shares between investors. In smaller companies capital stock is controlled through the maintenance of a stock certificate book and a stockholders ledger.

4. After the auditors obtain an understanding of the client's internal control over the financing cycle, they will often perform only limited tests of controls because of the limited number of transactions typically involved. It is usually more efficient to assess control risk at a high level and perform detailed substantive tests of transactions.

5. In the audit of interest-bearing debt, the auditors' primary substantive procedures will include vouching selected transactions occurring during the period, examining debt agreements, confirming balances and terms, and evaluating compliance with restrictive covenants.

6. The auditors' primary substantive procedures for equity transactions will typically include vouching the major equity transactions occurring during the period, confirming the number of shares outstanding with the registrar, and evaluating the company's compliance with stock option plan requirements and other restricting agreements.

Key Terms Introduced or Emphasized in Chapter 15

Debenture bond   An unsecured bond, dependent upon the general credit of the issuer.

Sinking fund   Cash or other assets set aside for the retirement of a debt.

Stock certificate book   A book of serially numbered certificates with attached stubs. Each stub shows the corresponding certificate number and provides space for entering the number of shares represented by the certificate, the name of the shareholder, and the serial number of the certificate surrendered in exchange for the new one. Surrendered certificates are canceled and replaced in the certificate book.

Stock registrar   An institution charged with responsibility for avoiding overissuance of a corporation's stock. Every new certificate must be presented to the registrar for examination and registration before it is issued to a stockholder.

Stock transfer agent   An institution responsible for maintaining detailed records of shareholders and handling transfers of stock ownership.

Stockholders ledger   A record showing the number of shares owned by each stockholder. This is the basic record used for preparing dividend payments and other communications with shareholders.

Treasury stock   Shares of its own stock acquired by a corporation for the purpose of being reissued at a later date.

Trust indenture   The formal agreement between bondholders and the issuer as to the terms of the debt.

Review Questions

15-1. What does the trust indenture used by a corporation in creating long-term bonded indebtedness have to do with the payment of dividends on common stock?

15-2. Long-term creditors often insist upon placing certain restrictions upon the borrowing company for the term of the loan. Give three examples of such restrictions, and indicate how each restriction protects the long-term creditor.

15-3. Most corporations with bonds payable outstanding utilize the services of a trustee. What relation, if any, does this practice have to the maintenance of adequate internal control?

15-4. What information should be requested by the auditors from the trustee responsible for an issue of debentures payable?

15-5. Palmer Company has issued a number of notes payable during the year, and several of these notes are outstanding at the balance sheet date. What sources of information should the auditors use in preparing a working paper analysis of the notes payable?

15-6. Is the confirmation of notes payable usually correlated with any other specific phase of the audit? Explain.

15-7. What is the principal reason for testing the reasonableness of the Interest Expense account in conjunction with the verification of notes payable?

15-8. In addition to verifying the recorded liabilities of a company, the auditors must also give consideration to the possibility that other unrecorded liabilities exist. What specific steps may be taken by the auditors to determine that all their client's interest-bearing liabilities are recorded?

15-9. Audit programs for examination of accounts receivable and notes receivable often include investigation of selected transactions occurring after the balance sheet date as well as transactions during the year under audit. Are the auditors concerned with notes payable transactions subsequent to the balance sheet date? Explain.

15-10. "Auditors are not qualified to pass on the legality of a bond issue; this is a question for the company's attorneys. It is therefore unnecessary for the auditors to inspect the bond indenture." Criticize the quotation.

15-11. Mansfield Corporation has outstanding an issue of 30-year bonds payable. There is no sinking fund for these bonds. Under what circumstances, if any, should this bond issue be classified as a current liability?

15-12. Two assistant auditors were assigned by the auditor-in-charge to the verification of long-term liabilities. Some time later, they reported to the auditor-in-charge that they had determined that all long-term liabilities were properly recorded and that all recorded long-term liabilities were genuine obligations. Does this determination constitute a sufficient examination of long-term liabilities? Explain.

15-13. Compare the auditors' examination of owners' equity with their work on assets and current liabilities. Among other factors to be considered are the relative amounts of time involved and the character of the transactions to be inspected.

15-14. What do you consider to be the most important control a corporation can adopt with respect to capital stock transactions?

15-15. What is the primary responsibility of an independent registrar with respect to capital stock?

15-16. In the audit of a small corporation not using the services of an independent stock registrar and stock transfer agent, what use is made of the stock certificate book by the auditors?

15-17. Describe the significant features of a stock certificate book, its purpose, and the manner in which it is used.

15-18. You have been retained to perform an audit of Valley Products, a small corporation which has not been audited during the previous 10 years of its existence. How will your work on the Capital Stock account in this initial audit differ from that required in a repeat engagement?

15-19. Your new client, Black Angus Valley Ranch, is a small corporation with fewer than 100 stockholders. It does not utilize the services of an independent stock registrar or transfer agent. For your first audit, you want to obtain or prepare a year-end list of stockholders showing the number of shares owned by each. From what source or record should this information be obtained? Explain.

15-20. Corporations sometimes issue their own capital stock in exchange for services and various assets other than cash. As an auditor, what evidence would you look for to determine the propriety of the values used in recording such transactions?

15–21. In your second annual audit of a corporate client, you find a new account in the general ledger called Treasury Stock, which has a balance of $306,000. Describe the procedures you would follow to verify this item.

15–22. In auditing the financial statements of Foster Company, you observe a debit entry for $200,000 labeled as Dividends in the Retained Earnings account. Explain in detail how you would verify this entry.

15–23. Name three situations that might place a restriction on retained earnings, limiting or preventing dividend payments. Explain how the auditors might become aware of each such restricting factor.

15–24. Comment on the desirability of audit work on the owners' equity accounts before the balance sheet date.

15–25. Delta Company has issued stock options to four of its officers permitting them to purchase 5,000 shares each of common stock at a price of $25 per share at any time during the next five years. The president asks you what effect, if any, the granting of the options will have upon the balance sheet presentation of the stockholders' equity accounts.

15–26. What errors are commonly encountered by the auditors in their examination of the capital and drawing accounts of a sole proprietor?

Questions Requiring Analysis

15–27. The only long-term liability of Range Corporation is a note payable for $1 million secured by a mortgage on the company's plant and equipment. You have audited the company annually for the three preceding years, during which time the principal amount of the note has remained unchanged. The maturity date is 10 years from the current balance sheet date. You are informed by the president of the company that all interest payments have been made promptly in accordance with the terms of the note. Under these circumstances, what audit work, if any, is necessary with respect to this long-term liability during your present year-end audit?

15–28. In an audit of a corporation that has a bond issue outstanding, the trust indenture is reviewed and confirmation as to the issue is obtained from the trustee. List eight matters of importance to the auditors that might be found either in the indenture or in the confirmation obtained from the trustee. Explain briefly the reason for the auditors' interest in each of the items.

15–29. During your annual audit of Walker Distributing Co., your assistant, Jane Williams, reports to you that, although a number of entries were made during the year in the general ledger account Notes Payable to Officers, she decided that it was not necessary to audit the account because it had a zero balance at year-end.

Required: Do you agree with your assistant's decision? Discuss.

15–30. You are engaged in the audit of the financial statements of Armada Corporation for the year ended August 31, 200X. The balance sheet, reflecting all your audit adjustments accepted by the client to date, shows total current assets, $8,000,000; total current liabilities, $7,500,000; and stockholders' equity, $1,000,000. Included in current liabilities are two unsecured notes payable—one payable to United National Bank in the amount of $900,000 due October 31, 200X; the other payable to First State Bank in the amount of $800,000 due September 30, 200X. On September 30, the last scheduled date for your audit fieldwork, you learn that Armada Corporation is unable to pay the $832,000 maturity value of the First State Bank note, that Armada executives are negotiating with First State Bank for an extension of the due date of the note, and that nothing definite has been decided as to the extension.

Required:

    a. Should this situation be disclosed in notes to Armada Corporation's August 31 financial statements?

    b. After the question of financial statement disclosure has been resolved to the auditors' satisfaction, might this situation have any effect upon the audit report?

15–31. You are retained by Columbia Corporation to audit its financial statements for the fiscal year ended June 30. Your consideration of internal control indicates a fairly satisfactory condition, although there are not enough employees to permit an extensive separation of duties. The company is one of the smaller units in its industry, but it has realized net income of about $500,000 in each of the last three years.

    Near the end of your fieldwork you overhear a telephone call received by the president of the company while you are discussing the audit with him. The telephone conversation indicates that on May 15 of the current year the Columbia Corporation made an accommodation endorsement of a 60-day, $430,000 note issued by a major customer, Brill Corporation, to its bank. The purpose of the telephone call from Brill was to inform your client that the note had been paid at the maturity date. You had not been aware of the existence of the note before overhearing the telephone call.

Required:

a. From an ethical standpoint, do you think the auditors would be justified in acting on information acquired in this manner?

b. Should the balance sheet as of June 30 disclose the contingent liability? Give reasons for your answer.

c. Prepare a list of auditing procedures that might have brought the contingency to light. Explain fully the likelihood of detection of the accommodation endorsement by each procedure listed.

15–32.   Stan Jones, CPA, the continuing auditor of Sussex, Inc., is beginning the audit of the common stock and treasury stock accounts. Jones has decided to design substantive tests with the risk of material misstatement specified at a high level.

Sussex has no par, no stated value common stock and acts as its own registrar and transfer agent. During the past year Sussex both issued and reacquired shares of its own common stock, some of which the company still owned at year-end. Additional common stock transactions occurred among the shareholders during the year.

Common stock transactions can be traced to individual shareholders' accounts in a subsidiary ledger and to a stock certificate book. The company has not paid any cash or stock dividends. There are no other classes of stock, stock rights, warrants, or option plans.

Required:

What substantive audit procedures should Jones apply in examining the common stock and treasury stock accounts?

(AICPA, adapted)

15–33.   Valley Corporation established a stock option plan for its officers and key employees this year. Because the options granted have a higher option price than the stock's current market price, the company has not recognized any cost for the options in the financial statements. However, a note to the financial statements includes all required disclosures.

Required:

a. Do you believe that Valley's management has appropriately accounted for the stock option plan? Explain your answer.

b. What responsibility do the auditors have for the information in the notes to the financial statements?

c. List the audit procedures, if any, that you believe should be applied to the stock option plan.

Multiple Choice Questions

15–34.   Select the best answer choice for each of the following, and justify your selection in a brief statement.

a. Which of the following is *least* likely to be an audit objective for interest-bearing debt?

(1) Determine the existence of recorded interest-bearing debt.

(2) Establish the completeness of recorded interest-bearing debt.

(3) Determine that the client has rights to receive proceeds relating to the redemption of interest-bearing debt.

(4) Determine that the valuation of interest-bearing debt is in accordance with generally accepted accounting principles.

b. The auditors may find unrecorded long term liabilities by analyzing:

(1) Interest payments.

(2) Discounts on long-term liabilities.

(3) Premiums on long-term liabilities.

(4) Recorded long-term liability accounts.

c. A likely reason that consideration of client compliance with debt provisions is important to an audit is that violation of such debt provisions may affect the total recorded:

(1) Number of debt restrictions.

(2) Current liabilities.

(3) Long term assets.

(4) Capital stock.

    d. A transfer agent and registrar is most likely to provide the auditor with evidence on:

       (1) Restrictions on the payment of accounts payable.

       (2) Shares issued and outstanding.

       (3) Preferred stock liquidation value.

       (4) Transfers occurring between management and related parties.

    e. The audit procedure of confirmation is least appropriate with respect to:

       (1) The trustee of an issue of bonds payable.

       (2) Holders of common stock.

       (3) Holders of notes receivable.

       (4) Holders of notes payable.

    f. An auditor is most likely to trace treasury stock purchase transactions to the:

       (1) Numbered stock certificates on hand.

       (2) Articles of incorporation.

       (3) Year's interest expense.

       (4) Minutes of the audit committee.

    g. In the continuing audit of a manufacturing company of medium size, which of the following areas would you expect to require the least amount of audit time?

       (1) Owners' equity.

       (2) Revenue.

       (3) Assets.

       (4) Liabilities.

    h. The auditors can best verify a client's bond sinking fund transactions and year-end balance by:

       (1) Recomputation of interest expense, interest payable, and amortization of bond discount or premium.

       (2) Confirmation with individual holders of retired bonds.

       (3) Confirmation with the bond trustee.

       (4) Examination and count of the bonds retired during the year.

    i. The auditors' program for the examination of long-term debt should include steps that require the:

       (1) Verification of the existence of the bondholders.

       (2) Examination of copies of debt agreements.

       (3) Inspection of the accounts payable subsidiary ledger.

       (4) Investigation of credits to the bond interest income account.

    j. All corporate capital stock transactions should ultimately be traced to the:

       (1) Minutes of the board of directors.

       (2) Cash receipts journal.

       (3) Cash disbursements journal.

       (4) Numbered stock certificates.

    k. Which of the following is most likely to be an audit objective in the audit of owners' equity?

       (1) Establish that recorded owners' equity includes all long-term debt and equity balances.

       (2) Determine that common stock is valued at current market value.

       (3) Determine that the presentation and disclosure of owners' equity is appropriate.

       (4) Determine that the existence of recorded owner's equity is in conformity with equity accounting rule valuations.

    l. When auditing a sole proprietorship a common difficulty is lack of:

       (1) Segregation of personal net worth and business capital.

       (2) Availability of the owner.

       (3) Agreement as to the distribution between retained earnings and owners' capital.

       (4) Proper measures of dividends.

(AICPA, adapted)

Problems

15–35. The following covenants are extracted from the indenture of a bond issue of Case Company. The indenture provides that failure to comply with its terms in any respect automatically advances the due date of the loan to the date of noncompliance (the regular due date is 20 years hence). Give any audit procedures or reporting requirements you think should be taken or recognized in connection with each of the following:

1. "The debtor company shall endeavor to maintain a working capital ratio of 2 to 1 at all times; and in any fiscal year following a failure to maintain said ratio, the company shall restrict compensation of officers to a total of $2 million. Officers for this purpose shall include chairman of the board of directors, president, all vice presidents, secretary, controller, and treasurer."

2. "The debtor company shall keep all property that is security for this debt insured against loss by fire to the extent of 100 percent of its actual value. Policies of insurance comprising this protection shall be filed with the trustee."

3. "The debtor company shall pay all taxes legally assessed against property that is security for this debt within the time provided by law for payment without penalty, and shall deposit receipted tax bills or equally acceptable evidence of payment of same with the trustee."

4. "A sinking fund shall be deposited with the trustee by semiannual payments of $900,000, from which the trustee shall, in its discretion, purchase bonds of this issue."

(AICPA, adapted)

15–36. You have been retained to audit the financial statements of Midwest Products, Inc., for the year ended December 31. During the current year, Midwest had obtained a long-term loan from its bank in accordance with a financing agreement which provided that:

1. The loan is secured by the company's inventory and accounts receivable.
2. The company must maintain a debt-to-equity ratio not to exceed 2 to 1.
3. The company may not pay dividends without permission from the bank.
4. Monthly installment payments will commence July 1 of the next year.

In addition, during the current year, Midwest Products, Inc., borrowed from its president on a short-term basis, including substantial amounts just prior to the year-end.

Required:

a. For the purpose of your audit of the financial statements of Midwest Products, Inc., what procedures would you employ in examining the above-described items? Do not discuss internal control.

b. What financial statement disclosures are appropriate with respect to the loans from the president?

(AICPA, adapted)

15–37. In your first audit of Hydrafoil Company, a manufacturer of specially designed boats capable of transporting passengers over water at very high speeds, you find that sales are made to commercial transportation companies. The sales price per unit is $400,000, and with each unit sold, the client gives the purchasing company a certificate reading as follows:

Hydrafoil Company promises to pay _____ the sum of $24,000 when the boat designated as Serial No. _____ is permanently retired from service and evidence of such retirement is submitted.

The president of Hydrafoil Company explains to you that the purpose of issuing the certificates is to ensure contact with customers when they are in the market for new equipment. You also learn that the company makes no journal entry to record a certificate when it is issued. Instead, the company charges an expense account and credits a liability account $200 per month for each outstanding certificate, based on the company's experience that its Hydrafoil boats will be rendered obsolete by new, more efficient models in approximately 10 years from the date of sale.

Required: Do you concur with Hydrafoil Company's accounting for the certificates? You may assume that the 10-year service life of the product (and therefore of the certificates) is an accurate determination. Explain your position clearly.

15–38. Robert Hopkins was the senior office employee in Griffin Equipment Company. He enjoyed the complete confidence of the owner, William Barton, who devoted most of his attention to sales, engineering, and production problems. All financial and accounting matters were entrusted to Hopkins, whose title was office manager. Hopkins had two assistants, but their only experience in accounting and financial work had been gained under Hopkins's supervision. Barton had informed Hopkins that it was his responsibility to keep him (Barton) informed on the financial position and operating results of the company but not to bother him with details.

The company was short of working capital and would occasionally issue notes payable in settlement of past-due open accounts to suppliers. The situations warranting issuance of notes were decided upon by Hopkins, and the notes were drawn by him for signature by Barton. Hopkins was aware of the weakness in internal control and finally devised a scheme for defrauding the company through understating the amount of notes payable outstanding. He prepared a note in the amount of $24,000 payable to a supplier to whom several invoices were past due. After securing Barton's signature on the note and mailing it to the creditor, Hopkins entered the note in the Notes Payable account of the general ledger as $4,000, with an offsetting debit of $4,000 to Accounts Payable. Subsequently, when funds became available to the company, he paid the $20,000 of accounts payable that remained on the books.

Several months later when the note matured, a check for $24,000 plus interest was issued and properly recorded, including a debit of $24,000 to the Notes Payable account. Hopkins then altered the original credit in the account by changing the figure from $4,000 to $24,000. He also changed the original debit to Accounts Payable from $4,000 to $24,000. This alteration caused the Notes Payable account to have a balance in agreement with the total of other notes outstanding. To complete the fraud, Hopkins called the supplier to whom the check had been sent and explained that the check should have been for only $4,000 plus interest.

Hopkins explained to the supplier that the note of $24,000 originally had been issued in settlement of a number of past-due invoices, but that while the note was outstanding, checks had been sent in payment of all the invoices. "In other words," said Hopkins over the telephone, "we made the mistake of giving you a note for those invoices and then going ahead and sending you checks for them as soon as our cash position had improved. Then we paid the note at maturity. So please excuse our mistakes and return the overpayment." After reviewing the record of invoices and checks received, the supplier agreed he had been overpaid by $20,000 plus interest and promptly sent a refund, which Hopkins abstracted without making any entry in the accounts.

Required:
a. Assuming that an audit by CPAs was made while the note was outstanding, do you think that the $20,000 understatement of the Notes Payable account would have been detected? Explain fully the reasoning underlying your answer.

b. If the fraud was not discovered while the note was outstanding, do you think that an audit subsequent to the payment of the note would have disclosed the fraud? Explain.

c. What controls would you recommend for Griffin Equipment Company to avoid fraud of this type?

15–39. You are engaged in the first audit of Microdent, Inc. The corporation has both a stock transfer agent and an independent registrar for its capital stock. The transfer agent maintains the record of stockholders, and the registrar determines that there is no overissue of stock. Signatures of both are required to validate stock certificates.

It has been proposed that confirmations be obtained from both the transfer agent and the registrar as to the stock outstanding at the balance sheet date. If such confirmations agree with the accounting records, no additional work is to be performed as to capital stock.

If you agree that obtaining the confirmations as suggested would be sufficient in this case, give the justification for your position. If you do not agree, state specifically all additional steps you would take and explain your reasons for taking them.

(AICPA, adapted)

15–40. You are engaged in the audit of Phoenix Corp., a new client, at the close of its first fiscal year, April 30, 20X1. The accounts had been closed before the time you began your year-end fieldwork.

You review the following stockholders' equity accounts in the general ledger:

Capital Stock

	5/1/X0 CR1	500,000
	4/28/X1 J12-5	50,000

Paid-in Capital in Excess of Stated Value

	5/1/X0 CR1	250,000
	2/2/X1 CR10	2,500

Retained Earnings

4/28/X1 J12-5	50,000	4/30/X1 J12-14	800,000

Treasury Stock

9/14/X0 CP5	80,000	2/2/X1 CR10	40,000

Income Summary

4/30/X1 J12-13	5,200,000	4/30/X1 J12-12	6,000,000
4/30/X1 J12-14	800,000		

Other informastion in your working papers includes the following:

1. Phoenix's articles of incorporation filed April 17, 20X0, authorized 100,000 shares of no-par-value capital stock.

2. Directors' minutes include the following resolutions:

   4/18/X0   Established $50 per share stated value for capital stock.

   4/30/X0   Authorized issue of 10,000 shares to an underwriting syndicate for $75 per share.

   9/13/X0   Authorized acquisition of 1,000 shares from a dissident holder at $80 per share.

   2/1/X1   Authorized reissue of 500 treasury shares at $85 per share.

   4/28/X1   Declared 10 percent stock dividend, payable May 18, 20X1, to stockholders of record May 4, 20X1.

3. The following costs of the May 1, 20X0, and February 2, 20X1, stock issuances were charged to the named expense accounts: Printing Expense, $2,500; Legal Fees, $17,350; Accounting Fees, $12,000; and SEC Fees, $150.

4. Market values for Phoenix Corp. capital stock on various dates were:

   9/13/X0 $78.50   2/2/X1   85.00

   9/14/X0   79.00   4/28/X1   90.00

5. Phoenix Corp.'s combined federal and state income tax rates total 55 percent.

Required:

a. Prepare the necessary adjusting journal entries at April 30, 20X1.

b. Prepare the stockholders' equity section of Phoenix Corp.'s April 30, 20X1, balance sheet.

In-Class Team Case

15–41. The following long-term debt working paper (indexed K-1) was prepared by client personnel and audited by Judith Dranertz, an audit assistant, during the calendar year 200X audit of American Widgets, Inc., a continuing audit client. The engagement supervisor is reviewing the working papers.

Required: Identify the deficiencies in the working paper that the engagement supervisor should discover.

(AICPA, adapted)

AMERICAN WIDGETS, INC.
Working Papers
December 31, 20X1

Lender	Interest Rate	Payment Terms	Collateral	Balance 12/31/X0
φ First Commercial Bank	12%	Interest only on 25th of month, principal due in full 1/1/20X5; no prepayment penalty	Inventories	$ 50,000 ✓
φ Lender's Capital Corp.	Prime plus 1%	Interest only on last day of month, principal due in full 3/5/X3	2nd mortgage on Park St. building	100,000 ✓
φ Gigantic Building & Loan Assoc.	12%	$5,000 principal plus interest due on 5th of month, due in full 12/31/20X8	1st mortgage on Park St. building	720,000 ✓
φ J. Lott, majority stockholder	0%	Due in full 12/31/20X4	Unsecured	300,000 ✓
				$1,170,000 ✓
				F

20X1 Borrowings	20X1 Reductions	Balance 12/31/X1	Interest Paid to	Accrued Interest Payable 12/31/X1	Comments
$300,000 A 1/31/X1	$100,000 ⊗ 6/30/X1	$ 250,000 CX	12/25/X1	$2,500 NR	Dividend of $80,000 paid 9/2/X1 (W/P N-3) violates a provision of the debt agreement, which thereby permits lender to demand immediate payment; lender had refused to waive this violation.
50,000 A 2/29/X1		200,000 C	12/31/X1		Prime rate was 8% to 9% during the year.
	60,000 ø	660,000 C	12/5/X1	5,642 R	Reclassification entry for current portion proposed (See RJE-3).
	100,000 N 12/31/X1	200,000 C			Borrowed additional $100,000 from J. Lott on 1/7/X2.
$350,000	$260,000	$1,310,000 T/B		$8,142 T/B	
F	F	F		F	

Interest costs from long-term debt

Interest expense for year	$ 281,333 T/B
Average loan balance outstanding	$1,406,667 R

Five-Year Maturities (for disclosure purposes)

Year-end		
	12/31/X2	$ 60,000
	12/31/X3	260,000
	12/31/X4	260,000
	12/31/X5	310,000
	12/31/X6	60,000
	Thereafter	360,000
		$1,310,000

Tickmark Legend

F	Readded foots correctly
C	Confirmed without exception, W/P K-2
CX	Confirmed without exception, W/P K-3
NR	Does not recompute correctly
A	Agreed to loan agreement, validated bank deposit ticket, and board of directors' authorization, W/P W-7
ø	Agreed to canceled checks and lender's monthly statements
N	Agreed to cash disbursements journal and canceled check dated 12/31/X1, clearing 1/8/X2
T/B	Traced to working trial balance
✓	Agreed to 12/31/X0 working papers
φ	Agreed interest rate, term, and collateral to copy of note and loan agreement
⊗	Agreed to canceled check and board of directors' authorization, W/P W-7

Overall conclusions

Long-term debt, accrued interest payable, and interest expense are correct and complete at 12/31/X1.

Chapter 16

Auditing Operations and Completing the Audit

Chapter learning objectives

After studying this chapter, you should be able to:

LO1. Identify the audit objectives for revenue and expense accounts.

LO2. Explain the relationships between revenue and expense accounts and balance sheet accounts.

LO3. Describe the nature of appropriate substantive audit procedures to accomplish the objectives for the audit of revenue and expense accounts.

LO4. Describe the fundamental controls over payroll.

LO5. Complete an audit program for payroll.

LO6. Explain the types of procedures that are necessary to complete the audit.

LO7. Describe the auditors' responsibilities for the detection and evaluation of various types of subsequent events.

LO8. Explain the steps involved in evaluating audit findings.

LO9. Discuss the auditors' post-audit responsibilities.

This chapter presents information about the manner in which auditors examine the client's income statement accounts and the procedures and considerations involved in completing the audit engagement. These procedures and judgments, completed at or near the last day of field-work, are important in determining the nature and content of the auditors' report.

Auditing Operations

Today, with great emphasis being placed upon corporate earnings as an indicator of the health and well-being of corporations as well as of the overall economy, the income statement is of fundamental importance to management, stockholders, creditors, employees, and government. The relative level of corporate earnings is often a key factor in the determination of such issues as wage negotiations, income tax rates, subsidies, and government fiscal policies. In fact, accountants generally agree that the measurement of income is the most important single function of accounting. While this text has emphasized the relationships of revenues and expenses to various balance sheet accounts, this section presents additional details on the auditing of operations.

The Auditors' Approach to Examining Operations

Learning Objective 1

The doctrine of **conservatism** is a powerful force influencing decisions on revenues and expenses. The concept remains important in large part due to the subjectivity involved with many accounting estimates (as for expected future credit losses on receivables, lives of assets, and the warranty liability for products sold). Conservatism in the valuation of assets means that when two (or more) reasonable alternative values are indicated, the accountant will choose the lower amount. For valuation of liabilities, the higher amount is chosen. Therefore, when applied to the income statement, the conservatism concept results in a low or "conservative" income figure.

Most auditors have a considerable respect for the doctrine of conservatism. In part, this attitude springs from the concept of legal liability to third parties. Financial statements that *understate* financial position and operating results almost never lead to legal action against the auditors involved. Nevertheless, auditors must recognize that overemphasis on conservatism in financial reporting is a narrow and shortsighted approach to meeting the needs of our society. To be of greatest value, financial statements should present fairly, rather than under-state, financial position and operating results.

Auditors obtain evidence about many income statement accounts concurrently with related balance sheet accounts. Depreciation expense, for example, is most conveniently verified along with the plant and equipment accounts. Once the existence and cost of depreciable assets are established, the verification of depreciation expense is merely an additional step. On the other hand, to verify depreciation expense without first establishing the nature and amount of assets owned and subject to depreciation would obviously be a cart-before-the-horse approach. The same line of reasoning suggests that the auditors' work on inventories, especially in determin-ing that inventory transactions were accurately cut off at the end of the period, is a major step toward the verification of the income statement figures for sales and cost of goods sold.

The auditors' examination of operations should, however, be much more than an incidental by-product of the examination of assets and liabilities. They use a combination of cross-referencing, analytical procedures, and analysis of specific transactions to bring to light errors, omissions, and inconsistencies not disclosed in the audit of balance sheet accounts.

Specifically, the objectives for the audit of revenues and expenses are to:

1. Consider *inherent risks* of revenue and expenses, including fraud risks.
2. Consider *internal control* over revenues and expenses.
3. Determine the *occurrence* of recorded revenue and expense transactions.
4. Establish the *completeness* of recorded revenue and expense transactions.
5. Determine that the *valuation* of revenue and expense transactions is in accordance with generally accepted accounting principles.

6. Determine that the *presentation* and *disclosure* of revenue and expense accounts are appropriate, including the proper classification of amounts and proper presentation of earnings-per-share data.

Revenue

Learning Objective 2

The auditors' review of revenue was considered in connection with accounts receivable in Chapter 11. In this section we consider (1) the relationship of revenue to various balance sheet accounts and (2) the miscellaneous revenue account.

Relationship of Revenue to Balance Sheet Accounts

As pointed out previously, most revenue accounts are verified by the auditors in conjunction with the audit of a related asset or liability. The following list summarizes the revenue verified in this manner:

Balance Sheet Item	Revenue
Accounts receivable	Sales
Notes receivable	Interest
Securities and other investments	Interest, dividends, gains on sales, share of investee's income
Property, plant, and equipment	Rent, gains on sale
Intangible assets	Royalties

Miscellaneous Revenue

Miscellaneous revenue, by its very nature, is a mixture of minor items, some nonrecurring and others likely to be received at irregular intervals. If the client's personnel receive a cash payment and are not sure of the source, it is likely that it will be recorded as miscellaneous revenue. Because of the nature of items often recorded in the Miscellaneous Revenue account, the auditors will obtain an analysis of the account. Among the items the auditors might find improperly included as miscellaneous revenue are the following:

1. Collections on previously written-off accounts or notes receivable.
2. Write-offs of old outstanding checks or unclaimed wages. In many states, unclaimed properties revert to the state after statutory periods; in such circumstances, these write-offs should be credited to a liability account rather than to miscellaneous revenue.
3. Proceeds from sales of scrap. Scrap sale proceeds generally should be applied to reduce cost of goods sold, under by-product cost accounting principles.
4. Rebates or refunds of insurance premiums. These refunds should be offset against the related expense or unexpired insurance.
5. Proceeds from sales of plant assets. These proceeds should be accounted for in the determination of the gain or loss on the assets sold.

The auditors should propose adjusting journal entries to classify correctly any material items of the types described above that have been included in miscellaneous revenue by the client. Before concluding the work on revenue, the auditors should perform analytical procedures and investigate unusual fluctuations. Material amounts of unrecorded revenue, as well as significant misclassifications affecting revenue accounts, may be discovered by these procedures.

Expenses

The auditors' work relating to purchases and cost of goods sold was covered in Chapter 12. We are now concerned with audit procedures for other types of expenses.

Relationship of Expenses to Balance Sheet Accounts

Let us consider for a moment the expense accounts for which we have already outlined audit procedures in the chapters dealing with balance sheet topics:

Balance Sheet Item	Expenses (and Costs)
Accounts and notes receivable	Uncollectible accounts and notes expense
Inventories	Purchases, cost of goods sold, and payroll
Property, plant, and equipment	Depreciation, repairs and maintenance, and depletion
Intangible assets	Amortization
Accrued liabilities	Commissions, fees, bonuses, product warranty expenses, and others
Interest-bearing debt	Interest

In the following sections, we shall complete our review of expenses by considering additional audit objectives and procedures for selling, general, and administrative expenses other than those listed above.

Substantive Tests for Selling, General, and Administrative Expenses

For other expenses not verified in the audit of balance sheet accounts, the following substantive tests are appropriate:

1. Perform analytical procedures related to the accounts.
   a. Develop an expectation of the account balance.
   b. Determine the amount of difference from the expectation that can be accepted without investigation.
   c. Compare the company's account balance with the expected account balance.
   d. Investigate significant deviations from the expected account balance.
2. Obtain or prepare analyses of selected expense accounts.
3. Obtain or prepare analyses of critical expenses in income tax returns.

1. Perform Analytical Procedures Related to the Accounts.

a. Develop an Expectation of the Account Balance.

Auditors develop an expectation of the account balance by considering factors such as budgeted amounts, the prior-year audited balances, industry averages, relationships among financial data, and relevant nonfinancial data.

An effective budgeting program will reduce control risk, since budgets provide management with information as to expected amounts. The existence of these expected expense amounts increases the likelihood that errors will be detected by management, since any significant discrepancy between budgeted and actual amounts receives timely attention.

The existence of a good budgeting program also helps the auditors in their audit of expense accounts. When the control over budgeting has been found to be effective, the budgeted amounts often provide the auditors with very good expected amounts for their analytical procedures.

One of the previously described audit objectives was to determine whether expenses had been correctly classified. The classification of such costs may affect net income. For example, manufacturing overhead costs may properly be carried forward as part of inventory cost, whereas the expenses of selling, general, and administrative functions usually are deducted from revenue in the period incurred. The auditors' review of the propriety of classification of expenses can be linked conveniently with the comparison of amounts of the various expenses. Comparison of yearly totals is accomplished by inclusion of amounts for the preceding year on the auditors' lead schedules or working trial balance, but this procedure may be supplemented by comparison of expenses on a month-by-month basis.

Comparison of expense (as well as revenue) accounts with industry and nonfinancial data is another means of bringing to light circumstances that require investigation. The auditors may also examine relationships between financial and nonfinancial information, such as between production records stated in gallons or pounds and the dollar amounts of sales.

b. Determine the Amount of Difference from the Expectation that Can Be Accepted without Investigation.

The auditors use their estimates of materiality to arrive at which differences are to be investigated and which might be expected to occur by chance. However, the extent of the assurance desired from the analytical procedure must also be considered.

c. Compare the Company's Account Balance with the Expected Account Balance.

Comparisons of the revenue and expense accounts with expected amounts may reveal significant differences that warrant investigation. Figure 16.1 illustrates a working paper that compares major income statement categories for the year under audit with the prior year amounts and industry averages.

d. Investigate Significant Deviations from the Expected Account Balance.

The starting point for investigating significant variations in expenses generally is inquiry of management. The auditors substantiate management's explanations for significant variations by various means, including analyses of accounts.

FIGURE 16.1 **Comparative Income Statement**

```
                          CHEVIOT CORPORATION
                    Comparative Income Statement          R-1-4
                     Year Ended December 31, 20X3

                    20X2                         20X3              Industry

               Amount    Percentage        Amount    Percentage   Percentage

Sales         $5,487,842 ✓    100%     $6,107,401 ⋁ ▽   100%         100%

Cost of        3,746,583 ✓     68       4,030,701 ⋁ ∅    66           65
goods sold

Gross profit   1,741,259       32       2,076,700 ∅      34           35

Selling          554,841 ✓     10         856,540 ⋁ △    14           15
expenses

General and      796,347       15         875,570 ⋁ ∅    14           12
administrative
expenses

Income before    390,071        7         344,590 ∅       6            8
taxes

Taxes            128,732 ✓       2          68,693 ⋁ ✗     1            3

Net income       261,339         5         275,897 ∅       5            5
                    ∧                         ∧
```

∧ *Footed.*

⋁ *Agreed to the general ledger.*

✓ *Agreed to the prior year working papers.*

∅ *Amount is reasonable in relation to prior year results and industry statistics.*

▽ *See audit procedures performed on sales, R-1-2.*

△ *Large increase in selling expenses is due to the addition of a salesperson to the sales staff. Based on a review*
   of the payroll records the increase in the amount appears reasonable.

✗ *Decrease in tax rate is due to the realization of several thousand dollars in tax credits. See tax accrual*
   working paper, O-3.

Conclusion:

The comparative analysis revealed no unusual fluctuations that could not be adequately explained.

UMH
2/21/X4

Concur
C.M.
2/25/X4

2. Obtain or Prepare Analyses of Selected Expense Accounts.

As a result of the above procedure, the auditors will have chosen certain expense accounts for further verification. The client should be requested to furnish analyses of the accounts selected, together with related vouchers and other supporting documents, for the auditors' review.

Which expense accounts are most important for the auditors to analyze? The American Institute of Certified Public Accountants (AICPA) has suggested investigation of (1) advertising, (2) research and development, (3) legal expenses and other professional fees, (4) maintenance and repairs, and (5) rents and royalties.[1]

The analyses of legal and other professional fees may disclose legal and audit fees properly chargeable to costs of issuing stock of debt instruments, or to costs of business combinations. Also, the analysis of professional fees expense furnishes the names of attorneys to whom letters should be sent requesting information as to pending litigation and other loss contingencies. Figure 16.2 illustrates an analysis of the professional fees expense account.

FIGURE 16.2 Professional Fees Analysis

```
                          CHEVIOT CORPORATION
Acct. No. 547             Professional Fees Expense                R-3-7
                          Year Ended December 31, 20X3

    Date        Reference      Payee        Description              Amount

Various         Various     Hale and     Monthly retainer for legal  $12,000
                            Hale         services—12 x $1,000

Mar. 5, X3      CD 411      Jay & Wall,  Fee for the audit           22,000 ✓
                            CPAs

May 2, X3       CD 602      Hale and     Fee for legal services       6,000 ✓
                            Hale         relating to acquisition of
                                         real property adjoining
                                         Vancouver plant

Sept. 18, X3    DC 1018     Hale and     Fee for legal services        800 ✓
                            Hale         relating to modification of
                                         installment sales contract
                                         forms

Dec. 31, X3                              Balance per Ledger          $40,800
```

Dec. 31, X3   AJE 41   To capitalize May 2, X3, disbursement   6,000
                         as part of cost of land   K-1

Dec. 31, X3   Adjusted balance $34,800 ∧

                                                                  to R-3

AJE 41
Land   6,000
    Professional Fees   6,000
    To capitalize legal fees
    for acquiring land

∧ Footed and agreed to general ledger balance.
✓ Examined billing and copy of client's check in payment thereof.
Conclusion:
    Professional fees expense is fairly presented in the adjusted amount of $34,800.

                        KGL   CMM
                        2/15/X4   2/20/X4

[1] See AICPA, *Audit and Accounting Manual* (New York, 2002), paragraph AAM 5400.170.

3. Obtain or Prepare Analyses of Critical Expenses in Income Tax Returns.

Income tax returns generally require schedules for officers' salaries, directors' fees, taxes, travel and entertainment, contributions, and casualty losses. In addition to these, officers' expense account allowances are presented in the analysis of officers' salaries. Accordingly, the auditors should obtain or prepare analyses of any of these expenses that were not analyzed when performing other audit steps. The auditors should bear in mind that details of these expenses will probably be closely scrutinized when the state or federal revenue agents examine the client's tax returns.

The Audit of Payroll

The payroll in many companies is the largest operating cost and therefore deserves the close attention of management as well as the auditors. In the past, payroll frauds were common and often substantial. Today, however, such frauds may be more difficult to conceal for several reasons: (1) extensive segregation of duties relating to payroll; (2) the use of computers, with proper controls, for preparation of payrolls; and (3) the necessity of filing frequent reports to the government listing employees' earnings and tax withholdings.

Internal Control over Payroll

Learning Objective 4

The establishment of strong internal control over payroll remains important for several reasons. Although payroll frauds are less frequent today, the possibility of large-scale payroll fraud still exists. Such frauds may involve listing fictitious persons on the payroll, overpaying employees, and continuing employees on the payroll after their separation from the company. A second reason for emphasizing internal control over payrolls is that a great mass of detailed information concerning hours worked and rates of pay must be processed quickly and accurately if workers are to be paid promptly and without error. Good employee relations demand that paychecks be ready on time and be free from error. As pointed out in previous chapters, internal control is a means of securing accuracy and dependability in accounting data as well as a means of preventing fraud.

Still another reason for emphasizing the importance of internal control over payrolls is the existence of various payroll tax and income tax laws that require that certain payroll records be maintained and that payroll data be reported to the employee and to governmental agencies. Complete and accurate records of time worked are also necessary if a company is to protect itself against lawsuits under the Fair Labor Standards Act.

To control payroll costs means to avoid waste and to obtain efficient production from the dollars expended for services of employees. As a means of establishing control over payroll costs, many companies delegate to department heads and other supervisors responsibility for the control of costs in their respective units of the business. Budgets are prepared using estimates of departmental labor costs for the coming period. As the year progresses and actual labor costs are compiled, the controller submits monthly reports to top management comparing the budgeted labor costs and the actual labor costs for each department. The effectiveness of this control procedure will depend largely upon the extent to which top management utilizes these reports and takes action upon variances from the budget.

Most important of all controls over payroll is the division of payroll work among several departments of the company. Payroll activities include the functions of (1) employment (human resources), (2) timekeeping, (3) payroll preparation and recordkeeping, and (4) distribution of pay to employees. For effective internal control, a separate department of the company should handle each of these functions. These several phases of payroll activities will now be considered individually.

Employment (Human Resources)

The first significant step in establishing strong internal control over payrolls should be taken by the human resources department when a new employee is hired. At this point, the authorized rate of pay should be entered on a pay-rate record. The employee also should sign a payroll deduction authorization specifying any amounts to be withheld and a withholding tax exemption certificate. These records should be kept in the human resources department, but a notice of the hiring of the new employee, the rate of pay, and the payroll deductions should be sent to the payroll department. When a computer is used, this information will be keyed into an employee payroll master file. The human resources department, the payroll department, or data processing will enter the data into the computer system.

Under no circumstances should a name be added to the payroll without having received the formal authorization notice from the human resources department. When an employee's rate of pay is changed, the new rate should be entered on the pay-rate record (often computerized) that is maintained in the human resources department. An authorization for the new rate should be sent to the payroll department before the change can be made effective on the payroll. Upon termination of an employee, notice of termination should be sent from the human resources department to the payroll department. The work of the payroll department and the propriety of names and pay raises used in preparing the payroll, therefore, rest upon formal documents or computer input originating outside the payroll department.

Adequate internal control demands that the addition and removal of names from the company payroll, as well as rate changes and reclassification of employees, be evidenced by written approval of an executive in the human resources department and by the head of the operating department concerned. To permit the payroll department to initiate changes in pay rates or to add names to the payroll without formal authorization from the human resources department increases the likelihood of fraud.

Timekeeping

The function of timekeeping consists of determining the number of hours (or units of production) for which each employee is to be paid. The use of electronic time-recording equipment is of considerable aid in establishing adequate internal control over the timekeeping function. In addition, supervisors should maintain contact with subordinates and prepare time reports summarizing the use of labor.

Internal control can be improved by the practice of regular comparison of the time reports prepared by timekeepers or supervisors with time clock records showing the arrival and departure times of employees. If pay is based on piecework, a comparison may be made between the reports of units produced and the quantities that are added to the perpetual inventory records.

Salaried employees receiving a fixed monthly or weekly salary may not be required to use time clocks. Some companies require salaried employees to fill out a weekly or semimonthly report indicating the time devoted to various activities. If a salaried employee is absent, the department head usually has authority to decide whether a pay reduction should be made.

Payroll Preparation and Recordkeeping

In a manual system, the payroll department has the responsibility for computing the amounts to be paid to employees and for preparing all payroll records. It is important that the payroll department *not* perform the related functions of timekeeping, employment, or distribution of pay to employees. The output of the payroll department may be thought of as: (1) the payroll checks or direct deposits (or pay envelopes, if wages are paid in cash); (2) individual employee statements of earnings and deductions; (3) a payroll journal; (4) an employees' ledger, summarizing earnings and deductions for each employee; (5) a payroll distribution schedule, showing the allocation of payroll costs to direct labor, overhead, and various departmental expense accounts; and (6) quarterly and annual reports to the government showing employees' earnings and taxes withheld. If the client utilizes a centralized computer, many of these functions may be delegated to data processing.

In a computerized system the payroll is calculated by the computer, using the work hours reported by the timekeeping department and the authorized pay rates and payroll deductions reported by the human resources department. In addition to preparing the payroll journal, the payroll department prepares the payroll checks or the pay envelopes, if wages are paid in cash. Checks are then forwarded to the treasurer for signature.

Regardless of the system used, the auditors should expect the client's system to include such basic records as time cards, payroll journals, labor distributions, and employee earnings records. In a computerized system some or all of these documents may exist only in computer-readable form.

Distributing Paychecks or Cash

The distribution of paychecks or pay envelopes to employees should be the task of the paymaster, an individual who performs no other payroll activity. If pay is deposited directly into employee bank accounts, controls over that process are necessary, such as authorization of deposits by personnel in the treasurer's department.

If employees are paid in cash, the paymaster will use a copy of the payroll journal and the information on the payroll envelopes (both prepared by the payroll department) to fill the payroll envelopes with cash. The paymaster will require proof of identity when distributing checks or cash to employees and require them to sign a receipt for any cash received. All checks or pay envelopes for an absent employee should be retained and neither returned to the payroll department nor turned over to another employee for delivery.

Most companies that pay employees by check use a special payroll bank account. A voucher for the entire amount of the weekly payroll may be prepared in the general accounting department based on the payroll summary prepared in the payroll department. This voucher is sent to the treasurer, who issues a check on the general bank account for the amount of the payroll. The check is deposited in the special payroll bank account and checks to individual employees are drawn on this account. It also is the practice of some companies to require dual signatures on large checks and to have printed on the check a statement that this type of check is not valid if issued for an amount in excess of a specified dollar amount.

If wages are paid in cash, any unclaimed wages should be deposited in the bank and credited to a special liability account. Subsequent disbursement of these funds to employees then will be controlled by the necessity of drawing a check and preparing supporting documents. The dangers inherent in permitting unclaimed pay envelopes to be retained by the paymaster, returned to the payroll clerk, or intermingled with petty cash are apparent.

Documentation of Internal Control for Payroll

Typical of the questions to be posed by the auditors prior to the completion of an internal control questionnaire, a systems flowchart, or other record of payroll controls are the following: Are employees paid by check or direct deposit? Is a payroll bank account maintained on an imprest basis? Are the activities of timekeeping, payroll compilation, payroll check signing, and paycheck distribution performed by separate departments or employees? Are all operations involved in the preparation of payrolls subjected to independent verification before the paychecks are distributed? Are employee time reports approved by supervisors? Is the payroll bank account reconciled monthly by an employee having no other payroll duties?

Audit Program for Payroll

Learning Objective 5

The following audit procedures are representative of the work generally completed to establish the propriety of payments for salaries, wages, bonuses, and commissions:

1. Obtain an understanding of the internal control over payrolls.
2. Perform tests of controls over payroll transactions for selected pay periods, including the following specific procedures:
   a. Compare names and wage or salary rates to records maintained by the human resources department.
   b. Compare time shown on payroll to time cards and time reports approved by supervisors.
   c. If payroll is based on piecework rates rather than hourly rates, reconcile earnings with production records.
   d. Determine basis of deductions from payroll and compare with records of deductions authorized by employees.
   e. Test extensions and footings of payroll.

FIGURE 16.3
Objectives of Major Substantive Tests of Payrolls

Substantive Tests	Primary Audit Objectives
Perform analytical procedures. Investigate fluctuations in salaries, wages, and commissions. Obtain a summary of amounts of officers' compensation and trace to authorization.	*Existence or occurrence Completeness Valuation*
Test computations of compensation under profit-sharing or bonus plans. Test commission earnings. Test pension obligations.	*Valuation*

    f. Compare total of payroll with total of payroll checks issued.

    g. Compare total of payroll with total of labor cost summary prepared by cost accounting department.

    h. If wages are paid in cash, compare receipts obtained from employees with payroll records.

    i. If wages are paid by check, compare paid checks with payroll and compare endorsements to signatures on withholding tax exemption certificates.

    j. Observe the use of time clocks by employees reporting for work and investigate time cards not used.

3. Perform analytical procedures to test the reasonableness of payroll expense; for example, develop an expectation about the amount of payroll expense by multiplying the amount of one pay period by the number of pay periods in the year.

4. Investigate any extraordinary fluctuations in salaries, wages, and commissions.

5. Obtain or prepare a summary of compensation of officers for the year and compare to contracts, minutes of directors' meetings, or other authorization.

6. Test computations of compensation earned under profit-sharing or bonus plans.

7. Test commission earnings by examination of contracts and detailed supporting records.

8. Test pension obligations by reference to authorized pension plans and supporting records.

    Figure 16.3 relates these procedures to their primary audit objectives.

    In addition to the above procedures, the auditors may plan a surprise observation of a regular distribution of paychecks to employees. The auditors' objective in observing the distribution of checks or cash to employees on a regular payday is to determine that every name on the company payroll is that of a bona fide employee presently on the job. This audit procedure is especially desirable if the various phases of payroll work are not sufficiently segregated by departments to afford good internal control. The history of payroll frauds shows that permitting one person to have custody of employment records, time cards, paychecks, and employees' earnings records has often led to the entering of fictitious names on the payroll and to other forms of fraud, such as use of excessive pay rates and continuance of pay after the termination of an employee. When performing this procedure the auditors first will determine that they have possession of all the checks or envelopes comprising the payroll. They will then accompany representatives of the client around the plant as all the checks or envelopes are distributed to employees. It is essential that the auditors establish the identity of each employee receiving payment.

Audit of the Statement of Cash Flows

The statement of cash flows is prepared from other financial statements and from analyses of increases and decreases in selected account balances. The amounts included in the statement of cash flows are audited in conjunction with the audit of balance sheet and income statement accounts. Thus, limited substantive testing is necessary. The auditors merely compare the amounts included in the statement of cash flows to other financial statement balances and amounts included in audit working papers.

    Since receipts and payments must be classified in the statement of cash flows as to whether they are from operating, investing, or financing activities, the presentation and disclosure audit objective is especially important. The auditors must determine that the concept of cash or cash and cash equivalents analyzed in the statement agrees with an amount shown on the balance sheet. Finally, the auditors should ascertain that a statement of cash flows is presented for each year for which an income statement is presented.

Completing the Audit

Learning Objective 6

The auditors' report should not be dated prior to the date they have gathered sufficient, competent evidence. This date is often the last day of fieldwork but it may be a later date. Therefore, the auditors' opinion on the financial statements is based on all evidence gathered by the auditors up to the date of the audit report and any other information that comes to their attention between that date and the issuance of the financial statements. To be effective, certain audit procedures described in previous chapters cannot be completed before the end of the audit. Among those procedures are the following:

1. Search for unrecorded liabilities.
2. Review the minutes of meetings.
3. Perform final analytical procedures.
4. Perform procedures to identify loss contingencies.
5. Perform the review for subsequent events.
6. Obtain the representation letter.

Search for Unrecorded Liabilities

As discussed in Chapter 14, auditors must be alert for unrecorded payables. The search for unrecorded liabilities includes procedures performed to near the date of auditors report, such as examining subsequent cash disbursements. These procedures are designed to detect liabilities that existed at year-end but were omitted from the liabilities recorded in the client's financial statements.

Review the Minutes of Meetings

The auditors should review the **minutes** of meetings of stockholders and directors, including important subcommittees of directors such as the audit committee and the investment committee. This review includes meetings held through the date of the audit report. In completing the audit the auditors must determine that they have considered all minutes, including those for meetings subsequent to year-end. They will also obtain written representation from management that all minutes have been made available.

Perform Final Analytical Procedures

The discussion of **analytical procedures** in Chapter 5 pointed out that they must be performed in planning as well as for overall review purposes at the completion of the audit. Analytical procedures performed as a part of the overall review assist the auditors in assessing the validity of the conclusions reached, including the opinion to be issued. This final review may identify areas that need to be examined further as well as provide a consideration of the adequacy of data gathered in response to unusual or unexpected relationships identified during the audit. *SAS No. 99,* "Consideration of Fraud in a Financial Statement Audit," specifically requires auditors to evaluate whether analytical procedures performed as substantive tests or in the overall review stage indicate a previously unrecognized risk of material misstatement due to fraud.

Perform Procedures to Identify Loss Contingencies

A **loss contingency** may be defined as a *possible* loss, stemming from past events that will be resolved as to existence and amount by some future event. Central to the concept of a contingent loss is the idea of uncertainty—uncertainty as to both the amount of loss and whether, in fact, any loss has been incurred. This uncertainty is resolved when some future event occurs or fails to occur.

Most loss contingencies may also appropriately be called **contingent liabilities.** Loss contingencies, however, is a broader term, encompassing the possible impairment of assets as well as the possible existence of liabilities. The audit problem with respect to loss contingencies is twofold. First, the auditors must determine the existence of the loss contingencies. Because of the uncertainty factor, most loss contingencies do not appear in the accounting records, and a systematic search is required if the auditors are to have reasonable assurance that no important loss contingencies have been overlooked. Second, the auditors must appraise the probability that a loss has been incurred and its amount. This is made difficult both by the uncertainty factor and also by the tendency of the client management to maintain at least an outward appearance of optimism.

In *FASB No. 5,* "Accounting for Contingencies," the Financial Accounting Standards Board set forth the criteria for accounting for loss contingencies. Such losses should be reflected in the accounting records when both of the following conditions are met: (1) information available prior to the issuance of the financial statements indicates that it is *probable* that a loss has been sustained before the balance sheet date, and (2) the amount of the loss can be *reasonably estimated.* Recognition of the loss may involve either recognition of a liability or reduction of an asset. When a loss contingency has been accrued in the accounts, it is usually desirable to explain the nature of the contingency in a note to the financial statements and to disclose any exposure to loss in excess of the amount accrued.

Loss contingencies that do not meet both of the above criteria should still be disclosed in a note to the financial statements when there is at least a *reasonable possibility* that a loss has been incurred. This disclosure should describe the nature of the contingency and, if possible, provide an estimate of the possible loss. If the amount of possible loss cannot be reasonably estimated, the disclosure should include either a range of loss or a statement that an estimate cannot be made.

Certain contingent liabilities traditionally have been disclosed in financial statement notes even though the possibility that a loss has occurred is remote. Such items include notes receivable discounted and guarantee endorsements. With the exception of those items for which disclosure is traditional, disclosure need not be made of loss contingencies when the possibility of loss is remote.

The procedures undertaken by auditors to identify the existence of loss contingencies and to assess the probability of loss vary with the nature of the contingent item. Regardless of the procedures performed, it is important that they be extended to near the date of the audit report, so that the auditors have the latest available information to evaluate the financial statement presentation and disclosure of loss contingencies. To illustrate these types of procedures, we will discuss several of the more frequent types of contingencies warranting financial statement disclosure.

Litigation

Perhaps the most common loss contingency appearing in financial statements is that stemming from pending or threatened litigation. A letter of inquiry (or **lawyer's letter**) to the client's legal counsel is the auditors' primary means of obtaining evidence regarding pending and threatened litigation, as well as **unasserted claims** for which no potential claimant has yet demonstrated the intent to initiate legal action.

SAS 12 (AU 337), "Inquiry of a Client's Lawyer Concerning Litigation, Claims, and Assessments," indicates that the auditors should generally obtain from management a list describing and evaluating threatened or pending litigation. The auditors then ask management to request the client's lawyers to corroborate the information and to comment on those areas where their views differ from those of management. The lawyers also are requested to identify any pending claims, litigation, and assessments that have been omitted from management's list. If management does not wish to prepare a list of pending litigation for review by the lawyers, the lawyers may be requested to provide an independent description of all pending claims, litigation, and assessments that they are handling.

Auditors must also inquire of the lawyers regarding the possibility of unasserted claims on which individuals have not yet taken legal action. An unasserted claim should be disclosed if it is (1) *probable* that a claim will be asserted and (2) *reasonably possible* that a loss will result. If management prepares a list of matters for review by the lawyers, it should include such unasserted claims. The lawyers will provide any relevant additional information related to those listed unasserted claims. However, if management fails to list the unasserted claim in the letter of inquiry, the lawyer is *not* required to describe the claim in the reply to the auditors;

the lawyer is, however, generally required to inform the client of the omission and to consider resignation if the client fails to inform the auditors of the unasserted claim. For this reason, auditors must always consider carefully the reasons for any lawyer's resignation.

Illustration of Disclosure

The following note to the financial statements of an aircraft manufacturer illustrates the disclosure of the contingent liability associated with pending litigation.

> A number of suits are pending against the Company as the result of accidents in prior years involving airplanes manufactured by the Company. It is believed that insurance carried by the Company is sufficient to protect it against loss by reason of suits involving the lives of passengers and damage to aircraft. Other litigation pending against the Company involves no substantial amount or is covered by insurance.

The note of another large corporation contained the following note concerning contingent liabilities:

> The Company is a party to a number of lawsuits and claims (some of which are for substantial amounts) arising out of the conduct of its business, including those relating to commercial transactions, product liability, and environmental, safety, and health matters. While the ultimate results of lawsuits or other proceedings against the Company cannot be predicted with certainty, management does not expect that these matters will have a material adverse effect on the consolidated financial position or results of operations of the Company.

A refusal by a lawyer to furnish the information requested in the auditors' letter of inquiry would be a limitation of the scope of the auditors' examination and would necessitate qualification of the audit report.

Income Tax Disputes

The necessity of estimating the income tax liability applicable to the year under audit was discussed in Chapter 14. In addition to the taxes relating to the current year's income, uncertainty often exists concerning the amount ultimately payable for prior years. A lag of two or three years often exists between the filing of income tax returns and the final settlement after review by the Internal Revenue Service (IRS). Disputes between the taxpayer and the IRS may create contingent liabilities not settled for several more years. The auditors should determine whether internal revenue agents have examined any returns of the client since the preceding audit and, if so, whether any additional taxes have been assessed. In addition, the auditors should review any correspondence with the IRS and any other regulatory agencies.

Accommodation Endorsements and Other Guarantees of Indebtedness

The endorsement of notes of other concerns or individuals is very seldom recorded in the accounts, but may be reflected in the minutes of directors' meetings. The practice is more common among small concerns—particularly when one person has a proprietary interest in several companies. Officers, partners, and sole proprietors of small organizations should be questioned as to the existence of any contingent liability from this source. Inquiry should also be made as to whether any collateral has been received to protect the company. The auditors may also decide to confirm written or oral guarantees or other contingent liabilities with appropriate financial institutions, using a specially designed confirmation letter.

Accounts Receivable Sold or Assigned with Recourse

When accounts receivable are sold or assigned *with recourse,* a guarantee of collectibility is given. Authorization of such a transaction should be revealed during the auditors' reading of the minutes, and evidence of such agreements also may be found during the examination of transactions and correspondence with financial institutions. Confirmation by direct communication with the purchaser or assignee is necessary for any receivables sold or assigned.

Environmental Issues

Environmental remediation liability laws, written at all levels of government, are increasingly leading to both contingent and accrued liabilities. The Resource, Conservation, and Recovery Act, Superfund, and various clean air and water acts create potential liability for companies, as illustrated in the following example focusing on the electronics industry.

Focus on the Electronics Industry

The electronics industry and other high-technology enterprises may find themselves liable for remediation of environmental contamination. As described in an AICPA industry *Audit Risk Alert,* Superfund legally empowers the United States Environmental Protection Agency to seek recovery from both current and previous owners or operators of a contaminated site, or anyone who generated or transported hazardous substances to or from such a site. The use of toxic or hazardous materials in the electronics industry or the manufacturing of by-products that adversely affect the environment may create environmental cleanup issues. Various professional pronouncements released interpret *FASB No. 5* for environmental matters to help companies determine when it is appropriate to disclose or possibly accrue liabilities for such matters.

Commitments

Closely related to contingent liabilities are obligations termed **commitments.** The auditors may discover during their audit any of the following commitments: inventory purchase commitments, commitments to sell merchandise at specified prices, contracts for the construction of plant and equipment, pension or profit-sharing plans, long-term operating leases of plant and equipment, employee stock option plans, and employment contracts with key officers. A common characteristic of these commitments is the contractual obligation to enter into transactions *in the future.*

To illustrate the relationship of a commitment to a loss contingency, assume that a manufacturer commits to sell a substantial part of its output at a fixed price over the next three years. At the time of forming the agreement, the manufacturer, of course, believes the arrangement to be advantageous. However, it is possible that rising price levels may transform the fixed price sales agreement into an unprofitable one, requiring sales to be made at prices below manufacturing cost. Such circumstances may warrant recognition of a loss in the financial statements.

All classes of material commitments may be described in a single note to financial statements, or they may be included in a "Contingencies and Commitments" note.

General Risk Contingencies

In addition to loss contingencies and commitments, all businesses face the risk of loss from numerous factors called **general risk contingencies.** A general risk contingency represents a loss that *might occur in the future,* as opposed to a loss contingency that *might have occurred in the past.* Examples of general risk contingencies are threat of a strike or consumer boycott, risk of price increases in essential raw materials, and risk of a natural catastrophe.

Since the events that might produce a loss actually have not occurred and they are part of the general business environment, general risk contingencies *need not be disclosed* in financial statements. The lack of insurance coverage is a general risk contingency. Neither the adequacy nor the lack of insurance coverage is required to be presented in financial statements.

The Auditors' Procedures for Loss Contingencies

An overview of the auditors' procedures to detect and evaluate loss contingencies is described below.

1. Review the minutes of directors' meetings to the date of completion of fieldwork. Important contracts, lawsuits, and dealings with subsidiaries are typical of matters discussed in board meetings that may involve loss contingencies.
2. Send a letter of inquiry to the client's lawyer requesting:
   a. A description (or evaluation of management's description) of the nature of pending and threatened litigation and of tax disputes.
   b. An evaluation of the likelihood of an unfavorable outcome in the matters described.

   c. An estimate of the probable loss or range of loss, or a statement that an estimate cannot be made.

   d. An evaluation of management's description of any unasserted claims that, if asserted, have a reasonable possibility of an adverse outcome.

   e. A statement of the amount of any unbilled legal fees.

3. Send confirmation letters to financial institutions to request information on contingent liabilities of the company.

4. Review correspondence with financial institutions for evidence of accommodation endorsements, guarantees of indebtedness, or sales or assignments of accounts receivable.

5. Review reports and correspondence from regulatory agencies to identify potential assessments or fines.

6. Obtain a representation letter from the client indicating that all liabilities known to officers are recorded or disclosed.

Perform the Review for Subsequent Events

Learning Objective 7

Evidence not available at the close of the period under audit often becomes available before the auditors finish their fieldwork and write their audit report. The CPA's opinion on the fairness of the financial statements may be changed considerably by these subsequent events. The term **subsequent event** refers to an event or transaction that occurs after the date of the balance sheet but prior to the completion of the audit and issuance of the audit report. Subsequent events may be classified into two broad categories: (1) those providing additional evidence about facts existing on or before the balance sheet date, and (2) those involving facts coming into existence after the balance sheet date.

Type 1 Subsequent Events

The first type of subsequent event provides additional evidence as to *conditions that existed at the balance sheet date* and affects the estimates inherent in the process of preparing financial statements. This type of subsequent event requires that the financial statement amounts be adjusted to reflect the changes in estimates resulting from the additional evidence.

As an example, let us assume that a client's accounts receivable at December 31 included one large account and numerous small ones. The large amount due from the major customer was regarded as fully collectible at the year-end, but during the course of the audit engagement the customer entered bankruptcy. As a result of this information, the auditors found it necessary to recommend an increase in the December 31 allowance for uncollectible accounts. The bankruptcy of the customer shortly after the balance sheet date indicates that the financial strength of the customer had probably deteriorated before December 31, and the client was simply in error in believing the receivable to be fully collectible at that date. Evidence becoming available after the balance sheet date through the date of issuance of the auditors' report should be used in making judgments about the valuation of receivables.

Other examples of this first type of subsequent event include the following:

1. Customers' checks included in the cash receipts of the last day of the year prove to be uncollectible and are charged back to the client's account by the bank. If the checks were material in amount, an adjustment of the December 31 cash balance may be necessary to exclude the checks now known to be uncollectible.

2. A new three-year union contract signed two weeks after the balance sheet date provides evidence that the client has materially underestimated the total cost to complete a long-term construction project on which revenue is recognized by the percentage-of-completion method. The amount of income (or loss) to be recognized on the project in the current year should be recomputed using revised cost estimates.

3. Litigation pending against the client is settled shortly after the balance sheet date, and the amount owed by the client is material. This litigation was to be disclosed in notes to the financial statements, but no liability had been accrued because at year-end no reasonable estimate could be made of the amount of the client's loss. Now that competent evidence exists as to the dollar amount of the loss, this loss contingency meets the criteria for accrual in the financial statements, rather than mere note disclosure.

Type 2 Subsequent Events

The second type of subsequent event involves conditions *coming into existence after the balance sheet date.* These events do not require adjustment to the dollar amounts shown in the financial statements, *but they should be disclosed if the financial statements otherwise would be misleading.* To illustrate, assume that shortly after the balance sheet date a client sustains an uninsured fire loss destroying most of its plant assets. The carrying value of plant assets should not be reduced in the balance sheet because these assets were intact at year-end. However, people analyzing the financial statements would be misled if they were not advised that most of the plant assets are no longer in a usable condition.

What types of events occurring after the balance sheet date warrant disclosure in the financial statements? To explore this question, assume that the following events occurred after the balance sheet date but prior to completion of the audit fieldwork:

1. Business combination with a competing company.
2. Early retirement of bonds payable.
3. Adoption of a new pension plan requiring large, near-term cash outlays.
4. Death of the company treasurer in an airplane crash.
5. Introduction of a new line of products.
6. Plant closed by a labor strike.

Although these events may be significant in the future operations of the company and of interest to many who read the audited financial statements, none of these occurrences has any bearing on the results of the year under audit, and their bearing on future results is not easily determinable.

It is generally agreed that subsequent events involving business combinations, substantial casualty losses, and other significant changes in a company's financial position or financial structure should be disclosed in notes. Otherwise the financial statements might be misleading rather than informative. Consequently, the first three of the preceding examples (combination with a competing company, early retirement of bonds payable, and adoption of a new pension plan) should be disclosed in notes to the financial statements. The last three subsequent events (personnel changes, product line changes, and strikes) are nonaccounting matters and are not disclosed in notes unless particular circumstances make such information essential to the proper interpretation of the financial statements.

Pro Forma Statements as a Means of Disclosure

Occasionally subsequent events may be so material that supplementary *pro forma financial statements* should be prepared giving effect to the events as if they had occurred as of the balance sheet date. The pro forma statements (usually a balance sheet only) may be presented in columnar form next to the audited financial statements. This form of disclosure is used only when the subsequent event has a significant effect upon the asset structure or capital structure of the business. An example would be a business combination.

Distinguishing between the Two Types of Subsequent Events

In deciding whether a particular subsequent event should result in an adjustment to the financial statements or a note disclosure, the auditor should carefully consider *when the underlying conditions came into existence.* For example, assume that shortly after the balance sheet date, a major customer of the audit client declares bankruptcy, with the result that a large receivable previously considered fully collectible now appears to be uncollectible. If the customer's bankruptcy resulted from a steady deterioration in financial position, the subsequent event provides evidence that the receivable actually was uncollectible at year-end, and the allowance for doubtful accounts should be increased. On the other hand, if the customer's bankruptcy stemmed from a casualty (such as a fire) occurring after year-end, the conditions making the receivable uncollectible came into existence after the balance sheet date. In this case, the subsequent event should be disclosed in a note to the financial statements.

Audit Procedures Relating to Subsequent Events

The period of time between the balance sheet date and the date of the audit report is called the *subsequent period*. During this period, the auditors should determine that proper cutoffs of cash receipts and disbursements and sales and purchases have been made, and they should examine data to aid in the evaluation of assets and liabilities as of the balance sheet date. In addition, the auditors should:

1. Review the latest available interim financial statements and minutes of directors, stockholders, and appropriate committee meetings.

2. Inquire about matters dealt with at meetings for which minutes are not available.

3. Inquire of appropriate client officials as to loss contingencies; changes in capital stock, debt, or working capital; changes in the current status of items estimated in the financial statements under audit; or any unusual adjustments made subsequent to the balance sheet date.

4. Obtain a letter from the client's lawyer describing as of the last day of fieldwork any pending litigation, unasserted claims, or other loss contingencies.

5. Include in the representation letter a representation from the client concerning subsequent events.

Generally, the auditors' responsibility for performing procedures to gather evidence as to subsequent events extends only through the date of the audit report. However, even after completing normal audit procedures, the auditors have the responsibility to evaluate subsequent events that come to their attention. Suppose, for example, that the auditors completed their work for a December 31 audit on February 3 and thereafter began drafting their report. On February 11, before issuing their report, the client informed the auditors that the client had settled a lawsuit on that day by a substantial payment. In such a circumstance, generally accepted accounting principles require that the liability be established in the December 31 balance sheet. If the adjustment does not also require a note disclosure, the audit report ordinarily would continue to be dated as of the date the auditor had sufficient audit evidence, February 3. If a related note disclosure is necessary, auditors have two methods available for dating the audit report. They may *dual-date* their report "February 3, except for Note X, as to which the date is February 11." Alternatively, they might decide to return to the client's facilities for further review of subsequent events through the date of the subsequent event, February 11; in this case, the audit report would bear that date only.

Dual-dating extends the auditors' responsibility for disclosure through the later date *only with respect to the specified item*. Using the later date for the date of the report extends the auditors' responsibility with respect to all areas of the financial statements. Finally, in the unusual circumstance in which the client did not agree to properly reflect the event, the departure from generally accepted accounting principles could result in either a qualified or adverse opinion.

Figure 16.4 summarizes the auditors' responsibilities for subsequent events with respect to the balance sheet date, the date of the audit report, and the date upon which the audit report is actually issued.

The Auditors' S-1 Review in an SEC Registration

The Securities Act of 1933 (Section 11 [a]) extends the auditors' liability in connection with the registration of new securities with the Securities and Exchange Commission (SEC) to the *effective date* of the registration statement—the date on which the securities may be sold to the public. In many cases, the effective date of the registration statement may be several weeks or even months later than the date the auditors completed their fieldwork. Accordingly, on or as close as practicable to the effective date, the auditors return to the client's facilities to conduct an **S-1 review**, so-called because of the "Form S-1" title of the traditional SEC registration statement for new securities issues. In addition to completing the subsequent events review described in the preceding section, the auditors should read the entire prospectus and other pertinent portions of the registration statement. They should also inquire of officers and other key executives of the client whether any events not reported in the registration statement have occurred that require amendment of the registration statement to prevent the audited financial statements therein from being misleading.

FIGURE 16.4
Subsequent Events

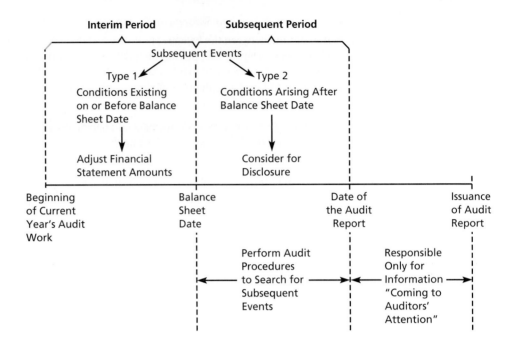

Obtain Representation Letter

Chapter 5 included a general description of the **representation letter** that the auditors must obtain from management. The primary purpose of the representation letter is to have the client's principal officers acknowledge that they are primarily responsible for the fairness of the financial statements. Since the financial statements must reflect all material subsequent events, the representation letter should be dated as of the date of the audit report.

Evaluate Audit Findings

Learning Objective 8

Throughout the course of the audit, the auditors will propose adjusting entries for all *material misstatements* (whether caused by error or fraud) that are discovered in the client's financial records. Any material misstatement that the auditors find must be corrected; otherwise, they cannot issue an unqualified opinion on the financial statements. In evaluating whether an individual misstatement is material, the auditors consider both quantitative and qualitative factors. For example, a $10,000 related party transaction might be considered material for a particular audit, whereas a misstatement of trade accounts receivable of the same amount would not be considered material. Immaterial misstatements that are discovered by the auditors are accumulated on a working paper with a title, such as "Adjusting Entries Passed."

Evaluation Materiality—Considering Quantitative Factors

To issue an unqualified opinion, the auditors must conclude that there is a low level of risk of material misstatement of the financial statements. In evaluating this risk the auditors develop an estimate of the **total likely misstatement in the financial statements,** which is made up of the following three components:

1. *Known misstatements* (adjusting entries passed) include those that the client has not corrected.
2. *Projected misstatements* include those that are calculated when the auditors employ audit sampling, as described in Chapter 9. For example, if the book value of accounts receivable is $6,250,000 and the auditors, using audit sampling, estimate the audited value to be $6,100,000, the projected misstatement would be the difference of $150,000. This projected misstatement should be decreased by the amount of known misstatement used to calculate it (either included above in item [1] or corrected).
3. *Other estimated misstatements* are those estimated by techniques other than audit sampling, such as analytical procedures. One significant source of these estimated misstatements is differences related to accounting estimates, such as those for inventory obsolescence,

uncollectible receivables, and warranty obligations. For these items, the estimated misstatement is the difference between the client's estimate and the closest amount that the auditors consider to be reasonable. An example would be a situation in which the management estimates the company's warranty liability to be $100,000, and the auditors develop an estimate of between $120,000 and $140,000 for the account. The estimated misstatement is $20,000 ($120,000 − $100,000).

Obviously, if the auditors estimate that the total of these three misstatements (the total likely misstatement) is material to the financial statements, they will conclude that the risk of material misstatement is too high to issue an unqualified opinion on the financial statements. Even if the total likely misstatement in the financial statements is estimated to be somewhat less than a material amount, the auditors, recognizing that the actual misstatement might be greater than their estimate, may still conclude that the risk of material misstatement of the financial statements is too high. In either case, the auditors will ask management to adjust the financial statements for the known misstatements, or they will perform additional audit procedures to further reduce detection risk. The auditors should never issue an unqualified opinion on financial statements in which the risk of material misstatement is considered to be excessive.

The auditors will conclude that the risk of material misstatement is sufficiently low to issue an unqualified opinion only when *total likely misstatement is significantly less than a material amount.* The relationship between total likely misstatement and materiality is often documented in a working paper similar to that shown in Figure 16.5. As illustrated, the auditors must consider the effects of the total likely misstatement on the various components of the financial statements, such as current assets and net income. As we have emphasized throughout, whether a misstatement is material depends on its specific effect on the financial statements.

Notice that the misstatements in Figure 16.5 are adjusted for the effects of income taxes. To illustrate, consider the first misstatement, which represents an overstatement of prepaid expenses of $6,500. If that adjustment is not made, net income before taxes is overstated by that amount. However, since taxable income is also overstated by $6,500, the company's income tax expense is overstated, in this case by $2,600 (40 percent of $6,500). The 40 percent rate was used because it represents the company's marginal tax rate.

Evaluation Materiality—Considering Qualitative Factors

While a schedule such as that presented in Figure 16.5 is helpful for assessing the quantitative effects of misstatements, auditors must also consider qualitative factors when evaluating the materiality of such misstatements. In Staff Accounting Bulletin No. 99, the Securities and Exchange Commission (SEC) provides examples of such qualitative factors. One or more misstatements are likely to be material from a qualitative perspective when they:

- Arise from an item capable of precise measurement (e.g., the amount of a sale) rather than from an estimate (e.g., the amount in the allowance for doubtful accounts).
- Mask a change in earnings or other trends.
- Hide a failure to meet analysts' consensus expectations for the company.
- Change a loss into income, or vice versa.
- Concern a particularly important segment or other portion of the registrant's business.
- Affect compliance with regulatory requirements, loan covenants, or other contractual requirements.
- Increase management's compensation.
- Involve concealment of an unlawful transaction.
- Are of an amount that management or the auditors believe would affect the stock's price.

In addition, the SEC requires that management and auditors apply a *reasonableness* standard when considering fairness of financial presentation. This somewhat ill-defined standard suggests that the need for proper presentation is not entirely a function of the above types of qualitative considerations. For example, the intentional misrecording of certain immaterial transactions might be considered unreasonable. Indeed, intentional misstatements may in some circumstances

FIGURE 16.5 Total Likely Misstatement

SOUTHMADE PRODUCTS, INC.
Total Likely Misstatement
December 31, 20X4
Overstatement (Understatement)

S-8

W/P ref.		Current Assets	Non-current Assets	Current Liabilities	Non-current Liabilities	Owners' Equity	Income Before Taxes	Tax Expense
	Uncorrected Known Misstatements							
D8	Overstatement of prepaid expenses	$ 6,500		$ 2,600		$ 6,500 (2,600)	$ 6,500	$ 2,600
F-6	Overstatement of prior year's depreciation		($10,000)	(4,000)		(10,000) 4,000		
M-4	Unrecorded liabilities			(11,215) 4,486		11,215 (4,486)	11,215	4,486
	Projected Misstatements							
C-5	Overstatement of accounts receivable (confirmation results)	30,000		12,000		30,000 (12,000)	30,000	12,000
	Other Estimated Misstatements							
C-10	Understatement of allowance for uncollectible accounts	5,000		2,000		5,000 (2,000)	5,000	2,000
	Total Likely Misstatements	$ 41,500	($10,000)	$ 5,871	–	$ 25,629	$52,715	$21,086
	Amount considered material	$100,000	$125,000	$100,000	$125,000	$200,000	$150,000	

Conclusion: Total likely misstatements are small enough in amount to result in a sufficiently low level of audit risk to justify our opinion.

2/17/X5 JW

be unlawful; as such, they may require auditor consideration, as discussed in Chapter 2. Note that the situation being considered by the SEC in this case is one in which a client intentionally mis-records items to manage earnings (e.g., reporting sales in the wrong year), as opposed to a situation in which an accounting expediency is being applied to an immaterial area (e.g., the expensing of immaterial office supplies rather than listing them as an asset).

Evaluating the Risks of Material Misstatement

At or near the completion of fieldwork, the auditors should evaluate whether the accumulated results of their procedures and observations affect the assessments of the risks of material misstatement made earlier in the engagement. In addition, the partner in charge of the engagement should determine that information or conditions indicative of risks of material misstatement due to fraud have been communicated to the audit team members.

Review the Financial Statement Disclosures

Throughout the audit the auditors must recognize the need to determine that financial statement note disclosures are adequate. These disclosure requirements arise in numerous pronouncements of the Financial Accounting Standards Board, such as *FASB No. 5* on contingencies and *FASB No. 131* on reporting on segmental information. In addition, the auditors should be aware of the requirements of *AICPA Statement of Position 94-6,* "Disclosure of Certain Significant Risks and Uncertainties." That statement establishes disclosure requirements concerning (1) the nature of company operations, (2) the use of estimates in preparation of financial statements, (3) certain significant estimates, and (4) current vulnerability due to concentrations (e.g., dependence upon a particular customer, supplier, or product).

It is not effective to rely on the auditors' memories to evaluate the adequacy of disclosures, and it is not efficient for them to research the required disclosures each time they review a set of financial statements. Thus, many CPA firms use **disclosure checklists** that list all specific disclosures required by the FASB, the GASB, the FASAC, and the SEC. The auditors complete the checklist as a part of their review of the completed financial statements.

Client Approval of Adjusting Entries and Disclosures

During the course of the audit, the auditors may suggest various adjustments and disclosures concerning the financial statements. However, because they are the representations of management, the financial statements are not modified to reflect these items until management approves them. In some circumstances, management may propose differing adjustments and disclosures. Since the auditors' responsibility is to express an opinion on the financial statements, unresolved differences between auditor and client with respect to such differences may result in modification of the auditors' report. If any adjusting entries are not recorded, management must represent to the auditors (in the representation letters) that management believes the adjustments are not material.

Review the Engagement

SAS 22 (AU 311), "Planning and Supervision," states that "the work performed by each assistant should be reviewed to determine whether it was adequately performed and to evaluate whether the results are consistent with the conclusions to be presented in the auditors' report." This review of the work of the audit staff is primarily accomplished through a review of the audit working papers. The seniors on audit engagements typically perform their review of the audit working papers as the papers are completed. While audit partners and managers will generally communicate with seniors and other staff members throughout the audit, their review of the working papers generally is not completed until near (or after) completion of fieldwork. The audit partner and manager will devote special attention to those accounts that have a higher risk of material misstatement, such as the significant accounting estimates of inventory obsolescence and warranty obligations. Also, a final consideration will be made of whether the results of procedures performed throughout the audit, including while completing the audit, identify conditions and events that indicate there could be substantial doubt about the company's ability to continue as a going concern. Finally, if a second partner review is required by the CPA firm's quality control policies, this review is usually performed just prior to issuance of the audit report.

Responsibilities for Other Information in the Financial Report

Audited financial statements generally are included in three types of reports: (1) annual reports to shareholders, (2) reports to the SEC, and (3) auditor-submitted financial reports. These documents may include a considerable amount of information in addition to the audited financial statements. In completing the audit engagement, the auditors must fulfill certain responsibilities regarding this other information. The auditors' responsibility for specific information depends on the type of report and the nature of the information.

GAAP-Required Supplementary Information

The auditors have a responsibility to perform review procedures on supplementary information that is required by generally accepted accounting principles (e.g., the FASB). These procedures, as set forth in *SAS 52* (AU 558), "Required Supplementary Information," include inquiries of management regarding the appropriate presentation of the supplementary information and comparisons of the information with audited and other data known to the auditors.

If required supplementary information is omitted or not appropriately presented, or the auditors are not able to complete their limited procedures, these facts should be described in an explanatory paragraph in the auditors' report. Since the information is not required for fair presentation of the financial statements, the inclusion of the additional paragraph does not constitute a qualification of the auditors' opinion.

If the supplementary information was subjected to audit procedures in conjunction with the audit of the financial statements, the auditors may express an opinion on whether the information is presented fairly in relation to the financial statements taken as a whole.

Other Information in Client-Prepared Documents

Audit reports on the financial statements of large companies usually are included in an annual report to shareholders and in reports to the SEC. These annual reports contain information other than audited financial statements and required supplementary information, as, for example, a discussion of the company's plans and prospects for the future. In *SAS 8* (AU 550), "Other Information in Documents Containing Audited Financial Statements," the AICPA sets forth guidelines for the independent auditors with respect to such information. The auditors should read the other information and consider whether it is materially inconsistent with information appearing in the audited financial statements or notes. If the other information is inconsistent and the auditors conclude that neither the audited financial statements nor the audit report requires revision, they should request the client to revise the other information. If the client refuses to do so, the auditors should consider: (1) revising the audit report to describe the inconsistency, (2) withholding use of their audit report by the client, or (3) withdrawing from the engagement. The auditors should also be alert for, and discuss with the client, any other types of material misstatements included in the other information.

The inclusion of company financial statements on Internet Web sites raises a question as to whether auditors should "read" all information on the Web site (e.g., other financial information, press releases, or product information), and if so, how frequently, given the dynamic nature of most sites. The Auditing Standards Board has issued an interpretation stating that auditors are not required to read information contained in such electronic sites or to consider the consistency of such information with the financial statements.

Information Accompanying Financial Statements in Auditor-Submitted Documents

The auditors often process and reproduce financial reports for their clients, particularly for small companies with few shareholders. These documents may contain information in addition to the audited financial statements and the auditors' report. This *accompanying information* generally supplements or analyzes the basic financial statements but is not necessary for the presentation of the statements in accordance with generally accepted accounting principles. When the auditors submit a document that contains audited financial statements and accompanying information to their clients or others, they should report on all the information. If the auditors have performed audit procedures on the information in conjunction with their audit of the financial statements, they should express an opinion on whether it is fairly stated in all material respects in relation to the financial statements taken as a whole. Otherwise, the auditors should provide a disclaimer of opinion on the information.

Opinion Formulation and Report Issuance

After the preceding procedures have been performed, the auditors will ordinarily be in a position to issue their audit report. When the auditors have obtained reasonable assurance that the financial statements follow generally accepted accounting principles and the audit has been performed in conformity with generally accepted auditing standards, including no significant scope limitations, an unqualified opinion will ordinarily be issued. As we will discuss in Chapter 17, when various circumstances have occurred (e.g., changes in accounting principles, substantial doubt about the entity's ability to continue as a going concern, and when other auditors are involved), explanatory language may be added to the audit report.

Communicate with the Audit Committee

Auditors must communicate certain matters relating to fraud, illegal acts, reportable conditions, and certain other matters to the audit committee or the equivalent group with responsibility for oversight of the financial reporting process. All the communications may be communicated either orally or in writing.

Fraud and Illegal Acts

SAS 99 (AU 316), "Consideration of Fraud in a Financial Statement Audit," and *SAS 54* (AU 317), "Illegal Acts," require that the audit committee be informed about fraudulent or illegal acts that the auditors become aware of, unless those acts are clearly inconsequential. Although these disclosures are also normally made to management, when management is believed to be involved with such an act, the communications should be made directly to the audit committee.

Significant Deficiencies

Recall from our discussion in Chapter 7 that *SAS 60* (AU 325), "Communication of Internal Control Related Matters Noted in an Audit," requires that the auditors communicate to the audit committee any significant deficiencies in internal control (previously known as reportable conditions).

Other Communications

SAS 61 (AU 380), "Communication with Audit Committees," requires that auditors communicate a variety of matters concerning the audit, the accounting principles followed by the company, and the auditors' relationship with management. The purpose of these communications is to aid the audit committee in its oversight role over the company's senior management. Audit-related communications include the auditors' responsibilities for the audit and other information included with the financial statements. In addition, the auditors will provide the committee with the schedule of significant audit adjustments proposed by the auditors but not made by management.

Regarding accounting matters, the auditors are required to communicate information on the client's selection of significant accounting policies, as well as information on significant accounting estimates made by management. In their discussions, the auditors will provide an assessment of the quality, not just acceptability, of the accounting principles and the estimates. Concerning their relationship with management, the auditors will discuss any disagreements and other difficulties encountered in performing the audit. If management contacted other auditors concerning an accounting or auditing matter, the auditors will present their viewpoint to the audit committee.

Post-Audit Responsibilities

The Auditors' Subsequent Discovery of Facts Existing at the Date of Their Report

After the issuance of its audit report, a CPA firm may encounter evidence indicating that the client's financial statements were materially misstated or lacked required disclosures. The auditors must immediately investigate such subsequently discovered facts. If the auditors determine that the facts are significant and existed at the date of the audit report, they should advise the client to make appropriate disclosure of the facts to anyone actually or likely to be relying upon the audit report and the related financial statements. If the client refuses to make appropriate disclosure, the CPAs should inform each member of the client's board of directors

Learning Objective 9

of such refusal. They should also notify regulatory agencies having jurisdiction over the client, and, if practicable, each person known to be relying upon the audited financial statements, that the CPAs' report can no longer be relied upon.

Subsequent Discovery of Omitted Audit Procedures

What actions should the auditors take if, after issuing an audit report, they find that they failed to perform certain significant audit procedures? The omission of appropriate audit procedures in a particular engagement might be discovered during a peer review or other subsequent review of the auditors' working papers. Unlike the situation described in the previous section, the auditors do not have information indicating that the financial statements are in error. Instead, the subsequent review has revealed that they may have issued their audit report without having gathered sufficient evidential matter. In addressing this sensitive problem, *SAS 46* (AU 390), "Consideration of Omitted Procedures After the Report Date," states that the auditors should assess the importance of the omitted procedures to their previously issued opinion. If they believe that the omitted procedures impair their ability to support their previously issued opinion, and their report is still being relied upon by third parties, they should attempt to perform the omitted procedures or appropriate alternative procedures. Because of the legal implications of these situations, the auditors should consider consulting their legal counsel.

Chapter Summary

This chapter explained auditing operations and the considerations and procedures involved in completing the audit. To summarize:

1. The analysis throughout the text has emphasized the need to consider revenue and expense accounts in conjunction with the audit of asset and liability accounts. However, vouching and other substantive procedures are generally necessary for revenue and expense accounts that are less directly associated with transaction cycles, such as miscellaneous revenue and selling, general, and administrative expenses.

2. Substantive tests for payroll accounts address the overall reasonableness of payroll costs and the proper allocation of these costs to the functional areas of manufacturing, selling, and administration. In addition, tests must be performed on the allocation of manufacturing costs to work in process, finished goods, and cost of goods sold.

3. Because of their objectives, certain audit procedures cannot be completed before the end of the audit. These procedures include: (a) search for unrecorded liabilities, (b) review the minutes of meetings, (c) perform final analytical procedures, (d) perform procedures to identify loss contingencies, (e) perform the review for subsequent events, and (f) obtain the representation letter.

4. The auditors must perform audit procedures to determine that loss contingencies have been properly presented and disclosed in conformity with *FASB No. 5*. To identify loss contingencies, auditors perform various procedures, such as reviewing minutes of directors' meetings, inquiring of the client's lawyer, reviewing correspondence with financial institutions and regulatory agencies, sending confirmations to financial institutions, and obtaining a representation letter from officers of the company.

5. Subsequent events may be classified into two broad categories: (a) those providing additional evidence about facts existing on or before the balance sheet date (which may require adjusting entries), and (b) those involving facts coming into existence after the balance sheet date (which may require note disclosures). Many of these subsequent events relate to loss contingencies, and the audit procedures involved are similar to the ones used to audit those items.

6. Also important to completing the audit are the procedures performed to evaluate audit findings and review the audit work. In evaluating audit findings, the auditors accumulate known misstatements, projected misstatements, and other estimated misstatements to determine if the aggregate results of their procedures support the fairness of the financial statements. In addition, the auditors should consider whether any audit results indicate a need to reassess the risks of material misstatement of the financial statements.

7. Auditors also have certain post-audit responsibilities. When auditors find, subsequent to the issuance of their audit report, that the financial statements are materially misleading, they should take steps to prevent continued reliance on their report. In some cases this might involve notification of regulatory agencies.

Key Terms Introduced or Emphasized in Chapter 16

Analytical procedures   Evaluations of financial information made by a study of plausible relationships between financial and nonfinancial information.

Commitment   A contractual obligation to carry out a transaction at specified terms in the future. Material commitments should be disclosed in the financial statements.

Conservatism   An accounting doctrine for asset valuation in which the lower of two alternative acceptable asset valuations is chosen.

Contingent liability   A possible liability, stemming from past events, that will be resolved as to existence and amount by some future event.

Disclosure checklist   A list of specific disclosures required by the FASB, GASB, FASAC, and the SEC that is used to evaluate the adequacy of the disclosures in a set of financial statements.

General risk contingency   An element of the business environment that involves some risk of a future loss. Examples include the risk of accident, strike, price fluctuations, or natural catastrophe. General risk contingencies should not be disclosed in financial statements.

Lawyer's letter   A letter of inquiry sent by auditors to a client's legal counsel requesting a description and evaluation of pending or threatened litigation, unasserted claims, and other loss contingencies.

Loss contingency   A possible loss, stemming from past events, that will be resolved as to existence and amount by some future event. Loss contingencies should be disclosed in notes to the financial statements if there is a reasonable possibility that a loss has been incurred. When loss contingencies are considered probable and can be reasonably estimated, they should be accrued in the accounts.

Minutes   A formal record of the issues discussed and actions taken in meetings of stockholders and the board of directors.

Representation letter   A single letter or separate letters prepared by officers of the client company at the auditors' request setting forth certain representations about the company's financial position or operations.

S-1 review   Procedures carried out by auditors at the client company's facilities on or as close as practicable to the effective date of a registration statement filed under the Securities Act of 1933.

Subsequent event   An event occurring after the date of the balance sheet but prior to completion of the audit and issuance of the audit report.

Total likely misstatement in the financial statements   Total misstatement in the financial statements that is estimated by the auditors based on the results of audit procedures. For example, the projected misstatement from an audited sample is an estimate of the likely misstatement in the audited population.

Unasserted claim   A possible legal claim of which no potential claimant has exhibited an awareness.

Review Questions

16–1.   Identify three revenue accounts that are verified during the audit of balance sheet accounts; also, identify the related balance sheet accounts.

16–2.   How are analytical procedures used in the verification of revenue?

16–3.   Identify three items often misclassified as miscellaneous revenue.

16–4.   Identify three expense accounts that are verified during the audit of balance sheet accounts; also, identify the related balance sheet accounts.

16–5.   For which expense accounts should the auditors obtain or prepare analyses to be used in preparation of the client's income tax returns?

16–6.   When you are first retained to audit the financial statements of Wabash Company, you inquire whether a budget is used to control costs and expenses. The controller, James Lowe, replies that he personally prepares such a budget each year, but that he regards it as a highly confidential document. He states that you may refer to it if necessary, but he wants you to make sure that no employee of the firm sees any of the budget data. Comment on this use of a budget.

16–7.   What auditing procedure can you suggest for determining the reasonableness of selling, general, and administrative expenses?

16–8.   Describe how the auditors use analytical procedures in the examination of selling, general, and administrative expenses.

16–9. What division of duties among independent departments is desirable to achieve maximum internal control over payroll?

16–10. What safeguards should be employed when the inaccessibility of banking facilities makes it desirable to pay employees in cash?

16–11. You are asked by a client to outline the procedures you would recommend for handling of unclaimed wages. What procedures do you recommend?

16–12. What specific procedures are suggested by the phrase "test of controls over payroll transactions"?

16–13. Should the auditors make a complete review of all correspondence in the client's files? Explain.

16–14. What is the purpose of analytical procedures performed as a part of the overall review?

16–15. List the audit procedures that must be completed near the date of the audit report. **597**

16–16. What are *loss contingencies?* How are such items presented in the financial statements? Explain.

16–17. What is the usual procedure followed by the CPA in obtaining evidence regarding pending and threatened litigation against the client?

16–18. Explain how a loss contingency exists with respect to an *unasserted* claim. Should unasserted claims be disclosed in the financial statements?

16–19. If the federal income tax returns for prior years have not as yet been reviewed by federal tax authorities, would you consider it necessary for the client to disclose this situation in a note to the financial statements? Explain.

16–20. What is the meaning of the term *commitment?* Give examples. Do commitments appear in financial statements? Explain.

16–21. What are *general risk contingencies?* Do such items require disclosure in the financial statements?

16–22. What are *subsequent events?*

16–23. Describe the manner in which the auditors evaluate their audit findings.

16–24. Describe a disclosure checklist. What is its purpose?

16–25. What is the independent auditors' obligation with respect to information in client-prepared annual reports to shareholders, other than the audited financial statements?

16–26. When auditors submit documents to their clients that contain audited financial statements, what are their responsibilities concerning information that accompanies the financial statements?

Questions Requiring Analysis

16–27. In your audit of the financial statements of Wolfe Company for the year ended April 30, you find that a material account receivable is due from a company in reorganization under Chapter 11 of the Bankruptcy Act. You also learn that on May 28 several former members of the bankrupt company's management formed a new company and that the new company had issued a note to Wolfe Company that would pay off the bankrupt customer's account receivable over a four-year period. What presentation, if any, should be made of this situation in the financial statements of Wolfe Company for the year ended April 30? Explain.

16–28. During an audit engagement, Robert Wong, CPA, has satisfactorily completed an examination of accounts payable and other liabilities and now plans to determine whether there are any loss contingencies arising from litigation, claims, or assessments.

What are the audit procedures Wong should follow with respect to the existence of loss contingencies arising from litigation, claims, or assessments? Do not discuss reporting requirements.

16–29. You are the audit manager in the audit of the financial statements of Midwest Grain Storage, Inc., a new client. The company's records show that, as of the balance sheet date, approximately 15 million bushels of various grains are in storage for the Commodity Credit Corporation, an agency of the U.S. government.

In your review of the audit senior's working papers, you ascertain the following facts:

a. All grain is stored under a Uniform Grain Storage Agreement, which holds Midwest responsible for the quantity and quality of the grain.

b. Losses due to shrinkage, spoilage, and so forth are inherent in the storage of grain. Midwest's losses, however, have been negligible due to the excellence of its storage facilities.

c. Midwest carries a warehouseman's bond covering approximately 20 percent of the value of the stored grain.

In the loss contingencies section of the working papers, the senior auditor has made the following notation: "I propose recommending to Midwest's controller that the contingent liability for grain spoilage and shrinkage be disclosed in a note to the financial statements."

Do you concur with the senior's proposal? Explain.

16–30. Warren Cook, CPA, is auditing the State University Bookstore and has obtained the following summary of revenues and cost of sales from the client's computer.

	New Course Books	Used Course Books	General Books	Supplies	Insignia Items	Other
Sales	543,400	234,100	45,500	63,400	45,300	34,200
Cost of sales	396,682	154,974	27,300	40,893	27,633	20,178

a. Calculate the gross margin for each of State University's product lines.

b. Compare State University's gross margins to those presented by the National Association of College Stores. Indicate any margins that appear out of line, in relation to the industry. The association statistics may be obtained at the following Internet address: www.nacs.org. To get to the statistics, select "Industry Information." Then select "College Store Margins."

16–31. The auditor's opinion on the fairness of financial statements may be affected by subsequent events.

Required:

a. Define what is commonly referred to in auditing as a subsequent event, and describe the two general types of subsequent events.

b. Identify those auditing procedures that the auditor should apply at or near the completion of fieldwork to disclose significant subsequent events.

16–32. Linda Reeves, CPA, receives a telephone call from her client, Lane Company. The company's controller states that the board of directors of Lane has entered into two contractual arrangements with Ted Forbes, the company's former president, who has recently retired. Under one agreement, Lane Company will pay the ex-president $7,000 per month for five years if he does not compete with the company during that time in a rival business. Under the other agreement, the company will pay the ex-president $5,000 per month for five years for such advisory services as the company may request from the ex-president.

Lane's controller asks Reeves whether the balance sheet as of the date the two agreements were signed should show $144,000 in current liabilities and $576,000 in long-term liabilities, or whether the two agreements should be disclosed in a contingencies note to the financial statements.

How should Linda Reeves reply to the controller's questions? Explain.

16–33. On July 27, 200X, Arthur Ward, CPA, issued an unqualified audit report on the financial statements of Dexter Company for the year ended June 30, 200X. Two weeks later, Dexter Company mailed annual reports, including the June 30 financial statements and Ward's audit report, to 150 stockholders and to several creditors of Dexter Company. Dexter Company's stock is not actively traded on national exchanges or over the counter.

On September 5, the controller of Dexter Company informed Ward that an account payable for consulting services in the amount of $170,000 had inadvertently been omitted from Dexter's June 30 balance sheet. As a consequence, net income for the year ended June 30 was overstated by $90,500, net of applicable federal and state income taxes. Both Ward and Dexter's controller agreed that the misstatement was material to Dexter's financial position at June 30, 200X, and operating results for the year then ended.

What should Arthur Ward's course of action be in this matter? Discuss.

Multiple Choice Questions

16–34. Select the best answer for each of the following and give reasons for your choice:

a. Which of the following is *least* likely to be considered a substantive test relating to payrolls?

  (1) Investigate fluctuations in salaries, wages, and commissions.

  (2) Test computations of compensation under profit-sharing for bonus plans.

  (3) Test commission earnings.

  (4) Test whether employee time reports are approved by supervisors.

b. Which of the following is the *best* way for the auditors to determine that every name on a company's payroll is that of a bona fide employee presently on the job?

  (1) Examine human resources records for accuracy and completeness.

  (2) Examine employees' names listed on payroll tax returns for agreement with payroll accounting records.

  (3) Make a surprise observation of the company's regular distribution of paychecks on a test basis.

  (4) Visit the working areas and verify that employees exist by examining their badge or identification numbers.

c. As a result of analytical procedures, the independent auditors determine that the gross profit percentage has declined from 30 percent in the preceding year to 20 percent in the current year. The auditors should:

  (1) Express an opinion that is qualified due to the inability of the client company to continue as a going concern.

  (2) Evaluate management's performance in causing this decline.

  (3) Require note disclosure.

  (4) Consider the possibility of a misstatement in the financial statements.

d. When auditing the statement of cash flows, which of the following would an auditor *not* expect to be a source of receipts and payments?

  (1) Capitalization.

  (2) Financing.

  (3) Investing.

  (4) Operations.

e. The search for unrecorded liabilities for a public company includes procedures usually performed through the

  (1) Day the audit report is issued.

  (2) End of the client's year.

  (3) The date of the auditors' report.

  (4) Date the report is filed with the SEC.

f. The total likely misstatement in the financial statements is made up of:

	Known Misstatements	Projected Misstatements	Other Misstatements
(1)	Yes	Yes	Yes
(2)	Yes	Yes	No
(3)	No	Yes	No
(4)	No	Yes	Yes

g. A possible loss, stemming from past events that will be resolved as to existence and amounts is referred to as a:

  (1) Analytical process.

  (2) Loss contingency.

  (3) Probable loss.

  (4) Unasserted claim.

h. Which of the following is most likely to be considered a Type 1 subsequent event?

    (1) A business combination completed after year-end, but for which negotiations began prior to year-end.

    (2) A strike subsequent to year-end due to employee complaints about working conditions which originated two years ago.

    (3) Customer checks deposited prior to year-end, but determined to be uncollectible after year-end.

    (4) Introduction of a new line of products after year-end for which major research had been completed prior to year-end.

i. An auditor accepted an engagement to audit the 20X8 financial statements of EFG Corporation and began the fieldwork on September 30, 20X8. EFG gave the auditor the 20X8 financial statements on January 17, 20X9. The auditor completed the audit on February 10, 20X9, and delivered the report on February 16, 20X9. The client's representation letter normally would be dated:

    (1) December 31, 20X8.

    (2) January 17, 20X9.

    (3) February 10, 20X9.

    (4) February 16, 20X9.

j. Which of the following procedures is most likely to be included in the final review stage of an audit?

    (1) Obtain an understanding of internal control.

    (2) Confirmation of receivables.

    (3) Observation of inventory.

    (4) Perform analytical procedures.

k. Subsequent to the issuance of the auditor's report, the auditor became aware of facts existing at the report date that would have affected the report had the auditor then been aware of such facts. After determining that the information is reliable, the auditor should next:

    (1) Notify the board of directors that the auditor's report must no longer be associated with the financial statements.

    (2) Determine whether there are persons relying or likely to rely on the financial statements who would attach importance to the information.

    (3) Request that management disclose the effects of the newly discovered information by adding a footnote to subsequently issued financial statements.

    (4) Issue revised pro forma financial statements taking into consideration the newly discovered information.

l. Which of the following events occurring on January 5 of 20X2 is most likely to result in an adjusting entry to the 20X1 financial statements?

    (1) A business combination.

    (2) Early retirement of bonds payable.

    (3) Settlement of litigation.

    (4) Plant closure due to a strike.

Problems

16–35. Rita King, your staff assistant on the April 30, 20X2, audit of Maxwell Company, was transferred to another assignment before she could prepare a proposed adjusting journal entry for Maxwell's Miscellaneous Revenue account, which she had analyzed per the working paper on the following page. You have reviewed the working paper and are satisfied with King's procedures. You are convinced that all the miscellaneous revenue items should be transferred to other accounts. Maxwell Company's state of incorporation has an Unclaimed Properties Law.

Draft a proposed adjusting journal entry at April 30, 20X2, for Maxwell Company's Miscellaneous Revenue account.

```
                              Maxwell Company
Acct. No. 430              Miscellaneous Revenue                      Q-2
                          Year Ended April 30, 20X2
                                                        C.M.
                                                     May 19, X2

Date                 Description                    Reference      Amount

May 8, 20X1,         Proceeds of sale of scrap from    Various CR    $5,843 ᵞ
through              manufacturing process (total of
April 7, 20X2        12 monthly sales)

July 18, 20X1        Write-off of old outstanding checks;   GJ 7-4    1,100 ᵞ
                       nos. 118-$500; 214-$400; 407-$200

Sept. 22, 20X1       Recovery of previously written off     CR 9-1    4,381 ᵞ
                     account receivable from Wilson
                     Company

Feb. 6, 20X2         Cash proceeds from sale of machine.    CR 2-1    3,500 ᵞ
                     Cost of $10,000 and accumulated
                     depreciation of $8,000 as of Feb. 6,
                     X2, not removed from accounts

April 28, 20X2       Refund of premium overcharge on        CR 4-1      600 ᵞ
                       fire insurance policy no. 1856,
                       for period April 1, 20X2-Mar. 31, 20X3

April 30, 20X2       Balance per ledger                             $15,424

               ᵞ—Traced to cash receipts journal or general journal;
                    vouched to appropriate supporting documents.

                                                            R.A.K.
                                                            May 18, X2
```

16–36. Your client is a company that owns a shopping center with 30 store tenants. All leases with the store tenants provide for a fixed rent plus a percentage of sales, net of sales taxes, in excess of a fixed dollar amount computed on an annual basis. Each lease also provides that the lessor may engage CPAs to audit all records of the tenant for assurance that sales are being properly reported to the lessor.

You have been requested by your client to audit the records of Traders Restaurant to determine that the sales totaling $390,000 for the year ended December 31, 20X2, have been properly reported to the lessor. The restaurant and the shopping center entered into a five-year lease on January 1, 20X1. Traders Restaurant offers only table service; no liquor is served. During mealtimes there are four or five waiters and waitresses in attendance who prepare handwritten prenumbered restaurant checks for the customers. Payment is made at a cash register, operated by the proprietor, as the customer leaves. All sales are for cash. The proprietor also is the accountant. Complete files are kept of restaurant checks and cash register tapes. A daily sales journal and general ledger are also maintained.

Required: List the auditing procedures that you would employ to verify the total annual sales of Traders Restaurant.

(AICPA, adapted)

16–37. The following are typical questions that might appear on an internal control questionnaire for payroll activities:

1. Is there adequate separation of duties between employees who maintain human resources records and employees who approve payroll disbursements?

2. Is there adequate separation of duties between personnel who maintain timekeeping or attendance records for employees and employees who distribute payroll checks?

Required:

a. Describe the purpose of each of the above controls.

b. Describe the manner in which each of the above controls might be tested.

c. Assuming that the operating effectiveness of each of the above controls is found to be inadequate, describe how the auditors might alter their substantive tests to compensate for the increased level of control risk.

16–38.   In connection with an audit of the financial statements of Olympia Company, the auditors are reviewing procedures for accumulating direct labor-hours. They learn that all production is by job order and that all employees are paid hourly wages, with time and a half for overtime hours.

Olympia's direct labor-hour input process for payroll and job-cost determination is summarized in the flowchart that is illustrated below. Steps A and C are performed in timekeeping, step B in the factory operating departments, step D in payroll audit and control, step E in data input, and step F in computer operations.

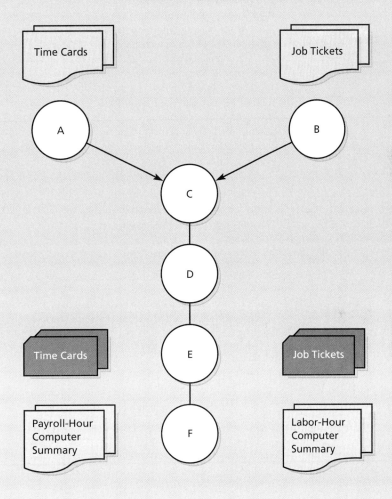

Required:

For each input processing step A through F:

a. List the possible errors or discrepancies that may occur.

b. Cite the corresponding control that should be in effect for each error or discrepancy.

Note: Your discussion of Olympia's procedures should be limited to the input for direct labor-hours, as shown in steps A through F in the flowchart. Do not discuss human resources procedures for hiring, promotion, termination, and pay-rate authorization. In step F do not discuss equipment, computer program, and general computer controls.

Organize your answer for each input-processing step as follows:

Step	Possible Misstatements or Discrepancies	Control
A		

(AICPA, adapted)

16–39. Rowe Manufacturing Company has about 50 production employees and uses the following payroll procedures.

The factory supervisor interviews applicants and on the basis of the interview either hires or rejects the applicants. After being employed, the applicant prepares a W-4 form (Employee's Withholding Exemption Certificate) and gives it to the supervisor. The supervisor writes the hourly rate of pay for the new employee in the corner of the W-4 form and then gives the form to a payroll clerk as notice that the applicant has been employed. The supervisor verbally advises the payroll department of pay-rate adjustments.

A supply of blank time cards is kept in a box near the entrance to the factory. Each employee takes a time card on Monday morning, signs it, and notes in pencil on the time card the daily arrival and departure times. At the end of the week, the employees drop the time cards in a box near the door to the factory.

The completed time cards are taken from the box on Monday morning by a payroll clerk. Two payroll clerks divide the cards alphabetically between them, one taking the A–L section of the payroll, the other taking the M–Z section. Each clerk is fully responsible for one section of the payroll. The payroll clerks compute the gross pay, deductions, and net pay; post the details to the employees' earnings records; and prepare and number the payroll checks. Employees are automatically removed from the payroll when they fail to turn in time cards.

The payroll checks are manually signed by the chief accountant and given to the supervisor, who distributes the checks to the employees in the factory and arranges for the delivery of the checks to the employees who are absent. The payroll bank account is reconciled by the chief accountant, who also prepares the various quarterly and annual payroll tax reports.

Required: List your suggestions for improving Rowe Manufacturing Company's internal control over factory hiring practices and payroll.

(AICPA, adapted)

16–40. City Loan Company has 100 branch loan offices. Each office has a manager and four or five employees who are hired by the manager. Branch managers prepare the weekly payroll, including their own salaries, and pay employees from cash on hand. The employees sign the payroll sheet signifying receipt of their salary. Hours worked by hourly personnel are inserted in the payroll sheet from time reports prepared by the employees and approved by the manager.

The weekly payroll sheets are sent to the home office, along with other accounting statements and reports. The home office compiles employee earnings records and prepares all federal and state payroll tax returns from the weekly payroll sheets.

Salaries are established by home office job-evaluation schedules. Salary adjustments, promotions, and transfers of full-time employees are approved by a home office salary committee based upon the recommendations of branch managers and area supervisors. Branch managers advise the salary committee of new full-time employees and terminations. Part-time and temporary employees are hired without referral to the salary committee.

Required: *a.* How might funds for payroll be diverted in the above system?

b. Prepare a payroll internal audit program to be used in the home office to audit the branch office payrolls of City Loan Company.

(AICPA, adapted)

16–41. The following "conditions" are excerpts from a report of an operational audit of a company's human resources department:

Condition I: The company's payroll is prepared by the human resources department.
Condition II: The firm's human resources manager is the proprietor's son, who has one year of experience in the human resources field.
Condition III: The distribution of payroll checks is made by the human resources department.
Condition IV: The human resources department makes a quarterly test of all personnel records to be assured that all required documentation is present.

Condition V: Personnel hiring is initiated by the human resources department only upon the receipt of a request from the user department. The request must be signed by the user department manager or assistant manager.

Condition VI: When documentation supporting a particular human resources action is received by the human resources department, a human resources clerk is assigned the task of making the appropriate changes on the file or files affected. No one, at any time, is assigned the task of verifying that the entries are correctly transcribed.

The internal auditor is preparing a "recommendations" section for the report. The following controls are to be used: (1) competence and integrity of personnel, (2) segregation of incompatible functions, (3) execution of activities, (4) proper recording of events, (5) appropriate limitation of access to assets, and (6) comparison of existing records with records required. The internal auditor notes that one of the controls is addressed by each of the six conditions identified.

Required:

a. Identify the control most directly addressed, using one policy or procedure per condition with no repeats.

b. State whether or not that control is violated by the condition.

c. If the control is violated, describe the possible consequences of any such violation.

d. If the control is violated, prescribe one corrective action for any such violation. Use the format shown below:

| | a. | b. | c. | d. |
| | | | Possible | Corrective |
Condition	Control (1)–(6)	Violated?	Consequences	Action Needed
I.				
II.				
III.				
IV.				
V.				
VI.				

(CIA, adapted)

16–42. Robertson Company had accounts receivable of $200,000 at December 31, 200X, and had provided an allowance for uncollectible accounts of $6,000. After performing all normal auditing procedures relating to the receivables and to the valuation allowance, the independent auditors were satisfied that this asset was fairly stated and that the allowance for uncollectible accounts was adequate. Just before completion of the audit fieldwork late in February, however, the auditors learned that the entire plant of Thompson Corporation, a major customer, had been destroyed by a flood early in February and that as a result Thompson Corporation was hopelessly insolvent.

The account receivable from Thompson Corporation in the amount of $44,000 originated on December 28; terms of payment were net 60 days. The receivable had been regarded as entirely collectible at December 31, and the auditors had so considered it in reaching their conclusion as to the adequacy of the allowance for uncollectible accounts. In discussing the news concerning the flood, the controller of Robertson Company emphasized to the auditors that the probable loss of $44,000 should be regarded as a loss of the following year, and not of 200X, the year under audit.

What action, if any, should the auditors recommend with respect to the receivable from Thompson Corporation?

16–43. In connection with your audit of the financial statements of Hollis Mfg. Corporation for the year ended December 31, 20X3, your review of subsequent events disclosed the following items:

a. January 7, 20X4: The mineral content of a shipment of ore en route to Hollis Mfg. Corporation on December 31, 20X3, was determined to be 72 percent. The shipment was recorded at year-end at an estimated content of 50 percent by a debit to Raw Materials Inventory and a credit to Accounts Payable in the amount of $82,400. The final liability to the vendor is based on the actual mineral content of the shipment.

b. January 15, 20X4: Culminating a series of personal disagreements between Ray Hollis, the president, and his brother-in-law, the treasurer, the latter resigned, effective immediately, under an agreement whereby the corporation would purchase his 10 percent stock ownership at book value as of December 31, 20X3. Payment is to be made in two equal amounts in cash on April 1 and October 1, 20X4. In December, the treasurer had obtained a divorce from his wife, who is Ray Hollis's sister.

c. January 31, 20X4: As a result of reduced sales, production was curtailed in mid-January and some workers were laid off. On February 5, 20X4, all the remaining workers went on strike. To date the strike is unsettled.

Required: Assume that the above items came to your attention before completion of your audit work. Indicate which of the items should be disclosed, and list all details that you would suggest should be disclosed. Indicate those items or details, if any, that should not be disclosed. Give your reasons for recommending or not recommending disclosure of the items or details.

(AICPA, adapted)

16–44.   In connection with her audit of the financial statements of Flowmeter, Inc., for the year ended December 31, 20X3, Joan Hirsch, CPA, is aware that certain events and transactions that have taken place after December 31, 20X3, but before she has issued her report dated February 28, 20X4, may affect the company's financial statements.

The following material events or transactions have come to her attention:

a. On January 3, 20X4, Flowmeter, Inc., received a shipment of raw materials from Canada. The materials had been ordered in October 20X3 and shipped FOB shipping point in December 20X3.

b. On January 15, 20X4, the company settled and paid a personal injury claim of a former employee as the result of an accident that had occurred in March 20X3. The company had not previously recorded a liability for the claim.

c. On January 25, 20X4, the company agreed to purchase for cash the outstanding stock of Porter Electrical Co. The business combination is likely to double the sales volume of Flowmeter, Inc.

d. On February 1, 20X4, a plant owned by Flowmeter, Inc., was damaged by a flood, resulting in an uninsured loss of inventory.

e. On February 5, 20X4, Flowmeter, Inc., issued to an underwriting syndicate $2 million in convertible bonds.

Required: For each of the above items, indicate how the event or transaction should be reflected in Flowmeter's financial statements and explain the reasons for selecting this method of disclosure.

(AICPA, adapted)

In-Class Team Case

16–45.   The audit staff of Adams, Barnes & Co. (ABC), CPAs, reported the following audit findings in their audit of Keystone Computers & Networks (KCN), Inc.:

1. Unrecorded liabilities in the amount of $6,440 for purchases of inventory. These inventory items were counted and included in the year-end total.

2. Projected misstatement from confirmation of accounts receivable in the amount of $2,042 understatement.

3. Projected misstatement from price tests of inventory of $9,510 overstatement.

4. The staff of ABC believes that the amount of KCN's allowance for uncollectible accounts should be increased by $5,000.

In addition, the audit staff has decided that for evaluating a material misstatement of the financial statements the following guidelines should be used:

Current assets—$50,000

Noncurrent assets—$75,000

Current liabilities—$50,000

Noncurrent liabilities—$75,000

Total owners' equity—$100,000

Net income before taxes—$65,000

Required: a. Prepare a schedule modeled after the one on page 606 to be used to evaluate the above audit findings, assuming that KCN's marginal tax rate is 25 percent.

b. Decide whether the results indicate that there is a sufficiently low risk of material misstatement to justify ABC's audit opinion.

Research and Discussion Case

16–46. Marshall and Wyatt, CPAs, have been the independent auditors of Interstate Land Development Corporation for several years. During these years, Interstate prepared and filed its own annual income tax returns.

During 2004 Interstate requested Marshall and Wyatt to audit all the necessary financial statements of the corporation to be submitted to the Securities and Exchange Commission (SEC) in connection with a multistate public offering of 1 million shares of Interstate common stock. This public offering came under the provisions of the Securities Act of 1933. The audit was performed carefully and the financial statements were fairly presented for the respective periods. These financial statements were included in the registration statement filed with the SEC.

While the registration statement was being processed by the SEC, but before the effective date, the Internal Revenue Service (IRS) obtained a federal court subpoena directing Marshall and Wyatt to turn over all its working papers relating to Interstate for the years 2001–2004. Marshall and Wyatt initially refused to comply for two reasons. First, Marshall and Wyatt did not prepare Interstate's tax returns. Second, Marshall and Wyatt claimed that the working papers were confidential matters subject to the privileged communications rule. Subsequently, however, Marshall and Wyatt did relinquish the subpoenaed working papers.

Upon receiving the subpoena, Wyatt called Dunkirk, the chairman of Interstate's board of directors, and asked him about the IRS investigation. Dunkirk responded, "I'm sure the IRS people are on a fishing expedition and that they will not find any material deficiencies."

A few days later Dunkirk received a written memorandum from the IRS stating that it was contending Interstate had underpaid its taxes during the period under review. The memorandum revealed that Interstate was being assessed $800,000, including penalties and interest for the three years. Dunkirk forwarded a copy of this memorandum to Marshall and Wyatt. This $800,000 assessment was material relative to the financial statements as of December 31, 2004. The amount for each year individually, exclusive of penalty and interest, was not material relative to each respective year.

Required:

a. In general terms discuss the extent to which a CPA firm's potential liability to third parties is increased in an SEC registration audit.

b. Discuss the implications of the IRS investigation, if any, relative to Marshall and Wyatt's examination of Interstate's 2004 financial statements. Discuss any additional investigative procedures that the auditors should undertake or any audit judgments that should be made as a result of this investigation.

c. Can Marshall and Wyatt validly refuse to surrender the subpoenaed working papers to the IRS? Explain.

(AICPA, adapted)

Suggested References

Part a:
This textbook, pp. 105–106.
Part b:
This textbook, pp. 601–602.
AICPA, Professional Standards, Statements on Auditing Standards, AU section 560.
FASB Statement No. 5, "Accounting for Contingencies."
Part c:
This textbook, pp. 78–79 and 147–148.

Chapter

17

Auditors' Reports

Chapter learning objectives

After studying this chapter, you should be able to:

LO1. Describe the standard audit report for nonpublic entity audits.

LO2. Describe the standard audit report for public company audits.

LO3. Identify the circumstances that result in the addition of explanatory language to the auditors' standard report, and describe the resulting report modification.

LO4. Identify the circumstances that may result in qualified opinions, adverse opinions, and disclaimers of opinion, and describe the resulting report modification.

LO5. Describe the auditors' responsibilities for reporting on comparative financial statements.

Expressing an independent and expert opinion on the fairness of financial statements is the most frequently performed attestation service rendered by the public accounting profession. This opinion, which is expressed in the auditors' report, provides users of financial statements with *reasonable assurance* that the statements are in conformity with generally accepted accounting principles. For users to understand the full implications of the auditors' opinion, it is important for the report to comply with the fourth standard of reporting, which states [emphasis added]:

> The [auditors'] report shall either contain an *expression of opinion* regarding the financial statements, taken as a whole, or an assertion to the effect that an opinion cannot be expressed. When an overall opinion cannot be expressed, the reasons therefor should be stated. In all cases where an auditor's name is associated with financial statements, the report should contain a clear-cut indication of the *character of the auditor's work,* if any, and the *degree of responsibility the auditor is taking.*

In Chapter 2 we saw that the auditors' **standard report** meets this reporting standard by (1) stating that the audit was performed in conformity with generally accepted auditing standards and (2) expressing an opinion that the client's financial statements are presented fairly in conformity with generally accepted accounting principles. However, if there are material deficiencies in the client's financial statements or limitations in the audit, or if there are other unusual conditions about which the readers of the financial statements should be informed, auditors *cannot* issue the standard report. Instead, they must carefully modify their report to make these problems or conditions known to users of the audited financial statements.

In this chapter, we describe the different types of reports that auditors may issue in order to indicate clearly the character of their work and the degree of responsibility they are taking.

Financial Statements

The reporting phase of an audit begins when the independent auditors have completed their fieldwork and have proposed any necessary adjustments to the client. Before drafting their report, the auditors will review the client-prepared financial statements for form and content or draft the financial statements on behalf of the client.

The *basic financial statements* on which the independent auditors customarily report are the balance sheet, the income statement, the statement of retained earnings, and the statement of cash flows. In some cases, the statement of retained earnings is combined with the income statement. In others, the statement of retained earnings is expanded to a statement of stockholders' equity. Financial statements generally are presented in comparative form for the current year and one or more preceding years and include explanatory notes. The financial statements for a parent corporation usually are consolidated with those of the subsidiaries.

Financial Statement Disclosures

To be in conformity with generally accepted accounting principles, the financial statements, including the notes, must disclose all matters that users need in order to interpret them. Just as the footnotes to a textbook are an integral part of that book, the notes to financial statements are an integral part of the financial statements. The purpose of notes to financial statements is to achieve adequate disclosure of information required by generally accepted accounting principles that cannot be adequately conveyed on the face of the financial statements. Although the notes are representations of management, the independent auditors generally assist in their drafting. The writing of notes to financial statements is a challenging task because complex issues must be summarized in a clear and concise manner. Adequate disclosure in the notes to the financial statements is necessary for the auditors to issue an unqualified opinion on the financial statements.

The Financial Accounting Standards Board (FASB), the Government Accounting Standards Board (GASB), the Federal Accounting Standards Advisory Board (FASAB), and the Securities and Exchange Commission (SEC) have issued numerous pronouncements that have added extensive disclosure requirements. Examples of these requirements include the disclosure of significant accounting policies, accounting changes, loss contingencies, and lease and post-retirement benefit information.

In addition to the note disclosures that are part of the basic financial statements, many clients are required by the FASB, the GASB, the FASAB, or the SEC to present *supplementary information.* Such information, while not a required part of the basic financial statements, is required to be presented as unaudited supplementary schedules accompanying the financial statements. As an example, large public companies are required to disclose selected interim financial data with their annual financial statements.

In evaluating financial reporting disclosures, the auditors should keep in mind that disclosures are meant to *supplement* the information on the face of the financial statements—not *correct* improper financial statement presentation. Thus, a note or supplementary schedule, no matter how skillfully drafted, does not compensate for the erroneous presentation of an item in the financial statements.

Comparative Financial Statements

The AICPA has long supported the presentation of comparative financial statements for a series of accounting periods in annual or interim reports to shareholders. Comparative statements show changes and trends in the financial position and operating results of a company over an extended period, and thus are more useful to investors and creditors than are financial statements for a single period. Publicly owned companies are required to include in their annual reports the balance sheets for each of the last two years and the related statements of income, retained earnings, and cash flows for each of the last three years. The auditors' report covers all financial statements that are presented. Throughout this chapter we will illustrate auditors' reports on comparative financial statements, because these are the types of reports that are most often encountered. Later in this chapter we will describe in detail the auditors' reporting responsibilities when management presents comparative financial statements.

The Auditors' Standard Report— Nonpublic Clients

In Chapter 2 we presented a standard audit report on the audit of one year's set of financial statements. The following is a standard report on *comparative financial statements* for two years:

Learning Objective 1

Report of Independent Public Accounting Firm

To the Board of Directors, Willingham Company:

We have audited the accompanying balance sheets of Willingham Company as of December 31, 20X6 and 20X5, and the related statements of operations, stockholders' equity, and cash flows for each of the three years in the period ended December 31, 20X6. These financial statements are the responsibility of the Company's management. Our responsibility is to express an opinion on these financial statements based on our audits.

We conducted our audits in accordance with generally accepted auditing standards (United States). Those standards require that we plan and perform the audit to obtain reasonable assurance about whether the financial statements are free of material misstatement. An audit includes examining, on a test basis, evidence supporting the amounts and disclosures in the financial statements. An audit also includes assessing the accounting principles used and significant estimates made by management, as well as evaluating the overall financial statement presentation. We believe that our audits provide a reasonable basis for our opinion.

In our opinion, the financial statements referred to above present fairly, in all material respects, the financial position of the Company as of December 31, 20X6 and 20X5, and the results of its operations and its cash flows for each of the three years in the period ended December 31, 20X6, in conformity with generally accepted accounting principles (United States).

Williams & Co., LLP

February 5, 20X7

Before continuing, let us mention a few details about this report. It has a title that includes the word *independent,* and it is ordinarily addressed to the person who retained the auditors. In the case of corporations, the audit committee of the board of directors ordinarily nominates the auditors and the stockholders approve that nomination. Therefore, these reports are usually addressed to the board of directors and stockholders of the corporation.

The first paragraph of the auditors' report is referred to as the **introductory paragraph.** It clearly states (1) the financial statements that have been audited, (2) that the financial statements are the responsibility of management, and (3) that the auditors' responsibility is to express an opinion on them. The second paragraph, which describes the nature of an audit, is called the **scope paragraph.** Finally, the **opinion paragraph** presents the auditors' opinion on whether the financial statements are in conformity with accounting principles generally accepted in the United States.

Historically, audit reports referred simply to generally accepted auditing standards and generally accepted accounting principles. Today, however, a number of nations have their own *generally accepted* standards (principles), and those standards usually differ from one another. To reduce confusion, audit reports issued in the United States now use terms such as "generally accepted auditing standards (United States)" or "auditing standards generally accepted in the United States." A similar modification is made relating to generally accepted accounting principles.

Notice that the audit report is signed with the name of the CPA firm, not the name of an individual partner in the firm. This signature stresses that it is the *firm,* not the individual, that takes responsibility for the audit report. If the CPA is practicing under his or her own name as a sole practitioner, the report is signed with the CPA's personal signature. In addition, a sole practitioner should use *I* instead of *we* in the audit report.

Also notice the date under the signature. The auditors' report should not be dated earlier than the date on which the auditors have obtained sufficient competent audit evidence to support their opinion on the financial statements. This date is normally the **last day of fieldwork**—that is, the date upon which the auditors conclude their investigative procedures. The date of the audit report is quite significant because the auditors have a responsibility to perform procedures through that date to search for any subsequent events that may affect the fairness of the client's financial statements (see Chapter 16), and due to requirements relating to changes in documentation that arise after that date (see Chapter 5).

An auditors' report with an unqualified opinion may be issued only when the following two conditions have been met:

1. The financial statements are presented in conformity with *generally accepted accounting principles,* including adequate disclosure.
2. The audit was performed in accordance with generally accepted auditing standards, with no significant *scope limitations* preventing the auditors from gathering the evidence necessary to support their opinion.

When considered material, a departure from either of these conditions results in a situation in which an unqualified opinion *cannot* be issued.

The Auditors' Standard Report—Public Clients

Learning Objective 2

Standard Nos. 1 and 2 of the Public Company Accounting Oversight Board[1] modify the wording of the standard audit report for audits of public companies. The resulting report is at the top of the following page.

There are a number of differences between this PCAOB audit report and the report used for audits of nonpublic companies. The primary differences are that the PCAOB report:

- Includes the word "Registered" in the title.
- References standards of the PCAOB rather than generally accepted auditing standards.

---

[1] Titles of Nos. 1 and 2 are *References in Auditors' Reports to the Standards of the Public Company Accounting Oversight Board* and *An Audit of Internal Control over Financial Reporting Performed in Conjunction with an Audit of Financial Statements,* respectively.

Report of Ernst & Young, LLP
Independent Registered Public Accounting Firm[2]

The Board of Directors and Stockholders, Amazon.com, Inc.:

We have audited the accompanying consolidated balance sheets of Amazon.com, Inc., as of December 31, 2004 and 2003, and the related consolidated statements of operations, stockholders' deficit, and cash flows for each of the three years in the period ended December 31, 2004. These financial statements are the responsibility of the Company's management. Our responsibility is to express an opinion on these financial statements based on our audits.

We conducted our audits in accordance with the standards of the Public Company Accounting Oversight Board (United States). Those standards require that we plan and perform the audit to obtain reasonable assurance about whether the financial statements are free of material misstatement. An audit includes examining, on a test basis, evidence supporting the amounts and disclosures in the financial statements. An audit also includes assessing the accounting principles used and significant estimates made by management, as well as evaluating the overall financial statement presentation. We believe that our audits provide a reasonable basis for our opinion.

In our opinion, the financial statements referred to above present fairly, in all material respects, the consolidated financial position of Amazon.com, Inc., at December 31, 2004 and 2003, and the consolidated results of its operations and its cash flows for each of the three years in the period ended December 31, 2004, in conformity with U.S. generally accepted accounting principles.

We also have audited, in accordance with the standards of the Public Company Accounting Oversight Board (United States), the effectiveness of Amazon.com, Inc.'s internal control over financial reporting as of December 31, 2004, based on criteria established in Internal Control–Integrated Framework issued by the Committee of Sponsoring Organizations of the Treadway Commission and our report dated February 24, 2005, expressed an unqualified opinion thereon.

Ernst & Young, LLP

Seattle, Washington
February 24, 2005

- Includes the city and state—or city and country in the case of non–U.S. auditors—where the auditors' report has been issued. (Historically, auditors have included this information, although it was not required.)
- Includes an additional paragraph indicating that the auditors have also issued a report on the client's internal control over financial reporting. (For a description of internal control over reporting, see Chapters 7 and 18.)

We will now turn our attention to modifications of auditors' standard reports. Although we will illustrate them, where applicable, using audit reports for nonpublic companies, the modifications require little or no changes to be used with the PCAOB audit report.

Expression of an Opinion

The auditors' options when expressing an opinion on financial statements may be summarized as follows:

1. *An unqualified opinion—standard report.* This report expresses a "clean opinion" and may be issued only when the two conditions listed in the preceding section have been met, and when no conditions requiring explanatory language exist.

2. *An unqualified opinion—with explanatory language.* In certain circumstances explanatory language is added to the auditors' report with no effect on the auditors' opinion. Examples of circumstances that require the addition of explanatory language include when the company changes accounting principles, or when there is substantial doubt about a company's ability to continue as a going concern.

---

[2] The actual report by Ernst & Young, LLP, also reported on certain schedules. We have removed the references to these schedules to illustrate the basic audit report.

3. *A qualified opinion.* A qualified opinion states that the financial statements are presented fairly in conformity with generally accepted accounting principles "except for" the effects of some matter. Qualified reports are issued when the financial statements depart materially from generally accepted accounting principles, or when limitations are placed on the scope of the auditors' procedures. The problems, while material, *do not overshadow the overall fairness* of the statements.

4. *An adverse opinion.* An adverse opinion states that the financial statements are *not* presented fairly in conformity with generally accepted accounting principles. Auditors issue an adverse opinion when the deficiencies in the financial statements are *so significant* that the financial statements taken as a whole are misleading. All significant reasons for the issuance of an adverse opinion should be set forth in an explanatory paragraph.

5. *A disclaimer of opinion.* A disclaimer of opinion means that due to a significant scope limitation, the auditors *were unable to form an opinion or did not form an opinion* on the financial statements. A disclaimer is not an opinion; it simply states that the auditor does not express an opinion on the financial statements.

The Unqualified Opinion

Auditors express an **unqualified opinion** on the client's financial statements when they have no material exceptions as to the fairness of the application of accounting principles, and there have been no unresolved restrictions on the scope of their engagement. The unqualified opinion is, of course, the most desirable report from the client's point of view. The client usually will make any necessary adjustments to the statements to enable the auditors to issue this type of opinion.

Learning Objective 3

Explanatory Language Added to the Auditors' Report

Under certain circumstances auditors add **explanatory language** to their audit report, even when issuing an unqualified opinion. Adding the explanatory language *is not regarded as a qualification;* rather, the language merely *draws attention* to a significant situation. Auditors add explanatory language to a report to (1) indicate that a part of the audit was performed by other auditors, (2) point out an uncertainty about the company's ability to continue as a going concern, (3) describe an inconsistency in the application of accounting principles, (4) emphasize a matter, and (5) describe a justified departure from officially recognized accounting principles.

Part of the Audit Performed by Other Auditors

In some audits the principal auditors of a company rely upon another CPA firm to perform a portion of the audit work. The most common situation in which CPAs rely upon the work of other auditors is in the audit of consolidated entities. If certain subsidiaries are audited by other CPA firms, the auditors reporting on the consolidated financial statements will usually decide to rely upon the work of these other CPAs rather than conduct another audit of the subsidiaries.

When more than one CPA firm participates in an engagement, the auditors' report is issued by the **principal auditors**—that is, by the CPA firm that did the majority of the audit work and has an overall understanding of the financial statements. The principal auditors have two basic alternatives in wording their report:

1. *Make no reference to the other auditors.* If the principal auditors *make no reference* in their report to the portions of the engagement performed by other CPAs, the principal auditors *assume full responsibility* for the other auditors' work. This approach is usually followed when the other CPA firm is well known, or when the principal auditors hired the other auditors. When no reference is made, the principal auditors should consider visiting the other auditors, reviewing the other auditors' audit programs and working papers, or performing additional audit procedures. If the principal auditors elect to make no reference, they will issue the standard auditors' report with no additional wording.

2. *Make reference to the other auditors.* Making reference to the work done by other auditors *divides* the responsibility for the engagement *among the participating CPA firms.* This type of report is called a **shared responsibility opinion,** even though it is signed only by the

principal auditors. This type of report is usually issued when the other auditors were engaged by the client, rather than by the principal auditors.

Report of Independent Auditors

To the Shareholders and Board of Directors of the Wellington Company:

We have audited the accompanying consolidated balance sheets of the Wellington Company and its subsidiaries as of December 31, 20X2 and 20X1, and the related consolidated statements of income, retained earnings, and cash flows for each of the three years in the period ended December 31, 20X2. These financial statements are the responsibility of Wellington Company's management. Our responsibility is to express an opinion on these consolidated statements based on our audits. *We did not audit the financial statements as of and for the year ended December 31, 20X2 of Glendo, Inc., which statements reflect total sales constituting 27 percent of total consolidated sales for 20X2. Those statements were audited by other auditors whose reports have been furnished to us, and our opinion, insofar as it relates to data included for Glendo, Inc. for 20X2, is based solely on the report of the other auditors.*

We conducted our audits in accordance with auditing standards generally accepted in the United States of America. Those standards require that we plan and perform the audit to obtain reasonable assurance about whether the financial statements are free of material misstatement. An audit includes examining, on a test basis, evidence supporting the amounts and disclosures in the financial statements. An audit also includes assessing the accounting principles used and significant estimates made by management, as well as evaluating the overall financial statement presentation. We believe that our audits *and the reports of other auditors* provide a reasonable basis for our opinion.

In our opinion, *based on our audits and the reports of other auditors,* the financial statements referred to above present fairly, in all material respects, the financial position of the Wellington Company and subsidiaries at December 31, 20X2 and 20X1, and the consolidated results of their operations and their cash flows for each of the three years in the period ended December 31, 20X2, in conformity with accounting principles generally accepted in the United States of America.

Williams & Co., LLP

Chicago, Illinois
February 5, 2003

A shared responsibility opinion indicates the portion of the engagement performed by the other auditors in terms of dollars or percentages. A typical shared responsibility opinion is illustrated in the accompanying box, with emphasis on the special wording added to the standard report.

The additional wording in the illustration is not a qualification, but rather an indication of the divided responsibility between the auditors who conducted the audits of the various portions of the overall financial statements.[3]

What if the other auditors qualify their report on a particular subsidiary? Are the principal auditors required to qualify the report on the consolidated financial statements? The answer to this question depends on the *materiality* of the matter. The consolidated financial statements will have much larger amounts and totals than those of the subsidiary. Matters that were material to the subsidiary's financial statements may be quite insignificant to the consolidated entity. To determine whether a qualification is in order, the principal auditors must evaluate the materiality of the matter *in relation to the consolidated financial statements.*

Regardless of whether the principal auditors plan to make reference to the work of the other auditors, they should make inquiries concerning the other auditors' *professional reputation and independence.* Inquiries concerning the other auditors' reputation might be made of the AICPA,

---

[3] Another acceptable, although less frequently used, option allows the principal auditor to obtain the permission of the other auditor to explicitly use that auditor's name in the audit report. In such circumstances the other auditor's report must also be presented with the report of the principal auditor.

other practitioners, or bankers. A letter should also be obtained from the other auditors stating that they are aware of the use of their report and that they meet the AICPA's and, for publicly traded clients, the SEC's standards of independence.

Principal auditors are never *forced* to rely on the work of other auditors. Instead, they may insist upon *personally* auditing any aspect of the client's operations. If the client refuses to permit them to do so, the auditors may regard this action as a **scope limitation** and, depending upon materiality, issue a qualified report or a disclaimer of opinion. As a practical matter, opinions are seldom modified for this reason. Satisfactory arrangements as to who will audit the various aspects of a client's business normally will be worked out before the audit begins.

Question about a Company's Going-Concern Status

SAS 59 (AU 341), "The Auditor's Consideration of an Entity's Ability to Continue as a Going Concern," requires that auditors evaluate whether there is substantial doubt about the client's ability to continue as a going concern for a reasonable period of time, which is defined as not to exceed one year beyond the date of the financial statements being audited. Going concern status is a significant issue for users of financial statements, because assets and liabilities are normally recorded and classified on the assumption that the company will continue to operate. Assets, for example, may be presented at amounts that are significantly greater than their liquidation values.

SAS 59 states that although the auditors are *not required to perform procedures specifically designed to test the going-concern assumption,* they must evaluate the assumption in relation to the results of the normal audit procedures. Conditions that may cause the auditors to question the going-concern assumption include negative cash flows from operations, defaults on loan agreements, adverse financial ratios, work stoppages, and legal proceedings. When such conditions or events are identified, the auditors should gather additional information and consider whether management's plans for dealing with the conditions are likely to mitigate the problem. If, after evaluating the information and management's plans, the auditors conclude that the substantial doubt is resolved, they may issue a standard unmodified report. If, on the other hand, substantial doubt still exists about the company's ability to continue as a going concern for a period of one year from the balance sheet date, the auditors should modify their report by adding a final paragraph. KPMG, LLP, included the following fourth paragraph in its audit report issued on Integrated Information Systems, Inc. (emphasis added):

> The accompanying consolidated financial statements have been prepared assuming that the Company will continue as a going concern. As discussed in note 1 to the consolidated financial statements, the Company has suffered negative cash flows from operations and has an accumulated deficit, [conditions] that raise *substantial doubt* about the Company's *ability to continue as a going concern.* Management's plans in regard to these matters are also described in note 1. The consolidated financial statements do not include any adjustments that might result from the outcome of this uncertainty.

Regardless of whether they decide to modify their report, the auditors should consider the adequacy of financial statement disclosures relating to the going-concern matters. Financial statement disclosures include:

- Pertinent conditions and events giving rise to the substantial doubt and their possible effects.
- Management's evaluation of the significance of the conditions and effect and management's plans for dealing with them.
- Possible discontinuance of operations.
- Information about the recoverability or classification of recorded asset amounts and the amounts and classification of liabilities.

When conditions and events indicate that there could be substantial doubt about the entity's ability to continue as a going concern, the auditors should document the conditions and events and significant management plans. In addition, they should document the auditing procedures performed to evaluate management's plans, the conclusion as to whether substantial doubt exists, and their consideration of the adequacy of financial statement disclosures. If those financial statement disclosures are inadequate, a qualified or adverse opinion is appropriate due to the departure from generally accepted accounting principles.

Generally Accepted Accounting Principles Not Consistently Applied

If a client company makes a **change in accounting principle** (including a change in the reporting entity), the nature of, justification for, and effect of the change are reported in a note to the financial statements for the period in which the change is made. The auditors evaluate such a change by determining that (1) the newly adopted principle is generally accepted, (2) the method of accounting for the effect of the change is in conformity with GAAP, and (3) management's justification for the change is reasonable.

When the auditors believe that the new principle is generally accepted, the accounting is proper, and the change is justified, the audit report is modified to *highlight the lack of consistent application of acceptable accounting principles,* but the opinion remains unqualified. A report modified for a change to an acceptable accounting principle includes an additional paragraph following the opinion paragraph, such as the following:

> As discussed in Note 15 to the consolidated financial statements, effective January 1, 2003, the Company changed its method for accounting for asset retirement obligations to conform with Statement of Financial Accounting Standards (SFAS) No.143, "Accounting for Asset Retirement Obligations."

The financial statement note referred to in the above example would describe the nature and justification for the change, as well as the effect on the financial statements.

The above discussion describes reporting in situations in which a material change in principle has occurred and (1) the principle is generally accepted, (2) the accounting is proper, and (3) the change is justified. If any of these three conditions is not met, a departure from generally accepted accounting principles exists. In such a circumstance the auditors should issue either a qualified or an adverse opinion.

Among situations that *do not* result in consistency modification are changes in accounting estimates (e.g., changing the life of a fixed asset) and changes in principles with an immaterial effect (even if expected to be material in the future); absent other circumstances, a standard unqualified opinion may be issued. Finally, because consistency is a between-periods concept, a consistency modification is not appropriate for a company in the first year of its existence.

Emphasis of a Matter

Auditors also may issue an unqualified opinion that departs from the wording of the standard report in order to emphasize a matter *regarding the financial statements.*[4] Auditors add an emphasis paragraph to their unqualified opinion calling attention to matters such as the following:

- Significant related party transactions described in a note to the financial statements.
- The company is a component of a larger business enterprise.
- Unusually important significant events.
- Accounting matters affecting comparability (other than changes in accounting principles) of financial statements with those of the preceding year.
- A risk or uncertainty.

A major assumption underlying the inclusion of an emphasis of a matter paragraph is that the matter is adequately disclosed in the notes to the financial statements. The auditor simply

---

[4] Emphasis of a matter paragraphs are *not used to describe details of the audit* (e.g., neither particular procedures followed during an audit nor a scope restriction would be described through an emphasis of a matter paragraph).

chooses to emphasize it. If the matter is not adequately disclosed, the financial statements contain a departure from GAAP; as described later in the chapter, either a qualified or an adverse opinion is then appropriate. Emphasis of a matter paragraphs are never required and are added solely at the auditor's discretion. The paragraph may either precede or follow the opinion paragraph.

The following is an example of an emphasis of a matter paragraph describing an uncertainty:

> As discussed in Note 19 to the financial statements, Honeywell is a defendant in litigation alleging (1) patent infringement, (2) market monopolization, and (3) interference with the plaintiff's markets and contractual relationships. A federal court jury has returned a verdict against Honeywell on the patent infringement and intentional interference claims in the case in the amount of $1.2 billion; however, the court has yet to rule on significant, complex, and interrelated issues that could alter or eliminate the jury verdict. The ultimate outcome of the litigation cannot presently be determined. Accordingly, no provision for any loss that may result from the resolution of this matter has been made in the accompanying financial statements.

Justified Departures from Officially Recognized Accounting Principles

FASB, GASB, and FASAB *Statements* and *Interpretations* and APB *Opinions* have the status of authoritative body pronouncements. They represent the highest level of generally accepted accounting principles. In unusual circumstances, however, clients may believe that it is appropriate for the financial statements to depart from these pronouncements in order to achieve the more important objective of a fair presentation. When the auditors agree, they may still issue an unqualified report, but they must disclose the departure in an explanatory paragraph, either before or after the opinion paragraph. Such reports are sometimes called "203 reports," because Rule 203 of the AICPA *Code of Professional Conduct* officially recognizes that in unusual circumstances a departure from authoritative accounting principles may be justified. The *Code of Professional Conduct* was discussed in Chapter 3. When the auditors do not agree that the departure is justified, as is discussed in the following section, a qualified or an adverse opinion is appropriate.

Qualified Opinions

A **qualified opinion** expresses the auditors' reservations or uncertainty about fair presentation in some areas of the financial statements. The opinion states that *except for* the effects of some deficiency in the financial statements, or some limitation in the scope of the auditors' examination, *the financial statements are presented fairly.* All qualified reports include a *separate explanatory paragraph* before the opinion paragraph disclosing the reasons for the qualification. The opinion paragraph of a qualified report includes the appropriate qualifying language and a reference to the explanatory paragraph.

Learning Objective 4

Qualified audit reports should be carefully worded to assure that the financial statement users understand that the auditors are qualifying their opinion. If the report includes ambiguous language such as "with the foregoing explanation as to inventories, the accompanying financial statements present fairly . . .," it will be difficult for the users to evaluate the degree of responsibility the auditors are taking. Qualified reports should always include precisely worded qualifying language that includes a phrase such as *except for* or *with the exception of.*

The materiality of the exception governs the use of the qualified opinion. The exception must be sufficiently significant to warrant mentioning in the auditors' report, but it must not be so significant as to necessitate a disclaimer of opinion or an adverse opinion. Consequently, the propriety of a qualified opinion in the event of a significant exception is a matter for careful professional judgment by the auditors.

Departure from Generally Accepted Accounting Principles

The auditors sometimes do not agree with the accounting principles used in preparing the financial statements—that is, they believe that the financial statements depart from GAAP. Auditors must consider the materiality of the effects of any departure from GAAP to determine the appropriate type of audit report. When the effects of the departures are *immaterial,* an unqualified opinion may be issued; when the effects are *material,* the auditors must issue either a qualified opinion or an adverse opinion.

The decision between a qualified opinion and an adverse opinion also is made based on the materiality of the effects of the departure from GAAP. When the effects of the departure are material, but not material enough to make the financial statements misleading, a qualified opinion is appropriate. When the effects of the departure are so material that the *financial statements taken as a whole are misleading,* an adverse opinion is appropriate. Accordingly, the auditors must use professional judgment to determine the effects of the departure on the financial statements, considering:

1. The dollar magnitude of the effects.
2. The significance of the item to the particular client.
3. The number of financial statement accounts and disclosures affected.
4. The effect of the departure on the financial statements taken as a whole.

The distinction between the effects of departures from generally accepted accounting principles that are material but do not overshadow the fairness of the statements and those departures that do overshadow the fairness of the statements is again a matter of professional judgment. In the discussions that follow, it will not be practical to present sufficient detail for readers to make these judgments. Therefore, we will use the term **material** to describe problems sufficient to require qualification of the auditors' report, but which do not overshadow the fairness of the statements. Problems overshadowing the fairness of the statements will be described as *very material* or as causing the statements to be *substantially misleading.*

When the report is qualified, the introductory and scope paragraphs of the standard report are unaffected. The modification involves adding an explanatory paragraph following the scope paragraph and qualifying the opinion paragraph. The **qualifying language** used in the opinion paragraph begins with a phrase such as *except for* or *with the exception of.* The following is an example of the explanatory and opinion paragraphs of an audit report qualified for a departure from generally accepted accounting principles. The introductory and scope paragraphs would contain standard wording.

> The company has excluded from property and debt in the accompanying balance sheets certain lease obligations that, in our opinion, should be capitalized in order to conform with accounting principles generally accepted in the United States. If these lease obligations were capitalized, property would be increased by $15,000,000, long-term debt by $14,500,000, and retained earnings by $500,000 as of December 31, 2006. Additionally, net income would be increased by $500,000 and earnings per share would be increased by $1.22 for the year then ended.
>
> In our opinion, except for the effects of not capitalizing certain lease obligations as discussed in the preceding paragraph, the financial statements referred to above present fairly, in all material respects, the financial position of Wend Company as of December 31, 2006, and the results of its operations and its cash flows for the year then ended in conformity with accounting principles generally accepted in the United States.

The third standard of reporting addresses a particular type of departure from generally accepted accounting principles—inadequate disclosures—and states that:

> Informative disclosures in the financial statements are to be regarded as reasonably adequate unless otherwise stated in the [auditors'] report.

Thus, auditors may need to issue a qualified or adverse opinion if they consider the disclosure in the client's financial statements to be inadequate.

SAS 32 (AU 431), "Adequacy of Disclosure in Financial Statements," requires auditors to include the omitted disclosure in an additional paragraph of their report, if it is practicable to do so. The word *practicable* in this context means that the information can reasonably be obtained and that its inclusion in the report would not cast the auditors in the role of the preparer of the information. For example, the omission by the client of the statement of cash flows from an otherwise complete set of financial statements would not cause the auditors to include the statement in their report, but would result in a qualified opinion.[5]

Ordinarily, a client that is reluctant to make a particular disclosure would rather make the disclosure in a note than have it highlighted in the auditors' report. Therefore, very few auditors' reports actually are qualified because of inadequate disclosure. Instead, the requirements of *SAS 32* usually convince the client to include the necessary disclosure among the notes to the financial statements.

Scope Limitations

Limitations on the scope of an audit arise when the auditors are unable to perform an essential audit procedure. Limitations may be imposed either by circumstances surrounding the audit (for example, the auditors were engaged too late in the year to observe the client's beginning inventory[6]), or by the client (for example, the client refused to allow the auditors to send confirmations to customers).

When a circumstance-imposed scope limitation is involved, the auditors will attempt to perform alternative procedures to gather sufficient competent evidential matter. If such evidential matter is collected and the auditors believe that it is sufficient, an unqualified opinion may be issued. In situations in which alternative procedures do not provide sufficient evidence, the auditors will either qualify the opinion to reflect the scope limitation or disclaim an opinion, depending on the importance of the omitted procedures to the auditors' ability to form an opinion on the financial statements. In assessing the importance of the omitted procedures, the auditors will consider the nature and magnitude of the potential effects of the matters in question, their significance to the financial statements, and the number of items involved.

If the auditors decide that a qualified opinion is appropriate, the report will contain a standard introductory paragraph. The scope paragraph will refer to, and be followed by, an explanatory paragraph that describes the scope limitation, and the opinion paragraph will be modified. The qualifying language and the explanatory paragraph that distinguish the qualified report from the auditors' standard report are shown below.

> *Except as discussed in the following paragraph,* we conducted our audit in accordance with generally accepted auditing standards (United States). Those standards require that we plan and perform the audit to obtain reasonable assurance about whether the financial statements are free of material misstatement. An audit includes examining, on a test basis, evidence supporting the amounts and disclosures in the financial statements. An audit also includes assessing the accounting principles used and significant estimates made by management, as well as evaluating the overall financial statement presentation. We believe that our audit provides a reasonable basis for our opinion.
>
> *We were unable to obtain audited financial statements supporting the Company's investment in a foreign affiliate stated at $20,500,000, or its equity in earnings of that affiliate of $6,250,450, which is included in net income, as described in Note 8 to the financial statements; nor were we able to satisfy ourselves as to the carrying value of the investment in the foreign affiliate or the equity in earnings by other auditing procedures.*
>
> In our opinion, *except for the effects of such adjustments, if any, as might have been determined to be necessary had we been able to examine evidence regarding the foreign affiliate investment and earnings,* the financial statements referred to above present fairly, in all material respects, the financial position of XYZ Company as of December 31, 20XX, and the results of its operations and its cash flows for the year then ended in conformity with accounting principles generally accepted in the United States of America.

[5] In this situation, the professional standards require issuance of a qualified opinion. The basis of the qualification is that when a balance sheet and statement of income are presented, a statement of cash flows is required. However, if only a balance sheet or a statement of income is presented, a statement of cash flows is not required.

[6] Note that even though this may be the "fault" of the client, it is considered a circumstance-imposed limitation because the client is not refusing to allow the auditor to perform a procedure which is possible to perform.

When a circumstance-imposed scope limitation affects a *very material* portion of the financial statements or when the client imposes a significant limitation, a qualified opinion would normally be considered inappropriate, and the auditors should issue a disclaimer of opinion. Disclaimers are discussed in detail later in this chapter.

Adverse Opinions

An **adverse opinion** is the opposite of an unqualified opinion; it is an opinion that states that the financial statements *do not* present fairly the financial position, results of operations, and cash flows of the client, in conformity with generally accepted accounting principles. When the auditors express an adverse opinion, they must have accumulated sufficient evidence to support this unfavorable opinion.

Adverse opinions result from *very material* departures from GAAP. The auditors express an adverse opinion when they believe that the departure causes the financial statements taken as a whole to be misleading. Whenever the auditors issue an adverse opinion, they should disclose in a separate paragraph of their report the reasons for the adverse opinion and the principal effects on the financial statements, if the effects can be determined.

An audit report that expresses an adverse opinion generally includes standard introductory and scope paragraphs, one or more explanatory paragraphs preceding the opinion paragraph and describing the reasons for the adverse opinion, and an opinion paragraph. Because the reasons for an adverse opinion are usually lengthy and complex, we illustrate only the opinion paragraph below.

> In our opinion, *because of the effects of the matters discussed in the preceding paragraph, the financial statements referred to above do not present fairly,* in conformity with accounting principles generally accepted in the United States of America, the financial position of XYZ Company as of December 31, 20X9, or the results of its operations or its cash flows for the year then ended.

Adverse opinions are rare because most clients follow the recommendations of the independent auditors with respect to fair presentation of financial statements. One possible source of adverse opinions is the actions of regulatory agencies that require organizations to use accounting practices that are not in accordance with generally accepted accounting principles.

Disclaimer of Opinion

A **disclaimer of opinion** is *no opinion.* Auditors issue a disclaimer whenever they are unable to form an opinion or have not formed an opinion as to the fairness of presentation of the financial statements. In an audit engagement, a disclaimer is issued when substantial or client-imposed scope restrictions preclude the auditors' compliance with generally accepted auditing standards. In rare circumstances, auditors issue disclaimers of opinion when a material uncertainty affects the financial statements.

Substantial Circumstance-Imposed Scope Restrictions

If a scope restriction is so severe that a qualified opinion is inappropriate, the auditors should issue a disclaimer of opinion. This might happen, for example, if the auditors were engaged after year-end and the client did not take a physical inventory. A disclaimer of opinion issued because of a scope limitation will omit the scope paragraph of the standard report and replace it with an explanatory paragraph describing the scope limitation. The wording of the opinion paragraph will change considerably, because the auditors are *not expressing an opinion*— rather, they are saying that *they have no opinion.* A disclaimer of opinion is illustrated below:

> *We were engaged* to audit the accompanying balance sheet of XYZ Company as of December 31, 20X2, and the related statements of income, retained earnings, and cash flows for the year then ended. These financial statements are the responsibility of the Company's management.
> *The Company did not make a count of its physical inventory, stated in the accompanying financial statements at $3,450,000 as of December 31, 20X2. Further, evidence supporting the cost*

> *of property and equipment acquired prior to December 31, 20X1, is no longer available. The Company's records do not permit the application of other auditing procedures to inventories or property and equipment.*
>
> *Since the Company did not take physical inventories and we were not able to apply other auditing procedures to satisfy ourselves as to inventory quantities and the cost of property and equipment, the scope of our work was not sufficient to enable us to express, and we do not express, an opinion on these financial statements.*

Disclaimers of opinion because of scope restrictions are relatively rare. The auditors should be able to foresee these types of problems in the planning stage of the engagement. The client usually will not want to incur the cost of an audit if it is apparent from the start that the auditors must issue a disclaimer of opinion.

Scope Restrictions Imposed by the Client

The professional standards state that when client-imposed restrictions significantly limit the scope of the audit, the auditor generally should *disclaim an opinion* on the financial statements. Two reasons exist for this requirement. First, a disclaimer is relatively useless to the client. Therefore, the fact that the auditors may have to issue a disclaimer is a substantial deterrent to the client's imposing any scope restrictions in the first place. Second, a client who imposes scope restrictions upon the auditors may have something to hide. An audit must be undertaken with an atmosphere of trust and cooperation. If the client is attempting to conceal information, no audit can ensure that all issues have been brought to light.

Uncertainties

Auditors should disclaim an opinion whenever they are unable to form an opinion on the financial statements. Another time when auditors may consider issuing a disclaimer is when the financial statements are affected by a significant uncertainty that is expected to be resolved at a future date, such as a significant lawsuit against the client. Occasionally, the uncertainty may be so significant to the financial statements that the auditors may not be able to form an overall opinion and, therefore, will issue a disclaimer of opinion.

Focus on the Financial Institution Industry

Because generally accepted accounting principles require extensive disclosure of risks and uncertainties in the notes to the financial statements, *few uncertainties would be expected to result in disclaimers of opinion.* One possible circumstance in which a disclaimer due to uncertainty might be considered appropriate is in the audit of a financial institution whose assets are primarily real estate loans to organizations in a geographical area that is undergoing a very major recession. The recession affects the value of the financial institution's loans both by increasing the debtor default rate and by reducing the value of the underlying collateral, which is primarily real estate in the depressed area. In such a circumstance the auditors might choose to issue a disclaimer due to the inability to make any realistic judgment as to the valuation of the loans.

Notice that this audit does not involve a scope restriction because the auditors are free to perform any and all possible audit procedures. The major uncertainty results in a situation in which the auditors cannot gather sufficient evidence.

Other Disclaimers Issued by CPAs

In this section, we have discussed only those disclaimers of opinion issued in *audit* engagements. CPA firms issue disclaimers of opinion in many other types of engagements; these disclaimers are dealt with in Chapter 19.

Disclaimers Are Not Alternatives to Adverse Opinions

A disclaimer can be issued *only* when the auditors do not have sufficient information to form an opinion on the financial statements. If the auditors have *already formed an opinion that the financial statements are not a fair presentation,* the disclaimer *cannot* be used as a way to avoid expressing an adverse opinion. In fact, even when auditors issue a disclaimer of opinion, they should express in explanatory paragraphs of their report *any and all material reservations* they have concerning the financial statements. These reservations would include any material departures from generally accepted accounting principles, including inadequate disclosure. In short, the issuance of a disclaimer can never be used to avoid warning financial statement users about problems that the auditors know to exist in the financial statements.

Summary of Auditors' Reports

Figure 17.1 summarizes the types of auditors' reports that should be issued under different conditions. The format and the modifying language found in each of the different reports is summarized in Figure 17.2.

Two or More Report Modifications

An audit report may be qualified for two or more situations. For example, the report may be qualified because of both a scope limitation and a separate problem involving a departure from generally accepted accounting principles. The wording of such a report would include the appropriate qualifying language and explanatory paragraphs for both types of qualifications.

When there are several situations requiring the qualification of an opinion, the auditors should consider the cumulative effects of these problems. If the effect of the problems is to overshadow the fairness of the statements viewed as a whole or to prevent the auditors from forming an overall opinion, a qualified opinion would be inappropriate. In such cases, the auditors should issue either an adverse opinion or a disclaimer of opinion, depending upon the circumstances.

When several situations requiring modification of the audit report exist, the explanatory language included in the report will ordinarily refer to each. As an example, consider the audit report for a company in extremely weak financial condition and with financial statements that include a material departure from generally accepted accounting principles. The audit report would be likely to include an explanatory paragraph describing substantial doubt about the ability of the company to continue as a going concern and an explanatory paragraph and opinion modification relating to the departure from generally accepted accounting principles.

Different Opinions on Different Statements

The fourth standard of reporting states that the auditors shall express an opinion on the financial statements "taken as a whole." This phrase may apply to an entire set of financial statements or to an individual financial statement, such as a balance sheet. Thus, it is acceptable for the auditors to express an unqualified opinion on one of the financial statements while expressing a qualified or adverse opinion, or a disclaimer of opinion, on the others.

One circumstance in which this may occur is when the auditors are retained *after* the client has taken its *beginning* inventory. In this case, the auditors can satisfy themselves as to the amounts in the year-end balance sheet, but they may not be able to satisfy themselves as to the statements of income, retained earnings, and cash flows. However, the auditors may be able to perform a useful service by issuing an unqualified opinion on the balance sheet and a disclaimer of opinion on the other financial statements.

Reporting on Comparative Financial Statements

As indicated previously, many companies present with the current year's financial statements comparative financial statements for one or more prior years. When comparative financial statements are presented by the client company, the auditors' report should cover the current year's financial statements as well as those for prior periods that were audited by their firm.

Learning Objective 5

The auditors may express different opinions on the financial statements of different years. In addition, auditors should update their reports for all prior periods presented for comparative purposes. *Updating* the report means either re-expressing the opinion originally issued or, depending upon the circumstances, revising the opinion from that originally issued. A different opinion on the prior-period financial statements may be warranted because new information may have come to light that causes the auditors to alter their original opinion. For example, the client may revise previously issued financial statements to correct a generally accepted accounting principles (GAAP) departure, indicating that a qualified opinion is no longer needed.

If the financial statements of prior comparative periods were unaudited, this fact should be stated on the applicable financial statements and the auditors' report should include a disclaimer of opinion on those financial statements.

FIGURE 17.1 Summary of Appropriate Auditors' Reports

*The auditors may decide to issue a disclaimer in this situation.

FIGURE 17.2 **Report Modifications**

Type of Report	Modifications Required in the Auditors' Report		
	Introductory or Scope Paragraph	Explanatory Paragraph	Opinion Paragraph
Unqualified Reports:			
Shared responsibility opinions	Describe work of other auditors (in introductory and scope paragraphs)	None	". . . based on our audit and the report of the auditors . . ."
Going concern uncertainty*	None	Describe going-concern uncertainty	None
GAAP not consistently applied	None	Describe change in accounting principle	None
Emphasis of a matter	None	Describe matter	None
Justified departure from official GAAP	None	Describe departure	None
Qualified Opinions:			
Exception as to GAAP, including disclosure	None	Describe departure or make disclosure	". . . except for (the problem) the financial statements present fairly . . ."
Scope restriction	"Except as explained in the following paragraph . . ." (in scope paragraph)	Describe scope restriction	". . . except for the effects of such adjustments as might have been determined to be necessary . . . the financial statements present fairly . . ."
Adverse Opinion:			
Very material exception as to GAAP	None	Describe substantial reasons for adverse opinion	". . . the financial statements do not present fairly . . ."
Disclaimer of Opinion:			
Scope restriction (client imposed or very material)	"We were engaged . . ." and omit "Our responsibility . . ." (in introductory paragraph) Omit scope paragraph	Describe scope restriction and any reservations	". . . we do not express an opinion on the financial statements."

*The auditors may decide to issue a disclaimer in this situation.

If prior-period financial statements were audited by another (predecessor) CPA firm, the current auditors' opinion will cover only the year or years that they have audited. For the financial statements audited by the predecessor auditors, there are two reporting options. First, the report of the predecessor auditors may be *reissued* by them bearing its original date. Alternatively, the current auditors may *refer to the report of the other auditors* by indicating in the introductory paragraph of their report (1) that the prior-period statements were audited by other auditors, (2) the date and type of report issued by the other auditors, and (3) if that report was other than standard, the reasons therefor. The current auditors should specifically describe any explanatory language included in the predecessor auditors' report.

An example of the introductory paragraph of a report in which another CPA firm's report on the prior year was qualified but not presented in the current year is illustrated on the next page, with the explanatory language emphasized.

> We have audited the balance sheet of XYZ Company as of December 31, 20X2, and the related statements of income, retained earnings, and cash flows for the year then ended. These financial statements are the responsibility of the Company's management. Our responsibility is to express an opinion based on our audit. *The financial statements of XYZ Company for the year ended December 31, 20X1, were audited by other auditors whose opinion, dated March 1, 20X2, on those statements was qualified as being presented fairly except for the effects on the 20X1 statements of the adjustments pertaining to the valuation of inventory, as discussed in Note X to the financial statements.*

Reports to the SEC

Most publicly owned corporations are subject to the financial reporting requirements of the federal securities laws, administered by the Securities and Exchange Commission (SEC). Many of the reports, or *forms,* filed with the SEC include audited financial statements for one or more years. Among the most important of these forms are the following:

- *Forms S-1 through S-11.* These are the "registration statements" for companies planning to issue securities to the public.
- *Forms SB-1 and SB-2.* These are more simplified registration forms for small businesses.
- *Form 8-K.* This is a "current report" filed for any month in which significant events occur for a company subject to the Securities Exchange Act of 1934. If the significant event is a business combination, audited financial statements of the acquired company often are required in the current report. An 8-K report is also used to notify the SEC of a change in auditors.
- *Form 10-Q.* This form is filed quarterly with the SEC by publicly owned companies. It contains unaudited financial information. The company's auditors perform reviews of this information, but their work is substantially less in scope than an audit.
- *Form 10-K.* This report is filed annually with the SEC by publicly owned companies. The report includes audited financial statements and other detailed financial information. It also includes management and the auditors' reports on internal controls over financial reporting.

Auditors dealing with these reports should be well versed on the requirements of each form, as well as in the provisions of the SEC's Regulation S-X, which governs the form and content of financial statements filed with the various forms.

The SEC, in conjunction with the Public Company Accounting Oversight Board (PCAOB), has the power to enforce a high quality of audit work on financial statements of public companies. The federal securities laws provide both civil and criminal penalties for any person, including auditors, responsible for misrepresentations of fact in audited statements filed with the SEC. The auditors' legal liability under the federal securities acts is discussed in Chapter 4.

Chapter Summary

This chapter explained the different types of reports that auditors issue to indicate the character of their audit and the degree of responsibility they are taking. To summarize:

1. The auditors' report should be viewed as a very carefully structured technical communication. The auditors' standard unqualified report includes an introductory paragraph, clarifying the responsibilities of management and the auditors; a scope paragraph, describing the nature of the audit; and an opinion paragraph, summarizing the auditors' opinion based on the audit. The report has a title that includes the word *independent,* is addressed to the company whose financial statements are being audited or to its board of directors or stockholders, and is signed with the name of the CPA firm.

2. The auditors' options when expressing an opinion are a standard unqualified opinion, an unqualified opinion with explanatory language, a qualified opinion, an adverse opinion, and a disclaimer of opinion. Figure 17.2 provides details on the appropriate modifications required for each of these types of reports.

3. When a client presents comparative financial statements for one or more prior periods with the current-period financial statements, the auditors should make certain that all periods are covered by an audit report. Audit reports on prior periods should be updated based on any new information that might affect the auditors' opinion. When predecessor auditors have audited the prior-period financial

statements, the current auditors may summarize the predecessor auditors' opinion in the current-year audit report, or the client may arrange to have the predecessor auditors reissue their audit report.

4. Auditors of publicly held corporations must understand the various reporting requirements of the SEC. The reports filed with the SEC must be in accordance with Regulation S-X, which governs the form and content of the corporation's financial statements.

Key Terms Introduced or Emphasized in Chapter 17

Adverse opinion   An opinion that the financial statements *do not* fairly present financial position, results of operations, and cash flows, in conformity with generally accepted accounting principles.

Change in accounting principle   Changes in accounting principles and reporting entities result in an explanatory paragraph being added to the auditors' report.

Disclaimer of opinion   A form of report in which the auditors state that they do not express an opinion on the financial statements.

Explanatory language   A paragraph inserted in an auditors' report to explain a matter or to describe the reasons for giving an opinion that is other than unqualified.

Introductory paragraph   The paragraph of the auditors' report in which the auditors indicate that they have audited the financial statements and that the financial statements are the responsibility of management.

Last day of fieldwork   The day upon which the auditors conclude their investigative procedures at the client's offices on a particular audit.

Material   Being of substantial importance. Significant enough to affect evaluations or decisions by users of financial statements. Information that should be disclosed in order for the financial statements to constitute a fair presentation. Determining what is material involves both quantitative and qualitative criteria.

Opinion paragraph   The paragraph of an auditors' report that communicates the degree of responsibility that the auditors are taking for the financial statements.

Principal auditors   Auditors who use the work and reports of other independent CPAs who have audited the financial statements of one or more subsidiaries, branches, or other segments of the principal auditors' client.

Qualified opinion   A modification of the auditors' standard report, employing a clause such as *except for* to limit the auditors' opinion on the financial statements. A qualified opinion indicates that except for the effects of some limitation on the scope of the audit or some departure from generally accepted accounting principles, the financial statements are fairly presented.

Qualifying language   Language inserted in the opinion paragraph, and sometimes in the scope paragraph, to express the auditors' reservations about some aspect of the client's financial statements.

Scope limitation   A restriction that prevents the auditors from being able to apply all of the audit procedures that they consider necessary under the circumstances. Scope limitations may be client imposed or may be imposed by other circumstances.

Scope paragraph   The paragraph of an auditors' report in which the auditors describe the character of their audit.

Shared responsibility opinion   An auditors' report in which the principal auditors decide to share responsibility with other auditors who have audited some segment of the client's business. The sharing of responsibility is done by making reference to the other auditors. Making reference is not, in itself, a qualification of the auditors' report.

Standard report   The "standard wording" of an unqualified auditors' report, not including such modifications as emphasis of a matter, substantial doubt about going-concern status, a change in accounting principle, departures from official GAAP, or a shared responsibility opinion.

Unqualified opinion   An opinion that the financial statements fairly present financial position, results of operations, and cash flows, in conformity with generally accepted accounting principles.

Review Questions

17–1.   Identify the three paragraphs of the standard audit report for a nonpublic company.

17–2.   What is the function of notes to financial statements?

17–3.   What basic conditions must be met before auditors can issue an unqualified auditors' report?

17–4.   Contrast the audit report for nonpublic entities with the audit report for public companies.

17–5.   Identify the basic types of opinions that an auditor may issue and explain when each is appropriate.

17–6.   Howard Green is a partner with Cary, Loeb, & Co. On February 20, Green completed the audit of Baker Manufacturing for the year ended last December 31. It is now March 1, and Green is about to sign the auditors' report. How should Green sign and date the report?

17–7.   Is a shared responsibility opinion a qualified opinion? Explain.

17–8.   Explain three situations in which the wording of an *unqualified* opinion might depart from the auditors' standard report.

17–9.   Wade Corporation has been your audit client for several years. At the beginning of the current year, the company changed its method of inventory valuation from average cost to last in, first out (LIFO). The change, which had been under consideration for some time, was in your opinion a logical and proper step for the company to take. What effect, if any, will this situation have on your audit report for the current year?

17–10.   What is meant by the term *qualifying language* in an auditors' report?

17–11.   Comment on the following: "If the financial statements contain a material departure from generally accepted accounting principles, the auditors may decide to add an explanatory paragraph to the audit report and, given that the information is included in that paragraph, issue an unqualified opinion on the financial statements."

17–12.   The auditors do not believe that certain lease obligations have been reflected in conformity with generally accepted accounting principles in the client's financial statements. What type of opinion should the auditors issue if they decide that the exceptions are immaterial? Material? Very material?

17–13.   Can the client change a set of financial statements to receive an unqualified opinion instead of an opinion qualified as to the adequacy of disclosure? Explain.

17–14.   Only one type of qualified opinion has qualifying language in both the scope paragraph and the opinion paragraph. What is the reason for this type of qualification?

17–15.   The auditors know that the client's accounting for deferred income taxes is not in accordance with generally accepted accounting principles, but because of a very significant scope limitation they have not been able to form an opinion on the financial statements taken as a whole. What type of report should they issue?

17–16.   Why are adverse opinions rare?

17–17.   What type of report should auditors issue when the client has imposed significant scope limitations?

17–18.   Assume that CPAs are attesting to comparative financial statements. Can the CPAs express differing opinions on the financial statements of two successive years?

17–19.   Assume that CPAs are attesting to comparative financial statements. Can the CPAs change their report on the prior year's statements?

17–20.   Describe the reports containing audited financial statements customarily filed by a company subject to the reporting requirements of the SEC.

Questions Requiring Analysis

17–21.   What type of audit report (unqualified opinion, qualified opinion, adverse opinion, disclaimer of opinion) should the auditors generally issue in each of the following situations? Explain.

a. Client-imposed restrictions significantly limit the scope of the auditors' procedures.

b. The auditors decide to make reference to the report of another CPA firm as a basis, in part, for the auditors' opinion.

c. The auditors believe that the financial statements have been presented in conformity with generally accepted accounting principles in all respects, except that a loss contingency that should be disclosed through a note to the financial statements is not included.

17–22.   The following statement is representative of attitudes and opinions sometimes encountered by CPAs in their professional practices: "It is important to read the notes to financial statements, even though they often are presented in technical language and are incomprehensible. The auditors may reduce their exposure to third-party liability by stating something in the notes that contradicts completely what they have presented in the balance sheet or income statement."

Required: Evaluate the above statement and indicate:

a. Areas of agreement with the statement, if any.

b. Areas of misconception, incompleteness, or fallacious reasoning included in the statement, if any.

(AICPA, adapted)

17–23.   Rowe & Myers is the principal auditor of Dunbar Electronics. During the audit, Rowe & Myers engaged Jones & Abbot, a Canadian public accounting firm, to audit Dunbar's wholly owned Canadian subsidiary.

Required: *a.* Must Rowe & Myers make reference to the other auditors in its audit report? Explain.

    b. Assume that Jones & Abbot issued a qualified report on the Canadian subsidiary. Must Rowe & Myers include the same qualification in its report on Dunbar Electronics?

17–24.   Lando Corporation is a domestic company with two wholly owned domestic subsidiaries. Michaels, CPA, has been engaged to audit the financial statements of the parent company and one of the subsidiaries and to act as the principal auditor. Thomas, CPA, has audited the financial statements of the other subsidiary whose operations are material in relation to the consolidated financial statements.

    The work performed by Michaels is sufficient for Michaels to serve as the principal auditor and to report as such on the financial statements. Michaels has not yet decided whether to make reference to the audit made by Thomas.

Required: *a.* There are certain required audit procedures that Michaels should perform with respect to the audit made by Thomas, whether or not Michaels decides to make reference to Thomas in Michaels' auditors' report. What are these audit procedures?

    b. What are the reporting requirements with which Michaels must comply if Michaels decides to make reference to the audit of Thomas?

(AICPA, adapted)

17–25.   While performing your audit of Williams Paper Company, you discover evidence that indicates that Williams may not have the ability to continue as a going concern.

Required: *a.* Discuss the types of information that may indicate a going-concern problem.

    b. Explain the auditors' reporting obligation in such situations.

Multiple Choice Questions

17–26.   Select the best answer for each of the following and explain fully the reason for your selection:

    a. A material departure from generally accepted accounting principles will result in auditor consideration of:

        (1) Whether to issue an adverse opinion rather than a disclaimer of opinion.

        (2) Whether to issue a disclaimer of opinion rather than an "except for" opinion.

        (3) Whether to issue an adverse opinion rather than an "except for" opinion.

        (4) Nothing, because none of these opinions is applicable to this type of exception.

    b. The auditors' report should be dated as of the date the:

        (1) Report is delivered to the client.

        (2) The auditors have accumulated sufficient evidence.

        (3) Fiscal period under audit ends.

        (4) Review of the working papers is completed.

    c. In the report of the principal auditor, reference to the fact that a portion of the audit was made by another auditor is:

        (1) Not to be construed as a qualification, but rather as a division of responsibility between the two CPA firms.

        (2) Not in accordance with generally accepted auditing standards.

        (3) A qualification that lessens the collective responsibility of both CPA firms.

        (4) An example of a dual opinion requiring the signatures of both auditors.

    d. Assume that the opinion paragraph of an auditors' report begins as follows: "With the explanation given in note 6, the financial statements referred to above present fairly. . . ." This is:

        (1) An unqualified opinion.

        (2) A disclaimer of opinion.

        (3) An "except for" opinion.

        (4) An improper type of reporting.

e. The auditor who wishes to indicate that the entity has significant transactions with related parties should disclose this fact in:

(1) An explanatory paragraph to the auditors' report.

(2) An explanatory note to the financial statements.

(3) The body of the financial statements.

(4) The "summary of significant accounting policies" section of the financial statements.

f. When restrictions that significantly limit the scope of the audit are imposed by the client, the auditor should generally issue which of the following opinions?

(1) Qualified.

(2) Disclaimer.

(3) Adverse.

(4) Unqualified.

g. Which of the following does not ordinarily involve addition of an explanatory paragraph to an audit report?

(1) A consistency modification.

(2) A qualified opinion.

(3) Part of the audit performed by other auditors.

(4) An adverse opinion.

h. An audit report for a public client indicates that the audit was performed in accordance with:

(1) Generally accepted auditing standards (United States).

(2) Standards of the Public Company Accounting Oversight Board (United States).

(3) Generally accepted accounting principles (United States).

(4) Generally accepted accounting principles (Public Company Accounting Oversight Board).

i. An audit report for a public client indicates that the financial statements were prepared in conformity with:

(1) Generally accepted auditing standards (United States).

(2) Standards of the Public Company Accounting Oversight Board (United States).

(3) Generally accepted accounting principles (United States).

(4) Generally accepted accounting principles (Public Company Accounting Oversight Board).

j. The likely result of substantial doubt about the ability of the client to continue as a going concern is the issuance of which of the following audit reports?

	Qualified	Unqualified with Explanatory Language
(1)	Yes	Yes
(2)	Yes	No
(3)	No	Yes
(4)	No	No

k. A change in accounting principles that the auditors believes is *not* justified is likely to result in which of the following audit reports?

	Adverse	Disclaimer
(1)	Yes	Yes
(2)	Yes	No
(3)	No	Yes
(4)	No	No

l. Which of the following is *least* likely to be considered as an "emphasis of a matter" in what remains an unqualified audit report?

(1) The company is a component of a larger business enterprise.

(2) An unusually important significant event.

(3) A decision not to confirm accounts receivable.

(4) A risk or uncertainty.

(AICPA, adapted)

Problems

17–27. The auditors' report below was drafted by a staff accountant of Williams & Co., CPAs, at the completion of the audit of the financial statements of Lenz Corporation (a nonpublic company) for the year ended March 31, 20X9. It was submitted to the engagement partner, who reviewed matters thoroughly and properly concluded that Lenz's disclosures concerning its ability to continue as a going concern for a reasonable period of time were adequate.

Independent Auditors' Report

To the Board of Directors of Lenz Corporation:

We have audited the accompanying balance sheet of Lenz Corporation, as of March 31, 20X9, and the related financial statements for the year then ended. Our responsibility is to express an opinion on these financial statements based on our audit.

We conducted our audit in accordance with standards that require that we plan and perform the audit to obtain reasonable assurance about whether the financial statements are in conformity with accounting principles generally accepted in the United States. An audit includes examining, on a test basis, evidence supporting the amounts and disclosures in the financial statements. An audit also includes assessing the accounting principles used and significant estimates made by management.

The accompanying financial statements have been prepared assuming that the Company will continue as a going concern. As discussed in Note X to the financial statements, the Company has suffered recurring losses from operations and has a net capital deficiency that raises substantial doubt about its ability to continue as a going concern. We believe that management's plans in regard to these matters, which are also described in Note X, will permit the Company to continue as a going concern beyond a reasonable period of time. The financial statements do not include any adjustments that might result from the outcome of this uncertainty.

In our opinion, subject to the effect on the financial statements of such adjustments, if any, as might have been required had the outcome of the uncertainty referred to in the preceding paragraph been known, the financial statements referred to above present fairly, in all material respects, the financial position of Lenz Corporation and the results of its operations and its cash flows in conformity with accounting principles generally accepted in the United States applied on a basis consistent with that of the preceding year.

Williams & Co., CPAs
April 28, 20X9

Required: Identify the deficiencies contained in the auditors' report as drafted by the staff accountant. Group the deficiencies by paragraph.

17–28. Sturdy Corporation (a nonpublic company) owns and operates a large office building in a desirable section of New York City's financial center. For many years, the management of Sturdy Corporation has modified the presentation of its financial statements by:

1. Reflecting a write-up to appraisal values in the building accounts.

2. Accounting for depreciation expense on the basis of such valuations.

Wyley, CPA, was asked to audit the financial statements of Sturdy Corporation for the year ended December 31, 20X3. After completing the audit, Wyley concluded that, consistent with prior years, an adverse opinion would have to be expressed because of the materiality of the deviation from the historical-cost principle.

Required: *a.* Describe in detail the appropriate content of the explanatory paragraph of the auditors' report on the financial statements of Sturdy Corporation for the year ended December 31, 20X3. Do not discuss deferred taxes.

          b. Write a draft of the opinion paragraph of the auditors' report on the financial statements of Sturdy Corporation for the year ended December 31, 20X3.

17–29. What type of auditors' report would be issued in each of the following cases? Justify your choice.

          a. Bowles Company is engaged in a hazardous trade and cannot obtain insurance coverage from any source. A material portion of the company's assets could be destroyed by a serious accident.

          b. Draves Company owns substantial properties that have appreciated significantly in value since the date of purchase. The properties were appraised and are reported in the balance sheet at the appraised values with full disclosure. The CPAs believe that the appraised values reported in the balance sheet reasonably estimate the assets' current values.

c. The CPA firm is auditing the financial statements that are to be included in the annual report to the stockholders of Eagle Company, a regulated company. Eagle's financial statements are prepared as prescribed by a regulatory agency of the U.S. government, and some items are not presented in accordance with generally accepted accounting principles. The amounts involved are somewhat material and are adequately disclosed in notes to the financial statements.

d. London Company has material investments in stocks of subsidiary companies. Stocks of the subsidiary companies are not actively traded in the market, and the CPA firm's engagement does not extend to any subsidiary company. The CPA firm is able to determine that all investments are carried at original cost, and the auditors have no reason to suspect that the amounts are not stated fairly.

e. Slade Company has material investments in stocks of subsidiary companies. Stocks of the subsidiary companies are actively traded in the market, but the CPA firm's engagement does not extend to any subsidiary company. Management insists that all investments shall be carried at original costs, and the CPA firm is satisfied that the original costs are accurate. The CPA firm believes that the client will never ultimately realize a substantial portion of the investments, and the client has fully disclosed the facts in notes to the financial statements.

(AICPA, adapted)

17–30.   Roscoe & Jones, CPAs, has completed the audit of the financial statements of Excelsior Corporation as of, and for, the year ended December 31, 20X4. Roscoe also audited and reported on the Excelsior financial statements for the prior year. Roscoe drafted the following report for 20X4.

We have audited the accompanying balance sheet of Excelsior Corporation Inc. as of December 31, 20X4, and the related statements of income and retained earnings for the year then ended. These financial statements are the responsibility of the Company's management. Our responsibility is to express an opinion on these financial statements based on our audit.

We conducted our audit in accordance with auditing standards generally accepted in the United States of America. Those standards require that we plan and perform the audit to obtain reasonable assurance about whether the financial statements are free of material misstatement. An audit includes examining, on a test basis, evidence supporting the amounts and disclosures in the financial statements. An audit also includes assessing the accounting principles used and significant estimates made by management, as well as evaluating the overall financial statement presentation. We believe that our audit provides a reasonable basis for our opinion.

In our opinion, the financial statements referred to above present fairly, in all material respects, the financial position of Excelsior Corporation as of December 31, 20X4, and the results of its operations for the year then ended in conformity with accounting principles generally accepted in the United States of America, applied on a basis consistent with that of the preceding year.

Roscoe & Jones, CPAs
March 15, 20X5

Other Information:

(1) Excelsior is a nonpublic company that presents comparative financial statements.

(2) Excelsior does not wish to present a statement of cash flows for either year.

(3) During 20X4, Excelsior changed its method of accounting for long-term construction contracts and properly reflected the effect of the change in the current year's financial statements and restated the prior year's statements. Roscoe is satisfied with Excelsior's justification for making the change. The change is discussed in Note 12.

(4) Roscoe was unable to perform normal accounts receivable confirmation procedures, but alternate procedures were used to satisfy Roscoe as to the validity of the receivables.

(5) Excelsior Corporation is the defendant in litigation, the outcome of which is highly uncertain. If the case is settled in favor of the plaintiff, Excelsior will be required to pay a substantial amount of cash that might require the sale of certain fixed assets. The litigation and the possible effects have been properly disclosed in Note 11.

(6) Excelsior issued debentures on January 31, 20X3, in the amount of $10 million. The funds obtained from the issuance were used to finance the expansion of plant facilities. The debenture agreement restricts the payment of future cash dividends to earnings after December 31, 20X3. Excelsior declined to disclose this essential data in the notes to the financial statements.

Required: Consider all facts given, and rewrite the auditors' report in an acceptable and complete format, incorporating any necessary departures from the standard report. Do not discuss the draft of Roscoe's report, but identify and explain any items included in *Other Information* that need not be part of the auditors' report.

(AICPA, adapted)

17–31.   Various types of accounting changes can affect the second reporting standard of the generally accepted auditing standards. This standard addresses whether accounting principles have been consistently observed in the current period in relation to the preceding period. Assume that the following list describes changes that have a material effect on a client's financial statements for the current year.

(1) A change from the completed-contract method to the percentage-of-completion method of accounting for long-term construction contracts.

(2) A change in the estimated service lives of previously recorded plant assets based on newly acquired information.

(3) Correction of a mathematical error in inventory pricing made in a prior period.

(4) A change from direct costing to full absorption costing for inventory valuation.

(5) A change from presentation of financial statements of individual companies to presentation of consolidated financial statements.

(6) A change from deferring and amortizing preproduction costs to recording such costs as an expense when incurred because future benefits of the costs have become doubtful. The new accounting method was adopted in recognition of the change in estimated future benefits.

(7) A change to including the employer's share of FICA taxes as "Retirement benefits" on the income statement. This information was previously included with "Other taxes."

(8) A change from the FIFO method of inventory pricing to the LIFO method of inventory pricing.

Required: For each item above, (a) identify the type of change described, (b) state whether any modification is required in the auditors' report as it relates to the second standard of reporting, and (c) state whether the prior year's financial statements should be restated when presented in comparative form with the current year's statements. Organize your answer sheet as follows.

For example, a change from the LIFO method of inventory pricing to the FIFO method of inventory pricing would appear as shown.

Item No.	Type of Change	Should Auditors' Report Be Modified?	Should Prior Year's Statements Be Restated?
Example	An accounting change from one generally accepted accounting principle to another generally accepted accounting principle	Yes	Yes

(AICPA, adapted)

17–32.   Brown & Brown, CPAs, was engaged by the board of directors of Cook Industries, Inc., to audit Cook's calendar year 20X8 financial statements. Cook Industries, Inc. is a nonpublic company. The following report was drafted by an audit assistant at the completion of the engagement. It was submitted to Brown, the engagement partner, for review on March 7, 20X9, the date of the completion of fieldwork. Brown has reviewed matters thoroughly and properly concluded that an adverse opinion was appropriate.

Brown also became aware of a March 14, 20X9, subsequent event which the client has properly disclosed in the notes to the financial statements. Brown wants responsibility for subsequent events to be limited to the specific event referred to in the applicable note to the client's financial statements.

The financial statements of Cook Industries, Inc., for the calendar year 20X7 were audited by predecessor auditors who also expressed an adverse opinion and have not reissued their report. The financial statements for 20X7 and 20X8 are presented in comparative form.

To the President of Cook Industries, Inc.:

We have audited the accompanying balance sheet of Cook Industries, Inc., as of December 31, 20X8, and the related statements of income, retained earnings, and cash flows for the year then ended. These financial statements are the responsibility of the Company's management. Our responsibility is to express an opinion on these financial statements based on our audit. As discussed in Note K to the financial statements, the Company has properly disclosed a subsequent event dated March 14, 20X9.

We conducted our audit in accordance with auditing standards generally accepted in the United States of America. Those standards require that we plan and perform the audit to obtain reasonable assurance about whether the financial statements are free of material misstatement. An audit includes examining, on a test basis, evidence supporting the amounts and disclosures in the financial statements. An audit also includes assessing the accounting principles used and significant estimates made by management, as well as evaluating the overall financial statement presentation. We believe that our audit provides a reasonable basis for our opinion.

In our opinion, except for the matters discussed in the first and the final paragraphs of this report, the financial statements referred to above present fairly, in all material respects, the financial position of Cook Industries, Inc., as of December 31, 20X8, and the results of its operations and its cash flows for the year then ended in conformity with accounting principles generally accepted in the United States of America applied on a basis consistent with that of the preceding year.

As discussed in Note G to the financial statements, the Company carries its property and equipment at appraisal values, and provides depreciation on the basis of such values. Further, the company does not provide for income taxes with respect to differences between financial income and taxable income arising because of the use, for income tax purposes, of the installment method of reporting gross profit from certain types of sales. We believe that these appraisal values are reasonable.

Brown & Brown, CPAs
March 7, 20X9

Required: Identify the deficiencies in the draft of the proposed report. Do *not* redraft the report or discuss corrections.

17–33.   Your client, Quaid Company, requests your assistance in rewriting the note presented below, to make it clearer and more concise.

Note 6. The indenture relating to the long-term debt contains certain provisions regarding the maintenance of working capital, the payment of dividends, and the purchase of the company's capital stock. The most restrictive of these provisions requires that: (*a*) working capital will be maintained at not less than $4,500,000; (*b*) the company cannot pay cash dividends or purchase its capital stock, if after it has done so, working capital is less than $5,000,000; and (*c*) cash dividends paid since January 1, 20X0, plus the excess of capital stock purchased over the proceeds of stock sold during the same period, cannot exceed 70 percent of net earnings (since January 1, 20X0) plus $250,000. At December 31, 20X1, $2,441,291 of retained earnings were available for the payment of dividends under this last provision, as follows:

Net earnings since January 1, 20X0	$5,478,127
70 percent of above	$3,834,688
Additional amount available under indenture	250,000
	$4,084,688
Cash dividends paid since January 1, 20X0	1,643,397
Retained earnings available December 31, 20X1	$2,441,291

Required: Rewrite the note in accordance with your client's instructions.

17–34.   On September 31, 20X1, White & Co., CPAs, was engaged to audit the consolidated financial statements of National Motors, Inc., for the year ended December 31, 20X1. National is a nonpublic company, and the prior year consolidated financial statements of National had not been audited. National's inadequate inventory records precluded White from forming an opinion as to the proper or consistent application of generally accepted accounting principles to inventory balances on January 1, 20X1. Therefore, White decided not to express an opinion on the results of operations for the year ended December 31, 20X1. National decided not to present comparative financial statements.

Rapid Parts Company, a consolidated subsidiary of National, was audited for the year ended December 31, 20X1, by Green & Co., CPAs. Green completed its fieldwork on February 28, 20X2, and submitted an unqualified opinion on Rapid's financial statements on March 7, 20X2. Rapid's statements reflect total assets and revenues of $7 million and $8 million, respectively, of the consolidated totals of National. White decided not to assume responsibility for the work of Green. Green's report on Rapid does not accompany National's consolidated statements.

White completed its fieldwork on March 28, 20X2, and submitted its auditors' report to National on April 4, 20X2.

Required: Prepare White & Company's auditors' report on the consolidated financial statements of National Motors, Inc.

17–35.   *Items 1 through 6* present various independent factual situations an auditor might encounter in conducting an audit.

Assume:
- The auditor is independent.
- The auditor previously expressed an unqualified opinion on the prior year's financial statements.
- Only single-year (not comparative) statements are presented for the current year.
- The conditions for an unqualified opinion exist unless contradicted in the factual situations.
- The conditions stated in the factual situations are material.
- No report modifications are to be made except in response to the factual situation.

Situations:
1. In auditing the long-term investments account, an auditor is unable to obtain audited financial statements for an investee located in a foreign country. The auditor concludes that sufficient competent evidential matter regarding this investment cannot be obtained.

2. Due to recurring operating losses and working capital deficiencies, an auditor has substantial doubt about an entity's ability to continue as a going concern for a reasonable period of time. However, the financial statement disclosures concerning these matters are adequate.

3. A principal auditor decides to take responsibility for the work of another CPA who audited a wholly owned subsidiary of the entity and issued an unqualified opinion. The total assets and revenues of the subsidiary represent 17 percent and 18 percent, respectively, of the total assets and revenues of the entity being audited.

4. An entity issues financial statements that present financial position and results of operations but omits the related statement of cash flows. Management discloses in the notes to the financial statements that it does not believe the statement of cash flows to be a useful financial statement.

5. An entity changes its depreciation method for production equipment from straight-line to a units-of-production method based on hours of utilization. The auditor concurs with the change, although it has a material effect on the comparability of the entity's financial statements.

6. An entity discloses certain lease obligations in the notes to the financial statements. The auditor believes that the failure to capitalize these leases is a departure from generally accepted accounting principles.

Required: List A represents the types of opinions the auditor ordinarily would issue and List B represents the report modifications (if any) that would be necessary. Select as the best answer for each situation (items 1 through 6) the type of opinion and modifications, if any, the auditor would normally select. The types of opinions in List A and the report modifications in List B may be selected once, more than once, or not at all.

(AICPA, adapted)

List A	List B
Types of Opinions	**Report Modifications**
A. An "except for" qualified opinion B. An unqualified opinion C. An adverse opinion D. A disclaimer of opinion E. Either an "except for" qualified opinion or an adverse opinion F. Either a disclaimer of opinion or an "except for" qualified opinion G. Either an adverse opinion or a disclaimer of opinion	H. Describe the circumstances in an explanatory paragraph preceding the opinion paragraph without modifying the three standard paragraphs. I. Describe the circumstances in an explanatory paragraph following the opinion paragraph without modifying the three standard paragraphs. J. Describe the circumstances in an explanatory paragraph preceding the opinion paragraph, and modify the opinion paragraph. K. Describe the circumstances in an explanatory paragraph following the opinion paragraph, and modify the opinion paragraph. L. Describe the circumstances in an explanatory paragraph preceding the opinion paragraph, and modify the scope and opinion paragraphs. M. Describe the circumstances in an explanatory paragraph following the opinion paragraph, and modify the scope and opinion paragraphs. N. Describe the circumstances within the scope paragraph without adding an explanatory paragraph. O. Describe the circumstances within the opinion paragraph without adding an explanatory paragraph. P. Describe the circumstances within the scope and opinion paragraphs without adding an explanatory paragraph. Q. Issue the standard auditors' report without modification.

17–36.   Johnson & Barkley, CPAs, audited the consolidated financial statements of Jordan Company (a nonpublic company) for the year ended December 31, 20X7, and expressed an adverse opinion because Jordan carried its plant and equipment at appraisal values and provided for depreciation on the basis of such values.

Johnson & Barkley also audited Jordan's financial statements for the year ended December 31, 20X8. These consolidated financial statements are being presented on a comparative basis with those of the prior year, and an unqualified opinion is being expressed.

Smith, the engagement supervisor, instructed Abler, an assistant on the engagement, to draft the auditors' report on May 3, 20X9, the date of completion of the fieldwork. In drafting the report below, Abler considered the following:

- Jordan recently changed its method of accounting for plant and equipment and restated its 20X7 financial statements to conform with GAAP. Consequently, the CPA firm's present opinion on those statements is different (unqualified) from the opinion expressed on May 12, 20X8.

- Larkin & Lake, CPAs, audited the financial statements of BX, Inc., a consolidated subsidiary of Jordan, for the year ended December 31, 20X8. The subsidiary's financial statements reflected total assets and revenues of 2 percent and 3 percent, respectively, of the consolidated totals. Larkin & Lake expressed an unqualified opinion and furnished Johnson & Barkley with a copy of the auditors' report. Johnson & Barkley has decided to assume responsibility for the work of Larkin & Lake insofar as it relates to the expression of an opinion on the consolidated financial statements taken as a whole.

- Jordan is a defendant in a lawsuit alleging patent infringement. This is adequately disclosed in the notes to Jordan's financial statements, but no provision for liability has been recorded because the ultimate outcome of the litigation cannot presently be determined.

Auditors' Report

We have audited the accompanying consolidated balance sheets of Jordan Company and subsidiaries as of December 31, 20X8 and 20X7, and the related consolidated statements of income, retained earnings, and cash flows for the years then ended. These financial statements are the responsibility of the Company's management. Our responsibility is to express an opinion on these financial statements based on our audits.

We conducted our audits in accordance with auditing standards generally accepted in the United States. Those standards require that we plan and perform the audit to obtain reasonable assurance about whether the financial statements are free of material misstatement. An audit includes examining, on a test basis, evidence supporting the amounts and disclosures in the financial statements. An audit also includes assessing the accounting principles used, as well as evaluating the overall financial statement preparation. We believe that our audits provide a reasonable basis for our opinion.

In our previous report, we expressed an opinion that the 20X7 financial statements did not fairly present financial position, results of operations, and cash flows in conformity with accounting principles generally accepted in the United States because the Company carried its plant and equipment at appraisal values and provided for depreciation on the basis of such values. As described in Note 12, the Company has changed its method of accounting for these items and restated its 20X7 financial statements to conform with accounting principles generally accepted in the United States. Accordingly, our present opinion on the 20X7 financial statements, as presented herein, is different from that expressed in our previous report.

The consolidated financial statements referred to above present fairly, in all material respects, the financial position of Jordan Company and subsidiaries as of December 31, 20X8 and 20X7, and the results of its operations and its cash flows for the years then ended in conformity with accounting principles generally accepted in the United States except for the change in accounting principles with which we concur.

The company is a defendant in a lawsuit alleging infringement of certain patent rights, the Company has filed a counteraction, and preliminary hearings and discovery proceedings are in progress. The ultimate outcome of the litigation cannot presently be determined. Accordingly, no provision for any liability that may result upon adjudication has been made in the accompanying financial statements.

Johnson & Barkley, CPAs
May 3, 20X9

Required:

Smith reviewed Abler's draft and stated in the *Supervisor's Review Notes* below that there were deficiencies in Abler's draft. Items 1 through 15 represent the deficiencies noted by Smith. For each deficiency, indicate whether Smith is correct or incorrect in the criticism of Abler's draft.

Supervisor's review notes:

1. The report is improperly titled.
2. All the basic financial statements are not properly identified in the introductory paragraph.
3. There is no reference to the American Institute of Certified Public Accountants in the introductory paragraph.
4. Larkin & Lake are not identified in the introductory and opinion paragraphs.
5. The subsidiary, BX, Inc., is not identified and the magnitude of BX's financial statements is not disclosed in the introductory paragraph.
6. The report does not state in the scope paragraph that generally accepted auditing standards require analytical procedures to be performed in planning an audit.
7. The report does not state in the scope paragraph that an audit includes assessing internal control.
8. The report does not state in the scope paragraph that an audit includes assessing significant estimates made by management.
9. The date of the previous report (May 12, 20X8) is not disclosed in the first explanatory paragraph.
10. It is inappropriate to disclose in the first explanatory paragraph the circumstances that caused Johnson & Barkley to express a different opinion on the 20X7 financial statements.

11. The fourth paragraph should begin with "In our opinion."

12. The concurrence with the accounting change is inappropriate in the opinion paragraph.

13. Uncertainties may no longer be mentioned in explanatory paragraphs and that paragraph must be deleted.

14. The letter of inquiry to Jordan's lawyer concerning litigation, claims, and assessments is not referred to in the second explanatory paragraph.

15. The report is not dual-dated, but it should be because of the change of opinion on the 20X7 financial statements.

In-Class Team Cases

17–37. For each of the following brief scenarios, assume that you are the CPA reporting on the client's financial statements. Reply as to the reporting circumstance involved, the type or types of opinion possible in the circumstance, and the appropriate report modifications. Since more than one report may be possible in several of the circumstances, a second "type of opinion" and "report modification" row is added for each circumstance. In most cases you will not need to use the second row. Do not read more into the circumstance than what is presented, and only reply "emphasis of a matter" in circumstances such as those suggested in the chapter. Unless stated otherwise, assume that the information presented is material to the financial statements.

Circumstance	Types of Opinion	Report Modifications and Paragraph(s) Modified
Consistency Emphasis of a matter Going concern Justified departure from GAAP Other auditors Scope limitation Unjustified departure from GAAP None	S. Standard unqualified U. Unqualified Q. Qualified D. Disclaimer A. Adverse	I. Introductory paragraph S. Scope paragraph O. Opinion paragraph E. Explanatory paragraph added N. No paragraphs added or modified

Scenarios:

1. A client has departed from GAAP for what you consider to be justified reasons, as following GAAP would result in misleading financial statements.

2. A client's financial statements follow GAAP, but you wish to emphasize a significant related party transaction in the audit report.

3. In auditing the long-term investments account of a new client, you are unable to obtain audited financial statements for the investee located in a foreign country. You conclude that sufficient competent evidential matter regarding this investment cannot be obtained.

4. Due to a very major lawsuit, you have substantial doubt about a client's ability to continue as a going concern for a reasonable period of time. The financial statement disclosures related to this lawsuit are adequate and you have decided *not* to issue a disclaimer of opinion.

5. You decide not to take responsibility for the work of another CPA who audited a 70 percent owned subsidiary and issued an unqualified opinion. The total assets and revenues of the subsidiary are 5 percent and 8 percent, respectively, of the total assets and revenues of the entity being audited.

6. A company has changed the remaining life of a significant asset from 12 to 10 years. You believe that the change is reasonable.

7. A company changes from FIFO to LIFO for inventory valuation and you concur with the change. The change has an immaterial effect on the comparability of the entity's financial statements this year, but it is expected to have a material effect in the future.

8. Your client is a defendant in a major lawsuit. It is probable that the company will lose a material amount due to this lawsuit, although it is impossible to calculate the likely amount. The financial statements include a note adequately describing the matter. You decide that a standard report is inappropriate.

9. Your client has declined to depreciate its assets this year since the depreciation expense would reduce the year's small income to a loss.

10. You decide to take responsibility for the work of another CPA who audited a 70 percent owned subsidiary and issued an unqualified opinion. The total assets and revenues of the subsidiary are 5 percent and 8 percent, respectively, of the total assets and revenues of the entity being audited.

	Circumstance	Type(s) of Opinion	Report Modifications and Paragraph(s) Modified
1			
2			
3			
4			
5			
6			
7			
8			
9			
10			

17–38. For each of the following brief scenarios assume that you are reporting on a client's financial statements. Reply as to the type or types of opinion possible in the circumstance:

S. Standard unqualified

U. Unqualified with explanatory language

Q. Qualified

D. Disclaimer

A. Adverse

Since more than one report may be possible in several of the circumstances, a second "type of opinion" column is added for each circumstance. In certain cases you will not need to use the second column. Do not read more into the circumstance than what is presented, and do not consider the possibility of an "emphasis of a matter" paragraph being added to the audit report. Unless stated otherwise, assume that the information presented is material to the financial statements.

Situation	Opinion	Opinion
1. A company in its first year of existence is valuing inventory at current replacement cost. While you believe that the inventory costs do approximate replacement costs, these costs do not approximate any GAAP inventory valuation method.		
2. Due to recurring operating losses and working capital deficiencies, you have substantial doubt about an entity's ability to continue as a going concern for a reasonable period of time. The notes to the financial statements adequately disclose the substantial doubt situation.		
3. You have discovered that a client has made illegal political payoffs to a candidate for president of the United States. You are unable to determine the amounts associated with the payoffs because of the client's inadequate record retention policies. The client has added a note to the financial statements to describe this, and has stated that the amounts of the payments are not determinable.		
4. In auditing the long-term investments account of a new client, you find that a large contingent liability exists that is material to the consolidated company. It is probable that this contingent liability will be resolved with a material loss in the future, and this amount is reasonably estimable as $2 million. Although no adjusting entry has been made, the client has provided a note to the financial statements that describes the matter in detail and includes the $2 million estimate in that note.		
5. A client is issuing two years of comparative financial statements. The first year was audited by another auditor who is *not* being asked to reissue her audit report. (Reply as to your report on the second year.)		
6. An entity changes its depreciation method for production equipment from straight-line to a units-of-production method based on hours of utilization. You concur with the change.		
7. A client has changed from the method it uses to calculate post-employment benefits from one acceptable method to another one. The effect of the change is immaterial this year, but it is expected to be material in the future.		
8. A client has departed from GAAP because both the client and you believe that because of relatively unique circumstances, following GAAP would lead to misleading results.		

Research and Discussion Case

17–39. Your firm audits Metropolitan Power Supply (MPS). The issue under consideration is the treatment in the company's financial statements of $700 million in capitalized construction costs relating to Eagle Mountain, a partially completed nuclear power plant.

Seven years ago, MPS began construction of Eagle Mountain, with an original cost estimate of $400 million and completion expected within five years. Cost overruns were enormous, and construction has been repeatedly delayed by litigation initiated by the antinuclear lobby. At present, the project is little more than 50 percent complete, and construction has been halted because MPS does not have the funds to continue.

If Eagle Mountain is ultimately completed, the state utilities commission will determine the extent to which MPS may recover its construction costs through its rate structure. The commission's rulings are difficult to predict, but it is quite possible that the commission will not allow MPS to include all of the Eagle Mountain construction costs in its "rate base." If Eagle Mountain were abandoned today, none of the construction costs would be recoverable. The related write-off would amount to over 70 percent of MPS's stockholders' equity, but the company would survive.

MPS's management, however, remains committed to the completion of the Eagle Mountain facility. Management has obtained authorization from the company's stockholders to issue $500 million in bonds and additional shares of common stock to finance completion of the project. If MPS incurs this additional debt and is still not able to make Eagle Mountain fully operational, it is doubtful that the company can avoid bankruptcy. In short, management has elected to gamble—all its chips are riding on Eagle Mountain.

Required:

a. Discuss the arguments for and against the auditors insisting that MPS begin expensing some portion of the construction costs rather than continuing to accumulate an ever-increasing asset. Indicate the position you would take as the auditor.

b. Discuss whether the auditors should modify their report because of uncertainty as to whether or not MPS can remain a going concern. Indicate the type of opinion that you would issue. (You need not limit yourself to a "going-concern" modification.)

Suggested References

Part a:
FASB Statement No. 144, "Accounting for the Impairment or Disposal of Long-Lived Assets."
FASB Statement No. 5, "Accounting for Contingencies," paragraph 31.

Part b:
Statement on Auditing Standards No. 59, "The Auditor's Consideration of an Entity's Ability to Continue as a Going Concern" (New York, 1988), AU 341.
Statement on Auditing Standards No. 58, "The Auditor's Standard Report" (New York, 1988), AU 508.

Integrated Audits of Public Companies

Chapter learning objectives

After studying this chapter, you should be able to:

LO1. Describe the nature of an integrated audit.

LO2. Discuss management's responsibility for reporting on internal control as required by the Sarbanes-Oxley Act of 2002.

LO3. Describe the auditors' responsibility for reporting on internal control through integrated audits as required by the Public Company Accounting Oversight Board.

LO4. Present the auditors' approach to analyzing internal control when performing an integrated audit.

LO5. Explain how findings relating to the audits of internal control and the financial statements may affect one another.

LO6. Discuss circumstances that require auditors to modify their report on internal control.

Learning Objective 1

In this chapter we provide information on **integrated audits** based on the provisions of Public Company Accounting Oversight Board (PCAOB) *Standard No. 2*, "An Audit of Internal Control over Financial Reporting Performed in Conjunction with an Audit of Financial Statements." Throughout this chapter, our emphasis is on presenting (1) details on audits of internal control over financial reporting and (2) information on how financial statement audits are modified when the auditors perform an integrated audit. Although we have referred to integrated audits earlier in the text, in this chapter we emphasize in detail the nature of a public company audit. While an integrated audit involves an enhanced consideration of internal control, the financial statement audit's various planning, evidence gathering, and reporting procedures remain largely unchanged. Accordingly, the focus of this chapter is on audits of internal control over financial reporting (hereafter, internal control).

Overview

Section 404 of the Sarbanes-Oxley Act of 2002 emphasizes that investors must have confidence not only in the financial statements issued by a company, but also in the underlying processes and controls that are relied upon to produce those statements. Consistently, PCAOB *Standard No. 2* recognizes this relationship and states that the internal control and financial statement audits should be viewed as integrated.

Section 404 is composed of two distinct sections.[1] Section 404(a) requires that each annual report filed with the Securities and Exchange Commission include an internal control report prepared by management in which management (1) acknowledges its responsibility for establishing and maintaining adequate internal control and (2) provides an assessment of internal control effectiveness as of the end of the most recent fiscal year. Section 404(b) requires the CPA firm to audit internal control and then report on the assessment made by management and express an opinion on the effectiveness of internal control. While the emphasis of this chapter is on the auditors' responsibility under Section 404(b), we will begin with an overview of management's responsibility.

Management's Responsibility for Internal Control

Learning Objective 2

Management has always been responsible for maintaining effective internal control. However, the **Sarbanes-Oxley Act of 2002** increases management's responsibility for demonstrating that controls are effective. As operationalized by the Securities and Exchange Commission (SEC), management is required to:

- Accept responsibility for the effectiveness of internal control.
- Evaluate the effectiveness of internal control using suitable control criteria.
- Support the evaluation with sufficient evidence.
- Provide a report on internal control.

Management's report and the auditors' opinion must be included in Form 10-K, the annual report filed with the SEC. The Sarbanes-Oxley Act requires management to perform the above steps in a meaningful manner. Indeed, if the auditors conclude that management has not

---

[1] While we emphasize Section 404 in this chapter, we also incorporate information from Section 103, which requires auditor reporting on internal control. In addition, other sections of the Sarbanes-Oxley Act are also relevant to the overall area of audits of financial statements. Section 302 requires each of a company's principal executives and financial officers to certify the financial and other information contained in the company's quarterly and annual reports. These certifications must indicate that, based on the officer's knowledge, the financial statements and other financial information included in the report fairly present, in all material respects, the financial condition and results of operations of the company as of, and for, the period presented in the report. Section 906 includes a similar certification requirement but amends the Federal Criminal Code and explicitly sets forth possible criminal penalties for certifications that do not comply with the requirements.

effectively fulfilled its responsibilities, they prepare a written communication to management and the audit committee in which they indicate that the audit of internal control cannot be completed and that a disclaimer of opinion will be issued.

While the exact wording of management's report on internal control is left to management's discretion, Section 404(a) of the Sarbanes-Oxley Act requires the report to:

- State that it is management's responsibility to establish and maintain adequate internal control.
- Identify management's framework for evaluating internal control.
- Include management's assessment of the effectiveness of the company's internal control over financial reporting as of the end of the most recent fiscal period, including a statement as to whether internal control over financial reporting is effective.
- Include a statement that the company's auditors have issued an attestation report on management's assessment.

Management's Assessment and Evaluation Process

For most SEC registrants, passage of Sarbanes-Oxley has resulted in a one-time major project of assessing, evaluating, and improving internal control to increase the likelihood that both management and the auditors will be able to conclude that the company's internal control is effective. The project is performed either by the company itself or by the company assisted by consultants—often personnel from a CPA firm that does not audit the company's financial statements. Subsequently, each year, results of the evaluation are updated.

What must be included in management's assessment process? *Standard No. 2* requires the auditors to determine whether management has considered controls such as the following:

- Controls over initiating, authorizing, recording, processing, and reporting significant accounts and disclosures and related assertions.
- Controls over the selection and application of accounting policies that are in conformity with generally accepted accounting principles.
- Antifraud programs and controls.
- Controls over significant nonroutine and nonsystematic transactions, such as accounts involving judgments and estimates.
- Company-level controls such as the control environment and controls over the period-end financial reporting process.

Management's process is one of identifying the controls and testing their design and operating effectiveness.

The company's external auditing firm may provide only very limited assistance to management to avoid a situation in which its assessment is in essence part of management's assessment, as well as its own. That is, the CPA firm performing the audit should not create a situation in which management relies in any way on the CPA firm's assessment in making its own assessment.

Figure 18.1 provides one way to consider management's responsibility relating to its assessment process and evaluation of internal control. As a starting point, the Securities and Exchange Commission, which provides operational guidance for implementing the Sarbanes-Oxley requirements, has adopted the following definition for internal control:

> Internal control over financial reporting is a process designed by, or under the supervision of, the company's principal executive and principal financial officers, or persons performing similar functions, and effected by the company's board of directors, management, and other personnel, to provide reasonable assurance regarding the reliability of financial reporting and the preparation of financial statements for external purposes in accordance with generally accepted accounting principles and includes those policies and procedures that:
>
> 1. Pertain to the maintenance of records that, in reasonable detail, accurately and fairly reflect the transactions and dispositions of the assets of the company;

2. Provide reasonable assurance that transactions are recorded as necessary to permit preparation of financial statements in accordance with generally accepted accounting principles, and that receipts and expenditures of the company are being made only in accordance with authorizations of management and directors of the company; and

3. Provide reasonable assurance regarding prevention or timely detection of unauthorized acquisition, use, or disposition of the company's assets that could have a material effect on the financial statements.

FIGURE 18.1
Management's Assessment Process and Evaluation of Internal Control

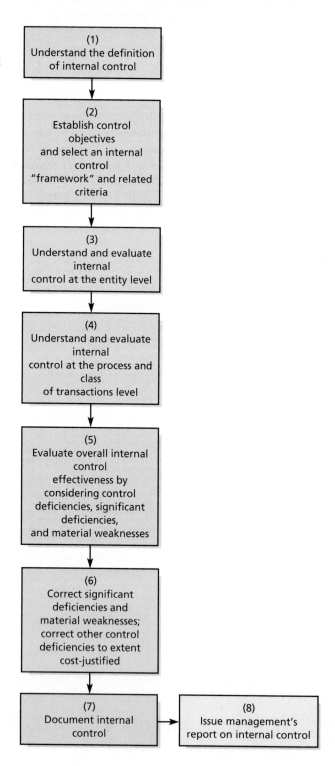

(1)
Understand the definition of internal control

(2)
Establish control objectives and select an internal control "framework" and related criteria

(3)
Understand and evaluate internal control at the entity level

(4)
Understand and evaluate internal control at the process and class of transactions level

(5)
Evaluate overall internal control effectiveness by considering control deficiencies, significant deficiencies, and material weaknesses

(6)
Correct significant deficiencies and material weaknesses; correct other control deficiencies to extent cost-justified

(7)
Document internal control

(8)
Issue management's report on internal control

Illustrative Case
Definitions of Terms

The definitions of *significant deficiencies* and *material weaknesses* include subjective terms relating to likelihoods and amounts. PricewaterhouseCoopers provided its staff with guidance suggesting that a 5–10 percent likelihood of occurrence should be considered *more than remote*, and that 4–5 percent of income is a *material amount*. A group of nine CPA firms (including the Big 4) arrived at a consensus that, for purposes of *Standard No. 2* reporting, 20 percent of overall annual or interim financial statement materiality would represent *more than an inconsequential misstatement*. See Chapter 6 of this text for more information on materiality.

Management's report must be based on the preceding definition of internal control and must result from an evaluation using an accepted "control framework." Although not required, the control framework ordinarily used is the *Internal Control–Integrated Framework,* created by the Committee of Sponsoring Organizations of the Treadway Commission (COSO). The COSO framework, discussed in detail in Chapter 7, is the internal control framework commonly used in audits of financial statements.

To evaluate internal control, steps (3) through (5) of Figure 18.1, management must understand the concepts of control deficiency, significant deficiency, and material weakness—concepts originally presented in Chapter 7 of this text. A **control deficiency** exists when the design or operation of a control does not allow management or employees, in the normal course of performing their functions, to prevent or detect misstatements on a timely basis.

A **significant deficiency** is a control deficiency (or a combination of control deficiencies) that adversely affects the company's ability to initiate, authorize, record, process, or report external financial data reliably in accordance with generally accepted accounting principles, such that there is *more than a remote likelihood* that a misstatement of the company's annual or interim financial statements (that is more than inconsequential) will not be prevented or detected.

A **material weakness** is a significant deficiency, or combination of significant deficiencies, that results in *more than a remote likelihood* that a material misstatement of the annual or interim financial statements will not be prevented or detected. Figure 18.2 compares the likelihood of occurrence and the potential amount of misstatement involved in the definitions of control deficiencies, significant deficiencies, and material weaknesses.

Figure 18.3 illustrates the relationships among control deficiencies, significant deficiencies, and material weaknesses. As the figure illustrates, all material weaknesses are significant deficiencies, but not all significant deficiencies are material weaknesses.

In evaluating the significance of identified deficiencies, both quantitative and qualitative factors are considered. Quantitative factors address the potential amount of loss. Qualitative factors include consideration of the nature of the accounts and assertions involved and the

FIGURE 18.2
Comparison of Control Deficiency, Significant Deficiency, and Material Weakness Definitions

	Likelihood	Potential Size of Misstatement
Control Deficiency	Likelihood not a consideration. Design or operation of control does not allow prevention or timely detection of misstatements.	Any misstatement (immaterial or material).
Significant Deficiency	More than remote.	More than inconsequential misstatement.
Material Weakness	More than remote.	Material misstatement.

FIGURE 18.3
Relationships among
Control Deficiencies,
Significant Deficiencies,
and Material Weaknesses

possible future consequences of the deficiency. Chapters 6 and 16 of this text include discussions of qualitative factors affecting materiality judgments.

Additionally, the consideration of a control deficiency should also include analysis of whether a **compensating control** exists to either prevent or detect the possible misstatement. For example, assume a company has a deficiency in control over cash disbursements. The compensating control of reconciliation of cash accounts by a competent individual who is otherwise independent of the cash function might make the likelihood of not detecting a significant misstatement remote. Therefore, while a deficiency might exist, it might not be a significant deficiency or a material weakness due to the existence of a compensating control.

Management must identify the significant financial statement accounts in order to evaluate the controls over major classes of transactions. Major classes of transactions are those that materially affect significant financial statement accounts—either directly through entries in the general ledger or indirectly through the creation of rights or obligations that may or may not be recorded in the general ledger. Major classes of transactions are classified as being *routine, nonroutine,* or *estimation transactions.*

In assessing controls, management focuses on the processes that impact the various classes of transactions. Processes generally involve a series of activities such as capturing input data, sorting and merging data, making calculations, updating records, and reporting information. The relationships among these activities are discussed later in this chapter when we discuss the auditors' responsibility to obtain an understanding of internal control.

As indicated in Figure 18.1, once deficiencies are identified (step 5), management takes actions to eliminate them (step 6). Management is well aware that when a material weakness exists at year-end, its publicly available internal control report must conclude that the company did not maintain effective internal control over financial reporting. Accordingly, eliminating material weaknesses is ordinarily a high priority. But as a practical matter, management also will ordinarily attempt to eliminate deficiencies of lesser consequence. Indeed, all significant deficiencies must be communicated by management to the audit committee, and all deficiencies must be communicated by management to the auditors.

A required part of management's assessment process is appropriate documentation of internal control. While this is shown late in the sequence of events in Figure 18.1, the documentation often occurs throughout the entire assessment and evaluation process. Virtually all of the documentation tools included in Chapters 7 and 8 of this text are relevant for both management's assessment and the external auditors' audit of internal control.

Management's assessment process culminates with the issuance of management's report on internal control. If management believes that no material weaknesses exist at year-end, it is able to issue a report concluding that the company maintained effective internal control over financial reporting. An illustration of such a report is included in Figure 18.4. In the next section, we will describe the auditors' process for evaluating and reporting on internal control.

FIGURE 18.4
Management Report on Internal Control

Management is responsible for establishing and maintaining adequate internal control over financial reporting. Carver Company's internal control system was designed to provide reasonable assurance to the company's management and board of directors regarding the preparation and fair presentation of published financial statements.

All internal control systems, no matter how well-designed, have inherent limitations. Therefore, even a system determined to be effective can provide only reasonable assurance with respect to financial statement preparation and presentation. [*Note: This paragraph is not required.*]

We assessed the effectiveness of the company's internal control over financial reporting as of December 31, 20X4. In making this assessment, we used the criteria set forth by the Committee of Sponsoring Organizations of the Treadway Commission (COSO) in *Internal Control–Integrated Framework*. Based on our assessment, we believe that, as of December 31, 20X4, the company's internal control over financial reporting is effective based on those criteria.

Carver Company's independent auditors have issued an audit report on our assessment of the company's internal control over financial reporting. This report appears on page xx.

Sally Jones
Chief Executive Officer
February 12, 20X5

John Hankson
Chief Financial Officer

The Auditors' Responsibility for Reporting on Internal Control in PCAOB Audits

Learning Objective 3

The auditors' objective in an audit of internal control is to express an opinion on management's assessment of the effectiveness of the company's internal control over financial reporting and to provide their own assessment of control effectiveness. To meet this objective, the auditors must plan and perform the audit to obtain reasonable assurance about whether the company has maintained, in all material respects, effective internal control as of the date specified in management's assessment. Reasonable assurance is obtained by (1) evaluating and testing management's assessment process, (2) evaluating and testing internal control testing performed by others [such as the work of internal auditors], and (3) performing tests of controls directly. Most of the guidance for the audit of internal control is presented in PCAOB *Standard No. 2*.[2]

The audit of internal control is performed to obtain reasonable assurance that no material weaknesses exist as of the date specified in management's assessment—normally the last day of the company's fiscal year. The audit may be viewed as consisting of the following six stages:

1. Plan the engagement.
2. Evaluate management's assessment process.
3. Obtain an understanding of internal control over financial reporting (internal control).
4. Test and evaluate design effectiveness of internal control.
5. Test and evaluate operating effectiveness of internal control.
6. Form an opinion on the effectiveness of internal control.

Plan the Engagement

Learning Objective 4

As indicated in Figure 18.5, the auditors first plan the engagement. Efficient planning requires coordination with the financial statement audit. For purposes of both audits, the auditors consider matters related to the client's industry, regulatory matters, the client's business, and any recent changes in the client's operations. The auditors' knowledge of a client's internal control at the planning stage of the engagement will differ significantly depending upon the nature

[2] *Standard No. 2* is available on the Public Company Accounting Oversight Board Web site at www.pcaobus.org.

FIGURE 18.5
An Audit of Internal Control over Financial Reporting

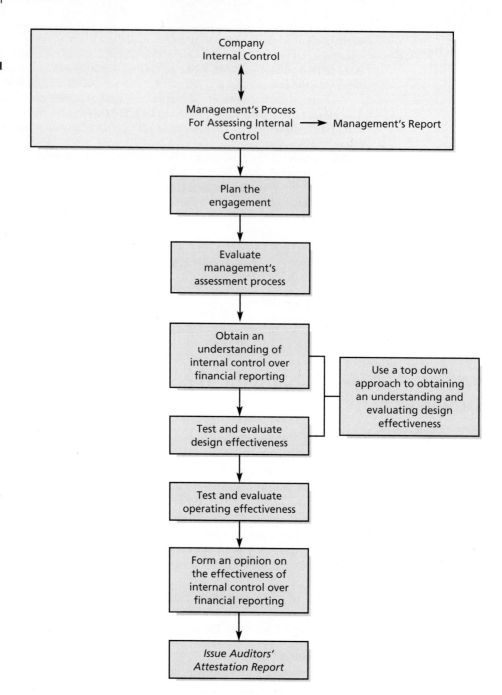

of the client and the auditors' experience with that client, and this in turn will affect the scope of the auditors' procedures. For example, when the auditors have previously performed audits of the client, the auditors begin the integrated audit with more information than in a circumstance in which the company is a new audit client. Accordingly, they only have to perform procedures to update their knowledge.

There is a subtle difference between the auditors' consideration of internal control for the audit of internal control as compared to the consideration in an audit of financial statements. In the audit of internal control, the focus is on whether internal control is effective at a point in time—the **as of date**—which is ordinarily the last day of the client's fiscal period. To express the internal control opinion, the auditors must obtain sufficient evidence on the effectiveness of controls only at the as of date. This would involve performing tests of controls for a period that is usually significantly less than the entire year. On the other hand, in a financial statement audit the consideration of internal control is performed to help plan the audit and to assess control risk for the entire financial statement period. Therefore, the auditors must perform tests of controls throughout the year to meet the objective of obtaining sufficient evidence to support the opinion on internal control and assess control risk. This distinction is discussed in more detail later in this chapter.

Evaluate Management's Assessment Process

As indicated in Figure 18.5, subsequent to planning, the auditors obtain an understanding of and evaluate management's process for assessing internal control effectiveness. As a starting point, the auditors must determine whether management has tested controls over all relevant assertions related to all significant accounts and disclosures in the financial statements. These controls vary in nature, but they must include controls over:

- Initiating, authorizing, recording, processing, and reporting significant accounts and disclosures.
- Selecting and applying appropriate accounting principles.
- Fraud through the implementation of antifraud programs.
- Various types of significant transactions, including overall company-level controls and information technology general controls, and those related to the period-end financial reporting process (e.g., consolidating adjustments, reclassifications, final adjustments).

In evaluating management's assessment process, the auditors also must examine its documentation of internal control to determine that it provides reasonable support for management's assessment. The documentation should include information about:

- The design of controls.
- How significant transactions are initiated, authorized, recorded, processed, and reported.
- The flow of transactions, which identifies points at which material misstatements could occur.
- Controls designed to prevent or detect fraud.
- Controls over the period-end financial reporting process.
- Controls over the safeguarding of assets.
- The results of management's testing and evaluation.

A finding by the auditors that management has not adequately documented its assessment process is considered to be a control deficiency and, possibly, a significant deficiency or a material weakness.

Antifraud Programs

PCAOB *Standard No. 2* emphasizes the need for controls specifically intended to address the risk of fraud. These controls may be a part of any of the five components of internal control, ranging from control activities, such as the reconciliation of cash accounts, to broad control environment–level controls, such as a corporate code of conduct. The lack of effective antifraud programs is considered at least a significant deficiency. Figure 18.6 provides examples of antifraud programs and elements.

Obtain an Understanding of Internal Control over Financial Reporting

Figure 18.5 indicates that the auditors obtain an understanding of internal control after evaluating management's assessment process. In actuality, the various steps are seldom as distinct as implied by this figure. The auditors will certainly have obtained a significant amount of information on internal control while evaluating management's assessment process. Regardless, it is in this phase of the process that emphasis shifts to more reliance on the auditors' own tests, including making inquiries of appropriate client personnel, inspecting company documents, observing the application of specific controls, and performing walk-throughs of transactions.

Walk-Throughs

A **walk-through,** a procedure long used in auditing but particularly emphasized in PCAOB *Standard No. 2,* involves literally tracing a transaction from its origination through the

FIGURE 18.6
Company-Level Antifraud Programs and Elements*

Antifraud Program or Element	Strong Indicator of Significant Deficiency
Management accountability	Senior management conducts ineffective oversight of antifraud programs and controls.
Audit committee	Audit committee passively conducts oversight. It does not actively engage the topic of fraud.
Internal audit	Inadequate scope of activities. Inadequate communication, involvement, and interaction with the audit committee.
Code of conduct/ethics	Nonexistent code or code that fails to address conflicts of interest, related party transactions, illegal acts, and monitoring by management and the board. Ineffective communication to all covered persons.
"Whistleblower" program**	No program for anonymous submissions. Inadequate process for responding to allegations of suspicions of fraud. Whistleblower program significantly defective in design or operation.
Hiring and promotion procedures	Failure to perform substantive background investigations for individuals being considered for employment or promotion to a position of trust.
Remediation	Failure to take appropriate and consistent remedial actions with regard to identified significant deficiencies, material weaknesses, actual fraud, or suspected fraud.

*Prepared using data from *Statement on Auditing Standard No. 99,* PCAOB *Statement No. 2,* and PricewaterhouseCoopers, "Key Elements of Antifraud Programs and Controls," 2003, pp. 25–26.
**A program for handling complaints and for accepting confidential submissions of concerns about questionable accounting, auditing, and other matters (e.g., hotlines).

company's information systems until it is reflected in the company's financial reports. Walk-throughs provide the auditors with evidence to:

- Confirm their understanding of the flow of transactions and the design of controls.
- Evaluate the effectiveness of the design of controls.
- Confirm whether controls have been placed in operation.

The auditors should perform at least one walk-through for each major class of transactions for the first year an integrated audit is performed. Also, the performance of walk-throughs should not be assigned to others (e.g., internal auditors).

While performing walk-throughs the auditors ask those involved to describe their understanding of the processing involved and to demonstrate what they do. In addition, follow-up inquiries should be made to help identify abuse of controls or indicators of fraud. Examples of such follow-up inquiries include:

- What do you do when you find an error?
- What kind of errors have you found?
- What happened as a result of finding the errors, and how were the errors resolved?
- Have you ever been asked to override the process or controls? If yes, why did it occur and what happened?

Walk-throughs need not be repeated every year. PCAOB *Standard No. 2* indicates that unless a significant change in the process flow of transactions occurs, the auditors may carry forward documentation to the next year after updating it for any changes that have taken place.

Additional Procedures for Obtaining an Understanding of Controls

As described in Chapter 7, during audits of financial statements auditors must obtain an understanding of the design of controls in each component of internal control—control environment, risk assessment, control activities, information and communication, and monitoring. Audits of internal control include this same process.

In obtaining an understanding of internal control, the auditors are aware of the fact that controls differ significantly in their broadness of coverage. Some are company-level controls that have a pervasive effect on the achievement of overall control objectives. Company-level controls often are included in the control environment or monitoring components. For example, the portions of the control environment dealing with the tone at the top, assignment of authority and responsibility, and corporate codes of conduct have a pervasive effect on internal control. Also, information technology general controls over program development program changes, computer operations, and access to programs have a pervasive effect in that they help ensure that specific controls over processing are operating effectively. Other controls are not pervasive in nature; they are designed to achieve specific objectives. As an example, management may establish a control requiring the accounting for all shipping documents to ensure that all sales are recorded; these specific controls often fit under the control activities component of internal control.

As indicated in Figure 18.5, the auditors usually take a "top down" approach to obtaining an understanding of internal control and evaluating design effectiveness. Using this approach, the auditors perform procedures to understand controls and identify the ones to test in a sequential manner. They start with the company-level controls and then drive down to significant accounts, significant processes, and finally controls at the transaction, process or application level. This approach helps to prevent the auditors from testing controls that may not be necessary to achieving particular control objectives.

Controls relating to audit committee effectiveness and the period-end financial reporting process are particularly emphasized in *Standard No. 2.* Ineffective audit committee oversight by itself is regarded as at least a significant deficiency and provides a strong indication that a material weakness in internal control exists.

The period-end financial reporting process (often referred to as "financial statement close") is also considered very significant. The period-end process involves the procedures used to enter transaction totals into the general ledger through the end of the financial statement reporting process. Auditors must thoroughly evaluate this process, including the manner in which financial statements are produced, the extent of information technology involved, who participates from management, the locations involved, and the types of adjusting entries and oversight by appropriate parties.

How do auditors determine which controls should be tested? The auditors first identify the significant financial statement accounts and disclosures and the relevant financial statement assertions. Next, they identify the classes of transactions and related processes that impact the assertions about the accounts. Finally, the auditors determine the control objectives for the classes of transactions and processes and identify the combination of pervasive and specific controls that are designed to meet those objectives.

Figure 18.7 graphically illustrates the links between significant financial statement accounts and controls to be tested.

Significant Accounts

As shown in Figure 18.7, the process of obtaining an understanding of internal control begins with an identification of **significant accounts** and disclosures. An account is significant if there is more than a remote likelihood that it could contain misstatements that individually, or when aggregated with others, could have a material effect on the financial statements. In making this determination, both the possibility of overstatement and understatement should be considered. In addition, the assessment should be made without giving any consideration to

FIGURE 18.7 **The Links between Significant Accounts and Controls to Be Tested**

Process	Identify significant accounts and disclosures	→	Identify relevant financial statement assertions	→	Identify significant processes and classes of transactions	→	Identify control objectives	→	Identify controls to test
Example	Accounts receivable	→	Completeness of accounts receivable	→	Cash receipt transactions and remittance process	→	Completeness of recording of cash remittances	→	Segregation of duties in handling cash remittances

the effectiveness of internal control. Factors that the auditors consider in deciding whether an account is significant include:

- Size and composition.
- Susceptibility of loss due to errors or fraud.
- Volume of activity, complexity, and homogeneity of individual transactions.
- Nature of the account.
- Accounting and reporting complexity.
- Exposure to losses.
- Likelihood of significant contingent liabilities.
- Existence of related party transactions.
- Changes from the prior period.

Identifying Relevant Financial Statement Assertions

Once they have determined the significant accounts and disclosures, the auditors must determine which financial statement assertions are relevant to the significant accounts: (1) existence or occurrence; (2) completeness; (3) valuation or allocation; (4) rights and obligations; and/or (5) presentation and disclosure. Relevant assertions for an account are those that have a meaningful bearing on whether the account is presented fairly. For example, valuation may be very relevant to determining the amount of receivables, but it is not ordinarily relevant to cash unless currency translation is involved.

Identifying Significant Processes and Major Classes of Transactions

After the auditors have identified the relevant assertions, they identify the significant major classes of transactions and related processes that affect the accounts or disclosures. **Major classes of transactions** (transaction cycles)[3] are those groupings of transactions that are significant to the financial statements. Consider a company whose sales may be initiated by customers either through the Internet or in a retail store. These types of sales represent two major classes of transactions within the sales processes.

When auditors consider the major classes of transactions it is helpful to classify them by what PCAOB *Standard No. 2* refers to as *transaction type*—routine, nonroutine, or estimation transactions. **Routine transactions** are for recurring activities, such as sales, purchases, cash receipts and disbursements, and payroll. **Nonroutine transactions** occur only periodically; they generally are not part of the routine flow of transactions and include transactions such as counting and pricing inventory, calculating depreciation expense, or determining prepaid expenses. **Estimation transactions** are activities involving management's judgments or assumptions, such as determining the allowance for doubtful accounts, establishing warranty reserves, and assessing assets for impairment.[4]

Throughout the audit of internal control auditors must be concerned about all three transaction types. However, the auditors must be aware that the unique nature of nonroutine transactions

---

[3] Because *Standard No. 2* consistently uses the term "classes of transactions," in this chapter we will also use it rather than the term "transaction cycles."

[4] Estimation transactions are referred to as "accounting estimates" in the AICPA Professional Standards.

and the subjectivity involved with estimation transactions makes them particularly prone to misstatement unless they are properly controlled.

After the auditors have identified the significant classes of transactions, they focus on the related processes. For each significant process, the auditors should:

- Understand the flow of transactions (initiation, authorization, recording, processing, and reporting).
- Identify points at which a misstatement could arise.
- Identify controls to address the potential misstatement.
- Identify controls to prevent or detect in a timely manner the unauthorized acquisition, use, or disposition of the company's assets.

Figure 18.8 provides an illustration of the relationships among significant accounts, processes, and transaction types emphasizing inventory processes; it presumes one major class of transactions for each process.

Considering Control Objectives and Identifying Controls to Test

After identifying significant accounts, relevant assertions, processes, and classes of transactions, the auditors should use this information to evaluate where errors or fraud could occur. This involves considering relationships among risks of errors and fraud and control objectives. Specifically, the auditors identify the controls to be tested by considering:

- The points at which errors or fraud could occur.
- The nature of the controls implemented by management.
- The significance of each control in achieving the objectives of the control criteria.
- The risk that controls might not be operating effectively.

FIGURE 18.8   Relationships among Processes, Transaction Types, and Significant Accounts

Example Processes	Transaction Types	Cash	Accounts Receivable	Allowance for Doubtful Accounts	Inventories (and I/S)	Inventory Reserves	Prepaid	Property, Plant, & Equipment	Other Accounts	Stockholders' Equity
Financial statement close	Nonroutine	X	X	X	X	X	X	X	X	X
Cash receipts	Routine	X	X						X	
Cash disbursements	Routine	X							X	
Payroll	Routine									
Inventory costing (CGS)	Routine	X			X					
Estimate purchase commitments	Estimation								X	
Estimate excess and obsolete inventory	Estimation					X				
Lower of cost or market calculation	Estimation					X				
LIFO calculation	Nonroutine					X				
Physical inventory count	Nonroutine					X				
Accounts receivable and sales	Routine		X							

Source: Adapted from Ernst & Young, *Evaluating Internal Control: Considerations for Documenting Controls at the Process, Transaction, or Application Level,* 2003.

In determining the risk that controls might not be operating effectively, the auditors consider factors such as changes in the volume or nature of transactions, changes in controls or personnel performing the control, the degree to which controls rely on the effectiveness of other controls, and the automation level and complexity of controls.

The auditors should determine appropriate control objectives for areas in which misstatements may occur and then test controls that are important to achieving each control objective. It is neither necessary to test all controls nor to test redundant controls (those that duplicate other controls), unless redundancy itself is a control objective. The auditors may decide to test preventive controls, detective controls, or a combination of both for the various assertions and significant accounts. Preventive controls have the objective of preventing errors or fraud from occurring; detective controls have the objective of detecting errors or fraud that has already occurred. Effective internal control generally involves "levels" of controls composed of a combination of both preventive and detective controls.

A question that arises when a client has multiple locations is: "Must the auditors perform tests at all locations?" The answer is "no." The auditors are required to perform tests of only those locations (or business units) that, individually or when aggregated, could create a material misstatement in the financial statements.

Test and Evaluate Design Effectiveness of Internal Control over Financial Reporting

As do other professional standards on internal control, PCAOB *Standard No. 2* distinguishes between design effectiveness and operating effectiveness. Figure 18.5 illustrates that the approach is to first test and evaluate the design, because if the design is ineffective it makes no sense to test whether the designed controls are operating effectively.

To test design, the auditors identify the company's control objectives for significant processes and classes of transactions. Next, they determine whether the related controls, if operating properly, can effectively prevent or detect misstatements that could be material. Procedures performed by the auditors to assess design effectiveness include inquiry, observation, walk-throughs, inspection of relevant documentation, and specific evaluation of whether the controls are likely to prevent or detect misstatements. Figure 18.9 provides an example of control objectives, risks, and controls using the COSO framework. The auditors specifically consider whether the controls, if functioning, would reduce the risks to an appropriately low level.

Test and Evaluate Operating Effectiveness of Internal Control over Financial Reporting

Tests of the operating effectiveness of a control determine whether the control functions as designed and whether the person performing the control possesses the necessary authority and qualifications. In deciding how to design tests of operating effectiveness, the auditors must focus on the nature, timing, and extent of the tests.

Nature of Tests of Operating Effectiveness

Tests of controls, in the order of increasing persuasiveness, include a combination of inquiries of appropriate personnel, inspection of relevant documents, observation of the company's operations, and reperformance of the application of controls. For example, to evaluate whether the second control objective in Figure 18.9, the accurate and complete recording of invoices, is achieved, the auditors might use generalized audit software to inspect electronic documents to determine that no gaps exist in the sequence of shipping documents. Also, *Standard No. 2* states that the auditors should vary the exact tests performed when possible to introduce unpredictability into the audit process.

Evaluating responses to inquiries represents a particular challenge in that the responses may range from formal written inquiries (e.g., representation letters) to informal oral inquiries. Because of the possibility of misrepresentations or misunderstanding of the responses, inquiry alone does not provide sufficient evidence to support the operating effectiveness of a control. Thus, auditors should substantiate the responses to inquiries by performing other procedures, such as inspecting reports or other documentation relating to the inquiries.

Timing of Tests of Controls

Tests of controls should be performed over a period of time sufficient to determine whether, as of the date specified in management's report, the controls operated effectively. The auditors are

FIGURE 18.9 **Process: Accounts Receivable**

Control Objective	Risks	Controls
1. Ensure that all goods shipped are accurately billed in the proper period.	Missing documents or incorrect information. Improper cutoff of shipment at the end of a period.	• Use standard shipping or contract terms. • Communicate nonstandard shipping or contract terms to accounts receivable department. • Identify shipments as being before or after period-end by means of a shipping log and prenumbered shipping documents.
2. Accurately record invoices for all authorized shipments and only for such shipments.	Missing documents or incorrect information.	• Prenumber and account for shipping documents and sales invoices. • Match orders, shipping documents, invoices, and customer information, and follow through on missing or inconsistent information. • Mail customer statements periodically and investigate and resolve disputes or inquiries, by individuals independent of the invoicing function. • Monitor number of customer complaints regarding improper invoices or statements.
3. Accurately record all authorized sales returns and allowances and only such returns and allowances.	Missing documents or incorrect information. Inaccurate input of data.	• Authorization of credit memos by individuals independent of accounts receivable function. • Prenumber and account for credit memos and receiving documents. • Match credit memos and receiving documents and resolve unmatched items by individuals independent of the accounts receivable function. • Mail customer statements periodically and investigate and resolve disputes or inquiries, by individuals independent of the invoicing function.
4. Ensure continued completeness and accuracy of accounts receivable.	Unauthorized input for nonexistent returns, allowances, and write-offs.	• Review correspondence authorizing returns and allowances. • Reconcile accounts receivable subsidiary ledger with sales and cash receipts transactions. • Resolve differences between the accounts receivable subsidiary ledger and the accounts receivable control account.
5. Safeguard accounts receivable records.	Unauthorized access to accounts receivable records and stored data.	• Restrict access to accounts receivable files and data used in processing receivables.

Source: Adapted from *Internal Control–Integrated Framework, Evaluation Tools.*

aware that some controls operate continuously (e.g., controls over routine transactions, such as sales), while others operate only periodically (e.g., controls over nonroutine transactions, such as the preparation and analysis of monthly or quarterly financial statements). For controls that operate only periodically, it may be necessary to wait until after the date of management's report to test them; for example, controls over period-end financial reporting normally operate only after the date of management's report. The auditors' tests can be performed only at the time the controls are operating.

Extent of Tests of Controls

PCAOB *Standard No. 2* requires the auditors to obtain sufficient evidence about the effectiveness of controls for all relevant assertions related to all significant accounts. This means that the auditors must design procedures to provide a high level of assurance that the controls related to each relevant assertion are operating effectively. For manual controls this generally involves more extensive testing than for automated controls. Generally, the more frequently controls operate, the more auditors should test them, and controls that are relatively more

Illustrative Case
Frequency of Testing

PricewaterhouseCoopers provided the following guidance to its auditors as to frequency of testing

Frequency of Control	Suggested Number of Items to Test
Annual	1
Quarterly	2
Monthly	3–6
Weekly	10–20
Daily	20–40
Multiple times per day	30–60

important should be tested more extensively. Also, the auditors cannot be satisfied with less-than-persuasive evidence because of a belief that management is honest.

When control exceptions are identified, the auditors should critically assess the nature and extent of testing and consider whether additional testing is appropriate. Also, a conclusion that an identified control exception does not represent a control deficiency is only appropriate if evidence beyond what the auditors had originally planned, and beyond inquiry, supports that conclusion. The issue of evaluating exceptions will be described in more detail later in this chapter.

While in all audits the auditors must perform enough of the work to provide the principal evidence for the engagement, the work of others—including internal auditors, company personnel, and third parties—may be used. It is expected that the work of others would be devoted more to testing low-risk, routine transactions rather than pervasive or control environment controls. In all cases in which the work of others is used, the auditors should evaluate the competence and objectivity of those individuals and test the work they have performed. Also, the auditors must perform the walk-throughs themselves and not use the work of others to reduce the work performed on control environment controls.

Another question related to the extent of testing that arises in practice is: "Must the auditors retest controls each year, or may they rotate areas so that not all controls are tested each year?" *Standard No. 2* provides that each year's audit must stand on its own and, accordingly, all relevant accounts and assertions must be tested annually. However, it is anticipated that natural efficiencies will occur as the auditors repeat the audit process. This is due to the concept referred to as "cumulative audit knowledge," or knowledge obtained from prior audits that remains relevant to the current audit. For example, the auditors will ordinarily spend less time obtaining the needed understanding of a company's internal control in subsequent years as compared to the first year's integrated audit. Also, the auditors may use the work of others to varying extents in particular years. Finally, to the extent that the auditors know of control weaknesses, the audit strategy should reflect that knowledge. However, the auditors must test controls every year, regardless of whether or not they have changed.

Relationship between Tests of Controls Performed for the Internal Control Audit and Those Performed for the Financial Statement Audit

Learning Objective 5

Are the types of tests of controls performed for an internal control audit the same as those performed for a financial statement audit? May the evidence from tests performed for an internal control audit be used for the financial statement audit? While the answer to both of these questions is "yes," the auditors must consider the differences in the objectives of the tests.

The objective of tests of controls in an audit of internal control is to obtain evidence about the effectiveness of controls to support the auditors' opinion on whether management's assessment of the effectiveness of internal control, taken as a whole, is fairly stated as of a point in time. Accordingly, to express this opinion the auditors must obtain evidence about the effectiveness of controls over all relevant assertions for all significant accounts and disclosures in the financial statements.

The objective of tests of controls for a financial statement audit is to assess control risk. If the auditors decide to assess control risk at less than the maximum, they are required to obtain evidence that the relevant controls operated effectively during the entire period upon which they plan to place reliance on those controls. However, the auditors are not required to assess control risk at less than the maximum for all assertions.

How may these two different approaches for tests of controls be reconciled in an integrated audit? PCAOB *Standard No. 2,* for purposes of the internal control audit, allows the auditors to obtain evidence about operating effectiveness at different times throughout the year—provided that the auditors update those tests or obtain other evidence that the controls still operated effectively at the end of the year. Thus, although the timing for issuing the internal control report will not ordinarily require tests from throughout the year, the integrated nature of the two audits suggests that testing should be spread throughout the year.

The requirements of *Standard No. 2* have had the effect of pushing auditors to perform financial statement audits using the systems approach—an approach with heavy reliance on internal control evidence. In essence, since extensive tests of controls are required for each significant account for the internal control audit, the auditors should have significant evidence about the effectiveness of internal control for the financial statement audit. The auditors generally must merely extend the tests to cover the financial statement period in order to assess control risk at a low level for purposes of the financial statement audit.

Effect of Tests of Controls on Financial Statement Audit Substantive Procedures

Historically, to enhance audit efficiency and effectiveness, auditors often have used a substantive audit approach that is not acceptable for integrated audits. Auditors have traditionally relied primarily (or completely) on evidence from substantive procedures rather than testing controls in audit areas when a substantive approach was considered the most cost effective approach. To illustrate, when only a financial statement audit is being performed, auditors often rely heavily upon substantive procedures to audit areas such as property, plant, and equipment, investments, and long-term debt. Since auditors must now report on the effectiveness of internal control, approaches limiting the testing of controls are not acceptable.

Historically, another efficiency that has developed in financial statement audits is minimizing the testing of controls aimed at **preventive controls** (e.g., transaction level controls), and emphasizing the testing of **detective controls** (e.g., various types of reconciliations and exception reports). When expressing an opinion on internal control, PCAOB *Standard No. 2* outlines an approach that involves the testing of both preventive and detective controls.

Since an integrated audit requires tests of controls for all major accounts and relevant assertions, circumstances in which controls are found to be effective will lead to a decreased scope of substantive procedures as compared to a situation in which tests of controls have revealed an ineffective system or a situation in which tests of controls have not been performed. However, when significant deficiencies or material weaknesses have been identified, the auditors must obtain assurance that such deficiencies have not resulted in undetected material misstatements. As an example, if controls over the recording of revenues are considered ineffective, the auditors must determine whether the audit procedures designed into their audit program must be modified to obtain more evidence about the fairness of revenue.

The extensive level of controls testing performed during an integrated audit leads to the question of whether substantive tests may be omitted completely in areas in which controls have been found to operate effectively. This is not acceptable. Regardless of the assessed level of control risk, the auditors must perform substantive procedures for all relevant assertions related to all significant accounts and disclosures.

Effect of Financial Statement Substantive Procedures on the Audit of Internal Control

We have shown that the audit of internal control may affect the scope of substantive procedures performed for the financial statement audit. Alternatively, the results of substantive procedures may affect the audit of internal control. The findings obtained while performing substantive procedures in the financial statement audit may provide evidence of the effectiveness or ineffectiveness of internal control over financial reporting. For example, identification of a material misstatement in the financial statements is considered indicative of at least a significant deficiency in internal control. Additional examples of substantive procedures findings that might affect the internal control audit are those relating to illegal acts, related party transactions, the reasonableness of accounting estimates, and the client's overall selection of accounting principles.

Form an Opinion on the Effectiveness of Internal Control over Financial Reporting

Learning Objective 6

In forming an opinion on internal control over financial reporting, the auditors evaluate all evidence, including:

1. The adequacy of the assessment performed by management.
2. The results of the auditors' evaluation of the design.
3. The results of tests of the operating effectiveness of controls.
4. Negative results of substantive procedures performed during the financial statement audit.
5. Any identified control deficiencies.

An unqualified audit opinion may be issued when no material weaknesses in internal control have been identified as existing at the as of date (year-end) and when there have been no restrictions on the scope of the auditors' work. One or more material weaknesses in internal control results in an adverse opinion.[5] Scope limitations may result in either a qualified opinion or a disclaimer of opinion.

Determining whether deficiencies have been identified and, if so, the likelihood and potential amount of misstatement, is key to identifying the proper opinion to issue. If no deficiencies have been identified and no scope limitations are involved, an unqualified opinion is appropriate.

Evaluating Deficiencies

The auditors must evaluate whether identified control deficiencies, individually or in combination, are significant deficiencies or material weaknesses. This involves a consideration of both quantitative and qualitative factors.

When a deficiency has been identified, the auditors will consider whether any other controls effectively mitigate the risk of potential misstatement and create a situation in which the deficiency is not significant or, at least, does not constitute a material weakness. Earlier in this chapter we used the example of a weakness in cash disbursements that was mitigated by the compensating control of reconciliation of the bank account by an individual otherwise independent of the cash function. Such a compensating control might cause the auditors to alter their assessment of a deficiency—reducing it from one that otherwise would be considered significant (or a material weakness) to one that is simply a control deficiency.

In evaluating the potential amount of misstatement related to a control deficiency, the auditors consider not only misstatements identified, but the amount that could occur with more than a remote chance. Although there are various possible approaches to this evaluation, one is to consider the potential magnitude of the misstatement that could result from the deficiency. That is, given the worst case scenario, how much dollar amount of misstatement could result? If that amount exceeds an inconsequential amount, the auditors consider how much of the potential misstatement could occur with more than a remote likelihood. If the more than remote likelihood of the potential misstatement exceeds an inconsequential amount, but is less than material, a significant deficiency is involved; if the amount is material, the deficiency is a material weakness.

The auditors must also consider qualitative factors when evaluating materiality, as is the case with financial statement audits. Examples of qualitative factors would include whether the weakness relates to related party transactions and the changes in account characteristics in relation to the prior year. Chapter 6 presents additional information on qualitative factors that are used by the auditors. In essence, the auditors should attempt to determine what a *prudent official in the conduct of his or her own affairs* would consider a significant deficiency and a material weakness.

PCAOB *Standard No. 2* provides several examples of deficiencies that are at least *significant deficiencies,* including the lack of effective:

---

[5] Notice that this is different from reports on audits of financial statements. In an audit of financial statements a departure from generally accepted accounting principles results in either a qualified opinion or an adverse opinion based on materiality.

Illustrative Case
Using Attributes Sampling to Consider Control Deficiencies

It is possible to use statistical attribute sampling (presented in Chapter 9) to consider control deficiency seriousness. Consider a control over authorization of sales transactions:

1% = Deviation rate in the auditors' sample
6% = Achieved upper deviation rate
5% = Risk of assessing control risk too low

If one further assumes that $3,000,000 of the transaction type occurred, the auditor may estimate that $180,000 (6% × $3,000,000) worth of transactions may not have been

properly approved. That is there is a remote chance (5%) that $180,000 in transactions were not properly approved.

If one assumes that the $180,000 represents possible misstatements, several conclusions are possible. If one considers that amount to be less than consequential, the deficiency is neither significant nor a material weakness from a quantitative measure of materiality. If $180,000 is consequential or greater, it may be considered significant or a material weakness. Note, however, that auditors must also take into account qualitative considerations.

- Controls over the selection and application of accounting principles that are in conformity with generally accepted accounting principles.
- Antifraud programs and controls.
- Controls over nonroutine and nonsystematic transactions.
- Controls over the period-end financial reporting process.

The standard also suggests that the following are at least significant deficiencies and *strong indicators* of the existence of a material weakness in internal control over financial reporting:

- Restatement of previously issued financial statements to reflect a correction.
- Identification by the auditors of a material misstatement that was not initially identified by the company's internal control.
- Ineffective oversight of external reporting by the audit committee.
- An ineffective internal audit function.
- An inadequate regulatory compliance function in highly regulated industries.
- Significant deficiencies previously communicated that have gone uncorrected for a reasonable period of time.
- An ineffective control environment.

Correcting a Material Weakness

Recall that the audit report is modified for material weaknesses that exist at the as of date (year-end). Consider a situation in which four months prior to year-end management identifies a material weakness. If management corrects this weakness prior to year-end, can the auditors issue an unqualified opinion on internal control? Yes, but only if the auditors have sufficient evidence to provide reasonable assurance that the new control is operating effectively. Obtaining such evidence is much easier for controls that operate frequently, in contrast to those that operate only monthly or quarterly (e.g., financial statement close). All in all, the timing of the identification of the material weakness is very important. For example, if the material weakness is not identified until after year-end, an adverse opinion must be issued even if the weakness is corrected: the control did not operate effectively on the date of management's report.

Two-Part Opinion

The auditors' opinions on internal control under PCAOB *Standard No. 2* have two distinct parts, both of which are based on the control criteria selected by management: (1) the auditors' opinion on whether management's assessment of the effectiveness of internal control is appropriate, and (2) the auditors' opinion on whether the company maintained, in all material respects, effective internal control over financial reporting. That is, the auditors report on both the appropriateness of management's assessment process and, more directly, on their own assessment of internal control. Figure 18.10 provides an unqualified report with opinions both on management's assessment and on internal control directly.

FIGURE 18.10   Report with Standard Unqualified Opinion on Internal Control over Financial Reporting

Report of Independent Registered Public Accounting Firm

To the Audit Committee and Stockholders of Carver Company:

[Introductory paragraph]

We have audited management's assessment, included in the accompanying Management Report on Internal Control, that Carver Company maintained effective internal control over financial reporting as of December 31, 20X3, based on criteria established in *Internal Control–Integrated Framework* issued by the Committee of Sponsoring Organizations of the Treadway Commission (COSO). Carver Company's management is responsible for maintaining effective internal control over financial reporting and for its assessment of the effectiveness of internal control over financial reporting. Our responsibility is to express an opinion on management's assessment and an opinion on the effectiveness of the company's internal control over financial reporting based on our audit.

[Scope paragraph]

We conducted our audit in accordance with the standards of the Public Company Accounting Oversight Board (United States). Those standards require that we plan and perform the audit to obtain reasonable assurance about whether effective internal control over financial reporting was maintained in all material respects. Our audit included obtaining an understanding of internal control over financial reporting, evaluating management's assessment, testing and evaluating the design and operating effectiveness of internal control, and performing such other procedures as we considered necessary in the circumstances. We believe that our audit provides a reasonable basis for our opinion.

[Definition paragraph]

A company's internal control over financial reporting is a process designed to provide reasonable assurance regarding the reliability of financial reporting and the preparation of financial statements for external purposes in accordance with generally accepted accounting principles. A company's internal control over financial reporting includes those policies and procedures that (1) pertain to the maintenance of records that, in reasonable detail, accurately and fairly reflect the transactions and dispositions of the assets of the company; (2) provide reasonable assurance that transactions are recorded as necessary to permit preparation of financial statements in accordance with generally accepted accounting principles, and that receipts and expenditures of the company are being made only in accordance with authorizations of management and directors of the company; and (3) provide reasonable assurance regarding prevention or timely detection of unauthorized acquisition, use, or disposition of the company's assets that could have a material effect on the financial statements.

[Inherent limitations paragraph]

Because of its inherent limitations, internal control over financial reporting may not prevent or detect misstatements. Also, projections of any evaluation of effectiveness to future periods are subject to the risk that controls may become inadequate because of changes in conditions, or that the degree of compliance with the policies or procedures may deteriorate.

[Opinion paragraph]

In our opinion, management's assessment that Carver Company maintained effective internal control over financial reporting as of December 31, 20X3, is fairly stated, in all material respects, based on criteria established in *Internal Control–Integrated Framework* issued by the Committee of Sponsoring Organizations of the Treadway Commission (COSO). Also in our opinion, Carver Company maintained, in all material respects, effective internal control over financial reporting as of December 31, 20X3, based on the *Internal Control–Integrated Framework* issued by the Committee of Sponsoring Organizations of the Treadway Commission (COSO) criteria.

[Explanatory paragraph]

We have also audited, in accordance with the standards of the Public Company Accounting Oversight Board (United States), the balance sheets of Carver Company as of December 31, 20X3, and December 31, 20X2, and the related statements of income, shareholders' equity, and cash flows for each of the three years for the period ended December 31, 20X3, of Carver Company and our report dated February 12, 20X4, expressed an unqualified opinion.

Willington & Co., CPAs

Bisbee, Arizona, United States of America
February 12, 20X4

FIGURE 18.11 **Abstract of Report with Adverse Opinion on Internal Control over Financial Reporting**

(Paragraphs 1–4 identical to Figure 18.10 standard unqualified report)

[*Explanatory paragraph*]

A material weakness is a control deficiency, or combination of control deficiencies, that results in more than a remote likelihood that a material misstatement of the annual or interim financial statements will not be prevented or detected. The following material weakness has been identified and included in management's assessment. [*Include a description of the material weakness and its effect on the achievement of the objectives of the control criteria.*] This material weakness was considered in determining the nature, timing, and extent of audit tests applied in our audit of the 20X3 financial statements, and this report does not affect our report dated [*date of report, which should be the same as the date of this report on internal control*] on those financial statements.

[*Opinion paragraph*]

In our opinion, management's assessment that Carver Company did not maintain effective internal control over financial reporting as of December 31, 20X3, is fairly stated, in all material respects, based on criteria established in *Internal Control–Integrated Framework* issued by the Committee of Sponsoring Organizations of the Treadway Commission (COSO). Also, in our opinion, because of the effect of the material weakness described above on the achievement of the objectives of the control criteria, Carver Company has not maintained effective internal control over financial reporting as of December 31, 20X3, based on criteria established in *Internal Control–Integrated Framework* issued by the Committee of Sponsoring Organizations of the Treadway Commission (COSO).

Audit Report Modifications

Existence of a Material Weakness

A material weakness in internal control that exists at year-end results in the issuance of an adverse opinion. When expressing an adverse opinion, the auditors' report must define a material weakness, indicate that one has been identified, and describe the material weakness. Because the audit opinion is on both the management's assessment and the internal control itself, the auditors may express both an unqualified opinion and an adverse opinion within the same report. For example, if management's report expresses an adverse assessment due to the existence of a material weakness, the auditors will agree with that assessment and provide an unqualified opinion on it. In the opinion on internal control itself, however, the auditors will issue an adverse opinion. Figure 18.11 provides an example of such an adverse opinion.

Scope Limitations

If a restriction on the scope of the audit is imposed by the circumstances, the auditors should withdraw from the engagement, disclaim an opinion, or express a qualified opinion. The decision made depends on the auditors' assessment of the importance of the omitted procedures to their ability to form an opinion on management's assessment of internal control over financial reporting. When restrictions are imposed by management, the auditors should withdraw from the engagement or disclaim an opinion on management's assessment of internal control over financial reporting and the effectiveness of internal control over financial reporting.

Earlier we discussed the situation in which the auditors identify a material weakness and management takes steps to correct that material weakness prior to year-end. If the auditors are unable to obtain sufficient evidence that the new controls are effective for a sufficient period of time, they will issue a disclaimer of opinion on internal control.

Management's Assessment Is Inadequate or Management's Report Is Inappropriate

When management's assessment is found to be inadequate, the auditors should modify their report for a scope limitation. If the auditors believe that management's report is inappropriate, they should modify their report to include, at a minimum, an explanatory paragraph describing their reasons for this conclusion. Figure 18.12 summarizes reporting for this and the preceding circumstances described in this section.

Reliance on Other Auditors

When other auditors have performed a portion of the audit, the auditors must decide whether they are able to serve as the principal auditors. The considerations and reporting requirements

FIGURE 18.12 Circumstances Affecting Auditors' Opinions on Management's Assessment and Internal Control

	Auditors' Opinions	
Circumstance	On Management's Assessment	On Internal Control
Material Weakness Exists at as of Date:		
Client agrees and modifies report.	Unqualified.	Adverse.
Client disagrees and does not modify report.	Adverse.	Adverse.
Material Weakness Existed During Year, System Changed Prior to as of Date:		
Auditors test new system and material weakness has been eliminated.	Unqualified.	Unqualified.
Auditors do not have sufficient time to test new system.	Treat as a scope limitation.	Same.
Scope Restriction*		
Circumstance-imposed.	Qualified or disclaimer (or withdraw from engagement).	Same.
Management-imposed.	Disclaimer (or withdraw from engagement).	Same.
Management's Assessment Process Is:		
Inadequate.	Treat as a scope restriction.	Same.
Inappropriate.	At a minimum, add an explanatory paragraph.	Same.

*If the auditors intend to issue a qualified opinion or disclaim an opinion, yet knows of a material weakness, the material weakness should be described in the report.

are essentially the same as when other auditors are involved in the financial statement audit. The auditors who are able to serve as the principal auditors of the financial statements ordinarily also serve as principal auditors of internal control. When the principal auditors decide to refer in their report to the work of the other auditors, this reference is included both in describing the scope of the audit and in expressing the opinion.

Subsequent Events

Subsequent events relevant to the internal control audit are changes in internal control subsequent to year-end but before the date of the auditors' report. The auditors have a responsibility to make inquiries of management about whether there have been any such changes. If the auditors obtain knowledge of subsequent events that materially and adversely affect the effectiveness of internal control, they should issue an adverse opinion. If the auditors are unable to determine the effect of the subsequent event, they should disclaim an opinion.

Issuing a Combined Report on the Financial Statements and Internal Control

PCAOB *Standard No. 2* allows auditors to either issue separate reports on their audits of the financial statements and internal control or issue one combined report. The illustrations in this chapter have been based on separate reports. Figure 18.13 provides an illustration of a combined unqualified report on both the financial statements and internal control.

Other Communication Requirements

PCAOB *Standard No. 2* requires the auditors to communicate in writing to the audit committee all significant deficiencies and material weaknesses of which the auditors are aware. This requirement exists even for those significant deficiencies and material weaknesses that have been corrected prior to year-end. The auditors also are required to communicate in writing to the company's management information on all control deficiencies that have not previously been communicated.

Report of Independent Registered Public Accounting Firm

To the Audit Committee and Stockholders of Carver Company:

[Introductory paragraph]

We have audited the accompanying balance sheets of Carver Company as of December 31, 20X3 and 20X2, and the related statements of income, stockholders' equity and comprehensive income, and cash flows for each of the years in the three-year period ended December 31, 20X3. We also have audited management's assessment, included in the accompanying Management Report on Internal Control over Financial Reporting, that Carver Company maintained effective internal control over financial reporting as of December 31, 20X3, based on criteria established in *Internal Control–Integrated Framework* issued by the Committee of Sponsoring Organizations of the Treadway Commission (COSO). Carver Company's management is responsible for these financial statements, for maintaining effective internal control over financial reporting, and for its assessment of the effectiveness of internal control over financial reporting. Our responsibility is to express an opinion on these financial statements, an opinion on management's assessment, and an opinion on the effectiveness of the company's internal control over financial reporting based on our audits.

[Scope paragraph]

We conducted our audits in accordance with the standards of the Public Company Accounting Oversight Board (United States). Those standards require that we plan and perform the audits to obtain reasonable assurance about whether the financial statements are free of material misstatement and whether effective internal control over financial reporting was maintained in all material respects. Our audit of financial statements included examining, on a test basis, evidence supporting the amounts and disclosures in the financial statements, assessing the accounting principles used and significant estimates made by management, and evaluating the overall financial statement presentation. Our audit of internal control over financial reporting included obtaining an understanding of internal control over financial reporting, evaluating management's assessment, testing and evaluating the design and operating effectiveness of internal control, and performing such other procedures as we considered necessary in the circumstances. We believe that our audits provide a reasonable basis for our opinions.

[Definition paragraph]

A company's internal control over financial reporting is a process designed to provide reasonable assurance regarding the reliability of financial reporting and the preparation of financial statements for external purposes in accordance with generally accepted accounting principles. A company's internal control over financial reporting includes those policies and procedures that (1) pertain to the maintenance of records that, in reasonable detail, accurately and fairly reflect the transactions and dispositions of the assets of the company; (2) provide reasonable assurance that transactions are recorded as necessary to permit preparation of financial statements in accordance with generally accepted accounting principles, and that receipts and expenditures of the company are being made only in accordance with authorizations of management and directors of the company; and (3) provide reasonable assurance regarding prevention or timely detection of unauthorized acquisition, use, or disposition of the company's assets that could have a material effect on the financial statements.

[Inherent limitations paragraph]

Because of its inherent limitations, internal control over financial reporting may not prevent or detect misstatements. Also, projections of any evaluation of effectiveness to future periods are subject to the risk that controls may become inadequate because of changes in conditions, or that the degree of compliance with the policies or procedures may deteriorate.

[Opinion paragraph]

In our opinion, the financial statements referred to above present fairly, in all material respects, the financial position of Carver Company as of December 31, 20X3 and 20X2, and the results of its operations and its cash flows for each of the years in the three-year period ended December 31, 20X3, in conformity with accounting principles generally accepted in the United States of America. Also in our opinion, management's assessment that Carver Company maintained effective internal control over financial reporting as of December 31, 20X3, is fairly stated, in all material respects, based on criteria established in *Internal Control–Integrated Framework* issued by the Committee of Sponsoring Organizations of the Treadway Commission (COSO). Furthermore, in our opinion, Carver Company maintained, in all material respects, effective internal control over financial reporting as of December 31, 20X3, based on the criteria established in *Internal Control–Integrated Framework* issued by the Committee of Sponsoring Organizations of the Treadway Commission (COSO).

Willington & Co., CPAs
Bisbee, Arizona, United States of America
February 12, 20X4

Chapter Summary

This chapter explained the nature of integrated audits of public companies performed in response to the Sarbanes-Oxley Act of 2002 and in accordance with Public Company Accounting Oversight Board *Standard No. 2*. To summarize:

1. Section 404(a) of the Sarbanes-Oxley Act requires management to acknowledge its responsibility for establishing and maintaining adequate internal control and provide an assessment of internal control effectiveness as of the end of the most recent fiscal year.

2. Section 404(b) of the Sarbanes-Oxley Act requires the auditors to attest to and report on the assessment made by management, as well as to provide their own opinion on the effectiveness of internal control.

3. Deficiencies relating to internal control are considered significant when there is more than a remote likelihood that a misstatement that is more than inconsequential may occur and be undetected. A deficiency is considered to be a material weakness when it involves a material amount.

4. An integrated audit includes an audit report on both the financial statements and internal control. To issue such a report the auditors perform procedures to test controls over all significant accounts, as well as substantive tests to support their opinion on the fairness of the financial statements.

5. Internal control audit reports are modified for a material weakness that exists at year-end. The report issued includes an adverse opinion indicating that effective internal control does not exist. If the scope of the auditors' work is limited, they should issue a qualified opinion or a disclaimer of opinion, or they should withdraw from the engagement.

Key Terms Introduced or Emphasized in Chapter 18

As of date   An audit of internal control over financial reporting assesses internal control as of a particular point in time, the "as of" date, as opposed to the entire period under audit. This date is ordinarily the last day of the client's fiscal period.

Compensating control   A control that reduces the risk that an existing or potential control weakness will result in a failure to meet a control objective (e.g., avoiding misstatements). Compensating controls are ordinarily controls performed to detect, rather than prevent, the misstatement from occurring. For example, a reconciliation of the bank account performed by an individual otherwise independent of the cash function serves to detect a variety of possible misstatements (both errors and fraud) that may have occurred in the processing of cash receipts and disbursements.

Complementary controls   Controls that function together to achieve the same control objective (e.g., avoiding misstatements).

Control deficiency   A weakness in the design or operation of a control that does not allow management or employees, in the normal course of performing their functions, to prevent or detect misstatements on a timely basis.

Detective controls   Policies and procedures that are designed to identify errors or fraud after they have occurred. Detective controls can be applied to groups of transactions (e.g., bank reconciliations).

Estimation transaction   A transaction involving management's judgments or assumptions, such as determining the allowance for doubtful accounts, establishing warranty reserves, and assessing assets for impairment.

Integrated audit (under PCAOB *Standard No. 2*)   An audit that includes audit reports on both a company's internal control over financial reporting and the financial statements.

Major classes of transactions   All classes of transactions that materially affect significant accounts or groups of accounts, either directly through entries in the general ledger or indirectly through the creation of rights or obligations that may not be recorded in the general ledger.

Material weakness   A significant deficiency or combination of significant deficiencies that results in more than a remote likelihood that a material misstatement of the annual or interim financial statements will not be prevented or detected.

Nonroutine transaction   A transaction that occurs only periodically, such as counting and pricing inventory, calculating depreciation expense, or determining prepaid expenses.

Preventive controls   Procedures designed to prevent an error or fraud. Preventive controls are normally applied at the individual transaction level.

Redundant controls   Duplicate controls that both achieve a control objective.

Routine transaction A transaction for a recurring financial activity recorded in the accounting records in the normal course of business, such as sales, purchases, cash receipts, cash disbursements, and payroll.

Sarbanes-Oxley Act of 2002 An act passed by the U.S. Congress to protect investors from the possibility of fraudulent accounting activities by corporations by improving the accuracy and reliability of corporate disclosures.

Section 404 The primary section of the Sarbanes-Oxley Act dealing with management and auditor reporting on internal control over financial reporting. Section 404(a) requires that each annual report filed with the Securities and Exchange Commission include an internal control report prepared by management in which management acknowledges its responsibility for establishing and maintaining adequate internal control and an assessment of internal control effective *as of the end of the most recent fiscal year*. Section 404(b) requires that the CPA firm attest to and report on the assessment made by management as well as provide its own opinion on internal control.

Significant account An account for which there is more than a remote likelihood that it could contain misstatements that individually, or when aggregated with others, could have a material effect on the financial statements.

Significant deficiency A control deficiency (or a combination of control deficiencies) that adversely affects the company's ability to initiate, authorize, record, process, or report external financial data reliably in accordance with generally accepted accounting principles, such that there is more than a remote likelihood that a more than inconsequential misstatement of the company's financial statements will not be prevented or detected.

Walk-through Tracing a transaction from origination through the company's information systems until it is reflected in the company's financial reports.

Review Questions

18–1. Section 404 of the Sarbanes-Oxley Act of 2002 includes two sections. Describe those sections.

18–2. Identify management's four overall responsibilities with respect to internal control over financial reporting that arise due to the Securities and Exchange Commission's implementation of the Sarbanes-Oxley Act of 2002.

18–3. What information must be included in management's report on internal control over financial reporting in the annual report filed with the Securities and Exchange Commission?

18–4. Describe the difference between a significant deficiency and a material weakness in internal control.

18–5. Comment on the accuracy of the following statement: "Just as all material weaknesses are significant deficiencies, all significant deficiencies are material weaknesses."

18–6. What is meant by the "as of" date when reporting on internal control over financial reporting?

18–7. What is a compensating control?

18–8. Provide examples of antifraud programs that the auditors might expect the client to have.

18–9. Describe what is meant by a "walk-through." Must walk-throughs be performed during audits of internal control over financial reporting? May the client perform a walk-through and the auditors then review the client's work?

18–10. While performing a walk-through, auditors ordinarily make certain inquiries of employees. Provide three examples of such inquiries.

18–11. When performing an audit of internal control over financial reporting, auditors distinguish among the following types of transactions: routine, nonroutine, and estimation. Distinguish between these three types of transactions and give an example of each.

18–12. When performing an integrated audit, auditors must identify significant accounts and disclosures. What makes an account significant? What factors should be considered in deciding whether an account is significant?

18–13. A client operates out of 25 locations. Must the CPA perform tests related to internal control at each of these locations?

18–14. Comment on the following: "Auditors must decide, based on cost considerations, whether to test the design effectiveness or operating effectiveness of controls."

18–15. Provide an example of a situation in which the design of controls may be effective but those controls do not operate effectively.

18–16. Comment on the following: "Inquiry alone does not provide sufficient evidence to support the operating effectiveness of a control."

18–17. Comment on the following: "All controls should be tested either prior to or on the 'as of' date."

18–18. What requirements exist when the auditors use the work of client personnel as a part of the evidence obtained for an audit of internal control? In which areas of the audit would one expect this to most likely occur?

18–19. Provide an example of a situation in which the performance of substantive tests for the financial statement audit might affect the internal control audit.

18–20. Provide an example of a situation in which the performance of tests of controls for the internal control audit might affect the performance of substantive tests in a financial statement audit.

18–21. Provide three examples of findings by the auditors that are at least significant deficiencies and strong indicators of the existence of a material weakness in internal control.

18–22. Auditors' opinions on internal control over financial reporting have two distinct parts. What are those two parts?

18–23. What type of report on internal control is likely to be issued when management imposes a scope limitation?

18–24. If an adverse internal control report is issued by the auditors, may an unqualified report be issued on the financial statements?

18–25. Which types of deficiencies must be communicated to the audit committee?

Questions Requiring Analysis

18–26. The CPA firm of Carson & Boggs LLP is performing an internal control audit in accordance with PCAOB standard no. 2. The partner in charge of the engagement has asked you to explain the process of determining which controls to test. Describe the process, presenting each of the links in this process and a short summary of how the auditors approach each of them.

18–27. Tests of controls are ordinarily performed for both financial statement audits and internal control audits.

a. What is the objective of tests of controls when performed for internal control audits?

b. What is the objective of tests of controls when performed for financial statement audits?

c. How are these different objectives reconciled in an integrated audit?

Multiple Choice Questions

18–28. Select the best answer for each of the following questions. Explain the reasons for your selection:

a. In an integrated audit, which of the following must the auditors communicate to the audit committee?

	Known Material Weaknesses	Known Significant Deficiencies
(1)	Yes	Yes
(2)	Yes	No
(3)	No	Yes
(4)	No	No

b. In an integrated audit, which of the following lead(s) to an adverse opinion on internal control?

	Known Material Weaknesses	Known Significant Deficiencies
(1)	Yes	Yes
(2)	Yes	No
(3)	No	Yes
(4)	No	No

c. In an integrated audit, which of the following must be communicated by management to the audit committee?

	Known Material Weaknesses	Known Significant Deficiencies
(1)	Yes	Yes
(2)	Yes	No
(3)	No	Yes
(4)	No	No

d. Which of the following is most likely to be considered a material weakness in internal control?

    (1) An ineffective control environment.

    (2) Restatement of previously issued financial statements due to a change in accounting principles.

    (3) Inadequate controls over nonsystematic transactions.

    (4) Weaknesses in risk assessment.

e. Which of the following is defined as a weakness in internal control that allows more than a remote likelihood of a misstatement that is more than inconsequential, but less than material?

    (1) Control deficiency.

    (2) Material weakness.

    (3) Reportable condition.

    (4) Significant deficiency.

f. The auditors identified a material weakness in internal control in August. The client was informed and the client corrected the material weakness prior to year-end (December 31); the auditors concluded that management eliminated the material weakness prior to year-end. The appropriate audit report on internal control is:

    (1) Adverse.

    (2) Qualified.

    (3) Unqualified.

    (4) Unqualified with explanatory language relating to the material weakness.

g. Which of the following need *not* be included in management's report on internal control under Section 404(a) of the Sarbanes-Oxley Act of 2002?

    (1) A statement that the company's auditors have issued an attestation report on management's assertion.

    (2) An identification of the framework used for evaluating internal control.

    (3) Management's assessment of the effectiveness of internal control.

    (4) Management's acknowledgement of its responsibility to establish and maintain internal control that detects all significant deficiencies.

h. Management's documentation of internal control ordinarily should include information on:

	Controls Designed To Prevent Fraud	Controls Designed to Ensure Employee Personal Integrity
(1)	Yes	Yes
(2)	Yes	No
(3)	No	Yes
(4)	No	No

i. A material weakness is a significant deficiency (or combination of significant deficiencies) that results in more than a remote likelihood that a misstatement of at least what amount will not be prevented or detected?

    (1) Any amount greater than zero.

    (2) A greater amount than zero, but at least inconsequential.

    (3) A greater amount than inconsequential.

    (4) A material amount.

j. A procedure that involves tracing a transaction from origination through the company's information systems until it is reflected in the company's financial report is referred to as a

    (1) Analytical analysis.

    (2) Substantive test.

    (3) Test of a control.

    (4) Walk-through.

k. Which of the following is *not* a typical question asked during a walk-through?

    (1) Have you ever been asked to override the process or controls?

(2) What do you do when you find an error?

(3) What is the largest fraudulent transaction you ever processed?

(4) What kind of errors have you found?

l. An audit of internal control over financial reporting ordinarily assesses internal control:

(1) As of the last day of the fiscal period.

(2) As of the last day of the auditor's fieldwork.

(3) For the entire fiscal period.

(4) For the entire period plus the period of the auditor's fieldwork.

Problems

18–29. Your working papers for an integrated audit being performed under PCAOB *Standard No. 2* include the narrative description below of the cash receipts and billing portions of internal control of Slingsdale Building Supplies, Inc. Slingsdale is a single-store retailer that sells a variety of tools, garden supplies, lumber, small appliances, and electrical fixtures to the public, although about half of Slingsdale's sales are to construction contractors on account. Slingsdale employs 12 salaried sales associates, a credit manager, three full-time clerical workers, and several part-time cash register clerks and assistant bookkeepers. The full-time clerical workers perform such tasks as cash receipts, billing, and accounting and are adequately bonded. They are referred to in the narrative as "accounts receivable supervisor," "cashier," and "bookkeeper."

Narrative: Retail customers pay for merchandise by cash or credit card at cash registers when merchandise is purchased. A contractor may purchase merchandise on account if approved by the credit manager, based only on the manager's familiarity with the contractor's reputation. After credit is approved, the sales associate files a prenumbered charge form with the accounts receivable (AR) supervisor to set up the receivable.

The AR supervisor independently verifies the pricing and other details on the charge form by reference to a management-authorized price list, corrects any errors, prepares the invoice, and supervises a part-time employee who mails the invoice to the contractor. The AR supervisor electronically posts the details of the invoice in the AR subsidiary ledger; simultaneously, the transaction's details are transmitted to the bookkeeper. The AR supervisor also prepares a monthly computer-generated AR subsidiary ledger (without a reconciliation with the AR control account) and a monthly report of overdue accounts.

The cash receipts functions are performed by the cashier, who also supervises the cash register clerks. The cashier opens the mail, compares each check with the enclosed remittance advice, stamps each check "for deposit only," and lists checks for deposit. The cashier then gives the remittance advices to the bookkeeper for recording. The cashier deposits the checks daily, separate from the daily deposit of cash register receipts. The cashier retains the verified deposit slips, to assist in reconciling the monthly bank statements, but forwards to the bookkeeper a copy of the daily cash register summary. The cashier does not have access to the journals or ledgers.

The bookkeeper receives the details of transactions from the AR supervisor and the cashier for journalizing and posting to the general ledger. After recording the remittance advices received from the cashier, the bookkeeper electronically transmits the remittance information to the AR supervisor for subsidiary ledger updating. The bookkeeper sends monthly statements to contractors with unpaid balances upon receipt of the monthly report of overdue balances from the AR supervisor. The bookkeeper authorizes the AR supervisor to write off accounts as uncollectible when six months have passed since the initial overdue notice was sent. At this time, the credit manager is notified by the bookkeeper not to grant additional credit to that contractor.

Required: a. Based only on the information in the narrative, describe the internal control deficiencies in Slingsdale's internal control over the cash receipts and billing functions. Organize the weaknesses by employee job function: Credit manager, AR supervisor, Cashier, and Bookkeeper.

b. Assume that you have performed your audit of internal control in conformity with PCAOB standards. Based on your results for Part (a), you believe that several of the deficiencies represent material weaknesses. What effect will this have on your report on Slingsdale's internal control? Which types of opinions may be appropriate?

c. What communication responsibilities do you have for any weaknesses that represent significant deficiencies?

18–30. While performing an internal control audit in conformity with PCAOB *Standard No. 2,* the auditors must be able to identify both control strengths and control weaknesses. Items (1) through (11) present various control strengths and deficiencies. For each item, select from the list below the appropriate response.

A. Control strength for the revenue cycle (including cash receipts).

B. Control deficiency for the revenue cycle (including cash receipts).

C. Control strength unrelated to the revenue cycle.

Items to be answered:

1. Credit is granted by a credit department.

2. Sales returns are presented to a sales department clerk who prepares a written, prenumbered shipping report.

3. Statements are sent monthly to customers.

4. Write-offs of accounts receivable are approved by the controller.

5. Cash disbursements over $10,000 require two signatures on the check.

6. Cash receipts received in the mail are received by a secretary with no recordkeeping responsibility.

7. Cash receipts received in the mail are forwarded unopened, with remittance advices, to accounting.

8. The cash receipts journal is prepared by the treasurer's department.

9. Cash is deposited weekly.

10. Support for disbursement checks is canceled after payment by the treasurer.

11. Bank reconciliation is prepared by individuals independent of cash receipts recordkeeping.

In-Class Team Case

18–31. For each of the following independent cases state the highest level of deficiency that you believe that circumstances represent—a control deficiency, a significant deficiency, or a material weakness. Explain your decision in each case.

Case 1: The company processes a significant number of routine intercompany transactions. Individual intercompany transactions are not material and primarily relate to balance sheet activity, for example, cash transfers between business units to finance normal operations. A formal management policy requires monthly reconciliation of intercompany accounts and confirmation of balances between business units. However, there is not a process in place to ensure performance of these procedures. As a result, detailed reconciliations of intercompany accounts are not performed on a timely basis. Management does perform monthly procedures to investigate selected large-dollar intercompany account differences. In addition, management prepares a detailed monthly variance analysis of operating expenses to assess their reasonableness.

Case 2: During its assessment of internal control over financial reporting, management identified the following deficiencies. Based on the context in which the deficiencies occur, management and the auditors agree that these deficiencies individually represent significant deficiencies:

- Inadequate segregation of duties over certain information system access controls.

- Several instances of transactions that were not properly recorded in the subsidiary ledgers; the transactions involved were not material, either individually or in the aggregate.

- No timely reconciliation of the account balances affected by the improperly recorded transactions.

Case 3: The company uses a standard sales contract for most transactions, although sales personnel are allowed to modify sales contract terms as necessary to make a profitable sale. Individual sales transactions are not material to the entity. The company's accounting personnel review significant or unusual modifications to the sales contract terms, but they do not review changes in the standard shipping terms. The changes in the standard shipping terms could require a delay in the timing of revenue recognition. Management reviews gross margins on a monthly basis and investigates any significant or unusual relationships. In addition, management reviews the reasonableness of inventory levels at the end of each accounting period. The company has experienced limited situations in which revenue has been inappropriately recorded in advance of shipment, but amounts have not been material.

Case 4: The company has a standard sales contract, but sales personnel frequently modify the terms of the contract. Sales personnel frequently grant unauthorized and unrecorded sales discounts to customers without the knowledge of the accounting department. These amounts are deducted by customers in paying their invoices and are recorded as outstanding balances on the accounts receivable aging. Although these amounts are individually insignificant, they are material in the aggregate and have occurred consistently over the past few years.

Case 5: The company has found it necessary to restate its financial statements for the past two years due to a material overstatement of revenues two years ago (and an equal understatement last year). The errors are due to sales of certain software that allowed the purchasers extremely lenient rights of return. The errors were discovered shortly following the end of the current accounting year. Members of management indicated that the misstatements occurred because they simply didn't know the accounting rules. Now they know the rules and they won't let it happen again.

Case 6: Assume the same facts exist as in Case (5) except that you, the auditor, has identified the misstatements at the end of June of the year currently under audit. Members of management acknowledged that the misstatements occurred because they simply didn't know the rules at the time, and now they know the rules. Management, within the last six months of the year under audit, hired a new financial accounting expert and believes that the control weakness has been corrected as of year-end. Management believes that it is extremely unlikely that such a misstatement could occur again with the new expert reviewing these matters.

Case 7: Assume the same facts exist as in Case (6), except that management has informed the chief financial officer that she must watch over these matters much more carefully. She has attended several CPE courses on accounting and seems to be caught up in the area in which the misstatements occurred.

Case 8: Subsequent to year-end, the auditors have determined that they believe that management has understated its warranty obligations. The auditors know that, according to AU 312.36, they should consider the difference between management's estimate and the closest reasonable estimate as "likely misstatement." The chief financial officer (CFO) has argued that this amount is reasonable. Yet, in fact, neither the auditors nor the CFO know which amount is right. The CFO is under no particular pressure to meet an earnings forecast; he just thinks that the warranty obligations for many of the products will expire and will not be exercised. Still, the CFO can't convince the auditors. Likewise, the auditors can't convince the CFO of their position. The CFO finally agrees to a material adjustment to get to the auditors' amount and "keep the peace."

(Adapted from PCAOB *Standard No. 2*)

19

Additional Assurance Services: Historical Financial Information

Chapter learning objectives

After studying this chapter, you should be able to:

LO1. Identify and describe the types of special reports that auditors issue.

LO2. Describe the auditors' responsibilities when auditing financial statements for use in other countries.

LO3. Explain the special considerations involved in auditing personal financial statements.

LO4. Describe the nature of a review of financial statements for public companies.

LO5. Describe the nature of a review of financial statements for nonpublic companies.

LO6. Discuss the issuance of letters for underwriters.

LO7. Explain the accountants' responsibilities when performing accounting services.

In the preceding chapters, we emphasized the CPA's principal type of attestation engagement—the audit of a company's financial statements prepared in accordance with accounting principles generally accepted in the United States. However, CPAs perform numerous other types of assurance and accounting services. Chapter 20 describes new types of assurance services involving subject matter other than historical financial information. In this chapter, we will focus on engagements other than audits of U.S. companies that involve historical financial information, including:

- Issuing special reports.
- Auditing financial statements prepared for use in other countries.
- Auditing personal financial statements.
- Reviewing historical information.
- Issuing comfort letters.
- Auditing condensed financial statements.
- Performing accounting services.

Accounting services are different than those listed above in that CPAs provide no explicit assurance in their reports as to whether the information follows the appropriate criteria (e.g., generally accepted accounting principles). The role is one of assisting the client, and not one of providing assurance. An example of an accounting service is assisting the client in preparing or *compiling* its financial information.

At this point it is helpful to distinguish among the way the terms "auditor," "accountant," and "practitioner" are used in the *professional literature*. *Auditor* is used for most engagements under the generally accepted auditing standards, although *accountant* is used for interim review and for agreed-upon procedure engagements. *Accountant* is also used for financial statement review and compilation engagements of nonpublic companies. *Practitioner* is the term used in the attestation standards and in most other assurance services. To avoid confusion over this terminology, throughout most parts of Chapters 19 and 20 we simply use the more general term "CPAs."

Special Reports

Learning Objective 1

Although the term **special reports** seems general, its use in the auditing literature is restricted to the following five types of information:

1. Financial statements prepared in accordance with a comprehensive basis of accounting *other than generally accepted accounting principles*. (Example: cash-basis financial statements.)
2. Specified elements, accounts, or items of financial statements. (Examples: amount of net sales or accounts receivable.)
3. Compliance with aspects of contractual agreements or regulatory requirements *related to audited financial statements*. (Example: client's compliance with a bond indenture contract.)
4. Special-purpose financial presentations to comply with contractual agreements or regulatory provisions. (Example: financial information presented on the basis of accounting prescribed by a purchase agreement.)
5. Audited financial information presented in prescribed forms or schedules that require a prescribed form of auditors' report. (Example: filings with a regulatory agency.)

SAS 62 (AU 623), "Special Reports," provides guidance to auditors in the issuance of these reports. In all special reports, the auditors must describe the scope of the engagement and clearly report their findings.

1. Other Comprehensive Bases of Accounting

Auditors are sometimes requested to audit financial statements that are prepared on a comprehensive basis of accounting *other than* generally accepted accounting principles. What qualifies as another comprehensive basis of accounting? Examples of acceptable other comprehensive bases of accounting include (*a*) any basis required by a governmental regulatory agency, (*b*) the income tax basis, (*c*) the cash basis, and (*d*) a definite set of criteria having substantial support, such as price-level adjusted financial statements.

An audit report on financial statements prepared using another comprehensive basis of accounting departs from the standard form in several ways. Most important, the report must describe the basis of accounting being used or refer to a financial statement note that provides such a description. Next, consider the first generally accepted auditing standard of reporting; that standard requires the auditors to state in their report *whether* the financial statements are presented in accordance with generally accepted accounting procedures (GAAP). Thus, if the statements are prepared using another comprehensive basis, the auditors' report must state that the financial statements follow a comprehensive basis of accounting other than GAAP.

Finally, the auditors should be cautious about the titles given to the financial statements. Titles such as "balance sheet," "income statement," and "statement of cash flows" are generally associated with financial statements presented in accordance with GAAP. Consequently, the professional standards require more descriptive titles for statements that are presented on some other basis. For example, a cash-basis "balance sheet" is more appropriately titled "statement of assets and liabilities arising from cash transactions." Perhaps the most common financial statements prepared on a basis other than GAAP are cash-basis statements. An unqualified special report on cash-basis statements is shown below with the distinctive wording emphasized.

We have audited the accompanying *statement of assets and liabilities arising from cash transactions* of XYZ Company as of December 31, 20X1, and the related *statement of revenue collected and expenses paid* for the year then ended. These financial statements are the responsibility of the Company's management. Our responsibility is to express an opinion on these financial statements based on our audit.

We conducted our audit in accordance with auditing standards generally accepted in the United States of America. Those standards require that we plan and perform the audit to obtain reasonable assurance about whether the financial statements are free of material misstatement. An audit includes examining, on a test basis, evidence supporting the amounts and disclosures in the financial statements. An audit also includes assessing the accounting principles used and significant estimates made by management, as well as evaluating the overall financial statement presentation. We believe that our audit provides a reasonable basis for our opinion.

As described in Note 1, these financial statements were prepared on the basis of cash receipts and disbursements, which is a comprehensive basis of accounting other than generally accepted accounting principles.

In our opinion, the financial statements referred to above present fairly, in all material respects, the *assets and liabilities arising from cash transactions* of XYZ Company as of December 31, 20X1, and the *revenue collected and expenses paid* during the year then ended, *on the basis of accounting described in Note 1.*

The essence of this special report is the expression of an opinion as to whether the statements fairly present what they purport to present. The wording of the note mentioned in the report will vary from case to case in order to give an accurate indication of the basis of accounting used.

2. Specified Elements, Accounts, or Items of Financial Statements

Auditors may be engaged to attest to specified elements, accounts, or items of a financial statement (hereafter, simply, specified accounts). For example, auditors may be requested by a lessee to provide reports on an account such as the lessee's revenue. Such reports are commonly required by the provisions of lease agreements and may be relied upon to compute lease payments that are contingent on the lessee's revenue. Although only audits of such information are considered special reports, the review and agreed-upon procedures types of engagements are also available; we discuss them here for the sake of completeness. The attestation standards (included in Chapter 20) provide overall guidance for review and agreed-upon procedures engagements for various types of information, including specified accounts.

When the CPAs are engaged to audit (express an opinion on) specified accounts they modify the standard audit report to indicate the information examined, the basis of accounting used, and whether the information is presented fairly on that basis. For example, in a situation in which rents are based in part on revenue generated, the landlord of a shopping center may request that the CPAs "express an opinion" on the revenue reported by tenants. It should be noted that materiality for such engagements is determined *in relation to the information presented* (e.g., the specific account); this is generally *less* than would be used in an audit of the complete financial statements.

On occasion, the client may request that the CPAs *not* apply sufficient procedures to express an opinion, but perform either *review* or *agreed-upon procedures* on specified accounts of financial statements. A review ordinarily consists of analytical procedures and inquiries. Again using the shopping center example, the landlord of a shopping center may request that the CPAs perform review procedures (analytical procedures and inquiry procedures) applied to the revenue account. Typical review procedures are presented later in this chapter.

Finally, a CPA may be engaged to perform agreed-upon procedures on specified accounts. Such engagements are designed for use by specified parties. Agreed-upon procedures engagements are "customer driven" services in that the "specified party(ies)" agrees with the CPAs on the procedures to be performed and takes responsibility for their *sufficiency.* In our example, these might include procedures such as substantiating the revenue reported by tenants by agreeing the figures with the tenants' internal financial statements and state sales tax returns. In this situation the CPAs will meet with representatives of the landlord (the specified party) to agree upon the procedures to be performed. The accountants' report is restricted to the specified party and lists the procedures performed and related findings. However, it *should not include negative assurance,* indicating that nothing came to the CPAs' attention to indicate that the financial statement element is not fairly presented. The report should also *disclaim an opinion* on the information.

Another common example of an agreed-upon procedures engagement is one in which a bankruptcy trustee (the specified party) is involved with creditors' claims. A CPA may in such a situation be engaged to perform agreed-upon procedures relating to accounts payable and issue a report such as the following (emphasis added):

Independent Accountant's Report on Applying Agreed-Upon Procedures

To the Trustee of Mardem Company:

We have performed the procedures described below, which were agreed to by the Trustee of Mardem Company, with respect to the claims of creditors to determine the validity of claims of Mardem Company as of May 31, 20X1, as set forth in accompanying Schedule A. This engagement to apply agreed-upon procedures was performed in accordance with standards established by the American Institute of Certified Public Accountants. The sufficiency of these procedures is solely the responsibility of the Trustee of Mardem Company. Consequently, *we make no representation regarding the sufficiency of the procedures* described below either for the purpose for which this report has been requested or for any other purpose.

The procedures and associated findings are as follows:

1. Compare the total of the trial balance of accounts payable at May 31, 20X1, prepared by Mardem Company, to the balance in the related general ledger account.

   The total of the accounts payable trial balance agreed with the balance in the related general ledger account.

2. Compare the amounts for claims received from creditors (as shown in claim documents provided by Mardem Company) to the respective amounts shown in the trial balance of accounts payable. Using the data included in the claims documents and in Mardem Company's accounts payable detail records, reconcile any differences found to the accounts payable trial balance.

   All differences noted are presented in column 3 of Schedule A. Except for those amounts shown in column 4 of the Schedule A, all such differences were reconciled.

3. Examine the documentation submitted by creditors in support of the amounts claimed and compare it to the following documentation in Mardem Company's files: invoices, receiving reports, and other evidence of receipt of goods or services.

   Invoices, receiving reports, and other evidence existed for all documents submitted by creditors.

(continued)

> We were not engaged to, and did not, perform an audit, the objective of which would be the expression of an opinion on the specified elements, accounts, or items. Accordingly, *we do not express such an opinion.* Had we performed additional procedures, other matters might have come to our attention that would have been reported to you.
> *This report is intended solely for the use of the Trustee of Mardem Company and should not be used by those who have not agreed to the procedures and taken responsibility for the sufficiency of the procedures for their purpose.*

3. Compliance Reports

Regulatory requirements and debt agreements often require companies to provide compliance reports prepared by their independent auditors—the third type of special report. A common example of such reports is one prepared for bond trustees as evidence of the company's compliance with restrictions contained in the bond indenture. For example, the auditors may provide assurance that the client has complied with indenture provisions relating to the maintenance of certain financial ratios and restrictions on the payment of dividends.

This type of service, while similar to an agreed-upon procedures engagement, does not fit precisely into any of the three general types of attest engagements (i.e., examinations, reviews, and agreed-upon procedures engagements). To provide the service, the auditors must *first have performed an audit* of the related financial statements. The report issued includes an introductory paragraph summarizing the audit report on the financial statements, a paragraph providing negative assurance with respect to compliance, and a paragraph limiting distribution of the report to the client and the appropriate third party. The paragraph providing negative assurance as to compliance is illustrated below.

> In connection with our audit, nothing came to our attention that caused us to believe that the Company was not in compliance with any of the terms, covenants, provisions, or conditions of Sections 8 to 15, inclusive, of the Indenture dated July 21, 20X1, with First National Bank. However, our audit was not directed primarily toward obtaining knowledge of such noncompliance.

4. Special-Purpose Financial Presentations

The fourth type of special report is essentially an audit level of service for financial statements prepared to comply with either a contractual agreement or regulatory provisions. These presentations are typically prepared for the parties that have entered into the agreement or for filing with the regulatory agency, and they must be restricted accordingly. The statements may be prepared following either (*a*) GAAP or another comprehensive accounting basis, or (*b*) a prescribed basis of accounting. When such statements follow GAAP or another comprehensive basis of accounting, the information required by the agreement or the regulatory provisions is generally less complete than the basic financial statements, but more substantial than specified accounts. For example, assume that a company is selling a portion of its assets to another company. A statement of net assets sold may be prepared following GAAP. The report issued on the statement by the CPA should include standard introductory and scope paragraphs modified to refer to the special-purpose presentation. The remainder of the report is illustrated below (emphasis added).

> *The accompanying statement was prepared to present the net assets of Warren Company sold to Easton Corporation pursuant to the purchase agreement described in Note 7, and is not intended to be a complete presentation of Warren Company's assets and liabilities.*
> In our opinion, the accompanying *statement of net assets sold* presents fairly, in all material respects, the net assets of Warren Company as of June 8, 20X1, sold pursuant to the purchase agreement referred to in Note 7, in conformity with generally accepted accounting principles.
> *This report is intended solely for the information and use of the boards of directors and managements of Warren Company and Easton Corporation and should not be used for any other purpose.*

5. Financial Information Presented in Prescribed Forms or Schedules

CPAs also may audit the fairness of information supplied by a client on a prescribed form, such as a loan application or a form filed with a regulatory agency. However, the language of some forms may call for the auditors to issue reports that do not conform to the applicable professional standards. For example, a loan application may require the auditors to sign a statement that the financial information is "true and correct." In such cases, the auditors should reword the form of the report to comply with generally accepted auditing standards. Alternatively, many CPAs suggest to the client that the form simply be marked "see attached," with the attachment being the client's audited financial statements and the audit report.

Financial Statements Prepared for Use in Other Countries

Learning Objective 2

A U.S.-based company may prepare financial statements for use in other countries. For example, the company may have a subsidiary in Germany and may prepare financial statements for that subsidiary as part of an effort to raise capital in Germany. *SAS 51* (AU 534), "Reporting on Financial Statements Prepared for Use in Other Countries," addresses the auditors' responsibility in this situation. The auditors need to be familiar with both the accounting and auditing standards used in the foreign country. They also need to obtain the client's written representations concerning the intended purpose and use of the financial statements.

When auditing the information, the auditors should follow the general and fieldwork standards of the AICPA to the extent the standards are appropriate. In addition, the auditors may apply the other country's auditing standards and indicate so in their report.

The audit report issued depends upon whether it is for use primarily outside the United States (most frequently the case) or within the United States. If it is for use outside the United States the auditors may issue (1) a U.S. report, modified to reflect the accounting principles of the other country, or (2) the report form of the other country, if the auditors understand the responsibilities relating to issuance of that report. In circumstances in which the report is for general use in the United States, the auditors should use the U.S. standard report, modifying it for any departures from U.S. generally accepted accounting principles. Frequently, two sets of financial statements and audit reports are prepared—one following generally accepted accounting principles for distribution in the United States, and the other following the accounting principles of the foreign country for distribution outside the United States.

Audits of Personal Financial Statements

Learning Objective 3

In recent years, a number of politicians have had their personal financial statements audited and have made them public. Audited personal financial statements also may be required with large loan applications, or when an individual seeks to purchase a business using his or her personal credit.

Generally accepted accounting principles applied to personal financial statements are quite different from those applicable to business entities. In personal financial statements, assets are shown at their *estimated current values* and liabilities are presented at their *estimated current amounts*. Thus, auditors must apply audit procedures that will substantiate these estimates, rather than substantiate historical costs. On occasion, the auditors may need to rely upon appraisers, following the guidelines set forth in *SAS 73*, "Using the Work of a Specialist."

The "balance sheet" for an individual is termed a *statement of financial condition.* This statement shows the individual's *net worth* in lieu of "owners' equity" and includes a liability for income taxes on the differences between the estimated current values of assets and liabilities and their income tax bases. The "income statement" for an individual is called the *statement of changes in net worth.* In addition to showing revenue and expenses, this statement includes the increases and decreases in the estimated current values of assets and in the estimated amounts of liabilities during the period.

The accounting principles for personal financial statements are described in *Statement of Position 82-1,* issued by the Accounting Standards Division of the AICPA.[1] In addition, the AICPA has issued the *Guide for Personal Financial Statements* to provide auditors with guidelines for auditing personal financial statements.[2] The reports issued on personal financial statements are standard in form, modified only for the change in financial statement names.

---

[1] AICPA, *Statement of Position 82-1,* "Accounting and Financial Reporting for Personal Financial Statements" (New York, 1982).

[2] AICPA, *Guide for Personal Financial Statements* (New York, 1996).

Completeness—A Special Problem in Personal Financial Statements

One of the assertions that a client makes regarding its financial statements is that the statements are complete—that is, that they reflect all of the client's assets, liabilities, and transactions for the period. Determining the completeness of financial statements may be especially difficult in the audit of personal financial statements for several reasons. First, there is generally poor internal control—all aspects of each transaction usually are under the control of the individual. Second, some individuals may seek to omit assets and income from their personal financial statements. The motivation to conceal earnings or assets may stem from income tax or estate tax considerations, anticipation of a divorce, or illegal sources of income.

The omission of assets and other items from financial statements is far more difficult for auditors to detect than is the overstatement of assets and other items. Thus, in deciding whether to accept a personal financial statements audit engagement, auditors should assess the risk that an individual may be concealing assets. If auditors conclude during an engagement that the individual is concealing assets, it is doubtful that they can ever develop confidence that their audit procedures have located all the concealed assets. Therefore, they should withdraw from the engagement.

Most engagements involving personal financial statements are *not* audits, because individuals seldom need audited financial statements. The approaches described for reviews and compilations later in this chapter are more commonly applied to personal financial statements.

Reviews of the Interim Information of Public Companies

Public companies are required to file interim (quarterly) financial information with the SEC on Form 10-Q. Unlike annual financial statements filed with the SEC, this interim information is reviewed rather than audited. Guidance for reviews is included in *SAS No. 100* (AU 722), "Interim Financial Information." This standard was adopted as an interim standard by the PCAOB who now has the authority over reviews of the interim financial statements of public companies.

The objective of a review is to provide the accountants with a basis for communicating whether they are aware of any material modifications that should be made to the interim financial information for it to conform to generally accepted accounting principles. As is the case with audits, a starting point for an interim review is to establish an understanding with the client regarding the nature of the engagement. The understanding, which preferably should be in writing, includes information on management's responsibilities, the accountants' responsibilities, and the nature of reviews. An engagement letter is often used to document the understanding. A review includes obtaining an understanding of the client's business and internal control, performing review procedures, and communicating results.

Understanding the Client's Business and Internal Control

To perform a review the accountants must have a sufficient understanding of the client's business and its internal control to identify types of potential material misstatements and their likelihood of occurrence. This understanding allows them to select appropriate procedures that serve as the basis for the review. To obtain or update their understanding, accountants perform procedures such as reading documentation of the preceding year's audit and of recent reviews, reading the most recent financial statements, considering the results of any audit procedures performed on the current year's financial statements, and inquiring of management about changes in the company's business activities.

When performing an initial review of a company for which the public accounting firm has not yet conducted an audit, additional planning and procedures are necessary. The accountants should obtain a sufficient understanding of the client's business and its internal control to determine the inquiries to be made and the analytical procedures to be performed. Ordinarily, the accountants should also make inquiries of the predecessor accountant and review that accountant's documentation for the preceding annual audit and for any prior interim periods in the current year.

Review Procedures

A review consists of analytical procedures, inquiries, and certain other procedures. Analytical procedures[3] are applied to interim financial information to identify and provide a basis for inquiries about relationships that appear unusual and that may indicate a misstatement. The

---

[3] Chapter 5 presents general guidance on analytical procedures.

approach is to compare recorded amounts and calculated ratios to expectations developed by the accountant and to consider the reasonableness of relationships. For example, revenue reported by month, product line, or business segment is compared to amounts from comparable prior periods.

Unexpected results obtained through the use of analytical procedures are followed up by inquiries to management and certain other procedures. While a review ordinarily does not require accountants to corroborate management's responses with other evidential matter, they should consider the consistency of management responses in light of the results of other review procedures and their knowledge of the client's business and internal control. Additional procedures should be performed if the accountants become aware that information may be incorrect, incomplete, or otherwise unsatisfactory. The accountants should perform these procedures to the extent considered necessary to provide limited assurance that there are no material modifications that should be made to the statements. For example, if review procedures lead an accountant to question whether a significant sales transaction is recorded in conformity with generally accepted accounting principles, it may become necessary to discuss the terms of the transaction with both senior marketing and accounting personnel and to read the sales contract.

A review also consists of inquiries to top management on matters such as:

- Whether the financial statements are in accordance with generally accepted accounting principles.
- Unusual or complex situations affecting the interim financial information.
- Significant transactions occurring around the end of the period.
- Subsequent events.
- Whether management has knowledge of fraud having been committed.
- Whether allegations of fraudulent financial reporting have been made by employees, former employees, or other individuals.

Other procedures performed in a review include reading available minutes of stockholder and director meetings, reading the interim financial information, and obtaining reports from other accountants who have reviewed significant components of the company. Evidence must also be obtained showing that the interim financial information agrees or reconciles with the accounting records.

Communicating Results

Although the SEC requires interim reviews before the information is filed, it does not require that the accountant issue a review report—the client decides whether it wishes to have one issued. But, if a client wishes to communicate that the accountant has performed a review, a review report may be issued and included with the interim financial information. When issued, the report is ordinarily worded as follows (emphasis added):

Report of Independent Registered Public Accounting Firm

We have *reviewed* the balance sheet and related statements of income, retained earnings, and cash flows of ABC Company and consolidated subsidiaries as of September 30, 20X2 and 20X1, and for the three-month and nine-month periods then ended. These financial statements are the responsibility of the company's management.

We conducted our review in accordance with the *standards of the Public Company Accounting Oversight Board*. A review of interim financial information consists principally of applying *analytical procedures* to financial data and making *inquiries* of persons responsible for financial and accounting matters. It is *substantially less in scope than an audit* conducted in accordance with generally accepted auditing standards, the objective of which is the expression of an opinion regarding the financial statements taken as a whole. Accordingly, *we do not express such an opinion*.

Based on our review, *we are not aware of any material modifications* that should be made to the accompanying financial statements for them to be in conformity with generally accepted accounting principles.

Warren & Warren LLP
Houston, Tx
April 12, 20X2

Illustrative Case
Difference between CPAs' Responsibilities

The difference between CPAs' responsibilities when performing audits and reviews of financial statements was dramatically illustrated by the ZZZZ Best case. ZZZZ Best, Inc., was a company engaged in the business of carpet cleaning and restoring fire- and flood-damaged buildings. The company, which was founded by sixteen-year-old Barry Minkow, reported operating results that were almost wholly fictitious.

In the review of the financial statements of ZZZZ Best, the partner-in-charge of the engagement insisted upon observing two major restoration jobs, a finished job, and a carpet warehouse. However, Minkow and other officers of the company cleverly faked these locations. As a result, the observations did not result in detection of the fraud, and the public accounting firm also agreed not to make follow-up contacts with the insurance companies and building owners involved.

The court ruled that the accounting firm was not liable for failing to detect the misstatements of the financial statements. The court noted that the accountants' review report specifically disclaimed an opinion on ZZZZ Best's financial statements.

The assurance provided by a review report is necessarily limited because of the limited scope of the accountants' procedures. Although these procedures may bring to the CPAs' attention significant departures from GAAP, they do not guarantee that the CPAs will become aware of all of the significant matters that would be discovered in an audit. A review is not sufficient to enable the accountants to express an opinion on the fairness of the financial statements. Therefore, the middle paragraph of the accountants' report concludes with a statement that the accountants do not express such an opinion. The report will be modified, however, to describe any departure from GAAP that comes to light during the review. In addition, the date of the report should be the date that the accountants completed the review procedures and each page of the interim financial data should be marked as "unaudited."

Review reports are modified for a departure from generally accepted accounting principles. An explanatory paragraph is added describing the nature of the departure, and the final paragraph of the report begins as follows:

> Based on our review, with the exception of the matter described in the preceding paragraph, we are not aware of any material modifications . . . .

Because reviews do not provide an opinion, issuance of an adverse opinion is inappropriate.

The existence of substantial doubt about the company's ability to continue as a going concern or a lack of consistency in the application of accounting principles will not require the accountant to add an additional paragraph to the report, provided that the interim financial information adequately discloses such matters. Although not required, the accountant may emphasize such matters in a separate explanatory paragraph to the report.

Other Communications

What do CPAs do when they obtain evidence that the information is materially misstated, particularly given that a report is often not issued? When CPAs believe that interim financial information filed or to be filed by the company with the SEC is materially misstated, they should communicate the matter to management as soon as is practicable. If management does not respond appropriately, the accountant should inform the audit committee. If the audit committee fails to take appropriate action, the CPAs should consider resigning as the company's accountants. In this way the auditors assure that they will not be associated with financial information that is materially misstated. Also, consideration should be given to consulting with an attorney in these circumstances.

As with annual financial statement audits, the CPAs should communicate to the audit committee the information about significant adjustments found during the review and the acceptability and quality of significant accounting policies and estimates. The audit committee should also be informed about any disagreements with management over accounting principles or review procedures, or any other difficulties encountered in performing the review. These communication responsibilities with respect to an audit were described in detail in Chapter 16. Finally, the CPAs should make sure that the audit committee is informed about any instances of fraud or illegal acts that come to their attention, as well as any reportable conditions related to the preparation of interim financial statements.

Documentation

Documentation of the review should include any findings or issues that in the accountant's judgment are significant. It should enable members of the engagement team with supervision and review responsibilities to understand the nature, extent, and timing of procedures performed, identify the engagement team members, and identify the evidence obtained in support of the conclusion that the interim financial information agreed or reconciled with the accounting records. Examples of documentation include review programs, analyses, memoranda, and representation letters.

Review Services for Nonpublic Companies

Learning Objective 5

For small companies, the cost of an annual audit may exceed the benefits derived. Consider the example of a small company applying for a $20,000 bank loan. If the bank were to require the company to supply annual audited financial statements as a condition of the loan, the company's annual audit fees might well exceed its annual interest expense for the loan. Audits should not be performed unless the benefits are expected to exceed the cost. Therefore, companies that do not offer their securities for sale to the public (**nonpublic companies**) are not required to have annual audits. These companies are free to engage CPAs only for those services that the company wants and can afford.

The needs of nonpublic companies may differ significantly from those of public companies. Whereas public companies have large accounting departments that can prepare financial statements internally, a small nonpublic company might not even employ a full-time accountant. Therefore, the nonpublic company may turn to a public accounting firm for the preparation of its financial statements. Whereas public companies may need annual audits and quarterly reviews, nonpublic companies may only occasionally need CPAs to add credibility to their financial statements. On these occasions, a review may meet the company's needs at a far lower cost than an audit.

Serving the needs of small business represents a sizable part of the practice of most public accounting firms. For a smaller public accounting firm, especially one with only a single office, nonpublic clients may represent the firm's entire practice. To provide CPAs with guidance in meeting the accounting needs of these nonpublic clients, the AICPA established the Accounting and Review Services Committee. This committee has the authority to set professional standards for CPAs associated with the *unaudited* financial statements of nonpublic companies. These standards are published in a sequentially numbered series called *Statements on Standards for Accounting and Review Services (SSARS)*.

Rule 202 of the AICPA *Code of Professional Conduct* requires members to comply with the standards set forth in the *SSARS*. Thus, the Accounting and Review Services Committee has authority comparable to that of the Auditing Standards Board (ASB) and the FASB.

SSARS 1 established standards for two types of engagements involving unaudited financial statements of nonpublic companies: (1) **compilations,** which involve the preparation of financial statements with no attempt to verify the fairness of the presentation; and (2) **reviews,** which are limited investigations of much narrower scope than an audit, undertaken for the purpose of providing limited (negative) assurance that the statements are presented in accordance with GAAP.[4] The following considerations regarding the screening of clients and

---

[4] AICPA, *Statement on Standards for Accounting and Review Services (SSARS) 1,* "Compilation and Review of Financial Statements" (New York, 1978), AR 100. *SSARS 8,* "Amendment to Statement on Standards for Accounting and Review Services No. 1, 'Compilation and Review of Financial Statements'" and *SSARS 10,* "Performance of Review Engagements," updated portions of *SSARS 1.*

engagement letters apply to both compilation and review services. Compilation services are accounting services that are described in detail in the final section of this chapter.

Screening Clients

One of the basic elements of quality control in a public accounting firm relates to the acceptance and continuance of clients. The purpose of policies and procedures in this area is to minimize the risk of association with a client whose management lacks integrity. One means of acquiring information about a prospective client is to contact the client's predecessor CPAs.

SSARS 4 provides guidelines for accountants who decide to make inquiries of the predecessor accountants before accepting a compilation or review engagement.[5] These inquiries should include questions regarding the integrity of management, disagreements over accounting principles, the willingness of management to provide or to revise information, and the reasons for the change in accountants. The decision of whether to contact the predecessor accountants is left to the judgment of the successor CPAs. However, if inquiries are made with the client's consent, the predecessor accountants are generally required to respond.

Engagement Letters for Compilation and Review Services

Compilations and reviews are quite different from audits. The need to establish a clear understanding with the client concerning the nature of such services was dramatically illustrated in the *1136 Tenants' Corporation* case discussed in Chapter 4. CPAs must avoid the implication that they are performing audits when they are engaged to perform other services. Accordingly, although not required by professional standards, it is very important that CPAs prepare an *engagement letter* clearly specifying the nature of the services to be provided and the degree of responsibility the CPAs are assuming. This letter should include a discussion of the limitations of the services and a description of the accountants' report to be issued.

Review Procedures

The procedures for a review of a nonpublic company's financial statements are similar to those for reviews of financial statements of public companies—inquiry and analytical procedures. However, the review of a nonpublic company's financial statements *does not require knowledge of the client's internal control* and the overall requirements are presented in more general terms, with less specific requirements set forth.

To evaluate the responses to their inquiries and the results of other review procedures, the independent accountants should develop a knowledge of the accounting principles and practice in the client's industry and a thorough understanding of the client's business. The CPAs' understanding of the client's business should include a general understanding of the company's organization, its methods of operation, and the nature of its financial statement accounts.

The procedures for a review of the financial statements of nonpublic companies include inquiries of officers and other executives; analytical procedures applied to the financial data by reference to prior financial statements, budgets, and other operating data; and inquiries concerning the actions taken in meetings of stockholders, the board of directors, and committees of the board.

The CPAs' *inquiries* should focus on whether the financial statements are in accordance with generally accepted accounting principles, changes in business activities, significant subsequent events, and knowledge of material fraud or suspected fraud. Additional procedures should be performed if the accountants become aware that information may be incorrect, incomplete, or otherwise unsatisfactory. The CPAs should perform these procedures to the extent considered necessary to provide limited assurance that there are no material modifications that should be made to the statements. Figure 19.1 summarizes analytical procedures, inquiries, and other review procedures.

---

[5] AICPA, *Statement on Standards for Accounting and Review Services 4,* "Communication between Predecessor and Successor Accountants" (New York, 1981), AR 400.

FIGURE 19.1   Nonpublic Company Analytical Procedures, Inquiries, and Other
Review Procedures

Analytical Procedures

- Develop *expectations* by identifying and using plausible relationships that are reasonably expected to exist.
- Compare recorded amounts or ratios developed from recorded amounts to *expectations.*
- Compare the consistency of management's responses in light of results of other review procedures and knowledge of business and industry.

Other Review Procedures

- Inquire as to actions taken at shareholder, board of director, and other committees of board of directors.
- Read financial statements.
- Obtain reports from other accountants, if any, that have reviewed significant components.

Inquiries of Management Members with Responsibility for Financial and Accounting Matters About:

- Whether financial statements are prepared in conformity with GAAP.
- Whether accounting principles, practices, and methods are applied.
- Any unusual or complex situations that might affect the financial statements.
- Significant transactions taking place near the end of the period.
- Status of uncorrected misstatements identified in a previous engagement.
- Questions that have arisen in applying review procedures.
- Subsequent events.
- Knowledge of potentially material fraud or suspected fraud.
- Significant journal entries and other adjustments.
- Communications from regulatory agencies.

Finally, the auditors must obtain a representation letter that is tailored to the circumstances of the particular engagement. However, all representation letters should include management's acknowledgement of its:

- Responsibility for the financial statements' conformity with generally accepted accounting principles and its belief that it has met this responsibility.
- Responsibility to prevent and detect fraud, as well as to divulge any knowledge that it has of any actual or suspected fraud that is material.
- Responsibility to respond fully and truthfully to all inquiries and to provide complete information, including that on subsequent events.

Review Reports

A review provides the accountants with a basis for expressing **limited assurance** that there are no required material modifications to the financial statements. The accountants' standard report on a review of a nonpublic company's financial statements reads as follows (emphasis added):

> We have *reviewed* the accompanying balance sheet of XYZ Company as of December 31, 20X1, and the related statements of income, retained earnings, and cash flows for the year then ended, in accordance with *Statements on Standards for Accounting and Review Services Issued by the American Institute of Certified Public Accountants.* All information included in these financial statements is the representation of the management of XYZ Company.
>
> A review consists principally of *inquiries* of company personnel and *analytical procedures* applied to financial data. *It is substantially less in scope than an audit in accordance with generally accepted auditing standards,* the objective of which is the expression of an opinion regarding the financial statements taken as a whole. *Accordingly, we do not express such an opinion.*
>
> Based on our review, *we are not aware of any material modifications* that should be made to the accompanying financial statements in order for them to be in conformity with generally accepted accounting principles.

The date of completion of the review procedures should be used as the date of the report, and each page of the financial statements should include the caption "See Accountants' Review Report."

To provide any degree of assurance about the fairness of information requires that the CPAs be independent. Thus, the accountants performing a review must be independent of the client.

Departures from Generally Accepted Accounting Principles

A modification of the report is required when the accountants are aware of a material departure from generally accepted accounting principles (or some other comprehensive basis of accounting). The departure is referred to in the report's third paragraph as illustrated below:

> With the exception of the matter described in the following paragraph, we are not aware of any material modifications . . . .

In a separate paragraph of the review report the departure will be described. The following is an example of a report paragraph that discusses a departure from generally accepted accounting principles:

> As disclosed in Note 5 to the financial statements, generally accepted accounting principles require that land be stated at cost. Management has informed us that the Company has stated its land at appraised value and that, if generally accepted accounting principles had been followed, the land account and stockholders' equity would have been decreased by $500,000.

Review reports are not altered in cases involving a lack of consistent application of generally accepted accounting principles or the existence of major uncertainties. Also, when an accountant is unable to perform the necessary review procedures due to a scope limitation, the review is considered incomplete and no review report should be issued.

Accountants' Reports on Comparative Statements

As with audited financial statements, accountants who have reviewed prior-period financial statements presented with those of the current period should report on both years. *SSARS 2* provides guidance on the format of the accountants' reports on comparative financial statements.[6] If the accountants have reviewed both sets of financial statements, they will merely update their review report on the prior year by issuing one review report covering both years. The report will be dated as of the completion of the current year's review procedures.

In certain situations, the accountants may be engaged to perform a lower level of service on the current year's financial statements than they performed on the prior year's financial statements (e.g., a review this year and an audit last year or a compilation this year and a review last year). In these situations, the CPAs should not update the prior year's report. This would imply that they have performed those types of services to the date of the current year's report. Instead, the CPAs should either reissue their prior year report bearing its original date and present it with the current year's report, or include a reference to the prior year's report in the current year's report. For example, the following paragraph could be added to a compilation report on the current year's financial statements to refer to a review of the comparative financial statements for the prior year.

> The accompanying 20X1 financial statements of XYZ Company were previously reviewed by us, and our report dated March 1, 20X2, stated that we were not aware of any material modifications that should be made to those statements in order for them to be in conformity with generally accepted accounting principles. We have not performed any procedures in connection with that review engagement after the date of our report on the 20X1 financial statements.

A reference similar to the one above should also be included in the current report when another public accounting firm, whose report is not presented, reviewed the comparative financial statements.

[6]AICPA, *Statement on Standards for Accounting and Review Services 2,* "Reporting on Comparative Financial Statements" (New York, 1979), AR 200.

Illustrative Case
Summary Annual Reports

A number of corporations have experimented with issuing summary annual reports to shareholders. These reports generally include condensed financial statements and refer shareholders desiring more detailed information to the annual report filed with the SEC (Form 10-K). The auditors of these companies, following *SAS 42,* issue a report on the condensed information that refers to the report included with the Form 10-K.

Letters for Underwriters

Learning Objective 6

Investment banking firms that underwrite a securities issue often request independent auditors who audited the financial statements and schedules in the registration statement to issue a letter for the underwriters. This letter is commonly called a **comfort letter,** and *SAS 72,* "Letters for Underwriters and Certain Other Requesting Parties," as amended by *SAS 86,* provides guidance on its content. It indicates that a comfort letter may include the following subjects:

1. The independence of the auditors.
2. Whether the audited financial statements and financial statement schedules included in the registration statement comply with the accounting requirements of the Securities Act of 1933 and related regulations.
3. Unaudited financial statements, condensed interim financial information, and pro forma financial information. The auditors can provide negative assurance on the historical financial information only if it has been reviewed in accordance with *SAS 71.*
4. Changes in selected financial statement items during a period subsequent to the date and period of the latest financial statements included in the registration statement.
5. Tables, statistics, and other financial information included in the registration statement.
6. **Negative assurance** as to whether certain nonfinancial statement information included in the registration statement complies with SEC regulations.

Comfort letters help the underwriters in fulfilling their obligation to perform a reasonable investigation of the securities registration statement. No definitive criteria exist for the underwriters' "reasonable investigation." Therefore, the underwriters should approve the adequacy of the CPAs' procedures serving as a basis for the comfort letter.

Condensed Financial Statements

Occasionally, a client-prepared document will include *condensed financial statements* developed from audited basic financial statements. These statements typically include considerably less detail than the basic financial statements. The CPAs who have issued an audit report on the basic financial statements may be asked to report on the condensed statements. In these circumstances, the auditors should issue a report indicating they have audited the basic financial statements, the date and type of opinion expressed, and whether the condensed information is fairly stated in all material respects in relation to the basic financial statements. *SAS 42* (AU 552), "Reporting on Condensed Financial Statements and Selected Financial Data," provides guidance for these types of reports.

Accounting Services

Learning Objective 7

Many clients request CPAs to perform accounting services either in addition to or instead of attestation services. Reports resulting from accounting services provide no explicit assurance that the information constitutes a fair presentation. Because no explicit assurance is provided, accountants performing such services need *not* be independent of their client, although a lack of independence must be indicated in their report. In this section we will discuss:

- Compilations of financial statements of nonpublic companies.

- "Association" with the financial statements of public companies.
- Compilations of prospective financial information.

Compilation Engagements for Financial Statements of Nonpublic Companies

A **compilation** involves the *preparation* of financial statements from the accounting records and other representations of the client. To perform a compilation, *SSARS 1* requires the accountants to have knowledge of the accounting principles and practices used within the client's industry and a general understanding of the client's business transactions and accounting records. The CPAs must evaluate the client's representations in light of this knowledge.

At a minimum, the accountants must read the compiled statements for appropriate format and obvious material misstatement. CPAs performing a compilation must not accept patently unreasonable information. If the client's information appears to be incorrect, incomplete, or otherwise unsatisfactory, the CPAs should insist upon revised information. If the client refuses to provide revised information, the CPAs should withdraw from the engagement. Beyond these basic requirements, CPAs have no responsibility to perform any investigative procedures to substantiate the client's representations.

Proper CPA reporting on compiled statements is dependent upon whether the financial statements are expected to be used by a third party—a party other than management. If no such third-party use is expected, an accountant may either (1) issue a compilation report (described below) or (2) not issue a report, but only document the understanding with the client through use of an engagement letter. The engagement letter, preferably signed by management, must make clear the services performed and the limitations on the use of the financial statements. A phrase such as "Restricted for Management's Use Only" should be included on each page of the financial statements.

If the financial statements are to be used by a third party (or reasonably might be expected to be used by a third party) a compilation report must be issued by the CPA. This report disclaims an opinion or any other form of assurance on the financial statements. The recommended wording for an accountants' report on the compilation of financial statements is shown below (emphasis added):

We have *compiled* the accompanying balance sheet of XYZ Company as of December 31, 20X1, and the related statements of income, retained earnings, and cash flows for the year then ended, in accordance with *Statements on Standards for Accounting and Review Services issued by the American Institute of Certified Public Accountants.*

A compilation is limited to presenting in the form of financial statements information *that is the representation of management.* We have not audited or reviewed the accompanying financial statements and, accordingly, *do not express an opinion or any other form of assurance on them.*

Each page of the unaudited financial statements should be marked "See Accountants' Compilation Report," and the accountants' report should be dated as of the completion of the compilation.

Accountants may issue a compilation report on one or more individual financial statements, without compiling a complete set of statements. Also, financial statements may be compiled on a comprehensive basis of accounting *other than* generally accepted accounting principles. In this case, the basis of accounting used must be disclosed either in the statements or in the accountants' report.

Departures from Generally Accepted Accounting Principles

Treatment of departures from generally accepted accounting principles parallels that for reviews of financial statements. A departure from generally accepted accounting principles requires the accountants to discuss the departure in a separate paragraph in the compilation report. Refusal of the client to provide additional or revised information requested by the accountant results in withdrawal from the engagement. A lack of consistency of application of generally accepted accounting principles or the existence of major uncertainties does not require modification of the report.

Compilations That Omit Substantially All Disclosures

The numerous disclosures required by generally accepted accounting principles may not be particularly useful in the financial statements of a nonpublic business, especially when the statements are intended for internal use by management. Therefore, a nonpublic client may request CPAs to compile financial statements that omit substantially all of the disclosures required by GAAP. CPAs may compile such statements, provided that the omission is clearly indicated in the accountants' report. In such situations the accountants should add the following last paragraph to their report:

> Management has elected to omit substantially all of the disclosures (and the statement of cash flows) required by generally accepted accounting principles. If the omitted disclosures were included in the financial statements, they might influence the user's conclusions about the company's financial position, results of operations, and cash flows. Accordingly, these financial statements are not designed for those who are not informed about such matters.

If the client wishes to include only some of the disclosures required by GAAP, these disclosures should be labeled "Selected Information—Substantially All Disclosures Required by Generally Accepted Accounting Principles Are Not Included."

Compilations of Information in Prescribed Forms

Prescribed forms refer to standard, preprinted forms designed or adopted by the institution or agency to which the form is to be submitted. An example is a bank loan application. Since these prescribed forms often require financial statement items to be presented on a basis other than generally accepted accounting principles, accountants compiling the forms under *SSARS 1* would have to point out all the GAAP departures in their reports. This would seem to be unnecessary because it can be presumed that the information requested by a prescribed form meets the needs of the institution that designed the form. Accordingly, *SSARS 3*[7] allows the accountants to use the following alternative compilation report when a prescribed form calls for departures from GAAP.

> We have compiled the (identification of financial statements, including period covered and name of entity) included in the accompanying prescribed form in accordance with *Statements on Standards for Accounting and Review Services issued by the American Institute of Certified Public Accountants.*
>
> Our compilation was limited to presenting in the form prescribed by (name of body) information that is the representation of management. We have not audited or reviewed the financial statements referred to above and, accordingly, do not express an opinion or any other form of assurance on them.
>
> These financial statements (including related disclosures) are presented in accordance with the requirements of (name of body), which differ from generally accepted accounting principles. Accordingly, these financial statements are not designed for those who are not informed about such differences.

The accountants should modify this report to point out material departures from the requirements of the prescribed form, or other GAAP departures not required by the form.

Compilations When the CPAs Are Not Independent

Since compilations are accounting and not attestation services, CPAs may perform them even when they are not independent of the client. The accountants should indicate their lack of independence by adding the following last paragraph to their compilation report:

> We are not independent with respect to XYZ Company.

---

[7]AICPA, *Statement on Standards for Accounting and Review Services 3,* "Compilation Reports on Financial Statements Included in Certain Prescribed Forms" (New York, 1981), AR 300.03.

Other "Association" with the Financial Statements of Public Companies

CPAs also may become "associated" with the financial statements of a public company by assisting the company in preparing those statements or submitting the statements to the client or another third party. In such cases, the CPAs have no responsibility for performing investigative procedures, except to read the statements for obvious material misstatements. When CPAs are associated with the statements of a public company, but have neither audited nor reviewed those statements, they should determine that each page of the statements is marked as "unaudited" and issue the following disclaimer of opinion:

> The accompanying balance sheet of XYZ Corporation as of December 31, 20X1, and the related statements of income, retained earnings, and cash flows for the year then ended were not audited by us and, accordingly, we do not express an opinion on them.

If the CPAs know that unaudited financial statements are not in accordance with generally accepted accounting principles, or do not contain adequate informative disclosures, they should insist upon appropriate revision or should state their reservations in the disclaimer of opinion. If necessary, the CPAs should withdraw from the engagement and refuse to be associated with the financial statements.

CPA Firm Not Independent

A public accounting firm that is not independent of a public company may be associated with *unaudited* financial statements of that company. In such cases, the CPAs must issue a special disclaimer of opinion, which discloses the lack of independence. The AICPA has suggested the following language for this report.

> We are not independent with respect to XYZ Company, and the accompanying balance sheet as of December 31, 20X1, and the related statements of income, retained earnings, and cash flows for the year then ended were not audited by us and, accordingly, we do not express an opinion on them.

Notice that the accountants' report does not explain *why* the public accounting firm is not independent of the client. The Auditing Standards Board believes it would be confusing to users of the report if these reasons were spelled out.

Chapter Summary

This chapter described CPA services on historical financial information other than audits of corporation financial statements in accordance with U.S. generally accepted accounting principles. To summarize:

1. Special reports by auditors refer to those on: (*a*) financial statements prepared in accordance with some other comprehensive basis of accounting; (*b*) specified elements, accounts, or items of financial statements; (*c*) compliance with contractual or regulatory requirements; (*d*) special-purpose financial presentations; and (*e*) financial information presented in prescribed forms or schedules.

2. There are several major differences between personal financial statements and those of other types of organizations. For example, assets and liabilities on personal financial statements are presented at their estimated current values and amounts. Accountants may audit, review, or compile personal financial statements.

3. Management of a public company must engage CPAs to review the company's interim financial statements. If they are also engaged to issue a report, it will provide limited assurance that the financial statements contain no material departures from GAAP. The procedures performed in a review engagement consist of performing analytical procedures, making inquiries of management, reviewing minutes, and obtaining written representations from management. The accountants will adjust the specific procedures based on their knowledge of the client's internal control and business.

4. Nonpublic companies may engage CPAs to review their annual or interim financial statements. The procedures involved are similar to those for the review of a public company, although the accountants are not required to obtain an understanding of internal control of a nonpublic company and the professional guidance provided is more general in nature.

5. Letters for underwriters (comfort letters) provide assurance about various information contained in registration statements used for the sale of securities. They are designed to help the underwriters establish their due diligence requirement in investigating the fairness of the registration statement.

6. When compiled financial statements are not expected to be used by a third party, either a compilation report may be issued or an understanding with the client may be documented through use of an engagement letter. When third-party reliance is anticipated, the accountants must issue a report that provides no explicit assurance. CPAs who are not independent may perform compilations.

Key Terms Introduced or Emphasized in Chapter 19

Comfort letter   A letter issued by the independent auditors to the underwriters of securities registered with the SEC under the Securities Act of 1933. Comfort letters deal with such matters as the auditors' independence and the compliance of unaudited data with requirements of the SEC.

Compilation   An accounting service that involves the preparation of information from client records. No assurance is provided in a compilation.

Limited assurance (negative assurance)   The level of assurance provided by CPAs who review historical financial statements.

Negative assurance   An assertion by CPAs that after applying limited investigative techniques to certain information, they are not aware of the need to modify the presentation of the information. Equivalent to limited or moderate assurance.

Nonpublic company   A company other than one whose securities are traded on a public market or one that makes a filing with a regulatory agency in preparation for the sale of securities on a public market.

Public company   A company whose stock is traded on a public market or a company in the process of registering its stock for public sale.

Review of financial statements   A form of attestation based on inquiry and analytical procedures applied for the purpose of expressing limited assurance that historical financial statements are presented in accordance with generally accepted accounting principles or some other appropriate bases.

Special report   An auditors' report issued on any of the following: (*a*) financial statements prepared on a comprehensive basis of accounting other than GAAP, (*b*) elements of financial statements, (*c*) compliance with regulatory or contractual requirements, (*d*) financial presentations to comply with contractual agreements or regulatory provisions, or (*e*) audited information presented in prescribed forms.

Review Questions

19–1.   Evaluate this statement: "All companies should be audited annually."

19–2.   Evaluate this statement: "Auditors perform attestation services and accountants perform accounting services."

19–3.   In communications with clients, should CPAs refer to themselves as auditors or as accountants? Explain.

19–4.   Can auditors express an unqualified opinion on financial statements that are not presented on the basis of generally accepted accounting principles? Explain.

19–5.   Does the issuance of a special report based on agreed-upon procedures indicate an audit engagement or an accounting service? Why?

19–6.   Explain why engagements to perform agreed-upon procedures are restricted to specified parties.

19–7.   Describe the possible forms of audit reports for a U.S.-based client that is issuing a report for use primarily outside the United States.

19–8.   Jane Wilson has prepared personal financial statements in which her assets are valued at her historical cost, less appropriate depreciation. Is this presentation in conformity with generally accepted accounting principles? Can a public accounting firm audit these statements and issue an unqualified opinion?

19–9.   What are the general types of procedures performed during a review of the quarterly financial statements of a public company?

19–10.   Describe the most unique reporting aspect about the CPAs' required review of the quarterly financial statements of public companies.

19–11.   How do CPAs of public companies assist audit committees in performing their oversight function with respect to quarterly financial statements?

19–12. What types of services may be performed by CPAs with respect to the financial statements of nonpublic companies?

19–13. How does a review of the financial statements of a nonpublic company differ from an audit?

19–14. What are the types of procedures performed during the review of the financial statements of a nonpublic company?

19–15. Are engagement letters needed for accounting and review services? Explain.

19–16. What is the purpose of a comfort letter? Discuss.

19–17. What form of opinion will the auditors normally issue with respect to *condensed financial statements* that the client has developed from the audited financial statements?

19–18. What procedures are required when a CPA performs a compilation of financial statements?

19–19. Can the CPAs report on a nonpublic client's financial statements that omit substantially all disclosures required by generally accepted accounting principles? Explain.

19–20. What should the accountants do if they discover that the financial statements they are compiling contain a material departure from generally accepted accounting principles?

19–21. Describe a CPA's reporting responsibility when compiling financial statements that are not expected to be used by a third party.

19–22. Assume that a public accounting firm is reviewing the financial statements of a nonpublic company and discovers that the firm is not independent. What alternatives are available to the firm?

Questions Requiring Analysis

19–23. An accountants' report was appended to the financial statements of Worthmore, Inc., a public company. The statements consisted of a balance sheet as of November 30 and statements of income and retained earnings for the year then ended. The first three paragraphs of the report contained the wording of the standard unqualified report, and a fourth paragraph read as follows:

> The wives of two partners of our firm owned a material investment in the outstanding common stock of Worthmore, Inc., during the fiscal year ending November 30. The aforementioned individuals disposed of their holdings of Worthmore, Inc., on December 3 in a transaction that did not result in a profit or a loss. This information is included in our report in order to comply with certain disclosure requirements of the *Code of Professional Conduct* of the American Institute of Certified Public Accountants.
>
> Bell & Davis
> Certified Public Accountants

Required:

a. Was the public accounting firm of Bell & Davis independent with respect to the audit of Worthmore, Inc.'s financial statements? Explain.

b. Do you find Bell & Davis's report satisfactory? Explain.

(AICPA, adapted)

19–24. You have been asked by Ambassador Hardware Co., a small nonpublic company, to submit a proposal for the audit of the company. After performing an investigation of the company, including its management and accounting system, you advise the president of Ambassador that the audit fee will be approximately $20,000. Ambassador's president was somewhat surprised at the fee, and after discussions with members of the board of directors, he concluded that the company could not afford an audit at this time.

Required:

a. Discuss management's alternatives to having their company's financial statements audited in accordance with generally accepted auditing standards.

b. What should Ambassador's management consider when selecting the type of service that you should provide? Explain.

19–25. Rose & Co., CPAs, has satisfactorily completed the audit of the financial statements of Dale, Booster & Co., a partnership, for the year ended December 31, 20X1. The financial statements that were prepared on the entity's income tax (cash) basis include notes that indicate that the partnership was involved in continuing litigation of material amounts relating to alleged infringement of a competitor's patent. The amount of damages, if any, resulting from this litigation could not be determined at the time of completion of the engagement. The prior years' financial statements were not presented.

Required: Prepare an auditors' unqualified special report on the financial statements of Dale, Booster & Co. Your report should include two "explanatory paragraphs": one to mention the basis of accounting used, and another to emphasize the matter of the pending litigation. Address your report to Dale, Booster & Co.

(AICPA, adapted)

19–26.   Occasionally, public accounting firms are engaged to report on specified elements, accounts, and items of financial statements.

Required:
a. Discuss three types of reports that may be provided for specified elements, accounts, and items of financial statements.

b. Why should reports on the application of agreed-upon procedures to information be restricted as to use?

19–27.   "When performing accounting services, accountants provide no assurance in their reports. These reports may therefore be considered *special reports*."

Required:
a. Do you agree or disagree with the above statement? Explain.

b. Discuss the major types of special reports.

c. Provide an example of an accounting service.

19–28.   You have been engaged by the management of Pippin, Inc., a nonpublic company, to review the company's financial statements for the year ended December 31, 20XX. To prepare for the engagement, you consult the *Statements on Standards for Accounting and Review Services.*

Required:
a. Discuss the procedures required for the performance of a review of financial statements.

b. Explain the content of the report on a review of financial statements.

c. Discuss your responsibilities if you find that the financial statements contain a material departure from generally accepted accounting principles.

19–29.   In connection with a public offering of first-mortgage bonds by Guizzetti Corporation, the bond underwriter has asked Guizzetti's CPAs to furnish it with a comfort letter giving as much assurance as possible on Guizzetti's unaudited financial statements for the three months ended March 31. The CPAs had expressed an unqualified opinion on Guizzetti's financial statements for the year ended December 31, the preceding year; they also performed a review of Guizzetti's financial statements for the three months ended March 31. Nothing has come to their attention that would indicate that the March 31 statements are not properly presented.

Required:
a. Explain what can be stated about the unaudited financial statements in the letter.

b. Discuss other matters that are typically included in comfort letters.

19–30.   Andrew Wilson, CPA, has assembled the financial statements of Texas Mirror Co., a small public company. He has not performed an audit of the financial statements in accordance with generally accepted auditing standards. Wilson is confused about the standards applicable to this type of engagement.

Required:
a. Explain where Wilson should look for guidance concerning this engagement.

b. Discuss the concept of association with financial statements.

c. Explain Wilson's responsibilities with respect to a preparation of unaudited financial statements.

Multiple Choice Questions

19–31.   Select the best answer for each of the following and explain fully the reason for your selection.

a. Which of the following is *not* typically performed when the auditors are performing a review of client financial statements?

(1) Analytical procedures applied to financial data.

(2) Inquiries about significant subsequent events.

(3) Confirmation of accounts receivable.

(4) Obtaining an understanding of accounting principles followed in the client's industry.

b. Which of the following must be obtained in a review of a nonpublic company?

	Engagement Letter	Representation Letter
(1)	Yes	Yes
(2)	Yes	No
(3)	No	Yes
(4)	No	No

c. The CPA who is *not* independent may perform which of the following services for a nonpublic company?

	Compilation	Review
(1)	Yes	Yes
(2)	Yes	No
(3)	No	Yes
(4)	No	No

d. When performing a review of a nonpublic company, which is *least* likely to be included in auditor inquiries of management members with responsibility for financial and accounting matters?

   (1) Subsequent events.

   (2) Significant journal entries and other adjustments.

   (3) Communications with related parties.

   (4) Unusual or complex situations affecting the financial statements.

e. The proper report by an auditor relating to condensed financial statements includes:

   (1) A statement about the type of opinion expressed in the prior year.

   (2) An adverse opinion.

   (3) An opinion on whether the condensed information is fairly stated in all material respects in relation to the basic financial statements.

   (4) No assurance on the information.

f. Concerning interim quarterly financial statements, management of public companies:

   (1) Must engage CPAs to audit the statements.

   (2) Must engage CPAs to review the statements.

   (3) May choose to engage CPAs to review the statements.

   (4) May not engage CPAs to become associated with the statements.

g. A proper compilation report on financial statements that omit note disclosures:

   (1) Includes an adverse opinion.

   (2) Includes a disclaimer of opinion on the accuracy of such note disclosures.

   (3) Indicates that management has omitted such information.

   (4) Indicates that note disclosures are not necessary for those not informed about such matters.

h. Which of the following forms of accountant association always leads to a restricted use report?

   (1) Compilation.

   (2) Review.

   (3) Examination.

   (4) Agreed-upon procedures.

i. Which assertion is generally most difficult to attest to with respect to personal financial statements?

   (1) Existence and occurrence.

   (2) Rights and obligations.

   (3) Completeness.

   (4) Valuation.

j. Special reports are appropriate for:

   (1) Reviews of interim statements.

      (2) Compliance with regulatory requirements related to audited financial statements.

      (3) Forecasts.

      (4) Projections.

  k. In which of the following reports should a CPA *not* express negative (limited) assurance?

      (1) A standard compilation report on financial statements of a nonpublic entity.

      (2) A standard review report on interim financial statements of a public entity.

      (3) A standard review report on financial statements of a nonpublic entity.

      (4) A comfort letter on financial information included in a registration statement filed with the Securities and Exchange Commission.

  l. Comfort letters to underwriters are normally signed by the:

      (1) Independent auditor.

      (2) Underwriter.

      (3) Client's lawyer.

      (4) Chief executive officer.

Problems

19–32.   Jiffy Clerical Services is a company that furnishes temporary office help to its customers. The company maintains its accounting records on a basis of cash receipts and cash disbursements. You have audited the company for the year ended December 31, 20X4, and have concluded that the company's financial statements represent a fair presentation on that basis.

Required: *a.* Draft the unqualified auditors' report you would issue covering the financial statements (a statement of assets and liabilities and the related statement of revenue collected and expenses paid) for the year ended December 31, 20X4.

  b. Briefly discuss and justify your modifications of the conventional standard auditors' report on GAAP financial statements.

19–33.   On March 12, 20X5, Brown & Brown, CPAs, completed the audit engagement of the financial statements of Modern Museum, Inc., for the year ended December 31, 20X4. Modern Museum presents comparative financial statements on a modified cash basis. Assets, liabilities, fund balances, support, revenues, and expenses are recognized when cash is received or disbursed, except that Modern includes a provision for depreciation of buildings and equipment. Brown & Brown believes that Modern's three financial statements, prepared in accordance with a comprehensive basis of accounting other than generally accepted accounting principles, are adequate for Modern's needs and wishes to issue an auditors' special report on the financial statements. Brown & Brown has gathered sufficient competent evidential matter in order to be satisfied that the financial statements are fairly presented according to the modified cash basis. Brown & Brown audited Modern's 20X3 financial statements and issued the auditors' special report expressing an unqualified opinion.

Required: Draft the auditors' report to accompany Modern's comparative financial statements.

(AICPA, adapted)

19–34.   Loman, CPA, who has audited the financial statements of the Broadwall Corporation, a publicly held company, for the year ended December 31, 20X6, was asked to perform a review of the financial statements of Broadwall Corporation for the period ending March 31, 20X7. The engagement letter stated that a review does not provide a basis for the expression of an opinion.

Required: *a.* Explain why Loman's review will *not* provide a basis for the expression of an opinion.

  b. What are the review procedures Loman should perform, and what is the purpose of each procedure? Structure your response as follows:

Procedure	Purpose of Procedure

(AICPA, adapted)

19–35.   The following report on the basic financial statements was drafted by a staff assistant at the completion of the review engagement of Delano Company, a nonpublic continuing client for the year ended September 30, 20X8.

To the Board of Directors of Delano Company:

We have reviewed the accompanying balance sheet of Delano Company as of September 30, 20X8, and the related statements of income and retained earnings for the year then ended, in accordance with auditing standards generally accepted in the United States of America. Our review included such tests of the accounting records as we considered necessary in the circumstances.

A review consists principally of inquiries of company personnel. It is substantially less in scope than an audit, but more in scope than a compilation. Accordingly, we express only limited assurance on the accompanying financial statements.

Based on our review, we are not aware of any material modifications that should be made to the accompanying financial statements in order for them to be in conformity with generally accepted accounting principles applied on a consistent basis.

Anston & Co., CPAs
November 2, 20X8

Required: Identify the deficiencies in the draft of the proposed report on the comparative financial statements. Group the deficiencies by paragraph.

19–36. Norman Lewis, an inexperienced member of your staff, has compiled the financial statements of Williams Grocery. He has submitted the following report for your review:

The accompanying financial statements have been compiled by us. A compilation is an accounting service, but we also applied certain analytical procedures to the financial data.

As explained in Note 3, the Company changed accounting principles for accounting for its inventories. We have not audited or reviewed the accompanying financial statements, but nothing came to our attention to indicate that they are in error.

Required: Describe the deficiencies in the report, give reasons why they are deficiencies, and briefly discuss how the report should be corrected. Do not discuss the addressee, signature, and date. Organize your answer sheet as follows:

Deficiency	Reason	Correction

19–37. The following report was drafted on October 25, 20X8, by Bill Major, CPA, at the completion of the engagement to compile the financial statements of Ajax Company for the year ended September 30, 20X8. Ajax is a nonpublic entity in which Major's child has a material direct financial interest. Ajax decided to omit substantially all of the disclosures required by generally accepted accounting principles because the financial statements will be for management's use only. The statement of cash flows was also omitted because management does not believe it to be a useful financial statement.

To the Board of Directors of Ajax Company:

I have compiled the accompanying financial statements of Ajax Company as of September 30, 20×8, and for the year then ended. I planned and performed the compilation to obtain limited assurance about whether the financial statements are free of material misstatements.

A compilation is limited to presenting information in the form of financial statements. It is substantially less in scope than an audit in accordance with generally accepted auditing standards, the objective of which is the expression of an opinion regarding the financial statements taken as a whole. I have not audited the accompanying financial statements and, accordingly, do not express any opinion on them.

Management has elected to omit substantially all of the disclosures required by generally accepted accounting principles. If the omitted disclosures were included in the financial statements, they might influence the user's conclusions about the Company's financial position, results of operations, and changes in financial position.

I am not independent with respect to Ajax Company. This lack of independence is due to my child's ownership of a material direct financial interest in Ajax Company.

This report is intended solely for the information and use of the Board of Directors and management of Ajax Company and should not be used for any other purpose.

Bill Major, CPA

Required: Identify the deficiencies contained in Major's report on the compiled financial statements. Group the deficiencies by paragraph where applicable. Do *not* redraft the report.

(AICPA, adapted)

19–38. The limitations on the CPAs' professional responsibilities when they are associated with unaudited financial statements are often misunderstood. These misunderstandings can be substantially reduced if the CPAs follow professional pronouncements in the course of their work and take other appropriate measures.

Required: The following list describes seven situations CPAs may encounter, or contentions they may have to deal with, in their association with and preparation of *unaudited* financial statements. Briefly discuss the extent of the CPAs' responsibilities and, if appropriate, the actions they should take to minimize any misunderstandings. Mark your answers to correspond to the letters in the following list.

a. The CPAs were engaged by telephone to perform write-up work including the compilation of financial statements. The client believes that the CPAs have been engaged to audit the financial statements and examine the records accordingly.

b. A group of investors who own a farm that is managed by an independent agent engage CPAs to compile quarterly unaudited financial statements for them. The CPAs prepare the financial statements from information given to them by the independent agent. Subsequently, the investors find the statements were inaccurate because their independent agent was embezzling funds. They refuse to pay the CPAs' fee and blame them for allowing the situation to go undetected, contending that the CPAs should not have relied on representations from the independent agent.

c. In comparing the trial balance with the general ledger, the CPAs find an account labeled Audit Fees in which the client has accumulated the CPAs' quarterly billings for accounting services including the compilation of quarterly unaudited financial statements.

d. Unaudited financial statements for a public company were accompanied by the following letter of transmittal from the CPAs:

> We are enclosing your company's balance sheet as of June 30, 20X1, and the related statements of income and retained earnings and cash flows for the six months then ended to which we have applied certain auditing procedures.

e. To determine appropriate account classification, the CPAs examined a number of the client's invoices. They noted in their working papers that some invoices were missing, but did nothing further because it was felt that the invoices did not affect the unaudited financial statements they were compiling. When the client subsequently discovered that invoices were missing, he contended that the CPAs should not have ignored the missing invoices when compiling the financial statements and had a responsibility to at least inform him that they were missing.

f. The CPAs compiled a draft of unaudited financial statements from the client's records. While reviewing this draft with their client, the CPAs learned that the land and building were recorded at appraisal value.

g. The CPAs are engaged to compile the financial statements of a nonpublic company. During the engagement, the CPAs learn of several items for which generally accepted accounting principles would require adjustments of the statements and note disclosure. The controller agrees to make the recommended adjustments to the statements, but says that she is not going to add the notes because the statements are unaudited.

(AICPA, adapted)

19–39. Brown, CPA, received a telephone call from Calhoun, the sole owner and manager of a small corporation. Calhoun asked Brown to compile the financial statements for the corporation and emphasized that the statements were needed in two weeks for external financing purposes. Calhoun was vague when Brown inquired about the intended use of the statements. Brown was convinced that Calhoun thought Brown's work would constitute an audit. To avoid confusion, Brown decided not to explain to Calhoun that the engagement would be to compile the financial statements only. Brown, with the understanding that a substantial fee would be paid if the work was completed in two weeks, accepted the engagement and started the work at once.

During the course of the work, Brown discovered an accrued expense account labeled Professional Fees and learned that the balance in the account represented an accrual for the cost of Brown's services. Brown suggested to Calhoun's bookkeeper that the account name be changed to Fees for Limited Audit Engagement. Brown also reviewed several invoices to determine whether accounts were being properly classified. Some of the invoices were missing. Brown listed the missing invoice numbers in the working papers with a note indicating that there should be a follow-up on the next engagement. Brown also discovered that the available records included the fixed asset values at estimated current replacement costs. Based on the records available, Brown compiled a balance sheet, income statement, and statement of stockholders' equity. In addition, Brown drafted the notes, but he decided that any mention of the replacement costs would only confuse the readers. Brown suggested to Calhoun that readers of the financial statements would be better informed if they received a separate letter from Calhoun explaining the meaning and effect of the estimated replacement costs of the fixed assets. Brown mailed the financial statements and notes to Calhoun with the following note included on each page:

> The accompanying financial statements are submitted to you without complete audit verification.

Required: Identify the inappropriate actions of Brown, and indicate what Brown should have done to avoid each inappropriate action. Organize your answer sheet as follows:

Inappropriate Action	What Brown Should Have Done to Avoid Inappropriate Action

(AICPA, adapted)

In-Class Team Case

19–40. Webstar, a nonpublic company, is owned by Ben Williams and three of his friends. Previously the company's financing has been internally generated, with limited equity contributions by the owners. The company has not been audited in the past, and Williams has said to you that while he generally understands the nature of an audit, he would like to discuss services other than an audit. Specifically, he read a brief article in a management journal which described briefly reviews, compilations, financial statements prepared following another comprehensive basis of accounting (other than generally accepted accounting principles), and auditing specified elements of financial statements. Among his questions are the following:

a. Review of financial statements:

(1) Is the review form of association available for Webstar's financial statements?

(2) What procedures are typically included in a review?

(3) What type of assurance is included in a review report?

(4) What will result in modification of a review report?

(5) Williams says that he heard something about there being a requirement that every company obtain a review of its financial statements. He has been concerned, since he never has had this done. What's the story with this?

b. Compilation of financial statements:

(1) Is the compilation form of association available?

(2) What procedures are typically included in a compilation?

(3) If a compilation is performed, must a compilation report be issued?

(4) What type of assurance would be provided in a compilation report?

(5) What will result in modification of a compilation report?

c. Financial statements: Williams says he isn't sure he wants to prepare financial statements following GAAP. He says he needs only statements based on the income tax method he uses to file his income taxes.

(1) Are you able to issue an audit report based on the income tax basis?

(2) What type of report is this?

(3) How will the report issued differ from that of a GAAP audit?

d. Auditing a small portion of financial statements: Williams has given some thought to having an audit of just his company's revenues for the year and receivables at year-end.

(1) May you perform an audit of only these two accounts?

(2) What types of engagements are possible here?

(3) What type of assurance will be provided in these reports?

e. *Auditing assets to be purchased:* Williams states that the owners are now considering selling a portion of Webstar's assets to another company.

(1) May you perform an audit form of service on those assets?

(2) What type of report will be issued?

Required: Draft brief answers to each of the above questions.

Research and Discussion Case

19–41.   You are a young CPA just starting your own practice in Hollywood, California, after five years' experience with a "Big 4" firm. You have several connections in the entertainment industry and hope to develop a practice rendering income tax, auditing, and accounting services to celebrities and other wealthy clients.

One of your first engagements is arranged by John Forbes, a long-established business manager for a number of celebrities and a personal friend of yours. You are engaged to audit the personal statement of financial condition (balance sheet) of Dallas McBain, one of Forbes's clients. McBain is a popular rock star, with a net worth of approximately $100 million. However, the star also has a reputation as an extreme recluse who is never seen in public except at performances.

Forbes handles all of McBain's business affairs, and all your communications with McBain are through Forbes. You have never met McBain personally and have no means of contacting the star directly. All of McBain's business records are maintained at Forbes's office. Forbes also issues checks for many of McBain's personal expenses, using a check-signing machine and a facsimile plate of McBain's signature.

During the audit, you notice that during the year numerous checks totaling approximately $500,000 have been issued payable to Cash. In addition, the proceeds of a $250,000 sale of marketable securities was never deposited in any of McBain's bank accounts. In the accounting records, all of these amounts have been charged to the account entitled "Personal Living Expenses." There is no further documentation of these disbursements.

When you bring these items to Forbes's attention, he explains that celebrities such as McBain often spend a lot of cash supporting various "hangers-on," whom they don't want identified by name. He also states, "Off the record, some of these people also have some very expensive habits." He points out, however, that you are auditing only the statement of assets and liabilities, not McBain's revenue or expenses. Furthermore, the amount of these transactions is not material in relation to McBain's net worth.

Required: a. Discuss whether the undocumented disbursements and the missing securities' proceeds should be of concern to you in a balance sheet-only audit.

b. Identify the various courses of action that you might at least consider under these circumstances. Explain briefly the arguments supporting each course of action.

c. Explain what you would do and justify your decision.

d. Assume that you are a long-established CPA, independently wealthy, and that the McBain account represents less than 5 percent of the annual revenue of your practice. Would this change in circumstances affect your conclusion in part (*c*)? Discuss.

Suggested References

This textbook, discussion of *1136 Tenants Corporation* case, pp. 111–112; "Audit of Partnerships and Sole Proprietorships," pp. 576–577; and "Audits of Personal Financial Statements," pp. 692–693.

AICPA, *Personal Financial Statements Guide* (New York, 1983), pp. 12–13 and 25–26. *Statement on Auditing Standards 60,* "Communication of Internal Control Related Matters Noted in an Audit" (New York, 1988) AU 325.

Chapter 20

Additional Assurance Services: Other Information

Chapter learning objectives

After studying this chapter, you should be able to:

LO1. Describe the differences among assurance services, attestation services, and audits.

LO2. Explain the applicability of the attestation standards.

LO3. Describe the nature of attestation engagements, including examinations, reviews, and agreed-upon procedures engagements.

LO4. Describe the fundamental attributes of attestation services for internal control over financial reporting.

LO5. Describe the fundamental attributes of attestation services for prospective financial statements.

LO6. Describe the fundamental attributes of attestation services for management discussion and analysis.

LO7. Describe the nature of *Trust Services*.

LO8. Describe the nature of *ElderCare/PrimePlus* services.

LO9. Describe the nature of *CPA Performance View*.

LO10. Describe the nature of *Risk Advisory Services*.

LO11. List several developing assurance services.

To this point, we have focused primarily on services involving historical financial information; but CPAs are being asked to provide a wide range of other assurance services. This chapter focuses on these new types of services, beginning with a discussion of the broad concept of assurance. Next, we will turn our attention to the attestation standards, which apply to a majority of these new assurance services. Finally, we will provide a detailed description of a number of existing and developing services.

Assurance Services

Learning Objective 1

The Special Committee on Assurance Services of the AICPA has defined **assurance services** as independent professional services that "improve the quality of information, or its context, for decision makers."[1] As illustrated in Figure 20.1, assurance services encompass audits of financial statements and all other attestation services but they are broader. Attestation services are restricted to those that involve issuing an examination, review, or agreed-upon procedures report on subject matter or an assertion about subject matter that is the responsibility of another party. In an attestation engagement, the practitioner[2] must evaluate the subject matter of the engagement against *suitable criteria.*[3]

FIGURE 20.1 The Relationship between Assurance Services and Attestation Services

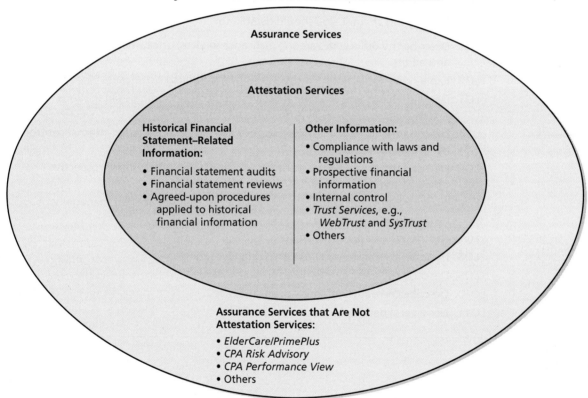

[1] International auditing standards define an assurance engagement as one in which the professional accountant evaluates subject matter, which is the responsibility of another party using identified suitable criteria, to express a conclusion that provides the intended users with a level of assurance about the subject matter. Therefore, in these standards, assurance services are equivalent to the AICPA's concept of attestation services.

[2] Because of the wide variety of assurance services provided by CPAs that are discussed in this chapter, we use the term *practitioner* rather than *auditor* throughout the chapter.

[3] Suitable criteria were previously referred to as "reasonable criteria." Some portions of the *AICPA Professional Standards* still use the term *reasonable criteria.*

FIGURE 20.2   Selected Characteristics of Assurance Services

| | **Assurance Services** | | |
| | **Assurance Services that Are Attestation Services** | | |
	Historical Financial Statement–Related Information*	**Other than Historical Financial Statements**	**Other Assurance Services**
Primary Source of Standards	Auditing standards. Review standards (SSARS).	Attestation standards.	General performance standards of *Code of Professional Conduct* (Rule 201).
Nature	Providing assurance on the reliability of historical financial statement information.	Providing assurance on the reliability of subject matter, or an assertion about subject matter, that is the responsibility of another party (other than historical financial information).	Independent professional services that improve the quality of information, or its context, for decision makers.
Forms of Engagements	Audits. Reviews. Agreed-upon procedures.	Examinations. Reviews. Agreed-upon procedures.	No specific forms have been developed; intended to be flexible.
Form of Report	Written.	Written.	Any reasonable form of communication.
Type of Conclusion	Reliability of information.	Reliability of information.	May be reliability of information, but may address broader concept such as relevance to a decision.
Is Independence Required?	Yes.	Yes.	Yes.

*Includes other services, such as agreed-upon procedures on portions of financial statements, special reports, and reports that are by-products of audits (e.g., communications with audit committees).

As discussed in Chapter 1, assurance services go beyond attestation services. They may involve analyzing data or putting them in a form to facilitate decision making. For example, CPAs may collect information that is generally considered to be relevant to a particular decision and synthesize it for the user. The CPA may also provide assurance that the user has a complete set of information with which to make a decision. In an assurance engagement, a report may or may not be issued and, if one is issued, it could be in oral, symbolic, or any other appropriate form. Figure 20.2 summarizes selected characteristics of the various types of assurance engagements.

The Demand for Assurance Services

The demand for new types of assurance services developed as a natural extension of the audit function. Management realized that contracting costs could be reduced in many situations by providing investors, creditors, customers, and others transacting with the company access to information that is *certified* as to its reliability. As with an audit, these new assurance services reduce information risk for the outside parties and, thereby, enable the company to contract at more favorable terms.

Fueling the demand for other assurance services are the developments in information technology, which have significantly changed the expectations of information users. Users can now instantaneously access a broad range of online information customized to their needs. Therefore, the value of a written audit report on standardized financial statements that are months old has diminished. Decision makers are demanding timely assurance about a wide range of financial and nonfinancial information. In addition, CPAs are using their expertise to place information in formats that improve decision making.

Illustrative Case
Types of Assurance Services

A wide variety of assurance services are currently being performed by accounting firms. In a survey of 21 large- and medium-sized CPA firms, the Special Committee on Assurance Services identified over 275 types of assurance services. A few examples will provide an indication of the breadth of the subject matter of these engagements:

- Customer satisfaction.
- Investment performance.

- Software functionality.
- Effectiveness of risk management.
- Clinical results of in-vitro fertilization.
- The distance that golf balls travel.

Over the last few years the accounting profession, through the AICPA, has been working on developing services that respond to these user demands. Two notable examples include *continuous auditing* and *assurance on system reliability*. **Continuous auditing** involves providing assurance using a series of reports provided simultaneously or shortly after the related information is released.[4] Continuous auditing is one way to provide more timely assurance about various types of information. Another way is by providing assurance about the reliability of the system that produces the information. Attesting to system reliability provides the user with timely assurance about any information generated by that system.

To facilitate the development of new assurance services, the AICPA established the *Assurance Services Executive Committee*, charged with the following responsibility:

> To identify, develop, and communicate new assurance service opportunities for the membership—that is, opportunities to provide new independent professional services that improve the quality of information, or its context, for decision makers. If performance standards are required, the committee will communicate and cooperate with appropriate senior technical committees or other bodies to assist in their formulation if the performance standards come within the latter's purview.

To date, the *Assurance Services Executive Committee* has facilitated the development of new services, and others are in process. Many of these new services are performed in accordance with the *Statements on Standards for Attestation Services*.

Attestation Standards

Learning Objective 2

Attestation standards, presented in *Statements on Standards for Attestation Engagements (SSAE) No. 10,* "Attestation Standards Revision and Recodification"[5] apply to engagements in which practitioners are engaged to issue or do issue an examination, a review, or an agreed-upon procedures report on subject matter, or an assertion about subject matter, that is the responsibility of another party. It is important to distinguish between the subject matter and the assertion about the subject matter.

The **subject matter** of an **attestation engagement** may take many forms, including:

- Historical or prospective performance or condition (e.g., historical prospective financial information, performance measurements, and backlog data).
- Physical characteristics (e.g., narrative descriptions, square footage of facilities).
- Historical events (e.g., price of a market basket of goods on a certain date).
- Analyses (e.g., break-even analyses).

[4] CICA and AICPA Research Report, *Continuous Auditing* (Toronto, 1999).

[5] *Statement No. 10* revises and recodifies the first nine SSAEs. References in this chapter will be entirely to this recodification.

- Systems or processes (e.g., internal control).
- Behavior (e.g., corporate governance, compliance with laws and regulations, and human resource practices).

The practitioners may attest to this subject matter at a point in time or for a period of time.

An **assertion** is a declaration about whether the subject matter is presented in accordance with certain criteria. To perform an attestation engagement, the practitioners generally must obtain an appropriate assertion from the party responsible for the subject matter. For example, in an engagement on a company's internal control over financial reporting, management (the responsible party) might assert that the company has maintained effective internal control.

While the practitioners generally must obtain an appropriate assertion about the subject matter, they ordinarily may report on either the *assertion about the subject matter,* or on the *subject matter* itself. Continuing with our internal control engagement example, if reporting on the assertion, the practitioner's opinion would include assurance on whether management's assertion about internal control is properly stated. Alternatively, when reporting on the subject matter, the practitioner's opinion would include assurance directly on the internal control. The following presents the two methods of reporting.

Reporting on Subject Matter	Reporting on Assertion
In our opinion, Welsing Corporation maintained effective internal control over financial reporting . . . based on [identify the criteria].	In our opinion, *management's assertion that* Welsing Corporation maintained effective internal control over financial reporting . . . based on [identify the criteria].

If the practitioners are reporting on an assertion about the subject matter, the assertion is presented with the subject matter or in the practitioners' report. If the practitioners are reporting *directly* on the subject matter, the assertion normally is included only in a representation letter that the practitioners obtain from the responsible party.

There is an exception to the option of reporting directly upon the subject matter *or* on management's assertion. When the examination reveals material departures from the suitable criteria, to most effectively communicate with the reader of the report, the practitioner should report directly upon the subject matter, and not on the assertion.

The 11 attestation standards provide a general framework for all such engagements. These standards, which were originally presented in Chapter 2, are shown again in Figure 20.3 for convenience. Many of these standards, such as independence, adequate knowledge and training, due professional care, and sufficient evidence, parallel the 10 generally accepted auditing standards. Therefore, we will focus on those aspects of the attestation standards that are unique.

The Criteria

Criteria are standards or benchmarks that are used to evaluate the subject matter of the engagement. Criteria are important in reporting the practitioners' conclusion to the users because they convey the basis on which the conclusion was formed. Without this frame of reference the practitioners' report is subject to misinterpretation. For example, generally accepted accounting principles are ordinarily used as the frame of reference—the criteria—to evaluate the financial statements.

In most areas, however, the criteria are not as well established as are generally accepted accounting principles. Accordingly, a practitioner must evaluate the criteria being followed. As indicated in the third general standard, the criteria used in an attestation engagement must be *suitable* and *available* to the users.

Suitable Criteria

Suitable criteria are those that are *objective* and permit reasonably *consistent measurements*. In addition, the criteria must be sufficiently *complete* such that no relevant factors are omitted that would affect a conclusion about the subject matter. Finally, the criteria must measure some characteristic of the subject matter that is *relevant* to a user's decision.

FIGURE 20.3
AICPA Attestation
Standards

General Standards

1. The engagement shall be performed by a practitioner having *adequate technical training and proficiency in the attest function.*
2. The engagement shall be performed by a practitioner having *adequate knowledge in the subject matter.*
3. The practitioner shall perform the engagement only if he or she has reason to believe that the *subject matter is capable of evaluation or measurement* against criteria that are suitable and available to users.
4. In all matters relating to the engagement, an *independence* in mental attitude shall be maintained by the practitioner.
5. *Due professional care* shall be exercised in the planning and performance of the engagement.

Standards of Fieldwork

1. The work shall be *adequately planned* and assistants, if any, shall be properly *supervised.*
2. *Sufficient evidence* shall be obtained to provide a reasonable basis for the conclusion that is expressed in the report.

Standards of Reporting

1. The report shall *identify the subject matter* or the assertion being reported on and state the *character of the engagement.*
2. The report shall state the *practitioner's conclusion* about the subject matter or the assertion in relation to the criteria against which the subject matter was evaluated.
3. The report shall state all of the practitioner's *significant reservations* about the engagement, the subject matter, and, if applicable, the assertion related thereto.
4. The use of an attest report shall be restricted to specified parties under the following circumstances:
   • When the criteria used to evaluate the subject matter are determined by the practitioner to be suitable only for a limited number of users who either participated in their establishment or can be presumed to have an adequate understanding of the criteria.
   • When the criteria used to evaluate the subject matter are available only to specified parties.
   • When reporting on subject matter and a written assertion has not been provided by the responsible party.
   • When the report is on an attest engagement to apply agreed-upon procedures to the subject matter.

Criteria are ordinarily suitable if they are developed by regulatory agencies or other bodies composed of experts that use due process, including exposing the proposed criteria for public comment. For example, the Committee of Sponsoring Organizations (COSO), discussed in Chapter 7, is an organization that followed due process in the development of its control criteria pertaining to internal control.

Criteria developed by management or industry groups without due process may be suitable, but the practitioner should carefully evaluate them in relation to the characteristics described in the previous paragraph. Criteria that are overly subjective should not be used in an attestation engagement. For example, an assertion that a particular software product is the *best on the market* is too subjective for an attestation engagement. There are no generally accepted criteria for what constitutes the *best* software product.

Some criteria may be suitable in evaluating subject matter only for those who established them (referred to as *specified parties*). As such, they are not suitable for *general use.* For example, criteria developed based on a lengthy, involved contract between two parties might result in a report whose use is restricted to the two parties. In such situations the attestation report should be *restricted* to the use of the specified parties.

Available Criteria

In addition to meeting the requirement that they be *suitable,* the criteria also must be available to users. This requirement of availability has two parts in that not only must the criteria be available, they must be understandable to users. The criteria may be made *available and understandable* to the users in a variety of ways. If the criteria were developed by a regulatory agency or an expert body using due process, it is likely that they are publicly available to users; it ordinarily is presumed that such criteria are understandable.

Alternatively, the criteria may be made available to the users in the presentation of the subject matter, in the assertion, or in the practitioners' report. Making the criteria available in one of these manners is particularly important when there is no "generally accepted" way of evaluating the related subject matter. Take for example the subject matter of customer satisfaction. There are a number of possible measures of customer satisfaction, including customer opinion, rate of customer referral, rate of return customer sales, and increase in dollar amount of sales to existing customers. Particular criteria might employ one or more of these or other customer satisfaction measures. If the practitioner found the criteria being followed to be suitable, the presentation of the subject matter on customer satisfaction would be likely to include the criteria describing the way in which customer satisfaction was defined and measured.

When criteria are available only to certain users, the practitioners' report should be restricted to those *specified parties.* Here again a contract between two parties provides a good illustration. In the preceding section on suitable criteria, we suggested that a contract may not be suitable for those who were not a party to the contract. This is because, even if available, it may not be understandable by others. Here we find the not too surprising conclusion that if the contract is not available, the report is restricted. These situations often have in common the fact that they have been developed by and agreed to by the parties to the engagement and are not generally understandable to those not so involved.

Attestation Risk and Materiality

Attestation risk is the risk that the practitioners will unknowingly fail to appropriately modify their report on subject matter that is materially misstated. Like audit risk, attestation risk consists of three components—inherent risk, control risk, and detection risk. In this context, *inherent risk* is the risk that the subject matter is materially misstated before considering any internal control. *Control risk* is the risk that internal control will fail to prevent or detect a material misstatement of the subject matter, and *detection risk* is the risk that the practitioners' procedures will fail to detect a material misstatement of the subject matter. In an attestation engagement, the practitioners assess inherent and control risks and design procedures to restrict detection risk to the appropriate level.

Determining materiality for an attestation engagement may be very difficult because the subject matter may not be financial in nature. In fact, the subject matter may not even be presented in quantitative terms. As an example, the practitioners may be attesting to material compliance with specific provisions of a regulation. To determine what is material for planning and reporting purposes, the practitioners must attempt to put themselves in the shoes of the intended users and must consider the extent and nature of misstatements of the subject matter that would be significant to their decisions.

Materiality for the engagement may be considered in the context of quantitative or qualitative factors. If the subject matter is quantitative, materiality should generally be a relative rather than an absolute amount. That is, as the quantitative amounts of the presentation increase, the amount considered to be material should also increase. For qualitative subject matter, the practitioners must use professional judgment to consider what omission or misstatement would have a significant effect on the presentation of the subject matter.

The Character of the Engagement

The practitioners should issue an attestation report that clearly describes the nature of the assurance being provided as an *examination,* a *review,* or the performance of *agreed-upon procedures.*

Examinations

Learning Objective 3

An **examination** is designed to provide the highest level of assurance that CPAs provide—the same level of assurance about other types of subject matter as an audit provides for financial statements. When performing an examination, practitioners select from all available

FIGURE 20.4
Standard Unqualified
Examination Report on
Subject Matter

Title	INDEPENDENT ACCOUNTANTS' REPORT
Introductory Paragraph	We have examined the accompanying schedule of investment performance statistics of Terrill Investment Fund for the year ended December 31, 20X2. This schedule is the responsibility of Terrill Investment Fund's management. Our responsibility is to express an opinion on this schedule based on our examination.
Scope Paragraph	Our examination was conducted in accordance with attestation standards established by the American Institute of Certified Public Accountants and, accordingly, included examining, on a test basis, evidence supporting the schedule and performing such other procedures as we considered necessary in the circumstances. We believe that our examination provides a reasonable basis for our opinion.
Opinion Paragraph	In our opinion, the schedule of investment performance statistics referred to above presents, in all material respects, the performance of Terrill Investment Fund for the year ended December 31, 20X2, in conformity with the measurement and disclosure criteria set forth by the Association of Investment Management Research, Inc., as described in Note 1.
	Wesley & Ward, LLP January 22, 20X3

procedures to gather sufficient evidence to allow the issuance of a report that includes positive assurance about whether the subject matter being examined follows some established or stated criteria. Sufficient evidence exists when it is enough to drive attestation risk to an appropriate *low level.*

At the completion of the examination, the practitioners issue an appropriate report. Figure 20.4 illustrates an annotated standard unqualified examination report *directly on the subject matter.* This standard report, however, is not appropriate in all cases. The following table illustrates circumstances that result in modification of the standard unqualified report.

Situation	Report Modification
1. Criteria are agreed-upon or only available to specified parties.	A statement of limitations on the use of the report.
2. Departure of subject matter from criteria.	Qualified or adverse opinion depending on materiality of the departure.
3. Limitation on scope of engagement.	Qualified opinion or disclaimer.
4. When reporting on subject matter and a written assertion is not obtained from the responsible party.	A statement of limitations on the use of the report.

Reviews

A **review** engagement involves performing limited procedures, such as inquiries and analytical procedures. In performing a review, the practitioners endeavor to gather sufficient evidence to drive attestation risk to a *moderate level.* Accordingly, the resulting report provides only limited assurance that the information is fairly presented. **Limited assurance** is also referred to as **negative assurance** because the practitioners' report disclaims an opinion on the reviewed information, but includes a statement such as "We are not aware of any material

FIGURE 20.5

Standard Unmodified
Review Report on
Subject Matter

Title	INDEPENDENT ACCOUNTANTS' REPORT
Introductory Paragraph	We have reviewed the accompanying schedule of investment performance statistics of Keller Investment Fund for the year ended December 31, 20X2. This schedule is the responsibility of Keller Investment Fund's management.
Nature of Review and Disclaimer Paragraph	Our review was conducted in accordance with attestation standards established by the American Institute of Certified Public Accountants. A review is substantially less in scope than an examination, the objective of which is the expression of an opinion on the schedule. Accordingly, we do not express such an opinion.
Negative Assurance Paragraph	Based on our review, nothing came to our attention that caused us to believe that the accompanying schedule of investment performance statistics of Keller Investment Fund for the year ended December 31, 20X2, is not presented, in all material respects, in accordance with the measurement and disclosure criteria set forth by the Association of Investment Management Research, Inc., as described in Note 1. *George Little & Associates, LLP* January 15, 20X3

modifications that should be made in order for the information to be in conformity with the criteria." Of course, when uncorrected material departures from the criteria are noted, the report must be modified to so indicate. An example of an annotated unmodified review report *directly on the subject matter* is presented in Figure 20.5. However, this unmodified report is not appropriate in all circumstances. The following table lists circumstances that result in modification of the practitioners' review report.

Situation	Report Modification
1. Criteria are agreed-upon or only available to specified parties.	A statement of limitations on the use of the report.
2. Departure of subject matter from criteria.	Modified report describing the departure.
3. Limitation on scope of the engagement.	Report cannot be issued.
4. When reporting on subject matter and a written assertion is not obtained from the responsible party.	A statement of limitations on the use of the report.

Agreed-Upon Procedures

Practitioners may also be engaged to perform procedures that were agreed upon by specified parties of the report. **Agreed-upon procedures** reports include a list of procedures performed (or reference thereto) and the related findings. Because specified parties have agreed upon the nature of the procedures, the reports for such engagements are intended only for those parties. Consequently, reports on agreed-upon procedures are referred to as *restricted use* reports, as contrasted to *general use* reports, such as those on examinations and reviews. As previously indicated, examination and review reports ordinarily may be used by all third parties. Only when the criteria have been agreed upon by the parties involved and such criteria are not generally understandable to those not involved with the information must an examination or review report be restricted.

Assurance Service Examples

Assurance on Internal Control over Financial Reporting

Learning Objective 4

Chapters 7 and 18 presented information on auditors' reports on internal control over financial reporting for public companies. In this section we will describe the standards for reporting on internal control for nonpublic companies.[6]

Section 501 of *Statements on Standards for Attestation Engagements (SSAE) No. 10* provides guidance for attesting to internal control over financial reporting for nonpublic companies. As is the case with public company internal control reporting, management must evaluate the company's internal control using a set of suitable criteria. These criteria, referred as **control criteria,** may be issued by various bodies, such as the Committee of Sponsoring Organizations of the Treadway Commission (COSO) or regulatory agencies. COSO's *Internal Control–Integrated Framework,* discussed in Chapters 7 and 19, is an example of a set of suitable criteria that may be used by management to report on a company's internal control.

Management Report on Internal Control

Wilson Company maintains internal control over financial reporting, which is designed to provide reasonable assurance to the Company's management and board of directors regarding the preparation of reliable published financial statements. Internal control contains self-monitoring mechanisms, and actions are taken to correct deficiencies as they are identified. Even effective internal control, no matter how well designed, has inherent limitations—including the possibility of the circumvention or overriding of controls—and therefore can provide only reasonable assurance with respect to financial statement preparation. Further, because of changes in conditions, internal control effectiveness may vary over time.

The Company assessed its internal control as of December 31, 20X2, in relation to criteria for effective internal control over financial reporting described in *Internal Control–Integrated Framework* issued by the Committee of Sponsoring Organizations of the Treadway Commission. Based on this assessment, the Company believes that, as of December 31, 20X2, its internal control over financial reporting met those criteria.

Wilson Company

Will Jones
Chief Executive Officer

Linda Beck
Chief Financial Officer
January 20, 20X3

In accordance with the attestation standards, practitioners may be engaged to examine or perform agreed-upon procedures on management's reports on internal control over financial reporting. However, the attestation standards *prohibit* reviews of internal control over financial reporting.

When examining the effectiveness of an entity's internal control over financial reporting, the CPAs should (1) plan the engagement, (2) obtain an understanding of internal control, (3) evaluate the design and operating effectiveness of internal control, and (4) form an opinion about the fairness of management's assertion. While these steps are similar to those used in the auditors' consideration of internal control for audit purposes, the scope of their performance ordinarily exceeds those of a financial statement audit because the internal control itself represents the subject matter of the engagement (rather than the financial statements).

While the practitioners generally must obtain an appropriate assertion about the internal control as provided above, as is the case generally with attestation engagements, they may report on *either* the *assertion* about the subject matter *or* the *subject matter* itself. The purpose

---

[6] The Federal Deposit Insurance Corporation Improvement Act of 1991, which applies to financial institutions with total assets of $500 million or more, requires a report similar to that described in this section.

of an examination of the effectiveness of a client's internal control is to express an opinion on either (1) the effectiveness of internal control, in all material respects, based on the control criteria, or (2) whether the written assertion about the effectiveness of control is fairly stated, in all material respects, based on the control criteria. All significant controls bearing on those issues must be tested. The practitioners' consideration of internal control in an audit of financial statements is designed to enable them to assess the risk of material misstatement and to determine the nature, timing, and extent of tests to be performed—the practitioners may decide that it is not efficient to test particular controls. Consequently, the auditors' consideration of internal control for audit purposes is seldom adequate to express an opinion on the effectiveness of the company's internal control over financial reporting.

The accompanying box, "Independent Accountants' Report," is an unqualified opinion on a company's internal control that may be issued when management's assertion about internal control is included in a separate report, such as the one presented previously (emphasis and annotations added), and when the accountants are reporting on that assertion:

Title	INDEPENDENT ACCOUNTANTS' REPORT
Introductory Paragraph	We have *examined management's assertion* in the accompanying Management Report on Internal Control that Wilson Company maintained *effective internal control over financial reporting* as of December 31, 20X2, based on the criteria for effective internal control over financial reporting established in *Internal Control–Integrated Framework,* issued by the Committee of Sponsoring Organizations of the Treadway Commission. Wilson Company's management is responsible for maintaining effective internal control over financial reporting. Our responsibility is to express an opinion on management's assertion based on our examination.
Scope Paragraph	Our examination was conducted in accordance with attestation standards established by the American Institute of Certified Public Accountants and, accordingly, included *obtaining an understanding of internal control* over financial reporting, *testing, and evaluating the design and operating effectiveness of internal control,* and performing such other procedures as we considered necessary in the circumstances. We believe that our examination provides a reasonable basis for our opinion.
Inherent Limitations Paragraph	Because of *inherent limitations* in any internal control, errors or fraud may occur and not be detected. Also, projections of any evaluation of internal control over financial reporting to future periods are subject to the risk that internal control may become inadequate because of changes in conditions, or that the degree of compliance with the controls may deteriorate.
Opinion Paragraph	In our opinion, *management's assertion* that Wilson Company maintained effective internal control over financial reporting as of December 31, 20X2, is *fairly stated, in all material respects,* based upon the criteria established in *Internal Control–Integrated Framework,* issued by the Committee of Sponsoring Organizations of the Treadway Commission.
	Owen & Co., CPAs
	February 15, 20X3

This unqualified opinion on management's assertions about internal control is not appropriate in all circumstances. The report should be modified in the following situations:

Situation	Report Modification
1. Existence of a material weakness.	Qualified or adverse opinion (depending upon the pervasiveness of the weakness or weaknesses).
2. Limitation on scope of engagement.	Qualified opinion or disclaimer of opinion (depending on importance of omitted procedure; generally disclaim for client-imposed scope limitations).

Assurance on Prospective Financial Statements

Learning Objective 5

Securities analysts and loan officers give considerable attention to prospective financial statements. Although such statements may be presented in various forms, CPAs most frequently are involved with *financial forecasts* and *financial projections*. A **financial forecast** presents information about the entity's *expected* financial position, results of operations, and cash flows. On the other hand, a **financial projection** presents expected results, *given one or more hypothetical assumptions*. For example, a projection might present expected results assuming the company expanded its plant. While a forecast may be issued for general use, a projection's use should be restricted to the party with whom the company is negotiating, for example, a bank that is considering loaning funds to the company to expand the plant. Both forecasts and projections must include certain minimum *prospective financial statement* items, background information, and a list of the major assumptions and accounting policies.[7]

Users of forecasts and projections often request assurance that this forward-looking information is properly presented and based upon reasonable assumptions. To provide such assurance, CPAs may be engaged to examine prospective statements, or they may be asked to perform certain agreed-upon procedures, but the attestation standards *prohibit* the review of prospective financial statements. Criteria for evaluation of the fairness of a forecast or projection are presented in Section 301 of *Statements on Standards for Attestation Engagements No. 10* and include a set of presentation guidelines.

Examinations of Prospective Financial Statements

In an examination of prospective financial statements, the practitioners gather evidence relating to the client's procedures for preparation of the statements, evaluate the underlying assumptions, obtain a written representation letter from the client, and evaluate whether the statements are presented in conformity with AICPA guidelines. The report issued is ordinarily on the subject matter and states whether, in the practitioners' opinion, the statements are presented in conformity with AICPA guidelines and whether the underlying assumptions provide a reasonable basis for the statements. In no circumstance is the practitioners' report to vouch for the achievability of the forecast or projection.

The accompanying box, "Independent Accountants' Report," is an example of an unqualified forecast examination report (emphasis added).

Independent Accountants' Report

We have *examined* the accompanying forecasted balance sheet, statements of income, retained earnings, and cash flows of Tyler Company as of December 31, 20X2, and for the year then ending. The management of Tyler Company is responsible for the preparation of the forecast. Our responsibility is to express an opinion on the forecast based on our examination.

Our *examination was conducted in accordance with attestation standards for an examination of a forecast established by the American Institute of Certified Public Accountants* and, accordingly,

---

[7] Details of required disclosures are presented in the AICPA's *Guide for Prospective Financial Information* (New York, 1999).

included such procedures as we considered necessary to evaluate both the assumptions used and the preparation and presentation of the forecast. We believe our examination provides a reasonable basis for our opinion.

In our opinion, the accompanying forecast is *presented in conformity with guidelines for presentation of a forecast established by the American Institute of Certified Public Accountants,* and *the underlying assumptions provide a reasonable basis for management's forecast.* However, there will usually be differences between the forecasted and actual results, because events and circumstances frequently do not occur as expected, and those differences may be material. We have no responsibility to update this report for events and circumstances occurring after the date of this report.

Owen & Co., CPAs
February 20, 20X3

As with other attestation reports, the standard report is not appropriate in all circumstances. The report should be modified in the following situations:

Situation	Report Modification
1. Material departure from presentation criteria.	Qualified or adverse opinion (if underlying assumptions are omitted, an adverse opinion should be issued).
2. One or more significant assumptions do not provide a reasonable basis for the prospective statements.	Adverse opinion.
3. Limitation on scope of engagement.	Disclaimer of opinion.

The report on a financial projection is similar to the one illustrated above, but a paragraph is added prior to the opinion paragraph indicating that the use of the report should be restricted to the specified party, and the opinion paragraph explicitly states the hypothetical assumptions.

Agreed-Upon Procedures on Prospective Financial Statements

Specific users may request the practitioners to perform certain agreed-upon procedures on prospective financial statements. In such circumstances the practitioners may perform the procedures and provide a summary of findings on the statements. As is the case with all engagements involving agreed-upon procedures, the report should indicate that its use is restricted to the specified parties.

Assurance on Compliance

Section 601, "Compliance Attestation," of *Statements on Standards for Attestation Engagements No. 10* provides guidance for two types of compliance attestation engagements:

1. Attesting to an entity's compliance with specified requirements of laws, regulations, rules, contracts, or grants.
2. Attesting to the effectiveness of an entity's internal control over compliance with specified requirements.

Practitioners are permitted to perform an examination or agreed-upon procedures on such matters, but they are *prohibited* from performing reviews of compliance or internal control over compliance. These types of engagements and reports are described in detail in Chapter 21.

Learning Objective 6

Assurance on Management's Discussion and Analysis

Management of a public company is required to provide a narrative explanation of financial results as reported in the financial statements filed with the SEC. This narrative explanation, referred to as **Management's Discussion and Analysis (MD&A),** is a required part of Form 10-K (for annual financial statements) and Form 10-Q (for interim financial statements) filed with the SEC. Practitioners may examine or review MD&A under the guidance of Section 701 of *Statements on Standards for Attestation Engagements No. 10.*

To accept an engagement to examine MD&A, the practitioners must have audited the most recent financial statement period to which the MD&A applies and the other financial statement periods also must have been audited by them or other auditors. The practitioners' objective in such an engagement is to provide assurance on whether (1) the presentation includes, in all material respects, the required elements of the rules and regulations adopted by the SEC; (2) the historical financial amounts included in the presentation have been accurately derived, in all material respects, from the entity's financial statements; and (3) the underlying information, determinations, estimates, and assumptions of the entity provide a reasonable basis for the disclosures contained in the presentation. Practitioners also may be engaged to perform a review of MD&A for an annual or interim period. However, if a review is performed and the report is not intended to be filed with the SEC, it should be restricted as to use.

Trust Services

Learning Objective 7

Information technology has a profound effect on the way in which companies do business. Increasingly, companies have developed technology-enabled systems that not only maintain historical information but also produce products and services, directly interact with customers and suppliers, and run portions of the business. As a result, system reliability is of major concern not only to management, but also stockholders, creditors, business partners, and other stakeholders in the company. The public accounting profession is developing a set of **Trust Services** that are intended to address user and preparer needs regarding issues of security, availability, processing integrity, online privacy, and confidentiality within e-commerce and other systems.

What is a *system?* Guidance on Trust Service Engagements states that a system consists of five key components organized to achieve specified objectives—infrastructure, software, people, procedures, and data. A system may be as simple as a personal computer–based payroll application with only one user, or as complex as a multiapplication, multicomputer banking system accessed by many users both within and outside the banks involved.

Trust Services are a set of services developed by the AICPA and the Canadian Institute of Chartered Accountants (CICA) in which a practitioner examines a system's controls and attests to the system's reliability. This is a part of a broader future vision of the accounting profession to supply real-time assurance on information databases and systems and is viewed as a natural extension of the CPA's audit and information technology consulting functions.

In a Trust Services engagement, management prepares and communicates a description of the aspects of the system that are to be included in the practitioner's engagement. Management's description can be included on the company's Web site, attached to the practitioners' report, or communicated to users in some other manner. It must clearly articulate the boundaries of the system so as to allow individuals to understand both the scope of management's assertions related to it and the practitioners' report.

Performing a Trust Services Engagement

In performing a Trust Services engagement the practitioner (1) performs procedures to determine that management's description of the system is fairly stated and (2) obtains evidence that the controls over the system are designed and operating effectively to meet the Trust Services Principles and Criteria—the suitable criteria required for an attest engagement. The evidence is on whether the system meets one or more of the following principles over a particular reporting period:

1. *Security.* The system (infrastructure, software, people, procedures, and data) is protected against unauthorized physical and logical access in conformity with the entity's security processes.
2. *Availability.* The system is available for operation and use as committed or agreed upon.
3. *Processing integrity.* System processing is complete, accurate, timely, and authorized.
4. *Online privacy.* Private information obtained as a result of electronic commerce is collected, used, disclosed, and retained as committed or agreed upon.
5. *Confidentiality.* Information designated as confidential is protected as committed or agreed upon.

Each of the principles has four criteria associated with it that fit into the following categories:

1. *Policies.* The entity has defined and documented its policies relevant to the particular principle. These policies are written statements that communicate management's intent, objectives, requirements, and responsibilities and/or standards for a particular subject.
2. *Communications.* The entity has communicated its defined policies to authorized users.
3. *Procedures.* The entity utilizes procedures to achieve the objectives in accordance with its defined policies.
4. *Monitoring.* The entity monitors the system and takes action to maintain compliance with its defined policies.

Types of Trust Services Engagements

At present CPAs offer two types of Trust Services, both providing either agreed-upon procedures or examination-level assurance. **WebTrust** provides assurance on electronic commerce systems, while **SysTrust** provides assurance on any system.

Reporting

Trust Services result in the issuance of a report. The reports issued for *SysTrust* and *WebTrust* are similar. The box below provides a *WebTrust* report example on security and confidentiality. Both *WebTrust* and *SysTrust* are designed to incorporate a seal management process by which a seal (logo) may be included on a client's Web site as an electronic representation of the practitioner's unqualified *WebTrust* report. If the client wishes to use the seal (logo) the engagement must be updated at least annually. Also, the initial reporting period must include at least two months.

Independent Practitioner's *WebTrust* Report on Consumer Protection

To the Management of E-Shop, Inc.

We have examined E-Shop, Inc.'s (E-Shop) compliance with the AICPA/CICA Trust Services Criteria for consumer protection, and based on these Criteria, the effectiveness of controls over the Online Privacy and Processing Integrity of the Customer Order Placement System during the period January 1, 20X2, through June 30, 20X2. The compliance with these criteria and maintaining the effectiveness of these controls is the responsibility of E-Shop's management. Our responsibility is to express an opinion based on our examination.

Within the context of AICPA/CICA Trust Services, consumer protection addresses the controls over personally identifiable information and the processing of electronic commerce transactions. The AICPA/CICA Trust Services Online Privacy and Processing Integrity Criteria are used to evaluate whether E-Shop's controls over consumer protection of its Customer Order Placement System are effective. Consumer protection does not address the quality of E-Shop's goods, nor their suitability for any customer's intended purpose.

Our examination was conducted in accordance with attestation standards established by the American Institute of Certified Public Accountants and, accordingly, included (1) obtaining an understanding of E-Shop's relevant online privacy and processing integrity controls; (2) testing and evaluating the operating effectiveness of the controls; (3) testing compliance with the Online Privacy and Processing Integrity Criteria; and (4) performing such other procedures as we considered necessary in the circumstances. We believe that our examination provides a reasonable basis for our opinion.

In our opinion, E-Shop complied, in all material respects, with the criteria for consumer protection and maintained, in all material respects, effective controls over the Customer Order Placement System to provide reasonable assurance that:

- Personal information obtained as a result of electronic commerce was collected, used, disclosed, and retained as committed or agreed, and
- System processing was complete, accurate, timely, and authorized during the period January 1, 20X2, through June 30, 20X2, based on the AICPA/CICA Trust Services Criteria for consumer protection.

Because of inherent limitations in controls, error or fraud may occur and not be detected. Furthermore, the projection of any conclusions, based on our findings, to future periods is subject to the risk that the validity of such conclusions may be altered because of changes made to

continued

> the system or controls, the failure to make needed changes to the system or controls, or a deterioration in the degree of effectiveness of the controls.
>
> The WebTrust Seal of assurance on E-Shop's Web site constitutes a symbolic representation of the contents of this report and it is not intended, nor should it be construed, to update this report or provide any additional assurance.
>
> This report does not conclude any representation as to the quality of E-Shop's goods nor their suitability for any customer's intended purpose.
>
> *Hartly & Warren, LLP*
> Certified Public Accountants
>
> Santa Fe, New Mexico
> July 16, 20X2

Competition

Several other organizations provide services that compete with the AICPA/CICA's *WebTrust* service. The Better Business Bureau's BBB*OnLine* program grants two different logos—a privacy seal and a reliability seal. The privacy seal is granted to companies that adopt appropriate standards regarding the safeguarding of customer information. Companies that employ appropriate business practices (e.g., follow Better Business Bureau truth-in-advertising and dispute resolution standards) can obtain the reliability seal. However, attestation is not part of the Better Business Bureau's program.

Another program, offered by *TRUSTe,* provides assurance that customer information will be protected. A company participating in *TRUSTe* must openly indicate what personal information is being gathered, how it will be used, with whom it will be shared, and whether the user has an option to control its dissemination. Based on such disclosure, users can make informed decisions about whether or not to release their personally identifiable information (e.g., credit card numbers) to the Web site. Finally, the International Computer Security Association (ICSA) certifies Web sites as using technology that protects customer data. ICSA's process includes a combination of self-reporting, on-site evaluation, remote testing, and spot-testing

The accounting profession believes that it can compete effectively in this area of *consumer-to-business* electronic commerce as well as in the area of *business-to-business* electronic commerce. The *WebTrust* service is more comprehensive in its scope than other electronic commerce services, and CPAs and chartered accountants have excellent reputations for evaluating controls and business practices.

ElderCare/ PrimePlus Services

Learning Objective 8

The population of the United States is aging, with the greatest increase in adults over 65 years of age expected to occur between 2010 and 2030. In response to these demographics, the AICPA and the Canadian Institute of Chartered Accountants (CICA) have developed ***ElderCare/ PrimePlus* services**[8] as a package of services to help older Americans maintain for as long as possible their lifestyle and financial independence. The profession sees three primary markets for these services:

- Older clients of the CPA who have the financial resources to avail themselves of the services.
- The children of older adults who have the resources and interest to see that their loved ones are cared for.
- Other professionals who deal with older adults (e.g., lawyers and health care professionals).

The services involved are of two types—financial and nonfinancial. Financial services include goal-setting, funding analysis, cost management, and needs assessment. Nonfinancial services may involve interpersonal and relationship management, as well as management of the interaction between service providers and the client. Figure 20.6 provides more detailed examples of each of these services.

---

[8] These services were originally referred to as *ElderCare* services. In 2002, the AICPA and CICA started the process of changing the name to *PrimePlus* services. Currently, the combined name, *ElderCare/PrimePlus* services, is most frequently used by CPAs.

FIGURE 20.6
Examples of
ElderCare/PrimePlus
Services

Financial Services	Nonfinancial Services
• Planning for fiduciary needs. • Evaluating financing options. • Receiving, depositing, and accounting for client receipts. • Ensuring that expected revenues are received. • Submitting claims to insurance companies. • Protecting the elderly from predators. • Estate planning. • Income tax planning and preparation. • Gift tax return preparation. • Evaluating investments and trust activity. • Portfolio management. • Risk management and insurance planning.	• Lifestyle planning. • Lifestyle management services. • Coordinating support and health care services. • Functioning as the "quarterback" or as a member of the *ElderCare/PrimePlus* team—which consists of health care, legal, and other professionals. • Helping family members monitor the elder's care. • Communicating family expectations to care providers. • Establishing, in concert with the family, appropriate standards of care. • Establishing performance monitoring systems.

CPA Performance View

Learning Objective 9

Many organizations track their success based solely on past financial performance (e.g., sales, net income, gross margin, return on assets, or asset turnover). It has been argued that while such an approach is an excellent way to see where the organization has *been,* it offers limited guidance on where it is *going.* **CPA Performance View** is a system that merges these standard financial measures with leading indicators, such as:

- Customer satisfaction.
- Employee training and satisfaction.
- Product quality.
- Sales calls and proposals delivered.

This service is based on performance measurement theory, including the **balanced scorecard approach,** which attempts to measure financial and nonfinancial dimensions of performance.

CPA Risk Advisory Services

Learning Objective 10

CPA Risk Advisory Services are intended to help organizations manage *risk,* which is defined as the chance of something happening that will affect the ability of an organization to meet its objectives. The overall approach may be viewed as one of (1) identifying and analyzing risks, (2) designing and implementing strategies related to risk, and (3) measuring, monitoring, and reporting on solutions. This service is in the early stages of development, as the profession is currently developing a common language and framework for considering risk as well as tools to assist CPAs providing the service.

Future Assurance Services

Learning Objective 11

The AICPA, through its various committees, continues to work on developing a host of other services to be provided by CPAs, including:

- *Health care performance measurement.* Health care recipients and their employers are increasingly concerned about the quality and availability of health care services. This service provides assurance about the effectiveness of health care services provided by health maintenance organizations, hospitals, doctors, and other providers.
- *Continuous auditing.* A demand exists for assurance beyond that provided with quarterly and annual financial statements. As indicated earlier in this chapter, continuous auditing provides assurance using a series of reports provided simultaneously or shortly after the related information is released. The area of continuous auditing is in its infancy but is expected to grow dramatically as companies provide more and more up-to-date financial information on their Web sites.

Chapter Summary

This chapter described assurance services, focusing on those that are governed by *Statements on Standards for Attestation Engagements.* To summarize:

1. Assurance services are defined as professional services that improve the quality of information, or its context, for decision makers.

2. The vast majority of currently provided assurance services are attestation services that are performed in accordance with *Statements on Standards for Attestation Engagements.* These services include examinations, reviews, and agreed-upon procedures engagements. An examination and a review involve providing assurance about the correspondence of subject matter with suitable criteria. An agreed-upon procedures engagement involves performing procedures and issuing a report of the findings.

3. CPAs may be engaged to examine a nonpublic entity's internal control over financial reporting based on suitable control criteria, such as those contained in *Internal Control–Integrated Framework,* developed by the Committee of Sponsoring Organizations of the Treadway Commission (COSO). However, practitioners are prohibited from providing a review service for controls over financial reporting.

4. CPAs may perform examinations, compilations, or agreed-upon procedures on prospective financial statements. Reviews of prospective financial statements are prohibited. Prospective financial statements include forecasts that reflect expected financial results and projections that reflect expected financial results given one or more hypothetical assumptions.

5. Practitioners may examine or review Management's Discussion and Analysis (MD&A). MD&A consists of a narrative explanation of financial results that must be included in annual and quarterly filings with the SEC. The practitioners' objective in an examination is to provide assurance on whether (1) the presentation includes all required elements, (2) any historical amounts have been accurately derived from the entity's financial statements, and (3) the underlying information, determinations, estimates, and assumptions provide a reasonable basis for the disclosures included.

6. Trust Services provide assurance on one or more of the following Trust Principles: (*a*) Security, (*b*) Availability, (*c*) Processing integrity, (*d*) Online privacy, and (*e*) Confidentiality. Currently two services have been developed—*WebTrust,* which provides assurance on electronic commerce systems, and *SysTrust,* which provides assurance on other systems.

7. Two other services that are being developed by the profession are *CPA Performance View* and *CPA Risk Advisory Services.* While *CPA Performance View* helps clients track success using a variety of financial and nonfinancial measures, *CPA Risk Advisory Services* help organizations to manage risk. Other assurance services being developed by the profession include health care performance measurement and continuous auditing.

Key Terms Introduced or Emphasized in Chapter 20

Agreed-upon procedures An attestation engagement in which the CPAs agree to perform specific procedures for a specified party or parties and issue a report that expresses the CPAs' findings. The report is restricted to use by the specified party or parties.

Assertion An assertion is a declaration about whether subject matter is presented in accordance with certain criteria.

Assurance services Professional services that improve the quality of information, or its context, for decision makers. Many assurance services involve some form of attestation.

Attestation engagement Providing assurance as to whether some subject matter, or an assertion about the subject matter, is in accordance with suitable criteria.

Attestation risk The risk that the practitioners will issue an unmodified report on subject matter that is materially misstated.

Balanced scorecard A management report that measures performance in relation to the following dimensions: financial, internal operations, innovation and learning, and customer perspectives.

Continuous auditing To provide assurance using a series of reports provided simultaneously or shortly after the related information is released.

Control criteria The suitable criteria required to be followed by a company requesting a CPA's report on the effectiveness of internal control, most commonly the *Internal Control–Integrated Framework,* developed by COSO.

CPA Performance View Services to help clients track success using a variety of financial and nonfinancial measures.

CPA Risk Advisory Services   Services intended to help organizations manage risk—the chance of something happening that will have an impact on the organization's objectives.

ElderCare/PrimePlus **services**   Services to help older Americans maintain, for as long as possible, their lifestyle and financial independence.

Examination   An attestation engagement designed to provide the highest level of assurance that CPAs provide on subject matter or an assertion about subject matter. An examination of financial statements is referred to as an audit.

Financial forecast   Prospective financial statements that present an entity's expected financial position, results of operations, and cash flows for one or more future periods.

Financial projection   Prospective financial statements that present expected results, given one or more hypothetical assumptions.

Limited assurance (negative assurance)   The level of assurance provided by CPAs who have performed a review of subject matter. Provides substantially less assurance than the reasonable assurance provided by an examination.

Management's Discussion and Analysis (MD&A)   Management's discussion of the company's operating results, liquidity, and financial position that is required in the regular financial statement filings with the SEC. CPAs may examine or review this information. However, if the information is reviewed, the report must be restricted as to its use.

Negative assurance   See *limited assurance.*

Review   An engagement designed to provide only a limited (moderate) degree of assurance about the conformance of subject matter, or an assertion about subject matter, with suitable criteria.

Subject matter   The underlying topic of the engagement. For example, subject matter may be prospective financial information or internal control.

Suitable criteria   Criteria that are objective and permit reasonably consistent measurement.

SysTrust   A Trust Service developed by the AICPA and CICA to provide assurance about the reliability of systems other than electronic commerce systems.

Trust Services   Engagements that provide assurance on systems. Trust Services provide assurance on one or more of the following Trust Principles: (1) Security, (2) Availability, (3) Processing integrity, (4) Online privacy, and (5) Confidentiality. Currently, two services have been developed. *WebTrust* provides assurance on electronic commerce systems; *SysTrust* provides assurance on other systems.

WebTrust   A Trust Service developed by the AICPA and CICA to provide assurance on electronic commerce systems.

Review Questions

20–1.   Explain the relationship between assurance services and attestation services.

20–2.   Describe what is meant by *decision context enhancement services*. How do they differ from traditional attestation services?

20–3.   Describe the forces that have fueled the demand for assurance services.

20–4.   Explain why continuous auditing is potentially of more value than periodic auditing.

20–5.   List and describe the three types of attestation engagements.

20–6.   Distinguish between forms of attestation engagements that result in reports that are designed for "general use" versus those that result in reports that are designed for "restricted use."

20–7.   Distinguish an attestation engagement in which the practitioners report directly on the subject matter from one in which the practitioners report on an assertion about the subject matter.

20–8.   Contrast a report on an examination under the attestation standards with a report on an audit under generally accepted auditing standards.

20–9.   Explain what is meant by *attestation risk*. What are its components?

20–10.   Can CPAs typically attest to management's assertion about a company's internal control over financial reporting based on the work performed during an audit? Explain.

20–11.   CPAs may issue several types of reports on management's assertion about a company's internal control (e.g., unqualified, qualified, disclaimer, modified, and adverse). Describe the circumstances in which each of these types of reports is appropriate.

20–12.   "A company would normally include a financial projection in its annual report rather than a financial forecast." Comment on the validity of this statement.

20–13.   Describe the major elements of a report on the examination of a financial forecast.

20–14. Describe the two types of compliance services that may be performed under *Statement on Standards for Attestation Engagements No. 10.*

20–15. Identify the circumstances under which CPAs may examine Management's Discussion and Analysis.

20–16. Describe the objectives of the practitioners' examination of Management's Discussion and Analysis.

20–17. List the principles that may be included in the criteria for a Trust Services engagement.

20–18. Contrast the types of systems on which assurance is provided in a *WebTrust* engagement as compared to a *SysTrust* engagement.

20–19. Discuss CPAs' competition for *WebTrust* in the market for consumer-to-business electronic commerce.

20–20. The attest standards provide guidance on agreed-upon procedures, review, and examination engagements. Which of these types of engagements are available for *WebTrust* and *SysTrust*?

20–21. What types of *ElderCare/PrimePlus* services do CPAs typically perform?

20–22. Identify three types of assurance services that are currently under development by the AICPA.

Questions Requiring Analysis

20–23. Other types of assurance services provided by CPAs developed as a natural extension of the audit function.

    a. Explain what is meant by the term *assurance services.*

    b. Describe the forces that have caused a demand for other types of assurance services.

Required: *c.* Describe the subset of assurance services governed by the *Statements of Standards for Attestation Engagements.*

20–24. The attestation standards provide guidance for three basic types of engagements.

Required: *a.* Describe these three types of engagements.

    b. Describe the types of procedures performed for each of these three types of engagements.

    c. Discuss the degree of assurance provided by each type of engagement.

    d. Identify when each of the three types of engagements results in reports that are appropriate for *general use.*

20–25. The management of Williams Co. is considering issuing corporate debentures. To enhance the marketability of the bond issue, management has decided to include a financial forecast in the prospectus. Management has requested that your CPA firm examine the financial forecast to add credibility to the prospective information.

Required: *a.* Explain what is involved in an examination of a financial forecast.

    b. Discuss the elements of a report on the examination of a financial forecast. (Do not write a report.)

20–26. Electronic commerce continues to grow rapidly, but many people believe that its growth has been somewhat inhibited by consumer concerns. The accounting profession developed *WebTrust* to address these concerns and facilitate electronic commerce.

Required: *a.* Present the principles on which a *WebTrust* engagement may be based.

    b. Contrast the *WebTrust* service with competing services provided by other organizations.

20–27. The third general attestation standard indicates that the subject matter of the engagement must be capable of reasonably consistent evaluation against criteria that are suitable and available to the user.

Required: *a.* Explain why criteria are needed for an attestation engagement.

    b. Describe what makes a particular set of criteria *suitable* for an attestation engagement.

    c. Explain how criteria are made *available* to users of the information.

20–28. Following are descriptions of potential needs of clients for assurance services. For each need, identify (1) the type of service that would best meet the client's need (i.e., attestation to prospective information, attestation to internal control, attestation to compliance, attestation to MD&A, *WebTrust, SysTrust, ElderCare/PrimePlus,* or other assurance service), (2) whether or not the service is an attestation service, and (3) the level of service that would be most appropriate (i.e., examination, review, agreed-upon procedures, or other).

Client Need	Type of Service	Attestation Service?	Level of Service
a. A computer manufacturing company wants to provide assurance about estimated future results to be included in the company's annual report.			
b. A company wants to provide positive assurance on its pension processing services for its retired employees.			
c. A financial institution wants to provide assurance to banking regulators that its internal control over financial reporting is adequate.			
d. A company that maintains a business-to-business electronic commerce portal wants to provide positive assurance about the reliability of its system to potential customers.			
e. The relative of an institutionalized uncle wants a CPA firm to oversee the uncle's financial affairs.			
f. A public company wants to provide its shareholders assurance about the narrative analysis of financial results provided in the company's Form 10-K.			
g. A grocery store wants to provide the highest level of assurance that its prices are less than the prices of its competitors.			
h. A bank wants a CPA firm to confirm the account receivables of a company that has pledged the receivables as collateral for a loan.			
i. A golf ball manufacturer wants to provide moderate assurance that its golf balls travel further than those of its competitors.			
j. Management of a technology company wants a CPA firm to provide assurance that its risk assessment process has identified all major business risks.			

Multiple Choice Questions

20–29. Select the best answer for each of the following and explain fully the reason for your selection.

    a. A report on an attestation engagement should:

        (1) State the nature of the client's control structure.

        (2) State the practitioner's conclusion about the subject matter or assertion.

        (3) Include a reasonable limitations section pertaining to data inputs.

        (4) Refer to the auditor's assertion concerning the subject matter.

    b. When an accountant examines a financial forecast that fails to disclose several significant assumptions used to prepare the forecast, the accountant should describe the assumptions in the accountant's report and issue a(n):

        (1) Qualified opinion.

        (2) Unqualified opinion with a separate explanatory paragraph.

        (3) Disclaimer of opinion.

        (4) Adverse opinion.

    c. Which of the following is *not* an objective of a CPA's examination of a client's MD&A?

        (1) The presentation includes, in all material respects, the required elements of the rules and regulations adopted by the Securities and Exchange Commission.

(2) The presentation is in conformity with rules and regulations adopted by the SEC.

(3) The historical amounts included in the presentation have been accurately derived, in all material respects, from the entity's financial statements.

(4) The underlying information, determinations, estimates, and assumptions provide a reasonable basis for the disclosures contained in the presentation.

d. A CPA's report relating to a *WebTrust* engagement is most likely to include:

(1) An opinion on whether the site is electronically secure.

(2) An opinion on management's assertion that the site meets one or more of the *WebTrust* criteria.

(3) Negative assurance on whether the site is electronically secure.

(4) No opinion or other assurance, but a summary of findings relating to the site.

e. Which type or types of report are appropriate when a material weakness in internal control has been identified in reporting on the results of an examination of a client's internal control over financial reporting?

	Disclaimer	Adverse
(1)	Yes	Yes
(2)	Yes	No
(3)	No	Yes
(4)	No	No

f. When reporting on the results of an examination of a client's internal control over financial reporting, a CPA should include a paragraph that describes the:

(1) Documentary evidence regarding the control environment factors.

(2) Changes in internal control since the prior report.

(3) Potential benefits from the CPA's suggested improvements.

(4) Inherent limitations of any internal control.

g. CPA services performed under ElderCare/PrimePlus Services may be:

	Financial	Nonfinancial
(1)	Yes	Yes
(2)	Yes	No
(3)	No	Yes
(4)	No	No

h. The performance measurement technique that attempts to measure financial and nonfinancial dimensions of performance is the:

(1) Balanced scorecard.

(2) Financial/nonfinancial trust.

(3) Income statement.

(4) Performance View.

i. Which is least *likely*?

(1) An assurance service that is also an attest service.

(2) A service that is not an assurance service, but is an attest service.

(3) A historical financial statement related assurance service.

(4) A nonhistorical financial information related assurance service.

j. Which of the following is *least* likely to be the subject matter of an attestation engagement?

(1) Behavior.

(2) Historical events.

(3) Suitable criteria.

(4) Systems or processes.

k. Which of the following is *not* a basic type of attestation engagement?

(1) Agreed-upon procedures.

(2) Compilation.

(3) Examination.

(4) Review.

l. The assurance services being developed that address user and preparer needs regarding issues of security, availability, processing integrity, online privacy and confidentiality within e-commerce and other systems are referred to as:

(1) *PrimePlus Services.*

(2) *Performance View services.*

(3) *Risk Advisory Services*

(4) *Trust Services.*

Problems

20–30. Assume that you are a partner with the CPA firm of Katherine Williams & Associates LLP. The following report was drafted by your staff at the conclusion of an engagement to examine management's assertion about internal control over financial reporting of First National Bank, a large financial institution. Assume that management's report on internal control over financial reporting will be presented with your firm's report.

We have examined management's assertion that First National Bank maintained effective internal control as of December 31, 20X2, included in the accompanying Management Report on Internal Control.

Our examination was made in accordance with generally accepted auditing standards and, accordingly, included obtaining an understanding of internal control over financial reporting, testing and evaluating the design and operating effectiveness of internal control, and such other procedures as we considered necessary in the circumstances.

In our opinion, management's assertion that First National Bank maintained effective internal control as of December 31, 20X2, is fairly stated.

Katherine Williams & Associates LLP
February 15, 20X3

Required:

a. Assuming that the examination revealed no weaknesses in internal control over financial reporting that would be considered material, describe any misstatements or omissions contained in the draft report.

b. Assuming that the examination revealed a material weakness in internal control over financial reporting that was acknowledged in management's report, describe the modification that would be required in the report.

c. Assuming that the examination revealed a material weakness in internal control over financial reporting that was not acknowledged in management's report, describe the modification that would be required in the report.

20–31. Effective internal control is of significant concern to regulators, stockholders, management, and other stakeholders in corporations. Therefore, CPAs are getting significant requests to provide assurance about the effectiveness of internal control.

Required:

a. Explain how providing assurance about internal control provides assurance about the reliability of other information provided by the company.

b. Describe the requirements of the FDIC as they relate to attestation to internal control by CPAs.

c. Describe the broad engagement activities that would be involved in performing an examination of the effectiveness of internal control.

20–32. *SysTrust* and *WebTrust* are Trust Services developed by the AICPA and the CICA.

Required:

a. Present and describe the Trust Services principles.

b. Present and describe the "criteria" related to Trust Services.

c. What is the relationship between the principles and criteria?

d. Must a *WebTrust* or *SysTrust* report provide assurance on all of the principles?

20–33. Assume that you are a partner with the firm of Slater & Lowe LLP. You have been asked by Grayson, Inc., an industrial supply company, to provide assurance about the change in existing customer satisfaction over the last three years. Grayson's management has indicated that the criteria it intends to use to evaluate customer satisfaction are a combination of customer retention rate and increase in dollar sales. Grayson's management will provide a schedule of the customer satisfaction measures and a note that describes the criteria used.

Required:

a. If Grayson wants to provide the presentation and CPA's report for general use by prospective customers, identify any available standards that provide guidance for such a service and the type or types of services that your firm could provide.

b. Describe the factors that you should consider in determining whether the criteria are suitable.

c. Assuming that you conclude that the criteria are suitable, draft your firm's report assuming that you perform an examination of the subject matter.

In-Class Team Case

20–34. Katherine Whipple of Food Queen Grocery, Inc., has asked you and your team to meet with her concerning a possible attest engagement relating to the assertion that Food Queen has the lowest overall prices of all grocery stores in the Salt Lake City area. Food Queen has just recently moved into the Salt Lake City area and is trying to establish a high volume, profitable position. Whipple has suggested to you that she believes that while Food Queen certainly doesn't have the lowest prices on all of the 25,000 types of items it sells, on most any rational basis she believes that its prices are "on the whole" lower than the competition—Albros, Kruegers, and Safest. In thinking about this, you realize that to perform such an attestation engagement, suitable criteria must be used to evaluate the subject matter.

Required:

a. For this engagement, what would you consider to be the subject matter?

b. Provide an approach on how one might derive suitable criteria for such an engagement, given that costs are considered lowest on an overall basis, but not necessarily for every item.

c. Discuss the nature of the required assertion from management for an engagement such as this.

Now consider the following: Whipple has suggested to you that when the engagement is completed she will use the results as part of an advertising campaign in which the ads suggest that Food Queen has the "certified lowest overall costs." When you asked her what would happen if the engagement revealed that Food Queen didn't have the lowest prices, she suggested that she would simply not use the report and wait a month or two and have you perform another engagement when she had had time to bring her prices even lower.

d. Are attestation engagements acceptable when the resulting report is to be used for advertising purposes?

e. Assume that your examination revealed that, based on the criteria developed, Whipple's assertion that Food Queen did have the lowest prices was fairly stated and that a general use report was proper. Outline the nature of the allowable presentation in the advertising materials.

Research and Discussion Case

20–35. Go to www.webtrust.org on the Internet and click on "Sites with Seals." Select a company listed as having a *WebTrust* site and reply to the following:

Required:

a. Explain why a company such as the one you selected would want to display the *WebTrust* seal.

b. Make copies of the following information from the Web site.

(1) Disclosures of Business Practices for electronic commerce.

(2) Management's assertion or assertions.

(3) The *WebTrust* report of the CPA firm.

c. On which WebTrust Principles does the *WebTrust* report include assurance?

d. Does the Web site include any other assurance services (e.g., *TRUSTe*)? If so, describe them.

Chapter 21

Internal, Operational, and Compliance Auditing

Chapter learning objectives

After studying this chapter, you should be able to:

LO1. Describe the functions performed by internal auditors.

LO2. Describe the internal auditors' role with respect to the Sarbanes-Oxley Act.

LO3. Identify the standards for the professional practice of internal auditing.

LO4. Explain the nature and the purpose of an operational audit.

LO5. Distinguish among the various types of compliance audits.

LO6. Describe the auditing and reporting requirements of *Government Auditing Standards* and the Single Audit Act.

To this point in the text we have focused primarily on audits and other types of assurance services provided by independent public accountants. This chapter describes several additional types of auditing: internal, operational, and compliance auditing.

Internal Auditing

Learning Objective 1

Virtually every large corporation in the United States today maintains an internal auditing staff. This staff function developed extremely rapidly as prior to 1940 few organizations had internal auditing departments. In 1941 the **Institute of Internal Auditors (IIA)** was founded with only 25 members. Now the IIA is a worldwide organization with over 80,000 members and with local chapters in principal cities throughout much of the world. The growth of the IIA has paralleled the recognition of internal auditing as an essential control function in all types of organizations.

What Is the Purpose of Internal Auditing?

The Institute of Internal Auditors (IIA) defines **internal auditing** as:

> An independent, objective assurance and consulting activity designed to add value and improve an organization's operations. It helps an organization accomplish its objectives by bringing a systematic, disciplined approach to evaluate and improve the effectiveness of risk management, control, and governance processes.

Internal auditors assist members of an organization in performing their responsibilities by furnishing them analyses, appraisals, recommendations, and counsel. In performing these functions, internal auditors can be thought of as a part of the organization's internal control. They represent a high-level control that functions by measuring and evaluating the effectiveness of other controls. As discussed in Chapter 7, auditing standards include the internal auditing function as part of the "monitoring component" of an organization's internal control.

Internal auditors are not merely concerned with the organization's financial controls. Their work encompasses all of the organization's internal control. They evaluate and test the effectiveness of controls designed to help the organization meet all its objectives. Also, many progressive internal auditing departments provide a wide range of other assurance and consulting services to the management of their organizations.

Evolution of Internal Auditing

Internal auditing has evolved to meet the needs of business and governmental and nonprofit organizations. Originally, a demand for internal auditing arose when managers of early large corporations recognized that annual audits of financial statements by CPAs were not sufficient. A need existed for timely employee involvement beyond that of the certified public accountants to ensure accurate and timely financial records and to prevent fraud. These original internal auditors focused their efforts on financial and accounting matters.

Subsequently, the role of internal auditors expanded as a result of demands by the major stock exchanges and the Securities and Exchange Commission (SEC) that management accept more responsibility for the reliability of published financial statements. These demands resulted in expanded internal auditor responsibilities, including more detailed analysis of internal control, as well as testing of interim and other accounting information not considered in annual audits performed by certified public accountants.

Gradually, the role of internal auditors expanded to encompass overall operational policies and procedures. Companies in the defense industry were among the first to demand such services. These companies recognized the need for reliable operating reports because they were used extensively by management to make decisions. The reports often were expressed not in dollars, but in terms of operating factors, such as quantities of parts in short supply, adherence to schedules, and quality of the product. Work by the internal auditors devoted to ensuring the dependability of these operating reports was better spent than additional audit effort devoted to financial and accounting matters.

As organizations became larger and more complex, they encountered additional operational problems that lent themselves to solutions by internal auditing. The internal auditors' role of determining whether operating units in the organization follow authorized accounting and financial policies was readily extended to include the determination of whether they follow all the organization's operating policies, and whether the established policies provide sound and effective control over all operations. The extension of internal auditing into these operational activities required internal auditors with specialized knowledge in other disciplines such as economics, law, finance, statistics, computer processing, engineering, and taxation.

Several relatively recent events have been important to the evolution of the internal auditing profession. The first was the enactment of the Foreign Corrupt Practices Act of 1977. The accounting provisions of that act require public companies to establish and maintain effective internal accounting control. To ensure compliance with these provisions, many companies established or augmented their internal auditing departments.

Another event that affected the internal auditing profession was the issuance in 1987 of the *Report of the National Commission on Fraudulent Financial Reporting*. This report contains the commission's findings and recommendations about preventing fraudulent financial reporting by public companies. Among its recommendations was a suggestion that public companies establish an internal auditing function staffed with appropriately qualified personnel and fully supported by top management. The commission also recommended that the companies help ensure the internal auditing function's objectivity by positioning it suitably within the organization, maintaining a director of the internal auditing function with appropriate stature, and establishing effective reporting relationships between the director of internal auditing and the audit committee of the board of directors. Consistently, in 1998 the Blue Ribbon Committee Report on Audit Committee Effectiveness concluded that appropriate responsibility for the oversight of financial integrity and accountability of public companies may be viewed as a three-legged stool consisting of (1) management and internal audit, (2) the board of directors and its audit committee, and (3) the external auditors.

The reengineering of companies in the mid-1990s led companies to *outsource* many of their noncore functions, including, in some cases, internal auditing. When outsourced, a specialized service provider other than company employees performs a portion or all of the internal auditing function. In some cases, CPA firms that also performed the audit of the financial statements provided major portions of the internal auditing function for companies. Providing both internal and external auditing services for SEC reporting clients has since been prohibited by the Sarbanes-Oxley Act of 2002.

Focus on Outsourcing the Internal Auditing Function

Prior to its elimination, CPA firm performance of all or a portion of the internal audit function for an audit client was extremely controversial. CPA firms argued that they could provide internal auditing services effectively and promised such benefits as lower costs and improved specialization, while allowing management to focus on core business issues. The AICPA positioned such services as "extended audit services" that were acceptable if the client understood its responsibility for establishing and maintaining internal control, and directing the internal auditing function. Representatives of the Institute of Internal Auditors questioned the propriety of CPAs' assuming responsibilities that are part of a corporation's internal control when they also audit that company.

The Internal Auditors' Role in Sarbanes-Oxley Compliance

Learning Objective 2

Internal auditors possess skills and experience that make them particularly valuable to a company's compliance efforts related to the Sarbanes-Oxley Act. As a result, many companies have involved their internal audit departments in documenting and testing controls to support management's assertion about the effectiveness of internal control over financial reporting. However, it is important to remember that it is management's responsibility to ensure the organization is in compliance with the requirements of the Sarbanes-Oxley Act. The internal auditors' role in documenting and testing controls can be significant, but it must be compatible with the overall mission and charter of the internal audit function, and it should not be seen as impairing the internal auditors' objectivity.

The work of the internal auditors may also be used by the external auditors in fulfilling the external audit function. PCAOB *Standard No. 2* allows the external auditors to use certain work of the internal auditors in fulfilling their responsibilities to provide an opinion on internal control over financial reporting.

Professional Standards of Internal Auditing

To maintain consistently high-quality services across the internal auditing profession, the IIA has issued *Standards for the Professional Practice of Internal Auditing.* These standards, as presented in Figure 21.1, set forth the criteria by which the operations of an internal auditing department should be evaluated and measured.

FIGURE 21.1 IIA *Standards for the Professional Practice of Internal Auditing*

ATTRIBUTE STANDARDS (AS)

AS1000—Purpose, Authority, and Responsibility
The purpose, authority, and responsibility of the internal auditing activity should be formally defined in a charter, consistent with the *Standards,* and approved by the board.

AS1100—Independence and Objectivity
The internal audit activity should be independent, and internal auditors should be objective in performing their work.
  AS1110—Organizational Independence
  The chief audit executive should report to a level within the organization that allows the internal audit activity to fulfill its responsibilities.
  AS1120—Individual Objectivity
  Internal auditors should have an impartial, unbiased attitude and avoid conflicts of interest.
  AS1130—Impairments to Independence or Objectivity
  If independence or objectivity is impaired in fact or appearance, the details of the impairment should be disclosed to appropriate parties. The nature of the disclosure will depend upon the impairment.

AS1200—Proficiency and Due Professional Care
Engagements should be performed with proficiency and due professional care.
  AS1210—Proficiency
  Internal auditors should possess the knowledge, skills, and other competencies needed to perform their individual responsibilities. The internal audit activity collectively should possess or obtain the knowledge, skills, and other competencies needed to perform its responsibilities.
  AS1220—Due Professional Care
  Internal auditors should apply the care and skill expected of a reasonably prudent and competent internal auditor. Due professional care does not imply infallibility.
  AS1230—Continuing Professional Development
  Internal auditors should enhance their knowledge, skills, and other competencies through continuing professional development.

AS1300—Quality Assurance and Improvement Program
The chief audit executive should develop and maintain a quality assurance and improvement program that covers all aspects of the internal audit activity and continuously monitors its effectiveness. The program should be designed to help the internal auditing activity add value and improve the organization's operations and to provide assurance that the internal audit activity is in conformity with the *Standards* and the Code of Ethics.
  AS1310—Quality Program Assessments
  The internal audit activity should adopt a process to monitor and assess the overall effectiveness of the quality program. The process should include both internal and external assessments.
    AS1311—Internal Assessments
    Internal assessments should include:
    • Ongoing reviews of the performance of the internal audit activity; and
    • Periodic reviews performed through self-assessment or by other persons within the organization, with knowledge of internal auditing practices and the *Standards.*
    AS1312—External Assessments
    External assessments, such as quality assurance reviews, should be conducted at least once every five years by a qualified, independent reviewer or review team from outside the organization.

(Continued)

FIGURE 21.1   *(Continued)*

ATTRIBUTE STANDARDS (AS)

AS1320—Reporting on the Quality Program
The chief audit executive should communicate the results of external assessments to the board.

AS1330—Use of "Conducted in Accordance with the *Standards*"
Internal auditors are encouraged to report that their activities are "conducted in accordance with the *Standards for the Professional Practice of Internal Auditing*." However, internal auditors may use the statement only if assessments of the quality improvement program demonstrate that the internal audit activity is in compliance with the *Standards*.

AS1340—Disclosure of Noncompliance
Although the internal audit activity should achieve full compliance with the *Standards* and internal auditors with the Code of Ethics, there may be instances in which full compliance is not achieved. When noncompliance impacts the overall scope or operation of the internal audit activity, disclosure should be made to senior management and the board.

PERFORMANCE STANDARDS (PS)

PS2000—Managing the Internal Audit Activity
The chief audit executive should effectively manage the internal audit activity to ensure it adds value to the organization.

PS2010—Planning
The chief audit executive should establish risk-based plans to determine the priorities of the internal audit activity, consistent with the organization's goals.

PS2020—Communication and Approval
The chief audit executive should communicate the internal audit activity's plans and resource requirements, including significant interim changes, to senior management and to the board for review and approval. The chief audit executive should also communicate the impact of resource limitations.

PS2030—Resource Management
The chief audit executive should ensure that internal audit resources are appropriate, sufficient, and effectively deployed to achieve the approved plan.

PS2040—Policies and Procedures
The chief audit executive should establish policies and procedures to guide the internal audit activity.

PS2050—Coordination
The chief audit executive should share information and coordinate activities with other internal and external providers of relevant assurance and consulting services to ensure proper coverage and minimize duplication of efforts.

PS2060—Reporting to the Board and Senior Management
The chief audit executive should report periodically to the board and senior management on the internal audit activity's purpose, authority, responsibility, and performance relative to its plan. Reporting should also include significant risk exposures and control issues, corporate governance issues, and other matters needed or requested by the board and senior management.

PS2100—Nature of Work
The internal audit activity evaluates and contributes to the improvement of risk management, control, and governance systems.

PS2110—Risk Management
The internal audit activity should assist the organization by identifying and evaluating significant exposures to risk and contributing to the improvement of risk management and control systems.

PS2120—Control
The internal audit activity should assist the organization in maintaining effective controls by evaluating their effectiveness and efficiency and by promoting continuous improvement.

PS2130—Governance
The internal audit activity should contribute to the organization's governance process by evaluating and improving the process through which (1) values and goals are established and communicated, (2) the accomplishment of goals is monitored, (3) accountability is ensured, and (4) values are preserved.

PS2200—Engagement Planning
Internal auditors should develop and record a plan for each engagement.

PS2201—Planning Considerations
In planning the engagement, internal auditors should consider:
- The objectives of the activity being reviewed and the means by which the activity controls its performance.

(Continued)

FIGURE 21.1 (*Concluded*)

PERFORMANCE STANDARDS (PS)

- The significant risks to the activity, its objectives, resources, and operations and the means by which the potential impact of risk is kept to an acceptable level.
- The adequacy and effectiveness of the activity's risk management and control systems compared to a relevant control framework or model.
- The opportunities for making significant improvements to the activity's risk management and control systems.

PS2210—Engagement Objectives
The engagement's objectives should address the risks, controls, and governance processes associated with the activities under review.

PS2220—Engagement Scope
The established scope of the engagement should be sufficient to satisfy the objectives of the engagement.

PS2230—Engagement Resources Allocation
Internal auditors should determine appropriate resources to achieve engagement objectives. Staffing should be based on an evaluation of the nature and complexity of each engagement, time constraints, and available resources.

PS2240—Engagement Work Program
Internal auditors should develop work programs that achieve the engagement objectives. These work programs should be recorded.

PS2300—Performing the Engagement
Internal auditors should identify, analyze, evaluate, and record sufficient information to achieve the engagement's results.

PS2310—Identifying Information
Internal auditors should identify sufficient, reliable, relevant, and useful information to achieve the engagement's objectives.

PS2320—Analysis and Evaluation
Internal auditors should base conclusions and engagement results on appropriate analyses and evaluations.

PS2330—Recording Information
Internal auditors should record relevant information to support the conclusions and engagement results.

PS2340—Engagement Supervision
Engagements should be properly supervised to ensure objectives are achieved, quality is assured, and staff is developed.

PS2400—Communicating Results
Internal auditors should communicate the engagement results promptly.

P2410—Criteria for Communicating
Communications should include the engagement's objectives and scope as well as applicable conclusions, recommendations, and action plans.

PS2420—Quality of Communications
Communications should be accurate, objective, clear, concise, constructive, complete, and timely.

PS2421—Errors and Omissions
If a final communication contains a significant error or omission, the chief audit executive should communicate corrected information to all individuals who received the original communication.

PS2430—Engagement Disclosure of Noncompliance with the *Standards*
When noncompliance with the *Standards* impacts a specific engagement, communication of the results should disclose the:
- Standard(s) with which full compliance was not achieved,
- Reason(s) for noncompliance, and
- Impact of noncompliance on the engagement.

PS2440—Disseminating Results
The chief audit executive should disseminate results to the appropriate individuals.

PS2500—Monitoring Progress
The chief audit executive should establish and maintain a system to monitor the disposition of results communicated to management.

PS2600—Management's Acceptance of Risks
When the chief audit executive believes that senior management has accepted a level of residual risk that is unacceptable to the organization, the chief audit executive should discuss the matter with senior management. If the decision regarding residual risk is not resolved, the chief audit executive and senior management should report the matter to the board for resolution.

Learning Objective 3

Purpose, Authority, and Responsibility

The purpose, authority, and responsibility of the internal auditing department should be set forth in the department's charter, as approved by the organization's board of directors. Its purpose should be consistent with the IIA's definition of internal auditing.

Independence and Objectivity

Since internal auditors are employees of the organization, they cannot have the perceived independence of external auditors. However, independence is still very important to internal auditors. They should maintain an impartial, unbiased attitude and avoid conflicts of interest. Independence of the internal auditing department is enhanced when the chief audit executive[1] reports to a level of management of sufficient stature to ensure broad audit coverage and adequate consideration and implementation of the auditors' recommendations. Ideally, the chief audit executive should report directly to the audit committee of the board of directors. Independence is also enhanced when potential conflicts of interest are considered in assigning staff to audit assignments. For example, it would be a conflict of interest for an internal auditor to audit an area in which that individual was recently employed. It is difficult, if not impossible, to remain objective in evaluating one's own operating decisions.

Proficiency and Due Professional Care

An internal auditing department should establish policies and procedures that ensure that staff members are competent to fulfill their assignments with professional proficiency. Ideally, the internal auditing department collectively should possess the skills and knowledge necessary to fulfill all the audit requirements of the organization. These skills and knowledge may be acquired through a combination of effective employment practices and continuing education programs.

Establishing appropriate staffing and supervisory policies also enhances professional proficiency. The department should establish policies for assigning staff members to audit areas so that the auditors will be competent to successfully complete those assignments. Once assigned to a task, the auditors should exercise the care and skill expected of reasonably prudent and competent professionals. Work by staff members should be adequately supervised and reviewed.

Quality Assurance and Improvement Program

The chief audit executive should establish a quality assurance system that covers all aspects of the internal audit activity and continuously monitors its effectiveness. Quality assurance policies and procedures should be communicated throughout the department, and the system should be monitored for effective design and application. The board of directors should receive a periodic assessment of the effectiveness of the quality assurance system.

Managing the Internal Auditing Activity

This group of standards provides guidance for the chief audit executive in managing the internal auditing function. The chief audit executive is responsible for properly administering the department to help assure that (1) audit work is planned, controlled, and coordinated to ensure that maximum value is provided to the organization, and (2) the resources of the internal auditing department are efficiently and effectively employed.

Nature of Work

The nature of the internal auditors' work should extend beyond accounting and financial controls to include compliance with all types of controls and operational auditing. The internal auditors should also perform work that contributes to the organization's risk assessment process and its system of governance.

Engagement Planning

The IIA's standards in this category recognize that if audit work is to be effective it must be adequately planned. Effective planning includes developing appropriate objectives, scope, resources, and work programs.

---

[1] This title, used by the IIA, is equivalent to the director of internal auditing.

Performing the Engagement

In performing every engagement the internal auditors should identify relevant information, perform appropriate analysis and evaluation of the information, prepare work papers that support their conclusions, and adequately supervise staff members assigned to the engagement.

Communicating Results

For audit work to have its intended effect, the results must be communicated to appropriate individuals, clearly, concisely, and on a timely basis. Communications should include the engagement's objectives as well as applicable conclusions and recommendations. When applicable, reports should indicate that the engagement was conducted in accordance with the IIA standards.

Monitoring Progress

This aspect of auditing standards involves monitoring progress of the organization with respect to the internal auditors' recommendations. The chief audit executive should follow up to determine that management has taken appropriate action on recommendations, or that management has decided to accept the risk of not taking any action.

Management's Acceptance of Risks

When the chief audit executive believes that an unacceptable level of risk exists, the matter should be discussed with management. If the matter remains unresolved, both the chief audit executive and senior management should report the matter to the board of directors.

Certification of Internal Auditors

Since 1974, the IIA has administered the **Certified Internal Auditor (CIA)** program. To become certified, a candidate must hold a bachelor's degree from an accredited college and successfully complete a two-day examination that is offered semiannually in principal cities throughout the world. The examination consists of four parts: internal audit process, internal audit skills, management control and information technology, and the audit environment. Another requirement of certification is at least two years of work experience in internal auditing or its equivalent, although an advanced academic degree may be substituted for one year of work experience in meeting this requirement. When internal auditors become certified, they must meet requirements for continuing professional education. More information on internal auditing and the CIA examination is available from the Institute of Internal Auditors, 247 Maitland Avenue, Altamonte Springs, Florida 32701 or at www.theiia.org.

Operational Auditing

Learning Objective 4

The term **operational auditing** refers to comprehensive examination of an operating unit or a complete organization to evaluate its systems, controls, and performance, as measured by management's objectives. Whereas a *financial audit* focuses on the measurement of financial position, results of operations, and cash flows of an entity, an operational audit focuses on the *efficiency, effectiveness,* and *economy* of operations. The operational auditor appraises management's operating controls and systems over such varied activities as purchasing, data processing, receiving, shipping, office services, advertising, and engineering.

Objectives of Operational Audits

Operational audits are often performed by internal auditors for their organizations. The major users of operational audit reports are managers at various levels, including the board of directors. Top management needs assurances that every component of an organization is working to attain the organization's goals. For example, management needs the following:

1. Assessments of the unit's performance in relation to management's objectives or other appropriate criteria.
2. Assurance that its plans (as set forth in statements of objectives, programs, budgets, and directives) are comprehensive, consistent, and understood at the operating levels.

3. Objective information on how well its plans and policies are being carried out in all areas of operations, as well as information on opportunities for improvement in effectiveness, efficiency, and economy.

4. Information on weaknesses in operating controls, particularly as to possible sources of waste.

5. Reassurance that all operating reports can be relied on as a basis for action.

Governmental auditors, such as those employed by the Government Accountability Office (GAO), perform operational audits of governmental programs that are administered by both governmental and nongovernmental organizations. Operational auditing is especially applicable to governmental programs where the effectiveness of the programs cannot be evaluated in terms of profits; they must be evaluated by measuring such elements as the number of families relocated, the number of individuals rehabilitated, and the extent of the improvement in environmental conditions. In addition to internal and governmental auditors, CPA firms perform operational audits for clients through their consulting services departments.

General Approach to Operational Audits

In many respects the auditor's work in performing an operational audit is similar to that of a financial statement audit, but there are some significant differences. The steps may be set forth as: (1) definition of purpose, (2) familiarization, (3) preliminary survey, (4) program development, (5) fieldwork, (6) reporting the findings, and (7) follow-up. The operational audit process is illustrated by Figure 21.2.

Definition of Purpose

The broad statement of purpose of an operational audit usually includes the intention to appraise the performance of a particular organization, function, or group of activities. However, this broad statement must be expanded to specify precisely the scope of the audit and the nature of the report. The auditors must determine specifically which policies and procedures are to be appraised and how they relate to the specific objectives of the organization.

FIGURE 21.2
The Operational Audit

Familiarization

Before starting an operational audit, the auditors must obtain a comprehensive knowledge of the objectives, organizational structure, and operating characteristics of the unit being audited. This familiarization process might begin with a study of organizational charts, statements of the functions and responsibilities assigned, management policies and directives, and operating policies and procedures. At this stage, the auditors may read some of the published material available on the subject to acquaint themselves as fully as possible with the functions performed. This background information equips the auditor to visit the organization's facilities and interview supervisory personnel to determine their specific objectives, the standards used to measure accomplishment of these objectives, and the principal problems encountered in achieving these objectives. During these visits, the auditors will also observe the operations and inspect the available records and reports.

In summary, the auditors attempt to familiarize themselves as thoroughly as possible with the function being performed, particularly from the standpoint of administrative responsibility and control. The auditors' understanding of the organization is documented with questionnaires, flowcharts, and written narratives.

Preliminary Survey

The auditors' preliminary conclusions about the critical aspects of the operations and potential problem areas are summarized as the auditors' preliminary survey. This survey serves as a guide for the development of the audit program.

Program Development

The operational audit program is tailor-made to the particular engagement. It contains all the tests and analyses the auditors believe are necessary to evaluate the organization's operations. Based on the nature and difficulty of the audit work, appropriate personnel will be assigned to the engagement, and the work will be scheduled.

Fieldwork

The fieldwork phase involves executing the operational audit program. The auditors select the items to be reviewed to determine the adequacy of the procedures and how well they are followed. Just as in financial statement audits, the auditors will frequently select representative samples of the transactions from the records and inspect them to determine whether proper procedures have been followed and to discover the nature and extent of the problems encountered. In other cases they may resort to inquiry or direct observation to satisfy themselves that the employees understand their instructions and are carrying out their work as intended.

Analysis is another important part of fieldwork. Actual performance by the organization is compared with various criteria, such as budgets, productivity goals, or performance by similar units. This analysis provides a basis for auditors' recommendations for improvements in effectiveness, efficiency, and economy.

As each phase of the fieldwork is completed, the auditors summarize the results and evaluate the material gathered. Deficiencies that appear to be significant are discussed with the supervisor involved. Frequently, corrective action may be taken at this time, although the primary purpose of this on-the-spot discussion is to make sure that all the relevant facts have been obtained.

During fieldwork, the auditors will document the planning, evidence gathered, analysis, interpretation, and findings in their *working papers*. The audit working papers should stand alone and support the auditors' report.

Reporting the Findings

On final completion of the fieldwork, the auditors should summarize their findings related to the basic purposes of the audit. The report will include suggested improvements in the operational policies and procedures of the unit and a list of situations in which compliance with existing policies and procedures is less than adequate. After they have completed the draft report, they should arrange an *exit conference* to review the findings with all persons directly concerned with the operations audited. The conference ensures that the auditors have an accurate and complete story; if there is a question about the facts, further investigation will be made until any doubt is resolved. If a serious disagreement on the interpretation of the facts remains, it is usually best to disclose both interpretations in the report. The conference also provides an opportunity for the affected management to consider and take timely action on the problems disclosed.

A formal report, such as the one illustrated by Figure 21.3, is then issued to top management. For each finding, a complete report will describe (1) the *criteria* used to evaluate the activity, (2) the *condition* (e.g., problem) that exists, (3) the *cause,* (4) the *effect,* and (5) *recommendations* for improvement.

Follow-up

The final stage in the operational auditors' work is the follow-up action to ensure that any deficiencies disclosed in the audit report are satisfactorily handled. This follow-up responsibility may be given to a line organization or staff group, but most frequently it is held to be a responsibility of the audit staff. In some instances the auditors find it desirable to make brief re-examinations after a reasonable lapse of time to ensure that all significant recommendations have been implemented.

FIGURE 21.3
Introductory Language for an Operational Audit Report

Neal McGregor
Vice President—Operations
Baxter Corporation
Kansas City, Missouri

Dear Mr. McGregor:

In September 20X1 we concluded an operational audit of the data processing operations.

Objectives, Scope, and Approach
The general objectives of this engagement, which were more specifically outlined in our letter dated June 30, 20X1, were as follows:

- To document, analyze, and report on the status of current operations.
- To identify areas that require attention.
- To make recommendations for corrective action or improvements.

Our operational audit encompassed the centralized data processing facilities and the on-site computer operations of the company's retailing division. Our evaluations included both the financial and operational conditions of the units. Financial data consulted in the course of our analyses were not audited or reviewed by us, and, accordingly, we do not express an opinion or any other form of assurance on them.

The operational audit involved interviews with management personnel and selected operations personnel in each of the units studied. We also evaluated selected documents, files, reports, systems, procedures, and policies as we considered appropriate. After analyzing the data, we developed recommendations for improvements. We then discussed our findings and recommendations with appropriate unit management personnel, and with you, prior to submitting this written report.

Findings and Recommendations
All significant findings are included in this report for your consideration. The recommendations in this report represent, in our judgment, those most likely to bring about improvements in the operations of the organization. The recommendations differ in such aspects as difficulty of implementation, urgency, visibility of benefits, and required investment in facilities and equipment or additional personnel. The varying nature of the recommendations, their implementation costs, and their potential impact on operations should be considered in reaching your decision on courses of action.

(Specific Findings and Recommendations)

Illustrative Cases
Compliance Auditing: Two Examples

COMPLIANCE WITH THE CLEAN AIR ACT

The Environmental Protection Agency has issued guidelines for Oxygenated Gasoline Credit Programs under the Clean Air Act, which requires CPAs (or internal auditors) to perform agreed-upon procedures regarding a company's compliance with an EPA regulation that requires gasoline to contain at least 2 percent oxygen. Management's assertion will indicate the company's compliance with the relevant requirements (which will be specifically listed) of the Clean Air Act.

COMPLIANCE WITH THE FDIC IMPROVEMENT ACT OF 1991

The Federal Depository Insurance Corporation (FDIC) Improvement Act of 1991 requires that CPAs be engaged to perform agreed-upon procedures engagements to test large financial institutions' compliance with certain provisions related to the "safety and soundness" of the institutions. The assertion in this case states management's belief that the institution has complied with the listed provisions of the act.

Compliance Auditing

Learning Objective 5

Society has always been concerned about compliance with laws and regulations by all types of organizations. As a result, compliance auditing has evolved to become an important part of the work of both external and internal auditors. **Compliance auditing** involves testing and reporting on whether an organization has complied with the requirements of various laws, regulations, and agreements. Congress and various regulators have adopted compliance auditing requirements for a wide variety of business, governmental, and nonprofit organizations. The Auditing Standards Board has developed general guidance for all types of engagements that involve attesting to compliance with laws and regulations, and more specific guidance for compliance auditing of federal financial assistance programs.

Attesting to Compliance with Laws and Regulations

Section 601 of *Statements on Standards for Attestation Engagements (SSAE) No. 10,* "Attestation Standards: Revision and Recodification,"[2] provides guidance for CPAs when they are engaged either to apply agreed-upon procedures or to perform an examination on an organization's compliance with laws and regulations. The *Statement* prohibits CPAs from performing *reviews* of compliance with laws and regulations.

In compliance attestation engagements CPAs address an organization's **compliance with specified requirements,** or its internal control over compliance with specific laws and regulations. Management[3] provides an assertion about compliance in writing in a representation letter to the CPAs. That assertion also may be presented in a formal report that accompanies the CPAs' report or be included in the CPAs' report. The CPAs' report provides assurance on either **management's assertion** or directly on compliance.

Applying Agreed-Upon Procedures to Specified Requirements

Engagements to apply agreed-upon procedures to test compliance with specified requirements are common compliance engagements. The objective of an agreed-upon procedures engagement is to assist users in evaluating an entity's compliance with specified requirements based on procedures agreed upon by the users of the report. A major advantage of agreed-upon procedures engagements results from the fact that since the users participate in designing the procedures to be performed by the CPAs, it is likely that the work performed will meet their needs.

---

[2] *Statement No. 10* revises and recodifies the first nine SSAEs. Guidance on compliance attestation was originally presented in *SSAE No. 3,* "Compliance Attestation."

[3] Section 101 of *SSAE No. 10* provides that the report should identify the party responsible for the assertion or the subject matter of the assertion. The responsible party is defined as the person or persons, either as individuals or representatives of the entity, responsible for the subject matter. Management is deemed to be the "responsible party" throughout this chapter.

Agreed-upon procedures reports are restricted use reports, intended for the audit committee, management, and other parties for whom the procedures were designed (e.g., the Environmental Protection Agency). The reports provide a summary of procedures performed and the CPAs' findings. The findings section of the report should set forth any instances of **noncompliance** with relevant laws and regulations noted by the CPAs, regardless of whether they became aware of them as a result of the procedures performed or in some other way, such as through an informal discussion with an internal auditor. The format of a report on the application of agreed-upon procedures to compliance is illustrated in the accompanying box.

Independent Accountant's Report

TO LENOS COMPANY:

We have performed the procedures enumerated below, which were agreed to by the Illinois Department of Education, solely to assist the users in evaluating Lenos Company's compliance with Section F.2. of Illinois Department of Education Regulation 74A of *Employment Health Requirements* during the period ended December 31, 20XX, included in the accompanying Management Report. Management is responsible for Lenos Company's compliance with these requirements. This agreed-upon procedures engagement was conducted in accordance with attestation standards established by the American Institute of Certified Public Accountants. The sufficiency of these procedures is solely the responsibility of those parties specified in this report. Consequently, we make no representation regarding the sufficiency of the procedures described below either for the purpose for which this report has been requested or for any other purpose.

[Include paragraphs to enumerate procedures and findings.]

We were not engaged to and did not conduct an examination, the objective of which would be the expression of an opinion on compliance. Accordingly, we do not express such an opinion. Had we performed additional procedures, other matters might have come to our attention that would have been reported to you.

This report is intended solely for the information and use of Illinois Department of Education and is not intended to be and should not be used by anyone other than these specified parties.

Applying Agreed-Upon Procedures to the Effectiveness of Controls over Compliance

As indicated previously, CPAs also may be engaged to test the effectiveness of the organization's internal control over compliance. An organization's **internal control over compliance** is the process by which management obtains reasonable assurance that the organization has complied with specific requirements. The CPAs' report on the application of agreed-upon procedures to test the effectiveness of controls over compliance is similar to the report on compliance that is presented above. It describes the tests of controls performed and the related findings and includes the appropriate limitations on the distribution of the report and other caveats.

Performing Examinations

CPAs are sometimes engaged to perform an examination of a client's compliance with specified requirements (the subject matter) or of management's assertion related thereto. In performing an examination engagement, the CPAs begin by obtaining a thorough understanding of the requirements. Then, they plan the engagement, consider the organization's internal control over compliance, perform sufficient procedures to form an opinion on compliance (or on management's assertion about compliance), and issue an opinion on compliance with specified requirements. An unqualified opinion on compliance with laws and regulations is shown in the accompanying box.

Independent Accountant's Report

TO LENOS COMPANY:

We have examined Lenos Company's compliance with Section F.2. of Illinois Department of Education Regulation 74A of *Employment Health Requirements* during the period ended December 31, 20X1. Management is responsible for Lenos Company's compliance with those

> requirements. Our responsibility is to express an opinion on the Company's compliance based on our examination.
>
> Our examination was conducted in accordance with standards established by the American Institute of Certified Public Accountants, and, accordingly, included examining, on a test basis, evidence about Lenos Company's compliance with those requirements and performing such other procedures as we considered necessary in the circumstances. We believe that our examination provides a reasonable basis for our opinion. Our examination does not provide a legal determination on Lenos Company's compliance with specified requirements.
>
> In our opinion, Lenos Company complied, in all material respects, with the aforementioned requirements for the year ended December 31, 20X1.

The CPAs' examination report should be modified in the following circumstances:

1. *Material noncompliance with specified requirements.* A qualified or adverse opinion should be issued when the auditors' procedures indicate that management's report is not fairly stated.

2. *Scope restriction.* A qualified opinion or disclaimer of opinion should be issued when the CPAs' procedures are restricted.

3. *Involvement of another CPA firm in the examination.* In these circumstances, the principal CPA firm generally issues a report that indicates a division of responsibility.

Although the CPAs' examination report may generally be on either the subject matter or on management's assertion, when it is other than unqualified the CPAs must report directly on the subject matter.

Compliance Auditing of Government Entities and Organizations Receiving Federal Financial Assistance

Learning Objective 6

SAS 74 (AU 801), "Compliance Auditing Applicable to Governmental Entities and Other Recipients of Governmental Financial Assistance," provides guidance on performing tests of compliance in the following types of audits:

1. Audits of the financial statements of entities receiving federal financial assistance in accordance with generally accepted auditing standards.

2. Audits conducted in accordance with *Government Auditing Standards.*

3. Audits conducted in accordance with the federal Single Audit Act.[4]

Audits in Accordance with Generally Accepted Auditing Standards

As discussed in Chapter 2, auditors have a responsibility to design all audits to obtain reasonable assurance of detecting material misstatements resulting from violations of laws and regulations that have a *direct and material effect* on line-item amounts in the financial statements. Governmental organizations are subject to a variety of laws and regulations that affect their financial statements—many more than typical business enterprises. An important aspect of generally accepted accounting principles for governmental organizations is the recognition of various legal and contractual requirements. These requirements pertain to bases of accounting, fund structure, and other accounting principles. Therefore, in performing an audit of a governmental organization's financial statements, auditors are more likely to encounter laws and regulations that have a direct and material effect on the amounts in the organization's financial statements.

Governmental organizations receive funds from various sources, including taxes, special assessments, and bond issues. Laws and regulations often dictate the way the funds may be spent. While certain funds may be used for general government purposes, others are restricted to specific purposes, such as schools, libraries, or highways.

---

[4] *SAS 74* refers to the Single Audit Act of 1984. This act was amended in its entirety by the Single Audit Act Amendments of 1996.

A governmental organization also may receive financial assistance from other governmental organizations in the form of grants, loans, loan guarantees, interest subsidies, insurance, and food commodities. This financial assistance often is provided subject to specified compliance requirements. For example, a federal agency may provide financial assistance to a governmental organization but require the organization to match the federal funding. In the event a governmental organization does not comply with the matching requirement, it may have to refund the federal financial assistance.

Auditors perform a number of procedures to identify the laws and regulations that have a direct effect on an organization's financial statements, including (1) discussing laws and regulations with management, program and grant administrators, and government auditors; (2) reviewing state and federal compliance requirement documents; (3) reviewing relevant grant and loan agreements; and (4) reviewing minutes of the legislative body of the governmental organization. Auditors also obtain written representations from management about the completeness of the laws and regulations identified and an acknowledgment of management's responsibility for compliance with them.

When auditors have an understanding of the important laws and regulations, they assess the risks that financial statement amounts might be materially affected by violations.[5] In making these assessments, they consider the controls designed to prevent violations, such as policies regarding acceptable operating practices, codes of conduct, and assignment of responsibility for complying and assessing compliance with legal and regulatory requirements. These risk assessments are then used to design the nature, timing, and extent of the auditors' substantive tests of compliance.

Audits in Accordance with Government Auditing Standards

The Government Accountability Office issues auditing standards for use in auditing federal entities and organizations that receive federal financial assistance. They include standards for financial audits and performance audits. These standards are included in a publication entitled **Government Auditing Standards,** which is commonly referred to as the "Yellow Book." The standards apply only when required by law, regulation, or agreement. These standards impose additional requirements related to (1) audit communication, (2) considering the results of previous audits, (3) noncompliance with provisions of contracts and grant agreements, (4) audit documentation, and (5) reporting.

Audit Communications

Government Auditing Standards require auditors to communicate information about the nature of the audit and level of assurance provided not only client management and the audit committee, but also to any outside individuals requiring the audit services. In making these communications the auditors should specifically address the planned work related to testing compliance with laws and regulations and internal control over financial reporting.

Considering the Results of Previous Audits

Government Auditing Standards require the auditors to consider the results of previous audits and follow up on known significant findings and recommendations in prior-year audit reports. The auditors' objective is to determine that client officers have taken appropriate corrective actions.

Noncompliance with Provisions of Contracts and Grants

As discussed in Chapter 2, generally accepted auditing standards require the auditors to plan an audit to provide reasonable assurance of detecting violations of laws and regulations that have a direct and material effect on the financial statements. *Government Auditing Standards*

---

[5] Generally, laws and regulations concerning compliance with financial assistance programs do not discuss compliance in terms of whether or not noncompliance might materially misstate the financial statements. These laws and regulations discuss the effect of noncompliance in terms of whether it has a direct and material effect on financial assistance programs.

make it clear that this responsibility extends to provisions of contracts and grants that have a direct and material effect on the financial statements.

Audit Documentation

Government Auditing Standards include several very specific requirements with respect to audit working papers, including documentation of:

1. The objectives, scope, and methodology used by the auditors, including sampling methods and other selection criteria used.
2. The auditor's determination that certain additional government auditing standards do not apply, or that an applicable standard was not followed and the reason therefor.
3. The work performed to support significant judgments and conclusions.
4. The consideration that the planned audit procedures are designed to achieve audit objectives when evidential matter obtained is highly dependent on computerized information systems and the auditors are not relying on the effectiveness of internal control.
5. Evidence of supervisory review, before the audit report is issued, of the work performed that supports findings, conclusions, and recommendations contained in the audit report.

Requirement 4 is designed to encourage auditors to rely upon internal control when financial statement assertions are significantly dependent upon computerized processing.

Reporting

In performing an audit of financial statements in accordance with *Government Auditing Standards,* in addition to issuing an independent auditor's report on the financial statements, the auditor must also issue written reports on compliance with laws and regulations and on internal control.[6]

Reporting on Compliance with Laws and Regulations

The report on compliance is based on the auditors' tests of compliance with laws, regulations, grants, and contracts that have a direct and material effect on the amounts in the financial statements—tests that are required by generally accepted auditing standards. The report describes the scope of the auditors' tests of compliance with laws and regulations and presents the auditors' findings.

Auditors may discover violations of provisions of laws, regulations, contracts, or grants that result in what they estimate to be a material misstatement of the organization's financial statements. In these circumstances, they must consider the effect of their opinion on the financial statements. The resulting misstatement, if left uncorrected, would normally require them to issue a qualified or adverse opinion. Of course, management will usually decide to correct the financial statements, allowing the auditors to issue an unqualified opinion. Even though the financial statements are corrected, the auditors must still modify their report on compliance with laws and regulations to include a description of the material instances of noncompliance. If the noncompliance resulted from a weakness in internal control considered by the auditors to be a reportable condition, they would also modify their report on internal control to describe the condition. The auditors should also report a description of any fraudulent or other illegal acts that they become aware of, unless they are clearly inconsequential.

Auditors also may be required to report fraudulent or illegal acts directly to a government agency or another third party. For example, when the client is required by law or regulation to notify specific external parties about a fraudulent or illegal act and fails to do so, the auditors

---

[6] *Government Auditing Standards* allow these reports on financial statements, internal control, and compliance to be presented separately or combined. The reporting options include (*a*) one report, all three combined; (*b*) two reports, with internal control and compliance combined; and (*c*) three separate reports.

are required to communicate the problem directly to the appropriate party. When the client fails to take appropriate steps to address fraudulent or illegal acts, auditors may also be required to notify a government agency.

Reporting on Internal Control

When performing an audit in accordance with *Government Auditing Standards,* information on reportable conditions (significant deficiencies) is included in the auditors' report on internal control. A report issued under *Government Auditing Standards* also identifies and discusses the implications of those reportable conditions that are considered to be material weaknesses. Other items in the report include (1) an indication that management is responsible for establishing and maintaining the internal control, (2) a description of the scope of the auditors' work in obtaining an understanding of internal control and in assessing control risk, and (3) a description of deficiencies in internal control not significant enough to be reportable conditions, or a reference to a separate letter to management that reported these conditions.[7]

Reference to Separate Reports

Government Auditing Standards also require that if an auditor issues separate reports on the financial statements, compliance, and internal control, the report on the financial statements must include a final paragraph that refers to the reports on compliance and internal control, as shown below:

> In accordance with *Government Auditing Standards,* we have also issued our reports dated July 15, 200X, on our consideration of the City of Springfield's internal control over financial reporting and on our tests of its compliance with certain provisions of laws, regulations, contracts, and grants. Those reports are an integral part of an audit performed in accordance with *Government Auditing Standards* and should be read in conjunction with this report in considering the results of our audit.

Audits in Accordance with the Single Audit Act

A major impetus for the demands for increased *compliance auditing* comes from the federal government, which provides more than $350 billion in financial assistance annually through various federal financial assistance programs. This federal financial assistance must be spent in accordance with the respective programs' requirements. Federal financial assistance is provided primarily to states and local governmental units, such as cities, counties, and school districts, and to nonprofit organizations, such as private colleges and universities and research institutes. Business organizations may also receive federal financial assistance.

Congress passed the **Single Audit Act** to provide a mechanism for improving the management of federal financial assistance programs by providing a statutory requirement to test controls over compliance and compliance with program requirements. The Single Audit Act applies to states, local governments, and nonprofit organizations that expend $500,000 or more within a fiscal year in federal financial assistance. Audits in accordance with the Single Audit Act[8] are specifically designed to assess whether the billions of dollars in federal financial assistance are being managed and spent in accordance with applicable laws and regulations. Consequently, audits under the Single Audit Act are more extensive than audits of an organization's financial statements in accordance with generally accepted auditing standards and *Government Auditing Standards.*

---

[7] Auditors of SEC registrants also issue reports on internal control as a part of the audit. Chapter 18 presents details.

[8] The Single Audit Act requires the Director of the Office of Management (OMB) to issue guidance for implementing the act. OMB Circular A-133, *Audits of States, Local Governments, and Non-Profit Organizations,* provides that guidance.

FIGURE 21.4   Schedule of Federal Financial Assistance

CITY OF ROSEBUD, NEW JERSEY Schedule of Federal Financial Assistance For the Year Ended June 30, 20X1				
Federal Grantor	**Federal CFDA Number**	**Program or Award Amount**	**Receipts**	**Disbursements**
Department of Housing and Urban Development, Community Development Block Grants/Entitlement Grants, CFDA number 14.218	—	$ 808,432	$ 562,453	$ 641,941
Passed through the New Jersey Department of Transportation: Federal Transit—Capital Investment Grants, CFDA number 20.500	21,300	483,993	483,993	483,993
Department of Education, Title I Grants to Local Education Agencies, CFDA number 84.010	66,418	158,700	—	30,910
		$1,451,125	$1,046,446	$1,156,844

The requirements of a Single Audit include determining and reporting on whether (1) the financial statements are presented fairly in all material respects in accordance with generally accepted accounting principles, (2) the schedule of expenditures of federal awards illustrated in Figure 21.4 is fairly presented in all material respects in relation to the financial statements taken as a whole, and (3) the entity complied with the provisions of laws, regulations, and contracts or grants that may have a direct and material effect on each major federal financial assistance program. The requirements also include obtaining an understanding of internal control pertaining to compliance with the provisions of laws, regulations, contracts, or grants that may have a material effect on each major federal financial assistance program; assessing control risk; and performing tests of controls. With respect to internal control, auditors must report on the procedures performed, including any reportable conditions identified with specific identification of reportable conditions that constitute material weaknesses.

Identification of Major Programs

An important aspect of performing an audit in accordance with the *Single Audit Act* is auditor identification of the **major federal financial assistance programs.** Major federal financial assistance programs are those programs to which the auditor must apply procedures to test for compliance and to test the effectiveness of controls. A major program is determined based on a risk-based approach considering both the amount of the program's expenditures and the risk of material noncompliance. However, the auditor must test compliance and controls of programs with expenditures that, in the aggregate, equal 50 percent of total federal financial assistance program expenditures.[9] The Illustrative Case on page 755 provides an example of how the auditors identify major programs.

Designing Compliance Procedures for Major Programs

Auditors approach a Single Audit in much the same way they approach an audit in accordance with generally accepted auditing standards, but they must consider the additional auditing requirements for individual major federal financial assistance programs. In performing an audit in accordance with generally accepted auditing standards, auditors are concerned with compliance with laws and regulations that could have a *direct* and *material* effect on the organization's financial statements. Under the Single Audit Act, auditors are also concerned with compliance with laws and regulations that could have a direct and material effect on each

---

[9] For low risk organizations, this percentage is reduced to 25 percent.

Illustrative Case
Identification of Major Programs

The City of Woodruff receives funds through four federal financial assistance programs. The following are the total amount of expenditures for the programs for the year and the auditors' assessments of the risk of material noncompliance of each program.

	Expenditures	Risk
Department of Education		
Title I—Grants to Local Education Agencies		
CFDA Number 84.010	$1,350,422	Moderate
Department of Transportation		
Highway Planning and Construction		
CFDA Number 20.205	787,900	Low
Department of Housing and Urban Development		
Community Development		
Block Grants/Entitlement Grants		
CFDA Number 14.218	340,000	High
Department of Health and Human Services		
Community Services Block Grant		
CFDA Number 93.569	95,200	Moderate
Total expenditures	$2,573,522	

Based on the amount of the expenditures and the risk of material noncompliance, the auditors have identified the first and third programs as major programs. Expenditures from these two programs total $1,690,422 ($1,350,422 + $340,000), which exceeds the required percentage of coverage of 50 percent of total federal financial assistance program expenditures. The second and fourth programs were not identified as major programs due to the auditors' assessments of the risk of material noncompliance and total amount, respectively.

major federal financial assistance program. Because materiality must be considered on a program-by-program basis, materiality for planning the compliance procedures will typically be much less than that for the financial statements. Further, an amount that is material to one major federal financial assistance program may not be material to another major program because of differences in program size and the differing significance of particular compliance requirements to each program. This lower level of planning materiality results in an increase in the extent of tests of compliance.

In designing the tests of compliance procedures, auditors first assess the inherent risk of material noncompliance with laws and regulations applicable to each major program by considering various factors, such as the amount of the program expenditures and any changes made in the program. Auditors then assess the *control risk* related to the organization's administration of the programs. When controls are considered likely to be effective, the Single Audit Act requires auditors to obtain an understanding of controls over compliance for major programs, assess control risk, and perform tests of controls sufficient to support an assessment of low control risk. But, when such controls are considered unlikely to be effective, auditors do not have to perform tests of controls.

Based on the auditors' assessments of the risks of material noncompliance and the related levels of control risk, they design sufficient substantive procedures to support an opinion on major program compliance with applicable laws and regulations. To provide assistance in designing these procedures, the Office of Management and Budget (OMB) issued the *OMB Circular A-133 Compliance Supplement (Compliance Supplement),* which specifies the compliance requirements and provides suggested audit procedures for a large number of federal financial assistance programs. For those major programs not included in the **Compliance Supplement,** auditors may determine the significant specific requirements to be tested by (1) following the *Compliance Supplement*'s guidance for such programs; (2) considering knowledge obtained from prior years' audits; (3) discussing laws and regulations with management, lawyers, program administrators, or federal, state, and local auditors; and (4) reviewing grant and loan agreements.

Compliance Requirements

Under the Single Audit Act, auditors must test for compliance with the specific requirements of all major programs. The **specific requirements** that must be audited are those that, if not complied with, could have a direct and material effect on a major program. These requirements and the related audit objectives are described below:

1. *Activities allowed or not allowed.* Determine that the organization complies with the specific requirements regarding the activities allowed or not allowed by the program.
2. *Allowable costs/cost principles.* Determine that the organization complies with federal cost accounting policies applicable to the program.
3. *Cash management.* Determine that the recipient/subrecipient followed procedures to minimize the time elapsing between the transfer of funds from the U.S. Treasury, or pass-through entity, and their disbursement.
4. *Davis-Bacon Act.* Determine that wages paid are not less than those established for the locality of the project (prevailing wage rates) by the Department of Labor.
5. *Eligibility.* Determine that individuals or groups of individuals that are being provided goods or services under a program are eligible for participation in and for the levels of assistance received under that program.
6. *Equipment and real property management.* Determine that the organization safeguards and maintains equipment purchased with federal assistance and uses the equipment for appropriate purposes.
7. *Matching, level of effort, earmarking.* Determine that the organization contributes the appropriate amount of its own resources to the program.
8. *Period of availability of federal funds.* Determine that federal funds were spent or obligated within the period of availability.
9. *Procurement and suspension and debarment.* Determine that the organization uses appropriate policies for purchases with federal funds, and that the organization does not contract with vendors that are suspended or debarred.
10. *Program income.* Determine whether program income is correctly recorded and used in accordance with the program requirements.
11. *Real property acquisition and relocation assistance.* Determine that the organization complied with property acquisition, appraisal, negotiation, and residential relocation requirements.
12. *Reporting.* Determine that the organization has complied with prescribed reporting requirements.
13. *Subrecipient monitoring.* Determine whether **recipients** monitor the compliance of **subrecipients.**
14. *Special tests and provisions.* Determine that the organization complies with other significant specific requirements that apply to the program.

Evaluating the Results of Compliance Procedures of Major Programs

In evaluating whether an entity's noncompliance is material to a major program, auditors should consider the frequency of noncompliance, and whether it results in a material amount of questioned costs. A **questioned cost** is an expenditure that the auditor questions on the grounds that it does not meet the criteria for allowability, program eligibility, other requirements, or is not adequately supported with documentation. An example of a questioned cost is a payment of financial assistance to an individual who does not meet the eligibility requirements of a program. In evaluating the effect of the questioned cost on their reports, auditors not only consider the actual amount, but also develop an estimate of the total amount of the

FIGURE 21.5
Schedule of Findings and Questioned Costs

CITY OF WAXVILLE, WASHINGTON
Schedule of Findings and Questioned Costs
April 30, 20X1

Program	Finding/Noncompliance	Questioned Cost
Department of Housing and Urban Development, Community Development Block Grants/Entitlement Grants Program		
1. Grant No. 85-C-7061 Project No. C-1 CFDA No. 14.218	Approximately $11,800 was expended for the payment of individual homeowners' property taxes and fire insurance. These are not allowable costs. The City intends to repay HUD for these costs.	$11,800
2. Grant No. 85-C-7071 Project No. C-1 CFDA No. 14.218	A request for reimbursement of funds was in excess of the actual documented expenditures. The City intends to repay HUD for these costs.	41,060
		$52,860

questioned costs. Thus, when auditors use audit sampling to select expenditures for testing, they consider the *projected amount* of questioned costs from the sample, as discussed in Chapter 9. Even if the estimated total questioned cost is not material enough to affect the auditors' opinion on compliance, they may be required to report the instances of noncompliance found and the resulting amounts of questioned costs. Auditors must report all questioned costs and likely questioned costs that exceed $10,000 in the Schedule of Findings and Questioned Costs, such as the example in Figure 21.5.

Reporting for a Single Audit

In addition to the reports required for an audit in accordance with *Government Auditing Standards,* auditors must report on:

- Whether the schedule of expenditures of federal awards is fairly presented in all material respects in relation to the financial statements taken as a whole.
- Whether the entity complied with the provisions of laws, regulations, and contracts or grants that may have a direct and material effect on each major federal financial assistance program.
- The work performed on internal control relating to major federal financial assistance programs.

In addition, an auditor must prepare a *summary report* that summarizes the results of the audit as described in the auditor's opinion on the financial statements, reports on internal control, reports on compliance, and the schedule of findings and questioned costs that accompanies these reports.

Compliance Auditing—A Summary

The auditors' compliance auditing and reporting requirements are summarized in Figure 21.6. Notice that the requirements build on each other. An audit in accordance with *Government Auditing Standards* includes the requirements of generally accepted auditing standards and a Single Audit includes the requirements of both standards.

FIGURE 21.6   Auditing and Reporting on Organizations Receiving Federal Financial Assistance—A Summary

---

Audit in Accordance with Generally Accepted Auditing Standards (GAAS)

Procedures Performed
- Audit procedures required by GAAS, including tests of compliance with laws and regulations having a direct and material effect on line-item amounts in the financial statements.

Report Issued
- Opinion on financial statements.

Audit in Accordance with Government Auditing Standards

Procedures Performed
- Some additional requirements, primarily related to communication and documentation.

Reports Issued
- Opinion on financial statements.
- Report(s) on compliance with applicable laws and regulations and internal control.

Audit in Accordance with the Single Audit Act

Procedures Performed
- Same as GAAS, plus:
  - Tests of compliance with the requirements applicable to major federal assistance programs.
  - Tests of the internal control over major federal assistance programs.

Reports Issued
- Same as *Government Auditing Standards,* plus:
  - Report on the schedule of expenditures of federal awards.
  - Summary report of audit results relating to financial statements, internal control, and compliance.
  - Report of findings and questioned costs.

Chapter Summary

This chapter described internal, operational, and compliance auditing. To summarize:

1. The Institute of Internal Auditors (IIA) defines *internal auditing* as an independent, objective assurance and consulting activity designed to add value and improve an organization's operations. It helps an organization accomplish its objectives by bringing a systematic, disciplined approach to evaluate and improve the effectiveness of risk management, control, and governance processes. The IIA's professional standards encompass attributes of internal auditors and performance of the internal audit function.

2. An *operational audit* is the examination of an operating unit or a complete organization to evaluate its performance, as measured by management's objectives. The stages of an operational audit might be summarized as definition of purpose, familiarization, preliminary survey, program development, fieldwork, reporting the findings, and follow-up.

3. *Compliance auditing* involves testing and reporting on whether an organization has complied with the requirements of various laws, regulations, and agreements.

4. The objective of a compliance audit engagement is the issuance of a report on the subject matter or an assertion by management regarding the organization's compliance with specified requirements, or regarding the organization's internal control over compliance with laws or regulations.

5. The objectives of compliance auditing of federal financial assistance programs are (*a*) to determine whether there have been violations of laws and regulations that may have a material effect on the organization's financial statements and major federal financial assistance programs, and (*b*) to provide a basis for additional reports on compliance and internal controls. Compliance auditing is involved in (*a*) audits of financial statements in accordance with generally accepted auditing standards, (*b*) audits

conducted in accordance with *Government Auditing Standards,* and (*c*) audits conducted in accordance with the federal Single Audit Act of 1984.

6. Audits of governmental organizations in accordance with generally accepted auditing standards must reflect the fact that such organizations are subject to a variety of laws and regulations that may have a direct and material effect on the amounts in the organization's financial statements.

7. In audits in accordance with *Government Auditing Standards,* the auditors issue a report on the financial statements and also report on compliance with laws and regulations and on internal control.

8. Audits in conformity with the Single Audit Act of 1984 are specifically designed to help ensure that the billions of dollars in federal financial assistance are appropriately spent. The focus of these audits is on organizations receiving significant amounts of federal assistance in a year. The auditors are required to report on requirements of major programs for which federal assistance has been received.

Key Terms Introduced or Emphasized in Chapter 21

Certified Internal Auditor (CIA)   An individual who has passed an examination administered by the Institute of Internal Auditors and has met the experience requirements necessary to become certified.

Compliance auditing   Performing procedures to test compliance with laws and regulations.

Compliance Supplement   A publication of the U.S. Office of Management and Budget that specifies audit procedures for federal financial assistance programs.

Compliance with specified requirements   An entity's compliance with specified requirements of laws, regulations, rules, contracts, or grants.

Government Auditing Standards   A document that contains standards for audits of government organizations, programs, activities, and functions and of government assistance received by contractors, and other nonprofit organizations. These standards, often referred to as generally accepted government auditing standards (GAGAS), are to be followed by auditors when required by law or other requirement.

Institute of Internal Auditors (IIA)   The international professional organization of internal auditors.

Internal auditing   An independent, objective assurance and consulting activity designed to add value and improve an organization's operations. It helps an organization accomplish its objectives by bringing a systematic, disciplined approach to evaluate and improve the effectiveness of risk management, control, and governance processes.

Internal control over compliance   The process by which management obtains reasonable assurance of compliance with specified laws and regulations.

Major federal financial assistance program (award)   A significant federal assistance program as determined by the auditors based on a risk-based approach. In a single audit, the auditors must provide an opinion on compliance related to major programs.

Management's assertion   Any declaration, or set of related declarations taken as a whole, made by management. In the context of compliance attestation, management's assertion deals with the entity's compliance with specified requirements, the effectiveness of the entity's internal control over compliance, or both.

Noncompliance   The failure to act in accordance with laws, regulations, agreements, or grants.

Operational auditing   The process of reviewing a department or other unit of a business, governmental, or nonprofit organization to measure the effectiveness, efficiency, and economy of operations.

Questioned costs   Those costs paid with federal assistance that appear to be in violation of a law or regulation, inadequately documented, unnecessary, or unreasonable in amount.

Recipient   An organization receiving federal financial assistance directly from the federal agency administering the program.

Single Audit Act   Legislation passed by the U.S. Congress that establishes uniform requirements for audits of federal financial assistance provided to state and local governments. The act was significantly amended in 1996.

Specific requirements (of laws, regulations, rules, contracts, or grants)   In compliance attestation engagements, management asserts that the organization is in compliance with specified requirements, and the CPAs attest to this assertion.

Subrecipient   An organization receiving federal financial assistance passed through from a recipient.

Review Questions

21–1. Define internal auditing.

21–2. Describe the scope of activities of an internal auditing function.

21–3. Nearly every large corporation now maintains an internal auditing department, but 50 years ago relatively few companies carried on a formal program of internal auditing. What have been the principal factors responsible for this rapid expansion?

21–4. Identify the knowledge and skills that are necessary to the performance of modern internal auditing.

21–5. "The principal distinction between public accounting and internal auditing is that the latter activity is carried on by an organization's own salaried employees rather than by independent professional auditors." Criticize this quotation.

21–6. Compare the objectives of internal auditors with those of external auditors.

21–7. Identify the eleven categories of the IIA's *Standards for the Professional Practice of Internal Auditing.*

21–8. Evaluate this statement: "Internal auditors cannot be independent of the activities that they audit."

21–9. Describe how the organizational status of the internal audit department affects its independence.

21–10. Briefly describe the factors that are important to the management of an internal auditing department.

21–11. Describe the requirements for becoming a Certified Internal Auditor.

21–12. Differentiate between financial statement audits and operational audits.

21–13. Describe the purpose of an operational audit.

21–14. Should the internal auditors generally disclose their findings to operating personnel of the department involved before transmitting the report to top management? Explain.

21–15. Describe the two types of agreed-upon procedures engagements that CPAs may perform relating to compliance with laws and regulations.

21–16. Evaluate this statement: "An agreed-upon procedures engagement on compliance with a law is designed to provide users with negative assurance on whether an entity has complied with that law."

21–17. Explain why tests of compliance with laws and regulations are considered to be substantive tests.

21–18. Explain the auditors' responsibility for testing compliance with laws and regulations in an audit in accordance with generally accepted auditing standards.

21–19. Identify the three types of audits that a governmental organization might obtain.

21–20. "In an audit in accordance with *Government Auditing Standards* the auditors must perform tests of compliance with all laws and regulations." Criticize this quotation.

21–21. Describe the additional audit report required by *Government Auditing Standards.*

21–22. The auditors' responsibility for reporting violations of laws and regulations under *Government Auditing Standards* differs from their responsibility under generally accepted auditing standards. Compare these responsibilities.

21–23. Contrast the requirements of an audit in accordance with *Government Auditing Standards* with the requirements of an audit in accordance with generally accepted auditing standards.

21–24. Explain why compliance with laws and regulations is so important in the audit of governmental organizations.

21–25. What is the purpose of the Single Audit Act?

21–26. When is a governmental organization required to have an audit in accordance with the Single Audit Act?

21–27. Explain how major federal assistance programs are identified.

21–28. Describe what is meant by a questioned cost.

21–29. Distinguish between a subrecipient and a primary recipient. Provide an example of each.

21–30. Identify the 14 requirements that may be applicable to federal financial assistance programs.

Questions Requiring Analysis

Required:

21–31. In order to function effectively, the internal auditor must often educate auditees and other parties about the nature and purpose of internal auditing.

  a. Define internal auditing.

      b. Briefly describe three possible benefits of an internal audit department's program to educate auditees and other parties about the nature and purpose of internal auditing.

(CIA, adapted)

21–32.   Steve Ankenbrandt, president of Beeb Corp., has been discussing the company's internal operations with the presidents of several other multidivision companies. Ankenbrandt discovered that most of them have an internal audit staff. The activities of the staffs at other companies include financial audits, operational audits, and sometimes compliance audits.

Required: Describe the meaning of the following terms as they relate to the internal auditing function:

      a. Financial auditing.

      b. Operational auditing.

      c. Compliance auditing.

(CIA, adapted)

21–33.   Throughout this book emphasis has been placed on the concept of independence as the most significant single element underlying the development of the public accounting profession. The term "independent auditor" is sometimes used to distinguish the public accountant from an internal auditor. Nevertheless, the Institute of Internal Auditors points to the factor of independence as essential to an effective program of internal auditing. Distinguish between the meaning of *independence* as used by the American Institute of Certified Public Accountants in describing the function of the certified public accountant and the meaning of *independence* as used by the Institute of Internal Auditors to describe the work of the internal auditor.

21–34.   You are conducting the first audit of the marketing activities of your organization. Your preliminary survey has disclosed indications of deficient conditions of a serious nature. You expect your audit work to document the need for substantial corrective action. You feel certain that your audit report will contain descriptions of a number of serious defects.

      Your preliminary meeting with the director of the marketing division and the principal subordinates gave you reason to believe that they will be defensive, that your audit report will receive a chilly reception, that your stated facts are likely to be challenged, and that any deficient conditions reported will be denied or minimized.

Required: *a.* Identify the aspect of the *Standards for the Professional Practice of Internal Auditing* that applies to the problems described above.

      b. Describe four techniques that you might use to improve the chances that your report will be well received and that appropriate corrective action will be taken.

(CIA, adapted)

21–35.   Matt Gunlock, CPA, is performing an audit of the City of Ryan in accordance with generally accepted auditing standards.

Required: *a.* Must Matt be concerned with the city's compliance with laws and regulations? Explain.

      b. How should Matt decide on the nature and extent of the tests of compliance that should be performed in the audit?

21–36.   Wixon & Co., CPAs, is performing an audit of the City of Brummet for the year ended June 30, 200X, in accordance with *Government Auditing Standards.* During the course of the audit, Gerald Yarnell, a senior auditor, discovers violations of laws and regulations that constitute material instances of noncompliance.

Required: *a.* Explain how these violations may affect the auditors' reports.

      b. How would your answer to (*a*) change if management elected to correct the financial statements for the violations?

21–37.   North County School District received $1,450,000 in federal financial assistance this year.

Required: *a.* Is North County School District required to have an audit in accordance with the Single Audit Act? Explain.

      b. What are the requirements of an audit in accordance with the Single Audit Act?

21–38.   The City of Westmore is confused about the type of audit that it should obtain: an audit in accordance with generally accepted auditing standards, an audit in accordance with *Government Auditing Standards,* or an audit in accordance with the Single Audit Act.

Required: *a.* Explain the differences between the three types of audits.

      b. How should the City of Westmore decide which type of audit it is required to obtain?

Multiple Choice Questions

21–39.   Select the best answer for each of the following questions. Explain the reasons for your selection.

   a. Internal auditing can best be described as:

   (1) An accounting function.

   (2) A compliance function.

   (3) An activity primarily to detect fraud.

   (4) A control function.

(CIA, adapted)

   b. The independence of the internal auditing department will most likely be assured if it reports to the:

   (1) Audit committee of the board of directors.

   (2) President.

   (3) Controller.

   (4) Treasurer.

(CIA, adapted)

   c. When performing an operational audit, the purpose of a preliminary survey is to:

   (1) Determine the objective of the activity to be audited.

   (2) Determine the scope of the audit.

   (3) Identify areas that should be included in the audit program.

   (4) All of the above.

(CIA, adapted)

   d. Operational auditing is primarily oriented toward:

   (1) Future improvements to accomplish the goals of management.

   (2) Ensuring the accuracy of the data in management's financial reports.

   (3) Determination of the fairness of the entity's financial statements.

   (4) Compliance with laws and regulations.

   e. Which of the following bodies promulgates standards for audits of federal financial assistance programs?

   (1) Governmental Accounting Standards Board.

   (2) Financial Accounting Standards Board.

   (3) Government Accountability Office.

   (4) Governmental Auditing Standards Board.

(AICPA, adapted)

   f. As compared to an audit in accordance with GAAS, an audit in accordance with *Government Auditing Standards* requires the auditors to:

   (1) Use a lower level of materiality.

   (2) Perform additional tests of internal control.

   (3) Issue an additional report on compliance with laws and regulations and internal control.

   (4) Fulfill all of the above requirements.

   g. In a compliance attestation engagement CPAs may address an organization's:

	Compliance with Specified Requirements	Internal Control Over Compliance with Specific Laws and Regulations
(1)	Yes	Yes
(2)	Yes	No
(3)	No	Yes
(4)	No	No

   h. The portion of internal control most directly related to a CPA's engagement to attest to compliance with laws and regulations is:

   (1) Internal control over compliance.

   (2) Internal control over financial reporting.

   (3) Internal control over laws and regulations.

   (4) Internal control over operations.

i. When issuing an unqualified audit report in a compliance attestation engagement, the CPA may report on:

	Management's Assertion	The Subject Matter
(1)	Yes	Yes
(2)	Yes	No
(3)	No	Yes
(4)	No	No

j. When issuing a qualified audit report in a compliance attestation engagement, the CPA may report on:

	Management's Assertion	The Subject Matter
(1)	Yes	Yes
(2)	Yes	No
(3)	No	Yes
(4)	No	No

k. An important aspect of performing an audit in accordance with the *Single Audit Act* is to identify:

(1) Major federal financial assistance programs.

(2) Government generally accepted assertions.

(3) Federal supplemental requirements.

(4) Title determination sub-acts.

l. The organization that administers the Certified Internal Auditor program is the:

(1) American Institute of Certified Public Accountants—Certified Internal Auditor Division.

(2) Institute of Internal Auditors.

(3) American Accounting Association

(4) Securities and Exchange Commission.

Problems

21–40. You are the chief audit executive for the internal auditing function of a large municipal hospital. You receive monthly financial reports prepared by the accounting department, and your review of them has shown that total accounts receivable from patients have steadily and rapidly increased over the past eight months.

Other information in the reports shows the following conditions:

1. The number of available hospital beds has not changed.

2. The bed occupancy rate has not changed.

3. Hospital billing rates have not changed significantly.

4. The hospitalization insurance contracts have not changed since the last modification 12 months ago.

Your internal audit department performed a financial and operational audit of the accounts receivable accounting function 10 months ago. The working papers file for that assignment contains financial information, a record of the preliminary survey, documentation of the study, evaluation of controls, documentation of the procedures used to produce evidence about the validity and collectibility of the accounts, and a copy of your report that commented favorably on the controls and collectibility of the receivables.

However, the current increase in receivables has alerted you to the need for another audit. You remember news stories last year about the manager of the city water system who lost his job because his accounting department double-billed all the residential customers for three months. You plan to perform a preliminary survey of the problem, if indeed a problem exists.

Required:

a. Write a memo to your senior auditor listing at least eight questions that should be used to guide and direct the preliminary survey. (Hint: The categories of questions used in the last preliminary survey were these: "Who does the accounts receivable accounting?" "What data processing procedures and policies are in effect?" and "How is the accounts receivable accounting done?" This time, you will use these categories and add a fourth category of questions: "What financial or economic events have occurred in the past 10 months?")

b. Describe the phases of the audit that would be performed after the preliminary survey is completed.

(CIA, adapted)

21–41. Devry Corporation has established an independent foundation for the purposes of community improvement. The foundation employs an executive director and eight staff people. The internal auditors of the company were requested to do an audit of the foundation in 20X1 to determine problems with the recording of transactions, the handling of cash, and documentation of transactions. The following items were found:

1. The foundation used the cash basis of reporting rather than the accrual basis.
2. The foundation lacked a copy of the plane ticket for airfare reimbursed for a trip taken by one of the volunteers.
3. Excess funds were invested in instruments other than those specified by the organization's policy manual.
4. The purchase of a desktop publishing system was expensed.
5. The foundation does not employ anyone with formal accounting training.
6. Many errors were made in recording transactions, which necessitated many year-end adjusting entries.
7. Numerous certificates of deposit were found in many different locations (e.g., filing cabinets, desk drawers, and safe deposit box).
8. The checking account was reconciled by the individual who wrote the checks.

Required: Write an internal audit report (in proper form) to the executive committee of the foundation indicating findings and recommendations.

(CIA, adapted)

21–42. In performing an audit in accordance with *Government Auditing Standards,* the auditors are required to issue an additional combined report on compliance with laws and regulations and on internal control.

Required:
a. Describe the nature of the procedures that the auditors must perform beyond those required by generally accepted auditing standards to provide a basis for this report.
b. Describe the specific contents of the auditors' combined report on compliance and internal control.

21–43. In performing an audit in accordance with both generally accepted auditing standards and *Government Auditing Standards,* the auditors are required to communicate information about weaknesses in the organization's internal control. However, the requirements are different.

Required:
a. Describe the differences between these requirements.
b. Describe the major aspects of the report on internal control required by *Government Auditing Standards.*

In-Class Team Case

21–44. Robert Myers, CPA, has been engaged to audit the City of Mystic in accordance with the Single Audit Act. Robert is aware that the Single Audit Act requires additional tests of major federal financial assistance programs, and he is trying to identify those programs for this audit. The City of Mystic participates in four federal financial assistance programs with the following amounts of expenditures and assessed risk of material noncompliance.

Grant Program	Expenditures	Risk
Department of Education, Title I Grants to Local Education Agencies	$ 2,370,000	High
Environmental Protection Agency Ford Creek Modification	6,780,000	Moderate
Department of Housing and Urban Development		
Project # C94-MC-08-0009	5,500,000	Low
Project # C94-MC-08-0010	350,000	Moderate
Total grant awards	$15,000,000	

Required:
a. Identify the major federal assistance programs.
b. Describe the compliance testing requirements for major federal financial assistance programs under the Single Audit Act.

Index

Note: Page numbers followed by *n* indicate material in footnotes.